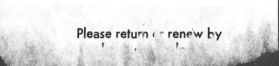

Please return or renew by

SCIENCE FICTION AND FANTASY REFERENCE INDEX, 1878-1985

SCIENCE FICTION AND FANTASY REFERENCE INDEX, 1878-1985

An International Author and Subject Index
to History and Criticism

Edited by H.W. Hall

Head, Special Formats Division
Sterling C. Evans Library
Texas A&M University

Volume 1:
Author Entries

GALE RESEARCH COMPANY • BOOK TOWER • DETROIT, MICHIGAN 48226

H. W. Hall, *Editor*

Gale Research Company

Amy Marcaccio, *Editorial Coordinator*
Linda George, *Editorial Assistant*

Mary Beth Trimper, *External Production Manager*
Linda Davis and Michael Vargas, *External Production Assistants*
Arthur Chartow, *Art Director*
Laura Bryant, *Internal Production Supervisor*
Louise Gagné, *Internal Production Associate*
Sandy Rock, *Senior Internal Production Assistant*
Candace Cloutier, *Internal Production Assistant*

Frederick G. Ruffner, *Chairman*
J. Kevin Reger, *President*
Dedria Bryfonski, *Publisher*
Ellen T. Crowley, *Associate Editorial Director*
Ann Evory, *Director, Indexes and Dictionaries Division*

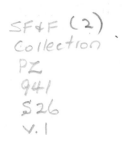
Library of Congress Cataloging-in-Publication Data

Science fiction and fantasy reference index, 1878-1985.

   Includes index.
   Contents: v. 1. Author entries — v. 2. Subject
entries
    1. Science fiction—History and criticism—Indexes.
2. Fantastic fiction—History and criticism—Indexes.
I. Hall, Halbert W.
Z5917.S36S297 1987 [PN3433.5] 016.8093'876 87-173
ISBN 0-8103-2129-7 (set)

Printed in the United States of America

For my mother, Edna Hall

And in memory of my father, H. T. Hall
(December 17, 1897-April 20, 1965)

Contents

Preface

The *Science Fiction and Fantasy Reference Index, 1878-1985,* is by far the most comprehensive index yet published to the secondary literature dealing with science fiction and fantasy. More than 19,000 individual books, articles, essays, news reports, and audiovisual items are indexed by over 42,000 author and subject citations. Although the earliest entry is an 1878 item on Jules Verne, most of the entries date from 1945 through 1985. More than 95 percent of the items indexed were personally examined; citations to the balance are based on secondary sources I judged reliable.

Scope

Fantastic literature is here defined as including science fiction, fantasy, and horror/supernatural/weird fiction. Science fiction generated the largest number of entries, followed by fantasy and horror. Approximately 90 percent of the indexed items are in English. Most of the citations to non-English material were supplied to me in 1981 by David Samuelson, Professor of English at California State University, Long Beach, and supplemented by contributions from several European contributors, notably Luk de Vos of the Netherlands, who is compiling a similar index to European secondary literature. Coverage of European material is representative, not comprehensive. The most significant non-English coverage is of French, German, and Italian material, but many other countries are represented. The non-English language entries are entered by author, with subject headings where subject analysis was possible. The citations list months in English to facilitate use by the English-speaking scholar. For a variety of reasons, involving both the background of this segment of the project and the lack of a multilingual word processing program, diacritical marks have been omitted.

History

This index began in 1967 in the form of 3x5-inch index cards, when no general indexes to the secondary literature existed. In 1980, I published a computer-output microfiche preliminary bibliography, *The Science Fiction Index,* which contained 4,350 citations, all reverified and included here. In 1972, the first book-length bibliography of science fiction secondary literature was published, Thomas D. Clareson's *Science Fiction Criticism: An Annotated Checklist* (Kent State University Press), which descriptively annotated more than 800 items, including book review columns from general magazines. Most of these entries, excluding the book reviews, are included here. Citations to reviews are contained in my *Science Fiction Book Review Index (SFBRI),* published by Gale Research and covering three periods, 1923-1973 (1975), 1974-1979 (1981), and 1980-1984 (1985). In addition to book reviews, the third volume of *SFBRI* cumulated my first five *Science Fiction and Fantasy Research Index (SFFRI)* annuals, 1980-1984, and all the citations to about 4,750 items in that portion of the volume, revised and corrected when necessary, are included in this new index. The annual *Science Fiction and Fantasy Research Index* will supplement and update this volume of *Science Fiction and Fantasy Reference Index, 1878-1985.*

While I was compiling and publishing the *SFFRI* annuals, Marshall Tymn was directing a parallel bibliographic project. The first cumulation of listings in the quarterly journal *Extrapolation* was edited by Tymn and Roger C. Schlobin and published as *The Year's Scholarship in Science Fiction and Fantasy: 1972-1975* (Kent State University Press, 1979). Supplements cover the 1976-1979 period (1983), and annuals for 1980, 1981, and 1982 appeared. Separate publication of the book ended in 1983. The listing was again published in *Extrapolation,* but the valuable descriptive annotations that had been the heart of the bibliography have been dropped. The Tymn-Schlobin bibliographies grouped citations in seven to ten subject sections, with author indexes. Subject indexing, except for author as subject, was therefore more general than the approach used here. Librarians and other readers should be aware that there is overlap between this index and the *Year's Scholarship* bibliographies; this volume, however, is much more comprehensive than the combined *Year's Scholarship* bibliographies.

Science Fiction and Fantasy Reference Index, 1878–1985

Methodology

A variety of methods were used to identify the items considered for indexing. A significant number were located by examination of my personal collection, and by intensive research in the Texas A&M University Library Science Fiction Research Collection. Bibliographic searching of published indexes, such as *Reader's Guide,* regular examination of almost 200 magazine titles, computer searches, citation analysis, help from fellow scholars, and good fortune were all significant tools in the growth of this index. Citation analysis proved to be one of the most fruitful methods. In effect, every scholar who wrote a footnote or provided a list of references became a contributor. More significantly, those citations led to other sources or hinted at new material in unexpected places. The value of citation analysis, and of such developing tools as *Arts and Humanities Citation Index,* can hardly be overemphasized. Users should note that the excellent "Primary and Secondary Bibliographies" for individual authors, published by G. K. Hall, are not fully analyzed in this index. Such author-specific bibliographies, which are cited here, will always be more inclusive than a general tool such as this one, and the scholar should always consult such specialty tools when researching a well-known writer.

Review of the historical files of magazines was a rewarding, if sometimes frustrating, activity. A new source, an uncited item, or a clue to a treasure trove of new material were the fruits of such labor. Missing issues are the bane of such effort; one never knows what might have been missed. In this volume, a gap in a sequential series of articles sometimes appears. While the existence of the item may be assumed, inadequate data existed to allow inclusion.

The coverage of news sources, particularly fan newspapers, deserves special notice. The runs of *Fantasy Times/Science Fiction Times, Locus,* and *Science Fiction Chronicle* are almost completely indexed and provide subject access to the fan newspapers from 1941 through 1985.

While *Fantasy Times/Science Fiction Times* is very valuable for its coverage of people and events, an even greater value lies in the overview it can provide the historical researcher. The definitive history of science fiction and fantasy is yet to be written, but whoever seeks to write that history must extensively research the files of *Fantasy Times/Science Fiction Times.* The sheer length of the historical record and the fairly consistent editorial slant provide the most complete contemporary record of the field existing in printed form. Certainly, this title does not provide all that is needed; the content should be supplemented with other contemporary professional and fan magazines to achieve a balanced overview.

Scholars, critics, bibliographers, and librarians over the years have questioned the value of the material published in "fanzines." In his 1985 Pilgrim Award acceptance speech, Samuel R. Delany emphasized the value and importance of this material:

> Fanzines—to take only one manifestation of this reader/writer relationship—have created a vast, "informal critical system" around science fiction amounting to many, many hundreds of thousands of pages—possibly even exceeding the actual number of pages of science fiction written! This energetic dialoguc has had its supportive and its destructive aspects, and any history of science fiction that does not research and theorize as to the scope and effect of this force on the way we read science fiction is ignoring an extraordinary historical influence on the field. (*SFRA Newsletter* No. 133: 7-15. August 1985.)

The *Science Fiction and Fantasy Reference Index* contains over 19,000 discrete bibliographic items. That total represents perhaps fifty to sixty percent of the directly applicable material published to date. The coverage of newspapers is significant but only touches the information available in the nation's newspapers. Coverage of the "fanzines" is the most comprehensive ever attempted but is necessarily very selective. The better fanzines of the 1930s and 1940s in particular are filled with valuable material, often the only critical commentary on many stories and books, yet these fanzines are essentially unindexed. Pavlat and Evan's *Fanzine Index* (Piser, 1965) lists hundreds of these unindexed fanzines published prior to 1952, and the majority of the "Fanzines" listed in the "Academic Periodicals and Major Fanzines" section of Tymn and Ashley's *Science Fiction, Fantasy and Weird Fiction Magazines* (Greenwood, 1985) are not indexed in any source, although work is underway to index them in future supplements to this volume.

Preface

Finally, as noted before, the publication of articles about fantastic literature knows no bounds. The secondary literature of science fiction and fantasy may appear in virtually any type of publication, and is found as frequently by serendipity as by systematic searching.

Materials Indexed

In addition to the several hundred books cited in the index itself, virtually all standard bibliographic sources were consulted, such as *Reader's Guide, Humanities Index, Social Sciences Index, Arts and Humanities Citation Index,* the MLA bibliographies, *Library Literature, ERIC, NewsBank,* and many others. Material from several thousand issues of magazines and newspapers was also indexed. The "List of Sources" indicates the titles that were systematically searched. The user should assume that coverage of the magazines listed is over 90 percent complete for each title. On occasion, issues were missing and will be included in supplements to this volume as they are located. The 20-year history of this project makes a more accurate statement of inclusive issues or years an impossibility.

Arrangement

The *Science Fiction and Fantasy Reference Index* is divided into two sections. The Author Entries volume provides access to authors and co-authors of all books, articles, and essays. By-lines of newspaper reports are not indexed by author. The Subject Entries volume provides access by subject headings. In both volumes, citations are printed in full, allowing the user immediate access to all information.

The *Science Fiction and Fantasy Reference Index* was compiled and sorted on a computer. The following examples illustrate the filing order:

La Barre
Labare

New York
Newark
Newyorker

Mac Donald
MacDonald
Mace
MacGregor
Malone
McAuley

In general, author names are truncated to two initials, such as Le Guin, U. K. An attempt was made to combine author entries when name variations, such as Robert and Bob, could be attributable to the same individual; if that information could not be verified, the names were left as they appeared on the sources.

Following each author heading or subject heading, items are subarranged in three categories: books, articles on specific books, and articles and news items. Within each category, items are arranged in title order.

Suggestions Are Welcome

Comments and suggestions from users are encouraged and should be directed to the editor:

H. W. Hall
3608 Meadow Oaks Lane
Bryan, TX 77802

Acknowledgments

Julie Hrachovy—typist par excellence; proofreader, spelling checker, and error checker extraordinary. Without her help, the index could not have been completed on schedule.

Bill Page—one of the most diligent and successful sleuths in the world. Using intuition, serendipity, and sheer persistence, he ferrets out unusual and elusive items at a phenomenal rate.

Geraldine Hutchins—reviewed and revised the subject heading list and proofread some segments of the index.

Dr. Evelyn King—Dr. King was always there: encouraging and supporting not only research projects such as this one, but also all other aspects of our library work.

Dr. Irene Hoadley—for her efforts to obtain research funding for the University Library.

Neil Barron—for his support, encouragement, contributions, and suggestions.

The Texas A&M University Library—for research support on the preliminary bibliography created in 1980 as a microfiche file, the seed project from which this volume germinated, and for research support to convert the massive historical file of data to a machine readable form which could be quickly revised into a publishable manuscript.

Thomas D. Clareson—a pioneer in the bibliographic control of the secondary literature of science fiction and fantasy in *Extrapolation*.

David Samuelson—for foreign language citations.

List of Sources

A comprehensive listing of all titles covered in an index of this size is impossible, particularly when the majority of the sources featured only one or two articles per title. The partial list provided here is designed to identify the more fruitful sources, and to offer the user assurance that major sources were included in the compilation of the index. The list includes collections of essays, magazines which were comprehensively indexed, and magazine issues which were devoted to the topics of science fiction and fantasy. Where a single issue is listed, the volume, issue, and date are given for the specific issue.

AB Bookman's Weekly (V. 72, No. 17, October 1983)

Aesthetics of Fantasy Literature and Art, by R. C. Schlobin. Notre Dame Press, 1982. 288p.

Algol

Alternative Futures

Amazing

America as Utopia, ed. by Kenneth M. Roemer. New York: Burt Franklin, 1981. 410 p.

American Cinematographer (1967-   )

Analog

Anatomy of Wonder: A Critical Guide to Science Fiction, ed. by Neil Barron. New York: Bowker, 1981. 724 p.

Arena Science Fiction

Art of the Essay, ed. by Leslie Fiedler. New York: Crowell, 1969.

Arthur C. Clarke, ed. by J. D. Olander and M. H. Greenberg. New York: Taplinger, 1977. 254 p.

Asimov on Science Fiction, by Isaac Asimov. Garden City, NY: Doubleday, 1981. 334 p.

Aurora: Beyond Equality, ed. by Susan Anderson. New York: Fawcett, 1976.

Black American Literature Forum (V. 18, No. 2, Summer 1984)

Blade of Conan, ed. by L. S. de Camp. New York: Ace, 1979. 310 p.

Bob Shaw: British Science Fiction Writers, Vol. 1, by Paul Kincaid and Geoff Rippington. Kent, Eng.: British Science Fiction Association, 1981. 38 p.

Book of Ellison, The, ed. by Andrew Porter. New York: Algol Press, 1978. 196 p.

Bridges to Science Fiction, by G. E. Slusser, G. R. Guffey, and Mark Rose. Carbondale: Southern Illinois Univ. Press, 1980. 168 p. (Eaton Conference on Science Fiction and Fantasy, 1st, Univ of California, Riverside, 1979.)

Bridges to Fantasy, ed. by G. E. Slusser, E. S. Rabkin, and Robert Scholes. Carbondale: Southern Illinois University Press, 1982. 231 p.

Chicago Tribune

Cinefantastique

Cinefex

Clockwork Worlds: Mechanized Environments in Science Fiction, ed. by R. D. Erlich and T. P. Dunn Westport, CT: Greenwood, 1983. 384 p.

Colloquy

Coming Attractions, ed. by M. H. Greenberg. New York: Gnome, 1957. 254 p.

Conan Reader, ed. by L. S. De Camp. Baltimore: Mirage, 1968.

Coordinates: Placing Science Fiction and Fantasy, ed. by G. E. Slusser, E. S. Rabkin, and Robert Scholes. Carbondale: Southern Illinois University Press. 1983. 209 p.

Craft of Science Fiction, ed. by Reginald Bretnor. New York: Harper, 1976.

Critical Encounters: Writers and Themes in Science Fiction, ed. by Dick Riley. New York: Ungar, 1978. 183 p.

Critical Encounters II: Writers and Themes in Science Fiction, by Tom Staicar. New York: Ungar, 1982. 162 p.

Cromlech

Current Contents Arts and Humanities

Dark Barbarian: The Writings of Robert E. Howard, a Critical Anthology, ed. by Don Herron. Westport, CT: Greenwood, 1984. 242 p.

Dark Brotherhood and Other Stories, by H. P. Lovecraft. Sauk City, WI: Arkham House, 1966.

Death and the Serpent: Immortality in Science Fiction and Fantasy, ed. by C. B. Yoke and D. M. Hassler. Westport, CT: Greenwood, 1985. 235 p.

Destinies

Disappearing Future: A Symposium of Speculation, ed. by George Hay. London: Panther, 1970. 156 p.

Discovering Modern Horror Fiction, by Darrell Schweitzer. Mercer Island, WA: Starmont, 1985. 156 p.

Discovering Stephen King, by Darrell Schweitzer. Mercer Island, WA: Starmont, 1985. 219 p.

Dream Makers: The Uncommon People Who Write Science Fiction, by Charles Platt. New York: Berkley, 1980. 284 p.

Dream Makers Volume II: The Uncommon Men and Women Who Write Science Fiction, by Charles Platt. New York: Berkley, 1983. 266 p.

Empire: For the SF Writer

Encyclopedia of Science Fiction, ed. by Robert Holdstock. London: Octopus, 1978.

End of the World, ed. by E. S. Rabkin, M. H. Greenberg, and J. D. Olander. Carbondale: Southern Illinois University Press, 1983. 204 p.

Engines of the Night, by Malzberg, B. N. Garden City, NY: Doubleday, 1982. 198 p.

ERIC

Mythlore

Neugier oder Flucht? Zu Poetik, Ideologie und Wirkung der Science Fiction, by Karl Eremrt. Stuttgart: Klett, 1980. 150 p.

New Orleans Times Picayune

New York Times

Newsbank

No Place Else: Explorations in Utopian and Dystopian Fiction, by E. S. Rabkin, M. H. Greenberg and J. D. Olander. Carbondale: Southern Illinois University Press, 1983. 278 p.

Noreascon Proceedings: The Twenty-Ninth World Science Fiction Convention, ed. by Leslie Turek, Boston, Massachusetts, September 3-6, 1971. Cambridge, MA: NESFA, 1976.

Oak Leaves

Omni's Screen Flights - Screen Fantasies: The Future According to Science Fiction Cinema, by Danny Peary. Garden City, NY: Doubleday Dolphin, 1984. 310 p.

Other Worlds: Fantasy and Science Fiction Since 1939,. ed. by J. J. Teunissen. Winnipeg, Canada: University of Manitoba, 1980. 225 p. (Also published as *Mosaic*, V. 13, No. 3/4, 1982)

Pale Shadow of Science, by B. W. Aldiss. Seattle: Serconia, 1985. 128 p.

Patchin Review

Patterns of the Fantastic II:. ed. by Donald Hassler. Mercer Island, WA: Starmont, 1984. 93 p.

Patterns of the Fantastic: Academic Programming at Chicon IV, ed. by Donald Hassler. Mercer Island, WA: Starmont, 1983. 105 p.

Pennsylvania English (V. 10, No. 2, Spring 1984)

Phantastik in Literatur und Kunst, by C. W. Thomas and J. M. Fischer. Darmstadt: Wissenschaftliche Buchgesellschaft, 1980. 563 p.

Philip K. Dick, ed. by M. H. Greenberg and J. D. Olander. New York: Taplinger, 1982. 256 p.

Philip K. Dick: Electric Shepherd, ed. by Bruce Gillespie. Melbourne, Aust: Nostrilia, 1975. 106 p.

Philosophers Look at Science Fiction, ed. by N. D. Smith. Chicago: Nelson-Hall, 1982. 204 p.

Philosophical Speculations on Science Fiction and Fantasy

Philosophy and Science Fiction, ed. by Michael Philips. Buffalo, NY: Prometheus, 1984. 392 p.

Polaris 6, ed. by Franz Rottensteiner. Frankfurt-am-Main: Suhrkamp, 1982. 331 p.

Popular Fiction and Social Change, ed. by Christopher Pawling. New York: St. Martins, 1984. 246 p.

PSFQ (Pretentious Science Fiction Quarterly)

Publishers Weekly

Pulp Voices, or Science Fiction Voices No. 6, by J. M. Elliot. San Bernardino, CA: Borgo, 1983. 64 p.

Quarber Merkur: Aufsatze zur Science Fiction und phantastischen Literatur, ed. by Franz Rottensteiner. Frankfurt-am-Main: Suhrkamp, 1979. 261 p.

Quark

Questar

Ray Bradbury, ed. by M. H. Greenberg et al. New York: Taplinger, 1980.

Restant (Belgium) (V. 10, No. 2, Spring 1982)

Rigel

Riverside Quarterly

Robert A. Heinlein, ed. by J. D. Olander and M. H. Greenberg. New York: Taplinger, 1978. 268 p.

Science Fiction and Fantasy Research Index

Science Fiction and Future Studies, by D. N. Samuelson. Bryan, TX: SFRA, 1975. 134 p. (SFRA Miscellaneous Publication No. 2; copy in Texas A&M University Library Science Fiction Research Collection)

Science Fiction and Space Futures, ed. by E. M. Emme. San Diego, CA: Univelt, for the American Astronautical Society, 1982. 270 p.

Science Fiction at Large, ed. by Peter Nicholls. New York: Harper, 1976.

Science Fiction Chronicle

Science Fiction Collector/Megavore

Science Fiction Dialogues, ed. by Gary Wolfe. Chicago: Academy Chicago, 1982. 227 p.

Science Fiction in the English Class, ed. by Ken Donnelson. [Special issue, *Arizona English Bulletin* 15(1):124. October 1972.]

Science Fiction Novel: Imagination and Social Criticism, ed. by Basil Davenport. Chicago: Advent, 1964.

Science Fiction Reference Book, by M. B. Tymn. Mercer Island, WA: Starmont, 1981. 536 p.

Science Fiction Review

Science Fiction Source Book, by David Wingrove. New York: Van Nostrand, 1984. 320 p.

Science Fiction Studies

Science Fiction the Academic Awakening, ed. by W. E. McNelly. Shreveport, LA: CEA, 1974. 57 p.

Science Fiction Times (Boston)

Science Fiction Times (Germany)

Science Fiction Times (New York)

Science Fiction Today and Tomorrow, ed. by Reginald Bretnor. New York: Harper, 1974.

Science Fiction Voices #1, by Darrell Schweitzer. San Bernardino, CA: Borgo, 1979. 64 p.

Science Fiction Voices #2, by J. M. Elliot. San Bernardino, CA: Borgo, 1979. 63 p.

Science Fiction Voices #3, by J. M. Elliot. San Bernardino, CA: Borgo, 1980. 64 p.

Science Fiction Voices #4, by J. M. Elliot. San Bernardino, CA: Borgo, 1982. 63 p.

Science Fiction Voices #5, by Darrell Schweitzer. San Bernardino, CA: Borgo, 1981. 64 p.

Science Fiction Writers: Critical Studies of the Major Authors from the Early Nineteenth Century to the Present Day, ed. by E. F. Bleiler. New York. Scribners, 1982. 623 p.

Science Fiction Yearbook, 1957 Edition. Vol. 1. Patterson, NJ: Fandom House, 1957. 42 p.

Science Fiction, Fantasy, and Weird Fiction Magazines, ed. by M. B. Tymn and Mike Ashley. Westport, CT: Greenwood, 1985. 970 p.

Science Fiction: A Collection of Critical Essays, ed. by Mark Rose. Englewood Cliffs: Prentice-Hall, 1976. 169 p.

Science Fiction: A Critical Guide, ed. by Patrick Parrinder. New York: Longman, 1979.

Science Fiction: A Review of Speculative Literature

Science Fiction: Contemporary Mythology, ed. by Patricia Warrick. New York: Harper, 1978.

Science Fiction: Its Meaning and Its Future, ed. by Reginald Bretnor. New York: Coward McCann, 1979.

Science Fiction: Today and Tomorrow, ed. by Reginald Bretnor. New York: Harper, 1974.

Science/Fiction Collections: Fantasy, Supernatural & Weird Tales, ed. by H. W. Hall. New York: Haworth, 1983. 181 p.

Scope of the Fantastic: Culture, Biography, Themes, Children's Literature, ed. by R. A. Collins and H. D. Pearce. Westport: Greenwood, 1985. 282 p.

Seekers of Tomorrow, by Sam Moskowitz. New York: Ballantine, 1967. 431 p.

Selected Proceedings of the 1978 SF Research Association National Conference, ed. by T. J. Remington. Cedar Falls, Iowa: Univ. of Northern Iowa, 1979. 281 p.

SF Commentary

SF Horizons

SF: The Other Side of Realism, ed. by T. D. Clareson. Bowling Green: Popular Press, 1971.

SFRA Newsletter

SFWA Bulletin

Shadowings: The Reader's Guide to Horror Fiction, 1981-1982, by D. E. Winter. Mercer Island, WA: Starmont, 1983. 148 p.

Shadows of the Magic Lamp: Fantasy and Science Fiction in Film, by G. E. Slusser and E. S. Rabkin. Carbondale: Southern Illinois University Press, 1985. 259 p.

Sound of Wonder: Interviews From "The Science Fiction Radio Show," Volume 1, by Daryl Lane, William Vernon, and David Carson. Phoenix: Oryx, 1985. 203 p.

Sound of Wonder: Interviews From "The Science Fiction Radio Show," Volume 2, by Daryl Lane, William Vernon, and David Carson. Phoenix: Oryx, 1985. 203 p.

Soviet Literature (No. 406, 1982)

Speaking of Science Fiction, by Paul Walker. Oradell, NJ: Luna Publications, 1978

Speculation

Starlog

Starship

Stellar Gauge, The, ed. by M. J. Tolley and Kirpal Singh. Carleton, Australia: Norstrilia. 1980. 281 p.

Strange Horizons: The Spectrum of Science Fiction, by Sam Moskowitz. New York: Scribners, 1976. 298 p.

Teaching Science Fiction: Education for Tomorrow, ed. by Jack Williamson. Philadelphia: Owlswick, 1980.

Texas Fandom 1981, by Becky Matthews. Dallas: Becky Matthews, 1981. 62 p.

This World and Nearer Ones: Essays Exploring the Familiar, by B. W. Aldiss. Kent, OH: Kent State University Press, 1981. 261 p.

Those Who Can, ed. by R. S. Wilson. New York: Mentor, 1973.

Thrust

Tolkien and the Critics: Essays on J. R. R. Tolkien's The Lord of the Rings, ed. by N. D. Isaacs and R. A. Zimbardo. Notre Dame, Indiana: University of Notre Dame Press, 1968. 296 p.

Tolkien Compass, ed. by Jared Lobdell. New York: Del Rey, 1980.

Tolkien Scrapbook, ed. by Alida Becker. New York: Grossett, 1978.

Tolkien: New Critical Perspectives, ed. by N. D. Isaacs and R. A. Zimbardo. Lexington: University Press of Kentucky, 1981. 175 p.

Transcendent Adventure: Studies of Religion in Science Fiction/Fantasy, ed. by Robert Reilly. Westport: Greenwood, 1985. 266 p.

Triviale Phantasie, Die: Beitrage zur vertwertbarkeit von Science Fiction, ed. by Joerg Wiegand. Bonn: Asgard, 1976. 160 p.

Turning Points: Essays on the Art of Science Fiction, ed. by Damon Knight. New York: Harper & Row, 1977. 303 p.

Twentieth Century American Science Fiction Writers, by David Cowart and Thomas Wymer. Detroit: Gale Research, 1981. 2 v.

Twilight Zone Magazine

Ursula K. Le Guin, ed. by J. D. Olander and M. H. Greenberg. New York: Taplinger, 1979. 258 p.

Ursula K. Le Guin, ed. by Harold Bloom. New York: Chelsea House, 1986. 274 p.

Ursula K. Le Guin: Voyager to Inner Lands and Outer Space, ed. by Joe De Bolt. New York: Kennikat, 1979.

Utopia/Dystopia?, ed. by P. E. Richter. Cambridge, MA: Schenkman, 1975. 151 p.

Utopias, ed. by Peter Alexander and Roger Gill. London: Duckworth, 1984. 218 p.

Vector

Viewpoint, by Ben Bova. Cambridge, MA: NESFA, 1977. 114 p.

Visual Encyclopedia of Science Fiction, ed. by Brian Ash. New York: Harmony, 1977. 352 p.

Voice of Youth Advocates

Voices for the Future, Vol. 1, ed. by T. D. Clareson. Bowling Green, OH: Popular Press, 1976.

Voices for the Future, Vol. 2, ed. by T. D. Clareson. Bowling Green, OH: Popular Press, 1979.

Voices for the Future, Vol 3, ed. by T. D. Clareson. Bowling Green, OH: Popular Press, 1979.

Volve. Scandinavian Views on Science Fiction. Selected Papers from the Scandinavian Science Fiction Festival 1977, ed. by Cay Dollerup. Copenhagen: Dept. of English, Univ. of Copenhagen: Dept of English, Univ. of Copenhagen, 1978. 123 p. (Anglica et Americana, 4)

Vonnegut in America, ed. by Jerome Klinkowitz. New York: Delacorte, 1977. 293 p.

Vonnegut Statement, ed. by Jerome Klinkowitz. New York: Delacorte, 1973.

World Future Society. Bulletin.

Writing and Selling Science Fiction, ed. by C. L. Grant. Cincinnati: Writer's Digest, 1976.

SCIENCE FICTION AND FANTASY REFERENCE INDEX, 1878-1985

Author Entries

A

Abadi-Nagy, Zoltan

"Skillful Seducer: of Vonnegut's brand of comedy, The," <u>Hungarian Studies in English</u> 8:45-56. December 1974.

Abbott, L. B.

"Magic for the 23rd century," <u>American Cinematographer</u> 57(6):642-643, 676-677, 700-701. June 1976.

Abby, Karen

"Science Fiction and fantasy: a collection proposal," <u>Wilson Library Bulletin</u> 55(8): 584-588. April 1981.

Abraham, Pierre

"Entretiens sur la science fiction," <u>Europe</u> No. 35:139-140. 1957.

Abrahm, P. M.

"Tik-Tok and the Three Laws of Robotics," by P. M. Abrahm and Stuart Kenter. <u>Science-Fiction Studies</u> 5(1): 67-80. March 1978.

Abramson, Marcia

"Vonnegut: humor with suffering," <u>Michigan Daily</u> (Ann Arbor) p. 2. January 22, 1969.

Abrash, Merritt

"Dante's Hell as an Ideal Mechanical Environment," in: Erlich, Richard D., ed. <u>Clockwork Worlds</u>. Westport, CT: Greenwood, 1983. pp. 21-26.

"Elusive Utopias: Societies as Mechanisms in the Early Fiction of Philip K. Dick," in: Erlich, Richard D., ed. <u>Clockwork Worlds</u>. Westport, CT: Greenwood, 1983. pp. 115-123.

"Hubris of Science: Wells' Time Traveler," in: Hassler, Donald M. <u>Patterns of the Fantastic II</u>. Mercer Island, WA: Starmont, 1984. pp. 5-12.

"Is there life after immortality?" in: Yoke, C. B. and Hassler, D. M., eds. <u>Death and the Serpent</u>. Westport, CT: Greenwood, 1985. pp. 19-28.

"Le Guin's 'The field of vision': a minority view on ultimate truth," <u>Extrapolation</u> 26(1): 5-15. Spring 1985.

"Missing the point in More's <u>Utopia</u>," <u>Extrapolation</u> 19(1):27-38. December 1977.

"Robert Silverberg's <u>The World Inside</u>," in: Rabkin, Eric S., et. al., eds. <u>No Place Else</u>. Carbondale: Southern Illinois University Press, 1983. pp. 225-243.

Abret, Helga

<u>Jahrhundert der Marsianer</u>, by Helga Abret and Lucian Boia. Munich: Heyne, 1984. 366 p.

"Herbert W. Frankes Roman Ypsilon Minus-eine negative Utopie?" in: Rottensteiner, Franz, ed. <u>Polaris 6</u>. Frankfurt-am-Main: Suhrkamp, 1982. pp. 287-300.

"Treffpunkt Mond: Zu Henri Stahls 'astronomischem Roman' <u>Ein Rumane auf dem Mond</u>," by Helga Abret and Lucian Boia. <u>Quarber Merkur</u> 55:3-13. July 1981.

Ackerman, F. J.

<u>Reference Guide to American Science Fiction Films, Volume 1</u>, by A. W. Strickland and F. J. Ackerman. Bloomington, IN: T. I. S., 1981. 397 p.

"<u>Weekend Magazine</u>: a checklist of <u>New York Post</u> science fiction," <u>Fantasy Times</u> No. 223:5. May (2) 1955.

"Bob Olsen dead at 71," <u>Fantasy Times</u> No. 248:1,6. June (1) 1956.

"Bradbury's Best," <u>Starlog</u> 84: 65, 96. July 1984.

1

Ackerman, F. J. (Continued)

"Brave nude world," <u>American Sunbather</u> 13(8):16-19. August 1961.

"Fantasy Foundation: Forrest J. Ackerman's Archive of the Fantastic," <u>Special Collections</u> 2(1/2): 111-118. Fall/Winter 1982.

"Karloff succumbs at 81," <u>Science Fiction Times</u> No. 464:1-4. March 1969.

"Lon Chaney's 100th Birthday," <u>Fantasy Newsletter</u> 6(5): 17. May 1983.

"Monsters made me," <u>Science Fiction Times</u> No. 369:24-26. September 1961.

"None came back, except Ack; on Rocketship XM," <u>Fantasy Times</u> No. 101:6. March (1) 1950.

"On Ray Cummings," <u>Fantasy Times</u> No. 265:1-2. February (2) 1957.

"Russian chronicles," <u>Science Fiction Chronicle</u> 4(1):9-10. October 1982.

"Saga of Shibano, The," <u>Science Fiction Times</u> No. 459:5,8. October 1968.

"Science fiction marquee: 1956," in: <u>Science Fiction Yearbook, 1957 Edition</u>. Vol. 1. Patterson, NJ: Fandom House, 1957. pp. 18-19.

"Science fiction, messenger of light," <u>Fantasy Times</u> No. 221:3-5. April (2) 1955.

"Week-end Magazine," <u>Fantasy Times</u> No. 245:5. April (2) 1956.

Adair, S. A.

<u>Science Fiction in Elementary Science Education</u>. Ph. D. Dissertation, Temple University, 1983. 186 p. (DAI 44: 68A)

Adam, Vera

"Once Upon a Time There Will Be...: Children as Science Fiction Readers and Writers," <u>Romanian Review</u> No. 1: 86-89. 1981.

Adamo, Susan

"Distant Stars: A New Approach to Illustrated Science Fiction," <u>Starlog</u> 52: 32-33. November 1981.

"Douglas Adams," <u>Starlog</u> 47: 28-30. June 1981.

"Here Comes the Greatest American Hero," <u>Starlog</u> 46: 29-30. May 1981.

"Starlog Interview: Mark Hamill," <u>Starlog</u> 65: 18-22. December 1982.

"Starlog Interview: Peter Barton," <u>Starlog</u> 64: 27-29. November 1982.

"Vincent DiFate," <u>Starlog</u> 48: 52-55. July 1981.

Adams, Claude

"Science fiction: more to it than meets the eye," <u>The Gazette</u> (Montreal) p. 45. October 9, 1971.

Adams, John

"Hal Hall and the Science Fiction Book Review Index," <u>Science Fiction Times (Boston)</u> 1(10): 7-8. 1981.

"Linkages: science fiction and science fantasy," <u>School Library Journal</u> 26(9): 23-28. May 1980.

Adams, Marion

"You've come a long way since Shortridge High, Kurt Vonnegut, jr.," <u>Indianapolis</u> p. 27-33. October 1976.

Adams, Phoebe

"Potpourri," (book review column.) <u>Atlantic</u> 192:120. January 1964.

Adams, R. M.

"H. G. Wells reconsidered," <u>Scientific American</u> 217:124-129. 1967.

"Hobbit Habit," in: Isaacs, N. D. <u>Tolkien: New Critical Perspectives</u>, ed. by N. D. Isaacs and R. A. Zimbardo. Lexington: University Press of Kentucky, 1981. pp. 168-175.

Adams, Robert

"Horseclans and me," <u>Empire: For the SF Writer</u> 3(4): 11. April 1978.

Adams, W. C.

"Before and After 'The Day After': a nationwide survey of a movie's impact," ERIC ED 245 288. 22 p. May 1984.

Adams, William

"Television vs. Science Fiction," <u>Questar</u> 3(2): 37, 57-58, 71. December 1980.

Adcock, Craig

"Dada cyborgs and the imagery of science fiction," Arts Magazine 58(2):66-71. October 1983.

Adcox, John

"Starlog Profile: Lloyd Alexander," Starlog No. 101: 40-41. December 1985.

Addeler, Geoffrey

"Faust in the Labyrinth: Burgess' Earthly Powers," Modern Fiction Studies 27(3): 517-531. Autumn 1981.

Adelberth, R.

"Science fiction; aventyrs-romanens renassans?" Biblioteksbladet 36(3):130-138. 1951.

Aden, R. C.

"Sociology taught by fiction," Social Studies 47(1):30. January 1956.

Adkins, N. F.

"Early American story of utopia, An," Colophon n.s. 1:123-132. Summer 1935.

"Introduction," in: Griffith, Mary. Three Hundred Years Hence. Boston: Gregg, 1975. pp. 5-20. (Introduction reprinted from Colophon, Summer 1935.)

Adkins, P. H.

Edgar Rice Burroughs Bibliography and Price Guide. New Orleans: P.D.A. Enterprises, 1974. 25 p.

"David H. Keller as pulp writer," in: Keller, D. H. The Human Termites. New Orleans: P.D.A. Enterprises, 1979. pp. 5-15.

Adlard, Mark

"Billion Year Spree; a labour of love," Foundation 6:61-69. May 1974.

"British SF: a British view of the American view," Vector 82:17. July/August 1977.

"D. G. Compton and new standards of excellence," Vector 66: 29-33. July/August 1973.

"Peter Tate: an interview," Vector 61: 24-27. September/October 1972.

"When work will have to be invented," International Management 28:54-56. May 1973.

Adler, Alan

Science Fiction and Horror Movies: Posters in Full Color. New York: Dover, 1977. 40 p.

Adler, Dick

"One man's monstrous menagerie,", The Daily Telegraph Magazine No. 492:29-33. April 10, 1974.

Adomites, P. D.

"Confessions of a special effects junkie," Questar 1(4):26-27. August 1979.

"Portrait: Caroline Munro," by P. D. Adomites and Tom Sciacca. Questar 2(3):34-41. June 1980.

"Retrospective: Night of the Living Dead," Questar 3(1):40-51. October 1980.

Agel, Jerome

Making of Kubrick's 2001, The. New York: New American Library, 1970. 367 p.

Aggeler, Geoffrey

Anthony Burgess: the artist as novelist. University: University of Alabama Press, 1979. 245 p.

"Wagnerian affirmation: Anthony Burgess's The Worm and the Ring," Western Humanities Review 27(4):401-410. Autumn 1973.

Ahearn, M. L.

"Science fiction in the mainstream novel: Doris Lessing," Extrapolation 20(4):355-367. Winter 1979.

Aho, G. L.

William Morris: A Reference Guide. Boston: G. K. Hall, 1985. 428 p.

Aiken, Joan

"Between Family and Fantasy," in: Haviland, Virginia, ed. The Openhearted Audience: Ten Authors Talk About Writing For Children. Washington, D. C.: Library of Congress, 1980. pp. 47-68.

Airey, Jean

"John Nathan-Turner's Who Confessions," by Jean Airey and Laurie Haldeman. Starlog No. 101: 49. December 1985.

Akey, Craig

"Getting it off the ground," _Wisconsin English Journal_ 18(3):9-12. April, 1976.

Akien, Arnold

"You Can Get There From Here," _Vector_ 101: 14-17. April 1981.

Albanese, J. S.

"Deviance in Utopia: the criminology of ideal society," _World Future Society Bulletin_. 16(1): 25-29. January/February 1982.

"Deviance in Utopia: The Criminology of Ideal Society," _World Future Society Bulletin_ 16(1): 25-29. January/February 1982.

Alberes, R. M.

"Faillite de la fiction scientifique," _Combat_ November 21, 1957.

Albrecht, W. T.

William Morris' The Well at Worlds End: An Explanation and a Study. Ph.D. Dissertation, University of Pennsylvania, 1970. 219 p.

Albright, Donn

"Ray Bradbury index part III," _Xenophile_ 36:R2-R7. November 1977.

"Ray Bradbury...index continued," _Xenophile_ 3(1):4-10. 1976.

Albright, William

"'Star Trek' Role Eclipses Koenig's Many Talents," _Houston Post_ Sec. E, p. 6. May 22, 1982.

Alcorn, Noeline

"Exploring our future: a look at science fiction," _Children's Literature Association Yearbook_ 1978. p. 37-45.

Aldani, Lino

Fantascienza, La. Piacenza: Tribuna, 1962.

Alderson, J. J.

"Trek of Burke and Wills, or, the triumphant march of Australian science fiction," _Aussiecon Fifth Anniversary Memorial Fanzine_ Vol. 2, pp. 5-7. January 1981.

Aldiss, B. W.

Billion Year Spree: The History of Science Fiction. London: Weidenfield, 1973. 339 p.; Garden City, NY: Doubleday, 1973. 456 p.

Hell's Cartographers: Some Personal Histories of Science Fiction Writers, ed. by B. W. Aldiss and Harry Harrison. London: Weidenfield, 1975. 246 p.

Pale Shadow of Science, The. Seattle: Serconia, 1985. 128 p.

Science Fiction Art. New York: Bounty, 1975. 128 p.

Science Fiction Art: The Fantasies of SF. New York: Crown, 1975. 128 p.

Science Fiction as Science Fiction. SL: Bran's Head, 1978. 39 p.

This World and Nearer Ones: Essays Exploring the Familiar. Kent, OH: Kent State University Press, 1981. 261 p.

"Dracula," in: Magill, Frank N., ed. _Survey of Modern Fantasy Literature_, Vol 1. Englewood Cliffs, NJ: Salem Press, Inc., 1983. pp. 404-409.

"Halcyon Drift," in: Magill, Frank N., ed. _Survey of Science Fiction Literature_, Vol. 2. Englewood Cliffs, NJ: Salem Press, 1979. pp. 936-939.

"Something Else," in: Tymn, M. B. and Ashley, Mike. _Science Fiction, Fantasy, and Weird Fiction Magazines._ Westport, CT: Greenwood, 1985. pp. 579-580.

"1951: Yesterday's Festival of the Future," in: Aldiss, B. W. _This World and Nearer Ones._ Kent, OH: Kent State University Press, 1981. pp. 129-132.

"After the Renaissance," _Vector_ 75: 47-50. July 1975.

"Art of SF magazine covers," _Private Library_ Series 2, V. 2:47-53. Summer 1969.

"At fandom," _New Statesman_ 95(2456):505. April 14, 1978.

"Atheist's Tragedy Revisited," in: Aldiss, B. W. _The Pale Shadow of Science._ Seattle: Serconia, 1985. pp. 91-93.

"Author's choice," _Vector_ 63: 29-31. January/February 1973.

"Barefoot: Its First Decade," in: Aldiss, B. W. _This World and Nearer Ones._ Kent, OH: Kent State University Press, 1981. pp. 86-89.

"Billion Year Spree," _Bookseller._ p. 108- . July 14, 1973. (Not seen)

Aldiss, B. W. (Continued)

"Billion year spree: I, Origin of the species," Extrapolation 14(2):167-191. May 1973.

"Blish and the mathematics of knowledge," in: Tolley, M. J., ed. The Stellar Guage. Carleton, Australia: Norstrilia, 1980. pp. 135-149.

"Brief History," in: Wingrove, David, ed. The Science Fiction Source Book. New York: Van Nostrand, 1984. pp. 9-20.

"British science fiction now," SF Horizons 2:13-37. Winter 1965.

"Burroughs: Less Lucid Than Lucian," in: Aldiss, B. W. This World and Nearer Ones. Kent, OH: Kent State University Press, 1981. pp. 198-200.

"California, Where They Drink Buck Rogers," in: Aldiss, B. W. This World and Nearer Ones. Kent, OH: Kent State University Press, 1981. pp. 220-223.

"Chinese perspective," Locus 12(11):1,12. December 1979.

"Conjuring Helliconia," Locus 18(3): 17-19. March 1985.

"Construzione di Helliconia, la," Cosmo informatore 14(3):14-16. Fall 1985.

"Cultural Totems in the Soviet Union," in: Aldiss, B. W. This World and Nearer Ones. Kent, OH: Kent State University Press, 1981. pp. 233-248.

"Dick's maledictory web," in: Aldiss, B. W. This World and Nearer Ones. Kent, OH: Kent State University Press, 1981. pp. 51-58. also in: Greenberg, M. H., ed. Philip K. Dick. NY: Taplinger, 1982. pp. 97-104.

"Dick's maledictory web: about and around Martian Time-Slip," Science Fiction Studies 2(1):42-47. March 1975.

"Distinguished Authors From the 'Foreign' Lands," Vector 105: 21-22. December 1981.

"Downward Journey: Orwell's 1984," Extrapolation 25(1): 5-11. Spring 1984. also in: Aldiss, B. W. The Pale Shadow of Science. Seattle: Serconia, 1985. pp. 61-69.

"Drei Ansichten des Films Solaris: Symbole der Verganglichkeit," Quarber Merkur 38:56-59. November 1974.

"Early one Oxford morning," Vector 69: 11-14. Summer 1975.

"Edmund Crispin: an appreciation," Locus 12(2):6. February 1979.

"Ever Since the Enlightenment," in: Aldiss, B. W. This World and Nearer Ones. Kent, OH: Kent State University Press, 1981. pp. 18-36.

"Fame and Helliconia," Focus: An SF Writer's Magazine 7: 27-29. Spring 1983.

"Film Tarkovsky Made, The," in: Aldiss, B. W. This World and Nearer Ones. Kent, OH: Kent State University Press, 1981. pp. 162-169.

"Fireby-Wireby Book," in: Aldiss, B. W. This World and Nearer Ones. Kent, OH: Kent State University Press, 1981. pp. 143-147.

"Flight Into Tomorrow," in: Aldiss, B. W. This World and Nearer Ones. Kent, OH: Kent State University Press, 1981. pp. 195-197.

"From History to Timelessness," in: Aldiss, B. W. This World and Nearer Ones. Kent, OH: Kent State University Press, 1981. pp. 120-124.

"Future and alternative histories," in: Ash, Brian, ed. Visual Encyclopedia of Science Fiction. New York: Harmony, 1977. pp. 116-123.

"Gulf and the Forest, The: Contemporary SF in Britain," Magazine of Fantasy and Science Fiction 54(4):4-11. April 1978.

"Gulf and the Forest: Contemporary SF in Britain," in: Aldiss, B. W. This World and Nearer Ones. Kent, OH: Kent State University Press, 1981. pp. 90-101.

"Guru number four," Summary 1(2):63-68. 1971.

"H. G. Well's 15re," in: Rejser i tid og rum. En Bog om science fiction, ed. by Tage La Cour. Copenhagen: Stig Verdelkaer, 1973.

"H. G. Wells," in: Bleiler, E. F., ed. Science Fiction Writers. New York: Scribners, 1982. pp. 25-30.

"Hand in the jar, The: metaphor in Wells and Huxley," Foundation 17:26-31. September 1979.

"Hashish Club," in: Aldiss, B. W. This World and Nearer Ones. Kent, OH: Kent State University Press, 1981. pp. 125-128.

"Helliconia: How and Why," in: Aldiss, B. W. The Pale Shadow of Science. Seattle: Serconia, 1985. pp. 121-128.

"Hiroshima Man," in: Aldiss, B. W. This World and Nearer Ones. Kent, OH: Kent State University Press, 1981. pp. 112-119.

"How We Work: Brian Aldiss," in: Aldiss, Brian. Hell's Cartographers, ed. by B. W. Aldiss and Harry Harrison. London: Weidenfeld and Nicholson, 1975. pp. 233-237.

Aldiss, B. W. (Continued)

"Immanent Will Returns," in: Aldiss, B. W. _The Pale Shadow of Science_. Seattle: Serconia, 1985. pp. 51-60.

"In memoriam: James Blish," _Extrapolation_ 17(1):5-7. December 1975.

"It Catechised From Outer Space: Politics in SF," in: Aldiss, B. W. _This World and Nearer Ones_. Kent, OH: Kent State University Press, 1981. pp. 188-193.

"James Blish and the Mathematics of Knowledge," in: Aldiss, B. W. _This World and Nearer Ones_. Kent, OH: Kent State University Press, 1981. pp. 37-50.

"James Blish: the mathematics of behavior," _Foundation_ 13:43-51. May 1978.

"Judgement at Jonbar," _SF Horizons_ 1:13-37. Spring 1964.

"Kissingers Have Long Ears," in: Aldiss, B. W. _This World and Nearer Ones_. Kent, OH: Kent State University Press, 1981. pp. 170-172.

"Long Cut to Burma," in: Aldiss, B. W. _The Pale Shadow of Science_. Seattle: Serconia, 1985. pp. 17-25.

"Looking Forward to 2001," in: Aldiss, B. W. _This World and Nearer Ones_. Kent, OH: Kent State University Press, 1981. pp. 104-110.

"Magic and Bare Boards," in: Aldiss, B. W. _Hell's Cartographers_, ed. by B. W. Aldiss and Harry Harrison. London: Weidenfeld and Nicholson, 1975. pp. 173-209.

"Man who could work miracles," _Vector_ 65:23-32. May/June 1973.

"Mary Wollstonecraft Shelley," in: Bleiler, E. F., ed. _Science Fiction Writers_. New York: Scribners, 1982. pp. 3-9.

"Modest Atmosphere With Monsters," in: Aldiss, B. W. _This World and Nearer Ones_. Kent, OH: Kent State University Press, 1981. pp. 224-232.

"Monster for All Seasons," in: Aldiss, B. W. _The Pale Shadow of Science_. Seattle: Serconia, 1985. pp. 105-120. also in: Wolfe, Gary. _Science Fiction Dialogues_. Chicago: Academy Chicago, 1982. pp. 9-23.

"Nesvadba: In the Footprints of the Admirable Capek," in: Aldiss, B. W. _This World and Nearer Ones_. Kent, OH: Kent State University Press, 1981. pp. 64-68.

"Old Bessie," in: Aldiss, B. W. _The Pale Shadow of Science_. Seattle: Serconia, 1985. pp. 27-34.

"On being a literary pariah," _Extrapolation_ 17(2):168-171. May 1976.

"On the age of the term 'science fiction'," _Science Fiction Studies_ 3(2):213. July 1976. Comment: S. Moskowitz. SFS 3(3):312-313. N. 1976.

"One that could control the moon: science fiction plain and coloured," _International Literary Annual_ No. 3:176-189. 1961.

"Origin of the species," in: McNelly, W. E., ed. _Science Fiction the Academic Awakening_. Shreveport, LA: CEA, 1974. pp. 35-37.

"Pale Shadow of Science," in: Aldiss, B. W. _The Pale Shadow of Science_. Seattle: Serconia, 1985. pp. 95-104.

"Peep," in: Aldiss, B. W. _The Pale Shadow of Science_. Seattle: Serconia, 1985. pp. 79-83.

"Philip K. Dick: A Whole New Can of Worms," _Foundation_ 26: 11-14. October 1982.

"Pilgrim Award: acceptance speech," in: Remington, T. J., ed. _Selected Proceedings of the 1978 Science Fiction Research Association National Conference_. Cedar Falls: Univ. of Northern Iowa. 1979. p. 242-244.

"Pilgrim fathers: Lucian and all that," in: Knight, Damon, ed. _Turning Points_. New York: Harper, 1977. p. 73-95.

"Preparation for What?" in: Aldiss, B. W. _The Pale Shadow of Science_. Seattle: Serconia, 1985. pp. 1-15.

"Profession of science fiction, VII: magic and bare boards," _Foundation_ 6:6-31. May 1974.

"Robots: Low-Voltage Ontological Currents," in: Dunn, Thomas P., ed. _The Mechanical God_. Westport: Greenwood, 1982. pp. 3-9.

"Science fiction as empire," _Algol_ 20:18-21. May 1973.

"Science Fiction Markets," _Author_ 86:131-134. Winter 1975.

"Science Fiction's Mother Figure," in: Aldiss, B. W. _The Pale Shadow of Science_. Seattle: Serconia, 1985. pp. 37-49.

"SF and HG," _Arena SF_ 13: 4-8. 1982.

"SF art," in: _The Saturday Book, 24_. New York: Macmillan, 1964. p. 170-183.

"SF Art: Strangeness With Beauty," in: Aldiss, B. W. _This World and Nearer Ones_. Kent, OH: Kent State University Press, 1981. pp. 148-162.

"SF Conferences in Poznan and Dublin," _Science Fiction Studies_ 4(2):211-212. July 1977.

"SF Market Today," _Bookseller_ 3116:1452. September 11, 1965.

Author Entries

Aldiss, B. W. (Continued)

"SF: serious, popular, and S-and-S," London Magazine 10:74-78. April 1970.

"Sleazo Inputs I Have Known," in: Aldiss, B. W. This World and Nearer Ones. Kent, OH: Kent State University Press, 1981. pp. 182-187.

"Sower of the Systems: Some Paintings by G. F. Watts," in: Aldiss, B. W. This World and Nearer Ones. Kent, OH: Kent State University Press, 1981. pp. 136-142.

"Spielberg: When the Mundane Breaks Down," in: Aldiss, B. W. This World and Nearer Ones. Kent, OH: Kent State University Press, 1981. pp. 173-180.

"Sturgeon remembered," Vector No. 127: 1. August/September 1985.

"Swim in Sumatra," in: Aldiss, B. W. This World and Nearer Ones. Kent, OH: Kent State University Press, 1981. pp. 249-255.

"To Barsoom and beyond," Vector 63: 7-21. January/February 1973.

"Transatlantic Harrison, Yippee!" in: Aldiss, B. W. The Pale Shadow of Science. Seattle: Serconia, 1985. pp. 85-88.

"Universe as Coal-Shuttle," in: Aldiss, B. W. This World and Nearer Ones. Kent, OH: Kent State University Press, 1981. pp. 211-217.

"Up against the Universe," Foundation 20: 9-15. October 1980.

"Verne: The Extraordinary Voyage," in: Aldiss, B. W. This World and Nearer Ones. Kent, OH: Kent State University Press, 1981. p. 69-78.

"Vonnegut: Guru Number Four," in: Aldiss, B. W. This World and Nearer Ones. Kent, OH: Kent State University Press, 1981. pp. 79-85.

"What dark non-literary passions (on the ouster of Lem from SFWA)," Science Fiction Studies 4(2):126-127. July 1977.

"Whole New Can of Worms," in: Aldiss, B. W. The Pale Shadow of Science. Seattle: Serconia, 1985. pp. 71-77.

"Why They Left Zirn Unguarded: The Stories of Robert Sheckley," in: Aldiss, B. W. This World and Nearer Ones. Kent, OH: Kent State University Press, 1981. pp. 59-63.

"Within the reach of storms," Vector 42:5-11. 1967. (also in SFWA Bulletin, August 1967.)

"Worst SF story ever published," Australian Science Fiction Review No. 15:13-15. April 1968.

"Wounded land: J. G. Ballard, The," in: Clareson, T. D., ed. SF: The Other Side of Realism. Bowling Green: Popular Press, 1971. p. 116-129.

"Yes, well, but..." in: Aldiss, B. W. This World and Nearer Ones. Kent, OH: Kent State University Press, 1981. pp. 201-210.

Aldiss, Margaret

Item Eighty-Three: Brian W. Aldiss, 1954-1972. Oxford: SF Horizons, 1973. 40 p.

Aldridge, Alexandra

Scientific Worldview in Dystopia, The. Ann Arbor: UMI Research Press, 1984. 97 p.

"Myths of origin and destiny in literature: Zamiatin's We," Extrapolation 19(1):68-75. December 1977.

"Origins of Dystopia: When the Sleeper Wakes and We," in: Erlich, Richard D., ed. Clockwork Worlds. Westport, CT: Greenwood, 1983. pp. 63-84.

"Science Fiction and Emerging Values," in: Myers, R. E., ed. The Intersection of Science Fiction and Philosophy. Westport: Greenwood, 1983. pp. 15-27.

Alessandri, Tom

"Holmes and a certain Mr. Spock," Baker Street Journal 26(1):23-25. March 1976.

Alexander, Charles

"Sculpture: science fiction machines," (Commentary on a sculpture; no content relating to SF) Leonardo 9(2):119-120. 1976.

Alexander, J. P.

"Biological Hazards of Time Travel," Aurora SF 8(3): 26-28. Winter 1982/83.

"Dinosauria, part 1: Gotterdammerung," Fantasy: A Forum for Science Fiction and Fantasy Artists. 2(4): 24-26. Winter 1980.

"Non-Human Communication," Aurora SF 7(1): 16-18. Summer 1981.

Alexander, Lloyd

"Fantasy as images; a literary view," Language Arts 55(4):440-446. April 1978.

"Flat heeled muse," Horn Book 41(2):141-145. April 1965.

Alexander, Lloyd (Continued)

"Grammer of Story, The," in: Hearne, Betsy and Kaye, Marilyn, eds. Celebrating Children's Books. New York: Lothrop, 1981. pp. 3-23.

"High fantasy and heroic romance," Horn Book 47(6):577-584. December 1971.

"Substance and fantasy," Library Journal 91(22):6157-6159. December 15, 1966.

"Truth about fantasy, The," Top of the News 24:168-174. January 1968. Excerpted: Texas Library Journal 43:101-102. Fall 1967.

"Wishful Thinking, or Hopeful Dreaming," in: Boyer, Robert H. and Zahorski, Kenneth J. Fantasists on Fantasy. New York: Avon Discus, 1984. pp. 137-150.

Alexander, Peter

Utopias, ed. by Peter Alexander and Roger Gill. London: Duckworth, 1984. 218 p.

"Grimm's Utopia: motives and justifications," in: Utopias, ed. by Peter Alexander and Roger Gill. London: Duckworth, 1984. pp. 31-42.

Alexandrescu, Sorin

"Dialektik des Phantastischen, Die," Quarber Merkur 62: 11-41. December 1984.

Alfreds, Mike

"Shared Experience: From Science Fiction to Shakespeare," by Mike Alfreds and Clive Barker. Theatre Quarterly 10(39): 12-22. 1981.

Algeo, John

"Secrets of Dr. Taverner, The," in: Magill, Frank N., ed. Survey of Modern Fantasy Literature, Vol 3. Englewood Cliffs, NJ: Salem Press, Inc., 1983. pp. 1375-1377.

"Strange Life of Ivan Osokin," in: Magill, Frank N., ed. Survey of Modern Fantasy Literature, Vol 4. Englewood Cliffs, NJ: Salem Press, Inc., 1983. pp. 1840-1842.

"Strange Story, A," in: Magill, Frank N., ed. Survey of Modern Fantasy Literature, Vol 4. Englewood Cliffs, NJ: Salem Press, Inc., 1983. pp. 1843-1847.

"Zanoni," in: Magill, Frank N., ed. Survey of Modern Fantasy Literature, Vol 5. Englewood Cliffs, NJ: Salem Press, Inc., 1983. pp. 2203-2205.

"'Haunted and the Haunters: Or, The House and the Brain, The'," in: Magill, Frank N., ed.

Survey of Modern Fantasy Literature, Vol 2. Englewood Cliffs, NJ: Salem Press, Inc., 1983. pp. 698-700.

Alkon, Paul

"Samuel Madden's Memoirs of the Twentieth Century," Science Fiction Studies 12(2): 184-201. July 1985.

Allan, Jim

Speculation on the Silmarillion. SL: S.N., no date. 20 p. (Copy in Texas A&M University SF Research Collection)

Allard, Yvon

"Merveilleux et le fantastique," Bulletin de bibliographie 5(4):783-863. January 1976.

"Roman de science fiction," Bulletin de bibliographie: Revue de bibliographie de la Centrale des bibliotheques du Quebec 5:3-84. October 1975.

Allen, D. C.

"Science and invention in Greene's prose," PMLA 53(4):1007-1018. December 1938.

Allen, Dick

"Poet looks at space, inner and outer, The," Arts in Society 6(2):185-193. Summer/Fall 1969.

"Pop ethics," Poetry 117:115-117. November 1970. (Book review of Holding your eight hands.)

"Science space speculative fantasy fiction," Yale Alumni Magazine p. 7-12. January 1971.

"What rough beast: SF-oriented poetry," Extrapolation 17(1):8-17. December 1975.

Allen, E. M.

Fellowship of Merlin: The Role of the Sorcerer in The Once and Future King and The Lord of the Rings. Master's Thesis, Baylor University, 1978. 145 p.

"Persian Influences in J. R. R. Tolkien's The Lord of the Rings," in: Reilly, Robert, ed. The Transcendent Adventure. Westport: Greenwood, 1984. pp. 189-206.

Allen, John

"Dolby sound system for recording Star Wars," American Cinematographer 58(7):709,748,761. July 1977.

Allen, L. D.

Asimov's Foundation Trilogy and Other Works.
Lincoln, Neb.: Cliffs Notes, 1977. 90 p.

Ballantine Teacher's Guide to Science
Fiction. New York: Ballantine, 1975. 346 p.

Herbert's Dune and Other Works. Lincoln, NE:
Cliffs Notes, 1975. 101 p.

Science Fiction Reader's Guide. Lincoln,
Nebraska: Centennial Press, 1974. 299 p.
(Reprint of Science Fiction: An Introduction)

Science Fiction: An Introduction. Lincoln:
Cliffs Notes, 1973. 187 p.

"Chad Oliver," in: Bleiler, E. F., ed.
Science Fiction Writers. New York:
Scribners, 1982. pp. 467-473.

"Isaac Asimov," in: Bleiler, E. F., ed.
Science Fiction Writers. New York:
Scribners, 1982. pp. 267-276.

Allen, Mel

"Witches and asprin," Writer's Digest
57(6):26-27. June 1977.

Allen, Nancy

Annotated Catalog of Unpublished Film and
Television Scripts at The University of
Illinois at Urbana-Champaign, by Nancy Allen
and R. L. Carringer. Urbana: University
Library, 1983. 129 p. (ERIC ED 233 704)

Allen, P. C.

"Fourth World Fantasy Convention," SFWA
Bulletin 14(1): 17-20. Spring 1979.

"Of swords and sorcery 3," Fantasy
Crossroads 10/11:42-46. March 1977. (Book
Reviews)

"Of swords and sorcery 4," Fantasy
Crossroads 12:21-27. November 1977. (Book
Reviews)

"Of swords and sorcery 5," Fantasy
Crossroads 13: 31-40. June 1978.

"Of swords and sorcery 6," Fantasy
Crossroads 15: 27-29. January 1979.

"Of swords and sorcery," Fantasy Crossroads
8: 40-42. May 1976.

"Of swords and sorcery: Fafhrd and the Gray
Mouser," Fantasy Crossroads 8:40-42. May
1976.

"Other health knowledge magazines,"
Science-Fiction Collector 3:40-42. 1977.

Allen, Paul

"Forgotten fantasy," Science Fiction
Collector 5:23-24. September 1977.

Allen, R. S.

Science Fiction: The Future. New York:
Harcourt, 1971. 345 p.

Allen, Thomas

"Incredible atomic muck, The," Media and
Methods 6:51-53, 70. October 1969.

"Three sci-fi films for three audiences,"
America 135(1):19-20. July 10, 1976.

Allen, Walter

"Wells, H. G.," in: Woodcock, George, ed.
20th Century Fiction. Chicago: St. James,
1985. pp. 711-716.

Alleva, Richard

"Haunting fo Julia," Cinefantastique
11(3):50. September 1981.

Allgood, D. E.

Truth in Faerie: J. R. R. Tolkien's Lord of
the Rings and The Silmarillion. Master's
Thesis, University of Idaho, 1978. 93 p.

Allott, Kenneth

Jules Verne. London: Cresset, 1940. 283 p.;
Reprinted, Port Washington, NY: Kennikat, 1970.

Alpers, H. J.

H. P. Lovecraft: der Poet des Grauens.
Meitingen: Corian, 1983. 201 p.

Isaac Asimov: der Tausendjahres-planer, ed.
by H. J. Alpers and Harald Pusch. Meitingen:
Corian, 1984. 199 p.

Lesebuch der deutschen Science Fiction 1984,
ed. by H. J. Alpers and T. M. Loock.
Meitingen: Corian, 1983. 264 p.

Lexikon der Science Fiction Literatur, ed.
by H. J. Alpers. Munchen: Heyne, 1980. 2 v.

Marion Zimmer Bradleys 'Darkover'.
Meitingen: Corian, 1983. 199 p.

Reclams Science Fiction Fuehrer, ed. by H.
J. Alpers, Werner Fuchs, R. M. Hahn and
Wolfgang Jeschke. Munich: Heyne, 1980. 503 p.

Alpers, H. J. (Continued)

Science Fiction Almanac 1986, ed. by H. J. Alpers. s.l.: Rastatt, 1985. 192 p.

"25 Jahre Science Fiction Times: the times they are a-changing," Science Fiction Times (Germany) 26(1):7-9. January 1984.

"Carson der Stuermer: Zu Burroughs' Venus-Romanen," Science Fiction Times (Bremerhaven) No. 122/123. 1971.

"Conan Schlagetot," Science Fiction Times (Bremerhaven) No. 122/123:18. 1971.

"H. G. Francis im Gespraech," by H. J. Alpers and T. M. Loock. Science Fiction Times (Germany) 25(8):5-9. August 1983.

"Lendenschurz, Doppelaxt und Magie heroic fantasy und verwandte Gattungen," in: Weigand, Jorg, ed. Die Triviale Phantasie. Bonn: Asgard, 1976. p. 29-58.

"Loincloth, double ax, and magic: 'Heroic fantasy' and related genres," Science Fiction Studies 5(1):19-32. March 1978. (Comment: N. R. Spinrad, Science Fiction Studies 5(2):198. July 1978.)

"Michael Weisser im Gesprach," by H. J. Alpers and T. M. Loock. Science Fiction Times (Germany) 25(10):5-12. October 1983.

"Reinmar Cunis im Gesprach," by H. J. Alpers and T. M. Loock. Science Fiction Times (Germany) 25(2):6-12. February 1983.

"Verne und Wells: zwei pioniere der science fiction?" in: Barmeyer, Eike, ed. Science fiction: theorie und geschichte. Munchen: Fink, 1972. p. 244-258.

Alpert, Hollis

"Day they did it," Saturday Review 45:35. February 10, 1962.

"Fantastic journey," Saturday Review 51(16):48. April 20, 1968.

"Offbeat Director in Outer Space," New York Times Magazine p. 14-15, 40-51. January 16, 1977.

Alterman, P. S.

Study of Four Science Fiction Themes and Their Function in Two Contemporary Novels. Ph.D. Dissertation, University of Denver, 1974. 247 p.

"Aliens in Golding's The Inheritors," Science-Fiction Studies 5(1):3-10. March 1978.

"Four Voices in Robert Silverberg's Dying Inside," in: Staircar, Tom, ed. Critical Encounters II. New York: Ungar, 1982. pp. 90-103.

"Neuron and Junction: Patterns of Thought in The Andromeda Strain," in: Dunn, Thomas P., ed. The Mechanical God. Westport: Greenwood, 1982. pp. 109-115.

"Of rocket and monster scholarship: class outlines," Cthulhu Calls 4(1):7-10. July 1976.

"Of rocket and monster scholarship: SF in schools," Cthulhu Calls 5(1):7-15. July 1977.

"Of rocket and monster scholarship: teaching," Cthulhu Calls 4(2)9-15. October 1976.

"Of rocket and monster scholarship; teaching SF, part 2," Cthulhu Calls 3(4):11-14. April 1976.

"Samuel R. Delany," in: Cowart, David, ed. Twentieth-Century American Science Fiction Writers, Part 1: A-L, Detroit: Gale, 1981. pp. 119-128. (Dictionary of Literary Biography, v. 8)

"Surreal translations of Samuel R. Delany, The," Science-Fiction Studies 4(1):25-34. March 1977.

"Teacher's corner: types of SF courses," Cthulhu Calls 3(2):32-35. October 1975.

"Ursula K. Le Guin: damsel with a dulcimer," in: Olander, Joseph D. and Martin Harry Greenberg, eds. Ursula K. Le Guin. New York: Taplinger, 1979. pp. 64-76.

Alting, M. C.

Het heelal van de dromers: een verkenning in de wereld van de science fiction. Amsterdam: Meulenhoff, 1978. 101 p.

Altner, Patricia

"Yarbro, Chelsea Quinn," in: Vinson, James, ed. Twentieth Century Romance and Gothic Writers. Detroit: Gale, 1982. pp. 726-728.

Altov, Genrikh

"Levels of narrative ideas: colors on the SF palette," Science-Fiction Studies 5(2):157-163. July 1978.

"Science fiction: attractions and limitations," Sputnik pp. 34-41. August 1968.

Alvarado, Manual

Doctor Who: the Unfolding Text, by John Tulloch, John and Manual Alvarado. New York: St. Martins, 1983. 342 p.

Alves, Joe

"Designing a world for UFO's, extraterrestrials, and mere mortals," American Cinematographer 59(1):34-35, 60-62,84-85. January 1978.

Amann, W. F.

"Pseudoscientific spirit in the treatment of literature, The," Journal of Higher Education 24:195-197. April 1953.

Amelio, R. J.

Hal in the Classroom: Science Fiction Films. Dayton, OH: Pflaum, 1974. 153 p.

Amis, Kingsley

New Maps of Hell: A Survey of Science Fiction. New York: Harcourt, 1960. 161 p.

"Adventures on a distant star," New York Times Book Review p. 60. November 24, 1963. (Book Review)

"Afterword," in: Wingrove, David, ed. The Science Fiction Source Book. New York: Van Nostrand, 1984. pp. 309-311.

"Cosmic despair, A," New York Times Book Review p. 6. October 22, 1967. (Book Review)

"Dracula, Frankenstein, Sons and Co.," Observer pp. 6-12. July 7, 1968. (not seen)

"Grundleggern," in: Rejser i tid og rum. En Bog om science fiction, ed. by Tage La Cour. Copenhagen: Stig Verdelkaer, 1973.

"Practical nightmare, A," Holiday 37:8-15. February 1965.

"Situation today, The," in: Fiedler, Leslie, ed. The Art of the Essay. New York: Crowell, 1969. pp. 297-313.

"Situation today, The," in: Knight, Damon, ed. Turning Points: Essays in the Art of Science Fiction. New York: Harper, 1977. pp. 100-116.

Amory, Cleveland

"Review/Star Trek," TV Guide 15(12):1. March 25, 1967.

Amory, Mary

Biography of Lord Dunsany. London: Collins, 1972. 288 p.

Anderson, Craig

Science Fiction Films of the Seventies. Jefferson, NC: McFarland, 1985. 256 p.

Anderson, Erland

"Three cheers for science fiction," College Composition and Communication 25(2):203-205. May 1974.

Anderson, H. A.

"Out-of-this-world special effects for Star Trek," by H. A. Anderson, G. D. Linwood, and Joseph Westheimer. American Cinematographer 48:714-717. October 1967.

Anderson, J. J.

"Foundation on sands, The," The Alien Critic 3(4): 23-28. November 1974.

Anderson, J. P.

Ray Bradbury's Theory of Writing: Principles and Practices. Master's Thesis, Ball State University, 1972. 70 p.

Anderson, Jack

"'The Games' Serious Science Fiction on Stage," New York Times p. H6. October 21, 1984.

Anderson, James

"Joseph Payne Brennan: An Interview," Fantasy Review 7(9): 9-10. October 1984.

Anderson, John

"Dark Crystal," Creative Computing 9(3): 168-174. March 1983.

Anderson, Jon

"NBC taking an 'Amazing' risk to win viewers," Chicago Tribune Sec. 5, p. 1, 11. September 12, 1985.

Anderson, K. A. T.

Christian Concepts and Doctrine in Selected Works of Science Fiction. Ph. D. Dissertation, University of Denver, 1981. 308 p. (DAI 42A:4829)

Anderson, Kay

"Nicholas Meyer: holding the reins on Star Trek II," Cinefantastique 12(4):14-17. May/June 1982.

"Silent Running," by Kay Anderson and Shirley Meech. Cinefantastique 2(2):8-15. Summer 1972.

"Star Trek: The Motion Picture," Cinefantastique 9(3/4):65-67. Spring 1980.

"Star Trek: The Wrath of Khan," Cinefantastique 12(5/6):51-75. July/August 1982.

"Streets of Fire," Cinefantastique 14(4/5):26-27. September 1984.

Anderson, Kristine

"Introduction: a woman's view," in: Lane, Mary E. B. Mizora: A Prophecy. Boston: Gregg, 1975. pp. xi-xiii.

Anderson, Laurie

"Letter from Smyrna," Riverside Quarterly 7(3): 189-192. May 1983.

Anderson, Leif

Index till de tio forsta argangarna av tidskriften Hapna (Arg. 1-10). Lind: Centauria, 1965. unpaged.

Index till de tio forsta argangarna av tidskriften Hapna. Supplement. (Arg. 11-13). Lind: Centauria, 1966. unpaged.

Anderson, Margo

"Spectacular visual effects for Damnation Alley," American Cinematographer 58(11):1182-1187, 1178. November 1977.

Anderson, Poul

"Adventures in futuristics," Texas Library Journal 56(2): 38-41. Spring 1980

"Art of Robert Ervin Howard," in: De Camp, L. S., ed. Blade of Conan. New York: Ace, 1979. pp. 85-89.

"Author's Choice," Vector 64: 24-26. March/April 1973.

"Concerning future histories," Science Fiction Writers of America. Bulletin. 14(3):7-14. Fall 1979.

"Concerning Jack Vance: an afterword," in: Underwood, Tim, and Miller, Chuck, eds. Jack Vance. New York: Taplinger, 1980. pp. 223-224.

"Creation of imaginary worlds, The," in: Bretnor, Reginald, ed. Science Fiction Today and Tomorrow. New York: Harper, 1974. pp. 235-258.

"Fantasy of Johannes V. Jensen," in: Schweitzer, Darrell, ed. Exploring Fantasy Worlds. San Bernardino, CA: Borgo, 1985. pp. 67-75.

"Future of mythology," Mythlore 8(2):3-5. Summer 1981.

"Geology, Meteorology, Oceanography, Geography, Nomenclature, Biology," in: Ellison, Harlan, ed. Medea. New York: Bantam, 1985. pp. 17-27.

"History and science fiction," Starship 17(1):8-14. Winter 1979-1980.

"How to build a planet," in: Knight, Damon, ed. Turning Points: Essays in the Art of Science Fiction. New York: Harper, 1977. pp. 205-214. (also in SFWA Bulletin, November 1966.)

"Introduction," in: Clement, Hal. Mission of Gravity. Boston: Gregg, 1978. pp. vii-xiii.

"John W. Campbell," Locus No. 90:4-5. July 12, 1971.

"L. Sprague de Camp: engineer and sorcerer," in: De Camp, L. S. The Best of L. Sprague de Camp. New York: Ballantine, 1978. pp. xi-xvii.

"Nebula Award science fiction, 1965-1970: the science," in: Biggle, Lloyd, ed. Nebula Award Stories Seven. New York: Harper, 1973. pp. 261-273.

"Nomenclature in science fiction," in: Grant, C. L., ed. Writing and Selling Science Fiction. Cincinnati, OH: Writers Digest, 1976. pp. 77-90.

"One Man's Work," in: Wingrove, David, ed. The Science Fiction Source Book. New York: Van Nostrand, 1984. pp. 70-71.

"Our many roads to the stars," in: Dann, Jack and George Zebrowski, eds. Faster Than Light. New York: Ace, 1976. pp. 298-313.

"Poul Anderson talar om science fiction," Algol 15(3):11-19. Summer/Fall 1978.

"Profession of science fiction: vi: entertainment, instruction or both, The?" Foundation 5:44-50. 1974.

"Richard the Lion-Hearted is alive and well in California," in: De Camp, L. S., ed. Blade of Conan. New York: Ace, 1979. pp. 275-290.

Anderson, Poul (Continued)

"Science fiction and science, part 1: reality, fiction and points between," Destinies 1(1):292-308. October 1978.

"Science fiction and science, part 3: on imaginary science," Destinies 1(3):304-320. April/June 1979.

"Science fiction and science, part 4: the science fiction in science," Destinies 1(4):304-320. August/September 1979.

"Science fiction and science, part 5: science fiction and reason," Destinies 1(5):303-320. October/December 1979.

"Spacecraft and star drives," in: Ash, Brian, ed. Visual Encyclopedia of Science Fiction. New York: Harmony, 1977. pp. 68-77.

"Star-flights and fantasies: sagas still to come," in: Bretnor, Reginald, ed. The Craft of Science Fiction. New York: Harper, 1976. pp. 22-36.

"Sublimated blood thirstiness," in: De Camp, L. S., ed. Blade of Conan. New York: Ace, 1979. pp. 233-234.

"Theorie cyclique de la science fiction", Marginal 7:201-211. 1975.

"Worth of words, The," Algol 11(2):11-12. May 1974.

"Writers: 1," Science Fiction Chronicle 6(3):22. December 1984.

Anderson, Ray

Persuasive Functions of Science Fiction: A Study of the Rhetoric of Science. Ph.D. Dissertation, University of Minnesota, 1968. 374 p.

Anderson, S. A.

"Evolutionary futurism in Stapledon's Star Maker," Process Studies 5(2): 123-128. Summer 1975.

Anderson, S. J.

"Feminism and science fiction: beyond BEMs and boobs," in: Anderson, Susan Janice, ed. Aurora: Beyond Equality. Greenwich, Connecticut: Fawcett, 1976. pp. 11-15.

Andrae, Thomas

"From Menace to Messiah: The Prehistory of the Superman in Science Fiction Literature," Discourse 2: 84-111. Summer 1980.

Andrejew, Kirill

"Sie vier Zukunften Stanislaw Lems," Quarber Merkur 41:18-27. September 1975.

Andrevon, J. P.

"Films d'aujourd'hui sur des themes de maintenant," J. P. Andrevon, Pierre Gires, and Evelyne Lowin. Cinema D'aujourd'hui. No. 7:91-98. Spring 1976.

"Reperes ideologiques pour une chronologie de la science fiction au cinema," Cinema D'aujourd'hui. No. 7:23-33. Spring 1976.

"Science fiction est-ce que c'est politique, ou pas?" Cahiers Pedagogiques 150:23-24. January 1977.

Andrews, C. S.

"Aldous Huxley: a bibliography, 1960-1964," by T. D. Clareson and C. S. Andrews. Extrapolation 6(1):2-21. December 1964.

Andrews, J. W.

"Short Fiction of Gennadiy Samoilovich Gor, The," in: Magill, Frank N., ed. Survey of Science Fiction Literature, Vol. 4. Englewood Cliffs, NJ: Salem Press, 1979. pp. 1965-1966.

Andrews, Nigel

"Space Gothic," by Nigel Andrews and Harlan Kennedy. American Film 4(5):17-22. March 1979.

Andreyev, Kirill

"Ray Bradbury," Soviet Literature Monthly 5:176-180. 1968.

Andruschak, H. J. N.

"Mythlore Issue Index, Volumes 1-7, whole numbers 1-26," by H. J. N. Andruschak and G. H. GoodKnight. Mythlore 8(1): 37-39. Spring 1981.

Anestopoulo, Catherine

"Would You Read it if it were in French?" A Foreign Fanzine 4: 36-38. August 1981.

Angelo, Les

"California scene (column)," Science Fiction Times No. 459:5,12. October 1968.

Angenot, Marc

"Absent paradigm: an introduction to the semiotics of science fiction, The," Science-Fiction Studies 6(1):9-19. March 1979. (a different version in French published in Poetique 33:74-90. 1978.)

"Emergence of the anti-utopian genre in France: Souvestre, Giraudeau, Robida, et al," Science Fiction Studies 12(2): 129-135. July 1985.

"International Bibliography of Prehistoric Fiction," by Marc Angenot and Nadia Khouri. Science-Fiction Studies 8(1): 38-53. March, 1981.

"Jules Verne and French literary criticism (II)," Science-Fiction Studies 3(1):46-49. March 1976.

"Jules Verne and French literary criticism," Science-Fiction Studies 1(1):33-37. Spring 1973.

"Jules Verne: the last happy utopianist," in: Parrinder, Patrick, ed. Science Fiction: a Critical Guide. New York: Longman, 1979. pp. 18-33.

"Not only but also: reflection on cognition and ideology in science fiction and SF criticism," by Marc Angenot and Darko Suvin. Science-Fiction Studies 6(2):168-179. July 1979.

"Science Fiction in France before Verne," Science-Fiction Studies 5(1):58-66. March 1978.

"Select bibliography of the sociology of literature, A," Science-Fiction Studies 4(3):295-308. November 1977.

Anker, Roger

"Artist's Profile: Stephen Gervais," Fantasy Review 8(10): 8-11. October 1985.

Annan, David

Cinefantastic: Beyond the Dream Machine. London: Lorrimer, 1974. 132 p.

Annas, P. J.

"Neue Welten, neue Worte: Androgynie in der Frauen-SF," in: Femistische Utopien: Aufbruch in dei postpatriarchale Gesellschaft, ed. by Barbara Holland-Cunz. Meitingen: Corian Verlag, 1985.

"New Welten, neue Worte: Androgynie in der Frauen Science Fiction," Science Fiction Times (Germany) 24(4):4-13. 1982.

"New worlds, new words: androgyny in feminist science fiction," Science-Fiction Studies 5(2):143-156. July 1978.

Anninski, L. A.

"Stanislaw Lems Das Hohe Schloss," Quarber Merkur 31:35-40. July 1972.

Ansen, David

"When You Wish Upon a Tron," Newsweek 100(1): 64-68. July 5, 1982.

Antczak, Janice

Mythos of a New Romance, The: A Critical Analysis of Science Fiction for Children as Informed by the Literary Theory of Northrop Frye. D.L.S., Columbia University, 1979. 376 p. (DAI 42:2080A)

Anthony, Piers

Index to Book Reviews in Science Fiction Magazines 1926-1963. Gainesville, Florida: Bacon, n.d. 119 p.

"Babble," Beabohema 5:9-20. 1969.

"Background of Chthon, The," Algol 14:9-14. Fall 1968.

Anton, Uwe

Seltsamen Welten des Philip K. Dick, Die. Meitingen: Corian, 1985. 160 p.

"Entropie und Hoffnung: Vier Romane von Philip K. Dick," Science Fiction Times (Germany) 27(2):4-10. February 1985.

"Philip Kendred Dick: 16.12.1928/2.3.1982," Science Fiction Times (Germany) 24(6):3. June 1982.

Apostolou, John L.

"Japanese Science Fiction in English Translation," Extrapolation 25(1): 83-86. Spring 1984.

Appel, Alfred, Jr.

"Vladimir Nabokov," Contemporary Literature 9:236-245. Spring 1968.

Appel, Benjamin

Fantastic Mirror: Science Fiction Across the Ages. New York: Pantheon, 1969. 145 p.

Apter, T. E.

Fantasy Literature.   London: Macmillan, 1982.   161 p.

Fantasy Literature: An Approach to Reality. Bloomington: Indiana University Press, 1982. 161 p.

Aquino, John

Fantasy in Literature. Washington, DC: National Education Association, 1977. 63 p.

Science Fiction as Literature. Washington, DC: National Education Association, 1976. 62 p.

"Shaw and C. S. Lewis's Space Trilogy," Shaw Review 18(1):28-32. January 1975.

Arab-Ogly, E.

"Dialoge mit der Zukunft," Quarber Merkur. No. 50:52-64. February 1979.

Arbogast, D. K.

"Science fiction and drugs,"   Fantastic 19(5):132-135. June 1970.

Arbur, Rosemarie

Leigh Brackett, Marion Zimmer Bradley, Anne McCaffrey: A Primary and Secondary Bibliography. Boston: G. K. Hall, 1982. 277 p.

Marion Zimmer Bradley. Mercer Island, WA: Starmont, 1985.   138 p.

"Darkover," in: Magill, Frank N., ed. Survey of Science Fiction Literature, Vol. 1. Englewood Cliffs, NJ: Salem Press, 1979. pp. 488-492.

"Ringworld," in: Magill, Frank N., ed. Survey of Science Fiction Literature, Vol. 4. Englewood Cliffs, NJ: Salem Press, 1979. pp. 1799-1804.

"Sword of Rhiannon, The," in: Magill, Frank N., ed.   Survey of Science Fiction Literature, Vol. 5. Englewood Cliffs, NJ: Salem Press, 1979. pp. 2201-2206.

"Ars Scientia = Ars Poetica," in: Hassler, Donald M. Patterns of the Fantastic II. Mercer Island, WA: Starmont, 1984. pp. 13-27.

"Beyond feminism, the self interest: woman's place in the work of Le Guin," in: Remington, T. J. Selected Proceedings: 1978 SFRA National Conference. Cedar Falls: Univ. of Northern Iowa, 1979. p. 146-163.

"Le Guin's 'Song' of Inmost Feminism," Extrapolation 21(3): 223-226. Fall 1980.

"Leigh Brackett: No 'Long Goodbye' Is Good Enough," in: Staircar, Tom, ed. The Feminine Eye. New York: Ungar, 1982. pp. 1-13.

"Not a genre but a movement: science fiction as a post-romantic phenomenon," Human Perspectives on Technology 7:3-6. September 1978.

"Teleology of Human Nature for Mentality?" in: Myers, R. E., ed. The Intersection of Science Fiction and Philosophy. Westport: Greenwood, 1983. pp. 71-91.

Archer, Anne

"In the Mind of Tron,"   Business Screen pp. 6-7, 42-43, 62. February/March 1982.

Archer, Dirce

"Surveying British science fiction," Astounding 52(1):135-146. September 1953. (Review Column)

Armstrong, D. D.

"Odyssey of Creative Sequel called '2010'," Milwaukee Jounal December 9, 1984. in: NewsBank. Film and Television. 72:F14-F15. January 1985.

Armytage, W. H. G.

Heavens Below: Utopian Experiments in England, 1560-1960. London: Routledge, 1961. 458 p.

Yesterday's Tomorrows: A Historical Survey of Future Societies. London: Routledge, 1968. 288 p.

"Disenchanted mechanophobes in twentieth century England," Extrapolation 9(2):33-62. 1968.

"Extrapolators and exegetes of evolution," Extrapolation 7(1):2-17. December 1965.

"Superman and the system (conclusion)," Riverside Quarterly 3(1): 44-51. August 1967.

"Superman and the system, part 2," Riverside Quarterly 3(1):44-51. August 1967.

"Superman and the system," Riverside Quarterly 2(4):232-241. March 1967.

"Utopias: the technological and educational dimension," in: Utopias, ed. by Peter Alexander and Roger Gill. London: Duckworth, 1984. pp. 85-94.

Arnold, A. M.

"Frankly Speaking: Today's Horror Movies are Just That: Horrible," <u>Seventeen</u> 41(7): 20. July 1982.

Arnold, Alan

<u>Once Upon a Galaxy: A Journal of the Making of the Empire Strikes Back.</u> New York: Ballantine/del Rey, 1980. 277 p.

"O Pioneers, or, inside I.L.M.," <u>American Cinematographer</u> 61(6):554-555. June 1980.

Arnold, Francis

"Out of this world," <u>Films and Filming</u> 9(9):14-18. June 1963.

Arnold, J. E.

"Science fiction on the drawing board: Arcturus IV project," <u>Science Digest</u> 34(3):39-43. September 1953.

Arnold, J. J.

"Rendezvous of Star Trekkies is Always Far-Out" <u>St. Louis (Mo.) Post-Dispatch</u> April 29, 1982. in: <u>NewsBank. Social Relations,</u> 3:G1. 1982.

Arnold, J. W.

"Musical Fantasy: The Little Prince," in: Slusser, George, ed. <u>Shadows of the Magic Lamp.</u> Carbondale: Southern Illinois University Press, 1985. pp. 122-140.

Arnold, John

"Movie Ticket to Immortality, A? Why Not?" <u>Miami Herald</u> July 4, 1985. in: <u>NewsBank. Film and Television.</u> 2:C2. July 1985.

Arthur, Anthony

"Uses of Bettelheim's <u>The Uses of Enchantment,</u> The" <u>Language Arts</u> 55(4):455-459. April 1978.

Arthurs, B. D.

"Interview: Terry Carr," <u>Science Fiction Review</u> 11(4): 40-42. November 1982.

Asadulleav, S.

"Naucnaja fantastika v estetike socialisticeskogo realizma," <u>Literaturnyjh Azerbajdzan</u> 10:26- . 1969.

Asahina, Robert

"On Screen: Mixed Effects," <u>New Leader</u> 65(14): 19-20. July 12-26, 1982.

Ascher, M.

"Computers in science fiction II," <u>Computers and Automation</u> 22(11):20-23. November 1973.

"Computers in science fiction," <u>Harvard Business Review</u> 41(6):40-50,188-192. November/December 1963.

"Fictional computers and their themes," <u>Computers and Automation</u> 11(12):59-66. December 1962.

Ash, Brian

<u>Faces of The Future: The Lessons of Science Fiction.</u> London: Elek, 1975. 213 p.; New York: Taplinger, 1975. 213 p.

<u>Visual Encyclopedia of Science Fiction.</u> New York: Harmony, 1977. 352 p.

<u>Who's Who in H. G. Wells.</u> London: Hamish Hamilton, 1976. 219 p.

<u>Who's Who in Science Fiction.</u> New York: Taplinger, 1976. 220 p.

"Faces of the future," <u>New Humanist</u> 90(10):335-337. February 19, 1975.

Ash, C. V.

<u>Master of Villany: A Biography of Sax Rohmer,</u> by C. V. Ash and E. S. Rohmer, ed. by R. E. Briney. Bowling Green, OH: Popular Press, 1972. 312 p.

Ash, L. M.

"WLB biography: Ray Bradbury," <u>Wilson Library Bulletin</u> 39(3):268,280. November 1964.

Asherman, Allan

<u>Making of Star Trek II: The Wrath of Khan.</u> New York: Pocket Books, 1982. 223 p.

<u>Star Trek Compendium, The.</u> New York: Simon and Schuster, 1981. 187 p.

Ashley, L. F.

"Children's reading interests and individualized reading," <u>Elementary English</u> 47(8):1088-1095. December 1970.

Ashley, Mike

Complete Index to Astounding/Analog, by Mike Ashley with Terry Jeeves. Oak Forest, IL: Weinberg, 1981. 253 p.

Fantasy Readers Guide to Ramsey Campbell. Wallsend: Cosmos Literary Agency, 1980. 62 p.

History of the Science Fiction Magazines, The: Part 1, 1926-1935. London: New English Library, 1974. 239 p.

History of the Science Fiction Magazines, The: Part 2, 1936-1945, by Mike Ashley. London: New English Library, 1975. 298 p.

History of the Science Fiction Magazines, The: Part 3, 1946-1955, by Mike Ashley. London: New English Library, 1976. 349 p.

History of the Science Fiction Magazines, The: Part 4, 1956-1965, by Mike Ashley. London: New English Library, 1978. 288 p.

Illustrated Book of Science Fiction Lists. London: Virgin Books, 1982. 190 p.

Illustrated Science Fiction Book of Lists. New York: Cornerstone Library, 1982. 190 p.

Monthly Terrors: An Index to the Weird Fantasy Magazines Published in the United States and Great Britain, by F. H. Parnell and Mike Ashley. Westport, CT: Greenwood, 1985. 602 p.

Science Fiction, Fantasy, and Weird Fiction Magazines, ed. by M. B. Tymn and Mike Ashley. Westport, CT: Greenwood, 1985. 970 p.

Who's Who in Horror and Fantasy Fiction. London: Elm Tree, 1977. 240 p.

Who's Who in Horror and Fantasy Fiction. New York: Taplinger, 1978. 240 p.

"Ace Mystery," in: Tymn, M. B. and Ashley, Mike. Science Fiction, Fantasy, and Weird Fiction Magazines. Westport, CT: Greenwood, 1985. pp. 6-7.

"Ad Astra," in: Tymn, M. B. and Ashley, Mike. Science Fiction, Fantasy, and Weird Fiction Magazines. Westport, CT: Greenwood, 1985. pp. 7-9.

"Adventures in Horror," by Mike Ashley and Frank Parnell. in: Tymn, M. B. and Ashley, Mike. Science Fiction, Fantasy, and Weird Fiction Magazines. Westport, CT: Greenwood, 1985. pp. 9-10.

"Air Wonder Stories," by Mike Ashley and R. J. Ewald. in: Tymn, M. B. and Ashley, Mike. Science Fiction, Fantasy, and Weird Fiction Magazines. Westport, CT: Greenwood, 1985. pp. 10-12.

"Alien Worlds," in: Tymn, M. B. and Ashley, Mike. Science Fiction, Fantasy, and Weird Fiction Magazines. Westport, CT: Greenwood, 1985. pp. 12-13.

"Amazing Science Stories," in: Tymn, M. B. and Ashley, Mike. Science Fiction, Fantasy, and Weird Fiction Magazines. Westport, CT: Greenwood, 1985. pp. 14.

"Amazing Stories," in: Tymn, M. B. and Ashley, Mike. Science Fiction, Fantasy, and Weird Fiction Magazines. Westport, CT: Greenwood, 1985. pp. 14-49.

"American Science Fiction Magazine," by Graham Stone and Mike Ashley. in: Tymn, M. B. and Ashley, Mike. Science Fiction, Fantasy, and Weird Fiction Magazines. Westport, CT: Greenwood, 1985. pp. 59-60.

"Analog Science Fiction/Science Fact," by A. I. Berger and Mike Ashley. in: Tymn, M. B. and Ashley, Mike. Science Fiction, Fantasy, and Weird Fiction Magazines. Westport, CT: Greenwood, 1985. pp. 60-103.

"Andromeda," in: Tymn, M. B. and Ashley, Mike. Science Fiction, Fantasy, and Weird Fiction Magazines. Westport, CT: Greenwood, 1985. pp. 783-784.

"Anduril," in: Tymn, M. B. and Ashley, Mike. Science Fiction, Fantasy, and Weird Fiction Magazines. Westport, CT: Greenwood, 1985. pp. 813.

"Argosy and All Story," in: Tymn, M. B. and Ashley, Mike. Science Fiction, Fantasy, and Weird Fiction Magazines. Westport, CT: Greenwood, 1985. pp. 103-108.

"Argosy Special," in: Tymn, M. B. and Ashley, Mike. Science Fiction, Fantasy, and Weird Fiction Magazines. Westport, CT: Greenwood, 1985. pp. 108-109.

"Astounding Stories Yearbook," in: Tymn, M. B. and Ashley, Mike. Science Fiction, Fantasy, and Weird Fiction Magazines. Westport, CT: Greenwood, 1985. pp. 123-124.

"Authentic Science Fiction," in: Tymn, M. B. and Ashley, Mike. Science Fiction, Fantasy, and Weird Fiction Magazines. Westport, CT: Greenwood, 1985. pp. 124-127.

"Beyond Infinity," in: Tymn, M. B. and Ashley, Mike. Science Fiction, Fantasy, and Weird Fiction Magazines. Westport, CT: Greenwood, 1985. pp. 142-143.

"Bizarre Fantasy Tales," in: Tymn, M. B. and Ashley, Mike. Science Fiction, Fantasy, and Weird Fiction Magazines. Westport, CT: Greenwood, 1985. pp. 145-146.

"Bizarre Mystery Magazine," in: Tymn, M. B. and Ashley, Mike. Science Fiction, Fantasy, and Weird Fiction Magazines. Westport, CT: Greenwood, 1985. pp. 146-147.

Ashley, Mike (Continued)

"Black Cat (1895-1923), in: Tymn, M. B. and Ashley, Mike. Science Fiction, Fantasy, and Weird Fiction Magazines. Westport, CT: Greenwood, 1985. pp. 147-149.

"Black Cat (1970-)," by Mike Ashley and F. H. Parnell. in: Tymn, M. B. and Ashley, Mike. Science Fiction, Fantasy, and Weird Fiction Magazines. Westport, CT: Greenwood, 1985. pp. 149-150.

"Book of Terror," by Mike Ashley and F. H. Parnell. in: Tymn, M. B. and Ashley, Mike. Science Fiction, Fantasy, and Weird Fiction Magazines. Westport, CT: Greenwood, 1985. pp. 150-151.

"Book of Weird Tales," in: Tymn, M. B. and Ashley, Mike. Science Fiction, Fantasy, and Weird Fiction Magazines. Westport, CT: Greenwood, 1985. pp. 151-152.

"Brief Fantastic Tales," by Grant Thiessen and Mike Ashley. in: Tymn, M. B. and Ashley, Mike. Science Fiction, Fantasy, and Weird Fiction Magazines. Westport, CT: Greenwood, 1985. pp. 152-153.

"Captain Future," by Mike Ashley and Robert Ewald. in: Tymn, M. B. and Ashley, Mike. Science Fiction, Fantasy, and Weird Fiction Magazines. Westport, CT: Greenwood, 1985. pp. 155-157.

"Centaur, The," in: Magill, Frank N., ed. Survey of Modern Fantasy Literature, Vol 1. Englewood Cliffs, NJ: Salem Press, Inc., 1983. pp. 217-221.

"Chillers," in: Tymn, M. B. and Ashley, Mike. Science Fiction, Fantasy, and Weird Fiction Magazines. Westport, CT: Greenwood, 1985. pp. 161-162.

"Chrysalis," in: Tymn, M. B. and Ashley, Mike. Science Fiction, Fantasy, and Weird Fiction Magazines. Westport, CT: Greenwood, 1985. pp. 784-785.

"Cosmic Science Stories," in: Tymn, M. B. and Ashley, Mike. Science Fiction, Fantasy, and Weird Fiction Magazines. Westport, CT: Greenwood, 1985. pp. 168.

"Cosmos Science Fiction and Fantasy Magazine (1953-1954)," in: Tymn, M. B. and Ashley, Mike. Science Fiction, Fantasy, and Weird Fiction Magazines. Westport, CT: Greenwood, 1985. pp. 170-173.

"Coven 13," in: Tymn, M. B. and Ashley, Mike. Science Fiction, Fantasy, and Weird Fiction Magazines. Westport, CT: Greenwood, 1985. pp. 175-178,

"Cypher," in: Tymn, M. B. and Ashley, Mike. Science Fiction, Fantasy, and Weird Fiction Magazines. Westport, CT: Greenwood, 1985. pp. 816.

"Dark Horizons," by Mike Ashley and J. L. Sanders. in: Tymn, M. B. and Ashley, Mike. Science Fiction, Fantasy, and Weird Fiction Magazines. Westport, CT: Greenwood, 1985. pp. 816-817.

"Destinies," in: Tymn, M. B. and Ashley, Mike. Science Fiction, Fantasy, and Weird Fiction Magazines. Westport, CT: Greenwood, 1985. pp. 785-788.

"Dime Mystery Magazine," in: Tymn, M. B. and Ashley, Mike. Science Fiction, Fantasy, and Weird Fiction Magazines. Westport, CT: Greenwood, 1985. pp. 180-183.

"Dynamic Science Fiction," in: Tymn, M. B. and Ashley, Mike. Science Fiction, Fantasy, and Weird Fiction Magazines. Westport, CT: Greenwood, 1985. pp. 196-198.

"Education of Uncle Paul, The," in: Magill, Frank N., ed. Survey of Modern Fantasy Literature, Vol 1. Englewood Cliffs, NJ: Salem Press, Inc., 1983. pp. 468-471.

"Eerie Mysteries," in: Tymn, M. B. and Ashley, Mike. Science Fiction, Fantasy, and Weird Fiction Magazines. Westport, CT: Greenwood, 1985. pp. 201-202.

"Eerie Stories," in: Tymn, M. B. and Ashley, Mike. Science Fiction, Fantasy, and Weird Fiction Magazines. Westport, CT: Greenwood, 1985. pp. 202-203.

"Erotic Science Fiction Stories," in: Tymn, M. B. and Ashley, Mike. Science Fiction, Fantasy, and Weird Fiction Magazines. Westport, CT: Greenwood, 1985. pp. 204-205.

"Etchings and Odysseys," in: Tymn, M. B. and Ashley, Mike. Science Fiction, Fantasy, and Weird Fiction Magazines. Westport, CT: Greenwood, 1985. pp. 205-206.

"Eternity Science Fiction," in: Tymn, M. B. and Ashley, Mike. Science Fiction, Fantasy, and Weird Fiction Magazines. Westport, CT: Greenwood, 1985. pp. 206-208.

"Extro Science Fiction," in: Tymn, M. B. and Ashley, Mike. Science Fiction, Fantasy, and Weird Fiction Magazines. Westport, CT: Greenwood, 1985. pp. 208-209.

"Famous Science Fiction," in: Tymn, M. B. and Ashley, Mike. Science Fiction, Fantasy, and Weird Fiction Magazines. Westport, CT: Greenwood, 1985. pp. 217-219.

"Fantastic," in: Tymn, M. B. and Ashley, Mike. Science Fiction, Fantasy, and Weird Fiction Magazines. Westport, CT: Greenwood, 1985. pp. 221-232.

"Fantastic Adventures," in: Tymn, M. B. and Ashley, Mike. Science Fiction, Fantasy, and Weird Fiction Magazines. Westport, CT: Greenwood, 1985. pp. 232-241.

Ashley, Mike (Continued)

"Fantastic Adventures Yearbook," in: Tymn, M. B. and Ashley, Mike. Science Fiction, Fantasy, and Weird Fiction Magazines. Westport, CT: Greenwood, 1985. pp. 240-241.

"Fantastic Story Quarterly," in: Tymn, M. B. and Ashley, Mike. Science Fiction, Fantasy, and Weird Fiction Magazines. Westport, CT: Greenwood, 1985. pp. 249-250.

"Fantastic Universe," in: Tymn, M. B. and Ashley, Mike. Science Fiction, Fantasy, and Weird Fiction Magazines. Westport, CT: Greenwood, 1985. pp. 250-254.

"Fantasy (1938-1939)," in: Tymn, M. B. and Ashley, Mike. Science Fiction, Fantasy, and Weird Fiction Magazines. Westport, CT: Greenwood, 1985. pp. 254-256.

"Fantasy (1946-1947)," in: Tymn, M. B. and Ashley, Mike. Science Fiction, Fantasy, and Weird Fiction Magazines. Westport, CT: Greenwood, 1985. pp.

"Fantasy Book (1981-)," in: Tymn, M. B. and Ashley, Mike. Science Fiction, Fantasy, and Weird Fiction Magazines. Westport, CT: Greenwood, 1985. pp. 264-266.

"Fantasy Fan," in: Tymn, M. B. and Ashley, Mike. Science Fiction, Fantasy, and Weird Fiction Magazines. Westport, CT: Greenwood, 1985. pp. 822-823.

"Fantasy Fiction (1950)," in: Tymn, M. B. and Ashley, Mike. Science Fiction, Fantasy, and Weird Fiction Magazines. Westport, CT: Greenwood, 1985. pp. 266-267.

"Fantasy Macabre," in: Tymn, M. B. and Ashley, Mike. Science Fiction, Fantasy, and Weird Fiction Magazines. Westport, CT: Greenwood, 1985. pp. 823.

"Fear!" in: Tymn, M. B. and Ashley, Mike. Science Fiction, Fantasy, and Weird Fiction Magazines. Westport, CT: Greenwood, 1985. pp. 272-273.

"Fireside Ghost Stories," by Mike Ashley and F. H. Parnell. in: Tymn, M. B. and Ashley, Mike. Science Fiction, Fantasy, and Weird Fiction Magazines. Westport, CT: Greenwood, 1985. pp. 273.

"Flash Gordon Strange Adventures Magazine," in: Tymn, M. B. and Ashley, Mike. Science Fiction, Fantasy, and Weird Fiction Magazines. Westport, CT: Greenwood, 1985. pp. 273-274.

"Future Fiction," in: Tymn, M. B. and Ashley, Mike. Science Fiction, Fantasy, and Weird Fiction Magazines. Westport, CT: Greenwood, 1985. pp. 277-284.

"Futurian/PseudoFuturian/Futurian War Digest/New Futurian," in: Tymn, M. B. and Ashley, Mike. Science Fiction, Fantasy, and

Weird Fiction Magazines. Westport, CT: Greenwood, 1985. pp. 825-826.

"Futuristic Science Stories," in: Tymn, M. B. and Ashley, Mike. Science Fiction, Fantasy, and Weird Fiction Magazines. Westport, CT: Greenwood, 1985. pp. 286-287.

"Futuristic Stories," in: Tymn, M. B. and Ashley, Mike. Science Fiction, Fantasy, and Weird Fiction Magazines. Westport, CT: Greenwood, 1985. pp. 287-288.

"Galileo," in: Tymn, M. B. and Ashley, Mike. Science Fiction, Fantasy, and Weird Fiction Magazines. Westport, CT: Greenwood, 1985. pp. 309-313.

"Gamma," in: Tymn, M. B. and Ashley, Mike. Science Fiction, Fantasy, and Weird Fiction Magazines. Westport, CT: Greenwood, 1985. pp. 313-314.

"Ghost Stories," in: Tymn, M. B. and Ashley, Mike. Science Fiction, Fantasy, and Weird Fiction Magazines. Westport, CT: Greenwood, 1985. pp. 315-317.

"Ghosts and Goblins," in: Tymn, M. B. and Ashley, Mike. Science Fiction, Fantasy, and Weird Fiction Magazines. Westport, CT: Greenwood, 1985. pp. 317-318.

"Golden Fleece Historical Adventure," in: Tymn, M. B. and Ashley, Mike. Science Fiction, Fantasy, and Weird Fiction Magazines. Westport, CT: Greenwood, 1985. pp. 319-320.

"Great Science Fiction," in: Tymn, M. B. and Ashley, Mike. Science Fiction, Fantasy, and Weird Fiction Magazines. Westport, CT: Greenwood, 1985. pp. 320-323.

"Gripping Terror," by Mike Ashley and F. H. Parnell. in: Tymn, M. B. and Ashley, Mike. Science Fiction, Fantasy, and Weird Fiction Magazines. Westport, CT: Greenwood, 1985. pp. 323-324.

"Horror Stories (1935-1941)," in: Tymn, M. B. and Ashley, Mike. Science Fiction, Fantasy, and Weird Fiction Magazines. Westport, CT: Greenwood, 1985. pp. 326-328.

"Human Chord, The," in: Magill, Frank N., ed. Survey of Modern Fantasy Literature, Vol 2. Englewood Cliffs, NJ: Salem Press, Inc., 1983. pp. 757-759.

"Impulse," in: Tymn, M. B. and Ashley, Mike. Science Fiction, Fantasy, and Weird Fiction Magazines. Westport, CT: Greenwood, 1985. pp. 350-352.

"Infinity," in: Tymn, M. B. and Ashley, Mike. Science Fiction, Fantasy, and Weird Fiction Magazines. Westport, CT: Greenwood, 1985. pp. 789-790.

Ashley, Mike (Continued)

"International Science Fiction," in: Tymn, M. B. and Ashley, Mike. Science Fiction, Fantasy, and Weird Fiction Magazines. Westport, CT: Greenwood, 1985. pp. 355-356.

"Interzone," in: Tymn, M. B. and Ashley, Mike. Science Fiction, Fantasy, and Weird Fiction Magazines. Westport, CT: Greenwood, 1985. pp. 356-358.

"Isaac Asimov's Science Fiction Magazine," by T. N. Hamilton and M. Ashley. in: Tymn, M. B. & Ashley, M. Science Fiction, Fantasy, and Weird Fiction Magazines. Westport, CT: Greenwood, 1985. pp. 358-363.

"Julius Le Vallon and The Bright Messenger," in: Magill, Frank N., ed. Survey of Modern Fantasy Literature, Vol 2. Englewood Cliffs, NJ: Salem Press, Inc., 1983. pp. 817-821.

"Kadath," in: Tymn, M. B. and Ashley, Mike. Science Fiction, Fantasy, and Weird Fiction Magazines. Westport, CT: Greenwood, 1985. pp. 367-368.

"Last Wave," in: Tymn, M. B. and Ashley, Mike. Science Fiction, Fantasy, and Weird Fiction Magazines. Westport, CT: Greenwood, 1985. pp. 371-372.

"Lore," in: Tymn, M. B. and Ashley, Mike. Science Fiction, Fantasy, and Weird Fiction Magazines. Westport, CT: Greenwood, 1985. pp. 829.

"Magazine of Horror," in: Tymn, M. B. and Ashley, Mike. Science Fiction, Fantasy, and Weird Fiction Magazines. Westport, CT: Greenwood, 1985. pp. 391-396.

"Man With the Hungry Eyes," in: Tymn, M. B. and Ashley, Mike. Science Fiction, Fantasy, and Weird Fiction Magazines. Westport, CT: Greenwood, 1985. pp. 788-789.

"Master Thriller Series," by Mike Ashley and W. G. Lofts. in: Tymn, M. B. and Ashley, Mike. Science Fiction, Fantasy, and Weird Fiction Magazines. Westport, CT: Greenwood, 1985. pp. 404-406.

"Mind Magic Magazine," by Mike Ashley and F. H. Parnell. in: Tymn, M. B. and Ashley, Mike. Science Fiction, Fantasy, and Weird Fiction Magazines. Westport, CT: Greenwood, 1985. pp. 409-410.

"Mind, Inc.," by Mike Ashley and Grant Thiessen. in: Tymn, M. B. and Ashley, Mike. Science Fiction, Fantasy, and Weird Fiction Magazines. Westport, CT: Greenwood, 1985. pp. 407-409.

"Mysterious Traveler Magazine," in: Tymn, M. B. and Ashley, Mike. Science Fiction, Fantasy, and Weird Fiction Magazines. Westport, CT: Greenwood, 1985. pp. 413-414.

"Mystery Adventures," in: Tymn, M. B. and Ashley, Mike. Science Fiction, Fantasy, and Weird Fiction Magazines. Westport, CT: Greenwood, 1985. pp. 416-417.

"Mystic Magazine," in: Tymn, M. B. and Ashley, Mike. Science Fiction, Fantasy, and Weird Fiction Magazines. Westport, CT: Greenwood, 1985. pp. 417-418.

"Nebula Science Fiction," in: Tymn, M. B. and Ashley, Mike. Science Fiction, Fantasy, and Weird Fiction Magazines. Westport, CT: Greenwood, 1985. pp. 419-423.

"New Dimensions," in: Tymn, M. B. and Ashley, Mike. Science Fiction, Fantasy, and Weird Fiction Magazines. Westport, CT: Greenwood, 1985. pp. 790-792.

"New Worlds," in: Tymn, M. B. and Ashley, Mike. Science Fiction, Fantasy, and Weird Fiction Magazines. Westport, CT: Greenwood, 1985. pp. 423-437.

"New Writings in SF," in: Tymn, M. B. and Ashley, Mike. Science Fiction, Fantasy, and Weird Fiction Magazines. Westport, CT: Greenwood, 1985. pp. 792-796.

"Nova," in: Tymn, M. B. and Ashley, Mike. Science Fiction, Fantasy, and Weird Fiction Magazines. Westport, CT: Greenwood, 1985. pp. 796-797.

"Occult," in: Tymn, M. B. and Ashley, Mike. Science Fiction, Fantasy, and Weird Fiction Magazines. Westport, CT: Greenwood, 1985. pp. 439-440.

"Orbit," in: Tymn, M. B. and Ashley, Mike. Science Fiction, Fantasy, and Weird Fiction Magazines. Westport, CT: Greenwood, 1985. pp. 797-799.

"Orbit Science Fiction," in: Tymn, M. B. and Ashley, Mike. Science Fiction, Fantasy, and Weird Fiction Magazines. Westport, CT: Greenwood, 1985. pp. 451-454.

"Oriental Stories," in: Tymn, M. B. and Ashley, Mike. Science Fiction, Fantasy, and Weird Fiction Magazines. Westport, CT: Greenwood, 1985. pp. 454-456.

"Other Times," in: Tymn, M. B. and Ashley, Mike. Science Fiction, Fantasy, and Weird Fiction Magazines. Westport, CT: Greenwood, 1985. pp. 457.

"Other Worlds Science Stories," in: Tymn, M. B. and Ashley, Mike. Science Fiction, Fantasy, and Weird Fiction Magazines. Westport, CT: Greenwood, 1985. pp. 457-466.

"Out of This World," in: Tymn, M. B. and Ashley, Mike. Science Fiction, Fantasy, and Weird Fiction Magazines. Westport, CT: Greenwood, 1985. pp. 466-467.

Ashley, Mike (Continued)

"Outlands," in: Tymn, M. B. and Ashley, Mike. Science Fiction, Fantasy, and Weird Fiction Magazines. Westport, CT: Greenwood, 1985. pp. 471-472.

"Perry Rhodan," in: Tymn, M. B. and Ashley, Mike. Science Fiction, Fantasy, and Weird Fiction Magazines. Westport, CT: Greenwood, 1985. pp. 799-801.

"Phantom," in: Tymn, M. B. and Ashley, Mike. Science Fiction, Fantasy, and Weird Fiction Magazines. Westport, CT: Greenwood, 1985. pp. 474-476.

"Prize Ghost Stories," in: Tymn, M. B. and Ashley, Mike. Science Fiction, Fantasy, and Weird Fiction Magazines. Westport, CT: Greenwood, 1985. pp. 482-483.

"Quark," in: Tymn, M. B. and Ashley, Mike. Science Fiction, Fantasy, and Weird Fiction Magazines. Westport, CT: Greenwood, 1985. pp. 801-802.

"Questar," by Jon Harvey and Mike Ashley. in: Tymn, M. B. and Ashley, Mike. Science Fiction, Fantasy, and Weird Fiction Magazines. Westport, CT: Greenwood, 1985. pp. 485-486.

"Rigel Science Fiction," in: Tymn, M. B. and Ashley, Mike. Science Fiction, Fantasy, and Weird Fiction Magazines. Westport, CT: Greenwood, 1985. pp. 487-488.

"Rod Serling's The Twilight Zone Magazine," in: Tymn, M. B. and Ashley, Mike. Science Fiction, Fantasy, and Weird Fiction Magazines. Westport, CT: Greenwood, 1985. pp. 490-491.

"S. F. Digest (1976)," in: Tymn, M. B. and Ashley, Mike. Science Fiction, Fantasy, and Weird Fiction Magazines. Westport, CT: Greenwood, 1985. pp. 534-535.

"Satellite Science Fantasy," in: Tymn, M. B. and Ashley, Mike. Science Fiction, Fantasy, and Weird Fiction Magazines. Westport, CT: Greenwood, 1985. pp. 493-497.

"Saturn: The Magazine of Science Fiction," by Joe Sanders and Mike Ashley. in: Tymn, M. B. and Ashley, Mike. Science Fiction, Fantasy, and Weird Fiction Magazines. Westport, CT: Greenwood, 1985. pp. 497-500.

"Science and Invention," in: Tymn, M. B. and Ashley, Mike. Science Fiction, Fantasy, and Weird Fiction Magazines. Westport, CT: Greenwood, 1985. pp. 500-504.

"Science Fantasy (1950-1966)," in: Tymn, M. B. and Ashley, Mike. Science Fiction, Fantasy, and Weird Fiction Magazines. Westport, CT: Greenwood, 1985. pp. 505-510.

"Science Fantasy (1970-1971)," in: Tymn, M. B. and Ashley, Mike. Science Fiction,

Fantasy, and Weird Fiction Magazines. Westport, CT: Greenwood, 1985. pp. 511.

"Science Fiction (Canadian)," in: Tymn, M. B. and Ashley, Mike. Science Fiction, Fantasy, and Weird Fiction Magazines. Westport, CT: Greenwood, 1985. pp. 519-520.

"Science Fiction," by Mike Ashley and R. H. Thompson. in: Tymn, M. B. and Ashley, Mike. Science Fiction, Fantasy, and Weird Fiction Magazines. Westport, CT: Greenwood, 1985. pp. 511-519.

"Science Fiction Adventures (1956-1958)," in: Tymn, M. B. and Ashley, Mike. Science Fiction, Fantasy, and Weird Fiction Magazines. Westport, CT: Greenwood, 1985. pp. 524-526.

"Science Fiction Adventures (1958-1963)," in: Tymn, M. B. and Ashley, Mike. Science Fiction, Fantasy, and Weird Fiction Magazines. Westport, CT: Greenwood, 1985. pp. 526-529.

"Science Fiction Adventures Yearbook," in: Tymn, M. B. and Ashley, Mike. Science Fiction, Fantasy, and Weird Fiction Magazines. Westport, CT: Greenwood, 1985. pp. 529-530.

"Science Fiction Classics," in: Tymn, M. B. and Ashley, Mike. Science Fiction, Fantasy, and Weird Fiction Magazines. Westport, CT: Greenwood, 1985. pp. 530-532.

"Science Fiction Classics Annual," in: Tymn, M. B. and Ashley, Mike. Science Fiction, Fantasy, and Weird Fiction Magazines. Westport, CT: Greenwood, 1985. pp. 533.

"Science Fiction Digest (1981-1982)," in: Tymn, M. B. and Ashley, Mike. Science Fiction, Fantasy, and Weird Fiction Magazines. Westport, CT: Greenwood, 1985. pp. 535-536.

"Science Fiction Library," in: Tymn, M. B. and Ashley, Mike. Science Fiction, Fantasy, and Weird Fiction Magazines. Westport, CT: Greenwood, 1985. pp. 536-537.

"Science Fiction Monthly (1974-1976)," in: Tymn, M. B. and Ashley, Mike. Science Fiction, Fantasy, and Weird Fiction Magazines. Westport, CT: Greenwood, 1985. pp. 539-540.

"Science Fiction Quarterly," in: Tymn, M. B. and Ashley, Mike. Science Fiction, Fantasy, and Weird Fiction Magazines. Westport, CT: Greenwood, 1985. pp. 545-550.

"Science Fiction Yearbook," in: Tymn, M. B. and Ashley, Mike. Science Fiction, Fantasy, and Weird Fiction Magazines. Westport, CT: Greenwood, 1985. pp. 551.

"Scientifiction," in: Tymn, M. B. and Ashley, Mike. Science Fiction, Fantasy, and Weird Fiction Magazines. Westport, CT: Greenwood, 1985. pp. 841.

Ashley, Mike (Continued)

"Scoops," in: Tymn, M. B. and Ashley, Mike. Science Fiction, Fantasy, and Weird Fiction Magazines. Westport, CT: Greenwood, 1985. pp. 562-565.

"Screen Chills and Macabre Stories," in: Tymn, M. B. and Ashley, Mike. Science Fiction, Fantasy, and Weird Fiction Magazines. Westport, CT: Greenwood, 1985. pp. 566-567.

"Shadow," in: Tymn, M. B. and Ashley, Mike. Science Fiction, Fantasy, and Weird Fiction Magazines. Westport, CT: Greenwood, 1985. pp. 842.

"Shock," in: Tymn, M. B. and Ashley, Mike. Science Fiction, Fantasy, and Weird Fiction Magazines. Westport, CT: Greenwood, 1985. pp. 576-577.

"Skyrack/Skyrack Newsletter," in: Tymn, M. B. and Ashley, Mike. Science Fiction, Fantasy, and Weird Fiction Magazines. Westport, CT: Greenwood, 1985. pp. 842.

"Skyworlds," in: Tymn, M. B. and Ashley, Mike. Science Fiction, Fantasy, and Weird Fiction Magazines. Westport, CT: Greenwood, 1985. pp. 577-579.

"Sorcerer's Apprentice," in: Tymn, M. B. and Ashley, Mike. Science Fiction, Fantasy, and Weird Fiction Magazines. Westport, CT: Greenwood, 1985. pp. 580-581.

"Space Adventures," in: Tymn, M. B. and Ashley, Mike. Science Fiction, Fantasy, and Weird Fiction Magazines. Westport, CT: Greenwood, 1985. pp. 581-582.

"Space and Time," by Mike Ashley and Gordon Linzner. in: Tymn, M. B. and Ashley, Mike. Science Fiction, Fantasy, and Weird Fiction Magazines. Westport, CT: Greenwood, 1985. pp. 582-584.

"Space Fact and Fiction," in: Tymn, M. B. and Ashley, Mike. Science Fiction, Fantasy, and Weird Fiction Magazines. Westport, CT: Greenwood, 1985. pp. 584-585.

"Space Science Fiction," in: Tymn, M. B. and Ashley, Mike. Science Fiction, Fantasy, and Weird Fiction Magazines. Westport, CT: Greenwood, 1985. pp. 585-587.

"Spaceway," in: Tymn, M. B. and Ashley, Mike. Science Fiction, Fantasy, and Weird Fiction Magazines. Westport, CT: Greenwood, 1985. pp. 599-602.

"Star Science Fiction Stories," in: Tymn, M. B. and Ashley, Mike. Science Fiction, Fantasy, and Weird Fiction Magazines. Westport, CT: Greenwood, 1985. pp. 802-804.

"Stardust (1940)," by R. A. Madle and Mike Ashley. in: Tymn, M. B. and Ashley, Mike. Science Fiction, Fantasy, and Weird Fiction Magazines. Westport, CT: Greenwood, 1985. pp. 606-607.

"Startling Mystery Stories," in: Tymn, M. B. and Ashley, Mike. Science Fiction, Fantasy, and Weird Fiction Magazines. Westport, CT: Greenwood, 1985. pp. 608-611.

"Stellar," in: Tymn, M. B. and Ashley, Mike. Science Fiction, Fantasy, and Weird Fiction Magazines. Westport, CT: Greenwood, 1985. pp. 804-806.

"Strange Adventures," in: Tymn, M. B. and Ashley, Mike. Science Fiction, Fantasy, and Weird Fiction Magazines. Westport, CT: Greenwood, 1985. pp. 620-621.

"Strange Fantasy," in: Tymn, M. B. and Ashley, Mike. Science Fiction, Fantasy, and Weird Fiction Magazines. Westport, CT: Greenwood, 1985. pp. 621-622.

"Strange Love Stories," in: Tymn, M. B. and Ashley, Mike. Science Fiction, Fantasy, and Weird Fiction Magazines. Westport, CT: Greenwood, 1985. pp. 622-623.

"Strange Tales," in: Tymn, M. B. and Ashley, Mike. Science Fiction, Fantasy, and Weird Fiction Magazines. Westport, CT: Greenwood, 1985. pp. 625-626.

"Strangest Stories Ever Told," in: Tymn, M. B. and Ashley, Mike. Science Fiction, Fantasy, and Weird Fiction Magazines. Westport, CT: Greenwood, 1985. pp. 628.

"Supernatural Stories," in: Tymn, M. B. and Ashley, Mike. Science Fiction, Fantasy, and Weird Fiction Magazines. Westport, CT: Greenwood, 1985. pp. 637-640.

"Sword & Sorcery Annual," in: Tymn, M. B. and Ashley, Mike. Science Fiction, Fantasy, and Weird Fiction Magazines. Westport, CT: Greenwood, 1985. pp. 642.

"Tales of Crime and Punishment," by Mike Ashley and F. H. Parnell. in: Tymn, M. B. and Ashley, Mike. Science Fiction, Fantasy, and Weird Fiction Magazines. Westport, CT: Greenwood, 1985. pp. 643-644.

"Tales of Ghosts and Haunted Houses," by Mike Ashley and F. H. Parnell. in: Tymn, M. B. and Ashley, Mike. Science Fiction, Fantasy, and Weird Fiction Magazines. Westport, CT: Greenwood, 1985. pp. 644.

"Tales of Magic and Mystery," in: Tymn, M. B. and Ashley, Mike. Science Fiction, Fantasy, and Weird Fiction Magazines. Westport, CT: Greenwood, 1985. pp. 644-647.

"Tales of Mystery and Detection," by Mike Ashley and F. H. Parnell. in: Tymn, M. B. and Ashley, Mike. Science Fiction, Fantasy, and Weird Fiction Magazines. Westport, CT: Greenwood, 1985. pp. 647-648.

Ashley, Mike (Continued)

"Tales of Terror," by Mike Ashley and F. H. Parnell. in: Tymn, M. B. and Ashley, Mike. Science Fiction, Fantasy, and Weird Fiction Magazines. Westport, CT: Greenwood, 1985. pp. 648-649.

"Tales of Terror From the Beyond," by Mike Ashley and F. H. Parnell. in: Tymn, M. B. and Ashley, Mike. Science Fiction, Fantasy, and Weird Fiction Magazines. Westport, CT: Greenwood, 1985. pp. 649.

"Tales of the Frightened," in: Tymn, M. B. and Ashley, Mike. Science Fiction, Fantasy, and Weird Fiction Magazines. Westport, CT: Greenwood, 1985. pp. 649-650.

"Tales of the Uncanny," by Mike Ashley and F. H. Parnell. in: Tymn, M. B. and Ashley, Mike. Science Fiction, Fantasy, and Weird Fiction Magazines. Westport, CT: Greenwood, 1985. pp. 650-651.

"Tales of Tomorrow," in: Tymn, M. B. and Ashley, Mike. Science Fiction, Fantasy, and Weird Fiction Magazines. Westport, CT: Greenwood, 1985. pp. 652.

"Tales of Wonder," in: Tymn, M. B. and Ashley, Mike. Science Fiction, Fantasy, and Weird Fiction Magazines. Westport, CT: Greenwood, 1985. pp. 652-654.

"Terror Tales," in: Tymn, M. B. and Ashley, Mike. Science Fiction, Fantasy, and Weird Fiction Magazines. Westport, CT: Greenwood, 1985. pp. 660-661.

"Thrill Book," in: Tymn, M. B. and Ashley, Mike. Science Fiction, Fantasy, and Weird Fiction Magazines. Westport, CT: Greenwood, 1985. pp. 661-664.

"Thriller," in: Tymn, M. B. and Ashley, Mike. Science Fiction, Fantasy, and Weird Fiction Magazines. Westport, CT: Greenwood, 1985. pp. 664-665.

"Thrilling Mystery," in: Tymn, M. B. and Ashley, Mike. Science Fiction, Fantasy, and Weird Fiction Magazines. Westport, CT: Greenwood, 1985. pp. 666-667.

"Thrilling Science Fiction," in: Tymn, M. B. and Ashley, Mike. Science Fiction, Fantasy, and Weird Fiction Magazines. Westport, CT: Greenwood, 1985. pp. 667-670.

"Thrilling Stories," in: Tymn, M. B. and Ashley, Mike. Science Fiction, Fantasy, and Weird Fiction Magazines. Westport, CT: Greenwood, 1985. pp. 670-671.

"Toadstool Wine." in: Tymn, M. B. and Ashley, Mike. Science Fiction, Fantasy, and Weird Fiction Magazines. Westport, CT: Greenwood, 1985. pp. 674-675.

"Treasury of Great Science Fiction Stories," in: Tymn, M. B. and Ashley, Mike. Science Fiction, Fantasy, and Weird Fiction Magazines. Westport, CT: Greenwood, 1985. pp. 677-678.

"True Twilight Tales," in: Tymn, M. B. and Ashley, Mike. Science Fiction, Fantasy, and Weird Fiction Magazines. Westport, CT: Greenwood, 1985. pp. 678-679.

"Uncanny Stories," by Mike Ashley and Robert Weinberg. in: Tymn, M. B. and Ashley, Mike. Science Fiction, Fantasy, and Weird Fiction Magazines. Westport, CT: Greenwood, 1985. pp. 683-684.

"Uncanny Tales (1939-1940)," in: Tymn, M. B. and Ashley, Mike. Science Fiction, Fantasy, and Weird Fiction Magazines. Westport, CT: Greenwood, 1985. pp. 684-685.

"Uncanny Tales (1940-1943)," by Mike Ashley and Grant Thiessen. in: Tymn, M. B. and Ashley, Mike. Science Fiction, Fantasy, and Weird Fiction Magazines. Westport, CT: Greenwood, 1985. pp. 685-688.

"Universe," in: Tymn, M. B. and Ashley, Mike. Science Fiction, Fantasy, and Weird Fiction Magazines. Westport, CT: Greenwood, 1985. pp. 805-806.

"Vargo Statten Science Fiction Magazine," in: Tymn, M. B. and Ashley, Mike. Science Fiction, Fantasy, and Weird Fiction Magazines. Westport, CT: Greenwood, 1985. pp. 703-705.

"Vector," in: Tymn, M. B. and Ashley, Mike. Science Fiction, Fantasy, and Weird Fiction Magazines. Westport, CT: Greenwood, 1985. pp. 843-844.

"Venture Science Fiction (1963-1965)," in: Tymn, M. B. and Ashley, Mike. Science Fiction, Fantasy, and Weird Fiction Magazines. Westport, CT: Greenwood, 1985. pp. 709-710.

"Vertex," in: Tymn, M. B. and Ashley, Mike. Science Fiction, Fantasy, and Weird Fiction Magazines. Westport, CT: Greenwood, 1985. pp. 711-714.

"Vision of Tomorrow," in: Tymn, M. B. and Ashley, Mike. Science Fiction, Fantasy, and Weird Fiction Magazines. Westport, CT: Greenwood, 1985. pp. 714-715.

"Void Science Fiction and Fantasy," in: Tymn, M. B. and Ashley, Mike. Science Fiction, Fantasy, and Weird Fiction Magazines. Westport, CT: Greenwood, 1985. pp. 716-718.

"Vortex (1947)," in: Tymn, M. B. and Ashley, Mike. Science Fiction, Fantasy, and Weird Fiction Magazines. Westport, CT: Greenwood, 1985. pp. 718-719.

"Vortex (1977)," in: Tymn, M. B. and Ashley, Mike. Science Fiction, Fantasy, and Weird Fiction Magazines. Westport, CT: Greenwood, 1985. pp. 719-720.

Ashley, Mike (Continued)

"Weird and Occult Library," in: Tymn, M. B. and Ashley, Mike. Science Fiction, Fantasy, and Weird Fiction Magazines. Westport, CT: Greenwood, 1985. pp. 723-724.

"Weird Horrors," in: Tymn, M. B. and Ashley, Mike. Science Fiction, Fantasy, and Weird Fiction Magazines. Westport, CT: Greenwood, 1985. pp. 806-807.

"Weird Mystery," in: Tymn, M. B. and Ashley, Mike. Science Fiction, Fantasy, and Weird Fiction Magazines. Westport, CT: Greenwood, 1985. pp. 724.

"Weird Pocket Library," in: Tymn, M. B. and Ashley, Mike. Science Fiction, Fantasy, and Weird Fiction Magazines. Westport, CT: Greenwood, 1985. pp. 725.

"Weird Shorts," in: Tymn, M. B. and Ashley, Mike. Science Fiction, Fantasy, and Weird Fiction Magazines. Westport, CT: Greenwood, 1985. pp. 725-726.

"Weird Story Magazine," in: Tymn, M. B. and Ashley, Mike. Science Fiction, Fantasy, and Weird Fiction Magazines. Westport, CT: Greenwood, 1985. pp. 726-727.

"Weird Terror Tales," in: Tymn, M. B. and Ashley, Mike. Science Fiction, Fantasy, and Weird Fiction Magazines. Westport, CT: Greenwood, 1985. pp. 736-737.

"Weird World," by Mike Ashley and Stephen Holland. in: Tymn, M. B. and Ashley, Mike. Science Fiction, Fantasy, and Weird Fiction Magazines. Westport, CT: Greenwood, 1985. pp. 737-738.

"Weirdbook," by Jon Harvey and Mike Ashley. in: Tymn, M. B. and Ashley, Mike. Science Fiction, Fantasy, and Weird Fiction Magazines. Westport, CT: Greenwood, 1985. pp. 738-740.

"Whispers," by Jon Harvey and Mike Ashley. in: Tymn, M. B. and Ashley, Mike. Science Fiction, Fantasy, and Weird Fiction Magazines. Westport, CT: Greenwood, 1985. pp. 740-742.

"Witch's Tales," by Mike Ashley and F. H. Parnell. in: Tymn, M. B. and Ashley, Mike. Science Fiction, Fantasy, and Weird Fiction Magazines. Westport, CT: Greenwood, 1985. pp. 742-743.

"Wonder Stories," by Robert Ewald and Mike Ashley. in: Tymn, M. B. and Ashley, Mike. Science Fiction, Fantasy, and Weird Fiction Magazines. Westport, CT: Greenwood, 1985. pp. 743-762.

"Wonder Stories Annual," in: Tymn, M. B. and Ashley, Mike. Science Fiction, Fantasy, and Weird Fiction Magazines. Westport, CT: Greenwood, 1985. pp. 766-768.

"Wonder Stories Quarterly," in: Tymn, M. B. and Ashley, Mike. Science Fiction, Fantasy, and Weird Fiction Magazines. Westport, CT: Greenwood, 1985. pp. 763-766.

"Wonders of the Spaceways," in: Tymn, M. B. and Ashley, Mike. Science Fiction, Fantasy, and Weird Fiction Magazines. Westport, CT: Greenwood, 1985. pp. 767-768.

"Worlds of Fantasy (1950-1954)," in: Tymn, M. B. and Ashley, Mike. Science Fiction, Fantasy, and Weird Fiction Magazines. Westport, CT: Greenwood, 1985. pp. 770-771.

"Worlds of the Universe," in: Tymn, M. B. and Ashley, Mike. Science Fiction, Fantasy, and Weird Fiction Magazines. Westport, CT: Greenwood, 1985. pp. 773-774.

"Worlds of Tomorrow," in: Tymn, M. B. and Ashley, Mike. Science Fiction, Fantasy, and Weird Fiction Magazines. Westport, CT: Greenwood, 1985. pp. 774-780.

"Yankee Weird Shorts," in: Tymn, M. B. and Ashley, Mike. Science Fiction, Fantasy, and Weird Fiction Magazines. Westport, CT: Greenwood, 1985. pp. 780-781.

"Algernon Blackwood: The Ghostly Tale's Great Visionary," Twilight Zone 5(2): 56-63. May/June 1985.

"Bibliography of fantasy anthologies," by Neil Barron, Mike Ashley and R. C. Schlobin. in: Magill, Frank N., ed. Survey of Modern Fantasy Literature, Vol 5. Englewood Cliffs, NJ: Salem Press, Inc., 1983. pp. 2532-2538.

"Bibliography," in: Kincaid, Paul, ed. Bob Shaw, British Science Fiction Writers, Volume 1. Kent, Eng.: British Science Fiction Association, 1981. pp. 32-38.

"Essential Writers: Blood Brothers," Twilight Zone 4(2): 63-70. May/June 1984.

"Essential writers: M. R. James," Twilight Zone 1(9):55-59. December 1981.

"Fiction of William Hope Hodgson, a Working Bibliography," Science Fiction Collector 15: 15-18. July 1981.

"IASFM: Welcome to the 100 Club," Fantasy Review 8(11): 6, 40. November 1985.

"Jack Williamson: pioneer behind the pen," Science Fiction Times (Boston) 1(4):1,14. August 1979.

"Mark Adlard interviewed," by Mike Ashley and Geoff Rippington. Arena 7:8-12. March 1978.

"Outer limits: the worldwide following," in: Holdstock, Robert, ed. Encyclopedia of Science Fiction. London: Octopus, 1978. pp. 152-161.

Ashley, Mike (Continued)

"Perils of bibliography: a look at the writing of E. C. Tubb, The," Science Fiction Collector 7:5-45. July 1979.

"Pulps and magazines: the history of the comics," in: Holdstock, Robert, ed. Encyclopedia of Science Fiction. London: Octopus, 1978. pp. 50-67.

"Short fiction of Blackwood, The," in: Magill, Frank N., ed. Survey of Modern Fantasy Literature, Vol 3. Englewood Cliffs, NJ: Salem Press, Inc., 1983. pp. 1441-1451.

Ashmead, John

Constructing Scientifiction & Fantasy, by John Ashmead, Darrell Schweitzer, and George Scithers. Lake Geneva, WI: TSR Hobbies, 1982. 31 p.

Ashmead, L. P.

"John W. Campbell," Locus No. 90:8-9. July 12, 1971.

"Specialized needs at Doubleday: mystery-suspense and science fiction," Writer 82(5):23 24. May 1969.

Asimov, Isaac

Asimov on Science Fiction. Garden City, NY: Doubleday, 1981. 334 p.

Hour With Isaac Asimov, An: Building a Firm Foundation, interviewed by Randall Garrett. Garden Grove, CA: Hourglass, 1979. 1 cassette.

In Joy Still Felt: The Autobiography of Isaac Asimov, 1954-1978. Garden City, NY: Doubleday, 1980. 828 p.

In Memory Yet Green: The Autobiography of Isaac Asimov 1920-1954. Garden City, NY: Doubleday, 1979. 732 p.

Isaac Asimov. Washington, DC: Tapes for Readers, 1980.

"1984" in: Asimov, Isaac. Asimov on Science Fiction. Garden City, NY: Doubleday, 1981. pp. 275-289.

"Adventure," in: Asimov, Isaac. Asimov on Science Fiction. Garden City, NY: Doubleday, 1981. pp. 34-38.

"And it will serve us right," Psychology Today 2(11):38-41,64. April 1969.

"Anniversaries," in: Asimov, Isaac. Asimov on Science Fiction. Garden City, NY: Doubleday, 1981. pp. 249-253.

"Answer to Star Wars?" in: Asimov, Isaac. Asimov on Science Fiction. Garden City, NY: Doubleday, 1981. pp. 295-299.

"Art of the tomorrow seekers, The," in: Encyclopedia Britannica. Britannica Yearbook of Science and the Future. Chicago, Encyclopedia Britannica, 1968. pp. 30-43.

"Arthur C. Clarke," in: Asimov, Isaac. Asimov on Science Fiction. Garden City, NY: Doubleday, 1981. pp. 227-229.

"Articles of Science Fiction," in: Asimov, Isaac. Asimov on Science Fiction. Garden City, NY: Doubleday, 1981. pp. 259-262.

"Asimov Connection," Locus 18(6): 19-21, 42. June 1985.

"Asimov ponders PCs," PC World 3(9):188-190. September 1985.

"Asimov's guide to Asimov," in: Olander, J. D. and M. H. Greenberg, eds. Isaac Asimov. New York: Taplinger, 1977. pp. 201-206.

"Beyond Our Brain," in: Asimov, Isaac. Asimov on Science Fiction. Garden City, NY: Doubleday, 1981. pp. 140-152.

"Big, Big, Big," in: Asimov, Isaac. Asimov on Science Fiction. Garden City, NY: Doubleday, 1981. pp. 196-202.

"Boom in Science Fiction," in: Asimov, Isaac. Asimov on Science Fiction. Garden City, NY: Doubleday, 1981. pp. 132-135.

"Brotherhood of Science Fiction," in: Asimov, Isaac. Asimov on Science Fiction. Garden City, NY: Doubleday, 1981. pp. 235-238.

"By No Means Vulgar," in: Asimov, Isaac. Asimov on Science Fiction. Garden City, N.Y.: Doubleday, 1981. pp. 46-50.

"By-products of science fiction, The," Chemical and Engineering News 34:3882-3886. August 13, 1956. also in: Magazine of Fantasy and Science Fiction 12(4):42-49. April 1957.

"Call It SF or Sci-Fi, It's Big," The 1980 World Book Year Book. Chicago: World Book, 1980. pp. 52-69.

"Campbell Touch," in: Asimov, Isaac. Asimov on Science Fiction. Garden City, NY: Doubleday, 1981. pp. 203-207.

"Cult of ignorance, The," in: Asimov, Isaac. Is Anyone There? New York: Ace Books, 1967. pp. 293-299.

"Dean of Science Fiction," in: Asimov, Isaac. Asimov on Science Fiction. Garden City, N.Y.: Doubleday, 1981. pp. 230-234.

Asimov, Isaac (Continued)

"Dreams of Science Fiction,"   in: Asimov, Isaac. Asimov on Science Fiction. Garden City, NY: Doubleday, 1981. pp. 87-95.

"Editorial: Book Reviews,"   Isaac Asimov's Science Fiction Magazine 5(2): 6-8, 10. February 16, 1981.

"Editorial: Plagiarism,"   Isaac Asimov's Science Fiction Magazine 9(8): 4-10. August 1985.

"Editorial: Religion and Science Fiction," Isaac Asimov's Science Fiction Magazine 8(6): 6-10. June 1984.

"Editorial: Science Fiction Poetry,"   Isaac Asimov's Science Fiction Magazine 5(3): 6-11. March 16, 1981.

"Escape into reality,"   Humanist 17(6):326-332. November/December 1957. also in: Asimov, Isaac. Is Anyone There? New York: Ace Books, 1967. pp. 285-292.

"Extraordinary Voyages,"   in: Asimov, Isaac. Asimov on Science Fiction. Garden City, N. Y.: Doubleday, 1981. pp. 12-24.

"Fact catches up with fiction,"   New York Times Magazine p. 34. November 19, 1961.

"Fairy Tales,"   Isaac Asimov's Science Fiction Magazine 9(10): 4-8. October 1985.

"Feminization of Sci-Fi,"   Vogue 172(10): 558, 608. October 1982.

"Final Thoughts: Why This World Loves Sci-Fi," Home Video 2(9): 84. September 1981.

"First Science Fiction Novel,"   in: Asimov, Isaac. Asimov on Science Fiction. Garden City, NY: Doubleday, 1981. pp. 181-183.

"First Science Fiction Writer,"   in: Asimov, Isaac. Asimov on Science Fiction. Garden City, NY: Doubleday, 1981. pp. 184-186.

"Foundation of SF success, The,"   Magazine of Fantasy and Science Fiction 6(1):69. January 1954.

"Golden Age Ahead,"   in: Asimov, Isaac. Asimov on Science Fiction. Garden City, N. Y.: Doubleday, 1981. pp. 136-139.

"H. G. Wells in 1931, Isaac Asimov Today," Next 2(1): 103-105. January/February 1981.

"Hints,"   in: Asimov, Isaac. Asimov on Science Fiction. Garden City, NY: Doubleday, 1981. pp. 41-45.

"Hole in the Middle,"   in: Asimov, Isaac. Asimov on Science Fiction. Garden City, N. Y.: Doubleday, 1981. pp. 187-189.

"Hollywood and I,"   in: Asimov, Isaac. Asimov on Science Fiction. Garden City, N. Y.: Doubleday, 1981. pp. 326-330.

"Horace,"   in: Asimov, Isaac. Asimov on Science Fiction. Garden City, NY: Doubleday, 1981. pp. 212-216.

"How Easy to See the Future,"   in: Asimov, Isaac. Asimov on Science Fiction. Garden City, NY: Doubleday, 1981. pp. 81-86.

"How not to build a robot,"   in: Asimov, Isaac. Is Anyone There? New York: Ace Books, 1967. pp. 303-307.

"How Science Fiction Came to Be Big Business," in: Asimov, Isaac. Asimov on Science Fiction. Garden City, NY: Doubleday, 1981. pp. 121-131.

"Hugo, The," in: Asimov, Isaac. The Hugo Winners. Garden City, NY: Doubleday, 1962. pp. 315-318.

"Hugo,"   in: Asimov, Isaac. Asimov on Science Fiction. Garden City, NY: Doubleday, 1981. pp. 245-248.

"If it's good science fiction the writers know some science," TV Guide 25:17-19. December 24, 1977.

"Imagination in orbit,"   Writer 74(3):16-18,37. March 1971. also in: Burack, A. S., ed. The Writer's Handbook. Boston: The Writer, 1966. pp. 309-315.

"Influence of Science Fiction,"   Isaac Asimov's Science Fiction Magazine 5(8):5-10. August 3, 1981.

"Insiduous Uncle Martin, The,"   in: Asimov, Isaac. Is Anyone There? New York: Ace Books, 1967. pp. 307-311.

"Isaac Asimov's Science Fiction Magazine," in: Asimov, Isaac. Asimov on Science Fiction. Garden City, NY: Doubleday, 1981. pp. 322-325.

"It's a Funny Thing,"   in: Asimov, Isaac. Asimov on Science Fiction. Garden City, N. Y.: Doubleday, 1981. pp. 56-59.

"John W. Campbell,"   Locus No. 90:7. July 12, 1971.

"Learning Device,"   in: Asimov, Isaac. Asimov on Science Fiction. Garden City, N. Y.: Doubleday, 1981. pp. 51-55.

"Letter Column,"   in: Asimov, Isaac. Asimov on Science Fiction. Garden City, NY: Doubleday, 1981. pp. 254-258.

"Life in 1990,"   Science Digest 58(2):63-70. August 1965.

"Living with 'the machine',"   Chicago Tribune Sec. 1, p. 19. February 21, 1985.

Asimov, Isaac (Continued)

"Lovely lost landscapes of Luna, The," in: Asimov, Isaac. Is Anyone There? New York: Ace Books, 1967. pp. 311-319.

"Machine and the robot, The," in: Warrick, Patricia, ed. Science Fiction: Contemporary Mythology. New York: Harper, 1978. pp. 244-254.

"Missed Opportunities," SciQuest 54(9): 33. November 1981.

"More Science Fiction From the Soviet Union," in: Asimov, Isaac. Asimov on Science Fiction. Garden City, NY: Doubleday, 1981. pp. 171-177.

"Mosaic and the Plate Glass," in: Asimov, Isaac. Asimov on Science Fiction. Garden City, NY: Doubleday, 1981. pp. 60-63.

"Mr. Spock is dreamy," TV Guide 15(17):9-11. April 29, 1967.

"My Own View," in: Asimov, Isaac. Asimov on Science Fiction. Garden City, NY: Doubleday 1981. pp. 17-20.

"Myth of the Machine," in: Asimov, Isaac. Asimov on Science Fiction. Garden City, N. Y.: Doubleday, 1981. pp. 153-163.

"Name of Our Field," in: Asimov, Isaac. Asimov on Science Fiction. Garden City, N. Y.: Doubleday, 1981. pp. 25-29.

"Next 100 years: science-based estimates of what the century ahead may bring, The," in: The World Almanac (Centennial Ed.), 1968. pp. 39-41.

"Other worlds to conquer," Writer 64(5):148-151. May 1951. also in: Writers Handbook. Boston: Writer, 1957. pp. 321-327.

"Our Conventions," in: Asimov, Isaac. Asimov on Science Fiction. Garden City, N. Y.: Doubleday, 1981. pp. 241-244.

"Pladoyer fur science-fiction," in: Der Spiegel no. 11:138-139. 1972.

"Prescientific Universe," in: Asimov, Isaac. Asimov on Science Fiction. Garden City, N. Y.: Doubleday, 1981. pp. 99-102.

"Prolific Writer," in: Asimov, Isaac. Asimov on Science Fiction. Garden City, N. Y.: Doubleday, 1981. pp. 331-334.

"Pumpkin is not a spaceship," Horizon 23(1):37. January 1980.

"Ray Bradbury," in: Asimov, Isaac. Asimov on Science Fiction. Garden City, NY: Doubleday, 1981. pp. 223-226.

"Reagan doctrine, The," Lone Star Review (Austin American Statesman) p. 4. May 1981.

"Rejection Slips," in: Asimov, Isaac. Asimov on Science Fiction. Garden City, N. Y.: Doubleday, 1981. pp. 263-266.

"Reluctant Critic," in: Asimov, Isaac. Asimov on Science Fiction. Garden City, N. Y.: Doubleday, 1981. pp. 305-310.

"Reminiscences of Peg," Locus 12(8):13. September 1979.

"Ring of Evil," in: Asimov, Isaac. Asimov on Science Fiction. Garden City, NY: Doubleday, 1981. pp. 290-294.

"Robots and androids," in: Ash, Brian, ed. Visual Encyclopedia of Science Fiction. New York: Harmony, 1977. pp. 172-180.

"Science Fiction and Society," in: Asimov, Isaac. Asimov on Science Fiction. Garden City, NY: Doubleday, 1981. pp. 103-111.

"Science fiction and society," in: Williamson, Jack, ed. Teaching Science Fiction: Education for Tomorrow. Philadelphia: Owlswick, 1980. pp. 26-32.

"Science Fiction Breakthrough," in: Asimov, Isaac. Asimov on Science Fiction. Garden City, NY: Doubleday, 1981. pp. 190-195.

"Science Fiction From the Soviet Union," in: Asimov, Isaac. Asimov on Science Fiction. Garden City, NY: Doubleday, 1981. pp. 164-170.

"Science fiction" in: Bild der Wissenschaft 7:112-119. February 1970.

"Science Fiction, 1938," in: Asimov, Isaac. Asimov on Science Fiction. Garden City, N. Y.: Doubleday, 1981. pp. 112-120.

"Science fiction, an aid to science, foresees the future," Smithsonian 1:41-47. May 1970.

"Science fiction: real-life mirror of social change," Prism. January 1974. (not seen)

"Science Fiction: 1938," in: Pohl, Frederik, ed. Nebula Winners Fourteen. New York: Harper, 1980; New York: Bantam, 1982. pp. 102-110.

"Scientist as Villain," in: Asimov, Isaac. Asimov on Science Fiction. Garden City, N. Y.: Doubleday, 1981. pp. 64-68.

"Second Nova," in: Asimov, Isaac. Asimov on Science Fiction. Garden City, NY: Doubleday, 1981. pp. 217-222.

"SF market still healthy," (Reply to Lupoff) SEE UNDER: Lupoff, R. "Whats left of the SF market."

"SF: clue to creativity," Library Journal 89(4):914-917. February 15, 1964.

Asimov, Isaac (Continued)

"So why aren't we rich?" in: Asimov, Isaac, ed. <u>Nebula Award Stories Eight</u>. New York: Berkley, 1973. pp. ix-xvii.

"Social science fiction," in: Bretnor, Reginald, ed. <u>Modern Science Fiction</u>. N. Y.: Coward, 1953; reprinted, Chicago: Advent, 1979. p. 157-196; also in: Knight, Damon, ed. <u>Turning Points</u>. NY: Harper, 1977. p. 29-61.

"Speculative Fiction," in: Asimov, Isaac. <u>Asimov on Science Fiction</u>. Garden City, N. Y.: Doubleday, 1981. pp. 300-304.

"Sword of Achilles," <u>Bulletin of the Atomic Scientists</u> 19:17-18. November 1963. also in: Asimov, I. <u>Is Anyone There?</u> New York: Ace Books, 1967. p. 299-303; as "SF: clue to creativity," <u>Library Journal</u> 89:914-917. 1964.

"Symbolism," <u>Isaac Asimov's Science Fiction Magazine</u> 9(6): 4-8. June 1985.

"Theodore Sturgeon in Memoriam, 2," <u>Locus</u> 18(7): 25. July 1985.

"There's nothing like a good foundation," <u>Science Fiction Writers of America Bulletin</u>. 14(3):31-34. Fall 1979 and 3(1):12-14. January 1967. also in: Knight, Damon, ed. <u>Turning Points</u>. New York: Harper, 1967. p. 273-276.

"There's Nothing Like a Good Foundation," in: Asimov, Isaac. <u>Asimov on Science Fiction</u>. Garden City, NY: Doubleday, 1981. pp. 313-317.

"They don't make monsters like they used to," <u>TV Guide</u> 22(23):13. 1974.

"Transportation: 21st century," <u>Dodge Adventurer</u> 7(2):28-30. Winter 1979.

"Try science fiction as a teaching aid," <u>Science Newsletter</u> (Prentice Hall) 3(3):1-2. Fall 1958.

"Try to Write," <u>Asimov on Science Fiction</u>. Garden City, NY: Doubleday, 1981. pp. 74-77.

"UFO," <u>TV Guide</u> 22:40. December 14, 1974.

"Universe of Science Fiction," in: Asimov, Isaac. <u>Asimov on Science Fiction</u>. Garden City, NY: Doubleday, 1981. pp. 30-33.

"Vocabulary of Science Fiction," in: Asimov, Isaac. <u>Asimov on Science Fiction</u>. Garden City, NY: Doubleday, 1981. pp. 69-73.

"Vor ensomme planet," in: <u>Rejser i tid og rum. En Bog om science fiction</u>, ed. by Tage La Cour. Copenhagen: Stig Verdelkaer, 1973.

"Wendell Urth Series," in: Asimov, Isaac. <u>Asimov on Science Fiction</u>. Garden City, N. Y.: Doubleday, 1981. pp. 318-321.

"What Makes Good Science Fiction?" in: Asimov, Isaac. <u>Asimov on Science Fiction</u>. Garden City, NY: Doubleday, 1981. pp. 269-274.

"When Aristotle fails, try science fiction," <u>Intellectual Digest</u> 2(4):75-77. December 1971.

"Women and Science Fiction," <u>Isaac Asimov's Science Fiction Magazine</u> 7(1):7-13. January 1983.

"Word Processor and I," <u>Popular Computing</u> 1(4): 32-36. February 1982.

Assayas, Olivier

"Effets Speciaux, 2e Partie: SPFX News, ou situation du cinema de science-fiction envisage en tant que secteur de pointe," <u>Cahiers du Cinema</u> 316: 36-40. October 1980.

"Effets Speciaux: SPFX News; ou situation du cinema de Science-Fiction envisage en tant que secteur de pointe," <u>Cahiers du Cinema</u> 318: 34-40. 1980.

"Effets Speciaux: SPFX News; ou situations du cinema de science fiction envisage en tant que secteur de pointe," <u>Cahiers du Cinema</u> 317: 22-33. November 1980.

Association francais d'etudes americaines

<u>Fantastique a la science fiction americaine</u>. Paris: Didier, 1973. 132 p.

Astle, Richard

"<u>Exile Waiting, The</u>," in: Magill, Frank N., ed. <u>Survey of Science Fiction Literature</u>, Vol. 2. Englewood Cliffs, NJ: Salem Press, 1979. pp. 739-743.

"<u>Martian Time Slip</u>," in: Magill, Frank N., ed. <u>Survey of Science Fiction Literature</u>, Vol. 3. Englewood Cliffs, NJ: Salem Press, 1979. pp. 1357-1361.

"<u>Melmoth the Wanderer</u>," in: Magill, Frank N., ed. <u>Survey of Modern Fantasy Literature</u>, Vol 2. Englewood Cliffs, NJ: Salem Press, Inc., 1983. pp. 998-1003.

"<u>Wanting Seed, The</u>," in: Magill, Frank N., ed. <u>Survey of Science Fiction Literature</u>, Vol. 5. Englewood Cliffs, NJ: Salem Press, 1979. pp. 2402-2406.

Astryx

"Prototypes of fact," <u>Times Educational Supplement</u> 2732:618. September 29, 1967.

Atchity, Kenneth

"Two views of J. R. R. Tolkien," in: Becker, Alida, ed. <u>The Tolkien Scrapbook</u>. New York: Grossett and Dunlap, 1978. pp. 96-100.

Atheling, William, Jr.

See: **Blish, James**

Atkins, Dorothy

"Star Trek: A Philosophical Interpretation," in: Myers, R. E., ed. <u>The Intersection of Science Fiction and Philosophy</u>. Westport: Greenwood, 1983. pp. 93-108.

Atkins, John

"Orwell in 1984," <u>College Literature</u> 11(1): 34-43. 1984.

Atkins, T. R.

<u>Science Fiction Films</u>. New York: Monarch, 1976. 101 p.

"Ray Bradbury: an interview," <u>Sight and Sound</u> 43:96-100. Spring 1974.

"Space: 1999," by T. R. Atkins and M. E. O'Brien. <u>Cinefantastique</u> 4(2):44-46. Summer 1975.

Atkinson, Geoffrey

<u>Extraordinary Voyage in French Literature Before 1700</u>. New York: Columbia University Press, 1920. 189 p.

<u>Extraordinary Voyage in French Literature from 1700 to 1720</u>. Paris: Librarie Ancienne Honore Champion, 1922. 147 p.

Atnally, Richard

"On past and future Brave New Worlds," <u>Alternative Futures</u> 2(2): 84-86. Spring 1979.

Attebery, Brian

<u>America and the Materials of Fantasy</u>. Ph. D. Dissertation, Brown University, 1979. 339 p. (DAI 40A: 5862)

<u>Fantasy Tradition in American Literature From Irving to Le Guin</u>. Bloomington: Indiana University Press, 1980. 212 p.

"<u>Beginning Place</u>: Le Guin's metafantasy," in: <u>Ursula K. Le Guin</u>, ed. by Harold Bloom. New York: Chelsea House, 1986. pp. 235-242.

"<u>Oz Books, The</u>," in: Magill, Frank N., ed. <u>Survey of Modern Fantasy Literature</u>, Vol 3. Englewood Cliffs, NJ: Salem Press, Inc., 1983. pp. 1196-1208.

"<u>Zimiamvian Trilogy, The</u>," in: Magill, Frank N., ed. <u>Survey of Modern Fantasy Literature</u>, Vol 5. Englewood Cliffs, NJ: Salem Press, Inc., 1983. pp. 2206-2213.

"On a Far Shore: The Myth of Earthsea," <u>Extrapolation</u> 21(3): 269-277. Fall 1980.

"Science Fantasy," in: Cowart, David, ed. <u>Twentieth Century American Science Fiction Writers</u>. Detroit: Gale, 1981. v. 2, pp. 236-242.

"Ursula K. Le Guin," in: Cowart, David, ed. <u>Twentieth-Century American Science-Fiction Writers, Part 1: A-L</u>. Detroit: Gale, 1981. pp. 263-280. (Dictionary of Literary Biography, v. 8)

Atwood, Margaret

"Superwoman drawn and quartered: the early forms of <u>She</u>," <u>Alphabet</u> 10:65-82. July 1965.

Aubrion, Michel

"Science fiction et l'avenir de l'homme," <u>Revue generale, Perspectives europeennes des sciences humaines, Bruxelles</u>. 106(5):1-32. May 1970.

Auden, W. H.

"At the end of the quest, victory," in: Becker, Alida, ed. <u>The Tolkien Scrapbook</u>. New York: Grossett and Dunlap, 1978. pp. 44-48.

Audiberti, Jacques

"Humain a l'abhumain, L'" <u>Cahiers du Sud</u> No. 317. June 1953.

Auer, Marilyn

"Look at science fiction and fantasy: from the author's view," by J. Vinay and Marilyn Auer. <u>Bloomsbury Review</u> 1(5):17-18,20. July/August 1981.

Auer, Tom

"Look at science fiction and fantasy: from the publishing point of view," by Tom Auer and J. Vinay. <u>Bloomsbury Review</u> 1(5):17,19. July/August 1981.

"Writing of one long novel: an interview with William S. Burroughs," <u>Bloomsbury Review</u> 1(3):13-16. March/April 1981.

Aukerman, C. W.

"SF in the classroom: developing a high school reading list," <u>Extrapolation</u> 18(2):155-161. May 1977.

Auld, William

"Utopioj, sitiroj, fantascienco," <u>Kontakto</u> 2: 8-12. 1981.

Australian Science Fiction Association

<u>Index to British Science Fiction Magazines, 1934-1953, Parts 1-7</u>. Canberra City: ASFA, 1970. 213 p.

<u>Science Fiction Book Reviews, 1969-1972</u>. Sydney: Australian Science Fiction Association, 1973. 60 p.

Autrey, M. W.

"Edgar Allan Poe's satiric view of evolution," <u>Extrapolation</u> 18(2):186-199. May 1977.

Auty, Chris

"Complete Spielberg?" <u>Sight and Sound</u> 51(4): 275-279. Autumn 1982.

Aylesworth, T. G.

"Witchcraft for kids," <u>Publishers Weekly</u> 221(9):80-81. February 26, 1982.

Aylward, David

"Checklist of Science Fiction and Fantasy Book Dealers," by David Aylward and Robert Hadji. <u>Special Collections</u> 2(1/2): 171-175. Fall/Winter 1982.

"Spaced Out Library: Toronto Public Library's Spaced Out Collection," <u>Special Collections</u> 2(1/2): 63-67. Fall/Winter 1982.

Azzopardi, John

"Death Ship (review)," <u>Cinefantastique</u> 10(2):39,42. Fall 1980.

"Watcher in the Woods (review)," <u>Cinefantastique</u> 10(2):39. Fall 1980.

B

Babcock, C. L.

"Tutankhamun and Star Trek," Vital Speeches 43(24):744-747. October 1, 1977.

Babrick, Jean

"Possible Gods: religion in science fiction," Arizona English Bulletin 51(1):37-42. October 1972.

Bacht, Heinrich

"Die Selbstzerstorung des menschen im spiegel des modernen zukunftsromans," Stimmen der Zeit 153:10-24. 1953/1954.

Bacia, H.

"Funfhundert jahrige Reich des Perry Rhodan und seine Junger," Konkret No. 11:22- . 1969.

Bacon, Leonard

"Imaginative power of C. S. Lewis, The," Saturday Review of Literature 17(15):9. April 8, 1944. (Review of Perelandra).

Badami, M. K.

"Feminist critique of science fiction, A," Extrapolation 18(1):6-19. December 1976.

"Science fiction aus feminischer Sicht," in: Alpers, H. J., ed. Science Fiction Almanach 1981. Moewig, 1980. pp. 325-346. (Tr. of "A Feminist critique of science fiction.")

Baddock, Barry

"SF in the classroom: 1, a look at student projects," Extrapolation 17(1):29-31. December 1975.

"SF in the classroom: 3, science fiction readership on campus," by Barry Baddock and James Gunn. Extrapolation 15(2):148-151. May 1974.

Bagalyakz, Boris

"Fandom in the USSR," Locus 18(12): 20, 29. December 1985.

Bailey, Chris

"So, Who Needs Characters, Anyway?" Vector 105: 19-21. December 1981.

Bailey, E. C., Jr.

"Shadows in Earthsea: Le Guin's Use of a Jungian Archetype," Extrapolation 21(3): 254-261. Fall 1980.

Bailey, Hilary

"Time and the space ship," Times (London) Educational Supplement 2947:19. November 12, 1971.

"Wave of Fantasy," New Scientist 1307: 596-597. May 27, 1982.

Bailey, J. O.

Pilgrims Through Space and Time: Trends and Patterns in Scientific and Utopian Fiction. New York: Argus Books, 1947, 341 p. Reprinted, Westport, Connecticut: Greenwood Press, 1972.

"Early American utopian fiction, An," American Literature 14(3):285-293. November 1942.

"Is science fiction art? A look at H. G. Wells," Extrapolation 2(1):17-19. December 1960.

"Shaw's life force and science fiction," Shaw Review 16(2):48-58. May 1973.

"Some comments on science fiction," Journal of General Education 28(1):75-82. Spring 1976.

Bailey, K. V.

"Evolution and Revolution: Some Theme-Origins in 'The War of the Worlds'," _Vector_ 119: 28-32. April 1984.

"Letter, on H. G. Wells," _Foundation_ 33: 62-70. Spring 1985.

"Play and Ritual in Science Fiction," _Foundation_ 27: 5-24. February 1983.

"Prized harmony: myth, symbol and dialectic in the novels of Olaf Stapledon, A," _Foundation_ 15:53-56. January 1979. Comment, Angus Taylor: _Foundation_ 16:24-25. May 1979.

"Spaceships, Little Nell, and the Sinister Cardboard Man," _Foundation_ 21: 34-47. February 1981.

"Sundering Sea: A Mid-Distant View of British SF," _Foundation_ 30: 14-25. March 1984.

"There Are No Nightmares At the Ritz: An Exploration of _The Drowned World_," _Vector_ 121: 24-28. August 1984.

Bailey, Mark

"Honour and glory of a mouse: Reepicheep of Narnia," _Mythlore_ 5(2): 35-36, 46. Autumn 1978.

Bailly, C.

Litteratures de science fiction: catalogue, collections communales et provinciales, by C. Lhoest and C. Bailly. Liege: Bibliotheque Centrale de la Ville de Liege, 1976. 91 p.

Bain, D. C.

"_Tao Te Ching_ as background to the novels of Ursula K. Le Guin," in: _Ursula K. Le Guin_, ed. by Harold Bloom. New York: Chelsea House, 1986. pp. 211-224.

"R. A. Lafferty: The Function of Archetype in the Western Mystical Tradition," _Extrapolation_ 23(2): 159-174. Summer 1982.

"_Tao Te Ching_ as Background to the Novels of Ursula K. Le Guin," _Extrapolation_ 21(3): 209-222. Fall 1980.

Bainbridge, W. S.

Dimensions of Science Fiction. Cambridge, MA: Harvard University Press, 1986. 278 p.

Spaceflight Revolution: a Sociological Study, The. New York: Wiley, 1976. 294 p.

"Analytical Laboratory, 1938-1976," _Analog_ 100(1): 121-134. January 1980.

"Impact of Science Fiction on Attitudes Toward Technology," in: Emme, Eugene M., ed. _Science Fiction and Space Futures_. San Diego: Univelt, 1982. pp. 121-135.

"New maps of science fiction," by W. S. Bainbridge and M. M. Dalziel. in: Bova, Ben, ed. _Analog Yearbook_. New York: Ace, 1978(c. 1977). pp. 277-299.

"Religions For a Galactic Civilization," in: Emme, Eugene M., ed. _Science Fiction and Space Futures_. San Diego: Univelt, 1982. pp. 185-201.

"Science fiction subculture, The," in: Bainbridge, W. S. _The Spaceflight Revolution: a Sociological Study_. New York: Wiley, 1976. pp. 198-234.

"Science fiction subculture, The," in: Bova, Ben, ed. _Analog Yearbook_. New York: Ace, 1978 (c. 1977). pp.277-299.

"Shape of science fiction as perceived by the fans, The," by W. S. Bainbridge and M. M. Dalziel. _Science Fiction Studies_ 5(2):164-171. July 1978.

"Women in Science Fiction," _Sex Roles_ 8(10): 1081-1091. October 1982.

Bains, William

"Scientifaction," _Vector_ 101: 18-19 April 1981.

Baird, N. D.

Key to Fredric Brown's Wonderland: a Study and an Annotated Bibliographical Checklist. Georgetown, CA: Talisman Literary Research, 1981. 63 p.

Baird, Newton

"Paradox and plot: the fiction of Frederic Brown," _Armchair Detective_ 10:33-38,85-87,151-159,249-260,370-375. No date.

Baker, B. B.

"Something in our midst," _South Carolina Librarian_. Spring 1971.

Baker, J. F.

"P. W. interviews: Judy Lynn del Rey," _Publishers Weekly_ 209(24):10-11. June 14, 1976.

Baker, R. A.

"Seers and prophets: tomorrow's private eyes," by R. A. Baker and M. T. Nietzel. in: Baker, R. A. and Nietzel, M. T. _Private Eyes: One Hundred and One Knights_. Bowling Green: Popular Press, 1985. pp. 341-354.

Baker, R. H.

"Bored with the good earth," _Saturday Review_ 36(32):18-20. August 8, 1953.

Bal, Sant Singh

George Orwell: The Ethical Imagination. Atlantic Highlands, NJ: Humanities Press, 1981. 254 p.

Balabukh, A.

"Science Fiction: Facts and Problems," by A.Balabukh and V. Smoriakov. _Soviet Studies in Literature_ 18(1): 70-79. Winter 1981/1982.

Balcerzan, Ewa

Stanislaw Lem. Warsaw: Paustwowy Instytut Wydawniczy, 1973. 179 p.

"Nichts: ausser den Menschen," _Quarber Merkur_ 38:43-47. November 1974.

"Polnische Sekundar literatur zu Stanislaw Lem," _Quarber Merkur_ 30:15-17. April 1972.

"Polnische Sekundar Literautur zu Stanislaw Lem II," _Quarber Merkur_ 31:55. July 1972.

"Seeking only man: language and ethics in _Solaris_," _Science Fiction Studies_ 2(2):152-156. July 1975.

Balfour, B. J.

"Interview: Alan Dean Foster," _Science Fiction Times_ (Boston) 1(5):1,6-7. November 1979.

Ball, James

Exotic, Historical, Escapist Sword and Sorcery Motion Pictures Produced in America. Ph. D. Dissertation, University of Southern California, 1977. 329 p.

Ball, Ted

"Bibliographic notes on some HPL books," _Science Fiction Collector_ 4:18-19. July 1977.

Ballantine, Betty

"Theodore Sturgeon in Memoriam, 7," _Locus_ 18(7): 26-28. July 1985.

Ballard, J. G.

"Cataclysms and dooms," in: Ash, Brian, ed. _Visual Encyclopedia of Science Fiction_. New York: Harmony, 1977. pp. 130-136.

"Crash," _Magazine Litteraire_ 88:10-12. May 1974.

"J. G. Ballard," _Books and Bookmen_ 15:6. July 1970.

"New metaphor for the future, A," _Algol_ 21:36-37. November 1973.

"Profession of Science Fiction, 26: From Shanghai to Shepperton," _Foundation_ 24: 5-23. February 1982.

"Some words about Crash," _Foundation_ 9:44-53. November 1975. (Part II of this article originally appeared in _Magazine Litteraire_, April 1974, No. 87.)

Balliett, Whitney

"Books," _New Yorker_ pp. 159-160. April 2, 1960. (Book review)

Ballif, Sandra

"Sindarin-Quenya dictionary, part 1," _Mythlore_ 1(1):41-44. January 1969.

"Sindarin-Quenya dictionary, part 2," _Mythlore_ 1(2):33-36. April 1969.

"Sindarin-Quenya dictionary, part 3," _Mythlore_ 1(4):23-26. October 1969.

Ballmer, T. T.

"Sprache in Science Fiction," in: Ermert, Karl, ed. _Neugier oder Flucht?_ Stuttgart: Klett, 1980. pp. 82-92.

Balter, Gerri

"Interview With C. J. Cherryh," _Rune_ No. 61: 5-10. Fall 1980.

Bammer, Angelika

"Utopian futures and cultural myopia," _Alternative Futures_ 4(2/3): 1-16. Spring/Summer 1981.

Bandler, M. J.

"King of the Macabre at Home," _Parents_
57(1): 68-72. January 1982.

Bandstetter, Gabriele

"Verhaeltnis von Traum und Phantastik in Alfred
Kubins Roman _Die andere Seite_," in:
Thomsen, C. W., ed. _Phantastik in Literatur
und Kunst_. Darmstadt: Wissenschaftliche
Buchgesellschaft, 1980. pp. 255-267.

Bangsund, John

John W. Campbell: an Australian Tribute.
Canberra: Ronald E. Graham and John Bangsund,
1972. 100 p.

"Aliens in the Spinifex: Australian SF writers
of the sixties," by Lee Harding and John
Bangsund. _Australian Science Fiction Review_
No. 3:3-10. September 1966.

"Psalms of Olaf Stapledon," _Australian
Science Fiction Review_ No. 7:3-7. February
1967.

Banham, Reyner

"Without mercy or metaphor: robot detectives
in SF," _Listener_ pp. 775-776. November
13, 1958.

Bankers, Peter

"Star Trek: The Motion Picture, the universe
and beyond," _American Cinematographer_
61(2):136-137, 176,202-204. February 1980.

Bankier, Jennifer

"Thoughts on: Darkover, Star Trek, and Canada,"
T-Negative 24: 3-6. September 1974.

Banks, Ann

"Symposium sidelights," _Novel: a Forum on
Fiction_ 3(3):208-211. Spring 1970.

Banks, M. A.

Understanding Science Fiction. Morristown,
NJ: Silver Burdett, 1982. 180 p.

"Starlog Interview: David A. Kyle," _Starlog_
47: 49-51, 63. June 1981.

Banks, R. J.

"Dystopian American futures of Frederik Pohl,
The," _Journal of the American Studies
Association of Texas_ 4:55-64. 1973.

Banks, W. H., Jr.

"Homework assignments," _The Science Teacher_
29:36,39. February 1962.

Bannon, B. A.

"Writer and SF," _Publishers Weekly_
209(24):46-48. June 14, 1976.

Baransczak, Stanislaw

"Elektrycerze i cyberchanioly," _Nurt_ No.
8:14-16. 1972.

Barbano, Nicholas

"Ray Harryhausen Interview," _A Foreign
Fanzine_ 4: 17-22. August 1981.

Barbier, Sandra

"Science fiction fans have big day at
convention," _New Orleans Times Picayune_
Sec. 1, p. 13. July 23, 1979.

Barbour, Douglas

_Worlds out of Words: The SF Novels of Samuel
R. Delany_. Somerset: Bran's Head, 1979.
171 p.

"_Doors of His Face, The Lamps of His Mouth,
and Other Stories, The_," in: Magill, Frank
N., ed. _Survey of Science Fiction
Literature_, Vol. 2. Englewood Cliffs, NJ:
Salem Press, 1979. pp. 583-586.

"_Early Hainish Novels, The_," in: Magill,
Frank N., ed. _Survey of Science Fiction
Literature_, Vol. 2. Englewood Cliffs, NJ:
Salem Press, 1979. pp. 681-686.

"_Lathe of Heaven_: Taoist dream," _Algol_
21:22-24. November 1973.

"_Nova_," in: Magill, Frank N., ed. _Survey
of Science Fiction Literature_, Vol. 4.
Englewood Cliffs, NJ: Salem Press, 1979. pp.
1560-1565.

"_Witches of Karres, The_," in: Magill, Frank
N., ed. _Survey of Science Fiction
Literature_, Vol. 5. Englewood Cliffs, NJ:
Salem Press, 1979. pp. 2482-2487.

"Cultural invention and metaphor in the novels
of Samuel R. Delaney," _Foundation_
7/8:105-121. March 1975.

"Multiplex misdemeanors: the figures of the
artist in the SF novels of Samuel R. Delany,"
Khatru No. 2: 21-24. May 1975.

"On Ursula Le Guin's _A Wizard of Earthsea_,"
Riverside Quarterly 6:119-123. 1974.

Author Entries

Barbour, Douglas (Continued)

"Samuel R. Delany and the Arts of Fiction," Khatru 1(5): 10, 12-22. April 1976.

"Samuel R. Delany," in: Bleiler, E. F., ed. Science Fiction Writers. New York: Scribners, 1982. pp. 329-336.

"Social role of SF: a reply, The," Algol 13(1):45-46. Winter 1976.

"Wholeness and balance in the Hainish novels of Ursula K. Le Guin," Science Fiction Studies 1(3):164-173. Spring 1974.

"Wholeness and Balance," in: Ursula K. Le Guin, ed. by Harold Bloom. New York: Chelsea House, 1986. pp. 23-34.

"Wholeness and balance: an addendum," Science Fiction Studies 2(3):248-249. November 1975.

Barclay, G. S. J.

Anatomy of Horror: The Masters of Occult Fiction. New York: St. Martins, 1978. 144 p.

Barets, Sophie

"D'un Futur deja Present: Dune. Entrien avec Alexandro Jodorowski," Cinema D'aujourd'hui. No. 7:105-110. Spring 1976.

Barets, Stan

Catalogue des ames et cycles de la S. F. Paris: Denoel, 1979. 298 p.

Barfield, Owen

"Some reflections of The Great Divorce of C. S. Lewis," Mythlore 4(1):7-8. September 1976.

Bargiac, Blaise

"Actualisation de virtuel, L'" Arguments 2(9):2-9. 1958.

Baring-Gould, W. S.

"Little superman, what now?" Harpers 193:283-288. September 1946.

Barjeval, Rene

"Science fiction c'est le vrai 'nouveau roman'," Les Nouvelles Litteraires p. 1. Oct. 11, 1962.

Bark, Ed

"Spielberg to Produce Series for NBC," Dallas Morning News July 31, 1984. NewsBank. Film and Television. FTV 11:B2. 1984.

Barker, Chris

"Citadel of the Autarch, and The New Sun," Vector 119: 35-37. April 1984.

Barker, Clive

"Shared Experience: From Science Fiction to Shakespeare," by Mike Alfreds and Clive Barker. Theatre Quarterly 10(39):12-22. 1981.

Barker, Jim

"I'm Not a Number; I'm a Freelance Artist," Focus 6: 24-26. Autumn 1982.

Barker, Lynn

"Submitting to Network Television," SFWA Bulletin 14(2): 72-73. Summer 1979.

Barker, Peter

"Omnilinguals," in: Smith, Nicholas D., ed. Philosophers Look at Science Fiction. Chicago: Nelson-Hall, 1982. pp. 75-85.

Barkley, Christine

"Donaldson as Heir to Tolkien," Mythlore 10(4): 50-57. Spring 1984.

"Predictability and Wonder: Familiarity and Recovery in Tolkien's Works," Mythlore 8(1): 16-18. Spring 1981.

"There But Not Back Again: The Road from Innocence to Maturity," by Christine Barkley and M. B. Ingham. Riverside Quarterly 7(2): 101-104. March 1982.

Barksdale, E. C.

"Back to the Future," by E. C. Barksdale and D. P. Pace. Cinefantastique 16(1):45,56-57. March 1986.

Barlow, George

"Anti-utopian moderne, L'" Esprit 29(3):381-396. 1961.

Barmeyer, Eike

Science Fiction: Theorie und geschichte. Munchen: Fink, 1972. 383 p.

Barmeyer, Eike (Continued)

"Kommunikationen," in: Barmeyer, Eike, ed.
Science fiction: theorie und geschichte.
Munchen: Fink, 1972 p. 203-219.

"SF ueber Worte, Worte ueber SF," in:
Rottensteiner, Franz, ed. Quarber Merkur.
Frankfurt: Suhrkamp, 1979. pp. 70-81.

"Zwischen mythos und gedankespiel,"
Suddeutsche Zeitung November 12, 1970.

Barnes, Harper

"Arthur C. Clarke: Dean of Outer Space Gurus,"
St. Louis (Mo.) Post Dispatch December 5,
1984. in: NewsBank. Film and Television.
72: F12-F13. January 1985.

Barnes, M. J. E.

Linguistics and Language in Science
Fiction-Fantasy. Ph.D. Dissertation, East
Texas State University, 1971. 196 p.

"Using science fiction to teach linguistics,"
College Composition and Communication
26(4):392-394. December 1975.

Barnes, Steven

"Science Fiction: Why Doesn't It Work on
Television?" Beyond 1: 10,17. Winter 1982.

Barnish, V. L.

Notes on Ray Bradbury's Science Fiction.
London: Methuen, 1978. 90 p.

Barnouw, Dagmar

Versuchte Realitaet oder von der Moeglichkeit,
gluecklichere Welten zu denken: Utopischer
Diskurs von Thomas Morus zur feministischen
Science Fiction. Meitingen: Corian, 1985.
277 p.

"Disorderly company: from The Golden Notebook
to The Four Gated City," Contemporary
Literature 14(4):491-514. Autumn 1973.

"Science fiction as a model for probabilistic
worlds: Stanislaw Lem's fantastic empiricism,"
Science Fiction Studies 6(2):153-167.
July 1979.

Barnsley, J. H.

"Island, Walden Two, and the utopian
tradition," World Future Society Bulletin.
16(5): 1-7. September/October 1982.

"Beguiling Visions: H. G. Wells's A Modern
Utopia and Men Like Gods," World Future
Society. Bulletin. 18(5): 27-40.
September/October 1984.

"Two Lesser Dystopias: We and A Clockwork
Orange," World Future Society. Bulletin
18(1): 1-10. January/February 1984.

Barnwell, W. C.

"A. J. Budrys," in: Cowart, David, ed.
Twentieth-Century American Science-Fiction
Writers, Part 1: A-L, Detroit: Gale, 1981.
pp. 83-86.

Baronian, J. B.

"S. F. et fantastique. b) Du surnaturel,"
Europe 580/581:91-96. August/September 1977.

Barr, George

"Where artists rarely tread," Locus No.
83:4a-b. May 13, 1971.

"Will awards reflect truth?" Locus No.
87:8a-b. June 25, 1971.

"Writing again regarding trophies," Locus
No. 147:5-6. August 18, 1973.

Barr, Marleen

Future Females: A Critical Anthology.
Bowling Green: Popular Press, 1981. 191 p.

"Charles Bronson, Samurai, and Other Feminine
Images," in: Barr, Marleen S., ed. Future
Females. Bowling Green, OH: Bowling Green
State University Popular Press, 1981. pp.
138-154.

"Feminist Fantasy: Unisex and the Patriarchy,"
Fantasy Newsletter 6(9): 37-38, 46.
October/November 1983.

"Holding Fast to Feminism and Moving Beyond:
Suzy McKee Charnas's The Vampire Tapestry,"
in: Staicar, Tom, ed. The Feminine Eye. New
York: Ungar, 1982. pp. 60-72.

"Immortal feminist communities of women: a
recent idea," in: Yoke, C. B. and Hassler, D.
M., eds. Death and the Serpent. Westport,
CT: Greenwood, 1985. pp. 39-48.

"Metalinguistic Racial Grammer of Bellona:
Ethnicity, Language, and Meaning in Samuel R.
Delany's Dhalgren," in: Hassler, Donald M.
Patterns of the Fantastic. Mercer Island,
WA: Starmont, 1983. pp. 57-62.

"Science Fiction and the Fact of Women's
Repressed Creativity: Anne McCaffrey Portrays a
Female Artist," Extrapolation 23(1):
70-76. Spring 1982.

Barr, Marleen (Continued)

"Utopia at the end of a male chauvinist dystopian world: Suzy McKee Charnas's feminist science fiction," in: Barr, Marleen, ed. Women and Utopia. New York: Lanham, 1983. pp. 43-66.

Barrett, C. L.

"SF and the $64,000?" Fantasy Times No. 253:4,6. August (2) 1956.

Barrett, D. V.

"Chris Evans Interviewed," Vector 119: 19-25. April 1984.

"Fire-Lizards is Cats; Dragons Ain't Horses: Anne McCaffrey," Vector 123: 3-7. 1984.

"Mary Gentle Interviewed," Vector 116: 7-12. September 1983.

"Personal Guide to Christopher Hodder-Williams," Vector 114: 6-15. 1983.

"Standpoint: A Reassessment of Reassessments," Vector 106: 15-15. February 1982.

"When Fact and Fiction Collide: Christopher Hodder-Williams Interviewed," Vector 114: 16-32. 1983.

Barron, A. S.

"Why do scientists read science fiction?" Bulletin of the Atomic Scientists 13:62-65. February 1957. reply: Asimov, Isaac. 13: inside back cover. May 1957.

Barron, Neil

Anatomy of Wonder: Science Fiction. New York: Bowker, 1976. 471 p.

Anatomy of Wonder: A Critical Guide to Science Fiction, ed. by Neil Barron. 2nd ed. New York: Bowker, 1981. 724 p.

"Mission of Gravity," in: Magill, Frank N., ed. Survey of Science Fiction Literature, Vol. 3. Englewood Cliffs, NJ: Salem Press, 1979. pp. 1424-1428.

"Unsleeping Eye, The," in: Magill, Frank N., ed. Survey of Science Fiction Literature, Vol. 5. Englewood Cliffs, NJ: Salem Press, 1979. pp. 2366-2369.

"Anatomy of wonder: a bibliographic guide to science fiction," Choice 6(11):1536-1545. January 1970.

"Annotated bibliography," in: Magill, Frank N., ed. Survey of Modern Fantasy Literature, Vol 5. Englewood Cliffs, NJ: Salem Press, Inc., 1983. pp. 2517-2531.

"Autobiography, Biography, and Author Studies," in: Barron, Neil, ed. Anatomy of Wonder. 2nd ed. New York: Bowker, 1981. pp. 549-566.

"Bibliography of fantasy anthologies," by Neil Barron, Mike Ashley and R. C. Schlobin. in: Magill, Frank N., ed. Survey of Modern Fantasy Literature, Vol 5. Englewood Cliffs, NJ: Salem Press, Inc., 1983. pp. 2532-2538.

"Bradbury Collection to Bowling Green," SFRA Newsletter 114: 16-17. September 1983.

"Core Collection Checklist," in: Barron, Neil, ed. Anatomy of Wonder. 2nd ed. New York: Bowker, 1981. pp. 624-645.

"History and Criticism," in: Barron, Neil, ed. Anatomy of Wonder. 2nd ed. New York: Bowker, 1981. pp. 531-548.

"Humanities Research Center Builds F&SF Collection," SFRA Newsletter 114: 17-18. September 1983.

"Huntington Library SF Holdings," SFRA Newsletter 111: 11. May 1983.

"Indexes and Bibliographies," in: Barron, Neil, ed. Anatomy of Wonder. 2nd ed. New York: Bowker, 1981. pp. 523-530.

"Launching the SF collection," Wilson Library Bulletin 52(1):56-60. September 1977.

"Library and reference resources," in: Williamson, Jack, ed. Teaching Science Fiction: Education for Tomorrow. Philadelphia: Owlswick, 1980. pp. 242-258.

"Pilgrim Award Acceptance Speech," SFRA Newsletter 105: 4S-8S. October 1982.

"Robert Plank Dies," SFRA Newsletter 114: 7-8. September 1983.

"Science Fiction Illustration," in: Barron, Neil, ed. Anatomy of Wonder. 2nd ed. New York: Bowker, 1981. pp. 571-574.

"Science Fiction on Film and Television," in: Barron, Neil, ed. Anatomy of Wonder. 2nd ed. New York: Bowker, 1981. pp. 567-570.

"Science Fiction Revisited," Choice 10(7): 920-928. September 1973.

"Science Fiction: The New Growth Industry," Choice 16(8): 963-980. October 1979.

"Secrets from the Vault: Building a Personal Reference Library," Fantasy Newsletter 4(9): 23-27. September 1981.

"Selection, Acquisition, and Cataloging of Science Fiction," in: Barron, Neil, ed. Anatomy of Wonder. 2nd ed. New York: Bowker, 1981. pp. 509-522.

Barron, Neil (Continued)

"SF: Fan to Scholar Industry," _Fantasy Newsletter_ 5(6): 34-36. July 1982.

"University of Queensland Collection Grows," _SFRA Newsletter_ 114: 20. September 1983.

"University of Queensland Library Holdings," _SFRA Newsletter_ 111: 9-10. May 1983.

Barrow, C. W.

"On Science Fiction," _Humanities in the South_ 47:3-4. Spring 1978.

Barshay, R. H.

Philip Wylie: The Man and His Work. Washington, DC: University Press of America, 1979. 127 p.

Bartelt, John

"John Varley Interviewed," _Digressions_ No. 4: 24-31, 36. February 1980.

"John Varley's Short Fiction, Part One: Eight Worlds," _Digressions_ No. 4: 5-10. February 1980.

"John Varley's Short Fiction, Part Two: Other Worlds," _Digressions_ No. 4: 14-16. February 1980.

"John Varley: An Interview," by M. P. Smith and John Bartelt. _Rune_ No. 70:35-44. 1982.

Barter, John

"Attitudes Toward Science Fiction," in: Malik, Rex, ed. _Future Imperfect._ London: Pinter, 1980. pp. 31-39.

Barth, Jack

"Fanzines," _Film Comment_ 21(2):24-30. April 1985.

Barth, M. E.

Problems in Generic Classification: Toward a Definition of Fantasy Fiction. Ph. D. Dissertation, Purdue University, 1981. 254 p.

"_Dead Father, The,_" in: Magill, Frank N., ed. _Survey of Modern Fantasy Literature,_ Vol 1. Englewood Cliffs, NJ: Salem Press, Inc., 1983. pp. 347-349.

"_Harvest Home,_" in: Magill, Frank N., ed. _Survey of Modern Fantasy Literature,_ Vol 2. Englewood Cliffs, NJ: Salem Press, Inc., 1983. pp. 690-694.

"_Other, The,_" in: Magill, Frank N., ed. _Survey of Modern Fantasy Literature,_ Vol 3. Englewood Cliffs, NJ: Salem Press, Inc., 1983. pp. 1169-1172.

"Short fiction of Barthelme, The," in: Magill, Frank N., ed. _Survey of Modern Fantasy Literature,_ Vol 3. Englewood Cliffs, NJ: Salem Press, Inc., 1983. pp. 1423-1427.

Barthell, R. J.

"Science fiction: a literature of ideas," _Extrapolation_ 13(1):56-63. December 1971.

"Staging a minicon," in: Williamson, Jack, ed. _Teaching Science Fiction: Education for Tomorrow._ Philadelphia: Owlswick, 1980. pp. 219-227.

Barthes, Roland

"Pour Roland Barthes il n'existe aucun discours qui ne soit une Fiction," _La Quinzaine Litteraire_ No. 225:9. January 16, 1976.

Bartholomew, Barbara

"C. J. Cherryh: A Corrupter of Minds," _Lan's Lantern_ No. 10: 34-36. June 1980.

"Women vs. Science Fiction, part 1," _Sumermorn_ 3: 31-35. Fall 1979.

Bartholomew, David

"Altered States," _Cinefantastique_ 11(1):14-25. Summer 1981.

"Altering states: creating the impossible with makeup; Dick Smith's incredible 35 year career," _Cinefantastique_ 11(1):26-43. Summer 1981.

"Basket Case (review)," _Cinefantastique_ 12(5/6):91-92. July/August 1982.

"Black moon," _Cinefantastique_ 5(1):5-12. Spring 1976.

"Capricorn One (review)," _Cinefantastique_ 7(3/4):58-59. Fall 1978.

"DePalma of the paradise," _Cinefantastique_ 4(2):8-15. Summer 1975.

"Dragonslayer (review)," _Cinefantastique_ 11(3):46. September 1981.

"Electric Grandmother (review)," _Cinefantastique_ 12(4):50. May/June 1982.

"ET: The Extraterrestrial," _Cinefantastique_ 13(2)/13(3):12-27. November/December 1982.

"Exorcist," _Cinefantastique_ 3(4):8-21. Winter 1974.

Bartholomew, David (Continued)

"Fantastic Planet (review)," _Cinefantastique_ 3(3):31. Fall 1974.

"Fog (review)," _Cinefantastique_ 10(1):15. Summer 1980.

"Golden Voyage of Sinbad," by Dan Scapperotti and David Bartholomew. _Cinefantastique_ 3(1):4,42-45. Spring 1974.

"Grendel, Grendel, Grendel (review)," _Cinefantastique_ 12(5/6):91. July/August 1982.

"Howling (review)," _Cinefantastique_ 11(2):46. Fall 1981.

"Pink Floyd The Wall (review)," _Cinefantastique_ 13(2)/13(3):89,92. November/December 1982.

"Polanski: The Tenant," _Cinefantastique_ 5(3):4-7,30-31. Winter 1976.

"Rollerball (review)," _Cinefantastique_ 4(3):31,35. Fall 1975.

"Secret of NIMH (review)," _Cinefantastique_ 13(2)/13(3):88. November/December 1982.

"Silent Running analyzed," _Cinefantastique_ 2(3):45-46. Winter 1973.

"Somewhere in Time (review)," _Cinefantastique_ 10(4):44. Spring 1981.

"Stepford Wives," _Cinefantastique_ 4(2):40-42. Summer 1975.

"Tenant (review)," _Cinefantastique_ 5(2):22-23,29. Fall 1976.

"Wicker Man," _Cinefantastique_ 6(3):4-19,32-47. Winter 1977.

Bartholomew, R. B.

"Science fiction: a unique tool for science teachers," by W. G. Lamb and R. B. Bartholomew. _Science Teacher_ 42(3):37-38. March 1975.

Bartkowski, Frances

Toward a Feminist Eros: Readings in Feminist Utopian Fiction. Ph. D. Dissertation, University of Iowa, 1982. 225 p.

Bartlett, Sally

"Invasion From Eternity: Time and Myth in Middle-Earth," _Mythlore_ 10(3): 18-22. Winter 1984.

Bartter, M. A.

"Times and Spaces: Exploring Gateway," _Extrapolation_ 23(2): 189-200. Summer 1982

"Up the Empire State Building: Satan and King Kong in Walter Tevis's _Mockingbird_," in: Reilly, Robert, ed. _The Transcendent Adventure_. Westport: Greenwood, 1984. pp. 177-187.

Baruch, E. H.

"Dystopia now," _Alternative Futures_ 2(3):55-67. Summer 1979.

"Natural and necessary monster: women in utopia," _Alternative Futures_ 2(1): 29-48. Winter 1979.

Basile, G. M.

"Utopia of Rebirth: Aleksandr Bogdanov's Krasnaia Zvezda," _Canadian-American Slavic Studies_ 18(1/2): 54-62. Spring/Summer 1984.

Basney, L.

"What about fantasy?" _Christianity Today_ 20:18. May 21, 1976.

Basney, Lionel

"Myth, History and Time in the Lord of the Rings," in: Isaacs, N. D. and R. A. Zimbardo. _Tolkien and the Critics_. Lexington: University Press of Kentucky, 1981. pp. 8-18.

Bastian, D. M.

"Over the edge: Denvention II," by David Doering and D. M. Bastian. _Leading Edge_ No. 2:44-50. 1981.

Batchelor, John

Mervyn Peake: a Biographical and Critical Exploration. London: Duckworth, 1976. 176 p.

"Chesterton as an Edwardian novelist," _Chesterton Review_ 1(1):23-35. 1974.

"H. G. Wells," in: Batchelor, John. _The Edwardian Novelists_. New York: St. Martins, 1982. pp. 119-144.

Bates, Susannah

Pendex: An Index of Pen Names and House Names. New York: Garland, 1981. 233 p.

Bathrick, Serafina

"Past as Future: Family and the American Home in Meet Me in St. Louis," Minnesota Review ns6, 1976. pp. 132-139.

Batman, Alex

"Leigh Brackett," in: Cowart, David, ed. Twentieth-Century American Science-Fiction Writers, Part 1: A-L. Detroit: Gale, 1981. pp. 58-60. (Dictionary of Literary Biography, v. 8)

Batory, D. M.

"'The Poison Belt' as a Morality Tale," Riverside Quarterly 7(2): 97-100. March 1982.

"Burroughs-Doyle Connection," Science Fiction Collector 15: 10-14. July 1981.

"Look behind Conan Doyle's 'Lost World', A," Riverside Quarterly 6(4):268-271. December 1977.

"Rime of the Polestar," Riverside Quarterly 7(4): 222-227. December 1985.

Battaglia, Beatrice

"Varieta formali della 'science fiction', Le," Quaderni di Filologia Germanica della Facolta di Lettere e Filosofia dell'Universita di Bologna. 2: 213-234. 1982.

Batteau, D. W.

"Science fiction, prophet and critic; Harvard's collection of an esoteric literary genre," Harvard Alumni Bulletin 60(5):209-211,223. November 30, 1957.

Battestini, Monique

"Nouvelle francaise de science-fiction et l'enseignment," Cahiers Pedagogiques 150: 5-8. January 1977.

"Origines de la mouvelle francaise de Science Fiction," Revue de Pacifique 3(1):3-23. spring, 1977. (California State Univ.)

Baudin, Henri

Monstres dans la science fiction. Paris: Lettres Modernes Minard, 1976. 74 p.

Science fiction: un univers en expansion. Paris: Bordas, 1971. 159 p.

"SF et fantastique. a) Un avatar de l'imaginaire," Europe 580/581:85-91. August/September 1977.

Baudrillard, Jean

"Simulacres et Science-fiction," in: Baudrillard, Jean. Simulacres et simulatoin. Paris: Galilee, 1981. pp. 179-188.

Bauenfeind, Bill

"Tracking Down the TZ Alumni," Twilight Zone 4(1): 75-79. March/April 1984.

Bauer, Eberhard

"Aus einer anderen Welt: die begegnung mit ausseririrdeschen lebewesen im lichte der science fiction," in: Neue Wissenschaft. Zeitschrift fur Grenzgebiete des Seelenlebens 15(1/2):32-53. 1967.

Baughman, Ronald

L. Frank Baum: the Wonderful Wizard of Oz. An Exhibition of his Published Writings, in Commemoration of the Centenary of his Birth, May 15, 1856, by J. Baum and R. Baughman. New York: Columbia Univ. Libraries, 1956. 50 p.

Baum, F. J.

To Please a Child, by F. J. Baum and R. P. McFall. Chicago: Reilly and Lee, 1962. 284 p.

Baum, Joan

L. Frank Baum: the Wonderful Wizard of Oz. An Exhibition of his Published Writings, in Commemoration of the Centenary of his Birth, May 15, 1856, by Joan Baum and Ronald Baughman. New York: Columbia Univ. Libraries, 1956. 50 p.

Baumann, H. D.

"Anmerkungen zur Science Fiction kunst," Science Fiction Times (Germany) 27(6):4-14. June 1985.

"Koepfe aus dem Feuer," Science Fiction Times (Germany) 27(5):7-9. May 1985.

"Sebastian F. Raumschiffkommandant," Science Fiction Times (Germany) 26(7):11-14. July 1984.

Baumgardner, G. B.

Cat's Cradle: An Archetypal Study in Satire. Masters Thesis, Chico State College, CA., 1968. 56 p.

Baumgartner, K. O.

"What's an Ubik? Science Fiction Reference
Sources," Reference Services Review 11(4):
81-92. Winter 1983.

Baumier, Jean

"Denis G...et la croisiere Mars," Europe
revue mensuelle No. 139/140:50-53.
July/August. 1957.

Bausinger, H.

"Wege zur erforschung der trivialen literatur,"
in: H. O. Burger, ed. Studien zur
Trivialliteratur. Frankfurt, 1968.

Baxter, John

Science Fiction in the Cinema. London:
Zwemmer, 1970, 240 p.; New York: A. S.
Barnes, 1970.

"Hornbook for critics, A," Niekas 9:31-34.
September 1964.

Baxter, Paul

"Time And Again And Again...," Vector 100:
33-34. December 1980.

Baxter, Sylvester

"Edward Bellamy," Books News 8(96):
416-417. August 1889/1890.

Bayley, B. J.

"Into the Arena: Who Owns the Noosphere,"
Vector 113: 27-31. 1983.

"Science, religion and the science fiction
idea: or, where would we be without Hitler?"
Foundation 17:50-57. September 1979.

"SF Novel and Basic Form," Vector 103:
19-23. August 1981.

"So What's New? My Thoughts on the Bomb,"
Vector 116: 29-33. September 1983.

Bazin, N. T.

"Androgeny or Catastrophe: The Vision of Doris
Lessing's Later Novels," Frontiers 5(3):
10-15. Fall 1980.

"Evolution of Doris Lessing's Art from a
Mystical Moment to Science Fiction," in:
Reilly, Robert, ed. The Transcendent
Adventure. Westport: Greenwood, 1984. pp.
157-167.

Beach, Sarah

"Mythopoesis: Style," Mythlore 11(3): 27.
Winter/Spring 1985.

Beagle, P. S.

"Edgar Pangborn: an appeciation," Locus
9(4):1-2. March 31, 1976.

"Tolkien's Magic Ring," in: Boyer, Robert H.
and Zahorski, Kenneth J. Fantasists on
Fantasy. New York: Avon Discus, 1984. pp.
125-136.

Beahm, George

Kirk's Works: an Index of the Art of Tim
Kirk. Newport News, VA: Heresy Press, n.d.
122 p.

"Fantasy and Science Fiction Art: The Limited
Edition Print," in: Hopkins, Mariane S., ed.
Fandom Directory 1982. Newport News, VA:
Fandom Computer Services, 1982. pp. 370-376.

Beale, Ken

"Arthur C. Clarke talks about 2001," Science
Fiction Times No. 454:1-4. May 1968.

"How Star Trek does it," Science Fiction
Times No. 450:5. January 1968.

"Motion pictures, stage and TV: the best of
1960, part 1," Science Fiction Times No.
358:5-6. March (2) 1961.

"Motion pictures, stage and TV: the best of
1960, part 2," Science Fiction Times No.
359:4-5. April (1) 1961.

"Motion pictures, stage and TV: the best of
1961, part 1," Science Fiction Times No.
382:2-3. March (2) 1962.

"Planet of the Apes," Science Fiction Times
No. 452:2. March 1968.

"Twenty years of imaginative entertainment,"
Science Fiction Times No. 369:13-14,39.
September 1961.

Bealmear, Robert

"Eerie effects for Lifeforce," American
Cinematographer 66(6): 60-67. June 1985.

Bealu, Marcel

"Multitude d'immensites par-dela la porte du
profond sommeil," in: H. P. Lovecraft.
Paris: Editions de l'Herne, 1969. pp. 177-181.

Bear, Greg

"Beneath the dream: tomorrow through the past," Science Fiction Writers of America. Bulletin. 14(3):38-41. Fall 1979.

"Nebula Awards give solid gains to science fiction authors," Los Angeles Times: Book Section p. 3. March 7, 1978.

"Science Fiction Feels the Force," Los Angeles Times. Calendar. pp. 40-43. June 8, 1980.

"Theodore Sturgeon in Memoriam, 1," Locus 18(7): 1, 25. July 1985.

Beard, Michael

"Jack Finney," in: Cowart, David, ed. Twentieth-Century American Science-Fiction Writers, Part 1, A-L. Detroit: Gale, 1981. pp. 182-185. (Dictionary of Literary Biography, v. 8)

Beare, Geraldine

Index to the Strand Magazine 1981-1950. Westport, CT: Greenwood, 1982. 859 p.

Beare, Rhona

"Charles Williams and the Angelicals," Mythlore 8(4): 31, 38. Winter 1982.

"Charles Williams and The Stone," Mythlore 8(3):34. Autumn 1981.

"Tolkien's Calendar and Ithildin," Mythlore 9(4): 23-24. Winter 1983.

Beatie, B. A.

"Narrative Technique in Stardance," Extrapolation 23(2): 175-184. Summer 1982

Beauchamp, Gorman

Jack London. Mercer Island, WA: Starmont, 1984. 96 p. (Starmont Reader's Guide, 15)

"Island of Doctor Moreau as Theological Grotesque," Papers on Language and Literature 15: 408-417. 1979.

"1984: Oceania as an ideal state," College Literature 11(1): 1-12. 1984.

"Anti-politics of utopia," Alternative Futures 2(1): 49-59. Winter 1979.

"Cultural primitivism as norm in the dystopian novel," Extrapolation 19(1):88-96. December 1977.

"Frankenstein Complex and Asimov's Robots," Mosaic 13(3/4): 83-94. Spring/Summer 1980.

"Future words: language and the dystopian novel," Style 8(3):437-451. Fall 1974.

"Jack London's Utopian Dystopia and Dystopian Utopia," in: Roemer, Kenneth M., ed. America As Utopia. New York: Franklin, 1981. pp. 91-107.

"Jack London," in: Cowart, David, ed. Twentieth-Century American Science-Fiction Writers, Part 1: A-L, Detroit: Gale, 1981. pp. 297-303. (Dictionary of Literary Biography, v. 8)

"Man as Robot: The Taylor System in We," in: Erlich, Richard D., ed. Clockwork Worlds. Westport, CT: Greenwood, 1983. pp. 85-93.

"Of man's last disobedience: Zamiatin's We and Orwell's 1984," Comparative Literature Studies 10(4):285-301. December 1973.

"Proto-Dystopia of Jerome K. Jerome," Extrapolation 24(2): 170-181. Summer 1983.

"Themes and uses of fictional utopias; a bibliography of secondary works in English," Science Fiction Studies 4(1):55-63. March 1977.

"Zamiatin's We," in: Rabkin, Eric S., et. al., eds. No Place Else. Carbondale: Southern Illinois University Press, 1983. pp. 56-77.

Beaumont, R. A.

"Weapons in Future Warfare," by R. A. Beaumont and R. S. Ficks. in: Bretnor, Reginald, ed. The Future at War: Vol. 1: Thor's Hammer. New York: Ace, 1979. pp. 147-172.

Bechtold, A. R.

"Be Your Own Agent," Empire: For the SF Writer 5(1): 9. Winter 1979.

Beck, C. F.

Hammer and Tongs. Lakeport, CA: Futile Press, 1937. 19 p.

Beck, C. T.

"Reader's forum: science fiction survey," Journal of Popular Film & Television 7(3):322-325. 1979.

Becker, Alida

Tolkien Scrapbook. Philadelphia: Running Press, 1975. 191 p.

Becker, M. L.

"Reader's guide; pseudo-scientific fiction,"
Saturday Review of Literature 7(1):13. July
26, 1930. (on Sherlock Holmes)

Becker, M. R.

Clifford D. Simak: A Primary and Secondary
Bibliography. Boston: G. K. Hall, 1980.
149 p.

Beharriell, F. J.

"Arthur Schnitzler and the fantastic," in:
Collins, R. A. and H. D. Pearce, eds. The
Scope of the Fantastic: Theory, Technique,
Major Authors. Westport, CT: Greenwood Press,
1985. pp. 207-214.

Behla, Paul

"Was is das: wissenschaftliche phantastik?"
Potsdamer Forschungen Wiss Schriftenreihe der
Padgogischen Hochschule "Karl Liebknecht"
Potsdam. Reihe A., No. 15, 65-74. 1975.

"Wissenschaftlich-Phantastische Literatur,
Die," in: Ludwig, Nadeshda, ed. Sowjetische
Kinder- und Jugendliteratur. Berlin:
Kinderbuchverlag, 1981. 324 p.

Behnke, R. I.

"H. P. Lovecraft," Quarber Merkur 30:43-58.
April 1972.

Behr, O. M.

"Forget science fiction," American Bar
Association Journal 55:316. April 1969.
(not about science fiction)

Beja, Morris

"2001: odyssey to Byzantium,"
Extrapolation 10(2):67-68. May 1969.

"Three perspectives of a film," by Morris
Beja, Robert Plank and Alex Eisenstein. in:
Clareson, Thomas D., ed. SF: The Other Side
of Realism. Bowling Green, Ohio: Bowling
Green University Popular Press, 1971. pp.
263-271.

Belcher, Susan

"Frankenstein's Mother," by Seon Manley and
Susan Belcher. in: Manley, Seon, and Belcher,
Susan, eds. O, Those Extraordinary Women.
Philadelphia: Chilton, 1972. pp. 31-56.

Belevan, Harry

Theorie du Fantastique: Notes pour une
dynamique de la litterature d'expression
fantastique. Bruxelles: Recto-Verso, 1980.
124 p. (Ides...et autres, 27)

Belgion, Montgomery

H. G. Wells. London: Longmans, 1953. 43 p.

Belisle, L. P.

Literary Treatment of Alienation in Isaac
Asimov's Foundation Trilogy. Masters Thesis,
Wayne State University, 1969. 58 p.

Bell, A. A., Jr.

"Origin of the name Narnia," Mythlore
7(2):29. Summer 1980.

Bell, John

"Charles R. Saunders Interview," Black
American Literature Forum 18(2): 90-92.
Summer 1984.

"James DeMille: Canadian pilgrim through space
and time," Borealis 1(2):6-9. Spring 1978.

"Persistence of Division: Further Examples of
English-Language Science Fiction Concerning
Canadian Separatist Conflicts,"
Science Fiction Studies 11(2): 190-193.
July 1984.

"Uneasy Union: A Checklist of English-Language
Science Fiction Concerning Canadian Separatist
Conflicts," Science Fiction Studies 9(1):
82-88. March 1982.

Bell, Joseph

Howard Phillips Lovecraft: The Books,
1915-1981. Toronto: Soft Books, 1981. 71 p.

Howard Phillips Lovecraft: The Books, Addenda
and Auxiliary. Toronto: Soft Books, 1983.
39 p.

Bell, M. J.

"Otis Adelbert Kline's Mars novels," Oak
Leaves 1(4):3-6. Summer 1971.

"Otis Adelbert Kline's Venus novels," Oak
Leaves 1(10):3-6. Winter 1972/73.

Bell, M. S.

"Report from NASFIC," Leading Edge No.
10:83-87. Fall 1985.

Bell, M. S. (Continued)

"Sheer joy of storytelling: an interview with C. J. Cherryh," <u>Leading Edge</u> No. 8:11-23. Fall 1984.

"View from the edge: free will and predestination in The Lord of the Rings," <u>Leading Edge</u> No. 2:92-95. 1981.

Bell, Michael

"Barsoom and Gor," <u>ERB-dom</u> No. 46:21-22. May 1971.

Bell, P. K.

"American fiction: forgetting ordinary truths," <u>Dissent</u> 20(1):26-34. Winter 1973.

Bellamy, Edward

"How and Why I Wrote Looking Backward," in: Roemer, Kenneth M., ed. <u>American As Utopia</u>. New York: Franklin, 1981. pp. 22-27.

Bellamy, J. D.

"Kurt Vonnegut for president: the making of an academic reputation," in: Klinkowitz, Jerome and John Somer, eds. <u>The Vonnegut Statement</u>. New York: Delacorte Press/Seymore Lawrence, 1973. pp. 71-89.

"Kurt Vonnegut, Jr.," by J. D. Bellamy and John Casey. in: Bellamy, Joe David, ed. <u>The New Fiction: Interviews with Innovative American Writers</u>. Urbana: University of Illinois Press, 1974. pp. 194-207.

Bellemin-Noel, Jean

"Formes fantastiques aux themes fantasmatiques," <u>Litterature</u> No. 2:103-118. 1971.

"Notes sur le fantastique," <u>Litterature</u> no. 8:3-23. December 1972.

Bello, F. P.

<u>Typecasting: A Study of the Directors of Televised Science Fiction</u>. Masters Thesis, California State University, Fullerton, 1979. 142 p.

Ben Yehuda, Nachman

"Science Fiction in Israel," <u>Science Fiction and Fantasy Research Index</u> 2: 63-64. 1982.

Benares, Camden

"Future unlimited: birth of a future history," <u>Science Fiction Writers of America. Bulletin</u>. 14(3):22-24. Fall 1979.

Benaton, Dena

"Battlestar Galactica: a review," <u>Locus</u> 11(8):10-11. October 1978.

Bendau, C. P.

<u>Colin Wilson: the Outsider and Beyond</u>. San Bernardino, CA: Borgo Press, 1979. 63 p.

<u>Still worlds collide: Philip Wylie and the end of the American dream</u>. San Bernardino, CA: Borgo Press, 1980. 63 p. (The Milford series: Popular writers of today, v. 30.)

"<u>Disappearance, The</u>," in: Magill, Frank N., ed. <u>Survey of Science Fiction Literature</u>, Vol. 2. Englewood Cliffs, NJ: Salem Press, 1979. pp. 543-547.

"<u>Half Past Human</u>," in: Magill, Frank N., ed. <u>Survey of Science Fiction Literature</u>, Vol. 2. Englewood Cliffs, NJ: Salem Press, 1979. pp. 940-944.

"<u>Sirens of Titan, The</u>," in: Magill, Frank N., ed. <u>Survey of Science Fiction Literature</u>, Vol. 5. Englewood Cliffs, NJ: Salem Press, 1979. pp. 2079-2084.

"<u>When Worlds Collide</u> and <u>After Worlds Collide</u>," in: Magill, Frank N., ed. <u>Survey of Science Fiction Literature</u>, Vol. 5. Englewood Cliffs, NJ: Salem Press, 1979. pp. 2463-2468.

Bender, Karen

"One Hundred Most Important People in Science Fiction/Fantasy: A. Merritt," <u>Starlog</u> No. 100: 76, 80. November 1985.

"One Hundred Most Important People in Science Fiction/Fantasy: Arthur C. Clarke," <u>Starlog</u> No. 100: 44. November 1985.

"One Hundred Most Important People in Science Fiction/Fantasy: Buster Crabbe," <u>Starlog</u> No. 100: 75. November 1985.

"One Hundred Most Important People in Science Fiction/Fantasy: George Orwell," <u>Starlog</u> No. 100: 52. November 1985.

"One Hundred Most Important People in Science Fiction/Fantasy: J. R. R. Tolkien," <u>Starlog</u> No. 100: 53. November 1985.

"One Hundred Most Important People in Science Fiction/Fantasy: Jim Henson," <u>Starlog</u> No. 100: 81-82. November 1985.

Benedict, Joan

Stanley Kubrick's A Clockwork Orange.   M.A. Thesis, McGill University, 1978.

Benet, W. R.

"Some pleasing horrors,"   Saturday Review of Literature   p. 18.   September 12, 1942.

Benevento, J. O.

"Introduction to the realities of fiction: teaching magic realism in three stories by Borges, Fuentes, and Marquez,"   Kansas Quarterly   16(3): 125-131.   Summer 1984.

Benfey, Theodor

"Seeds and the Vonneguts,"   Chemistry   45:2. November 1972.

Benford, Gregory

Proceedings of the Day Program and Nebula Awards Banquet: 1970.   Philadelphia: Terminus, Owlswick and Ft. Mudge Electrick Street Railway Gazette, 1970.

"Aliens and Knowability,"   Starship   19(1): 25-27.   November 1982.

"Aliens and Knowability: A Scientist's Perspective,"   in: Slusser, George E., ed. Bridges to Science Fiction.   Carbondale: Southern Illinois University Press, 1980.   pp. 53-63.

"Aliens I have Known,"   Future Life   21: 71-73.   September 1980.

"Awe and the awful, The,"   in: Bova, Ben, ed. Analog Yearbook.   New York: Ace, 1978 (c. 1977).   pp. 13-21.

"Cobblestones into highways,"   Locus 10(8):6,9.   October 1977.

"Hard Science Fiction in the Real World," Science Fiction Review   13(1): 29-34. February 1985.

"Hard science fiction in the real world,"   in: Pournelle, Jerry, ed.   The Science Fiction Yearbook.   New York: Baen, 1985.   pp. 52-72.

"In the Wave's Wake,"   Foundation   30: 5-9. March 1984.

"Is There a Technological Fix for the Human Condition?"   Vector   119: 5-15.   April 1984.

"Journey to the Genre's Core,"   Vector   121: 22-23.   August 1984.

"Journey to the Genre's Core: A Reply to Damon Knight,"   Science Fiction Review   13(3): 32. August 1984.

"On reviewing SF,"   Locus   11(2):8-10. March 1978.

"Profession of Science Fiction, 22: A String of Days,"   Foundation   21: 5-17.   February 1981.

"Putting Science Into Science Fiction," Writer   96(7): 7-10.   July 1983.

"Science and science fiction,"   in: McNelly, W. E., ed.   Science Fiction the Academic Awakening.   Shreveport, LA: CEA, 1974.   pp. 30-34.

"Science, science fiction and all that . . ." Algol   13(1):29-31.   Winter 1976.

"String of Days,"   Science Fiction Review 10(1): 14-20.   February 1981.

"Teaching physics with science fiction,"   Fan Plus   1(1):13-14.   January 1980.

"Time-word path: building SF, The,"   Algol 15(3):31-33.   Summer/Fall 1978.

"To borrow or not to borrow: Benford and Faulkner,"   Fantasy Review   8(4): 9-10, 12. April 1985.

"Why is There So Little Science in Literature," in: Pournelle, Jerry, ed.   Nebula Award Stories Sixteen.   New York: Bantam, 1983.   pp. 22-30.

"Why Is There So Little Science in Literature?" Isaac Asimov's Science Fiction Magazine 6(2): 43-50.   February 15, 1982.

Bengels, Barbara

"'Read History': Dehumanization in Karel Capek's R. U. R.,"   in: Dunn, Thomas P., ed. The Mechanical God.   Westport: Greenwood, 1982.   pp. 13-17.

"Flights into the Unknown: Structural Similarities in Two Works by H. G. Wells and Henry James,"   Extrapolation   21(4): 361-366.   Winter 1980.

"Olaf Stapledon's 'Odd John' and 'Sirius': ascent into bestiality,"   Foundation 9:57-61.   November 1975.

"Teaching of science fiction: another view, The,"   HPT News: Newsletter of the Lehigh University Perspectives on Technology Program 3:4-6.   December 1977.

Bengston, Goran

"Billion Year Spree: an open letter," Foundation   6:69-75.   May 1974.

Benidt, Jennifer

"Fright Night," by Jennifer Benidt and Janine Pourroy. Cinefex No. 25:54-71. February 1986.

"Terminator, The," Cinefex No. 21:4-23. April 1985.

Benison, Jonathan

"Jean Baudrillard on the Current State of SF," Foundation 32: 25-42. November 1984.

Bennett, Arnold

"Sci-Fi," Logos (Montreal, Canada) 5(1): 4-5. April 1972.

Bennett, Carl

"Ballantine books: a checklist of science fiction, fantasy, and weird fiction, 1953-1976," Science Fiction Collector 6:3-47. May 1978.

Bennett, M. A.

"Theme of responsibility in Miller's A Canticle for Leibowitz, The," English Journal 59:484-489. April 1970.

Bennett, M. J.

"Edgar Allan Poe and the Literary Tradition of Lunar Speculation," Science-Fiction Studies 10(2): 137-147. July 1983.

Bennett, Sister M.

"Science fact or fiction; which, and why?" Catholic Library World 25:179-181. March 1954.

Bennetts, Leslie

"Spielberg to Produce New TV Adventure Series," New York Times p. 21. July 31, 1984.

Benoit, Monique

"La vie est le reve d'un reve," Etudes Litteraires 7(1): 109-125. April 1974.

Benson, Gordon, Jr.

Anne Inez McCaffrey: Dragonlady and More, a Working Bibliography. Albuquerque: Galactic Central, 1986. 9 p.

Arthur Bertram Chandler: Master Navigator of Space. Albuquerque: Galactic Central, 1985. 14 p.

Arthur Wilson "Bob" Tucker. Albuquerque: Galactic Central, 1985. 5 p.

Catherine Lucille Moore and Henry Kuttner: A Working Bibliography, by Virgil Utter and Gordon Benson, Jr. Albuquerque: Galactic Central, 1986. 45 p.

Edgar Pangborn: A Bibliography. Albuquerque: Galactic Central, 1985. 4 p.

Eric Frank Russell: A Working Bibliography. Albuquerque: Galactic Central, 1986. 18 p.

Gordon Rupert Dickson: First Dorsai. Albuquerque: Galactic Central, 1986. 20 p.

H. Beam Piper. Albuquerque: Galactic Central, 1985. 5 p.

Hal Clement (Harry Clement Stubbs). Albuquerque: Galactic Central, 1985. 5 p.

Harry Maxwell Harrison. Albuquerque: Galactic Central, 1985. 17 p.

James White: Doctor to Aliens: A Working Bibliography. Albuquerque: Galactic Central, 1986. 9 p.

John Kilian Houston Brunner. Albuquerque: Galactic Central, 1985. 25 p.

Leigh Douglass Brackett and Edmond Hamilton: A Working Bibliography. Albuquerque: Galactic Central, 1986. 16 p.

Manly Wade Wellman: The Gentleman From Chapel Hill; A Memorial Working Bibliography. Albuquerque: Galactic Central, 1986. 17 p.

Margaret St. Clair. Albuquerque: Galactic Central, 1986. 10 p.

Poul Anderson: Myth-Maker and Wonder-Weaver: An Interim Bibliography (1947-1982). Albuquerque, NM: Galactic Central, 1982. 29 p.

Poul Anderson: Myth-Master and Wonder-Weaver, an Interim Bibliography 1947-1986, Fourth revised edition. Albuquerque: Galactic Central, 1986. 46 p.

William Tenn (Philip Klass). Albuquerque: Galactic Central, 1985. 7 p.

Williamson, Jack (John Stewart): Child and Father of Wonder. Albuquerque: Galactic Central, 1985. 14 p.

Benson, Michael

Vintage Science Fiction Films, 1896-1949. Jefferson, NC: McFarland, 1985. 219 p.

Bentcliffe, Eric

Checklist, Part 1: Magazines, Original &
Reprint. Stockbridge: Norwest Science
Fantasy Club, n.d. 12 p.

Benthail, J.

"Architectural fantasy of Jules Verne,"
Architectural Design 49(2):69-70. 1974.

Beraducci, M. C.

Content Analysis of the Science Fiction
Writing of Arthur C. Clarke, Lester Del Rey,
and Isaac Asimov. Research paper, Long Island
University, 1970.

Beranek, Martin

"Weird fiction," Science Fiction Times
(Bremerhaven) No. 137:8-14. October 1975.

Bereit, V. F.

"Genre of science fiction, The," Elementary
English 46:895-900. November 1969.

Berenguer, Andres

"Adventure of photographing Jules Verne's
Fabulous Journey to the Center of the Earth,"
American Cinematographer
58(12):1294-1296,1308. December 1977.

Beres, Stanislaw

"Universum des Stanislaw Lem, Das," Quarber
Merkur 62: 42-47. December 1984.

Berg, J. H.

"Norwegian Fandom Are You Serious?" Thule
1(1): 1-2. 1982.

"Situation Today," Thule 1(1): 3-4. 1982.

Berg, Serge

"Verne's fiction as strange as truth," Los
Angeles Times Sec. 1-B, p. 7. March 31, 1978.

Berger, A. A.

"Personal Response to Whetmore's 'A Female
Captain's Enterprise'," in: Barr, Marlene S.,
ed. Future Females. Bowling Green, OH:
Bowling Green State University Popular Press,
1981. pp. 162-163.

Berger, A. I.

Magic That Works: John W. Campbell and the
American Response to Technology. Masters
Thesis, Northern Illinois University, 1972.
151 p.

Science Fiction and the Ideology of Changee in
America, 1935-1975. Ph.D. Dissertation,
Northern Illinois University, 1978. 411 p.

"Analog Science Fiction/Science Fact," by A.
I. Berger and Mike Ashley. in: Tymn, M. B.
and Ashley, Mike. Science Fiction, Fantasy,
and Weird Fiction Magazines. Westport, CT:
Greenwood, 1985. pp. 60-103.

"Bug Jack Barron," in: Magill, Frank N.,
ed. Survey of Science Fiction Literature,
Vol. 1. Englewood Cliffs, NJ: Salem Press,
1979. pp. 265-271.

"Davy," in: Magill, Frank N., ed. Survey
of Science Fiction Literature, Vol. 1.
Englewood Cliffs, NJ: Salem Press, 1979. pp.
493-496.

"Dhalgren," in: Magill, Frank N., ed.
Survey of Science Fiction Literature, Vol. 2.
Englewood Cliffs, NJ: Salem Press, 1979. pp.
533-538.

"Dispossessed, The," in: Magill, Frank N.,
ed. Survey of Science Fiction Literature,
Vol. 2. Englewood Cliffs, NJ: Salem Press,
1979. pp. 548-553.

"Iron Dream, The," in: Magill, Frank N.,
ed. Survey of Science Fiction Literature,
Vol. 3. Englewood Cliffs, NJ: Salem Press,
1979. pp. 1062-1067.

"Space Merchants, The," in: Magill, Frank
N., ed. Survey of Science Fiction
Literature, Vol. 5. Englewood Cliffs, NJ:
Salem Press, 1979. pp. 2127-2131.

"Love, Death, and the Atomic Bomb: Sexuality
and Community in Science Fiction, 1935-55,"
Science-Fiction Studies 8(3): 280-295.
November 1981. .

"Magic that works: John W. Campbell and the
American response to technology, The,"
Journal of Popular Culture 5(4):867-943.
Spring 1972.

"Nuclear energy: science fiction's metaphor of
power," Science Fiction Studies
6(2):121-128. July 1979.

"Science fiction critiques of the American
space program, 1945-1958," Science Fiction
Studies 5(2):99-109. July 1978.

"SF fans in socio-economic perspective:
factors in the social consciousness of a
genre," Science Fiction Studies
4(3):232-246. November 1977.

Berger, A. I. (Continued)

"Triumph of prophecy: science fiction and nuclear power in the post-Hiroshima period, The," Science Fiction Studies 3(2):143-150. July 1976.

Berger, H. L.

Anti-Utopian Science Fiction of the Mid-Twentieth Century. Ph.D. Dissertation, University of Tennessee, 1970. 234 p.

Science Fiction and the New Dark Age. Bowling Green, Ohio: Bowling Green University Popular Press, 1976. 231 p.

Berger, Meyer

"Space fever hits the small fry," New York Times Magazine p. 17. March 16, 1952.

Bergeron, Philippe

"Dream Flight," American Cinematographer 65(8): 49-51. August/September 1984.

Berghahn, K. K.

Literarische Utopien von Morus bis Gegenwart, by K. K. Berghahn and H. U. Seeber. Koenigstein: Sthenaeum, 1983. 308 p.

Berghaus, Edgar

"Ostblock Science Fiction," Hectographed special supplement to Science Fiction Times No. 75, 1967.

Bergier, Jacques

"Bornes du possible reculent," Arguments 2(9):9-11. 1958.

"H. P. Lovecraft, ce grand genie venu d'ailleurs," in: H. P. Lovecraft. Paris: Editions de l'Herne, 1969. pp. 121-125.

"Litterature Sovietique d'avant-garde," Planete no. 2. December 1961/January 1962.

"Longue quete dans la nuit cosmique," Planete 23:19. July/August 1965.

"Science fiction et critique sociale," Critique (Paris) 82. March 1954.

"Science fiction sovietique," Magazine Litteraire 88:19-20. May 1974.

"Science fiction," in: Encyclopedie de la Pleiade. Histoire de la litterature vol. 3. (Ed. Raymond Queneau). Paris, 1958, 1963. pp. 1671-1689.

Berglund, E. P.

Reader's Guide to the Cthulhu Mythos, by Robert Weinberg and E. P. Berglund. Albuquerque: Silver Scarab Press, 1973. Revised edition, 88 p.

Bergmann, Frank

"Roots of Tolkien's tree: the influence of George Macdonald and German romanticism upon Tolkien's essay, 'On Fairy Stories', The," Mosaic 10(2):5-14. Winter 1977.

Bergonzi, Bernard

Early H. G. Wells: a Study of the Scientific Romances, The. Toronto: University of Toronto Press, 1961. 226 p.

H. G. Wells: a Collection of Critical Essays. Englewood Cliffs, New Jersey: Prentice-Hall, 1976. 182 p.

"The Time Machine, an ironic myth," Critical Quarterly 2:293-305. 1960.

"Another early Wells item," Nineteenth Century Fiction 13:72-73. 1958.

"Battle of Dorking, The," Notes and Queries 206:346-347. September 1961.

"Publication of The Time Machine, 1894-1895," Review of English Studies 11:42-51. 1960. also in: Clareson, T. D., ed. SF: The Other Side of Realism. Bowling Green: Bowling Green Popular Press, 1971. pp. 204-215.

Bergvall, Ake

"Myth Retold: C. S. Lewis' Till We Have Faces," Mythlore 11(1): 5-12, 22. Summer 1984.

Berkenwald, M.

"Interview: Norman Spinrad," by M. Berkenwald, John Christopher. Future Life 23: 22-25. December 1980.

Berkowitz, Stan

"Computers Create the Animation for Disney's Video Game Movie," New Orleans Times Picayune p. 6-7. July 9, 1982.

Berkvist, Robert

"Science fiction for boys," New York Times Book Review p. 38. June 9, 1963.

Berman, B. L.

"Confidence-Man: His Masquerade, The," in:
Magill, Frank N., ed.   Survey of Modern
Fantasy Literature, Vol 1. Englewood Cliffs,
NJ: Salem Press, Inc., 1983. pp. 308-313.

"Ixion in Heaven," in: Magill, Frank N.,
ed.   Survey of Modern Fantasy Literature,
Vol 2. Englewood Cliffs, NJ: Salem Press,
Inc., 1983. pp. 791-793.

"Steppenwolf," in: Magill, Frank N., ed.
Survey of Modern Fantasy Literature, Vol 4.
Englewood Cliffs, NJ: Salem Press, Inc., 1983.
pp. 1821-1825.

"Strange Case of Dr. Jekyll and Mr. Hyde,
The," in: Magill, Frank N., ed.   Survey of
Modern Fantasy Literature, Vol 4. Englewood
Cliffs, NJ: Salem Press, Inc., 1983. pp.
1834-1839.

"Trilby," in: Magill, Frank N., ed.
Survey of Modern Fantasy Literature, Vol 4.
Englewood Cliffs, NJ: Salem Press, Inc., 1983.
pp. 1969-1971.

Berman, Jeffrey

"Forster's other cave: the platonic structure
of 'The Machine Stops',"   Extrapolation
17(2):172-181. May 1976.

"Where's All the Fiction in Science Fiction?"
in: Barr, Marlene S., ed. Future Females.
Bowling Green, OH: Bowling Green State
University Popular Press, 1981. pp. 164-176.

Berman, Ruth

Suspending Disbelief: The Development of
Fantasy as a Literary Genre in Nineteenth
Century British Fiction as Represented by Four
Leading Periodicals.   Ph. D. Dissertation,
University of Minnesota, 1979. 358 p.

"Bibliography of Fantasy and Fantasy-Criticism
in Four Leading Nineteenth-Century
Periodicals,"   Extrapolation 22(3):
277-290. Fall 1981.

"Dragons for Tolkien and Lewis,"   Mythlore
11(1): 53-58. Summer 1984.

"Here an orc, there an orc,"   Mythlore
1(1):8-10. January 1969.

"White knight and leech gatherer: the poet as
boor,"   Mythlore 9(3):29-31. Autumn 1982.

"Who's Lleu?" Mythlore 4(4): 20-21. June
1977.

Bern, Kunsthalle

Science Fiction, ausstellung, Kunsthalle Bern,
8 Juli-17 September 1967. Katalog. Bern:
Kunsthalle Bern, 1967. 24 p.

Bernabeau, E. P.

"Science fiction: a new mythos,"
Psychoanalytical Quarterly 26(4):527-535.
October 1957.

Bernari, C.

"Litteriature la science et la SF," Lettres
Nouvelles July 1967.

Bernheim, Mark

"I. B. Singer's Yenne Velt," in: Collins, R.
A. and H. D. Pearce, eds. The Scope of the
Fantastic: Theory, Technique, Major Authors.
Westport, CT: Greenwood Press, 1985. pp.
193-200.

Bernstein, Jeremy

"Out of the ego chamber,"   New Yorker pp.
40-46,51-65. August 9, 1969.

"Science and science fiction," in: Bernstein,
Jeremy. A Comprehensible World: on Modern
Science and its Origins. New York: Random
House, 1967. pp. 207-269.

Berri, Kenneth

"Les cinq cents millions de la Begum ou la
technologie de la fable," Stanford French
Review 3(1):29-40. Spring 1979.

Berry, Eliot

Poetry of Force and Darkness: the Fiction of
John Hawkes, A. San Bernardino, California:
Borgo Press, 1979. 64 p. (Popular Writers of
Today, v. 22)

Berst, Jesse

"Catering to science fiction buffs means big
business at fantasy castles," Publishers
Weekly 215(24):89-90. June 11, 1979.

Berton, Claude

"Souvenirs de la vie 1: Heraire de J. H.
Rosny," La Vie des Peuples 4:385-395. 1921.

Science Fiction and Fantasy Reference Index, 1878-1985

Bertoni, Alfio

Catalogo generale della fantascienza, by Alfio Bertoni and Gianluigi Missiaja. Venezia: CCSF, 1968.

Bertrand, F. C.

"Encounters with Reality: P. K. Dick's A Scanner Darkly," Philosphical Speculations in Science Fiction and Fantasy 1(1): 12-17. March 1981.

"Kant's 'Noumenal Self' and Doppelganger in P. K. Dick's A Scanner Darkly," Philosophical Speculations in Science Fiction and Fantasy 2: 69-80. Summer 1981.

"Stanislaw Lem, Science Fiction, and Kitsch," Riverside Quarterly 7(3): 161-164. May 1983.

Bessiere, Irene

Recit fantastique. La poetique de l'incertain. Paris: Larousse, 1973. 256 p.

Bessy, Maurice

"From 'Melies'," in: Johnson, William, ed. Focus on the Science Fiction Film. Englewood Cliffs, NJ: Prentice Hall, 1972. pp. 26-30.

Bester, Alfred

"Gourmet dining in outer space," Holiday 27:30. May 1960. also in: Knight, Damon, ed. Turning Points: Essays in the Art of Science Fiction. New York: Harper, 1977. pp. 259-266.

"Here come the clones," Publishers Weekly 209(24):56-57. June 14, 1976.

"How we work: Alfred Bester," in: Aldiss, Brian W. and Harry Harrison, eds. Hell's Cartographers: Some Personal Histories of Science Fiction Writers. London: Weidenfeld and Nicholson, 1975. pp. 217-219.

"Isaac Asimov," Publishers Weekly 201(16):18-19. April 17, 1972.

"My affair with science fiction," in: Aldiss, Brian W. and Harry Harrison, eds. Hell's Cartographers: Some Personal Histories of Science Fiction Writers. London: Weidenfeld and Nicholson, 1975. pp. 46-75.

"Robert Heinlein," Publishers Weekly 204(1):44-45. July 2, 1973.

"Science fiction and the renaissance man," in: Davenport, Basil, ed. The Science Fiction Novel: Imagination and Social Criticism. Chicago: Advent, 1964. pp. 102-125.

"Writing and The Demolished Man," Algol 18:4-9. May 1972. also in: Experiment Perilous: Three Essays on Science Fiction. New York: Algol Press, 1976. pp. 29-34.

Bestuzhev-Lada, Igor

"Kakie zvezdy svetiat fantastike?" by Arkady Strugatsky, Dmitrii Bilenkin, and Igor Bestuzhev-Lada. Literaturnoe obozrenie No. 8:100-106. 1977. in: Soviet Studies in Literature 14(4):3-26. Autumn 1978.

"Kogda lishim stanovitsya shelovechestvo," Foreword to Utopiia 14 (Utopia 14 trans. by M. Bruhnov from the retitled Bantam edition of Player Piano). Moscow: Molodaia gvardiia, 1967. pp. 5-24.

"What stars gleam in SF?" by A. Strugatsky, D. Bilenkin and I. Bestuzhev-Lada. Soviet Studies in Literature 14(4):3-26. Autumn 1978. (tr. of "Kakie zuezdy Svetiat fantastike?" Literaturnoe Obozrenie 8:100-106. 1977.)

Betancourt, John

"Note for Desperate TV Watchers," Fantasy Newsletter 6(1): 26. January 1983.

Bettelheim, Bruno

Uses of Enchantment: the Meaning and Importance of Fairy Tales, The,. New York: Knopf, 1976. 328 p.

Betts, G. R.

"Ray Bradbury," (Illus.) in: Betts, G. R. Writers in Residence: American Authors at Home. New York: Viking, 1981. pp. 156-159.

Beum, Robert

"Literature and Machinisme," Sewanee Review 86(2):217-244. Spring 1978.

Bezeredy, Agnes

Tudomanyos fantasztikus, tipiisztikus fantasztikus muvek bibliografiaja, ed. by Agnes Bezeredy and Jolan Cziszar. Miskolc: Rakoczi, 1979. 434 p.

Bharuch, Fershid

Richard Corben: Flights Into Fantasy. Brooklyn: Thumb Tack Books, 1982. 200 p.

Biamonti, Francesco

Harry Harrison: Bibliographia (1951-1965).
Trieste: Editoriale Libraria, 1965. 12 p.

"Italian SF," SF Horizons 2:52-54. Winter
1965.

Bianchi, Ruggero

"I parametri della controutopia," in: Utopia
e fantascienza. Torino: Giappichelli, 1975.
p. 159+.

Bianculli, David

"'Star Wars' Fits Small Screen," Houston
Post, p. D7. June 15, 1982.

"Vonnegut: New book, new mood," Philadelphia
Inquirer May 6, 1985. in: NewsBank.
Literature. 125:G5-G7. June 1985.

Bickman, Martin

"Le Guin's The Left Hand of Darkness: form
and content," Science Fiction Studies
4(1):42-47. March 1977.

Diederwell, Bruce

"Grotesque in Wells's The Invisible Man,"
Extrapolation 24(4): 301-310. Winter 1983.

Bieger, Marcel

"Berserker und Kloester: ueber die Neue
Phantistik Reihe bei Fischer," Science
Fiction Times (Germany) 27(6):15-16. June
1985.

"Corian Verlag: Interview mit den
Herausbegean," Science Fiction Times
(Germany) 25(8):13-15. August 1983.

"Drache in schwarzen Auge," Science Fiction
Times (Germany) 26(7):5-10. July 1984.

"Gesprach mit Fritz Leiber," Science Fiction
Times (Germany) 25(3):5-10. March 1983.

"Indiziert!" by Harald Pusch and Marcel
Bieger. Science Fiction Times (Germany)
26(5):15-17. May 1984.

"Interview mit Dr. Helmut W. Pesch," Science
Fiction Times (Germany) 26(7):24. July 1984.

"Interview mit Horst Pukallus," Science
Fiction Times (Germany) 26(3):9-12. March
1984.

"Interview mit Jorg Weigand," by Marcel Bieger
and Harald Pusch. Science Fiction Times
(Germany) 26(5):5-14. May 1984.

"Interview mit Marion Zimmer Bradley,"
Science Fiction Times (Germany) 27(1):4-11.
January 1985.

"Interview mit Wolfgang Hohlbein," by Marcel
Bieger and Harald Pusch. Science Fiction
Times (Germany) 25(7):14-15. July 1983.

"Mann als Alien," by Marcel Bieger and Rainer
Goetz. Science Fiction Times (Germany)
26(2):5-7. February 1984.

"Potemkinsche Doerfer," Science Fiction
Times (Germany) 25(5):9-10. May 1983.

"Two Oogly L'il Aliens in America; Impressionen
vom World Con 1982 in Chicago," Science
Fiction Times (Germany) 25(1):20-21. January
1983.

"Zukunft aus der Glaskugel," Science Fiction
Times (Germany) 26(2):16-17. February 1984.

Biemiller, Lawrence

"Scholars Consider Galactic Empires and the
Future of Science Fiction," Chronicle of
Higher Education 24(21): 15-16. July 21,
1982.

Bier, Jesse

"The masterpiece in science fiction: power or
parody?" Journal of Popular Culture
12(4):604-610. Spring 1979.

Bierbaum, D. I.

"Aus jenen Tagen: Rezensionen alter
phantastischer Romane: In purpurner
Finsternis," Quarber Merkur 24:7-9.
September 1970.

Bierman, Judah

"Ambiguity in utopia: The Dispossessed,"
Science Fiction Studies 2(3):249-255.
November 1975.

Biesterfeld, W.

Literarische Utopie. Stuttgart: Metzler,
1974.

Bigelow, Charles

"Science fiction and the future of anarchy:
conversations with Ursula K. Le Guin," by
Charles Bigelow and J. McMahon. Oregon
Times (Portland) pp. 24-29. December 1974.

Biggers, Cliff

"Interview with Piers Anthony, An," Science Fiction Review 23:56-62. November 1977. (Reprinted from Future Retrospective.)

Biggle, Lloyd, Jr.

"Morasses of academe revisited, The" Analog 98(9):146-163. September 1978.

"On Being a Writer," Lan's Lantern No. 8: 21-23. March 1979.

"Roots: A Taxicab Tour of Science-Fiction History," in: Jarvis, Sharon, ed. Inside Outer Space. New York: Ungar, 1985. pp. 119-130.

"Science fiction goes to college: Groves and the morasses of academe," Riverside Quarterly 6:100-109. 1974.

Bilenkin, Dmitrii

"Kakie zvezdy svetiat fantastike?" by Arkady Strugatsky, Dmitrii Bilenkin, and Igor Bestuzhev-Lada. Literaturnoe obozrenie No. 8:100-106. 1977. in: Soviet Studies in Literature 14(4):3-26. Autumn 1978.

"What stars gleam in SF?" by A. Strugatsky, D. Bilenkin and I. Bestuzhev-Lada. Soviet Studies in Literature 14(4):3-26. Aut. 1978. (tr. of "Kakie zuezdy Svetiat fantastike?" Literaturnoe Obozrenie 8:100-106. 1977.)

Bilker, Audrey

Writing Science Fiction that Sells, by H. L. Bilker and Audrey Bilker. Chicago: Contemporary Books, 1982. 159 p.

Bilker, H. L.

Writing Science Fiction that Sells, by H. L. Bilker and Audrey Bilker. Chicago: Contemporary Books, 1982. 159 p.

Billam, E. R.

"Science Fiction," New Statesman p. 406. March 27, 1954.

Billeter, Fritz

"Science fiction. Ausstellung in Bern," Artis 19(9):28-31. 1967.

Bilyeu, Richard

Tanelorn Archives, The: A Primary and Secondary Bibliography of the Works of Michael Moorcock 1949-1979. Altona, Canada: Pandora's Books, 1981. 108 p.

"Avon and Daw Problem, The," Megavore 11: 25. October 1980.

Binder, Lambert

"Losung der Liechname," Quarber Merkur No. 51:42-44. November 1979.

Binder, Otto

"Space World," SF Times No. 334:3-4. March (1) 1960.

"New frontier of science 'fiction'," Science Fiction Times No. 369:7-9. September 1961.

"To Frank R. Paul," Science Fiction Times No. 405:8. August 1963.

Bing, John

"Lawyer in utopia, A," in: Dollerup, Cay, ed. Volve. Scandinavian Views on Science Fiction. Copenhagen: Dept. of English, University of Copenhagen, 1978. pp. 70-78.

Bing, Jon

"Karavane," in: Magill, Frank N., ed. Survey of Science Fiction Literature, Vol. 3. Englewood Cliffs, NJ: Salem Press, 1979. pp. 1114-1117.

Bingenheimer, Heinz

Transgalaxis: katalog der deutschsprachigen utopish-phantastischen literatur 1460-1960. Friedrichsdorf: Transgalaxis, 1959. 124 p.

Bingham, J. M.

"Enchantment revisited: or why teach fantasy?" by J. M. Bingham and Grayce Scholt. CEA Critic 40(2):11-15. January 1978.

Bingham, Sallie

"Rudy Rucker's New Novel is Set on a Kentucky Farm," Louisville Courier-Journal December 9, 1984. in: NewsBank. Literature. 70:D12. January 1985.

Binkin, Irving

Catalog of Lovcraftiana: The Grill/Binkin Collection, by Mark Owings and Irving Binkin. Baltimore: Mirage, 1975. 71 p.

Author Entries

Biodrowski, Steve

"Return of the Living Dead,"
Cinefantastique 15(4):16-29. October 1985.

Birchby, Sid

"Sexual symbolism in W. H. Hodgson,"
Riverside Quarterly 1:70-71. November 1964.

Bisbee, Sam

"Lust in Space," Future Life 17: 30-33.
March 1980.

Bisceglia, Jacques

Tresors du roman policier, de la
science-fiction et du fantastique: catalogue
encyclopedique. Paris: Les editiions de
l'amateur, 1981. 431 p.

Bischoff, David

"Essaying: cross pollination and SF,"
Thrust 11:22-25. Fall 1978.

"Essaying: Doctor Who," Thrust 16: 18-21.
Fall 1980.

"Essaying: why I write science fiction,"
Thrust 10:26-29. Spring 1978.

"Kirby McCauley interview, The," Thrust
10:7-12. Spring 1978.

Bischoff, Murray

"Rich man, poor man, space man, thief,"
Prevue 2(12):28-33. June/July 1983.

Bisenieks, Dainis

"Children, magic and choices," Mythlore
6(1): 13-16. Winter 1979.

"Finder of the Welsh gods," Mythlore
3(3):29-31. 1976.

"International news: Latvia," Science
Fiction Times No. 460:4-5. November 1968.

Bishop, C. H.

"Children and science fiction,"
Commonwealth 63:172-174. November 18, 1955.

Bishop, Gerald

New British Science Fiction and Fantasy Books
Published During 1970 & 1971. San
Bernardino, CA: Borgo, 1980. 40 p.

New SF Published in Great Britain 1968-1969.
Lake Jackson, Texas: Joanne Burger, 1970.

Science Fiction Books Published in Britain,
1972 & 1973. San Bernardino, CA: Borgo, 1980
c1975. 33 p.

Science Fiction Books Published in Britain,
1974-1978. San Bernardino, CA: Borgo, 1980
c1979. 82 p.

Venture Science Fiction Magazine: A
Checklist. Exeter: Aardvark House, 1970.
30 p.

"British scene, The," Science Fiction Times
No. 461:8. December 1968.

"First world SF writers conference," Locus
9(13):1. October 30, 1976.

"International news: from England," Science
Fiction Times No. 460:4. November 1968.

"International SF writers organization
proposed," Locus 9(13):1-2. October 30,
1976.

"SF Publishing Statistics, 1980," World SF
Newsletter 5: 2-4. Winter 1982.

Bishop, Michael

"All That Glitters is Not Golding...Or Bishop
Either," Thrust 22: 9-12. Spring/Summer
1985.

"Believers and heretics: an Episcopal Bull
(which last word may be defined as the reader
likes)," Foundation 19: 54-61. June 1980.

"Evangels of hope," Foundation 14:35-43.
September 1978.

"Evangels of Hope: Some Thoughts on Alexei and
Cory Panshin's SF in Dimension," Shayol
1(4): 12-15. Winter 1980.

"Gene Wolfe as hero," Thrust 16: 10-13.
Fall 1980.

"In Pursuit of Ubik," in: Greenberg, M.
H., ed. Philip K. Dick. New York:
Taplinger, 1982. pp. 137-147.

"In pursuit of Ubik," Starship
17(3):25-28. Summer 1980.

"Interview with Michael Bishop," Pretentious
Science Fiction Quarterly 2: 6-7. Summer 1978.

"Introduction," in: Dick, P. K. Ubik.
Boston: Gregg, 1979. pp. v-xvi.

"Knack and how to get it. See?" SFWA
Bulletin 13(4):14-16. Fall 1978.

"On reviewing and being reviewed," Shayol
1: 24-27. November 1977.

Bishop, Michael (Continued)

"Philip K. Dick: auf Ubiks spuren," _Science Fiction Times_ (Germany) 24(6):5-9. June 1982.

"Pitching Pennies Against the Starboard Bulkhead: 'A Reverie for Mister Ray'," _Thrust_ 17: 14-17. Summer 1981.

"Potpourri," _Thrust_ No. 23: 5-8. Fall/Winter 1985.

"Viewpoint: Light Years and Dark: Science Fiction Since 1960," _Isaac Asimov's Science Fiction Magazine_ 8(4): 46-64. April 1984.

Bishop, Nancy

"Michael Nesmith is Still Swinging," _Dallas Morning News_ January 25, 1983. in: _NewsBank. Film and Television_ 79:G3-4. 1982/1983.

Bishop, Pete

"Jim Henson Has Taken Muppets From Ed Sullivan to World Fame," _Pittsburgh Press_ January 2, 1983. in: _NewsBank. Film and Television_ 75:E2. 1982/1983.

Biskind, Peter

"Pods, Blobs, and Ideology in American Films of the Fifties," in: Slusser, George, ed. _Shadows of the Magic Lamp._ Carbondale: Southern Illinois University Press, 1985. pp. 58-72.

"War of the Worlds," _American Film_ 9(3): 37-42. December 1983.

Bittner, J. W.

Approaches to the Fiction of Ursula K. Le Guin., Ph. D. Dissertation, University of Wisconsin, Madison, 1979. 511 p.

"Chronosophy, Aesthetics, and Ethics in Le Guin's _The Dispossessed_," in: Rabkin, Eric S., et. al., eds. _No Place Else._ Carbondale: Southern Illinois University Press, 1983. pp. 244-270.

"Persuading us to rejoice and teaching us how to praise: Le Guin's _Orsinian Tales_," _Science Fiction Studies_ 5(3):215-242. November 1978.

"Persuading us to rejoice and teaching us how to praise: Le Guin's _Orsinian Tales_," in: _Ursula K. Le Guin_, ed. by Harold Bloom. New York: Chelsea House, 1986. pp. 119-144.

"Survey of Le Guin criticism, A," in: De Bolt, Joe, ed. _Ursula K. Le Guin: Voyager_

to Inner Lands and to Outer Space. Port Washington, New York: Kennikat, 1979. pp. 31-49.

Bixby, Jerome

"STF editor as scientist (or, who, me?), The," _Fantasy Times_ No. 138:15-17. September (2) 1951.

Bizzell, Patricia

"Lloyd Biggle, Jr.," in: Cowart, David, ed. _Twentieth-Century American Science-Fiction Writers, Part 1: A-L._ Detroit: Gale, 1981. pp. 37-39. (Dictionary of Literary Biography, v. 8)

Black, B. S.

"Mapping Middle-Earth," Worcester, MA: Undergraduate Report, Worcester Polytechnic Institute, 1981. Report No. 81D3601. 75 p.

Black, E.

"Relationship of science fiction reading to reasoning abilities," by E. Black and E. K. Weaver. _Science Education_ 49:293-296. April 1965.

Black, Nancy

Exploring Science Fiction. O'Fallon, MO: Book Lures, 1983. 30 p.

Black, S. J.

"Utopia as reality," _College English_ 33(3):304-316. December 1971.

Blackbeard, Bill

"Anthony Boucher," in: Cowart, David, ed. _Twentieth-Century American Science-Fiction Writers, Part 1: A-L._ Detroit: Gale, 1981. pp. 53-54. (Dictionary of Literary Biography, v. 8)

"C. M. Kornbluth," in: Cowart, David, ed. _Twentieth-Century American Science-Fiction Writers, Part 1: A-L._ Detroit: Gale, 1981. pp. 242-245. (Dictionary of Literary Biography, v. 8)

"Eight Year Shaft: The Grand Scam of Comic Book Reprints Since The Turn of the Century," _Riverside Quarterly_ 7(2): 119-121. March 1982.

"Eighty Year Shaft Part II: The Grab Bag Packages," _Riverside Quarterly_ 7(3): 165-169. May 1983.

Blackbeard, Bill (Continued)

"Famed Los Angeles fan center closes doors forever," _Fantasy Times_ No. 249:FTM3-FTM4. June (2) 1956.

"Hugo Gernsback," in: Cowart, David, ed. _Twentieth-Century American Science-Fiction Writers, Part 1: A-L_. Detroit: Gale, 1981. pp. 186-189. (Dictionary of Literary Biography, v. 8)

"Pipsqueak Prometheus: Some remarks on the writings of L. Ron Hubbard," _Inside_ No. 1: 23-31. October 1962.

"SF & fantasy, 1941-1956," _Fantasy Times_ No. 254:25-27. September (1) 1956.

Blackford, Jenny

"Ebony: the festival of colours," by Russell Blackford and Jenny Blackford. _Science Fiction: A Review of Speculative Literature_ 6(2): 45-47. 1984.

Blackford, Russell

"Damien Broderick Interview," _Science Fiction: A Review of Speculative Literature_ 4(3): 94-105. September 1982.

"Definition of love: Kurt Vonnegut's Slapstick," _Science Fiction: a Review of Speculative Literature_. 2(3): 208-228. August 1980.

"Ebony: the festival of colours," by Russell Blackford and Jenny Blackford. _Science Fiction: A Review of Speculative Literature_ 6(2): 45-47. 1984.

"Myth and the Art of Science Fiction Commentary," _Science Fiction: A Review of Speculative Literature_ 3(2): 52-56. May 1981.

"Sexuality in science fiction," _Science Fiction: A Review of Speculative Literature_ 6(2): 41. 1984.

"Warriors of the Tao: David Lake's Xuma novels," _Science Fiction: A Review of Speculative Literature_ 6(1): 16-18. 1984.

Blades, John

"Vonnegut: Society's critic still wonders if we'll make it," _Chicago Tribune_ Sec. 5, p. 1, 3. October 4, 1985.

"Will videotapes spur the sales of books, or drive a nail in bookstores' coffin?" _Chicago Tribune_ Sec. 13, p. 10-11. November 13, 1985.

Blair, Karin

Meaning in Star Trek. New York: Warner Books, 1977. 208 p.

"Garden in the machine: the why of _Star Trek_, The," _Journal of Popular Culture_ 13(2):310-319. Fall 1979.

"Sex and Star Trek," _Science Fiction Studies_ 10(3): 292-297. November 1983.

Blake, C. H.

"Will the real Sloth please stand up?" _Cinefantastique_ 15(5):32-34. January 1986.

Blalack, Robert

"Composite optical and photographic effects for Star Wars," by Robert Blalack and Paul Roth. _American Cinematographer_ 58(7):706-708,772. July 1977.

Blanc, Bernard

Pourqui j'ai tue Jules Verne. Paris: Stock, 1978. 358 p.

Blanchot, Maurice

"Bon usage de la science fiction," _Nouvelle Revue Francaise_ 7(73):91-100. January 1959.

Bland, Jay

"Up Against the Wall: The Ethical Limits of Rational Objectivity," _Science Fiction: A Review of Speculative Literature_ 5(3): 96-101. September 1983.

Blank, E. W.

"Alchemy and chemistry in literature," _School Science and Mathematics_ 42:550-558. June 1942.

Blankenship, R. W.

"What was the red star Frodo saw over Rivendell?" _Leading Edge_ No. 9:60-63. Winter 1985.

Blasius, Jurgen

"Absolute Bibliothek: Phantastische Sinnfiguren des Exakten," _Quarber Merkur_ 55:48-58. July 1981.

Blau, Robert

"Dr. Who convention to preview stage version," Chicago Tribune Sec. 5, p. 7. November 28, 1985.

Bleiler, E. F.

Checklist of Fantastic Literature: a Bibliography of Fantasy, Weird and Science Fiction Books Published in the English Language, The. Chicago: Shasta, 1948, 455 p. Reprinted, West Linn, Oregon: Fax Collector's Editions, 1972.

Checklist of Science Fiction and Supernatural Fiction, The,. Revised edition. Glen Rock, New Jersey: Firebell Books, 1978. 265 p.

Guide to Supernatural Fiction: A Full Description of 1,775 Books From 1750 to 1960. Kent, OH: Kent State University Press, 1983. 723 p.

Science Fiction Writers: Critical Studies of the Major Authors from the Early Nineteenth Century to the Present Day. New York: Scribners, 1982. 623 p.

"A. Merritt," in: Bleiler, E. F., ed. Science Fiction Writers. New York: Scribners, 1982. pp. 65-71.

"Edgar Allan Poe," in: Bleiler, E. F., ed. Science Fiction Writers. New York: Scribners, 1982. pp. 11-18.

"Edgar Rice Burroughs," in: Bleiler, E. F., ed. Science Fiction Writers. New York: Scribners, 1982. pp. 59-64.

"John W. Campbell, Jr.," in: Bleiler, E. F., ed. Science Fiction Writers. New York: Scribners, 1982. pp. 151-159.

"Jules Verne," in: Bleiler, E. F., ed. Science Fiction Writers. New York: Scribners, 1982. pp. 573-582.

"Luis Philip Senarens," in: Bleiler, E. F., ed. Science Fiction Writers. New York: Scribners, 1982. pp. 53-58.

"Luncheon With John Wyndham," Extrapolation 25(4): 314-317. Winter 1984.

"M. P. Shiel," in: Bleiler, E. F., ed. Science Fiction Writers. New York: Scribners, 1982. pp. 31-37.

"Pilgrim Award Acceptance Address," SFRA Newsletter 123: 7-19. July/August 1984.

"S. Fowler Wright," in: Bleiler, E. F., ed. Science Fiction Writers. New York: Scribners, 1982. pp. 83-89.

"Who was Moxon's master?" Extrapolation 26(3): 181-189. Fall 1985.

Bleymehl, Jakob

Beitrage zur Geschichte und Bibliographie der Utopischen und Phantastischen Literatur. Furth/Saar: Offizin Bleymehl, 1965. 352 p.

"Chronologie und Bibliographie," in: Bleymehl, Jakob. Beitrage zur Geschichte und Bibliographe der Utopischen und phantastischen Literatur. Furth/Saar: Offizin Bleymehl, 1965. pp. 85-352.

"SF in East Europe," Fantasy Times No. 193:3. January (1) 1954.

Blish, James

Issue at Hand: Studies in Contemporary Magazine Science Fiction, The, by William Atheling, Jr. Chicago: Advent, 1964. 136 p.

More Issues at Hand: Critical Studies in Contemporary Science Fiction, by William Atheling, Jr. Chicago: Advent, 1970. 154 p.

"Admonitory exercises," Australian Science Fiction Review No. 11:22-24. August 1967.

"Aristotelean Spheres," Vector 120: 5-7. June 1984.

"Arts in science fiction, The," in: Chauvin, Cy, ed. Multitude of Visions. Baltimore: T-K Graphics, 1975. pp. 58-67.

"Arts in science fiction," Vector 61: 5-14. September/October 1972.

"Bad Idea Trampled to Death by Ducks," Vector 120: 7-9. June 1984.

"Blish on Moskowitz," Australian Science Fiction Review No. 16:8-16. June 1968.

"Cathedrals in space," in: Knight, Damon, ed. Turning Points: Essays in the Art of Science Fiction. New York: Harper, 1977. pp. 144-162.

"Cents of Wonder," Inside and Science Fiction Advertiser No. 12: 11-12. November 1955.

"Change, SF and Marxism: open or closed universes? a reply to Mr. Rottensteiner," Science Fiction Studies 1(2):86-88. Fall 1973.

"Development of a science fiction writer: II, The," Foundation 2:17-22. June 1972.

"Future recall," in: Hay, George, ed. The Disappearing Future; a Symposium of Speculation. London: Panther, 1970. pp. 97-105.

"Is this thinking?" SF Horizons 1:54-57. Spring 1964.

Blish, James (Continued)

"John Brunner: a colleague's view," in: De Bolt, Joe, ed. <u>Happening Worlds of John Brunner</u>. Port Washington, NY: Kennikat, 1975. pp. 3-7.

"Kleine Okie-Musik," <u>Australian Science Fiction Review</u> No. 12:10-12. October 1967.

"Look, Dear, he found my lost necklace," <u>SFWA Bulletin</u> 10(3): 14-15. Winter 1974/1975.

"Moskowitz on Kuttner," <u>Riverside Quarterly</u> 5(2):140-143. February 1972.

"Nachruf auf die prophetie," in: Barmeyer, Eike, ed. <u>Science fiction: theorie und geschichte</u>. Munchen: Fink, 1972. pp. 118-128.

"New Totemism?" <u>Vector</u> No. 120: 11-13. June 1984.

"On science fiction criticism," <u>Riverside Quarterly</u> 3(3):214-217. August 1968. also in: Clareson, Thomas D., ed. <u>SF: The Other Side of Realism</u>. Bowling Green, Ohio: Bowling Green University Popular Press, 1971. pp. 166-170.

"Probapossible prolegomena to ideareal history," <u>Foundation</u> 13:6-12. May 1978.

"Reply to Norman Spinrad," <u>Science Fiction Times</u> pp. 8-9. ca. October 1967.

"Science in science fiction," <u>Vector</u> 69: 5-10. Summer 1975.

"Second pair of decades, and the third," <u>Science Fiction Times</u> No. 369:27-29. September 1961.

"SF: the critical literature," <u>SF Horizons</u> 2:38-50. Winter 1965.

"Strange Career of Dr. Mirabilis," <u>Vector</u> 120: 9-10. June 1984.

"Tale that wags the god: the function of science fiction, The," <u>American Libraries</u> 1(11):1029-1033. December 1970.

"Theodore Sturgeon's macrocosm," <u>Magazine of Fantasy and Science Fiction</u> 23(3):42-45. September 1962.

"Think me to your leader," <u>Sunday Times Magazine</u> pp. 30-31. November 22, 1970.

"Transatlantic view," <u>Vector</u> 63: 25-28. January/February 1973.

"Wiederentdeckung James Branch Cabells, Die" <u>Quarber Merkur</u> 26:30-32. February 1971.

Bloch, E.

"Okkulte phantastik und heidentum," in: Bloch, E. <u>Erbschaft dieser Zeit</u>. Frankfurt, 1962. pp. 186- .

Bloch, R. N.

<u>Bibliographie der utopischen und phantastischen Literatur 1750-1950</u>. Giessen: Munniksma, 1984. 143 p.

Bloch, Robert

<u>Eigth Stage of Fandom, The; Selections from 25 years of Fan Writing</u>, by Robert Bloch and Earl Kemp, ed. Chicago: Advent, 1962. 176 p.

"Fantastic Adventures With Amazing," (autobiographical) <u>Amazing</u> 57(5):89-102. January 1984.

"Gremlins (review)," <u>Starlog</u> 88: 40-42. November 1984.

"How to be a SF critic," <u>Inside</u> No. 1: 16-17. October 1962.

"Imagination and modern social criticism," in: Davenport, Basil, ed. <u>The Science Fiction Novel: Imagination and Social Criticism</u>. Chicago: Advent, 1964. pp. 126-155.

"Poe and Lovecraft," in: Joshi, S. T., ed. <u>H. P. Lovecraft: Four Decades of Criticism</u>. Athens, OH: Ohio University Press, 1980. pp. 158-160.

"Science fiction and film: men, myths, and monsters." <u>Algol</u> 11(2):7-10. May 1974.

"SUP full of horrors," <u>Cthulhu Calls</u> 3(1):26-32. July 1975.

"Traditions of science fiction and conventions, The," <u>The Alien Critic</u> 3(3):33-37. August 1974.

Block, A. B.

"Film Rights to '2010' May be Legal Odyssey in the Making," <u>Los Angeles Herald Examiner</u> December 22, 1982. in: <u>NewsBank. Film and Television</u>. 69:D8. January 1983.

"Little Guy Wasn't Pretty, But What He Achieved in Filmdom Was Out of This World," <u>Los Angeles Herald Examiner</u> January 2, 1983. in: <u>Newsbank. Business</u>. 7:C1. 1983.

Block, D. Z.

"Paperback Originals of Philip K. Dick," <u>Paperback Quarterly</u> 5(3): 44-50. Fall 1982.

Blonski, Jan

"Chancen der Science-Fiction," <u>Quarber Merkur</u> 31:21-25. July 1972.

"Kon trojanski czyli o powiesci przysclosciowej i Szanse science fiction," <u>Zycie Literackie</u> 30:31. 1961.

Blonski, Jan (Continued)

"Szanse science fiction," <u>Azcie Literackie</u> No. 31. 1961.

Bloom, Harold

<u>Mary Shelley</u>. New York: Chelsea House, 1985. 205 p.

<u>Ursula K. Le Guin</u>. New York: Chelsea House, 1986. 274 p.

"Clinamen: Towards a Theory of Fantasy," in: Slusser, George E., ed. <u>Bridges to Fantasy</u>. Carbondale: Southern Illinois University Press, 1982. pp. 1-19.

Bloomfield, Masse

"Reaching for the stars: goals for the library profession," <u>Special Libraries</u> 62:265-267. July/August 1971.

Bloomfield, Paul

<u>Imaginary Worlds; or, the Evolution of Utopia</u>. London: Hamilton, 1932. 283 p.

Bloomquest, Jane

"Science Fiction Theater the Moebius Way," by Jane Bloomquest and William McMillan. in: Hassler, Donald M. <u>Patterns of the Fantastic</u>. Mercer Island, WA: Starmont, 1983. pp. 81-90.

Blotner, Joseph

"Novel of the future, The," in: Blotner, Joseph. <u>The Modern American Political Novel: 1900-1960</u>. Austin: University of Texas Press, 1966. pp. 139-163.

Bloxom, M. D.

"Bibliography: Selected references," in: <u>George Orwell and Nineteen Eighty-Four</u>. Washington, DC: Library of Congress, 1985. pp. 123-150.

Blue, Tyson

"King Directs 'Overdrive'," <u>Twilight Zone</u> 5(6): 30-31. February 1986.

Bluedorn, A. C.

"Winning the race: report on the use of science fiction in the classroom," <u>Exchange</u> (Pennsylvania State University) 4(1):7-11. Spring 1979.

Blum, I. D.

"English utopias from 1551 to 1699: a bibliography," <u>Bulletin of Bibliography</u> 21:143-144. January/April 1955.

Blum, Walter

"Day With Frank Herbert," <u>San Francisco Examiner</u> December 5, 1982. in: <u>NewsBank. Film and Television</u>. 51:C4-6. January 1983.

Blumenfeld, Ralph

"Novelist into playwright," <u>New York Post</u> p. 38. November 11, 1970.

Bly, J. I.

"Sonata Form in Tremor of Intent," <u>Modern Fiction Studies</u> 27(3): 489-504. Autumn 1981.

Boardman, John

"Barsoom confidential," <u>AMRA</u> 2(62):12-14. October 1974.

"In memoriam: David Mason (1924-1974)," <u>Science Fiction Review</u> 4(1):13. February 1975.

"Novels of Eric Ruecker Eddison," in: De Camp, L. S., ed. <u>Blade of Conan</u>. New York: Ace, 1979. pp. 171-176.

"Ocean trade in the Hyborian Age," in: De Camp, L. S., ed. <u>Blade of Conan</u>. New York: Ace, 1979. pp. 45-50.

"Ray Bradbury off Broadway," <u>Riverside Quarterly</u> 3(3): 229-230. August 1968.

"Warlords of Krishna, The," <u>Foundation</u> 1:42-47. March 1972.

Bodem, M. M.

"Role of fantasy in children's reading, The," <u>Elementary English</u> pp. 470-471. April 1975.

Bodtke, Richard

"Great sorrows, small joys: the world of Kurt Vonnegut, Jr.," <u>Cross Currents</u> 20:120-125. Winter 1970.

Boehm, G. A. W.

"Futurism," <u>Think</u> (I. B. M.) 36:16-27. July/August 1970.

Boenig, R. E.

"C. S. Lewis' The Great Divorce and the Medieval Dream Vision," _Mythlore_ 10(2): 31-35. Summer 1983.

"Lewis' Time Machine and his trip to the moon," _Mythlore_ 7(2):6-9. Summer 1980.

Boerem, R.

"Continuity of the Fungi from Yuggoth," in: Joshi, S. T., ed. _H. P. Lovecraft: Four Decades of Criticism_. Athens, OH: Ohio University Press, 1980. pp. 222-225.

"Lovecraftian Nightmare," in: Joshi, S. T., ed. _H. P. Lovecraft: Four Decades of Criticism_. Athens, OH: Ohio University Press, 1980. pp. 217-221.

Boese, W. E.

"Chariots of the gods? and all that: pseudohistory in the classroom," by H. E. Legrand and W. E. Boese. _History Teacher_ 8(3):359-370. May 1975.

Boettcher, H. U.

"Ostern in Leeds," _Science Fiction Times_ (Germany) 27(7):22-23. July 1985.

Bogdanoff, Grichka

Effet science fiction, L': a la recherche d'une definition,, by Igor and Grichka Bogdanoff. Paris: Laffont, 1979. 424 p.

Science fiction, La, by Igor and Grichka Bogdanoff. Paris: Seghers, 1976. 378 p.

Bogdanoff, Igor

Effet science fiction, L': a la recherche d'une definition, by Igor and Grichka Bogdanoff. Paris: Laffont, 1979. 424 p.

Science fiction, La, by Igor and Grichka Bogdanoff. Paris: Seghers, 1976. 378 p.

"SF et poesie. a) Structure," _Europe_ 580/581:96-100. August/September 1977.

Boggs, W. A.

"Looking backward at the utopian novel, 1888-1900," _New York Public Library Bulletin_ 64:329-336. June 1960.

Bogle, Charles

"Remaking of _Star Trek_, The," _Future Life_ 9:28-29,64. March 1979.

Bogle, Edra

"David Gerrold," in: Cowart, David, ed. _Twentieth-Century American Science-Fiction Writers, Part 1: A-L_. Detroit: Gale, 1981. pp. 189-191. (Dictionary of Literary Biography, v. 8)

Bogstad, Janice

"Beyond Childhood's End: A Look at Post-1950's Evolutionary Topics in Science Fiction," _Aurora SF_ 7(2): 15-19. Winter 1981/1982.

"Chelsea Quinn Yarbro interviewed," _Janus_ 5(2):6-9. Autumn 1979.

"Fantastic Fictions... ; Genre Definitions and the Contemporary Cross-Genre Novel," in: Hassler, Donald M., ed. _Patterns of the Fantastic II_. Mercer Island, WA: Starmont, 1985. pp. 81-90.

"Interview: John Varley," _Janus_ 5(1): 20, 24-25. Spring 1979.

"Interview: Suzy McKee Charnas," _Janus_ 5(1): 20-23. Spring 1979.

"Jo Clayton interviewed," _Janus_ 5(2):10-12. Autumn 1979.

"On the Women in Science Fiction 1982," _Women Library Worker's Journal_ p. 3-8. January/March 1983.

"Science Fiction Fan Conventions," in: Wolfe, Gary, ed. _Science Fiction Dialogues_. Chicago: Academy Chicago, 1982. pp. 210-213.

Bohdanowicz, Ladislaw

"European scene: Poland, The," by Ladislaw Bohdanowicz and Francelia Butler. _Extrapolation_ 11(2):79-81. May 1970.

Boia, Lucian

Jahrhundert der Marsianer, Das, by Helga Abret and Lucian Boia. Munich: Heyne, 1984. 366 p.

"Treffpunkt Mond: Zu Henri Stahls 'astronomischem Roman' _Ein Rumane auf dem Mond_," by Helga Abret and Lucian Boia. _Quarber Merkur_ 55:3-13. July 1981.

Boies, J. J.

"Existential exchange in the novels of Charles Williams," _Renascence_ 26:219-229. 1974.

Bold, Alan

"Hobbit Verse Versus Tolkien's Poem," in: Giddings, Robert, ed. J. R. R. Tolkien: This Far Land. London: Vision, 1983. pp. 137-153.

Boldt, R. D.

"Chad Oliver: interview," by H. W. Hall and R. D. Boldt. in: Hall, H. W. Chad Oliver: A Peliminary Bibliography. Bryan, TX: Dellwood, 1985. pp. 50-86.

Boleman, J. S.

"Teaching science with science fiction," Bulletin of the American Physical Society 21(2):177. February 1976.

Bolick, Phil

"Thick thews & busty babes," Shayol 2: 24-25. February 1978.

Bolling, Douglass

"Structure and theme in Briefing For a Descent Into Hell," Contemporary Literature 14(4):550-564. Autumn 1973.

Bolton, W. F.

"Sources and non-sources: politics and the English language," College Literature 11(1): 71-77. 1984.

Boly, J. R.

"Cosmic graffiti," in: Remington, Thomas, J. ed. Selected Proceedings of the 1978 Science Fiction Research Association National Conference. Cedar Falls, Iowa: University of Northern Iowa, 1979. pp. 164-168.

Bombard, A.

"Jules Verne: seer of the space age," Unesco Courier 31:31-36. March 1978.

Bond, B. C.

"Unity of word: language in C. S. Lewis' trilogy," Mythlore 2(4):13-15. Winter 1972.

Bond, N.

"Vital factor," Senior Scholastic 72:21. March 7, 1958.

Bonds, M. J.

"Ultimate Fantasy Report," Starlog 64: 84-93. November 1982.

"Walter Koenig: American actor, heroic Russian," Starlog No. 91:40-41. February 1985.

Boni, John

"Analogous form: black comedy and some Jacobean plays," Western Humanities Review pp. 201-215. Summer 1974.

Bonn, T. L.

Under Cover: An Illustrated History of American Mass Market Paperbacks. New York: Penguin, 1982. 144 p.

Bonnefoy, Cl.

"Publique populaire est prive de legende, Le," Arts No. 908:3. March 20, 1963.

Bonnefoy, Jean

"Urbanifiction: les villes imaginees de la SF," Cahiers Pedagogiques 150: 17-22. January 1977.

Bono, Barbara

"Prose fictions of William Morris: a study in the literary aesthetic of a Victorian social reformer, The," Victorian Poetry 13(3/4):43-59. 1975.

Boone, A. R.

"Hollywood planets wage space war," Popular Science 165:168-169. November 1954.

"How movies take you on a trip to the moon," Popular Science 156:124-129. May 1950.

"Prehistoric monsters roar and hiss for sound film," Popular Science 122:20+. April 1933.

Borel, Yogi

"Notes on science fiction and the symbolist tradition," Riverside Quarterly 3(4): 256-265. March 1969.

Borges, J. L.

Literatura fantastica, La: conferencia..., ed. by J. L. Borges. Buenos Aires: Ediciones Culturales Olivetti, 1967. 19 p.

Borgmeier, Raimund

Science Fiction: Theorie and Geschichte. Themen und Typen, Form und Weltbild, by Ulrich Suerbaum, Ulrich Broich, and Raimund Borgmeier. Stuttgart: Plilipp Reclam, 1981. 215 p.

"Religion in der science-fiction," Die Neueren Spracken 24:121-135. 1975.

Borie, Bertrand

"Sting: man, myth, and monster," by Bertrand Borie, Randy Lofficier and J. M. Lofficier. Starlog No. 101:16-18. December 1985.

Borinski, Ludwig

"Kritik der utopie in der modernen englischen literatur," in: Die Neueren Sprachen. N.F. Beiheft 2. 1958.

Borman, Gilbert

"New Look At Eugene Zamiatin's We," Extrapolation 24(1): 57-65. Spring 1983.

Born, Daniel

"Character as Perception: Science Fiction and the Christian Man of Faith," Extrapolation 24(3): 251-271. Fall 1983.

Born, Franz

Man who invented the future: Jules Verne. New York: Scholastic Book Service, 1971. 143 p. (Abridged) (Translation of: Der Mann der die Zukunft erfand.)

Born, Nicolas

"Schwache Bilder anderen Welt: Science Fiction und ihre mogliche Rechtfertigung," in: Born, Nicolas. Die Welt der Maschine. Hamburg: Rowohlt, 1980. pp. 221.

Borner, Albrecht

"Verlauf der Ding- und Werkzeugwelt: Alfred Doblins 'Berge, Meere, und Giganten," Quarber Merkur 24:17-28. September 1970.

"Welt der geausserten Innerlichkeit, Die: Franz Werfel's Stern der Ungeborenen," Quarber Merkur 27:3-21. July 1971.

"Welt des aristokratischen Gestes: Ernst Jungers 'Heliopolis'," Quarber Merkur 26:3-25. February 1971.

"Welt des perfekten Defekts: Walter Jen's Nein: Die Welt der Angeklagten, Hans Erich

Nossaks Nach dem letzten Aufstand, Arno Schmidts Die Gelehrlenrepublik," Quarber Merkur 28:3-17. November 1971.

"Welt des reinen Geistes: Hermann Hesses 'Glasperlinspiel'," Quarber Merkur 25:3-25. January 1971.

Borrello, Alfred

H. G. Wells: Author in Agony. Carbondale, Illinois: Southern Illinois University Press, 1972. 129 p.

"Inferno: the science fiction," in: Borrello, Alfred. H. G. Wells: Author in Agony. Carbondale, Illinois: Southern Illinois University Press, 1972. pp. 54-77.

Borroughs, J.

"Science and literature," North American Review 199:415-424. March 1914.

Borski, Lech

"Co dalej?" Nowe Ksiazki November 30, 1971.

Bosky, Bernadette

"Stephen King and Peter Straub: fear and friendship," in: Schweitzer, Darrell, ed. Discovering Stephen King. Mercer Island: Starmont, 1985. pp. 55-82.

Boss, J. E.

"Elements of style in science fiction: Andre Norton compared with others," Extrapolation 26(3): 201-211. Fall 1985.

"Season of Becoming: Ann Maxwell's Change," Science Fiction Studies 12(1): 51-65. March 1985.

Bossay, L. D.

Religious Themes and Motifs in Science Fiction. Ph. D. Dissertation, University of Texas Austin, 1979. 151 p. (DAI 40A:5854)

Bossetto, Roger

"Pierre Very: un rencontre avec la science-fiction," Europe 60(636): 78-85. 1982.

Boston, Richard

"Tintin, Asterix, and Barbarella," New Society pp. 673-674. November 9, 1967.

Boswell, G. W.

"Tolkien as litterateur," South Central Bulletin 32:188-197. 1972.

Bosworth, Patricia

"To Vonnegut, the hero is the man who refuses to kill," New York Times sec. 2, p. 5. October 25, 1970.

Bothorel, Nicole

"Notes sur certains problemes de science fiction," Interferences 5:38-45. 1975.

Bott, W.

"Politische bildung durch science-fiction-romanhefte?" Das Forum: Zietschrift der Volkshochschulen Bayerns 11:36- . 1971.

Boucher, Anthony

"All star survey," Magazine of Fantasy and Science Fiction 15(4):50-54. October 1958.

"Criminals at large," New York Times Book Review p. 68. November 8, 1964. (Book review)

"Footnote," Fantasy Times No. 254:24-25. September (1) 1956.

"In step with science," New York Times Book Review p. 18. February 27, 1966. (Book review)

"Publishing of science fiction, The," in: Bretnor, Reginald, ed. Modern Science Fiction: its Meaning and its Future. New York: Coward McCann, 1953. Reprinted, Chicago: Advent, 1979. pp. 23-42.

"Science and fantasy,", New York Herald Tribune Book Review p. 60. December 4, 1960. (Book review)

"Science fiction still leads science fact," New York Times Magazine pp. 56,58,63-64. December 1, 1957.

"Wizards of a small planet," Playboy 5:21-22,46. May 1958.

Boucher, Yvon

"Introduction a la litterature fantastique," Le Devoir p. 16, col. 4. April 24, 1976.

Bouissy, M.

"Fantastique et l'anticipation dans la litterature italienne d'aujourd'hui. Petit

Lexique," in: Ministere de l'Education Nationale. Centre National de Tele-Enseignement. Paris. Texte Serie 4. A Gt. 457.

Bounds, S. J.

"Openings for new writers," Focus: An SF Writers' Magazine No. 11: 7-9. 1985.

Bouquet, J. L.

"Science fiction et fiction tout court," Arts Spectacles No. 553:6. February 1-7, 1956.

"SF et rhetorique des idees," Arts 1.2. 1956.

Bourgeois, Jacques

"Theatre lyrique: un opera de science fiction," Arts Spectacles No. 554:4. February 8-14, 1956.

Bourges, Philippe

"Science fiction de Vladimir Pozner, La," Magazine Litteraire 94:36-37. November 1974.

Bourjaily, Vance

"What Vonnegut is and isn't," New York Times Book Review pp. 3,10. August 13, 1972.

Bourquin, D. R.

Work of Bruce McAllister: An Annotated Bibliography and Guide. San Bernardino, CA: Borgo, 1985. 30 p.

Bousfield, Wendy

"Dream World," in: Tymn, M. B. and Ashley, Mike. Science Fiction, Fantasy, and Weird Fiction Magazines. Westport, CT: Greenwood, 1985. pp. 190-194.

"Fantastic Science Fiction (1952)," in: Tymn, M. B. and Ashley, Mike. Science Fiction, Fantasy, and Weird Fiction Magazines. Westport, CT: Greenwood, 1985. pp. 244-248.

"Fantasy Book (1947-1951)," in: Tymn, M. B. and Ashley, Mike. Science Fiction, Fantasy, and Weird Fiction Magazines. Westport, CT: Greenwood, 1985. pp. 258-264.

"Out of This World Adventures," in: Tymn, M. B. and Ashley, Mike. Science Fiction, Fantasy, and Weird Fiction Magazines. Westport, CT: Greenwood, 1985. pp. 467-471.

"Science Stories," in: Tymn, M. B. and Ashley, Mike. Science Fiction, Fantasy, and Weird Fiction Magazines. Westport, CT: Greenwood, 1985. pp. 551-552.

Bousfield, Wendy (Continued)

"Space Stories," in: Tymn, M. B. and Ashley, Mike. Science Fiction, Fantasy, and Weird Fiction Magazines. Westport, CT: Greenwood, 1985. pp. 591-599.

"Ten Story Fantasy," in: Tymn, M. B. and Ashley, Mike. Science Fiction, Fantasy, and Weird Fiction Magazines. Westport, CT: Greenwood, 1985. pp. 654-659.

Bouson, J. B.

"Poet 'Taught by Dreams and Fantasies,' A: Muir's dual vision of human nature," in: Collins, R. A., ed. Scope of the Fantastic: Culture, Biography, Themes, Children's Literature. Westport: Greenwood, 1985. pp. 115-128.

Bouyxou, J. P.

Science fiction au cinema, La. Paris: Union Generale d'Editions, 1971. 514 p.

Bova, Ben

Notes to a Science Fiction Writer. New York: Charles Scribner's Sons, 1975. 177 p.

Notes to a Science Fiction Writer. 2nd ed., revised. Boston: Houghton, 1981. 193 p.

Viewpoint. Cambridge, MA: NESFA, 1977. 114 p.

Vision of the Future: The Art of Robert McCall. New York: Abrams, 1982. 191 p.

"By their fruits," in: Bova, Ben. Viewpoint. Cambridge, MA: NESFA, 1977. pp. 73-80.

"Challenge of Science Fiction Writing," Writer 95(9): 9-12. September 1982.

"Conflict in science fiction stories," Writer 89:15-17. August 1976.

"From mad professors to brilliant scientists: the evolution of a genre," Library Journal 98:1646-1649. 1973.

"Future of science: Prometheus, Apollo, Athena, The," in: Wilhelm, Kate, ed. Nebula Award Stories Nine. New York: Harper, 1975. pp. 117-131.

"Giant step backward," in: Bova, Ben. Viewpoint. Cambridge, MA: NESFA, 1977. pp. 21-28.

"Idea factory," in: Bova, Ben. Viewpoint. Cambridge, MA: NESFA, 1977. pp. 63-72.

"Inside Analog or How I learned to stop worrying and love my job," in: Bova, Ben. Viewpoint. Cambridge, MA: NESFA, 1977. pp. 1-10.

"Many worlds of science fiction, The," Elementary English 47:799-804. October 1970.

"Mental energy crisis," in: Bova, Ben. Viewpoint. Cambridge, MA: NESFA, 1977. pp. 29-37.

"Mystic west, The," in: Bova, Ben. Viewpoint. Cambridge, MA: NESFA, 1977. pp. 11-20.

"New worlds for old," in: Bova, Ben. Viewpoint. Cambridge, MA: NESFA, 1977. pp. 97-103.

"Plot in science fiction," Writer 88:17-20,46. 1975.

"Right Stuff (review)," Starlog No. 88: 59-61. November 1984.

"Role of science fiction, The," in: Bretnor, Reginald, ed. Science Fiction Today and Tomorrow. New York: Harper, 1974. pp. 3-16.

"SF game, The," in: Bova, Ben. Viewpoint. Cambridge, MA: NESFA, 1977. pp. 89-96.

"Space: 1999, marked down from 2001," in: Bova, Ben. Viewpoint. Cambridge, MA: NESFA, 1977. pp. 104-114.

"Teaching science fiction," in: Bova, Ben. Viewpoint. Cambridge, MA: NESFA, 1977. pp. 38-45.

Kelvin Throop fights back," in: Bova, Ben. Viewpoint. Cambridge, MA: NESFA, 1977. pp. 81-88.

Bowden, J. H.

"Exlit," College English 38:287-291. 1976.

Bowen, Elizabeth

"Things to Come: a critical appreciation," in: Johnson, William, ed. Focus on the Science Fiction Film. Englewood Cliffs, NJ: Prentice Hall, 1972. pp. 43-45.

Bowen, John

"Virtues of science fiction, The," Listener 72:1063. December 31, 1967.

Bowen, M. E.

"Introduction," in: Mercier, L. S. Memoirs of the Year 2500. Boston: Gregg, 1977. pp. v-xxv.

"Introduction," in: Russen, David. Iter Lunare. Boston: Gregg, 1976. pp. v-xiv.

Bowen, Roger

"Science, myth, and fiction in H. G. Wells's Island of Dr. Moreau," Studies in the Novel 8(3):318-333. Fall 1976.

Bower, M. J.

"Miniature World of Outland," Starlog 47: 40-43. June 1981.

Bowers, Bill

Double: Bill Symposium, by Bill Bowers and Bill Mallardi. Akron, OH: D:B Press, 1969. 111 p.

"Making of a fanzine, The," Outworlds 20:764-767. Second Quarter 1974.

Bowers, D. W.

"Science fiction for college libraries," Choice 6(4):478-483. June 1969.

Bowie, Robert

"Freedom and Art in A Clockwork Orange. Anthony Burgess and the Christian Premises of Dostoevsky," Thought 56(220): 402-416. December 1981.

Bowman, Harry

"NBC sneaks three new series," Dallas Morning News Sec. B, p. 11. September 9, 1966.

Bowman, S. E.

"Utopian views of Man and the Machine," Studies in the Literary Imagination 6(2): 105-120. Fall 1973.

Bowron, A. W.

"Boredom of fantasy," Ontario Library Review 38:19-21. Fall 1954.

Boyajian, Jerry

Index to the Science Fiction Magazines, 1977. by Jerry Boyajian and K. R. Johnson. Cambridge: Twaci Press, 1982. 28 p.

Index to the Science Fiction Magazines, 1978, by Jerry Boyajian and K. R. Johnson. Cambridge: Twaci Press, 1982. 28 p.

Index to the Science Fiction Magazines, 1979, by Jerry Boyajian and K. R. Johnson. Cambridge, MA: Twaci Press, 1981. 32 p.

Index to the Science Fiction Magazines, 1980, by Jerry Boyajian and K. R. Johnson. Cambridge, MA: Twaci Press, 1981. 27 p.

Index to the Science Fiction Magazines, 1981, by Jerry Boyajian and K. R. Johnson. Cambridge, MA: Twaci Press, 1982. 32 p.

Index to the Science Fiction Magazines, 1982, by Jerry Boyajian and K. R. Johnson. Cambridge, MA: Twaci, 1983. 35 p.

Index to the Science Fiction Magazines, 1983, by Jerry Boyajian and K. R. Johnson. Cambridge, MA: Twaci, 1984. 31 p.

Index to the Science Fiction Magazines. 1984. by Jerry Boyajian and K. R. Johnson. Cambridge, MA: Twaci, 1985. 31 p.

Index to the Semi-Professional Fantasy Magazines 1982, by Jerry Boyajian and K. R. Johnson. Cambridge: Twaci, 1983. 27 p.

Index to the Semi-Professional Fantasy Magazines 1983, by Jerry Boyajian and K. R. Johnson. Cambridge, MA: Twaci, 1983. 27 p.

Boyar, Jay

"Disney bets 'Cauldron' will put new movement in animation," Chicago Tribune May 5, 1985. in: NewsBank. Film and Television. 109:A5-A6. May 1985.

Boyd, Beulah

"Science fiction and films about the future," Arizona English Bulletin 51(1):62. October 1972.

Boyd, David

"Mode and meaning in 2001," Journal of Popular Film 6(3):202-215. 1978.

Boyd, Ian

Novels of G. K. Chesterton: a Study in Art and Propaganda, The. New York: Barnes & Noble, 1975. 241 p.

Boyd, John

"What it means to write science fiction," in: McNelly, W. E., ed. Science Fiction the Academic Awakening. Shreveport, LA: CEA, 1974. pp. 44-46.

Boyer, Paul

By the Bomb's Early Light: American Thought and Culture at the Dawn of the Atomic Age. New York: Pantheon, 1985. 440 p.

Boyer, R. H.

Fantasists on Fantasy: A Collection of Critical Reflections, by R. H. Boyer and K. J. Zahorski. New York: Avon Discus, 1984. 287 p.

Fantasy Literature: A Core Collection and Reference Guide, by M. B. Tymn, K. J. Zahorski, and R. H. Boyer. New York: Bowker, 1979. 273 p.

Lloyd Alexander, Evangeline Walton Ensley, Kenneth Morris: A Primary and Secondary Bibliography, by K. J. Zahorski and R. H. Boyer. Boston: G. K. Hall, 1981. 291 p.

"On fantasy," by R. H. Boyer and K. J. Zahorski. in: Tymn, Marshall B., Kenneth J. Zahorski, and Robert H. Boyer. _Fantasy Literature: a Core Collection and Reference Guide_. New York: Bowker, 1979. pp. 3-83.

"Science fiction and fantasy literature: clarification through juxtaposition," by R. H. Boyer and K. J. Zahorski. _Wisconsin English Journal_ 18(3):2-8. April 1976.

"Secondary Worlds of High Fantasy," by K. J. Zahorski and R. H. Boyer. in: Schlobin, Roger C., ed. _The Aesthetics of Fantasy Literature and Art_. Notre Dame, IN: University of Notre Dame Press, 1982. pp. 56-81.

Boylan, J. H.

"Hal in '2001: A Space Odyssey': the lover sings his song," _Journal of Popular Culture_ 18(4):53-56. Spring 1985.

Boyno, E. A.

"Mathematics in Science Fiction: Of Measure Zero," in: Hassler, Donald M., ed. _Patterns of the Fantastic II_. Mercer Island, WA: Starmont, 1985. pp. 39-44.

Boytinck, Paul

Anthony Burgess: an Enumerative Bibliography with Selected Annotations. Norwood, Pennsylvania: Norwood Editions, 1974. 43 p.

Boyum, J. G.

"Clockwork Orange: Viddying metaphor," in: Boyum, J. G. _Double Exposure: Fiction into Film_. New York: Universe, 1985. pp. 162-169.

"Close encounters (review)," by David Sterritt and J. G. Boyum. _Science Digest_ 83(2):16-18. February 1978.

"Slaughterhouse Five: Pilgrim's Progress through Time and Space," by J. G. Boyum. in: Boyum, J. G. _Double Exposure: Fiction into Film_. New York: Universe, 1985. pp. 197-205.

Bozzetto, Roger

"Lucien de Samosate, precurseur de modernite," _Change_ (Paris) 40: 55-67. 1981.

"Mouvements, gestes et science fiction," _Cahiers du Vingtieme Siecle_ 2:21-32. 1974.

"Pierre Very: une rencontre avec la science fiction," _Europe_ 60(636): 78-86. April 1982.

"Point de vue des specialistes," _Cahiers Pedagogiques_ 150:27-39. January 1977.

"SF et Poesie. b) Fonction," _Europe_ 580/581:100-103. August/September 1977.

Brabazon, James

Dorothy L. Sayers: The Life of a Courageous Woman. London: Gollancz, 1981. 308 p.

Bracken, Michael

"Grant Carrington: More Than Amazing," _Night Voyages_. 1(8): 18-22. Fall 1981.

"Monteleone Connection, The," _Night Voyages_ 1(7): 10-19. Spring 1981.

Brackett, Leigh

"And as for the admixture of cultures on imaginary worlds," in: De Camp, L. S., ed. _Blade of Conan_. New York: Ace, 1979. pp. 235-242.

"Introduction: Beyond Our Narrow Skies," in: Brackett, Leigh, ed. _The Best of Planet Stories No. 1_. New York: Ballantine, 1975. pp. 1-8.

"John W. Campbell," _Locus_ No. 91:9. July 22, 1971.

Bradbrook, B. R.

"Chesterton and Karel Capek: a study in personal and literary relationship," _The Chesterton Review_ 4:89-103. 1978.

Bradbury, Ray

American Film Institute Seminar With Ray Bradbury Held October 1, 1969. Beverly Hills, CA: Center for Advanced Film Studies, c1978. 84 p. on 1 microfiche. (The American Film Institute Seminars, Pt. 1, No. 23)

"At what temperature do books burn," _Writer_ 80:18-20. July 1967.

"Beaumont remembered," in: Beaumont, Charles. _Best of Beaumont_. New York: Bantam, 1982. pp. ix-xvi.

Bradbury, Ray (Continued)

"Day after tomorrow," <u>Nation</u> 176:364-367. May 2, 1953.

"Death warmed over," <u>Cthulhu Calls</u> 3(2):36-43. October 1975.

"God in science fiction, The," <u>Saturday Review</u> 5(6):36-38,43. December 10, 1977.

"Here there by tygers," <u>Mother Earth News</u> 49:77. January 1978.

"How I Was Always Rich But Was Too Dumb to Know It," in: <u>Pages The World of Books, Writers, and Writing. 1.</u> Detroit: Gale, 1976. pp. 189-193.

"How, instead of being educated in college, I was graduatd from libraries, or, thoughts from a chap who landed on the moon in 1932," <u>Wilson Library Bulletin</u> 45(9):842-851. May 1971.

"Impatient Gulliver above our roofs, An," <u>Life</u> 63:31-37. November 24, 1967.

"Inspiration for the Zen writer," <u>Writer's Digest</u> 54(11):15. November 1974.

"Literature for the space age," <u>California Librarian</u> 21:159-164. July 1960.

"Miracles and miracles: pass it on!" <u>Galileo</u> 1:12-14. 1976.

"Science fiction as modern romance; excerpts from address," <u>Intellect</u> 104:490. April 1976.

"Secret Mind," in: Wingrove, David, ed. <u>The Science Fiction Source Book</u>. New York: Van Nostrand, 1984. pp. 72-74.

"Shaw as influence; Laughton as teacher," <u>Shaw Review</u> 16(2):98-99. May 1973.

"We must choose: darkness or light," <u>Houston Chronicle</u> sec. 4, p. 13. May 28, 1972.

Bradham, J. A.

"Case in James Blish's <u>A Case of Conscience</u>, The," <u>Extrapolation</u> 16(1):67-80. December 1974.

Bradley, M. Z.

<u>Men, Halfings and Hero Worship</u>. Baltimore: T-K Graphics, 1973. 51 p.

"And strange-sounding names," in: De Camp, L. S., ed. <u>Blade of Conan</u>. New York: Ace, 1979. pp. 293-299.

"Evolution of consciousness: twenty-five years of writing about women in science fiction, An," <u>Science Fiction Review</u> 6(3):34-45. August 1977.

"Experiment perilous: the art and science of anguish in science fiction," <u>Algol</u> 19:4-11. November 1972. also in: <u>Experiment Perilous: Three Essays on Science Fiction</u>. New York: Algol Press, 1976. pp. 7-20.

"Faking it," <u>Empire for the SF Writer</u> 9(3): 12-13. Spring 1985.

"Fandom: Its Value to the Professional," in: Jarvis, Sharon, ed. <u>Inside Outer Space</u>. New York: Ungar, 1985. pp. 69-84.

"Fantasy and the contemporary occult novel, social and intellectual approaches, 1," <u>Fantasy Review</u> 9(6)(eg v. 8 #6): 10-12. June 1985.

"Fantasy and the contemporary occult novel: social and intellectual approaches, II," <u>Fantasy Review</u> 8(7): 31-32. July 1985.

"Feminine imperative, The," <u>Viva</u> 4(3):44-46,48,104,108. December 1976.

"How to prepare a manuscript," <u>Empire: For the SF Writer</u> 3(2): 21-26. August 1977.

"I know you're busy, but please help me," <u>Empire: For the SF Writer</u> 3(3): 37-39. November 1977.

"Maverick view, The," <u>Science Fiction Writers of America</u>. <u>Bulletin</u>. 14(3):17-21. Fall 1979.

"My trip through science fiction," <u>Algol</u> 15(1):10-20. Winter 1977/1978.

"Respectfully to Differ..." <u>Fantasy Newsletter</u> 5(8): 19-21. September 1982.

"So You Want to be a Science Fiction Writer!" <u>Empire For the SF Writer</u> 32: 6-9. Winter 1984.

"Something worse than fantasy: rape in science fiction," <u>Thrust</u> No. 13:13-15,45. Fall 1979.

"Two worlds of fantasy," <u>Haunted: Studies in Gothic Fiction</u> 1:82-85. June 1968.

Bradshaw, F. H.

"Popular literature: matrix of science fiction," <u>Arizona English Bulletin</u> 51(1):54-57. October 1972.

Bradshaw, Steve

"Against Darwin," <u>New Society</u> pp. 660-661. March 13, 1975.

Author Entries

Brady, C. A.

"Lunatics and selenophiles," _America_ pp. 448-449. July 26, 1958.

"Some notes on C. S. Lewis's _The Dark Tower and Other Stories_," _CSL: The Bulletin of the New York C. S. Lewis Society_ 8(11):1-10. 1977.

Brady, C. J.

"Computer as a symbol of God: Ellison's macabre exodus, The," _Journal of General Education_ 28(1):55-62. Spring 1976.

Brady, Frank

"Lost film of Orson Welles, The," _American Film_ 4(2):63-69. November 1978.

Brady, Thomas

"Toujours Tarzan," _New York Times Magazine_ pp. 22-23. January 5, 1947.

Braff, L. C.

"To Con or Not to Con," _Fantasy Newsletter_ 6(3): 20. March 1983.

"To Con or Not To Con?" by Sharon Jarvis and Lea Braff. _Fantasy Newsletter_ 6(8): 26, 38. September 1983.

Bragg, Roy

"Aggiecon XIII: Science Fiction's True Believers Abound," _Bryan-College Station Eagle_, Sec. 1, p. 1. March 27, 1982.

Brague, P. E.

"Escapism plus,", _Library Journal_ p. 1603. April 15, 1968.

Brain, Bonnie

"Saviors and scientists: Extraterrestrials in recent science fiction films," _Et Cetera_ 40(2): 218-229. Summer 1983.

Brajer, Peter

"_Deathworld Trilogy, The_," in: Magill, Frank N., ed. _Survey of Science Fiction Literature_, Vol. 2. Englewood Cliffs, NJ: Salem Press, 1979. pp. 519-523.

Branch, D. R.

"Flying nonesuch, The," _Writer's Digest_ 57(8):41. August 1977.

Brandis, Evgeni

Sovetskii nauchno fantasticheskii roman. Leningrad: 1959. 44 p. (LCC 60-29095)

Zhiul Verne. Leningrad: 1956. 246 p. (LCC 57-17667)

Zwerkalo trevog i somnenii: o sovremennom sostoknzi i nugyak pazvntiya anglo amerikanskoi nauchnoya fantastiki. Moscow: Zpanio, 1959.

"Fantascienza e l'uomo nel mondo conterporaneo, La," in: Petronio, Giuseppe, ed. _Letteratura di massa, letteratura de consumo: Guida storica e critica._ Bari: Laterza, 1979. pp. 121-147.

"Fantastika v dvizuscemsja mire," by E. Brandis and V. Dmitrevski. _Inostrannaja literatura_ 1: 216-1967.

"Fantasy pisut dlja vsech!" by E. Brandis and V. Dmitrevski. _Literaturnaja gazeta_ Feb. 1, 1966.

"Fantasy Writers Write for Everyone," by Y. Brandis and V. Dmitrevsky. _Current Digest of the Soviet Press_ 18(6): 17-20. March 2, 1966.

"Future, its promoters and false prophets, The," by Evgeni Brandis and Vladimir Dmitrevskiy. _Magazine of Fantasy and Science Fiction_ 29(4):62-80. October 1965.

"Im reich der phantastik," by J. Brandis and Wladimir Dmitrijewski. in: Barmeyer, Eike, ed. _Science fiction: theorie und geschichte._ Munchen: Fink, 1972. pp. 128-133.

"In the land of science fiction," by Evgeni Brandis and Vladimir Dmitrevsky. _Soviet Literature_ 5:145-150. 1968. also in: Magidoff, Robert, ed. _Russian Science Fiction, 1969._ NY: New York Univ. Press, 1969. pp. 3-10.

"Naucnaja fantastika i celovek v segodn jasnem mire," _Vosprosy Literatury._ vi:97-126. 1977.

"Wissenschaft-phantastische Literatur und die Gesaltung von Zukunftsmodellen," _Sowjetwissenschaft_ 17(8):798-813. 1969.

"Wissenschaftliche Phantastik lebt weiter," by J. Brandis and W. Dmitrewski. _Kunst und Literatur_ 24:792-807. 1976.

Brandon, Carl

"Apogee effects," _Cinefantastique_ 15(3):9,57. July 1985.

Brandstetter, Gabriele

"Phantastik in der Musik," by Gabriele Brandstetter and Norbert Brandstetter. in: Thomsen, C. W., ed. <u>Phantastik in Literatur und Kunst</u>. Darmstadt: Wissenschaftliche Buchgesellschaft, 1980. pp. 514-530.

Brandstetter, Norbert

"Phantastik in der Musik," by Gabriele Brandstetter and Norbert Brandstetter. in: Thomsen, C. W., ed. <u>Phantastik in Literatur und Kunst</u>. Darmstadt: Wissenschaftliche Buchgesellschaft, 1980. pp. 514-530.

Branham, R. J.

"Fantasy and Ineffability: Fiction at the Limits of Language," <u>Extrapolation</u> 24(1): 66-79. Spring 1983.

"Principles of the Imaginary Milieu: Argument and Idea in Fantasy Fiction," <u>Extrapolation</u> 21(4): 328-337. Winter 1980.

"Stapledon's 'Agonostic Mysticism'," <u>Science-Fiction Studies</u> 9(3): 249-256. November 1982.

Branon, M. M.

"Future: an exhibit of science fiction, The," <u>Texas Library Journal</u> 44:155-156. Winter 1968.

Brantlinger, Patrick

"Gothic Origins of Science Fiction," <u>Novel</u> 14(1): 30-43. Autumn 1980.

Brashear, M. G.

"Novel of transcendence: Silverberg's <u>Downward to Earth</u>, The," <u>Riverside Quarterly</u> 7(1):17-26. March 1980.

Braswell, L.

"Visionary Voyage in Science Fiction and Medieval Allegory," <u>Mosaic</u> 14(1): 125-142. Winter 1981.

Bratman, D. S.

"Books about J. R. R. Tolkien and his works," <u>Science Fiction Collector</u> 5:26-28. September 1977.

"Mythcon XII report," <u>Mythlore</u> 8(3):37. Autumn 1981.

"Subject Index to <u>Mythlore</u> no. 1-30," <u>Mythlore</u> 9(1): 42-47. Spring 1982.

"Subject index to <u>Mythlore</u> no. 31-39," <u>Mythlore</u> 11(2):61-63. Autumn 1984.

Braucourt, Guy

"Interview with Don Siegel," in: Johnson, William, ed. <u>Focus on the Science Fiction Film</u>. Englewood Cliffs, NJ: Prentice Hall, 1972. pp. 74-76.

Braude, Anne

"Malthoms," <u>Niekas</u> 25: 12-13. February 1981.

Braude, Nan

"Sion and Parnassus: three approaches to myth," <u>Mythlore</u> 1(1):6-8. January 1969.

Braudy, Leo

"Genre Life/Historical Death," in: Slusser, George, ed. <u>Shadows of the Magic Lamp</u>. Carbondale: Southern Illinois University Press, 1985. pp. 1-13.

Braun, Saul

"Shazam! Here comes captain relevant," <u>New York Times Magazine</u> pp. 32,36,38,41,43-44, 46,48,55. May 2, 1971. Discussion, p. 6. May 30, 1971.

Braun, Wolfgang

"'Von Mitternacht kommt die Macht': Technik und Ideologie in Hans Dominiks 'Die Macht der Drei'," in: Ermert, Karl, ed. <u>Neugier oder Flucht?</u> Stuttgart: Klett, 1980. pp. 116-125.

Bravard, R. S.

<u>Samuel R. Delany: a Primary and Secondary Bibliography</u>, by M. W. Peplow and R. S. Bravard. Boston: G. K. Hall, 1980. 112 p.

"Samuel R. Delany: A Selective Primary and Secondary Bibliography, 1979-1983," Peplow, M. W.; Bravard, R. S. <u>Black American Literature Forum</u> 18(2): 75-77. Summer 1984.

"Through a Glass Darkly: Bibliographing Samuel R. Delany," by R. S. Bravard and M. W. Peplow. <u>Black American Literature Forum</u> 18(2): 69-75. Summer 1984.

Bray, M. K.

"Mandalic activism: an appproach to structure, theme and tone in four novels by Philip K. Dick," <u>Extrapolation</u> 21(2):146-157. Summer 1980.

Bray, M. K. (Continued)

"Rites of Reversal: Double Consciousness in Delany's Dhalgren," Black American Literature Forum 18(2): 57-61. Summer 1984.

Brecher, Harold

"Top Psychiatrists Explain: The Amazing Appeal of 'Return of the Jedi'," by Harold Brecher and Peter Judd. National Enquirer p. 12. June 21, 1983.

Breen, J. L.

"On science fiction detective stories," Isaac Asimov's Science Fiction Magazine 3(6):69-78. June 1979.

Breen, Jennifer

"Anthony Burgess's guide to novels," Meanjin 44(1): 142-145. March 1985.

Breen, Walter

Darkover Concordance: a Reader's Guide, The. Berkeley, California: Pennyfarthing Press, 1979. 163 p.

Gemini Problem: a Study in Darkover, The. Berkeley: by the author, 1973. Reprinted, Baltimore: T-K Graphics, 1976. 39 p.

Breit, Harvey

"Lunar man," New York Times Book Review p. 8. March 14, 1954.

"Talk with Mr. Bradbury," New York Times Book Review p. 11. August 5, 1951.

Brender, Alan

"Harry Hamlin: A Young Star Among the Giants of Clash of the Titans," Starlog 46: 17-21. May 1981.

"Outland," Starlog 45: 47-51. April 1981.

"Science Fiction in Production," Starlog 44: 30-31, 63. March 1981.

"Star Wars' Latest Incarnation: It's a Radio Play," Starlog 47: 23-24. June 1981.

"Starlog Interview: Blair Brown," Starlog 46: 35-37, 62. May 1981.

"Starlog Interview: Frances Sternhagen," Starlog 47: 17-20. June 1981.

"Starlog Interview: Jeremy Bulloch," Starlog 50: 17-21. September 1981.

"Starlog Interview: Mark Lenard: Star Trek's Other Alien," Starlog 43: 24-27. January 1981.

"Starlog Interview: Mike Hodges, Director of the New 'Flash Gordon'" Starlog 44: 59-61. March 1981.

"Starlog Interview: Thom Christopher," Starlog. 45: 16-19. April 1981.

"Starlog Interview: Verna Fields: The Studio Executive Who Halted the Expanding Budget on 'The Incredible Shrinking Woman,'" Starlog 44: 24-29. March 1981.

"Starlog Interview: Wilfrid Hyde-White," Starlog 47: 44-46. June 1981.

Brennan, J. P.

"Macabre," in: Tymn, M. B. and Ashley, Mike. Science Fiction, Fantasy, and Weird Fiction Magazines. Westport, CT: Greenwood, 1985. pp. 375-376.

"Anarchism and utopian tradition in The Dispossessed," by J. P. Brennan and M. C. Downs. in: Olander, Joseph D. and Martin Harry Greenberg, eds. Ursula K. Le Guin. New York: Taplinger, 1979. pp. 116-152.

"Mechanical Chicken: Psyche and Society in The Space Merchants," Extrapolation 25(2): 101-114. Summer 1984.

Brenner, Malcolm

"Interview: Poul Anderson," Future Life 26: 26-28. May 1981.

Brennert, Alan

"Confessions of a Story Editor," Starlog 48: 86-89, July 1981.

Bretnor, Reginald

Craft of Science Fiction, The. New York: Harper & Row, 1976. 321 p.

Modern Science Fiction: Its Meaning and Its Future. New York: Coward-McCann, 1953. 294 p.

Science Fiction, Today and Tomorrow. New York: Harper & Row, 1974. 342 p.

"Future of science fiction, The," in: Bretnor, Reginald, ed. Modern Science Fiction: Its Meaning and Its Future. New York: Coward McCann, 1953. Reprinted, Chicago: Advent, 1979. pp. 265-294.

"How to build a science fiction story," Writers Digest 56:24-25. July 1976.

Bretnor, Reginald (Continued)

"On taking science fiction seriously," Science Fiction Advertiser 7:3-8. Winter 1954.

"One man's BEM," in: De Camp, L. S., ed. Blade of Conan. New York: Ace, 1979. pp. 301-310.

"Science fiction in the age of space," in: Bretnor, Reginald, ed. Science Fiction Today and Tomorrow. New York: Harper, 1974. pp. 150-179.

"SF: the challenge to the writer," in: Bretnor, Reginald, ed. The Craft of Science Fiction New York: Harper, 1976. pp. 3-21.

Bretz, Mark

"Entering another dimension," St. Louis Globe-Democrat April 2, 1981. in: NewsBank. Film and Television. 15: F7. July/December 1981.

"Versatile Mr. Nimoy Might Surprise Fans of Stoic Mr. Spock," St. Louis Globe-Democrat January 1-2, 1983. in: NewsBank. Film and Television 77:E13. 1982/1983.

Brewer, D. S.

"The Lord of the Rings as romance," in: Salu, Mary and Robert T. Farrell, eds. J. R. R. Tolkien: Scholar and Storyteller. Essays in Memoriam. Ithaca, New York: Cornell University Press, 1979. pp. 249-264.

Brewer, F. J.

James Branch Cabell: a Bibliography of his Writings, Biography and Criticism. Charlottesville, Virginia: University of Virginia Press, 1957. 206 p.

Brewer, Jeutonne

Anthony Burgess: a bibliography. Metuchen, NJ: Scarecrow, 1980. 175 p. (Scarecrow Author Bibliographies, 47)

Brewster, Anne

"Interview with Stanislaw Lem," Science Fiction: A Review of Speculative Literature 4(1): 6-8. March 1982.

Brice, W. R.

"Exploration of space: fact and fiction," Journal of College Science Teaching 7(2):107-110. November 1977.

Bridgstock, Martin

"Psychological Approach to "Hard" Science Fiction," Science-Fiction Studies 10(1): 50-57. March 1983.

Bridienne, J. J.

Litterature francais d'imaginations scientifique, La. Paris: Dassonville, 1950. 294 p.

"J. H. Rosny Aine, romancier des possibles cosmiques," Fiction No. 27:108-110. Februrary 1956.

"Science fiction, nouveau genre litteraire?" Lectures Culturelles May 1952.

Brien, Alan

"Adam beyond the stars," Spectator 201:379. September 19, 1958.

"Science fiction: an inter-galactic trip among the paperbacks," Sunday Times Magazine pp. 16-17. July 24, 1977. (Book review)

Brigg, Peter

J. G. Ballard. Mercer Island, WA: Starmont, 1985. 138 p.

"Andromeda Strain, The," in: Magill, Frank N., ed. Survey of Science Fiction Literature, Vol. 1. Englewood Cliffs, NJ: Salem Press, 1979. pp. 63-66.

"Beginning Place, The," in: Magill, Frank N., ed. Survey of Modern Fantasy Literature, Vol 1. Englewood Cliffs, NJ: Salem Press, Inc., 1983. pp. 81-83.

"Dream Play, A," in: Magill, Frank N., ed. Survey of Modern Fantasy Literature, Vol 1. Englewood Cliffs, NJ: Salem Press, Inc., 1983. pp. 428-430.

"Drowned World, The," in: Magill, Frank N., ed. Survey of Science Fiction Literature, Vol. 2. Englewood Cliffs, NJ: Salem Press, 1979. pp. 634-638.

"Fu Manchu Stories, The," in: Magill, Frank N., ed. Survey of Modern Fantasy Literature, Vol 2. Englewood Cliffs, NJ: Salem Press, Inc., 1983. pp. 585-589.

"Gravity's Rainbow," in: Magill, Frank N., ed. Survey of Science Fiction Literature, Vol. 2. Englewood Cliffs, NJ: Salem Press, 1979. pp. 915-920.

"Macroscope," in: Magill, Frank N., ed. Survey of Science Fiction Literature, Vol. 3. Englewood Cliffs, NJ: Salem Press, 1979. pp. 1308-1311.

Brigg, Peter (Continued)

"Six Characters in Search of an Author," in: Magill, Frank N., ed. Survey of Modern Fantasy Literature, Vol 4. Englewood Cliffs, NJ: Salem Press, Inc., 1983. pp. 1757-1759.

"Watch the Northwind Rise," in: Magill, Frank N., ed. Survey of Modern Fantasy Literature, Vol 5. Englewood Cliffs, NJ: Salem Press, Inc., 1983. pp. 2067-2068.

"Analogies of scale in Piers Anthony's Macroscope," Science Fiction Studies 2(2):119-130. July 1975.

"Archetype of the journey in Ursula Le Guin's fiction, The," in: Olander, Joseph D. and Martin Harry Greenberg, eds. Ursula K. Le Guin. New York: Taplinger, 1979. pp. 36-63.

"Consistent extrapolation: a critical approach, The," in: Remington, Thomas, J., ed. Selected Proceedings of the 1978 SFRA National Conference. Cedar Falls, Iowa: Univ. of Northern Iowa, 1979. pp. 9-21.

"Fantasy and modern drama," in: Magill, Frank N., ed. Survey of Modern Fantasy Literature, Vol 5. Englewood Cliffs, NJ: Salem Press, Inc., 1983. pp. 2422-2446.

"Frank Herbert and Bill Ranson's The Jesus Incident: Variations on the Godgame," Philosophical Speculations on Science Fiction and Fantasy. 1(1): 26-34. March 1981.

"Frank Herbert: On Getting Our Heads Together," Mosaic 13(3/4): 193-202. Spring/Summer 1980.

"Three styles of Arthur C. Clarke: the projector, the wit, and the mystic," in: Olander, Joseph D. and Martin Harry Greenberg, eds. Arthur C. Clarke. New York: Taplinger, 1977. pp. 15-51.

Briggs, Julia

Night Visitors: the Rise and Fall of the English Ghost Story. London: Faber & Faber, 1977. 238 p.

Brincy, R. E.

Master of Villany: A Biography of Sax Rohmer, by C. V. Ash and E. S. Rohmer, ed. by R. E. Briney. Bowling Green, OH: Popular Press, 1972. 312 p.

SF Bibliographies: an Annotated Bibliography of Bibliographical Works on Science Fiction and Fantasy Fiction, by R. E. Briney and Edward Wood. Chicago: Advent Publishers, 1972. 49 p.

"Professional Works and Miscellany," in: Wetzel, George. Howard Phillips Lovecraft: Memoirs, Critiques, & Bibliographies. North Tonowonda, NY: SSR, 1955. pp. 59-83.

Brissenden, R. F.

"Phenomenon of Science Fiction," "Meanjin (Melbourne,Aust.) 57: 203-213. Winter 1954.

Britikov, A. F.

Russkij sovietskij naucno fantasticeskij roman. Leningrad: Nauka, 1970. 448 p.

"Sovetskaia nauchnaia fantastika," in: Poliak, L. and Kovskii, V., eds. Zhanrovo-stilevye iskania sovremennoi sovetskoi prozy. Moscow: 1971. pp. 308-350.

Problemy i zucenija naucnoj fantastike," Ruskaia Literatura. No. 1:193-202. 1980.

Brizzi, M. T.

Philip Jose Farmer. Mercer Island, Washington: Starmont Houst, 1980. 80 p. (Starmont Reader's Guide 3)

"C. J. Cherryh and Tomorrow's New Sex Roles," in: Staicar, Tom, ed. The Feminine Eye. New York: Ungar, 1982. pp. 32-47.

"Narcissism and Romance in McCaffrey's Restoree," in: Hassler, Donald M. Patterns of the Fantastic. Mercer Island, WA: Starmont, 1983. pp. 41-46.

Broad, W. J.

"Science fiction writers speak up over real-life Star Wars," Chicago Tribune Sec. 5, p. 10. March 21, 1985.

Brochon, Pierre

"Entretien sur la science fiction," Europe No. 4:3-28. 1957.

"Surnaturel a la fabrique d'absolu, Du," Europe revue mensuelle No. 139/140:20-28. July/August 1957.

Brock, E. H.

Projected Societies in American Science Fiction, 1945-1970. Ph.D. Dissertation, Ohio State University, 1976. 165 p.

"Heroes and villains in projected societies in American science fiction: 1945-1970," Unpublished (?) paper, cited in Sociological Abstracts on-line search. Citation MiSSA 1977 0091. No date.

Brock, E. M.

"Twentieth-century anti-utopian fiction: a critical analysis," Southeastern Librarian 17:221-232. No date.

Broderick, D. M.

"Science fiction and sexism," Moccasin Telegraph 17:29-31. Summer 1975.

Brodkin, S. Z.

Science Fiction: Teacher's Manual, by S. Z. Brodkin and E. J. Pearson. Evanston: McDougal, 1974. 56 p.

Brodskey, S. L.

"Psy-Fi," Human Behavior 5:65-68. January 1976.

Brody, Alan

"2001 and the paradox of the fortunate fall," Hartford Studies in Literature 1(1):7-19. 1969.

Brody, Sidney

"Future perfect," Today's Education 60:23. February 1971.

Broege, Valerie

"Electric Eve: Images of Female Computers in Science Fiction," in: Erlich, Richard D., ed. Clockwork Worlds. Westport, CT: Greenwood, 1983. pp. 183-191.

Broer, Lawrence

"Pilgrim's Progress: Is Kurt Vonnegut, Jr. Winning His War With Machines?" in: Erlich, Richard D., ed. Clockwork Worlds. Westport, CT: Greenwood, 1983. pp. 137-161.

Brohaugh, William

"SF Tiltin," Questar 3(4): 36-39. June 1981.

Broich, Ulrich

Science Fiction: Theorie und Geschichte. Themen und Typen, Form und Weltbild. by Ulrich Suerbaum, Ulrich Broich, and Raimund Borgmeier. Stuttgart: Plilipp Reclam, 1981. 215 p. 81-137889

"Robinsonade und science fiction," Anglia 94(1/2). 1976.

Bromley, Robin

"Tube Fantastic, The," Twilight Zone 5(6): 54-55, 95. February 1986.

Bronner, S. E.

"Revolutionary Anticipation and Tradition," Minnesota Review ns6, 1976. pp. 88-95.

Brooke-Rose, Christine

Rhetoric of the Unreal, A. Cambridge: Cambridge University Press, 1981. 446 p.

Brooks, C. W.

Revised Hannes Bok Checklist. Baltimore: T-K Graphics, 1974. 46 p.

Brooks, D. E.

"Elmo Lincoln, Tarzan extraordinaire," Barsoomian No. 15:7-14. October 1969.

Brophy, Brigid

"Rare books," New Statesman pp. 904-905. June 14, 1963.

Brophy, L.

"Grave new worlds," Catholic World 179(1069):40-43. April 1954.

Brosnan, John

Future Tense: the Cinema of Science Fiction. New York: St. Martins, 1978. 320 p.

Horror People, The. New York: St. Martin's Press, 1976. 304 p.

"Special Effects in science fiction cinema," in: Wingrove, David. Science Fiction Film Source Book. Harlow: Longman Green, 1985. pp. 301-308.

Brotman, S.

"Out of this world: recommended science fiction," School Library Journal 23:30-31. December 1976.

Brower, B.

"Vulgarization of American demonology," Esquire 61:94-99. June 1964.

Brown, A. M.

"Boom!" Fantasy Times No. 100:12-13. February (2) 1950.

"Confidentially: The Beginning of the End," Fantasy Times No. 42:27. March 16, 1947.

Brown, Barbara

"Left Hand of Darkness: androgyny, future, present and past," in: Ursula K. Le Guin, ed. by Harold Bloom. New York: Chelsea House, 1986. pp. 225-234.

"Left Hand of Darkness: Androgyny, Future, Present, and Past," Extrapolation 21(3): 227-235. Fall 1980.

Brown, C. A.

"Once upon a Narnia," CSL: The Bulletin of the New York C. S. Lewis Society 8(8):1-4. 1977.

Brown, C. N.

"Book summary, 1984," Locus 18(2): 1, 26-28. February 1985.

"Conversation with Ian Ballantine," Locus 11(10):10-11. December 1978.

"I remember Jack Gaughan," Locus 18(9): 51. September 1985.

"Magazine report, 1984," Locus 18(2): 1, 28-29. February 1985.

"On Books: The Best of 1981," Isaac Asimov's Science Fiction Magazine 6(6): 12-17. June 1982.

"Recommended Reading, 1984," Locus 18(2): 1, 4-5. February 1985.

"SF in the Soviet Union, part 1," Locus 15(8):1,14-15. August 1982.

Brown, E. C.

"Snapshot," Vector 117: 5-9, 38. December 1983.

Brown, E. J.

Brave New World, 1984, and We: an Essay on Anti-Utopia. Ann Arbor: Ardis Publishers, 1976. 61 p.

"Zamiatin and English literature," American Contributions to the Fifth International Congress of Slavists, II: Literary Contributions. The Hague, 1963.

Brown, Judith

"Pilgrimage from deep space, The," Mythlore 4:13-15. March 1977.

Brown, L. W.

"Analogue Men," in: Magill, Frank N., ed. Survey of Science Fiction Literature, Vol. 1. Englewood Cliffs, NJ: Salem Press, 1979. pp. 48-52.

Brown, R. G.

Conflict and Confluence: The Art of Anthony Burgess. Ph.D. Dissertation, University of Iowa, 1971. 351 p.

Brown, Rich

"Criticism: Budrys Over the Coals," Thrust 18: 15-17. Winter/Spring 1982.

"Friday: A Personal Reaction," Science Fiction Review 11(4): 38-39. November 1982.

Brown, Rupert

World of the Dark Crystal. by Brian Froud, J. J. Llewelyn, and Rupert Brown. New York: Knopf, 1983. 128 p.

Brown, S. P.

"Secretly hidden behind the pen name of Richard Bachman was Stephen King," New York Daily News May 19, 1985. in: NewsBank. Literature. 110:A1-A2. June 1985.

"Stephen King, shining through," Washington Post p. C1, C4. April 9, 1985.

Brown, Steve

"Two Tractates of Philip K. Dick," Science Fiction Review 10(2): 11-12. Summer 1981.

Browne, Howard

"Fantastic," Fantasy Times No. 149:3-4. March (1) 1952.

"Profit Without Honor," Amazing 58(1): 71-81. May 1984.

"So what's a little blood?" Inside and Science Fiction Advertiser No. 10: 19-20, 23. July 1955.

Browne, R. L.

"Flatland: A Romance of Many Dimensions," by Jane Hipolito and R. L. Browne. in: Magill, Frank N., ed. Survey of Science Fiction Literature, Vol. 2. Englewood Cliffs, NJ: Salem Press, 1979. pp. 792-796.

Browne, W. P.

"Government and politics in selected works of John Brunner," in: De Bolt, Joe, ed. Happening Worlds of John Brunner. Port Washington, NY: Kennikat, 1975. pp. 130-144.

Browning, Gavin

"Scientism in science fiction," Foundation 33: 24-36. Spring 1985.

Brownstein, Stu

"Worldcon: A Prejudicial View," P*S*F*Q* 6: 7. Fall 1981.

Broxon, M. D.

SFWA Handbook, The. S. L.: Science Fiction Writers of America, 1976. 147 p.

Broyles, L. D.

Who's Who in Science Fandom. Waco, Texas: by the author, No Date.

Bruccoli, M. J.

Notes on the Cabell Collection at the University of Virginia. Charlottesville, Virginia: University of Virginia Press, 1957. 178 p.

Brueil, Suzanne

"Anticipations ou escroquerie allasscience," Les Lettres Francaises Juillet 21-28, 1955.

Brunet, Roger

Mystic Vision of Olaf Stapledon: The Spirit in Crisis. M. A. Thesis, Carleton University, Ottawa, 1968.

Brunner, John

"Actual Fall, The," Science Fiction Chronicle 5(3):1,19-24. December 1983.

"Art & craft of writing SF, The," Algol 21:27-28. November 1973.

"Building four-dimensional people in science fiction," Writer 84(12):21-24. December 1971.

"Coming events: an assessment of Thomas Pynchon's 'Gravity's Rainbow'," Foundation 10:20-27. June 1976.

"Conjugation of the Verb 'Tomorrow'," Arena Science Fiction 11: 27-33. November 1980.

"Dealing in futures," Author 81:83-86. Summer 1970.

"Development of a science fiction writer, The," Foundation 1:5-12. March 1972.

"Educational relevance of science fiction, The," Physics Education 6(6):389-391. November 1971.

"Evolution of a science fiction writer, The," in: Brunner, John. The Book of John Brunner. New York: Daw, 1976.

"Genesis of Stand on Zanzibar, and digressions in the remainder of its pentateuch," Extrapolation 11(2):34-43. May 1970.

"Noise level: on writing," Science Fiction Review 14(3): 14-15. August 1985.

"On Going From L to XLIX and Related Matters," Science Fiction Review 14(1): 16-17. February 1985.

"One sense of wonder, slightly tarnished," Books and Bookmen 12:19-20. July 1967.

"One Writer and the Next War," Science Fiction Review 11(1): 22-23. February 1982.

"Parallel worlds," Foundation 3:6-14. March 1973.

"Reference Books," Focus: an SF Writers' Magazine. 4: 21-23. Spring 1981.

"Researching The Great Steamboat Race," Focus: An SF Writers' Magazine No. 8: 12-15. Autumn 1983.

"Science fiction and the larger lunacy," in: Nicholls, Peter, ed. Science Fiction at Large. New York: Harper, 1976. pp. 73-104.

"Through a glass darkly," Vector 60: 5-12. June 1972.

"Utopias and nightmares," in: Ash, Brian, ed. Visual Encyclopedia of Science Fiction. New York: Harmony, 1977. pp. 124-129.

"When I was halfway up who should I bump into but myself coming down, or, We have met the eminent and he is us," in: De Bolt, Joe, ed. Happening Worlds of John Brunner. Port Washington, NY: Kennikat, 1975. pp. 179-194.

"Work of Philip K. Dick, The," New Worlds 166:142-149. September 1966.

"Yesterdata: the future considered as an obsolete assumption," Vector 97:24-32. April 1980.

Brunsdale, M. M.

"Norse Mythological Elements in The Hobbit," Mythlore 9(4): 49-50. Winter 1983.

Brutenhuis, Peter

"Battle between the sexes was the answer, A," New York Times Book Review p. 4. October 27, 1963. (Book review)

Bruzenak, Ken

"Conan," Prevue 2(46): 52-57, 65. November/December 1981.

"Dragonslayer," Prevue 2(4): 27-31. February/March 1981.

"Making of Conan," Prevue 22(46):52-57,65. November/December 1981.

"Outland," Prevue 2(4): 38-42. February/March 1981.

Bryan, C. D. B.

"Kurt Vonnegut on target," New Republic pp. 21-26. October 8, 1966.

"Kurt Vonnegut, head bokonist," New York Times Book Review pp. 2,25. April 6, 1969.

Bryant, Ed

"Breaking waves: the latest look at SF," Cthulhu Calls 2(2):14-26. January 1975.

Bryant, Edward

"Dangerous visions of Harlan Ellison: an interview, part II," by L. C. Harper and Edward Bryant. Bloomsbury Review 5(5):17-19,24. February 1985.

"Dangerous visions of Harlan Ellison: an interview," by L. C. Harper and Edward Bryant. Bloomsbury Review 5(4):12-15. January 1985.

Bryce, Lynn

"Use of Christian Iconography in Selected Marginalia of J. R. R. Tolkien's Lothlorien Chapters," Extrapolation 25(1): 51-59. Spring 1984.

Brynes, Asher

"Adventure to the moon," New Republic pp. 25-26. October 23, 1961.

Bryning, F. B.

"Australian Writers and Science Fiction," Overland (Melbourne, Aust.) No. 61:23-25. August 1975.

"What Has Science Fiction to Say?" Meanjin (Melbourne, Aust.) No. 13(2): 214-218. Winter 1954.

Brzustowitcz, R., Jr.

"Some notes on sources," Kalki 7(1):25-27. 1975.

Buccleugh, Stephen

"Piers Anthony," by Stephen Buccleugh and Beverly Rush. in: Cowart, David, ed. Twentieth-Century American Science-Fiction Writers, Part 1: A-L. Detroit: Gale, 1981. pp. 13-15. (Dictionary of Literary Biography, v. 8)

Buchanan, Ginjer

"Clarion: a personal view," Locus No. 118:5-6. August 4, 1972.

Buchen, I. H.

"Frankenstein and the alchemy of creation and evolution," Wordsworth Circle 8:103-112. 1977.

"Science fiction futures," Intellect 103(2365):459. April 1975.

"Science fiction: the literature in transition," in: Samuelson, D. N. Science Fiction and Future Studies. Bryan, TX: SFRA, 1975. pp. 85-93.

Buchner, Hermann

Programmiertes Gluck: Sozialkritik in der utopischen Sowjetliteratur. Wein: Europa, 1970. 184 p.

"Echo aus der Zukunft," Sozialistische Zeitschrift fur Kunst und Gesellschaft. No. 18/19. July 1973.

Buck, Lynn

"Vonnegut's world of comic futility," Studies in American Fiction 3:181-198. Autumn 1975.

Buckley, Kathryn

"How do we evaluate a work of science fiction," Foundation 1:13-20. March 1972.

Bucknall, B. J.

Ursula K. Le Guin. New York: Ungar, 1981. 175 p.

Bucknall, B. J. (Continued)

"Androgynes in outer space," in: Riley, Dick, ed. Critical Encounters: Writers and Themes in Science Fiction. New York: Ungar, 1978. pp. 56-69.

"Ursula K. Le Guin," in: Mainiero, Lina, ed. American Women Writers. New York: Ungar, 1982. v. 2, pp. 546-547.

Budrys, Algis

Benchmarks: Galaxy Bookshelf. Carbondale: Southern Illinois University Press, 1985. 349 p.

Non-Literary Influences on Science Fiction (An Essay). Polk City, IA: Drumm, 1983. 24 p.

"1984, Nineteen Eighty-Four, and other SF novels, signs, and protents," in: Pournelle, Jerry, ed. The Science Fiction Yearbook. New York: Baen, 1985. pp. 4-20.

"Can Speculative-Fiction Writers and Scholars Do Each Other Good?" Extrapolation 25(4): 306-314. Winter 1984.

"Clarifying Clarion," Isaac Asimov's Science Fiction Magazine 8(6): 56-67. June 1984.

"Empire Talks Back," Isaac Asimov's Science Fiction Magazine. 4(11): 44-59. November 1980.

"Fiction in the Chain Mode: Nonliterary Influences on Science Fiction," in: Wolfe, Gary. Science Fiction Dialogues. Chicago: Academy Chicago, 1982. pp. 58-70.

"John W. Campbell," Locus No. 90:8. July 12, 1971.

"Literatures of milieux," Missouri Review 7(2): 49-63. 1984.

"Obstacles and Ironies in Science Fiction Criticism," Patchin Review 2: 5-15. September 1981.

"On being a bit of a legend," Science Fiction Review (Portland) 7(1):69-71. February 1978.

"On writing, part 10," Locus 11(5):4-6. July 1978.

"On writing, part 11," Locus 11(6):17-18. August 1978.

"On writing: action," Locus 10(10):5,7. December 1977.

"On writing: getting started," Locus 11(9):4-6. November 1978.

"On writing: kinematic prose," Locus 11(3):6-8. April 1978.

"On writing: kinematic technique," Locus 11(2):5-6. March 1978.

"On writing: motivation," Locus 10(6):2-3. August 1977.

"On writing: technique," Locus 11(1):1,15. January/February 1978.

"On writing: technique," Locus 12(6):13-14. July/August 1979.

"On writing: the basic story," Locus 10(9):12. November 1977.

"On writing: the column," Locus 10(4):5. May 1977.

"On writing: the writer," Locus 10(5):1,15-16. July 1977.

"On writing: validation, continued," Locus 12(5):1,6. June 1979.

"On writing: validation," Locus 12(1):8. January 1979.

"On writing: workshops," Locus 11(7):21-22. September 1978.

"On writing: writers," Locus 10(8):1,6. October 1977.

"Outlook from Limbo," SFWA Bulletin 16(2): 57-61. Spring 1981.

"Paradise Charted," TriQuarterly 49: 5-75. Fall 1980.

"Pulp!" Science Fiction Review 11(4): 16-20. November 1982.

"Revenge of the Empire," Amazing 57(6): 59-76. March 1984.

"Science fiction in the marketplace," in: Dickson, G. R., ed. Nebula Winners Twelve. New York: Harper, 1978. pp. 99-113.

"State of the Art," Analog 100(10): 107-114. October 1980.

"Tom Reamy: A Rare and Masterful Fantasist," Trumpet 12: 46-48. Summer 1981.

"What Did 1980 Mean," in: Pournelle, Jerry, ed. Nebula Award Stories Sixteen. New York: Bantam, 1983. pp. 192-209.

Buechner, F.

"If not good, old scratch," New York Times Book Review p. 3. May 6, 1973.

Bufkin, E. C.

"Ironic art of William Golding's The Inheritors, The," Texas Studies in Language and Literature 9:567-578. Winter 1968.

Buhle, Paul

"Dystopia as utopia: Howard Phillips Lovecraft and the unknown content of American horror literature," The Minnesota Review 6:118-131. Spring 1976.

"Dystopia as Utopia: Howard Phillips Lovecraft and the Unknown Content of American Horror Literature," in: Joshi, S. T., ed. H. P. Lovecraft: Four Decades of Criticism. Athens, OH: Ohio U. P., 1980. pp. 196-210.

Buhler, Walter

"Sekundarliteratur zu Perry Rhodan," Andromeda Science Fiction Magazine 103: 13-14. 1981.

Bukato, Wiktor

"Not only Stanislaw Lem," Locus 18(8): 36, 38. August 1985.

Buller, N. G.

"Totonto's spaced out library: a science fiction collection," Ontario Library Review 57:167-170. September 1973.

Bullinger, Cara

"Longing for Eressea: a theme in Elvish poetry," Leading Edge 9:31-33. Winter 1985.

Bullock, R. D.

"Importance of free will in the Lord of the Rings," Mythlore 11(3): 29-58. Winter/Spring 1985.

Bulman, L. T.

"Using science fiction as bait," Library Journal 80:2885-2886. December 15, 1955.

Bulmer, Ken

"Guest of Honor speech, 1968 SF Convention," Vector 50: 3-9. July 1968.

"Technologies and artefacts," in: Ash, Brian, ed. Visual Encyclopedia of Science Fiction. New York: Harmony, 1977. pp. 154-163.

"Tubb replaces Campbell as editor of Britain's Authentic SF," Fantasy Times No. 237:1,6. December (2) 1955.

Bulmer, Pamela

"SF criticism in theory and practice," Vector 59: 36-48. Spring 1972.

Burden, Brian

"Philip K. Dick and the Metaphysics of American Politics," Foundation 26: 41-46. October 1982.

Burek, Tomasz

"Powrot do Galicji," Tworczosc No. 7. 1967.

Burger, D. A.

"Animal Farm," in: Magill, Frank N., ed. Survey of Modern Fantasy Literature, Vol 1. Englewood Cliffs, NJ: Salem Press, Inc., 1983. pp. 45-47.

"Book of the Dun Cow, The," in: Magill, Frank N., ed. Survey of Modern Fantasy Literature, Vol 1. Englewood Cliffs, NJ: Salem Press, Inc., 1983. pp. 149-153.

"Tolkien's elvish craft and Frodo's mithril coat," in: Collins, R. A. and H. D. Pearce, eds. The Scope of the Fantastic: Theory, Technique, Major Authors. Westport, CT: Greenwood Press, 1985. pp. 255-262.

"Use of the past in The Lord of the Rings," Kansas Quarterly 16(3): 23-28. Summer 1984.

Burger, Joanne

SF Published in 1967. Lake Jackson, TX: Author, 1968. 12 p.

SF Published in 1968. Lake Jackson, TX: Author, 1969. 50 p.

SF Published in 1969. Lake Jackson, TX: Author, 1970. 61 p.

SF Published in 1970. Lake Jackson, TX: Author, 1971. 48 p.

SF Published in 1971. Lake Jackson, TX: Author, 1972. 48 p.

SF Published in 1972. Lake Jackson, TX: Author, 1973. 42 p.

SF Published in 1973. Lake Jackson, TX: Burger, 1975. 46 p.

SF Published in 1974. Lake Jackson, TX: Author, 1975. 40 p.

SF Published in 1975. Lake Jackson, TX: Author, 1976. 45 p.

SF Published in 1976. Lake Jackson, TX: Author, 1977. 48 p.

Burgess, A. J.

"Concept of Eden," in: Reilly, Robert, ed. The Transcendent Adventure. Westport: Greenwood, 1984. pp. 73-81.

"Science fiction and religion," in: Williamson, Jack ed. Teaching Science Fiction: Education for Tomorrow. Philadelphia: Owlswick, 1980. pp. 168-176.

"SF in the classroom: 2. Teaching religion through science fiction," Extrapolation 13(2):112-115. May 1972.

Burgess, Anthony

"Big Nation Needs Big Books," San Francisco Examiner December 28, 1980. in: Newsbank. Literature. 41:c4-5. July 1980/June 1981.

"H. G. Wells," New York Times Book Review pp. 1,18. August 3, 1969. (Book review)

"Utopias and dystopias," in: The Novel Now: A Guide to Contemporary Fiction. New York: W. W. Norton, 1967. pp. 38-47.

Burgess, Eric

"Making of Moonraker, The," New Scientist No. 1160:984-987. June 21, 1979.

Burgess, M. A.

Future Visions: The New Golden Age of the Science Fiction Film, by Douglas Menville and R. Reginald. Van Nuys, CA: Newcastle, 1985. 192 p.; San Bernardino, CA: Borgo, 1985. 192 p.

Guide to Science Fiction and Fantasy in the Library of Congress Classification Scheme. San Bernardino, CA: Borgo, 1984. 86 p.

Science Fiction and Fantasy Awards, by R. Reginald. San Bernardino, California: Borgo Press, 1980. 64 p.

Science Fiction and Fantasy Literature: A Checklist, 1700-1974 with Contemporary Science Fiction Authors II, by R. Reginald. Detroit: Gale, 1979. 2 v.

Stella Nova: The Contemporary Science Fiction Authors, by R. Reginald. Los Angeles: Unicorn & Son, 1970. Second edition: Contemporary Science Fiction Authors, by R. Reginald. New York: Arno Press, 1975. 368 p.

Things to Come: An Illustrated History of the Science Fiction Film, by Douglas Menville and Robert Reginald. New York: New York Time Books, 1977. 212 p.

Work of Julian May, The: An Annotated Bibliography and Guide, by Thaddeus Dikty and R. Reginald. San Bernardino, CA: Borgo, 1985. 66 p.

Work of R. Reginald: An Annotated Bibliography & Guide, by Michael Burgess and J. M. Elliot. San Bernardino, CA: Borgo, 1985. 48 p.

"Aladore," by Robert Reginald and M. A. Burgess. in: Magill, Frank N., ed. Survey of Modern Fantasy Literature, Vol 1. Englewood Cliffs, NJ: Salem Press, Inc., 1983. pp. 4-6.

"Bring the Jubilee," by R. Reginald. in: Magill, Frank N., ed. Survey of Science Fiction Literature, Vol. 1. Englewood Cliffs, NJ: Salem Press, 1979. pp. 260-264.

"Face in the Frost, The," in: Magill, Frank N., ed. Survey of Modern Fantasy Literature, Vol 1. Englewood Cliffs, NJ: Salem Press, Inc., 1983. pp. 508-510.

"Hasan," by R. Reginald. in: Magill, Frank N., ed. Survey of Modern Fantasy Literature, Vol 2. Englewood Cliffs, NJ: Salem Press, Inc., 1983. pp. 695-697.

"House on the Strand, The," in: Magill, Frank N., ed. Survey of Modern Fantasy Literature, Vol 2. Englewood Cliffs, NJ: Salem Press, Inc., 1983. pp. 749-751.

"House-Boat on the Styx, A and Pursuit of the House-Boat," by Robert Reginald and M. A. Burgess. in: Magill, F. N., ed. Survey of Modern Fantasy Literature, Vol 2. Englewood Cliffs: Salem Press, 1983. pp. 752-756.

"Melusine: Or, Devil Take Her!" by R. Reginald. in: Magill, Frank N., ed. Survey of Modern Fantasy Literature, Vol 2. Englewood Cliffs, NJ: Salem Press, Inc., 1983. pp. 1004-1006.

"Monk's Magic," by R. Reginald. in: Magill, Frank N., ed. Survey of Modern Fantasy Literature, Vol 3. Englewood Cliffs, NJ: Salem Press, Inc., 1983. pp. 1057-1059.

"Neustrian Cycle, The," by R. Reginald. in: Magill, Frank N., ed. Survey of Modern Fantasy Literature, Vol 3. Englewood Cliffs, NJ: Salem Press, Inc., 1983. pp. 1099-1104.

"Pavane," by R. Reginald. in: Magill, Frank N., ed. Survey of Science Fiction Literature, Vol. 4. Englewood Cliffs, NJ: Salem Press, 1979. pp. 1660-1664.

"So Love Returns," by R. Reginald. in: Magill, Frank N., ed. Survey of Modern Fantasy Literature, Vol 4. Englewood Cliffs, NJ: Salem Press, Inc., 1983. pp. 1766-1768.

"Thing from the Lake, The," by Robert Reginald and M. A. Burgess. in: Magill, Frank N., ed. Survey of Modern Fantasy Literature, Vol 4. Englewood Cliffs, NJ: Salem Press, Inc., 1983. pp. 1901-1903.

Burgess, M. A. (Continued)

"University of Cosmopoli Tales, The," by R. Reginald. in: Magill, Frank N., ed. Survey of Modern Fantasy Literature, Vol 4. Englewood Cliffs, NJ: Salem Press, Inc., 1983. pp. 1999-2001.

"Wonderful Adventures of Phra the Phoenician, The," by R. Reginald. in: Magill, Frank N., ed. Survey of Modern Fantasy Literature, Vol 5. Englewood Cliffs, NJ: Salem Press, Inc., 1983. pp. 2156-2158.

"You're All Alone," by R. Reginald. in: Magill, Frank N., ed. Survey of Modern Fantasy Literature, Vol 5. Englewood Cliffs, NJ: Salem Press, Inc., 1983. pp. 2200-2202.

"Ace numbering system, The," by R. Reginald. unpublished article in: Science Fiction: Collected Papers, by R. Reginald. Texas A&M University, p. 1829. No date.

"Looking back on films that look far ahead," by R. Reginald and Douglas Menville. Science Digest 83(2):12-13. February 1978.

"Short fiction of Knowles, The," by R. Reginald. in: Magill, Frank N., ed. Survey of Modern Fantasy Literature, Vol 4. Englewood Cliffs, NJ: Salem Press, Inc., 1983. pp. 1589-1591.

Burgstaler, J. L.

Character and Theme in J. R. R. Tolkien's The Lord of the Rings. Masters Thesis, St. Cloud State University, 1978. 123 p.

Burgum, E. B.

"Freud and fantasy in contemporary fiction," Science and Society 29(2):224-231. Spring 1965.

"Science Fiction: Menace or Marvel?" New Foundations 7: 30-35. Spring 1954.

Burhans, C. S., Jr.

"Hemingway and Vonnegut: diminishing vision in a dying age," Modern Fiction Studies 21(2):173-191. Summer 1975.

Burk, J. K.

"Lin Carter in the Land of Lost Boys," Trumpet 12: 38-41. Summer 1981.

Burke, M. C.

"Free-fall sex and golden eggs," Science Teacher 45:33-34. March 1978.

Burleson, D. R.

H. P. Lovecraft: A Critical Study. Westport, CT: Greenwood, 1983. 243 p.

"At the Mountains of Madness," by D. W. Mosig and D. R. Burleson. in: Magill, Frank N., ed. Survey of Science Fiction Literature, Vol. 1. Englewood Cliffs, NJ: Salem Press, 1979. pp. 97-101.

"Case of Charles Dexter Ward, The," in: Magill, Frank N., ed. Survey of Modern Fantasy Literature, Vol 1. Englewood Cliffs, NJ: Salem Press, Inc., 1983. pp. 203-206.

"Dream-Quest of Unknown Kadath, The," in: Magill, Frank N., ed. Survey of Modern Fantasy Literature, Vol 1. Englewood Cliffs, NJ: Salem Press, Inc., 1983. pp. 431-435.

"Lovecraft Mythos, The," in: Magill, Frank N., ed. Survey of Science Fiction Literature, Vol. 3. Englewood Cliffs, NJ: Salem Press, 1979. pp. 1284-1288.

"H. P. Lovecraft: The Hawthorne Influence," Extrapolation 22(3): 262-269. Fall 1981.

"Humour beneath horror: some sources for The Dunnich Horror and The Whisperer in Darkness," Lovecraft Studies 1(2):5-15. Spring 1980.

"Short Fiction of H. P. Lovecraft, The," in: Magill, Frank N., ed. Survey of Science Fiction Literature, Vol. 4. Englewood Cliffs, NJ: Salem Press, 1979. pp. 1973-1977.

"Short fiction of Lovecraft, The," in: Magill, Frank N., ed. Survey of Modern Fantasy Literature, Vol 4. Englewood Cliffs, NJ: Salem Press, Inc., 1983. pp. 1621-1628.

Burns, Arthur

"Paul Linebarger," Algol 20:8-10. May 1973.

"Paul Linebarger," Australian Science Fiction Review No. 11:3-7. August 1967.

Burns, E. J.

"Nostalgia isn't what it used to be: the Middle Ages in literature and film," in: Slusser, George, ed. Shadows of the Magic Lamp. Carbondale: Southern Illinois University Press, 1985. pp. 86-97.

Burns, Fred

"Achieving the Fantastic in Animated Films," in: Slusser, George, ed. Shadows of the Magic Lamp. Carbondale: Southern Illinois University Press, 1985. pp. 112-121.

Burns, G. C.

Utopia and Dystopia in Popular Song Lyrics:
Rhetorical Visions in the United States,
1963-1972. Ph. D. Dissertation, Northwestern
University, 1981. 300 p. (DAI 42A:1839)

Burns, Grant

"Art of Fission, The: Novels and stories with
nuclear themes," in: Burns, Grant. The
Atomic Papers. Metuchen, NJ: Scarecrow, 1984.
pp. 259-291.

Burns, J. H.

"Flash Gordon We May Never See," Starlog
43: 21-22. January 1981.

"Greatest American Hero: First Season Episode
Guide," Starlog 54: 38-39. January 1982.

"Starlog Interview: Director Jeannot Szwarc,"
Starlog 43: 60-62. Febraury 1981.

"Starlog Interview: George Takei, part 1,"
Starlog 47: 36-39, 62. June 1981.

"Starlog Interview: George Takei, part 2,"
Starlog 49: 44-47. August 1981.

"Starlog Interview: Harrison Ford," Starlog
48: 17-20. July 1981.

"Starlog Interview: Juanita Bartlett, part 1,"
Starlog 53: 32-34. December 1981.

"Starlog Interview: Juanita Bartlett, part 2,"
Starlog 54: 45-47. Janurary 1982.

"Starlog Interview: Julian Glover," Starlog
52: 38-40. November 1981.

"Starlog Interview: Ken McMillian," Starlog
56: 22-24. March 1982.

"Starlog Interview: Lawrence Kasdan, part 1,"
Starlog 50: 32-35. September 1981.

"Starlog Interview: Lawrence Kasdan, part 2,"
Starlog 51: 56-59. October 1981.

"Starlog Interview: Sarah Douglas," Starlog
47: 32-35, 62. June 1981.

"TZ Interview: Burgess Meredith:
Multidimensional Man," Twilight Zone 4(1):
26-31, 80. March/April 1984.

Burns, M. B.

"Books by Kurt Vonnegut," Hollins Critic
3:7. October 1966. updated in: Dillard, R.
H. W., et al. The Sounder Few: Selected
Essays from the Hollins Critic. Athens: Univ.
of Georgia Press, 1971. pp. 192-193.

Burroughs, John

"Science and literature," North American
Review 199:415-424. 1914.

Burroughs, William

"Hallucinatory operators are real, The," SF
Horizons 2:3-11. Winter 1965.

"William Burroughs discusses science fiction,"
SF Horizons 2:3-12. Winter 1965.

Burt, D. C.

"Poe, Bradbury, and the science fiction tale of
terror," Mankato State College Studies
3:76-84. 1968.

"Well-Mannered Landscape: Nature in Utopia,"
in: Roemer, Kenneth M., ed. American As
Utopia. New York: Franklin, 1981. pp.
175-185.

Burton, S. H.

"Introduction," in: Burton, S. H. Science
Fiction. London: Longman, 1967.

Bush, C. K.

Splintered Shards: Reality and Illusion in the
Novels of Philip K. Dick. Master's Thesis,
Idaho State University, 1975. 112 p.

Bush, D. F.

"Futurama: World's Fair as Utopia,"
Alternative Futures 2(4): 3-20. Fall 1979.

Bush, John

"Gollancz/Sunday Times science fiction
competition, A," Bookseller pp. 1936-1937.
March 31, 1973.

"Keeping a Tight Ship," Focus: An SF
Writers' Magazine No. 8: 31-37. Autumn 1983.

"Publishers: men or monsters," Vector
Supplement pp. 2-7. May/June 1979.

Bushmaker, Keith

"Mycenae to Mars: science fiction in the ninth
grade curriculum," by Keith Bushmaker and
Richard Onesti. Wisconson English Journal
18(3):13-14,21. April 1976.

Bushyager, L.

"Fans and fanzines," Publishers Weekly
209(24):52. June 14, 1976.

Butler, Bill

"Real people, The," _Spectator_ pp. 281-282. September 3, 1963.

Butler, Francelia

"European scene: Poland, The," by Ladislaw Bohdanowicz and Francelia Butler. _Extrapolation_ 11(2):79-81. May 1970.

Butler, P.

"Ages of heroes," _Saturday Review_ 53:4. July 11, 1970.

Butler, R. R.

"Todorov's fantastic, Kayser's grotesque, and West's _Miss Lonelyhearts_," in: Collins, R. A. and H. D. Pearce, eds. _The Scope of the Fantastic: Theory, Technique, Major Authors_. Westport, CT: Greenwood Press, 1985. pp. 41-48.

Butler, Ted

"Algol interview: Michael Moorcock," _Algol_ 15(1):29-31. Winter 1977/1978.

Butor, Michel

"Crise de croissance de la science fiction, La," _Cahiers du Sud_ p. 223-237. 1964; also in: Butor, Michel. _Essais sur les modernes_. Paris: Gallimard, 1964. p. 223-237.

"Golden Age in Jules Verne," in: Butor, Michel. _Inventory_. New York: Simon & Schuster, 1968. pp. 114-145.

"Goldene Zeitalter und der Hochste Punkte in einigen Werken von Jules Verne, Das," in: Butor, Michel. _Michel Butor, Repertoire 3, Aufsatze zur modernen Literatur und Musik_. Munchen: Biederstein, 1972. pp. 172-219.

"Growing pains in science fiction," _Carleton Miscellany_ 4(3):113-120. Summer 1963.

"Krise der science fiction, Die," in: Barmeyer, Eike, ed. _Science fiction: theorie und geschichte_. Munchen: Fink, 1972. pp.7 6-85. Also in: Butor Michel, _Repertoire 3_. Munchen: Biederstein, 1965. pp. 220-232.

"On fairy tales," in: Butor, Michel. _Inventory_. New York: Simon & Schuster, 1968. pp. 211-223.

"Point surpreme et l'age d'or a travers quelques oeuvres de Jules Verne, Le," in:

Butor, Michel. _Essais sur les modernes_. Paris: Gallimard, 1964. p. 35-94.

"Science fiction: the crisis of its growth," _Partisan Review_ 34:595-602. Fall 1967. also in: Clareson, Thomas D., ed. _SF: The Other Side of Realism_. Bowling Green, Ohio: Bowling Green Popular Press, 1971. pp. 157-165.

Butrym, A. J.

"For Suffering Humanity: The Ethics of Science in Science Fiction," in: Reilly, Robert, ed. _The Transcendent Adventure_. Westport: Greenwood, 1984. pp. 55-70.

Button, Bob

"Are we fleeing reality? Or escaping into it? And what's behind this fascination with alien life?" _Science Digest_ 83(2):14-15. February 1978.

Button, D. E.

"Asimov at 60," _Future Life_ 18: 54-56. May 1980.

Byars, Jackie

"Introduction to Some Ideological Readings of Alien," _Science-Fiction Studies_ 7(3): 278-282. November 1980.

Byfield, Bruce

"The Bones of Contention," _Empire For the SF Writer_ 32: 10-11. Winter 1984.

Byrd, Donald

"Science Fiction's Intelligent Computers," _Byte_ 6(9): 200-214. September 1981.

Byrne, Janet

"Moving Toward Entropy: Anna Kavan's Science Fiction Mentality," _Extrapolation_ 23(1): 5-11. Spring 1982.

Byron, Stuart

"Kong is nice guy: Dino de Laurentis," _Film Comment_ 13(1):18. January/February 1977.

"Something wicker this way comes," _Film Comment_ 13(6):29. November/December 1977.

C

Cacha, F. B.

"Children create fiction using science," Science and Children 15(3):21-22. November/December 1977.

Cadigan, Pat

"14 Questions: Michael Whelan," by Pat Cadigan and Arnie Fenner. Shayol No. 5: 12-19. Winter 1982.

"Genie-us of Tom Reamy," by Pat Cadigan and Arnie Fenner. Shayol 1: 33-40. November 1977.

"Has success spoiled Stephen King? Naaah!" by Pat Cadigan, Marty Ketchum and Arnie Fenner. Shayol 6:17-19. 1982.

Caen, Michel

"Lovecraft cinema," in: H. P. Lovecraft. Paris: Editions de l'Herne, 1969. pp. 182-185.

Caillet, G.

"Roman peut-il etre scientifique, Le?" France Illustration No. 358:186. August 23, 1952.

Caillois, Roger

"Analyse du fantastique," La Nef 19:67-71. July/August 1958.

"C'el le fantastique," Bulletin de l'Academic Royale de Langue et de litterautre Francaises. Bruxelles 53:249-259. 1974.

"Dalla fiaba alla fantasciencza," L'Europa Letteraria 20/21:81-104. April 1963.

"De la f'eerie a la science fiction. L'Image fantastique" in: Caillois, Roger. Anthologie du Fantastique. 1958. also in Callois, R. Obliques precede de Images, Images. Paris: Gallimard, 1975; Also in Prevues 118:136-148. 1960.

"Science fiction," Diogenes No. 89:87-105. Spring 1975.

"Science Fiction," in: Caillois, Roger. Obliques precede de Images, Images. Paris: Gaillimard, 1975. 75-504640.

"Un nouveau fantastique," Bulletin de l'Academie Royale de Langue et de Litterature francaises Bruxelles. 52:260-268. 1974.

Caimmi, Giuseppie

"John Brunner: bibliografia Italiana," Alternativa: per una critica della Science Fiction pp. 32-33. Gennaio 1978.

"John Brunner: una carriera," Alternativa: per una critica della Science Fiction pp. 7-11. Gennaio 1978.

Cain, Scott

"Cocoon has young director in happy daze," Atlanta Journal June 19, 1985. in: NewsBank. Film and Television. 2:C7-C8. July 1985.

"Ken Marshall hopes Krull will lead him out of the unknowns," Atlanta Journal. July 29, 1983. in: NewsBank. Films and Television FTV-14:D12. 1983.

Calabrese, Fabio

"Italian SF: trends and authors," Foundation 34: 49-57. Autumn 1985.

Calame, G. P.

"Science in science fiction; a seminar course," American Journal of Physics 41(2):184-187. February 1973.

Calder, Jenni

"Orwell the Man," in: George Orwell and Nineteen Eighty-Four. Washington, DC: Library of Congress, 1985. pp. 25-38.

Caldwell, Jean

"I'm Not Fully Human Unless I'm Writing, Says Madeleine L' Engle, Reaching for Her Notebook," Writer's Digest 62(3): 40-42. March, 1982.

Calife, J. L.

"Science fiction in Brazil," Locus 18(12): 23, 32. December 1985.

Calkins, Elizabeth

Teaching Tomorrow: A Handbook of Science Fiction for Teachers, A, by Barry McGhan and Elizabeth Calkins. Dayton, Ohio: Plaum Publishing Company, 1972. 103 p.

"Science fiction in the high school," by Elizabeth Calkins and Barry McGhan. in: Williamson, Jack, ed. Teaching Science Fiction: Education for Tomorrow. Philadelphia: Owlswick, 1980. pp. 82-96.

Callahan, P. J.

"Animism and magic in Tolkien's The Lord of the Rings," Riverside Quarterly 4(4): 240-249. March 1971.

"Frankenstein, Bacon, and the 'Two Truths'," Extrapolation 14(1):39-47. December 1972.

"Tolkien, Beowulf, and the Barrowwights," Notre Dame English Journal 7(2):4-13. Spring 1972.

"Two Gardens in C. S. Lewis's That Hideous Strength, The," in: Clareson, Thomas D., ed. SF: the Other Side of Realism. Bowling Green, Ohio: Bowling Green University Popular Press, 1971. pp. 147-156.

Callaway, David

"Gollum: A Misunderstood Hero," Mythlore 10(3): 14-17, 22. Winter 1984.

Callow, A. J.

The Chronicles of Moorcock (A Bibliography). United Kingdom: privately printed, 1978.

Calloway, James

"Trials and Tribulations of Creating 'Star Trek'," Raleigh (N. C.) News and Observer October 24, 1982. in: NewsBank. Film and Television. 57:B4-5. December 1982.

Calverley, Ross

"Vulcan's Spanner: How I Wrote a Novel by Accident," Focus: An SF Writer's Magazine No. 9: 30-36. Autumn 1984.

Cameron, Alastair

Fantasy Classification System. St. Vital, Manitoba: Canadian Science Fiction Association, 1952. 52 p.

Cameron, Eleanor

"High fantasy: A Wizard of Earthsea," Horn Book 47(2):129-138. April 1971.

"Into something rich and strange: of dreams," Quarterly Journal of the Library of Congress 35(2):92-107. April 1978.

Campbell, Bebe

"Superman, Bat Man, Archie and me," Essence 8(7):54-58. November 1977.

Campbell, F. F.

"Necessary heresies," in: Samuelson, D. N. Science Fiction and Future Studies. Bryan, TX: SFRA, 1975. pp. 71-74.

Campbell, Glenn

"Baring the soul of Lifeforce," Cinefex No. 23:34-53. August 1985.

Campbell, Ian

"Science fiction of John Leslie Mitchell, The," Extrapolation 16(1):53-63. December 1974.

Campbell, J. L., Sr.

"Garrett P. Serviss," in: Bleiler, E. F., ed. Science Fiction Writers. New York: Scribners, 1982. pp. 39-44.

"John Taine," in: Bleiler, E. F., ed. Science Fiction Writers. New York: Scribners, 1982. pp. 75-82.

"Olaf Stapledon," in: Bleiler, E. F., ed. Science Fiction Writers. New York: Scribners, 1982. pp. 91-100.

"Sir Arthur Conan Doyle," in: Bleiler, E. F., ed. Science Fiction Writers. New York: Scribners, 1982. pp. 45-50.

Campbell, J. W., Jr.

"Concerning science fiction," <u>Writer</u>
59(5):149-150. May 1946.

"Introduction," in: Campbell, John W., Jr.
<u>The Astounding Science Fiction Anthology</u>.
New York: Simon, 1952. pp. ix-xv.

"No copying allowed," in: Knight, Damon, ed.
<u>Turning Points: Essays in the Art of Science
Fiction</u>. New York: Harper, 1977. pp.
171-174.

"Non-escape literature," in: Campbell, John
W. <u>Collected Editorials from Analog</u>, No date.

"Place of science fiction, The," in: Bretnor,
Reginald, ed. <u>Modern Science Fiction: Its
Meaning and Its Future</u>. New York: Coward
McCann, 1953. Reprinted, Chicago: Advent,
1979. pp. 3-22.

"Reply to Norman Spinrad," <u>Science Fiction
Times</u> pp. 7-8. ca. October 1967.

"Science fact, science fiction," <u>Writer</u>
77(8):26-27. August 1964.

"Science fiction and the opinion of the
universe," <u>Saturday Review</u>
39(19):9-10,42-43. May 12, 1956. Discussion:
39(23):26. June 9, 1956. Discussion:
39(24):29. June 16, 1956.

"Science fiction we can buy," <u>The Writer</u>
81(9):27-28. September 1968.

"Science of science fiction," Atlantic
181(5):97-98. May 1948.

"Value of science fiction," in: Stokley,
James, ed. <u>Science Marches On</u>. Washburn,
1951. pp. 43-47.

Campbell, Mary

"Hilarious New Musical Features Ravenous Plant
Life,"(AP) <u>Austin American Statesman</u> Sec.
H, p. 46. May 30, 1982.

Campbell, Mrs. J. W.

"Postscriptum," in: Campbell, John W. <u>The
Best of John W. Campbell</u>. New York:
Ballantine, 1976. pp. 360-364.

Campbell, R. A.

"Charles Kingsley: a bibliography of secondary
studies," <u>Bulletin of Bibliography</u>
33(2):78-91,104,127-130. February/March 1976.

Campbell, Ramsey

"Beyond the pale," <u>Fantasy Review</u> 8(8):
33-34, 42. August 1985.

"Commentary: Rebuttal: 'Fiedler on the Roof',"
<u>Fantasy Review</u> 7(8): 17-18. September
1984.

"Contemporary horror: a mixed bag," <u>Fantasy
Review</u> 9(6)(eg v. 8 #6): 37-38. June 1985.

"James Herbert: Notes toward a reappraisel,"
<u>Fantasy Review</u> 8(2): 9-10. February 1985.

"Small dose of reality, A," <u>Fantasy Review</u>
8(11): 13-14. November 1985.

Campra, Rosalba

"Il fantastico: Una isotopia della
transgressione," <u>Strumenti Critici</u> (Italy)
15(2): 199-231. June 1982.

Canary, R. H.

"On David Ketterer's <u>New Worlds for Old</u>: new
worlds for old?" <u>Science Fiction Studies</u>
2(2):130-137. July 1975.

"Science fiction as fictive history,"
<u>Extrapolation</u> 16(1):81-93. December 1974.
also in: Clareson, T. D., ed. <u>Many Futures,
Many Worlds</u>. Kent, Ohio: Kent State
University Press, 1977. pp. 164-181.

"Utopian and fantastic dualities in Robert
Graves' <u>Watch the North Wind Rise</u>,"
<u>Science Fiction Studies</u> 1(4):248-255. Fall
1974.

"Whatever happened to the Cabell revival,"
<u>Kalki</u> 6(2):55-60. 1974.

Canemaker, John

"Vladimir William Tytla (1904-1968);
animation's Michelangelo," <u>Cinefantastique</u>
5(3):8-19. Winter 1976.

Canestri, J.

"Science fiction: reality and psychoanalysis,"
<u>Acta Psiquiatrica y Psicologica de America
Latina</u> 16(4):405. 1970. (not seen)

Canney, J. R.

<u>Bibliography of First Printings of the
Writings of Edgar Allan Poe</u>, by C. F.
Heartman and J. R. Canney. Hattiesburg,
Mississippi: Book Farm, 1943. Revised
edition, 294 p.

Cannon, Peter

"H. P. Lovecraft in Hawthornian Perspective,"
in: Joshi, S. T., ed. <u>H. P. Lovecraft: Four
Decades of Criticism</u>. Athens, OH: Ohio
University Press, 1980. pp. 161-165.

Cannon, Peter (continued)

"In Search of Lovecraft's Newburyport," P*S*F*Q 6: 18-20. Fall 1981.

"Influence of Vathek on H. P. Lovecraft's The Dream-Quest of the Unknown Kadath," in: Joshi, S. T., ed. H. P. Lovecraft: Four Decades of Criticism. Athens, OH: Ohio University Press, 1980. pp. 153-157.

Cansler, R. L.

"Stranger in a strange land: science fiction as literature of creative imagination, social criticism and entertainment," Journal of Popular Culture 5(4):944-954. Spring 1972.

Cantey, W. W.

"Triumph of Star Wars, The," Questar 1:6-13. 1978.

Cantril, Hadley

Invasion From Mars: A Study in the Psychology of Panic, by Herta Herzog, Hazel Gaudet and Hadley Cantril. Princeton: Princeton University Press, 1983. 224 p.

Cantrill, Dante

"It's a Chimera: an introduction to John Barth's latest fiction," Rendezvous 10(2):17-30. Winter 1975.

Capace, Louis

"Communistes abordent la SF, Les," France-Observateur 29,8,1957.

"Deux pamplemousses Contre La SF," France-Observateur 9,1,1958.

"Un nouveau genre litteraire: la science fiction," L'Observateur November 25, 1951.

Capanna, Pablo

Sentido de la ciencia ficcion, El. Buenos Aires: Editorial Columbia, 1966. 271 p.

Capeland, T. A.

"Francis Godwin's The Man in the Moone: a Picaresque satire," Extrapolation 16(2):156-163. May 1975.

Capella, Ray

"Hyborians, be seated," in: De Camp, L. S., ed. Blade of Conan. New York: Ace, 1979. pp. 177-181.

Caplan, J. M.

"Amour dans la SF, L'" France-Observateur 12,8,1954.

Caras, Roger

"Our Man in the Future," Science Digest 90(3): 54-59. March 1982.

Card, O. S.

"Fantasy and the Believing Reader," Science Fiction Review 11(3): 45-50. August 1982.

"Heroes and villains," SFWA Bulletin 14(1):21-23. Spring 1979.

"How to be a Science Fiction Critic," Science Fiction Review 11(2): 15-17. May 1982.

"Immutable laws of science fiction, The," SFWA Bulletin 14(3):82-83. Fall 1979.

"On Sycamore Hill, A Personal View," Science Fiction Review 14(2): 6-11. May 1985.

"Well-Ground Axe: On Themes," SFWA Bulletin 15(1): 10-12. Spring 1980.

"Well-Ground Axe: The Illusion of Truth," SFWA Bulletin 16(1): 45-48. Winter 1981.

"Well-Ground Axe: Using Criticism," SFWA Bulletin 15(2): 43-45. Winter 1980.

Cardinal, Roger

"Mapping the fantastic," Queen's Quarterly 92(3): 549-560. Autumn 1985.

Carducci, M. P.

"Flesh Gordon," by Mark Carducci and Douglas Olson. Cinefantastique 3(4):4-7,38. Winter 1974.

"Making Alien; behind the scenes; interviews," by M. P. Carducci and Glen Lovell. Cinefantastique 9(1):10-39. Fall 1979.

Care, Ross

"Futureworld (review)," Cinefantastique 5(3):25. Winter 1976.

Carew, Virginia

"Le Guin: artistic and formal maturity," in: Turek, Leslie, ed. Noreascon Proceedings. Cambridge, MA: NESFA, 1976. pp. 115-119.

Carey, Graham

"Real world of science fiction: (reply to Krim, Seymour)," Commonweal 58(12):300. June 26, 1953.

Carey, J. L.

"Art and reality in The Golden Notebook," Contemporary Literature 14(4):437-456. Autumn 1973.

Cargill, Oscar

"Science and the literary imagination in the United States," College English 13(2):90-94. November 1978.

Carilla, Emilio

Cuento fantasico, El. Buenos Aires: Editorial Nova, n.d. 75 p.

Carl, L. S.

"Roots of fantasy, The," Empire for the SF Writer 9(3): 10-11. Spring 1985.

Carl, M. J.

Science Fiction: Our Heritage of the Future. Dubuque, Iowa: Kendall/Hunt Publishing Company, 1974. 62 p.

Carlile, Tom

"Starlog retrospective: Barbarella," Starlog No. 92:34-37,65. March 1985.

Carlsen, M. M.

"What Stoker saw: an introduction to the literary vampire," Folklore Forum 10(2):26-32. Fall 1978.

Carmody, Larry

"1982: the SF year in review, events," Science Fiction Chronicle 4(6):1,19-20. March 1983.

"1983: the SF year in review; events," Science Fiction Chronicle 5(6):1,21-22. March 1984.

"1984: the SF year in review, events," Science Fiction Chronicle 6(6): 1, 30-31. March 1985.

Carneiro, Andre

Introducao ao estudio la science fiction. Sao Paulo: Conseho Estadual de Cultura, 1968. 140 p.

"Ciudad, La," in: Magill, Frank N., ed. Survey of Science Fiction Literature, Vol. 1. Englewood Cliffs, NJ: Salem Press, 1979. pp. 383-385.

"Noites marcianas, As," in: Magill, Frank N., ed. Survey of Science Fiction Literature, Vol. 4. Englewood Cliffs, NJ: Salem Press, 1979. pp. 1545-1547.

Carnell, C. S.

"C. S. Lewis: an appraisal," Mythlore 1(4):18-20. October 1969.

"Ransom in C. S. Lewis' Perelandra as hero in transformation," Studies in the Literary Imagination 14(2):67-72. Fall 1981.

"Ransom in Perelandra: Jungian hero?" Mythlore 8(2):9-10. Summer 1981.

Carnell, John

"Birth of New Worlds, The," Fantasy Review 1(4):5-6. August/September 1947.

Caron, Evelyne

"Structures et organisation de quelques themes dans les oeurves D'Arthur Machen," Litteratur No. 8:36-40. December 1972.

Caronia, Antonio

"Incarnazioni dell'immaginario," in: Nei labirinti della fantascienza. Milano: Feltrinelli, 1979. p. 9-30.

Carpenter, Humphrey

Inklings, The. Boston: Houghton Mifflin, 1979. 287 p.

Letters of J. R. R. Tolkein by Humphrey Carpenter and Christopher Tolkien. Boston: Houghton, 1981. 453 p.

Tolkien: a Biography. Boston: Houghton Mifflin, 1977. 287 p.

Carpenter, Lynette

"Benevolent fantasy and the imagination in...the 1940's," in: Collins, R. A., ed. Scope of the Fantastic: Culture, Biography, Themes, Children's Literature. Westport: Greenwood, 1985. pp. 51-60.

Carr, J. D.

"Alsidige Conan Doyle, Den," in: Rejser i tid og rum. En Bog om science fiction, ed. by Tage La Cour. Copenhagen: Stig Verdelkaer, 1973.

Carr, J. F.

"Future history chronology: the first hundred years, A," SFWA Bulletin 14(3):25-27. Fall 1979.

"In the heat of the light," SFWA Bulletin 14(3):28-29. Fall 1979.

"Outtakes: a look at science fiction future histories," SFWA Bulletin 14(3):4, 55. Fall 1979.

"Terrohuman future history of H. Beam Piper, The," SFWA Bulletin 14(3):42-51. Fall 1979.

Carr, J. L.

Leigh Brackett: American Writer. Polk City, Iowa: Chris Drumm, 1986. 67 p.

Carr, John

"Larry Niven," by Richard Finholt and John Carr. in: Bleiler, E. F., ed Science Fiction Writers. New York: Scribners, 1982. pp. 459-465.

Carr, Marion

"Classic hero in a new mythology," Horn Book 47:508-513. October 1971.

Carr, Nick

America's Secret Service Ace: The Operator 5 Story. Mercer Island, WA: Starmont, 1985. 63 p.

"Pulp villains, The," Xenophile No. 42:19,126. September/October 1979.

Carr, Terry

"Greater Realities, or, How to Write Science Fiction Without Knowing Much About Science," Isaac Asimov's Science Fiction Magazine 7(1):32-43. January 1983.

"Instant crunchy karma," Locus No. 128:5-6. December 1, 1972.

"Instant karma," Locus No. 126:5-6. November 4, 1972.

"Instant karma: Peter Beagle," Locus No. 127:5-6. November 17, 1972.

"Quality of science fiction," Science Fiction Chronicle 5(10):22. July 1984.

Carringer, R. L.

Annotated Catalog of Unpublished Film and Television Scripts at The University of Illinois at Urbana-Champaign, by Nancy Allen and R. L. Carringer. Urbana: University Library, 1983. 129 p. (ERIC ED 233 704)

"Circumscription of space and the form of Poe's Arthur Gordon Pym," PMLA 89:506-516. 1974.

Carrington, Grant

"Cook's Broth," Night Voyages 1(9): 14-16. Winter/Spring 1983.

"Stirring Up the Natives," Thrust 18: 25-26. Winter/ Spring 1982.

Carroll, Ed

"Spider-Man at the Library," by Larry Dorrell and Ed Carroll. School Library Journal 27(10): 17-19. August 1981. (Comment: 28(4):3. Dec. 1981.)

Carroll, Peter

"Does somebody out there like us?" San Francisco Bay Guardian 12(14):10-12. January 19, 1978.

Carrouges, Michel

"Apocalypse et anticipation," Lumiere et Vie September 1953.

"Perspectives sur le mondes futurs," Cahiers du Sud No. 317. June 1953.

"Ray Bradbury, le martiens et nous," Monde Nouveau 79:62. May 1954.

"Soif du futur, La," Arguments 2(9):22-25. September 1958.

"Spectroscope des anticipations, Le," Cahiers du Sud No. 317:7-16. June 1953.

Carson, David

Sound of Wonder: Interviews From "The Science Fiction Radio Show," Volume 1, by Daryl Lane, William Vernon and David Carson. Phoenix: Oryx, 1985. 203 p.

Sound of Wonder: Interviews From "The Science Fiction Radio Show," Volume 2, by Daryl Lane, William Vernon and David Carson. Phoenix: Oryx, 1985. 203 p.

Carson, Julie

"Pronominalization in <u>A Clockwork Orange</u>," <u>Papers on Language and Literature</u> 12(2):202-205. Spring 1976.

Carson, Ronald

"Kurt Vonnegut: matter-of-fact moralist," <u>Listening</u> 6(3):182-195. Autumn 1971.

Cartano, Tony

"Science Fiction depassee par la 'Speculative Fiction, La," <u>La Quinzaine Litteraire</u> No. 225:13-15. January 16, 1976.

"Science fiction francaise d'aujourd'hui, La," in: Bonnefoy, Claude, ed. <u>Dictionnaire de litterature francaise contemporaine</u>. Paris: Delarge, 1977. p. 411.

"Science fiction francaise, d'aujourd'hui, La," in: <u>Dictionnaire de litterature francaise contemporaine</u>. Paris: Delarge, 1977. pp. 361-363.

Carter, A. H., III

<u>Fantasy in the Work of Italo Calvino</u>. Ph.D. Dissertation, University of Iowa, 1971. 196 p.

Carter, Angela

"Fools Are My Theme, Let Satire By My Song," <u>Vector</u> 109: 27-36. 1982.

Carter, Lin

<u>Imaginary Worlds: the Art of Fantasy</u>. New York: Ballantine Books, 1973. 278 p.

<u>Lovecraft: a Look Behind the "Cthulhu Mythos"</u>. New York: Ballantine Books, 1972. 198 p.

<u>Tolkien: a Look Behind "The Lord of the Rings"</u>. New York: Ballantine Books, 1969. 211 p.

"Andre Norton; a profile," in: Norton, Andre. <u>Star Guard</u>. New York: Harcourt, 1955.

"H P L: The History," in: Wetzel, George. <u>Howard Phillips Lovecraft: Memoirs, Critiques, & Bibliographies</u>. North Tonowonda, NY: SSR, 1955. pp. 38-40.

"Real Hyborian Age, The," in: De Camp, L. S., ed. <u>Blade of Conan</u>. New York: Ace, 1979. pp. 67-76.

"That letter from the kid in Podunk," <u>Science Fiction Times</u> No. 456:3-4. July 1968.

Carter, M. L.

"Shadow of a Shade: a Survey of Vampirism in Literature. New York: Gordon Press, 1975. 176 p.

"Cosmic Gospel: Lewis & L'Engle," <u>Mythlore</u> 8(4): 10-12. Winter 1982.

"Note on moral concepts in Lewis' fiction," <u>Mythlore</u> 5(1):35. May 1978.

"Psychological symbolism of the magic fountain and the giant herdsman in Yvain," <u>Mythlore</u> 11(3): 30-31. Winter/Spring 1985.

Carter, P. A.

<u>The Creation of Tomorrow: Fifty Years of Magazine Science Fiction</u>. New York: Columbia University Press, 1977. 318 p.

"Extravagant fiction today: cold fact tomorrow: a rationale for the first American science fiction magazines," <u>Journal of Popular Culture</u> 5(4):842-857. Spring 1972.

"Rockets to the moon 1919-1944: a dialogue between fiction and reality," <u>American Studies</u> 15(1):31-46. Spring 1974.

Carter, S. R.

"Harry Harrison's <u>The Adventures of the Stainless Steel Rat</u>: a study in multiple interfaces," <u>Extrapolation</u> 21(2):139-145. Summer 1980.

Carter-Day, Deborah

"'Coinhere' and 'The Terrible Good': A Soul's Journey to Awareness and Responsibility," <u>Mythlore</u> 7(4): 27-30. Winter 1981.

Cartnal, Alan

"Premier convention: a first for fantasy films," <u>Los Angeles Times</u> Sec. 4, p. 2. November 29, 1972.

Cartwright, J. R.

"Lawyer's reading of Chesterton, A," <u>Chesterton Review</u> 2(1):22-38. Fall/Winter 1975.

Caruba, David

"Starlog Profile: Patrick Macnee," <u>Starlog</u> No. 101: 68-69. December 1985.

Cary, J.

"Horror comics," _Spectator_ 6608:177.
February 18, 1955. Discussion: 6609:220.
February 25, 1955.

Casebeer, E. F.

"If," in: Tymn, M. B. and Ashley, Mike.
_Science Fiction, Fantasy, and Weird Fiction
Magazines_. Westport, CT: Greenwood, 1985.
pp. 329-343.

"Rocket Stories," in: Tymn, M. B. and
Ashley, Mike. _Science Fiction, Fantasy, and
Weird Fiction Magazines_. Westport, CT:
Greenwood, 1985. pp. 488-490.

"Science Fiction Digest (1954)," in: Tymn,
M. B. and Ashley, Mike. _Science Fiction,
Fantasy, and Weird Fiction Magazines_.
Westport, CT: Greenwood, 1985. pp. 533-534.

"Star Science Fiction," in: Tymn, M. B. and
Ashley, Mike. _Science Fiction, Fantasy, and
Weird Fiction Magazines_. Westport, CT:
Greenwood, 1985. pp. 604-606.

"Tops in Science Fiction," in: Tymn, M. B.
and Ashley, Mike. _Science Fiction, Fantasy,
and Weird Fiction Magazines_. Westport, CT:
Greenwood, 1985. pp. 675-677.

"Universe Science Fiction," in: Tymn, M. B.
and Ashley, Mike. _Science Fiction, Fantasy,
and Weird Fiction Magazines_. Westport, CT:
Greenwood, 1985. pp. 692-694.

"Vanguard Science Fiction," in: Tymn, M. B.
and Ashley, Mike. _Science Fiction, Fantasy,
and Weird Fiction Magazines_. Westport, CT:
Greenwood, 1985. pp. 701-703.

"Vortex Science Fiction," in: Tymn, M. B.
and Ashley, Mike. _Science Fiction, Fantasy,
and Weird Fiction Magazines_. Westport, CT:
Greenwood, 1985. pp. 720-721.

"Worlds Beyond," in: Tymn, M. B. and
Ashley, Mike. _Science Fiction, Fantasy, and
Weird Fiction Magazines_. Westport, CT:
Greenwood, 1985. pp. 768-770.

Casey, John

"Interview with Kurt Vonnegut, Jr., An," in:
Bellamy, Joe David, ed. _Apocalypse:
Dominant Contemporary Forms_. Philadelphia:
Lippencott, 1972.

"Kurt Vonnegut, Jr.," by J. D. Bellamy and
John Casey. in: Bellamy, Joe David, ed.
_The New Fiction: Interviews with Innovative
American Writers_. Urbana: University of
Illinois Press, 1974. pp. 194-207.

"Kurt Vonnegut, Jr.: a subterranean
conversation," _Confluence_ 2:3-5. Spring
1969.

Casillo, Robert

"Olaf Stapledon and John Ruskin,"
Science-Fiction Studies 9(3): 306-321.
November 1982.

Casper, Gary

"Whither science fiction?" _Small Press
Review_ 9:1. October/November 1977.

Cassutt, Michael

"Interview: Gregory Benford," _Future Life_
24: 40-42. February 1981.

Castagnino, R. H.

"Ciencia-ficcion y teoria literaria," _La
Prensa_ (Buenos Aires) Secciones Ilustradas.
p. 3. August 29, 1971.

Castle, George

"TV science fiction a victim of cheap thrills,"
Chicago Tribune Sec. 3, p. 14. July 18,
1976.

Catalano, Frank

"SFU method for successful writing," by Cyn
Mason and Frank Catalano. _Science Fiction
Chronicle_ 4(2):14. November 1982.

Cataldi, Margherita

"Mito edenico, utopia e fantascienza nella
narrativa di Flann O'Brien," in: _Utopia e
fantascienza_. Torino: Giappichelli, 1975. p.
142-158.

Cater, William

"Filial duty of Christopher Tolkien, The," in:
Becker, Alida, ed. _The Tolkien Scrapbook_.
New York: Grossett & Dunlap, 1978. pp. 90-95.

Cathcart, R. B.

Un-earthly, Non-human Architecture.
Monticello, Illinois: Vance Bibliographies,
1980. 11 p. (Architecture series:
Bibliography A-182)

Catizone, Rick

"Interview: David Allen," _Questar_
3(1):26-29. October 1980.

Caulfield, Deborah

"Horrifying Duo: King and Romero," Los Angeles Times October 27, 1982. in: NewsBank. Film and Television. 50:B7. December 1982.

"Two real-life doctors cure sci-fi movies' ills," Los Angeles Times Sec. 6, p. 11. July 9, 1982.

Cavaliero, Glen

Charles Williams: Poet of Theology. Grand Rapids, MI: Eerdmans, 1983. 199 p.

Cawelti, J. G.

Adventure, Mystery and Romance: Formula Stories as Art and Popular Culture. Chicago and London: University of Chicago Press, 1976. 336 p.

Cawley, Rusty

"Comics are Passion for 'Con Traders," Bryan-College Station (Texas) Eagle Sec. A, p. 11. March 27, 1981.

"Sky's the Limit for Roger Zelazny," (Interview) Bryan-College Station Eagle. Sec. C. p. 14. April 10, 1982.

"Weird Tales not uncommon on A&M Library Shelves," Bryan Eagle p. 1D. July 30, 1981.

Cazedessus, Camille, Jr.

ERB-dom: A Guide to Issues No. 1-25, by J. F. Roy, John Harwood, and Camille Cazedessus, Jr. Evergreen, CO: Opar Press, 1964. 23 p.

Ghost Stories . . . . Evergreen, Colorado: Opar Press, 1973. 32 p.

"2001: A Space Odyssey," ERB-dom No. 36:4-5. July 1970.

"2001: A Space Odyssey; what does it mean?" ERB-dom No. 36:17-18. July 1970.

"Building a Burroughs collection, part II: A. L. Burt Co.," ERB-dom No. 23:14. April 1968.

"Building a Burroughs collection," ERB-dom No. 22:12. November 1967.

"Tarzan of the Apes: the play," ERB-dom No. 28:4-5. November 1969.

Cederstrom, Lorelei

"'Inner Space' Landscape: Doris Lessing's Memoirs of a Survivor," Mosaic 13(3/4): 116-132. Spring/Summer 1980.

Cerasini, M. A.

"Howard in the Eighties," by M. A. Cerasini and Charles Hoffman. Cromlech 1(1): 37-42. Spring 1985.

Cerf, Bennett

"Trade winds: the literary scene," Saturday Review p. 4. January 27, 1951.

Cernysheva, Tatyana

"Ostaroj skazke i Novejsej fantastike," Vosprosy Literatury i:229-448. 1977.

Cersowsky, Peter

"Copernican revolution in the history of fantastic literature ...," in: Collins, R. A., ed. Scope of the Fantastic: Theory, Technique, Major Authors. Westport: Greenwood, 1985. pp. 19-26.

Cetron, Marvin

Encounters with the Future: A Forecast of Life into the 21st Century. by Marvin Cetron and Thomas O'Toole. New York: McGraw-Hill, 1982.

Chalfant, F. E.

"Fearful Pleasures," in: Magill, Frank N., ed. Survey of Modern Fantasy Literature, Vol 2. Englewood Cliffs, NJ: Salem Press, Inc., 1983. pp. 543-548.

"Wessex Tales and A Changed Man, The Waiting Supper, and Other Tales," in: Magill, Frank N., ed. Survey of Modern Fantasy Literature, Vol 5. Englewood Cliffs, NJ: Salem Press, Inc., 1983. pp. 2107-2111.

Chalker, J. L.

In Memoriam Clark Ashton Smith. Baltimore: Anthem, 1963. 98 p.

Index to the Science Fantasy Publishers, by Mark Owings and J. L. Chalker. Baltimore: Chalker and Owings, 1966. 78 p.

Index to the Science Fantasy Publishers: A Bibliography of the Science Fiction and Fantasy Specialty Houses, The, by M. Owings and J. L. Chalker. Baltimore: The Anthem Series, 1966. Second Edition, 76 p.

Revised H. P. Lovecraft Bibliography, The, by M. Owings and J. L. Chalker. Baltimore: Mirage Press, 1973. 43 p.

"Correcting Some Odd Ideas..." Fantasy Newsletter 6(9): 13-14. October/November 1983.

Chalker, J. L. (Continued)

"Howard Phillips Lovecraft: a bibliography," in: Lovecraft, H. P. The Dark Brotherhood and Other Pieces. Sauk City, Wisconsin: Arkham House, 1966. pp. 198-241.

"Inside the Whale responses to Christopher Priest's 'Outside the Whale'," by Jack Williamson, Jerry Pournelle, and Jack Chalker. Science Fiction Review 9(4): 18-23. November 1980.

"Jack Chalker's guide to Baltimore's inner harbor," Science Fiction Chronicle 4(12):1,22-23. September 1983.

"Little Fish Swim On and On: On Specialty Publishing," Fantasy Review 7(6): 20-22. July 1984.

"On SF Publishing: Old Testament," Fantasy Newsletter 6(2): 5-7. February 1983.

"On SF Publishing: Son of Daddy!" Fantasy Newsletter 6(8): 14-16. September 1983.

"On Small Press Publishing: 'Daddy' Dies & The Show Goes On," Fantasy Review of Fantasy and Science Fiction 7(3): 13-14, 42. April 1984.

"On Small Presses: We Didn't Call It 'Mirage' For Nothing," Fantasy Review 7(9): 11-12, 42. October 1984.

"On specialty presses: Mirage Press bibliographica & other stories," Fantasy Reveiw 8(4): 43-44. April 1985.

"On specialty presses: a look back at the basics," Fantasy Review 8(8): 31-32, 36. August 1985.

"On specialty presses: Advent," Fantasy Review 9(6)(eg v. 8 #6): 40-41. June 1985.

"On Specialty Presses: Random Notes and Conventional Thought," Fantasy Review 7(1): 35-36. January 1984.

"On specialty presses: the state of the art," Fantasy Review 8(11): 11-12, 40. November 1985.

"On Specialty Publishers: Modern Times," Fantasy Newsletter 6(3): 21-23. March 1983.

"On Specialty Publishers: Still More Little Fish," Fantasy Review 7(4): 15-16, 40. May 1984.

"On Specialty Publishing: Daddy," Fantasy Newsletter 6(7): 16-18. August 1983.

"On Specialty Publishing: Young Whippersnappers," Fantasy Newsletter 6(6): 21-22, 43. June/July 1983.

"On Specialty Publishing: Grand Dreams and Little Fish," Fantasy Review 7(2): 11-12, 42. March 1984.

"On Specialty Publishing: Philadelphia Story," Fantasy Newsletter 6(4): 10-12. April 1983.

"Philadelphia Fables: The Old Bibliographer's Prologue," Fantasy Review 7(8): 15-17, 19. September 1984.

"Reflections on the Franklin Mint," Fantasy Newsletter 6(5): 9-11. May 1983.

Chalpin, Lila

"Anthony Burgess's gallows humor in dystopia," Texas Quarterly 16(3):73-84. Autumn 1973.

Chamberlain, G. B.

"Angenot-Khouri Bibliography of Prehistoric Fiction: Additions, Corrections, and Comment," Science-Fiction Studies 9(3): 342-346. November 1982.

"Pasts That Might Have Been: An Annotated Bibliography of Alternate History," by B. C. Hacker and G. B. Chamberlain. Extrapolation 22(4): 334-379. Winter 1981.

Chambers, John

"Changing beasts into men, almost," American Cinematographer 58(7):854-856, 864-867. August 1977.

"Cult of science fiction, The," Dalhousie Review 40:78-86. Spring 1960.

Chambron, Jacques

"Voyages dens le temps ou voyages dans L'espace?" Change (Paris) 40:121-131. 1981.

Champlin, Charles

"Gary Kurtz Crystallizes His Fantasy," Los Angesle Times November 4, 1982. in: NewsBank. Film and Television. 50:E14-F1. December 1982.

Champlin, Chuck

"Flying effects for The Greatest American Hero," American Cinematographer 64(1):42-44. January 1983.

Chan, Mei-Mei

"'2010' Stars," _USA Today_ p. 6D. December 12, 1984.

Chanady, A. B.

"Structure of the fantastic in Cortazar's _Cambio de luces_," in: Collins, R. A., ed. _Scope of the Fantastic: Theory, Technique, Major Authors_. Westport: Greenwood, 1985. pp. 159-164.

Chandler, A. B.

"Appreciation of Jack Vance," _Science Fiction: A Review of Speculative Literature_ 4(2): 53-54. June 1982.

"Around the world in 23,741 days," _Algol_ 15(2):21-30. Spring 1978.

"My Life and Grimes," in: World Science Fiction Convention, 40th, Sept. 2-6, 1982. _Program Book_. Chicago: Chicon IV, 1982. pp. 10-19.

"Sea and Science Fiction," by A. B. Chandler and J. M. Elliot. _Owlflight_ 3:25-31. 1982.

Chant, Joy

"Niggle and Numenor," _Children's Literature in Education_ No. 19:161-171. Winter 1975.

Chapman, E. L.

Magic Labyrinth of Philip Jose Farmer. San Bernardino, CA: Borgo, 1984. 96 p.

"Arthur Rex," in: Magill, Frank N., ed. _Survey of Modern Fantasy Literature_, Vol 1. Englewood Cliffs, NJ: Salem Press, Inc., 1983. pp. 57-60.

"_Dr. Bloodmoney, or How We Got Along After the Bomb_," in: Magill, Frank N., ed. _Survey of Science Fiction Literature_, Vol. 2. Englewood Cliffs, NJ: Salem Press, 1979. pp. 564-568.

"_Fellowship of the Talisman, The_," in: Magill, Frank N., ed. _Survey of Modern Fantasy Literature_, Vol 2. Englewood Cliffs, NJ: Salem Press, Inc., 1983. pp. 549-552.

"_Jimgrim Series, The_," in: Magill, Frank N., ed. _Survey of Modern Fantasy Literature_, Vol 2. Englewood Cliffs, NJ: Salem Press, Inc., 1983. pp. 801-804.

"_Lud-in-the-Mist_," in: Magill, Frank N., ed. _Survey of Modern Fantasy Literature_, Vol 2. Englewood Cliffs, NJ: Salem Press, Inc., 1983. pp. 926-931.

"_Om: The Secret of Ahbor Valley_," in: Magill, Frank N., ed. _Survey of Modern Fantasy Literature_, Vol 3. Englewood Cliffs, NJ: Salem Press, Inc., 1983. pp. 1142-1145.

"_Riverworld Series, The_," in: Magill, Frank N., ed. _Survey of Modern Fantasy Literature_, Vol 3. Englewood Cliffs, NJ: Salem Press, Inc., 1983. pp. 1325-1331.

"_World of Tiers, The_," in: Magill, Frank N., ed. _Survey of Modern Fantasy Literature_, Vol 5. Englewood Cliffs, NJ: Salem Press, Inc., 1983. pp. 2171-2175.

"Anima figures in a demonic comedy in the Lewis tradition: E. E. Y. Hales' _Chariot of Fire_," _Mythlore_ 6(3):19-23. Summer 1979.

"From Rebellious Rationalist to Mythmaker and Mystic: The Religious Quest of Philip Jose Farmer," in: Reilly, Robert, ed. _The Transcendent Adventure_. Westport: Greenwood, 1984. pp. 127-144.

"Sex, Satire, and Feminism in the Science Fiction of Suzette Haden Elgin," in: Staicar, Tom, ed. _The Feminine Eye_. New York: Ungar, 1982. pp. 89-102.

"Shaman as hero and spiritual leader: Richard Adams' mythmaking in _Watership Down_ and _Shardik_, The," _Mythlore_ 5:7-11. Autumn 1978.

"_Tros Series, The_," in: Magill, Frank N., ed. _Survey of Modern Fantasy Literature_, Vol 4. Englewood Cliffs, NJ: Salem Press, Inc., 1983. pp. 1975-1978.

Chapman, Ed

"Images of the Numinous in T. H. White and C. S. Lewis," _Mythlore_ 4(4): 3-10. June 1977.

"Toward a sacremental ecology: technology, nature and transcendance in C. S. Lewis' Ransom Trilogy," _Mythlore_ 3(4):10-17. June 1976.

Chapman, R. S.

"Science Fiction in den Fuenfzigern: Billy Graham, MacCarthy und die Bombe, part 1," _Science Fiction Times_ (Germany) 27(3):8-12. March 1985.

"Science Fiction in den Fuenfzigern: Billy Graham, MacCarthy und die Bombe, part 2,' _Science Fiction Times_ (Germany) 27(4):15-17. April 1985.

"Science fiction of the 1950's: Billy Graham, McCarthy and the bomb," _Foundation_ 7/8:38-52. March 1975.

Chapman, Vera

"Forerunner to Tolkien? Walter de la Mare's _The Three Royal Monkeys_," _Mythlore_ 8(2):32-33. Summer 1981.

Chapuis, Alfred

Automates dans les oeuvres d'imagination, Les. Nuechatel: Editions du Griffon, 1947. 276 p.

Chapwick, Morris

"California scene, The (column)," _Science Fiction Times_ No. 462:4-6. January 1969.

"California scene, The," _Science Fiction Times_ No. 465:5. April 1969.

Chard, J. M.

"Some elements of myth and mysticism in C. S. Lewis' novel _Til We Have Faces_," _Mythlore_ 5(2): 15-18. Autumn 1978.

Charnas, S. M.

"Mostly, I Want to Break Your Heart," by S. M. Charnas and Douglas Winter. _Fantasy Review_ 7(8): 5-6, 41. September 1984.

"Woman Appeared," in: Barr, Marlene S., ed. _Future Females_. Bowling Green OH: Bowling Green State University Popular Press, 1981. pp. 103-108.

Charters, L. I.

"Binary First Contact," in: Hassler, Donald M., ed. _Patterns of the Fantastic II_. Mercer Island, WA: Starmont, 1985. pp. 51-58.

"Hugo and Nebula Award trends," _Locus_ 12(1):6,8. January 1979.

Chase, Donald

"Peter Weller," _New York Daily News_ August 5, 1984. _NewsBank. Film and Television_. FTV 21:A9-A10. 1984.

"War of the Wizards," _American Film_ 7(8): 52-59. June 1982.

Chatham, G. N.

"Haruspicating with science fiction, or, through the looking glass: dimly," Washington, DC: Library of Congress Congressional Research Service, 1978. 6 p. (ERIC ED 166 065)

Chauvin, Cy

Multitude of Visions: Essays on Science Fiction. Baltimore: T-K Graphics, 1975. 67 p.

"Aspects of Ursula K. Le Guin," _Vector_ 97:15-18. April 1980.

"Cliche: The Freedom of Science Fiction," _Vector_ 113: 6-10. 1983.

"Doris Lessing: briefing," _Vector_ 78:50-54. November/December.

"Ian Watson's Miracle Men," in: Staircar, Tom, ed. _Critical Encounters II_. New York: Ungar, 1982. pp. 44-59.

"Transatlantic Literature, Hurrah!" _Foundation_ 30: 42-47. March 1984.

Cheatwood, Derral

"Tarzan Films: An Analysis of Determinants of Maintenance and Change in Conventions," _Journal of Popular Culture_ 16(2): 127-142. Fall 1982.

Cheetham, Anthony

"Publisher's lot," _Vector_ 48:2-5. February 1968.

Chernyshev, Andrej

"Anatomiya nauchnoj fantastiki," by Vladislav Pronin and Andrej Chernyshev. _Detskaya Literatura_ 4(100):32-37. 1974.

Chernysheva, Tatyana

"Chelovek i sreda v sovremennoi nauchnofantasticheskoi literature," _Fantastika_ pp. 299-320. 1968.

"Folktale, Wells and modern science fiction, The," in: Suvin, Darko and Robert M. Philmus, eds. _H. G. Wells and Modern Science Fiction_. Lewisburg: Bucknell University Press, 1977. pp. 35-47.

("Utopia and its evolution in the example of the work of the Sturgatskiis,") (In Russian) _Canadian-American Soviet Studies_ 18(1/2):76-84. Spring/Summer 1984.

Cherryh, C. J.

"Female Characters in SF and Fantasy," _SFWA Bulletin_ 16(3): 22-29. March 1982.

Cherryh, C. J. (Continued)

"Goodbye Star Wars, Hellow Alley-Oop," in: Jarvis, Sharon, ed. Inside Outer Space. New York: Ungar, 1985. pp. 17-26.

"Linguistic Sexism in SF and Fantasy: A Modest Proposal," SFWA Bulletin 15(1): 7-9, 26. Spring 1980.

"Romantic/Science Fiction: The Oldest Form of Literature," Lan's Lantern No. 10: 30-33. June 1980.

"Use of archaeology in worldbuilding, The," SFWA Bulletin 13(4):5-10. Fall 1978.

Chesneaux, Jean

The Political and Social Ideas of Jules Verne. London: Thames and Hudson, 1972. 224 p.

"Auteur americain, Un: P. J. Farmer fascine par la regression," La Quinzaine Litteraire No. 225:10-11. January 16, 1976.

"Rupture dans la S. F.," La Quinzaine Litteraire No. 16. February 28, 1978.

Chesterton, G. K.

"Fairy Tales," in: Boyer, Robert H. and Zahorski, Kenneth J. Fantasists on Fantasy. New York: Avon Discus, 1984. pp. 23-30.

Chevrier, Yves

"Blade Runner; or, The Sociology of Anticipation," Science-Fiction Studies 11(1): 50-60. March 1984.

Childs, Mike

"Clash of the Titans," by Mike Childs and Alan Jones. Cinefantastique 9(2):22-27. Winter 1979.

"DePalma has the power; interviews," by Mike Childs and Alan Jones. Cinefantastique 6(1):4-13. Summer 1977.

"Hawk the Slayer (review)," Cinefantastique 11(1):45. Summer 1981.

Chilvers, Colin

"Physical and mechanical special effects for Superman," American Cinematographer 60(1):42-45,60. January 1979.

Chomet, R.

"Bestiaire digest de la science fiction," by R. Chomet and G. Klein. Bizarre No. 11:61, 63, 65-67. October 1955.

Chown, M.

"Is today tomorrow? with miniguide," Scholastic Teacher Jr./Sr. High p. 32. March 1973.

Christensen, B. M.

"J. R. R. Tolkien: a bibliography," Bulletin of Bibliography 27(3):61-67. July-September 1970.

"Tolkien bibliography, A," in: Becker, Alida, ed. The Tolkien Scrapbook. New York: Grossett & Dunlap, 1978. pp. 180-190.

Christensen, Bonniejean

"Gollum's character transformation in The Hobbit," in: Lobdell, Jared, ed. A Tolkien Compass. New York: Ballantine/Del Rey, 1980. pp. 9-28.

Christensen, J. M.

"New Atlantis revisited: science and the victorian tale of the future," Science Fiction Studies 5(3):243-249. November 1978.

Christian, Gary

"Some predictions worked: top writer sees sci-fi losing its peculiar brand of monopoly as science becomes growth industry," Houston Post Sec. AA, p. 9. March 27, 1977.

Christianson, G. E.

"Kepler's Somnium: science fiction and the renaissance scientist," Science Fiction Studies 3(1):79-90. March 1976. Comment: D. Suvin, 3(2):211-212. July 1976. Reply: G. E. Christianson, 3(2):213. July 1976.

Christman, Richard

"Star Trek," San Francisco 19:25. April 1977.

Christopher, J. D.

Science Fiction is Kid's Stuff: A Guide to the Teaching of Science Fiction in the High School English Class. (No publication data; copy in Texas A&M University Library, Science Fiction Research Collection) 85 p.

Christopher, J. R.

C. S. Lewis: an Annotated Checklist of Writings About Him and His Works, by J. R. Christopher and J. K. Ostling. Kent, Ohio: Kent State University Press, 1973. 389 p.

"C. S. Lewis Dances Among the Elves," Mythlore 9(1): 11-17, 47. Spring 1982.

"C. S. Lewis: a bibliographic supplement," by J. R. Christopher and J. K. Ostling. CSL: the Bulletin of the New York C. S. Lewis Society 5(8):4-6. 1974.

"Climbing Jacob's ladder: a hierarchical approach to imagistic mysticism," Mythlore 3(3):10-19. 1976.

"Dorothy Sayers and the inklings," Mythlore 4(1):8-9. September 1976.

"In the C. S. Lewis tradition: two short stories by Anthony Boucher," Mythlore 2(3):25. Winter 1971.

"Inklings Bibliography (1)," Mythlore 3(4):30-38. June 1976.

"Inklings Bibliography (2)," Mythlore 4(1):33-39. September 1976.

"Inklings Bibliography (3)," Mythlore 4(2):33-38. December 1976.

"Inklings Bibliography (4)," Mythlore 4(3): 33-38. March 1977.

"Inklings Bibliography (5)," Mythlore 4(4): 40-46. June 1977.

"Inklings Bibliography (6)," Mythlore 5(1):40-46. May 1978.

"Inklings Bibliography (7)," Mythlore 5(2): 43-46. Autumn 1978.

"Inklings Bibliography (8)," Mythlore 6(1): 46-47. Winter 1979.

"Inklings Bibliography (10)," Mythlore 6(3):38-45. Summer 1979.

"Inklings Bibliography (11)," Mythlore 6(4):44-47. Fall 1979.

"Inklings Bibliography (12)," Mythlore 7(1):41-45. March 1980.

"Inklings Bibliography (13)," Mythlore 7(2):42-47. Summer 1980.

"Inklings Bibliography, (14)," Mythlore 7(3): 43-47. Autumn 1980.

"Inklings Bibliography, (15)," Mythlore 7(4): 42-46. Winter 1981.

"Inklings Bibliography, (16)," Mythlore 8(1): 43-47. Spring 1981.

"Inklings Bibliography, (17)," Mythlore 8(2): 43-47. Summer 1981.

"Inklings Bibliography, (18)," Mythlore 8(3): 45-47. Autumn 1981.

"Inklings Bibliography, (19)," Mythlore 8(4): 43-47. Winter 1982.

"Inklings Bibliography, (20)," Mythlore 9(1): 37-41. Spring 1982.

"Inklings Bibliography, (21)," Mythlore 9(2): 42-46. Summer 1982.

"Inklings Bibliography, (22)," Mythlore 9(3): 42-46. Autumn 1982.

"Inklings Bibliography, (23)," Mythlore 9(4): 51-55. Winter 1983.

"Inklings Bibliography, (24)," Mythlore 10(1): 50-54. Spring 1983.

"Inklings Bibliography, (25)," Mythlore 10(2): 51-55. Summer 1983.

"Inklings Bibliography, (26)," Mythlore 10(3): 51-55. Winter 1984.

"Inklings Bibliography, (27)," Mythlore 10(4): 58-63. Spring 1984.

"Inklings Bibliography, (28)," Mythlore 11(1): 59-63. Summer 1984.

"Introduction to Narnia, part 1: the chronology of the Chronicles," Mythlore 2(2):23-25. Autumn 1970.

"Introduction to Narnia, part 2: the geography of the Chronicles," Mythlore 2(3):12-15,27. Winter 1971.

"Introduction to Narnia, part 3: the genre of the Chronicles," Mythlore 2(4):17-20. Winter 1972.

"Lazarus, come forth from that tomb," Riverside Quarterly 6(3):190-197. August 1975.

"Lewis Carroll, scientifictionist, Part II," Mythlore 9(4): 45-48. Winter 1983.

"Lewis Carroll, scientifictionist," Mythlore 9(3):25-28,41. Autumn 1982.

"Methuselah, out of Heinlein by Shaw," Shaw Review 16(2):79-86. May 1973.

"Moore meaning: in fact, a lot," Riverside Quarterly 6(2):124-133. April 1974.

"Sir Gawain's missing day," Mythlore 6(1): 39-41. Winter 1979.

"Three letters by J. R. R. Tolkien at the University of Texas," Mythlore 7(2):5. Summer 1980.

Christopher, J. R. (Continued)

"Touring the Dark Tower," CSL: the Bulletin of the New York C. L. Lewis Society 9:9-13. April 1978.

"Transformed nature: 'where is it now, the glory and the dream?'" CSL: the Bulletin of the C. S. Lewis Society 7(11):1-7. 1976.

"Trying to capture white magic," Mythlore 5(1):36. May 1978.

Christopher, John

"Decline and fall of the bug-eyed monster, The," Magazine of Fantasy and Science Fiction 11(4):74-76. October 1956.

"Interview: Norman Spinrad," by M. Berkenwald and John Christopher. Future Life 23: 22-25. December 1980.

"Not what-if but how-he," Writer 81(11):15-17,45. November 1968.

Chruszczewski, C.

"Slowo wstepne," in: Kaczmarka, Jerzego, ed. Materialy z Miedzynarodowego Spotkania Pisarzy-Tworcow Literatury Fantastyczno-Naukowej. Poznan: Wyndawnictwo Poznanskie, 1974. pp. 11-16.

Churchill, R. C.

"Henry James on the moon," Humanist 85:144-145. May 1970.

"Man who was Sunday: G. K. Chesterton, 1874-1936, The," Contemporary Review 224:12-15. January 1974.

Churchman, C. W.

"Design of a perfect society," in: Utopias, ed. by Peter Alexander and Roger Gill. London: Duckworth, 1984. pp. 43-49.

Chute, David

"A Pair of Holy Terrors Join Forces To Create 'Talisman'," Los Angeles Herald Examiner March 12, 1983. in: NewsBank. Literature 80:G6-7. 1983.

"Joe Dante Brings Out 'Dark Side of E. T.' in 'Gremlins'," Los Angeles Herald Examiner June 10, 1984. NewsBank. Film and Television. FTV 3:D5-D6. 1984.

Ciardi, John

"Manner of speaking," Saturday Review 50(38):16-17. September 30, 1967.

Ciment, Michel

Kubrick. New York: Holt, 1983. 239 p.

"Odyssey of Stanley Kubrick: part 3: toward the infinite, 2001," in: Johnson, William, ed. Focus on the Science Fiction Film. Englewood Cliffs, NJ: Prentice Hall, 1972. pp. 134-141.

Cioffi, Frank

Formula Fiction? An Anatomy of American Science Fiction, 1930-1940. Westport, CT: Greenwood, 1982. 181 p.

"Gilbert Sorrentino's Science Fiction World in Mulligan Stew," Extrapolation 22(2): 140-145. Summer 1981.

Cirino, Chuck

"Lights! Camera! Aliens!" by Chuck Cirino and David Nichols. Home Video 2(9): 32-33. September 1981.

Cirne, Moacy

"FC: A/Z," Vozes 70(9):57-66. November 1976.

Clancy, L. J.

"'If the accident will': the novels of Kurt Vonnegut," Meanjin Quarterly 30(1):37-45. Autumn 1971.

Clancy-Hepburn, Ken

"Sexism and sci-fi," Human Ecology Forum 4(2):28-30. 1973.

Clarens, Carlos

Illustrated History of the Horror Film. New York: Capricorn Books, 1967. 256 p.

"Sci-fi hits the big time," Film Comment 14(2):49-53. April 1978.

Clareson, T. D.

Many Futures, Many Worlds: Theme and Form in Science Fiction. Kent, Ohio: Kent State University Press, 1977. 303 p.

Robert Silverberg. Mercer Island, WA: Starmont, 1983. 96 p.

Robert Silverberg: A Primary and Secondary Bibliography. Boston: G. K. Hall, 1983. 321 p.

Clareson, T. D. (Continued)

Science Fiction Criticism: an Annotated Checklist. Kent, Ohio: Kent State University Press, 1972. 225 p.

Science Fiction in America, 1870s-1930s: An Annotated Bibliography of Primary Sources. Westport, CT: Greenwood, 1984. 305 p.

SF: A Dream of Other Worlds. College Station, Texas: Texas A&M University Library, 1973. 15 p.

SF: The Other Side of Realism: Essays on Modern Fantasy and Science Fiction. Bowling Green, Ohio: Bowling Green University Popular Press, 1971. 356 p.

Some Kind of Paradise: The Emergence of American Science Fiction. Westport, CT: Greenwood, 1985. 248 p.

Spectrum of Worlds. Garden City, New York: Doubleday, 1972.

Voices for the Future: Essays on Major Science Fiction Writers. Bowling Green, Ohio: Bowling Green University Popular Press, 1976. 283 p.

Voices for the Future: Essays on Major Science Fiction Writers, Vol 2 Bowling Green, OH: Bowling Green State University Popular Press, 1979. 208 p.

Voices For the Future: Essays on Major Science Fiction Writers, Vol 3. Bowling Green, OH: Popular Press, 1984. 219 p.

"Avon Fantasy Reader," in: Tymn, M. B. and Ashley, Mike. Science Fiction, Fantasy, and Weird Fiction Magazines. Westport, CT: Greenwood, 1985. pp. 127-132.

"Avon Science Fiction and Fantasy Reader," in: Tymn, M. B. and Ashley, Mike. Science Fiction, Fantasy, and Weird Fiction Magazines. Westport, CT: Greenwood, 1985. pp. 132-134.

"Avon Science Fiction Reader," in: Tymn, M. B. and Ashley, Mike. Science Fiction, Fantasy, and Weird Fiction Magazines. Westport, CT: Greenwood, 1985. pp. 134-135.

"City," in: Magill, Frank N., ed. Survey of Science Fiction Literature, Vol. 1. Englewood Cliffs, NJ: Salem Press, 1979. pp. 369-373.

"Downward to the Earth," in: Magill, Frank N., ed. Survey of Science Fiction Literature, Vol. 2. Englewood Cliffs, NJ: Salem Press, 1979. pp. 591-594.

"Famous Fantastic Mysteries," in: Tymn, M. B. and Ashley, Mike. Science Fiction, Fantasy, and Weird Fiction Magazines. Westport, CT: Greenwood, 1985. pp. 211-216.

"Fantastic Novels, in: Tymn, M. B. and Ashley, Mike. Science Fiction, Fantasy, and Weird Fiction Magazines. Westport, CT: Greenwood, 1985. pp. 241-244.

"Magazine of Fantasy and Science Fiction," in: Tymn, M. B. and Ashley, Mike. Science Fiction, Fantasy, and Weird Fiction Magazines. Westport, CT: Greenwood, 1985. pp. 377-391.

"Planet Stories," in: Tymn, M. B. and Ashley, Mike. Science Fiction, Fantasy, and Weird Fiction Magazines. Westport, CT: Greenwood, 1985. pp. 476-481.

"Unknown," in: Tymn, M. B. and Ashley, Mike. Science Fiction, Fantasy, and Weird Fiction Magazines. Westport, CT: Greenwood, 1985. pp. 694-698.

"Aldous Huxley: a Bibliography, 1960-1964," by T. D. Clareson and C. S. Andrews. Extrapolation 6(1):2-21. December 1964.

"Annotated bibliography of critical materials dealing with science fiction," Extrapolation 12(2):109-145. May 1971.

"Annotated checklist of American science fiction, 1880-1915," Extrapolation 1(1):5-20. December 1959.

"Arthur C. Clarke: the man and writer: the early novels," Algol 12(1):7-10. November 1974.

"Checklist of articles dealing with science fiction, A," by T. D. Clareson and E. S. Lauterbach. Extrapolation 1(2):29-34. May 1960.

"Classic: Aldous Huxley's Brave New World," Extrapolation 2(2):33-40. May 1960.

"Clifford D. Simak: the inhabited universe," in: Clareson, Thomas D., ed. Voices for the Future: Essays on Major Science Fiction Writers, Vol. 1. Bowling Green, Ohio: Bowling Green Univ. Popular Press, 1976. pp. 64-88.

"Cosmic loneliness of Arthur C. Clarke, The," in: Clareson, Thomas D., ed. Voices for the Future: Essays on Major Science Fiction Writers, Vol. 1. Bowling Green, Ohio: Bowling Green Univ. Popular Press, 1976. pp. 216-237.

"Currents and directions in SF from the 50's to the 80's," by G. Dickson, J. Haldeman, and T. Clareson. in: Remington, T. J., ed. Selected Proceedings of the 1978 SFRA Nat'l Conference. Univ. of North. Iowa, 1979. pp. 222-240.

"Early novels, The," Algol 12(1):7-10. November 1974.

Clareson, T. D. (Continued)

"Emergence of Science Fiction: The Beginnings to the 1920's," in: Barron, Neil, ed. <u>Anatomy of Wonder</u>. 2nd ed. New York: Bowker, 1981. pp. 3-87.

"Fictions of Robert Silverberg, The," in: Clareson, T. D., ed. <u>Voices for the Future: Essays on Major Science Fiction Writers</u>, Vol. 2. Bowling Green, Ohio: Bowling Green University Popular Press, 1979. pp. 1-33.

"First installment: an annotated bibliography of critical writings dealing with science fiction," <u>Extrapolation</u> 11(2):56-78. May 1970.

"Interplay of science and fiction: the canals of Mars, The," by W. B. Johnson and T. D. Clareson. <u>Extrapolation</u> 5(2):37-39. May 1964.

"Introduction," in: Silverberg, Robert. <u>The Best of Robert Silverberg, Volume 2</u>. Boston: Gregg, 1978. pp. vii-xxi.

"Introduction," in: Sutphen, V. T. <u>The Doomsman</u>. Boston: Gregg, 1975. pp. v-xiii.

"Introduction," in: Tymn, M. B. and Ashley, Mike. <u>Science Fiction, Fantasy, and Weird Fiction Magazines</u>. Westport, CT: Greenwood, 1985. pp. xv-xxvii.

"John A. Mitchell's <u>Drowsy</u>: a most unusual country," <u>Extrapolation</u> 12:99-105. May 1971.

"Lost lands, lost races: a pagan princess of their very own," <u>Journal of Popular Culture</u> 8(4):714-723. Spring 1975.

"Lost lands, lost races: a pagan princess of their very own," in: Clareson, T. D., ed. <u>Many Futures, Many Worlds</u>. Ohio: Kent State Univ. Press, 1977. pp. 117-139. (revised from <u>J. of Popular Culture</u> 8:714-723. Spring 1975.)

"M. L. A. Forum: science fiction: the new mythology," ed. by T. D. Clareson. <u>Extrapolation</u> 10(2):69-115. May 1969.

"Major trends in American science fiction, 1880-1915," <u>Extrapolation</u> 1(1):2-4.

"Many futures, many worlds," in: Clareson, Thomas D., ed. <u>Many Futures, Many Worlds</u>. Kent, Ohio: Kent State University Press, 1977. pp. 14-26.

"More issues at hand: critical studies in contemporary science fiction," <u>Journal of Popular Culture</u> 5:247-249. Summer 1971. (Book review)

"Note on Voltaire's <u>Micromegas</u>, A," <u>Extrapolation</u> 2(1):4. December 1960.

"Now That We Are Twenty-Five," <u>Extrapolation</u> 25(4): 291-301. Winter 1984.

"Review and brief mention: reprints, reprints galore," <u>Extrapolation</u> 17(2):133-138. May 1976.

"Robert Silverberg: the complete writer," <u>Magazine of Fantasy and Science Fiction</u> 46(4):73-80. April 1974.

"Science fiction and literary tradition," in: Simak, Clifford D., ed. <u>Nebula Award Stories Six</u>. Garden City, New York, 1971. pp. xi-xxvii.

"Science fiction, literary tradition, and intellectual history," in: Williamson, Jack, ed. <u>Teaching Science Fiction: Education for Tomorrow</u>. Philadelphia: Owlswick, 1980. pp. 44-51.

"Science fiction: the new mythology," <u>Extrapolation</u> 10:69-115. May 1969.

"Scientist as hero in American science fiction 1880-1920, The," <u>Extrapolation</u> 7(1):18-28. December 1965.

"Scientist, The," by L. S. De Camp and T. D. Clareson. in: Warrick, Patricia, ed. <u>Science Fiction: Contemporary Mythology</u>. New York: Harper, 1978. pp. 196-206.

"Second installment: an annotated bibliography of critical writings dealing with science fiction," <u>Extrapolation</u> 12(1):35-59. December 1970.

"SF criticism: an annotated bibliography," in: McNelly, W. E., ed. <u>Science Fiction the Academic Awakening</u>. Shreveport, LA: CEA, 1974. pp. 50-53.

"SF in the classroom: English 390: special topics," <u>Extrapolation</u> 14(1):64-66. December 1972.

"SF: the other side of realism," in: Clareson, Thomas D., ed. <u>SF: The Other Side of Realism</u>. Bowling Green, Ohio: Bowling Green University Popular Press, 1971. pp. 1-28.

"SFRA Conference at Pennsylvania State University," <u>SFWA Bulletin</u> 9(5): 5-8. 1974.

"SFRA, academe, and science fiction criticism..." <u>Noreascon Program Book</u> (29th World Science Fiction Convention) Boston: Noreascon, 1971. pp. 81-86.

"Speculations," in: Turek, Leslie, ed. <u>Noreascon Proceedings</u>. Cambridge, MA: NESFA, 1976. pp. 119-122.

"Toward A History of Science Fiction," in: Tymn, Marshall B., ed. <u>The Science Fiction Reference Book</u>. Mercer Island, WA: Starmont House, 1981. pp. 3-18.

Clareson, T. D. (Continued)

"Two contrasting studies of science fiction: a review," English Literature in Transition 11(4):226-229. 1968. (Book review)

"Variations and Design: The Fiction of Gene Wolfe," in: Clareson, Thomas D., ed. Voices For the Future, Vol. 3. Bowling Green: Popular Press, 1984. pp. 1-29.

"Whose Castle?: Speculations as to the Parameters of Science Fiction," Essays in Arts and Sciences 9(2): 139-143. August 1980.

Clark, J. A.

"Big Ball of Wax," in: Magill, Frank N., ed. Survey of Science Fiction Literature, Vol. 1. Englewood Cliffs, NJ: Salem Press, 1979. pp. 213-217.

"Dragonflight," in: Magill, Frank N., ed. Survey of Science Fiction Literature, Vol. 2. Englewood Cliffs, NJ: Salem Press, 1979. pp. 605-607.

"Little Fuzzy," in: Magill, Frank N., ed. Survey of Science Fiction Literature, Vol. 3. Englewood Cliffs, NJ: Salem Press, 1979. pp. 1230-1234.

"Midsummer Tempest, A," in: Magill, Frank N., ed. Survey of Modern Fantasy Literature, Vol 2. Englewood Cliffs, NJ: Salem Press, Inc., 1983. pp. 1025-1028.

Clark, J. D.

"Informal biography of Conan the Cimmerian," by J. D. Clark, P. S. Miller, and L. S. de Camp. in: De Camp, L. S., ed. Blade of Conan. New York: Ace, 1979. pp. 9-44.

Clark, J. H.

"New map of the mind, A," Foundation 2:24-28. June 1972.

Clark, Jeff

"Frankenstein Unbound: the regeneration of a myth," in: Chauvin, Cy, ed. Multitude of Visions. Baltimore: T-K Graphics, 1975. pp. 49-57.

"Labors of Stableford (Response to Stableford's 'SF: The Nature of the Medium')," Khatru No. 2: 11-20. May 1975.

Clark, Jim

"Nightmare on Elm Street: Part II," Cinefantastique 15(5):14,55. January 1986.

Clark, Judith

"Xanth Novels, The," in: Magill, Frank N., ed. Survey of Modern Fantasy Literature, Vol 5. Englewood Cliffs, NJ: Salem Press, Inc., 1983. pp. 2185-2191.

Clark, Mike

"Frank Ashmore: filling his own shoes in V," Starlog No. 95: 40-41, 72. June 1985.

"Irwin Allen remembers 'Lost in Space', Part One," Starlog No. 100: 26-29. November 1985.

"June Chadwick: she's evil in the second degree," Starlog No. 94:16-18. May 1985.

"Men Who Made the Monsters," by Mike Clark and David Hutchison. Starlog 74: 34-41, 64. September 1983.

"Michael Ironside: he's Ham Tyler: friend or foe?" Starlog No. 90:54-56. January 1985.

"Starlog Exclusive: Bill Mumy," by Bill Cotter and Mike Clark. Starlog 48: 77, 80-81. July 1981.

"Starlog interview: Jonathan Harris," Starlog No. 96: 78-81. July 1985.

"Steven Paul: 'I Rewrote Kurt Vonnegut'," Starlog 80: 24-26. March 1984.

"Warning! Warning!" by Mike Clark and Bill Cotter. Starlog 57: 36-40. April 1981.

Clark, V. M.

Aldous Huxley and Film. Ph. D. Dissertation, Maryland, 1983. 182 p. (DAI 44A(10):3069)

Clark, W. H.

"Drugs and utopia/dystopia," in: Richter, P. E., ed. Utopia/Dystopia?. Cambridge, MA: Schenkman, 1975. pp. 109-124.

Clark, W. J.

Author Index to the Doc Savage Magazine. Los Angeles: M&B, 1971. 21 p.

Clarke, A. C.

Ascent To Orbit: A Scientific Autobiography (The Technical Writings of Arthur C. Clarke). New York: Wiley, 1984. 226 p.

Odyssey File by A. C. Clarke and Peter Hyams. New York: Del Rey, 1984. 132 p.

Clarke, A. C. (Continued)

View From Serendip. New York: Ballantine, 1978. 245 p.

"Beyond Babel; laying the foundation of the first global society," *Unesco Courier* 23(3):32-37. March 1970.

"Computers and cybernetics," in: Ash, Brian, ed. *Visual Encyclopedia of Science Fiction*. New York: Harmony, 1977. pp. 181-189.

"Conquest of space," *Fortnightly* 173:161-167. March 1950.

"Defensa e ilustracion do la fantasia cientifica," *El Correo de la Unesco* (Paris) 15(11). Nov. 1962.

"Einstein and Science Fiction," in: *Einstein: The First Hundred Years*, ed. by Maurice Goldsmith, Alan Mackay, and James Woudhuysen. New York: Pergamon, 1980. pp. 159-161.

"History lesson," *Social Education* 36(3):250-254. March 1972. (Fiction)

"In defence of science fiction; excerpt from address," *Unesco Courier* 15(11):14-17. November 1962.

"Making of a Writer: In the Beginning Was Jupiter," *New York Times Book Review* p. 14, 34. March 6, 1983.

"Professor Irwin and the Deeks affair," *Science Fiction Studies* 5(1):90-92. March 1978.

"Russian odyssey, A," *Locus* 15(9):1,15. September 1982.

"Science fiction: preparation for the age of space," in: Bretnor, Reginald, ed. *Modern Science Fiction: Its Meaning and Its Future*. New York: Coward McCann, 1953. Reprinted, Chicago: Advent, 1979. pp. 197-220.

"Son of Dr. Strangelove," in: Knight, Damon, ed. *Turning Points: Essays in the Art of Science Fiction*. New York: Harper, 1977. pp. 277-284.

"When earthman and alien meet," *Playboy* 15:118-121,126,210-212. January 1968.

"When Worlds Collide (review)," in: Johnson, William, ed. *Focus on the Science Fiction Film*. Englewood Cliffs, NJ: Prentice Hall, 1972. pp. 66-67.

Clarke, Boden

Work of Jeffery M. Elliot: An Annotated Bibliography and Guide. San Bernardino, CA: Borgo, 1984. 50 p.

Clarke, E. R.

"Utopie, L',: Tentative de reintegration universelle," *Studies in Eighteenth-Century Culture*, Vol. 6, 1977. pp. 417-426.

Clarke, F. S.

"3D explosion," *Cinefantastique* 13(6)/14(1):28-43. September 1983.

"Beneath The Planet of the Apes (review)," *Cinefantastique* 1(1):26-27. Fall 1970.

"Cinefantastique in review," *Science Fiction Times* No. 465:8-9. April 1969.

"Escape From the Planet of The Apes (review)," *Cinefantastique* 1(4):28. Fall 1971.

"Forbidden Planet," by F. S. Clarke and Steve Rubin. *Cinefantastique* 8(2/3):4-67. Spring 1979.

"George Pal's production of The Disappearance," by P. S. Perakos and F. S. Clarke. *Cinefantastique* 8(4):4-6. Summer 1979.

"Production: Logan's Run," by F. S. Clarke, Steve Rubin and W. A. Wyss. *Cinefantastique* 5(2):16-21. Fall 1976.

"Rasputin in film," *Cinefantastique* 1(1):6-20. Fall 1970.

"Whatever happened to Jim Danforth's Timegate?" *Cinefantastique* 8(4):9-11. Summer 1979.

"When Dinosaurs Ruled the Earth," *Cinefantastique* 1(3):26-27. Summer 1971.

Clarke, Gerald

"Empire strikes back, The!" *Time* 115(20):66-73. May 19, 1980.

"Great Galloping Galaxies," *Time* 121(21): 62-65. May 23, 1983.

"I've Got to Get My Life Back Again," *Time* 121(21): 66-68. May 23, 1983.

Clarke, I. F.

Pattern of Expectation 1644-2001. New York: Basic Books, 1979. 344 p. also, London: Jonathan Cape, 1979. 344 p.

Tale of the Future from the Beginning to the Present Day. London: The Library Association, 1979. Third ed.

Tale of the Future from the Beginning to the Present Day. London: The Library Association, 1961. 165 p.

Clarke, I. F. (Continued)

Tale of the Future from the Beginning to the Present Day. London: The Library Association, 1972. Second ed. 196 p.

Voices Prophesying War 1763-1984. London: Oxford University Press, 1966. 254 p.

"Almanac of anticipations," Futures 17(2):170-184. April 1985.

"Almanac of Anticipations: A Prospect of Probabilities, 1830-1890," Futures 16(3): 315-324. June 1984.

"Almanac of Anticipations: From the Balloon to Big Brother, 1783-1984," Futures 16(2): 183-193. April 1984.

"Almanac of Anticipations: Journeys Through Time and Space, From the Santa Maria to the 'Last Columbus'," Futures 16(4): 425-434. August 1984.

"Almanac of Anticipations: Oldspeak, the Language of the Future," Futures 16(5): 533-542. October 1984.

"Almanac of Anticipations: The Great War That Never Was, 1871-1914," Futures 16(6): 637-647. December 1984.

"Battle of Dorking 1871-1914, The," Victorian Studies 8(4):308-328. June 1965.

"First forecast of the future, The," Futures 1:325-330. June 1969. also in: Hay, George, ed. The Disappearing Future; a Symposium of Speculation. London: Panther, 1970. pp. 11-15.

"From prophecy to prediction, 15: the idea of the future," Futures 8(6):537-543. December 1976.

"Future as History," in: Malik, Rex, ed. Future Imperfect. London: Pinter, 1980. pp. 11-25.

"Nineteenth Century Utopia," Quarterly Review 296: 80-91. January 1958.

"Pattern of prediction 1763-1973: anxious anticipations: 1918-1939, The," Futures 3(1):72-76. March 1971.

"Pattern of prediction 1763-1973: forecasts of future wars, 1871-1914, The," Futures 1(6):553-557. December 1969.

"Pattern of prediction 1763-1973: the first forcast of the future, The," Futures 1(4):325-330. June 1969.

"Pattern of prediction; forecasting: facts and fallibilities, The," Futures 3(3):302-305. September 1971.

"Patterns of prediction: Jules Verne and the vision of the future," Futures 1(5):464-468. September 1969.

"Prophets and predictors: 1. the utility of utopia," Futures 3(4):396-401. December 1971.

"Prophets and predictors: 2. the primacy of Plato," Futures 4(1):75-80. March 1972.

"Science and society, 1915-1945: the best and the worst," Futures 17(1):57-67. February 1985.

"Science fiction past and present," Quarterly Review 295:260-270. July 1957.

"Shape of wars to come, The," in: Clareson, Thomas D., ed. SF: The Other Side of Realism. Bowling Green, Ohio: Bowling Green University Popular Press, 1971. pp. 216-228.

"Shape of wars to come," History Today 15(2):108-116. February 1965. also in: Clareson, Thomas D., ed. SF: The Other Side of Realism. Bowling Green, Ohio: Bowling Green University Popular Press, 1971. pp. 216-228.

"Voices prophesying war: problems in research," Extrapolation 9(2):26-32. May 1968.

Claus, P. J.

"Structuralist appreciation of Star Trek," in: Arens, W., ed. American Dimension: Cultural Myths and Social Realities. Port Washington, NY: Alfreds, 1976. pp. 15-32.

Clausen, Christopher

"'Lord of the Rings' and 'The Ballad of the White Horse'," South Atlantic Bulletin 39(2):10-16. 1974.

Claypool, Bob

"His 'Wildest Dreams' are now coming true," Houston Post p. 10B. October 23, 1978.

Clayton, David

"On Realistic and Fantastic Discourse," in: Slusser, George E., ed. Bridges to Fantasy. Carbondale: Southern Illinois University Press, 1982. pp. 59-78.

Clayton, John

"Fiction meets fact: designing a space station," Starlog No. 95: 59-60. June 1985.

Cleary, R. D.

Study of Marriage in Doris Lessing's Fiction.
Ph. D. Dissertation, State University of New
York at Stony Brook, 1981. 454 p. (DAI 42:
4831A)

Cleaver, Pamela

"Haggard, H. Rider," in: Vinson, James, ed.
Twentieth Century Romance and Gothic Writers.
Detroit: Gale, 1982. pp. 323-326.

Cleaver, T. M.

"Christopher Lambert," Starlog 84: 55-58,
96. July 1984.

"Fred Ward: Splashing Down as Gus Grissom,"
Starlog 81: 59-61, 66. April 1984.

"Meet Kate Capshaw," Starlog 83: 51-53.
June 1984.

"Starlog Interview: David Loughery,"
Starlog 88: 30-32. November 1984.

"Starlog Interview: Frank Marshall Adventure
Alongside Indiana Jones and the Temple of
Doom," Starlog 83: 36-39. June 1983.

"Starlog Interview: James Cameron," Starlog
89: 56-57, 66. December 1984.

"Starlog Interview: Lance Hendriksen,"
Starlog 78: 51-53. January 1983.

Clegg, Cyndia

"Problems of Realizing Medieval Romance in
Film: John Boorman's Excalibur," in:
Slusser, George, ed. Shadows of the Magic
Lamp. Carbondale: Southern Illinois
University Press, 1985. pp. 98-111.

Clem, R. S.

"City, The," by T. R. Cogswell and R. S. Clem.
in: Warrick, Patricia, ed. Science
Fiction: Contemporary Mythology. New York:
Harper, 1978. pp. 359-365.

Clement, Hal

"Basic Concepts: Astrophysics, Geology," in:
Ellison, Harlan, ed. Medea. New York:
Bantam, 1985. pp. 14-16.

"Chips on Distant Shoulders," in: Bretnor,
Reginald, ed. The Future at War: Vol. 3:
Orion's Sword. New York: Ace, 1980. pp.
40-60.

"Creation of imaginary beings, The," in:
Bretnor, Reginald, ed. Science Fiction Today
and Tomorrow. New York: Harper, 1974. pp.
259-277.

"Hard sciences and tough technologies," in:
Bretnor, Reginald, ed. The Craft of Science
Fiction. New York: Harper, 1976. pp. 37-53.

"John W. Campbell," Locus No. 90:5-6.
July 12, 1971.

"Whirligig world," in: Clement, Hal.
Mission of Gravity. Boston: Gregg, 1978.
pp. 242-256. (Reprinted from Astounding,
June 1953)

Clements, W. M.

"Formula as genre in popular horror
literature," Research Studies (Washington
State University) 49(2):116-122. June 1981.

Clemmer, R. O.

"Mythic process, evolution, and science
fiction," SFWA Bulletin 13(4):19-25, 29.
Fall 1978.

Clifford, Gay

"Caleb Williams and Frankenstein: first-person
narrative and 'Things as They Are'," Genre
10(4):601-617. Winter 1977.

Clifton, Mark

"But they want to write them," Inside and
Science Fiction Advertiser No. 9: 33-37. May
1955.

Cline, W. C.

In the Nick of Time: Motion Picture Sound
Serials. Jefferson, NC: McFarland, 1984.
281 p.

Clinton, Timothy

"Through a TV Screen Darkly," by Timphy
Clinton and R. G. Salter. Home Video 2(9):
43-45. September 1981.

Clipper, L. J.

G. K. Chesterton. New York: Twayne, 1974.
190 p.

Close, Peter

"Fantasms, magics, and unfamiliar sciences: the
early fiction of Jack Vance, 1945-1950," in:
Underwood, Tim, and Miller, Chuck, eds. Jack
Vance. New York: Taplinger, 1980. pp. 23-66.

Close, Peter (Continued)

"Interview with Jack Vance, An," _Science Fiction Review_ 6(4):36-42. November 1977.

Cluny, C. M.

"Robur le Conquerant, de la terre a la lune," _Magazine Litteraire_ No. 31:10-12. August 1969.

Clute, John

"Chronicles of Thomas Covenant the Unbeliever, The and The Second Chronicles of Thomas Covenant," in: Magill, Frank N., ed. _Survey of Modern Fantasy Literature_, Vol 1. Englewood Cliffs, NJ: Salem Press, 1983. pp. 266-274.

"Crock of Gold, The," in: Magill, Frank N., ed. _Survey of Modern Fantasy Literature_, Vol 1. Englewood Cliffs, NJ: Salem Press, Inc., 1983. pp. 324-327.

"Elidor," in: Magill, Frank N., ed. _Survey of Modern Fantasy Literature_, Vol 1. Englewood Cliffs, NJ: Salem Press, Inc., 1983. pp. 472-474.

"Eternal Champion Series, The," in: Magill, Frank N., ed. _Survey of Modern Fantasy Literature_, Vol 1. Englewood Cliffs, NJ: Salem Press, Inc., 1983. pp. 489-496.

"Fantastica," in: Magill, Frank N., ed. _Survey of Modern Fantasy Literature_, Vol 2. Englewood Cliffs, NJ: Salem Press, Inc., 1983. pp. 524-525.

"Giles Boat-Boy or, The Revised New Syllabus," in: Magill, Frank N., ed. _Survey of Science Fiction Literature_, Vol. 2. Englewood Cliffs, NJ: Salem Press, 1979. pp. 873-877.

"Green Child, The," in: Magill, Frank N., ed. _Survey of Modern Fantasy Literature_, Vol 2. Englewood Cliffs, NJ: Salem Press, Inc., 1983. pp. 654-657.

"Jagged Orbit, The," in: Magill, Frank N., ed. _Survey of Science Fiction Literature_, Vol. 3. Englewood Cliffs, NJ: Salem Press, 1979. pp. 1094-1097.

"King of Elfland's Daughter, The," in: Magill, Frank N., ed. _Survey of Modern Fantasy Literature_, Vol 2. Englewood Cliffs, NJ: Salem Press, Inc., 1983. pp. 848-851.

"Lady into Fox," in: Magill, Frank N., ed. _Survey of Modern Fantasy Literature_, Vol 2. Englewood Cliffs, NJ: Salem Press, Inc., 1983. pp. 863-866.

"Michaelmas," in: Magill, Frank N., ed. _Survey of Science Fiction Literature_, Vol. 3.

Englewood Cliffs, NJ: Salem Press, 1979. pp. 1387-1390.

"Titus Groan Trilogy, The," in: Magill, Frank N., ed. _Survey of Modern Fantasy Literature_, Vol 4. Englewood Cliffs, NJ: Salem Press, Inc., 1983. pp. 1947-1953.

"C. S. Lewis," in: Bleiler, E. F., ed. _Science Fiction Writers_. New York: Scribners, 1982. pp. 243-248.

"E. E. Smith," in: Bleiler, E. F., ed. _Science Fiction Writers_. New York: Scribners, 1982. pp. 125-130.

"Fred Hoyle," in: Bleiler, E. F., ed. _Science Fiction Writers_. New York: Scribners, 1982. pp. 387-392.

"Gordon R. Dickson," in: Bleiler, E. F., ed. _Science Fiction Writers_. New York: Scribners, 1982. pp. 345-350.

"Identity of E. V. Odle," _Science-Fiction Studies_ 8(3): 343. November 1981.

"James Blish," in: Bleiler, E. F., ed. _Science Fiction Writers_. New York: Scribners, 1982. pp. 291-296.

"Karel Capek," in: Bleiler, E. F., ed. _Science Fiction Writers_. New York: Scribners, 1982. pp. 583-589.

"Margaret St. Clair," in: Bleiler, E. F., ed. _Science Fiction Writers_. New York: Scribners, 1982. pp. 491-495.

"Murray Leinster," in: Bleiler, E. F., ed. _Science Fiction Writers_. New York: Scribners, 1982. pp. 111-117.

"Posthumous fantasy," in: Magill, Frank N., ed. _Survey of Modern Fantasy Literature_, Vol 5. Englewood Cliffs, NJ: Salem Press, Inc., 1983. pp. 2383-2390.

"Short fiction of de la Mare, The," in: Magill, Frank N., ed. _Survey of Modern Fantasy Literature_, Vol 3. Englewood Cliffs, NJ: Salem Press, Inc., 1983. pp. 1492-1495.

"Sturgeon remembered," _Vector_ No. 127: 2. August/September 1985.

Coale, Samuel

Anthony Burgess. New York: Ungar, 1981.

"Criticism of Anthony Burgess: A Selected Checklist," _Modern Fiction Studies_ 27(3): 533-536. Autumn 1981.

"Interview With Anthony Burgess," _Modern Fiction Studies_. 27(3): 429-452. Autumn 1981.

"Ludic Loves of Anthony Burgess," _Modern Fiction Studies_ 27(3): 453-463. Autumn 1981.

Cobb, J. P.

"Medium and Message in Ellison's 'I Have No Mouth, and I Must Scream,'" in: Myers, R. E., ed. The Intersection of Science Fiction and Philosophy. Westport: Greenwood, 1983. pp. 159-167.

Cobb, Lawrence

"Beginning of the real story: images of heaven in C. S. Lewis and Dante, The," CSL: the Bulletin of the New York C. S. Lewis Society 7(2):1-5. December 1975.

Cobbs, A. L.

"Tin Drum, The," in: Magill, Frank N., ed. Survey of Modern Fantasy Literature, Vol 4. Englewood Cliffs, NJ: Salem Press, Inc., 1983. pp. 1943-1946.

Coblentz, S. E.

"In the Beginning," by S. E. Coblentz with J. M. Elliot. SFWA Bulletin 17(2): 9-11, 23. Summer 1983.

Cochell, S.

"Martians in the classroom," Senior Scholastic (Teacher Edition) 82:9T-10T. March 10, 1963.

Cockcroft, T. G. L.

Index to Fiction in Radio News and Other Magazines. Lower Hutt, New Zealand: by the author, 1970. 12 p.

Index to the Verse in Weird Tales. Lower Hutt, New Zealand: by the author, 1960. 17 p.

Index to the Weird Fiction Magazines. Lower Hutt, New Zealand: by the author, 1962-1964, 2 volumes. 55 and 47 p. Revised edition, 1967. Reprinted, New York: Arno Press, 1975, 2 volumes in 1.

The Tales of Clark Ashton Smith: a Bibliography. Melling, Lower Hutt, New Zealand: by the author, 1951. 5 p.

"Some bibliographic notes on CAS," Nyctalops No. 7:60-64. August 1972.

Cockrum, Kurt

Fantasms II: a Bibliography of the Literature of Jack Vance, compiled by Kurt Cockcrum, D. J. H. Levack, and Tim Underwood. Riverside, California: K. Cockrum, 1979. 99 p.

Cocks, Geoffrey

"War, man, and gravity: Thomas Pynchon and science fiction," Extrapolation 20(4):368-377. Winter 1979.

Cocteau, Jean

"Realite copie le reve, Le," Les Lettres Francaises 561. Mars 24/31, 1955.

Coffey, Warren

"Slaughterhouse-Five," Commonweal pp. 347-348. June 6, 1969. (Book review)

Cogell, E. C.

Ursula K. Le Guin: A Primary and Secondary Bibliography. Boston: G. K. Hall, 1983. 224 p.

"Hopeful Art or An Artful Hope?: Darko Suvin's Aesthetics for Science Fiction," Essays in Arts and Sciences 9(2): 235-246. August 1980.

"Middle-landscape myth in science fiction, The," Science Fiction Studies 5(2):134-142. July 1978.

"Science Fiction and Fantasy Collections in U. S. and Canadian Libraries," in: Tymn, Marshall B., ed. The Science Fiction Reference Book. Mercer Island, WA: Starmont House, 1981. pp. 378-452.

"Setting as analogue to characterization in Ursula Le Guin," Extrapolation 18(2):131-141. May 1977.

"Taoist configurations: The Dispossessed," in: De Bolt, Joe, ed. Ursula K. Le Guin: Voyager to Inner Lands and to Outer Space. Port Washington, New York: Kennikat, 1979. pp. 153-179.

Cogell, Wayne

"Absurdity of Sartre's Ontology, The: A Response by Ursula K. Le Guin," in: Smith, Nicholas D., ed. Philosophers Look at Science Fiction. Chicago: Nelson-Hall, 1982. pp. 143-151.

Cogswell, T. R.

"City, The," by T. R. Cogswell and R. S. Clem. in: Warrick, Patricia, ed. Science Fiction: Contemporary Mythology. New York: Harper, 1978. pp. 359-365.

Cohan, R. H.

"Images of horror and fantasy: Bronx Museum," Arts Magazine 52(6):16. February 1978.

Cohen, D. R.

"Great escapes through fantasy," Crawdaddy 85:51. June 1978.

Cohen, M. N.

Rider Haggard: His Life and Works. London: Hutchinson, 1960. 327 p. Reprinted, New York: Walker, 1961.

Colbath, M. L.

"Worlds as they should be: Middle-earth, Narnia and Prydain," Elementary English 48(8):937-945. December 1971.

Colbert, R. E.

"Case of Conscience, A: The Literary Criticism of James Blish," Essays in Arts and Sciences 9(2): 247-256. August 1980.

"Unbinding Frankenstein: The Science Fiction Criticism of Brian Aldiss," Extrapolation 23(4): 333-344. Winter 1982.

Cole, E. H.

"Ave Atque Vale," in: Wetzel, George. Howard Phillips Lovecraft: Memoirs, Critiques, & Bibliographies. North Tonowonda, NY: SSR, 1955. pp. 10-17.

Cole, R. N.

"Edu-perfection or edu-disaster? science fiction visions of tomorrow," Instructional Innovator 25(3):24-26. March 1980.

Cole, S. A.

"Evolutionary fantasy: Shaw and utopian fiction," Shaw Review 16(2):89-97. May 1973.

Cole, W. R.

A Checklist of Science Fiction Anthologies. Brooklyn, New York: by the author, 1964. 374 p. Reprinted, New York: Arno Press, 1975.

"2001: A Space Odyssey," Science Fiction Times No. 453:2. April 1968.

"Nudity and Heinlein," Science Fiction Times No. 448:5. November 1967.

"On science fiction anthologies," Science Fiction Times No. 369:21-23. September 1961.

"On SF anthologies, 1962," Science Fiction Times No. 399/400:6-8. January/February 1963.

"Planet of the Apes, a review," Science Fiction Times No. 452:2. March 1968.

Colker, David

"Clouded TV debut for Star Wars," Los Angeles Herald Examiner. September 3, 1982. in: NewsBank. Film and Television. FTV-35:D10. 1982/1983.

Collectif

"Pensee anticipatrice, La; par dela la science ficiton," Arguments September 1958.

Collettivo "Un'Ambigua Utopia".

Nei labirinti della fantascienza. Milan: Feltrinelli, 1979. 251 p.

Collier, J.

"Star Wars in the Comics," Amazing Heroes 13: 40-53. July 1982.

Collings, M. K.

"Refracted Visions and Future Worlds: Mormonism and Science Fiction," Dialogue 17(3): 107-116. Autumn 1984.

Collings, M. R.

Many Facets of Stephen King, The. Mercer Island, WA: Starmont, 1985. 190 p.

Piers Anthony. Mercer Island, WA: Starmont, 1983. 96 p. (Starmont Reader's Guide, 20)

Shorter Works of Stephen King, The, by Michael Collings and David Engebretson. Mercer Island, WA: Starmont, 1985. 202 p.

Stephen King as Richard Bachman. Mercer Island, WA: Starmont, 1985. 168 p.

"Stand, The: science fiction into fantasy," in: Schweitzer, Darrell, ed. Discovering Stephen King. Mercer Island: Starmont, 1985. pp. 83-90.

"E. T. and the Christmas Tree," Fantasy Newsletter 5(10): 31-32. November 1982.

"James P. Hogan's Inherit the Stars: A Paradigm for Communication," Extrapolation 25(2): 138-145. Summer 1984.

"Mechanics of immortality, The," in: Yoke, C. B. and Hassler, D. M., eds. Death and the Serpent. Westport, CT: Greenwood, 1985. pp. 29-38.

Collings, M. R. (Continued)

"Mechanisms of Fantasy, The" Lamp-post of the Southern California C. S. Lewis Society 4(3/4): 13-14, 16. August/November 1980.

"Words and worlds: the creation of a fantasy universe in Zelazny, Lee, and Anthony," in: Collins, R. A., ed. Scope of the Fantastic: Theory, Technique, Major Authors. Westport: Greenwood, 1985. pp. 173-182.

Collins, Christopher

"Zamyatin, Wells and the utopian literary tradition," Slavonic and East European Review 44(103):351-360. July 1966.

Collins, R. A.

Scope of the Fantastic: Culture, Biography, Themes, Children's Literature, ed. by R. A. Collins and H. D. Pearce. Westport: Greenwood, 1985. 282 p.

Thomas Burnett Swann: A Brief Critical Biography and Annotated Bibliography. Boca Raton: Thomas Burnett Swann Fund, 1979. 29 p.

"Fantasy and 'Forestructures': The Effect of Philosophical Climate upon Perceptions of the Fantastic," in: Slusser, George E., ed. Bridges to Fantasy. Carbondale: Southern Illinois U. P., 1982. pp. 108-120.

"Interview With David Hartwell, An" by R. A. Collins and David Pettus. Fantasy Newsletter 6(7): 8-10. August 1983.

"Julian May Interview," Fantasy Newsletter 6(3): 24-27. March 1983.

"New Haven, 1982: Crowley, Godwin, King, Etchison Take Top Awards; FN Wins Too!" Fantasy Newsletter 6(1): 20-21. January 1983.

"Retrospective/Thomas Burnett Swann: Swann on Swann: The Author's Conscious Use of Fantasy," Fantasy Newsletter 6(4): 18-20. April 1983.

"Thomas Burnett Swann: A Retrospective," Fantasy Newsletter 6(3): 6-9. March 1983.

Collins, R. G.

"Star Wars: the pastiche of myth and the yearning for a past future," Journal of Popular Culture 11(1):1-10. Summer 1977.

Collins, Tom

"TZ Interview: Robert Bloch," Twilight Zone 1(3): 13-17. June 1981.

Colombo, J. R.

Blackwood's Books: A Bibliography Devoted to Algernon Blackwood. Toronto: Houslow Press, 1981. 119 p.

CDN SF & F: A Bibliography of Canadian Science Fiction and Fantasy. Toronto: Hounslow, 1979. 85 p.

Years of Light: A Celebration of Leslie A. Croutch. Toronto: Hounslow Press, 1982. 194 p.

"Stardust (1975-)," in: Tymn, M. B. and Ashley, Mike. Science Fiction, Fantasy, and Weird Fiction Magazines. Westport, CT: Greenwood, 1985. pp. 607-608.

"Canadian science fiction and fantasy," Science Fiction Studies 12(3): 348-349. November 1985.

"Science Fiction in Bulgaria," Science-Fiction Studies. 8(2): 187-190. July 1981.

Colquitt, B. F.

"Orwell: traditionalist in wonderland," Discourse 8(4):370-383. Autumn 1965.

Comfort, Alex

"Warrior and the suffragette: notes on the science fiction of John Norman, The," Paunch 48/49:6-17. 1977.

Como, J. T.

C. S. Lewis at the Breakfast Table and Other Reminiscences. New York: Macmillan, 1979. 352 p.

Compere, Daniel

Approach de l'ile chez Jules Verne. Paris: Lettres Moderne, 1977. 171 p.

Developpement des etudes sur Jules Verne, by Francois Raymond and Daniel Compere. Paris: Lettres Modernes, 1976. 93 p.

Vie amienoise de Jules Verne, La. Amiens: Centre de documentation Jules Verne, 1978. 14 p.

Voyage imaginaire de Jules Verne, Un: Voyage ou centre de la terre. Paris: Lettres Modernes, 1977. 79 p.

"Anticipation populaire, L'" Europe 542:148-153. June 1974.

"Introuvables Jules Verne, Les" Magazine Litteraire No. 132:65. January 1978.

Compere, Daniel (Continued)

"Vision et Prevision," Europe 60(636): 87-92. 1982.

Compton, D. D.

Comic Universe: Humor in the Science Fiction Short Story, 1940-1960. Ph.D. Dissertation, Texas Christian University, 1982. 252 p.

Compton, D. G.

"Profession of science fiction: XVI: by chance out of conviction, The," Foundation 17:5-12. September 1979.

Coney, M. G.

"Period of transition," Vector 75: 44-46. July 1975.

"Whatever happened to Fay Wray?" Science Fiction Review 5(1):39-41. 1976.

Coney, Michael

"Profession of Science Fiction, 32: Thank You For the Music," Foundation 32: 61-68. November 1984.

Conger, L.

"Excursions out of the ordinary," Writer 89:9-10. March 1976. (cited in other sources but not about SF)

Conklin, Groff

"On SF anthologies," Fantasy Times No. 200:22-23,27. June (1) 1954.

"Science in science fiction," Science Illustrated 1(4):44-45,109-111. July 1946.

"What is good science fiction?" Library Journal 83(8):1256-1258. April 15, 1958.

Conley, G. W.

"John W. Campbell, Jr.," in: Cowart, David, ed. Twentieth-Century American Science Fiction Writers, Part 1: A-L Detroit: Gale, 1981. pp. 97-101. (Dictionary of Literary Biography, v. 8)

Connelly, J. F.

"Science fiction short story: excitement, adventure, and discovery, The," Exercise Exchange 19(2):21-22. 1975. (not seen)

Connelly, Wayne

"H. G. Wells' The Time Machine: its neglected mythos," Riverside Quarterly 5(3):178-191. August 1972.

"Optimism in Anthony Burgess' A Clockwork Orange," Extrapolation 14(1):25-29. December 1972.

"Science fiction and the mundane egg," Riverside Quarterly 5(4):260-267. April 1973.

Conner, Anne

"Implications for the Future: Today's Science Fiction," School Library Journal 31(2): 110-111. October 1984.

Conner, Edward

"Return of the dead, The," Films in Review 15(3):146-160. March 1964.

Conner, Mike

"Norwescon report," Locus 14(4):12. May 1981.

Conners, James

"'Do it to Julia': thoughts on Orwell's 1984," Modern Fiction Studies 16(4):463-473. Winter 1970/1971.

"Zamyatin's We and the genesis of 1984," Modern Fiction Studies 21(1):107-124. Spring 1975.

Conners, Mike

"Rejection! Rejection!" Thrust 18: 18-19, 33. Winter/Spring 1982.

Conover, Willis

Lovecraft at Last, by H. P. Lovecraft and Willis Conover. Arlington, Virginia: Carrollton, Clark, 1975. 272 p.

Conquest, Robert

"Beyond the moon," Encounter 32(6):48-50. June 1969.

"Science fiction and literature," The Critical Quarterly 5(4):355-367. Winter 1963.

Constantine, John

"Judgement day," Vector 96:25-36. December 1979/January 1980.

Contento, William

Index to Science Fiction Anthologies and Collections. Boston: G. K. Hall, 1978. 608 p.

Index to Science Fiction Anthologies and Collections 1977-1983. Boston: G. K. Hall, 1984. 503 p.

Conti, Laura

"Alla ricerca delle radici storiche e psicologiche del racconto di fantascienza," Problemi del socialismo February 1961. pp. 171-188.

Cook, Bruce

Science Fiction and Film: A Study of the Interaction of Science, Science Fiction Literature, and the Growth of Cinema. Ph. D. Dissertation, University of Southern California, 1976.

"Ray Bradbury and the Irish," Catholic World 200(1198):224-230. January 1965.

"When Kurt Vonnegut talks, and he does, the young all tune in," National Observer p. 21. October 12, 1970.

Cook, Fred

Collector's Index to Weird Tales, by Sheldon Jaffery and Fred Cook. Bowling Green, OH: Bowling Green State University Popular Press, 1985. 162 p.

Fred Cook's Index to the Wonder Group. Grand Haven, Michigan: n.p., 1966. 239 p.

Cook, J. T.

Student Attitude: A Comparison of Science Fiction Literature and Reading Values. Ph.D. Dissertation, Brigham Young University, 1979. 156 p.

Cook, M. L.

Mystery, Detective and Espionage Magazines. Westport, CT: Greenwood, 1983. 795 p.

Cook, Monte

"Tips for Time Travel," in: Smith, Nicholas D., ed. Philosophers Look at Science Fiction. Chicago: Nelson-Hall, 1982. pp. 47-55.

"Who Inhabits Riverworld?" in: Smith, Nicholas D., ed. Philosophers Look at Science Fiction. Chicago: Nelson-Hall, 1982. pp. 97-104.

Cook, W. P.

H. P. Lovecraft: a Portrait. Baltimore: Mirage Press, 1968. 66 p.

In Memoriam Howard Phillips Lovecraft: Recollections, Appreciations, Estimates. S. L.: Driftwood Press, 1941. 76 p.

Coombes, Harry

"John Cowper Powys: a modern Merlin," Southern Review 11:779-793. 1976.

Cooper, B. L.

"Beyond Flash Gordon and 'Star Wars': science fiction and history instruction," Social Education 42(5):392-397. May 1978.

Cooper, Basil

The Werewolf Legend, Fact & Art. New York: St. Martin's, 1977.

Cooper, Edmund

"Violence in SF," Vector 70: 10-16. Autumn, 1975.

Cooper, J. C.

Fantasy and the Human Spirit. New York: Seabury, 1975. 178 p. (not applicable)

Cooper, J. E.

"Original science fiction useful in teaching geologic time table; with two of the stories which were written in this project," American Biology Teacher 16:17-19. October 1954.

Cooper, Susan

"Escaping into Ourselves," in: Boyer, Robert H. and Zahorski, Kenneth J. Fantasists on Fantasy. New York: Avon Discus, 1984. pp. 277-287.

"Newbery award acceptance," The Horn Book Magazine 52:361-366. 1976.

Copeland, Joe

"From the Arizona Desert: I Was Mark Hammill's Stand-In," Starlog 65: 42-45. December 1982.

Copenhagen. Kongelige Bibliotek

Triviallitteratur, kriminalromaner, science fiction. Kobenhavn: Kongelige Bibliotek, 1980. 62 p.

Coppard, Audrey

Orwell Remembered, by Audrey Coppard and Bernard Crick. New York: Facts on File, 1984. 287 p.

Cordesse, Gerard

"Double et le robot, Le" Recherches anglaises et Americaines 6:32-42. 1973.

"Impact of American science fiction on Europe, The," in: Bigsby, C. W. E., ed. Superculture: American Popular Culture and Europe. Bowling Green, Ohio: Bowling Green Popular Press, 1975. pp. 160-174,222-223.

"Informations et documents," Science fiction, by G. Cordesse and Patrick Duvic. Paris, Services americains d'information et de relations culturelles, 1972. 35p.

"S. F. et mythe," Europe 580/581:73-79. August/September 1977.

Corley, James

"Book Reviewing, The Objective Critique," Vector 99: 10-11. October 1980.

"Heartache, hardware, sex and the system: the science fiction of Bob Shaw," Vector 91:3-9. January/February 1979.

"Interview with Bob Shaw, An," by James Corley and David Wingrove. Vector 91:10-12. January/February 1979.

"Serpent in the Garden," Arena 12: 4-9. Summer 1981.

Corliss, Richard

"Future imperfect," New Times 8(1):78-80. January 7, 1977.

"Lover From Another Planet, The (Review of Starman)," Time 124(26): 65. December 24, 1984.

"Steve's Summer Magic," Time 119(22): 54-60. May 31, 1982.

Corn, J. J.

Yesterday's Tomorrows: Past Visions of the American Future, by J. J. Corn and Brian Harrigan. New York: Summit, 1984. 158 p.

Correy, John

"Something About 'Star Trek' Talks to Everyman," New York Times p. H25. June 10, 1984.

Corrick, Jim

"Chronology of the universe of Andre Norton," Collector's Bulletin No. 9:17. June 1968.

"Events in the universe of Andre Norton," Collector's Bulletin No. 9:18-19. June 1968.

Corriell, Vernell

"Open letter to Ray Palmer," Fantasy Times No. 249:FTM1-FTM3. June (2) 1956.

Corrin, J. P.

"Formulation of the distributist circle, The," Chesterton Review 1(2):52-83. 1975.

Cosem, Michel

Decouvrir la science fiction. Paris: Seghers, 1975. 320 p.

Cosgrave, J. O.

"Gates of conjecture," Saturday Review of Literature 8:597-598. March 19, 1932.

Cosman, Max

"Post World War III," Commonweal pp. 157-158. May 5, 1961. (Book review)

Cossato, G. P.

"Science fiction in Italy," Algol 16:12-15. December 1970.

Costa, R. H.

H. G. Wells. New York: Twayne, 1967. 181 p.

"Afterword: Letter to George Orwell," in: The Future in Peril: 1984 and the Anti-Utopians. College Station: Honors Program, Texas A&M University, [1985]. pp. 51-53.

"Edwardian intimations of the shape of fiction to come: Mr. Britling/Job Huss as Wellsian central intelligence," English Literature in Transition 18(4):229-242. 1975.

Costello, J. H.

"H. Beam Piper: an infinity of worlds, part I," Renaissance 4(4):1-3. 1972.

"H. Beam Piper: an infinity of worlds, part II," Renaissance 5(1):1-5. Winter 1973.

"H. Beam Piper: an infinity of worlds, part III," Renaissance 5(2):1-8. Spring 1973.

Costello, Peter

Jules Verne: Inventor of Science Fiction. New York: Scribners, 1978. 239 p.

Cotter, Bill

"David Hasselhoff as the 'Knight Rider'," Starlog 79: 19-22. February 1984.

"Starlog Exclusive: Bill Mumy," by Bill Cotter and Mike Clark. Starlog 48: 77, 80-81. July 1981.

"V," Starlog 88: 82-84. November 1984.

"Warning! Warning!" by Mike Clark and Bill Cotter. Starlog 57: 36-40. April 1981.

Cotton, G. B.

"Science fiction and fantasies," by G. B. Cotton and H. M. McGill. in: Fiction Guides, General: British and American. London: Clive Bingley, 1967.

Couch, F. A., Jr.

"Orlando," in: Magill, Frank N., ed. Survey of Modern Fantasy Literature, Vol 3. Englewood Cliffs, NJ: Salem Press, Inc., 1983. pp. 1164-1168.

Coulson, Robert

"Paperback Science Fiction," in: Cowart, David, ed. Twentieth Century American Science Fiction Writers. Detroit: Gale, 1981. v. 2, pp. 254-262.

"Recent fantasies of Manly Wade Wellman," in: Schweitzer, Darrell, ed. Discovering Modern Horror Fiction I. Mercer Island: Starmont, 1985. pp. 92-105.

Counts, Kyle

"All of Me (review)," Cinefantastique 15(2):51,59. May 1985.

"Brainstorm," by Charlotte Wolter and Kyle Counts. Cinefantastique 14(2):16-21,54-59. December 1983/January 1984.

"Cat People (review)," Cinefantastique 12(5/6):93. July/August 1982.

"Children of the Corn (review)," Cinefantastique 14(4/5):102,108. September 1984.

"Cujo (review)," Cinefantastique 14(2):50. December 1983/January 1984.

"Fire and Ice," Cinefantastique 12(5/6):18-19. July/August 1982.

"Fright Night (review)," Cinefantastique 15(5):38-39. January 1986.

"Goonies (review)," Cinefantastique 15(5):35. January 1986.

"Heartbeeps (review)," Cinefantastique 12(2/3):85. April 1982.

"Heartbeeps," Cinefantastique 11(3):14-15. September 1981.

"How to build a werewolf," Cinefantastique 11(3):42-45. September 1981.

"Ice Pirates (review)," Cinefantastique 14(4/5):104. September 1984.

"Jacob's Ladder," Cinefantastique 16(1):19-21,60-61. March 1986.

"Making of Alfred Hitchcock's The Birds," Cinefantastique 10(2):14-35. Fall 1980.

"Nightmare on Elm Street (review)," Cinefantastique 15(3):43. July 1985.

"Of Unknown Origin (review)," Cinefantastique 14(3):59-60. May 1984.

"Omen (review)," Cinefantastique 5(2):27. Fall 1976.

"Poltergeist (review)," Cinefantastique 13(1):47. September/October 1982.

"Psycho II (review)," Cinefantastique 13(6)/14(1):96,98. September 1983.

"Resurrection (review)," Cinefantastique 11(1):45. Summer 1981.

"Starman (review)," Cinefantastique 15(3):47-49,56. July 1985.

"Sword and The Sorcerer (review)," Cinefantastique 12(5/6):89. July/August 1982.

"Virus," Cinefantastique 13(6)/14(1):102. September 1983.

"Weird Science (review)," Cinefantastique 16(1):48. March 1986.

"Who really wrote Starman," Cinefantastique 15(3):47,56. July 1985.

Counts, Kyle (Continued)

"Wizards (review)," _Cinefantastique_ 5(4):19,21. Spring 1977.

Cousin, Clara

"Advice to the Alienated," _Patchin Review_ 1: 14-15. July 1981.

Covell, Ian

"Interview with Bob Shaw, An," _Science Fiction Review_ 7(1):8-12. February 1978.

"Interview with John Brunner," _Science Fiction Review_ 8(1):8-15. January 1979.

"Interview with Michael Moorcock," _Science Fiction Review_ 8(1):18-25. January 1979.

"Some notes on British authors," _Science Fiction Collector_ 4:28-30. July 1977.

Cover, A. B.

"Of Misery, And Guilt, and Spam," _Starship_ 20(1): 29-30. Winter 1983/84.

"Vertex interviews Philip K. Dick," _Vertex_ 1(6):34-37,96-98. February 1974.

Cowan, M. E.

"Alien: An Analytical Commentary," _Lan's Lantern_ No. 10: 27-30. June 1980.

Cowan, S. A.

"Track of the Hound: Ancestors of Kazak in _The Sirens of Titan_," _Extrapolation_ 24(3): 280-287. Fall 1983.

Cowart, David

Twentieth Century American Science Fiction Writers by David Cowart and Thomas Wymer. Detroit: Gale Research, 1981. 2 v. (Dictionary of Literary Biography, 8)

Cowper, Richard

"A rose is a rose is a rose . . . in search of Roger Zelazny," _Foundation_ 11/12:142-147. March 1977.

"Apropos 'The White Bird of Kinship'," _Vector_ 110: 6-11. 1982.

"Is There A Story In It Somewhere?" in: Wingrove, David, ed. _The Science Fiction Source Book_. New York: Van Nostrand, 1984. pp. 74-75.

"Profession of science fiction: X: backwards across the frontier, The," _Foundation_ 9:4-20. November 1975.

"Writers, The: Is there a story in it somewhere?" _Science Fiction Chronicle_ 6(11): 37-38. August 1985.

"Yorcon speech," _Vector_ 96:20-24. December 1979/January 1980.

Cox, A. J.

"A. E. Van Vogt; ein Portraet," _Science Fiction Times_ (Germany) 25(1):5-9. January 1983.

"Anatomy of science fiction, The," _Inside_ No. 2. June 1963. (not seen)

"Boredom of fantasy," _Inside-Riverside Quarterly_ p. 6-10. Summer 1964.

"Charles Schneeman," _Fantasy Times_ No. 156:2. June (2) 1952.

"Cosmic reporter: new Siodmak film," _Fantasy Times_ No. 169:6-7. January (1) 1953.

"Critics and science fiction," _Fantasy Times_ No. 200:9-10. June (1) 1954.

"Debut of a new Tarzan," _Jong_ 1(1):1-2. April (2) 1949. (Supplement to _Fantasy Times_)

"Deus ex machina: a study of A. E. Van Vogt, part I," _Science Fiction Advertiser_ 5(6):3-20. March 1952.

"Deus ex machina: a study of A. E. Van Vogt, part II," _Science Fiction Advertiser_ 6(1):3-18. July 1952.

"Dutch SF mag out," _Fantasy Times_ No. 77: 1-3. March 1, 1949.

"Fabulous magician turned out 4,000 fantasy films," _Fantasy Times_ No. 78:1-2. March 15, 1949.

"Fritz Lang, pioneer of science fiction movies," _Fantasy Times_ No. 81:3. May (1) 1949.

"Interesting sidelights on the movie Mighty Joe Young," _Fantasy Times_ No. 88: 1, 7. August (2) 1949.

"Interview with Richard A. Hoen," _Fantasy Times_ No. 93:3-5. November (1) 1949.

"Jack Vance: der Weltenschoepfer," _Science Fiction Times_ (Germany) 24(7):5-9. July 1982.

"Jack Vance: the world-thinker," in: Underwood, Tim, and Miller, Chuck, eds. _Jack Vance_. New York: Taplinger, 1980. pp. 67-86.

"LASFS member was undercover agent for FBI," _Fantasy Times_ No. 155:1,4. June (1) 1952.

Cox, A. J. (Continued)

"Moon story cycle starts in movies," Fantasy Times No. 77: 1-2. March 1, 1949.

"Nat Schachner dead at 60," Fantasy Times No. 236:1. December (1) 1955.

"Science fiction 15 years ago and today," Fantasy Times No. 254:21-23. September (1) 1956.

"Set of Destination Moon televised," Fantasy Times No. 97:4,8. January (1) 1950.

"SF Con report: Cleveland in 1955," Fantasy Times No. 205:1-3. August (2) 1954.

"World SF Convention report," Fantasy Times No. 206:2. September (1) 1954.

Cox, C. L.

"Fan Club Listing,", in: Hopkins, Harry A., ed. Fandom Directory 1981. Langley AFB, Virginia: Fandom Computer Services, 1981. pp. 116-127.

"Fan Club Listing," in: Hopkins, Mariane S., ed. Fandom Directory 1982. Newport News, VA: Fandom Computer Services, 1982. pp. 14-19.

"Why Publish?" in: Hopkins, Harry A., ed. Fandom Directory 1980. Langley AFB, Virginia: Fandom Computer Servicews, 1980. pp. 273-274.

Cox, Jeff

"Tolkien, the man who created nine languages," Quinto Lingo 6(8/9):8-11. August/September 1969.

Cox, Vic

"Ray Harryhausen: Acting Without the Lumps," Cinefex 5: 4-19. July 1981.

Coyle, Wallace

Stanley Kubrick: A Guide to References and Sources. Boston: G. K. Hall, 1980. 160 p.

Coyle, William

"Ruskin's King of the Golden River: a Victorian fairy tale," in: Collins, R. A., ed. Scope of the Fantastic: Culture, Biography, Themes, Children's Literature. Westport: Greenwood, 1985. pp. 85-90.

Crabbe, K. F.

J. R. R. Tolkien New York: Ungar, 1981. 180 p.

Craft, Carole

"Author Explains Sci-Fi, Fantasy," Battalion (Texas A&M Univ.) p. 5. November 10, 1982.

Craig, Charles

"Son of slave slut," (Humor) Empire for the SF Writer 9(3): 26-27. Spring 1985.

Craig, Kent

"Slan," in: Magill, Frank N., ed. Survey of Science Fiction Literature, Vol. 5. Englewood Cliffs, NJ: Salem Press, 1979. pp. 2096-2100.

Crain, Bradford

"Masks, mirrors, and magic: fantasy as autobiography in the works of Hesse and Yeats," in: Collins, R. A., ed. Scope of the Fantastic: Culture, Biography, Themes, Children's Literature. Westport: Greenwood, 1985. pp. 91-98.

Cramer, J. G.

"Alternate Universes II," Analog 104(11): 141-145. November 1984.

"Other Universes I," Analog 104(9): 95-100. September 1984.

Crane, J. K.

T. H. White. New York: Twayne Publishers, 1974. 202 p.

"T. H. White: the fantasy of the here and now," Mosaic 10(2):33-46. Winter 1977.

Crane, Lyell

"Francais, attention! Voici la science fiction," Fantasy Times No. 148:3. February (2) 1952.

Cranis, Alan

From H. G. Wells to George Pal. Master's Thesis, University of Southern California, 1976.

Cranny-Francis, Anne

"Sexuality and Sex-Role stereotyping in Star Trek," Science Fiction Studies 12(3): 274-284. November 1985.

Craven, David

"Science fiction and the future of art,"
Arts Magazine 58(9):125-129. May 1984.

Crawford, G. W.

"Night-Side: Eighteen Tales," in: Magill,
Frank N., ed. Survey of Modern Fantasy
Literature, Vol 3. Englewood Cliffs, NJ:
Salem Press, Inc., 1983. pp. 1124-1126.

"Parasite, The," in: Magill, Frank N., ed.
Survey of Modern Fantasy Literature, Vol 3.
Englewood Cliffs, NJ: Salem Press, Inc., 1983.
pp. 1209-1211.

"Short fiction of Aickman, The," in: Magill,
Frank N., ed. Survey of Modern Fantasy
Literature, Vol 3. Englewood Cliffs, NJ:
Salem Press, Inc., 1983. pp. 1412-1416.

"Short fiction of Campbell, The," in: Magill,
Frank N., ed. Survey of Modern Fantasy
Literature, Vol 3. Englewood Cliffs, NJ:
Salem Press, Inc., 1983. pp. 1485-1488.

"Short fiction of Le Fanu, The," in: Magill,
Frank N., ed. Survey of Modern Fantasy
Literature, Vol 4. Englewood Cliffs, NJ:
Salem Press, Inc., 1983. pp. 1600-1606.

"Stephen King's American gothic," in:
Schweitzer, Darrell, ed. Discovering Stephen
King. Mercer Island: Starmont, 1985. pp.
41-45.

"Urban Gothic: the fiction of Ramsey
Campbell," in: Schweitzer, Darrell, ed.
Discovering Modern Horror Fiction I. Mercer
Island: Starmont, 1985. pp. 13-20.

Crawford, J. H.

"333": A Bibliography of the Science-Fantasy
Novel, by J. H. Crawford, J. J. Donahue, and
D. M. Grant. Providence, Rhode Island: The
Grandon Company, 1953. 80 p.

Crawford, J. W.

"Utopian Eden of Lost Horizon,"
Extrapolation 22(2): 186-190. Summer 1981.

Crawley, Tony

Steven Spielberg Story, The. New York:
Morrow, 1984. 159 p.

Creech, Heather

"Who Reads Science Fiction?" Emergency
Librarian 9(3): 6-9. January/February 1982.

Cremaschi, Inisero

Collina, La. Milan: Editrice Nord, 1980.
157 p.

Collina, La, rassegna di critica e narativa
insolita, fantascienza e neofantistico, v. 3.
Milano: Editrice Nord, 1982. 176 p.

Futuro: il meglio di una mitica rivista de
fantascienza, ed. by Insisero Cremaschi.
Milan, 1976.

"Chronistoria della fantascienza italiana,"
in: Cremaschi, Inisero, ed. Universo e
dintorni: 29 autori italiani di fantascienza.
Milano: Garzanti, 1978.

Creteaux, M.

"Science fiction gagne ses letters de noblesse,
La" Notes bibliographiques, 1974, 4, p.
327-332.

"Science fiction", Notes bibliographiques,
1973, 3, p. 195-199.

Crichton, J. M.

"Sci-fi and Vonnegut," New Republic
160:33-35. April 26, 1969.

Crichton, Jennifer

"Ballantine/Del Rey is Feeling the Force,"
Publishers Weekly 224(5): 35-37. July 29,
1983.

"Del Rey Sets to Launch Footfall, A Novel of
Alien Invasion," Publishers Weekly
227(10): 75-76. March 8, 1985.

"Douglas Adams's Hitchhiker Trilogy,"
Publishers Weekly 223(1): 47-49. January
14, 1983.

"Hardcover SF: A Bestseller List Staple Now,"
Publishers Weekly 227(10): 76. March 8,
1985.

Crick, Bernard

Orwell Remembered, by Audrey Coppard and
Bernard Crick. New York: Facts on File, 1984.
287 p.

"Reception of Nineteen Eighty-Four," in:
George Orwell and Nineteen Eighty-Four.
Washington, DC: Library of Congress, 1985.
pp. 97-103.

Crider, A. B.

Mass Market Publishing in America. Boston:
G. K. Hall, 1982. 294 p.

Crider, Bill

"SF Writers in Other Fields," Paperback Quarterly. 4(3): 24-27. Fall 1981.

Crispin, A. C.

"Search for Spock (review)," Starlog 88: 36,37. November 1984.

"Theodore Sturgeon in Memoriam, 6," Locus 18(7): 25-26. July 1985.

Crispin, Ann

"Universe Not Your Own: Writing Novelizations and Tie-ins," Starlog 83: 41-43. June 1984.

Crispin, E.

"Science fiction," Times Literary Supplement 3217:865-866. October 25, 1963.

Crispin, Edmund

"Makrokosmos," New Statesman 49(1267):854. June 18, 1955. (Book review)

Crist, J. K.

"Horror in the nursery," Collier's 121:22-23. March 27, 1948.

Critelli, J. W.

"Analysis of a Modern Myth: The Star Trek Series," by J. E. Ellington and J. W. Critelli. Extrapolation 24(3): 241-250. Fall 1983.

Cro, Stelio

"New World in Spanish utopianism," Alternitive Futures 2(3): 39-54. Summer 1979.

Crochet, Bruce

"Explorers (review)," Cinefantastique 15(5):42-43. January 1986.

Croghan, Antony

Science Fiction and the Universe of Knowledge: The Structure of An Aesthetic Form. London: Coburgh, 1981. 47 p.

Crohmalneceanu, O. S.

"Roman als science fiction," in: Wort in der Zeit. Osterreichesche Literaturzeitschrift no. 12:24-27. 1965.

Cronel, Herve

"Approches de la science fiction," La Nouvelle Revue Francaise (Paris) 260:114-117. August 1974.

Cronimus, J. P.

"From France," Science Fiction Times No. 462:3. January 1969.

"International news: from France," Science Fiction Times No. 460:4. November 1968.

Crook, David

"They're in the running for Runner," Los Angeles Times. July 12, 1983. in: NewsBank. Film and Television. FTV-10:E9. 1983.

Cross, T. P.

"Day After, The: report of a survey of effects of viewing and beliefs about nuclear war," by T. P. Cross and Leonard Saxe. 12 p. ERIC ED 260 951.

Crosse, Gordon

"Alan Garner: Librettist," Labrys No. 7: 129-132. November 1981.

Crossette, Barbara

"Making a Plant Grow: A Hidden Art on Stage," New York Times Sec. 3, p. 3. October 8, 1982.

Crossley, Robert

"From the Earth to the Moon," in: Magill, Frank N., ed. Survey of Science Fiction Literature, Vol. 2. Englewood Cliffs, NJ: Salem Press, 1979. pp. 850-854.

"Lost Horizon," in: Magill, Frank N., ed. Survey of Science Fiction Literature, Vol. 3. Englewood Cliffs, NJ: Salem Press, 1979. pp. 1265-1269.

"Modern Utopia, A," in: Magill, Frank N., ed. Survey of Science Fiction Literature, Vol. 3. Englewood Cliffs, NJ: Salem Press, 1979. pp. 1429-1434.

Crossley, Robert (Continued)

"Education and fantasy," College English 37(3):281-293. November 1975.

"Famous Mythical Beasts: Olaf Stapledon and H. G. Wells," Georgia Review 36(3): 619-635. Fall 1982.

"Letters of Olaf Stapledon and H. G. Wells, 1931-1942, ed. by Robert Crossley," in: Wolfe, Gary. Science Fiction Dialogues. Chicago: Academy Chicago, 1982. pp. 27-57.

"Long Day's Dying, A: the elves of J. R. R. Tolkien and Sylvia Townsend Warner," in: Yoke, C. B. and Hassler, D. M., eds. Death and the Serpent. Westport, CT: Greenwood, 1985. pp. 57-70.

"Olaf Stapledon Collection at the University of Liverpool," SFRA Newsletter 117: 8-10. December 1983.

"Politics and the Artist: The Aesthetic of Darkness and the Light," Science-Fiction Studies 9(3): 294-305. November 1982.

"Pure and Applied Fantasy, or From Faerie to Utopia," in: Schlobin, Roger C., ed. The Aesthetics of Fantasy Literature and Art. Notre Dame, IN: University of Notre Dame Press, 1982. pp. 176-192.

"Short Fiction of H. G. Wells, The," in: Magill, Frank N., ed. Survey of Science Fiction Literature, Vol. 4. Englewood Cliffs, NJ: Salem Press, 1979. pp. 1967-1972.

"Teaching the Course in Fantasy: An Elvish Counsel," Extrapolation 22(3): 242-251. Fall 1981.

Crouch, L. E.

Scientist in American Science Fiction, 1843-1912. Masters Thesis, University of Texas, 1970. 49 p.

Scientist in English Literature: Domingo Gonsales (1638) to Victor Frankenstein (1817). Ph. D. Dissertation, University of Oklahoma, 1975. 275 p. (DAI 36:2181A)

Crouch, Marcus

"Practical fantasist, The," The Junior Bookshelf 36(2):81-86. April 1972.

Crouch, T. D.

"'To Fly to the World in the Moon': Cosmic Voyaging in Fact and Fiction From Lucian to Sputnik," in: Emme, Eugene M., ed. Science Fiction and Space Futures. San Diego: Univelt, 1982. pp. 7-26.

Crouch, William

"William Friedkin," Cinefantastique 3(3):6-13. Fall 1974.

Croucher, Michael

"Making of To Kill a King, The" Labrys No. 7: 127-128. November 1981.

Crouchet, Bruce

"2010 (review)," Cinefantastique 15(2):51,56. May 1985.

"Dune (review)," Cinefantastique 15(3):46. July 1985.

"Invaders from Mars," Cinefantastique 16(1):32-35. March 1986.

Crow, C. L.

Haunted Dusk, The: American Supernatural Fiction, 1820-1920. by Howard Kerr, J. W. Crowley, and C. L. Crow. Athens, GA: University of Georgia Press, 1983. 236 p.

Occult in America, The: New Historical Perspectives. by Howard Kerr and C. L. Crow. Urbana: University of Illinois Press, 1983. 246 p.

Crow, J. H.

"Words of binding: patterns of integration in the Earthsea trilogy," by J. H. Crow and R. D. Erlich. in: Olander, J. D. and M. H. Greenberg, eds. Ursula K. Le Guin. New York: Taplinger, 1979. pp. 200-224.

Crow, John

"Mythic patterns in Ellison's A Boy and His Dog," by John Crow and Richard Erlich. Extrapolation 18(2):162-166. May 1977.

Crowe, Edith

"Many Faces of Heroism in Tolkien, The," Mythlore 10(2): 5-8. Summer 1983.

Crowley, C. P.

"Failure of nerve: H. G. Wells," University of Windsor Review 2(2):1-8. Spring 1967.

Crowther, Bosley

"Don't look now, but..." New York Times Sec. II, p. 1. May 6, 1951.

Crowther, Bosley (Continued)

"Outer space comes of age," Atlantic 189:91-92. March 1952.

"Passing wonders: Destination Moon," New York Times Sec. II, p. 1. July 9, 1950.

Crozier, I. J.

"Olympic con to be held in Australia," Fantasy Times No. 253:5-6. August (2) 1956.

Cruickshank, Art

"Photographing miniatures on a massive scale," American Cinematographer 61(1):48-49, 72-76,98-99. January 1980.

Cruse, Amy

"Science and romance," in: Cruse, Amy. After the Victorians. London: Allyn and Unwin, 1938. pp. 163-173.

Csernai, Zoltan

"Renyi Alfred es a science fiction," SF Tajekoztato p. 48-50. September 1971.

Csicsery-Ronay, Istvan, Jr.

"Book is the Alien, The: On Certain and Uncertain Readings of Lem's Solaris," Science Fiction Studies 12(1): 6-21. March 1985.

Cuddy, Page

"Report from the bunker," Science Fiction Chronicle 4(10):1,18-20. July 1983.

Cude, Wilfred

"What literary criticism needs to learn from scientific methodology," Mosaic 17(4): 1-16. Fall 1984.

Culhane, John

Special Effects in the Movies. New York: Ballantine, 1981. 184 p.

"George Lucas: Skywalker Supreme," Reader's Digest 121(725): 66-70. September 1982. (Condensed from Families, April 1982)

"Last of the 'Nine Old Men,' The," American Film 2(8):10-16. June 1977.

Cullinan, John

"Anthony Burgess' A Clockwork Orange: two versions," English Language Notes 9:287-292. 1972.

"Anthony Burgess' The Muse: a sort of SF story," Studies in Short Fiction 9:213-220. 1972.

"Art of fiction XLVIII: Anthony Burgess, The," Paris Review 56:119-163. 1973.

"Burgess' The Wanting Seed," Explicator 31(7):51-53. March 1973.

Cullum, Paul

"Tony Rothman: a man with his mind on the future," Images (the Daily Texan, University of Texas). October 16, 1978.

Cummings, Sherwood

"Connecticut Yankee in King Arthur's Court, A," in: Magill, Frank N., ed. Survey of Science Fiction Literature, Vol. 1. Englewood Cliffs, NJ: Salem Press, 1979. pp. 428-432.

"Science in fiction and belles-lettres," in: Roucek, Joseph Slabey, ed. The Challenge of Science Education. New York: Philosophical Library, 1959. pp. 411-423.

Cunha, Fausto

"Quen e Vonnegut e Por Que Dizem Essas Coisas dele?" Suplemento do Journal do Brasil. 2(19):2. July 29, 1972.

Cunis, Reinmar

"Wunschbild und Alptraum. Eine soziologische betrachtung moderner literarischer utopien," in: Die neue Gesellschaft 8:219-225. May 1961.

Cunningham, A. M.

"We have seen the future and it is feminine," Mademoiselle 76:140-141,169-170. February 1973.

Cunningham, L. W.

"Chesterton as mystic," American Benedictine Review 26(1):16-24. March 1975.

Curren, Patrick

"Amityville 3D (review)," Cinefantastique 14(3):58. May 1984.

Currey, L. W.

Index to Stories in Thematic Anthologies of Science Fiction, ed. by M. B. Tymn, M. H. Greenberg, L. W. Currey and J. D. Olander. Boston: G. K. Hall, 1978. 193 p.

Research Guide to Science Fiction Studies: An Annotated Checklist of Primary and Secondary Sources for Fantasy and Science Fiction, A, ed. by M. B. Tymn, R. C. Schlobin and L. W. Currey. New York: Garland, 1977. 165 p.

Science Fiction and Fantasy Authors: a Bibliography of First Editions of Their Fiction and Selected Non-fiction. Boston: G. K. Hall, 1979. 571 p.

"Introduction," in: Harben, William N. The Land of the Changing Sun. Boston: Gregg, 1975. pp. v-xiv.

"Reference sources for science fiction," by L. W. Currey and M. B. Tymn. A. B. Bookman's Weekly 76(18):3062-3100. October 28, 1985.

"Science Fiction," in: Carbonneau, Denis, ed. Annual Report of the American Rare, Antiquarian and Out-Of-Print Book Trade, 1978/1979. New York: BCAR Publications, 1979. pp. 80-86.

Curtis, J. L.

"Nouveau genre litteraire, la science fiction, Un," Le Flambeau 54:1-22. 1971.

"Pascal de nos jours lirait de la SF," Arts 15,7,1959.

Curtis, Keith

"Chronological Jack Vance Crime Checklist," Science Fiction: A Review of Speculative Literature 4(2): 79. June 1982.

"Conversation with Roger Zelazny, A," by Terry Dowling and Keith Curtis. Science Fiction: A Review of Speculative Literature 1(2):11-23. June 1978.

"Roger Zelazny: a selected checklist," Science Fiction: a Review of Speculative Literature 1(2):25-26. June 1978.

Curtis, Richard

How to be Your Own Literary Agent. Boston: Houghton, 1983. 162 p.

"Agent's corner, #15," Locus 15(5):7-28. May 1982.

"Agent's corner, No. 10: warranty and idemnity clauses," Locus 14(11):7,28,30. December 1981.

"Agent's corner, No. 19," Locus 15(9):20-21. September 1982.

"Agent's corner," Locus 14(10):9. November 1981.

"Agent's corner," Locus 14(8):9,18. September 1981.

"Agent's Corner: A model royalty statement," Locus 18(4): 9, 44. April 1985.

"Agent's Corner: A Modest Wager," Locus 17(12): 9-11. December 1984.

"Agent's Corner: Acceptability," Locus 18(6): 9-10. June 1985.

"Agent's corner: all about advances," Locus 15(12):7,28. December 1982.

"Agent's Corner: Audits," Locus 18(5): 9-11. May 1985.

"Agent's Corner: Belly-up," Locus 18(11): 9-11. November 1985.

"Agent's Corner: Books Into Movies," Locus 17(10): 9-11. October 1984.

"Agent's Corner: Brand Names," Locus 17(7): 9, 42. July 1984.

"Agent's corner: breaking out," Locus 18(8): 19-21, 48. August 1985.

"Agent's Corner: Building careers," Locus 18(12): 9-11. December 1985.

"Agent's Corner: Clout," Locus 17(8): 9-11. August 1984.

"Agent's corner: collaboration, part 1," Locus 16(2):7-9. February 1983.

"Agent's corner: collaborations, part 2," Locus 16(3):7-8. March 1983.

"Agent's corner: conflicts of interest," Locus 16(9):10. September 1983.

"Agent's corner: contracts," Locus 13(12):1,9,24. December 1980/January 1981.

"Agent's corner: copublishing," Locus 16(11):13-15. November 1983.

"Agent's corner: courtesy," Locus 16(12):13-17. December 1983.

"Agent's corner: dinosaurs," Locus 16(8):7. August 1983.

"Agent's Corner: Good News About Death," Locus 17(4): 9-11. April 1984.

"Agent's corner: Guidelines," Locus 18(10): 9-11. October 1985.

"Agent's Corner: Hardcover vs. Softcover vs. Hard-Soft," Locus 18(7): 9-11. July 1985.

Curtis, Richard (Continued)

"Agent's corner: let's have lunch," <u>Locus</u> 16(10):9,33. October 1983.

"Agent's corner: miscellaneous contractual provisions," <u>Locus</u> 15(7):7,22. July 1982.

"Agent's corner: movie deals, part 1," <u>Locus</u> 15(4):9,20. April 1982.

"Agent's corner: movie deals, part 3," <u>Locus</u> 15(6):7,19. June 1982.

"Agent's Corner: Movies Into Books," <u>Locus</u> 17(11): 9-11. November 1984.

"Agent's corner: multiple submissions and auctions," <u>Locus</u> 15(10):13-14. October 1982.

"Agent's Corner: Multiple-Book Deals," <u>Locus</u> 17(6): 9-11. June 1984.

"Agent's corner: o.p. and reversion," <u>Locus</u> 14(5):9-15. June 1981.

"Agent's corner: on the decline of Western Literature," <u>Locus</u> 17(5):13. May 1984.

"Agent's corner: orphans," <u>Locus</u> 16(4):13,26. April 1983.

"Agent's Corner: Outlines," <u>Locus</u> 17(9): 9-11. September 1984.

"Agent's corner: P & L," <u>Locus</u> 18(2): 9-11, 36. February 1985.

"Agent's corner: Pet Peeves," <u>Locus</u> 18(9): 9-11. September 1985.

"Agent's corner: printings," <u>Locus</u> 15(8):7,19. August 1982.

"Agent's corner: render my statement, tender my check; towards reform, part 2," <u>Locus</u> 16(7):13-15. July 1983.

"Agent's corner: rights," <u>Locus</u> 14(6):9,22. July 1981.

"Agent's Corner: Rivals," <u>Locus</u> 18(1): 11-13. January 1985.

"Agent's corner: royalty rates, part 1," <u>Locus</u> 15(2):7,14. February 1982.

"Agent's corner: royalty rates, part 2," <u>Locus</u> 15(3):9,20. March 1982.

"Agent's corner: royalty statements, part II," <u>Locus</u> 14(2):7-10. March 1981.

"Agent's corner: royalty statements," <u>Locus</u> 14(1):7-10. February 1981.

"Agent's Corner: Sales Conferences," <u>Locus</u> 18(3): 9-11. March 1985.

"Agent's corner: toward reform, part 1," <u>Locus</u> 16(6):7,9. June 1983.

"Agent's Corner: Union Now, Part 1," <u>Locus</u> 17(1): 9-11. January 1984.

"Agent's Corner: Union Now, Part 2," <u>Locus</u> 17(4): 7-8. February 1984.

"Agent's Corner: Union Now, Part 3," <u>Locus</u> 17(3): 9-11. March 1984.

"Agent's corner: warrenty and indemnity clauses, part 1," <u>Locus</u> 15(1):7. January 1982.

"Agent's corner: writers and taxes," <u>Locus</u> 16(1):7-8. January 1983.

Curtoni, Vittorio

<u>Frontiere dell'ignoto, Le: vent'anni de fantascienza italiana</u>. Milan: Nord, 1977. 227 p. (Revision of the author's thesis: La fantascienza italiana dal 1952 a oggi.)

<u>Guida alla fantascienza</u>, by Vittorio Curtoni and Guiseppe Lippe. Milan: Gammalibri, 1978. 221 p.

Curtright, Bob

"Philadelphia Experiment, The," <u>Wichita Eagle Beacon</u> August 24, 1984. in: <u>NewsBank. Film and Television</u> FTV 28:A4. 1984.

Curval, Philippe

"France, terre d'election de la S.F., La," <u>Monde (des Livres)</u> No. 10018:17 April 15, 1977.

"Nouveau desir de lire: Science fiction a la francaise, Un," <u>Monde des Livres</u> No. 10018:1. April 15, 1977.

"Science fiction: Les Maitres actuals du genre," <u>Monde des Livres</u> No. 10018:16. April 15, 1977.

Cziszar, Jolan

<u>Tudomanyos fantasztikus, tipiisztikus fantasztikus muvek bibliografiaja</u>, ed. by Agnes Bezeredy and Jolan Cziszar. Miskolc: Rakoczi, 1979. 434 p.

<u>Utopisztikus, tudomanyos, fantasztikus Muvek bibliografiaja</u>. Miszkolc: Rakoczi, 1970. 159 p.

D

D'Ammassa, Don

"Articulate Eye: Arsan Darnay," <u>Empire: For the SF Writer</u> 4(2): 23-24. February 1979.

"Articulate Eye: Card Tricks," <u>Empire: For the SF Writer</u>. 4(4): 6-7. September 1979.

"Articulate Eye: Humor," <u>Empire: For the SF Writer</u> 3(4): 22. April 1978.

"Articulate Eye: Kevin O'Donnell," <u>Empire: For the SF Writer</u> 4(1): 25. July 1978.

"Articulate Eye: P. J. Plauger," <u>Empire: For the SF Writer</u> 3(1): 12-13. June 1977.

"Articulate Eye: problem stories," <u>Empire for the SF Writer</u> 9(3): 14-15. Spring 1985.

"Articulate Eye: Short Years with Longyear," <u>Empire: For the SF Writer</u> 23: 15-16. Spring 1981.

"Articulate Eye: the Varley variations," <u>Empire: For the SF Writer</u> 3(3): 28-29. November 1977.

"Autoclave Two GOH Speech," <u>Lan's Lantern</u> No. 8: 26-29. March 1979.

"1984: the SF year in review, the best novels of 1984," <u>Science Fiction Chronicle</u> 6(6): 32. March 1985.

"Three by Bachman," in: Schweitzer, Darrell, ed. <u>Discovering Stephen King</u>. Mercer Island: Starmont, 1985. pp. 123-130.

"Young worlds," <u>Mythologies</u> No. 10:5-9. January 1977.

D'Angelo, Carr

"One Hundred Most Important People in Science Fiction/Fantasy: Kurt Vonnegut, jr.," <u>Starlog</u> No. 100: 16. November 1985.

"Science fiction media 1984/85: Television, books, comics," by Robert Greenberger, Chris Henderson, and Carr D'Angelo. <u>Starlog</u> No. 96: 33-37, 92. July 1985.

D'Astorg, Bertrand

"Du Roman d'anticipation," <u>Esprit</u> 202:657-673. May 1953.

"Mensonges et verites de nos anticipations. Du roman d'anticipation," <u>Esprit</u> 21:657-673. 1953.

D'Ivray, Jehan

"J. H. Rosny aine," <u>La Revue Mondiale</u> 150:394-405. 1922.

D'Orso, Mike

"Teenager Computes a Role in Sci-Fi Convention," <u>Norfolk Virginian-Pilot</u> August 15, 1984. in: <u>NewsBank. Social Relations</u> SOC 56:F5-F6. 1984.

Dadoun, Roger

"King Kong: du monstre comme de-monstration," <u>Litteratur</u> No. 8:107- . December 1972.

"Science fiction court apres l'impossible, La," <u>La Quinzaine Litteraire</u> No. 225:7. January 16, 1976.

Daetz, Lily

"Science fiction: a discussion in the Soviet press," <u>Bulletin of the Institute for the Study of the History and Culture of the U. S. S. R.</u> (Munchen) 17(5):36-40. 1970.

Dahlin, Robert

"Ballantine and Random House join their imaginations to publish a fantasy of epic size," <u>Publishers Weekly</u> 211(1):38-39. January 3, 1977.

"Brothers Hildebrandt create first novel: Bantam to publish it in September," <u>Publishers Weekly</u> 215(20):196. May 14, 1979.

"Interview: David Hartwell," <u>Publishers Weekly</u> 221(26): 12-13. June 25, 1982.

Dahlin, Robert (Continued)

"PW interview: Frederik Pohl," <u>Publishers Weekly</u> 214(5):10-11. July 31, 1978.

"Science Fiction: Without Apologies and Without Scrimping on Production," <u>Christian Science Monitor</u> p. B2. March 2, 1984.

Dailey, J. O. M.

<u>Modern Science Fiction</u>. Ph.D. Dissertation, University of Utah, 1974. 75 p.

Dalby, Richard

<u>Bram Stoker: A Bibliography of First Editions</u>. London: Dracular Press, 1983. 156 p.

Dalgaard, Niels

"Den fortraengte natur: Wulff: Danske fanzines," <u>Proxima</u> No. 19, sect. I:12-15. March 1979.

"Kurt Vonnegut interviewed," <u>Arena</u> 8:4-8. October 1978.

"Profeten og symbolerne: tanker omkring <u>Havet</u>," <u>Proxima</u> No. 19, sect. I:25-28. March 1979.

Dalton, Dirk

"Synthesized sound effects for Star Trek: The Motion Picture," <u>American Cinematographer</u> 61(2):160-161,198-199. February 1980.

Dalziel, M. M.

"New maps of science fiction," by W. S. Bainbridge and M. M. Dalziel. in: Bova, Ben, ed. <u>Analog Yearbook</u>. New York: Ace, 1978(c. 1977). pp. 277-299.

"Shape of science fiction as perceived by the fans, The," by W. S. Bainbridge and M. M. Dalziel. <u>Science Fiction Studies</u> 5(2):164-171. July 1978.

Dan, S. P.

<u>Proza fantastica romaneasca</u>. Bucuresti: Minerva, 1975. 354 p.

"Phantastische Prosa Rumaniens, Die," <u>Quarber Merkur</u>. No. 45:62-67. December 1976.

Dand, E.

"Science Fiction in the Novels of Michel Butor," <u>Forum for Modern Language Studies</u>. 18(1): 47-62. January 1982.

Dane, C.

"American fairy tales; science fiction," <u>Fortnightly</u> 145(ns 139):465-470. April 1936. Same, revised: <u>North American Review</u> 242:143-152. September 1936.

Daniels, D.

"2001: a new myth," <u>Film Heritage</u> 3(4):1-11. Summer 1968.

"Skeleton key to 2001," <u>Sight and Sound</u> 40(1):28-33. Winter 1970/1971.

Daniels, Steve

"Warp,", <u>Prevue</u> 2(4):43-46. February/March 1981.

Dann, Jack

"A Few Sparks in the Dark," <u>Starship</u> 19(1): 7-13. November 1982.

"Dreaming again," by Jack Dann and George Zebrowski. in: Dann, Jack and George Zebrowski, eds. <u>Faster Than Light</u>. New York: Ace, 1976. pp. xiii-xviii.

Darby, George

"World Beyond Star Wars," <u>The Sunday Times Magazine</u> p. 38-43. April 11, 1982.

Dard, Roger

"Science fiction boom on in Australia," <u>Fantasy Times</u> No. 236:3,8. December (1) 1955.

"Science fiction in Australia," <u>Fantasy Times</u> No. 254:11-13. September (1) 1956.

Darlington, Andy

"Knight without limit: an overview of the work of Barrington Bayley," <u>Arena</u> 10:4-12. April 1980.

"M. John Harrison: The Condition of falling; Interview," <u>Vector</u> 122: 3-5. 1984.

"Many faces of Adlard, The," <u>Arena</u> 7:12-25. March 1978.

"Philip E. High: the man who created the wooden spaceships," <u>Vector</u> 83:26-29. September/October 1977.

"Terminal choreography: an overview of Michael Moorcock's Dancers at the End of Time stories," <u>Vector</u> 88:20-25. July/August 1978.

Darlington, Andy (Continued)

"Two Days in Leeds with Kurt Vonnegut," Science Fiction Review 13(1): 8-11. February 1984.

Darnay, Arsen

"Future is the past, The," SFWA Bulletin 13(4):11-13. Fall 1978.

Darrach, Brad

"Back to the gore of yore; reprinting of Doc Savage stories," Time 98(1):70-71. July 5, 1971.

"It's an Asimovalanche: the one man book-a-month club has just published his 179th," People pp. 110-112,117-118. November 22, 1976.

Darvell, M.

"High on sci-fi: LRG encounters with Strick, Philip," Film 60:9. April 1978.

Daso, Don

"Special Effects in Star Wars," by Peter Lehman and Don Daso. Wide Angle 1(1): 72-77. 1979. (Revised)

Dautzenberg, J. A.

"Science Fiction en literatuurwetenschap: geschiedenis, problemen, bibliografie," Forum der Lettern 21(1):1-27. 1980.

"Survey of Dutch and Flemish Science Fiction, A," Science-Fiction Studies 8(2): 173-186. July 1981.

"Theorien over de fantastische literatuur," Revisor (Netherlands) 8(5): 2-9. October 1981.

Davenport, Basil

Inquiry Into Science Fiction. New York: Longmans, Green, 1955. 87 p.

Science Fiction Novel: Imagination and Social Criticism, The. Chicago: Advent, 1959. 128 p.

"Devil is not dead," Saturday Review of Literature 13:3-4. February 15, 1936.

"Vision of Olaf Stapledon," in: Stapledon, Olaf. To The End of Time. New York: Funk, 1953. pp. viii-xvi. (Reprinted, Gregg, 1975.)

Davenport, Guy

"Hobbitry," in: Davenport, Guy. The Geography of the Imagination. San Francisco: North Point Press, 1981. pp. 336-338.

David, B. R.

"Anthony Burgess: a checklist (1956-1971)," Twentieth Century Literature 19(3):181-188. July 1973.

David, Saul

"Behind the scene of Logan's Run," American Cinematographer 57(6):636-637, 674-675,702-705. June 1976.

Davidson, Avram

"Clarion Call," Science Fiction Review 13(3): 39-41. August 1984.

Davidson, Bill

"From the pages of comic books . . . ." TV Guide 25(5):24-26. January 29, 1977.

Davidson, D. A.

"Fantasy literature: a high interest unit for junior high," Cthulhu Calls 4(4):30-31. April 1977.

"Sword and sorcery fiction: an annotated book list," English Journal 61(1):43-51. January 1972.

Davidson, E. S.

"Doc Savage Series," in: Magill, Frank N., ed. Survey of Modern Fantasy Literature, Vol 1. Englewood Cliffs, NJ: Salem Press, Inc., 1983. pp. 401-403.

"Empire of the East," in: Magill, Frank N., ed. Survey of Modern Fantasy Literature, Vol 1. Englewood Cliffs, NJ: Salem Press, Inc., 1983. pp. 478-482.

"Peter Ibbetson," in: Magill, Frank N., ed. Survey of Modern Fantasy Literature, Vol 3. Englewood Cliffs, NJ: Salem Press, Inc., 1983. pp. 1227-1229.

"Sorcerer's Skull, The," in: Magill, Frank N., ed. Survey of Modern Fantasy Literature, Vol 4. Englewood Cliffs, NJ: Salem Press, Inc., 1983. pp. 1777-1779.

Davidson, Laurence

"Interview with Stanton A. Coblentz," by Lawrence Davidson and R. A. Lupoff. <u>Locus</u> 12(11):10-11. December 1979.

"Rigel Interviews Anne McCaffrey," by Richard Wolinsky and Laurence Davidson. <u>Rigel Science Fiction</u> 3: 19-24. Winter 1982.

Davidson, Mark

"Look forward to encountering new neighbors, A," by Mark Davidson and Nirmali Ponnamperuma. <u>Science Digest</u> 83(2):8-11. February 1978.

Davies, Dorothy

"What Every Good Writer Should Know," <u>Focus: An SF Writers' Magazine</u> No. 8: 21-22. Autumn 1983.

"Who Needs Writing Organizations?" <u>Focus</u> 6: 26-27. Autumn 1982.

Davies, H. N.

"<u>Symzonia</u> and <u>The Man in the Moon</u>," <u>Notes and Queries</u> 213:342-345. September 1968.

"Bishop Godwin's 'Lunatique Language'," <u>Warburg and Courtauld Institute Journal</u> 30:296-316. 1967.

Davies, Owen

"Scenes of future perfect," <u>Omni</u> 7(8): 76-78. May 1985.

Davis, Chandler

"Change, SF and Marxism: open or closed universes? Thesis, antithesis, synthesis," <u>Science Fiction Studies</u> 1(2):92-94. Fall 1973.

Davis, D. D.

"Aldous Huxley: a bibliography 1965-1973," <u>Bulletin of Bibliography</u> 31(2):67-70. April/June 1974.

Davis, Grania

"Japanese microcon," <u>Locus</u> 12(11):11-12. December 1979.

Davis, Hassold

"Lord Dunsany tells how," <u>Writer's Digest</u> 9(7):26-27. June 1929.

Davis, Howard

"Ainulindale: Music of Creation," <u>Mythlore</u> 9(2): 6-10. Summer 1982.

Davis, Ivor

"Cutting 'Close Encounters' a bit too close," <u>Los Angeles</u> 22:250-251. November 1977.

Davis, J. C.

"History of Utopia: the chronology of Nowhere," in: <u>Utopias</u>, ed. by Peter Alexander and Roger Gill. London: Duckworth, 1984. pp. 1-18.

Davis, J. L.

<u>James Branch Cabell</u>. New York: Twayne Publishers, 1962. 174 p.

Davis, K. C.

<u>Two-Bit Culture: The Paperbacking of America</u>. Boston: Houghton Mifflin, 1984. 430 p.

Davis, K. W.

"You're the only ones who'll talk about the <u>really</u> terrific changes going on: speculative fiction and rites of passage," in: Samuelson, D. N. <u>Science Fiction and Future Studies</u>. Bryan, TX: SFRA, 1975. pp. 94-99.

Davis, Ken

"<u>Shape of Things to Come, The</u>: H. G. Wells and the Rhetoric of Protest," in: Rabkin, Eric S., et. al., eds. <u>No Place Else</u>. Carbondale: Southern Illinois University Press, 1983. pp. 110-124.

Davis, R. M.

"Frontiers of Genre, The: Science Fiction Westerns," <u>Science Fiction Studies</u> 12(1): 33-41. March 1985.

Davis, Richard

<u>Encyclopedia of Horror</u>. London: Octopus, 1981. 192 p.

Davis, Scott

"'Triffids' Revisited," by S. J. Maronie and Scott Davis. <u>Starlog</u> 56: 46-47. March 1982.

Davis, Wolfgang

"Brutalitat in der Gormenghast-Trilogie des Mervyn Peake," Quarber Merkur 61: 11-28. July 1984.

Davison, Peter

"What Orwell really wrote," in: George Orwell and Nineteen Eighty-Four. Washington, DC: Library of Congress, 1985. pp. 5-21.

Day, B. M.

Bibliography of Adventure: Mundy, Burroughs, Rohmer, Haggard. Denver, New York: Science Fiction and Fantasy Publications, 1964. 125 p.

Checklist of Fantastic Literature in Paperbound Books, The. Denver, New York: Science Fiction and Fantasy Publications, 1965. 128 p. Reprinted, New York: Arno Press, 1975.

Complete Checklist of Science Fiction Magazines, The. Woodhaven, New York: Science Fiction and Fantasy Publications, 1961. 63 p.

Edgar Rice Burroughs Biblio. Materials Toward a Bibliography . . . . New York: Science Fiction and Fantasy Publications, 1956. 28 p.

Edgar Rice Burroughs, a Bibliography. Woodhaven, New York: Science Fiction and Fantasy Publications, 1962. 45 p.

Index on the Weird & Fantastica in Magazines, An. South Ozone Park, New York: by the author, 1953. 162 p.

Sax Rohmer: a Bibliography. Denver, New York: Science Fiction and Fantasy Publications, 1963. 34 p.

Supplemental Checklist of Fantastic Literature, The. Denver, New York: Science Fiction and Fantasy Publications, 1963. 155 p.

Talbot Mundy Biblio. Materials Toward a Bibliography of the Works of Talbot Mundy. New York: Science Fiction and Fantasy Publications, 1955. 28 p.

Day, D. B.

Index to the Science Fiction Magazines 1926-1950. Portland, Oregon: Perri Press, 1952. 184 p.

Index to the Science Fiction Magazines: 1926-1950, Revised ed. Boston: G. K. Hall, 1982. 289 p.

Day, David

Tolkien Bestiary. New York: Ballantine, 1979. 287 p.

Day, F. W.

Role and Purpose of the Map in Science Fiction and Fantasy Literature. Masters Thesis, Bowling Green State University, 1979. 47 p.

Day, M. S.

"Imaginary vs. imaginative literature," English in Texas 1:75-83. 1965.

Day, N. G.

"Freaking the Mundane: A Sociological Look at Science Fiction Conventions, and Vice Versa," by P. J. Day and N. G. Day. in: Hassler, Donald M. Patterns of the Fantastic. Mercer Island, WA: Starmont, 1983. pp. 91-102.

Day, P. J.

"Earthmother/Witchmother: Feminism and Ecology Renewed," Extrapolation 23(1): 12-21. Spring 1982.

"Freaking the Mundane: A Sociological Look at Science Fiction Conventions, and Vice Versa," by P. J. Day and N. G. Day. in: Hassler, Donald M. Patterns of the Fantastic. Mercer Island, WA: Starmont, 1983. pp. 91-102.

"Love and the Technocracy: Dehumanization in Social Welfare," in: Erlich, Richard D., ed. Clockwork Worlds. Westport, CT: Greenwood, 1983. pp. 195-211.

De Araujo, Victor

Short Story of Fantasy: Henry James, H. G. Wells and E. M. Forster. Ph.D. Dissertation, University of Washington, 1965. 276 p.

De Bolt, Denise

"Brunner bibliography, A," by Joe de Bolt and Denise de Bolt. in: De Bolt, Joe, ed. Happening Worlds of John Brunner. Port Washington, NY: Kennikat, 1975. pp. 195-209.

De Bolt, Joe

Happening Worlds of John Brunner, The. Port Washington, New York: Kennikat Press, 1975. 216 p.

Ursula K. Le Guin: Voyager to Inner Lands and to Outer Space. Port Washington, NY: Kennikat, 1979. 221 p.

"Brunner bibliography, A," by Joe de Bolt and Denise de Bolt. in: De Bolt, Joe, ed. Happening Worlds of John Brunner. Port Washington, NY: Kennikat, 1975. pp. 195-209.

De Bolt, Joe (Continued)

"Computer and man, The: the human use of non-human beings in the works of John Brunner," by E. L. Lamie and Joe de Bolt. in: De Bolt, Joe, ed. Happening Worlds of John Brunner. Port Washington, NY: Kennikat, 1975. pp. 167-176.

"Development of John Brunner, The," in: Clareson, Thomas D., ed. Voices for the Future: Essays on Major Science Fiction Writers, vol. 2. Bowling Green, Ohio: Bowling Green University Popular Press, 1979. pp. 106-135.

"Introduction to John Brunner and his works, An," in: De Bolt, Joe, ed. Happening Worlds of John Brunner. Port Washington, NY: Kennikat, 1975. pp. 11-59.

"Le Guin biography, A," in: De Bolt, Joe, ed. Ursula K. Le Guin: Voyager to Inner Lands and to Outer Space. Port Washington, New York: Kennikat, 1979. pp. 13-28.

"Le Guin Biography," Empire: For the SF Writer 3(4): 23-28. April 1978.

"Modern Period, The: 1938-1980," by Joe De Bolt and John Pfeiffer. in: Barron, Neil, ed. Anatomy of Wonder. 2nd ed. New York: Bowker, 1981. pp. 125-334.

"Outstanding Science Fiction Books: 1927-1979," in: Tymn, Marshall B., ed. The Science Fiction Reference Book. Mercer Island, WA: Starmont House, 1981. pp. 291-337.

"Patterns of science fiction readership among academics," Extrapolation 19(2):112-125. May 1978.

"Sam Moskowitz: Scholar of the Sense of Wonder," in: Wolfe, Gary, ed. Science Fiction Dialogues. Chicago: Academy Chicago, 1982. pp. 172-180. (Reprinted from SFRA Newsletter)

"Sam Moskowitz: Scholar With A Sense of Wonder," SFRA Newsletter 97:(insert) p. 3-9. December 1981.

De Bono, Edward

"Lateral thinking and science fiction," in: Nicholls, Peter, ed. Science Fiction at Large. New York: Harper, 1976. pp. 35-56.

De Camp, L. S.

Blade of Conan. New York: Ace, 1979. 310 p.

Blond Barbarians and Noble Savages. Baltimore: T-K Graphics, 1975. 45 p.

Conan Grimore, The, ed. by L. S. De Camp and G. H. Scithers. Baltimore: Mirage Press, 1972. 263 p.

Conan Reader, The. Baltimore: Mirage Press, 1968. 149 p.

Conan Swordbook: 27 Examinations of Heroic Fiction, The. Baltimore: Mirage Press, 1969. 259 p.

Literary Swordsmen and Sorcerers: the Makers of Heroic Fantasy. Sauk City, Wisconsin: Arkham House, 1976. 313 p.

Lovecraft: A Biography. Garden City: Doubleday, 1975. 510 p.

Miscast Barbarian: A Biography of Robert E. Howard (1906-1936), The. Saddle River, New Jersey: Gerry De La Ree, 1975. 43 p.

Science Fiction Handbook: the Writing of Imaginative Fiction. New York: Hermitage House, 1953. 328 p. Revised edition: Science Fiction Handbook, Revised. Philadelphia: Owlswick Press, 1975. 220 p.

"Care & feeding of mad scientists, The," Astounding 47(5):128-140. July 1951.

"Compleat duelist," in: De Camp, L. S., ed. Blade of Conan. New York: Ace, 1979. pp. 261-262.

"Development of a science fiction writer: V, The," Foundation 4:25-27. July 1973.

"Editing Conan," in: De Camp, L. S., ed. Blade of Conan. New York: Ace, 1979. pp. 113-121.

"Fletcher Pratt, a friend," Fantasy Times No. 250:1,4-5. July (1) 1956.

"Howard and the races," in: De Camp, L. S., ed. Blade of Conan. New York: Ace, 1979. pp. 127-129.

"Hyborian technology," in: De Camp, L. S., ed. Blade of Conan. New York: Ace, 1979. pp. 51-65.

"Imaginative fiction and creative imagination," in: Bretnor, Reginald, ed. Modern Science Fiction: Its Meaning and Its Future. New York: Coward McCann, 1953. Reprinted, Chicago: Advent, 1979. pp. 119-154.

"Informal biography of Conan the Cimmerian," by J. D. Clark, P. S. Miller, and L. S. de Camp. in: De Camp, L. S., ed. Blade of Conan. New York: Ace, 1979. pp. 9-44.

"J. R. R. Tolkien," Locus No. 149:2. September 14, 1973.

"John W. Campbell," Locus No. 91:8. July 22, 1971.

"Language for time travelers," in: Greenberg, M. H., ed. Coming Attractions. New York: Gnome, 1957. pp. 52-61.

De Camp, L. S. (Continued)

"Memories of R.E.H.," in: De Camp, L. S., ed. <u>Blade of Conan</u>. New York: Ace, 1979. pp. 91-98.

"Mundy's Vendhya," in: De Camp, L. S., ed. <u>Blade of Conan</u>. New York: Ace, 1979. pp. 183-188.

"Professionalism," <u>Algol</u> 14(4):17-20. Fall 1976/Winter 1977.

"R. E. Howard notes (letter)," <u>Fantasy Times</u> No. 262:5,7. January (1) 1957.

"Range," in: De Camp, L. S., ed. <u>Blade of Conan</u>. New York: Ace, 1979. pp. 227-232.

"Ranging afterthoughts," in: De Camp, L. S., ed. <u>Blade of Conan</u>. New York: Ace, 1979. pp. 243-247.

"Recurrent concepts," in: Ash, Brian, ed. <u>Visual Encyclopedia of Science Fiction</u>. New York: Harmony, 1977. pp. 263-271.

"Scientist, The," by L. S. De Camp and T. D. Clareson. in: Warrick, Patricia, ed. <u>Science Fiction: Contemporary Mythology</u>. New York: Harper, 1978. pp. 196-206.

"Stirrups and scholarship," in: De Camp, L. S., ed. <u>Blade of Conan</u>. New York: Ace, 1979. pp. 139-141.

De Faccio, Jerry

"MAD," <u>Science Fiction Times</u> No. 369:15-16. September 1961.

De la Ree, Gerry

<u>After Ten Years: A Tribute to Stanley G. Weinbaum, 1902-1935</u>, ed. by Gerry de la Ree and Sam Moskowitz. Westwood, New Jersey: Gerry de la Ree, 1945. 30 p.

<u>Index to Novels in the SF Mags, An</u>. River Edge, New Jersey: by the author, 1962. (not seen)

<u>Virgil Finlay Remembered</u>. Saddle River, NJ: de la Ree, 1981. 127 p.

"Dean of the science fiction illustrators," <u>Science Fiction Times</u> No. 405:3-4,10. August 1963.

"Introduction," in: Hamilton, Edmond. <u>The Horror on the Asteroid</u>. Boston: Gregg, 1975. pp. v-ix.

"Virgil Finlay checklist, A," in: Finley, Virgil. <u>Virgil Finlay</u>. West Kingston, RI: Grant, 1971. pp. 95-153.

"Virgil Finlay: master of fantasy," <u>Starlog</u> 14:28-33. June 1978.

De Lacy, Justine

"Orwell Literary Cache Discovered," <u>New York Times</u> p. 25. June 12, 1984.

De Larber, N. S.

"<u>Venture Science Fiction</u> (1957-1958; 1969-1970)," in: Tymn, M. B. and Ashley, Mike. <u>Science Fiction, Fantasy, and Weird Fiction Magazines</u>. Westport, CT: Greenwood, 1985. pp. 705-709.

De Turris, Gianfranco

"Uncommon market: toward a European SF," by Gianfranco de Turris and Sebastino Fusco. <u>Australian Science Fiction Review</u> No. 14:3-5. February 1968.

De Vos, Luk

<u>Science Fiction: Status of Status Quo?</u> Antwerpen/Gent: Restant Uitgaven, 1977. 214 p.

<u>Zucht van de Zombie, De</u>. Antwerp: EXA, 1985. 112 p.

"Science fiction as trivialliteratur: some methodological considerations," <u>Comparative Literature Studies</u> 14(1):4-19. March 1977.

De Voto, B.

"Doom beyond Jupiter: the science pulps," <u>Harper</u> 179:445-448. September 1939.

De Wohl, L.

"Religion, philosophy and outer space," <u>America</u> 151:420-421. July 24, 1954.

Dean, J. F.

"Between 2001 and Star Wars: science fiction films," <u>Journal of Popular Film and Television</u> 7(1):32-41. 1978. Comment: 7(3):322-325. 1979.

Dean, John

"French science fiction: the intergalactic European connection," <u>Stanford French Review</u> 3(3):405-416. Winter 1979.

"Immigrant of darkness, The: the vampire in American fiction," <u>Foundation</u> 33: 19-24. Spring 1985.

"Science Fiction City, The" <u>Foundation</u> 23: 64-72. October 1981.

Dean, John (Continued)

"Uses of Wilderness in American Science Fiction, The," <u>Science Fiction Studies</u> 9(1): 68-81. March 1982.

Dean, Martyn

<u>Guide to Fantasy Art Techniques</u>. New York: Arco, 1984. 111 p.

Deasy, Philip

"God, space, and C. S. Lewis," <u>Commonweal</u> 68(18):421-423. August 1, 1958.

Decker, Andreas

"Cabbage setzt sich zur Wehr, Der, or, The Kraut Strikes Back: A Survey of SF in West Germany, 1950 to Now," <u>Fantasy Review</u> 7(1): 37-38, 54. January 1984

Decottignies, Jean

"Reflexions sur un genre appele 'fantastique'," in: Colin, A. <u>Le Reel et le texte</u> pp. 243-252.

Decoufle, A. C.

"S. F. et prospective," <u>Europe</u> 580/581:53-57. August/September 1977.

Deeb, Gary

"NBC Taking Science-Fiction Trip to Better Ratings," <u>New Orleans Times-Picayune</u> Sec. D, p. 5. August 22, 1984.

"NBC Will Grab For Sci-Fi Brass Ring," <u>New Orleans Times-Picayune</u> Sec. EP, p. 6. July 3, 1984.

DeFord, M. A.

"Science fiction comes of age," <u>Humanist</u> 17(6):323-326. November/December 1950.

"Word in advance, A," in: Deford, Miriam Allen. <u>Elsewhere, Elsewhen, Elsehow</u>. New York: Walker, 1971. pp. ix-v.

DeForest, Lee

"Introduction," in: Gernsback, Hugo. <u>Ralph 24C41+: A Romance of the Year 2660</u>. New York: Frederick Fell, 1950. pp. 15-19.

Degaudenzi, J. L.

"Mythe et realite: le veritable Dracula," <u>Midi-Minuit Fantastique</u> No. 27:74.

Deisch, Noel

"Navigation of space in early speculation and in modern research, The," <u>Popular Astronomy</u> 38(1):73-88. January 1930.

Deitz, T. F.

"<u>Foundling and Other Tales of Prydain, The</u>," in: Magill, Frank N., ed. <u>Survey of Modern Fantasy Literature</u>, Vol 2. Englewood Cliffs, NJ: Salem Press, Inc., 1983. pp. 571-574.

"<u>Merman's Children, The</u>," in: Magill, Frank N., ed. <u>Survey of Modern Fantasy Literature</u>, Vol 2. Englewood Cliffs, NJ: Salem Press, Inc., 1983. pp. 1021-1024.

DeJaynes, R. L.

"Making of things other than the self," <u>Mythlore</u> 9(3):15-18. Autumn 1982.

Del Rey, J. L.

"Science fiction explosion, The," <u>Top of the News</u> 34(1):53-58. Fall 1977.

Del Rey, Lester

<u>World of Science Fiction, The</u>. New York: Ballantine/Del Rey, 1979. 416 p.

"Best of sci-fi," <u>Chemistry</u> 51:28-30. November 1978.

"Farewell to the master," <u>Locus</u> No. 90:2-4. July 12, 1971.

"Forum: the siren song of academe," <u>Galaxy</u> 36(3):69-80. March 1975.

"Frederik Pohl, frontiers man," <u>Magazine of Fantasy and Science Fiction</u> 45(3):55-64. September 1973.

"Galactic empires," in: Ash, Brian, ed. <u>Visual Encyclopedia of Science Fiction</u>. New York: Harmony, 1977. pp. 110-115.

"Hand at issue, The," <u>Magazine of Fantasy and Science Fiction</u> 42(4):72-77. April 1972.

"J. R. R. Tolkien," <u>Locus</u> No. 149:2. September 14, 1973.

"Of destiny and wonder," in: Campbell, John W. <u>John W. Campbell Anthology: Three Novels</u>. Garden City, NY: Doubleday, 1973. pp. xi-xv.

Del Rey, Lester (Continued)

"Rebellion: the new wave and art,"
Starship 16(4):25-28. Fall 1979.

"Three Careers of John W. Campbell," in:
Campbell, John W. The Best of John W.
Campbell. New York: Ballantine, 1976. pp.
ix-xv.

Del Valle, Cezar

"Steely-Eyed Workaholics Dance Across the
Screen," InfoWorld 4(48): 30-32, 34.
December 6, 1982.

Delany, S. R.

American Shore: Meditations on a Tale of
Science Fiction by Thomas M. Disch.
Elizabethtown, NY: Dragon, 1978. 243 p.

Jewel-Hinged Jaw: Notes on the Language of
Science Fiction, The. Elizabethtown, New
York: Dragon Press, 1977. 326 p. Reprinted,
New York: Berkley, 1978. 303 p.

Starboard Wine: More Notes on the Language of
Science Fiction. Hastings-on-Hudson, NY:
Dragon, 1984. 244 p.

"1985 Pilgrim Award acceptance speech," SFRA
Newsletter 133: 7-15. August 1985.

"About five thousand one hundred and seventy
five words," Extrapolation 10(2):52-66.
May 1969. also in: Hay, George, ed. The
Disappearing Future. pp. 130-145. Clareson,
T. D., ed. SF: The Other Side of Realism.
pp. 130-146.

"Critical methods: speculative fiction," in:
Delany, S. R., ed. Quark #1. N. Y.:
Paperback Library, 1970. pp. 182-195. also
in: Clareson, T. D., ed. Many Futures, Many
Worlds. Kent State Univ. Press, 1977. pp.
278-291.

"Discourse of Science Fiction, The" SFWA
Bulletin 16(2): 27-35. Spring 1981.

"In the once upon a time city," Locus
18(2): 21-22. February 1985.

"Profession of science fiction: VIII:
shadows: part 1, The," Foundation
6:31-60. May 1974.

"Profession of science fiction: VIII:
shadows: part 2, The," Foundation
7/8:122-154. March 1975.

"Reflections on historical models of modern
English language science fiction," Science
Fiction Studies 7(2):135-149. July 1980.

"Science fiction and 'literature', or, the
conscience of the king," Analog 99(5):
59-78. May 1979.

"Significance of Science Fiction,, The"
Michigan Quarterly Review 20(3): 224-235.
Spring 1981.

"Some Reflections on SF Criticism," Science
Fiction Studies 8(3): 233-239. November
1981.

"Theodore Sturgeon in Memoriam, 10," Locus
18(7): 29. July 1985.

"Thickening the plot," in: Wilson, Robin
Scott, ed. Those Who Can. New York:
Mentor/New American Library, 1973. pp. 70-77.

"When is a paradox not a paradox?"
Foundation 7/8:100-102. March 1975.

Delap, Richard

"Smoke and glass: a nonfiction fantasy about
Harlan Ellison," Science Fiction Review
4:6-12. February 1975.

"Tomorrow's libido: sex and science fiction,"
The Alien Critic 3(1):5-12. February 1974.

Delcourt, Christian

"Quelques aspects do la science fiction et du
fantasique," Ecritures 73:7-20. 1973.

"S. F. et recit. c) Metamorphoses de la S.
F.," Europe 580/581:113-119.
August/September 1977.

Delcourt, Xavier

"Pour Michel Butor, les frontieres entre
science fiction et litterature tendent a
s'effacer," (Interview) La Quinzaine
Litteraire No. 225:5-7. January 16, 1976.

DelFattore, Joan

"James Bond fantasy, The," in: Magill, Frank
N., ed. Survey of Modern Fantasy
Literature, Vol 5. Englewood Cliffs, NJ:
Salem Press, Inc., 1983. pp. 2492-2500.

Dell, F.

"Phantasy and fiction," Child Study
9:187-190. March 1932.

Delmas, Henri

Rayon SF, Le. Catalogue bibliogaphique de
science-fiction, utopies, voyages
extraordinaires. by Henri Delmas and Alain
Julian. Toulouse: Editions Milan, 1983. 331 p.

Delson, James

"Arts, The: film," _Omni_ 2(2):20-24. November 1979.

DeLuca, Geraldine

"State of the field in contemporary children's fantasy, an interview with George Woods, The," _The Lion and the Unicorn_ 1(2):4-16. 1978.

DeMott, Benjamin

"Vonnegut's otherworldly laughter," _Saturday Review_ 54(18):29-32,38. May 1, 1971.

Dempewolff, R. F.

"2001; backstage magic for a trip to Saturn," _Popular Mechanics_ 127:106-109. April 1967.

"How they made 2001," _Science Digest_ 63:34-39. May 1968. (Reprint from _Popular Mechanics_)

Demuth, Michel

"Voyage a Ellisonland," _Magazine Litteraire_ 88:16-18. May 1974.

Denholm, W. J., III

"Lancer Science Fiction Checklist (Including Lodestone and Magnum Books)," _Megavore_ 10: 4-31. August, 1980.

"Robert E. Howard Lancer paperback collector's checklist, The," _P. S. F. Q._ (Cupertino, California) No. 3/4:16-20. 1978/1979.

Denkena, K. S.

"Dragon oder 'Sein Ziel war es, die Alter Ordnung wieder herzustellen," _Science-Fiction Times_ (Bremerhaven) No. 136:11-16. May 1975.

Dennerstein, Robert

"Defender of unbridled imagination," _Rocky Mountain News_ November 8, 1981. in: _NewsBank. Film and Television._ 56: B1-2. July/December 1981.

Denny, R.

"Reactors of the imagination," _Bulletin of the Atomic Scientists_ 9:206-210. July 1953.

DePrez, Daniel

"Interview with John Varley, An," _Science Fiction Review_ 6:8-14. August 1977.

"Interview with Philip K. Dick: conducted September 10, 1976, An," _Science Fiction Review_ No. 19:6-12. August 1976. (issue identified on contents page as vol. 5, no. 3, whole no. 18)

Derleth, A. W.

100 Books by August Derleth. Sauk City, Wisconsin: Arkham House, 1962. 121 p.

H. P. L.: A Memoir. New York: Ben Abramson, 1945. 123 p.

Some Notes on H. P. Lovecraft. Sauk City, Wisconsin: Arkham House, 1959, 62 p. Reprinted, Folcroft, Pennsylvania: Folcroft Press, 1974.

Thirty Years of Arkham House 1939-1969. Sauk City, Wisconsin: Arkham House, 1970. 99 p.

Twenty-five years of writing, 1925-1951. Sauk City, Wisconsin: Arkham House, 1952.

"Bibliography of representative science fiction since 1940," _English Journal_ 41:7-8. January 1952.

"Contemporary science fiction," _College English_ 13(4):187-194. January 1952. also in: _English Journal_ 41(1):7-8. January 1952.

"Fantastic Story, The" in: Boyer, Robert H. and Zahorski, Kenneth J. _Fantasists on Fantasy._ New York: Avon Discus, 1984. pp. 95-110.

"Fantastic story, The," in: Derleth, August W. _Writing Fiction._ Boston: Writer, 1946. pp. 130-143.

"Final notes," in: Lovecraft, H. P. _The Dark Brotherhood and Other Pieces._ Sauk City, Wisconsin: Arkham House, 1966. p. 302.

"H. P. Lovecraft, outsider," _River_ 1:88-90,95. 1937. (not seen)

"H. P. Lovecraft: the making of a literary reputation, 1937-1971," _Books at Brown_ 25:13-25. 1977.

"Horror fiction," _Writer_ 58(5):134-137. May 1945.

"Making of a hoax, The," in: Lovecraft, H. P. _The Dark Brotherhood and Other Pieces._ Sauk City, Wisconsin: Arkham House, 1966. pp. 262-267.

"Science fiction story, The," in: Derleth, August W. _Writing Fiction._ Boston: Writer, 1946. pp. 119-130.

Dermon, E. S.

"Happiness in Vonnegut's Euphio," Media & Methods 13(3):36-37. November 1976.

Derry, Charles

"Horror of personality," Cinefantastique 3(3):15-27. Fall 1974.

Derus, D. L.

"Chesterton and W. B. Yeats: vision, system and rhetoric," Chesterton Review 3:197-214. 1976.

Dervin, Daniel

"Primal conditions and Conventions: The Genres of Comedy and Science Fiction," Film Psychology Review 4(1): 115-147. Winter/Spring 1980.

Descamps, Cristian

"Speculative Fiction active les 'productions desirantes, La," La Quinzaine Litteraire No. 225:15-16. January 16, 1976.

Desimond, Michel

"Afterword," Riverside Quarterly 4(1): 48-51. August 1969.

Desmond, W. H.

Science Fiction Magazine Checklist 1961-1972. South Boston, MA: Desmond, 1973. 16 p.

"SF magazine checklist, The," Science Fiction Times (Boston) 1(5):22. November 1979.

"SF magazine checklist," Science Fiction Times (Boston) 1(7):22. March 1980.

"SF magazine checklist: A. Merritt's Fantasy Magazine; Ace Mystery Magazine, Air Wonder Stories, Amazing Stories, The," Science Fiction Times (Boston) 1(4):15. August 1979.

Desroches, H.

"Petite bibliotheque de l'utopie," Esprit 42:663-670. 1974.

Detter, J. W.

"Recommended: Rosemary Sutcliff," English Journal 74(7):83-84. November 1985.

Deutsch, Michael

"Lovecraft ou la mythologie," Esprit September 1957.

"Ray Bradbury et la poesie du futur," Critique No. 22:608-609. July 1957.

Devaux, Pierre

"Colonisation de planetes est-elle possible, La?" La Revue Francaise No. 56:21-25. May 1954.

DeVitis, A. A.

Anthony Burgess. New York: Twayne, 1972.

Devoe, A.

"Scientification," American Mercury 77:26-29. August 1953.

DeVore, Howard

"Bizarre," in: Tymn, M. B. and Ashley, Mike. Science Fiction, Fantasy, and Weird Fiction Magazines. Westport, CT: Greenwood, 1985. pp. 143-145.

"Fanciful Tales of Time and Space," in: Tymn, M. B. and Ashley, Mike. Science Fiction, Fantasy, and Weird Fiction Magazines. Westport, CT: Greenwood, 1985. pp. 219-221.

"Miracle Science and Fantasy Stories," in: Tymn, M. B. and Ashley, Mike. Science Fiction, Fantasy, and Weird Fiction Magazines. Westport, CT: Greenwood, 1985. pp. 410-413.

"Hugos Nobody Knows, The," World Science Fiction Convention, 34th Kansas City. MidAmericon Program Book. Kansas City: MidAmericon, 1976. pp. 39-40.

"Literary Awards in Science Fiction," in: Tymn, Marshall B., ed. The Science Fiction Reference Book. Mercer Island, WA: Starmont House, 1981. pp. 215-224.

"T. L. Sherred: An Appreciation," Locus 18(7): 52. July 1985.

Dezso, Toth

"Roviden a science fictionrol," SF Tajekoztato p. 8-9. July 1971.

Dick, P. K.

"Android and the Human," Vector 64: 5-20. March/April 1973.

Dick, P. K. (Continued)

"How to build a universe that doesn't fall apart two days later," in: Dick, P. K. I Hope I Shall Arrive Soon. Garden City, NY: Doubleday, 1985. pp. 1-23.

"Introduction: The Golden Man," in: Dick, P. K. The Golden Man. New York: Berkley, 1980. pp. xv-xxvii.

"Letters from Amerika," Vector 75: 16-20. July 1975.

"Man, android and machine," in: Nicholls, Peter, ed. Science Fiction at Large. New York: Harper, 1976. pp. 199-224.

"Now Wait For This Year," in: Greenberg, Martin H., ed. Philip K. Dick. New York: Taplinger, 1982. pp. 215-227.

"Profession of science fiction: XVII: the lucky dog pet store, The," Foundation 17:41-49. September 1979.

"Who is an SF writer," in: McNelly, W. E., ed. Science Fiction the Academic Awakening. Shreveport, LA: CEA, 1974. pp. 46-50.

"[Unpublished] forward to The Preserving Machine," Science Fiction Studies 2(1):22-23. March 1975.

Dickholtz, Daniel

"One Hundred Most Important People in Science Fiction/Fantasy: Andre Norton," Starlog No. 100: 14-15. November 1985.

"One Hundred Most Important People in Science Fiction/Fantasy: E. E. Smith," Starlog No. 100: 31-32. November 1985.

"One Hundred Most Important People in Science Fiction/Fantasy: Fritz Lang," Starlog No. 100: 62-63. November 1985.

"One Hundred Most Important People in Science Fiction/Fantasy: H. G. Wells," Starlog No. 100: 45. November 1985.

"One Hundred Most Important People in Science Fiction/Fantasy: Isaac Asimov," Starlog No. 100: 52-53. November 1985.

"One Hundred Most Important People in Science Fiction/Fantasy: Judy-Lynn Del Rey," Starlog No. 100: 63. November 1985.

"One Hundred Most Important People in Science Fiction/Fantasy: Lester Del Rey," Starlog No. 100: 63. November 1985.

"One Hundred Most Important People in Science Fiction/Fantasy: Roger Zelazny," Starlog No. 100: 80. November 1985.

"One Hundred Most Important People in Science Fiction/Fantasy: William Shatner," Starlog No. 100: 41. November 1985.

Dickinson, Mike

"Blue Hawk, The," in: Magill, Frank N., ed. Survey of Modern Fantasy Literature, Vol 1. Englewood Cliffs, NJ: Salem Press, Inc., 1983. pp. 132-136.

"Land of Mist, The," in: Magill, Frank N., ed. Survey of Modern Fantasy Literature, Vol 2. Englewood Cliffs, NJ: Salem Press, Inc., 1983. pp. 867-869.

"Merlin," in: Magill, Frank N., ed. Survey of Modern Fantasy Literature, Vol 2. Englewood Cliffs, NJ: Salem Press, Inc., 1983. pp. 1007-1009.

"Silverlock and The Moon's Fire-Eating Daughter," in: Magill, Frank N., ed. Survey of Modern Fantasy Literature, Vol 4. Englewood Cliffs, NJ: Salem Press, Inc., 1983. pp. 1749-1753.

"Romance and hardening arteries: a reappraisal of the SF of Jack Vance," Vector 95:22-25. October 1979.

"Short fiction of Doyle, The," in: Magill, Frank N., ed. Survey of Modern Fantasy Literature, Vol 3. Englewood Cliffs, NJ: Salem Press, Inc., 1983. pp. 1504-1506.

"Three aspects of fantasy," Vector 96:10-14. December 1979/January 1980.

"Why They're All Crying Wolfe: A Few Thoughts on The Book of the New Sun," Vector 118: 13-20. February 1984.

Dickson, G. R.

"Childe Cycle: status 1979, The," SFWA Bulletin 14(3):65-74. Fall 1979.

"Concerning Sandra Miesel," in: Miesel, Sandra. Dreamrider. New York: Ace, 1982. pp. v-xv.

"Currents and directions in SF from the 50's to the 80's," by G. Dickson, J. Haldeman, and T. Clareson. in: Remington, T. J., ed. Selected Proceedings of the 1978 SFRA Nat'l Conference. Univ. of North. Iowa, 1979. pp. 222-240.

"John W. Campbell," Locus No. 90:6. July 12, 1971.

"LACon II guest of honor speech," Science Fiction Chronicle 6(3):1,28-35. December 1984.

"Plausibility in science fiction," in: Bretnor, Reginald, ed. Science Fiction Today and Tomorrow. New York: Harper, 1974. pp. 295-308.

Dickson, L. L.

"H. G. Wells upside down: fantasy as allegory in William Golding's <u>Inheritors</u>," in: Collins, R. A. and H. D. Pearce, eds. <u>The Scope of the Fantastic</u>. Westport, CT: Greenwood Press, 1985. pp. 151-157.

Dickson, Lovat

<u>H. G. Wells: His Turbulent Life and Times</u>. London: Macmillan, 1969. 330 p.

Dickstein, Morris

"Black humor and history: fiction in the sixties," <u>Partisan Review</u> 43(2):185-211. 1976.

"Time Bandits," <u>American Film</u> 7(11): 39-43. October 1982.

Diederichs, Ulf

"Zeitgemasses und Unzeitgemasses," in: Schmide-Henkel, Gerhard, ed. <u>Trivialleratur</u>. Berlin: Literarisches Colloquim, 1963. pp. 111-141.

Diehl, Digby

"And now the movies: Vonnegut vogue is in high gear, but if it flops . . ." <u>Showcase/Chicago Sun-Times</u> p. 2. February 28, 1971.

Dietz, Frank

"Countdown (movie review)," <u>Science Fiction Times</u> No. 455:5. June 1968.

Dietz, Kirsten

"Obscenity OK in Stories Says Local Sci-Fi Writer," <u>Battalion</u> (Texas A&M University) p. 6. April 16, 1985.

"Science Fiction Writer to Give Presentation," <u>Battalion</u> (Texas A&M Univ.) p. 7. April 15, 1985.

Dietz, Ludwig

"Zukunftsroman als jugendlekture," <u>Der Deutschunterricht</u> 13:79-98. 1961.

Dietz, T. F.

<u>Use of Song and Poetry in Lord of the Rings</u>. Masters Thesis, University of Georgia, 1978. 130 p.

"Sorcerer's Ship, The," in: Magill, Frank N., ed. <u>Survey of Modern Fantasy Literature</u>, Vol 4. Englewood Cliffs, NJ: Salem Press, Inc., 1983. pp. 1774-1776.

DiFate, Vincent

"Hubert Rogers: an appreciation," <u>Locus</u> 15(7):24,25. July 1982.

"John W. Campbell," <u>Locus</u> No. 91:9. July 22, 1971.

"Science Fiction Art: Some Contemporary Illustrators," in: Tymn, Marshall B., ed. <u>The Science Fiction Reference Book</u>. Mercer Island, WA: Starmont House, 1981. pp. 33-55.

"SF art," <u>Locus</u> No. 176:7-8. July 20, 1975.

"Sketches: a conversation with the artist Paul Lehr," <u>Starship</u> 17(3):29-33. Summer 1980.

"Sketches: an interview with Richard Powers: part I," <u>Algol</u> 14(3):27-31. Summer/Fall 1977.

"Sketches: an interview with Richard Powers: part II," <u>Algol</u> 15(1):35-36. Winter 1977/1978.

"Sketches: John Schoenherr interview," <u>Algol</u> 15(3):41-49. Summer/Fall 1978.

"Sketches: Society of Illustrators, a commentary," <u>Science Fiction Chronicle</u> 5(12):22-24. September 1984.

"Sketches: the dark side of tomorrow: another look at surrealism in science fiction art," <u>Starship</u> 16(3):59-62. Summer 1979.

"Sketches: the dark side, part II: surrealism in SF art," <u>Starship</u> 16(4):41-47. Fall 1979.

"Sketches: the evolution of a science fiction cover painting; part I," <u>Algol</u> 16(1):39-42. Winter 1978/1979.

"Sketches: Awards," <u>Science Fiction Chronicle</u> 6(10): 34-38. July 1985.

"Sketches: Out of the Void," <u>Starship</u> 20(1): 35-38. Winter 1983/84.

"Sketches: William Cameron Menzies and the Dreams of Childhood," <u>Starship</u> 19(1): 28-31. November 1982.

"Tantalizing Images," <u>Starship</u> 18(2): 29-31. Summer/Fall 1981.

Diffloth, G.

<u>Science fiction, La</u>. Paris: Gamma Presse, 1964. 96 p.

Digby, Joan

"Realizing Paper Tigers: The Fantastic Collages of John Digby," Fantasy Newsletter 5(1): 18-21, 36. January 1982.

Dikty, Thaddeus

Work of Julian May, The: An Annotated Bibliography and Guide. by Thaddeus Dikty and R. Reginald. San Bernardino, CA: Borgo, 1985. 66 p.

Dilley, Frank

"Multiple Selves and Survival of Brain Death," in: Smith, Nicholas D., ed. Philosophers Look at Science Fiction. Chicago: Nelson-Hall, 1982. pp. 105-116.

Dillingham, Peter

"Preliminary bibliography of science fiction poetry," Cthulhu Calls 3(4):43-50. April 1976.

"Science factual, science figurative and science fiction poetry," Cthulhu Calls 4(1):50-54. July 1976.

Dillingham, T. F.

"Harlan Ellison," in: Cowart, David, ed. Twentieth-Century American Science-Fiction Writers, Part 1: A-L Detroit: Gale, 1981. pp. 161-169. (Dictionary of Literary Biography, v. 8)

Dilov, Ljuben

"Bulgarian Science Fiction," SFRA Newsletter 111: 5-8. May 1983.

Dimeo, R. S.

Mind and Fantasies of Ray Bradbury. Ph.D. Dissertation, University of Utah, 1970. 227 p.

Dimeo, Steven

"Amityville II: The Possession," Cinefantastique 13(2)/13(3):91. November/December 1982.

"Battle Beyond the Stars (review)," Cinefantastique 10(3):33. Winter 1980.

"Black Hole (review)," Cinefantastique 9(3/4):68-69. Spring 1980.

"Brave New World (review)," Cinefantastique 10(1):16-17. Summer 1980.

"Cocoon (review)," Cinefantastique 15(5):40,53. January 1986.

"Entity (review)," Cinefantastique 13(5):56,60. June/July 1983.

"Friday the 13th: The Final Chapter (review)," Cinefantastique 14(4/5):101,107. September 1984.

"Incredible Shrinking Woman (review)," Cinefantastique 11(1):44,46. Summer 1981.

"Man and Apollo: religion in Bradbury's science fantasies," in: Greenberg, M. H. and J. D. Olander, eds. Ray Bradbury. NY, Taplinger, 1980. pp. 156-164. also in: Journal of Popular Culture 5(4):970-978. Spring 1972.

"Martian Chronicles," Cinefantastique 10(1):19-23. Summer 1980.

"Meteor (review)," Cinefantastique 9(3/4):70. Spring 1980.

"Nightmares (review)," Cinefantastique 14(2):52. December 1983/January 1984.

"Outland (review)," Cinefantastique 11(3):47-48. September 1981.

"Psychological symbolism in three early tales of invisibility," Riverside Quarterly 5(1): 20-27. July 1971.

"Silver Bullet (review)," Cinefantastique 16(1):43,54. March 1986.

"Spacehunter (review)," Cinefantastique 13(6)/14(1):97. September 1983.

"Star Trek: The Motion Picture," Amazing 27(7): 23-29. May 1980.

Ding-bo, Wu

"Chinese SF in trouble," Locus 17(3):17. March 1984.

"SF report from China, part 2, Chinese SF," Locus 14(10):18-20. November 1981.

"SF report from China," Locus 16(2):1,15. February 1983.

Dirac, Hugh

Profit of Doom, The. London: Sidgwick, 1971.

Dirda, Michael

"Galactic Night's Entertainment," Washington Post Book World p. 6, 8. April 26, 1981.

Dirda, Michael (Continued)

"Gene Wolfe Talks About 'The Book of the New Sun'," Washington Post Book World p. 11. January 30, 1983.

"Genre Ghetto, The," Nation 234(20): 635-636. May 22, 1982.

"Letter From the World Science Fiction Convention," Washington Post Book World p. 8, 10. September 25, 1983.

"Science fiction, growing pairs, and future shocks," Washington Post Book World p. 12. November 11, 1984.

Disch, T. M.

"Buck Rogers in the New Jerusalem," in: Roemer, Kenneth M., ed. America As Utopia. New York: Franklin, 1981. pp. 52-54.

"Closer look at Close Encounters, A," Foundation 15:50-53. January 1979.

"Embarrassments of science fiction, The," in: Nicholls, Peter, ed. Science Fiction at Large. New York: Harper, 1976. pp. 139-156.

"Fact of Magic, The; Thomas Disch Interviews John Crowley," Science Fiction Digest 1(2): 101-105. January/February 1982.

"Ideas: a popular misconception," Foundation 14:43-47. September 1978.

"Introduction," in: Dick, P. K. Solar Lottery. Boston: Gregg, 1976. pp. v-xvi.

"Representation in SF," in: Chauvin, Cy, ed. Multitude of Visions. Baltimore: T-K Graphics, 1975. pp. 8-13.

"Road to Heaven: science fiction and the militarization of space," Nation 242(18): 650-656. May 10, 1986.

"Science Fiction as a Church," Foundation 25: 53-58. June 1982.

"Science Fiction vs. Literature: the Prosecution's Case," Patchin Review 2: 18-23. September 1981.

"Toward the Transcendent: An Introduction to Solar Lottery and Other Works," in: Greenberg, Martin H., ed. Philip K. Dick. New York: Taplinger, 1982. pp. 13-25.

Diskin, L. F.

Teaching and Reading Science Fiction in College. Ph.D. Dissertation, 1975. 478 p.

Theodore Sturgeon. (Starmont Reader's Guide, 7) Mercer Island, WA: Starmont, 1981. 72 p.

Theodore Sturgeon: A Primary and Secondary Bibliography. Boston: G. K. Hall, 1980. 105 p.

"Gray Matters," in: Magill, Frank N., ed. Survey of Science Fiction Literature, Vol. 2. Englewood Cliffs, NJ: Salem Press, 1979. pp. 921-925.

"Bradbury on children," in: Greenberg, M. H. and J. D. Olander, eds. Ray Bradbury. New York: Taplinger, 1980. pp. 127-155.

"New Disciple, A," Fantasy Review 8(5): 8, 32. May 1985.

Dispa, M. F.

Heros de la science fiction. Brussels: De Boeck, 1976. 160 p.

Divey, Steve

"'Metropolis': the first great science fiction film," Vector 83:25-26. September/October 1977.

"Star Wars," Vector 82:4-5. July/August 1977.

Dixon, Buzz

"Lathe of Heaven (review)," Cinefantastique 10(1):14. Summer 1980.

"Of Christians, censorship, and science fiction," Farrago No. 9: 23-25. 1978.

Dizer, J. T.

Tom Swift & Company: 'Boy's Books' by Stratemeyer and Others. Jefferson, NC: McFarland, 1982. 183 p.

Dmitrevski, Vladimir

"Fantastika v dvizuscemsja mire," by E. Brandis and V. Dmitrevski. Inostrannaja literatura 1: 216-1967.

"Fantasy pisut dlja vsech!" by E. Brandis and V. Dmitrevski. Literaturnaja gazeta. February 1, 1966.

"Fantasy Writers Write for Everyone," by Y. Brandis and V. Dmitrevsky. Current Digest of the Soviet Press 18(6): 17-20. March 2, 1966.

"Future, its promoters and false prophets, The," by Evgeni Brandis and Vladimir Dmitrevskiy. Magazine of Fantasy and Science Fiction 29(4):62-80. October 1965.

Dmitrevski, Vladimir (Continued)

"Im reich der phantastik," by J. Brandis and Wladimir Dmitrijewski. in: Barmeyer, Eike, ed. Science fiction: theorie und geschichte. Munchen: Fink, 1972. pp. 128-133.

"Wissenschaftliche Phantastik lebt weiter," by J. Brandis and W. Dmitrewski. Kunst und Literatur 24:792-807. 1976.

Doberer, K. K.

"Drei ebenen der science fiction," in: Geist und Tat. Monatsschrift fur Recht, Freiheit und Kultur 17:274-277. 1962.

Dobson, Michael

"To Canvass the Solar System: An Interview with Astronomical Artist Ron Miller," Future 6: 59-65. November 1978.

Dobzynski, Charles

"Bradbury, fabuliste de norte temps," Europe revue mensuelle No. 139-140:76-87. July/August 1957.

"Une machine a decerveler," Les Lettres Francaises No. 618:9. May 1956.

Dodd, A. L.

"Science fiction in the elementary school," Science Teacher 25:463-464. December 1958. also in: Education Digest 24:38-39. March 1959.

Dodd, Sandra

"Jack Williamson: an interview," Luna Monthly No. 53:1-3. September 1974.

Dodds, Richard

"She made Time Bandits just for fun," New Orleans Times-Picayune November 6, 1981. in: NewsBank. Film and Television. 56: B3. July/December 1981.

Dodge, R. K.

Influence of Machines and Technology on American Literature of the Late Ninteenth and Early Twentieth Centuries. Ph.D. Dissertation, University of Texas, 1967. 209 p.

Doe, Jane

"Have you Hugged Your Editor Today?" Patchin Review 1: 24-25. July 1981.

Doering, David

"Approaching the edge: interview with David Michael Bastian, October 29, 1981," Leading Edge No. 2:5-7. 1981.

"Brushing up with Don Maitz," Leading Edge No. 7:39-41. undated.

"Heritage of greatness: an interview with Real Musgrave," Leading Edge No. 10:52-56. Fall 1985.

"Over the edge: Denvention II," by David Doering and D. M. Bastian. Leading Edge No. 2:44-50. 1981.

"Painting that crazy stuff: an interview with James Christensen," Leading Edge No. 6:41-52. undated.

Doherty, G. D.

"Use of language in SF, The," SF Horizons 1:43-53. Spring 1964.

Doherty, Thomas

"Mad Max Beyond Thunderdome (review)," Cinefantastique 15(5):37,54. January 1986.

"Purple Rose of Cairo (review)," Cinefantastique 15(4):51-52. October 1985.

"Runaway (review)," Cinefantastique 15(3):45,56. July 1985.

Dohner, Jan

"Literature of change: science fiction and women," Top of the News 34(3):261-265. Spring 1978.

Dollens, M. S.

"Recollections of science fiction magazine art," Cthulhu Calls 4(1):28-35. July 1976.

Dollerup, Cay

Volve. Scandinavian Views on Science Fiction. Selected Papers from the Scandinavian Science Fiction Festival 1977. Copenhagen: Dept. of English, Univ. of Copenhagen, 1978. 123 p. (Anglica et Americana, 4)

"Fremtidskrigene og roman cerne," Proxima No. 19, sect. II:44-47. March 1979.

"On the criticism of science fiction: caveats and trends," in: Dollerup, Cay, ed. Volve. Scandinavian Views on Science Fiction. Copenhagen: Department of English, University of Copenhagen, 1978. pp. 108-115.

Dollerup, Cay (Continued)

"Science fiction and mainstream: a discussion," edited by Annemette Goldberg and Cay Dollerup. in: Dollerup, Cay, ed. Volve. Scandinavian Views on SF. Copenhagen: Dept. of English, Univ. of Copenhagen, 1978. pp. 11-16.

"Science(?) fiction in the classroom. On the pedagogical uses of science fiction," in: Dollerup, Cay, ed. Volve. Scandinavian Views on Science Fiction. Copenhagen: Dept. of English, Univ. of Copenhagen, 1978. pp. 96-107.

"Teknologidyrkerne: Jules Verne," Proxima No. 19, sect. 2:42-44. March 1979.

"Ur science fiction," Proxima No. 7:15-18. March 1976.

Dominianni, Robert

"Ray Bradbury's 2026: A Year With Current Value," English Journal 73(7): 49-51. November 1984.

Dominquez, Ivo, Jr.

"High school reading club writes a novel, A," Journal of Reading 21(8):698-700. May 1978.

Domjan, L. K.

"Sci-Fi Fans List Stars, Gripes," St. Louis (Mo.) Post-Dispatch July 26, 1982. in: NewsBank. Social Relations 33: F4. 1982.

Donaho, Bill

"Baycon and the art show," Science Fiction Times No. 455:4. June 1968.

"Hugo Awards," Science Fiction Times No. 421:5-7. November 1964.

Donahue, J. J.

"333": A Bibliography of the Science-Fantasy Novel, by J. H. Crawford, J. J. Donahue, and D. M. Grant. Providence, Rhode Island: The Grandon Company, 1953. 80 p.

Donahue, T. S.

"Linguist Looks at Tolkien's Elvish, A," Mythlore 10(3): 28-34. Winter 1984.

Donelson, K. L.

"Science fiction, fantasy, and utopias," in: Donelson, Kenneth L. and Nilsen, Alleen Pace.

Literature for Today's Young Adults. Glenview, IL: Scott, Foresman, 1980. pp. 258-282.

Donlan, D.

"Developing a reading participation guide for a novel; Fahrenheit 451," Journal of Reading 17(6):439-443. March 1974.

"Experiencing The Andromeda Strain," English Journal 63:72-73. September 1974.

Donnelly, Jerome

"Humanizing Technology in The Empire Strikes Back: Theme and Values in Lucas and Tolkien," Philosophy in Context 11: 19-32. 1982.

Donner, Wolf

"Science fiction anhanger in Heidelberg. Ruckschritte in den fortschritt," in: Die Ziet no. 35:20. August 28, 1970.

Donoghue, Denis

"Nineteen Eighty-Four: Politics and fable," in: George Orwell and Nineteen Eighty-Four. Washington, DC: Library of Congress, 1985. pp. 57-69.

Donovan, J.

"Writer criticizes fantasy fare," Biography News 1:1228. November 1974.

Donovan, R. A.

"Future According to Hoyle, The: A Footnote On the Two Cultures," South Atlantic Quarterly 81(2): 178-187. Spring 1982.

Donovan, R. M.

"Bug eyed monsters," Ontario Library Review 36(1):28-30. February 1952.

Donovan, Richard

"Morals from Mars," Reporter 4(13):38-40. June 26, 1951.

Dooley, L. R.

"Larry Niven: immortality and unstable equilibrium," in: Yoke, C. B. and Hassler, D. M., eds. Death and the Serpent. Westport, CT: Greenwood, 1985. pp. 153-162.

Dooley, Patricia

"Finding Fantasy," _School Libary Journal_ 27(4): 32-33. December 1980.

Doremieux, Alain

Histories fantastiquest de demain quinze recits de science fiction choisis et presentes par Alain Doremieux. Tournai: Casterman, 1966.

"Defense et illustration de la SF," by Gerard Klein, Alain Doremieux, and Jacques Goimard. _Le Monde_ 28.6.1967.

"Savanturiers, Les," _Nouvel Ubservateur_ 21.6.1967.

Dorey, Alan

"Standpoint: SF in the Modern World," _Vector_ 107: 5-8. April 1982.

"Telegram for Vector," _Vector_ 100: 10-13. December 1980.

"Unlimited dreams: J. G. Ballard," _Vector_ 96:4-9. December 1979/January 1980.

Dorfles, Gillo

"Fantascienza e suo miti, La," in: Dorfles, Gillo. _Nuovi riti, nuovi miti._ Turin: s. n., 1965. pp. 207-230.

Dorgeles, Roland

"Rosny aine," in: Dorgeles, Roland. _Images._ Paris: A. Michel, 1975. pp. 163-173.

Dorrell, Larry

"Spider-Man at the Library," by Larry Dorrell and Ed Carroll. _School Library Journal_ 27(10): 17-19. August 1981. (Comment: 28(4):3. Dec. 1981.)

Douay, Dominique

"Dream and the Reality, The," _Foundation_ 32: 42-44. November 1984.

"S. F. et ideologie: une quete absurde," by Dominique Douay and Pierre Guiliani. _Europe_ 580/581:79-84. August/September 1977.

"Un regard terroriste sur L'histoire," _Change_ (Paris) 40:45-53. 1981.

Double, Richard

"There Are No Persons," in: Myers, R. E., ed. _The Intersection of Science Fiction and Philosophy._ Westport: Greenwood, 1983. pp. 109-120.

Dougherty, P. H.

"Advertising: Guccione's new aim with _Omni_," _New York Times_ p. D13. August 2, 1979.

Douglas, C. N.

"Texas, the state of the SF art," in: _First Occasional Lone Star Science Fiction Convention and Chili Cookoff._ Austin: Lone Star Con, 1985. pp. 53-55.

Douglas, Geoffrey

"Brothers Hildebrandt Are Not Grim, The," _TWA Ambassador_ 12(10): 97-103. October 1979.

Douglas, J. C.

"Krull star Marshall longs to be villain," _Grand Rapids Press._ July 31, 1983. in: NewsBank. _Film and Television_ FTV-14:D14. 1983.

Doumic, R.

"Romans de Rosny, Les," _Revue des Deux-Mondes_ 129:936-947. 1895.

Dovey, I.

"Sister, board that space ship," _Elementary English_ 31:345-346. October 1954.

Dow, James

"Magicam miniatures constructed for Star Trek: The Motion Picture," _American Cinematographer_ 61(2):152-154, 178-179,186-187. February 1980.

Dowd, Alice

"Science Fiction Microfilming Project at the New York Public Library, The," _Microform Review_ 14(1): 15-20. Winter 1985.

Dowdy, D. A.

"Figure of Taliessin," _Mythlore_ 7(1):6-13. March 1980.

Dowelson, Annette

"Out in third field with Robert A. Heinlein," by Betty Whetton and Annette Dowelson. Arizona English Bulletin 51(1):97-105. October 1972.

Dowie, William

"Gospel of Middle-Earth according to J. R. R. Tolkien, The," in: Salu, Mary, ed. J. R. R. Tolkien: Scholar and Storyteller. Ithaca: Cornell Univ. Press, 1979. pp. 265-285. also in: Heythrop Journal 15:37-52. January 1974.

Dowling, E.

"Pterodactyl for breakfast," New Republic 157(21):39-43. November 18, 1967.

Dowling, Terry

"'Man' with the off-white light-sabre, The," Science Fiction: A Review of Speculative Literature 1(3):4-9. December 1978.

"Alternative reality and deviant logic in J. G. Ballard's second 'Disaster' trilogy," Science Fiction: A Review of Speculative Literature 1(1):6-18. June 1977.

"Art of xenography: Jack Vance's 'General Culture' novels, The," Science Fiction: A Review of Speculative Literature 1(3):13-98. December 1978.

"Catharsis among the Byzantines: Delany's Driftglass," Science Fiction: A Review of Speculative Literature 6(2): 42-44. 1984.

"Conversation with Roger Zelazny, A," by Terry Dowling and Keith Curtis. Science Fiction: A Review of Speculative Literature 1(2):11-23. June 1978.

"Frank Herbert Interviewed," Science Fiction: A Review of Speculative Literature 3(3): 96-108. September 1981.

"Jack Vance's "General Culture" novels: a synoptic survey," in: Underwood, Tim, and Miller, Chuck, eds. Jack Vance. New York: Taplinger, 1980. pp. 131-178.

"Kirth Gersen: The Other Demon Prince," Science Fiction: A Review of Speculative Literature 4(2): 55-66. June 1982.

"Lever of Life, The: Winning and Losing in the Fiction of Cordwainer Smith," Science Fiction: A Review of Speculative Literature 4(1): 9-37. March 1982.

"Much richer phenomenon, A," Science Fiction: A Review of Speculative Literature 2(2):174-183. December 1979.

"Peter Weir: Master of Unease; Interview," by Terry Dowling and George Mannix. Science Fiction: A Review of Speculative Literature 3(1):7-27. January 1981.

"Timewinds: Terry Dowling and George Mannix talk with Dennis Collins and Mark Salwowski," by Terry Dowling and George Mannix. Science Fiction: A Review of Speculative Literature 2(1):67-73. May 1979.

"What is science fiction?" Science Fiction: A Review of Speculative Literature 2(1):4-19. May 1979.

"Xenographical Postscript, A," Science Fiction: A Review of Speculative Literature. 2(3): 243-250. August 1980.

Downey, A. L.

Life and Works of J. H. Rosny Aine, 1856-1940. Ph.D. Dissertation, University of Michigan, 1950. 283 p.

Downs, H.

"Computer that sweated," Science Digest 59:88-93. June 1966. (fiction; some sources cite as secondary article)

Dowst, Kenneth

"'Commonplaces' in Utopian Fiction," Journal of General Education 33(1): 58-68. Spring 1981.

Doxey, W. S.

"Vonnegut's Cats' Cradle," The Explicator 37(4):6. Summer 1979.

Doyle, R. J.

"Science fiction as an early warning system," in: Samuelson, D. N. Science Fiction and Future Studies. Bryan, TX: SFRA, 1975. pp. 31-36.

Doyno, V. A.

"2001 (squared): years and shapes," Hartford Studies in Literature 1(2):131-132. 1969.

Dozois, Gardner

Fiction of James Tiptree, Jr., The. New York: Algol Press, 1977. 36 p.

"1982: the SF year in review, short fiction," Science Fiction Chronicle 4(6):1,13,19. March 1983.

Dozois, Gardner (Continued)

"1983: the SF year in review; short fiction," Science Fiction Chronicle 5(6):1,19-21. March 1984.

"1984: the SF year in review, short fiction," Science Fiction Chronicle 6(6): 1, 26-28. March 1985.

"Beyond the Golden Age, Part II: The New Wave Years," Thrust 19: 10-14. Winter/Spring 1983.

"Beyond the Golden Age," Starship 18(2): 7-13. Summer/Fall 1981.

"Damon Knight," in: Bleiler, E. F., ed. Science Fiction Writers. New York: Scribners, 1982. pp. 393-400.

"Foreword: summation 1976," in: Dozois, Gardner, ed. Best Science Fiction Stories of the Year, Sixth Annual Collection. New York: Ace, 1977. pp. xi-xxvii.

"Introduction," in: Tiptree, James, Jr. 10,000 Light-Years From Home. Boston: Gregg, 1976. pp. v-xxxvi.

"Introduction: summation 1977," in: Dozois, Gardner, ed. Best Science Fiction Stories of the Year, Seventh Annual Collection. New York: Dell, 1978. pp. 9-20.

"Living in the future: you are what you eat," in: Grant, C. L., ed. Writing and Selling Science Fiction. Cincinnati, Ohio: Writers Digest, 1976. pp. 111-128.

"Looking at 1980; the anthologies," Science Fiction Chronicle 2(11):1,18,20. August 1981.

"Science fiction in the eighties," Washington Post Book World p. 9. December 30, 1984.

"SF retrospective: 1979," Thrust 15:6-13. Summer 1980. also in: Dozois, Gardner, ed. Best Science Fiction Stories of the Year, Ninth Annual Collection. New York: Dutton, 1980.

"Summation: 1978," in: Dozois, Gardner, ed. Best Science Fiction Stories of the Year, Eighth Annual Collection. New York: Dell, 1980. pp. 9-31.

"Writing science fiction: think like an alien, write like an angel; with list of markets; excerpt from Writing and Selling Fiction," Writers Digest 56:26-28. February 1976.

Drabble, Margaret

"Doris Lessing: Cassandra in A World Under Seige," Ramparts 10(8):50-54. February 1972.

Drake, C. V.

"Psycho III," Cinefantastique 16(1):24-30. March 1986.

"Santa Claus: The Movie," Cinefantastique 15(5):16-19. January 1986.

Drake, H. L.

"A. E. Van Vogt's 'Unreality' and Formula Writing," Paper presented at the Annual Meeting of the Mid-West Popular Culture Association, Kalamazoo, MI., October 23-25, 1980. 11 p. ERIC ED 197 380.

"A. E. Van Vogt: In Search of Meaning," 1980. 23 p. ERIC ED 193 738.

"Algol profile, A. E. van Vogt," Algol 14(2):17-19. Spring 1977.

"General semantics and science fiction in the speech communication classroom," Paper presented at the annual meeting of the Speech Communication Association, 59th, New York. November 1973. 34 p. (ERIC ED 084 580)

Drake, Phyllis

"Homer in 2001," English Journal 59(9): 1270-1271. December 1970.

Draper, R. P.

"Lessing, Doris," in: Woodcock, George, ed. 20th Century Fiction. Chicago: St. James, 1985. pp. 377-380.

Drennan, K. M.

"Show by show guide to Night Gallery, part 2," by J. M. Straczynski and K. M. Drennan. Twilight Zone 5(2): 83-89. May/June 1985.

"Show by show guide to Night Gallery, part 3," by K. M. Drennan and P. M. Straczynski. Twilight Zone 5(3): 78-85. July/August 1985.

"Show by show guide to Night Gallery, part 4," by J. M. Straczynski and K. M. Drennan. Twilight Zone 5(4): 74-80. October 1985.

"Show by show guide to Night Gallery, part 5," by J. M. Straczynski and K. M. Drennan. Twilight Zone 5(5):82-87. December 1985.

"Show by show guide to Night Gallery, part 6," by K. M. Drennan and J. M. Straczynski. Twilight Zone 5(6): 72-75. February 1986.

"Show by show guide to Night Gallery," by J. M. Straczynski and K. M. Drennan. Twilight Zone 5(1): 54-60. March/April 1985.

Drescher, H. W.

"Aussenseiter im utopischen roman der moderne: George Orwell, Nineteen eighty-four, und Ray Bradbury, Fahrenheit 451," Anglia: zeitschrift fur englische philologie 96(3/4):430-446. 1978.

Drevdahl, J. E.

"Personality & creativity in artists & writers," Journal of Clinical Psychology 14(2):107-111. April 1958.

Drew, B. A.

"Turn-ons of yesteryear, The," Gallery 7(13):61-63. December 1979.

Dreyfuss, Joel

"Asimov: Intellectual Protrusions," Washington Post p. B1, B17. October 22, 1973.

Drost, Wolfgang

"Logik des Absurden: Zur Phantastik in Baudelaires Dichtung und Kunsttheorie," in: Thomsen, C. W., ed. Phantastik in Literatur und Kunst. Darmstadt: Wissenschaftliche Buchgesellschaft, 1980. pp. 182-200.

Drumm, Chris

Algis Budrys Checklist. Polk City, IA: Drumm, 1983. 16 p.

Hal Clement Checklist. Polk City, IA: Drumm, 1983. 7 p.

James Gunn Checklist. Polk City, IA: Drumm, 1984. 24 p.

Larry Niven Checklist. Polk City, IA: Drumm, 1983. 24 p.

Mack Reynolds Checklist. Polk City, IA: Drumm, 1983. 24 p.

R. A. Lafferty Checklist: A Bibliographical Chronology with Notes and Index. Polk City, IA: Drumm, 1983. 30 p.

Tom Disch Checklist. Polk City, IA: Drumm, n.d. 22 p.

Drury, R. W.

"Realism plus fantasy equals magic," Horn Book 48(2):113-119. April 1972.

Drury, Roger

"Providence at Elrond's Council," Mythlore 7(3): 8-9. Autumn 1980.

Du Bois, William

"Books of the times," New York Times p. 23. August 27, 1953. (Book review)

Du Brow, Rich

"No space fiction on fall television," Dallas Morning News p. C-11. July 21, 1969.

"This 23-year old tells an amazing story," Los Angeles Herald Examiner June 30, 1985. in: NewsBank. Film and Television. 1:B2-B3. July 1985.

Duane, Diane

"Watching the Sparks Fly Upward: Six Months After the Door Into Fire," Empire: For the SF Writers. 4(4): 10-12. September 1979.

Dubanski, Ryszard

"Last man theme in modern fantasy and SF, The," Foundation 16:26-31. May 1979.

Dubourg, Maurice

"Pierre Very et la fantastique," Europe 60(636): 32-46. 1982.

Duchac, K. F.

"Books in orbit," Wisconsin Library Bulletin 55(1):3-8. January/February 1959.

Ducharme, E.

"Canticle for Miller," English Journal 55(8):1042-1044. November 1966.

Duda, Harry

"Imie przyszlosci," Opole No. 11. 1971.

Dudar, Helen

"Stephen King: His Principled Price," Los Angeles Times Sec. CA1, p. 52. August 1, 1982.

Duke, Maurice

"Baroque waste land of James Branch Cabell, The," in: French, Warren, ed. The Twenties: Fiction, Poetry, Drama. Deland, Florida: Everett/Edwards, 1975. pp. 75-86

"Cabell's and Glasgow's Richmond: the intellectual background of the city," Mississippi Quarterly 27(4):375-391. Fall 1974.

"Ornate wasteland of James Branch Cabell, The," Kalki 6(3):79-89. 1974.

Dumbleton, D. D.

"Science fiction and cultural understanding," Trends in Social Education 24:14-19. February 1977.

Dumont, J. P.

"Egy komputer pszichologiaja," by J. P. Dumont and Jean Monod. Helikon 18(1): 94-104. 1972.

Dumonties, M.

"B. P. 1: La science fiction pour un reve centenaire," Beaubourg-Pont des Arts No. 1:19-21. March 1977.

Dunbar, D. L.

Unique Motifs in Brazilian Science Fiction. Ph.D. Dissertation, University of Arizona, 1976. 148 p.

Duncan, Larry

"Theodore Sturgeon interview, The," Thrust 11:6-11. Fall 1978.

Duncan, Pamela

"Silent Running," Cinefex No. 8:36-66. April 1982.

Dunlap, Frank

"God and Kurt Vonnegut, Jr., at Iowa City," Chicago Tribune Magazine pp. 48,84,86,88. May 7, 1967.

Dunn, L. G.

"Creating film magic for the original King Kong," American Cinematographer 58(1):64-65,91-99. January 1977.

Dunn, R. J.

"Narrative distance in Frankenstein," Studies in the Novel 6(4):408-417. Winter 1974.

Dunn, T. P.

Clockwork Worlds: Mechanized Environments in Science Fiction. by R. D. Erlich and T. P. Dunn. Westport, CT: Greenwood, 1983. 384 p.

Mechanical God, The: Machines in Science Fiction, by T. P. Dunn and R. D. Erlich. Westport, CT: Greenwood, 1982. 284 p.

"Machine Stops, The," in: Magill, Frank N., ed. Survey of Science Fiction Literature, Vol. 3. Englewood Cliffs, NJ: Salem Press, 1979. pp. 1299-1303.

"A Vision of Dystopia: Beehives and Mechanization," Journal of General Education 33(1): 45-57. Spring 1981.

"Creation Unfinished: Astronomical Realities in the Hainish Fiction of Ursula K. Le Guin," in: Hassler, Donald M., ed. Patterns of the Fantastic II. Mercer Island, WA: Starmont, 1985. pp. 59-67.

"Existential Pilgrims and Comic Catastrophe in the Fiction of Robert Sheckley," Extrapolation 26(1): 56-65. Spring 1985.

"List of Works Useful For the Study of Machines in Science Fiction," by T. P. Dunn and R. D. Erlich. in: Dunn, Thomas P., ed. The Mechanical God. Westport: Greenwood, 1982. pp. 225-273.

"List of Works Useful for the Study of Mechanized Environments in SF." by R. D. Erlich and T. P. Dunn. in: Erlich, Richard D., ed. Clockwork Worlds. Westport, CT: Greenwood, 1983. pp. 263-359.

"Mechanical Hive, The: Urbmon 116 as the Villain-Hero of Silverberg's The World Inside," by T. P. Dunn and R. D. Erlich. Extrapolation 21(4): 338-347. Winter 1980.

"Pilgrim Award Presentation Speech: America as Bruce Franklin," SFRA Newsletter 115: p. c-e. October 1983.

"Short Fiction of Robert Sheckley, The," in: Magill, Frank N., ed. Survey of Science Fiction Literature, Vol. 4. Englewood Cliffs, NJ: Salem Press, 1979. pp. 2046-2050.

"Social Science Fiction of Robin Cook, The," in: Hassler, Donald M. Patterns of the Fantastic. Mercer Island, WA: Starmont, 1983. pp. 67-72.

Dunne, Mike

"Ray Bradbury, Cosmic Optimist," Sacramento Bee, Feb. 6, 1982. in: Newsbank Review of Literature. 54: G10-11. 1981/1982.

Dunsany, Lord

Patches of Sunlight. London: Heinemann. No date.

DuPlessis, R. B.

"Feminist Apologies of Lessing, Piercy, and Russ, The," Frontiers 4: 1-8. Spring 1979.

Durand, Gilbert

Structures anthropologiques de l'imaginaire, Les. 3rd. ed. Paris: Bondas, 1969. 536 p.

Durant, F. C., III

Worlds Beyond: The Art of Chesley Bonestell, by F. C. Durant, III and Ron Miller. Norfolk: Starblaze, 1983. 133 p.

Durgnat, Raymond

"Subconscious: from pleasure castle to libido motel, The," Films and Filming pp. 13-15,41,46. January 1962.

Durie, A. J. L.

Index to the British Editions of the Magazine of Fantasy and Science Fiction with a Cross Reference to the Original American Edition. Wisbech: Fantast, 1966. 44 p.

Duriez, Colin

"Leonardo, Tolkien and Mr. Baggins," Mythlore 1(2):18-28. April 1969.

Durkin, M. B.

Dorothy L. Sayers. Boston: Twayne, 1980. 204 p.

Durzak, Manfred

"Science Fiction unterwegs zur E-Literatur," in: Ermert, Karl, ed. Neugier oder Flucht? Stuttgart: Klett, 1980. pp. 33-42.

Dutcher, R. F.

"Short Walk to the End, A: Some Notes on Suzy McKee Charnas," Pretentious Science Fiction Quarterly 2: 4-5. Summer 1978.

Duval, R. P.

"Dans la jungle litteraire, un labyrinthe: la science fiction," Notes bibliographiques, 1963, 6, pp. 564-570.

Duvic, Patrice

"Informations et documents," Science fiction, by G. Cordesse and Patrick Duvic. Paris, Services americains d'information et de relations culturelles, 1972. 35p.

"Intervista con Harlan Ellison," Robot: Rivista di fantascienza 1(1):95-99. April 1976.

Duvoli, J. R.

"Latitude Zero (review)," Cinefantastique 1(1):37. Fall 1970.

Dyal, D. H.

"Science Fiction Research Collection at Texas A&M University, The," Special Collections 2(1/2): 39-48. Fall/Winter 1982.

Dyer, P. J.

"All manner of fantasies,", Films and Filming 4(9):13-15,34. June 1958.

Dykstra, John

"Miniature and mechanical special effects for Star Wars," American Cinematographer 58(7):702-705,732, 742-745,750-757. July 1977.

"Special effects for Silent Running," American Cinematographer 53(7):756-757, 808-809. July 1972.

E

Eads, Bill

"Roger Zelazny: The New Wave King of Science Fiction," by Michael Vance and Bill Eads. Media Sight 3(1): 39-42. Summer 1984.

Eaglen, A. B.

"Alternatives: A Bibliography of Books and Periodicals on Science Fiction and Fantasy," Top of the News 39(1): 96-102. Fall 1982.

Eastman, D. R.

"Strategies of Survival, The: Cybernetic Differences in the Einstein Intersection," Extrapolation 22(3): 270-276. Fall 1981.

Ebel, Henry

"Psychohistory in the cinema: I. The new theology: Star Wars, Close Encounters, and the crisis of pseudo-rationality," Journal of Psychohistory 5(4):487-508. Spring 1978.

Ebeling, Gerhard

"Zeit und Wort," in: Meyer, R. W. Das Zeitproblem im 20. Jahrhundert. Bern-Munchen, 1964. pp. 342-361.

Eberle, R. R.

"Checklist (1928-1965) of E. E. Smith," Science Fiction Times No. 433:8-9. November 1965.

Ebert, Roger

"Cockroaches and Giant Crabs Color 'Creepshow'," Salt Lake Tribune November 11, 1982. in: Newsbank. Film and Television. 50:B13-14. December 1982.

"Just another horror movie, or is it?" Readers Digest 94(566):127-128. June 1969.

"Orwell's '1984' Should Make It," New Orleans Times Picayune Sec. 7 p. 6. July 20, 1984.

"Thar's gold in that thar space," New Orleans Times Picayune Sec. 5, p. 10. June 7, 1979.

Ebert, T. L.

"Convergence of Postmodern Innovative Fiction and Science Fiction, The: An Encounter with Samuel R. Delany's Technophobia," Poetics Today 1(4): 91-104. 1980.

Eckley, Grace

"Absolute at Large, The," in: Magill, Frank N., ed. Survey of Science Fiction Literature, Vol. 1. Englewood Cliffs, NJ: Salem Press, 1979. pp. 6-10.

"Barefoot in the Head," in: Magill, Frank N., ed. Survey of Science Fiction Literature, Vol. 1. Englewood Cliffs, NJ: Salem Press, 1979. pp. 125-129.

"Beasts," in: Magill, Frank N., ed. Survey of Science Fiction Literature, Vol. 1. Englewood Cliffs, NJ: Salem Press, 1979. pp. 133-137.

"Black Easter," in: Magill, Frank N., ed. Survey of Science Fiction Literature, Vol. 1. Englewood Cliffs, NJ: Salem Press, 1979. pp. 233-237.

"Blessing of Pan, The," in: Magill, Frank N., ed. Survey of Modern Fantasy Literature, Vol 1. Englewood Cliffs, NJ: Salem Press, Inc., 1983. pp. 129-131.

"Can Such Things Be?," in: Magill, Frank N., ed. Survey of Science Fiction Literature, Vol. 1. Englewood Cliffs, NJ: Salem Press, 1979. pp. 283-287.

"Case of Conscience, A," in: Magill, Frank N., ed. Survey of Science Fiction Literature, Vol. 1. Englewood Cliffs, NJ: Salem Press, 1979. pp. 303-307.

Eckley, Grace (Continued)

"Clipper of the Clouds and The Master of the World," in: Magill, Frank N., ed. Survey of Science Fiction Literature, Vol. 1. Englewood Cliffs, NJ: Salem Press, 1979. pp. 386-392.

"Day After Judgement, The," in: Magill, Frank N., ed. Survey of Science Fiction Literature, Vol. 1. Englewood Cliffs, NJ: Salem Press, 1979. pp. 497-501.

"Devil Rides Out, The," in: Magill, Frank N., ed. Survey of Modern Fantasy Literature, Vol 1. Englewood Cliffs, NJ: Salem Press, Inc., 1983. pp. 383-386.

"Doctor Mirabilis," in: Magill, Frank N., ed. Survey of Science Fiction Literature, Vol. 2. Englewood Cliffs, NJ: Salem Press, 1979. pp. 569-573.

"Etidorhpa," in: Magill, Frank N., ed. Survey of Modern Fantasy Literature, Vol 1. Englewood Cliffs, NJ: Salem Press, Inc., 1983. pp. 497-500.

"I, Robot," in: Magill, Frank N., ed. Survey of Science Fiction Literature, Vol. 2. Englewood Cliffs, NJ: Salem Press, 1979. pp. 995-999.

"Finnegans wake in the work of James Blish," Extrapolation 20(4):330-342. Winter 1979.

"Short fiction of Dunsany, The," in: Magill, Frank N., ed. Survey of Modern Fantasy Literature, Vol 3. Englewood Cliffs, NJ: Salem Press, Inc., 1983. pp. 1507-1510.

Eckley, Wilton

"Gladiator," in: Magill, Frank N., ed. Survey of Science Fiction Literature, Vol. 2. Englewood Cliffs, NJ: Salem Press, 1979. pp. 888-893.

"It Can't Happen Here," in: Magill, Frank N., ed. Survey of Science Fiction Literature, Vol. 3. Englewood Cliffs, NJ: Salem Press, 1979. pp. 1089-1093.

"Mysterious Stranger, The," in: Magill, Frank N., ed. Survey of Modern Fantasy Literature, Vol 3. Englewood Cliffs, NJ: Salem Press, Inc., 1983. pp. 1081-1085.

"Pollinators of Eden, The," in: Magill, Frank N., ed. Survey of Science Fiction Literature, Vol. 4. Englewood Cliffs, NJ: Salem Press, 1979. pp. 1705-1709.

"Rakehells of Heaven, The," in: Magill, Frank N., ed. Survey of Science Fiction Literature, Vol. 4. Englewood Cliffs, NJ: Salem Press, 1979. pp. 1746-1750.

"Retief: Ambassador to Space," in: Magill, Frank N., ed. Survey of Science Fiction Literature, Vol. 4. Englewood Cliffs, NJ: Salem Press, 1979. pp. 1775-1789.

"Star Rover," in: Magill, Frank N., ed. Survey of Science Fiction Literature, Vol. 5. Englewood Cliffs, NJ: Salem Press, 1979. pp. 2159-2162.

Eco, Umberto

"Science Fiction and the Art of Conjecture," Times Literary Supplement 4257: 1257-1258. November 2, 1984.

Edelhart, Mike

"More fiction writing tips: interview with Anthony Burgess," Writer's Digest 55(8):13. August 1975.

Edelheit, S. J.

Dark Prophecies: Essays on Orwell and Technology. Ph.D. Dissertation, Brandeis University, 1975. 186 p.

"Language of Le Guin, The," New Boston Review 5(1):5-6,13. September/October 1979.

Edelson, Edward

Visions of Tomorrow: Great Science Fiction From the Movies. Garden City, NY: Doubleday, 1975. 117 p.

Edelstein, Arnold

"Slaughterhouse Five: time out of joint," College Literature 1(2):128-139. Spring 1974.

Edelstein, J. M.

"Future without humanity, The," New Republic 145(15):24-25. October 9, 1961. (Book review)

Edelstein, Scott

"Big Aurora ripoff," by Mark McGarry and Scott Edelstein. Empire: For the SF Writer 3(4): 13-15. April 1978.

"Interview: Joanna Russ," Empire: For the SF Writer 3(2): 6-12. August 1977.

Eder, Alois

"'...ein ins Groteske umgekipper Kafka': Herzmanovsky-Orlando," Quarber Merkur 55:13-20. July 1981.

Eder, Alois (Continued)

"Christlichsoziale Utopie, Eine," <u>Quarber Merkur</u> 19(2):3-22. October 1981.

Eder, K.

"Feind vom fremden stern: science fiction auf deutschen Bildschirmen, " <u>Deutsche Zeitung</u> No. 43:11. 1971.

Edkins, E. A.

"Idiosyncracies of H P L," in: Wetzel, George. <u>Howard Phillips Lovecraft: Memoirs, Critiques, & Bibliographies</u>. North Tonowonda, NY: SSR, 1955. pp. 5-7.

Edlin, G. K.

"Researches in Tollan," <u>Kalki</u> 7:103-107. 1977.

"Researches into the dirghagama," <u>Kalki</u> 7(1):31-33. 1975.

Edlund, Richard

"Creating the special visual effects for Raiders," <u>American Cinematographer</u> 62(11):1106-1108, 1144-1151. November 1981.

"Jedi Journal," by Richard Edlund, Dennis Muren, and Ken Ralston. <u>Cinefex</u> 13: 4-67. July 1983.

"Special Visual Effects for The Empire Strikes Back," <u>American Cinematographer</u> 61(6): 552-553, 564-567, 604-606. June 1980.

Edson, Laurie

"Fantastic travel adventures of Henri Michaux," in: Collins, R. A. and H. D. Pearce, eds. <u>The Scope of the Fantastic: Theory, Technique, Major Authors</u>. Westport, CT: Greenwood Press, 1985. pp. 215-220.

Edwards, B. L.

<u>Rhetoric of Reading, A: A Study of C. S. Lewis's Approach to the Written Text</u>. Ph. D. Dissertation, University of Texas at Austin, 1981. 235 p.

"Towards a Rhetoric of Fantasy Criticism: C. S. Lewis's Reading of MacDonald and Morris," <u>Literature and Belief</u> 3:63-73. 1983.

Edwards, Malcolm

<u>Complete Book of Science Fiction and Fantasy Lists, The</u>, by Maxim Jakubowski and Malcolm Edwards. London: Granada, 1983. 350 p. (US Ed. as <u>The SF Book of Lists</u>.)

<u>Realms of Fantasy</u>, by Malcolm Edwards and Robert Holdstock. Garden City, NY: Doubleday, 1983. 120 p.

<u>SF Book of Lists, The</u>, by Maxim Jakubowski and Malcolm Edwards. New York: Berkley, 1983. 352 p.

"C. M. Kornbluth," in: Bleiler, E. F., ed. <u>Science Fiction Writers</u>. New York: Scribners, 1982. pp. 401-407.

"Eric Frank Russell," in: Bleiler, E. F., ed. <u>Science Fiction Writers</u>. New York: Scribners, 1982. pp. 197-202.

"Jack Vance," in: Bleiler, E. F., ed. <u>Science Fiction Writers</u>. New York: Scribners, 1982. pp. 543-549.

"Robert Silverberg interview," <u>Vector</u> 72: 16-20. February 1976.

"Robert Silverberg," in: Bleiler, E. F., ed. <u>Science Fiction Writers</u>. New York: Scribners, 1982. pp. 505-511.

"SF Publishing: The Economics," in: Wingrove, David, ed. <u>The Science Fiction Source Book</u>. New York: Van Nostrand, 1984. pp. 289-292.

"William Tenn," in: Bleiler, E. F., ed. <u>Science Fiction Writers</u>. New York: Scribners, 1982. pp. 525-530.

"Yesterday, today & tomorrow: the modern era," in: Holdstock, Robert, ed. <u>Encyclopedia of Science Fiction</u>. London: Octopus, 1978. pp. 174-189.

Edwards, Phil

"Mad Max Beyond Thunderdome," <u>American Cinematographer</u> 66(9):68-78. September 1985.

Edwards, Ray

"Movie gothick: a tribute to James Whale," <u>Sight and Sound</u> 27(2):95-98. Autumn 1957.

Edwards, Suzanne

"Best of C. L. Moore, The," in: Magill, Frank N., ed. <u>Survey of Science Fiction Literature</u>, Vol. 1. Englewood Cliffs, NJ: Salem Press, 1979. pp. 173-177.

"Syndic, The," in: Magill, Frank N., ed. <u>Survey of Science Fiction Literature</u>, Vol. 5. Englewood Cliffs, NJ: Salem Press, 1979. pp. 2211-2214.

Effinger, G. A.

"Writing Through Adversity," in: Jarvis, Sharon, ed. _Inside Outer Space_. New York: Ungar, 1985. pp. 133-148.

Efremov, Ivan

"Controversy over ideology in science fiction works," _Current Digest of the Soviet Press_ 18(6):16-17. March 2, 1966.

"Geneigte horizont," in: _Kunst und Literatur_ 11:1150-1167. 1962.

"Nauka i naucnaja fantastika," _Fantastika, 1962_. Moskva, 1962.

"Planet Zirda, The," _Soviet Life_ p. 62. June 1963.

"Problems, Searches and Polemics: The Billion Facets of the Future. _Current Digest of the Soviet Press_ 18(6): 16-17. March 2, 1966.

"Von der phantastik in der literatur," in: _Sovietliteratur_ no. 1:190-194. 1960.

Egan, James

"Apocalypticism in the Fiction of Stephen King," _Extrapolation_ 25(3): 214-227. Fall 1984.

"Dark Apocalyptic: Lovecraft's Cthulhu Mythos as a Parody of Traditional Christianity," _Extrapolation_ 23(4): 362-376. Winter 1982.

Egan, Thomas

"Tolkien and Chesterton: Some Analogies," _Mythlore_ 12(1): 28-35. Autumn 1985.

Egelhof, Joseph

"Sci-fi light years ahead of NASA: science fiction writers turn to inner space," _Chicago Tribune_ pp. 1,4. September 17, 1975.

Eggeling, John

"Battle of the Dorking, The," in: Magill, Frank N., ed. _Survey of Science Fiction Literature_, Vol. 1. Englewood Cliffs, NJ: Salem Press, 1979. pp. 130-132.

"Crystal Age, A," in: Magill, Frank N., ed. _Survey of Science Fiction Literature_, Vol. 1. Englewood Cliffs, NJ: Salem Press, 1979. pp. 449-452.

Eghoff, S. A.

"Tomorrow plus X: some thoughts on science fiction," _Ontario Library Review_ 46:77-80.

May 1962. also in: _Top of the News_ 19:31-35. December 1962.

Egoff, Sheila

"Science fiction," in: Egoff, Sheila, ed. _Only Connect: Readings on Children's Literature_. New York: Oxford University Press, 1969. pp. 384-398.

Eichler, Margaret

"Science Fiction as Desirable Feminist Scenarios," _Women's Studies International Quarterly_. 4(1): 51-64. 1981.

Eichner, H. M.

Atlantean Chronicles. Alhambra, California: Fantasy Publishing Company, 1971. 230 p.

"Bibliography," in: Eichner, Henry M. _Atlantean Chronicles_. Alhambra, California: Fantasy Publishing Co., 1971. pp. 135-228.

Eisele, Martin

"Zeitkugel, oder: das reisen auf altern wellen... Reflexionen zu einer 'neuen' romanserie," _Science Fiction Times_ (Bremerhaven) No. 136:17-19. May 1975.

Eisenberg, Adam

"Explorers," _Twilight Zone_ 5(4): 50-53. October 1985.

"Galaxina," _Cinefantastique_ 10(2):36-37. Fall 1980.

"Ghostbusters," _Cinefex_ No. 17:4-53. June 1984.

"Howling, The," by J. R. Fox and Adam Eisenberg. _Cinefantastique_ 10(3):18-23. Winter 1980.

"Jupiter revisited: The Odyssey of 2010," by Adam Eisenberg and Don Shay. _Cinefex_ No. 20:4-67. January 1985.

"Low tech effects: The Right Stuff," _Cinefex_ No. 14:4-25. October 1983.

"Stuff that dreams are made of," _Cinefex_ No. 23:4-33. August 1985.

"Waging a four minute war," _Cinefex_ No. 15:28-49. January 1984.

"What dreams are made of," _Cinefex_ No. 19:60-71. November 1984.

Eisenstein, Alex

"The Time Machine and the end of man," Science Fiction Studies 3(2):161-165. July 1976.

"Three perspectives of a film," by Morris Beja, Robert Plank and Alex Eisenstein. in: Clareson, Thomas D., ed. SF: The Other Side of Realism. Bowling Green, Ohio: Bowling Green University Popular Press, 1971. pp. 263-271.

"Very early Wells: origins of some major physical motifs in The Time Machine and The War of the Worlds," Extrapolation 13(2):119-126. May 1972.

Eisenstein, Phyllis

"Profession of Science Fiction, The, 28: Science Fiction and Me," Foundation 25: 31-35. June 1982.

Eisfeld, Rainer

"25 Jahre Science Fiction Times: Those were the days, my friend," Science Fiction Times (Germany) 26(1):5-7. January 1984.

Eiogruber, Frank, Jr.

Gangland's Doom: The Shadow of the Pulps. Oak Lawn, Illinois: Robert Weinberg, 1974. 64 p.

Eisler, Riane

"Beyond feminism: the Gylan future," Alternative Futures 4(2/3):122-130. Spring/Summer 1981.

Eisler, Steven

Space Wars: Worlds and Weapons. New York: Crescent, 1979. 96 p.

Eisner, Greta

"'Canterville Ghost, The'," in: Magill, Frank N., ed. Survey of Modern Fantasy Literature, Vol 1. Englewood Cliffs, NJ: Salem Press, Inc., 1983. pp. 190-192.

"Castle, The," in: Magill, Frank N., ed. Survey of Modern Fantasy Literature, Vol 1. Englewood Cliffs, NJ: Salem Press, Inc., 1983. pp. 207-210.

"Citizen of the Galaxy," in: Magill, Frank N., ed. Survey of Science Fiction Literature, Vol. 1. Englewood Cliffs, NJ: Salem Press, 1979. pp. 363-368.

"Does Anyone Else Have Something Further to Add?," in: Magill, Frank N., ed. Survey of Science Fiction Literature, Vol. 2. Englewood Cliffs, NJ: Salem Press, 1979. pp. 574-578.

"Haunting of Hill House, The," in: Magill, Frank N., ed. Survey of Modern Fantasy Literature, Vol 2. Englewood Cliffs, NJ: Salem Press, Inc., 1983. pp. 710-714.

"Shape of Things to Come, The," in: Magill, Frank N., ed. Survey of Science Fiction Literature, Vol. 4. Englewood Cliffs, NJ: Salem Press, 1979. pp. 1902-1907.

"Lester del Rey," in: Cowart, David, ed. Twentieth-Century American Science-Fiction Writers, Part 1: A-L. Detroit: Gale, 1981. pp. 129-133. (Dictionary of Literary Biography, v. 8)

Eizykman, Boris

Bande dessinee de science fiction americaine, by Boris Eizykman and Daniel Riche. Paris: Michel, 1976. 126 p.

Inconscience fiction. Paris: Kesselring, 1979. 319 p.

Science fiction et capitalismus: critique de la position de desir de la science. Paris: Mame, 1974. 253 p.

"Chance and Science Fiction: SF as Stochastic Fiction," Science-Fiction Studies 10(1): 24-34. March 1983.

"On science fiction," Science Fiction Studies 2(2):164-166. July 1975. (Originally published in Les Nouvelles Litteraires. April 1, 1974.)

"Temporality in Science Fiction Narrative," Science Fiction Studies 12(1): 66-87. March 1985.

Ekkehard, H.

"Ideologie und unterhaltung? literatur uber science fiction." Buch und Bibliothek 23:141-143. February 1971.

Eklund, Sven

"Science fiction in Scandinavia," Australian Science Fiction Review No. 14:15-19. February 1968.

Elbow, G. S.

"Science fiction for geographers: selected works," by G. S. Elbow and T. L. Martinson. Journal of Geography. 79(1):23-27. January 1980.

Elchlepp, Elizabeth

"Adam and Eve," in: Magill, Frank N., ed. _Survey of Modern Fantasy Literature_, Vol 1. Englewood Cliffs, NJ: Salem Press, Inc., 1983. pp. 1-3.

"Temptation of Saint Anthony, The," in: Magill, Frank N., ed. _Survey of Modern Fantasy Literature_, Vol 4. Englewood Cliffs, NJ: Salem Press, Inc., 1983. pp. 1891-1894.

"Turnabout," in: Magill, Frank N., ed. _Survey of Modern Fantasy Literature_, Vol 4. Englewood Cliffs, NJ: Salem Press, Inc., 1983. pp. 1983-1985.

"Venetian Glass Nephew, The," in: Magill, Frank N., ed. _Survey of Modern Fantasy Literature_, Vol 4. Englewood Cliffs, NJ: Salem Press, Inc., 1983. pp. 2029-2032.

Elflandsson, Galad

"David Lindsay and the quest for muspel-fire," _AB Bookman's Weekly_ 74(14):2131-2147. October 1, 1984.

Elgin, D. D.

Comedy of the Fantastic, The: Ecological Perspectives in the Fantasy Novel. Westport, CT: Greenwood, 1985. 204 p.

Elgin, S. H.

Science Fiction Poetry Handbook. Huntsville, Arizona: Science Fiction Poetry Association, 1986. 81 p.

"Teach Yourself Alien," _Aurora SF_ 7(1): 10-13. Summer 1981.

"Why a Woman is Not Like a Physicist," _Aurora SF_ 8(1): 30-34. Summer 1982.

Eliade, Mircea

"Los mitos en el mundo moderno," _La Torre, Rev. de la Universidad de Puerto Rico_ 2(6). April/June 1954.

Elis-Vetter, Ingeborg

"Vampir-Motiv in einigen deutschen Horror-Geschichten," in: Rottensteiner, Franz, ed. _Quarber Merkur_. Frankfurt: Suhrkamp, 1979. pp. 239-259.

Elkins, Charles

"Food of the Gods and How It Came to Earth, The," in: Magill, Frank N., ed. _Survey of_

Science Fiction Literature, Vol. 2. Englewood Cliffs, NJ: Salem Press, 1979. pp. 807-812.

"Island," in: Magill, Frank N., ed. _Survey of Science Fiction Literature_, Vol. 3. Englewood Cliffs, NJ: Salem Press, 1979. pp. 1073-1078.

"Star Maker," in: Magill, Frank N., ed. _Survey of Science Fiction Literature_, Vol. 5. Englewood Cliffs, NJ: Salem Press, 1979. pp. 2150-2155.

"Approach to the social functions of American science fiction, An," _Science Fiction Studies_ 4(3):228-232. November 1977.

"Approach to the social functions of science fiction and fantasy," in: Collins, R. A., ed. _Scope of the Fantastic: Culture, Biography, Themes, Children's Literature_. Westport: Greenwood, 1985. pp. 23-32.

"Asimov's 'Foundation' novels: historical materialism distorted into cyclical psycho-history," _Science Fiction Studies_ 3(1):26-36. March 1976. expanded: Olander, J. O., ed. _Isaac Asimov_. NY: Taplinger, 1977. pp. 97-110.

"Beyond reality's barriers: new dimensions," by Robert Silverberg and Charles Elkins. in: Warrick, Patricia, ed. _Science Fiction: Contemporary Mythology_. New York: Harper, 1978. pp. 92-100.

"E. M. Forster's 'The Machine Stops': Liberal-Humanist Hostility to Technology," in: Erlich, Richard D., ed. _Clockwork Worlds_. Westport, CT.: Greenwood, 1983. pp. 47-62.

"George Orwell," in: Bleiler, E. F., ed. _Science Fiction Writers_. New York: Scribners, 1982. pp. 233-241.

"Kurt Vonnegut," in: Bleiler, E. F., ed. _Science Fiction Writers_. New York: Scribners, 1982. pp. 551-561.

"Preliminary reflections on teaching science fiction critically," by Charles Elkins and Darko Suvin. _Science Fiction Studies_ 6(3):263-270. November 1979.

"Science fiction and future studies: dramatic and rational models," in: Samuelson, D. N. _Science Fiction and Future Studies_. Bryan, TX: SFRA, 1975. pp. 6-21.

"Science fiction versus futurology: dramatic versus rational models," _Science Fiction Studies_ 6(1):20-31. March 1979.

"Worlds of Olaf Stapledon, The: Myth or Fiction?" _Mosaic_ 13(3/4): 145-152. Spring/Summer 1980.

Elkins, M. J.

"Ada or Ardor: A Family Chronicle," in: Magill, Frank N., ed. Survey of Science Fiction Literature, Vol. 1. Englewood Cliffs, NJ: Salem Press, 1979. pp. 16-21.

Elkins, Merry

"Steven Spielberg on Indiana Jones and the Temple of Doom," American Cinematographer 65(7):50-60. July 1984.

Elleman, Barbara

"Popular reading: time fantasy update," Booklist 81(19): 1407-1408. June 1, 1985.

"Time fantasy," Booklist 74(19):1558-1560. June 1, 1978.

Ellenshaw, Harrison

"Creating the Matte Paintings for The Empire Strikes Back," American Cinematographer 61(6): 582-584, 607-611. June 1980.

Ellerbrock, Beate

Perry Rhodan: untersuchen einer science fiction heftromanserie, by Beate Ellerbrock, Jurgend Ellerbrock, and Frank Thiesse. Giessen: Anabas, 1976. 152 p.

Ellerbrock, Jurgend

Perry Rhodan: untersuchen einer science fiction heftromanserie, by Beate Ellerbrock, Jurgend Ellerbrock, and Frank Thiesse. Giessen: Anabas, 1976. 152 p.

Ellik, Ronald

Universes of E. E. Smith, by Ronald Ellik and William Evans. Chicago: Advent, 1966. 272 p.

Ellingsen, Peter

"Sci-Fi Guru Takes Off On Another 'Odyssey'," St. Petersburg (FL.) Times. April 11, 1982. in: Newsbank. Film and Television. 130: C1-2. 1982.

Ellington, J. E.

"Analysis of a Modern Myth: The Star Trek Series," by J. E. Ellington and J. W. Critelli. Extrapolation 24(3): 241-250. Fall 1983.

Elliot, J. M.

Fantasy Voices #1. San Bernardino, CA.: Borgo Press, 1982. 64 p.

Future of the Space Program/Large Corporations & Society: Discussions with 22 Science Fiction Writers. San Bernardino, CA: Borgo Press, 1981. 64 p.

Pulp Voices: Interviews with Pulp Magazine Writers and Editors, or, Science Fiction Voices No. 6. San Bernardino, CA: Borgo Press, 1983. 64 p.

Science Fiction Voices #2. San Bernardino, CA: Borgo Press, 1979. 62 p. (The Milford Series: Popular Writers of Today, Vol. 25.)

Science Fiction Voices #3. San Bernardino, CA: Borgo Press, 1980. 64 p.

Science Fiction Voices #4. San Bernardino, CA: Borgo Press, 1982. 63 p.

Work of R. Reginald: An Annotated Bibliography & Guide. Burgess, Michael; Elliot, J. M. San Bernardino, CA: Borgo, 1985. 48 p.

"Book of Ptath, The," in: Magill, Frank N., ed. Survey of Modern Fantasy Literature, Vol 1. Englewood Cliffs, NJ: Salem Press, Inc., 1983. pp. 146-148.

"A. E. Van Vogt: 'Making It'," Science Fiction Chronicle 2(8):1,20. May 1981.

"A. E. Van Vogt: A Writer with a Winning Formula," in: Elliot, J. M., ed. Science Fiction Voices #2. San Bernardino, CA.: Borgo Press, 1979. pp. 30-40.

"A. E. Van Vogt: master craftsman," Questar 2(3):22-26,58. June 1980.

"Amazing interview: Bob Shaw," Amazing 28(1): 14-21. July 1981.

"Bob Shaw: Science Fiction Traditions," in: Elliot, J. M. Science Fiction Voices #4. San Bernardino, CA: Borgo, 1982. pp. 26-37.

"Bradbury chronicles, The," Future No. 5:22-26. 1978.

"Brian M. Stableford: An Academic Looks at Science Fiction," in: Elliot, J. M. Science Fiction Voices #4. San Bernardino, CA: Borgo, 1982. p. 51-63.

"By Chance, Out of Conviction: D. G. Compton," Thrust 18: 5-7. Winter/Spring 1982.

"C. L. Moore: Poet of Far-Distant Futures," in: Elliot, J. M. Pulp Voices. San Bernardino, CA: Borgo, 1983. pp. 45-51.

"C. L. Moore: tales of drama and wonder, an interview," PSFQ (Cupertino, California) No. 3/4:28-31. 1978/1979.

Elliot, J. M. (Continued)

"Charles D. Hornig: A Question of Conscience," in: Elliot, J. M. Science Fiction Voices #4. San Bernardino, CA: Borgo, 1982. pp. 11-25.

"Colin Wilson: the Outsider," by Colin Wilson and J. M. Elliot. Fantasy Newsletter 3(11): 4-7, 31. November 1980.

"David Gerrold: His Star Trek Continues," in: Elliot, J. M., ed. Science Fiction Voices #3. San Bernardino, CA: Borgo Press, 1980. pp. 19-32.

"Forty-five years and five months," by R. A. Lupoff and J. M. Elliot. Questar 3(1):18-20,53-56. October 1980.

"Frank Kelly Freas: Portrait of an Artist," in: Elliot, J. M. Science Fiction Voices #4. San Bernardino, CA: Borgo, 1982. pp. 38-50. (Reprinted from Thrust, 1980).

"Future Forum: How do You Envisage First Contact With an Alien Race?" Future Life 22: 53-57. November 1980.

"Future Interview: A. E. Van Vogt," by J. M. Elliot and Al Flyn. Future 7: 22-24, 74. January 1979.

"Gardening Words: An Interview With Ian Watson," Foundation 30: 51-66. March 1984.

"Gregory Benford: A Scientist Looks at Science Fiction," in: Elliot, J. M., ed. Science Fiction Voices #3. San Bernardino, CA: Borgo Press, 1980. pp. 44-52. (An earlier version appeared in Galileo, 1978.)

"Harlan Ellison," Future Life No. 9:23-25,56-57. March 1979.

"Harlan Ellison: Outspoken, Outrageous, Outstanding," in: Elliot, J. M., ed. Science Fiction Voices #3. San Bernardino, CA: Borgo Press, 1980. pp. 9-18. (An earlier version appeared in Future Life, 1979.)

"Horace L. Gold: Galaxy's Pioneering Editor," in: Elliot, J. M. Pulp Voices. San Bernardino, CA: Borgo, 1983. pp. 25-31.

"Hugh B. Cave: Master of Vintage Horror," in: Elliot, J. M. Fantasy Voices #1. San Bernardino, CA: Borgo, 1982. pp. 31-44. (Reprinted from Fantasy Newsletter, 1980)

"Interview essay," by Katherine Kurtz and J. M. Elliot. in: Boyer, R. H. and Zahorski, K. J. Fantasists on Fantasy. New York: Avon Discus, 1984. pp. 231-260.

"Interview with a super man," Questar 2(1):36-39. November 1979.

"Interview with A. E. van Vogt, An," Science Fiction Review 6(4):19-23. November 1977.

"Interview with Bob Shaw," Amazing 28(1): 14-21. July 1981.

"Interview with Larry Niven, An," Science Fiction Review 7(3):24-27. July 1978.

"Interview with Octavia Butler," Thrust No. 12:19-22. Summer 1979.

"Interview with Ray Bradbury, An," Science Fiction Review 6(4):48-50. November 1977. (Reprinted from San Francisco Review of Books, June 1977)

"Interview: 'Take me home, little boy . . . '" Questar 2(3):45-47,61-63. June 1980.

"Interview: A. E. Van Vogt," Questar 2(3):22-26,58. June 1980.

"Interview: Brian Aldiss," Future Life 21: 44-46, 67. September 1980.

"Interview: Brian Stableford," Starship 18(2): 15-20. Summer/Fall 1981.

"Interview: Chelsea Quinn Yarbro," Fantasy Newsletter 4(12): 10-15, 30. December 1981.

"Interview: David Gerrold," Thrust No. 13:6-12. Fall 1979.

"Interview: Diane Duane," Starship 17(4): 17-24. Fall 1980.

"Interview: Forrest Ackerman," Questar 2(3):45-47,61-63. June 1980.

"Interview: Frank Belknap Long," Fantasy Newsletter 27:16-22,30. August 1980.

"Interview: Frank Kelly Freas," Thrust 15:14-19. Summer 1980.

"Interview: John Norman; The Chronicles of Gor," Questar 2(2):12-16. February 1980.

"Interview: Juanita Coulson," Fantasy Newsletter 4(10): 18-25, 34. October 1981.

"Interview: Karl Edward Wagner," Fantasy Newsletter 4(7): 17-22, 34. July 1981.

"Interview: Katherine Kurtz, part 1," Fantasy Newsletter 3(5):16-21. May 1980.

"Interview: Pamela Sargent," Fantasy Newsletter 5(9): 18-23. October 1982.

"Interview: Poul Anderson," Galileo 11/12:12-18. 1979.

"Interview: Raymond Gallun," Thrust 17: 6-13. Summer 1981.

"Interview: Richard Cowper," Fantasy Newsletter 4(5): 17-24, 30. May 1981.

"Interview: Robert Anton Wilson," Starship 18(1): 15-22. Spring 1981.

Elliot, J. M. (Continued)

"Interview: Robert Bloch," _Questar_ 2(4): 19-21, 52. August 1980.

"Interview: Robert Reginald," _Fantasy Newsletter_ 4(1): 18-23, 30. January 1981.

"Interview: Stanton A. Coblentz," _Fantasy Newsletter_ 3(10): 11-16. October 1980.

"Interview: The Making of a Professional: A. E. Van Vogt," _Amazing_ 28(5): 6-14. March 1982.

"Interview: William F. Nolan," _Fantasy Newsletter_ 4(2): 10-13. February 1981.

"Jack Williamson," _Future Life_ 22: 32-33, 65. November 1980.

"Jack Williamson: In At the Creation," in: Elliot, J. M. _Pulp Voices_. San Bernardino, CA: Borgo, 1983. pp. 9-24.

"Jerry Pournelle: From Space Program to Space Opera," in: Elliot, J. M., ed. _Science Fiction Voices #3_. San Bernardino, CA: Borgo Press, 1980. pp. 53-64. (An earlier version appeared in _Starship_, 1979).

"John Norman: Chronicles of Gor," in: Elliot, J. M. _Fantasy Voices #1_. San Bernardino, CA: Borgo, 1982. pp. 18-30. (Reprinted from _Questar_, 1980).

"John Norman: The Chronicles of Gor," _Questar_ 2(2):12-16. February 1980.

"Katherine Kurtz: Tapestries of Medieval Wonder," in: Elliot, J. M. _Fantasy Voices #1_. San Bernardino, CA: Borgo, 1982. pp. 44-64. (Reprinted from _Fantasy Newsletter_, 1980).

"Larry Niven: science fiction's master world-builder," _Questar_ 1(4):9-11. August 1979. also in: Elliot, J. M.. _Science Fiction Voices No. 2_. San Bernardino, California: Borgo Press, 1979. pp. 9-19.

"Larry Niven: Soothsayer of Known Space," _Future_ 3: 31-33. July 1978.

"Looking Back: My Life in Science Fiction; Charles D. Hornig," _Thrust_ 20: 11-16. Spring/Summer 1984.

"Manly Wade Wellman: Better Things Waiting," in: Elliot, J. M. _Fantasy Voices #1_. San Bernardino, CA: Borgo, 1982. pp. 5-18. (Reprinted from _Fantasy Newsletter_, 1980).

"Many faces of Don Post, Sr.," _Questar_ 2(3):17-21. June 1980.

"Meet the Editor: Donald A. Wollheim," _SFWA Bulletin_ 18(1): 29-30. Spring 1984.

"Meet the Editor: Elinor Mavor," _SFWA Bulletin_ 18(2): 11-13. Summer 1983.

"Meet the editor: George H. Scithers," _SFWA Bulletin_ 19(4): 21-24. Winter 1985.

"Meet the editor: Lou Aronica," _SFWA Bulletin_ 19(2): 6-9. Summer 1985.

"Meet the Editor: Robert Reginald, Borgo Press," _SFWA Bulletin_ 18(4): 6-10. Winter 1984.

"Meet the Editor: Ruth K. Hapgood," _SFWA Bulletin_ 18(2): 8-11. Summer 1984.

"Meet the Editor: Shawna McCarthy," _SFWA Bulletin_ 18(3): 10-13. Fall 1984.

"Meet the Editor: Stanley Schmidt," _SFWA Bulletin_ 19(1): 52-55. Spring 1985.

"Nolan's Run," _Night Voyages_ 1(9):46-48. Winter/Spring 1983.

"Nolan's Run: Interview," _Questar_ 3(4): 62-64, 73-74. June 1981.

"Pamela Sargent: Woman of Wonder: An Interview," _Foundation_ 26: 56-72. October 1981.

"Portfolio: Morris Scott Dollens," _Future Life_ 19: 58-63. June 1980.

"Poul Anderson: Seer of Far-Distant Futures," in: Elliot, J. M., ed. _Science Fiction Voices #2_. San Bernardino, CA: Borgo Press, 1979. pp. 41-50. (An earlier version appeared in _Galileo_, 1979.)

"Profession of Science Fiction, The, 25: Perfecting Visions, Slaying Cynics (an interview with George Zebrowski)," _Foundation_ 23: 44-64. October 1981.

"Ray Bradbury: Poet of Fantastic Fiction," in: Elliot, J. M., ed. _Science Fiction Voices #2_. San Bernardino, CA: Borgo Press, 1979. pp. 20-29.

"Raymond Z. Gallun: Seeker of Tomorrow," in: Elliot, J. M. _Pulp Voices_. San Bernardino, CA: Borgo, 1983. pp. 52-63.

"Richard Lupoff: On the Verge...," in: Elliot, J., ed. _Science Fiction Voices #3_. San Bernardino, CA: Borgo Press, 1980. pp. 33-43. (An earlier version appeared in _Starship_, 1979.)

"Robert Silverberg: Next Stop: Lord Valentine's Castle, an interview," _PSFQ_ 5:18-24. Spring 1981.

"Robert Silverberg: Next Stop: Lord Valentine's Castle," in: Elliot, J., ed. _Science Fiction Voices #2_. San Bernardino, CA: Borgo Press, 1979. pp. 51-62.

"Sea and Science Fiction," by A. B. Chandler and J. M. Elliot. _Owlflight_ 3: 25-31. 1982.

Elliot, J. M. (Continued)

"Songs sweet and haunting," Foundation 33: 5-19. Spring 1985.

"Stanton A. Coblentz: 'I Pant for the Music Which is Divine," in: Elliot, J. M. Pulp Voices. San Bernardino, CA: Borgo, 1983. pp. 32-44.

"Starship interview: Jerry Pournelle," Starship 16(4):11-17. Fall 1979.

"Starship interview: Larry Niven," Starship 16(4):11,17-23. Fall 1979.

"Starship interview: Richard Lupoff," Starship 16(3):21-26. Summer 1979.

"Visions of the future," Questar 3(1):21-25. October 1980.

"What Writers Watch," Questar 3(4): 56-59. June 1981.

Elliott, David

"Android Role Opens Bright New Path for Don Opper," San Diego Union June 28, 1984. NewsBank. Film and Television. FTV 1:C4. 1984.

"Howard puts all into a Cocoon," San Diego Union June 23, 1985. in: NewsBank. Film and Television. 2:B12-B13. July 1985.

"New Life Scored into 'Metropolis'," San Diego Union August 17, 1984. in: NewsBank. Film and Television FTV 26: E12-E13. 1984.

Elliott, E. T.

"Interview with Poul Anderson," Science Fiction Review 7(2):32-37. May 1978.

"Raising Hackles, 1984: The Science Fiction Year," Science Fiction Review 14(1): 60-62. February 1985.

"Raising Hackles: Science Fiction is Dying: Can the Patient be Saved?" Science Fiction Review 12(1): 47-48. February 1983.

"Raising Hackles: Fantasy as Cancer, Part 1," Science Fiction Review 11(3): 43-44. August 1982.

"Raising Hackles: Fantasy as Cancer, part II," Science Fiction Review 11(4): 60-61. November 1982.

"Raising Hackles: SF and Business," Science Fiction Review 12(4): 42. November 1983.

"Raising Hackles: The Old Float Game," Science Fiction Review 13(3): 21-22. August 1984.

Elliott, R. C.

Shape of Utopia: Studies in a Literary Genre. Chicago and London: University of Chicago Press, 1970. 158 p.

"Saturnalia, satire, and utopia," Yale Review 55(4):535-536. June 1966.

Elliott, R. W.

"Cheshire Voice, A," Labrys No. 7: 109-114. November 1981.

Ellis, H. F.

"Queen of visceronoonia," New Yorker 45(45):54-56. December 27, 1969.

Ellis, James

"Leigh Brackett: storyteller," Xenophile No. 42:27-28. September/October 1979.

Ellis, P. B.

H. Rider Haggard: a Voice From the Infinite. London: Routledge & Kegan Paul, 1978. 291 p.

Last Adventurer, The: The Life of Talbot Mundy. West Kinston,RI: Grant, 1984. 279 p.

Ellis, S. M.

Wilkie Collins, Le Fanu and Others. London: Constable, 1931. 343 p.

Ellison, Harlan

All the Lies That Are My Life. Columbia, PA: Underwood/Miller, 1980. 130 p.

American Film Institute Seminar With Harlan Ellison, The. Beverly Hills, CA: Center for Advanced Film Studies, c1978. 87 p. on 1 microfiche.

Medea: Harlan's World. New York: Bantam, 1985. 532 p.

"3 faces of fear," Cinema 3(2):1-8,13-14. March 1966. (not seen)

"Ellison on Ellison," in: Porter, Andrew, ed. The Book of Ellison. New York: Algol Press, 1978. pp. 67-78.

"Few (hopefully final) words about the New Wave," in: McNelly, W. E., ed. Science Fiction the Academic Awakening. Shreveport, LA: CEA, 1974. pp. 40-43.

"Glass Teat, The, Part 1," Los Angeles Free Press p. 7-8. May 9, 1969. (Underground Newspaper Collection, Reel 21, Title 3)

Ellison, Harlan (Continued)

"Glass Teat, The, Part 2," <u>Los Angeles Free Press</u> p. 7-8. May 23, 1969. (<u>Underground Newspaper Collection</u>, Reel 21, Title 3)

"Hans Stefan Santesson, 1914-1975," <u>Locus</u> No. 170:1-2. March 15, 1975.

"Hard Truths," <u>Fantasy Newsletter</u> 5(4): 5-8. April/May 1982.

"How you stupidly blew fifteen million dollars a week, avoided having an adenoid-shaped swimming pool . . . and otherwise pissed me off," <u>Algol</u> 15(2):9-14. Spring 1978.

"Introduction," in: Ellison, Harlan, ed. <u>Medea</u>. New York: Bantam, 1985. pp. 9-13.

"Memoir: 'I have no mouth and I must scream'," <u>Starship</u> 17(3):6-13. Summer 1980.

"Memoir: I Have No Mouth, and I Must Scream," in: Greenberg, Martin H., ed. <u>Fantastic Lives: Autobiographical Essays by Notable Science Fiction Writers</u>. Carbondale: Southern Illinois University Press, 1981. pp. 1-19.

"Profession of Science Fiction, The,20: Mortal Dreads," <u>Foundation</u> 20: 28-32. October 1980.

"Punk is not a Pistolero, A," <u>Patchin Review</u> 1: 6-13. July 1981.

"Re: the 1978 World Science Fiction Convention," <u>Locus</u> 10(10):3. December 1977.

"Science fiction is . . . " <u>New Times</u> 3:60. October 18, 1974. (not seen)

"Special Dreamer, A," <u>Starship</u> 17(4): 27-29. Fall 1980.

"Speculative fiction: out of the ghetto," <u>Writer's Yearbook</u> pp. 30-34,112. 1972.

"Voice from the styx: comment on the art of speculative fiction, A," <u>Psychotic</u> 27:5-11. September 1968.

"Whore with a heart of iron pyrites, The; or, where does a writer go to find a maggie?" in: Wilson, R. S. ed. <u>Those Who Can: a Science Fiction Reader</u>. New York: Mentor, 1973. pp. 123-134.

"Why a top fantasy writer hates 'Star Wars'," <u>Los Angeles</u> 22:236-237. August 1977.

"With the eyes of a demon: seeing the fantastic as a video image," in: Bretnor, Reginald, ed. <u>The Craft of Science Fiction</u>. New York: Harper, 1976. pp. 236-291.

"With the eyes of a demon: writing for television today," <u>Writer's Digest</u> 56(7):15+. July 1976.

Ellwood, G. F.

<u>In a Faraway Galaxy: A Literary Approach to a Film Saga</u>, by Doris Robin, Lee Vibber, and G. F. Ellwood. Pasadena, CA: Extequer Press, 1984. 149 p.

"Matters of Grave Import: Gems; the Power and the Glory," <u>Mythlore</u> 10(1): 46, 54. Spring 1983.

"Of creation and love," <u>Mythlore</u> 6(4):19,42. Fall 1979.

"On myth," <u>Mythlore</u> 1(2):14-16. April 1969.

"To adore and to obey," <u>Mythlore</u> 7(1):18-19. March 1980.

Elrick, G. S.

<u>Science Fiction Handbook for Readers and Writers</u>. Chicago: Chicago Review Press, 1978. 315 p.

"Armageddon 2419 A. D.," in: Magill, Frank N., ed. <u>Survey of Science Fiction Literature</u>, Vol. 1. Englewood Cliffs, NJ: Salem Press, 1979. pp. 84-88.

"Before Adam," in: Magill, Frank N., ed. <u>Survey of Science Fiction Literature</u>, Vol. 1. Englewood Cliffs, NJ: Salem Press, 1979. pp. 144-148.

Elsberg, Iakov

"V bitve za cheloveka," <u>Literaturnaia gazeta</u>. January 1, 1972. p. 4.

Elsen, Claude

"Du roman fantastique a la science fiction; les chroniqueurs de l'Impossible," <u>La Gazette des lettres</u> February 15, 1951.

Emme, E. M.

<u>Science Fiction and Space Futures</u> San Diego, CA: Univelt, for the American Astronautical Society, 1982. 270 p.

"Eclectic Bibliography on the History of Space Futures, An," in: Emme, Eugene M., ed. <u>Science Fiction and Space Futures</u>. San Diego: Univelt, 1982. pp. 213-245.

Emmerova, Jarmila

"Doslov," in: Bradbury, Ray. <u>Illustrovana zena.</u> Praha: Ceskoslovensky Spisovatel, 1968. pp. 243-245.

Emmons, W. S., Jr.

"Bibliography of H. P. Lovecraft, A,"
Extrapolation 3(1):2-25. December 1961.

"H. P. Lovecraft as a mythmaker,"
Extrapolation 1(2):35-37. May 1960.

Enders, Carl

"Bucher uber Geistergeschichten, Vampyre, und
Robinsonaden," by Rudolf Furst, Egon von
Momorzynski, and Carl Enders. Quarber Merkur
39:51-55. Jan. 1975.

Enders, H.

"Zukunftsroman," Jugendschriften-Warte
1955. pp. 19-20.

Enders-Dragaesser, Uta

Frauen bei Marion Zimmer Bradley," by Uta
Enders-Dragaesser and Brigitte Sellach. in:
Femistische Utopien: Aufbruch in dei
postpatriarchale Gesellschaft, ed. by Barbara
Holland-Cunz. Meitingen: Corian Verlag, 1985.

Eney, Dick

Proceedings: Discon. Chicago: Advent, 1965.
191 p.

Eng, Steve

"Arkham Collector," in: Tymn, M. B. and
Ashley, Mike. Science Fiction, Fantasy, and
Weird Fiction Magazines. Westport, CT:
Greenwood, 1985. pp. 111-112.

"Arkham Sampler," in: Tymn, M. B. and
Ashley, Mike. Science Fiction, Fantasy, and
Weird Fiction Magazines. Westport, CT:
Greenwood, 1985. pp. 112-115.

"Barbarian Bard: the poetry of Robert E.
Howard," in: Herron, Don, ed. Dark
Barbarian: The Writings of Robert E. Howard, a
Critical Anthology. Westport, CT: Greenwood,
1984. pp. 23-64.

"Fantasy genre poetry," in: Magill, Frank N.,
ed. Survey of Modern Fantasy Literature,
Vol 5. Englewood Cliffs, NJ: Salem Press,
Inc., 1983. pp. 2415-2421.

"Songs of Science, Songs of Weird: A Review of
Fantastic Poetry," Fantasy Review 7(9):
15-16. October 1984.

Engdahl, S. L.

"Changing role of science fiction in children's
literature, The," Horn Book 47(5):449-455.
October 1971.

"Prospective on the Future: The Quest of Space
Age Young People," in: Lentz, Millicent, ed.
Young Adult Literature: Background and
Criticism. Chicago: ALA, 1980. pp. 425-433.

"Why write for today's teenagers?" Horn
Book 48(3):249-254. June 1972.

Engebretson, David

Shorter Works of Stephen King, The, by
Michael Collings and David Engebretson. Mercer
Island, WA: Starmont, 1985. 202 p.

Engel, David

"On the question of foma: a study of the
novels by Kurt Vonnegut," Riverside
Quarterly 5(2):119-128. February 1972.

Engel, Peter

"Interview with Stanislaw Lem, An," Missouri
Review 7(2): 218-237. 1984.

"Lem: Science Fiction's Passionate Realist,"
New York Times Book Review p. 7, 34. March
20, 1983.

Engelhard, Hubert

"Science fiction est un genre litteraire, La,"
La Reforme Juillet 3, 1954.

Engholm, Ahrvid

"Land of the Midnight Zine," A Foreign
Fanzine. 4: 25-26. August 1981.

England, Jim

"Consolations for Disappointed Writers,"
Focus: An SF Writer's Magazine No. 7: 23-26.
Spring 1983.

"SF and Reality," Vector 103: 14-16.
August 1981.

Engle, Paul

"Point that must be raised: the equalization
of fiction, A," Chicago Tribune Book World
p. 1. June 10, 1973. (not seen)

Englert, L.

"Gefahrdung des Menschen im Spiegel des
zeitgenossischen Zukunftsromans," Der
Hessische Erzieher 8:33-48. 1959.

Enquete

"Faut-il bruler lea recits d'anticipation scientifique," <u>Les Nouvelles Litteraires</u> August 29, 1957.

Enright, D. J.

"Decline of Science Fiction, The," (Poem) <u>Times Literary Supplement</u> 4078: 594. May 29, 1981.

Epperson, W. R.

"Repose of very delicate balance: postulants and celebrants in the sacrement of marriage in the detective fiction of Dorothy L. Sayers," <u>Mythlore</u> 6(4):33-36. Fall 1979.

Epstein, E. L.

"Novels of J. R. R. Tolkien and the ethnology of medieval Christendom, The," <u>Philological Quarterly</u> 48(4):517-525. October 1969.

Eremrt, Karl

<u>Neugier oder Flucht? Zu Poetik, Ideologie und Wirkung der Science Fiction</u>. Stuttgart: Klett, 1900. 150 p.

Erickson, Hal

"Censorship: Another dimension behind The Twilight Zone," <u>Twilight Zone</u> 5(4): 70-73. October 1985.

Ericson, J. V.

"Image of Robots in Science Fiction," Worcester, MA: Undergraduate Report, Worcester Polytechnic Institute, 1982. Report No. 82C0341. 59 p.

Erisman, R. O.

"Trolls and witches of a coexistent cosmos," <u>New York Times Book Review</u> p. 27. August 27, 1961. (Book revew)

Erlich, R. D.

<u>Clockwork Worlds: Mechanized Environments in Science Fiction</u>. by R. D. Erlich and T. P. Dunn. Westport, CT: Greenwood, 1983. 384 p.

<u>Mechanical God, The: Machines in Science Fiction</u>, by Thomas P. Dunn and Richard D. Erlich. Westport, CT: Greenwood, 1982. 282 p.

"Colossus," in: Magill, Frank N., ed. <u>Survey of Science Fiction Literature</u>, Vol. 1. Englewood Cliffs: Salem, 1979. pp. 409-414.

"Earthsea Trilogy, The," in: Magill, Frank N., ed. <u>Survey of Modern Fantasy Literature</u>, Vol 1. Englewood Cliffs, NJ: Salem Press, Inc., 1983. pp. 447-459.

"Left Hand of Darkness, The," in: Magill, Frank N., ed. <u>Survey of Science Fiction Literature</u>, Vol. 3. Englewood Cliffs, NJ: Salem Press, 1979. pp. 1171-1177.

"List of Works Useful For the Study of Machines in Science Fiction," by T. P. Dunn and R. D. Erlich. in: Dunn, Thomas P., ed. <u>The Mechanical God</u>. Westport: Greenwood, 1982. pp. 225-273.

"List of Works Useful for the Study of Mechanized Environments in SF." by R. D. Erlich and T. P. Dunn. in: Erlich, Richard D., ed. <u>Clockwork Worlds</u>. Westport, CT: Greenwood, 1983. pp. 263-359.

"Mechanical Hive, The: Urbmon 116 as the Villain-Hero of Silverberg's The World Inside," by T. P. Dunn and R. D. Erlich. <u>Extrapolation</u> 21(4): 338-347. Winter 1980.

"Moon-Watcher, Man and Star-Child: <u>2001</u> as Paradigm," in: Hassler, Donald M. <u>Patterns of the Fantastic</u>. Mercer Island, WA: Starmont, 1983. pp. 73-80.

"Mythic patterns in Ellison's <u>A Boy and His Dog</u>," by John Crow and Richard Erlich. <u>Extrapolation</u> 18(2):162-166. May 1977.

"Niven and Pournelle's 'Oath of Fealty': A Case of Improvement?" <u>Foundation</u> 27: 64-70. February 1983.

"Odysseus in grey flannel: the heroic journey in two dystopias by Pohl and Kornbluth," <u>Par Rapport</u> 1:126-131. Summer 1978.

"SF in the classroom: strange odyssey: from Dart and Ardrey to Kubrick and Clarke," <u>Extrapolation</u> 17(2):118-124. May 1976.

"Trapped in the bureaucratic pinball machine: a vision of dystopia in the twentieth century," in: Remington, T. J., ed. <u>Selected Proceedings of the 1978 SFRA Nat'l Conference</u>. Cedar Falls: Univ. of North. Iowa, 1979. pp. 30-45.

"Womb With a View, A,: Domesticating the Fantastic in Pohl and Kornbluth's <u>Gladiator-at-Law</u>," <u>Foundation</u> 23: 31-29. October 1981.

"Words of binding: patterns of integration in the Earthsea trilogy," by J. H. Crow and R. D. Erlich. in: Olander, J. D. and M. H. Greenberg, eds. <u>Ursula K. Le Guin</u>. New York: Taplinger, 1979. pp. 200-224.

Ernoult, Claude

"Science Fiction et rhetorique des idees," <u>Bizarre</u> No. 11:60, 62, 64. October 1955.

Ertal, Claude

"Demons et Merveilles Reve ou Ecriture," in: H. P. Lovecraft. Paris: Editions de l'Herne, 1969. pp. 75-90.

Ervasti, Kaarle

Aikataika: Fantastica Fennica, 1867-1981. Helsinki: Ervasti, 1982. 66 p.

Escarpit, Robert

Litteraire et le Social, Le. Paris: Flammion, 1970.

"Ghetto de la science fiction, Le," Le Monde August 31, 1954.

Eschelbach, C. J.

Aldous Huxley: a Bibliography, 1916-1959, by C. J. Eschelbach and J. L. Shober. Berkeley: University of California Press, 1961. 150 p.

Eschmann, E. W.

"Grossen Gehirne. Vom Computer in Utopie und Wirklichkeit," Merkur; Deutsche Zeitschrift fur Europaisches Denken 19:720-735. 1965.

"Raumsucher. Zur amerikanischen Literatur der Space-Fiction," Merkur; Deutsches Zeitschrift fur Europaisches Denken 12:368-378. April 1958.

Eshbach, L. A.

Of Worlds Beyond: the Science of Science Fiction Writing. Reading, Pennsylvania: Fantasy, Press, 1947. 96 p. Reprinted, Chicago: Advent, 1964. 104 p.

Over My Shoulder: Reflections on a Science Fiction Era. Philadelphia: Train, 1983. 417 p.

"Fantasy Press Story, The," Starship 20(1): 11-15. Winter 1983/84.

"Shasta Publishers," Fantasy Commentator 5(1): 34-40. Winter 1983.

"Wanted: 1500 STF collectors," Fantasy Times No. 138:18. September (2) 1951.

Esmonde, M. P.

"After Armageddon: the post cataclysmic novel for young readers," Children's Literature 6:211-220. 1977.

"After Armageddon: The Postcataclysmic Novel for Young Readers," in: Lentz, Millicent, ed. Young Adult Literature: Background and Criticism. Chicago: ALA, 1980. pp. 440-448.

"Death and deathlessness in children's fantasy," Fantasiae 7(4):1,8-11. April 1979.

"From Little Buddy to Big Brother: The Icon of the Robot in Children's Science Fiction," in: Dunn, Thomas P., ed. The Mechanical God. Westport: Greenwood, 1982. pp. 85-98.

"The master pattern: the psychological journey in the Earthsea trilogy," in: Olander, J. D. and M. H. Greenburg, eds. Ursula K. Le Guin. New York: Taplinger, 1979. pp. 15-35.

Espeland, Mecedes

"Star Trek as Recreational Reading for Children," Research Paper, Glassboro State College, 1979. 53 p. ERIC ED 195 967

Espley, J. L.

"H. Beam Piper: an annotated bibliography," Extrapolation 21(2):172-181. Summer 1980.

Estes, Jane

"Mars is exciting, but millions have already visited Frank Herbert's planet 'Dune'," People 6(7):86-87. August 16, 1976.

Estrabau, G. D. de

"Ciencia ficcion en la narrativa de Edgar A. Poe," Plural 6(78):88-90. March 1978.

"Wodehouse y Graves: extranos companeros de cama," Plural 6(77):47-48. February 1978.

Estrada, Jackie

"Science fiction market, The," Writers Digest 49(4):49-52,80-81. April 1969.

Etherington, N. A.

Rider Haggard. Boston: Twayne, 1984. 138 p.

"Rider Haggard, imperialism, and the layered personality," Victorian Studies 22(1): 71-87. Autumn 1978.

Ettlin, Michael

"Close Encounter with Sci-Fi Fans," Los Angeles Times. Sec. 6, p. 5. September 4, 1980.

Eurich, Nell

Science in Utopia: a Mighty Design.
Cambridge, Massachusetts: Harvard University
Press, 1967. 332 p.

Evans, Christopher

Science Fiction as Religion. by Stan Gooch
and Christopher Evans. Somerset: Bran's Head,
1981. 15 p.

"Arts, The: Books," Omni 3(8): 34. May
1981.

"Long Time Coming," Vector 98: 16-19.
June 1980.

"Sense and sensibility: the short stories of
Thomas M. Disch," Vector 93:12-15.
May/June 1979.

"Wrestling With Words," in: Wingrove, David,
ed. The Science Fiction Source Book. New
York: Van Nostrand, 1984. pp. 76-77.

Evans, I. O.

"Founder of science fiction," in: Evans, I.
O. Jules Verne and His Work. New York:
Twayne Publishers, 1966. pp. 155-164.

Evans, John

(Letter outlining SF course to be taught at
McGill University), Analog 86(3):173-174.
November 1970.

Evans, R. O.

"Nouveau Roman, Russian dystopias, and Anthony
Burgess, The," Studies in the Literary
Imagination 6(2):27-37. Fall 1973.

Evans, Richard

"On fiction editing," Focus (BSFA) No.
2:4-6. Spring 1980.

Evans, Robley

J. R. R. Tolkien. New York: Warner
Paperback Library, 1973. 206 p. Reprinted,
New York: Crowell, 1976.

Evans, W. H.

"Fantasy in The Idler Magazine: A
Bibliography," by W. H. Evans and A. L.
Searles. Fantasy Commentator 1(11):
302-304. Summer 1946.

"Thumbing the Munsey Files," Fantasy
Commentator 1(11): 300-301. Summer 1946.

Evans, William

Fanzine Index...Listing Most Fanzines From the
Beginning Through 1952 Including Titles,
Editors' Names and Data on Each Issue, ed. by
Robert Pavlat and William Evans. Flushing, New
York: Harold Palmer Piser, 1965. 143 p.

Universes of E. E. Smith, by Ronald Ellik
and William Evans. Chicago: Advent, 1966.
272 p.

Evdokimov, Aleksandr

"Sovetskaia fantastika (opyt bibliografii)," in
Fantastika 1967. Moskva: Molodaia gvardiia,
1968. pp. 379-399.

"Sovetskaia fantastika (opyt bibliografii)," in
Fantastika 1968. Moskva: Molodaia gvardiia,
1969. pp. 323-348.

"Sovetskaia fantastika voennykh let (1941-1945
gg.)," in Fantastika 69/70. Moskva:
Molodaia gvardiia, 1970. pp. 315-318.

Everett, R. P.

"Hell and high water," Cinefex No.
18:4-41. August 1984.

Everett, Todd

"Giorgio Moroder Scores a Silent Classic,"
Los Angeles Herald Examiner August 16, 1984.
in: NewsBank. Film and Television FTV
26:E10-E11. 1984.

Everitt, David

"3-D: The Second Coming," Starlog 54:
32-36. 64. January 1982.

"Art of Chris Achilleos, The" Starlog 60:
48-52. July 1982.

"Starlog Interview: Alan Ladd, Jr.," by Kerry
O'Quinn and David Everitt. Starlog 55:
40-43. February 1982.

"Starlog Interview: Scott Glenn: Actor as
Astronaut," Starlog 78: 54-55. January
1984.

Evers, Richard

"Round Table Interview/Discussion: Vonda
McIntyre, Joanna Russ, Jessica Amanda
Salmonson," P*S*F*Q 6: 9-13, 21-24, 35.
Fall 1981.

Everson, William

"Family tree of monsters, A," Film Culture
1(1):24-30. January 1955.

Everson, William (Continued)

"Horror films," <u>Films in Review</u>
5(1):12-23. January 1954.

Ewald, R. J.

"<u>Air Wonder Stories</u>," by Mike Ashley and R.
J. Ewald. in: Tymn, M. B. and Ashley, Mike.
<u>Science Fiction, Fantasy, and Weird Fiction</u>
<u>Magazines</u>. Westport, CT: Greenwood, 1985.
pp. 10-12.

"<u>Captain Future</u>," by Mike Ashley and Robert
Ewald. in: Tymn, M. B. and Ashley, Mike.
<u>Science Fiction, Fantasy, and Weird Fiction</u>
<u>Magazines</u>. Westport, CT: Greenwood, 1985.
pp. 155-157.

"<u>Startling Stories</u>," in: Tymn, M. B. and
Ashley, Mike. <u>Science Fiction, Fantasy, and</u>
<u>Weird Fiction Magazines</u>. Westport, CT:
Greenwood, 1985. pp. 611-617.

"<u>Wonder Stories</u>," by Robert Ewald and Mike
Ashley. in: Tymn, M. B. and Ashley, Mike.
<u>Science Fiction, Fantasy, and Weird Fiction</u>
<u>Magazines</u>. Westport, CT: Greenwood, 1985.
pp. 743-762.

Eyman, Scott

"Forry Ackerman's fantastic, horrific museum,"
<u>Plain Dealer Magazine</u> pp. 44-46,54-56.
(date not available, C. 1980; copy in Texas A&M
University Science Fiction Research Collection)

Ezine, J. L.

"Science fiction nous interroge. Entretien avec
Jean-Claude Amyl, La," <u>Les Nouvelles</u>
<u>litteraires</u> (Paris) 2427:3. April 1, 1974.

F

Fabbricante, L. V.

J. H. Rosny Aine and His Novels: Social, Analytical and Pre-Historical. Ph.D. Dissertation, Columbia, 1953. 251 p.

Fabian, Stephen

"Lucky Me," Fantasy Commentator 4(4): 216-221. Winter 1982.

Fabozzi, Antonio

Il cinema della paura: orrore e fantascienza nel cinema americano degli anni '70 e '80. Napoli: Liguori, 1982. 235 p.

Fabrini, Julius

"Starlog Interview: DeForest Kelley, Part 1," by Randy Lofficier, J. M. Lofficier, and Julius Fabrini. Starlog 87: 18-20, 67. October 1984.

"Starlog Interview: DeForest Kelley, Part 2," by Randy Lofficier, J. M. Lofficier, and Julius Fabrini. Starlog 88: 22-23. November 1984.

"Starlog Profile: George Takei," Starlog No. 101: 12-13, 62. December 1985.

Fabun, Don

"Science fiction in motion pictures, radio, and television," in: Bretnor, Reginald, ed. Modern Science Fiction: Its Meaning and Its Future. New York: Coward McCann, 1953. Reprinted, Chicago: Advent, 1979. pp. 43-70.

Fackler, Mark

"Cooley and Clarke: A Study in Comparative Futurology." Paper presented at the Annual Meeting of the Association for Education in Journalism, Boston, MA., August 9-13, 1980. 21 p. ERIC ED 191 028.

Fadiman, Clifton

"Party of one," Holiday 11(6):14,16,146. June 1952.

"Wild child," in: Fadiman, Clifton. Party of One. New York: World, 1955. pp. 324-333.

Faery, R. B.

"Earthsea Trilogy, The," in: Magill, Frank N., ed. Survey of Science Fiction Literature, Vol. 2. Englewood Cliffs, NJ: Salem Press, 1979. pp. 692-697.

Faig, K. W., Jr.

"H. P. Lovecraft: His Life and Work," by K. W. Faig, Jr. and S. T. Joshi. in: Joshi, S. T., ed. H. P. Lovecraft: Four Decades of Criticism. Athens, OH: Ohio University Press, 1980. pp. 1-19.

Fainburg, Z. I.

"Auf der Suche nach einer Formel fur das Menschliche," Quarber Merkur 38:36-39. Novvember 1974.

"Sovremennoe obschchestvo i nauchnaya fantastika," Voprosy Filosofii 21(6):32-43. 1967.

Falconer, L. N.

Gazeteer of the Hyborian World of Conan, Including Also the World of Kull and an Ethnogeographical Dictionary of the Principal Peoples of the Era. West Linn, Oregon: Starmont House, 1977. 119 p.

Falessi, Cesare

"Oltre il cielo," Robot No. 12/13/14. 1977.

Falk, Andre

"Science et science fiction," <u>Arts</u>
February 1956.

Falster, C.

"Rejse til mjanen," in: <u>Rejser i tid og rum.</u>
<u>En Bog om science fiction</u>, ed. by Tage La
Cour. Copenhagen: Stig Verdelkaer, 1973.

Fanzo, D. A.

<u>Inquiry Into the Literature of Science</u>
<u>Fiction: Its Development, Maturation, and</u>
<u>Significance as a Literary Genre</u>. Masters
Thesis, Texas Technological College, 1965.
108 p.

Farber, Jim

"Man With Two Brains (review),"
<u>Cinefantastique</u> 13(6)/14(1):98. September
1983.

Farber, Stephen

"End of the World, The, Take 1," <u>American</u>
<u>Film</u> 8(1): 61-63. October 1982.

Farley, E. E.

"Which does not touch upon mirror and pigeon,"
<u>The Eildon Tree</u> 1(1):19-21. 1974.

Farley, Ellen

"Is the Sky the Limit for Science-Fiction
Movies," <u>Los Angeles Times</u> p. 102-103.
February 26, 1978.

Farmer, P. J.

<u>Doc Savage: His Apocalyptic Life</u>. New York:
Bartam, 1975. 269 p.

"Baum, L. Frank," in: Woodcock, George, ed.
<u>20th Century Fiction</u>. Chicago: St. James,
1985. pp. 65-68.

"Burroughs, Edgar Rice," in: Woodcock,
George, ed. <u>20th Century Fiction</u>. Chicago:
St. James, 1985. pp. 117-119.

"Charles R. Tanner," <u>Locus</u> No. 155:2.
February 12, 1974.

"Maps and Spasms," in: Greenberg, Martin H.,
ed. <u>Fantastic Lives: Autobiographical Essays</u>
<u>by Notable Science Fiction Writers</u>.
Carbondale: Southern Illinois University Press,
1981. pp. 20-56.

"Religion and myths," in: Ash, Brian, ed.
<u>Visual Encyclopedia of Science Fiction</u>. New
York: Harmony, 1977. pp. 222-236.

"Remarkable adventure, The," by P. J. Farmer
and Beverly Friend. in: Warrick, Patricia,
ed. <u>Science Fiction: Contemporary</u>
<u>Mythology</u>. New York: Harper, 1978. pp.
39-49.

"Tarzan lives," <u>Esquire</u> 77:127-131. April
1972.

Farmer, Penelope

"Patterns on a wall," <u>Horn Book</u>
50:169-176. October 1974.

Farquahar, J.

"American Horror Myth, An: Night of the Living
Dead," <u>Semiotica</u> 38(1-2): 1-15. 1982.

Farrell, Patricia

"Amazing Mr. Asimov, The," <u>Writer's Digest</u>
53(7):20. July 1973.

Farrell, R. T.

<u>J. R. R. Tolkien: Scholar and Storyteller</u>,
ed. by Mary Salu and R. T. Farrell. Ithaca:
Cornell University Press, 1979. 325 p.

Farrelly, J. P.

"Promised land, The: Moses, Nearing, Skinner,
and Le Guin," <u>Journal of General Education</u>
33(1): 15-23. Spring 1981.

Farson, Daniel

<u>The Man Who Wrote Dracula: a Biography of</u>
<u>Bram Stoker</u>. London: Michael Joseph, 1975.
240 p. Reprinted, New York: St. Martin's
Press, 1976.

Fauconnier, Denise

"Voyage spatial dans la science fiction, Le"
in: Societe des Anglicistes de l'Enseignement
Superieur. <u>Le Voyage dans la Litterature</u>
<u>Anglo-Saxonne</u>. Actes du congres de Nice, 1971.
Paris: Didier, 1973. pp. 181-203.

Faulkner, Peter

<u>Against the Age: An Introduction to William</u>
<u>Morris</u>. London: Allen, 1980. 193 p.

Favier, Jacques

<u>Nouvelle de science fiction angloamericaine de 1950 a 1970, Le.</u> Thesis, Universite de Paris VIII. June 29, 1972.

"Getting there: transits in speculative fiction," <u>San Jose Studies</u> 7(3): 43-55. November 1981.

"Jeux de la temporalite en science fiction, Les" <u>Litterautr</u> No. 8:53-71. December 1972.

"S. F. et recit. b) Place privilegiee de la nouvelle," <u>Europe</u> 580/581:108-113. Aug/Sept. 1977.

"Space and settor in short science fiction," in: Johnson, Ira D. and Johnson, Christione, eds. <u>Les Americanistes: New French Criticism on Modern American Fiction</u>. Port Washington, New York: Kennikat, 1978. pp. 182-201.

Faye, Barry

"<u>Ape and Essence</u>," in: Magill, Frank N., ed. <u>Survey of Science Fiction Literature</u>, Vol. 1. Englewood Cliffs, NJ: Salem Press, 1979. pp. 78-83.

Faye, I. S.

"<u>Pilgrimage: The Book of the People</u> and <u>The People: No Different Flesh</u>," in: Magill, Frank N., ed. <u>Survey of Science Fiction Literature</u>, Vol. 4. Englewood Cliffs, NJ: Salem Press, 1979. pp. 1682-1686.

Federman, Raymond

"Interview With Stanislaw Lem," <u>Science-Fiction Studies</u> 10(1): 2-14. March 1983.

Feeley, Gregory

"Cages of Conscience from Seedling Stories: The Development of Blish's Novels," <u>Foundation</u> 24: 59-68. February 1982.

"Correcting the Record on Blish," <u>Foundation</u> 29: 52-61. November 1983.

"Dann's Disjunctions," <u>Foundation</u> 25: 36-42. June 1982.

"Davidson Apocrypha, The," <u>Foundation</u> 27: 60-64. February 1983.

"Echoes From the Future: An Interview With Jack Dann," <u>Vector</u> 107: 9-18. April 1982.

"Echos of the Future: Interview with Jack Dann," <u>Thrust</u> 21: 5-9, 15. March/April 1984.

"Nursery Within The Last Dangerous Visions," <u>Thrust</u> 20: 22-24. Spring/Summer 1984.

"Unglimpsed Reign of <u>King Log</u>, The," <u>Vector</u> 120: 14-21, 38. June 1984.

Feeley, M. P.

"Warp and weft: patterns of artistry in Nabokov's <u>Pale Fire</u>," in: Collins, R. A., ed. <u>Scope of the Fantastic: Theory, Technique, Major Authors</u>. Westport: Greenwood, 1985. pp. 239-246.

Feenberg, Andrew

"End to history: science fiction of the nuclear age," <u>Johns Hopkins Magazine</u> 28(2):13-22. March 1977.

"Politics of survival: science fiction in the nuclear age, The," <u>Alternative Futures</u> 1(2):3-23. Summer 1978.

Fehrenbach, T. R.

"Ultimate Weapon, The," in: Bretnor, Reginald, ed. <u>The Future at War: Vol. 2: The Spear of Mars</u>. New York: Ace, 1980. pp. 271-297.

Feibiger, D. J.

"Adventures of Mark Twain," <u>Cinefantastique</u> 15(5):49. January 1986.

Feinleib, Sidney

"Uses of the future," by Frederik Pohl and Sidney Feinleib. in: Turek, Leslie, ed. <u>Noreascon Proceedings</u>. Cambridge, MA: NESFA, 1976. pp. 128-137.

Fekete, John

"<u>The Dispossessed</u> and <u>Triton</u>: tyranny and the decay of language," <u>Science Fiction Studies</u> 6(2):129-143. July 1979.

Feldman, Silvia

"Projections of the Terminal Man," <u>Human Behavior</u> 3(2):64-69. February 1974.

Fenichel, R. R.

"Comment," <u>Hartford Studies in Literature</u> 1:133-135. 1969.

Fenner, Arnie

"14 Questions: Michael Whelan," by Pat Cadigan and Arnie Fenner. <u>Shayol</u> No. 5: 12-19. Winter 1982.

Fenner, Arnie (Continued)

"Artist Profile: Alicia Austin," <u>Fantasy Newsletter</u> 6(6): 24-27, 45. June/July 1983.

"Blackshear is Here," <u>Shayol</u> No. 5: 45-48. Winter 1982.

"Dillons, The," <u>Fantasy Review</u> 7(6): 14-17. July 1984.

"Genie-us of Tom Reamy, The," by Pat Cadigan and Arnie Fenner. <u>Shayol</u> 1: 33-40. November 1977.

"Has success spoiled Stephen King? Naaah!" by Pat Cadigan, Marty Ketchum and Arnie Fenner. <u>Shayol</u> 6:17-19. 1982.

"Profile: Hank Jankus," <u>Fantasy Newsletter</u> 6(5): 18-21. May 1983.

"Punchatz: A Barnstormer in Texas," <u>Shayol</u> No. 6: 20-27. Winter 1982.

"Richard Corbin profile," <u>Fantasy Review</u> 9(6)(eg v. 8 #6): 6-9. June 1985.

"Tim Kirk: Artist Profile," <u>Fantasy Newsletter</u> 6(2): 20-23. February 1983.

Fenton, R. W.

<u>The Big Swingers</u>. Englewood Cliffs, New Jersey: Prentice-Hall, 1967. 258 p.

Ferebee, A.

"Statement: success is spoiling Buck Rogers," <u>Industrial Design</u> 10:82-83. November 1963.

Fergus, George

"Checklist of SF novels with female protagonists, A," <u>Extrapolation</u> 18(1):20-27. December 1976.

"Sex roles, biology, & science fiction, or there's no vinism like chau-vinism," <u>Mythologies</u> 11:16-35. February 1977.

Fergus, Michael

"Sci-fi approach to planning, The," <u>Royal Town Planning Institute Journal</u> 58:245-246. June 1972.

Ferguson, A. R.

"Newspeak, the first edition: tyranny and the decay of language," <u>Michigan Quarterly Review</u> 14(4):445-453. 1975.

Ferguson, Bruce

"Slaughterhoused: the books of Kurt Vonnegut," <u>Vector</u> 87: 18-24. May/June 1978.

"Songs of the southern weyr: a look at the SF music of New Zealand," <u>Pacific Quarterly Moana</u> 4(3):346-349. July 1979.

Ferguson, Mary

"Ambrosio: Or, The Monk," in: Magill, Frank N., ed. <u>Survey of Modern Fantasy Literature</u>, Vol 1. Englewood Cliffs, NJ: Salem Press, Inc., 1983. pp. 36-41.

"Italian, The," in: Magill, Frank N., ed. <u>Survey of Modern Fantasy Literature</u>, Vol 2. Englewood Cliffs, NJ: Salem Press, Inc., 1983. pp. 787-790.

"Mysteries of Udolpho, The," in: Magill, Frank N., ed. <u>Survey of Modern Fantasy Literature</u>, Vol 3. Englewood Cliffs, NJ: Salem Press, Inc., 1983. pp. 1075-1080.

"Private Memoirs and Confessions of a Justified Sinner, The," in: Magill, Frank N., ed. <u>Survey of Modern Fantasy Literature</u>, Vol 3. Englewood Cliffs, NJ: Salem Press, Inc., 1983. pp. 1291-1296.

"Stand, The," in: Magill, Frank N., ed. <u>Survey of Modern Fantasy Literature</u>, Vol 4. Englewood Cliffs, NJ: Salem Press, Inc., 1983. pp. 1801-1806.

Ferguson, Neil

"Man From the Future, A," <u>Foundation</u> 27: 32-35. February 1983.

Ferman, E. L.

"Editorial: Profile of an F&SF Reader," <u>Magazine of Fantasy and Science Fiction</u> 62(6): 5-6. June 1982.

Ferns, C. S.

<u>Aldous Huxley: Novelist</u>. London: Athlone, 1980. 240 p.

Ferran, Pierre

"Averir de la science fiction, L'" <u>Quinzaine Litteraire</u> No. 123:13-14. August 1, 1971.

"Forts en themes, Les," <u>Cahiers Pedagogiques</u> 150: 12-14. January 1977.

"Science fiction, La," <u>B. T. 2</u> 49:1-36. May 1973.

Author Entries

Ferrari, A. M.

Jack Williamson. Dissertation, Universita
'Degli Studi de Torino, 1974/1975.

Ferrell, Keith

George Orwell: The Political Pen. New York:
Evans, 1985. 180 p.

H. G. Wells: First Citizen of the Future.
New York: Evans, 1983. 121 p.

Ferren, Bran

"Creating special visual effects for Altered
States," American Cinematographer
62(3):236-239, 260-266,296-298. March 1981.

Ferreras, J. I.

Novela de ciencia ficcion, La: interpretacion
de una novela marginal. Madrid: Siglo
Vientiuno de Espania Editores, 1972. 240 p.

Ferrini, Franco

Che cosa e la fantascienza. Rome: Ubaldini,
1970. 150 p.

Ferry, Jean

"Proust et la science fiction," Cahiers du
College de Pataphysique 28:54-68. 1964.

Ferry, M. G.

"Chronicles of Prydain, The: an inexhaustible
source for literature classes," Illinois
English Bulletin 72(2): 52-56. Winter 1985.
(ERIC ED 252 860)

Fesenkov, Vasil

"Civilization on other planets?" Soviet
Life p. 46. January 1964. (not seen)

Fesperman, Dan

"E. T., Phone Your Broker," Miami Herald.
December 12, 1982. in: Newsbank. Business
and Economic Development. 111:E7-8. December
1982.

Festa, Conrad

"Vonnegut's satire," in: Klinkowitz, Kurt,
ed. Vonnegut in America. New York:
Delacorte, 1977. pp. 133-149.

Fetzer, Leland

"H. G. Wells' first Russian admirer,"
Foundation 11/12:39-47. March 1977.

Feuer, Jane

"Cine-Scene," Common Sense (Bloomington,
IN) 3(1):8. October 1-15, 1972.

Ffloker, Michael

"Sci-fi sex," Playboy 23:140. March 1976.

Ficks, R. S.

"Weapons in Future Warfare," by R. A. Beaumont
and R. S. Ficks. in: Bretnor, Reginald, ed.
The Future at War: Vol. 1: Thor's Hammer.
New York: Ace, 1979. pp. 147-172.

Ficowski, Jerzy

"Brund Schulz," Quarber Merkur 24:53-56.
September 1970.

Fiedel, Robert

"And the beast goes on," American Film
2(5):71-72. March 1977.

Fiedler, Jean

Isaac Asimov, by Jean Fiedler and Jim Mele.
New York: Ungar, 1982. 122 p.

"Asimov's robots," by Jean Fiedler and Jim
Mele. in: Riley, Dick, ed. Critical
Encounters: Writers and Themes in Science
Fiction. New York: Ungar, 1978. pp. 1-22.

Fiedler, L. A.

Olaf Stapledon: A Man Divided. New York:
Oxford University Press, 1983. 236 p.

"Criticism of Science Fiction, The," in:
Slusser, George E., ed. Coordinates.
Carbondale: Southern Illinois University Press,
1983. pp. 1-13.

"Divine stupidity of Kurt Vonnegut, Jr., The,"
Esquire 74:195-197,199-200,202-204.
September 1970.

"Who was William Olaf Stapledon?" Galileo
11/12:34-36. 1979.

Field, R. R.

"Browsing without the BEM's," Alabama
Librarian 8:5-8. January 1957.

Fiene, D. M.

"Kurt Vonnegut as an American dissident: his popularity in the Soviet Union and his affinities with Russian literature," in: Klinkowitz, Kurt, ed. Vonnegut in America. New York: Delacorte, 1977. pp. 258-293.

"Vonnegut's The Sirens of Titan," Explicator 34:item 27. December 1975.

Fifield, Merle

"Fantasy in and for the sixties: The Lord of the Rings," English Journal 55:841-844. October 1966.

Filipov, Vladimir

"'Klanica pet': tretata senzacija," Literaturen Front (2):11. January 1973.

Filmer, Kathy

"Speaking in parables," Mythlore 11(2):15-20. Autumn 1984.

"That hideous 1984: the influence of C. S. Lewis' That Hideous Strength on Orwell's 1984," Extrapolation 26(2): 160-169. Summer 1985.

Finch, Christopher

Making of the Dark Crystal, The: Creating A Unique Film. New York: Holt, 1983. 96 p.

Special Effects: Creating Movie Magic. New York: Abbeville, 1984. 252 p.

Finch, Hardy

"Goodby Earth and all that," Scholastic Teacher 66(1):37T. February 2, 1955. (Popular Science and UFO books only)

Finch, Sheila

"Oath of Fealty: No thud, some blunders," Science Fiction Review 14(4): 28-30. November 1985.

"Paradise lost: The prison at the heart of Le Guin's Utopia," Extrapolation 26(3): 240-249. Fall 1985.

Finch-Reyner, Sheila

"Unseen Shore: Thoughts on the popularity of fantasy," Journal of Popular Culture 18(4): 127-134. Spring 1985.

Fine, D. M.

"California as dystopia: Los Angeles fiction in the 1930's," Alternative Futures 2(4): 21-30. Fall 1979.

Finer, S. E.

"Profile of science fiction, A," Sociological Review 2(2):239-255. December 1954.

Fingesten, P.

"Myth of science fiction," by S. Mandel and P. Fingesten. Saturday Review 38(35):7-8. August 27, 1955.

Finholt, Richard

"Larry Niven," by Richard Finholt and John Carr. in: Bleiler, E. F., ed Science Fiction Writers. New York: Scribners, 1982. pp. 459-465.

Fink, Beatrice

"Narrative techniques and utopian structures in Sade's Aline et Valcour," Science-Fiction Studies 7(1): 73-79. March 1980.

Fink, Howard

"'Coming up for air' in Orwell's ambiguous satire on the Wellsian utopia," Studies in the Literary Imagination 6(2):51-60. Fall 1973.

"Shadow of Men Like Gods: Orwell's Coming Up for Air as parody," in: Suvin, Darko and R. M. Philmus, eds. H. G. Wells and Modern Science Fiction. Lewisburg: Bucknell University Press, 1977. pp. 144-158.

Finkelstein, Sidney

"World of science fiction, The," Masses and Mainstream 8(4):48-57. April 1955.

Finlay, Virgil

Virgil Finlay. West Kingston, RI: Grant, 1971. 153 p.

Finley, Nancy

"Fantasy paintings," School Arts 76(1):62-63. September 1976.

Finney, K. D.

"Days of Future Past, The, or Utopians Lessing and Le Guin Fight Future Nostalgia," in: Hassler, Donald M. Patterns of the Fantastic. Mercer Island, WA: Starmont, 1983. pp. 31-40.

Firchow, P. E.

End of Utopia: A Study of Aldous Huxley's Brave New World. Cranbury, NJ: Bucknell University Press, 1984. 154 p.

"Science and conscience in Huxley's Brave New World," Contemporary Literature 16(3):301-316. 1975.

Firsching, L. J.

"J. G. Ballard's ambiguous apocalypse," Science Fiction Studies 12(3): 297-310. November 1985.

Fischer, Dennis

"Keep, The (review)," Cinefantastique 14(3):55. May 1984.

"Michael Crichton on robots, writing and directing, and Runaway," Cinefantastique 15(2):6,59. May 1985.

"On the Set of The Philadelphia Experiment," Starlog 85: 42-44, 65. August 1984.

"One Hundred Most Important People in Science Fiction/Fantasy: Theodore Sturgeon," Starlog No. 100: 80-81. November 1985.

"Otherworld," Starlog No. 91:48-52. February 1985.

"Possession (review)," Cinefantastique 14(4/5):106. September 1984.

"Profile: Ernie Hudson," Starlog No. 98:40-43. September 1985.

"Starlog Interview/Portfolio: Ron Cobb," by James Van Hise and Dennis Fisher. Starlog 57: 30-33, 64. April 1982.

"Starlog Interview: Jane Badler," Starlog 89: 27-29, 55. December 1984.

"Starlog interview: Toby Hooper," Starlog No. 96: 44-46, 96. July 1985.

"Troll," Cinefantastique 16(1):14-17. March 1986.

"Visit to Otherworld," Starlog No. 94:72-73. May 1985.

"Writers on Writing," To The Stars 2: 9, 39. 1984.

Fischer, J. M.

Phantastik in Literatur und Kunst, by C. W. Thomsen and J. M. Fischer. Darmstadt: Wissenschaftliche Buchgesellschaft, 1980. 563 p.

"Bibliographie der Sekundarliteratur," in: Thomsen, C. W., eds. Phantastik in Literatur und Kunst. Darmstadt: Wiss. Buchgesellschaft, 1980. pp. 531-548.

"Deutschsprachige Phantastik zwischen Decadence und Faschismus," in: Zondergeld, R. A. Phaicon 3. Frankfurt: Suhrkamp, 1978. pp. 93-130.

"Produktiver Ekel. Zum Werk Howard Phillips Lovecraft," in: Thomsen, C. W., ed. Phantastik in Literatur und Kunst. Darmstadt: Wissenschaftliche Buchgesellschaft, 1980. pp. 314-332.

"Science Fiction-Phantastik-Fantasy," in: Ermert, Karl, ed. Neugier oder Flucht? Stuttgart: Klett, 1980. pp. 8-17.

Fischer, W. B.

Between Fantastic Fabulation and Didactic Disquisition: Kurd Lasswitz, Hans Deminik, and the Development of German Science Fiction, 1871 1945. Ph.D. Dissertation, Yale, 1979. 408 p.

Empire Stikes Out, The: Kurd Lasswitz, Hans Dominik, and the Development of German Science Fiction. Bowling Green, OH: Bowling Green State University Popular Press, 1984. 335 p.

"German theories of science fiction: Jean Paul, Kurd Lasswitz, and after," Science Fiction Studies 3(3):254-265. November 1976.

Fish, R. S.

Oral Interpretation of the Horror Stories of H. P. Lovecraft. Masters Thesis, University of Oklahoma, 1965. 157 p.

Fishburn, Katherine

Unexpected Universe of Doris Lessing. Westport, CT: Greenwood, 1985. 184 p.

Fisher, B. F., IV

"Twilight Stories," in: Magill, Frank N., ed. Survey of Modern Fantasy Literature, Vol 4. Englewood Cliffs, NJ: Salem Press, Inc., 1983. pp. 1989-1991.

"Wagner, The Wehr-Wulf," in: Magill, Frank N., ed. Survey of Modern Fantasy Literature, Vol 4. Englewood Cliffs, NJ: Salem Press, Inc., 1983. pp. 2049-2053.

Fisher, Bob

"Visual effects for 2010," <u>American Cinematographer</u> 66(1): 65-76. January 1984.

Fisher, David

"Angel, the devil, and the space travellers: variations on a traditional theme, The," <u>Sight and Sound</u> 23(3):155-157. January/March 1954.

Fisher, J. L.

"Trouble in Paradise: The Twentieth-Century Utopian Ideal," <u>Extrapolation</u> 24(4): 329-339. Winter 1983.

Fishman, Robert

"Utopia in three dimensions," in: <u>Utopias</u>, ed. by Peter Alexander and Roger Gill. London: Duckworth, 1984. pp. 95-108.

Fishwick, Marshall

"Evolution of monsters: adapted from Faust revisited," <u>Saturday Review</u> 46:32. September 14, 1963.

Fiske, John

"Popularity and Ideology: a structuralist reading of Dr. Who," in: Rowland, W. D., jr. <u>Interpreting Television: Current Research Perspectives</u>. Beverly Hills: Sage, 1984. pp. 165-198.

Fison, Peter

"That thing from another world," <u>Twentieth Century</u> 158:280-288. September 1955.

Fissore, Valerio

"Modi narrativi comparati dei racconti di utopia e di SF," In: <u>Utopia e fantascienza</u>. Torino: Giappichelli, 1975. p. 45-62.

"Poe e la fantascienza," In: Ruggero Bianche, ed. <u>E. A. Poe: dal gotico alla fantascienza</u>. Milan: Mursia, 1978. pp. 69-76.

Fitting, Peter

"<u>Ubik</u>: the deconstruction of bourgeois SF," <u>Science Fiction Studies</u> 2(1):47-54. March 1975.

"<u>Ubik</u>: The Deconstruction of Bourgeois SF," in: Greenberg, Martin H., ed. <u>Philip K. Dick</u>. New York: Taplinger, 1982. pp. 149-159.

"Modern Anglo-American SF novel: utopian longing and capitalist cooptation, The," <u>Science Fiction Studies</u> 6(1):59-76. March 1979.

"Orientations actuelles de la science fiction," <u>Etudes Litteraires</u> (Quebec) 7(1):61-95. April 1974.

"Reality as Ideological Construct: A Reading of Five Novels by Philip K. Dick," <u>Science-Fiction Studies</u> 10(2): 219-236. July 1983.

"Second Alien, The," <u>Science-Fiction Studies</u> 7(3): 285-293. November 1980.

"SF criticism in France," <u>Science Fiction Studies</u> 1(3):173-181. Spring 1974.

"SF in France," <u>Locus</u> No. 159:8. May 11, 1974.

"So we all became mothers: new roles for men in recent utopian Fiction," <u>Science Fiction Studies</u> 12(2): 156-183. July 1985.

"Two new books from France," <u>Science Fiction Studies</u> 1(4):276-279. Fall 1974.

Fitzgerald, M. G.

"Television's giant step; what's right with <u>Space: 1999</u>," <u>Questar</u> 1(2):32-37. Summer 1978.

Flammarion, Camille

<u>Mondes imaginaires et les mondes reels, Les</u>. Paris: Didier, 1872. 577 p.

Flanagan, Graeme

<u>Robert Bloch: a bio-bibliography</u>. Canberra City, Aust.: Flanagan, 1979. 63 p.

Flanery, Karen

<u>Fandom Is For the Young</u>, by Karen Flanery and Nana Grasmick. New York: Vantage, 1981. 160 p.

Flaszen, Ludwik

"O <u>Obloku Magellana</u>," <u>Zycie literackie</u> No. 7. 1956.

Flautz, J. T.

"American demagogue in Barsoom," <u>Journal of Popular Culture</u> 1(3):263-275. Winter 1967.

Flechtner, H. J.

"Phantastische literatur. Eine literarasthetische untersuchung," in: Zeitschrift fur Asthetik und allgemeine Kunstwissenschaft 24:37-46. 1934.

Fleck, L. M.

"Science fiction as a tool of speculative philosophy," in: Remington, T. J., ed. Selected Proceedings of the 1978 SFRA National Conference. Cedar Falls, Iowa: University of Northern Iowa, 1979. pp.133-145.

Fleischer, Leonore

"Futuristic Visions," Publishers Weekly 226(14): 101. October 5, 1984.

"Milestone: DAW Books," Publishers Weekly 227(19):225. May 10, 1985.

"Talk of the Trade: Off to Fantastica," Publishers Weekly 244(15): 95. October 7, 1983.

"Twist of Fate, A: Harlan Ellison," Publishers Weekly 226(6): 79. August 10, 1984.

Fleming, G. J.

"Science Fiction and High School Students' Attitudes Toward Science," by P. A. Rubba, G. B. Lockwood, and G. J. Fleming. Hoosier Science Teacher 7(3): 85-88. February 1982.

Fleming, Linda

Science Fiction Subculture: Bridge Between the Two Cultures. Ph.D. Dissertation, University of North Carolina, 1976. 479 p.

"American SF subculture, The," Science Fiction Studies 4(3):263-271. November 1977.

Fletcher, Jo

"Interview (of sorts) with Harry Adam Knight, An," by Stephen Jones and Jo Fletcher. Fantasy Review 8(7): 41. July 1985.

Fletcher, John

"Cultural Pessimists: The Tradition of Christopher Priest's Fiction," International Fiction Review 3: 20-24. 1979.

Fletcher, M. P.

Science Fiction Story Index 1950-1979. 2nd ed. Chicago: American Library Association, 1981. 610 p.

"Science fiction magazines and annual anthologies: an annotated checklist," Serials Librarian 7(1): 65-71. Fall 1982.

Fletcher, V. J.

Dream and Nightmares: Utopian Visions in Modern Art. Washington, DC: Hirshhorn Museum and Sculpture Garden 1983. 201 p.

Flieger, Verlyn

Medieval Epic and Romance Motifs in J. R. R. Tolkien's The Lord of the Rings. Ph. D. Dissertation, Catholic University of America, 1977. 163 p.

Splintered Light: Logos and Language in Tolkien's World. Grand Rapids, MI: Eerdman's, 1983. 167 p.

"Barfield's Poetic Diction and splintered light," Studies in the Literary Imagination 14(2):47-66. Fall 1981.

"Frodo and Aragorn: The Concept of the Hero," in: Isaacs, Neil D. Tolkien: New Critical Perspectives, ed. by N. D. Isaacs and R. A. Zimbardo. Lexington: University Press of Kentucky, 1981. pp. 40-62.

"Wright's Islandia: utopia with problems," in: Barr, Marleen, ed. Women and Utopia. New York: Lanham, 1983. pp. 96-107.

Flora, J. M.

"Cabell as precursor: reflections on Cabell and Vonnegut," Kalki 6(4):118-137. 1975.

"Cabell, James Branch," in: Woodcock, George, ed. 20th Century Fiction. Chicago: St. James, 1985. pp. 122-123.

Flyn, Al

"Future Interview: A. E. Van Vogt," by J. M. Elliot and Al Flyn. Future 7: 22-24, 74. January 1979.

Flynn, George

Mack Reynolds Checklist, A, by Chris Drumm and George Flynn. Polk City, IA: Drumm, 1983. 24 p.

"Noreascon releases Hugo nominee, winner counts," Science Fiction Chronicle 2(5):1-3. February 1981.

Flynn, J. L.

Future Threads: Costume Design for the Science Fiction World. Studio City, CA: New Media, 1985. 80 p.

Flynn, J. L. (Continued)

"Costuming for Fun and Fandom," in: Hopkins, Mariane S., ed. Fandom Directory 1982. Newport News, VA: Fandom Computer Services, 1982. pp. 366-369.

Flynn, Randal

"Darkness and Grace," Focus: an SF Writers' Magazine 4: 12-13. Spring 1981.

Fogel, Stan

"Investigation: Stanislaw Lem's pynchonesque novel," Riverside Quarterly 6:268-289. 1977.

"Investigation, The: Stanislaw Lem's Pynchonesque Novel," Riverside Quarterly 7(2): 123-126. March 1982.

"Ludic Temperament of John Barth, The," Fantasy Newsletter 5(6): 13-16. July 1982.

Fogg, W. L.

"Technology and dystopia," in: Richter, P. E., ed. Utopia/Dystopia. Cambridge, Mass.: Schenkman, 1975. pp. 70-71.

"Technology and utopia," in: Richter, P. E., ed. Utopia/Dystopia?. Cambridge, MA: Schenkman, 1975. pp. 57-74.

Foldeak, Hans

Neuere tendenzen der sowjetischen science fiction. Munchen: Sagner, 1975. 208 p.

"Ideologische Phantastik: I. Efremov, CAS BYKA," Quarber Merkur 42:28-41. December 1975.

"Philosophische Phantastik: Gennadi Gor," Quarber Merkur 41:41-48. September 1975.

Foltin, H. F.

"Minderwertige prosaliteratu. Einteilung und bezeichnungen," Deutsche Vierteljahresschrift 39:288-324. 1965.

Fonstad, K. W.

Atlas of Middle-Earth. Boston: Houghton, 1981. 208 p.

Atlas of Pern, The. New York: Del Rey, 1984. 169 p.

Fontana, J. P.

"Science fiction sovietique: le point!" Fiction No. 290:185-190. May 1978.

Forbes, A. B.

"Literary quest for utopia, 1880-1900, The," Social Forces 6:179-189. December 1927.

Forbes, Cheryl

"Charles Williams: substituted love," Christianity Today 19(23):16-19. August 29, 1975.

"For Tolkien fans (letter)," Christianity Today 21(5):31. December 3, 1976.

"Frodo decides: or does he?" Christianity Today 20(6):10-13. December 19,1975.

"Narnia: fantasy but . . . " Christianity Today 20(15):6-10. April 23, 1976.

Ford, D. E.

"Fandom: 1941-1956," Fantasy Times No. 254:27-29. September (1) 1956.

"Midwestcon report," Fantasy Times No. 249:2. June (2) 1956.

Ford, J. E.

"Battlestar Galactica and Mormon Theology," Journal of Popular Culture 17(2): 83-87. Fall 1983.

Ford, P. F.

Companion to Narnia. New York: Harper, 1980. 313 p.

Foreman, Michael

"Illustrating Garner," Labrys No. 7: p. 123-126. November 1981.

Forester, E. M.

"Fantasy," in: Forester, E. M. Aspects of the Novel. New York: Harcourt, 1954. pp. 155-180.

Forkan, J. P.

"Scout ship to control: ready ad guns; we are now entering sci-fi boom era," Advertising Age 47(6):20,41. February 9, 1976.

Forrester, Kent

"Dangers of being earnest: Ray Bradbury and The Martian Chronicles, The," Journal of General Education 28(1):50-54. Spring 1976.

Forster, Werner

"Time travelling into the present: science fiction in the GDR," _Journal of Popular Culture_ 18(3):71-82. Winter 1984.

Fortunati, Vita

Letteratura utopica inglese, La. Ravenna: Longo, 1979. 222 p.

"Fantastico, Il: La letteratura come sintomo," by Vita Fortunati and G. Franci. _Quaderni di Filologia Germanica della Facolta di Lettere e Filosofia dell'Universita di Bologna._ 1980; 1: 11-22. 1982.

Fossati, Franco

"Buck Rogers, il primo," _Robot: rivista de fantascienza._ 1(1):100-102. April 1976.

Foster, A. D.

"Critique of Return of the Jedi," _Amazing_ 57(5): 141-145. January 1984.

"E.T. (Review)" _Starlog_ 64: 49-54. November 1982.

"Indiana Jones and the Temple of Doom (review)," _Starlog_ 88: 50-52. November 1984.

"Racism in the media and science fiction subtlety and the faithful dog syndrome, or is Mr. T a wookie?" _Science Fiction Review_ 14(3): 20-21. August 1985.

Foster, D. L.

"Women on the Edge of Narrative: Language in Marge Piercy's Utopia," in: Hassler, Donald M. _Patterns of the Fantastic._ Mercer Island, WA: Starmont, 1983. pp. 47-56.

Foster, D. W.

Jorge Luis Borges: An Annotated Primary and Secondary Bibliography. New York: Garland, 1984. 328 p.

Foster, E. H.

"Vonnegut, Kurt," in: Woodcock, George, ed. _20th Century Fiction._ Chicago: St. James, 1985. pp. 688-689.

Foster, F. S.

"Octavia Butler's Black Female Future Fiction," _Extrapolation_ 23(1): 37-49. Spring 1982.

Foster, M. A.

Write the Other Way: The Correlation of Style and Theme in Selected Prose Fiction of Ray Bradbury. Ph.D. Dissertation, Florida State University, 1973. 139 p.

Foster, Robert

Complete Guide to Middle-Earth From the Hobbit to the Silmarillion. New York: Del Rey, 1978. 575 p.

Guide to Middle Earth. Baltimore: Mirage, 1971. 291 p.

Teacher's Guide to the Hobbit New York: Ballantine, 1981. 40 p.

"Frank Herbert," in: Cowart, David, ed. _Twentieth-Century American Science-Fiction Writers, Part 1:A-L._ Detroit: Gale, 1981. pp. 232-239. (Dictionary of Literary Biography, v. 8)

Foust, R. E.

"Eater of Darkness, The," in: Magill, Frank N., ed. _Survey of Modern Fantasy Literature_, Vol 1. Englewood Cliffs, NJ: Salem Press, Inc., 1983. pp. 460-464.

"Face in the Abyss, The," in: Magill, Frank N., ed. _Survey of Modern Fantasy Literature_, Vol 1. Englewood Cliffs, NJ: Salem Press, Inc., 1983. pp. 504-507.

"Mistress Masham's Repose," in: Magill, Frank N., ed. _Survey of Modern Fantasy Literature_, Vol 3. Englewood Cliffs, NJ: Salem Press, Inc., 1983. pp. 1052-1055.

"Phantom Ship, The," in: Magill, Frank N., ed. _Survey of Modern Fantasy Literature_, Vol 3. Englewood Cliffs, NJ: Salem Press, Inc., 1983. pp. 1246-1249.

"Sin Eater and Other Tales and Episodes, The," in: Magill, Frank N., ed. _Survey of Modern Fantasy Literature_, Vol 4. Englewood Cliffs, NJ: Salem Press, Inc., 1983. pp. 1754-1756.

"'Vampyre, The'," in: Magill, Frank N., ed. _Survey of Modern Fantasy Literature_, Vol 4. Englewood Cliffs, NJ: Salem Press, Inc., 1983. pp. 2013-2016.

"Fabulous paradigm: fantasy, metafantasy, and Peter S. Beagle's _The Last Unicorn_," _Extrapolation_ 21(1):5-20. Spring 1980.

Fowler, Chris

"Harlan Ellison interview," _Vector_ 75: 5-24. July 1975.

Fowler, Chris (Continued)

"Last Rebel, The: An Interview With M. John Harrison," Foundation 23: 5-30. October 1981.

"Robert Silverberg, interview," Vector 76/77:5-13. August/September.

"Roger Elwood interview," by Martin Hatfield, Christopher Fowler, and Ian Thomson. Vector 79: 10-14. January/February 1977.

"Star Wars: a personal view," Vector 82:5-6. July/August 1977.

Fowler, George

"Case against The Acorn, II, The," ERB-dom No. 19:20. December 1966.

"Case against The Acorn, The," ERB-dom No. 18:7. August 1966.

Fox, Andrew

"Dearest Ms. McCaffrey: letters from Andrew Fox," Voices of Youth Advocates 1(4):5-6. October 1978.

Fox, D. M.

"Weird tales in the library," Library Journal 66(14):652-653. August 1941.

Fox, Geoff

"Notes on teaching A Wizard of Earthsea," in: Fox, Geoff, ed. Writers, Critics, and Children: Articles From Children's Literature in Education. New York: Agathon Press, 1976. pp. 211-223.

Fox, J. R.

"Altered States (review)," Cinefantastique 11(1):46. Summer 1981.

"Blade Runner (review)," Cinefantastique 13(1):44. September/October 1982.

"Changeling, The (review)," Cinefantastique 10(1):13,15. Summer 1980.

"Howling, The," by J. R. Fox and Adam Eisenberg. Cinefantastique 10(3):18-23. Winter 1980.

"Incubus (review)," Cinefantastique 13(2)/13(3):90,92. November/December 1982.

"Quest For Fire," Cinefantastique 12(1):10-13. February 1982.

"Riding high on horrors," Cinefantastique 10(1):5-11,40-44. Summer 1980.

"Somewhere in Time," Cinefantastique 10(4):14-19. Spring 1981.

"Stalker (review)," Cinefantastique 13(6)/14(1):104. September 1983.

"Tanya's Island," Cinefantastique 10(1):24-31. Summer 1980.

"Time Bandits (review)," Cinefantastique 12(1):50. February 1982.

"Who is Michele Burke?" Cinefantastique 12(2/3):72-73. April 1982.

Fox, Jordan

"Rick Baker: maker of monsters, master of the apes," Cinefex No. 16:4-70. April 1984.

"Roy Arbogast," Cinefex 5: 42-53. July 1981.

"Walter Murch: Making Beaches Out of Grains of Sand," Cinefex 3: 42-57. December 1980.

Fox, R. E.

"Politics of Desire in Delany's Triton and The Tides of Lust, The," Black American Literature Forum 18(2): 49-56. Summer 1984.

Fox, T. C.

"Star Wars war II: star drek, The," Film Comment 13(4):22-23. July/August 1977.

Foyster, John

"Cordwainer Smith,", Australian Science Fiction Review No. 11:8-14. August 1967.

"Cordwainer Smith," in: Exploring Cordwainer Smith. New York: Algol, 1975. pp. 10-17.

"Editorials of John Campbell," Australian Science Fiction Review No. 4:5-23. October 1966.

"Science fiction in the classroom," Australian Science Fiction Review No. 13:7-10. December 1967.

"Worldcon for sale," Locus No. 60:6a-b. July 23, 1970.

Francavilla, J. V.

"Disching It Out: an interview with Thomas Disch," Science Fiction Studies 12(3): 241-251. November 1985.

"Empire Strikes Back," Cinefantastique 10(2):40-41. Fall 1980.

Francavilla, J. V. (Continued)

"Evil Dead (review)," _Cinefantastique_ 14(2):51-52. December 1983/January 1984.

"Excalibur (review)," _Cinefantastique_ 11(2):47. Fall 1981.

"Octopussy (review)," _Cinefantastique_ 13(6)/14(1):99. September 1983.

"Promethean Bound: Heroes and Gods in Roger Zelazny's Science Fiction," in: Reilly, Robert, ed. _The Transcendent Adventure_. Westport: Greenwood, 1984. pp. 207-222.

"Ray Bradbury Theatre (review)," _Cinefantastique_ 16(1):46. March 1986.

"Return of the Jedi (review)," _Cinefantastique_ 13(6)/14(1):4,7. September 1983.

"These Immortals: An Anternative View of Immortality in Roger Zelazny's Science Fiction," _Extrapolation_ 25(1): 20-33. Spring 1984.

Franci, G.

"Fantastico, Il: La letteratura come sintomo," by V. Fortunati and G. Franci. _Quaderni di Filologia Germanica della Facolta di Lettere e Filosofia dell'Universita di Bologna_. 1980; 1: 11-22. 1982.

Francis, Davy

"Lifting the Lid off XIMOC," by Hilary Robinson and Davy Francis. _Focus: An SF Writer's Magazine_ No. 9: 37-39. Autumn 1984.

Frane, Jeff

Fritz Leiber. Mercer Island, WA: Starmont House, 1980. 64 p. (Starmont Reader's Guide, 4)

"Year in Fantasy, The," in: Carr, Terry, ed. _Fantasy Annual V_. New York: Timescape, 1982. pp. 257-263.

Frank, A. G.

Science Fiction and Fantasy Film Handbook. Totawa, NJ: Barnes and Noble, 1982. 194 p.

Sci-Fi Now: 10-Exciting Years of Science Fiction from 2001 to Star Wars and Beyond. London: Octopus Books, 1978. 80 p.

"Screen trips: celluloid protagonists and friends," in: Holdstock, Robert, ed. _Encyclopedia of Science Fiction_. London: Octopus, 1978. pp. 68-85.

Frank, A. P.

"Where laughing is the only way to stop it from hurting," _Summary_ 1(2):51-62. 1971.

Frank, Eduard

"Probleme um Gustav Meyrinks Roman _Der Engel vom westlichen Fenster_," _Quarber Merkur_ 51:52-55. November 1979.

Frank, F. S.

"_Castle of Otranto: A Gothic Story, The_," in: Magill, Frank N., ed. _Survey of Modern Fantasy Literature_, Vol 1. Englewood Cliffs, NJ: Salem Press, Inc., 1983. pp. 211-216.

"_Vathek: An Arabian Tale_," in: Magill, Frank N., ed. _Survey of Modern Fantasy Literature_, Vol 4. Englewood Cliffs, NJ: Salem Press, Inc., 1983. pp. 2023-2028.

"_Wieland: Or, The Transformation_," in: Magill, Frank N., ed. _Survey of Modern Fantasy Literature_, Vol 5. Englewood Cliffs, NJ: Salem Press, Inc., 1983. pp. 2126-2131.

"Bibliography of writings about Ann Radcliffe, A," _Extrapolation_ 17(1):54-62. December 1975.

"Gothic at absolute zero: Poe's _Narrative of Arthur Gordon Pym_, The," _Extrapolation_ 21(1):21-30. Spring 1980.

Frank, Howard

1977 Science Fiction and Fantasy Magazine Checklist and Price Guide, by Howard Frank and Roy Torgeson. Port Washington, NY: Science Fiction Resources, 1977. 50 p.

Frank, Janrae

"Doctors and the Devils," by Greg Mank and Janrae Frank. _Cinefantastique_ 15(5):28-30. January 1986.

"Dungeonmaster (review)," _Cinefantastique_ 15(4):50. October 1985.

"Sex, Swords, and Superstition: A Close Look at Phyllis Ann Karr's _Thorn and Frostflower_," _Thrust_ 22: 15-17. Spring/Summer 1985.

Frank, S.

"Out of this world," _Nations Business_ 40(3):40-42,80-81. March 1952.

Frank, Sam

"Restoration of Capra's 'Lost' Classic is on the Horizon," San Francisco Examiner August 26, 1984. in: NewsBank. Film and Television FTV 26:C9-C10. 1984.

Franke, H. W.

"Denkmodelle als prognostisches Training. Vernachlassigte Moglichkeiten der Literatur," Quarber Merkur 51:38-41. November 1979.

"Kybernetische aspekte der literatur," Zeitschrift fur Literaturwissenschaft und Linguistik 16. 1974.

"Literatur der technischen Welt," Quarber Merkur 29:51-56. January 1972. Also in: Barmeyer, Eike, ed. Science fiction: theorie und geschichte. Munchen: Fink, 1972. pp. 105-118.

"Masstabe fur science fiction," in: Weigand, Jorg, ed. Die Triviale Phantasie. Bonn: Asgard, 1976. pp. 85-90.

"Science fiction und die technische innovation," Angewandte Informatik 6:265-268. 1971.

"Science Fiction und technische Intelligenz," in: Rottensteiner, Franz, ed. Polaris 6. Frankfurt-am-Main: Suhrkamp, 1982. pp. 149-157.

"Science Fiction: Grenzen and Moglichkeit," in: Rottensteiner, Franz, ed. Polaris 6. Frankfurt-am-Main: Suhrkamp, 1982. pp. 141-148.

"Science Fiction: fur und wider," in: Ermert, Karl, ed. Neugier oder Flucht? Stuttgart: Klett, 1980. pp. 70-76.

Frankel, G.

"Science fiction: mimarobens smygiektyr," Biblioteksbladet 53(9):1161-1169. 1968.

Franklin, H. B.

Future Perfect: American Science Fiction of the Nineteenth Century. New York: Oxford University Press, 1966. 402 p.

Robert A. Heinlein: America as science fiction. New York: Oxford University Press, 1980. 232 p.

"America as Science Fiction: 1939," Science Fiction Studies 9(1): 38-50. March 1982.

"Change, SF, and Marxism: open or closed universes? a response from a Marxist," Science Fiction Studies 1(2):90-92. Fall 1973.

"Don't Look Where We're Going: The Vision of the Future in Science Fiction Films, 1970-82," Science-Fiction Studies 10(1): 70-80. March 1983.

"Don't Look Where We're Going: Vision of the Future in Science Fiction Films, 1970-1982," in: Slusser, George, ed. Shadows of the Magic Lamp. Carbondale: Southern Illinois University Press, 1985. pp. 73-85.

"Fiction of the future," Stanford Today Series 1, No. 17:28-30. Summer 1966. also in: The Futurist 4(1):26-28. February 1970.

"Foreword to J. G. Ballard's 'The Subliminal Man'," in: Clareson, Thomas D., ed. SF: The Other Side of Realism. Bowling Green, Ohio: Bowling Green University Popular Press, 1971. pp. 199-203.

"Future imperfect," American Film 8(5): 47-49, 75-76. March 1983.

"Pilgrim Award Acceptance Speech: The Critical Task of Science Fiction Criticism," SFRA Newsletter 115: p. f-r. October 1983.

"Science fiction as an index to popular attitudes toward science: a danger, some problems, and two possible solutions," Extrapolation 6(2):23-31. May 1965.

"Science fiction before Gernsback," in: Knight, Damon, ed. Turning Points: Essays in the Art of Science Fiction. New York: Harper, 1977. pp. 96-99.

"Viewpoint: Don't Worry, It's Only Science Fiction," Isaac Asimov's Science Fiction Magazine 8(13): 26-39. mid-December 1984.

"What are we to make of J. G. Ballard's apocalypse," in: Clareson, T. D., ed. Voices for the Future: Essays on Major Science Fiction Writers, Vol. 2. Bowling Green, Ohio: Bowling Green Univ. Popular Press, 1979. pp. 82-105.

Franklin, Michael

Reader's Guide to Fantasy, by Baird Searles, Beth Meacham, and Michael Franklin. New York: Facts on File, 1982. 196 p.

Reader's Guide to Science Fiction, A, by Baird Searles, Martin Last, Beth Meacham and Michael Franklin. New York: Avon, 1979. 266 p.

Franson, Donald

A History of the Hugo, Nebula and International Fantasy Awards, revised edition, by Donald Franson and Howard DeVore. Dearborn Heights, Michigan: Howard DeVore, 1975. 104 p. (new edition issued each year)

Franson, Donald (Continued)

Science Fiction Title Changes: A Guide to the Changing Titles of Science Fiction and Fantasy Stories Published in Magazines and Books, by Michael Vigiano and Donald Franson. Seattle: National Fantasy Fan Federation, 1965. 47 p.

"Short History of Creation Science Fiction, The," Fantasy Review 7(6): 13, 46. July 1984.

Frantz, R. J.

"Fandom Glossary," by Ron J. Frantz and Harry A. Hopkins. in: Hopkins, Harry A., ed. Fandom Directory 1980. Langley AFB, Virginia: Fandom Computer Services, 1980. pp. 7-11.

"Movie Memories: Fond and Technical," in: Hopkins, Harry A., ed. Fandom Directory 1981. Langley AFB, Virginia: Fandom Computer Services, 1981. pp. 96-100.

Franza, August

"Growing up with 1984," English Journal 72(6): 30-31. October 1983.

Fraser, B. M.

"Faster than light: the ways and means of space travel," Questar 3(3): 26-30. February 1981.

"Frederik Pohl of 'The Future'," Questar 3(4): 24-27. June 1981.

"Future, The: subject to change without notice," Amazing 27(12): 125-130. May 1981.

"Profile: Hal Clement," Algol 17(2):19-23. Spring 1980.

"Putting the past into the future: interview with Andre Norton," Fantastic 27(11): 4-9. October 1980.

"Spectrum: Vincent Di Fate-All the Colors of Space and Time," Quest/Star 4(1): 33-36. October 1981.

"Writer as an artist, The," Algol 17(2):22-23. Spring 1980.

Fraser, Brian

"Up, up, and away: a look at writing science fiction," Canadian Author and Bookman 53(2):3-13. 1978.

Fraser, G. S.

"New novels," New Statesman p. 390. September 28,1957. (Book reviews)

Fratz, Doug

"Alienated critic, The: Theodore Sturgeon and me," Thrust No. 23: 5-26. Fall/Winter 1985.

"Norman Spinrad interview, The," Thrust 8:7-11. Fall 1977.

"Ted White interview, The," Thrust 8:12-17. Spring 1977.

Frazier, Joel

"20,000 Leagues Under the Sea: the filming of Jules Verne's classic science fiction novel," by Joel Frazier and Harry Hathorne. Cinefantastique 14(3):32-53. May 1984.

Frazier, Robert

"Interview: Gene Wolfe," Thrust 19: 5-9. Winter/Spring 1983.

"Interview: Joan Vinge," Thrust 16: 6-9, 43. Fall 1980.

"Silent Evolution: Speculative Verse," by Robert Frazier and Terry Hansen. PSFQ 5: 10-13. Spring 1981.

"Stars and Blisters," Empire For the SF Writer 32: 18 20. Winter 1984.

Freas, F. K.

Separate Star, A. Virginia Beach: Greenswamp, 1984. 128 p.

"In the beginning . . . was Campbell," Analog 100(6): 98-102. June 1980.

"John W. Campbell," Locus No. 90:9-10. July 12, 1971.

"Six to go: NASA posters," Locus No. 102:2-3. November 19, 1971.

Frederick, R. D.

"With 'Ark', Geo. Lucas Retains 'King Midas' Role," Variety 305: 15. January 13, 1982.

Fredericks, S. C.

Future of Eternity, The: Mythologies of Science Fiction and Fantasy. Bloomington: Indiana University Press, 1982. 229 p.

"Incomplete Enchanter, The," in: Magill, Frank N., ed. Survey of Science Fiction Literature, Vol. 3. Englewood Cliffs, NJ: Salem Press, 1979. pp. 1031-1035.

Fredericks, S. C. (Continued)

"Strange Relations," in: Magill, Frank N., ed. Survey of Science Fiction Literature, Vol. 5. Englewood Cliffs, NJ: Salem Press, 1979. pp. 2190-2194.

"David Ketterer on SF as apocalyptic literature," Science Fiction Studies 1(3):217-219. Spring 1974.

"Fantastic pastoral of Thomas Burnett Swann," in: Collins, R. A. and H. D. Pearce, eds. The Scope of the Fantastic: Theory, Technique, Major Authors. Westport, CT: Greenwood Press, 1985. pp. 201-205.

"Lucian's 'true history' as SF," Science Fiction Studies 3(1):49-60. March 1976.

"Myth of descent in Vincent King's Light a Last Candle, The," Riverside Quarterly 6(1):20-28. August 1973.

"On Alexei Panshin and Heinlein criticism," Science Fiction Studies 4(2):212-215. July 1977.

"On David Ketterer's New Worlds for Old: a Unique Critical Method," Science-Fiction Studies 2(2): 134-137. July 1975.

"Philip Jose Farmer and the White Goddess," Riverside Quarterly 7(3): 141-148. May 1983.

"Problems of fantasy," Science Fiction Studies 5(1):33-44. March 1978.

"Revivals of ancient mythologies in current science fiction and fantasy," in: Clareson, T. D., ed. Many Futures, Many Worlds. Kent, Ohio: Kent State University Press, 1977. pp. 50-65.

"Roger Zelazny and the trickster myth," Journal of American Culture 2(2):271-278. Summer 1979.

"Sci-Fi," Indiana Alumni, p. 8-11. April/May 1981.

"Science fiction and the world of Greek myth," Helios 2:1-22. 1975.

Freedman, Carl

"Towards a Theory of Paranoia: The Science Fiction of Philip K. Dick," Science-Fiction Studies 11(1): 15-24. March 1984.

Freedman, R. A.

"Physics-13: Teaching Modern Physics Through Science-Fiction," American Journal of Physics 48(7): 548-551. July 1980.

Freedman, Russell

2000 Years of Space Travel. New York: Holiday House, 1963. 256 p.

Jules Verne: Portrait of a Prophet. New York: Holiday House, 1965. 256 p.

"To the moon with Jules Verne," Catholic Digest 31(2):60-65. December 1966. (Condensed from "Jules Verne: portrait of a prophet").

Freeland, Nat

"Special effects expert Doug Trumball: a cinematic Peter Max," Show Magazine pp. 44-45. July 23, 1970.

Freeman, Jon

"World of the Wars," in: Bretnor, Reginald, ed. The Future at War: Vol. 3: Orion's Sword. New York: Ace, 1980. pp. 166-181.

Freeman, Keith

"Word processing," Focus: An SF Writers' Magazine No. 11: 13-15. 1985.

Freeman, W. L.

"Bloody fight," Inside and Science Fiction Advertiser No. 9: 26-33. May 1955.

"Fire the critic: the strange science fiction attitude of the business people," Inside and Science Fiction Advertiser No. 12: 2-4. November 1955.

"She ain't what she used to be," Inside and Science Fiction Advertiser No. 8: 12-17. March 1955.

Freff

"Dave Francis interview," Khatru No. 6: 22-31. 1977.

"From the moment I reached out to hold: an interview with Jon Anderson," Khatru No. 7: 26-37. 1978.

"Interview with Frank Kelly Freas, An," Science Fiction Review 19:42-46. November 1976. (Note: issue incorrectly identified on contents page as v. 5, no. 3, whole no. 18, August, 1976.)

Freiberg, Karen

"Kate Wilhelm," in: Mainiero, Lina, ed. American Women Writers. New York: Ungar, 1982. v. 4, pp. 422-423.

Freiberg, S. K.

"La belle dame and the sestina," <u>Kalki</u>
7(1):19-22. 1975.

Freibert, L. M.

"World Views in Utopian Novels by Women,"
<u>Journal of Popular Culture</u> 17(1): 49-60.
Summer 1983.

"World views in utopian novels by women," in:
Barr, Marleen, ed. <u>Women and Utopia</u>. New
York: Lanham, 1983. pp. 67-84.

Freitas, R. A., Jr.

"Extraterrestrial zoology," <u>Analog</u> 101(8):
53-67. July 20, 1981.

Fremont-Smith, Eliot

"Books of the times," <u>New York Times</u> p.
212. January 13, 1967. (Book reviews)

French, Jim

"Boskone report," <u>Science Fiction Chronicle</u>
2(8):18-20. May 1981.

"Interview with John Brunner," <u>Locus</u>
11(3):15. April 1978.

"Lunacon '81," <u>Science Fiction Chronicle</u>
2(9):14-15. June 1981.

French, Lawrence

"Ray Harryhausen retires," <u>Cinefantastique</u>
15(5):11. January 1986.

French, Rod

"Gene Wolfe and the Tale of Wonder: The End of
an Apprenticeship," <u>Science Fiction: A
Review of Speculative Literature</u>. 5(2):
43-47. June 1983.

French, Warren

"Lovecraft, H. P.," in: Woodcock, George,
ed. <u>20th Century Fiction</u>. Chicago: St.
James, 1985. p. 403-404.

Frenkel, James

"Afterword," in: Dick, Philip K. <u>Dr.
Bloodmoney</u>. New York: Bluejay, 1985. pp.
307-314.

Frentz, T. S.

"Inferential model criticism of The Empire
Strikes Back," by T. S. Frentz and M. E. Hale.
<u>Quarterly Jounal of Speech</u> 69(3): 278-289.
August 1983.

Frentzen, Jeffrey

"Battlestar Galactica (review),"
<u>Cinefantastique</u> 8(1):17-18. Winter 1978.

"Herk Harvey's Carnival of Souls,"
<u>Cinefantastique</u> 13(6)/14(1):91-95.
September 1983.

"Show by show guide: The Outer Limits, Part 3,"
by D. J. Schow and Jeffrey Frentzen. <u>Twilight
Zone</u> 4(2): 84-87. May/June 1984.

"Show by show guide: The Outer Limits, part 4,"
by D. J. Schow and Jeffrey Frentzen.
<u>Twilight Zone</u> 4(3):85-88. July/August 1984.

"Show by show guide: The Outer Limits, part 5,"
by D. J. Schow and Jeffrey Frentzen.
<u>Twilight Zone</u> 4(4):83-86. September/October
1984.

"Show by show guide: The Outer Limits, part 6,"
by D. J. Schow and Jeffrey Frentzen.
<u>Twilight Zone</u> 4(6):83-86. November/December
1984.

"Show by show guide: The Outer Limits, part 7,"
by D. J. Schow and Jeffrey Frentzen.
<u>Twilight Zone</u> 4(6):101-104.
January/February 1985.

Freund, B. L.

"Who's on top?" <u>Harper's Bazaar</u> 105:52-53.
July 1972. (not seen)

Freund, Rudolf

"Rettung aus dem Schrotthaufen? Nur
einschneidende sofortmassnahmen konnen die
drohende rohstoffverknappung aufhalten," <u>Die
Zeit</u> no. 24:46. June 16, 1972.

Frewin, Anthony

<u>One Hundred Years of Science Fiction
Illustration, 1840-1940</u>. London: Jupiter,
1974. 128 p.

Freyberg, J. T.

"Hold high the cardboard sword," <u>Psychology
Today</u> 8(9):63-64. February 1975. (not seen)

Friedenreich, Kenneth

"Kurt Vonnegut: the PR man turned novelist," Newsday (magazine section) p. 12. August 11, 1975.

Friedman, A. J.

"Contemporary American Physics Fiction," American Journal of Physics 47(5): 392-395. May 1979.

"Toward convergence in science and literature," Discussion paper, seminar 152, "Science and Literature: Correlations and Divergences," Modern Language Association, San Francisco. December 1975. Unpublished.

Friedman, B. R.

"Fabricating history: narrative strategy in 'The Lord of the Rings'," Clio No. 2:123-144. 1973.

Friedman, Barton

"Tolkien and David Jones: The Great War and The War of the Ring," Clio 11(2): 115-136. Winter 1982.

Friedrich, Otto

"Ultra Vonnegut," Time pp. 65-69. May 7, 1973.

Friend, Beverly

Science Fiction Fan Cult. Ph.D. Dissertation, Northwestern University, 1975. 243 p.

Science Fiction: The Classroom in Orbit. Glassboro, NJ: Educational Impact, 1974. 92 p.

"Babel 17," in: Magill, Frank N., ed. Survey of Science Fiction Literature, Vol. 1. Englewood Cliffs, NJ: Salem Press, 1979. pp. 113-119.

"Female Man, The," in: Magill, Frank N., ed. Survey of Science Fiction Literature, Vol. 2. Englewood Cliffs, NJ: Salem Press, 1979. pp. 766-769.

"Flatland: A Romance of Many Dimensions," in: Magill, Frank N., ed. Survey of Modern Fantasy Literature, Vol 2. Englewood Cliffs, NJ: Salem Press, Inc., 1983. pp. 561-565.

"Malevil," in: Magill, Frank N., ed. Survey of Science Fiction Literature, Vol. 3. Englewood Cliffs, NJ: Salem Press, 1979. pp. 1317-1322.

"Mirror, The," in: Magill, Frank N., ed. Survey of Modern Fantasy Literature, Vol 3.

Englewood Cliffs, NJ: Salem Press, Inc., 1983. pp. 1034-1036.

"Rite of Passage," in: Magill, Frank N., ed. Survey of Science Fiction Literature, Vol. 4. Englewood Cliffs, NJ: Salem Press, 1979. pp. 1805-1808.

"Reaching the future through paperback fiction," Media & Methods 11:35-36. November 1974.

"Remarkable adventure, The," by P. J. Farmer and Beverly Friend. in: Warrick, Patricia, ed. Science Fiction: Contemporary Mythology. New York: Harper, 1978. pp. 39-49.

"Strange bedfellows: science fiction, linguistics and education," English Journal 62(7):998-1003. October 1973.

"Sturgeon connection, The," in: Clareson, Thomas D., ed. Voices for the Future: Essays on Major SF Writers, Vol 1. Bowling Green, Ohio: Bowling Green University Popular Press, 1976. pp. 153-166.

"Syllabus for a Proposed Course: The Treatment of Women in Science Fiction," SFRA Newsletter 103: 12-17. August 1982.

"Time Travel as a Feminist Didactic in Works by Phyllis Eisenstein, Marlys Millhiser, and Octavia Butler," Extrapolation 23(1): 50-55. Spring 1982.

"Virgin territory: the bonds and boundaries of women in SF," in: Clareson, T. D., ed. Many Futures, Many Worlds. Kent State Univ. Press, 1977. pp. 140-163. also in: Extrapolation, Dec. 1972, and in her SF: Classroom in Orbit.

"Virgin territory: women and sex in science fiction," Extrapolation 14(1):49-58. December 1972.

Frierson, Meade

HPL: A Tribute to Howard Phillips Lovecraft 1890-1937. Birmingham, AL: Frierson, 1979. 143 p.

"Science fiction and radio," Diversity No. 3:18-22. August 1972.

Fries, Maureen

"Rationalization of the Arthurian matter in T. H. White and Mary Stewart, The," Philological Quarterly 56(2):258-265. Spring 1977.

Frisby, E. S.

Nietzsche's Influence on the Superman in Science Fiction Literature. Ph.D. Dissertation, Florida State University, 1979. 176 p.

Frisch, A. J.

"Language Fragmentation in Recent Science-Fiction Novels," in: Myers, R. E., ed. The Intersection of Science Fiction and Philosophy. Westport: Greenwood, 1983. pp. 147-158.

"Religious Imagination and Imagined Religion," by A. J. Frisch and Joseph Martos. in: Reilly, Robert, ed. The Transcendent Adventure. Westport: Greenwood, 1984. pp. 11-26.

"Toward New Sexual Identities: James Tiptree, Jr.," in: Staircar, Tom, ed. The Feminine Eye. New York: Ungar, 1982. pp. 48-59.

Frisch, S. L.

"Poetics of the uncanny: E. T. A. Hoffmann's 'Sandman'," in: Collins, R. A. and H. D. Pearce, eds. The Scope of the Fantastic: Theory, Technique, Major Authors. Westport, CT: Greenwood Press, 1985. pp. 49-55.

Fromental, J. L.

"Science fiction et bande dessinee," by J. L. Fromenthal and F. Landon. Magazine litteraire (Paris) 88:25-27. May 1974.

Frommlet, Wolfram

"Science fiction und soziale utopie im kinderund jugenbuch," Kurbiskern 1:101-111. 1975.

Frost, Gregory

"John Kessel: literary vampire," Fantasy Review 8(4): 41-42, 46. April 1985.

"With friends like these, who needs critics?" Fantasy Review 8(9): 4. September 1985.

Frost, Naomi

"Life after death: visions of Lewis and Williams," CSL: The Bulletin of the New York C. S. Lewis Society 6(6):2-6. 1975.

Froud, Brian

World of the Dark Crystal, The, by Brian Froud, J. J. Llewelyn, and Rupert Brown. New York: Knopf, 1983. 128 p.

Frye, Northrop

"Varieties of literary utopia," Daedalus 94(3):323-347. Spring 1965.

Fryxell, D. A.

"Galaxy of SF Stars," by W. J. Reynolds and D. A. Fryxell. TWA Ambassador 12(10): 94-95, 124-127. October 1979.

Fuchs, W. J.

Comics: Anatomie eines Massenmediums, by W. J. Fuchs and R. C. Reitberger. Hamburg: Rowohlt, 1971. 333 p.

Fuchs, Werner

Reclams Science Fiction Fuehrer, ed. by H. J. Alpers, Werner Fuchs, R. M. Hahn and Wolfgang Jeschke. Munich: Heyne, 1980. 503 p.

Fuks, L.

"Kilka uwag o literaturze fantastyczno-naukowej z punktu widzenia gnoseologii logiki i etyki," in: Kaczmarka, J., ed. Materialy z Miedzynarodowego Spotkania Pisarzy-Tworcow Lit. Fantastyczno-Naukowej. Poznan: Wyn. Poz., 1974. pp. 53-58.

Fuller, Edmund

"Affectionate and muted exchange anent Lewis," by Alan Jones and Edmund Fuller. Studies in the Literary Imagination 14(2):3-12. Fall 1981.

Fuller, Florence

"Is God science fiction?" Colloquy, Education in Church & Society 4(5):26-27. May 1971.

Fuller, Richard

"Fuller's earth," Colloquy, Education in Church & Society 4(5):37-45. May 1971.

Fulmer, Gilbert

"Time Travel, Determinism, and Fatalism," Philosophical Speculations in Science Fiction and Fantasy. 1(1): 41-47. March 1981.

Fulton, Ken

"Dealer's Defense, A: The Case for Science Fiction and Fantasy," AB Bookman's Weekly 71(9): 1495-1510. February 28, 1983.

Fulwiler, William

"Tarzan, Kull, and Conan," AMRA 2(62):15-19. October 1974.

Fulwiler, William (Continued)

"Who Wrote Poltergeist?"   Fantasy Newsletter
5(10): 33. November 1982.

Fuoroli, Caryn

"Doris Lessing's game: referential language and
fictional form,"   Twentieth Century
Literature 27(2):146-165. Summer 1981.

Furst, Rudolf

"Bucher uber Geistergeschichten, Vampyre, und
Robinsonaden," by Rudolf Furst, Egon von
Momorzynski, and Carl Enders. Quarber Merkur
39:51-55. Jan. 1975.

Furter, Pierre

Strategies de l'utopie. Colloque organis'e au
Centre Thomas More, by Pierre Furter and
Gerard Raulet.   Paris: Editions Galilee, 1979.
269 p.

Furuya, D. M.

"Conan the Barbarian: The Heroic Spirit and the
Sword," Martial Arts Movies 2(6): 12-24.
June 1982.

Fusco, Sebastino

"Uncommon market: toward a European SF," by
Gianfranco de Turris and Sebastino Fusco.
Australian Science Fiction Review No.
14:3-5. February 1968.

Fuson, B. W.

"Poetic precursor of Bellamy's 'Looking
Backward,' A,"   Extrapolation 5(2):31-36.
May 1964. also in: Clareson, T. D., ed. SF:
The Other Side of Realism. Bowling Green,
Ohio: Bowling Green Popular Press, 1971. pp.
282-288.

"Three Kansas utopian novels of 1890,"
Extrapolation 12(1):7-24. December 1970.

Fuzellier, Etienne

"Science fiction a-t-elle une valeur educative,
La?" L'Anneau d'or, 126, 1965, pp. 453-459.

"Science fiction, La," Education Nationale
24e annee, No. 848:26-28. January 25, 1968.

"SF et son role dans Le monde moderne, La,"
Technique Art Science (Revue de l'Enseign,
Technique). March 1963.

G

Gaar, A. C.

German Science Fiction: Variation on the Theme of Survival in the Space-Time Continuum. Ph.D. Dissertation, University of North Carolina, 1973. 312 p.

"Singular man in the perfect future," in: Samuelson, D. N. Science Fiction and Future Studies. Bryan, TX: SFRA, 1975. pp. 100-107.

"Two new books from Germany," Science Fiction Studies 1(4):285-287. Fall 1974.

"Zufall in den Romanen und Zwei Kurzgeschichten Herbert W. Frankes," Quarber Merkur 41:11-18. September 1975.

Gaasbeek, Rinus

Fantasfeer, by Arnold Spiank, Rinus Gaasbeek, and George Gorremans. Amsterdam: Meulenhoff, 1979. 278 p.

Gabard, E. C.

Contributions Toward a History of Science Fiction in English, 1920 to 1950, With Emphasis on the Science Novel. Masters Thesis, University of Southern California, 1952. 219 p.

Gabbard, G. N.

"Dance version of Jurgen, The," Kalki 6(4):115-117. 1975.

Gabbard, Krin

"Religious and Political Allegory in Robert Wise's The Day the Earth Stood Still," Film/Literature Quarterly 10(3): 150-154. July 1982.

Gabriel, Judy

"Movie Robot is Born," American Cinematographer 63(2): 128-129, 184-190. February 1982.

Gaddis, V. H.

"New science of space speech, The," Worlds of Tomorrow 1(3):115-123. August 1963.

Gaffo, Mauro

"Gian luigi Zuddas: L'Iceberg Rivelato," Cosmo informatore 14(1):64-65. spring 1985.

"Il mio amico stone," Cosmo informatore 14(12):52-54. spring 1985.

"XI Italcon: Caccia alle streghe," Cosmo informatore 14(2):17-19. summer 1985.

Gagne, P. R.

"Creepshow," Cinefantastique 13(1):16-35 September/October 1982.

"Creepshow," Cinefantastique 12(2/3):16-21. April 1982.

"Dick Smith on The Hunger," Cinefantastique 13(4):16-23. April/May 1983.

"Ghost Stories: the novels of Peter Straub," Cinefantastique 12(1):14-19. February 1982.

"Ghost Story," Cinefantastique 12(1):20-39. February 1982.

"Science fiction typographics," Cinefantastique 10(4):36-41. Spring 1981.

"Stephen King," Cinefantastique 14(2):4-5. December 1983/January 1984.

Gagne, Paul

"Interview With Peter Straub," American Fantasy 1(1): 8-26. February 1982.

Gagnon, C. M.

"Bibliographie selective et indicative de la paralitterature," by C. M. Gagnon and Sylvie Provost. Cahiers de l'institut superieur des sciences humaines (Laval Univ.) No. 24. October 1978.

Gaillard, Dawson

Dorothy L. Sayers.   New York: Ungar, 1981.
124 p.

Gakov, Vladimir

Vitok spirali.   Moskva: Znanie, 1980 64 p.

"Far Rainbow," in: Magill, Frank N., ed.
Survey of Science Fiction Literature, Vol. 2.
Englewood Cliffs, NJ: Salem Press, 1979. pp.
756-760.

"Final Circle of Paradise, The," in:
Magill, Frank N., ed.   Survey of Science
Fiction Literature, Vol. 2. Englewood Cliffs,
NJ: Salem Press, 1979. pp. 776-781.

"Hard to Be a God," in: Magill, Frank N.,
ed.   Survey of Science Fiction Literature,
Vol. 2. Englewood Cliffs, NJ: Salem Press,
1979. pp. 950-955.

"Leopard s vershini Kilimandzharo," in:
Magill, Frank N., ed.   Survey of Science
Fiction Literature, Vol. 3. Englewood Cliffs,
NJ: Salem Press, 1979. pp. 1188-1192.

"Noon: Twenty-Second Century," in: Magill,
Frank N., ed.   Survey of Science Fiction
Literature, Vol. 4. Englewood Cliffs, NJ:
Salem Press, 1979. pp. 1548-1554.

"Short Fiction of Dmitri Bilenkin, The," in:
Magill, Frank N., ed.   Survey of Science
Fiction Literature, Vol. 4. Englewood Cliffs,
NJ: Salem Press, 1979. pp. 1934-1938.

"Short Fiction of Kirill Bulychev, The," in:
Magill, Frank N., ed.   Survey of Science
Fiction Literature, Vol. 4. Englewood Cliffs,
NJ: Salem Press, 1979. pp. 2019-2022.

"Sozdan dla busi," in: Magill, Frank N.,
ed.   Survey of Science Fiction Literature,
Vol. 5. Englewood Cliffs, NJ: Salem Press,
1979. pp. 2117-2121.

"1982: one year in Soviet science fiction,"
Locus 15(12):11-12. December 1982.

"1984: One year of Soviet science fiction,"
Locus 18(3): 23-24. March 1985.

"1984: One Year of Soviet Science Fiction,"
Locus 18(3): 23-24. March 1985.

"Conversations in Maleyevka,"   Soviet
Literature No. 6 (447):173-179. 1985.

"Laser Ray in 1926: Alexei Tolstoy's Science
Fiction,"   Soviet Literature No. 418:
161-169. 1983.

"New generation of Soviet science fiction: old
themes, new conclusions)," (in Russian) by V.
Gakov and V. Gopman.   Canadian-American
Slavic Studies 18(1/2):85-96. Spring/Summer
1984.

"One Year in Soviet SF,"   Locus 17(8):
24-26. August 1984.

"Soviet science fiction in Wonderland,"
Soviet Literature No. 428: 175-184. 1983.

"Soviet science fiction, IV,"   Locus 18(4):
19-21. April 1985.

"Soviet science fiction: origin of the
species,"   Locus 16(3):11,18. March 1983.

"Soviet Science Fiction: The Golden Age, Part
One,"   Locus 17(3): 22-24. March 1984.

"Soviet Science Fiction: The Golden Age, Part
Two,"   Locus 17(4): 22-23. April 1984.

Galbreath, Robert

"Ambiguous Apocalypse: Trancendental Versions
of the End," in: Rabkin, Eric S., ed. The
End of the World. Carbondale: Southern
Illinois University Press, 1983. pp. 53-72.

"Holism, openness, and the other: Le Guin's use
of the occult,"   Science-Fiction Studies
7(1): 36-48. March 1980.

"Introduction to the Ketterer forum,"
Science Fiction Studies 3(1):60-64. March
1976.

"Redemption and Doubt in Philip K. Dick's Valis
Trilogy,"   Extrapolation 24(2): 105-115.
Summer 1983.

"Salvation Knowledge: Ironic Gnosticism in
Valis and Flight to Lucifer," in: Wolfe,
Gary, ed. Science Fiction Dialogues.
Chicago: Academy Chicago, 1982. pp. 115-132.

"Taoist Magic in the Earthsea Trilogy,"
Extrapolation 21(3): 262-268. Fall 1980.

Gales, H. H.

Selection of Science Fiction For the Public
Library. Masters Thesis, Catholic University
of America, 1961. 74 p.

Galey, M.

"Essais sur le fantastique," Revue de Paris
72(10):103-108. October 1965.

Gallagher, E. J.

Annotated Guide to Fantastic Adventures.
Mercer Island, WA: Starmont, 1985. 170 p.

Jules Verne: A Primary and Secondary
Bibliography, by E. J. Gallagher, J. A.
Mistichelli, and J. A. Van Eerde. Boston: G.
K. Hall, 1980. 544 p.

Gallagher, E. J. (Continued)

"From folded hands to clenched fists: Kesey and science fiction," Lex et Scientia: Journal of Law and Science 13(1/2):46-50. 1977.

"Lem's lunatic robots: charting The Cyberiad," Science, Technology & Society No. 15:ll-13. December 1979.

"Science fiction for the STS teacher," Humanities Perspectives on Technology No. 10:10. February 1979.

"Science fiction odds and ends," Humanities Perspectives on Technology No. 13:7. October 1979.

"Thematic structure of The Martian Chronicles, The," in: Greenberg, M. H. and J. D. Olander, eds. Ray Bradbury. New York: Taplinger, 1980. pp. 55-82.

Gallagher, Steve

"Blind Man's Movies," Vector 105: 7-14. December 1981.

"Building a Novel," Focus 6: 7-10. Autumn 1982.

"Dust in the Archives, a Tear in the Eye," Vector 115: 28-31. 1983.

"Media Maze," Focus 5: 20-26, 33. Spring 1982.

"Putting the Feathers on the Indians," Focus: An SF Writers' Magazine No. 8: 18-21. Autumn 1983.

"Science fiction and the cinema," Vector No 94:15-18C. July/August 1979.

Gallant, J. W.

"Proposal for the reading of science fiction," High Points 33:20-27. April 1951.

Gallant, Joseph

"Literature, science and the manpower crisis," Science 125(3252):787-791. April 26, 1957. Discussions: Science 125:1212-1214,1261; 126:856,1421. also in: Saturday Review 40:56. May 4, 1957.

Galle, H. J.

"Annie France-Harrar," Quarber Merkur 30:18-42. April, 1972.

"Mark Twain oder Lache Bajazzo," Quarber Merkur 26:33-62. February 1971.

Galle, J. W.

Archetypal Patterns in J. R. R. Tolkien's The Lord of the Rings. Masters Thesis, Louisiana Tech University, 1979. 89 p.

Gallet, G. H.

"On Verne and Bailey," Fantasy Times No. 269:7-8. April (2) 1957.

Gallix, Francois

"T. H. White et la legende du roi Arthur," Mosaic 10(2):47-63. Winter 1977.

Gallot, G. H.

"History of French science fiction, part 1," Fantasy Times No. 172:5,7. February (2) 1953.

"History of French science fiction, part 2," Fantasy Times No. 173:5-6. March (1) 1953.

Gallun, R. Z.

"Profession of Science Fiction, The, 24: The Making of a Pulp Writer," Foundation 22: 35-48. June 1981.

Gans, H. J.

"Star Wars; the teen-ager as democracy's savior," Social Policy 8(4):54-55. January/February 1978.

Garagnon, Jean

"Abbe, L', Prevose et l'utopie," Studies in Eighteenth-Century Culture, Vol. 6, 1977. pp. 439-458.

Garber, Eric

Uranian Worlds: A Reader's Guide to Alternative Sexuality in Science Fiction And Fantasy, by Eric Garber and Lyn Paleo. Boston: G. K. Hall, 1983. 177 p.

Garci, J. L.

Ray Bradbury, humanista del futuro. Madrid: Helios, 1971. 372 p.

Garcia, Frank

"James P. Hogan: an interview," Fantasy Review 8(9): 11-12. September 1985.

Gardiner, H. J.

American Utopian Fiction, 1885-1910: The Influence of Science and Technology. Ph.D. Dissertation, University of Houston, 1978. 198 p.

"Images of the waste land in Delaney's The Einstein Intersection," Extrapolation 18(2):116-123. May 1977.

Gardner, C. S.

"Unearth," in: Tymn, M. B. and Ashley, Mike. Science Fiction, Fantasy, and Weird Fiction Magazines. Westport, CT: Greenwood, 1985. pp. 688-692.

"Lin Carter interviewed, part 1," Science Fiction Times (Boston) 1(7):1,4-5. March 1980.

"Things That Go Bump in the Movies: Horror Film in the 1980s," In: Winter, Douglas E. Shadowings: The Reader's Guide to Horror Fiction 1981-1982. Mercer Island, WA: Starmont, 1983. pp. 111-118.

Gardner, J. H.

"Mary Shelley's divine tragedy," Essays in Literature (Western Illinois University) 4(2):182-197. Fall 1977.

Gardner, M.

"Anne McCaffrey," Biography News 2:830. July 1975.

"Humorous science fiction," Writer 62(5):148-151. May 1949.

Gardner, Martin

The Wizard of Oz and Who He Was, by Martin Gardner and R. B. Nye. East Lansing: Michigan State University Press, 1957. 208 p.

"Unter falscher flagge. Sektierer der Wissenschaft," in: Der Monat 6(62):162-171. 1953.

Gardner, T. S.

"Avon Fantasy Reader, a review," Fantasy Times No. 94: 4. November (2) 1949.

"1946 in science fiction, part 1: Fantastic Adventures and Amazing Stories," Fantasy Times No. 55:7-8. August 1947.

"1946 in science fiction, part 2: Weird Tales and Planet Stories," Fantasy Times No. 56:5,14. September 1947.

"1946 in science fiction, part 4: Thrilling Wonder Stories," Fantasy Times No. 58:7. November 1947.

"1946 in science fiction, part 5: Astounding Science Fiction and conclusion," Fantasy Times No. 60:7-8. December 1947.

"1947 in science fiction, part 1: Amazing Stories," Fantasy Times No. 63:3-4. March 1948.

"1947 in science fiction, part 2: Fantastic Adventures," Fantasy Times No. 64:3-4. April 1948.

"1947 in science fiction, part 3: Weird Tales," Fantasy Times No. 65:3. May 1948.

"1947 in science fiction, part 4: Famous Fantastic Mysteries," Fantasy Times No. 66:6. June 1948.

"1947 in science fiction, part 5: Planet Stories," Fantasy Times No. 67:8. July 1948.

"1947 in science fiction, part 6: Thrilling Wonder Stories and Startling Stories," Fantasy Times No. 68:15,18-19. August 1948.

"1947 in science fiction, part 7: Astounding Science Fiction," Fantasy Times No. 69:6-8. September 1948.

"1948 in science fiction, part 1: Fantastic Adventures," Fantasy Times No. 74:3-4. January 1, 1949.

"1948 in science fiction, part 2: Weird Tales," Fantasy Times No. 75:3,8. February 1, 1949.

"1948 in science fiction, part 3: Planet Stories," Fantasy Times No. 76:2. February 15, 1949.

"1948 in science fiction, part 4: Startling Stories," Fantasy Times No. 77: 3, 7. March 1, 1949.

"1948 in science fiction, part 4: Startling Stories," Fantasy Times No. 77:3,8. March 1, 1949.

"1948 in science fiction, part 5: Thrilling Wonder Stories," Fantasy Times No. 78:3,8. March 15, 1949.

"1948 in science fiction, part 6: Amazing Stories," Fantasy Times No. 79:3-4. April (1) 1949.

"1948 in science fiction, part 7: Famous Fantastic Mysteries," Fantasy Times No. 80:3. April (2) 1949.

"1948 in science fiction, part 8: Fantastic Novels," Fantasy Times No. 81:1,3. May (1) 1949.

Gardner, T. S. (Continued)

"1948 in science fiction, part 9a:
Astounding," Fantasy Times No. 82:1.
May (2) 1949.

"1948 in science fiction, part 9b:
Astounding," Fantasy Times No. 83:4.
June (1) 1949.

"1949 in science fiction, part 10a:
Astounding," Fantasy Times No. 108:9-10.
June (2) 1950.

"1949 in science fiction, part 10b:
Astounding Science Fiction," Fantasy
Times No. 109:8,10. July (1) 1950.

"1949 in science fiction, part 10c:
Astounding Science Fiction," Fantasy
Times No. 110:7-8. July (2) 1950.

"1949 in science fiction, part 11: conclusion,"
Fantasy Times No. 111:7. August (1) 1950.

"1949 in science fiction, part 1: Fantastic
Novels," Fantasy Times No. 97:2. January
(1) 1950.

"1949 in science fiction, part 2: Famous
Fantastic Mysteries," Fantasy Times No.
98:7-8. January (2) 1950.

"1949 in science fiction, part 3: Planet
Stories," Fantasy Times No. 99:7-8.
February (1) 1950.

"1949 in science fiction, part 4: Thrilling
Wonder Stories," Fantasy Times No.
100:24,28. February (2) 1950.

"1949 in science fiction, part 5: Startling
Stories," Fantasy Times No. 101:4. March
(1) 1950.

"1949 in science fiction, part 6: Weird
Tales," Fantasy Times No. 102:7. March
(2) 1950.

"1949 in science fiction, part 7: Super
Science Stories," Fantasy Times No.
103:2,8. April (1) 1950.

"1949 in science fiction, part 8a: Amazing
Stories," Fantasy Times No. 104:2,9-10.
April (2) 1950.

"1949 in science fiction, part 8b: Amazing
Stories," Fantasy Times No. 105:10,12.
May (1) 1950.

"1949 in science fiction, part 9a: Fantastic
Adventures," Fantasy Times No. 106:7.
May (2) 1950.

"1949 in science fiction, part 9b: Fantastic
Adventures," Fantasy Times No. 107:9.
June (1) 1950.

"1952 in science fiction, addendum," Fantasy
Times No. 176:4-5. April (2) 1953.

"1952 in science fiction," Fantasy Times
No. 169:3-5,9. January (1) 1953.

"1953 in science fiction, part 1," Fantasy
Times No. 194:1-2. January (2) 1954.

"1953 in science fiction, part 2," Fantasy
Times No. 195:2,5. February (1) 1954.

"1953 in science fiction, part 3," Fantasy
Times No. 196:2-3. February (2) 1954.

"1953 in science fiction, part 4," Fantasy
Times No. 197:2. March (2) 1954.

"1954 in science fiction, part 1," Fantasy
Times No. 214:2,4. January (1) 1955.

"1954 in science fiction, part 2," Fantasy
Times No. 215:2,4. January (2) 1955.

"1955 in science fiction, part 1," Fantasy
Times No. 239:1-2,6. January (2) 1956.

"1955 in science fiction, part 2," Fantasy
Times No. 240:3-4,6. February (1) 1956.

"1956 in science fiction, part 1," Fantasy
Times No. 262:1-2. January (1) 1957.

"1956 in science fiction, part 2," Fantasy
Times No. 263:5. January (2) 1957.

"1956 in science fiction, part 3," Fantasy
Times No. 264:4-5. February (1) 1957.

"1956 in science fiction," in: Science
Fiction Yearbook, 1957 Edition. Vol. 1.
Patterson, NJ: Fandom House, 1957. pp. 14-17.

"1957 in science fiction, part 1," Science
Fiction Times No. 287:2-3. January 1958.

"1957 in science fiction, part 2," Science
Fiction Times No. 288:2-3. February 1958.

"1957 in science fiction, part 3," Science
Fiction Times No. 289:2. February 1958.

"1957 in science fiction, part 4," Science
Fiction Times No. 290:2. March 1958.

"Are science fiction fans suckers," Fantasy
Times No. 56:1,14. September 1947.

"Bridge between science and science fiction,"
Science Fiction Times No. 369:19-20.
September 1961.

"Broken record," Fantasy Times No. 56:8-9.
September 1947.

"Congratulations to Fantasy Times on its
100th issue," Fantasy Times No. 100:9-11.
February (2) 1950.

"Is science fiction a normal casualty of the
times?" Fantasy Times No. 254:19-21.
September (1) 1956.

Gardner, T. S. (Continued)

"Psychological quirks of writers," _Fantasy Times_ No. 10:5-6. June 1944.

"Psychology of the science fiction fan," _New Fandom_. April 1939. (not seen)

"Sex in science fiction," _Fantasy Times_ 1(10):6-8. December 1945.

"Solution strictly phoney," _Fantasy Times_ No. 67:12-13. July 1948.

"What's your guess," _Fantasy Times_ No. 138:13-14. September (2) 1951.

"Whither?" _Fantasy Times_ No. 200:16-17. June (1) 1954.

Garmon, Gerald

"Edmond Hamilton," in: Coward, David, ed. _Twentieth-Century American Science-Fiction Writers, Part 1: A-L._ Detroit: Gale, 1981. pp. 201-203. (Dictionary of Literary Biography, v. 8)

Garner, Alan

"Inner time," in: Nicholls, Peter, ed. _Science Fiction at Large._ New York: Harper, 1976. pp. 119-138.

Garnett, David

"Interview: Arthur C. Clarke," _Locus_ 11(5):9-11. July 1978.

"Milford 1982: The Truth," _Focus: An SF Writer's Magazine_ 7: 29-32. Spring 1983.

Garr, A. C.

"Human as machine analog: the big daddy of interchangeable parts in the fiction of Robert A. Heinlein, The," in: Olander, J. D. and M. H. Greenberg, eds. _Robert A. Heinlein._ New York: Taplinger, 1978. pp. 64-82.

Garrett, Randall

Hour With Isaac Asimov. See under: Asimov, Isaac.

Garrison, Webb

"Science fiction stories described atom bomb 17 months before first one was dropped," _National Enquirer._ January 3, 1971. (not seen)

Garsault, Alain

"Manifestations fantastiques," _Positif_ 230:53-59. May 1980.

"Recit d'aventures et la fable metaphysique (sur zardoz), Le," _Positif_ 157:20-24. March 1974.

"S. F. et image: le recit cinematographique," _Europe_ 580/581:119-125. August/September 1977.

"XVIIIe festival international du film de science fiction, Trieste, 1979," _Positif_ 225:57-58. December 1979.

Gasca, Luis

Cine y ciencia ficcion. Barcelona: Libres de Sinera, 1969.

Cine y ciencia ficcion (1898-1973). Barcelona: Editorial Planeta, 1975. 246 p.

Fantascienza e cinema. Lessico delle opere, storie e personaggi dal 1898 ai nostri giorni. Milan: Mazzotta, 1972. 317 p. (Tr. of _Cine y ciencia ficcion._)

Imagen y ciencia ficcion. San Sebastian: XIV Festival International dl Cine, 1966.

Gasparetto, P. F.

"Un archetipo di fantautopia lunare nel '600 inglese," In: _Utopia e fantascienza._ Torino: Giappichelli, 1975. p. 81-98.

Gattegno, Jean

Lewis Carroll: Fragments of a Looking Glass. New York: Thomas Y. Crowell, 1976. 327 p.

Science Fiction, La. 2nd ed. Paris: Presses universitaires de France, 1973. 128 p.

Science Fiction, La. Paris: Presses universitaires de France, 1971. 126 p.

"Date de naissance, La. b) 1818," _Europe_ 580-581:38-43. August/September 1977.

"Folie, Groyance et fantastique dans 'Dracula'," _Litteratur_ No. 8:72-83. December 1972.

Gatts, Strawberry

"Use of holograms in Logan's Run," _American Cinematographer_ 57(6):650-659, 669,706. June 1976.

Gaudet, Hazel

Invasion From Mars: A Study in the Psychology of Panic, by Hadley Cantril, Hazel Gaudet, and Herta Herzog. Princeton: Princeton University Press, 1983. 224 p.

Gaughan, Jack

"Everything you wanted to know about the elements of style," Locus No. 165:7-8. September 26, 1974.

"John W. Campbell," Locus No. 91:9. July 22, 1971.

"Notes from the belfrey, art," Locus No. 102:5a-b. December 10, 1971.

"Notes from the belfrey," Locus No. 139:5-6. April 14, 1973.

"Notes from the belfrey: the art game," Locus No. 108:5-6. February 25, 1972.

"Notes from the belfrey: volunteer fire department," Locus No. 110:12-13. March 25, 1972.

"One-eyed man is king," Locus No. 120:5-6. August 25, 1972.

Gaumann, G. V.

"Year of utopias, A," English Journal 61:234-238,251. February 1972.

Gauthier, Guy

Villes imaginaires: le theme de la ville dans l'utopie et la science fiction. Paris: CEDIC, 1978. 192 p.

"Science fiction's museum of the imagination," in: Johnson, William, ed. Focus on the Science Fiction Film. Englewood Cliffs, NJ: Prentice Hall, 1972. pp. 97-103.

Gawron, J. M.

"Introduction," in: Delany, S. R. Dhalgren. Boston: Gregg, 1977. pp. v-xliii.

Gechter, A. E.

"Lands at the center of the Earth," Barsoomian No. 4:3-4. January 1953.

"Weapons of choice, II," in: De Camp, L. S., ed. Blade of Conan. New York: Ace, 1979. pp. 211-214.

Geddes, G. T.

Miracles of Rare Device: An Introductory Selection of Science Fiction. Glasgow: Jordanhill College Library, 1972. 24 p.

Geddie, Tom

"Interview: Peter Straub," Fantasy Newsletter 5(3): 18-23. March 1982.

"Walt Miller and the Wandering Jew," Sumermorn 3: 20-25. Fall 1979.

Geduld, Carolyn

Filmguide to 2001: A Space Odyssey. Bloomington, Indiana: Indiana University Press, 1973. 87 p.

Geduld, H. M.

Definitive Dr. Jekyll and Mr. Hyde Companion, The. New York: Garland, 1983. 219 p.

"Close encounters with nonhuman humanists," Humanist 38(5):51. September/October 1978.

"Nothing new under the sun," Humanist 38(2):57. March/April 1978.

"Return to Melies: reflections on the science fiction film," in: Johnson, William, ed. Focus on the Science Fiction Film. Englewood Cliffs, NJ: Prentice Hall, 1972. pp. 142-147.

Geer, Caroline

"Land of Faerie: the disappearing myth," Mythlore 5(2): 3-5. Autumn 1978.

Geffe, P. R.

"Scientists in SF: a debate," by P. R. Geffe, M. A. Rothman, J. W. Campbell, and J. V. McConnell. in: Knight, Damon, ed. Turning Points: Essays in the Art of Science Fiction. New York: Harper, 1977. pp. 175-196.

Gegenheimer, A. F.

"Language in two recent imaginary voyages," PMLA 61(2):603. June 1946. (Response to Seeker, E. D. PMLA 60:586+. June 1945)

Gehman, R. B.

"Deadwood Dick to Superman," Science Digest 25:52-57. June 1949.

"Imagination runs wild," New Republic 120(3):15-18. January 17, 1949.

Gehres, M. A.

"Madeleine L'Engle: author with a homely, holy touch," Church and Synagogue Libraries 12(3):4,6. January/February 1979.

Geis, R. E.

"Interview with Alan Burt Akers, An," Science Fiction Review 5(3):32-34. 1976.

"Interview with Donald Wollheim, part two, An," Science Fiction Review 9(2):23-24. February 1980.

"Interview with Donald Wollheim," Science Fiction Review 9(1):13-15. February 1980.

"Interview with Jerry Pournelle, An," Science Fiction Review 5(1):6-14. 1976.

"Interview with Philip Jose Farmer, An," by D. A. Kraft, Mitch Scheele, and R. E. Geis. Science Fiction Review 4(3):7-21. 1975.

"Interview with Stephen Fabian, An," Science Fiction Review 7(4):24-28. September/October 1978.

"Interview with: L. Sprague de Camp, An," by Darrell Schweitzer and R. E. Geis. Science Fiction Review 4(4):11-14. 1975.

Gelinas, M.

"Romans de science fiction por les jeunes," Documentation et Bibliotheques 23:99-105. June 1977.

Gelmis, Joseph

"Fountain of youth," Long Island N. Y. Newsday June 23, 1985. in: NewsBank. Film and Television. 5:C4-C6. July 1985.

Genciova, Miroslava

Vedickofantasticka literatura: Stovnavad zanrova studie. Praha: Albatros, 1980. 177 p.

Gendolla, Peter

"Todliche Blick des Automaten," Quarber Merkur 19(2):37-63. October 1981.

"Wissenschaft und Phantasie. Zu texten vor Stanislaw Lem," Quarber Merkur 42:3-28. December 1975.

Geng, Veronica

"Dancing in Space," Vogue 172(10): 559-560, 606. October 1982.

Gentle, Mary

"Bright Walls of the Universe," Vector 104: 15-17. October 1981.

"Godmakers and Worldshapers: Fantasy and Metaphysics," Vector 106: 8-14. Fall 1982.

"Horror, The! The Horror!" Vector 107: 19-25. April 1982.

"Power of the pagan," Vector No. 126: 6-9. June/July 1985.

"Real Writers Don't Publish Fanzines," Focus (BSFA) No. 10: 5-11. February 1985.

Gentry, Rick

"Alan Splet and sound effects for Dune," American Cinematographer 65(11):62-72. December 1984.

George, Bill

"Empire strikes gold," Cinefantastique 10(2):40. Fall 1980.

"Eroticism in the Fantasy Cinema," Quest/Star 4(1): 25-28, 46-47. October 1981.

"Friday the 13th: A New Beginning (review)," Cinefantastique 15(4):46-47. October 1985.

George, Jim

"Gagging it up with The Man With One Red Shoe," Starlog No. 96: 22-24. July 1985.

"Interview: James Doohan," by Jim George and J. C. McDowell. Starlog No. 94:27-29. May 1985.

"Starlog Interview: Edward Andrews," Starlog 87: 30-32. October 1984.

George, Rambert

"Litterature d'anticipation, La," Le Progres; journal republicain quotidien. 95(33,041):6. May 14, 1954.

Gerani, Gary

Fantastic Television, by Gary Gerani and P. H. Schulman. New York: Harmony Books, 1977. 192 p.

"Incredible Hulk, The: episode guide," Starlog 43: 34-42. February 1981.

Author Entries

Gerasimov, Genadii

"Vstrecha nad planetoi Zemlia: dialog sovetskogo i amerikanskogo pistelei-Chingiz Aitmatov, Kurt Vonnegut," <u>Literaturnaia gazeta</u> p. 2. July 23, 1975.

Gerber, Richard

<u>Utopian Fantasy: A Study of English Utopian Fiction Since the End of the Nineteenth Century</u>, Second Edition. New York: McGraw-Hill, 1973. 168 p.

<u>Utopian Fantasy: A Study of English Utopian Fiction Since the End of the Nineteenth Century</u>. London: Routledge & Kegan Paul, 1955. 162 p. Reprinted, Folcroft Press, n.d.

"Wells: the country of the blind," in: Goller, Karl Heinz, ed. <u>Die Englische Kurzgeschichte</u>. Dusseldorf: Bagel Verlag, 1973. pp. 98-108.

Gerhard, Joseph

"Frankenstein's dream: the child as father of the monster," <u>Hartford Studies in Literature</u> 7(2):97-115. 1975.

Gerlach, John

"Logic of Wings, The: Garcia Marquez, Todorov, and the Endless Resources of Fantasy," in: Slusser, George E., ed. <u>Bridges to Fantasy</u>. Carbondale: Southern Illinois University Press, 1982. pp. 121-129.

Gernsback, Hugo

<u>Evolution of Modern Science Fiction</u>. New York: by the author, 1952. 12 p.

"Celestial television," <u>Fantasy Times</u> No. 147:3. February (1) 1952.

"Concrete science fiction," <u>Science Fiction Times</u> No. 358:3-5. March (2) 1961.

"Concrete science fiction; an address," presented March 12, 1961, Eastern Science Fiction Association. Typedraft in Texas A&M University Library Science Fiction Research Collection.

"Frank R. Paul," <u>Science Fiction Times</u> No. 405:2,7. August 1963.

"Impact of science fiction on world progress," <u>Fantasy Times</u> No. 170:inset following p. 2. January 1953.

"Prophets of doom," <u>Science Fiction Times</u> No. 409/410:3-6. December 1963.

"Science fiction vs. reality, an address," presented October 21, 1960, MIT Science Fiction Society. Typedraft in Texas A&M University Library Science Fiction Research Collection.

"Science fiction vs. reality," <u>Science Fiction Times</u> No. 350:1-5. November (2) 1960.

Gerrold, David

<u>The World of Star Trek</u>. New York: Ballantine/Del Rey, 1973. 276 p.

<u>World of Star Trek, The</u>. Revised Edition. New York: Bluejay, 1984. 209 p.

"7000 more words about Harlan Ellison," in: Porter, Andrew, ed. <u>The Book of Ellison</u>. New York: Algol Press, 1978. pp. 29-44.

"Anne McCaffrey: The Dragon Lady of Science Fiction," <u>Starlog</u> 80: 32-33. March 1984.

"Chuck's Latest Bucket," <u>Science Fiction Review</u> 10(4): 22-23. November 1981.

"Dreamscape (review)," <u>Starlog</u> 88: 53-55. November 1984.

"Farewell, Ted Sturgeon," <u>Starlog</u> 97: 73. August, 1985.

"Right Stuff, The: Film vs. Reality," <u>Starlog</u> 79: 58-59. February 1984.

"Science Fiction Authors Reappraise Role of Computers," <u>Infoworld</u> 4(26): 12, 14-15. July 5, 1982.

"Star Trek Experience, The," <u>Starlog</u> 64: 40-43. November 1982.

"Theodore Sturgeon in Memoriam, 4," <u>Locus</u> 18(7): 25. July 1985.

Gerson, Villiers

"Science fiction," <u>New York Times</u> Sec. 7, p. 4:1. September 24, 1950.

Geyh, M. A.

"Wissenschaftliche Spelaologie und die Arbeit Herbert W. Frankes," in: Rottensteiner, Franz, ed. <u>Polaris 6</u>. Frankfurt-am-Main: Suhrkamp, 1982. pp. 305-310.

Giachino, Enzo

"Per recuperare il miracolo," In: <u>Utopia e fantascienza</u>. Torino: Giappichelle, 1975. p. 63-80.

Giannone, Richard

Vonnegut: A Preface to His Novels. Port Washington, New York: Kennikat Press, 1977. 136 p.

"Violence in the Fiction of Kurt Vonnegut," Thought 56(220): 58-76. March 1981.

Gibb, Jocelyn

Light on C. S. Lewis. London: Geoffrey Bles, 1965. 160 p.

Gibbons, Tom

"H. G. Wells's fire sermon: The War of the Worlds and the Book of Revelation," Science Fiction: A Review of Speculative Literature 6(1): 5-14. 1984.

Gibbs, A.

"Onward and upward with the arts; inertrum, neutronium, chromaloy, and p-p-p-proot!" New Yorker 18(52):42-53. February 13, 1943.

Giblin, J. C.

"Does it have to be fantasy to be imaginative?" Children's Literature in Education 9:151-155. Autumn 1978.

Gibson, E. K.

C. S. Lewis, Spinner of Tales: A Guide to His Fiction. Grand Rapids, MI: Eerdmans, 1980. 284 p.

Gibson, Joe

"Gone to the Dogma," Inside and Science Fiction Advertiser No. 8:9-11. March 1955.

"Ray Palmer's medicine show," Inside and Science Fiction Advertiser No. 10: 21-23. July 1955.

Gibson, R. W.

Thomas More: A Preliminary Bibliography of His Works and Moreana to the Year 1750 . . . with a Bibliography of Utopiana Compiled by R. W. Gibson and J. Max Patrick. New Haven: Yale University Press, 1961. 499 p.

Giddings, Robert

J. R. R. Tolkien: The Shores of Middle-Earth, by Robert Giddings and Elizabeth Holland. London: Junction Books, 1981. 289 p.

J. R. R. Tolkien: This Far Land, ed. by Robert Giddings. London: Vision, 1983. 206 p.

"Introduction," in: Giddings, Robert, ed. J. R. R. Tolkien: This Far Land. London: Vision, 1983. pp. 7-24.

Giese, Berthold

"Biblischen geschichten des Norman Spinrad," Science Fiction Times (Germany) 26(8):10-13. August 1984.

Giesen, Rolf

Phantastische Film, Der: zur Sociologie von Horror, Science-Fiction und Fantasy im Kino. Schoendorf: Programm Roloff & Seesslen, 1980.

"Trickfilm, der: a survey of German special effects," Cinefex No. 25:38-53. February 1986.

Giffin, S. F.

"On reading science fiction," Alabama Librarian 8:2-3. January 1957.

Gifford, Denis

Science Fiction Film. London: Studio Vista, 1971. 160 p.

Gilbert, Fulmer

"Cosmological Implications of Time Travel," in: Myers, R. E., ed. The Intersection of Science Fiction and Philosophy. Westport: Greenwood, 1983. pp. 31-44.

Gilbert, J. B.

"Wars of the worlds," Journal of Popular Culture 10(2):326-336. Fall 1976.

Gilbert, L. S.

"Short fiction of Maupassant, The," in: Magill, Frank N., ed. Survey of Modern Fantasy Literature, Vol 4. Englewood Cliffs, NJ: Salem Press, Inc., 1983. pp. 1652-1656.

"Short fiction of Saki, The," in: Magill, Frank N., ed. Survey of Modern Fantasy Literature, Vol 4. Englewood Cliffs, NJ: Salem Press, Inc., 1983. pp. 1679-1683.

Gilbert, Mike

"Sabers, lasers and starships; an introduction and review of science fiction and fantasy wargaming, part two," Science Fiction Review No. 33:32. November 1979.

Gilbert, S. M.

"Rider Haggard's Heart of Darkness," in: Slusser, George E., ed. Coordinates. Carbondale: Southern Illinois University Press, 1983. pp. 124-138.

Gilden, Mel

"Martian Invasion of Television, A," Los Angeles Times. Calendar. p. 52. January 27, 1980.

"Special Effects Behind 'The Empire', The," Los Angeles Times. Sec. 6, p. 9. September 29, 1980.

Gill, R. B.

"Bargaining in Good Faith: The Laughter of Vonnegut, Grass, and Kundera," Critique 25(2): 77-91. Winter 1984.

Gill, Roger

"In England's green and pleasant land," in: Utopias, ed. by Peter Alexander and Roger Gill. London: Duckworth, 1984. pp. 109-118.

Gill, Stephen

Scientific Romances of H. G. Wells: A Critical Study. Cornwall, Ontario: Vesta Publications, 1977. 160 p. (First edition, 1975)

Gillespie, B. R.

"Vector zero: the SF story in the seventies," in: Chauvin, Cy, ed. Multitude of Visions. Baltimore: T-K Graphics, 1975. pp. 14-23.

Gillespie, Bruce

Philip K. Dick: Electric Shepherd. Melbourne, Australia: Nostrilla Press, 1975. 106 p.

S F Commentary Reprint Edition: First Year, 1969. Melbourne: Gillespie, 1982. 152 p.

"Cryptozoic!," in: Magill, Frank N., ed. Survey of Science Fiction Literature, Vol. 1. Englewood Cliffs, NJ: Salem Press, 1979. pp. 443-448.

"Greybeard," in: Magill, Frank N., ed. Survey of Science Fiction Literature, Vol. 2. Englewood Cliffs, NJ: Salem Press, 1979. pp. 926-931.

"Long Loud Silence, The," in: Magill, Frank N., ed. Survey of Science Fiction Literature, Vol. 3. Englewood Cliffs, NJ: Salem Press, 1979. pp. 1238-1241.

"Short Fiction of Thomas M. Disch, The," in: Magill, Frank N., ed. Survey of Science Fiction Literature, Vol. 5. Englewood Cliffs, NJ: Salem Press, 1979. pp. 2059-2064.

"Year of the Quiet Sun, The," in: Magill, Frank N., ed. Survey of Science Fiction Literature, Vol. 5. Englewood Cliffs, NJ: Salem Press, 1979. pp. 2520-2524.

"Australian SF: Contemporary Perspectives," Science Fiction: A Review of Speculative Literature 5(1): 12-16. March 1983.

"Best of Philip K. Dick, The," in: Magill, Frank N., ed. Survey of Science Fiction Literature, Vol. 1. Englewood Cliffs, NJ: Salem Press, 1979. pp. 196-201.

"Cheerfulness keeps breaking in," by Bruce Gillespie and Lee Harding. SF Commentary 54:12-21. Reprinted from Yggdrasil No. 3. 1978.

"Frenzied living space: Kobo Abe's future," Vector 60: 25-29. June 1972.

"Hidden heroes: the science fiction novels of Wilson Tucker," SF Commentary 43:26-51. August 1975.

"Literature which awakens us: the science fiction of Brian W. Aldiss," in: Tolley, M. J., ed. The Stellar Gauge. Carleton, Australia: Norstrilia, 1980. pp. 151-185.

"Mad, mad worlds: seven novels of Philip K. Dick," SF Commentary p. 1. January, 1969. also in: Gillespie, Bruce, ed. Philip K. Dick: Electric Shepherd. 1975.

"Smack that Pulpit!" Vector 123: 8-10. 1984.

"Why read science fiction," The Education Magazine (Victoria, Australia) pp. 306. October 1971.

Gillespie, G. V.

"Irish Mythological Cycle and Tolkien's Eldar, The," Mythlore 8(4): 8-9, 42. Winter 1982.

Gillings, W. H.

"New British market for science fiction," Fantasy Times No. 9:5-6. May 1944.

Gillings, Walter

"Man from minehead, The," Algol 12(1):12-14. November 1974.

Gilmore, Maeve

A World Away. London: Gollancz, 1970. 157 p.

Gilpatrick, E. E.

"Interview: Philip Jose Farmer," _Fantasy Newsletter_ 5(7): 27-30. August 1982.

"Thrust Profile: Philip Jose Farmer," _Thrust_ 22: 13-14, 22. Spring/Summer 1985.

Gindin, James

"Lessing criticism," _Contemporary Literature_ 14(4):586-589. Autumn 1973.

Giorgi, Piero

"SF in Italien," _Andromeda_ 102: 22-28. July 1980.

Gipple, Cindy

"Alarming Politics: A Clockwork Orange," _Pandora_ (Seattle, WA) p. 10. May 16, 1972.

Gire, Dan

"Reanimator," _Cinefantastique_ 15(4):10,60. October 1985.

Gires, Pierre

"Films d'aujourd'hui sur des themes de maintenant," J. P. Andrevon, Pierre Gires, and Evelyne Lowin. _Cinema D'aujourd'hui_. No. 7:91-98. Spring 1976.

"Quelques films d'hier sur les themes de toujours," _Cinema D'aujourd'hui_. No. 7:41-52. spring 1976.

Girley, O. C.

"Andre Norton, mistress of adventure," _Collector's Advocate_ No. 1:3-10. August 1965.

Giuffrida, Sergio

"_Cosmo_," _Wow_ No. 10. 1977.

"_Fantascienza_," _Wow_ No. 3. 1976.

"_Futuria_," _Wow_ No. 7. 1977.

"_Galassia_," _Wow_ No. 11. 1977.

"_Galaxy_," _Wow_ No. 6. 1977.

"_Gamma_," _Wow_ No. 5. 1976.

"_Oltre il Cielo_," _Wow_ No. 4. 1976.

"_Scienza fantastica_," _Wow_ No. 9. 1977.

Glad, J. P.

Extrapolations from Dystopia: A Critical Study of Soviet Science Fiction. Princeton: Kingston Press, 1982. 223 p.

Russian Soviet Science Fiction and Related Critical Activity. Ph.D. Dissertation, New York University, 1971. 177 p.

Glad, John

"Brave New Worlds," _Wilson Quarterly_ 7(4): 68-78. Autumn 1983.

Gladish, Christine

"_October Country, The_," in: Magill, Frank N., ed. _Survey of Science Fiction Literature_, Vol. 4. Englewood Cliffs, NJ: Salem Press, 1979. pp. 1571-1573.

Glass, H. B.

"Scientist in contemporary fiction," _Scientific Monthly_ 85(6):288-293. December 1957.

Glastonbury, Marion

"E. B. White's unexpected items of enchantment," in: Fox, Geoff, ed. _Writers, Critics, and Children: Articles From Children's Literature in Education_. New York: Agathon Press, 1976. pp. 104-115.

Glazebrook, Philip

"Anti-heroes of horror, The," _Films and Filming_ 13(1):36-37. October 1966.

Glazer, J. I.

"Modern fantasy," by J. I. Glazer and Gurney Williams, III. in: Glazer, Joan I. and Gurney Williams, III. _Introduction to Children's Literature_. New York: McGraw-Hill, 1979. pp. 258-301.

Glenn, K. M.

"Martin Gaite, Todorov, and the fantastic," in: Collins, R. A. and H. D. Pearce, eds. _The Scope of the Fantastic: Theory, Technique, Major Authors_. Westport, CT: Greenwood Press, 1985. pp. 165-172.

Glenn, Louis

Charles W. S. Williams: a Checklist. Kent, Ohio: Kent State University Press, 1975. 128 p.

Glick, Seth

"Tentative bibliography of S&S," _AMRA_
2(62):7-11. October 1974.

Glicksberg, C. I.

"Anti-utopianism in modern literature,"
Southwest Review 37(3):221-228. Summer 1952.

Glicksohn, S. W.

"City of which the stars are suburbs, A," in:
Clareson, T. D., ed. _SF: The Other Side of
Realism_. Bowling Green, Ohio: Bowling Green
University Popular Press, 1971. pp. 334-347.

"Martian point of view, The," _Extrapolation_
15(2):161-173. May 1974.

Glover, D. E.

C. S. Lewis: The Art of Enchantment.
Athens, OH: Ohio University Press, 1981.
235 p.

Glover, David

"Utopia and fantasy in the late 1960s:
Burroughs, Moorcock, Tolkien," in: Pawling,
Christopher, ed. _Popular Fiction and Social
Change_. New York: St. Martins, 1984. pp.
185-211.

Glover, R. A.

"Evil Dead," by R. A. Glover and Dan
Scapperotti. _Cinefantastique_
13(6)/14(1):24-27. September 1983.

"Final Conflict (review)," _Cinefantastique_
11(2):50. Fall 1981.

Glut, D. F.

Classic Movie Monsters. Metuchen, NJ:
Scarecrow Press, 1978.

Dracula Book, The. Metuchen, New Jersey:
Scarecrow Press, 1975. 388 p.

Frankenstein Catalog, The. Jefferson, NC:
McFarland, 1984. 525 p.

_Frankenstein Legend, The: A Tribute to Mary
Shelley and Boris Karloff_. Metuchen, New
Jersey: Scarecrow Press, 1973. 372 p.

Glyer, Michael

"1984: The Fifty-Candle Blowout," in:
Pournelle, Jerry, ed. _The Science Fiction
Yearbook_. New York: Baen, 1985. pp. 328-344.

"Directory to Science Fiction Fan Clubs,"
Starlog 57: 22-27. April 1982.

Glyer, Mike

"Through time and space with CAS,"
Nyctalops No. 7:13-16. August 1972.

Gnaedinger, Mary

"Aims of _Famous Fantastic Mysteries_,"
Fantasy Times No. 2:2. October 1941.

"Look into the future of _Famous Fantastic
Mysteries_ and _Fantastic Novels_," _Fantasy
Times_ No. 100:21-22. February (2) 1950.

"Lost and fabled: a remembrance," _Fantasy
Times_ No. 200:20-21,27. June (1) 1954.

Gobetz, G. E.

"Teaching about utopian ideas and practices,"
Improving College and University Teaching
19(1):26-32. Winter 1971.

Goble, Neil

Asimov Analyzed. Baltimore: Mirage Press,
1972. 174 p.

Goddard, James

J. G. Ballard: the First Twenty Years, ed.
by James Goddard and David Pringle. Hayes,
England: Bran's Head Books, 1976. 99 p.

"J. G. Ballard interview," by James Goddard and
David Pringle. _Vector_ 73/74:28-29. March
1976.

Godshalk, W. L.

"Alfred Bester," in: Cowart, David, ed.
_Twentieth-Century American Science-Fiction
Writers, Part 1; A-L_. Detroit: Gale, 1981.
p. 30-36. (Dictionary of Literary Biography,
v. 8)

"Alfred Bester: science fiction or fantasy?"
Extrapolation 16(2):149-155. May 1975.

"Cabell's mirrors and (incidentally) pigeons,"
Kalki 6(2):63-67. 1974.

"Kurt Vonnegut's renaissance hero," _Clifton:
Magazine of the University of Cincinnati_
1:41-45. 1973. (not seen)

"Recurring characters of Kurt Vonnegut, Jr.,
The," _Notes on Contemporary Literature_
3(1):2-3. 1973.

"Vonnegut and Shakespeare: Rosewater at
Elsinore," _Critique_ 15(2):37-48. 1973.

Godwin, K. G.

"David Lynch retrospective: Eraserhead," Cinefantastique 14(4/5):41-50,55-72. September 1984.

Godwin, Parke

"Conversation with Al Sarrantonio," Thrust 22: 5-8. Spring/Summer 1985.

"Road to Camelot, The: A Conversation With Marion Zimmer Bradley," Fantasy Review of Fantasy and Science Fiction 7(3): 6-9. April 1984.

"Road to Hill House, The: Pat LoBrutto," Fantasy Review 7(8): 9-10. September 1984.

"State of the artless," by Parke Godwin and Howard Roller. Amazing 27(11): 19-23. March 1981.

"There Goes Deuteronomy," in: Jarvis, Sharon, ed. Inside Outer Space. New York: Ungar, 1985. pp. 3-15.

Goeller, K. H.

"Spektrum von science fiction zwischen trivial- und hochliteratur," Neusprachliche Mitteilungen 30:136-144. 1977.

Goerlich, E. J.

"Science Fiction. Zur Gestaltung der modernen technischen Dichtung," Jahresbericht 1952/53 des Technologischen Gewerbemuseums (Technische BundesLehr- und Versuchsanstalt). Wien, 1953. pp.33- .

Goetz, Rainer

"Mann als Alien," by Marcel Bieger and Rainer Goetz. Science Fiction Times (Germany) 26(2):5-7. February 1984.

Goff, Penrith

"Other Side, The," in: Magill, Frank N., ed. Survey of Modern Fantasy Literature, Vol 3. Englewood Cliffs, NJ: Salem Press, Inc., 1983. pp. 1176-1178.

"Short fiction of Kafka, The," in: Magill, Frank N., ed. Survey of Modern Fantasy Literature, Vol 4. Englewood Cliffs, NJ: Salem Press, Inc., 1983. pp. 1575-1580.

Goimard, Jacques

Annee 1977-1978 de la science-fiction et du fantastique, L'. Paris: Julliard, 1978.

Annee 1978-1979 de la science-fiction et du fantastique, L'. Paris: Julliard, 1979. 314 p.

Annee 1979-1980 de la science-fiction et du fantastique, L'. Paris: Julliard, 1980. 302 p.

Annee 1980-1981 de la science fiction et du fantastique, L'. Paris: Julliard, 1981. 283 p.

Annee 1981-1982 de la science-fiction et du fantastique, L'. Paris: Julliard, 1982. 334 p.

"50 films cles du cinema de science fiction: dictionnaire critique," by Jacques Goimard, Jean-Claude Michel, and Alain Schlockoff. Cinema d'aujourd'hui. No. 7:65-84. Spring 1976.

"Chronologie generale de la S. F.," Europe 580/581:156-169. August/September 1977.

"Defense et illustration de la SF," by Gerard Klein, Alain Doremieux, and Jacques Goimard. Le Monde 28.6.1967.

"France. Des lecteurs, mais ou sont les auteurs?" Magazine litteraire (Paris) 88:21-23. May 1974.

"Les Noms," by Yves Olivier-Martin and Jacques Goimard. Europe 580/581:20-22. August/September 1977.

"Litterature et cinema de science fiction: le malentendu," Cinema d'aujourd'hui. No. 7:34-40. Spring 1976.

"Poetique de la science fiction. I. Hier et avant-hier," Positif 160:24-29. June 1974.

"Poetique de la science fiction. II. demain et apres-demain," Positif 162:35-44. October 1974.

"Presence de la science fiction (a propos du festival de Trieste 1973)," Positif 156:58-60. February 1974.

"Prologue dans le logos," Europe 580/581:3-13. August/September 1977.

"Qu'est ce que la science fiction," La Quinzaine Litteraire 123:12-13. August 1, 1971.

"Science fiction au pays de Descartes, La," Magazine Litteraire No. 31:22-25. August 1969.

"Une definition, une definition de la definition, et ainse de suite," Cinema D'aujourd'hui. No. 7:11-22. Spring 1976.

Gold, H. L.

"Beyond," Fantasy Times No. 175:1-2. April 1953.

"Its all yours," Fantasy Times No. 113:2. September (1) 1950.

Author Entries

Goldberg, Annemette

"Science fiction and mainstream: a discussion," edited by Annemette Goldberg and Cay Dollerup. in: Dollerup, Cay, ed. Volve. Scandinavian Views on SF. Copenhagen: Dept. of English, Univ. of Copenhagen, 1978. pp. 11-16.

"Science fiction, computers, and reality: a discussion," in: Dollerup, Cay, ed. Volve. Scandinavian Views on SF. Copenhagen: Department of English, University of Copenhagen, 1978. pp. 89-95.

Goldberg, Jan

"Starlog Interview: Dame Judith Anderson," Starlog 85: 34-36. August 1984.

Goldberg, Joshua

"What's in a name? or playfully on a tangent," Armchair Detective 7:122-124. 1974.

Goldberg, Lee

"Back to the Future," Starlog No. 97: 44-47. August 1985.

"Bob Zemeckis: It's a wonderful time," Starlog 99: 47-49. October 1985.

"Death Duel on the Small Screen: Blue Thunder Battles Airwolf," Starlog 81: 38-39. April 1984.

"Elya Baskin: Russian actor, American citizen, movie cosmonaut," Starlog No. 91:17-19. February 1985.

"Ewok Adventure, The," Starlog 89: 61-63, 67. December 1984.

"Forgotten James Bond, The," Starlog 75: 32-34. October 1983.

"In Brief: George Lucas, the new projects," Starlog No. 100: 42-43. November 1985.

"John Korty, director of The Ewok Adventure," Starlog No. 90:27-29. January 1985.

"John Lithgow: it's more fun being the villain," Starlog No. 93:28-31. April 1985.

"Let's Make a 'Deal of the Century'," Starlog 77: 60-62. December 1983.

"Lewis Smith," Starlog 87: 52-53, 68. October 1984.

"Michael Crichton: the business of moviemaking is science fiction," Starlog No. 91:43-47,68. February 1985.

"Now reentering the Twilight Zone," Starlog No. 99:38-41. October 1985.

"On location with A View to Kill," Starlog No. 92:27-30,66. March 1985.

"On the Set of 2010," Starlog 87: 24-28, 68. October 1984.

"On the Set of Buckaroo Banzai," Starlog 81: 44-46. April 1984.

"On the Set of Iceman," Starlog 80: 51-53, 65. March 1984.

"Peter Weller," Starlog 86: 19-22. September 1984.

"Producing Space," Starlog No. 94:47-49. May 1985.

"Profile: Bob Zemeckis," Starlog No. 99:47-49. October 1985.

"Richard Donner: directing is believing," Starlog No. 93:18-22. April 1985.

"Robert Englund," Starlog No. 93:34-36. April 1985.

"Robert Zemeckis," Starlog 85: 58-59, 66. August 1984.

"Roger Moore: His name is Bond," Starlog No. 96: 40-43. July 1985.

"Roy Scheider: making contact in 2010," Starlog No. 90:19-22. January 1985.

"Rutger Hauer: Knight Wolf to a Ladyhawke," Starlog No. 95: 65-67. June 1985.

"Special Preview: Alfred Hitchcock Presents," Starlog 99: 32-33. October 1985.

"Starlog Interview: W. D. Richter," Starlog No. 89: 19-22. December 1984.

"Starlog Interview: Billy Dee Williams," Starlog 80: 28-30. March 1984.

"Starlog Interview: Bob Balaban," Starlog 89: 35-37. December 1984.

"Starlog Interview: Christopher Lloyd," Starlog 82: 20-23. May 1984.

"Starlog Interview: Earl MacRauch," Starlog 84: 66-68. July 1984.

"Starlog Interview: Harlan Ellison, next stop, 'The Twilight Zone'," Starlog No. 100: 58-60, 93. November 1985.

"Starlog Interview: Harlan Ellison, part two," Starlog No. 101: 34-36. December 1985.

"Starlog Interview: Jeff Goldblum," Starlog 85: 22-23. August 1984.

195

Goldberg, Lee (Continued)

"Starlog Interview: Keir Dullea," _Starlog_ 88: 73-75. November 1984.

"Starlog Interview: Richard Donner, Part 2," _Starlog_ No. 97: 40-42. August 1985.

"Starlog profile: Michael J. Fox," _Starlog_ No. 98:23-25. September 1985.

"Tom Selleck: tracking the action of Runaway," _Starlog_ No. 92:60-61,65. March 1985.

Goldblatt, Burt

Cinema of the Fantastic, by Chris Steinbrunner and Burt Goldblatt. New York: Saturday Review Press, 1972. 282 p.

Goldin, Stephen

"_Mindswap,_" in: Magill, Frank N., ed. _Survey of Science Fiction Literature,_ Vol. 3. Englewood Cliffs, NJ: Salem Press, 1979. pp. 1413-1416.

"_Stray Lamb, The,_" in: Magill, Frank N., ed. _Survey of Modern Fantasy Literature,_ Vol 4. Englewood Cliffs, NJ: Salem Press, Inc., 1983. pp. 1848-1850.

"_Topper_ and _Topper Takes a Trip,_" in: Magill, Frank N., ed. _Survey of Modern Fantasy Literature,_ Vol 4. Englewood Cliffs, NJ: Salem Press, Inc., 1983. pp. 1958-1962.

"_Way Station,_" in: Magill, Frank N., ed. _Survey of Science Fiction Literature,_ Vol. 5. Englewood Cliffs, NJ: Salem Press, 1979. pp. 2429-2432.

"SFWAward Ho!" _Empire: For the SF Writer_ 23: 18-19. Spring 1981.

"SFWAward Ho," _Empire: For the SF Writer_ 4(3): 14. July 1979.

Golding, William

"Androids all," _Spectator_ 6922:263-264. February 24, 1961.

"Astronauts by gaslight," _Spectator_ 6937:841-842. June 9, 1961.

"Astronauts by gaslight," in: Golding, William. _The Hot Gates._ New York: Harcourt, 1966. pp. 111-115.

Goldman, S. H.

"_I Am Legend,_" in: Magill, Frank N., ed. _Survey of Science Fiction Literature,_ Vol. 2. Englewood Cliffs, NJ: Salem Press, 1979. pp. 986-990.

"_Immortals, The,_" in: Magill, Frank N., ed. _Survey of Science Fiction Literature,_ Vol. 2. Englewood Cliffs, NJ: Salem Press, 1979. pp. 1014-1018.

"_Journey to the Center of the Earth,_" in: Magill, Frank N., ed. _Survey of Science Fiction Literature,_ Vol. 3. Englewood Cliffs, NJ: Salem Press, 1979. pp. 1102-1105.

"_Languages of Pao, The,_" in: Magill, Frank N., ed. _Survey of Science Fiction Literature,_ Vol. 3. Englewood Cliffs, NJ: Salem Press, 1979. pp. 1135-1139.

"_Listeners, The,_" in: Magill, Frank N., ed. _Survey of Science Fiction Literature,_ Vol. 3. Englewood Cliffs, NJ: Salem Press, 1979. pp. 1226-1229.

"_Love and Napalm: Export U. S. A.,_" in: Magill, Frank N., ed. _Survey of Science Fiction Literature,_ Vol. 3. Englewood Cliffs, NJ: Salem Press, 1979. pp. 1274-1277.

"_Omnivore,_" in: Magill, Frank N., ed. _Survey of Science Fiction Literature,_ Vol. 4. Englewood Cliffs, NJ: Salem Press, 1979. pp. 1596-1602.

"_Ophiuchi Hotline, The,_" in: Magill, Frank N., ed. _Survey of Science Fiction Literature,_ Vol. 4. Englewood Cliffs, NJ: Salem Press, 1979. pp. 1608-1612.

"_Puppet Masters, The,_" in: Magill, Frank N., ed. _Survey of Science Fiction Literature,_ Vol. 4. Englewood Cliffs, NJ: Salem Press, 1979. pp. 1730-1734.

"_Sheep Look Up, The,_" in: Magill, Frank N., ed. _Survey of Science Fiction Literature,_ Vol. 4. Englewood Cliffs, NJ: Salem Press, 1979. pp. 1913-1916.

"_Shockwave Rider, The,_" in: Magill, Frank N., ed. _Survey of Science Fiction Literature,_ Vol. 4. Englewood Cliffs, NJ: Salem Press, 1979. pp. 1922-1925.

"_Squares of the City, The,_" in: Magill, Frank N., ed. _Survey of Science Fiction Literature,_ Vol. 5. Englewood Cliffs, NJ: Salem Press, 1979. pp. 2132-2135.

"_Synthetic Man, The,_" in: Magill, Frank N., ed. _Survey of Science Fiction Literature,_ Vol. 5. Englewood Cliffs, NJ: Salem Press, 1979. pp. 2215-2217.

"_Venus Plus X,_" in: Magill, Frank N., ed. _Survey of Science Fiction Literature,_ Vol. 5. Englewood Cliffs, NJ: Salem Press, 1979. pp. 2370-2372.

"_When Harlie Was One,_" in: Magill, Frank N., ed. _Survey of Science Fiction Literature,_ Vol. 5. Englewood Cliffs, NJ: Salem Press, 1979. pp. 2455-2458.

Goldman, S. H. (Continued)

"Immortal man and mortal overlord: the case for intertextuality," in: Yoke, C. B. and Hassler, D. M., eds. Death and the Serpent. Westport, CT: Greenwood, 1985. pp. 193-208.

"John Brunner's dystopias: heroic man in unheroic society," Science Fiction Studies 5(3):260-270. November 1978.

"Polymorphic worlds of John Brunner, The: how do they happen?" Science Fiction Studies 3(2):103-112. July 1976.

Goldman, Stephen

Teacher's Manual: The Road to Science Fiction, by James Gunn and Stephen Goldman. New York: New American Library, 1980. 45 p.

"American Science Fiction of the Twentieth Century: Metaphors for American Attitudes Toward the Future," Studia Anglica Posmaniensia 13: 163-176. 1982.

"Isaac Asimov," in: Cowart, David, ed. Twentieth-Century American Science-Fiction Writers, Part 1: A-L. Detroit: Gale, 1981. pp. 15-29. (Dictionary of Literary Biography, v. 8)

Goldsmith, A. L.

Golem Remembered, The, 1909-1980: Variations of a Jewish Legend. Detroit: Wayne State University Press, 1981. 181 p.

Goldsmith, Cele

"Amazing future, The," Science Fiction Times No. 369:17-19. September 1961.

"Dean of SF artists," Science Fiction Times No. 405:8-9. August 1963.

Goldsmith, D. H.

Kurt Vonnegut: Fantasist of Fire and Ice. Bowling Green, Ohio: Bowling Green University Popular Press, 1972. 44 p.

Goldsmith, M.

"Soviet SF," Spectator 6843:226-227. August 21, 1959.

Goldstein, R. M.

"Fantasy," by R. M. Goldstein and Edith Zornow. in: Goldstein, R. M. and Zornow, Edith. The Screen Image of Youth: Movies About Children and Adolescents. Metuchen, NJ: Scarecrow, 1980. pp. 271-278.

Goldstone, Adrian

Bibliography of Arthur Machen, A, by Adrian Goldstone and Wesley Sweetser. Austin: University of Texas, 1965. 180 p.

Goldstone, Louis, Jr.

Science Fiction Index No. 1, 1926. San Francisco, CA: Goldstone, n.d. 7 p.

Goldthwaite, Thomas

"Time to Ponder Ozma and Astroblemes, and if Fred Pohl Will win another Hugo," Arizona Republic August 27, 1978. in: NewsBank. Literature. 81:A5-A6. 2 pages. 1978.

Golemba, H. L.

Frank R. Stockton. Boston: Twayne, 1981. 182 p.

Golemba, Henry

"Rockets rise on the Wabash," Great Lakes Review 5(1):1-6. Summer 1979.

Coligorcky, Eduardo

Ciencia ficcion: realidad y psicoanalisis, by Eduardo Goligorsky and Marie Langer. Buenos Aires: Paidos, 1969. 185 p.

Golowin, Sergius

Science Fiction, ed. by Sergius Golowin and Walter Zuercher. Gurtendorf: Zuercher, 1967. 68 p.

Gomoll, Jeanne

"Doris Lessing: Canopus in Argos," P*S*F*Q* 6: 14, 17. Fall 1981.

Gondor, L. H.

"Fantasy of utopia, The," American Journal of Psychotherapy 17(4):606-618. October 1963.

Gooch, Stan

Science Fiction as Religion, by Stan Gooch and Christopher Evans. Somerset: Bran's Head, 1981. 15 p.

Good, Graham

"Ideology and personality in Orwell's criticism," College Literature 11(1): 78-93. 1984.

Goodavage, J. F.

"UFOs and Stranger Intruders," in: Bretnor, Reginald, ed. <u>The Future at War: Vol. 2: The Spear of Mars</u>. New York: Ace, 1980. pp. 82-100.

Goodheart, Eugene

"Olaf Stapledon's <u>Last and First Men</u>," in: Rabkin, Eric S., et. al., eds. <u>No Place Else</u>. Carbondale: Southern Illinois University Press, 1983. pp. 78-93.

Goodknight, G. H.

"Counsel of Elrond: first encounters with Tolkien," <u>Mythlore</u> 8(2):5. Summer 1981.

"Enlargement of being," <u>Mythlore</u> 3(3):9,28. 1976.

"Going on in the great dance," <u>Mythlore</u> 5(1):25-26. May 1978.

"Mythlore Issue Index, Volumes 1-7, whole numbers 1-26," by H. J. N. Andruschak and G. H. Goodknight. <u>Mythlore</u> 8(1): 37-39. Spring 1981.

"Tolkien at eighty: an appreciation," <u>Mythlore</u> 2(4):3-4. Winter 1972.

"Tolkien in Translation," <u>Mythlore</u> 9(2): 22-27. Summer 1982.

Goodman, M. B.

<u>William S. Burroughs: an Annotated Bibliography of His Works and Criticism</u>. New York: Garland Publishing, 1975. 96 p.

Goodman, R. C.

"Filming the Aerials for The Empire Strikes Back," <u>American Cinematographer</u> 61(6): 594-595, 621-626. June 1980.

Goodstone, Tony

<u>Pulps, The: 50 Years of American Pop Culture</u>. New York: Chelsea House, 1970.

Goodwin, Archie

"Interview: The Brothers Hildebrandt," <u>Epic Illustrated</u> 1(5): 51-66, 76. April 1981.

Goodwin, Barbara

"Economic and social Innovation in Utopia," in: <u>Utopias</u>, ed. by Peter Alexander and Roger Gill. London: Duckworth, 1984. pp. 69-84.

Goodwin, Pearl

"Elements of utopias in young adult literature," <u>English Journal</u> 74(6): 66-69. October 1985.

Goorden, Bernard

<u>S. F., fantastique et ateliers creatifs</u>. Brussels: J. E. B, 1978. 221 p.

"Etude: nouvear monde, mondes nouveaux," <u>Fiction</u> 299:185-190. March 1979.

Goossens, R.

<u>Fantasfeer: bibliografie van science fiction en fantasy in het Nederlands</u>, by A. Spaink, G. Gorremans, and R. Goossens. Amsterdam: Meulenhoff, 1979. 279 p.

Gopman, Vladimir

"Category of Time in the Writings of J. G. Ballard, The," <u>Foundation</u> 30: 34-42. March 1984.

"New generation of Soviet science fiction: old themes, new conclusions)," (in Russian) by V. Gakov and V. Gopman. <u>Canadian-American Slavic Studies</u> 18(1/2): 85-96. Spring/Summer 1984.

Gopnik, A.

"Brief and biased guide to the philosophy of science for students of science fiction, A," by I. Gopnik and A. Gopnik. <u>Science Fiction Studies</u> 7(2):200-207. July 1980.

Gopnik, I.

"Brief and biased guide to the philosophy of science for students of science fiction, A," by I. Gopnik and A. Gopnik. <u>Science Fiction Studies</u> 7(2):200-207. July 1980.

Gorden, J. L.

<u>Inside Science Fiction and the Fiction of Joe Haldeman</u>. Ph. D. Dissertation, University of Iowa, 1981. 162 p.

Gordon, Ambrose, Jr.

"Quiet betrayal: some mirror work in Borges, A," <u>Texas Studies in Literature and Language</u> 17(1):207-218. Spring 1975.

Author Entries

Gordon, Andrew

"Close Encounters: the gospel according to Steven Spielberg," in: Remington, T. J., ed. Selected Proceedings of the 1978 SFRA National Conference. Cedar Falls, Iowa: University of Northern Iowa, 1979. pp. 169-177.

"Star Wars: myth for our time," Literature/Film 6(4):314-326. Fall 1978.

"E. T. as Fairy Tale," Science Fiction Studies 10(3): 298-305. November 1983.

"Empire Strikes Back, The: Monsters from the Id," Science-Fiction Studies 7(3): 313-318. November 1980.

"Human, More or Less: Man-Machine Communion in Samuel R. Delany's Nova and Other Science Fiction Stories," in: Dunn, Thomas P., ed. The Mechanical God. Westport: Greenwood, 1982. pp. 193-202.

"Silverberg's Time Machine," Extrapolation 23(4): 345-361. Winter 1982.

Gordon, Bruce

"Tomorrowland 1986, part 2," by Bruce Gordon and David Mumford. Starlog No. 99:50-53. October 1985.

"Tomorrowland 1986," by Bruce Gordon and David Mumford. Starlog 99: 50-53. October 1985.

Gordon, Joan

Joe Haldeman Mercer Island, WA: Starmont House, 1980. 64 p. (Starmont Reader's Guide, 4)

"Interview with Gene Wolfe," Science Fiction Review 10(2): 18-22. Summer 1981.

Goreniowa, Anna

"Funcje ideologiczne narracyjmej formy utopii," in: Literatura I Metodologia Warszawa: Ossolineum, 1970.

"Proza fantastyczno-naukowa St. Lema," Tygodnik Kulturalny No. 17. 1971.

Gorer, Geoffrey

"There is a happy land," Encounter 1:83-86. July 1962.

Gorlier, C.

"Il romanzo e la scienza," Ulisse revista di cultura internazionale 10:1020-1027. 1956/1957.

Gorlovskij, A.

"Vremja fantastiki," Junost' 1:73-78. 1967.

Gorman, Ed

"Interview with Algis Budrys," Science Fiction Review (Portland) 7(1):62-68. February 1978.

Gorner, Peter

"...And Herbert Saw the Sand and Called It Dune," Chicago Tribune Sec. 2, p. 1-2. March 15, 1977.
"Unabridged king of the paperbacks," Chicago Tribune. Sec. 5, p. 1, 4. June 5, 1985.

Gorney, Cynthia

"Ray Bradbury: The Martian Chronicles," Washington Post Sec. B, p. 1, 11. January 28, 1980.

Gorra, Michael

"Fanpublishing symposium," Outworlds 24:918-924. Second quarter 1975.

Gorremans, George

Fantasfeer: bibliografie van science fiction en fantasy in het Nederlands, by A. Spaink, G. Gorremans, and R. Goossens. Amsterdam: Meulenhoff, 1979. 279 p.

Gorton, Mark

"Some Say in Ice: The Apocalyptic Fears of Women in Love," Foundation 28: 56-60. July 1983.

Goselin, P. D.

"Two faces of Eve: Galadriel and Shelob as anima figures," Mythlore 6(3):3-4,28. Summer 1979.

Goshgarian, Gary

"Three syllibi," by Dave Samuelson, Gary Goshgarian and James Gunn. in: Williamson, Jack, ed. Teaching Science Fiction: Education for Tomorrow. Philadelphia: Owlswick, 1980. pp. 194-202.

Goslicki, Janusz

"Jozio rozszyfrowany," Zycie Literackie No. 2. Jan. 14, 1962.

Goss, G. L.

"Selfless Billy Pilgrim, The," <u>Buffalo Spree</u> 5:34-35,44-45,47,52-53,60-61. Fall 1971.

Goswami, Amit

<u>Cosmic Dancers: Exploring the Physics of Science Fiction</u>, by Amit Goswami and Maggie Goswami. New York: Harper, 1983. 292 p.

Goswami, Maggie

<u>Cosmic Dancers: Exploring the Physics of Science Fiction</u>, by Amit Goswami and Maggie Goswami. New York: Harper, 1983. 292 p.

Gotschalk, F. C.

"Getting inside the author's mind," <u>SFWA Bulletin</u> 17(4): 9-11. Winter 1983.

Gottlieb, S. A.

"Reading of Williams' Arthurian cycle, A" <u>Mythlore</u> 4(2):3-6. December 1976.

Gotz, I. L.

"Commune as symbol, The," <u>Alternative Futures</u> 2(1): 97-106. Winter 1979.

Gouanvic, J. M.

"Herbe Rouge, L'," in: Magill, Frank N., ed. <u>Survey of Science Fiction Literature</u>, Vol. 2. Englewood Cliffs, NJ: Salem Press, 1979. pp. 965-968.

"Boris Vian et la science fiction: L'univers romanesque de Vian dans ses realtions avec la science fiction," <u>Fiction</u> No. 290:175-184. Mai 1978.

"Enquete sur l'irruption de la science fiction americaine en Europe dans les annees 50," <u>Imagine</u> 1(1):95-110. September/October/November 1979.

"Etude textuelle de quelques structures de l'imaginaire de science fiction chez J. H. Rosny Aine (premiere partie)," <u>Fiction</u> No. 332:181-191. Juin 1979.

"Positions de l'histoire dans la science fiction," <u>Change</u> (Paris) 40:85-103. 1981.

"Science Fiction and Teaching in Quebec," <u>Science Fiction Studies</u> 9(1): 107-108. March 1982.

Goudriaan, Roelof

"Where Once the Sea Has Guzzled: a Look at Fandom in the Netherlands," <u>Matrix</u> 35: 10-11. April/May 1981.

Gougaud, Henri

<u>Demons et marveilles de la science fiction</u>. Paris: Julliard, 1974. 189 p.

Gough, John

"C. S. Lewis and the problem of David Holbrook," <u>Children's Literature in Education</u> 8(2):51-62. Summer 1977.

Goulart, Ron

<u>Cheap Thrills: An Informal History of the Pulp Magazines</u>. New Rochelle, NY: Arlington House, 1972. 192 p.

"Ghostbusters (review)," <u>Starlog</u> 88: 38-39. November 1984.

"Historical Hysteria or Humor in Science Fiction," in: Jarvis, Sharon, ed. <u>Inside Outer Space</u>. New York: Ungar, 1985. pp. 29-34.

"Poltergeist (Review)," <u>Starlog</u> 64: 65-66. November 1982.

"Saga of Skyrocket Steele, The," <u>Empire: For the SF Writer</u> 23: 8. Spring 1981.

"SF in the Comics, Part 5: The Big Fifties Boom," <u>Starlog</u> 45: 54-57. April 1981.

"SF in the Comics, part 6: the 60s and 70s: a summing up," <u>Starlog</u> 46: 42-45. May 1981.

"SF in the comics. Part II: the 30's boomtime for SF heroes," <u>Starlog</u> 42: 32-35. January 1981.

"SF in the comics: part 3, the 'Super' 40's," <u>Starlog</u> 43: 56-59. February 1981.

"SF in the Comics; Part IV: From 'Flash Gordon' to 'Wash Tubbs'," <u>Starlog</u>. 44: 56-58. March 1981.

"Sheena, Queen of the Comics," <u>Starlog</u> 87: 54-55. October 1984.

Gould, Ella

"Edward Bryant: Definitely an Original Type of Wyoming Writing," <u>Wyoming State Tribune</u> March 3, 1982. in: NewsBank. Literature. 68:G5. 1981/82.

Gould, Helen

"Scientific films staging comeback," _New York Times_ Sec. II, p. 4. May 21, 1950.

Gould, Jeff

"Destruction of the Social by the Organic in Alien, The," _Science Fiction Studies_ 7(3): 282-285. November 1980.

Gould, S. J.

"Misunderstood Monsters," _Psychology Today_ 15(12): 97-103. December 1981.

Gould, Steve

"The Dallas Futurian Society," by Al Jackson and Steve Gould. in: _First Occasional Lone Star Science Fiction Convention and Chili Cookoff_. Austin: Lone Star Con, 1985. pp. 27-28.

Goupil, Armand

Jules Verne. Paris: Larousse, 1975. 191 p.

Govan, S. Y.

"Connections, Links, and Extended Networks: Patterns in Octavia Butler's Science Fiction," _Black American Literature Forum_ 18(2): 82-87. Summer 1984.

"Insistent Presences of Black Folk in the Novels of Samuel R. Delany," _Black American Literature Forum_ 18(2): 43-48. Summer 1984.

Gove, P. B.

Imaginary Voyage in Prose Fiction, The. A History of Its Criticism and a Guide for Its Study, with an Annotated Checklist of 215 Imaginary Voyages from 1700 to 1800. NY: Columbia Univ. Press, 1941. 445 p. Repr., NY: Arno Press, 1975.

Gower, Kathy

"Science fiction and women," in: Andersen, Margaret, ed. _Mother Was Not a Person_. Montreal: Continent Publishing Ltd. and Black Rose Books, 1972. pp. 98-101.

Grabnar, Boris

"Abadon," in: Magill, Frank N., ed. _Survey of Science Fiction Literature_, Vol. 1. Englewood Cliffs, NJ: Salem Press, 1979. pp. 1-5.

Graff, Vera

Homo futurus: eine Analyse der modernen Science Fiction. Hamburg: Claassen, 1971. 238 p.

Graham, Jefferson

"'The Twilight Zone' Returns," _Twilight Zone_ 5(1): 84-85. March/April 1985.

Graham, Keith

"Consensus in social decision making: why is it Utopian?" in: _Utopias_, ed. by Peter Alexander and Roger Gill. London: Duckworth, 1984. pp. 49-60.

Graham, L. R.

"Bogdanov's inner message," in: Bogdonov, A. _Red Star_. Bloomington: Indiana University Press, 1984. pp. 241-253.

Graman, Jean

"Yefremov's _Andromeda_: plot summary and commentary," _Vector_ 25: 9-15. March 1964.

Grand, Gilbert

"Dix exploration (possibles) du futur: bilan: science fiction," _Le Devoir_ p. 9, col. 1, art. 2. January 3, 1976.

"Mutants, paranormal et vieux classiques," _Le Devoir_ p. 20, col. 1, art 1. May 3, 1975.

"Nouvelle vague americaine dans toute sa richesse, La," _Le Devoir_ p. 14, col. 1, art. 2. September 13, 1975.

"Un retour a la 'hard science' chez les Americanis," _Le Devoir_ p. 29, col. 4, art. 1. May 17, 1975.

Granin, Daniil

"Journey into the future, A," in: Magidoff, Robert, ed. _Russian Science Fiction, 1969_. New York: New York University Press, 1969. pp. 11-20. also in: _Soviet Literature_ 5:151-158. 1968.

Grannis, C. B.

"Updated book output statistics 1978: title production, average prices," _Publishers Weekly_ 216(10):44-48. September 3, 1979.

Grant, Allan

"When a camera gets under the skin," <u>Popular Photography</u> 59(4):118-119. October 1966.

Grant, B. K.

<u>Planks of Reason: Essays on the Horror Film</u>, ed. by Barry K. Grant. Metuchen, NJ: Scarecrow, 1984. 442 p.

Grant, C. L.

<u>Writing and Selling Science Fiction</u>, ed. by C. L. Grant. Cincinnati: Writers Digest, c. 1976. 191 p.

"Grey Arena, The," in: Underwood, Tim, and Miller, Chuck, eds. <u>Fear Itself</u>. Columbia, PA: Underwood/Miller 1982. pp. 145-151.

"Introduction; getting your feet wet," in: Grant, C. L., ed. <u>Writing and Selling Science Fiction</u>. Cincinnati, Ohio: Writers Digest, 1976. pp. 1-18.

"Many Years Ago, When We All Lived in the Forest...," In: Winter, Douglas E. <u>Shadowings: The Reader's Guide to Horror Fiction 1981-1982</u>. Mercer Island, WA: Starmont, 1983. pp. 30-32.

"Stephen King: 'I Like to go for the Jugular'." <u>Twilight Zone</u> 1(1): 18-23. April 1981.

Grant, D. M.

"333": A Bibliography of the Science-Fantasy Novel, by J. H. Crawford, J. J. Donahue, and D. M. Grant. Providence, Rhode Island: The Grandon Company, 1953. 80 p.

<u>Rhode Island on Lovecraft</u>, ed. by D. M. Grant and T. P. Hadley. Providence, Rhode Island: Grant-Hadley, 1945. 26 p.

<u>Talbot Mundy: Messenger of Destiny</u>. West Kingston, RI: Donald M. Grant, 1983. 253 p.

"Robert E. Howard, Darrel Crombie and the adventure school," <u>Borealis</u> 1(1):6-7. Summer 1978.

Grant, Nigel

"Education for AD 2001: Science Fiction, Futurology and Education Planning," <u>Scottish Educational Review</u> 13(2): 91-104. November 1981.

Grant, Patrick

"Tolkien: archetype and word," <u>Cross Currents</u> 22:365-380. Winter 1973.

"Tolkien: Archetype and Word," in: Isaacs, Neil D. <u>Tolkien: New Critical Perspectives</u>, ed. by N. D. Isaacs and R. A. Zimbardo. Lexington: University Press of Kentucky, 1981. pp. 87-105.

Grant, Richard

"Bibliography of Avram Davidson, A," <u>Megavore</u> 9:4-20. June 1980.

Grasmick, Nana

<u>Fandom Is For the Young</u>, by Karen Flanery and Nana Grasmick. New York: Vantage, 1981. 160 p.

Gravely, W. H., Jr.

<u>Lunar Voyage in Literature From Lucian To Poe, The</u>. Master's Thesis, University of Virginia, 1934. 189 p.

Graves, Robert

"Det frosvunde Atlantis," in: <u>Rejser i tid og rum. En Bog om science fiction</u>, ed. by Tage La Cour. Copenhagen: Stig Verdelkaer, 1973.

Gray, Francine du Plessix

"Visiting Italo Calvino," <u>New York Times Book Review</u> p. 1, 22-23. June 21, 1981.

Gray, Paul

"Master of Postliterate Prose," <u>Time</u> 120(9):87. Aug. 10, 1982.

Gray, Thomas

"Bureaucratization in The Lord of the Rings," <u>Mythlore</u> 7(2):3-4. Summer 1980.

Greaves, G. K.

"Unfettered mind roams the universe, An," <u>Portales News-Tribune</u> Sec. 2, p. 1. July 6, 1975.

Grebens, G. V.

See: Grebenschikov, G. V.

Grebenschikov, G. V.

<u>Ivan Efremov's Theory of Soviet Science Fiction</u>. Ph.D. Dissertation, Michigan State University, 1972. 188 p.

Grebenschikov, G. V. (Continued)

"Efremov's science fiction: a reexamination of his major works," Russian Language Journal No. 106:105-113. n.d.

Greeley, A. M.

"Varieties of apocalypse in science fiction," Journal of American Culture 2(2):279-287. Summer 1979.

Green, D. L.

"Children's literature periodicals on individual authors, dime novels, fantasy," Phaedrus 3(1):22-24. Spring 1976.

Green, Frank

"He Looks to the Stars," San Diego Union April 2, 1981. in: Newsbank. Literature. 67:C2. July 1980-June 1981.

Green, H. E.

"Bringing up Baby," Cinefex No. 22:42-67. June 1985.

Green, M.

"Science and sensibility," Kenyon Review 25(4):700-728. Autumn 1963.

Green, M. B.

"Two surveys of the literature of science," in: Green, M. B. Science and the Shabby Curate of Poetry. New York: Norton, 1965. pp. 120-155.

Green, Martin

"Distaste for the contemporary," Nation 190(21):451-452. May 21, 1960.

Green, R. J.

"Modern science fiction and fantasy: a frame of reference," Illinois Schools Journal 57(3):45-53. Fall 1977.

Green, R. L.

C. S. Lewis: A Biography, by R. L. Green and Walter Hooper. London: Collins, 1974. 320 p.; Glasgow: Fount, 1979.

Into Other Worlds: Space-Flight in Fiction, from Lucian to Lewis. London and New York: Abelard-Schuman, 1957. 190 p. Reprinted, New York: Arno Press, 1975.

"C. S. Lewis and Andrew Lange," Notes & Queries 22(5):208-209. May 1975.

"Venus' nattevagt," in: Rejser i tid og rum. En Bog om science fiction, ed. by Tage La Cour. Copenhagen: Stig Verdelkaer, 1973.

Green, S. E.

"Amazing Up for Sale," Science Fiction Times (Boston) 1(10): 1,11. 1981.

"Marketing Science Fiction and Fantasy Poetry," Empire For the SF Writer 32: 16-17. Winter 1984.

"New Science Fiction Anthology Announced," Science Fiction Times (Boston) 1(10): 9. 1981.

"SFPA Starts Publishing Program," Science Fiction Times (Boston) 1(10): 9. 1981.

Green, T. M.

"Philip K. Dick: a parallax view," Science Fiction Review 5(2):12-15. 1976.

"What Rough Beast?" Thrust 20: 20-21, 32. Spring/Summer 1984.

Green, W. H.

Hobbit and Other Fiction by J. R. R. Tolkien: Their Roots in Medieval and Heroic Literature and Language. Ph. D. Dissertation, Louisiana State University, 1969. 188 p.

"Ring at the center: Eaca in The Lord of the Rings, The," Mythlore 4(2):17-19. December 1976.

Green, William

"Legendary and historical time in Tolkien's Farmer Giles of Ham," Notes on Contemporary Literature 5(3):14-15. 1975.

Greenberg, M. H.

Arthur C. Clarke, ed. by J. D. Olander and M. H. Greenberg. New York: Taplinger, 1977. 254 p.

Coming Attractions. New York: Gnome, 1957. 254 p.

End of the World, The, by Eric S. Rabkin, Martin H. Greenberg, and Joseph D. Olander. Carbondale: Southern Illinois University Press, 1983. 204 p.

Fantastic Lives: Autobiographical Essays by Notable Science Fiction Writers. Carbondale: Southern Illinois University Press, 1981. 215 p.

Greenberg, M. H. (Continued)

Index to Stories in Thematic Anthologies of
Science Fiction, ed. by M. B. Tymn, M. H.
Greenberg, L. W. Currey and J. D. Olander.
Boston: G. K. Hall, 1978. 193 p.

Isaac Asimov, ed. by J. D. Olander and M. H.
Greenberg. New York: Taplinger, 1977. 247 p.

No Place Else: Explorations in Utopian and
Dystopian Fiction, by Eric S. Rabkin, Martin
H. Greenberg, and Joseph D. Olander.
Carbondale: Southern Illinois University Press,
1983. 278 p.

Philip K. Dick, by Martin H. Greenberg and
Joseph O. Olander. New York: Taplinger, 1982.
256 p.

Ray Bradbury, by Joseph D. Olander, and
Martin H. Greenberg. New York: Taplinger,
1980. 248 p.

Robert A. Heinlein, ed. by J. D. Olander and
M. H. Greenberg. New York: Taplinger, 1978.
268 p.

Science Fiction: Contemporary Mythology,
ed. by Patricia Warrick, M. H. Greenberg and
Joseph Olander. New York: Harper, 1978.
476 p.

Ursula K. Le Guin, ed. by J. D. Olander and
M. H. Greenberg. New York: Taplinger, 1979.
258 p.

"Teaching political science fiction," by M. H.
Greenberg and J. D. Olander. in: Williamson,
Jack, ed. Teaching Science Fiction:
Education for Tomorrow. Philadelphia:
Owlswick, 1980. pp. 145-156.

"Utopias and dystopias," by Frederik Pohl, M.
H. Greenberg and J. D. Olander. in: Warrick,
Patracia, ed. Science Fiction: Contemporary
Mythology. New York: Harper, 1978. pp.
393-400.

Greenberger, Robert

"Charm of Khan, The: An Interview with Ricardo
Montalban," Starlog 62: 16-20, 65.
September 1982.

"Conan the Barbarian (Review)," Starlog 64:
46-47. November 1982.

"Heavy Metal Story, The," Starlog 50:
24-27, 61. September 1981.

"Jennifer Beals: the man-made Bride,"
Starlog No. 98:11-13. September 1985.

"Jeremy Leven: creating Creator," Starlog
No. 92:40-42. March 1985.

"Karen Allen, beloved of John Carpenter's
Starman," Starlog No. 90:51-53,58.
January 1985.

"Kevin McCarthy: And For His Next Trick...,"
Starlog 79: 60-63. February 1984.

"One Hundred Most Important People in Science
Fiction/Fantasy: Alex Raymond," Starlog
No. 100: 82. November 1985.

"One Hundred Most Important People in Science
Fiction/Fantasy: Jerry Siegel & Joe Shuster,"
Starlog No. 100: 83. November 1985.

"One Hundred Most Important People in Science
Fiction/Fantasy: Julius Schwartz," Starlog
No. 100: 83-84. November 1985.

"Paper Tiger's Dramatic Debut," Starlog
45: 44-45. April 1981.

"Ridley Scott," Starlog 60: 60-64. July
1982.

"Roy Thomas and Gerry Conway, Scribes to Conan
the Barbarian," Starlog 84: 50-51, 94.
July 1984.

"Science Fiction in the Comics Today,"
Starlog 48: 42-43. July 1981.

"Science fiction media 1984/85: Television,
books, comics," by Robert Greenberger, Chris
Henderson, and Carr D'Angelo. Starlog No.
96: 33-37, 92. July 1985.

"Science Fiction Television 1980-81,"
Starlog 48: 60-61. July 1981.

"Science Fiction Television in Review
1981-1982.," Starlog 60: 43-46. July 1982.

"Secret Force Behind 'The Greatest American
Hero'," Starlog 64: 24-26, 64. November
1982.

"Simon Jones: a guide to this hitchhiker's
galaxy," Starlog No. 93:23-25,65. April
1985.

"Sky's the Limit," Video Action 1(7):
64-70. June 1981.

"Sneak Peek at the Heavy Metal Movie,"
Starlog 48: 50-51. July 1981.

"Starlog Interview: Faye Grant," Starlog
82: 42-43, 67. May 1984.

"Starlog Interview: Hugh Hudson," Starlog
81: 19-23. April 1984.

"Starlog Interview: Scatman Crothers,"
Starlog 77: 52-53. December 1983.

"Starlog Interview: Chuck Yeager," Starlog
77: 44-46, 65. December 1983.

"Starlog Interview: Connie Sellecca,"
Starlog 54: 20-22. January 1982.

"Starlog Interview: Dennis Quaid," Starlog
79: 51-54. February 1984.

Greenberger, Robert (Continued)

"Starlog Interview: Jimmy Doohan," Starlog 62: 43-44, 64. September 1982.

"Starlog Interview: Lance Guest," Starlog 85: 60-62. August 1984.

"Starlog Interview: Nicholas Meyer," Starlog 78: 16-18. January 1984.

"Starlog Interview: Phoebe Cates," Starlog 84: 26-28. July 1984.

"Starlog interview: Red Sonja, Brigitte Nielsen," Starlog No. 96: 41-49. July 1985.

"Starlog Profile: Nichelle Nichols," Starlog No. 100: 66-68. November 1985.

"Superman II: The Adventure Continues," Starlog 46: 31-33, 63. May 1981.

"TV Preview: 'Alien' on Earth: The Making of 'Panic Offshore'," Starlog 45: 31-33. April 1981.

"Twilight Zone Comes Home," Starlog 75: 52-54. October 1983.

"Veronica Cartwright is Betty Grissom," Starlog 81: 62-63, 66. April 1984.

"Whiz Kids," Starlog 79: 34-35. February 1984.

"Year at a Glance (Starlog index, issues 35-46)," Starlog 48: 44-47. July 1981.

Greene, E. E.

"Teaching futuristics in the classroom today: a multi-media journey," Previews 4(6):5-9. February 1976.

Greenhut, D. S.

"Damon Knight," in: Cowart, David, ed. Twentieth-Century American Science-Fiction Writers, Part 1: A-L. Detroit: Gale, 1981. pp. 239-242. (Dictionary of Literary Biography, v. 8)

Greenland, Colin

Entropy Exhibition: Michael Moorcock and the British 'New Wave' in Science Fiction. London: Routledge, 1983. 244 p.

Entropy Exhibition: New Worlds 1964-70 and the Literary Development of Science Fiction. Thesis, Pembroke College, Oxford University, England, 1981. 363 p.

"From Beowulf to Kafka: Mervyn Peake's 'Titus Alone'," Foundation 21: 48-53. February 1981.

"Highly Desirable Residence," Focus 5: 6-15. Spring 1982.

"Martial Lore: Thoughts on 'Battlestar Galactica'" Foundation 18: 35-37. January 1980.

"Queen of Counters, The, Reversed," Vector 116: 13-15. September 1983.

"Times themselves talk nonsense: language in Barefoot in the Head, The," Foundation 17:32-41. September 1979.

Greenlaw, M. J.

Study of the Impact of Technology on Human Values as Reflected in Modern Science Fiction For Children. Ph.D. Dissertation, Michigan State University, 1970. 190 p.

"Profile: Lloyd Alexander," Language Arts 61(4): 406-413. April 1984.

"Science fiction as a mode for interdisciplinary education," by James Quina and M. J. Greenlaw. Journal of Reading 19(2):104-111. November 1975.

"Science Fiction: Images of the Future, Shadows of the Past," Top of the News 39(1): 64-71. Fall 1982.

"Science fiction: impossible, improbable, or prophetic?" Elementary English 48(4):196-202. April 1971.

Gregg, Stephen

"Hugo Awards and poetry," Cthulhu Calls 3(3):9-12. January 1976.

Gregory, Jay

"Peter Straub: Interview," Twilight Zone 1(2): 13-16. May 1981.

Gregory, M. W.

"Act of Faith: George Orwell's socialist thought and 1984," South Atlantic Quarterly 84(4):368-378. Autumn 1985.

Gregory, Sinda

"Interview With Ursula K. Le Guin," by Larry McCaffrey and Sinda Gregory. Missouri Review 7(2): 64-85. 1984.

Greiner, D. J.

"Vonnegut's Slaughterhouse Five and the fiction of atrocity," Critique 14(3):38-51. 1973.

Greiner, Pat

"Magnifico giganticus: Asimov's Shakspearean fool," Extrapolation 26(1): 29-35. Spring 1985.

Grenier, Christian

Jeunesse et science fiction. Paris: Magnard, 1972. 122 p.

Grennan, M. R.

"Lewis trilogy: a scholar's holiday, The," Catholic World 167:337-344. July 1948.

Grennell, D. A.

"How are the fallen mighty dept.: Captain Satan," Xenophile No. 42:9-10,20. September/October 1979.

Gresham, Stephen

"Interview with Mary Elizabeth Counselman, An," Weird Tales Collector 6:11-13. 1980.

Griffey, W. H.

"Weapons of choice, I," in: De Camp, L. S., ed. Blade of Conan. New York: Ace, 1979. pp. 207-210.

Griffin, Brian

"Moving towards Chaos: Aldiss's Hothouse," Foundation. 20: 15-27. October 1980.

Griffin, J. W.

Dark Valley Destiny: The Life of Robert E. Howard, by L. S. de Camp, Catherine Crook de Camp and J. W. Griffin. New York: Bluejay, 1984. 377 p.

Griffin, R. M.

"Medievalism in A Canticle for Leibowitz," Extrapolation 14(2):112-125. May 1973.

Griffith, John

"Personal fantasy in Andersen's fairy tales," Kansas Quarterly 16(3): 81-88. Summer 1984.

Griffiths, John

Three tomorrows: American, British, and Soviet science fiction. London: Macmillan, 1980. 217 p.; Totowa, NJ: Barnes & Noble, 1980. 217 p.

Grigorescu, Dan

"Forecasts, not prophecies," Romanian Review 22:57-58. 1968.

Grigsby, J. L.

"Asimov's Foundation Trilogy and Herbert's Dune Trilogy: A Vision Reversed," Science-Fiction Studies 8(2): 149-155. July 1981.

"Herbert's Reversal of Asimov's Vision Reassessed: Foundation's Edge and God Emperor of Dune," Science-Fiction Studies 11(2): 174-180 July 1984.

Grimsley, Juliet

"The Martian Chronicles: a provocative study," English Journal 59(9):1239-1242. December 1970.

Grin, P. E.

"Sind Sie schon SF-Leser?" Geist und Tat 7:283- . 1952.

Griset, Antoine

"Panorama de la science fiction," Magazine Litteraire No. 125:57. June, 1977.

"S. F. Panorama," Magazine Litteraire No. 109:58-61. February 1976.

"S. F. Panorama," Magazine Litteraire No. 122:53-55. March 1977.

"S. F. Panorama," Magazine Litteraire No. 135:52-53. April 1978.

"Science fiction va bien, merci..., La," Magazine Litteraire (Paris) 88:34-36. May 1974.

"Une chronique de la science fiction," Magazine Litteraire No. 85:62-63. February 1974. (Book review)

Grobman, M. K.

"Myth, Cultural Differences, and Conflicting Worldviews in New Wave Science Fiction," by M. K. Grobman and N. R. Grobman. Extrapolation 23(4): 377-384. Winter 1982.

Grobman, N. R.

"Myth, Cultural Differences, and Conflicting Worldviews in New Wave Science Fiction," by M. K. Grobman and N. R. Grobman. Extrapolation 23(4): 377-384. Winter 1982.

Grochowiak, Stanislaw

"How funny this Lem is!" _Kultura_ No. 39.
1965.

"Nad _Solaris_," _Nowa Kultura_ No. 39.
1961.

Groeger, Erika

"Burgerliche atomwissenschaftler im
englisch-amerikanischen roman von 1945 bis zur
gegenwart," _Zeitschrift fur Anglistik und_
Amerikanistik. 16:25-48. 1968.

Gromova, Ariadna

"Naucnaja fantastika- cto eto takoe?"
Detskaja literatura 5:11-14. 1966.

"Zigzagi fantstiki," _Literaturnaja gazeta_
April 19, 1972.

Gropper, E. C.

"Disenchanted turn to Hesse, The," _English_
Journal 61(7):979-984. October 1972.

Gros-Louis, D. K.

"Slaughterhouse Five: Pacifism vs.
Passiveness," _Ball State University Forum_
18(2): 3-8. Spring 1977.

Grose, C. R.

"Eros and the ghoul: necrophilia in the prose
and poetry of Clark Ashton Smith,"
Nyctalops No. 7:34-36. August 1972.

Grose, Tim

"1984 and _Caves of Steel_: Two views of the
Machine," in: _The Future in Peril: 1984 and_
the Anti-Utopians. College Station: Honors
Program, Texas A&M University, [1985]. pp. 1-5.

Gross, E. H.

"Science fiction as a factor in science
education," by E. H. Gross and J. H. Woodburn.
Science Education 43(1):28-31. February
1959.

Gross, Edward

"Psycho II," _Cinefantastique_ 16(1):31,53.
March 1986.

"Roddy McDowall," _Starlog_ No.
101:52-53,71. December 1985.

"Starlog Interview: Don Jokoby," _Starlog_
99: 34-37. October 1985.

Grossman, Edward

"Vonnegut and his audience," _Commentary_
58(1):40-46. July 1974.

Grotjahn, Martin

"Horror: yes, it can do you good," _Films and_
Filming 5(2):9. November 1958.

Grotta, Daniel

See: Grotta-Kurska, Daniel

Grotta-Kurska, Daniel

Biography of J. R. R. Tolkien. 1978.
Reprint of _J. R. R. Tolkien: Architect of_
Middle Earth.

J. R. R. Tolkien: Architect of Middle Earth.
Philadelphia: Running Press, 1976. 165 p.
Reprinted, 1978, as _The Biography of J. R. R._
Tolkien.

"Conversation with Colin Wilson," _Oui_
2(12):71,74,92,129-130. December 1973.

Gruber, Frank

Pulp Jungle. Los Angeles: Sherbourne, 1967.
189 p.

Grunwald, H. A.

"From Eden to the nightmare," _Horizon_
5(4):73-79. March 1963.

Guardamagna, Daniela

Analisi dell'incubo. L'utopia negativa da
Swift alla fantascienza. Rome: Bulzoni,
1980. 240 p.

Gubar, Susan

"_She_ in _Herland_: Feminism as Fantasy,"
in: Slusser, George E., ed. _Coordinates_.
Carbondale: Southern Illinois University Press,
1983. pp. 139-149.

"C. L. Moore and the conventions of women's
science fiction," _Science-Fiction Studies_
7(1): 16-27. March 1980.

Gubko, N.

"Antivoennyi roman Vonneguta," _Zvezda_
6:220-222. 1971.

Gudelius, Barbel

"Grenze, Die," in: _Femistische Utopien: Aufbruch in dei postpatriarchale Gesellschaft_, ed. by Barbara Holland-Cunz. Meitingen: Corian Verlag, 1986.

Guffey, G. R.

Bridges to Science Fiction, by G. E. Slusser, G. R. Guffey, and Mark Rose. Carbondale: Southern Illinois University Press, 1980. 168 p.

"_Fahrenheit 451_ and the 'Cubby-Hole Editors' of Ballantine Books," in: Slusser, George E., ed. _Coordinates_. Carbondale: Southern Illinois University Press, 1983. pp. 99-106.

"Literature and Science," by G. E. Slusser and G. R. Guffey. in: Barricelli, Jean-Pierre, ed. _Interrelations of Literature_. New York: Modern Language Association, 1982. pp. 176-204.

"Unconscious, Fantasy, and Science Fiction," in: Slusser, George E., ed. _Bridges to Fantasy_. Carbondale: Southern Illinois University Press, 1982. pp. 142-159.

Guiffrida, Sergio

"_Proxima_," _Wow_ No. 8. 1977.

Guiliani, Pierre

"Az SF Franciaorszagban," _SF Tajekoztato_ 7:37-41. November 1972.

"Litterature de science fiction et politique," _Revue Politique et Parlementaire_ 853:68-81. (1974?)

"S. F. et ideologie: une quete absurde," by Dominique Douay and Pierre Guiliani. _Europe_ 580/581:79-84. August/September 1977.

"Science fiction et histoire," _Change_ (Paris) 40: 20-44. 1981.

Guitar, M. A.

"Why they love monsters," _New York Times Magazine_ p. 109. October 25, 1964.

Gulbin, Suzanne

"Parallels and contrasts in _Lord of the Flies_ and _Animal Farm_," _English Journal_ 55(1):86-88. January 1966.

Guld, Jens

Bibliografi over litteratur pa dansk om science fiction intil 1976. Copenhagen: Science Fiction Cirklen, 1977. 37 p.

"Critical works on science fiction in Danish," in: Dollerup, Cay, ed. _Volve. Scandinavian Views on Science Fiction_. Copenhagen: Department of English, University of Copenhagen, 1978. pp. 63-65.

Gummell, Bryn

"Fantasy of Mervyn Peake," _Malahat Review_ 58: 17-35. April 1981.

Gunew, Sneja

"'Mythic reversals' the evolution of the shadow motif," in: Olander, J. D. and M. H. Greenberg, eds. _Ursula K. Le Guin_. New York: Taplinger, 1979. pp. 178-199.

"Forms of Power in Recent Australian Science Fiction," _Meanjin_ 41(2): 277-286. June 1982.

"To light a candle is to cast a shadow: the shadow as identity touchstone in Ursula K. Le Guin's Earthsea trilogy and in the _Left Hand of Darkness_," _SF Commentary_ 48/49/50:32-39. October/December 1976.

Gunn, Eileen

"_Martians, Go Home_," in: Magill, Frank N., ed. _Survey of Science Fiction Literature_, Vol. 3. Englewood Cliffs, NJ: Salem Press, 1979. pp. 1362-1365.

Gunn, James

Alternate Worlds: the Illustrated History of Science Fiction. Englewood Cliffs, New Jersey: Prentice-Hall, 1975. 256 p. Reprinted, New York: A&W Visual Library, 1976.

Discovery of the Future: the Ways Science Fiction Developed, The. College Station, Texas: Texas A&M University Library, 1975. 17 p.

Isaac Asimov: The Foundations of Science Fiction Success. New York: Oxford University Press, 1982. 236 p.

Teacher's Manual: The Road to Science Fiction, by J. E. Gunn and Stephen Goldman. New York: New American Library, 1980. 45 p.

"_Foundation Trilogy, The_," in: Magill, Frank N., ed. _Survey of Science Fiction Literature_, Vol. 2. Englewood Cliffs, NJ: Salem Press, 1979. pp. 819-831.

"_Fury_," in: Magill, Frank N., ed. _Survey of Science Fiction Literature_, Vol. 2. Englewood Cliffs, NJ: Salem Press, 1979. pp. 855-857.

Gunn, James (Continued)

"Humanoids, The and 'With Folded Hands'," in: Magill, Frank N., ed. Survey of Science Fiction Literature, Vol. 2. Englewood Cliffs, NJ: Salem Press, 1979. pp. 981-985.

"Tower of Glass," in: Magill, Frank N., ed. Survey of Science Fiction Literature, Vol. 5. Englewood Cliffs, NJ: Salem Press, 1979. pp. 2303-2306.

"World of Null-A, The," in: Magill, Frank N., ed. Survey of Science Fiction Literature, Vol. 5. Englewood Cliffs, NJ: Salem Press, 1979. pp. 2501-2505.

"1984: Novel of the Year," Fantasy Review 7(4): 17-19. May 1984.

"Academic viewpoint, The," in: Dickson, Gordon R., ed. Nebula Winners Twelve. New York: Harper, 1978. pp. 114-124.

"Aliens," by Pamela Sargent and James Gunn. in: Warrick, Patricia, ed. Science Fiction: Contemporary Mythology. New York: Harper, 1978. pp. 146-157.

"Author watches his brain child die on television," TV Guide 19(6):7-12. February 13, 1971.

"Commentary: Inner Concerns in Outer Space: The Real and the Surreal," Fantasy Newsletter 5(1): 5-7. January 1982.

"From the pulps to the classroom," Algol 14(1):8-14. Winter 1976/1977.

"From the Pulps to the Classroom: The Strange Journey of Science Fiction," in: Tymn, Marshall B., ed. The Science Fiction Reference Book. Mercer Island, WA.: Starmont House, 1981. pp. 233-245.

"Gatekeepers, The," Science-Fiction Studies 10(1): 15-23. March 1983

"Grand Master, The: Robert A. Heinlein," Starship 18(1): 31-34. Spring 1981.

"Henry Kuttner, C. L. Moore, Lewis Padgett et al," in: Clareson, T. D., ed. Voices for the Future: Essays on Major SF Writers, Vol. 1. Bowling Green, Ohio: Bowling Green University Popular Press, 1976. pp. 185-215.

"Heroes, heroines, villains: the characters in science fiction," in: Bretnor, Reginald, ed. The Craft of Science Fiction. New York: Harper, 1976. pp. 161-177.

"History and Transcendance; From Inner Space to Exotic Parable," Fantasy Newsletter 5(9): 25-26, 38. October 1982.

"I remember Ted," Fantasy Review 8(5): 7. May 1985.

"I, Asimov," Extrapolation 21(4): 309-327. Winter 1980.

"Immortals: from print to film and back again, The," Destinies 1(5):230-253. October/December 1979.

"Literature of science fiction visualized," Educational Screen & AV Guide 50(9):4-9. September 1971.

"On style," in: Scott, Robin, ed. Those Who Can: A Science Fiction Reader. New York: Mentor/New American Library, 1973. pp. 303-312.

"On the Foundations of Science Fiction," Isaac Asimov's Science Fiction Magazine 4(4): 64-84. April 1980.

"On the Lem Affair," Science-Fiction Studies 4(3): 314-316. November 1977.

"On the Robot Novels," Isaac Asimov's Science Fiction Magazine 5(1): 60-90. January 19, 1981.

"On the Tinsel Screen: Science Fiction and the Movies," Isaac Asimov's Science Fiction Magazine 4(2): 112-126. February 1980.

"On Variations on a Robot," Isaac Asimov's Science Fiction Magazine 4(7): 56-81. July 1980.

"Philosophy of Science Fiction, The, part 1," Dynamic Science Fiction 1(2): 104-113. March 1953.

"Philosophy of Science Fiction, The, part 2," Dynamic Science Fiction 1(3): 83-91. June 1953.

"Polishing the Robots," Fantasy Review 7(6): 9-11. July 1984.

"Reader Reaction and Science Fiction Writers: The New Wave and the Labor Day Group," Fantasy Newsletter 5(11): 11-13. December 1982.

"Retrospective: Science Fiction's 'New Wave', " Fantasy Newsletter 5(3): 11-16. March 1982.

"Science and Fiction: Fiction and Science," Fantasy Newsletter 5(7): 5-7. August 1982.

"Science fiction and the future," Algol 16(1):36-37. Winter 1978-1979.

"Science fiction and the mainstream," in: Bretnor, Reginald, ed. Science Fiction Today and Tomorrow. New York: Harper, 1974. pp. 183-216.

"Science Fiction in the Eighties," in: Wolfe, Gary. Science Fiction Dialogues. Chicago: Academy Chicago, 1982. pp. 1-6.

"Science Fiction year, 1984," SFWA Bulletin 19(3): 10-12. Fall 1985.

Gunn, James (Continued)

"Science fiction: the shape of the future," Kansas English 59(2):6-15. 1974. (not seen)

"SF in the classroom: III, science fiction readership on campus," by Barry Baddock and James Gunn. Extrapolation 15(2):148-151. May 1974.

"Son of Foundation," Fantasy Newsletter 6(4): 15-17. April 1983.

"Strange journey, 1984," in: Pournelle, Jerry, ed. The Science Fiction Yearbook. New York: Baen, 1985. pp. 156-165.

"Stuff Itself, The," Isaac Asimov's Science Fiction Magazine 5(4): 48-77. April 13, 1981.

"Teaching science fiction revisited," Analog 94(3):6-10,175-178. November 1974.

"Teaching science fiction revisited," in: Bova, Ben. Viewpoint. Cambridge, MA: NESFA, 1977. pp. 46-55.

"Teaching science fiction," Publishers Weekly 209(24):62-63. June 14, 1976.

"Three syllibi," by Dave Samuelson, Gary Goshgarian and James Gunn. in: Williamson, Jack, ed. Teaching Science Fiction: Education for Tomorrow. Philadelphia: Owlswick, 1980. pp. 194-202.

"Tinsel screen: science fiction and the movies, The," in: Williamson, Jack, ed. Teaching Science Fiction: Education for Tomorrow. Philadelphia: Owlswick, 1980. pp. 205-218.

"View From Outside, The: Form and Content," Fantasy Newsletter 5(5): 15-16. June 1982.

"Where do You Get Those Crazy Ideas?" in: Brady, John. Fiction Writer's Market, ed. by John Brady and Jean M. Fredette. Cincinnati, OH: Writer's Digest Books, 1981. pp. 284-293.

"Where do you get those crazy ideas?" in: Grant, C. L., ed. Writing and Selling Science Fiction. Cincinnati, Ohio: Writers Digest, 1976. pp. 59-76.

Gunn, S.

"Science and literature," Science 34(878):550-556. October 27, 1911.

Gunn, Steve

"Sci-fi's evolution: odyssey that's stranger than fiction," Chicago Tribune Sec. 1, p. 9. July 8, 1978.

Gunther, Gotthard

Entdeckung Amerikas und die sache der amerikanischen weltraumliteratur, Die. Dusseldorf: Karl Rauch Verlag, 1952. 24 p.

Gunther, Henry

Wissenschaftliche phantastik: authoren der Deutschen Demokratischen Republik. s.l.: Schriftstellerverband der DDR, 1978. 64 p.

Gunther, John

"Outside our world," McCalls 78(1):40,157-160. October 1950.

Gury, Jacques

"Thomas More entre la science fiction et Ivan Illich!" Moreana: Bulletin Thomas More. 58:41-42. 1978.

Guseva, Elena

"Chesterton on the centenary of his birth," Chesterton Review 1(1):19-22. 1974.

Gussow, Mel

"Musical: A Cactus Owns 'Little Shop of Horrors'," New York Times Sec. 1, p. 47. May 30, 1982.

"Theater: 'The Games' Space Opera Time Trip," New York Times p. 22. October 11, 1984.

"Vonnegut is having fun doing a play," New York Times p. 56. October 6, 1970.

Gustafson, Jon

"Gimlet eye: commentary on science fiction and fantasy art, The," Science Fiction Review 4(2):48-52. 1975.

"Interview with Tim Kirk, An," Science Fiction Review 21:50-51. May 1977.

"Jack Gaughan: An Appreciation," Locus 18(9): 51. September 1985.

Gutheil, Monika

"Utopia in Leben und Werk von Charlotte Perkins Gilman," in: Femistische Utopien: Aufbruch in dei postpatriarchale Gesellschaft, ed. by Barbara Holland-Cunz. Meitingen: Corian Verlag, 1986.

Guthery, Tom, IV

"Animation in Fandom,"   in: Hopkins, Harry A.,
ed. <u>Fandom Directory 1981</u>. Langley AFB,
Virginia: Fandom Computer Services, 1981. pp.
13-28.

Guthke, K. S.

<u>Mythos der Neuzeit, Der: das Thema der
Mehrheit der Welten in der Literatur- und
Geistesgeschichte von der kopernikanischen
Wende bis zur Science Fiction</u>. Bern:
Francke, 1983. 1983.

Guthmann, Edward

"'Brother' Hits Harlem in a Spaceship,"   <u>San
Francisco Examiner</u> September 30, 1984. in:
<u>NewsBank. Film and Television</u> FTV
33:G10-G11. 1984/1985.

Gutsch, Juergen

<u>Science Fiction: Materialien und Hinweise</u>, by
Freidrich Leiner and Juergen Gutsch.
Frankfurt: Diesterweg, 1980. 114 p.

<u>Science Ficton: eine Textsammlung fuer die
Schule</u>, by Freidrich Leiner and Juergen
Gutsch. Frankfurt: Diesterweg, 1973. 150 p.

"Literarische Systeme fur den Moglichkeitssinn.
Einige Aspekte der Science-Fiction-Literatur,"
<u>Diskussion Deutsch</u> 2:335-350. 1971.

Gyorgy, Szepe

"Hozzaszolas a sci fi myelvenek kerdesehaz,"
<u>SF Tajekoztato</u>   p. 63-68. January 1972.

"Science Fiction nyelveszeti problemai,"   <u>SF
Tajekoztato</u> No. 7:12-32. November 1972.

Gyory, Jean

<u>Phantastiches Ostereich</u>. Wein: Zsolnay,
1976. 430 p.

H

H. G. Wells Society

H. G. Wells: A Comprehensive Bibliography.
London: H. G. Wells Society, 1966. 61 p.

H. G. Wells: A Comprehensive Bibliography.
Revised Ed. London: H. G. Wells Society, 1968.
70 p.

Haac, O. A.

"Toward a Definition of Utopia," Studies in
Eighteenth-Century Culture, Vol. 6, 1977.
pp. 407-416.

Haack, F. W.

"Jungste tag der mananen. Ist science fiction
ein religionsersatz?" Christ und Welt
19(5):12. 1966.

Haan, Kalju

"Dramateater alustab hooaega," Sirp ja Vasar
36. September 3, 1976.

Haas, George

"Memories of Klarkash-Ton," Nyctalops No.
7:70-74. August 1972.

Haase, D. P.

"Heinrich von Ofterdingen," in: Magill,
Frank N., ed. Survey of Modern Fantasy
Literature, Vol 2. Englewood Cliffs, NJ:
Salem Press, Inc., 1983. pp. 720-724.

Hackenberry, Charles

"Interview With a Time Traveler,"
Pennsylvania English 10(2): 5-13. Spring
1984.

"Painter at the Keyboard," Extrapolation
26(1): 50-55. Spring 1985.

Hacker, B. C.

"Pasts That Might Have Been: An Annotated
Bibliography of Alternate History," by Barton
C. Hacker and Gorgon B. Chamberlain.
Extrapolation 22(4): 334-379. Winter 1981.

Hacker, Marilyn

"Science fiction and feminism: the work of
Joanna Russ," Chrysalis No. 4:67-69. 1977.

Hackford, T. R.

"Fantastic Visions: British Illustrations of
the Arabian Nights," in: Schlobin, Roger C.,
ed. The Aesthetics of Fantasy Literature and
Art. Notre Dame, IN: University of Notre Dame
Press, 1982. pp. 143-175.

Haden-Guest, Anthony

"Out here in the Hamptons: snapshots of the
literary life," New York pp. 43-47.
September 1, 1975.

"Star Trek wars," New Times 9:10.
November 11, 1977.

Hadfield, A. M.

Charles Williams: An Exploration of His Life
and Work. New York: Oxford University Press,
1983. 268 p.

Hadji, Robert

"Checklist of Science Fiction and Fantasy Book
Dealers," by David Aylward and Robert Hadji.
Special Collections 2(1/2): 171-175.
Fall/Winter 1982.

Hadley, T. P.

Rhode Island on Lovecraft, ed. by D. M.
Grant and T. P. Hadley. Providence, Rhode
Island: Grant-Hadley, 1945. 26 p.

Hagemann, E. R.

Comprehensive Index to Black Mask, 1920-1951.
Bowling Green: Bowling Green University
Popular Press, 1982. 236 p.

Hagen, Randall

"Possible subconscious source of Philip Jose
Farmer's Riverwold, The," Moebius Trip
22:22-27. April 1975. (not seen)

Hager, Margit

"Aspekte des Phantastischen, 4. Teil und
Schluss," Quarber Merkur 61: 3-11. July
1984.

Hager, Stanton

"Palaces of the looking glass: Borges's
deconstruction of metaphysics," in: Collins,
R. A., ed. Scope of the Fantastic: Theory,
Technique, Major Authors. Westport:
Greenwood, 1985. pp. 231-238.

Hahn, Oscar

Cuento fantastico hispanoamericano en el siglo
XIX, El. Mexico, D.F.: Premia Editoria,
1978. 183 p.

Hahn, R. M.

Reclams Science Fiction Fuehrer, ed. by H.
J. Alpers, Werner Fuchs, R. M. Hahn and
Wolfgang Jeschke. Munich: Heyne, 1980. 503 p.

"25 Jahre Science Fiction Times: Memorien,
geschrieben in der Badewanne," Science
Fiction Times (Germany) 26(1):9. January
1984.

"Die Lust an Spekulativen," by Ronald Hahn and
Werner Fuchs. Buchmarkt No. 11/12. 1972.

"Interview mit G. F. Unger," Science Fiction
Times (Bremerhaven) No. 136:9-10. May 1975.

"Mit Frank Herbert an der Alster," Science
Fiction Times (Germany) 26(12):8-9. December
1984.

"Perry Rhodan as a social and idealogical
phenomenon," by Sylvia Pukallus, R. M. Hahn
and Horst Pukallus. Science Fiction Studies
6(2):190-200. July 1979.

"Science fiction in West Germany," Fantasy
Media 2(2): 10-11. May/June 1980.

"Welt der roten Sonne, Die: Der Private Kosmos
der Marion Zimmer Bradley," in: Alpers, H.
J., ed. Science Fiction Almanach 1981.
Moewig, 1980. pp. 308-324.

"Wissenschaft & technik-zukunft. Geschichte
und ideologie der SF hefte," in: Barmeyer,
Eike, ed. Science fiction: theorie und
geschichte. Munchen: Fink, 1972. pp. 219-243.

"Zwischen Kosmos und Kommerz," Science
Fiction Times (Germany) 25(12):8-14.
December 1983.

Haiblum, Isidore

"Confessions of a freelance fantasist, part 1,"
Twilight Zone 3(2):62-66. May/June 1983.

"Confessions of a freelance fantasist, part 2,"
Twilight Zone 3(3):56-60. July/August
1983.

"Confessions of a freelance fantasist, part 3,"
Twilight Zone 3(5):62-65.
November/December 1983.

"Isaac Bashevis Singer: portrait of a
magician," Twilight Zone 3(6):24-27.
January/February 1984.

Haight, Gordon

"H. G. Wells: 'The Man of the Year Million',"
Nineteenth Century Fiction 12(4):323-326.
March 1958.

Haile, H. G.

"Faust figure, The," in: Magill, Frank N.,
ed. Survey of Modern Fantasy Literature,
Vol 5. Englewood Cliffs, NJ: Salem Press,
Inc., 1983. pp. 2316-2330.

Haining, Peter

Doctor Who: A Celebration. London: Allen,
1983. 256 p.

Doctor Who: The Key to Time; a Year by Year
Record. London: Allen, 1984. 264 p.

H. G. Wells Scrapbook, The. London: New
English Library, 1978. 144 p.

Jules Verne Companion. New York: Baronet,
1978. 128 p.

Terror! A History of Horror Illustrations
from the Pulp Magazines. New York: A&W
Visual Library, 1977.

Haldeman, Greg

"AggieCon XII," Locus 14(5):17. June
1981.

Haldeman, Joe

"Another world of science fiction," _Analog_ 103(8): 87-91. August 1983.

"Currents and directions in SF from the 50's to the 80's," by G. Dickson, J. Haldeman, and T. Clareson. in: Remington, T. J., ed. _Selected Proceedings of the 1978 SFRA Nat'l Conference._ Univ. of North. Iowa, 1979. pp. 222-240.

"Forms of science fiction (a course outline)," _Tabebuian_ No. 22:6-19. Summer 1975.

"Introduction," in: Heinlein, R. A. _Double Star._ Boston: Gregg, 1978. pp. v-xviii.

"On Surviving Freelancing," _Empire: For the SF Writer_ 23: 12-13. Spring, 1981.

"Starry-Eyed Boy Comes Down to Earth," _Los Angeles Times._ Sec. 6, p. 5. December 7, 1980.

Haldeman, Laurie

"John Nathan-Turner's Who Confessions," by Jean Airey and Laurie Haldeman. _Starlog_ No. 101: 49. December 1985.

Hale, M. E.

"Inferential model criticism of The Empire Strikes Back," by T. S. Frentz and M. E. Hale. _Quarterly Jounal of Speech_ 69(3): 278-289. August 1983.

Haleff, Maxine

"Reviving the Lost World of Sci-fi Film Pioneer," _Los Angeles Times Calendar_, p. 20. October 10, 1982. in: _Newsbank. Film and Television._ 42: B5-6. 1982.

Hall, D. L.

"Irony and anarchy: the utopian sensibility," _Alternative Futures_ 2(2): 3-24. Spring 1979.

Hall, Graham

Robert Bloch Bibliography. Tewkesbury, Gloucestershire: by the author, 1965. 31 p.

Hall, H. W.

Chad Oliver: A Preliminary Bibliography. Bryan, TX: Dellwood Press, 1985. 86

Science Fiction and Fantasy Book Review Index, 1980-1984. Detroit: Gale Research, 1985. 761 p.

Science Fiction and Fantasy Research Index, Vol. 2. Bryan, TX. SFBRI, 1982. 72 p.

Science Fiction and Fantasy Research Index, Vol. 3. Bryan, TX: SFBRI, 1983. 74 p.

Science Fiction and Fantasy Research Index, Vol. 4, by H. W. Hall and Geraldine Hutchins. Bryan, TX: SFBRI, 1985. 71 p.

Science Fiction Book Review Index, Vol. 1, 1970. Bryan, TX: SFBRI, 1971. 36 p.

Science Fiction Book Review Index, Vol. 2, 1971. Bryan, TX: SFBRI, 1972. 33 p.

Science Fiction Book Review Index, Vol. 3, 1972. Bryan, TX: SFBRI, 1973. 35 p.

Science Fiction Book Review Index, Vol. 4, 1973. Bryan, TX: SFBRI, 1974. 31 p.

Science Fiction Book Review Index, Vol. 5, 1974. Bryan, TX: SFBRI, 1975. 40 p.

Science Fiction Book Review Index, Vol. 6, 1975. Bryan, TX: SFBRI, 1976. 58 p.

Science Fiction Book Review Index, Vol. 7, 1976. Bryan, TX: SFBRI, 1977. 40 p.

Science Fiction Book Review Index, Vol. 8, 1977. Bryan, TX: SFBRI, 1978. 39 p.

Science Fiction Book Review Index, Vol. 9, 1978. Bryan, TX: SFBRI, 1979. 37 p.

Science Fiction Book Review Index, Vol. 10, 1979. Bryan, TX: SFBRI, 1980. 61 p.

Science Fiction Book Review Index, Vol. 11, 1980. Bryan, TX: SFBRI, 1981. 40 p.

Science Fiction Book Review Index, Vol. 12, 1981. Bryan, TX: SFBRI, 1982. 46 p.

Science Fiction Book Review Index, Vol. 13, 1982. Bryan, TX: SFBRI, 1983. 52 p.

Science Fiction Book Review Index, Vol. 14, 1983. Bryan, TX: SFBRI, 1984. 61 p.

Science Fiction and Fantasy Book Review Index, Vol. 15, 1984. Bryan, TX: SFBRI, 1985. 46 p.

Science Fiction Book Review Index. Pilot Issue (1969). Huntsville, TX: s.n., 1970. 12 p.

Science Fiction Book Review Index, 1923-1973. Detroit: Gale Research, 1975. 438 p.

Science Fiction Book Review Index, 1974-1979. Detroit: Gale Research, 1981. 391 p.

Science Fiction Index, The: An Index to English Language Books and Articles About Science Fiction and Fantasy. Bryan, TX: SFBRI, 1980. (Microfiche)

Hall, H. W. (Continued)

Science Fiction Magazines, The: A Bibliographical Checklist of Titles and Issues Through 1982. Bryan, TX: SFBRI, 1983. 89 p.

Science Fiction Research Index, Vol. 1. Bryan, TX: SFBRI, 1981. 27 p.

Science/Fiction Collections: Fantasy, Supernatural, & Weird Tales. New York: Haworth Press, 1982. 181 p. (Also issued as Special Collections, Volume 1, No. 1/2, Fall/Winter 1982.)

"Announcing the future: science fiction at Texas A&M University," Texas Library Journal 50(5):221-223,257. December 1974.

"Bibliographic control of science fiction, The," Extrapolation 15(1):42-50. December 1973.

"Brief Directory of Science Fiction Research Collections," Special Collections 2(1/2): 177-181. Fall/Winter 1982.

"Chad Oliver: interview," by H. W. Hall and R. D. Boldt. in: Hall, H. W. Chad Oliver: A Preliminary Bibliography. Bryan, TX: Dellwood, 1985. pp. 50-86.

"Introduction: The State of the Art," Special Collections 2(1/2): 3-8. Fall/Winter 1982.

"Library and Private Collections of Science Fiction and Fantasy," in: Barron, Neil, ed. Anatomy of Wonder. 2nd ed. New York: Bowker, 1981. pp. 602-623.

"Popular literature periodicals," Journal of Popular Culture 7(4):882-883. Spring 1974.

"Science Fiction Magazines," in: Barron, Neil, ed. Anatomy of Wonder. 2nd ed. New York: Bowker, 1981. pp. 590-601.

"Science Fiction Sources in Microform," Extrapolation 21(4): 379-385. Winter 1980.

"SF: the other side of the coin," Library Journal 95:2240-2241. June 15, 1970.

"Texas and science fiction," Southwestern American Literature 1:144-148. 1972.

Hall, J. N.

James Branch Cabell: A Complete Bibliography. New York: Revisionist Press, 1974. 245 p.

Hall, M. M.

"Amazing Interview: Gene Wolfe," Amazing 28(2): 125-130. September 1981.

"Interview: Robert Silverberg," Fantasy Newsletter 6(6): 16-17, 46. June/July 1983.

"Interview: Ed Bryant," Fantasy Newsletter 5(5): 29-34. June 1982.

"Riding the Changes," Starship 18(2): 21-22. Summer/Fall 1981.

"Stephen Donaldson: the Pursuit of Wonder," Sumermorn 3: 27-29. Fall 1979.

Hall, Margaret

"I Often Wonder Why I Write," Focus: An SF Writer's Magazine No. 9: 24-29. Autumn 1984.

Hall, Peter

"Utopian thought," in: Utopias, ed. by Peter Alexander and Roger Gill. London: Duckworth, 1984. pp. 189-196.

Hall, R. A., Jr.

"Silent Commands? Frodo and Gollum at the Cracks of Doom," Mythlore 10(3): 5-7. Winter 1984.

"Tolkien's Hobbit tetraology as 'anti-Nibelungen'," Western Humanities Review 32(4):351-359. Autumn 1978.

"Who is Master of the Precious," Mythlore 11(3): 34-35. Winter/Spring 1985.

Hall, T. H.

Dorothy L. Sayers: Nine Literary Studies. London: Duckworth, 1980.

Hall, Thomas

Science and Pseudoscience in Poe's Works. Master's Thesis, North Texas State Teachers College, 1938. 145 p.

Hall, Tord

"Aniara," in: Magill, Frank N., ed. Survey of Science Fiction Literature, Vol. 1. Englewood Cliffs, NJ: Salem Press, 1979. pp. 72-77.

"Harry Martinson 'Aniara' c. eposzarol," Helikon 18(1): 73-88. 1972.

"Introduction: Aniara," in: Martinson, Harry. Aniara. New York: Avon, 1976. pp. vii-xviii.

Hallenberger, Gerd

Macht und Herrschaft in den Welten der Science Fiction: die politische Seite der SF. Meitingen: Corian, 1985. 300 p.

Hallenberger, Gerd (Continued)

"Entwicklung der anglo-amerikanischen SF," by Gerd Hallenberger and Heinrich Kelm. <u>Science Fiction Times</u> (Bremerhaven) No. 136:4-9. May 1975.

"Zukunft als ware," by Gerd Hallenberger and Heinrich Kelm. <u>Kurbiskern</u> 1:76-90. 1975.

Hallett, Vic

"2001; review," <u>Vector</u> 49: 7-8. June 1968.

Halperin, Danny

"Beauty and the sci-fi beasts," <u>Daily Telegraph Magazine</u> pp. 56-57,59,62. November 7, 1975. (not seen)

Halpern, F. M.

<u>International Classified Directory of Dealers in Science Fiction and Fantasy Books and Related Materials</u>. Haddonfield, New Jersey: Haddonfield House, 1975. 90 p.

Hamblen, C. F.

"Bradbury's <u>Fahrenheit 451</u> in the classroom," <u>English Journal</u> 57(6):818-819. September 1968.

Hamblin, W. L.

"Outer space," <u>Space Travel</u>. November 1958.

Hamburger, Philip

"Television: now I lay me down to sleep," <u>New Yorker</u> pp. 57-59. December 22, 1951.

"Television; Captain Video and his video rangers," <u>New Yorker</u> 27(45):57-59. December 22, 1951.

Hamermesh, Madeline

"Persisting ideal: the mythic hero in SF," <u>SFWA Bulletin</u> 10(3): 26-27, 31. Winter 1974/1975.

Hamil, R. E.

"When science fiction becomes history," in: Samuelson, D. N. <u>Science Fiction and Future Studies</u>. Bryan, TX: SFRA, 1975. pp. 53-55.

Hamilton, Edmond

"John W. Campbell," <u>Locus</u> No. 91:8. July 22, 1971.

Hamilton, J. B.

"Notes toward a definition of science fiction," <u>Extrapolation</u> 4(1):2-13. December 1962.

Hamilton, T. W.

"<u>Asimov's SF Adventure Magazine</u>," in: Tymn, M. B. and Ashley, Mike. <u>Science Fiction, Fantasy, and Weird Fiction Magazines</u>. Westport, CT: Greenwood, 1985. pp. 115-117.

"<u>Cosmos Science Fiction and Fantasy Magazine (1977)</u>," in: Tymn, M. B. and Ashley, Mike. <u>Science Fiction, Fantasy, and Weird Fiction Magazines</u>. Westport, CT: Greenwood, 1985. pp. 173-175.

"<u>Isaac Asimov's Science Fiction Magazine</u>," by T. W. Hamilton and Mike Ashley. in: Tymn, M. B. and Ashley, Mike. <u>Science Fiction, Fantasy, and Weird Fiction Magazines</u>. Westport, CT: Greenwood, 1985. pp. 358-363.

Hamit, Francis

"Science Fiction Convention Lures Chicagoans and Alien Fans, too," <u>Chicago Tribune</u> Sec. 3, p. 1, 2. September 3, 1982.

Hamling, Bill

"They don't hardly write them no more," <u>Inside and Science Fiction Advertiser</u> No. 8: 20-22. March 1955.

Hamling, W. L.

"Alas, what boom?" <u>Fantasy Times</u> No. 200:15-17. June (1) 1954.

"Decade of thrills," <u>Fantasy Times</u> No. 138:19-21. September (2) 1951.

Hammett, Chris

"Science fiction's urban vision," <u>Vector</u> 70: 17-33. Autumn, 1975.

Hammond, Asenath

"Jupiter," <u>Locus</u> 12(3):1,5,8. April 1979.

Hammond, Azenata

"Saturn Flyby," <u>Locus</u> 13(11):1-2,7. November 1980.

Hammond, David

"Concerning the persona of King Kong; in two sizes," <u>American Cinematographer</u> 58(1):42-43,52-53. January 1977.

Hammond, J. R.

<u>George Orwell Companion: A Guide to the Novels, Documentaries, and Essays</u>. New York: St. Martins, 1982. 278 p.

<u>H. G. Wells: Interviews and Recollections</u>. New York: Harper, 1980. 121 p.

<u>Herbert George Wells: An Annotated Bibliography of His Works</u>. New York: Garland Publishing, 1977. 257 p.

Hammond, W. G.

"Addenda to J. R. R. Tolkien: a bibliography," <u>Bulletin of Bibliography and Magazine Notes</u> 34(3):119-127. July/September 1977.

Hand, Jack

"Traditionalism of women's roles in Frank Herbert's <u>Dune</u>," <u>Extrapolation</u> 26(1): 24-28. Spring 1985.

Handke, Ryszard

<u>Polska proza fantastyczno naukowa: problemy poetyki</u>. Warsaw: Zaklad, 1969. 176 p.

"Neologizm a jezyknauki i techniki w stylizacji prozy fantastyczno-naukowej St. Lema," in: <u>Styl i Kompozycja</u>. Wroclaw: 1965. pp. 234-247.

"Rola katagorii adresata narracji w fantastyce naukowej," in: <u>Prace a poetyki</u>. Poswiecone VI Myadzynarodowamu Kongresowi Slawietow. Szerk. M. R. Mayenowa es J. Slawinski. Wroclaw-Varso-Krakko, 1968. pp. 133-148.

"Science fiction dzis: Perspektywy ewolugi," in: Kaczmarka, J., ed. <u>Materialy z Miedzynarodowego Spotkania Pisarzy-Tworcow Literatury Fantastyczno-Naukowej</u>. Poznan: Wyndawnictwo Poznanskie, 1974. pp. 59-68.

"W sprawie stylistycznej wartosci neologizmow Lema," in: <u>Jezyk Polski</u> XLIV/5, 288-293. Varso, 1971.

Handy, P. M.

"Zenna Henderson," in: Cowart, David, ed. <u>Twentieth-Century American Science-Fiction Writers, Part 1: A-L</u>. Detroit: Gale, 1981. pp. 228-232. (Dictionary of Literary Biography, V. 8)

Handy, W. J.

"Science, literature, and modern criticism," <u>Texas Quarterly</u> 1(2):147-153. Spring 1958.

Hanff, P. E.

<u>Bibliographia Oziana: A Concise Bibliographical Checklist of the Oz Books by L. Frank Baum and His Successors</u>, by P. E. Hanff and D. G. Greene. Demorest, Georgia: International Wizard of Oz Club, 1976. 103 p.

Hanger, N. C.

"Excellent Absurdity, The: Substitution and Co-Inheritance in C. S. Lewis and Charles Williams," <u>Mythlore</u> 9(4): 14-18. Winter 1983.

Hanlon, M.

"Needed: science stories for young readers," <u>School Science and Mathematics</u> 58(515):677-689. December 1958.

Hanna, Judith

"Neglected Heroine, The," <u>Vector</u> 116: 16-18. September 1983.

"Two-Foot Square of Gene Wolfe; Interview," by Judith Hanna and Joseph Nicholas. <u>Vector</u> 118: 5-12. February 1984.

Hannay, M. P.

<u>C. S. Lewis</u>. New York: Ungar, 1981. 299 p.

"Arthurian and cosmic myth in <u>That Hideous Strength</u>," <u>Mythlore</u> 2(2):7-9. Autumn 1970.

"C. S. Lewis collection at Wheaton College," <u>Mythlore</u> 2(4):20. Winter 1972.

"C. S. Lewis' theory of mythology," <u>Mythlore</u> 1(1):14-24. January 1969.

"Head versus heart in Dorothy L. Sayers' <u>Gandy Night</u>," <u>Mythlore</u> 6(3):33-37. Summer 1979.

"Mythology of <u>Out of the Silent Planet</u>," <u>Mythlore</u> 1(4):11-14. October 1969.

"Orual: the search for justice," <u>Mythlore</u> 2(3):5-6. Winter 1971.

"Surprised by joy: C. S. Lewis' changing attitudes toward women," <u>Mythlore</u> 4(1):15-20. September 1976.

Hannigan, J. A.

"Youth and Future Studies: Science Fiction
Visual Images as a Source for Change," in:
<u>Frontiers of Library Service for Youth</u> New
York: Columbia University, School of Library
Service, 1979. pp. 43-56.

Hansen, A. J.

"Celebration of solipsism: a new trend in
American fiction, The," <u>Modern Fiction
Studies</u> 19(1):5-15. Spring 1973.

"Meeting of Parallel Lines, The: Science,
Fiction, and Science Fiction," in: Slusser,
George E., ed. <u>Bridges to Fantasy</u>.
Carbondale: Southern Illinois University Press,
1982. pp. 51-58.

Hansen, Terry

"Myth-Adventure in Leigh Brackett's
'Enchantress of Venus'," <u>Extrapolation</u>
23(1): 77-82. Spring 1982.

"Silent Evolution: Speculative Verse," by
Robert Frazier and Terry Hansen. <u>PSFQ</u> 5:
10-13. Spring 1981.

Hansen, Zia

<u>American Films of the 1970s: "Star Wars"
(1977) ("Network," 1976), ("Annie Hall," 1977),
("Coming Home," 1978)</u>. Ph. D. Dissertation,
Oklahoma State University, 1980. 137 p.

Hanu, Lucian

"Eurocon-80: An Interview With Ion Hobana,"
<u>Romanian Review</u> No. 1: 128-131. 1981.

Hanus, R. A.

"<u>Slaughterhouse-Five</u>: Kurt Vonnegut's idea of
theatre," <u>Illinois English Bulletin</u> 72(2):
5-10. Winter 1985. (ERIC ED 252 860)

Hanzo, T. A.

"Past of Science Fiction," in: Slusser,
George E., ed. <u>Bridges to Science Fiction</u>.
Carbondale: Southern Illinois University Press,
1980. pp. 131-146.

Harbottle, Philip

<u>Multi-Man, The: A Biographic and
Bibliographic Study of John Russell Fearn
(1908-60)</u>. Wallsend, Northumberland, England:
by the author, 1968. 69 p.

Hardesty, W. H., III

"<u>After Many a Summer Dies the Swan</u>," in:
Magill, Frank N., ed. <u>Survey of Science
Fiction Literature</u>, Vol. 1. Englewood Cliffs,
NJ: Salem Press, 1979. pp. 33-37.

"<u>Birthgrave Trilogy, The</u>," in: Magill,
Frank N., ed. <u>Survey of Modern Fantasy
Literature</u>, Vol 1. Englewood Cliffs, NJ:
Salem Press, Inc., 1983. pp. 116-121.

"<u>Collected Ghost Stories of M. R. James,
The</u>," in: Magill, Frank N., ed. <u>Survey of
Modern Fantasy Literature</u>, Vol 1. Englewood
Cliffs, NJ: Salem Press, Inc., 1983. pp.
289-293.

"<u>Gods Themselves, The</u>," in: Magill, Frank
N., ed. <u>Survey of Science Fiction
Literature</u>, Vol. 2. Englewood Cliffs, NJ:
Salem Press, 1979. pp. 909-914.

"<u>Moon Is Hell, The</u>," in: Magill, Frank N.,
ed. <u>Survey of Science Fiction Literature</u>,
Vol. 3. Englewood Cliffs, NJ: Salem Press,
1979. pp. 1444-1448.

"<u>Rendezvous with Rama</u>," in: Magill, Frank
N., ed. <u>Survey of Science Fiction
Literature</u>, Vol. 4. Englewood Cliffs, NJ:
Salem Press, 1979. pp. 1759-1763.

"<u>Volkhavaar</u>," in: Magill, Frank N., ed.
<u>Survey of Modern Fantasy Literature</u>, Vol 4.
Englewood Cliffs, NJ: Salem Press, Inc., 1983.
pp. 2036-2038.

"<u>You Shall Know Them</u>," in: Magill, Frank
N., ed. <u>Survey of Science Fiction
Literature</u>, Vol. 5. Englewood Cliffs, NJ:
Salem Press, 1979. pp. 2529-2533.

"Nomad of the timestreams: Moorcock's Oswald
Bastable, A," in: Remington, T. J., ed.
<u>Selected Proceedings of the 1978 SFRA National
Conference</u>. Cedar Falls, Iowa: Univ. of
Northern Iowa, 1979. pp. 105-113.

"Programmed Utopia of R. A. Lafferty's <u>Past
Master</u>," in: Erlich, Richard D., ed.
<u>Clockwork Worlds</u>. Westport, CT: Greenwood,
1983. pp. 105-113.

"Science Fiction and the American Dream,"
<u>Essays in Arts and Humanities</u> 9(2): 203-215.
August 1980.

"Semiotics, Space Opera, and Babel-17,"
<u>Mosaic</u> 13(3/4): 63-69. Spring/Summer 1980.

Hardin, N. S.

"Doris Lessing and the Sufi way,"
<u>Contemporary Literature</u> 14(4):565-581.
Autumn 1973.

"Sufi teaching story and Doris Lessing,"
<u>Twentieth Century Literature</u> 23(3):314-326.
October 1977.

Hardin, Nils

"Science-Fiction Fanzines: the Time Binders,"
in: Cowart, David ed. Twentieth Century
American Science Fiction Writers. Detroit:
Gale, 1981. v. 2, pp. 280-294.

Harding, Lee

Altered I, The: Ursula K. Le Guin's Science
Fiction Writing Workshop. New York: Berkley,
1978. 181 p. (Originally published by
Norstrilia Press, 1976)

"Aliens in the Spinifex: Australian SF writers
of the sixties," by Lee Harding and John
Bangsund. Australian Science Fiction Review
No. 3:3-10. September 1966.

"Cheerfulness keeps breaking in," by Bruce
Gillespie and Lee Harding. SF Commentary
54:12-21. Reprinted from Yggdrasil No. 3.
1978.

"Cosmological eye: the new SF," Australian
Science Fiction Review No. 13:11-13.
December 1967.

Hardy, D. A.

"Painting: impact of astronautics and science
fiction on my work," Leonardo 9(2):95-98.
1976. Letter: Leonardo 9(3):262. 1976.
Reply: Leonardo 9(3):262. 1976.

Hardy, David

"Art and artists: the startling and
provocative skills of the artists," in:
Holdstock, Robert, ed. Encyclopedia of
Science Fiction. London: Octopus, 1978. pp.
122-141.

Hardy, Gene

"More Than a Magic Ring," in: Street,
Douglas, ed. Children's Novels and the
Movies. New York: Ungar, 1983. pp. 131-140.

Hardy, Phil

Science Fiction. New York: Morrow, 1984.
400 p.

Hare, D. E.

In This Land There Be Dragons: Carl G. Jung,
Ursula K. Le Guin, and Narrative Prose
Fantasy. Ph. D. Dissertation, Emory
University, 1982. 231 p.

Harfst, Betsy

"Of myths and polynominoes: mythological
content in Clarke's fiction," in: Olander,
Joseph D. and Martin Harry Greenberg, eds.
Arthur C. Clarke. New York: Taplinger,
1977. pp. 87-120.

Hark, I. R.

"Fantasy Worlds of Peter Beagle, The," in:
Magill, Frank N., ed. Survey of Modern
Fantasy Literature, Vol 2. Englewood Cliffs,
NJ: Salem Press, Inc., 1983. pp. 526-534.

"Revolt of Man, The," in: Magill, Frank N.,
ed. Survey of Modern Fantasy Literature,
Vol 3. Englewood Cliffs, NJ: Salem Press,
Inc., 1983. pp. 1311-1312.

"Science Fiction Films," in: Cowart, David,
ed. Twentieth Century American Science
Fiction Writers. Detroit: Gale Research,
1981. v. 2, pp. 263-270.

"Star Trek and television's moral universe,"
Extrapolation 20(1):20-37. Spring 1979.

"Unity in the composite novel: triadic
patterning in Asimov's The Gods Themselves,"
Science Fiction Studies 6(3):281-286.
November 1979.

Harkavy, Jerry

"Castle Rock monthly puts Stephen King on
map," Chicago Tribune Sec. 5, p. 10. June
27, 1985.

Harlung, Asger

"Om Erwin Neutzsky-Wulffs Oiufaels,"
Proxima No. 19 sect. I:20-22. March 1979.

Harmetz, Aljean

"Conan flexes its muscles," Los Angeles
Herald Examiner. March 17, 1982. in:
NewsBank. Film and Television FTV-115:F4.
1981/1982.

"Empire Video Rights Bought for $12 Million,"
New York Times p. 20. August 30, 1984.

"Handshake Seals Film Deal for Pet Sematary,"
New Orleans Times Picayune Sec. E, p. 12.
July 4, 1984.

"Little Shop of Horrors in Pittsburgh," Los
Angeles Herald Examiner November 7, 1982.
in: Newsbank. Film and Television.
50:B8-10. December 1982.

Harmon, Jim

"Birth of a Galaxy," _Inside and Science Fiction Advertiser_ No. 7: 20-22, 29. January 1955.

Harms, J. M.

"Children's responses to fantasy in literature," _Language Arts_ 52(7):942-946. October 1975.

Harness, C. L.

"What Works For Me: Waiting For Things to Work," _SFWA Bulletin_ 18(1): 14-20. Spring 1984.

Harper, Andrew

Michael Moorcock: A Bibliography, by Andrew Harper and George McAulay. Baltimore: T-K Graphics, 1976. 29 p.

Harper, L. C.

"Dangerous visions of Harlan Ellison: an interview, part II," by L. C. Harper and Edward Bryant. _Bloomsbury Review_ 5(5):17-19,24. February 1985.

"Dangerous visions of Harlan Ellison: an interview," by L. C. Harper and Edward Bryant. _Bloomsbury Review_ 5(4):12-15. January 1985.

Harper, M.

"Utopias you wouldn't like," _Harper_ 210(1259):87-88. April 1955.

Harrigan, Brian

Yesterday's Tomorrows: Past Visions of the American Future, by J. J. Corn and Brian Harrigan. New York: Summit, 1984. 158 p.

Harrington, Curtis

"Ghoulies and ghosties," _Sight and Sound_ 21(4):157-161. April/June 1951. Reprinted, _Quarterly of Film, Radio, & Television_ 7(2):191-202. Winter 1952.

Harris, D. M.

"Confessions of a wage slave," _Science Fiction Review_ 4(1):26-28. February 1975.

Harris, J. P.

"Fugitive From the Empire (review)," by Dan Scapperotti and J. P. Harris. _Cinefantastique_ 11(2):45. Fall 1981.

"Of precocious pigs, singing cabbages, and a little frog named Kermit," _Cinefantastique_ 13(4):25-31. April/May 1983.

"Tales From the Darkside (review)," _Cinefantastique_ 15(3):44,59. July 1985.

Harris, Kathryn

"What will MCA do with all that cash from ET?" _Los Angeles Times_ Sec. 4, pp. 1-2. August 4, 1982.

Harris, Mason

"Science fiction as the dream and nightmare of progress (part one)," _West Coast Review_ 9(4):3-9. April 1975.

"Science fiction as the dream and nightmare of progress (part two)," _West Coast Review_ 10(1):19-26. June 1975.

Harrison, Harry

Great Balls of Fire. London: Pierrot Publishing, 1977. 117 p.

"_Long Afternoon of Earth, The_," in: Magill, Frank N., ed. _Survey of Science Fiction Literature_, Vol. 3. Englewood Cliffs, NJ: Salem Press, 1979. pp. 1235-1237.

"Beginning of the affair, The," in: Aldiss, Brian W. and Harry Harrison, eds. _Hell's Cartographers: Some Personal Histories of Science Fiction Writers_. London: Weidenfeld and Nicholson, 1975. pp. 76-95.

"Benford, Wolfe, Silverberg. . . & literature," _Fantasy Review_ 8(7): 33. July 1985.

"Footnote to the economics of SF," _Australian Science Fiction Review_ No. 12:13-15. October 1967.

"From the easy chair," _Vector_ 63: 22-23. January/February 1973.

"How we work: Harry Harrison," in: Aldiss, Brian W. and Harry Harrison, eds. _Hell's Cartographers: Some Personal Histories of Science Fiction Writers_. London: Weidenfeld and Nicholson, 1975. pp. 220-224.

"Inventing New Worlds I," in: Malik, Rex, ed. _Future Imperfect_. London: Pinter, 1980. pp. 73-80.

"John W. Campbell," _Locus_ No. 90:9. July 12, 1971.

Harrison, Harry (Continued)

"Life at 12 1/2 to one," Science Fiction Times No. 278:3-4. September 1957.

"Machine as hero: the vital and exotic hardware ingredient," in: Holdstock, Robert, ed. Encyclopedia of Science Fiction. London: Octopus, 1978. pp. 86-103.

"Science fiction: short story and novel," Writer 83(5):16-18. May 1970. also in: Burick, A. S., ed. Writer's Handbook. Boston: Writer, 1972. pp. 468-472.

"Sturgeon remembered," Vector No. 127: 2. August/September 1985.

"Term defined, The," in: McNelly, W. E., ed. Science Fiction the Academic Awakening. Shreveport, LA: CEA, 1974. pp. 37-39.

"Warfare and weaponry," in: Ash, Brian, ed. Visual Encyclopedia of Science Fiction. New York: Harmony, 1977. pp. 100-109.

"We are sitting on our . . . . " SF Horizons 1:39-42. Spring 1964.

"Why Heinlein's Glory Road is a bad, bad book," Vector 25: 6-8. March 1964.

"With a piece of twisted wire," SF Horizons 2:55-63. Winter 1965.

"Worlds beside worlds," in: Nicholls, Peter, ed. Science Fiction at Large. New York: Harper, 1976. pp. 105-114.

Harrison, J. F. C.

"Millennium and Utopia," in: Utopias, ed. by Peter Alexander and Roger Gill. London: Duckworth, 1984. pp. 61-68.

Harrison, M. J.

"Introduction," in: Disch, T. M. 334. Boston: Gregg, 1976. pp. v-xiii.

Harrison, T. P.

"Birds in the moon," Isis 45(4):323-330. December 1954.

Harrod, Elizabeth

"Trees in Tolkien, and What Happened Under Them," Mythlore 11(1): 47-52, 58. Summer 1984.

Harryhausen, Ray

Film Fantasy Scrapbook. 3rd ed., rev. and enlarged. San Diego, CA: Barnes, 1981. 150 p.

Film Fantasy Scrapbook. New York: Barnes, 1974. Second edition, revised, 142 p.

Harsh, D. J.

"Aslan in Filmland: The Animation of Narnia," in: Street, Douglas, ed. Children's Novels and the Movies. New York: Ungar, 1983. pp. 163-170.

Hart, C. W., Jr.

"'Pseudo-science' and the reader's guide," Magazine of Fantasy and Science Fiction 12(3):47-50. March 1957.

Hart, Lyn

"Science fiction," Booklist 46:73-75. November 1, 1949.

Hart, Rose

"Sexism in the Cinema," Common Sense (Bloomington, IN) p. 6. October 16, 1972.

Hartl, John

"Dune," Seattle Times December 2, 1984. in: NewsBank. Film and Television. 66: E13-E14. January 1985.

"Retrospect: The Incredible Shrinking Man," Cinefantastique 4(2):26-29. Summer 1975.

"Sci-Fi Oldies and Oddies Are Featured At X-Po," Seattle Times January 14, 1983. in: NewsBank. Film and Television 78:D13. 1982/1983.

Hartlaub, Geno

"Phantasie und Drogen," Die Neue Rundschau. 83(3):574-584. 1972.

Hartley, M. L.

"Is science fiction subversive," Southwest Review 38(3):244-250. Summer 1953.

Hartmann, Christel

"Literarische Konflikt in der Utopisch phantastischen Literatur, gezeight am Beispiel der Bruder Strugazki," Quarber Merkur 28:48-65. November 1971.

Hartmann, W. K.

"A 'What-If' World Comes to Life in Los Angeles," Smithsonian 12(12): 86-94. March 1982.

Hartt, Jon

"Hack prolific," Inside and Science Fiction Advertiser No. 9: 40-43. May 1955.

Hartt, W. F.

"Godly influences: the theology of J. R. R. Tolkien and C. S. Lewis," Studies in the Literary Imagination 14(2):21-30. Fall 1981.

Hartung, A. E.

"Polite and the Popular, The: different uses of fantasy in two Bluebeard tales," Kansas Quarterly 16(3): 65-84. Summer 1984.

Hartwell, D. G.

Age of Wonders: Exploring the World of Science Fiction. New York: Walker, 1984. 201 p.

"Big boom," Locus No. 168:5-6. December 24, 1974.

"Golden Age of Science Fiction is 12, The," Top of the News 39(1): 39-53. Fall 1982.

"Introduction," in: Compton, D. G. The Steel Crocodile. Boston: Gregg, 1976. pp. v-xiii.

"Introduction," in: Delany, S. R. Empire Star. Boston: Gregg, 1977. pp. v-xiii.

"Introduction," in: Disch, T. M. The Genocides. Boston: Gregg, 1978. pp. v-xv.

"Introduction," in: Shiel, M. P. The Purple Cloud. Boston: Gregg, 1977. pp. v-xviii.

"Introduction," in: Tucker, George. A Voyage to the Moon. Boston: Gregg, 1975. pp. vii-ix.

"Science Fiction for the Book Collector," Washington Post Book World p. 11. August 28, 1983.

"T. W. S. (i.e. thrilling wonder stories) Robert Heinlein has 'time enough for love'," Crawdaddy p. 16. July 1973.

"T. W. S. 32nd world science fiction convention," Crawdaddy p. 20. December 1973.

"T. W. S. a sci-fi round-up: what to look for in the near future," Crawdaddy p. 20. September 1974. (not seen)

"T. W. S. introducing some of the new talents in sci fi," Crawdaddy p. 20. May 1974. (not seen)

"T. W. S. SF dealers," Crawdaddy p. 18. July 1975. (not seen)

"T. W. S. SF in the mainstream, the mainstream in SF current trends," Crawdaddy p. 16. February 1974. (not seen)

"T. W. S. SF in U. S. and in England," Crawdaddy p. 20. October 1973. (not seen)

"T. W. S. what to look for in the Hugo awards in 1974," Crawdaddy p. 18. March 1974.

"T. W. S.: a school's out seminar in science fiction," Crawdaddy p. 20. August 1974.

"Thrilling wonder stories, beyond Star Trek: visit to a fantastic planet," Crawdaddy p. 22. April 1974. (not seen)

Hartwell, David

"Science fiction: into an orbit of its own," Book Collector's Market 2(3):19-20. August 1976.

Harvey, David

Song of Middle Earth, The: J. R. R. Tolkien's Themes, Myths, and Symbols. London: Allen & Unwin, 1985. 143 p.

Harvey, Jon

"Ariel, The Book of Fantasy," in: Tymn, M. B. and Ashley, Mike. Science Fiction, Fantasy, and Weird Fiction Magazines. Westport, CT: Greenwood, 1985. pp. 109-110.

"Copper Toadstool," in: Tymn, M. B. and Ashley, Mike. Science Fiction, Fantasy, and Weird Fiction Magazines. Westport, CT: Greenwood, 1985. pp. 166-167.

"Dark Fantasy," in: Tymn, M. B. and Ashley, Mike. Science Fiction, Fantasy, and Weird Fiction Magazines. Westport, CT: Greenwood, 1985. pp. 179-180.

"Dragonfields," in: Tymn, M. B. and Ashley, Mike. Science Fiction, Fantasy, and Weird Fiction Magazines. Westport, CT: Greenwood, 1985. pp. 189-190.

"Literary Magazine of Fantasy and Terror," by Jon Harvey and Mike Ashley. in: Tymn, M. B. and Ashley, Mike. Science Fiction, Fantasy, and Weird Fiction Magazines. Westport, CT: Greenwood, 1985. pp. 372-374.

"Midnight Sun," in: Tymn, M. B. and Ashley, Mike. Science Fiction, Fantasy, and Weird Fiction Magazines. Westport, CT: Greenwood, 1985. pp. 406-407.

"Phantasy Digest," in: Tymn, M. B. and Ashley, Mike. Science Fiction, Fantasy, and Weird Fiction Magazines. Westport, CT: Greenwood, 1985. pp. 473-474.

Harvey, John (Continued)

"Questar," by Jon Harvey and Mike Ashley. in: Tymn, M. B. and Ashley, Mike. Science Fiction, Fantasy, and Weird Fiction Magazines. Westport, CT: Greenwood, 1985. pp. 485-486.

"Weirdbook," by Jon Harvey and Mike Ashley. in: Tymn, M. B. and Ashley, Mike. Science Fiction, Fantasy, and Weird Fiction Magazines. Westport, CT: Greenwood, 1985. pp. 738-740.

"Whispers," by Jon Harvey and Mike Ashley. in: Tymn, M. B. and Ashley, Mike. Science Fiction, Fantasy, and Weird Fiction Magazines. Westport, CT: Greenwood, 1985. pp. 740-742.

Harvey, Steve

"Contest is Out of this World," Los Angeles Times p. B1. November 25, 1978.

Harwood, John

ERB-dom: A Guide to Issues No. 1-25, by J. F. Roy, John Harwood, and Camille Cazedessus, Jr. Evergreen, CO: Opar Press, 1964. 23 p.

Literature of Burroughsiana, The: A Listing of Magazine Articles, Book Commentaries, News Items, and Related Items Concerning the Life and/or Works of Edgar Rice Burroughs. Baton Rouge, Louisiana: Camille Cazedessus, 1963. 105 p.

"Literature of Burroughsania," Barsoomian No. 7:5-11. January/April 1954.

Haselkorn, M. P.

"Interview with Ursula K. Le Guin," Science Fiction Review (Portland) No. 25: 72-74. May 1978.

Haskell, J. D., Jr.

"Addendum to Pieratt and Klinkowitz: Kurt Vonnegut, Jr.," Papers of the Bibliographic Society of America 70:122. 1976.

Hassan, Ihab

"Beyong arcadians and technophiles: new convergences in culture?" The Massachusetts Review 17(1):7-18. Spring 1976.

"Fiction and future: an extravaganza for voice and tape," in: Liberations. Middletown, Connecticut: Wesleyan University Press, 1971. pp. 193-194. (Reprinted in Paracriticisms. Urbana: University of Illinois Press, 1975.)

"Toward a transhumanized earth: imagination, science and the future," Georgia Review 32(4):777-807. Winter 1978.

Hasse, D. P.

"Romantic theory of the fantastic," in: Magill, Frank N., ed. Survey of Modern Fantasy Literature, Vol 5. Englewood Cliffs, NJ: Salem Press, Inc., 1983. pp. 2247-2258.

Hasselblatt, Dieter

Gruene Maennchen vom Mars: science fiction fur leser und macher. Dusseldorf: Droste, 1974. 234 p.

"Dieter Hasselblatt im gesprach mit Stanislaw Lem," Quarber Merkur 48:9-25. March 1978.

"Kien happy-end am daisy-day: analysen zum science fiction market," in: Weigand, Jorg, ed. Die Triviale Phantasie. Bonn: Asgard, 1976. pp. 103-122.

"Reflections from West Germany on the science fiction market," Science Fiction Studies 4(3):256-263. November 1977.

"Schielen, Lugen, Stehlen," in: Ermert, Karl, ed. Neugier oder Flucht? Stuttgart: Klett, 1980. pp. 43-52.

"Science fiction ist eine Ware," Akzente 4(1):86-94. 1974.

"Science Fiction Literatur und ihre Stellig in der heutigen Diskussion," Universitas 35:1167-1172. 1980.

"Signale aus dem Dunkelfeld," in: Rottersteiner, Franz, ed. Polaris 6. Frankfurt-am-Main: Suhrkamp, 1982. pp. 270-286.

"Stanislaw Lems phantastisches kunstfigurenkabinett," Quarber Merkur 43:59-64. May 1976.

Hassler, D. M.

Death and the Serpent: Immortality in Science Fiction and Fantasy, by C. B. Yoke and D. M. Hassler. Westport, CT: Greenwood, 1985. 235 p.

Comic Tones in Science Fiction: The Art of Compromise with Nature. Westport, CT: Greenwood, 1982. 143 p.

Hal Clement. Mercer Island, WA: Starmont, 1982. 64 p. (Starmont Reader's Guide, 11)

Patterns of the Fantastic II. Mercer Island, WA: Starmont, 1984. 93 p.

Patterns of the Fantastic: Academic Programming at Chicon IV, ed. by Donald Hassler. Mercer Island, WA: Starmont, 1983. 105 p.

Walden Two," in: Magill, Frank N., ed. Survey of Science Fiction Literature, Vol. 5. Englewood Cliffs, NJ: Salem Press, 1979. pp. 2392-2395.

Author Entries

Hassler, D. M. (Continued)

"Giles Goat-Boy: Or, The Revised New Syllabus," in: Magill, Frank N., ed. Survey of Modern Fantasy Literature, Vol 2. Englewood Cliffs, NJ: Salem Press, Inc., 1983. pp. 616-618.

"Inheritors, The," in: Magill, Frank N., ed. Survey of Science Fiction Literature, Vol. 3. Englewood Cliffs, NJ: Salem Press, 1979. pp. 1036-1039.

"Lord of the Flies," in: Magill, Frank N., ed. Survey of Science Fiction Literature, Vol. 3. Englewood Cliffs, NJ: Salem Press, 1979. pp. 1257-1260.

"Omni," in: Tymn, M. B. and Ashley, Mike. Science Fiction, Fantasy, and Weird Fiction Magazines. Westport, CT: Greenwood, 1985. pp. 444-448.

"Asimov's golden age: the ordering of an art," in: Olander, Joseph D. and Martin Harry Greenberg, eds. Isaac Asimov. New York: Taplinger, 1977. pp. 111-119.

"Eighteenth century and science fiction, The: a symbiosis?" Science Fiction: A Review of Speculative Literature 2(1):75-82. May 1979.

"Erasmus Darwin and enlightenment origins of science fiction," Studies on Voltaire and the Eighteenth Century No. 153:1045-1056. 1976.

"Hard Science Fiction of Hal Clement," Gamut 3: 46-54. Spring-Summer 1981.

"Images for an ethos, images for change and style," Extrapolation 20(2):176-188. Summer 1979.

"Introduction," in: Yoke, C. B. and Hassler, D. M., eds. Death and the Serpent. Westport, CT: Greenwood, 1985. pp. 3-7.

"Introduction: Dangerous Tastes: Science and Fiction," in: Hassler, Donald M., ed. Patterns of the Fantastic II. Mercer Island, WA: Starmont, 1985. pp. 1-3.

"Irony in Hal Clement's World Building," in: Wolfe, Gary, ed. Science Fiction Dialogues. Chicago: Academy Chicago, 1982. pp. 85-98.

"Muted Use of Irony in Hard Science Fiction: Hal Clement's Needle," Ball State University Forum 23(1): 57-60. Winter 1982.

"Science at the Crossroads in Hal Clement's The Nitrogen Fix," in: Staicar, Tom, ed. Critical Encounters II. New York: Ungar, 1982. pp. 60-72.

"Short Fiction of Theodore Sturgeon, The," in: Magill, Frank N., ed. Survey of Science Fiction Literature, Vol. 5. Englewood Cliffs, NJ: Salem Press, 1979. pp. 2056-2058.

"What the Machine Teaches: Walter Tevis's Mockingbird," in: Dunn, Thomas P., ed. The Mechanical God. Westport: Greenwood, 1982. pp. 75-82.

Hasson, Judi

"Unifying Interest in Science Fiction, A," Washington Post p. C4. December 29, 1974.

Hasty, Mara

"How the Isle of Ransom reflects an actual Icelandic setting," Mythlore 5(2): 44. Autumn 1978.

Hatch, Robert

"Lucky Jim and the Martians," Nation 190(12):257-258. March 19, 1960. (Book review)

Hatcher, Jack

"Fuel for the future," in: Greenberg, M. H., ed. Coming Attractions. New York: Gnome, 1957. pp. 206-231.

Hatfield, Martin

"Roger Elwood interview," by Martin Hatfield, Christopher Fowler, and Ian Thomson. Vector 79: 10-14. January/February 1977.

Hathorne, Harry

"20,000 Leagues Under the Sea: the filming of Jules Verne's classic science fiction novel," by Joel Frazier and Harry Hathorne. Cinefantastique 14(3):32-53. May 1984.

Hatlen, Burton

"Mad Dog and Maine, The," In: Winter, Douglas E. Shadowings: The Reader's Guide to Horror Fiction 1981-1982. Mercer Island, WA: Starmont, 1983. pp. 33-37.

Haunert, R. M.

Mythic Female Heroes in the High Fantasy Novels of Patricia McKillip. Ph. D. Dissertation, Bowling Green State University, 1983. 260 p. (DAI 44: 1085A)

Hauptfuhrer, Fred

"Wizardry of Frank Oz: his 'empire' began pre-Yoda with Miss Piggy, The," by Fred Hauptfuhrer and Karne Peterson. People Weekly 13(23):38-41. June 9, 1980.

Haus, I. N.

"Marchen, Das," in: Magill, Frank N., ed. Survey of Modern Fantasy Literature, Vol 2. Englewood Cliffs, NJ: Salem Press, Inc., 1983. pp. 973-975.

Hauser, Frank

"Science fiction films," in: Whitebait, William, ed. International Film Annual. New York: Doubleday, 1958. pp. 87-90.

Hausermann, H. W.

"Weltraumliteratur. Science Fiction, eine neue Literaturgattung," in: Hausermann, H. W. Moderne amerikanische Literatur. Kritische Aufzeichnungen. Bern-Munchen: Francke, 1965.

Hawthorne, Julian

"Introduction," in: Bradshaw, William R. The Goddess of Atvatabar. New York: Douthitt, 1892. pp. 9-12.

Hay, George

Disappearing Future, The: A Symposium of Speculation. London: Panther, 1970. 158 p.

"For the record: what the Science Fiction Foundation ought to be about," Foundation 5:63-66. January 1974.

"Science fiction: mankind's early warning system," Futures 5(3):491-494. October 1973.

"Science of fiction, A?" Foundation 3:35-43. March 1973.

"Sleep No More," Foundation 24: 68-76. February 1982.

Hay, Sheridan

"Interview With David Ireland," Science Fiction: A Review of Speculative Literature 3(3): 109-116. September 1981.

Hayakawa, S. I.

"From science fiction to fiction science (review of Dianetics, by L. Ron Hubbard)," Etc., a Review of General Semantics 8:280-293. Summer 1951. (Book review)

Hayes, N. L.

"Mooting of the minds: why fans enjoy Tolkien," by N. L. Hayes, Jonathan Langford and S. C. Walker. Leading Edge No. 9:78-84. Winter 1985.

Hayes, Noreen

"Of Hobbits: The Lord of the Rings," Critique 9(2):58-66. 1967.

Hayford, Jack

"Subtle Strike of the Empire, The," Christian Life 42(6): 34-36. October 1980.

Haykin, Michael

"Note on Charles Williams' The Place of the Lion," Mythlore 5(2): 37-38. Autumn 1978.

Hayles, N. B.

"Androgyny, ambivalence, and assimilation in The Left Hand of Darkness," in: Olander, Joseph D. and Martin Harry Greenberg, eds. Ursula K. Le Guin. New York: Taplinger, 1979. pp. 97-115.

"Imperfect Art: Competing Patterns in More Than Human," Extrapolation 22(1): 13-24. Spring 1981.

"Metaphysics and Metafiction in The Man in the High Castle," in: Greenberg, Martin H., ed. Philip K. Dick. New York: Taplinger, 1982. pp. 53-71.

Hayman, David

"Jolly mix: notes on techniques, style and decorum in Slaughterhouse Five, The," Summary 1(2):44-50. 1971.

Haynes, Jack

"Eros in That Hideous Strength," CSL: The Bulletin of the New York C. S. Lewis Society 5(6):2-4. April 1974.

Haynes, R. D.

H. G. Wells: Discoverer of the Future. The Influence of Science on His Thought. New York: New York University Press, 1980. 238 p.

Haynes, Renee

"Utopia: SF: doomsday," Contemporary Review 230:201-205. April 1977.

Hazelton, Dick

"Clockwork Orange," Outlaw (St. Louis, MO) p. 6-7. March 10, 1972.

Heald, Tim

Making of Space: 1999. New York: Ballantine, 1976. 259 p.

Healy, Michael

"Kelly: Mr. Nice Guy," Denver Post Sec. F, p. 1, 13. June 10, 1984.

"Shatner: New Enthusiasm," Denver Post Sec. F, p. 1, 13. June 10, 1984.

Heard, Colin

"Hammering the box office," Films and Filming 15(9):17-19. June 1969.

Heard, Gerald

"Science fiction, morals and religion," in: Bretnor, Reginald, ed. Science Fiction: Its Meaning and Its Future. New York: Coward McCann, 1953. Reprinted, Chicago: Advent, 1979. pp. 243-264.

Heartland, Harold

"Science fiction," Antiques Journal 31(10):36-37,56. October 1976.

Heartman, C. F.

Bibliography of First Printings of the Writings of Edgar Allan Poe, by C. F. Heartman and J. R. Canney. Hattiesburg, Mississippi: Book Farm, 1943. Revised edition, 294 p.

Hedegaard, Erik

"Stephen King," Rolling Stone 367: 52-57. April 15, 1982.

Heffelfinger, Charles

"To the Devil: A Daughter," in: Magill, Frank N., ed. Survey of Modern Fantasy Literature, Vol 4. Englewood Cliffs, NJ: Salem Press, Inc., 1983. pp. 1954-1957.

Heffeman, Harold

"Vonnegut likes a change of scenery," Star-Ledger (Trenton, New Jersey) p. 26. June 8, 1971.

Heidtmann, Horst

Utopisch-phantastische Literatur in der DDR: Untersuchungen zur Entwicklung eines unterhaltungsliterarischen Genres von 1945-1979. Munich: Fink, 1982. 280 p.

"Survey of science fiction in the German Democratic Republic, A," Science Fiction Studies 6(1):92-99. March 1979.

"Triebwerke statt Triebleben: Ueber Liebe und Sexualitaet in der DDR Science Fiction," Science Fiction Times (Germany) 25(9):5-14. September 1983.

"Triebwerke statt Triebleben: ueber Liebe und Sexualitaet in der DDR-Science-Fiction," Canadian-American Slavic Studies 18(1/2): 124-141. Spring/Summer 1984.

Hein, Rolland

Harmony Within, The: the Spiritual Vision of George MacDonald. Grand Rapids: Chrisitan University Press/Eerdmans, 1982. 163 p.

Heinen, Edward

"Big Brother Not Needed," English Journal 72(6): 42-43. October 1983.

Heinlein, R. A.

"Baedeker of the solar system," Saturday Review of Literature 32(52):9-10. December 24, 1949. (Book review)

"Making of Destination Moon, The," Starlog 6:19-24,54,56. 1977.

"On the writing of speculative fiction," in: Knight, Damon, ed. Turning Points: Essays in the Art of Science Fiction. New York: Harper, 1977. pp. 199-204.

"Pandora's box," in: Knight, Damon, ed. Turning Points: Essays in the Art of Science Fiction. New York: Harper, 1977. pp. 238-258.

"Ray guns and rocket ships," School Library Association of California Bulletin 24:11-15. November 1952. also in : Library Journal 78(13):1188-1191. July 1953.

"Science fiction futures; keynote address," SFWA Bulletin 14(3):5-6. Fall 1979.

"Science fiction," in: Rejser i tid og rum. En Bog om science fiction, ed. by Tage La Cour. Copenhagen: Stig Verdelkaer, 1973.

"Science fiction: its nature, faults and virtues," in: Davenport, Basil, ed. The Science Fiction Novel. Chicago: Advent, 1964. pp. 17-63. also in: Knight, Damon. Turning Points. NY: Harper, 1977. pp. 3-28.

"Shooting Destination Moon," in: Johnson, William, ed. Focus on the Science Fiction Film. Englewood Cliffs, NJ: Prentice Hall, 1972. pp. 52-65.

Heinlein, R. A. (Continued)

"Theodore Sturgeon: An Appreciation, 2," Locus 18(6): 50. June 1985.

"To read SF is to read Simak," Algol 14(3):11. Summer/Fall 1977.

"Where to: life in 2000 A. D.," Galaxy 3(5):13-22. February 1952.

Heins, E. L.

"Second look: 'The Sherwood Ring'," Horn Book 51(6):613. December 1975.

Heins, H. H.

Golden Anniversary Bibliography of Edgar Rice Burroughs. Albany, New York: N. p., 1962. 122 p.

Golden Anniversary Bibliography of Edgar Rice Burroughs. West Kingston, Rhode Island: Donald M. Grant, 1964. 418 p.

"Golden anniversary bibliography of Edgar Rice Burroughs, official supplement no. 1: the continuity problem," ERB-dom No. 11:12-13. August 1964.

"Golden anniversary bibliography of Edgar Rice Burroughs, official supplement no. 2," ERB-dom No. 12:7. January 1965.

"Golden anniversary bibliography of Edgar Rice Burroughs, official supplement no. 3" ERB-dom No. 13:10. 1965. (not seen)

"Golden anniversary bibliography of Edgar Rice Burroughs, official supplement no. 4," ERB-dom No. 14:16. 1965. (not seen)

"Golden anniversary bibliography of Edgar Rice Burroughs, official supplement no. 5," ERB-dom No. 15:15. February 1966.

"Golden anniversary bibliography of Edgar Rice Burroughs, official supplement no. 6," ERB-dom No. 17:10. 1966. (not seen)

"Golden anniversary bibliography of Edgar Rice Burroughs, official supplement no. 7," ERB-dom No. 18:6. August 1966.

"Golden anniversary bibliography of Edgar Rice Burroughs, official supplement no. 8," ERB-dom No. 19:21. December 1966.

Heintz, B. L.

Tomorrow, and Tomorrow, and Tomorrow. New York: Holt, 1974. 619 p.

Heisig, J. W.

"Bruno Bettelheim and the fairy tales," Children's Literature 6:93-114. 1977.

Heissenbuttel, H.

"Parabel oder die Lust am Alptraum? Prototypen der Science Fiction Literatur," Universitas: Zeitschrift fur Wissenschaft, Kunst und Literatur. 27(6):643-646. 1972.

Helbig, A. K.

"Madeleine L'Engle," in: Mainiero, Lina, ed. American Women Writers. New York: Ungar, 1982. v. 2, pp. 548-550.

Held, George

"Men on the moon: American novelists explore lunar space," The Michigan Quarterly Review 18(2):318-342. Spring 1979.

Heldreth, L. G.

"'Love is the Plan, the Plan is Death': The Feminism and Fatalism of James Tiptree, Jr.," Extrapolation 23(1): 22-30. Spring 1982.

"Clockwork Reels: Mechanized Environments in Science Fiction Films," in: Erlich, Richard D., ed. Clockwork Worlds. Westport, CT: Greenwood, 1983. pp. 213-261.

"Commentary: Ray Harryhausen," Fantasy Review 8(12): 13-14. December 1985.

"In Search of the Ultimate Weapon: The Fighting Machine in Science Fiction Novels and Films," in: Dunn, Thomas P., ed. The Mechanical God. Westport: Greenwood, 1982. pp. 129-152.

"Ultimate horror, the: the dead child in Stephen King's stories and novels, The," in: Schweitzer, Darrell, ed. Discovering Stephen King. Mercer Island: Starmont, 1985. pp. 141-152.

Heldreth, L. M.

"Darkover Novels, The," in: Magill, Frank N., ed. Survey of Modern Fantasy Literature, Vol 1. Englewood Cliffs, NJ: Salem Press, Inc., 1983. pp. 341-346.

Heller, Leonid

De la science-fiction sovietique: par dela le dogme, un univers. Lausanne: L'Age l'Homme, 1979. 296 p.

Historie de la science fiction sovietique. Lausanne: l'Age d'Homme, 1979. 350 p.

Heller, Leonid (Continued)

Science Fiction Sovietique, La. Paris: Presses Pocket, 1983. 317 p.

Hellin, F. P.

"Der Plan des Josef Popper-Lynkeus. Part 1," by F. P. Hellin and Robert Plank. Quarber Merkur 39:14-39. January 1975.

"Der Plan des Josef Popper-Lynkeus. Part 2," by F. P. Hellin and Robert Plank. Quarber Merkur 40:3-26. March 1975.

Hellman, Christian

"Day After," Science Fiction Times (Germany) 26(4):19. April 1984.

"Flucht in Fabelwelten: Eskapistisches Kino Zwischen Mythen und Marchen, part 2," Science Fiction Times (Germany) 26(11):9-14. November 1984.

"Flucht in Fabelwelten: Eskapistisches Kino Zwischen Mythen und Marchen, part 1," Science Fiction Times (Germany) 26(10):5-10. October 1984.

Hellmann, Christian

"Super," Science Fiction Times (Germany) 26(7):18-19. July 1984.

Helms, Philip

"Evolution of Tolkien fandom, The," in: Becker, Alida, ed. The Tolkien Scrapbook. New York: Grossett & Dunlap, 1978. pp. 104-109.

Helms, Randel

Tolkien and the Silmarils. Boston: Houghton, 1981. 104 p.

Tolkien's World. Boston: Houghton Mifflin, 1974. 167 p.

"All tales need not come true," Studies in the Literary Imagination 14(2):31-46. Fall 1981.

Helson, Ravenna

"Creative spectrum of authors of fantasy, The," Journal of Psychology 45:310-326. 1977.

"Experiences of authors in writing fantasy: two relationships between creative process and product," Altered States of Consciousness 3(3):235-238. 1977-1978.

"Heroic, comic, and tender: patterns of literary fantasy and their authors," Journal of Personality 41(2):163-184. June 1973.

"Imaginative process in children's literature: a quantitative approach, The," Poetics 7(2):135-153. June 1978.

"Sex-specific patterns in creative literary fantasy," Journal of Personality 38(3):344-363. September 1970.

Helton, H. P.

Use of Science Fiction as a Stimulus to a Guided Reading Program in High School. Masters Thesis, University of Southern California, 1956. 67 p.

Hemenway, L. R.

"Science fiction primer for teachers," Journal of Reading 19(4):337. 1976. (Book review)

Hemmings, J. D.

"Convention Index,", in: Hopkins, Harry A., ed. Fandom Directory 1981. Langley AFB, Virginia: Fandom Computer Services, 1981. pp. 66 95.

"Fanzine Index," in: Hopkins, Harry A., ed. Fandom Directory 1980. Langley AFB, Virginia: Fandom Computer Services, 1980. pp. 12-27.

"Fanzine Index," in: Hopkins, Mariane S., ed. Fandom Directory 1982. Newport News, VA: Fandom Computer Services, 1982. pp. 26-46.

Henderson, C. J.

"Buck Rogers: the once and future king of space," Questar 1(4):60-61. August 1979.

"Lord of the Rings," Questar 1(3):32-34,62. March 1979.

"Marvel's leap to television," Questar 1(2):38-39. Summer 1978.

"SF cinema," Questar 1(2):7-9. Summer 1978.

"Star Blazers: a Japanese Import with Quality," Questar 3(4): 60-61, 74. June 1981.

"Starlog Interview: Fritz Leiber," Starlog 83: 54-58, 63. June 1984.

"Superman: the legend, the movie, the magic," by C. J. Henderson and Kevin Hyde. Questar 1(3):11-17,39. March 1979.

"Walter Koenig on Star Trek," Questar 2(2):59. February 1980.

Henderson, Chris

"Castles," Starlog 88: 18-20. November 1984.

"One Hundred Most Important People in Science Fiction/Fantasy: Anne McCaffrey," Starlog No. 100: 22. November 1985.

"One Hundred Most Important People in Science Fiction/Fantasy: Donald A. Wollheim," Starlog No. 100: 16-17. November 1985.

"One Hundred Most Important People in Science Fiction/Fantasy: Edgar Rice Burroughs," Starlog No. 100: 41, 44. November 1985.

"One Hundred Most Important People in Science Fiction/Fantasy: Frank Frazetta," Starlog No. 100: 82-83. November 1985.

"One Hundred Most Important People in Science Fiction/Fantasy: Frank Herbert," Starlog No. 100: 32. November 1985.

"One Hundred Most Important People in Science Fiction/Fantasy: Frank Kelly Freas," Starlog No. 100: 75. November 1985.

"One Hundred Most Important People in Science Fiction/Fantasy: Frederik Pohl," Starlog No. 100: 83. November 1985.

"One Hundred Most Important People in Science Fiction/Fantasy: Fritz Leiber," Starlog No. 100: 15. November 1985.

"One Hundred Most Important People in Science Fiction/Fantasy: Harry Harrison," Starlog No. 100: 15. November 1985.

"One Hundred Most Important People in Science Fiction/Fantasy: Ian Ballantine," Starlog No. 100: 17. November 1985.

"One Hundred Most Important People in Science Fiction/Fantasy: Philip K. Dick," Starlog No. 100: 45, 52. November 1985.

"One Hundred Most Important People in Science Fiction/Fantasy: Robert E. Howard," Starlog No. 100: 82. November 1985.

"One Hundred Most Important People in Science Fiction/Fantasy: Terry Carr," Starlog No. 100: 30-31. November 1985.

"One Hundred Most Important People in Science Fiction/Fantasy: Virgil Finlay," Starlog No. 100: 41. November 1985.

"Science fiction media 1984/85: Television, books, comics," by Robert Greenberger, Chris Henderson, and Carr D'Angelo. Starlog No. 96: 33-37, 92. July 1985.

"Starlog interview: Joe Morton," Starlog No. 90:16-18. January 1985.

Henderson, Scott

"Far out production design for Star Trek: The Motion Picture," American Cinematographer 61(2):138-141,189-191. February 1980.

Hendin, Josephine

"Writer as cult hero, the father as son, The," Harper's 249:82-87. July 1974.

Hendrickson, Dyke

"Threads takes a horrifying look at nuclear war," Boston Herald June 24, 1985. in: NewsBank. Film and Television. 11:E1. July 1985.

Henighan, Tom

"Tarzan and Rima, the myth and the message," Riverside Quarterly 3(4): 256-265. March 1969.

Henkle, Roger

"Wrestling (American style) with Proteus," Novel: a Forum on Fiction 3(3):197-207. Spring 1970.

Hennelly, M. M., Jr.

"The Time Machine: a romance of 'the human heart'," Extrapolation 20(2):154-167. Summer 1979.

"Reader Vivisection in The Island of Dr. Moreau," Essays in Arts and Sciences 9(2): 217-233. August 1980.

"Road and the ring: solid geometry in Tolkien's Middle-Earth," Mythlore 9(3):3-13. Autumn 1982.

Hennesy, Dale

"Visualizing lifestyle 300 years in the future," American Cinematographer 57(6):640-641, 670-673, 686-689. June 1976.

Henning, C. M.

"'Star Wars' and 'Close Encounters'," Theology Today 35(2):202-206. July 1978.

Henry, B.

"Horror on the newsstands," American Mercury 43(172):432-439. April 1938.

Hensley, C. C.

Andre Norton's Science Fiction and Fantasy, 1950-1979.. Ph. D. Dissertation, University of Colorado at Boulder, 1980. 240 p. (DAI 41:3580-A)

Herbert, Frank

Dune: An Interview with Frank Herbert, by Frank Herbert and David Lynch. Stamford, CT: Waldentapes, 1984. 1 cassette, 50 min.

"Dune genesis," Omni 2(10):72-74. July 1980.

"Men on other planets," in: Bretnor, Reginald, ed. The Craft of Science Fiction. New York: Harper, 1976. pp. 121-135.

"Science fiction and a world in crisis," in: Bretnor, Reginald, ed. Science Fiction Today and Tomorrow. New York: Harper, 1974. pp. 96-97.

"Science fiction and you," in: Heintz, Bonnie L., ed. Tomorrow, and Tomorrow, and Tomorrow ... New York: Holt, 1974. pp. 1-8.

Herbert, G. B.

"Tolkien's Tom Bombadil and the platonic ring of Gyges," Extrapolation 26(2): 152-159. Summer 1985.

Herbert, Kathleen

"Owl Service, The, and the Fourth Branch of the Mabinogi," Labrys No. 7: p. 115-122. November 1981.

Herbert, Rosemary

"Brian W. Aldiss: Maverick," Bloomsbury Review 6(3):12,14. February 1986.

Herbert, Wray

"(Real) Secret of NIMH, The," Science News 122(6): 92-93. August 7, 1982.

Hermand, Jost

"Brecht on Utopia," Minnesota Review ns6, 1976. pp. 96-113

Herndon, Ben

"Ellison's Rules," Twilight Zone 5(5): 12A. December 1985.

"New Adventures in the Scream Trade," Twilight Zone 5(5): 6A-7A. December 1985.

"Real Tube Terror," Twilight Zone 5(5): 10A-11A. December 1985.

"Twilight Zone," Cinefantastique 16(1):22-23. March 1986.

Hernig, K. H.

"Fliegende Untertassen, Marsmenschen und Superman. Science Fiction Ausstellung begeistert in Dusseldorf," Artis 20(5):10-14. 1968.

Herrera, Rudy

"Will the real Human beings please stand up!" in: The Future in Peril: 1984 and the Anti-Utopians. College Station: Honors Program, Texas A&M University, [1985]. pp. 46-50.

Herron, Don

Dark Barbarian: The Writings of Robert E. Howard, a Critical Anthology. Westport, CT: Greenwood, 1984. 242 p.

"Carnacki the Ghost-Finder," in: Magill, Frank N., ed. Survey of Modern Fantasy Literature, Vol 1. Englewood Cliffs, NJ: Salem Press, Inc., 1983. pp. 193-196.

"Merlin's Godson and Merlin's Ring," in: Magill, Frank N., ed. Survey of Modern Fantasy Literature, Vol 2. Englewood Cliffs, NJ: Salem Press, Inc., 1983. pp. 1015-1020.

"Biggest horror fan of them all, The," in: Schweitzer, Darrell, ed. Discovering Stephen King. Mercer Island: Starmont, 1985. pp. 26-40.

"Dark barbarian," in: Herron, Don, ed. Dark Barbarian: The Writings of Robert E. Howard, a Critical Anthology. Westport, CT: Greenwood, 1984. pp. 149-181.

"Double shadow, The: the influence of Clark Ashton Smith," in: Underwood, Tim, and Miller, Chuck, eds. Jack Vance. New York: Taplinger, 1980. pp. 87-102.

"Horror Springs in the Fiction of Stephen King," in: Underwood, Tim, and Miller, Chuck, eds. Fear Itself. Columbia, PA: Underwood/Miller, 1982. pp. 57-82.

Hersey, H. B.

Pulpwood Editor. Westport, CT: Greenwood, 1974. 301 p.

Hersh, R. E.

"Lemuel Gulliver's Seven Pillars of Wisdom,"
in: Collins, R. A., ed.   Scope of the
Fantastic: Culture, Biography, Themes,
Children's Literature. Westport: Greenwood,
1985. pp. 99-106.

Hertz, B. K.

"Satire and psychosexual fantasy
in...Disraeli's Voyage of Captain Popanilla,"
in: Collins, R. A., ed.   Scope of the
Fantastic: Culture, Biography, Themes,
Children's Literature. Westport: Greenwood,
1985. pp. 79-84.

Hertzler, J. O.

History of Utopian Thought, The. New York:
Macmillan, 1923. 321 p.

Herzberg, Bruce

"Hal Clement," in: Cowart, David, ed.
Twentieth-Century American Science Fiction
Writers, Part 1: A-L. Detroit: Gale, 1981.
pp. 101-105. (Dictionary of Literary
Biography, v. 8)

Herzberg, M.

"Fiction that outstrips science," Senior
Scholastic 61:23T. October 8, 1952.

Herzog, Bert

"Aus wunsch wurde abwehr. Der vorzeichenwechsel
im utopieschen roman der letzen jahrzehnte,"
Schweizer Rundschau 60:1056-1064. 1961.

Herzog, Herta

Invasion From Mars, The: A Study in the
Psychology of Panic. by Hadley Cantril, Hazel
Gaudet and Herta Herzog. Princeton: Princeton
University Press, 1983. 224 p.

Hes, J. A.

Amerikaanse toekomstrverwachtingen in de
science fiction. Amersfoort: Werkgroep 2000,
1966. 33 p.

Hester, R. M.

"Interview: Doug Chaffee," by David Pettus and
R. M. Hester. Parsec No. 1:39-45. June
1982.

Hetzler, L. A.

"Chesterton and the man in the forest,"
Chesterton Review 1(1):11-18. 1974.

"George MacDonald and G. K. Chesterton,"
Durham University Journal 68(new series
37):172-182. 1976.

Heuer, R.

"Utopie als Antiquitat. Das Neueste von morgen
is von gestern, Kritische Anmerkungen zu drei
Science Fiction Serien," Die Welt der
Literatur 17:10- . 1967.

Heung, Marina

"Why E. T. Must Go Home: The New Family in
American Cinema," Journal of Popular Film
and Television 11(2): 79-85. Summer 1983.

Hevesi, Ludwig

"Aus jenen Tagen: Rezensionen alter
phantastischer Romane: Anatole France als
Utopist," Quarber Merkur 24:3-7. September
1970.

Hewitt, Tim

"Cat's Eye," Cinefantastique 15(2):8-11.
May 1985.

"Overdrive," Cinefantastique 16(1):9.
March 1986.

"Stephen King's Cat's Eye," Cinefantastique
15(4):34-39. October 1985.

"Steven King's Silver Bullet,"
Cinefantastique 15(5):4-7. January 1986.

Heyde, Konrad

"Private Science Fiction des Christian Wagner
von Warmbronn," Quarber Merkur 55:58-61.
July 1981.

Heydron, V. A.

"Women under Fire," in: Bretnor, Reginald,
ed. The Future at War: Vol. 2: The Spear of
Mars. New York: Ace, 1980. pp. 229-247.

Hickey, Neil

"Between time and Timbuktu," TV Guide
20(11):24-26. March 11, 1972.

Hicks, G.

"From out of this world: contemporary scene," Saturday Review 49:23-24. August 20, 1966.

Hicks, J. S.

"Joe Haldeman," in: Cowart, David, ed. Twentieth-Century American Science-Fiction Writers, Part 1: A-L. Detroit: Gale, 1981. pp. 198-201. (Dictionary of Literary Biography, v. 8)

"Science Fiction Fandom and Conventions," in: Cowart, David, ed. Twentieth Century American Science Fiction Writers. Detroit: Gale, 1981. v. 2, pp. 273-279.

Hicks, Jack

"Burroughs, William," in: Woodcock, George, ed. 20th Century Fiction. Chicago: St. James, 1985. pp. 120-122.

Hiemstra, M. R.

"Five approaches to the achievement of Clark Ashton Smith, cosmic master artist," Nyctalops No. 7:6-12. August 1972.

Hienger, Jorg

Literarische Zukunftsphantastik. Eine studie uber Science Fiction. Gottingen: Van der Hoek, 1972. 274 p.

"Entertainment and challenge in science fiction," Science Fiction Studies 7(2):166-173. July 1980.

"Uncanny and science fiction, The," Science Fiction Studies 6(2):144-152. July 1979.

Hieronimus, Ekkehard

"Ideologie und Unterhaltung? Literatur uber Science Fiction," Buss 23(2):141-143. 1971.

"Utopie und science fiction", Leserzeitschrift 5:4-11. 1965.

Higgins, D. S.

Private Diaries of Sir H. Rider Haggard 1914-1925, The, ed. by D. S. Higgins. London: Cassell, 1980. 299 p.

Rider Haggard: A Biography. Briarcliff Manor, NY: Stein & Day, 1983. 266 p.

Higgins, J. E.

Beyond Words: Mystical Fancy in Children's Literature. New York: Teacher's College Press, 1970. 112 p.

Higgins, Steve

"Descending on a point of flame: the spaceship in science fiction," Vector 85:13-17. January/February 1978.

Higgs, William

"Some Objections to Mr. Bellamy's Utopia," New Englander 52(ns 16): 231-239. March 1890.

Highet, Gilbert

"From world to world," in: Highet, G. People Places and Books. Oxford, 1953. pp. 130-137.

"Perchance to dream," in: Highet, G. Clerk of Oxenford. Oxford, 1964. pp. 3-10.

Hildebrand, Tim

"Two or three things I know about Kurt Vonnegut's imagination," in: Klinkowitz, Jerome and John Somer, eds. The Vonnegut Statement. New York: Delacorte Press/Seymour Lawrence, 1973. pp. 121-132.

Hildebrand, W. H.

"On three prometheuses: Shelley's two and Mary's one," Serif 11(2):3-11. 1974.

Hill, D. W.

"Science fiction and modern literature: is there a generic difference?" Unpublished paper. No date. (copy in Texas A&M University Science Fiction Research Collection)

Hill, Derek

"Face of horror, The," Sight and Sound 28(1):6-11. Winter 1958-1959.

Hill, Douglas

"Major themes: ideas, attitudes and idioms," in: Holdstock, Robert, ed. Encyclopedia of Science Fiction. London: Octopus, 1978. pp. 28-49.

"Science Fiction for Young People," Writer 97(1): 15-18. January 1984.

Hill, E. D.

"Place of the Future, The: Louis Marin and His Utopiques," <u>Science-Fiction Studies</u> 9(2): 167-180. July 1982.

Hill, Helen

"Corruption of power, The," by Agnes Perkins and Helen Hill. in: Lobdell, Jared, ed. <u>A Tolkien Compass</u>. New York: Ballantine/Del Rey, 1980. pp. 60-72.

Hill, J. M.

"Frankenstein and the physiognomy of desire," <u>American Imago</u> 32:335-358. 1975.

Hill, R.

"Posing the future," <u>Media & Methods</u> 8(7):54-55. March 1972.

"Was ist 'Science Fiction'?" <u>Frankfurter Allgemeine Zeitung</u> Nr. 57. March 7, 1964.

Hillegas, M. R.

<u>Future as Nightmare: H. G. Wells and the Anti-Utopians</u>. New York: Oxford University Press, 1967. 200 p. Reprinted, Carbondale: Southern Illinois University Press, 1974.

<u>Shadows of Imagination: the Fantasies of C. S. Lewis, J. R. R. Tolkien, and Charles Williams</u>. Carbondale: Southern Illinois University Press, 1969. 170 p. Reprinted, 1976.

"Annotated bibliography of Jules Verne's voyages extraordinaires," <u>Extrapolation</u> 3(2):32-47. May 1962.

"Bibliography of secondary materials on Jules Verne, A," <u>Extrapolation</u> 2(1):5-16. December 1960.

"Clarkson collection of science fiction at Harvard, The," <u>Extrapolation</u> 5(1):2-14. December 1963.

"Cosmic pessimism in H. G. Wells' scientific romances," <u>Papers of the Michigan Academy of Science, Arts, and Letters</u> 46:655-663. 1961.

"Course in science fiction: a hope deferred, The," <u>Extrapolation</u> 9(1):18-23. December 1967.

"Draft of the science fiction canon to be proposed at the 1961 MLA conference on science fiction, A," <u>Extrapolation</u> 3(1):26-30. December 1961.

"Dystopian science fiction: new index to the human situation," <u>New Mexico Quarterly</u> 31(3):238-249. Autumn 1961.

"First invasion from Mars, The," <u>Michigan Alumnus Quarterly Review</u> pp. 107-112. February 1960.

"Literary background to science fiction, The," in: Parrinder, Patrick, ed. <u>Science Fiction: A Critical Guide</u>. New York: Longman, 1979. pp. 2-17.

"Martians and mythmakers: 1877-1938," in: Browne, R. B., L. N. Landrum, and W. K. Bottoroff, eds. <u>Challenges in American Culture</u>. Bowling Green, Ohio: Bowling Green Univ. Popular Press, 1970. pp. 150-177.

"Other worlds to conjure," <u>Saturday Review</u> 49(13):33-34. March 26, 1966. (Book reviews)

"Satiric fantasies," <u>Nation</u> 206(4): 120-121. January 22, 1968. (Book review)

"Science fiction and the idea of progress," <u>Extrapolation</u> 1(2):25-28. May 1960.

"Science fiction as cultural phenomenon: a re-evaluation," <u>Extrapolation</u> 4(2):26-33. May 1963. also in: Clareson, T. D., ed. <u>SF: The Other Side of Realism</u>. Bowling Green: Bowling Green Popular Press, 1971. pp. 272-281.

"Science fiction as satire: a selected bibliography," <u>Satire Newsletter</u> 1(1):20-23. Fall 1965.

"Science fiction in the English department," in: Williamson, Jack, ed. <u>Teaching Science Fiction: Education for Tomorrow</u>. Philadelphia: Owlswick, 1980. pp. 97-101.

"Second thoughts on the course in science fiction," in: McNelly, W. E., ed. <u>Science Fiction the Academic Awakening</u>. Shreveport, LA: CEA, 1974. pp. 15-17.

"Victorian 'extraterrestrials'," in: Buckley, J. H., ed. <u>The Worlds of Victorian Fiction</u>. Harvard University Press, 1975. pp. 391-414.

Hillman, Tony

"Hooked," <u>Summary</u> 1(2):60-72. 1971.

Hills, N. L.

"Charles L. Harness: the flowering of melodrama," <u>Extrapolation</u> 19(2):141-148. May 1978.

"Fritz Leiber," in: Cowart, David, ed. <u>Twentieth-Century American Science-Fiction Writers, Part 1: A-L</u>. Detroit: Gale, 1981. pp. 281-290. (Dictionary of Literary Biography, v. 8)

Hilton-Young, Wayland

"Contented Christian, The," <u>Cambridge Journal</u> 5(10):603-612. July 1952.

Hinckley, David

"Jim Henson Creates a Bold New Fantasy World For His Film 'The Dark Crystal'," New York Daily News December 12, 1982. in: NewsBank. Film and Television. 63:C8-9. January 1983.

Hinson, Hal

"Stephen King Moves Beyond Horror," Los Angeles Herald Examiner Aug. 24, 1982. in: Newsbank. Literature 27: E7. 1982/1983.

Hinz, E. J.

"Introduction to the greater trumps, An," English Studies in Canada 1(2):217-229. Summer 1975.

"Life beyond life: Cabell's theory and practice of romance," Genre 10:229-327. 1977.

"Pieta as Icon in The Golden Notebook," by E. J. Hinz and J. J. Teunissen. Contemporary Literature 14(4):457-470. Autumn 1973.

Hipolito, Jane

"Carson of Venus," in: Magill, Frank N., ed. Survey of Science Fiction Literature, Vol. 1. Englewood Cliffs, NJ: Salem Press, 1979. pp. 298-302.

"Dark Is Rising Series, The," in: Magill, Frank N., ed. Survey of Modern Fantasy Literature, Vol 1. Englewood Cliffs, NJ: Salem Press, Inc., 1983. pp. 331-335.

"Flatland: A Romance of Many Dimensions," by Jane Hipolito and R. L. Browne. in: Magill, Frank N., ed. Survey of Science Fiction Literature, Vol. 2. Englewood Cliffs, NJ: Salem Press, 1979. pp. 792-796.

"Islander," in: Magill, Frank N., ed. Survey of Science Fiction Literature, Vol. 3. Englewood Cliffs, NJ: Salem Press, 1979. pp. 1084-1088.

"Norstrilia," in: Magill, Frank N., ed. Survey of Science Fiction Literature, Vol. 4. Englewood Cliffs, NJ: Salem Press, 1979. pp. 1555-1559.

"Princess of Mars, A," in: Magill, Frank N., ed. Survey of Science Fiction Literature, Vol. 4. Englewood Cliffs, NJ: Salem Press, 1979. pp. 1720-1725.

"Stars My Destination, The," in: Magill, Frank N., ed. Survey of Science Fiction Literature, Vol. 5. Englewood Cliffs, NJ: Salem Press, 1979. pp. 2168-2172.

"Flatland and beyond: characterization in science fiction," in: McNelly, W. E., ed. Science Fiction the Academic Awakening. Shreveport, LA: CEA, 1974. pp. 18-20.

"Last and first starship from earth, The," in: Clareson, T. D., ed. SF: The Other Side of Realism. Bowling Green, Ohio: Bowling Green University Popular Press, 1971. pp. 186-192.

"Statement is the self, The: Alfred Bester's science fiction," by Jane Hipolito and W. E. McNelly. in: Tolley, M. J., ed. The Stellar Guage. Carleton, Australia: Norstrilia, 1980. pp. 63-90.

Hirsch, David

"Britain's 'Triffids' To Invade U. S.," by Bill Pearson and David Hirsch. Starlog 56: 15-17, 64. March 1982.

"Commander Straker Speaks! An Interview With Ed Bishop," Starlog 55: 52-54. February 1982.

"Constructing the Miniatures for 'Flash Gordon'" by Bill Pearson and David Hirsch. Starlog 44: 48-51. March 1981.

"Doctor Who Episode Guide, 1982 Season," Starlog 64: 32-33. November 1982.

"Impressions of a Soundtrack-filled Summer," Starlog 64: 34-35, 96. November 1982.

"New Doctor Who," Starlog 62: 40-42, 65. Septeber 1982.

"Return of Doctor Who," Starlog 47: 52-53. June 1981.

"Science Fiction Toys & Games for 81-82," Starlog 48: 62-63. July 1981.

"Shuttles in Space: a Visionary Concept in Fact and on film," Starlog 48: 64-67. July 1981.

Hirsch, G. D.

"Monster Was A Lady, The: On the Psychology of Mary Shelley's Frankenstein," Hartford Studies in Literature 7(2): 116-153. 1975.

Hirsch, Walter

"Image of the scientist in science fiction," Science Newsletter 73:296. May 10, 1958.

"Image of the scientist in science fiction: a content analysis," American Journal of Sociology 63(5):506-512. March 1958.

"Science fiction . . . a study," Scope 13:12. October 1959.

Hitchcock, Chip

"Earthlight Closes Store," Science Fiction Times (Boston) 1(10): 1. 1981.

Hitchens, Gordon

"Breathless eagerness in the audience: historical notes on Dr. Frankenstein and his monster, A," Film Comment 6(1):49-51. Spring 1970.

Hlavaty, A. D.

"Engineer and Me, The," Megavore 11: 3-15. October 1980.

Ho, Tisa

"Childlike Hobbit, The," Mythlore 9(4): 3-9. Winter 1983.

Hobana, Ion

20,000 de pagini in cautarea lui Jules Verne. Bucharest: Editura Univers, 1979.

Douazeci de mii de pagini in cautarea lui Jules Verne. Bucarest: Editura Univers, 1979. 237 p.

Imaginile posibilului. Bucharest: Editura Meridiane, 1968.

Odiseea Martiana Maestrii Anticipatiei. Bucharest: Editura Minerva, 1975.

Viitorul a inceput ieri. Bucharest: Editura Tinerctului, 1966.

Viitorul? Atentie! Bucharest: Editura Tinerctului, 1968.

Virsta de aur a anticipatiei romanesti. Bucharest: Editura Tinerctului, 1969. 359 p.

"Dum o tisici patrech," in: Magill, Frank N., ed. Survey of Science Fiction Literature, Vol. 2. Englewood Cliffs, NJ: Salem Press, 1979. pp. 644-646.

"Futuristik und Phantistik in der rumaenischen Science Fiction," in: Rottensteiner, Franz, ed. Polaris 3. Frankfurt: Insel, 1975. pp. 123-146.

"Man with the Broken Ear, The," in: Magill, Frank N., ed. Survey of Science Fiction Literature, Vol. 3. Englewood Cliffs, NJ: Salem Press, 1979. pp. 1340-1343.

"Orasele Inecate," in: Magill, Frank N., ed. Survey of Science Fiction Literature, Vol. 4. Englewood Cliffs, NJ: Salem Press, 1979. pp. 1613-1616.

"Pe marginea colectiei de literatura stiintifico fantastica," Viata Romineasca 12(4):146-154. April 1959.

"Rumunska literatura fantastyczno-naukowa," in: Kaczmarka, J., ed. Materialy z Miedzynarodowego Spotkania Pisarzy-Tworcow Literatury Fantastyczno-Naukowej. Poznan: Wyndawnictwo Poznanskie, 1974. pp. 31-45.

"Survey of Romanian science fiction, A," Romanian Review 22:46-51. 1968.

"Unbekannte Jules Verne," in: Rottensteiner, Franz, ed. Polaris 4. Suhrkamp, 1978. pp. 42-55. Originally published: "Jules Verne, acest necunoscut," Secolul 20 No. 4. 1975.

Hobbs, Andy

"Hobbsspeak," Focus: An SF Writers' Magazine No. 11: 3-6. 1985.

Hoberman, J.

"They Come From Outer Space," Home Video 2(9): 39-43. September 1981.

Hobson, John

"Pastel City, The," Vector 104: 20. October 1981.

"Punk SF," Vector 101: 17-18. April 1981.

Hoch, D. G.

"Mythic patterns in 2001: A Space Odyssey," Journal of Popular Culture 4(4):961-965. Spring 1971.

Hockett, C. F.

"How to learn Martian," Astounding Science Fiction 55(3):97-106. May 1955.

"How to learn Martian," in: Greenberg, M. H., ed. Coming Attractions. New York: Gnome, 1957. pp. 38-51.

Hodenfield, Chris

"Sky is full of questions: science fiction in Steven Spielberg's suburbia, The (the making of 'Close Encounters of the Third Kind')," Rolling Stone 257:33-37. January 26, 1978.

Hodes, R. M.

"Tarzan phenomenon. Success in overseas market but not in the United States, letter to the editor," Library Journal 92(10):1876. May 15, 1967.

Hodge, J. L.

"Tolkien: formulas of the past," Mythlore 8(3):15-18. Autumn 1981.

Hodgell, Pat

"Night journey motif in twentieth century English fantasy, The," Riverside Quarterly 6(4):272-278. December 1977.

Hodgens, R. M.

"Sleeping beauty and Darko Suvin," Riverside Quarterly 5(3):202-205. August 1972.

Hodgens, Richard

"Brief, tragical history of the science fiction film, A," in: Johnson, William, ed. Focus on the Science Fiction Film. Englewood Cliffs, NJ: Prentice Hall, 1972. pp. 78-90.

"Brief, tragical history of the science fiction film," Film Quarterly 13(2):30-39. Winter 1959.

"Deep World of Hodgson's Nightland, The," Trumpet 12:14-18, 44. Summer 1981.

"Short tragical history of the science fiction film, A," Clareson, T. D., ed. SF: The Other Side of Realism. Bowling Green, Ohio: Bowling Green University Popular Press, 1971. pp. 248-262.

Hodges, Richard

"Notes on Lewis' The Dark Tower," CSL: The Bulletin of the New York C. S. Lewis Society 9:1-8. April 1978.

Hoefner, Harald

"Endgueltige Existenznachweis einer Eigenstaendigen Deutschen SF," Science Fiction Times (Germany) 26(10):11-12. October 1984.

Hoehl, Egbert

"Erfahrungen mit science fiction," Deutsche Rundschau 90:89-94. 1964.

Hoffeld, Laura

"Where magic begins," The Lion and the Unicorn 3(1):4-13. Spring 1979.

Hoffman, Charles

"Conan the Existential," Cromlech 1(1): 4-13. Spring 1985.

"Howard in the Eighties," by Marc A. Cerasini and Charles Hoffman. Cromlech 1(1): 37-42. Spring 1985.

Hoffman, F. W.

"Science Fiction: Reaching for the Stars," in: Hoffman, F. W. Popular Culture and Libraries. s.l.: Library Professional Publications, 1984. pp. 55-66.

Hoffman, Lee

"Essence of Ellison," in: Porter, Andrew, ed. The Book of Ellison. New York: Algol Press, 1978. pp. 11-13.

Hoffman, Rah

"Arcana of Arkham Anburn," Nyctalops No. 7:77-80. August 1972.

Hoffman, Stuart

Index to Unknown and Unknown Worlds by Author and by Title. Black Earth, Wisconsin: Sirius Press, 1955. 34 p.

Hoffman, T. P.

"Theme of Mechanization in Player Piano, The," in: Erlich, Richard D., ed. Clockwork Worlds. Westport, CT: Greenwood, 1983. pp. 125-135.

Hoffmeister, Adolf

"Tudomanyos fantasztikus irodalom: avagy Utikalaus a Labirintushoz. Part 2," SF Tajekoztato p. 17-39. September 1971.

"Tudomanyos fantasztikus irodalom: avagy Utikalauz a Labirintushoz. Part 1," SF Tajekoztato p. 48-54. July 1971.

Hofstede, B. P.

"Tussen utopia en apokalips: Science Fiction als pseudoreligie," Restant (Belgium) 10(2):7-12. Summer 1982.

Hogan, D. J.

"Blue Thunder (review)," <u>Cinefantastique</u> 13(5):59. June/July 1983.

"Body Double (review)," <u>Cinefantastique</u> 15(2):45. May 1985.

"Brainstorm (review)," <u>Cinefantastique</u> 14(3):59-60. May 1984.

"Christine (review)," <u>Cinefantastique</u> 14(3):56. May 1984.

"Creepshow (review)," <u>Cinefantastique</u> 13(4):56. April/May 1983.

"Day After (review)," <u>Cinefantastique</u> 14(3):54. May 1984.

"Dead Zone (review)," <u>Cinefantastique</u> 14(2):51. December 1983/January 1984.

"Endangered Species (review)," <u>Cinefantastique</u> 13(2)/13(3):88,92. November/December 1982.

"ET," <u>Cinefantastique</u> 13(1):51-54. September/October 1982.

"Final Countdown (review)," <u>Cinefantastique</u> 10(3):34. Winter 1980.

"Firestarter," <u>Cinefantastique</u> 14(3):28-31. May 1984.

"Friday the 13th, Part II (review)," <u>Cinefantastique</u> 11(2):48. Fall 1981.

"Happy birthday to me," <u>Cinefantastique</u> 11(3):48. September 1981.

"I Married a Monster From Outer Space (review)," <u>Cinefantastique</u> 3(1):20-23. Spring 1974.

"Jaws 3D," <u>Cinefantastique</u> 13(6)/14(1):56-73. September 1983.

"Kurt Vonnegut's Slapstick," <u>Cinefantastique</u> 13(1):4-9. September/October 1982.

"Making of The Thing," <u>Cinefantastique</u> 13(2)/13(3):48-58,63-74. November/December 1982.

"Night of the Comet (review)," <u>Cinefantastique</u> 15(2):48,54. May 1985.

"Quest for fire (review)," <u>Cinefantastique</u> 12(5/6):90,91. July/August 1982.

"Red Dawn (review)," <u>Cinefantastique</u> 15(2):46. May 1985.

"Shining, The (review)," <u>Cinefantastique</u> 10(2):38. Fall 1980.

"Spacehunter," <u>Cinefantastique</u> 13(5):18-25. June/July 1983.

"Splash (review)," <u>Cinefantastique</u> 14(4/5):106. September 1984.

"Swamp Thing (review)," <u>Cinefantastique</u> 12(4):48. May/June 1982.

"Tron (review)," <u>Cinefantastique</u> 13(1):48. September/October 1982.

"Tron," <u>Cinefantastique</u> 12(4):18-20. May/June 1982.

"View to Kill (review)," <u>Cinefantastique</u> 15(5):37,53. January 1986.

"War Games (review)," <u>Cinefantastique</u> 13(6)/14(1):101. September 1983.

Hogan, P. G., Jr.

"Philip K. Dick," in: Cowart, David, ed. <u>Twentieth-Century American Science Fiction Writers, Part 1: A-L</u>. Detroit: Gale, 1981. pp. 134-140. (Dictionary of Literary Biography, v. 8)

"Philosophical limitations of science fiction," <u>Journal of General Education</u> 28(1):1-15. Spring 1976. also in: Clareson, T. D. <u>Many Futures, Many Worlds</u>. Kent: Kent State Univ. Press, 1977. pp. 260-277.

"Philosophical limitations of utopian science fiction," <u>Journal of the American Studies Association of Texas</u> 6:55-62. 1975.

"SF in the classroom: 1. opportunities and limitations," <u>Extrapolation</u> 13(2):106-111. May 1972.

Hohman, J. R.

"Bookseller's list of basic science fiction," <u>Publishers Weekly</u> 209(24):61. June 14, 1976.

"Stocking and selling science fiction," <u>Publishers Weekly</u> 209(24):60-61. June 14, 1976.

Hoisington, T. H.

"Ein Abend mit Stanislaw Lem," <u>Quarber Merkur</u> 38:16-20. November 1974.

Hokenson, Jan

"Todorov and the existentialists," in: Collins, R. A. and H. D. Pearce, eds. <u>The Scope of the Fantastic: Theory, Technique, Major Authors</u>. Westport, CT: Greenwood Press, 1985. pp. 33-39.

Holan, Peter

"SF in Czechoslovakia," by Jaroslav Olsa, Jr. and Peter Holan. Locus 18(3): 25-26, 33. March 1985.

Holbing, Walter

"Dystopie der gegenwart: science fiction und schizophrenie in Vonnegut's Slaughterhouse Five," Arbeiten aus Anglistik und Amerikanistik 2:39-62. 1977.

Holbrook, David

"Problem of C. S. Lewis, The," in: Fox, Geoff, ed. Writers, Critics, and Children: Articles from Children's Literature in Education. New York: Agathon Press, 1976. pp. 116-124.

Holcomb, C.

"SF phenomenon in literature," Saturday Review of Literature 32(22):9-10,36-37. May 28, 1949.

Holder, R. C.

"Art and the artist in the fiction of Charles Williams," Renascence 27:81-87. 1975.

Holder, S. C.

"John Brunner's short fiction: the more things change...," in: De Bolt, Joe, ed. Happening Worlds of John Brunner. Port Washington, NY: Kennikat, 1975. pp. 78-95.

Holdom, Lynn

Capsule Reviews. San Bernardino, CA: Borgo, 1980. 51 p.

Holdstock, Rob

"Notes on an Unfinished Career," Focus: an SF Writers' Magazine 4:6-8. Spring 1981.

Holdstock, Robert

Encyclopedia of Science Fiction. London: Octopus Books, 1978. 224 p.

Realms of Fantasy, by Malcolm Edwards and Robert Holdstock. Garden City, NY: Doubleday, 1983. 120 p.

"Locations: a modern perspective of science fiction," in: Holdstock, Robert. Encyclopedia of Science Fiction. London: Octopus, 1978. pp. 8-17.

Holdsworth, Peter

"BSFA Survey," by Peter Holdsworth and Ken Lake. Matrix (BSFA) 45:8-10. December 1982/January 1983.

Holland, Elizabeth

J. R. R. Tolkien: The Shores of Middle-Earth, by Robert Giddings and Elizabeth Holland. London: Junction Books, 1981. 289 p.

Holland, N. N.

"2001: a psychosocial explanation," Hartford Studies in Literature 1(1):20-25. 1969.

"You, U. K. Le Guin," in: Barr, Marlene S., ed. Future Females. Bowling Green, OH: Bowling Green State University Popular Press, 1981. pp. 125-137.

Holland, Paul

"Michael Moorcock: ein Rustloser Arbeiter," Science Fiction Times (Germany) 27(7):10-18. July 1985.

Holland, Stephen

"Weird World," by Mike Ashley and Stephen Holland. in: Tymn, M. B. and Ashley, Mike. Science Fiction, Fantasy, and Weird Fiction Magazines. Westport, CT: Greenwood, 1985. pp. 737-738.

Holland, T. R.

Vonnegut's Major Works. Lincoln, Nebraska: Cliff's Notes, 1973. 58 p.

Holland-Cunz, Barbara

Feministische Utopien: Aufbruch in die post-patriarchale Gesellschaft, ed. by Barbara Holland-Cunz. Meitingen: Corian, 1986. 200 p.

"Doris Lessings Pentalogie Canopus im Argos: Archive," in: Femistische Utopien: Aufbruch in dei postpatriarchale Gesellschaft, ed. by Barbara Holland-Cunz. Meitingen: Corian Verlag, 1985.

"Frauen SF, oder Feministische Utopie," Science Fiction Times (Germany) 27(1):14-17. January 1985.

"Politische Struktur und Machtverhaeltnisse in der feminische Utopie," in: Femistische Utopien: Aufbruch in dei postpatriarchale Gesellschaft, ed. by Barbara Holland-Cunz. Meitingen: Corian Verlag, 1986.

Holland-Cunz, Barbara (Continued)

"PR fur PR," Science Fiction Times (Germany) 26(11):15-17. November 1984.

Hollander, Hans

"Bild in der Theorie des Phantastischen, Das," in: Thomsen, C. W., ed. Phantastik in Literatur und Kunst. Darmstadt: Wiss. Buchgesellschaft, 1980. pp. 52-78.

"Konturen einer Ikonographie des Phantastischen," in: Thomsen, C. W., ed. Phantastik in Literatur und Kunst. Darmstadt: Wiss. Buchgesellschaft, 1980. pp. 387-403.

"Zur phantastischen Architektur," in: Thomsen, C. W., ed. Phantastik in Literatur und Kunst. Darmstadt: Wiss. Buchgesellschaft, 1980. pp. 404-438.

Hollie, P. G.

"Zam! Science fiction zaps its giant robots, stresses 'relevance'," Wall Street Journal 48(82):1,23. October 26, 1971.

Hollington, Michael

"Great books and great wars: J. G. Ballard's Empire of the Sun," Meanjin 44(2): 269-275. June 1985.

Hollister, B. C.

"Holy cow! Science fiction comes to the classroom; interview," Media & Methods 10(7):8-9. April 1974.

"Martian perspective: analyzing American culture," Media & Methods 10(3):26-28,56-65. November 1973.

"Paperbacks: grokking the future," Media & Methods 9(4):23-27. December 1972.

"Teaching American history with science fiction," Social Education 39(2):81-86. February 1975.

"Tune in yesterday," English Journal 63(7):77-80. 1974.

Hollister, Bernard

Grokking the Future: Science Fiction in the Classroom, by Bernard Hollister and D. C. Thompson. S. L.: Pflaum/Standard, 1973. 167 p.

You and Science Fiction: A Humanistic Approach to Tomorrow. Skokie, Illinois: National Textbook Company, 1976. 349 p.

Hollow, John

Against the Night, The Stars: The Science Fiction of Arthur C. Clarke. San Diego: Harcourt, 1983. 197 p.

"2001 in perspective: the fiction of Arthur C. Clarke," Southwest Review 61(2):113-129. Spring 1976.

"Edgar Rice Burroughs," in: Cowart, David, ed. Twentieth-Century American Science-Fiction Writers, Part 1: A-L. Detroit: Gale, 1981. pp. 87-92. (Dictionary of Literary Biography, v. 8)

"Last resort: The End of August at the Ozone Hotel," Extrapolation 18(1):52-56. December 1976.

"Rereading Tarzan of the Apes; or 'what is it,' Lady Alice whispered, 'a man'," Dalhousie Review 56(1):83-92. Spring 1976.

Holloway, Mark

"Necessity of Utopia," in: Utopias, ed. by Peter Alexander and Roger Gill. London: Duckworth, 1984. pp. 179-188.

Hollwitz, J. C.

Mythopoeic Art of C. S. Lewis, The. Ph. D. Dissertation, Northwestern University, 1980. 235 p.

Hollwitz, John

"Wonder of passage, the making of Gold," Mythlore 11(3): 17-24. Winter/Spring 1985.

Holm, P. J.

Syzygy og den sorte stjerne. Copenhagen: Notabene, 1975. 51 p.

Holman, C. H.

"Lewis, C. S.," in: Woodcock, George, ed. 20th Century Fiction. Chicago: St. James, 1985. pp. 382-321.

Holmberg, J. H.

Drommar om evigheten: science fiction historia. Vanersborg: Askild, 1974. 186 p.

"European scene, The: Sweden," Extrapolation 11(2):76-79. May 1970.

"Letter from Sweden, October 1984," Science Fiction Chronicle 6(1):6-7. October 1984.

"Letter," Science Fiction Chronicle 3(12):11-12. September 1982.

Holmberg, J. H. (Continued)

"Scandinavian letter," _Science Fiction Chronicle_ 5(1):5,7. October 1983.

"SF notes from Sweden," _Science Fiction Chronicle_ 2(12):4. September 1981.

"Sf: report from Scandinavia," _Algol_ 12(1):19-20. November 1974.

Holmes, H. H.

See: Boucher, Anthony

Holmes, J. E.

"Science fiction and fantasy games," _Locus_ 14(11):9,24-28. December 1981.

Holsopple, Barbara

"'V' Spells Victory in Weekly Format," _Pittsburgh Press_ September 7, 1984. in: _NewsBank. Film and Television_ FTV 30:G3. 1984.

Holt, M. J.

"Joanna Russ," in: Bleiler, E. F., ed. _Science Fiction Writers_. New York: Scribners, 1982. pp. 483-490.

Holt, Patricia

"Interview: Alfred Coppel," _San Francisco Examiner_ February 27, 1983. in: _NewsBank. Literature_ 74:G6-7. 1983.

"Interview: Marion Bradley," _San Francisco Examiner_ February 27, 1983. in: _NewsBank. Literature_ 74:A7. 1983.

Holt, W. A.

"Olaf Stapledon, neglected titan," _Christianity Today_ 20(25):24-25. September 24, 1976.

Holte, Carleton

"Additions to _Anthony Burgess: A Checklist (1956-1971),_" _Twentieth Century Literature_ 20(1):44-52. January 1974.

Holtkamp, Jurgen

"Dossier 2: Die Eroffnung des rhodesischen Zeitalters oder Einubung in die Freie Welt. Science Fiction Literatur in Deutschland," in: Enzenberger, H. M., ed. _Kursbuch 14_. Frankfurt-am-Main, 1968. pp. 45-63.

Holton, Scott

Fantastic Worlds, by Scott Holton and Robert Skotak. New York: Starlog, 1978. 98 p.

"SF Graphics: The Advertising Posters for Star Wars," _Future_ 1: 48-50. April 1978.

"Shape of things to come, The," by Scott Holton and Ed Naha. _Future_ 2:30-33. 1978.

Holtsmark, E. B.

Tarzan and Tradition: Classical Myth in Popular Literature. Westport, CT.: Greenwood, 1981. 197 p.

Holtzman, Marcia

Teacher's Manual: Science Fiction. New York: New American Library, 1975. 60 p.

Home, W. S.

"Lovecraft 'books;' some addenda and corrigenda, The," in: Lovecraft, H. P. _The Dark Brotherhood and Other Pieces_. Sauk City, Wisconsin: Arkham House, 1966. pp. 134-152.

Homer, David

"Science Fiction and Teaching: Science, Science Fiction, and a Radical Science Education, by E. E. Nunan and David Homer. _Science-Fiction Studies_ 8(3): 311-330. November 1981.

Hooper, F. W.

"Narnia: the author, the critics, and the tale," in: Butler, Francelia. _Children's Literature: the Great Excluded_, Vol. 3. Storrs, Connecticut: Children's Literature Association, 1974. pp. 12-22.

Hooper, Walter

C. S. Lewis: A Biography, by R. L. Green and Walter Hooper. London: Collins, 1974. 320 p.

C. S. Lewis: A Biography, by R. L. Green and Walter Hooper. Glasgow: Fount, 1979.

Of Other Worlds; Essays and Stories, by C. S. Lewis and ed. by Walter Hooper. New York: Harper, 1966.

Past Watchful Dragons: The Narnian Chronicles of C. S. Lewis. New York: Collier, 1979. 140 p.

Through Joy and Beyond: A Pictorial Biography of C. S. Lewis. New York: Macmillan, 1982. 176 p.

Hooper, Walter (Continued)

"Reminiscences," _Mythlore_ 3(4):5-9. June 1976.

Hooton, D. D.

"Computers and Science Fiction: An Annotated Bibliography," Worcester, MA: Undergraduate Report, Worcester Polytechnic Institute, 1982. Report No. 82:C0491. 69 p.

Hoover, H. M.

"SF: out of this world," _Language Arts_ 57(4):425-428. April 1980.

"Where Do You Get Your Ideas?" _Top of the News_ 39(1): 57-61. Fall 1982.

Hope, Adrian

"Star wars' technical victory," _New Scientist_ 75: 460. August 25, 1977.

Hopkins, D. F.

"Impacts of literary science," _Chemistry and Industry_ pp. 440-442. March 16, 1963.

Hopkins, H. A.

Fandom Directory 1980. Hampton, VA: Fandom Computer Services, 1980. 304 p.

Fandom Directory 1981. Langley AFB, Virginia: Fandom Computer Services, 1981. 380 p.

Fandom Directory, Number 5, 1983-84 Edition. by Harry A. Hopkins and Mariane S. Hopkins. San Bernardino, CA: Fandom Computer Services, 1983. 448 p.

"Fandom Glossary," by Ron J. Frantz, Ron J. and Harry A. Hopkins. in: Hopkins, Harry A., ed. _Fandom Directory 1980._ Langley AFB, Virginia: Fandom Computer Services, 1980. pp. 7-11.

Hopkins, M. S.

Fandom Directory No. 6, 1984/1985 Edition. Baltimore, MD: Diamond Distributors, 1984. 384 p.

Fandom Directory No. 8, 1986-1987 Edition. San Bernardino, CA: Fandom Computer Services, 1986. 448 p.

Fandom Directory, 1982. Newport News, VA: Fandom Computer Services, 1982. 408 p.

Fandom Directory, Number 7, 1985-1986 Edition. San Bernardino, CA: Fandom Computer Services, 1985. 416 p.

Hopkins, Tom

"From the twisted mind of Kevin Yagher," _Dayton (OH) Daily News_ May 5, 1985. in: _NewsBank. Film and Television._ 130:A2-A6. June 1985.

Hopley, Claire

"Orwell's language of wasteland and trench," _College Literature_ 11(1): 59-70. 1984.

Hornum, B. G.

American Values and World View as Reflected in Science Fiction. Ph.D. Dissertation, Bryn Mawr, 1977. 378 p.

Horowitz, Carey

"Interview with Kurt Vonnegut, Jr, An," _Library Journal_ 98(8):1311. April 15, 1973.

Horrigan, Jeremiah

"Creating An Elfin World From Fabric and Fantasy," _Miami Herald_ December 12, 1982. in: _NewsBank. Film and Television._ 61: A11-12. January 1983.

Houghton, John

"Rochester the Renewer: The Byronic Hero and the Messiah as Elements in the King Elessar," _Mythlore_ 11(1): 13-16, 45. Summer 1984.

Houston Public Library

Future, The: Science Fiction Book Exhibit. Houston: Houston Public Library, 1968. 18 p.

Houston, David

"50's, The: golden age of science fiction television. Part II: Space Patrol and Tom Corbett," _Starlog_ 42: 64-65. January 1981.

"Arthur C. Clarke: at a turning point in paradise," _Future_ No. 2:20-26. 1978.

"Battlestar Galactica," _Future_ 6: 42-46. November 1978.

"Black Hole, The," by David Houston and Ed Naha. _Future Life_ 16: 52-55, 63. February 1980.

Houston, David (Continued)

"Chesley Bonestell, Space Painter: The Master at 90," <u>Future</u> 1: 66-74. April 1978.

"Chesley Bonestell: conqueror of space," <u>Starlog</u> 12:64-67. 1978.

"Creating the space fantasy universe of Star Wars," <u>Starlog</u> 7:19-28. 1977.

"Flash Gordon! Conqueror of Space and Screen," <u>Future</u> 3: 20-25. July 1978.

"Interview with the Logan Man: William F. Nolan," <u>Future</u> 4: 20-25. August 1978.

"Man of light & vision: Ralph McQuarrie," <u>Starlog</u> 17:36-41,70. 1978.

"One Hundred Most Important People in Science Fiction/Fantasy: A. E. Van Vogt," <u>Starlog</u> 100: 16. November 1985.

"One Hundred Most Important People in Science Fiction/Fantasy: Fredric Brown," <u>Starlog</u> 100: 76-77. November 1985.

"Other voices: Beginnings," <u>Starlog</u> 100: 12-13. November 1985.

"SFX, part 36: Have 'Monster Planet,' Will Travel," <u>Starlog</u> 46: 56-60. May 1981.

Houston, Penelope

"Glimpses of the moon," <u>Sight and Sound</u> 22(4):185-188. April/June 1953.

Howard, Allan

"Howard on crusade," in: De Camp, L. S., ed. <u>Blade of Conan</u>. New York: Ace, 1979. pp. 99-106.

Howard, Andrew

"<u>Till We Have Faces</u> and its mythological and literary precursors," <u>Mythlore</u> 4:30-32. March 1977.

Howard, Claire

"Vented spleen," <u>Mythlore</u> 2(3):9-11. Winter 1971.

Howard, June

"Widening the Dialogue on Feminist Science Fiction," in: Wole, Gary, ed. <u>Science Fiction Dialogues</u>. Chicago: Academy Chicago, 1982. pp. 155-168.

Howard, Nic

<u>Masters of Fantasy, 2: August Derleth</u>. Birmingham: British Fantasy Society, 1984. 24 p.

Howard, R. E.

"Spectres in the Dark," <u>Cromlech</u> 1(1): 24-36. Spring 1985.

Howard, Richard

<u>Fantastic: A Structural Approach to a Literary Genre, The</u>, by Tzvetan Todorov and Richard Howard. Cleveland and London: The Press of Case Western Reserve University, 1973. 179 p.

Howard, Thomas

<u>Achievement of C. S. Lewis, The</u>. Wheaton, IL: Shaw, 1980. 195 p.

<u>Novels of Charles Williams, The</u>. New York: Oxford University Press, 1983. 224 p.

"'Moral mythology' of C. S. Lewis, The," <u>Modern Age</u> 22(4):384-392. Fall 1978.

"Charles Williams' use of Arthurian materials," <u>Mythlore</u> 5(1):6-10. May 1978.

"Granting Charles Willimas his donee," <u>Mythlore</u> 8(2):13-14. Summer 1981.

"Shadows of ecstasy," <u>Studies in the Literary Imagination</u> 14(2):73-94. Fall 1981.

"Uses of myth," <u>Mythlore</u> 7(1):20-23. March 1980.

Howe, Florence

"Conversation with Doris Lessing (1966)," <u>Contemporary Literature</u> 14(4):413-417. Autumn 1973.

Howe, Irving

<u>1984 Revisited: Totalitarianism in our Century</u>. New York: Harper, 1983. 276 p.

"Fiction of anti-utopia, The," <u>New Republic</u> 146(17):13-16. April 23, 1962.

"Orwell: history as nightmare," <u>American Scholar</u> 25(2):193-207. Spring 1956.

Howell, J. M.

<u>John Gardner: A Bibliographical Profile</u>. Carbondale: Southern Illinois University Press, 1980. 172 p.

Howes, A. B.

"Expectation and surprise in Children's End," in: Olander, Joseph D. and Martin Harry Greenberg, eds. Arthur C. Clarke New York: Taplinger, 1977. pp. 149-171.

Hristov, Venko

"I nakraja: az avtora," in: Bradbury, Ray. Zdravej i sbogom. Plavdiv, Bulgaria: Danov, n. d. pp. 210-220.

Huddleston, Tony

"Mod SF author speaks lightly on writing art," Battalion (Texas A&M University) p. 1. April 23, 1969.

Hudgeons, T. E.

Official 1981 Price Guide to Comic and Science Fiction Books, The. Orlando, FL: House of Collectibles, 1981. 437 p.

Official 1982 Price Guide to Comic and Science Fiction Books, The. by Thomas E. Hudgeons and William Roger. Orlando, FL: House of Collectibles, 1982. 501 p.

Official Price Guide to Science Fiction and Fantasy Collectibles. Orlando, FL: House of Collectibles, 1985. 537 p.

Hudson, Derek

Lewis Carroll. London: Constable, 1954. 354 p.

"Study of Algernon Blackwood, A," in: Hudson, Derek, ed. Essays and Studies for 1961. London: John Murray, 1961. 14:102-114.

Hudson, Jacob

"David H. Keller: story teller," Fantasy Times No. 64:4-6. April 1948.

Hudson, W. M.

"Shapes of future America in Vonnegut's science fiction," Journal of the American Studies Association of Texas 4:74-82. 1973.

Huet, M. H.

"Itineraire du texte," Stanford French Review 3(1):17-28. Spring 1979.

Hughes, D. Y.

"Bergonzi and after in the criticism of Wells' SF," Science Fiction Studies 3(2):165-174. July 1976.

"Criticism in English of H. G. Wells' science fiction," Science Fiction Studies 6(3):309-319. November 1979.

"Early science journalism of H. G. Wells: a chronological survey, The," by D. Y. Hughes and R. M. Philmus. Science Fiction Studies 1(2):98-114. Fall 1973.

"Early science journalism of H. G. Wells: addenda, The," by D. Y. Hughes and R. M. Philmus. Science Fiction Studies 2(1):98-99. March 1975.

"Garden in Wells' early science fiction, The," in: Suvin, Darko and Robert M. Philmus, eds. H. G. Wells and Modern Science Fiction. Lewisburg: Bucknell University Press, 1977. pp. 48-69.

"Ghost in the Machine, The: The Theme of Player Piano," in: Roemer, Kenneth M., ed. American As Utopia. New York: Franklin, 1981. pp. 108-114.

"H. G. Wells: ironic romancer," Extrapolation 6(2):32-38. May 1965.

"Mood of a modern utopia, The," Extrapolation 19(1):59-67. December 1977.

Hughes, Daniel

"Pieties and Giant Forms in the Lord of the Rings," in: Isaacs, Neil D. Tolkien: New Critical Perspectives, ed. by N. D. Isaacs and R. A. Zimbardo. Lexington: University Press of Kentucky, 1981. pp. 72-86.

Hull, E. A.

"Fire and Ice: The Ironic Imagery of Arthur C. Clarke's Childhood's End," Extrapolation 24(1): 13-32. Spring 1983.

"Justifying the ways of man to God; the novels of Robert A. Heinlein," Extrapolation 20(1):38-49. Spring 1979.

"Lest We Forget: A Reminder of Some Good Reasons & Real Reasons for Teaching SF," Essays in Arts and Sciences. 9(2): 123-130. August 1980.

"Little Professor, Intuitionist, The: A Transactional Analysis of Isaac Asimov's The Gods Themselves," Extrapolation 22(2): 146-154. Summer 1981.

"Merging Madness: Rollerball as a Cautionary Tale," in: Erlich, Richard D., ed. Clockwork Worlds. Westport, CT: Greenwood, 1983. pp. 163-180.

"Orientation," Locus 15(3):1,13-14. March 1982.

Hull, E. A. (Continued)

"SFRA meets at Kent State," Fantasy Review 8(7): 39. July 1985.

"The World(con) according to Hull," Locus 18(11): 26-27. November 1985.

"World SF at Fanano," Fantasy Review 8(8): 34. August 1985.

Hulme, H. M.

"Middlemarch as science fiction: notes on language and imagery," Novel 2(1):36-45. Fall 1968.

Hume, B. R.

"LA Con II," Leading Edge No. 8:93-98. Fall 1984.

Hume, Kathryn

"C. S. Lewis' trilogy: a cosmic romance," Modern Fiction Studies 20(4):505-517. Winter 1974.

"Edifice Complex, The: Motive and Accomplishment in The Fountains of Paradise," Extrapolation 24(4): 380-388. Winter 1983.

"Hidden Dynamics of "The War of the Worlds,' The," Philological Quarterly 62(3): 279-292. Summer 1983.

"Medieval Romance and Science Fiction: The Anatomy of a Resemblance," Journal of Popular Culture 16(1): 15-26. Summer 1982.

Humel, Letty

"Market report: children's magazines," Science Fiction Times (Boston) 1(4):4-5. August 1979.

Humphries, Reynold

"Westworld (review)," Cinefantastique 3(3):33. Fall 1974.

Hundertmarck, Rosemarie

"Frau ale Stoerfaktor, Die," in: Rottensteiner, Franz, ed. Quarber Merkur. Frankfurt: Suhrkamp, 1979. pp. 111-140.

"Frau als Storfaktor," Quarber Merkur. 45:13-32. December 1976.

"Rollentausch: Frauen in der Science-Fiction," in: Alpers, H. J., ed. Science Fiction Almanach 1981. Moewig, 1980. pp. 268-307.

Hunt, L. I.

Symbols and Mysticism in the Novels of Thomas Burnett Swann. Masters Thesis, Florida Atlantic University, 1981. 80 p.

Hunt, Robert

"Science Fiction for the Age of Inflation: Reading Atlas Shrugged in the 1980s," in: Slusser, George E., ed. Coordinates. Carbondale: Southern Illinois University Press, 1983. pp. 80-98.

"Visionary States and the Search for Trancendence in Science Fiction," in: Slusser, George E., ed. Bridges to Science Fiction. Carbondale: Southern Illinois University Press, 1980. pp. 64-77.

Hunter, Alan

"F.A.S.," Blunt No. 2:24-26. November 1973.

Hunter, C. B.

"Selling Fantasy to the Mystery Magazines," SFWA Bulletin 15(1): 15-16. Spring 1980.

Hunter, Doris

"Siddhartha and A Clockwork Orange: two images of man in comtemporary literature and cinema," by Doris Hunter and Howard Hunter. in: Richter, P. E., ed. Utopia/Dystopia?. Cambridge, MA: Schenkman, 1975. pp. 125-142.

Hunter, Frank

"King of Horror Tries His Hand at Moviemaking," St. Louis (MO.) Globe Democrat November 6/7, 1982. in: Newsbank. Film and Television 53:F9-10. December 1982.

Hunter, Howard

"Siddhartha and A Clockwork Orange: two images of man in comtemporary literature and cinema," by Doris Hunter and Howard Hunter. in: Richter, P. E., ed. Utopia/Dystopia?. Cambridge, MA: Schenkman, 1975. pp. 125-142.

Hunter, Lynette

"Reading of The Napoleon of Notting Hill, A," Chesterton Review 3:118-128. 1976.

Hunter, Mollie

"One world, part II," Horn Book 52(1):32-38. February 1976.

Hunter, Mollie (Continued)

"One world," Horn Book 51(6):557-563. December 1975.

"One World," in: Boyer, Robert H. and Zahorski, Kenneth J. Fantasists on Fantasy. New York: Avon Discus, 1984. pp. 211-230.

Hunter, Stephen

"'The Prisoner' in disguise: what does it all mean?" Crawdaddy p. 16. April 1978. (not seen)

"Ladyhawke started well, but will it last?" Baltimore Sun April 21, 1985. in: NewsBank. Film and Television. 113:B2. May 1985.

Hunter, Tim

"2001: A Space Odyssey," Film Heritage 3(4):12-20. Summer 1968.

Huntington, John

Logic of Fantasy: H. G. Wells and Science Fiction, The. New York: Columbia University Press, 1982. 192 p.

"From man to overmind: Arthur C. Clarke's myth of progress," in: Olander, Joseph D. and Martin Harry Greenberg, eds. Arthur C. Clarke. New York: Taplinger, 1977. pp. 211-222.

"Impossible Love in Science Fiction," Raritan 4(2): 85-99. Fall 1984.

"Olaf Stapledon and the Novel About the Future," Contemporary Literature 22(3): 349-365. Summer 1981.

"Public and private imperatives in Le Guin's novels," Science Fiction Studies 2(3):237-243. November 1975.

"Remembrance of Things to Come: Narrative Technique in Last and First Men," Science-Fiction Studies 9(3): 257-264. November 1982.

"Science fiction and the future," College English 37(4):345-352. December 1975.

"Science fiction of H. G. Wells, The," in: Parrinder, Patrick, ed. Science Fiction: A Critical Guide. New York: Longman, 1979. pp. 34-51.

"Thinking by Opposition: The 'Two-World' Structure in H. G. Wells's Short Fiction," Science-Fiction Studies 8(3): 240-254. November 1981.

"Unity of Childhood's End, The," Science Fiction Studies 1(3):154-164. Spring 1974.

"Utopian and Anti-Utopian Logic: H. G. Wells and His Successors," Science-Fiction Studies 9(2): 122-146. July 1982.

Huntly, Randy

"Three monthly escapes," Arizona English Bulletin 51(1):63-65. October 1972.

Hupp, P. R.

"Petie monde des fanzines, Le," Magazine Litteraire No. 88:32-33. May 1974.

Hurley, N. P.

"Coming of the humanoids: android fiction," Commonweal 91(10):297-300. December 5, 1969.

Hurley, R. J.

"Librarian looks at science fiction, A," Books on Trial 11(8):318,350. June 1953.

"Step into space," Scholastic 63(2):42T. September 23, 1953. (Book review)

Hurst, L. J.

"Face of the Robots," Vector No. 128: 3-4. October/November 1985.

"Homeopathy for the Cranks: Three Studies of Pseudo-Science," Foundation 28: 60-77. July 1983.

"John Norman: the literature of difference," Foundation 33: 36-55. Spring 1985.

"Material World, The," Vector 119: 38-40. April 1984.

"Timeless dance: Keith Roberts' Pavane re-examined," Vector 124/125: 17-19. 1985.

Hutchens, J. K.

"On an author," New York Herald Tribune Book Review p. 3. August 10, 1952.

Hutchins, Geraldine

Science Fiction and Fantasy Research Index, Vol. 4, by H. W. Hall, and Geraldine Hutchins. Bryan, TX: SFBRI, 1985. 71 p.

Hutchison, David

Special Effects, Vol. 3. New York: Starlog, 1981. 98 p.

Special Effects, Vol. 4. New York: Starlog, 1984. 98 p.

Hutchison, David (Continued)

"Behind the Genesis Effect," _Starlog_ 64: 17-21. November 1982.

"Black Cauldron, The," _Starlog_ 96: 50-51. July 1985.

"Disney's 'Brave Little Toaster' to a New World of Animation," _Starlog_ 77: 34-35. December 1983.

"Dream is Alive, The," _Starlog_ 101: 60. December 1985.

"E.T.: The Little FX Movie That Made Good," _Starlog_ 65: 46-51, 63. December 1982.

"Hobbit (review)," _Cinefantastique_ 7(2) 28-31. Summer 1978.

"Haunting Special Effects of Ghostbusters, The," _Starlog_ 87: 34-37. October 1984.

"Incredible Effects World of Douglas Trumbull, The," _Future_ 1: 54-59, 62. April 1978.

"Men Who Made the Monsters, The" by Mike Clark and David Hutchison. _Starlog_ 74: 34-41, 64. September 1983.

"Music for a Barbarian," _Starlog_ 62: 24-25, 65. September 1982.

"On Location With Doug Trumbull and Brainstrom," _Starlog_ 55: 55-59, 64. February 1982.

"One Hundred Most Important People in Science Fiction/Fantasy: Albert Whitlock," _Starlog_ 100: 33. November 1985.

"One Hundred Most Important People in Science Fiction/Fantasy: Douglas Trumbull," _Starlog_ 100: 38-39. November 1985.

"One Hundred Most Important People in Science Fiction/Fantasy: Georges Melies," _Starlog_ 100: 24. November 1985.

"One Hundred Most Important People in Science Fiction/Fantasy: Ralph McQuarrie," _Starlog_ 100: 22. November 1985.

"One Hundred Most Important People in Science Fiction/Fantasy: Ray Bradbury," _Starlog_ 100: 74. November 1985.

"One Hundred Most Important People in Science Fiction/Fantasy: Syd Mead," _Starlog_ 100: 32. November 1985.

"One Hundred Most Important People in Science Fiction/Fantasy: Walt Disney," _Starlog_ 100: 81. November 1985.

"SFX Part XLII: The Matte Artist; An Interview With Albert Willock," _Starlog_ 60: 81-84. July 1982.

"SFX Part xxxvii: Storyboarding Special Effects," _Starlog_ 49: 20-23. August 1981.

"SFX, part 37: Star Trek: the Motion Picture Props," _Starlog_ 47: 57-61. June 1981.

"SFX, part XL: Spirits of the Lost Ark," _Starlog_ 54: 57-63. January 1982.

"SFX, Part xxxix: The Ultimate Dragon," _Starlog_ 53: 57-61. December 1981.

"SFX, Part XXXV: Flying Down to Mongo, or, The Traveling Matte Blues," _Starlog_ 45: 60-65. April 1981.

"SFX, part xxxviii: The Flash of His Pencil," _Starlog_ 52: 57-61. November 1981.

"Special Effects of Return of the Jedi, Part 3," _Starlog_ 84: 60-61. July 1984.

"Special Effects of Return of the Jedi, Part 4," _Starlog_ 86: 35-37. September 1984.

"Special effects of Return of the Jedi, part 6," _Starlog_ No. 94:52-54,62. May 1985.

"Special effects of Return of the Jedi, part 7," _Starlog_ No. 96: 64-67. July 1985.

"Special effects of Return of the Jedi," _Starlog_ No. 93:59-62,65. April 1985.

"Special Effects of Star Wars: Return of the Jedi, Part 2," _Starlog_ 82: 59-63. May 1984.

"Special Effects of Star Wars: Return of the Jedi, Part One," _Starlog_ 80: 18-22. March 1984.

"Special Effects: Among the Minds of Brainstorm," _Starlog_ 78: 36-39, 43. January 1984.

"Special FX: Patching the Pandemonium of Dark's Shadow Show," _Starlog_ 76: 66-70, 87. November 1983.

"Starlog Interview: Arthur C. Clarke, Beyond 2010," _Starlog_ 78: 30-34. January 1984.

"Starlog Interview: Doug Trumbull," _Starlog_ 77: 36-42, 62. December 1983.

"Starlog Interview: Peter Hyams," _Starlog_ 85: 52-55. August 1984.

"Steven Spielberg: The Making of Raiders of the Lost Ark," _Starlog_ 50: 41-45. September 1981.

"Tron: Changing the Laws of Physics," _Starlog_ 62: 50-55. September 1982.

"V: the special effects," _Starlog_ No. 91:61-64. February 1985.

"Videolog: Restoring the Classics," _Starlog_ 99: 27-28. October 1985.

Hutchison, David (Continued)

"Vincent Di Fate," <u>Future Life</u> No. 9: 58-63. March 1979.

Huttar, C. A.

"Hell and the city: Tolkien and the traditions of western literature," in: Lobdell, Jared, ed. <u>A Tolkien Compass</u>. New York: Ballantine/Del Rey, 1980. pp. 126-155.

Hutton, Muriel

"George Macdonald collection, The," <u>The Yale University Library Gazette</u> 51(2):74-85. October 1976.

Huxley, Aldous

"Chemical persuasion," in: Knight, Damon, ed. <u>Turning Points: Essays in the Art of Science Fiction</u>. New York: Harper, 1977. pp. 231-237.

Huxley, Julian

"My brother Aldous," <u>Humanist</u> 25(1):25. January/February 1965.

Hyams, Peter

<u>Odyssey File, The</u>, by Arthur C. Clarke and Peter Hyams. New York: Del Rey, 1984. 132 p.

Hyatt, Mike

"George Pal: father of modern science fiction," by Leslie Zador and Mike Hyatt. <u>Los Angeles Free Press</u> p. 36. August 20, 1971.

Hyde, Ann

"Library of the Future, The: Science Fiction and the Department of Special Collections," <u>Books and Libraries at the University of Kansas</u> p. 1-5. Spring 1976.

Hyde, Kevin

"Disney's calculated risk: The Black Hole," by W. G. Wilson, Jr. and Kevin Hyde. <u>Questar</u> 2(2):17-21. February 1980.

"George Romero: cinema's dark dreamer steps into the light," <u>Questar</u> 1(4):18-22,30. August 1979.

"Mike Gornick: the eyes of George Romero," <u>Questar</u> 2(1):11-13. November 1979.

"Rick Catizone: animation's low-key contender," <u>Questar</u> 1(4):28-29. August 1979.

"Superman: the legend, the movie, the magic," by C. J. Henderson and Kevin Hyde. <u>Questar</u> 1(3):11-17,39. March 1979.

"Tom Savini: the world is putty in his hands," <u>Questar</u> 1(4):23-25. August 1979.

Hyde, P. N.

<u>Linguistic Techniques Used in Character Development in the Works of J. R. R. Tolkien</u>. (Vol. 1-III) Ph. D. Dissertation, Purdue University, 1982. 1230 p.

"Quenti Lambardillion: a column on Middle-Earch linguistics: Tolkien's vowel structures," <u>Mythlore</u> 11(2):34-36. Autumn 1984.

"Quenti Lambardillion: A Column on Middle-earth Linguistics," <u>Mythlore</u> 9(4): 19-20, 32. Winter 1983.

"Quenti Lambardillion: a column on Middle-Earth linguistics: title page inscriptions," <u>Mythlore</u> 12(1):26-27,42. Autumn 1985.

"Quenti Lambardillion: Tolkien's linguistic aesthetic," <u>Mythlore</u> 11(3): 42-45. Winter/Spring 1985.

I

Idrizovic, Muris

"Bogatstvo svjetova u bajkama Vladimira Nazora," Zivot: Casopis za Knjizevnost i Kulturu 61(1/2): 163-168. January/February 1982.

Ikin, Van

"Answers to seventeen questions: an interview with Peter Carey," Science Fiction: A Review of Speculative Literature 1(1): 30-54. June 1977.

"Australian science fiction; the state of the art," Science Fiction: A Review of Speculative Literature 2(2):112-127. December 1979.

"Australian SF in 1982: A Checklist," Science Fiction: A Review of Speculative Literature 5(1): 11. March 1983.

"Australian SF in 1983, a checklist," Science Fiction: A Review of Speculative Literature 6(1): 15. 1984.

"George Turner: the man, the writer, the critic," Science Fiction: A Review of Speculative Literature 1(3):119-138. December 1978.

"Introduction: The History of Australian Science Fiction," in: Ikin, Van, ed. Australian Science Fiction. Chicago: Academy Chicago, 1984. pp. ix-xl.

"Lee Harding: an interview," Science Fiction: A Review of Speculative Literature 1(2):46-56. June 1978.

"Novels of Lee Harding: a survey, The," Science Fiction: A Review of Speculative Literature 1(2):28-44. June 1978.

"Paul Collins Interview," Science Fiction: A Review of Speculative Literature 3(2): 57-62. May 1981.

"Peter Carey: the stories," Science Fiction: A Review of Speculative Literature 1(1):19-29. June 1977.

"Science in science fiction: an interview with Frank Bryning, The," Science Fiction: A Review of Speculative Literature 2(1):21-39. May 1979.

Ileshin, B.

"Za politseiskimi bar'erami: roman 'Boinia nomer piat' i amerikanskaia deistvitel'nost'," Izvestiia November 28, 1970.

Illuminati, Augusto

"SF americana ovvero l'idologia del possible," Il Contemporaneo pp. 58-75. December 1961.

Immig, Rudolf

"Science Fiction im Unterricht (Religionsunterricht)," Zeitschrift fur Religionspadagogik. 27(11/12):367-372. 1972.

"Science Fiction," Zeitschrift fur Religionspadagogik. 27(11/12):354-366. 1972.

Indick, B. P.

"A. Merritt: a personal reappraisal," Farrago No. 9: 5-12. 1978.

Drama of Ray Bradbury, The. Baltimore: T-K Graphics, 1977. 23 p.

"King and the Literary Tradition of Horror and the Supernatural," in: Underwood, Tim, and Miller, Chuck, eds. Fear Itself. Columbia, PA: Underwood/Miller 1982. pp. 153-167.

"Lights, camera, inaction: unfilmed film scripts of Ray Bradbury," Xenophile No. 36:R25,R31. November 1977.

"Portrait of Nathan," in: Schweitzer, Darrell, ed. Exploring Fantasy Worlds. San Bernardino, CA: Borgo, 1985. pp. 89-96.

"Stephen King as an epic writer," in: Schweitzer, Darrell, ed. Discovering Modern Horror Fiction I. Mercer Island: Starmont, 1985. pp. 56-67.

Indick, B. P. (Continued)

"Western fiction of Robert E. Howard," in: Herron, Don, ed. Dark Barbarian: The Writings of Robert E. Howard, a Critical Anthology. Westport, CT: Greenwood, 1984. pp. 99-116.

"What makes him so scary?" in: Schweitzer, Darrell, ed. Discovering Stephen King. Mercer Island: Starmont, 1985. pp. 9-14.

Ing, Dean

"Military Vehicles: Into the Third Millennium," in: Bretnor, Reginald, ed. The Future at War: Vol. 1: Thor's Hammer. New York: Ace, 1979. pp. 220-248.

"Science fiction: no time like the past/present/future," Missouri English Bulletin 35(7):13-16. November 1977.

"Vehicles for future wars," Destinies 1(4):237-277. August/September 1979.

Inge, M. T.

"American comic art: a bibliographic guide," Choice 11(11):1581-1588. January 1975. Erratum Choice 12:364. May 1975.

"Science fiction in the EC comic books," Questar 1(2):18-20. Summer 1978.

Ingersoll, D. W., Jr.

"Machines Are Good to Think: A Structural Analysis of Myth and Mechanization," in: Erlich, Richard D., ed. Clockwork Worlds. Westport, CT: Greenwood, 1983. pp. 235-262.

Ingham, M. B.

"There But Not Back Again: The Road from Innocence to Maturity," by Christine Barkley and Muriel B. Ingham. Riverside Quarterly 7(2): 101-104. March 1982.

Inglis, Fred

"Cult and Culture: A Political-Psychological Excurses," in: Inglis, Fred. The Promise of Happiness. Cambridge: Cambridge University Press, 1981. pp. 182-210.

"Gentility and Powerlessness: Tolkien and the New Class," in: Giddings, Robert, ed. J. R. R. Tolkien: This Far Land. London: Vision, 1983. pp. 25-41.

"History Absolves Nobody: Ritual and Romance," in: Inglis, Fred. The Promise of Happiness. Cambridge: Cambridge University Press, 1981. pp. 213-231.

"Rumors of Angels and Spells in the Suburbs," in: Inglis, Fred. The Promise of Happiness. Cambridge: Cambridge University Press, 1981. pp. 232-250.

Inouye, Jon

"Four strata of science fiction," Empire: For the SF Writer 3(1): 8-9. June 1977.

Insulander, P.

"Scandinavian award," Science Fiction Times No. 465:4. April 1969.

Ioakimidis, Demetre

"Definitions, Les. a) une ideologie du progres," Europe 580/581:22-24. August/September 1977.

"S. F. et science," Europe 580/581:49-53. August/September 1977.

Iosefescu, Silvian

"Wanted a Dante," Romanian Review 22:52-55. 1968. (not seen)

Irving, S. L., Jr.

"Fury: a location journal," Cinefantastique 7(2):4-9. Summer 1978.

Irwin, Martha

"Satellite stimulates science fiction stories," by Margaret Sewell and Martha Irwin. Florida Libraries 8:11. December 1957.

Irwin, W. R.

Game of the Impossible, The: A Rhetoric of Fantasy. Urbana: University of Illinois Press, 1976. 215 p.

"From Fancy to Fantasy: Coleridge and Beyond," in: Schlobin, Roger C., ed. The Aesthetics of Fantasy Literature and Art. Notre Dame, IN: University of Notre Dame Press, 1982. pp. 36-55.

Irwin, Walter

Best of Trek, The, ed. by Walter Irwin and G. B. Love. New York: Signet, 1978. 239 p.

Best of Trek, No. 2, The, ed. by Walter Irwin and G. B. Love. New York: Signet, 1980.

Best of Trek, No. 3, The, ed. by Walter Irwin and G. B. Love. New York: Signet, 1981. 196 p.

Irwin, Walter (Continued)

Best of Trek, No. 4, The, ed. by Walter Irwin and G. B. Love. New York: Signet, 1981. 214 p.

Best of Trek, No. 5, The, ed. by Walter Irwin and G. B. Love. New York: Signet, 1982. 201p.

Best of Trek, No. 6, The, ed. by Walter Irwin and G. B. Love. New York: Signet, 1983. 191 p.

Best of Trek, No. 7, The, ed. by Walter Irwin and G. B. Love. New York: Signet, 1984. 205 p.

Best of Trek, No. 8, The, ed. by Walter Irwin and G. B. Love. New York: Signet, 1985. 221 p.

Best of Trek, No. 9, The, ed. by Walter Irwin and G. B. Love. New York: Signet, 1985. 207 p.

Best of Trek, No. 10, The, ed. by Walter Irwin and G. B. Love. New York: Signet, 1986. 198 p.

Isaacs, Leonard

Darwin to Double Helix: The Biological Theme in Science Fiction. London: Butterworths, 1977. 64 p.

Isaacs, N. D.

Tolkien and the Critics: Essays on J. R. R. Tolkien's The Lord of the Rings, ed. by N. D. Isaacs and R. A. Zimbardo. Notre Dame, Indiana: University of Notre Dame Press, 1968. 296 p.

Tolkien: New Critical Perspectives, by N. D. Isaacs and R. A. Zimbardo. Lexington: University Press of Kentucky, 1981. 175 p.

"On the Need for Writing Tolkien Criticism," in: Isaacs, N. D. Tolkien: New Critical Perspectives, ed. by N. D. Isaacs and R. A. Zimbardo. Lexinton: University Press of Kentucky, 1981. pp. 107.

"Unstuck in time: 'Clockwork Orange' and 'Slaughterhouse-Five'," Literature/Film Quarterly 1:122-131. 1973.

Isajenko, Fred

"John Varley Bibliography," Megavore 12: 29-31. December 1980.

Ischreyt, H.

"Science fiction. Die technische utopie?" VDI-Nachrichten no. 12:7. 1958.

Isherwood, Christopher

"Literary scene; why science fiction is enjoying a revival of popularity," Saturday Review of Literature 34(4):4. January 27, 1951.

"Science fiction: revival of popularity (excerpt from a review)," Writer 66(5):145. May 1953.

Ishihara, Fujio

(SF tosho kaisetsu somokuroku). Tokyo: Shambleau, 1969. 534 p. (Bibliography of stories translated into Japanese, 1945-1971.) (LCCN 70-823599)

Ishikawa, Takashi

(SF no jidai). s.l.: s. n., 1977. 350 p. (LCCN 78-801830)

Ivanescu, Mircea

"Lovecraft vizionarul," Secolul 20(4):78-80. 1973.

Iwamoto, Iwao

"Clown's say: a study of Kurt Vonnegut, Jr.'s Slaughterhouse-Five, A," Studies in English Literature (Tokyo), English Number, pp. 21-23. 1975.

Izaguirre, G. C.

"Overview of Science Fiction in South America," World SF Newsletter 2: 5-6. April 1981.

J

Jackson, Al

"The Dallas Futurian Society," by Al Jackson and Steve Gould. in: First Occasional Lone Star Science Fiction Convention and Chili Cookoff. Austin: Lone Star Con, 1985. pp. 27-28.

Jackson, Anthony

"Science and literature," Times Literary Supplement pp. 667-668. July 27, 1967.

Jackson, D. G.

Changing Myth of Frankenstein, The: A Historical Analysis of the Interaction of a Myth, Technology, and Society. Ph. D. Dissertation, University of Texas, Austin, 1976. 257 p. (DAI 37:4664A)

Jackson, Frank

"Sinbad and the Eye of the Tiger (review)," Cinefantastique 6(2):26-27. Fall 1977.

"Zardoz (review)," Cinefantastique 3(3):28,44. Fall 1974.

Jackson, K. R.

"Science fiction pornography," Science Fiction Collector 4:4-18. 1977.

Jackson, Rosemary

Fantasy: The Literature of Subversion. London: Methuen, 1981. 211 p.

Jacobs, Bob

"Bradbury on Bradbury: and beyond," in: Brady, John. Fiction Writer's Market, ed. by John Brady and Jean M. Fredette. Cincinnati, OH: Writer's Digest Books, 1981. pp. 88-100.

Jacobs, I. L.

"Mexican science fiction news," Fantasy Times No. 254:8,10. September (1) 1956.

Jacobs, L. B.

"Science fiction for children," Instructor 79(5):71-72. January 1970.

Jacobs, Lee

"British convention a huge success," Fantasy Times No. 130:1-2. May (2) 1951.

Jacobs, Madeleine

"Yesterday's predictions: the way the future was," Futurist 19(1): 42-45. February 1985.

Jacobs, R. M.

"Some notes on 'science fiction and the American dream'," CEA Critic 36(3):37-39. 1974.

Jacobs, Robert

"Writer's digest interview: Ray Bradbury," Writers Digest 56(2):18-25. February 1976.

Jacquemin, Georges

Litterature fantastique. Paris: Nathan, 1974. 179 p.

"Chateau des carpathes ou le fantastique a la maniere de Jules Verne, Le," Marche Romane 18:67-70. 1968.

Jacquemin, J.

"Maudite SF," Parole (Revue publiee a Louvain) No. 8. 1963.

Jaeger, Vel

"Star Trek Protraits: Vel Jaeger Gives Helpful Hints," Fantasy: A Forum for Science Fiction and Fantasy Artists. 2(4): 28-30. Winter 1980.

Jaen, D. T.

"Mysticism, Esoterism, and fantastic literature," in: Collins, R. A., ed. Scope of the Fantastic: Theory, Technique, Major Authors. Westport: Greenwood, 1985. p.p 105-112.

Jaffery, Sheldon

Collector's Index to Weird Tales, by Sheldon Jaffery and Fred Cook. Bowling Green, OH: Bowling Green State University Popular Press, 1985. 162 p.

Horrors and Unpleasantries: A Bibliographical History and Collectors Guide to Arkham House. Bowling Green, OH: Bowling Green State University Popular Press, 1983. 142 p.

Jager, Gottfied

"Ziele zwischen Wissenschaft und Kunst," in: Rottensteiner, Franz, ed. Polaris 6. Frankfurt-am-Main: Suhrkamp, 1982. pp. 301-304.

Jago, David

"Metaphysician as fiction writer: G. K. Chesterton's narrative techniques, The," Antigonish Review 22:85-99. Summer 1975.

Jakes, John

"Some notes on a theatrical vampire," Science Fiction Times No. 465:7, 14. April 1969.

Jakiel, S. J.

"Laws of time travel, The," by S. J. Jakiel and R. E. Levinthal. Extrapolation 21(2):130-138. Summer 1980.

"Of what use: science fiction in the junior high school," Arizona English Bulletin 51(1):58-61. October 1972.

Jakubowski, Maxim

Complete Book of Science Fiction and Fantasy Lists, by Maxim Jakubowski and Malcolm Edwards. London: Granada, 1983. 350 p. (US Ed. as The SF Book of Lists.)

Nebula: An Index. s.l.: BSFA, 1963. 18 p.

SF Book of Lists, by Maxim Jakubowski and Malcolm Edwards. New York: Berkley, 1983. 352 p.

"Afterword," in: Dick, Philip K. The Zap Gun. New York: Bluejay, 1985. pp. 253-258.

"Essex House: the rise and fall of speculative erotica," Foundation 14:50-64. September 1978.

"French SF," in: Barron, Neil, ed. Anatomy of Wonder. 2nd ed. New York: Bowker, 1981. pp. 399-425.

"Introduction: travelling toward epsilon," in: Jakubowski, Maxim, ed. Travelling Toward Epsilon. London: New English Library, 1976. pp. 9-27.

"Keeping a Tight Ship," Focus: An SF Writers' Magazine 8: 38-43. Autumn 1983.

"Ouvrages critiques consacres a la science fiction forment deja une bibliotheque, Les," La Quinzaine Litteraire No. 225:8-9. January 16, 1976.

"Passe compose de J. G. Ballard, Le," Magazine Litteraire 219:92-97. May 1985.

James, B. H.

"Bond vs. Bond," Cinefantastique 14(3):4-5. May 1984.

James, Leon

"Common practice in science fiction: aspects of the writing of Henry Kuttner," Xenophile No. 42:147-150. September/October 1979.

Jameson, Fredric

"After Armageddon: character systems in Dr. Bloodmoney," Science Fiction Studies 2(1):31-42. March 1975.

"Change, SF, and Marxism: open or closed universes? in retrospect," Science Fiction Studies 1(4):272-276. Fall 1974.

"Generic discontinuities in SF: Brian Aldiss' Starship," Science Fiction Studies 1(2):57-68. Fall 1973.

"Introduction/Prospectus: To Reconsider the Relationship of Marxism to Utopian Thought," Minnesota Review ns6, 1976. pp. 53-58.

"Progress Versus Utopia; or, Can We Imagine the Future?" Science-Fiction Studies 9(2): 147-159. July 1982.

"Science fiction as politics: Larry Niven," New Republic 175(18):34-38. October 30, 1976.

Jameson, Fredric (Continued)

"World reduction in Le Guin: the emergence of utopian narrative," <u>Science Fiction Studies</u> 2(3):221-230. November 1975.

"World reduction in Le Guin: the emergence of Utopian narrative," in: <u>Ursula K. Le Guin</u>, ed. by Harold Bloom. New York: Chelsea House, 1986. pp. 57-70.

Jameson, Malcolm

"Space war tactics," in: Greenberg, M. H., ed. <u>Coming Attractions</u>. New York: Gnome, 1957. pp. 186-205.

Jamroziak, Wojciech

"Historical SF of Teodor Parnicki, The," <u>Science Fiction Studies</u> 5(2):130-133. July 1978.

Janes, A.

"Status of science fiction as literature," in: Illinois University, Graduate School of Library Science. <u>Collecting Science Literature for General Reading</u>. Champaign: Illini Union Bookstore, 1961. pp. 171-180.

Janeway, Elizabeth

"End of the world is coming, The," <u>Atlantic Monthly</u> 228(2):87-90. August 1971.

Janifer, L.

"He saw another mountain," <u>Triumph</u> 9:39-40. October 1974.

Janifer, L. M.

"Fearless you," <u>Amazing Stories</u>. 42(6):4-5,134. March 1969.

"Theodore Sturgeon in Memoriam, 3," <u>Locus</u> 18(7): 25. July 1985.

Jannone, Claudia

"Venus on the half shell as structuralist activity," <u>Extrapolation</u> 17(2):110-117. May 1976.

Janos, L.

"Special science creates illusions in sci-fi spectacles," <u>Smithsonian</u> 9(1):56-64. April 1978.

Janowski, Jack

"Disciplined Writing Brings Author of Fantasy Novels Wide Acclaim," <u>Albuquerque Journal</u> August 15, 1980. in: <u>Newsbank. Literature.</u> 5: B4-5. 1980/81.

Janssens, F. J. B.

<u>Science fiction</u>. Antwerpen: De Sikkel, 1974. 32 p.

Japenga, Ann

"Frank Kelly: Back into Outer Space," <u>Los Angeles Times</u>. Sec. 5, p. 1, 6. July 21, 1980.

Japp, Uwe

"Neue Taschenbucher zur phantastischen Literatur und Science Fiction," <u>Quarber Merkur</u> 39:48-51. January 1975.

"Phantastische Literatur und das Wissen," in: Rottensteiner, Franz, ed. <u>Polaris 3</u>. Frankfurt: Insel, 1975. pp. 11-24.

Jarvis, Sharon

<u>Inside Outer Space: Science Fiction Professionals Look at Their Craft</u>. New York: Ungar, 1985. 148 p.

"Case of the Vanishing Vacation and Other Strange Tales," <u>Fantasy Newsletter</u> 6(2): 18-19. February 1983.

"To Con or Not To Con?" by Sharon Jarvis and Lea Braff. <u>Fantasy Newsletter</u> 6(8): 26, 38. September 1983.

"What Does a Woman Know About Science Fiction, Anyway?" in: Jarvis, Sharon, ed. <u>Inside Outer Space</u>. New York: Ungar, 1985. pp. 107-116.

"Who is this Woman? Why is She Unemployed and Smiling?" <u>Fantasy Newsletter</u> 5(11): 16. December 1982.

Jarzebski, Jerzy

"Stanislaw Lem, rationalist and visionary," <u>Science Fiction Studies</u> 4(2):110-126. July 1977.

Jasinski, R. P.

"Science Fiction in East Germany, 1949-1982." unpublished mss, Texas A&M University Library, Science Fiction Research Collection. 1982. 10 p.

Jasinski, R. P. (Continued)

"Science Fiction Fandom in Eastern Europe," in: Hopkins, Marianne S., ed. Fandom Directory 1982. Newport News, VA: Fandom Computer Services, 1982. pp. 20-25.

Jean-Aubry, G.

"Origines et de quelques aspects du roman moderne a hypothese scientifique, Des," La Revue des Idees 3:945-953. December 15, 1906.

Jeanes, Geoff

"Other worlds in fiction: reflections on a body of literature," CSL: The Bulletin of the New York C. S. Lewis Society 6(8):1-4. June 1975.

Jebb, Reginald

"Note on G. K. C., A," Chesterton Review 1(1):5-6. 1974.

Jeffrey, D. L.

"Recovery: Name in The Lord of the Rings," in: Isaacs, N. D. Tolkien: New Critical Perspectives, ed. by Neil D. Isaacs and Rose A. Zimbardo. Lexington: University Press of Kentucky, 1981. pp. 106-116.

Jehmlich, Reimer

Deformierte Zukunft, Die: untersuchungen zur Science Fiction, by Reimer Jehmlich und Harmut Luck. Munchen: Goldmann, 1974. 208 p.

Science Fiction. Darmstadt: Wissenschaftliche Buchgesellschaft, 1980. 170 p.

"Cog-Work: The Organization of Labor in Edward Bellamy's Looking Backward and in Later Utopian Fiction," in: Erlich, R. D., ed. Clockwork Worlds. Westport, CT: Greenwood, 1983. pp. 27-46.

"Phantastic-Science Fiction-Utopie: Begriffsgeschichte und Begriffsabgrenzung," in: Thomsen, C. W., ed. Phantastik in Literatur und Kunst. Darmstadt: Wiss. Buchgesellschaft, 1980. pp. 11-33.

Jenkins, Stephen

Fritz Lang: The Image & The Look. New York: Zoetrope, 1981. 173 p.

Jenkins, Sue

"Spock, Avon and the Decline of Optimism," Foundation 25: 43-45. June 1982.

Jenkinson, Karl

"Science fiction in high school; with list of anthologies and single stories," Wilson Library Bulletin 26:158-159. October 1951.

Jennings, Lane

"Future as Fiction," June 1984. 11 p. (Speech, World Future Society General Assembly, June 14, 1984.) ERIC ED 250 238.

Jennings, R. M.

"Science fiction and insurance themes," Best Review Life/Health Insurance Edition 77(1):16-18,61-62. July 1976.

Jensen, M. D.

"Fantasy and Science Fiction: Means of Anticipating Human Relationships in the Future," Paper presented at the Annual Meeting of the Speech Communication Association, Anaheim, CA, Nov. 12-15. 1981. ERIC ED 211 992.

Jensen, Paul

"Metropolis," Film Heritage 3(2):22-28. Winter 1967/1968.

Jerome, R. L.

"Colossus; the Forbin Project (review)," Cinefantastique 1(1):29. Fall 1970.

"Disappearance of The Damned," Cinefantastique 1(1):21-24. Fall 1970.

"Lost Horizon (review)," Cinefantastique 3(3):31. Fall 1974.

Jeschke, Wolfgang

Reclams Science Fiction Fuehrer, ed. by H. J. Alpers, Werner Fuchs, R. M. Hahn and Wolfgang Jeschke. Munich: Heyne, 1980. 503 p.

"Fundamentale probleme des Verlags buchhandels," Science Fiction Times (Germany) 24(7):9-10. July 1982.

"Pegasus und die rakete oder, was ist eigentlich: science fiction?" in: Weigand, Jorg, ed. Die triviale phantasie. Bonn: Asgard, 1976. pp. 9-28.

"Science fiction aus der sicht der macher," in: Weigand, Jorg, ed. Die Triviale Phantasie. Bonn: Asgard, 1976. pp. 91-102.

Jeschke, Wolfgang (Continued)

"Science-Fiction-Literatur in der Bundesrepublik," in: Ermert, Karl, ed. Neugier oder Flucht? Stuttgart: Klett, 1980. pp. 53-59.

"Sf: a publisher's view," Science Fiction Studies 4(3):283-287. November 1977.

Jeury, Michel

"Un plaisir de toutes les couleurs," Magazine litteraire (Paris) 88:33-34. May 1974.

Jewell, Jane

"Aussiecon II: Part II," Locus 18(11): 27-28. November 1985.

"My L.A.con," Locus 17(12): 23-26. December 1984.

Jianzhong, Guo

"Brief History of Chinese SF," Fantasy Review of Fantasy and Science Fiction 7(3): 11-12. April 1984.

Joachim, A.

"Curl up and read," Seventeen 27:134. August 1968. (Book reviews)

Johnson, A.

"Authors and editors," Publishers Weekly 195:20-21. April 21, 1969.

Johnson, D. S.

"Doc Savage: The Man of Bronze," by D. S. Johnson and Dale Winogura. Cinefantastique 3(3):4-5,38. Fall 1974.

"Five faces of George Pal," Cinefantastique 1(4):10-27. Fall 1971.

"Portrait of Jennie; a retrospect," Cinefantastique 1(3):12-19. Summer 1971.

Johnson, G. C.

"Brainstorm (review)," Starlog No. 88: 56-58. November 1984.

"Writing for the Twilight Zone," Twilight Zone 1(5): 45-50. August 1981.

Johnson, Gordon

"Bradbury and Asimov: a contrast," Library Review 24(2):65-67. Summer 1973.

"Science and the fiction," Library Review 23(1/2):17-19. Spring/Summer 1971.

Johnson, Janice

"Celeblain of Celeborn and Galadriel, The," Mythlore 9(2): 11-19. Summer 1982.

Johnson, K. H.

"Cocoon," Starlog 96: 52-54. July 1985.

"Hello, Brazil, the movie that wouldn't die," Starlog No. 92:54-56. March 1985.

"John Cleese," Starlog 96: 88-90. July 1985.

"On the set with Cocoon," Starlog 95: 50-54. June 1985.

"Science fiction according to Monty Python, part one," Starlog No. 91:21-24. February 1985.

"Science fiction according to Monty Python, part two," Starlog No. 93:43 46. April 1985.

"Star crossed lovers of Cocoon: Steve Guttenberg," Starlog No. 98:47-49. September 1985.

"Starlog Interview: Derek Meddings," Starlog 83: 59-62. June 1984.

"Starlog Interview: Ron Howard," Starlog 97: 15-17, 28. August 1985.

"Terry Gilliam and The Time Bandits," Prevue 2(4):24-26. February/March 1981.

Johnson, K. R.

Index to the Science Fiction Magazines: 1977, by Jerry Boyajian and K. R. Johnson. Cambridge: Twaci Press, 1982. 28 p.

Index to the Science Fiction Magazines: 1978, by Jerry Boyajian and K. R. Johnson. Cambridge: Twaci Press, 1982. 28 p.

Index to the Science Fiction Magazines: 1979, by Jerry Boyajian and K. R. Johnson. Cambridge, MA: Twaci Press, 1981. 32 p.

Index to the Science Fiction Magazines: 1980, by Jerry Boyajian and K. R. Johnson. Cambridge, MA: Twaci Press, 1981. 27 p.

Index to the Science Fiction Magazines: 1981, by Jerry Boyajian and K. R. Johnson. Cambridge, MA: Twaci Press, 1982. 32 p.

Johnson, K. R. (Continued)

Index to the Science Fiction Magazines: 1982, by Jerry Boyajian and K. R. Johnson. Cambridge, MA: Twaci, 1983. 35 p.

Index to the Science Fiction Magazines: 1983, by Jerry Boyajian and K. R. Johnson. Cambridge, MA: Twaci, 1984. 31 p.

Index to the Science Fiction Magazines: 1984, by Jerry Boyajian and K. R. Johnson. Cambridge, MA: Twaci, 1985. 31 p.

Index to the Semi-Professional Fantasy Magazines: 1982, by Jerry Boyajian and K. R. Johnson. Cambridge: Twaci, 1983. 27 p.

Index to the Semi-Professional Fantasy Magazines: 1983, by Jerry Boyajian and K. R. Johnson. Cambridge, MA: Twaci, 1983. 27 p.

"M. I. T. Science Fiction Society Library, The," Special Collections 2(1/2): 69-77. Fall/Winter 1982.

"Science fiction pornography," Science Fiction Collector 4:4-18. July 1977. Addendum: Science Fiction Collector 5:45-46. September 1977.

Johnson, Kepler

"Primacy of freedom in 1984 and A Canticle for Leibowitz," in: The Future in Peril: 1984 and the Anti-Utopians. College Station: Honors Program, Texas A&M University, [1985]. pp. 38-40.

Johnson, Paul

"Actress would reject immortality of Cocoon for her grandchildren," Arkansas Gazette June 24, 1985. in: NewsBank. Film and Television. 2:B10. July 1985.

"Still-young Howard gets perspective on aging," Arkansas Gazette June 21, 1985. in: NewsBank. Film and Television. 2:B11. July 1985.

Johnson, W. B.

"Checklist to articles on the Martian 'canal' controversy, A," Extrapolation 5(2):40-48. May 1964.

"Interplay of science and fiction: the canals of Mars, The," by W. B. Johnson and T. D. Clareson. Extrapolation 5(2):37-39. May 1964.

Johnson, W. L.

Ray Bradbury. New York: Ungar, 1980. 173 p.

"Invasion stories of Ray Bradbury, The," in: Riley, Dick, ed. Critical Encounters: Writers and Themes in Science Fiction. New York: Ungar, 1978. pp. 23-40.

Johnson, William

Focus on the Science Fiction Film. Englewood Cliffs, NJ: Prentice Hall, 1972. 182 p.

"Journey into science fiction," in: Johnson, William, ed. Focus on the Science Fiction Film. Englewood Cliffs, NJ: Prentice Hall, 1972. pp. 1-12.

"Lively arts, The: man of many worlds; Arthur C. Clarke," Senior Scholastic 92(13):21. May 9, 1968.

Jonas, Gerald

"Onward and upward with the arts: SF," The New Yorker 48(23):33-52. July 29, 1972.

Jones, A. H.

"Alexei Panshin's Almost Non-sexist Rite of Passage," in: Barr, Marline S., ed. Future Females. Bowling Green, OH: Bowling Green State University Popular Press, 1981. pp. 26-33.

"Cyborg (R)Evolution in Science Fiction, The," in: Dunn, Thomas P., ed. The Mechanical God. Westport: Greenwood, 1982. pp. 203-209.

"Feminist Science Fiction and Medical Ethics: Piercy's Woman On the Edge of Time," in: Myers, R. E., ed. The Intersection of Science Fiction and Philosophy. Westport: Greenwood, 1983. pp. 171-183.

"Women in Science Fiction: An Annotated Secondary Bibliography," Extrapolation 23(1): 83-90. Spring 1982.

Jones, Alan

"Affectionate and muted exchange anent Lewis," by Alan Jones and Edmund Fuller. Studies in the Literary Imagination 14(2):3-12. Fall 1981.

"Black Moon Rising," Cinefantastique 16(1):13. March 1986.

"Clash of the Titans," by Mike Childs and Alan Jones. Cinefantastique 9(2):22-27. Winter 1979.

"Dark Crystal," Cinefantastique 13(4):32-55. April/May 1983.

"DePalma has the power; interviews," by Mike Childs and Alan Jones. Cinefantastique 6(1):4-13. Summer 1977.

Jones, Alan (Continued)

"Dream Child," _Cinefantastique_ 15(3):32-35. July 1985.

"Inferno," _Cinefantastique_ 11(2):45. Fall 1981.

"Legend," _Cinefantastique_ 15(4):9,53. October 1985.

"Return to Oz," _Cinefantastique_ 15(3):27-31. July 1985.

Jones, Bob

"Strange Tales of Mystery and Terror," _Xenophile_ No. 42:127-130. September/October 1979.

"Thrill Book, The," _Xenophile_ 30:4-10. 1977.

Jones, D. W.

"Shape of the Narrative in The Lord of the Rings, The," in: Giddings, Robert, ed. _J. R. R. Tolkien: This Far Land_. London: Vision, 1983. pp. 87-107.

Jones, Gordon

"Jules Verne at Home," _Temple Bar_ 129: 664-671. 1904.

Jones, Jerene

"Fission impossible? for 19 years Barbara's been the bain of Martin Landau's existence," _People_ pp. 54-58. June 14, 1976.

Jones, P. N.

"Ghost of Hans J. Salter," _Cinefantastique_ 7(2):10-27. Summer 1978.

"Star Trek: The Motion Picture; interviews," _Cinefantastique_ 9(2):41-47. Winter 1979.

Jones, R. K.

Shudder Pulps, The: A History of the Weird Menace Magazines of the 1930's. West Linn, Oregon: Fax Collector's Editions, 1975. 238 p.

Jones, R. L.

"Gordon R. Dickson," in: Cowart, David, ed. _Twentieth-Century American Science-Fiction Writers, Part 1: A-L_. Detroit: Gale, 1981. pp. 141-147. (Dictionary of Literary Biography, v. 8)

"Harry Harrison," in: Cowart, David, ed. _Twentieth-Century American Science-Fiction Writers, Part 1: A-L_. Detroit: Gale, 1981. pp. 205-208. (Dictionary of Literary Biography, v. 8)

Jones, Stephen

"Better things waiting: an interview with Manly Wade Wellman," _Fantasy Media_ 2(2): 14-16. May/June 1980.

"Interview (of sorts) with Harry Adam Knight, An," by Stephen Jones and Jo Fletcher. _Fantasy Review_ 8(7): 41. July 1985.

"Versions of Arrakis you'll never see," by P. M. Sammon, Stephen Jones and F. A. Levy. _Cinefantastique_ 14(4/5):32-34. September 1984.

Jones, W. M.

"Iago of _Brave New World_, The," _Western Humanities Review_ 15(3):275-278. Summer 1961.

Jordan, L.

"Expanding horizons," _Junior Bookshelf_ 24(2):71-77. March 1960.

Jordin, Martin

"Contemporary futures: the analysis of science fiction," in: Pawling, Christopher, ed. _Popular Fiction and Social Change_. New York: St. Martins, 1984. pp. 50-75.

Joshi, S. T.

H. P. Lovecraft. Mercer Island, WA: Starmont, 1982. 83 p. (Starmont Reader's Guide, 13)

H. P. Lovecraft and Lovecraft Criticism. Kent, OH: Kent State University Press, 1981. 473 p.

H. P. Lovecraft: Four Decades of Criticism Athens, OH: Ohio University Press, 1980. 247 p.

Index to the Selected Letters of H. P. Lovecraft. West Warwick, RI: Necronomicon Press, 1980. 78 p.

Lovecraft's Library: A Catalogue, by S. T. Joshi and M. A. Michand. West Warwick, RI: Necronomicon, 1980. 92 p.

"Chronology of Selected Works by H. P. Lovecraft," in: Joshi, S. T., ed. _H. P. Lovecraft: Four Decades of Criticism_. Athens, OH: Ohio University Press, 1980. pp. 27-41.

Joshi, S. T. (Continued)

"H. P. Lovecraft: His Life and Work," by K. W. Faig, Jr. and S. T. Joshi. in: Joshi, S. T., ed. H. P. Lovecraft: Four Decades of Criticism. Athens, OH: Ohio University Press, 1980. pp. 1-19.

"Lovecraft Criticism: a Study," in: Joshi, S. T., ed. H. P. Lovecraft: Four Decades of Criticism. Athens, OH: Ohio University Press, 1980. pp. 20-26.

"Sources for the chronology of Lovecraft's fiction," Lovecraft Studies 1(2):21-29. Spring 1980.

"Topical References in Lovecraft," Extrapolation 25(3): 247-265. Fall 1984.

Joyce, William

"Space: 1999, The Excitement Still Lives," Media Sight 4: 24-27. Winter 1983.

Judd, Peter

"Top Psychiatrists Explain: The Amazing Appeal of 'Return of the Jedi'," by Harold Brecher and Peter Judd. National Enquirer p. 12. June 21, 1983.

Juhren, Marcella

"Mileage in Middle-Earth," Mythlore 1(4):22. October 1969.

Juin, Hubert

"Fantastique en litterature, Du," Les Lettres Francaises p. 6. March 5, 1964.

"Potencao de Salem, Les," in: H. P. Lovecraft. Paris: Editions de l'Herne, 1969. pp. 111-116.

"Science fiction es az irodalom," Helikon 18(1): 28-35. 1972. (Tr. from Europe No. 139/140, July 1957.)

"Science fiction et litterature," Europe revue mensuelle No. 139/140:53-63. July/August 1957.

"SF Sovietique, La," Combat 17.9.1959.

"SF," Informations et Documents 1.5.1960.

Jules-Verne, Jean

Jules Verne: A Biography. New York: Taplinger, 1976. 245 p.

Julian, Alain

Rayon SF, Le. Catalogue bibliogaphique de science-fiction, utopies, voyages extraordinaires, by Henri Delmas and Alain Julian. Toulouse: Editions Milan, 1983. 331 p.

Jungk, Robert

"Wo sind die erfinder einer menschenwurdigen zukunft? Pladoyer fur eine zukunftsliteratur: science creation," Pardon no. 2:27. 1969.

"Zukunftsforschung und imagination," in: Futurum 3:507-517. 1970.

Jurkeiwicz, Kenneth

"Technology in the Void: Politics and Science in Four Contemporary Space Movies," New Orleans Review 9(1): 16-20. 1982.

Just, K. G.

"Aspekte der Zukunft. Uber Luftfahrt und Literatur," Antaios 11:393- . 1969.

Justice, K. L.

"Background and Checklist: Don Elliott/Robert Silverberg Erotic Fiction Titles," Megavore 13: 18-24. March 1981.

"Failed Experiment, A: Laser Books, History and Checklist," Science Fiction Collector 15: 4-7. July 1981.

"Publisher's Codes and Collecting Contemporary Editions," Megavore 11: 23-24. October 1980.

"SF Writer aptitude test," Empire: For the SF Writer 3(1): 10-11, 26. June 1977.

Justus, D. R.

"Doctoral Dissertations in Science Fiction and Fantasy, 1970-1979," in: Tymn, Marshall B., ed. The Science Fiction Reference Book. Mercer Island, WA: Starmont House, 1981. pp. 483-488.

K

Kaczmarka, Jerzego

Materialy z Miedzynarodowego Spotkania
Pisarzy-Tworcow Literatury
Fantastyczno-Naukowej, ed. by Jerzego
Kaczmarka and Bronislalwa Kledzika. Poznan:
Wyndawnictwo Poznanskie, 1974. 269 pp.

Kadinsky, Margot

"Uber science fiction," in: David Kadinsky.
Der Mythos der Maschine. Stuttgart, Wien:,
1969. pp. 221-232.

Kadrey, Richard

"...But Does T. S. Eliot belong in Little
Plastic Eggs?" SFWA Bulletin 16(2): 43-48.
Spring 1981.

Kael, P.

"Are movies going to pieces?" Atlantic
214:61-66. December 1964.

Kael, Pauline

"Current cinema," New Yorker 46(49):76-78.
January 23, 1971.

Kaempffert, W.

"Speaking of books," New York Times Sec.
7, 2:2. May 11, 1952.

Kafer, Joachim

"Interview mit Michael Klett," by Thomas
Tilsner and Joachim Kafer. Andromeda Science
Fiction Magazine. 103: 5-9. 1981.

Kafka, Janet

"Why science fiction?" English Journal
64(5):46-53. May 1975. also in: Varlejs,
Jana. Adult Literature in the Seventies.
New York: Scarecrow, 1978. pp. 313-326.

Kagan, Janet

"Natural heroine of James H. Schmitz," in:
Owings, Mark. James H. Schmitz: A
Bibliography. Baltimore: Croatan House, 1973.
pp. 1-19.

Kagarlisky, Julii

Chto takoe fantastika? Moscow: s. n., 1974.
349 p.

Life and Thought of H. G. Wells, The.
London: Sedgewick and Jackson, 1966. 210 p.

Was ist phantastik? East Berlin: Das Neue
Berlin, 1977. 339 p.

"Bernard Shaw and science Fiction: why raise
the question?" Shaw Review 16(2)159-66.
May 1973.

"Byl li Svift naucmyn fantastom?," in:
Fantistika. Moskva, s.n., 1965. pp. 209-222.

"Fantastic in Theater and Cinema,"
Extrapolation 22(1): 5-12. Spring 1981.

"Fantasy and realism," in: Clareson, T. D.,
ed. SF: The Other Side of Realism.
Bowling Green, Ohio: Bowling Green University
Popular Press, 1971. pp. 29-52.

"Kak popast' na lunu?" in: Fantastika 68.
Moskva, 1969. pp. 251-269.

"Realizm i fantastika" Voprosy literatury
1:101-117. 1971.

"Realizmus es fantasztikum," Helikon 18(1):
12-27. 1972. (Tr. from Vosprosy Literatury
No. 1, 1971.)

"Russian translations of foreign science
fiction," Soviet Literature No. 5:159-165.
1968.

Kagle, S. E.

"Societal quest, The," Extrapolation
12(2):79-85. May 1971.

Kagle, Steven

"Science fiction as simulation game," in: Clareson, T. D., ed. Many Futures, Many Worlds. Kent, Ohio: Kent State University Press, 1977. pp. 224-236.

Kahn, Paul

"An experimental study to determine the effect of ... teaching the science attitudes to 7th and 8th grade boys through ... current events in science," Creston Jr. HS, Bronx, NY, 1957. (cf. Black, Eldred, Thesis, Atlanta Univ., 1959.)

Kallis, S. A., Jr.

"Attention science fiction fans (letter)," Scholastic 65(5):5. October 13, 1954.

Kam, R. S.

"SF in the classroom: I. science fiction in the high school," Extrapolation 15(2):140-143. May 1974.

"Silverberg & Conrad: explorers of inner darkness," Extrapolation 17(1):18-28. December 1975.

Kaminsky, S. M.

"Kolchak: The Night Stalker (review)," Cinefantastique 4(1):40-42. Spring 1975.

"Terminal Man (review)," Cinefantastique 3(4):28. Winter 1974.

Kandel, Michael

"Aur 'Kyberiade'," Quarber Merkur 39:3-5. November 1974.

"Lem in review (June 2238)," Science Fiction Studies 4(1):65-68. March 1977.

"Stanislaw Lem on men and robots," Extrapolation 14(1):13-24. December 1972.

"Stanislaw Lem uber menschen und roboter," in: Barmeyer, Eike, ed. Science fiction: theorie und geschichte. Munchen: Fink, 1972. p. 304-318.

"Zu Stanislaw Lems Kyberiade," in: Rottensteiner, Franz, ed. Quarber Merkur. Frankfurt: Suhrkamp, 1979. pp. 65-69.

Kane, Joe

"Nuclear films," Take One 2(6):9-11. July/August 1969.

Kankowski, Joseph

"Fiction by Edmond Hamilton," Xenophile 30:14-15. 1977.

Kano, Ichiro

Suiri SF enga shi. 335 p. (cf. Library of Congress. Books: Subjects.)

Kansy, Jan

"Sowjetische science fiction Gadkie Lebedi der Bruder Strugackie," Quarber Merkur 55:21-48. July 1981.

Kanters, R.

"Ou en est la SF?" Le Monde 7.5.1967.

Kanters, Robert

"Amateur de fantastique, L'" Revue de Paris 73(5):121-129. May 1966.

"Fantomes et martiens, on la litterature entre la magie et la science," Revue de Paris 65(5):122-131. May 1958.

Kaplan, E. A.

Fritz Lang: A Guide to References and Resources. Boston: G. K. Hall, 1981. 488 p.

Kaplan, Justin

"Shape of H. G. Wells, The," Atlantic Monthly 232(4):112-115. 1973.

Kaplan, Mike

"Materializing the ghost of Maxie at illusion arts," Cinefantastique 16(1):42. March 1986.

"Maxie (review)," Cinefantastique 16(1):43. March 1986.

"Swamp Thing," Cinefantastique 12(2/3):74-81. April 1982.

Kaplan, R. B.

"First Israeli SF convention," Locus 14(4):13. May 1981.

Kaplan, S. J.

"Limits of consciousness in the novels of Doris Lessing," Contemporary Literature 14(4):536-549. Autumn 1973.

Karawacka, H.

"O trylogii fantastycznej Jerzcgo Zutawskiego," Zeszyty Naukowe UL 1(25):81-106. Lodz, 1962.

Karbach, Walter

"Phantastik des Obskuren als Obskuritaet des Phantastischen. Okkultistische Quellen phantastischer Literatur," in: Thomsen, C. W., ed. Phantastik in Literatur und Kunst. Darmstadt: Wiss. Buchgesellschaft, 1980. pp. 281-298.

Karlinger, Felix

"Paradies und Holle im spiegel des science fiction romans," Quarber Merkur 44:3-15. July 1976.

Karloff, Boris

"My life as a monster," Films and Filming 4(2):11,34. November 1957.

Kasack, Wolfgang

Science Fiction in Osteuropa. Berlin: Arno Spitz, 1984. 150 p.

Kasprowski, Piotr

"SF in Poland," Locus 18(5): 24-30. May 1985.

Kass, Carole

"Actor Fascinated by Background of His Characters," Richmond Times-Dispatch December 9, 1984. in: NewsBank. Film and Television. 70:A8-A9. January 1985.

"Film's Stars Hope to Grab Brass Ring," Richmond Times-Dispatch July 29, 1984. NewsBank. Film and Television. 1984. FTV 18:D8-D9.

"Search for fire inspires film," Richmond Times Dispatch. March 14, 1982. in: NewsBank. Film and Television FTV-109:G8-9. 1981/1982.

Kast, Pierre

"Don't play with fire," in: Johnson, William, ed. Focus on the Science Fiction Film. Englewood Cliffs, NJ: Prentice Hall, 1972. pp. 68-70.

"Terres vierges de l'espace, Les," Magazine Litteraire No. 31:18-21. August 1969.

Katzantsev, Alexander

"Men of the future," Contemporary Review 233:203-204. October 1978.

Kauffman, Stanley

"1953: year of the blast off," Publisher's Weekly 164(25):2393-2396. December 19, 1953.

"Lost in the stars: a review of '2001: A Space Odyssey'," New Republic 158(18):24,41. May 4, 1968.

Kaufman, Jerry

"Man Who Fell to Earth, a review," Locus 9(10):11. August 31, 1976.

Kaufman, V. M.

"Aspects of the paradisiacal in Tolkien's work," in: Lobdell, Jared, ed. A Tolkien Compass. New York: Ballantine/Del Rey, 1980. pp. 156-167.

"Brave new improbable worlds: critical notes on 'Extrapolation' as a mimetic technique in science fiction," Extrapolation 5(1):17-24. December 1963.

Kaufmann, Felix

"Nonreproductive male/female differences," Alternative Futures 4(2/3): 36-46. Spring/Summer 1981.

Kaveney, Roz

"Science Fiction in the 1970's," Foundation 22: 5-35. June 1981.

"SF in the eighties," Vector 95:14-16. October 1979.

Kaveny, P. E.

"From Pessimism to Sentimentality: Do Androids Dream... becomes Blade Runner," in: Hassler, Donald M., ed. Patterns of the Fantastic II. Mercer Island, WA: Starmont, 1985. pp. 77-80.

"Quadruple Dose of Dr. Kaneny's Terrestrial Pessimism," Aurora SF 7(2): 26-27. Winter 1981/1982.

Kawano, R. M.

"C. S. Lewis: the public poet," _Mythlore_ 9(3):20-21. Autumn 1982.

Kawin, Bruce

"Children of the Light," in: Slusser, George, ed. _Shadows of the Magic Lamp_. Carbondale: Southern Illinois University Press, 1985. pp. 14-29.

Kay, Joseph

"Dreams For a Dollar and a Bit," _Future_ 4: 36-39. August, 1978.

"Great Flash Gordon Revival!" _Future Life_ 18: 32-33, 69. May 1980.

"How to Market a Myth: The Saga of the Hobbit," _Future_ 1: 64-65. April 1978.

"Living in the Future: An Interview with Artist Shisei Nagaoka," _Future_ 5: 36-41. October 1978.

Kaye, Lenny

"Flying saucers rock and roll: SF in rock music," _Locus_ No. 122:6. September 16, 1972.

Kaye, Marvin

"Immortalism: The Long-range view," _Thrust_ No. 23: 14-15. Fall/Winter 1985.

Kazin, Alfred

"Not one of us: George Orwell and _Nineteen Eighty-Four_," in: _George Orwell and Nineteen Eighty-Four_. Washington, DC: Library of Congress, 1985. pp. 70-78.

"War novel: from Mailer to Vonnegut, The," _Saturday Review_ 54:13-15,36. February 6, 1971.

Keeling, T. H.

"Science Fiction and the Gothic," in: Slusser, George E., ed. _Bridges to Science Fiction_. Carbondale: Southern Illinois University Press, 1980. pp. 107-119.

Keim, Heinrich

New Wave: die Avantgarde der modernen anglo-amerikanischen Science Fiction? Meitingen: Corian, 1983. 605 p.

Keller, D. H.

"_Titus Groan_: An Appreciation," in: Schweitzer, Darrell, ed. _Exploring Fantasy Worlds_. San Bernardino, CA: Borgo, 1985. pp. 83-88.

"Hugo Gernsback," _Fantasy Times_ No. 100:5-7. February (2) 1950.

Keller, Elaine

"Yesterday and tomorrow: a study of the utopian and dystopian vision," by Elaine Keller and Deborah Rosen. _Arizona English Bulletin_ 51(1):5-24. October 1972.

Keller, Georges

"Essai de synopsis, d'apres _L'Affaire Charles Dexter Ward_," by Georges Keller and Francois Kienzle. in: _H. P. Lovecraft_. Paris: Editions de l'Herne, 1969. pp. 191-194.

"Royaume noir, Le," in: _H. P. Lovecraft_. Paris: Editions de l'Herne, 1969. pp. 139-140.

Keller, Ken

"Checking in With C. J. Cherryh," _Shayol_ No. 5: 36-48. Winter 1982.

"Franklin Booth: The Forgotton Fantasist," _Trumpet_ 12: 28-31. Summer 1981.

Keller, M. M.

"History and biology in Poul Anderson's _Fire Time_: exploring some aspects of the two-phase biosphere," _Mythologies_ No. 9:13-24. June 1976.

Kelley, Bill

"Amazing Spielberg," _Cinefantastique_ 15(5):20-21. January 1986.

"At the Earth's Core (review)," _Cinefantastique_ 5(2):30-31. Fall 1976.

"Beastmaster (review)," _Cinefantastique_ 13(2)/13(3):90. November/December 1982.

"Carrie (review)," _Cinefantastique_ 5(3):20. Winter 1976.

"Case of the missing Sherlock Holmes," _Cinefantastique_ 13(6)/14(1):87-89. September 1983.

"Close Encounters of the Third Kind (review)," _Cinefantastique_ 7(2):30-31. Summer 1978.

"Ewok Adventure (review)," _Cinefantastique_ 15(2):49,60. May 1985.

Kelley, Bill (Continued)

"Jack is back," Cinefantastique 4(2):16-25. Summer 1975.

"King Kong (review)," Cinefantastique 5(4):20-21. Spring 1977.

"My Science Project (review)," Cinefantastique 15(5):41-42,54. January 1986.

"Salem's Lot," Cinefantastique 9(2):9-21. Winter 1979.

"Steven Spielberg's Amazing Stories," Cinefantastique 15(4):6. October 1985.

"Tobe Hooper's Funhouse," by Bill Kelley and Glenn Lovell. Cinefantastique 10(3):26-31. Winter 1980.

Kelley, L. P.

Fantasy: The Literature of the Marvelous. New York: McGraw Hill, 1973.

Kelley, M. R.

"Chaucer's House of Fame: England's earliest science fiction," Extrapolation 16(1):7-16. December 1974.

Kelly, M. R.

"Recommended reading, 1984," Locus 18(2): 26, 30. February 1985.

Kelly, R. G.

"Ideology in some modern science fiction novels," Journal of Popular Culture 2(2):211-227. Fall 1968.

Kelly, W. P.

"Henry Kuttner," in: Cowart, David, ed. Twentieth-Century American Science-Fiction Writers, Part 1: A-L. Detroit: Gale, 1981. pp. 245-250. (Dictionary of Literary Biography, v. 8)

Kemball-Cook, Jessica

"Earthsea and others," New Society 38(736):314-315. November 11, 1976.

"Enter the apes," New Society 32:660-661. June 12, 1975.

"Male chauvinist lions: part 1. Sex discrimination in Tolkien," Mallorn 10:14-19. 1976.

Kemp, Earl

Eigth Stage of Fandom, The; Selections from 25 years of Fan Writing, by Robert Bloch and Earl Kemp, ed. Chicago: Advent, 1962. 176 p.

Proceedings: Chicon III. Chicago: Advent, 1963. 208 p.

Who Killed Science Fiction? An Affectionate Autopsy. Chicago: by the editor, 1960. 107 p.

Why is a Fan: The Second SaFari Annual. Chicago: by the editor, 1961. 64 p.

Kemp, Peter

H. G. Wells and the Culminating Ape. New York: St. Martins, 1982. 225 p.

Kemske, Floyd

"End of fiction at Heavy Metal," Science Fiction Times (Boston) 1(5):1,19. November 1979.

Kendall, Douglas

"Trip through middle-earth: a chronology of The Hobbit and The Lord of the Rings, A," in: Becker, Alida, ed. The Tolkien Scrapbook. New York: Grossett & Dunlap, 1978. pp. 56-73.

Kenedy, R. C.

"Kurt Vonnegut, Jr.," Art International 15(5):20-25. May 20, 1971.

Kenkel, W. F.

"Marriage and the family in modern science fiction," Journal of Marriage and the Family 31(1):6-14. February 1969. condensed version in: Mental Health Digest 1:17-20. July 1969.

Kennard, J. E.

Number and Nightmare: Forms of Fantasy On Contemporary Fiction. Hamden, CT: Archon, 1975. 244 p.

Kennard, Jean

"MF: a separable meaning," Riverside Quarterly 6(3):200-206. August 1975.

Kennebeck, Edwin

"Future church, The," Commonweal 71(23):632-634. March 4, 1960. (Book review)

Kennedy, Doug

"Mind Alteration in 1984 and A Clockwork Orange," in: The Future in Peril: 1984 and the Anti-Utopians. College Station: Honors Program, Texas A&M University, [1985]. pp. 6-13.

Kennedy, Harlan

"Space Gothic," by Nigel Andrews and Harlan Kennedy. American Film 4(5):17-22. March 1979.

"Things That Go Howl in the Night," Film Comment 18(2): 37-39. March/April 1982.

Kennedy, Sanford

"Special equipment for filming Star Trek: The Motion Picture," American Cinematographer 61(2):156-157,184-185. February 1980.

Kenney, A. P.

"Mistress of Creation," Mythlore 11(1): 18-20, 45. Summer 1984.

Kenny, Anthony

Thomas More. Oxford: Oxford University Press, 1983. 111 p.

Kensicki, N. E.

Principles and Practice in Course Design for Science Fiction. D. A. Dissertation, Catholic University of America, 1979. 239 p.

Kent, G.

"Mister imagination: Jules Verne," Saturday Review 37:9-10. June 5, 1954. also in (abbreviated with title): "Around todays world with Jules Verne," Readers Digest 65:50-54. July 1954.

Kent, Joan

"Writers: Out of this World, Down to Earth," New Orleans Times-Picayune, August 1, 1982. in: Newsbank Review of Literature, 1982/1983, 8:G6-7.

Kent, Lloyd

"Cinematography of E.T.," American Cinematographer 64(1):54-58,85-90. January 1983.

Kenter, Stuart

"Tik-Tok and the Three Laws of Robotics," by P. M. Abrahm and Stuart Kenter. Science-Fiction Studies 5(1): 67-80. March 1978.

Kenwood, Michael

"Disch on Disch: interview," Vector 51: 3-12. October 1968.

Keogh, J. G.

"Slaughterhouse-Five & the future of science fiction," Media and Methods 7(5):38-39. January 1971.

Kepinski, Z. B.

"Mavo team, or the anti-astronautics of Stanislaw Lem," Nurt No. 8:25-29. 1972.

Kerel, F. K.

"Karel Capek," Europe Revue Mensuelle No. 139/140:63-76. July/August 1957.

Kerman, J. B.

"Private Eye: A Semiotic Comparison of the Film Blade Runner and the Book...", in: Hassler, Donald M., ed. Patterns of the Fantastic II. Mercer Island, WA: Starmont, 1985. pp. 69-75.

Kern, Gary

"Aelita," in: Magill, Frank N., ed. Survey of Science Fiction Literature, Vol. 1. Englewood Cliffs, NJ: Salem Press, 1979. pp. 28-32.

"Bedbug, The," in: Magill, Frank N., ed. Survey of Science Fiction Literature, Vol. 1. Englewood Cliffs, NJ: Salem Press, 1979. pp. 138-143.

"City of Truth, The," in: Magill, Frank N., ed. Survey of Science Fiction Literature, Vol. 1. Englewood Cliffs, NJ: Salem Press, 1979. pp. 378-382.

"R.U.R.," in: Magill, Frank N., ed. Survey of Science Fiction Literature, Vol. 4. Englewood Cliffs, NJ: Salem Press, 1979. pp. 1837-1843.

"Republic of the Southern Cross, The," in: Magill, Frank N., ed. Survey of Science Fiction Literature, Vol. 4. Englewood Cliffs, NJ: Salem Press, 1979. pp. 1768-1774.

Kern, Gary (Continued)

"Second War of the Worlds, The," in:
Magill, Frank N., ed. Survey of Science
Fiction Literature, Vol. 4. Englewood Cliffs,
NJ: Salem Press, 1979. pp. 1879-1883.

"Vosstanie veshchei," in: Magill, Frank N.,
ed. Survey of Science Fiction Literature,
Vol. 5. Englewood Cliffs, NJ: Salem Press,
1979. pp. 2373-2377.

"We," in: Magill, Frank N., ed. Survey
of Science Fiction Literature, Vol. 5.
Englewood Cliffs, NJ: Salem Press, 1979. pp.
2433-2441.

"'Dream of a Ridiculous Man, The'," in:
Magill, Frank N., ed. Survey of Science
Fiction Literature, Vol. 2. Englewood Cliffs,
NJ: Salem Press, 1979. pp. 618-624.

"Search for Fantasy: From Primitive Man to
Pornography," in: Slusser, George E., ed.
Bridges to Fantasy. Carbondale: Southern
Illinois University Press, 1982. pp. 175-194.

Kernbach, Victor.

"Modern Moralist: The Science Fiction Writer,"
Romanian Review No. 1:71-77. 1981.

Kerr, Howard

Haunted Dusk: American Supernatural Fiction,
1820-1920. by Howard Kerr, J. W. Crowley, and
C. L. Crow. Athens, GA: University of Georgia
Press, 1983. 236 p.

Occult in America: New Historical
Perspectives, by Howard Kerr and C. L. Crow.
Urbana: University of Illinois Press, 1983.
246 p.

Kerr, S. T.

Bibliographical Guide to Soviet Fantasy and
Science Fiction, 1957-1968. New York: n.p.,
1969. 92 p.

Kerr, Walter

"'Little Shop of Horrors' and the Terrors of
Special Effects," New York Times Sec. 2,
p. 3. August 22, 1982.

Kessel, John

"Greg Frost: jaundiced view of technology,"
Fantasy Review 9(6)(eg v. 8 #6): 42-44.
June 1985.

Kessler, C. F.

Daring to Dream: Utopian Stories by United
States Women 1836-1919. Boston: Pandora,
1984. 265 p.

"Heavenly utopia of Elizabeth Stuart Phelps,"
in: Barr, Marleen, ed. Women and Utopia.
New York: Lanham, 1983. pp. 85-94.

Kessler, H. F.

Female Archetype in George MacDonald's
Fantasy. Masters Thesis, Florida Atlantic
University, 1981. 62 p.

Ketchum, Marty

"Has success spoiled Stephen King? Naaah!" by
Pat Cadigan, Marty Ketchum and Arnie Fenner.
Shayol 6:17-19. 1982.

"Stephen King, a Bibliography," by Marty
Ketchum, D. J. H. Levack. and Jeff Levin. in:
Underwood, Tim, and Miller, Chuck, eds. Fear
Itself. Columbia, PA: Underwood/Miller, 1982.
pp. 231-246.

Ketterer, David

New Worlds for Old: The Apocalyptic
Imagination, Science Fiction, and American
Literature. Bloomington and London: Indiana
University Press, 1974. 347 p.

"Frankenstein in wolf's clothing," Science
Fiction Studies 6(2):216-220. July 1979.
(Review)

"Frozen Year, The: 'A Piece of Spoiled Goods'
by James Blish?" Extrapolation 26(1):
36-42. Spring 1985.

"Left Hand of Darkness: Ursula K. Le Guin's
archetypal Winter Journey," Riverside
Quarterly 5(4): 288-297. April 1973.

"Rite de Passage: a reading of Rogue
Moon," Foundation 5:50-56. January 1974.

"Solaris and the illegitimate suns of science
fiction," Extrapolation 14(1):73-89.
December 1972. also in: Foundation
3:50-63. March 1973.

"Solaris und die illegitimen sonnen der
Science Fiction," Quarber Merkur 31:40-54.
July 1972.

"Apocalypse," by Jack Williamson and David
Ketterer. in: Warrick, Patricia, ed.
Science Fiction: Contemporary Mythology.
New York: Harper, 1978. pp. 435-441.

"Canadian science fiction; a survey,"
Canadian Children's Literature 10:18-23.
1977/1978.

Ketterer, David (Continued)

"Covering <u>A Case of Conscience</u>," <u>Science-Fiction Studies</u> 9(2): 195-214. July 1982.

"Epoch-eclipse and apocalypse: special 'effects' in <u>A Connecticut Yankee</u>," <u>PMLA</u> 88(5):1104-1114. 1973.

"Fathoming <u>Twenty Thousand Leagues Under the Sea</u>," in: Collins, R. A., ed. <u>Scope of the Fantastic: Theory, Technique, Major Authors</u>. Westport: Greenwood, 1985. p. 263-275.

"Fathoming '20,000 Leagues Under the Sea'," in: Tolley, M. J., ed. <u>The Stellar Guage</u>. Carleton, Australia: Norstrilia, 1980. pp. 5-24.

"Grokking science fiction," <u>Canadian Review of American Studies</u> 12(3):361-373. Winter 1981. (Book Reviews)

"Historical Survey of Canadian Science Fiction," <u>Science-Fiction Studies</u> 10(1): 87-100. March 1983.

"Imprisoned in a tesseract: <u>Black Easter</u> and <u>The Day After Judgement</u> by James Blish," <u>Missouri Review</u> 7(2): 243-263. 1984.

"Last Inspirational Gasp of James Blish, The: <u>The Breath of Brahma</u>," <u>Science-Fiction Studies</u> 11(1): 45-49. March 1984.

"Letter, on James Blish," <u>Foundation</u> 33: 100. Spring 1985.

"Mary Shelley and science fiction: a select bibliography selectively annotated," <u>Science Fiction Studies</u> 5(2):172-178. July 1978.

"Metaphoric matrix: magnetism in <u>Frankenstein</u>," in: Remington, T. J., ed. <u>Selected Proceedings of the 1978 SFRA National Conference</u>. Cedar Falls, Iowa: University of Northern Iowa, 1979. pp. 55-67.

"New worlds for old: the apocalyptic imagination, science fiction, and American literature," <u>Mosaic</u> 5:37-57. October 1971.

"On David Ketterer's <u>New Worlds for Old</u>: in response," <u>Science Fiction Studies</u> 2(2):139-146. July 1975.

"Patropy, Polyploidy and Tectogenesis in the Fiction of James Blish and Norman L. Knight," <u>Science-Fiction Studies</u> 10(2): 199-218. July 1983.

"Power Fantasy in the 'Science Fiction' of Mark Twain," in: Slusser, George E., ed. <u>Bridges to Fantasy</u>. Carbondale: Southern Illinois University Press, 1982. pp. 130-141.

"Science fiction and allied literature," <u>Science Fiction Studies</u> 3(1):64-75. March 1976.

"Science fiction and fantasy in English and French," in: <u>The Oxford Companion to Canadian Literature</u>. Toronto: Oxford University Press, 1983. pp. 730-739.

"Science Fiction of Mark Twain, The" <u>Mosaic</u> 16(4): 59-82. Fall 1983.

"SF element in the work of Poe: a chronological survey, The," <u>Science Fiction Studies</u> 1(3):197-213. Spring 1974.

"Take off to Cosmic Irony: Science Fiction, Humor, and the Absurd," in: Cohen, Sarah Blacker, ed. <u>Comic Relief: Humor in Contemporary American Literature</u>. Urbana: University of Illionis Press, 1983. pp. 70-80.

"Ursula K. Le Guin's archetypal Winter Journey," in: <u>Ursula K. Le Guin</u>, ed. by Harold Bloom. New York: Chelsea House, 1986. pp. 11-22.

"Utopian fantasy as millenial motive and science fiction motif," <u>Studies in the Literary Imagination</u> 6(2):79-103. Fall 1973.

Keyes, Daniel

"How much does a character cost?" in: Wilson, Robin Scott, ed. <u>Those Who Can: A Science Fiction Reader</u>. New York: Mentor/New American Library, 1973. pp. 101-104.

Khanna, L. C.

"Truth and art in women's worlds: Doris Lessing's <u>Marriages Between Zones Three, Four, and Five</u>," in: Barr, Marleen, ed. <u>Women and Utopia</u>. New York: Lanham, 1983. pp. 121-133.

"Women's worlds: new directions in utopian fiction," <u>Alternative Futures</u> 4(2/3):47-60. Spring/Summer 1981.

Khmelnitskaia, Tamara

"Slozhnyi put' k prosteishim istinam," <u>Novyi Mir</u> 4:245-250. 1971.

Khouri, Nadia

"Clockwork and Eros: Models of Utopia in Edward Bellamy and William Morris," <u>CLA Journal</u> 24(3): 376-399. March 1981.

"Dialectics of power: Utopia in the science Fiction of Le Guin, Jeury and Piercy," <u>Science-Fiction Studies</u> 7(1): 49-60. March 1980.

"International Bibliography of Prehistoric Fiction," by Marc Angenot and Nadia Khouri. <u>Science-Fiction Studies</u> 8(1): 38-53. March, 1981.

Khouri, Nadia (Continued)

"Lost Worlds and the Revenge of Realism,"
Science-Fiction Studies 10(2): 170-190.
July 1983.

"Reaction and Nihilism: the political genealogy
of Orwell's 1984," Science Fiction
Studies 12(2): 136-147. July 1985.

"Utopia and epic: ideological confrontation in
Jack London's The Iron Heel," Science
Fiction Studies 3(2):174-181. July 1976.

Khutorskaia, L. N.

Mechta i kosmosj. s. l.: s. n., 1975. 113 p.

Kibbey, R. A.

"A. W. library pathfinder: literature: science
fiction," Addison Wesley Publishing Company,
No date. 2 p.

Kidd, Virginia

"Where 'To Milford' Became a Verb,"
Pennsylvania English 10(2): 21-23. Spring
1984.

Kiely, Robert

"Satire as fantasy," Summary 1(2):41-43.
1971.

Kienzle, Francois

"Lovecraftiana," in: H. P. Lovecraft.
Paris: Editions de l'Herne, 1969. pp. 135-136.

Kievitt, F. D.

"Walter M. Miller's A Canticle For Leibowitz
as a Third Testament," in: Reilly, Robert,
ed. The Transcendent Adventure. Westport:
Greenwood, 1984. pp. 169-175.

Kijowski, Andrzej

"Fantaszja i realizm," Zycie literackie No.
12. 1952. Also in: Kijowski, Andrzej. Rozowe
i Czarne. Krakow: Wydawnictwo Literackie,
1957. p. 82-87.

"Powrot na ziemie," Nowa Kultura No. 6:4.
1955. Also in: Kijowski, A. Rozone i Czone.
Krakow: Wyndawnictwo Literackiej, 1957. p.
124-129.

Kilby, C. S.

Tolkien & the Silmarillion. Wheaton,
Illinois: Harold Shaw, 1976. 89 p.

"Lost myth, The," Arts in Society
6(2):155-163. Summer/Fall 1969.

"Note on the Wade Collection," Studies in
the Literary Imagination 14(2):117-119. Fall
1981.

"Outer Dimension of Myth," Mythlore 10(4):
28-30. Spring 1984.

Kilday, Gregg

"Close Encounters with Douglas Trumbull,"
Home Video 2(9): 27-30. September 1981.

Kilker, D. K.

"Mirror for Observers, A," in: Magill,
Frank N., ed. Survey of Science Fiction
Literature, Vol. 3. Englewood Cliffs, NJ:
Salem Press, 1979. pp. 1417-1423.

"Rogue Queen," in: Magill, Frank N., ed.
Survey of Science Fiction Literature, Vol. 4.
Englewood Cliffs, NJ: Salem Press, 1979. pp.
1827-1831.

Killough, H. P.

"What is this thing called copyright,"
Empire for the SF Writer 9(3): 22 Spring
1985.

Kilman, Buzz

"Interview: Herald Movie Freak," Daily
Planet p. 1. March 10, 1972.

"Rat in a Box, A," Daily Planet p. 33.
June 10, 1972.

Kilpatrick, C. E.

"Mystery, horror, western and SF roundup no.
2," Library Journal 83(17):2628-2630.
October 1, 1958.

"Roundup of westerns, mysteries, horror and
SF," Library Journal 83(8):356-360.
February 1, 1958.

Kilworth, Garry

"Banana in Each Ear, A," Focus: An SF
Writer's Magazine 7: 40-46. Spring 1983.

"Famous Five Go Shoplifting," Focus: An SF
Writer's Magazine 10: 18-21. February 1985.

"Profession of Science Fiction, 31:
Confessions of a Bradbury Eater,"
Foundation 29: 5-10. November 1983.

Kincaid, Paul

Bob Shaw: British Science Fiction Writers, Volume 1 by Paul Kincaid and Geoff Rippington. Kent, England: British Science Fiction Association, 1981. 38 p.

"Aliens: a personal view," Vector 95:17-21. October 1979.

"And Torture One Poor Word Ten Thousand Ways; Interview," Vector No. 121: 12-21. August 1984.

"Guest Editorial: The Death of Science Fiction," Vector 105: 5-6. December 1981.

"Mouse, the lion, and Riddley Walker: Russell Hoban interviewed," Vector No. 124/125: 5-9. 1985.

"Novels of Robert Holdstock, The," Arena 9:27-32. August 1979.

"O Happy Days: an interview with Geoff Ryman," Vector No. 128: 5-7. October/November 1985.

"Of Men and Machines: Keith Roberts Interviewed," Vector 108: 6-12. 1982.

"Realms of Fantasy," Vector 117: 10-14. December 1983.

"Science and Fiction," Vector 119: 16-18. April 1984.

Kinders, Mark

"Science Fiction Buffs Watching the Future," Bismarck (N. D.) Tribune February 15, 1982. in: Newsbank, Social Relations. 7: A3. 1982.

King, A. S.

"On the Set of Starman," Starlog No. 89: 58-60. December 1984.

King, Betty

Women of the Future: The Female Main Character in Science Fiction. Metuchen, NJ: Scarecrow, 1984. 273 p.

King, Bill

"Nimoy's New Treks," Atlanta Journal January 21, 1983. in: NewsBank. Film and Television 77: E11-12. 1982/1983.

King, Don

"Narnia and the Seven Deadly Sins," Mythlore 10(4): 14-19. Spring 1984.

King, J. N.

"Theology, science fiction, and man's future," in: Clareson, T. D., ed. Many Futures, Many Worlds. Kent, Ohio: Kent State University Press, 1977. pp. 237-259.

King, Jeanne

"Science fiction for fun and profit," Arizona English Bulletin 51(1):43-48. October 1972.

King, Lindi

"World of only women," San Francisco Examiner April 14, 1985. in: NewsBank. Film and Television. 115:G5-G6. May 1985.

King, Marsha

"Vonda McIntyre's Stories are Out of This World," Seattle Times August 3, 1984. in: Newsbank. Literature. 26:D14. 1984.

King, Roger

"Recovery, Escape, Consolation: Middle-earth and the English Fairy Tale," in: Giddings, Robert, ed. J. R. R. Tolkien: This Far Land. London: Vision, 1983. pp. 42-55.

King, Stephen

Danse Macabre. New York's Everest House, 1981. 400 p.

"Cannibal and the Cop," In: Winter, Douglas E. Shadowings: The Reader's Guide to Horror Fiction 1981-1982. Mercer Island, WA: Starmont, 1983. pp. 27-29.

"Horror market and the ten bears, The," Writer's Digest 53(11):10-13. November 1973.

"Last Waltz: Horror and Morality, Horror and Magic," in: Fredette, Jean M., ed. 1983/84 Fiction Writer's Market. Cincinnati: Writer's Digest, 1983. pp. 172-185.

"On Becoming a Brand Name," in: Underwood, Tim, and Miller, Chuck, eds. Fear Itself. Columbia, PA: Underwood/Miller, 1982. pp. 15-42.

"Theodore Sturgeon, 1918-1985," SFWA Bulletin 19(2): 14-15. Summer 1985.

King, Tappan

"Science fiction and fantasy explosion, The," by Tappan King and Beth Meacham. American Bookseller 2(11):42-58. July 1979.

Kinnaird, John

"Frankenstein or The Modern Prometheus," in: Magill, Frank N., ed. Survey of Science Fiction Literature, Vol. 2. Englewood Cliffs, NJ: Salem Press, 1979. pp. 832-839.

"Sirius: A Fantasy of Love and Discord," in: Magill, Frank N., ed. Survey of Science Fiction Literature, Vol. 5. Englewood Cliffs, NJ: Salem Press, 1979. pp. 2085-2090.

Kiplinger, Christina

"Interview: Dennis Etchison," Science Fiction Chronicle 5(8):1,19-20. May 1984.

"Interview: J. N. Williamson," Fantasy Review 8(8): 11-13, 42. August 1985.

"Interview: Peter Tremayne," Fantasy Review 7(1): 13-14. January 1984.

Kirchbaum, Jorg

"'Es ware falsch, uber die zukunft zu schrieben (J. G. Ballard im gesprach mit Jorge Kirchbaum und Rein A. Zondergeld," by Jorg Kirschbaum and R. A. Zondergeld. Quarber Merkur 44:60-68. July 1976.

"Disch, Ballard, and Bradbury: eine hypotaktische vision," Quarber Merkur 39:3-6. January 1975.

"Einige Gedanken zur Phantastik," Quarber Merkur 41:27-30. September 1975.

"Sehnsucht der sirene nach dem wasser. Die welt des Maurice Renard," by Jorg Kirschbaum and R. A. Zondergeld. Quarber Merkur 43:50-58. May 1976.

"Stanislaw Lem; und Jahre nach Solaris," Quarber Merkur 38:39-42. November 1974.

Kirk, Malcom

"Interview: Arthur C. Clarke," Omni 1(6):100-103,139-141. March 1979.

Kirk, Russell

"Chesterton and T. S. Eliot," Chesterton Review 2:184-196. 1976.

Kirkpatrick, Hope

"Hierarchy in C. S. Lewis," CSL: The Bulletin of the New York C. S. Lewis Society 6(4):1-6. February 1975.

Kirkpatrick, John

"Great dance in Perelandra, The," CSL: The Bulletin of the New York C. S. Lewis Society 7(4):1-6. 1976.

Kirkpatrick, Mary

"Introduction to the Curdie books by George MacDonald including parallels between them and the Narnia chronicles," CSL: The Bulletin of the New York C. S. Lewis Society 5(5):1-6. March 1974.

"Lewis and MacDonald," CSL: The Bulletin of the New York C. S. Lewis Society 5(11):10-12. May 1974.

Kirman, J. H.

"Teaching about science, technology and society," History and Social Science Teacher 13:54-56. February 1977.

Kirpal, Singh

"Technology in George Orwell's '1984'," in: Tolley, M. J., ed. The Stellar Guage. Carleton, Australia: Norstrilia, 1980. pp. 43-61.

Kishi, David

"Fantasy in the theatre," Fantasy Times No. 56:4,18. September 1947.

Kitaigorodzki, Mauricio

"Science fiction in Argentina," Australian Science Fiction Review No. 14:20-22. February 1968.

Kittredge, Mary

"Interview with Jim Baen," Empire: For the SF Writer 25: 4-6. Fall 1981.

"Other side of magic: a few remarks about Shirley Jackson, The" in: Schweitzer, Darrell, ed. Discovering Modern Horror Fiction I. Mercer Island: Starmont, 1985. pp. 3-12.

Kivu, Dinu

"Hybrid genres?" Romanian Review 22:59-60. 1968.

Klages, Helmut

"Models for a Future Society: Literature and the Sociologist," Comparative Literature Studies 10(1): 323-333. March 1973.

Klass, Morton

"Artificial Alien: Transformations of the Robot in Science Fiction," in: Miller, R. J., ed. Robotics: Future Factories, Future Workers. Beverly Hills, CA: Sage, 1983. pp. 171-179. (Annals of the Am. Academy of Political and Social Science 470)

Klass, Philip

"Innocent in time: Mark Twain in King Arthur's court, An," Extrapolation 16(1):17-32. December 1974.

"John W. Campbell, Jr.: A Memoir," Pennsylvania English 10(2): 15-19. Spring 1984.

Klaus, Darla

"Science fiction and women," by Darla Klaus and Lori Korleski. The Cougar (University of Houston), Nova Supplement 43(11):2. September 16, 1976.

Klawans, Stuart

"Vonnegut, Bradbury and the fantastic company they keep," Book World (Chicago Tribune) p. 4. May 19, 1974.

Klein, Arnold

"Destination: Void," Harpers 265(1591): 64-67. December 1982.

Klein, G.

"Bestiaire digest de la science fiction," by R. Chomet and G. Klein. Bizarre No. 11:61, 63, 65-67. October 1955.

Klein, Gerard

Malaise dans la science fiction. Metz: l'Aube enclavee, 1978. 78 p.

"Defense et illustration de la SF," by Gerard Klein, Alain Doremieux, and Jacques Goimard. Le Monde 28.6.1967.

"Discontent in American science fiction," Science Fiction Studies 4(1):3-13. March 1977.

"Entre la fantastique et la science fiction, Lovecraft," Cahiers de l'Herne No. 12:47-74. 1969.

"Le Guin's 'aberrant' opus: escaping the trap of discontent," Science Fiction Studies 4(3):287-295. November 1977.

"Le Guin's Aberrant Opus: escaping the trap of discontent," in: Ursula K. Le Guin, ed. by Harold Bloom. New York: Chelsea House, 1986. pp. 85-98.

"Petition by agents of the dominant culture for the dismissal of science fiction, A," SF Studies 7(2):115-123. July 1980. Originally "Proces en dissolution de las SF," Europe pp. 145-155. August/September 1977.

"Proces en dissolution de la S. F., Le," Europe 580/581:145-155. August/September 1977.

"Prospective et science fiction," Les Nouvelles Litteraires (Paris) 2427:6-7. April 1, 1974.

"Science fiction et theologie," Fiction No. 167:141-150. 1967.

Klein, J. E.

"Artist draws on nightmares for a living," Chicago Tribune Sec. 5, p. 10. July 4, 1985.

Klein, J. K.

"Star Wars pro and con," by J. K. Klein and Jeff Rovin. Galaxy 38(8):63-72. October 1977.

"1983 World Fantasy Convention," SFWA Bulletin 17(4): 2-4. Winter 1983.

"1984 World Fantasy Award," SFWA Bulletin 18(4): 2, 10. Winter 1984.

"1984 World Fantasy Convention," SFWA Bulletin 18(4): 3-6. Winter 1984.

"Astounding/Analog 50th anniversary," Locus 14(5):1,20. June 1981.

"Biolog: Alison Tellure," Analog 104(5): 91. May 1984.

"Biolog: Andrew J. Offutt," Analog 102(8): 47. August 1982.

"Biolog: Arthur C. Clarke," Analog 102(4): 46-47. March 29, 1982.

"Biolog: Barry Longyear," Analog 101(5): 85. April 27, 1981.

"Biolog: Ben Bova," Analog 100(9):149. September 1980.

"Biolog: Bob Buckley," Analog 100(3):59. March 1980.

"Biolog: Brad Hamann," Analog 103(7): 48. July 1983.

"Biolog: Broeck Steadman," Analog 99(7): 97. July 1979.

Klein, J. K. (Continued)

"Biolog: Chad Oliver," _Analog_ 103(10): 28. mid-September 1983.

"Biolog: Charles L. Harness," _Analog_ 101(4): 85. March 30, 1981.

"Biolog: Charles Sheffield," _Analog_ 100(10): 41. October 1980.

"Biolog: Clifford D. Simak," _Analog_ 99(10): 145. October 1979.

"Biolog: David Bischoff," _Analog_ 101(12): 135. November 9, 1981.

"Biolog: David Brin," _Analog_ 103(12): 119. November 1983.

"Biolog: David R. Palmer," _Analog_ 103(2): 61. February 1983.

"Biolog: Dean Ing," _Analog_ 100(7):83. July 1980.

"Biolog: Don Sakers," _Analog_ 105(1): 71. January 1985.

"Biolog: Doug Beekman," _Analog_ 105(7): 79. July 1985.

"Biolog: Edward A. Byers," _Analog_ 101(10): 91. September 14, 1981.

"Biolog: Eric G. Iverson," _Analog_ 105(2): 115. February 1985.

"Biolog: Eric Vinicoff," _Analog_ 102(2): 149. February 1, 1982.

"Biolog: F. Paul Wilson," _Analog_ 101(1): 52. January 5, 1981.

"Biolog: G. Harry Stine," _Analog_ 99(9): 143. September 1979.

"Biolog: George O. Smith," _Analog_ 100(5):61. May 1980.

"Biolog: George W. Harper," _Analog_ 102(11):55. October 1982.

"Biolog: Gordon R. Dickson," _Analog_ 100(8):39. August 1980.

"Biolog: Grant D. Callin," _Analog_ 104(7): 61. July 1984.

"Biolog: Greg Bear," _Analog_ 103(6): 37. June 1983.

"Biolog: Hayford Peirce," _Analog_ 103(9): 77. September 1983.

"Biolog: Hilbert Schenck," _Analog_ 104(9): 94. September 1984.

"Biolog: Ian Stewart," _Analog_ 101(3): 39. March 2, 1981.

"Biolog: Isaac Asimov," _Analog_ 100(1):166. January 1980.

"Biolog: J. Brian Clarke," _Analog_ 105(5): 112. May 1985.

"Biolog: James E. Gunn," _Analog_ 104(1): 89. January 1984.

"Biolog: James White," _Analog_ 102(1): 131. January 4, 1982.

"Biolog: Janet Aulisio," _Analog_ 102(7): 106. July 1982.

"Biolog: Jayge Carr," _Analog_ 103(8): 50. August 1983.

"Biolog: Jerry E. Pournelle," _Analog_ 99(12): 161. December 1979.

"Biolog: Jerry Oltion," _Analog_ 105(4): 61. April 1985.

"Biolog: John Gribbin," _Analog_ 101(13): 59. December 7, 1981.

"Biolog: John Varley," _Analog_ 99(1):49. January 1979.

"Biolog: Joseph Green," _Analog_ 101(8): 84. July 20, 1984.

"Biolog: Kevin O'Donnell, jr.," _Analog_ 99(11): 65. November 1979.

"Biolog: Larry Niven," _Analog_ 103(13): 159. December 1983.

"Biolog: Laurence M. Janifer," _Analog_ 99(4): 139. April 1979.

"Biolog: Leo Summers," _Analog_ 104(3): 102. March 1984.

"Biolog: Lester Del Rey," _Analog_ 105(10): 97. October 1985.

"Biolog: Lyon Sprague de Camp," _Analog_ 100(2): 91. December 1980.

"Biolog: Marcia Martin," _Analog_ 104(11): 82. November 1984.

"Biolog: Margaret L. Silber," _Analog_ 102(10): 65. mid-September 1982.

"Biolog: Michael Kube-McDowell," _Analog_ 104(2): 106. Februray 1984.

"Biolog: Michael McCollum. _Analog_ 100(11):53. November 1980.

"Biolog: Milton A. and Tony Rothman," _Analog_ 101(6): 58. May 25, 1981.

"Biolog: Orson Scott Card," _Analog_ 99(2):175. February 1979.

"Biolog: Paul J. Nahin," _Analog_ 99(6): 111. June 1979.

Klein, J. K. (Continued)

"Biolog: Paul Lehr," <u>Analog</u> 99(5): 99. May 1979.

"Biolog: Ray Brown," <u>Analog</u> 102(12): 41. November 1982.

"Biolog: Raymond Z. Gallun," <u>Analog</u> 100(2): 137. February 1980.

"Biolog: Richard K. Lyon," <u>Analog</u> 102(9): 161. September 1982.

"Biolog: Rob Chilson," <u>Analog</u> 104(4): 90. April 1984.

"Biolog: Robert L. Forward," <u>Analog</u> 102(3): 98. March 1, 1982.

"Biolog: Robert Silverberg," <u>Analog</u> 103(3): 88. March 1983.

"Biolog: Stephen L. Gillett," <u>Analog</u> 104(12): 82. December 1984.

"Biolog: Steven Gould," <u>Analog</u> 101(9): 85. August 17, 1981.

"Biolog: Ted Reynolds," <u>Analog</u> 99(3):73. March 1979.

"Biolog: Thomas A. Easton," <u>Analog</u> 100(4):115. April 1980.

"Biolog: Thomas F. Monteleone," <u>Analog</u> 101(11): 161. October 12, 1981.

"Biolog: Thomas R. Dulski," <u>Analog</u> 102(13): 82. December 1982.

"Biolog: Timothy Zahn," <u>Analog</u> 101(7): 70. June 22, 1981.

"Biolog: Val Lakey," <u>Analog</u> 102(5): 163. May 1982.

"Biolog: Vernor Vinge," <u>Analog</u> 104(6): 146. June 1984.

"Biolog: Vincent Di Fate," <u>Analog</u> 101(2): 87. February 2, 1981.

"Biolog: W. R. Thompson," <u>Analog</u> 105(8): 79. August 1985.

"Biolog: Walter B. Hendrickson, jr.," <u>Analog</u> 103(11): 57. October 1983.

"Biolog: William E. Cochrane/S. Kye Boult," <u>Analog</u> 99(8): 156. August 1979.

"Biolog: William F. Wu," <u>Analog</u> 105(9): 119. September 1985.

"ConStellation," <u>SFWA Bulletin</u> 17(3): 2-3, 8. Fall 1983.

"Frank R. Paul, an appreciation," <u>Science Fiction Times</u> No. 405:9. August 1963.

"In Memoriam: Jack Gaughan, 1930-1985," <u>SFWA Bulletin</u> 19(3): 16. Fall 1985.

"LACon II: The World Science Fiction Convention, 1984," <u>SFWA Bulletin</u> 18(3): 3-6. Fall 1984.

"Nebula Award Weekend," <u>SFWA Bulletin</u> 17(1): 5-6, 27. Spring 1983.

"Nineteenth Annual Nebula Awards Banquet," <u>SFWA Bulletin</u> 18(2): 3-6. Summer 1984.

Klein, K. P.

<u>Zukunft zwischen trauma und mythos: science fiction. Zur wirkungsaesthetik, sozialpsychologie und didaktik eines literarischen massenphaenomens.</u> Suttgart: Keltt, 1976. 248 p.

Klein, Marcus

"Slouch toward Bethlehem, A," <u>Nation</u> 191(17):398-402. November 19, 1960. (Book review)

Klein, Ted

"Twilight Zone, The Movie (review)," <u>Cinefantastique</u> 13(6)/14(1):105-106. September 1983.

Kleiner, E. L.

"Introduction," in: Conrad, Jospeh and F. M. Hueffer. <u>The Inheritors</u>. Boston: Gregg, 1976. pp. v-xv.

"Joseph Conrad's forgotten role in the emergence of science fiction," <u>Extrapolation</u> 15(1):25-34. December 1973.

Kleinman, K. C.

"Quest of the Adult Trekker," <u>Fantasy Newsletter</u> 6(8): 29-36. September 1983.

Kline, O. A.

"Kline-Howard collaboration?" by Glenn Lord and O. A. Kline. <u>Oak Leaves</u> 1(10):13. Winter 1972/73.

"Reflections," <u>Oak Leaves</u> 1(11):3-4. 1975.

"Short autobiography," <u>Oak Leaves</u> 1(1):12. Fall 1970.

Kline, R. H.

"Behind the camera on Star Trek: The Motion Picture," _American Cinematographer_ 61(2):134, 180-181,187-188. February 1980.

"Challenges of photographing King Kong," _American Cinematographer_ 58(1):36-39, 68-70,92-95. January 1977.

Kling, Bernt

"Perry Rhodan," _Science Fiction Studies_ 4(2):159-161. July 1977.

"On SF comics: some notes for a future encyclopedia," _Science Fiction Studies_ 4(3):277-282. November 1977.

Klingberg, Gote

Frammande varldama i barn- och ungdomslitteraturen, De, [The Strange World of Children's Fiction]. Stockholm: Raben, 1980. 147 p.

Klinger, Werner

"So war Dominik nicht!" _Quarber Merkur_ 19(2):64-69. October 1981.

Klinkowitz, Jerome

Kurt Vonnegut. London: Methuen, 1982. 96 p.

Kurt Vonnegut, Jr.: A Descriptive Bibliography and Annotated Checklist, by A. B. Pieratt, Jr. and Jerome Klinkowitz. Hamden, Connecticut: Archon Books, 1974. 138 p.

Vonnegut in America: An Introduction to the Life and Work of Kurt Vonnegut. New York: Delacorte, 1977. 304 p.

Vonnegut Statement, The, ed. by Jerome Klinkowitz and John Somer. New York: Delacorte Press, 1973. 286 p.

"Mother Night, Cat's Cradle, and the crimes of our time," in: Klinkowitz, Jerome and John Somer, eds. The Vonnegut Statement. New York: Delacorte Press/Seymour Lawrence, 1973. pp. 18-30.

"Do-it-yourself story collection by Kurt Vonnegut, A," in: Klinkowitz, Kurt, ed. Vonnegut in America. New York: Delacorte, 1977. pp. 53-60.

"Dramatization of Kurt Vonnegut, Jr., The," _Players_ 50(3):62-64. February/March 1975.

"Kurt Vonnegut checklist, A," by Stanley Schatt and Jerome Klinkowitz. _Critique_ 12(3):70-76. 1971.

"Kurt Vonnegut, Jr. and the crime of his times," _Critique_ 12(3):38-53. 1971.

"Kurt Vonnegut, Jr.'s superfiction," _Revue Francaise d'Etudes Americaines_ No. 1: 115-124. April 1976.

"Kurt Vonnegut, Jr.," in: Literary Disruptions/The Making of a Post-Contemporary American Fiction. Urbana: University of Illinois Press, 1975. pp. 33-61.

"Kurt Vonnegut, Jr.: the canary in a cathouse," in: Klinkowitz, Jerome and John Somer, eds. The Vonnegut Statement. New York: Delacorte Press/Seymour Lawrence, 1973. pp. 7-17.

"Kurt Vonnegut: a chronology," in: Klinkowitz, Kurt, ed. Vonnegut in America. New York: Delacorte, 1977. pp. 3-6.

"Literary career of Kurt Vonnegut, Jr., The," _Modern Fiction Studies_ 19(1):57-67. Spring 1973.

"Lost in the cat house," _The Falcon_ No. 5:110-113. December 1972. (Book review)

"Vonnegut bibliography, The," by Jerome Klinkowitz and Stanley Schatt. in: Klinkowitz, Jerome and John Somer, eds. The Vonnegut Statement. New York: Delacorte Press/Seymour Lawrence, 1973. pp. 255-277.

"Vonnegut bibliography, The," in: Klinkowitz, Kurt, ed. Vonnegut in America. New York: Delacorte, 1977. pp. 217-252.

"Vonnegut in America," in: Klinkowitz, Kurt, ed. Vonnegut in America. New York: Delacorte, 1977. pp. 7-36.

"Vonnegut statment, The," by Jerome Klinkowitz and John Somer. in: Klinkowitz, Jerome and John Somer, eds. The Vonnegut Statement. New York: Delacorte Press/Seymour Lawrence, 1973. pp. 1-3.

"Why they read Vonnegut," in: Klinkowitz, Jerome and John Somer, eds. The Vonnegut Statement. New York: Delacorte Press/Seymour Lawrence, 1973. pp. 158-177.

Klinkowitz, Kurt

Vonnegut in America. New York: Delacorte, 1977. 293 p.

Klose, Kevin

"In Whovian Heaven," _Washington Post_ p. C1, C4. November 26, 1984.

Knapp, Bettina

"Jungian Reading of the Kalevala 500-1300? Finnish Shamanism: The Patriarchal Senex Figure, Part III: The Anima Archetype," Mythlore 9(1):35-36. Spring 1982.

"Jungian Reading of the Kalevala 500-1300? Finnish Shamanism: The Patriarchal Senex Figure," Mythlore 8(4): 33-36. Winter 1982.

"Jungian Reading of the Kalevala 500-1300? Finnish Shamanism: The Patriarchal Senex Figure, part 1, Introduction," Mythlore 8(3): 25-28. Autumn 1981.

"Jungian Reading of the Kalevala 500-1300? Finnish Shamanism: The Patriarchal Senex Figure, Part IV, Conclusion," Mythlore 9(2): 38-41. Summer 1981.

Knapp, J. V.

"Dance to a creepy minuet: Orwell's Burmese Days, precursor of Animal Farm," Modern Fiction Studies 21(1):11-29. Spring 1975.

Knapp, Lawrence

First Editions of Philip Jose Farmer, The. Menlo Park, California: David G. Turner, 1976. 8 p.

Knapp, Mona

Doris Lessing. New York: Ungar, 1985, c1984. 210 p.

Knepper, B. G.

"Coming Race: Hell? or Paradise Foretasted?" in: Rabkin, Eric S., et. al., eds. No Place Else. Carbondale: Southern Illinois University Press, 1983. pp. 11-32.

"Shaw's debt to The Coming Race," Journal of Modern Literature 1(3):339-353. March 1971.

Knight, Chris

"Amicus empire," Cinefantastique 2(4):4-19. Summer 1973.

"Chat with Peter Cushing about Dracula today," by Chris Knight and Peter Nicholson. Cinefantastique 2(2):5-7. Summer 1972.

"Mike Raven," Cinefantastique 3(1):44-45. Fall 1973.

"Tyburn," Cinefantastique 4(4):40-45. Winter 1976.

"Vampire with the golden gun; Christopher Lee interviewed," Cinefantastique 4(1):39. Spring 1975.

Knight, Damon

Creating Short Fiction. Cincinnati: Writer's Digest, 1981. 215 p.

Futurians. New York: John Day, 1977. 282 p.

In Search of Wonder: Essays on Modern Science Fiction. Chicago: Advent, 1956. 180 p. Chicago: Advent, 1967. Revised edition, 306 p.

Turning Points: Essays on the Art of Science Fiction. New York: Harper & Row, 1977. 303 p.

"Annotated 'masks'," in: Wilson, Robin Scott, ed. Those Who Can: A Science Fiction Reader. New York: Mentor/New American Library, 1973. pp. 209-231.

"Art of book reviewing, The," Science Fiction Times No. 278:5. September 1957.

"How we work: Damon Knight," in: Aldiss, Brian W. and Harry Harrison, eds. Hell's Cartographers: Some Personal Histories of Science Fiction Writers. London: Weidenfeld and Nicholson, 1975. pp. 225-227.

"In the beginning," SFWA Bulletin 10(4): 10-11. July 1975.

"Introduction," in: Knight, Damon, ed. A Century of Science Fiction. New York: Simon & Schuster, 1963. pp. 9-13.

"Kate and Damon in Brazil," Locus 18(6): 33-34. June 1985.

"Knight piece," in: Aldiss, Brian W. and Harry Harrison, eds. Hell's Cartographers: Some Personal Histories of Science Fiction Writers. London: Weidenfeld and Nicholson, 1975. pp. 96-143.

"My Father's House," Vector 47: 2-7. November 1967.

"Next ten years in science fiction, The," Fantasy Times No. 138:7-10. September (2) 1951.

"Notes on The Man in the Tree," Science Fiction Review 13(2): 29-31. May 1984.

"On touchstones: It's the picture, not the words," Fantasy Review 8(12): 6. December 1985.

"Project Boskone," Australian Science Fiction Review No. 12:5-9. October 1967.

"Reply to Gregory Benford," Vector No. 121: 21-22. August 1984.

"Science fiction basics," Library Journal 91(11):2777-2779. June 1, 1966.

Knight, Damon (Continued)

"SFWA Contract Survey (1)," <u>SFWA Bulletin</u> 16(2): 22-26. Spring 1981.

"SFWA Contract Survey (2)," <u>SFWA Bulletin</u> 16(3): 18-20. March 1982.

"SFWA Contract Survey (3)," <u>SFWA Bulletin</u> 16(4): 13-15. May 1982.

"SFWA contract survey, The," <u>SFWA Bulletin</u> 14(1):30-41. Spring 1979.

"What is science fiction?" in: Knight, Damon, ed. <u>Turning Points: Essays in the Art of Science Fiction</u>. New York: Harper, 1977. pp. 62-69.

"Writing and selling science fiction," in: Knight, Damon, ed. <u>Turning Points: Essays in the Art of Science Fiction</u>. New York: Harper, 1977. pp. 218-228.

"Yardstick for science fiction, A," <u>Future Science Fiction</u> No. 37:108-114. June 1958.

Knight, George

"Robert E. Howard: hard-boiled heroic fantasist," in: Herron, Don, ed. <u>Dark Barbarian: The Writings of Robert E. Howard, a Critical Anthology</u>. Westport, CT: Greenwood, 1984. pp. 117-134.

Knight, I. F.

"Alienations, eros, and work," <u>Alternative Futures</u> 2(1): 3-28. Winter 1979.

"Feminist scholar and the future of gender, The," <u>Alternative Futures</u> 4(2/3): 17-35. Spring/Summer 1981.

"Utopian Dream as Psychic Reality," <u>Studies in Eighteenth-Century Culture</u>, Vol. 6, 1977. pp. 427-438.

Knighten, M. A.

"<u>Caves of Steel, The</u>," in: Magill, Frank N., ed. <u>Survey of Science Fiction Literature</u>, Vol. 1. Englewood Cliffs, NJ: Salem Press, 1979. pp. 318-321.

"<u>Naked Sun, The</u>," in: Magill, Frank N., ed. <u>Survey of Science Fiction Literature</u>, Vol. 3. Englewood Cliffs, NJ: Salem Press, 1979. pp. 1476-1479.

"Gulag gateway: critical approaches to science fiction, The," <u>Extrapolation</u> 21(2):167-171.

"Short Fiction of John W. Campbell, Jr., The," in: Magill, Frank N., ed. <u>Survey of Science Fiction Literature</u>, Vol. 4. Englewood Cliffs, NJ: Salem Press, 1979. pp. 2003-2007.

Knoblauch, Mary

"Sci-fi launches trek toward mass appeal," <u>Chicago Tribune</u> Sec. 2, p. 1. February 10, 1977.

Knoepflmacher, U. C.

<u>Endurance of Frankenstein: Essays on Mary Shelley's Novel</u>, ed. by George Levine and U. C. Knoepflmacher. Berkeley: University of California Press, 1979. 341 p.

Knoles, William

"Girls for the slime god," <u>Playboy</u> 7(11):70-71,80,144,147-149. November 1960.

Knowlson, J. R.

"Communication with other worlds in fiction," <u>Philosophical Journal</u> 5(1):61-74. January 1968.

Knox, George

"Apocalypse and sour utopias," <u>Western Humanities Review</u> 16(1):11-22. Winter 1962.

Knucewicz, Piotr

"Przymierze z dzieckiem," <u>Miesiecznik Literacki</u> No. 1. 1966.

Knudsen, Steen

"Adam Hart & Co." <u>Proxima</u> No. 19 sect. I:15-19. March 1979.

Kobayashi, Yoshio

"Science Fiction in Japan," by Yoshio Kobayashi, S. Maki, and Edward Lipsett. <u>Locus</u> 18(1): 31-32. January 1985.

"SF in Japan: An Overview," by Yoshio Kobayashi and Edward Lipsett. <u>Locus</u> 17(3): 21. March 1984.

Kobel, Peter

"Author takes his fans on a galactic joyride: Douglas Adams," <u>Chicago Tribune</u> Sec. 5, p. 1-2. March 13, 1985.

Kobil, D. T.

"Elusive appeal of fantasy," <u>Mythlore</u> 4(4): 17-19. June 1977.

Kobler, J.

"Master of movie horror," <u>Saturday Evening Post</u> 232(38):30-31. March 19, 1960.

Koch, Nynne

"Med patriardatet mod stjernerne: Kvinder og science fiction," in: Koch, Nynne, ed. <u>Kvindestudier V: Utopi of Subkultur.</u> Copenhagen: Delta, 1981. pp. 252-282.

Kocher, P. H.

<u>Master of Middle-Earth: The Achievement of J. R. R. Tolkien.</u> Boston: Houghton Mifflin, 1972. 247 p.

<u>Reader's Guide to the Silmarillion.</u> Boston: Houghton Mifflin, 1980. 286 p.

"Druedain," <u>Mythlore</u> 10(3): 23-25. Winter 1984.

"Iluvatar and the secret fire," <u>Mythlore</u> 12(1): 36-37. Autumn 1985.

"J. R. R. Tolkien and George MacDonald," <u>Mythlore</u> 8(3): 3-4. Autumn 1981.

"Middle Earth: An Imaginary World?" in: Isaacs, Neil D. <u>Tolkien: New Critical Perspectives,</u> ed. by Neil D. Isaacs and Rose A. Zimbardo. Lexington: University Press of Kentucky, 1981. pp. 117-132.

"Tale of the Nolder, The," <u>Mythlore</u> 4:3-7. March 1977.

Koelb, Clayton

"Language of Presence in Varley's <u>The Persistence of Vision</u>," <u>Science-Fiction Studies</u> 11(2): 154-165. July 1984.

Koenen, Anne

"Maenner: die uebelsten Primaten der Erde; die Kurzgeschichten von James Tiptree, jr.," in: <u>Femistische Utopien: Aufbruch in dei postpatriarchale Gesellschaft,</u> ed. by Barbara Holland-Cunz. Meitingen: Corian Verlag, 1985.

Koenig, P. W.

"Interviews with two German science fiction writers," <u>Extrapolation</u> 18(2):150-154. May 1977.

"Science fiction in German universities," Unpublished paper. No date. (Texas A&M Univ. SF Research Collection)

Koenig, Walter

<u>Checkov's Enterprise: A Personal Journal of The Making of Star Trek: The Motion Picture.</u> New York: Pocket Books, 1980. 222 p.

"Where Have You Gone, Gene Roddenberry?," <u>Starlog</u> 62: 21-23. September 1982.

Koepke, C. A., III

"Close encounters of the reading kind," <u>Claremont Reading Conference Yearbook</u> pp. 121-128. 1979.

Koerber, Joachim

<u>Bibliographisches Lexikon der utopisch-phantastischen Literatur,</u> ed. by Joachim Koerber. Meitingen: Corian, 1984. 654 p.

<u>J. G. Ballard: der Visionaer des Phantastischen,</u> ed. by Joachim Koerber. Mietingen: Corian, 1985. 176 p.

"An der Schwelle zum Computerzeitalter: ein Gespraech mit John Sladek," <u>Science Fiction Times</u> (Germany) 25(9):16-18. September 1983.

"Brot and Steine," <u>Science Fiction Times</u> (Germany) 25(11):15-16. November 1983.

"Mr. Dicks Halluzinationen: zum Kurzgeschicktenwerk Philip K. Dicks," <u>Science Fiction Times</u> (Germany) 24(6):18-20. June 1982.

"SF Star: ein ainkender Stern," <u>Science Fiction Times</u> (Germany) 25(3):13. March 1983.

Koestler, Arthur

"Boredom of fantasy," in: Koestler, A. <u>Trail of the Dinosaur and Other Essays.</u> Macmillan, 1955. pp. 142-147.

"Ennui de l'imaginaire, L'" <u>L'ombre du dinosaure.</u> Paris, Calmann-Levy, 1956, pp. 175-182.

"Ennui nait de la fantaisie, L'" <u>Preuves</u> 32. October 1953.

Kolakowski, Leszek

"Informacja i utopia," <u>Tworczosc</u> No. 11. 1964.

Kolbe, M. E.

<u>Three Oxford Dons as Creators of Other Worlds for Children: Lewis Carroll, C. S. Lewis, and J. R. R. Tolkien.</u> Ph. D. Dissertation, University of Virginia, 1981. 274 p. (DAI 43: 1535A)

Koll, Elizabeth

"Movie Review: Clockwork Orange," <u>Lincoln Gazette</u> (Nebraska) 1(11):3. August 10, 1972.

Kollman, J. J.

"Charles Williams, <u>The Place of the Lion</u>, and neoplatonic fantasy," <u>Kansas Quarterly</u> 16(3): 35-44. Summer 1984.

Kollmann, Judith

"Charles Williams and second-hand paganism," <u>Mythlore</u> 11(2):5-7,20. Autumn 1984.

"Legend of the Grail and War in Heaven," <u>Mythlore</u> 10(4): 20-22, 44. Spring 1984.

Kolodney, D.

"Peace in Middle Earth; paintings . . . " <u>Ramparts Magazine</u> 9(4):35-38. October 1970.

Kondratiev, Alexi

"New Myths For Old: The Legacy of Iolo Morgannwg and Hersard de le Villemarque," <u>Mythlore</u> 10(1): 31-34. Spring 1983.

"New Myths for Old: The Legacy of Iolo Morgannwg and Hersard de le Villegarque," <u>Mythlore</u> 10(2): 43-46. Summer 1983.

Konig-Kurowski, Gerhard

"Konflikte und Konfliktlosungen in Science Fiction Romanen," <u>Quarber Merkur</u>. No. 45:32-51. December 1976.

Konner, Alfred

"Wirklichkeit und utopie: zum problem der Zukunftsromane fur kinder," <u>Deutschunterricht</u> (Berlin/DDR) No. 4:190-201. 1958.

Konrad, Helga

<u>Science fiction in der darstellung der Raumfahrt: aufgezeigt an Beispielen der franzoesischen Kinder- und Jungendliteratur</u>. Dissertation, Karl Franzens Universitat Graz, 1974. 128 p.

Konstantinowa, Elka

"Bulgarska literatura fantastyczno-naukowa," in: Kaczmarka, Jerzego, ed. <u>Materialy z Miedzynarodowego Spotkania Pisarzy-Tworcow Literatury Fantastyczno-Naukowej</u>. Poznan: Wyndawnictwo Poznanskie, 1974. pp. 17-24.

Kontaratos, A. N.

"Amazing 1865 moon shot of Jules Verne, The," <u>Look</u> 33(11):74-78. May 27, 1969.

Koontz, D. R.

"Science fiction and fantasy," in: Koontz, D. R. <u>Writing Popular Fiction</u>. Cincinnati: Writers Digest, 1972. pp. 14-70.

Koper, P. T.

"Science and rhetoric in the fiction of Ursula K. Le Guin," in: De Bolt, Joe, ed. <u>Ursula K. Le Guin: Voyager to Inner Lands and to Outer Space</u>. Port Washington, New York: Kennikat, 1979. pp. 66-86.

Kopley, Richard

"<u>Narrative of Arthur Gordon Pym, The</u>," in: Magill, Frank N., ed. <u>Survey of Modern Fantasy Literature</u>, Vol 3. Englewood Cliffs, NJ: Salem Press, Inc., 1983. pp. 1092-1095.

"Early illustrations of <u>Pym</u>'s 'Shrouded Human Figure'," in: Collins, R. A., ed. <u>Scope of the Fantastic: Culture, Biography, Themes, Children's Literature</u>. Westport: Greenwood, 1985. pp. 155-170.

Korber, Joachim

"Philip K. Dick ist tot," <u>Heyne Science Fiction Magazine</u> 4: 31-38. 1982.

Korleski, Lori

"Science fiction and women," by Darla Klaus and Lori Korleski. <u>The Cougar</u> (University of Houston), Nova Supplement 43(11):2. September 16, 1976.

Kornbluth, C. M.

"Failure of the science fiction novel as social criticism, The," in: Davenport, Basil, ed. <u>The Science Fiction Novel: Imagination and Social Criticism</u>. Chicago: Advent, 1964. pp. 64-101.

"Time travel and the law," in: Greenberg, M. H., ed. <u>Coming Attractions</u>. New York: Gnome, 1957. pp. 104-109.

Kosek, Steven

"'Blade Runner' May Mean a Second Coming for Sci-Fi Marvel Philip K. Dick," <u>Chicago Tribune</u>, July 4, 1982. in: <u>Newsbank Review of Literature</u>, 1982/83, 9:D5-6.

Koseler, Michael

"Ein Klassiker der englischen Phantastik: M. R. James," *Quarber Merkur* No. 62: 47-66. December 1984.

Kostolefsky, J.

"Science, yes; fiction, maybe," *Antioch Review* 13(2):236-240. June 1953.

Kotljar, Ju.

"Fantasika i podrostok," *Molodoj kommunist* 6:119- . 1964.

Kottak, C. P.

"Father strikes back," in: Kottak, C. P., ed. *Researching American Culture*. Ann Arbor: University of Michigan Press, 1982. pp. 98-104.

"Social science fiction," *Psychology Today* 11:12-18,106. February 1978.

"Structural and psychological analysis of popular American fantasy films," in: Kottak, C. P., ed. *Researching American Culture*. Ann Arbor: University of Michigan Press, 1982. pp. 87-97.

Kottner, Lee

"Disney's Haunted Mansion: SPFX: Live," *Questar* 3(4): 78-81. June 1981.

Kotzin, M. C.

"C. S. Lewis and George MacDonald: The Silver Chair and the Princess Books," *Mythlore* 8(1): 5-15. Spring 1981.

Kovaly, Pavel

"Marxism and utopia," in: Richter, P. E., ed. *Utopia/Dystopia?*. Cambridge, MA: Schenkman, 1975. pp. 75-92.

Kozak, E. M.

"Enterprising Trekkies Lobby for Their Ship," *USA Today* p. D1. June 13, 1984.

"Who Owns Those Letters," *Fantasy Newsletter* 6(4): 36. April 1983.

Kraft, D. A.

Compleat OAK Leaves. Clayton, GA: Fictioneer, 1980. ca. 188 p.

"Howard and Kline: men of the pulps," *Oak Leaves* 1(12):7-8. Autumn 1979.

"Interview with Philip Jose Farmer, An," by D. A. Kraft, Mitch Scheele, and R. E. Geis. *Science Fiction Review* 4(3):7-21. 1975.

"Otis Adelbert Kline: an appreciation," in: Kraft, D. A., ed. *The Compleat OAK Leaves*. Clayton, GA: Fictioneer, 1980. pp. 1-2.

"Two-gun Bart, Dr. Dorp, and 'The Ferret': Otis Adelbert Kline's three early series," *Oak Leaves* 1(12):4-5. Autumn 1979.

Kraft, K. T.

"Incorporating Divinity: Platonic Science Fiction in the Middle Ages," in: Slusser, George E., ed. *Bridges to Science Fiction*. Carbondale: Southern Illinois University Press, 1980. pp. 22-40.

Kramer, Carol

"Kurt's college cult adopts him as literary guru at 48," *Chicago Tribune* Sec. 5, p. 1. November 15, 1970.

Krammer, H.

"In sieben Fortstzungen durch das Weltall. Die Science-Fiction-Welle brandet uber Mattscheibe, Filmleinwand und Groschenliteratur," *Suddeutsche Zeitung* No. 277. 1966.

Krasner, Barbara

"Cannell Revisited," *Video Action* 1(7): 56-59. June 1981.

Krasnoff, Barbara

"From Housewife to Heroine: Women in SF Media," *Future Life* 26: 52-55. May 1981.

"Portfolio: Dale M. Figley," *Future Life* 26: 58-63. May 1981.

"Portfolio: Don Dixon," *Future Life* 18: 58-63. May 1980.

"Portfolio: Karl Kofoed," *Future Life*. 20: 58-63, 74. August 1980.

"Portfolio: Keith Page," *Future Life* 29: 58-63. September 1981.

"Portfolio: Ronald F. Hall," *Future Life* 30: 58-63. November 1981.

"Steve R. Dodd," *Future Life* 25: 58-63. March 1981.

Krauss, Heinrich

"Religiose Themen und Katagorien in der Science Fiction," in: Ermert, Karl, ed. Neugier oder Flucht? Stuttgart: Klett, 1980. pp. 95-105.

Krauss, Werner

"Geist und widergeist der utopien," Sinn und Form 14:764- . 1962. also in: Barmeyer, Eike, ed. Science fiction: theorie und geschichte. Munchen: Fink, 1972. pp. 23-47.

Kreischer, Edith

"Henry James The Turn of the Screw," in: Thomsen, C. W., ed. Phantastik in Literatur und Kunst. Darmstadt: Wissenschaftliche Buchgesellschaft, 1980. pp. 219-236.

Krementz, Jill

"Pictorial," Summary 1(2):between pp. 34 and 35. 1971.

Krenz, Claudia

"Philip K. Dick Forum, Part Two: Staying Alive in a Fifteen Cent Universe," SF Commentary 62/66: 20-22, 69. June 1981.

Kress, Susan

"In and Out of Time: The Form of Marge Piercy's Novels," in: Barr, Marlene S., ed. Future Females. Bowling Green, OH: Bowling Green State University Popular Press, 1981. pp. 109-122.

Kretzmann, E. M. J.

"German technological utopias of the pre-war period," Annals of Science 3(4):417-430. October 15, 1938.

Kreuziger, F. A.

Apocalypse and Science Fiction: A Dialectic of Religious and Secular Soteriologies. Chico, CA: Scholars Press, 1982. 247 p.

Krichbaum, Joerg

"Einige Gedanken zur Phantastik," in: Rottensteiner, Franz, ed. Quarber Merkur. Frankfurt: Suhrkamp, 1979. pp. 177-182.

"Es waere ein Irrtum, ueber die Zukunft zu schreiben: J. G. Ballard," in: Rottensteiner, Franz, ed. Quarber Merkur. Frankfurt: Suhrkamp, 1979. pp. 141-155.

Krieg, L. J.

"Levels of symbolic meaning in Pearl," Mythlore 5(2): 21-23. Autumn 1978.

Krim, Seymour

"Modern science fiction: its meaning and its future," Commonweal 58:252-254. June 12, 1953.

"Real world of science fiction, The," Commonweal 58(10):252-254. June 12, 1953. (Book review)

Krishnamoorthy, P. S.

Scholar's Guide to Modern American Science Fiction. Hyderabad, India: American Studies Research Centre, 1983. 182 p.

Kroeber, Karl

"Sisters and science fiction," The Little Magazine 10:87-90. Spring/Summer 1976.

Kroitor, H. P.

"Special demands of point of view in science fiction, The," Extrapolation 17(2):153-159. May 1976.

Krueger, J. R.

"Language and techniques of communication as theme or tools in science fiction," Linguistics 39: 68-86. May 1968.

"Names and nomenclatures in science fiction," Names 14(4):203-214. December 1968.

Kruger, K. J.

"Imaginary war fiction in Colorado State University Libraries: a bibliography," by John Newman and K. J. Kruger. Bulletin of Bibliography and Magazine Notes 35(4):157-168,171. December 1978.

Krulik, Ted

"Science Fiction Adventures (1952-1954)," by Ted Krulik and Bruce Tinkel. in: Tymn, M. B. and Ashley, Mike. Science Fiction, Fantasy, and Weird Fiction Magazines. Westport, CT: Greenwood, 1985. pp. 520-524.

"Bounded by Metal," in: Myers, R. E., ed. The Intersection of Science Fiction and Philosophy. Westport: Greenwood, 1983. pp. 121-132.

Krulik, Ted (Continued)

"Disease of longevity: James Gunn's <u>The Immortals</u>," in: Yoke, C. B. and Hassler, D. M., eds. <u>Death and the Serpent</u>. Westport, CT: Greenwood, 1985. pp. 175-184.

"Reaching for Immortality: Two Novels of Richard Matheson," in: Staicar, Tom, ed. <u>Critical Encounters II</u>. New York: Ungar, 1982. pp. 1-14.

"Science Fiction in the Classroom: Can Its Essence be Preserved?" <u>Extrapolation</u> 22(2): 155-163. Summer 1981.

Krupkat, Guenther

"Literatura fantastyczno-naukowa w NRD," in: Kaczmarka, J., ed. <u>Materialy z Miedzynarodowego Spotkania Pisarzy-Tworcow Literatury Fantastyczno-Naukowej</u>. Poznan: Wyndawnictwo Poznanskie, 1974. pp. 25-30.

Kruse, Jens

"Science Fiction in der BRD: Utopie oder Ideologie?" <u>Neue Germanistik</u> 1(2): 37-44. Spring 1981.

Krysmanski, H. J.

"Eigenart des utopischen romans," in: Barmeyer, Eike, ed. <u>Science fiction: theorie und geschichte</u>. Munchen: Fink, 1972. pp. 47-57.

"Wissenschaftmarchen. Der science fiction boom in der Bundesrepublik," <u>Die Zeit</u> 39:14-15 (Lit. Beil.) September 29, 1972.

Kuczewski, Maciej

"Mlot na science fiction," <u>Nowe Ksiazki</u> No. 11. n. d.

Kuczka, Peter

"<u>Elza Pilota, vagy a tokeletes tarsadalom</u>," in: Magill, Frank N., ed. <u>Survey of Science Fiction Literature</u>, Vol. 2. Englewood Cliffs, NJ: Salem Press, 1979. pp. 708-711.

"<u>Kazohinia</u>," in: Magill, Frank N., ed. <u>Survey of Science Fiction Literature</u>, Vol. 3. Englewood Cliffs, NJ: Salem Press, 1979. pp. 1118-1121.

"<u>Sempiternin</u>," in: Magill, Frank N., ed. <u>Survey of Science Fiction Literature</u>, Vol. 4. Englewood Cliffs, NJ: Salem Press, 1979. pp. 1892-1895.

"English Science Fiction: From a Distance," <u>Foundation</u> 30: 10-13. March 1984.

"Fifty questions: an interview with the Strutgatsky Brothers," <u>Foundation</u> 34: 16-22. Autumn 1985.

"Galaktika," <u>Science Fiction and Fantasy Research Index</u> 2: 70-71. 1982.

"Latod, baratom, mive, lett a Fold," <u>Helikon</u> 18(1): 3-11. 1972.

"Prolemy wegierskiej literatury fantastyczno-naukowej," in: Kaczmarka, J., ed. <u>Materialy z Miedzynarodowego Spotkania Pisarzy-Tworcow Literatury Fantastyczno-Naukowej</u>. Poznan: Wyndawnictwo Poznanskie, 1974. pp. 69-80.

"Science Fiction in Hungary" <u>SFWA Bulletin</u> 16(4): 27-28, 37-38. May 1982.

"Science fiction in Hungary," <u>Books from Hungary</u> 12(1): 32-33. January/March 1970.

"Science Fiction in Hungary," <u>Extrapolation</u> 23(3): 213-220. Fall 1982.

Kudlay, R. R.

<u>Burroughs' Science Fiction; with an Analytical Subject and Name Index</u>, by R. R. Kudlay and Joan Leiby. Geneseo, New York: School of Library & Information Science, State University College, 1973. 236 p.

Kuehn, R. E.

<u>Aldous Huxley: A Collection of Critical Essays</u>. Englewood Cliffs, New Jersey: Prentice-Hall, 1974. 188 p.

Kuhl, Rand

"Owen Barfield in southern California," <u>Mythlore</u> 1(4):8-10. October 1969.

Kuhn, H. B.

"Fantasy: in search of reality?" <u>Christianity Today</u> 20(10):77-78. February 13, 1976.

Kull, G.

"I remember Palmer," <u>Fantasy Times</u> No. 58:6-7. November 1947.

Kumar, Kristan

"Primitivism in feminist utopias," <u>Alternative Futures</u> 4(2/3): 61-66. Spring/Summer 1981.

Kuncewicz, Piotr

"Bezdroza okrutnej nieskonczonosci" Wspolczesnosc No. 13. July 1-15, 1962.

"Klopoty prorokow," Zycie Literackie No. 29. 1968.

"Science fiction: a real problem; Un problem reel: la science fiction," Polish Literature/Litterature Polonaise 4 Jg., nr. 2(12), p. 3-5. summer 1971.

Kunkel, Klaus

"Marchen fur ubermorgen," Planet 1:133-143. 1969.

Kurth, R. J.

"Realism in children's books of fantasy," California Librarian 39:39-40. July 1978.

Kurtz, Katherine

"Historian as mythmaker, and vice-versa," SFWA Bulletin 13(4):16-18. Fall 1978.

"Interview essay," by Katherine Kurtz and Jeffrey Elliot. in: Boyer, Robert H. and Zahorski, Kenneth J. Fantasists on Fantasy. New York: Avon Discus, 1984. pp. 231-260.

Kurtz, P.

"Media messiahs, psychic saviors, and space gurus," Humanist 38(1):4-5. January/February 1978.

Kusche, Helmut

"Literarischer horror: uber die chancen der horror literatur," Science Fiction Times (Bremerhaven) No. 137:15-18. October 1975.

"Utopische kriminalromane," Science Fiction Times (Bremerhaven) No. 137:24-26. October 1975.

Kuttner, Henry

"Science in fiction," Science Fiction Advertiser 2:3-6. January 1953. (not seen)

"Selling science fiction," Writer's Digest 19(11):34-38. October 1939.

"Selling the fantasy story," Writer's Digest 18(4):29-33. March 1938.

Kuzmenko, P.

"A kto ubil Billi?" Moskovskii komsomolets February 8, 1976.

Kuznets, L. R.

"Games of dark: psychofantasy in children's literature," The Lion & the Unicorn 1(2):17-24. 1978.

"Tolkien and the Rhetoric of Childhood," in: Isaacs, Neil D. Tolkien: New Critical Perspectives, ed. by N. D. Isaacs and R. A. Zimbardo. Lexington: University Press of Kentucky, 1981. pp. 150-162.

Kwiatkowski, Jerzy

"Rakieta na wirazu," Tworczosc No. 5. 1958.

Kwiecien, Fred

"Man's best friend," Barsoomian No. 15:4. October 1969.

Kwiryn, J.

"Freud w wersji kosmicznej," Nowe Ksiazki No. 12. 1961.

Kyle, D. A.

"A. C. Clarke lauds new color SF film 'War of the Worlds'," Fantasy Times No. 175:5. April 1953.

"Britain confirms hope for '57 World Con," Fantasy Times No. 244:3. April (1) 1956.

Kyle, David

Illustrated Book of Science Fiction Ideas and Dreams. London: Hamlyn, 1977. 173 p.

Pictorial History of Science Fiction, A. London: Hamlyn, 1976. 173 p.

Kyle, Richard

"Out of Time's Abyss: the Martian stories of Edgar Rice Burroughs," Riverside Quarterly 4(2): 110-122. January 1970.

Kyrou, Ado

"Science and fiction," in: Johnson, William, ed. Focus on the Science Fiction Film. Englewood Cliffs, NJ: Prentice Hall, 1972. pp. 91-96.

L

La Bar, Martin

"Arthur C. Clarke: humanism in science fiction," Christianity Today 22(17):27. June 2, 1978.

La Bossiere, C. R.

"Scarlet empire, The: two visions in one," Science Fiction Studies 1(4):290-292. Fall 1974.

"Under strabismic western eyes: a translation of Romanian SF," Riverside Quarterly 7(1):31-36. March 1980.

"Zamiatin's We: a caricature of utopian symmetry," Riverside Quarterly 6(1):40-43. August 1973.

La Chapelle, Dolores

"Go, go Gandalf," Ave Maria 104:12-15. November 19, 1966.

La Cour, Tage

Rejser i tid og rum. En Bog om science fiction. Copenhagen: Stig Verdelkaer, 1973. 188 p.

"Rejsen til mjanen: fra lukianos til H. G. Wells," in: Rejser i tid og rum. En Bog om science fiction, ed. by Tage La Cour. Copenhagen: Stig Verdelkaer, 1973.

La Faille, Eugene

"Computers in science fiction," Voice of Youth Advocates 8(2): 103-106. June 1985.

"Pawprints Across the Galaxy: Dogs in Science Fiction," Kliatt Young Adult Paperback Book Guide 18(6): 2-3, 76. September 1984.

La Polla, Franco

"Reale, fantastico, merce," Quaderni di Filologia Germanica della Facolta di Lettere e Filosofia dell'Universita di Bologna. 1980; 1: 151-155. 1982.

La Rocque, Geraldine E.

"Once Upon a Future," English Journal 70(3): 79-81. March 1981.

La Valley, A. J.

"Traditions of Trickery: The Role of Special Effects in the Science Fiction Film," in: Slusser, George, ed. Shadows of the Magic Lamp. Carbondale: Southern Illinois University Press, 1985. pp. 141-158.

Labarthe, A. S.

Images de la science fiction, by J. Siclier and S. A. Labarthe. Paris: Cerf, 1958. 137 p.

Labisch, W. E.

"Erotic Science Fiction?" Frankfurter Rundschau Nr. 241:12. 1971.

Lacassin, Francis

"Bandes dessinees et science fiction," Magazine Litteraire No. 31:15-17. August 1969.

"Lovecraft et les trous de la toile peinte," in: H. P. Lovecraft. Paris: Editions de l'Herne, 1969. pp. 106-110.

"Que la science fiction soit et la science fiction fut," Magazine Litteraire No. 31:7-10. August 1969.

"Science-fiction, La," by Juliette Raabe and Francis Lacassin. La bibliotheque ideale des litteratures d'evasion (La bibliotheque ideale). Paris: Ed. universitaires, 1969. pp. 155-178.

Lachg, Eric

"TV Hero For the Ages," _San Jose Mercury_ August 5, 1984. in: _NewsBank. Social Relations_ SOC 56:D13. 1984.

Lackey, D. P.

"Logic and Ethics of Asimovian Reality Changes," _Philosophical Speculations in Science Fiction and Fantasy_ 1(1): 35-40. March 1981.

Lacombe, Michele

"Feminist Science Fiction: A Commentary," _The Spinx: A Magazine of Literature and Society_ 4: 138-143. 1982.

LaFarge, Oliver

"Alien races in fiction," _North American Review_ 244(1):202-205. Autumn 1937.

Lafferty, R. A.

"Case of the Moth-eaten Magician," in: Greenberg, Martin H., ed. _Fantastic Lives: Autobiographical Essays by Notable Science Writers_. Carbondale: Southern Illinois University Press, 1981. pp. 57-78.

"Day After the World Ended," _Philosophical Speculations in Science Fiction and Fantasy_. 2: 61-68. Summer 1981.

"How to: It's down the slippery cellar stairs," _SFWA Bulletin_ 10(3):10-12. Winter 1974/1975.

"Profession of Science Fiction, 21: True Believers," _Foundation_ 20: 43-46. October 1980.

Laffly, Georges

"Science fiction, La," _Revue des Deux Mondes_ No. 3:394-405. January/February 1968.

Lafleur, L. J.

"Errors in 'Marvelous Voyages, IV'," _Popular Astronomy_ 50(8):431-433. October 1942.

"Marvelous Voyages, 1: Jules Verne's _Journey to the Center of the Earth_," _Popular Astronomy_ 50(1):16-21. January 1942.

"Marvelous Voyages, 2: the scientific romances of Edgar Rice Burroughs," _Popular Astronomy_ 50(2):69-73. February 1942.

"Marvelous Voyages, 3: Jules Verne's _From the Earth to the Moon_," _Popular Astronomy_ 50(4):196-198. April 1942.

"Marvelous Voyages, 4: Jules Verne, around the moon," _Popular Astronomy_ 50(7):377-379. August 1942.

"Marvelous Voyages, 5: errors in H. G. Wells' _The First Men in the Moon_, part I," _Popular Astronomy_ 51(2):80-83. February 1943.

"Marvelous Voyages, 6: errors in H. G. Wells' _First Men in the Moon_, part II," _Popular Astronomy_ 51(3):145-147. March 1943.

"Marvelous Voyages, 7: H. G. Wells' _The War of the Worlds_," _Popular Astronomy_ 51(7):359-362. August 1943.

"Marvelous Voyages, 8: errors in H. G. Wells' _The Time Machine_," _Popular Astronomy_ 51(8):438-440. October 1943.

"Marvelous Voyages, 9: J. B. S. Haldane's _The Last Judgement_," _Popular Astronomy_ 53(9):447-453. November 1945.

Lahalle, B. A.

Jules Verne et le Quebec (1837-1889): Famillesans-nom. Sherbrooke, Quebec: Naaman, 1979. 189 p.

Lahana, Jacqueline

Les mondes paralleles de la science-fiction sovietique. Lausanne: L'Age l'Homme, 1979. 160 p.

Laitin, J.

"Monsters made to order," _Colliers_ 134(12):52-53. December 10, 1954.

Lake, D. J.

"Le Guin's Twofold Vision: Contrary Image-Sets in The Left Hand of Darkness," _Science-Fiction Studies_ 8(2): 156-164. July 1981.

"Making the Two One: Language and Mysticism in _Riddley Walker_," _Extrapolation_ 25(2): 157-170. Summer 1984.

"Well's Time Traveller: An Unreliable Narrator," _Extrapolation_ 22(2): 117-126. Summer 1981.

"White sphinx and albino griffin: images of death in the scientific romances of H. G. Wells," in: Tolley, M. J., ed. _The Stellar Guage_. Carleton, Australia: Norstrilia, 1980. pp. 25-42.

"White sphinx and the whitened lemur: images of death in _The Time Machine_, The," _Science Fiction Studies_ 6(1):77-84. March 1979.

Lake, D. J. (Continued)

"Whiteness of Griffin and H. G. Wells's Images of Death, 1897-1914," Science-Fiction Studies 8(1): 12-18. March 1981.

Lake, Ken

"BSFA Survey," by Peter Holdsworth and Ken Lake. Matrix (BSFA) 45: 8-10. December 1982/January 1983.

"Haldeman interview, part one," by Ken Lake and Geoff Rippington. Vector 126: 3-5. June/July 1985.

"Haldeman interview, part two," by Ken Lake and Geoff Rippington. Vector 127: 6-8. August/September 1985.

"Penny plain, twopence coloured," Vector 124/125: 11. 1985.

Laker, C. R.

"Spuds to microchips," Focus: An SF Writers' Magazine 11: 10-13. 1985.

Lalli, C. G.

"Amazing Years," Amazing 56(5): 116-117. March 1983.

Lamb, J. E.

"Space biology: bringing the far out into focus," Science Teacher 43(6):19-21. September 1976.

Lamb, P. A.

"Race to the moon," English Journal 46(8):503-505. November 1957.

Lamb, W. G.

"Classroom environmental value clarification," Journal of Environmental Education 6(4):14-17. Summer 1975.

"Science fiction: a unique classroom tool," in: Lamb, William G. A Sourcebook for Secondary Environmental Education. Austin: University of Texas Science Education Center, 1973. (ERIC ED 095 682)

"Science fiction: a unique tool for science teachers," by W. G. Lamb and R. B. Bartholomew. Science Teacher 42(3):37-38. March 1975.

Lambe, D. R.

"Reflection on the science in science fiction creating alien races," Rigel 8: 21-23. Summer 1983.

"Science & Sense: Reflections on the Science in Science Fiction," Rigel 6: 55-58. Winter 1982.

"Science and Sense: Reflections on the Science in Science Fiction," Rigel 5: 50-52. Fall 1982.

Lambert, P. C.

"Wonderful journey, The," Alabama Librarian 8(1):3-5. January 1957.

Lambert, R.

"Underground paperbacks; A. Burgess' A Clockwork Orange," Media & Methods 6(1):22. September 1969.

Lambilliotte, M.

"Fantastique et L'Imaginaire, Le," Syntheses 189:221-232. February 1962.

Lamie, E. L.

"Computer and man, The: the human use of non-human beings in the works of John Brunner," by E. L. Lamie and Joe de Bolt. in: De Bolt, Joe, ed. Happening Worlds of John Brunner. Port Washington, NY: Kennikat, 1975. pp. 167-176.

Lanahan, William

"Slave girls and strategies: John Norman's Gor series," Algol 12(1):22-26. November 1974.

Lancy, L. J.

"Running experiments off: an interview," Meanjin Quarterly 30(1):46-54. Autumn 1971.

Landa, Suzanne

"Computers in American Movies: The Fears, the Dreams, the Reality," in: Malik, Rex, ed. Future Imperfect. London: Pinter, 1980. pp. 101-112.

Landers, C. E.

"Science fiction in the political science classroom: a comment," Teaching Political Science 4(4):475-480. July 1977.

Landers, C. E. (Continued)

"Teaching political science through science fiction," <u>Politics</u> 6:17-32. February 1976.

Landon, Brooks

"At Swim-Two-Birds," in: Magill, Frank N., ed. <u>Survey of Modern Fantasy Literature</u>, Vol 1. Englewood Cliffs, NJ: Salem Press, Inc., 1983. pp. 61-62.

"Heresiarch and Co., The," in: Magill, Frank N., ed. <u>Survey of Modern Fantasy Literature</u>, Vol 2. Englewood Cliffs, NJ: Salem Press, Inc., 1983. pp. 728-729.

"Insect Play, The," in: Magill, Frank N., ed. <u>Survey of Modern Fantasy Literature</u>, Vol 2. Englewood Cliffs, NJ: Salem Press, Inc., 1983. pp. 773-775.

"Magic Goes Away, The and The Magic May Return," in: Magill, Frank N., ed. <u>Survey of Modern Fantasy Literature</u>, Vol 2. Englewood Cliffs, NJ: Salem Press, Inc., 1983. pp. 938-941.

"Time and Again," in: Magill, Frank N., ed. <u>Survey of Modern Fantasy Literature</u>, Vol 4. Englewood Cliffs, NJ: Salem Press, Inc., 1983. pp. 1938-1942.

"Yellow Back Radio Broke-Down," in: Magill, Frank N., ed. <u>Survey of Modern Fantasy Literature</u>, Vol 5. Englewood Cliffs, NJ: Salem Press, Inc., 1983. pp. 2197-2199.

"Lifeforce (review)," <u>Cinefantastique</u> 15(5):37,52. January 1986.

"Short fiction of Bowen, The," in: Magill, Frank N., ed. <u>Survey of Modern Fantasy Literature</u>, Vol 3. Englewood Cliffs, NJ: Salem Press, Inc., 1983. pp. 1468-1470.

"Short fiction of Coover, The," in: Magill, Frank N., ed. <u>Survey of Modern Fantasy Literature</u>, Vol 3. Englewood Cliffs, NJ: Salem Press, Inc., 1983. pp. 1489-1491.

"Short fiction of Leiber, The," in: Magill, Frank N., ed. <u>Survey of Modern Fantasy Literature</u>, Vol 4. Englewood Cliffs, NJ: Salem Press, Inc., 1983. pp. 1611-1615.

Landow, G. P.

"King of the Golden River: Or, The Black Brothers, A Legend of Stiria, The," in: Magill, Frank N., ed. <u>Survey of Modern Fantasy Literature</u>, Vol 2. Englewood Cliffs, NJ: Salem Press, Inc., 1983. pp. 852-854.

"Portent: A Story of the Inner Vision of the Highlanders, Commonly Called 'The Second Sight'," in: Magill, F. N., ed. <u>Survey of Modern Fantasy Literature</u>, Vol 3. Englewood Cliffs: Salem Press, 1983. pp. 1271-1275.

"Story of the Glittering Plain, The," in: Magill, Frank N., ed. <u>Survey of Modern Fantasy Literature</u>, Vol 4. Englewood Cliffs, NJ: Salem Press, Inc., 1983. pp. 1831-1833.

"World's Desire, The," in: Magill, Frank N., ed. <u>Survey of Modern Fantasy Literature</u>, Vol 5. Englewood Cliffs, NJ: Salem Press, Inc., 1983. pp. 2176-2179.

"And the world became strange: realms of literary fantasy," <u>Georgia Review</u> 33(1):7-42. Spring 1979.

"And the World Became Strange: Realms of Literary Fantasy," in: Schlobin, R. C., ed. <u>The Aesthetic of Fantasy Literature and Art</u>. Notre Dame, IN: University of Notre Dame Press, 1982. pp. 105-142.

Landrum, L. N.

"Checklist of materials about science fiction films of the 1950's, A," <u>Journal of Popular Films</u> 1(1):61-63. Winter 1972.

"English 242: Popular literary forms (science fiction)," in: Gordon, Mark. <u>Currents of Warm Life: Popular Culture in American Higher Education</u>. Bowling Green: Popular Press, 1980. pp. 86-92.

"Science fiction film criticism in the seventies: a selected bibliography," <u>Journal of Popular Film</u> 6(3):278-289. 1978.

Landsman, Ben

"Starlog Interview: Patrick Troughton," by Ben Landsman and P. D. O'Neill. <u>Starlog</u> 89: 40-41. December 1984.

Landsman, Gail

"Science fiction: the rebirth of mythology," <u>Journal of Popular Culture</u> 5(4):989-996. Spring 1972.

Lane, Daryl

<u>Sound of Wonder: Interviews From "The Science Fiction Radio Show," Volume 1</u>, by Daryl Lane, William Vernon and David Carson. Phoenix: Oryx, 1985. 203 p.

<u>Sound of Wonder: Interviews From "The Science Fiction Radio Show," Volume 2</u>, by Daryl Lane, William Vernon and David Carson. Phoenix: Oryx, 1985. 203 p.

Lane, Dwight

"Helping children feel confident about the future," by Margaret Lane and Dwight Lane. <u>Family Circle</u> 88(2):22,26,29. February 1976.

Lane, Elizabeth

"Lloyd Alexander's Chronicles of Prydain and the Welsh tradition," Orcrist 7:25-28. 1973.

Lane, Margaret

"Helping children feel confident about the future," by Margaret Lane and Dwight Lane. Family Circle 88(2):22,26,29. February 1976.

Lang, L. A.

Impact of Classical Science on American Literature: The Creation of an Epic American Hero in Science Fiction. Ph.D. Dissertation, University of Minnesota, 1978. 200 p.

Langer, Marie

Ciencia ficcion: realidad y psicoanalisis, by Eduardo Goligorsky and Marie Langer. Buenos Aires: Paidos, 1969. 185 p.

Langford, David

"Sladek At Random: John Sladek Interviewed," Vector 112: 6-15. 1983.

Science in Science Fiction, The, by Peter Nicholls, David Langford and Brian Stableford. London: Joseph, 1982. 208 p.

"Albion writ: the final drips," Vector No. 128: 8-10. October/November 1985.

"Digging up the Future," Vector 100: 20-25. December 1980.

"Hey Prestel: Electronic SF," SFWA Bulletin 17(1): 10-12. Spring 1983.

"Ian Watson Interviewed," Science Fiction Review 11(1): 8-14. February 1982.

"Interview: John Sladek," Science Fiction Review 12(1): 8-14. February 1983.

"SF For the People: A New SF Magazine, Anyone?" Vector 103: 116-18. August 1981.

Langford, Jonathan

"Mooting of the minds: why fans enjoy Tolkien," by N. L. Hayes, Jonathan Langford and S. C. Walker. Leading Edge No. 9:78-84. Winter 1985.

Langford, M. K.

"Concept of freedom in surrealism, extentialism, and science fiction," Extrapolation 26(3): 249-256. Fall 1985.

Langton, Jane

"Weak Place in the Cloth," in: Boyer, Robert H. and Zahorski, Kenneth J. Fantasists on Fantasy. New York: Avon Discus, 1984. pp. 163-180.

"Weak place in the cloth: a study of fantasy for children," Horn Book 49(5):433-441. October 1973.

Langway, Lynn

"Turn Left at the Nebula," Newsweek 100(20): 119. November 15, 1982.

Lanier, Ellery

"Psychoanalysis by telepathy," Fantastic 7(9):95-102. September 1958.

Lanier, S. E.

"J. R. R. Tolkien," Locus No. 149:2. September 14, 1973.

Lanoux, Armand

"Univers de la science fiction, L'" Les Oeuvres Libres 144. 1958.

Lantero, E. H.

"What is man? Theological aspects of contemporary science fiction," Religion in Life 38(2):242-255. Summer 1969.

"What is time? More theological aspects of science fiction," Religion in Life 40(3):423-435. Autumn 1971.

Lapidus, Jerry

"Illustrated Man shows promise," Science Fiction Times No. 465:3. April 1969.

Laquer, W. Z.

"SF in Russland," Der Monat 11(112):88-91. 1958.

Lareau, Chris

"Epic struggles to marvelous premiere," Science Fiction Times (Boston) 1(5):1,4. November 1979.

"Seacon biggest overseas convention ever," Science Fiction Times (Boston) 1(4):4. August 1979.

Larkin, Gordon

"Chacal," in: Tymn, M. B. and Ashley, Mike. Science Fiction, Fantasy, and Weird Fiction Magazines. Westport, CT: Greenwood, 1985. pp. 159-161.

"Fantasy Tales," in: Tymn, M. B. and Ashley, Mike. Science Fiction, Fantasy, and Weird Fiction Magazines. Westport, CT: Greenwood, 1985. pp. 270-272.

"Shayol," in: Tymn, M. B. and Ashley, Mike. Science Fiction, Fantasy, and Weird Fiction Magazines. Westport, CT: Greenwood, 1985. pp. 573-575.

Larsen, Christopher

"Conversation with Douglas Adams," Bloomsbury Review 3(1):21-23. December 1982.

Larsen, Dave

"Sci-Fi Buff Has Closet Encounter, He Donates Burgeoning Collection to the City," Los Angeles Times Sec. 5, p. 1-2, 6. April 26, 1982.

Larsen, P. M.

"Synthetic Myths in Aldous Huxley's Brave New Worlds," English Studies 62(6): 506-508. December 1981.

Larson, D. M.

"Science fiction, novel, and continuity of condemnation," Journal of General Education 28(1):63-74. Spring 1976.

"Thematic Structure and Conventions in Science Fiction," The Spinx: A Magazine of Literature and Society 4(1): 38-47. 1981.

"Two-cultures split and the science fiction course, The," HPTNews: Newsletter of the Lehigh University Perspectives on Technology Program 3:1-4. 1977.

Larson, R. D.

Musique Fantastique: A Survey of Film Music in the Fantastic Cinema. Metuchen, NJ: Scarecrow, 1985. 602 p.

"Cycle of the Werewolf and the moral tradition of horror," in: Schweitzer, Darrell, ed. Discovering Stephen King. Mercer Island: Starmont, 1985. pp. 102-108.

"Joseph Payne Brennan: Old Cities and the Stream of Time," Threshold of Fantasy 1: 5-13. Spring 1982.

Larson, Ross

Fantasy and Imagination in the Mexican Narrative. Tempe: Arizona State University, Center for Latin American Studies, 1977. 154 p.

"Literatura de ciencia-ficcion en Mexico," Cuadernos Hispanoamericanos No. 284:425-430. February 1974.

"Utopia and science fiction," in: Larson, Ross. Fantasy and Imagination in the Mexican Narrative. Tempe: Center for Latin American Studies, University of Arizona, 1977. pp. 51-61.

Lascault, Gilbert

"Avenir redoute, Un. Les recits d'anticipation," Esprit 346:259-270. February 1966.

Laski, M.

"Horror comics," New Statesmen and Nation 48:612. November 13, 1954. Discussion, 48:647,696. November 20-27, 1954.

Laskowski, G. J.

"Cosmos Science Fiction and Fantasy Magazine (1977)," in: Tymn, M. B. and Ashley, Mike. Science Fiction, Fantasy, and Weird Fiction Magazines. Westport, CT: Greenwood, 1985. pp. 173-175.

"Forgotten Fantasy," in: Tymn, M. B. and Ashley, Mike. Science Fiction, Fantasy, and Weird Fiction Magazines. Westport, CT: Greenwood, 1985. pp. 275-276.

"Stanley Schmidt; interview," Lan's Lantern 8:11-16. March 1979.

Lasseter, R. A.

"Four letters about Le Guin," in: De Bolt, Joe, ed. Ursula K. Le Guin: Voyager to Inner Lands and to Outer Space. Port Washington, New York: Kennikat, 1979. pp. 89-114.

Lassman, Alfred

"Utopien und ihre leser," Neue Volksbildung, Buch und Bucherei N.F. VIII. pp. 327-335. 1957.

Last, Martin

Reader's Guide to Science Fiction, A, by Baird Searles, Martin Last, Beth Meacham and Michael Franklin. New York: Avon, 1979. 266 p.

Last, Richard

"Quartermass and the horrors of Earth,"
Daily Telegraph p. 9. September 3, 1973.

Lathouwers, M. A.

"Critique de la culture dans la litterature
Sovietique contemporaine, La," Irenikon
48(2):147-169. 1975.

Latil, Pierre

"Science et science fiction," La Reforme
July 3, 1954.

Lattery, R.

"Tolkien as Christian?" Triumph 9:35-37.
March 1974.

Lauber, Volkmar

"Efficiency and after: the dilemna of the
technological state," Alternative Futures
2(4): 47-65. Fall 1979.

Laughlin, Charlotte

De Camp: An L. Sprague de Camp Bibliography.
by Charlotte Laughlin and D. J. H. Levack.
Columbia, PA: Underwood/Miller, 1983. 328 p.

"Conan in Paperback," Paperback Quarterly
5(1): 13-24. Spring 1982.

Laumer, Keith

"Couldn't We All Just Be Dear, Dear Friends?"
in: Bretnor, Reginald, ed. The Future at War:
Vol. 3: Orion's Sword. New York: Ace, 1980.
pp. 100-105.

"How to collaborate without getting your head
shaved," in: Knight, Damon, ed. Turning
Points: Essays in the Art of Science Fiction.
New York: Harper, 1977. pp. 215-217.

Laura, E. G.

"Invasion of the Body Snatchers," in:
Johnson, William, ed. Focus on the Science
Fiction Film. Englewood Cliffs, NJ: Prentice
Hall, 1972. pp. 71-73.

Laurence, Alice

"Zenna Henderson, In Memoriam," SFWA
Bulletin 17(3): 6-8. Fall 1983.

Lautentaler, R.

"Begriff und geschichte utopischen Denkens,"
Sozialistische Zeitschrift fur Kunst und
Gesellschaft 18/19:17- . July 1973.

Lauterbach, E. S.

"Checklist of articles dealing with science
fiction, A," by T. D. Clareson and E. S.
Lauterbach. Extrapolation 1(2):29-34. May
1960.

Lauterbach, Edward

"Some Notes on Cthulhuian Pseudobiblia," in:
Joshi, S. T., ed. H. P. Lovecraft: Four
Decades of Criticism. Athens, OH: Ohio
University Press, 1980. pp. 96-103.

Lavender, Ralph

"Other Worlds: Myth and Fantasy, 1970-1980,"
Children's Literature in Education. 12(3):
140-150. 1981.

Laverty, C. D.

"Poe's vision of the future," Journal of the
American Studies Association of Texas
4:38-45. 1973.

Lavery, D. L.

"Genius of the sea: Walace Stevens' 'The Idea
of Order at Key West,' Stanislaw Lem's
Solaris and the Earth as muse, The,"
Extrapolation 21(2):101-105. Summer 1980.

Law, Richard

"Absurd in Science Fiction," Pennsylvania
English 10(2): 27-34. Spring 1984.

"Joanna Russ and the Literature of Exhaustion,"
Extrapolation 25(2): 146-156. Summer 1984.

"Joanna Russ: Conflict and Dying Alone,"
Fantasy Newsletter 6(4): 34-35. April 1983.

"Science Fiction Women: Victims, Rebels,
Heroes," in: Hassler, Donald M. Patterns
of the Fantastic. Mercer Island, WA:
Starmont, 1983. pp. 11-20.

"Science Fiction: The Urgency of Style,"
Extrapolation 22(4): 325-333. Winter 1981.

Lawing, J. V., Jr.

"Kurt Vonnegut: charming nihilist,"
Christianity Today 19:17-20,22. February
14, 1975.

Lawler, A. C.

"St. Germain Series, The," by A. C. Lawler and D. L. Lawler. in: Magill, Frank N., ed. Survey of Modern Fantasy Literature, Vol 3. Englewood Cliffs, NJ: Salem Press, Inc., 1983. pp. 1343-1346.

Lawler, D. L.

"Beyond Fantasy Fiction," in: Tymn, M. B. and Ashley, Mike. Science Fiction, Fantasy, and Weird Fiction Magazines. Westport, CT: Greenwood, 1985. pp. 137-142.

"Biography of the Life of Manuel, The," in: Magill, Frank N., ed. Survey of Modern Fantasy Literature, Vol 1. Englewood Cliffs, NJ: Salem Press, Inc., 1983. pp. 95-115.

"Darker Than You Think," in: Magill, Frank N., ed. Survey of Modern Fantasy Literature, Vol 1. Englewood Cliffs, NJ: Salem Press, Inc., 1983. pp. 336-340.

"Day of the Triffids, The," in: Magill, Frank N., ed. Survey of Science Fiction Literature, Vol. 1. Englewood Cliffs, NJ: Salem Press, 1979. pp. 502-507.

"Do Androids Dream of Electric Sheep?," in: Magill, Frank N., ed. Survey of Science Fiction Literature, Vol. 2. Englewood Cliffs, NJ: Salem Press, 1979. pp. 554-559.

"Dracula Tape Series, The," in: Magill, Frank N., ed. Survey of Modern Fantasy Literature, Vol 1. Englewood Cliffs, NJ: Salem Press, Inc., 1983. pp. 410-417.

"Exorcist, The," in: Magill, Frank N., ed. Survey of Modern Fantasy Literature, Vol 1. Englewood Cliffs, NJ: Salem Press, Inc., 1983. pp. 501-503.

"Galaxy Science Fiction," in: Tymn, M. B. and Ashley, Mike. Science Fiction, Fantasy, and Weird Fiction Magazines. Westport, CT: Greenwood, 1985. pp. 290-309.

"Grimus," in: Magill, Frank N., ed. Survey of Modern Fantasy Literature, Vol 2. Englewood Cliffs, NJ: Salem Press, Inc., 1983. pp. 680-683.

"Imperial Earth," in: Magill, Frank N., ed. Survey of Science Fiction Literature, Vol. 3. Englewood Cliffs, NJ: Salem Press, 1979. pp. 1019-1025.

"Interview with the Vampire," in: Magill, Frank N., ed. Survey of Modern Fantasy Literature, Vol 2. Englewood Cliffs, NJ: Salem Press, Inc., 1983. pp. 776-780.

"Man Who Folded Himself, The," in: Magill, Frank N., ed. Survey of Science Fiction Literature, Vol. 3. Englewood Cliffs, NJ: Salem Press, 1979. pp. 1333-1339.

"Man Who Was Thursday, The," in: Magill, Frank N., ed. Survey of Modern Fantasy Literature, Vol 2. Englewood Cliffs, NJ: Salem Press, Inc., 1983. pp. 961-965.

"Nerves," in: Magill, Frank N., ed. Survey of Science Fiction Literature, Vol. 3. Englewood Cliffs, NJ: Salem Press, 1979. pp. 1510-1515.

"October the First is Too Late," in: Magill, Frank N., ed. Survey of Science Fiction Literature, Vol. 4. Englewood Cliffs, NJ: Salem Press, 1979. pp. 1574-1582.

"Pastel City, The," in: Magill, Frank N., ed. Survey of Science Fiction Literature, Vol. 4. Englewood Cliffs, NJ: Salem Press, 1979. pp. 1655-1659.

"Peer Gynt," in: Magill, Frank N., ed. Survey of Modern Fantasy Literature, Vol 3. Englewood Cliffs, NJ: Salem Press, Inc., 1983. pp. 1216-1220.

"Picture of Dorian Gray, The," in: Magill, Frank N., ed. Survey of Modern Fantasy Literature, Vol 3. Englewood Cliffs, NJ: Salem Press, Inc., 1983. pp. 1257-1261.

"Science Fiction Plus," in: Tymn, M. B. and Ashley, Mike. Science Fiction, Fantasy, and Weird Fiction Magazines. Westport, CT: Greenwood, 1985. pp. 541-545.

"Silmarillion," in: Magill, Frank N., ed. Survey of Modern Fantasy Literature, Vol 4. Englewood Cliffs, NJ: Salem Press, Inc., 1983. pp. 1733-1743.

"Sirens of Titan, The: Vonnegut's metaphysical shaggy-dog story," in: Klinkowitz, Kurt, ed. Vonnegut in America. New York: Delacorte, 1977. pp. 61-86.

"Storm of Wings, A," in: Magill, Frank N., ed. Survey of Modern Fantasy Literature, Vol 4. Englewood Cliffs, NJ: Salem Press, Inc., 1983. pp. 1826-1830.

"Varney the Vampyre," in: Magill, Frank N., ed. Survey of Modern Fantasy Literature, Vol 4. Englewood Cliffs, NJ: Salem Press, Inc., 1983. pp. 2017-2022.

"Voyage to Arcturus, A," in: Magill, Frank N., ed. Survey of Science Fiction Literature, Vol. 5. Englewood Cliffs, NJ: Salem Press, 1979. pp. 2383-2388.

"War with the Newts," in: Magill, Frank N., ed. Survey of Science Fiction Literature, Vol. 5. Englewood Cliffs, NJ: Salem Press, 1979. pp. 2424-2428.

"Worlds of the Imperium," in: Magill, Frank N., ed. Survey of Science Fiction Literature, Vol. 5. Englewood Cliffs, NJ: Salem Press, 1979. pp. 2511-2515.

Lawler, D. L. (Continued)

"Best of C. M. Kornbluth, The," in: Magill, Frank N., ed. Survey of Science Fiction Literature, Vol. 1. Englewood Cliffs, NJ: Salem Press, 1979. pp. 178-185.

"Best of Henry Kuttner, The," in: Magill, Frank N., ed. Survey of Science Fiction Literature, Vol. 1. Englewood Cliffs, NJ: Salem Press, 1979. pp. 191-195.

"Certain assistances: the utilities of science fiction and fantasy in shaping the future," 21 p. 1975. ERIC ED 112 424.

"Certain Assistances: The Utilities of Speculative Fictions in Shaping the Future," Mosaic 13(3/4): 1-13. Spring/Summer 1980.

"Certain assistances: utilities of science fiction and fantasy in shaping the future," in: Samuelson, D. N. Science Fiction and Future Studies. Bryan, TX: SFRA, 1975. pp. 75-84.

"She Series, The," in: Magill, Frank N., ed. Survey of Modern Fantasy Literature, Vol 3. Englewood Cliffs, NJ: Salem Press, Inc., 1983. pp. 1396-1401.

"Short Fiction of Larry Niven, The," in: Magill, Frank N., ed. Survey of Science Fiction Literature, Vol. 4. Englewood Cliffs, NJ: Salem Press, 1979. pp. 2023-2029.

"St. Germain Series, The," by A. C. Lawler and D. L. Lawler. in: Magill, Frank N., ed. Survey of Modern Fantasy Literature, Vol 3. Englewood Cliffs, NJ: Salem Press, Inc., 1983. pp. 1343-1346.

Lawling, J. V.

"Refiner's fire: Kurt Vonnegut; charming nihilist," Christianity Today 19(10):17-19. February 14, 1975.

"Sniffing out science fiction," Christianity Today 20(11):18-20. February 27, 1976.

Lawrence, Mark

"Freedom, for what? 1984 and Anthem," in: The Future in Peril: 1984 and the Anti-Utopians. College Station: Honors Program, Texas A&M University, [1985]. pp. 41-45.

Lawrence, Seymour

"Publisher's dream, A," Summary 1(2):73-75. 1971.

Lazarus, Joseph

"E. T. and All of That," Pulpsmith 3(1): 54-57. Spring 1983.

Le Bris, Michel

"Lettre et le desir, La," in: H. P. Lovecraft. Paris: Editions de l'Herne, 1969. pp. 91-105.

Le Guin, U. K.

Dreams Must Explain Themselves. New York: Algol Press, 1975. 37 p.

Language of the Night: Essays on Fantasy and Science Fiction, The, by U. K. Le Guin and ed. by Susan Wood. New York: Putnam, 1979. 270 p.

"American SF and the other," Science Fiction Studies 2(3):208-210. November 1975. Comment, SFS 3(1):97. March 1976. Replies, SFS 3(1):98. Mr. 1976; SFS 3(2):211-212. Jl. 1976. (Also in her Language of the Night.)

"Brauchen wir das Geschlecht? in: Femistische Utopien: Aufbruch in dei postpatriarchale Gesellschaft, ed. by Barbara Holland-Cunz. Meitingen: Corian Verlag, 1985.

"Change, SF, and Marxism: open or closed universes? Surveying the battlefield," Science Fiction Studies 1(2):88-90. Fall 1973.

"Child and the shadow, The," Quarterly Journal of the Library of Congress 32(2):139-148. April 1975. (Also in her Language of the Night.)

"Child and the Shadow, The," in: Haviland, Virginia, ed. The Openhearted Audience: Ten Authors Talk About Writing for Children. Washington, DC: Library of Congress, 1980. pp. 101-113.

"Citizen of Mondath, A; the development of a science fiction writer: IV," Foundation 4:20-24. July 1973. (Also in her Language of the Night.)

"Concerning the 'Lem affair'," Science Fiction Studies 4(1):100. March 1977. Comment, Darko Suvin, Science Fiction Studies 4(1):101-102. March 1977.

"Crab nebula, the paramecium, and Tolstoy, The," Riverside Quarterly 5(2):89-96. February 1972.

"Creative spirit and children's literature: a symposium, The," Wilson Library Bulletin 53(2):166-169. October 1978.

"Do-it-yourself cosmology," in: Le Guin, U. K. Language of the Night. New York: Putnam, 1979. pp. 121-125.

Le Guin, U. K. (Continued)

"Dreams must explain themselves," <u>Algol</u> 21:7-14. November 1973. also in: <u>Signal</u> 19:3-11. January 1976. (Also in her <u>Language of the Night</u>.)

"Dreams Must Explain Themselves," in: Boyer, R. H. and Zahorski, K. J. <u>Fantasists on Fantasy</u>. New York: Avon Discus, 1984. pp. 181-194.

"Escape routes," <u>Galaxy</u> 35(12):40-44. December 1974. (Also in her <u>Language of the Night</u>.)

"European SF: Rottensteiner's anthology, the Strugatskys, and Lem," <u>Science Fiction Studies</u> 1(3):181-185. Spring 1974.

"From Elfland to Poughkeepsie," in: Boyer, R. H. and Zahorski, K. J. <u>Fantasists on Fantasy</u>. New York: Avon Discus, 1984. pp. 195-210. (Also in her <u>Language of the Night</u>.)

"Introduction to <u>City of Illusions</u>," in: Le Guin, U. K. <u>Language of the Night</u>. New York: Putnam, 1979. pp. 145-148.

"Introduction to <u>Planet of Exile</u>," in: Le Guin, U. K. <u>Language of the Night</u>. New York: Putnam, 1979. pp. 139-144.

"Introduction to <u>Rocannon's World</u>," in: Le Guin, U. K. <u>Language of the Night</u>. New York: Putnam, 1979. pp. 133-138.

"Introduction to <u>Star Songs of an Old Primate</u>," in: Le Guin, U. K. <u>Language of the Night</u>. New York: Putnam, 1979. pp. 179-184.

"Introduction to <u>The Altered I</u>," in: Le Guin, U. K. <u>Language of the Night</u>. New York: Putnam, 1979. pp. 191-194.

"Introduction to <u>The Left Hand of Darkness</u>," in: Le Guin, U. K. <u>Language of the Night</u>. New York: Putnam, 1979. pp. 155-161.

"Introduction to <u>The Word for World is Forest</u>," in: Le Guin, U. K. <u>Language of the Night</u>. New York: Putnam, 1979. pp. 149-154.

"Is gender necessary?" in: McIntyre, Vonda, ed. <u>Aurora: Beyond Equality</u>. Greenwich, Connecticut: Fawcett, 1976. pp. 11-15. (Also in her <u>Language of the Night</u>.)

"Lathe of Heaven, The," <u>Horizon</u> 23(1):32-36. January 1980.

"Mapping Imaginary Countries," in: Wingrove, David, ed. <u>The Science Fiction Source Book</u>. New York: Van Nostrand, 1984. pp. 77-79.

"Modest one," in: Le Guin, U. K. <u>Language of the Night</u>. New York: Putnam, 1979. pp. 175-178.

"Myth and archetype in science fiction," <u>Parabola</u> 1(4):42-47. Fall 1976. (Also in her <u>Language of the Night</u>.)

"National Book Award acceptance speech," in: Le Guin, U. K. <u>Language of the Night</u>. New York: Putnam, 1979. pp. 57-58.

"New book by the Strugatskys, A," <u>Science Fiction Studies</u> 4(2):157-159. July 1977.

"On David Ketterer's <u>New Worlds for Old</u>: Ketterer on <u>The Left Hand of Darkness</u>," <u>Science Fiction Studies</u> 2(2):137-139. July 1975.

"On Norman Spinrad's <u>The Iron Dream</u>," <u>Science Fiction Studies</u> 1(1):41-44. Spring 1973.

"On teaching science fiction," in: Williamson, Jack, ed. <u>Teaching Science Fiction: Education for Tomorrow</u>. Philadelphia: Owlswick, 1980. pp. 21-25.

"On theme," in: Wilson, Robin Scott, ed. <u>Those Who Can: A Science Fiction Reader</u>. New York: Mentor/New American Library, 1973. pp. 203-209.

"Prophets and mirrors," <u>Living Light</u> 7(3):111-121. Fall 1970.

"Response to the Le Guin issue, A," <u>Science Fiction Studies</u> 3(1):43-46. March 1976.

"Science fiction Americaine et L'autre," <u>Change</u> (Paris) 40:132-135. 1981.

"Science fiction and Mrs. Brown," in: Nicholls, Peter, ed. <u>Science Fiction at Large</u>. New York: Harper, 1976. pp. 13-34. (Also in her <u>Language of the Night</u>.)

"Science fiction as prophesy: Philip K. Dick," <u>New Republic</u> 175(18):33-34. October 30, 1976.

"Science-fiction americaine et L=l'autre," <u>Change</u> (Paris) 40: 132-135. 1981.

"Stalin in the soul," in: Le Guin, U. K. <u>Language of the Night</u>. New York: Putnam, 1979. pp. 211-222.

"Staring eye," <u>Vector</u> 75: 5-7. July 1975.

"Staring eye," in: Le Guin, U. K. <u>Language of the Night</u>. New York: Putnam, 1979. pp. 171-174.

"Stone Ax and the Musk Oxen," <u>Vector</u> 71: 5-13. December 1975.

"Stone ax and the muskoxen," in: Le Guin, U. K. <u>Language of the Night</u>. New York: Putnam, 1979. pp. 223-236.

"Talking about writing," in: Le Guin, U. K. <u>Language of the Night</u>. New York: Putnam, 1979. pp. 195-201.

Le Guin, U. K. (Continued)

"View in, The," in: Chauvin, Cy, ed. Multitude of Visions. Baltimore: T-K Graphics, 1975. pp. 5-8.

"Why are Americans afraid of dragons?" Pacific Northwest Library Association Quarterly 38(2):14-18. February 1974. (Also in her Language of the Night.)

"Writers, The: Mapping Imaginary Countries," Science Fiction Chronicle 6(11): 36-37. August 1985.

Le Vot, Andre

"S. F. et recit. a) L'anti-roman," Europe 580/581:103-108. August/September 1977.

Lea, S. L. W., Jr.

Gothic to Fantastic: Readings in Supernatural Fiction. New York: Arno, 1980. 190 p.

Leach, James

"Man Who Fell to Earth, The: adaptation by omission," Literature/Film Quarterly 6(4):371-379. Fall 1978 .

Leahy, J. T.

"Science fiction: from space opera to imaginative literature," The Trend in Engineering at the University of Washington 23(4):16-19,31. October 1971.

Lear, J.

"Let's put some science in science fiction," Popular Science Monthly 165(2):135-137. August 1954.

Lear, John

"Is there a lunar microbe stranger than science fiction?" Saturday Review 52:29-31. June 26, 1969. (Review)

Leary, D. J.

"Ends of childhood: eschatology in Shaw and Clarke, The," Shaw Review 16(2):67-78. May 1973.

Leavitt, D. B.

"Speculative Approaches to Consciousness in Science Fiction," in: Valle, R. S., ed. The Metaphors of Consciousness. New York: Plenum, 1981. pp. 395-415.

Leavy, M. A.

"Embryo," Cinefantastique 5(3):21,23. Winter 1976.

Leayman, C. D.

"They Came From Within (review)," Cinefantastique 5(3):22-23. Winter 1976.

Lebedev, A. A.

"Realisticeskaja fantastika i fantasticeskaja real'nost'" Novyj mir 11:261-266. 1968.

"Traditsii Svifta v tvorchestve Herbert Wells," Uchenye zapiski Gor'kovskogo universiteta, Gorky 160:140-154. 1973.

Lebedew, A.

"Realistische Phantastik und phantastische Realitat," Quarber Merkur 39:7-14. January 1975.

Leblond, M. A.

"Epopee evolutionniste de l'energie humaine, L'" Revue des Revues 46:641-655. 1903.

Lecaye, Alexis

Pirates du Paradis: essai sur la science-fiction, Les. Paris: Denoel/Gonthier, 1981. 250 p.

LeClair, Thomas

"Death and black humor," Critique 17(11):5-46. 1975.

"Essential Opposition: The Novels of Anthony Burgess," Critique 12(3): 77-94. 1971.

Lederer, Richard

"Shaping the dystopian nightmare," English Journal 56(8):1132-1135. November 1967.

Lee, Clayton

"Cognitive Approaches to Alien," Science-Fiction Studies 7(3): 299-304. November 1980.

Lee, G. F.

"Quest of Arthur Gordon Pym, The," Southern Literary Journal 4:22-33. 1972.

Lee, George

"And the Darkness Grasped It Not: the struggle for good and evil in Charles Williams," Mythlore 6(1): 18-20. Winter 1979.

Lee, L. L.

"Fantasy as comic American morality: The Circus of Dr. Lao," Markham Review 10: 53-56. Summer 1981.

Lee, Nora

"Across the eighth dimension with Buckaroo Banzai," Cinefex No. 19:44-59. November 1984.

"Creating dinosaurs for Baby," American Cinematographer 67(3): 57-63. March 1985.

"Crystal Palace set for War Games," American Cinematographer 64(9):64-67,82-87. September 1983.

"Rescher + Figueroca = Space," American Cinematographer 66(6): 68-86. June 1985.

"Spacehunter," by G. G. Turner and Nora Lee. American Cinematographer 64(7):56-59,88-91. July 1983.

"Star Trek III: The Search for Spock," American Cinematographer 65(8):54-63. August/September 1984.

"Video effects for 2010," American Cinematographer 66(1): 57-64. January 1984.

Lee, R. A.

Orwell's Fiction. Notre Dame, Indiana: University of Notre Dame Press, 1969. 188 p.

Lee, Vernon

"Rosny and the analytical novel in France," Cosmopolis 7:289-296. 1897.

Lee, Walt

Reference Guide to Fantastic Films: Science Fiction, Fantasy & Horror. Los Angeles: Chelsea-Lee Books, 1972-1974. 3 volumes.

Leeper, Geoffrey

"Happy utopias of Aldous Huxley and H. G. Wells, The," Meanjin Quarterly 24(1):120-124. 1965.

Lees, Gene

"Spaced-out world of Douglas Trumball," American Film 3:70. February 1978.

Lefebvre, Henri

"Vers un romantisme revolutionnaire," Nouvelles Revue Francaise October 1957.

Leff, Leonard

"Science and destruction in Vonnegut's Cat's Cradle," Rectangle (Sigma Tau Delta) 46:28-32. Spring 1971.

"Utopia reconstructed: alienation in Vonnegut's God Bless You, Mr. Rosewater," Critique 12(3):29-37. 1971.

Leflar, Donna

"Bibliography; novels of post-holocaust America: an annotated bibliography," by John Newman and Donna Leflar. Alternative Futures 1(3/4):110-116. Fall 1978.

Lefranc, Bolivar

"Brian Aldiss," Books and Bookmen 15(10):18,20. July 15, 1970.

LeGacy, Arthur

"Invasion of the Body Snatchers, The: a metaphor for the fifties," Literature/Film Quarterly 6(3):285-292. Summer 1978.

Legman, G.

"Folk literature and folklore with a few words on science fiction," in: Legman, G. The Horn Book: Studies in Erotic Folklore and Bibliography. New York: University Books, 1964. pp. 289-335.

Legrand, G.

"Barbarella, the comic-strip vamp," Atlas 10:120-121. August 1965.

Legrand, H. E.

"Chariots of the gods? and all that: pseudohistory in the classroom," by H. E. Legrand and W. E. Boese. History Teacher 8(3):359-370. May 1975.

Lehan, Terri

"Fantasy: A Reader's List," by Terri Lehan and Peggy Murray. Voice of Youth Advocates 5(4): 28-34. October 1982.

Lehman, Peter

"Special Effects in Star Wars," by Peter Lehman and Don Daso. Wide Angle 1(1):72-77. 1979. (Revised)

Lehman, Steven

"Ruddick on Rama: an amplification," Science Fiction Studies 12(2): 237. July 1985.

Lehman-Wilzig, S. N.

"Science fiction as futurist prediction: alternative visions of Heinlein and Clarke," Literary Review (Fairleigh Dickinson University) 20:133-151. Winter 1977.

Leibacher-Ouvard, L. H.

Utopian Imaginary Journeys in the Reign of Louis XIV. (French Text) Ph. D. Dissertation, Stanford University, 1982. 367 p.

Leiber, Fritz

"Anima Archetype in Science Fiction," in: Schweitzer, Darrell, ed. Exploring Fantasy Worlds. San Bernardino, CA: Borgo, 1985. pp. 76-82.

"Business, Bereavement, Flight: My Life and Writings, Part 7," Fantasy Review 7(6): 19, 30. July 1984.

"Controlled anachronism," in: De Camp, L. S., ed. Blade of Conan. New York: Ace, 1979. pp. 151-170.

"Enzenbacker's eight Norse gods," Locus 12(10):10-12. November 1979.

"Horror Hits a High," in: Underwood, Tim and Miller, Chuck, eds. Fear Itself. Columbia, PA: Underwood/Miller 1982. pp. 85-103.

"Howard's fantasy," in: Herron, Don, ed. Dark Barbarian: The Writings of Robert E. Howard, a Critical Anthology. Westport, CT: Greenwood, 1984. pp. 3-16.

"J. R. R. Tolkien," Locus No. 149:2-3. September 14, 1973.

"Lankhmar & lands around," Anduril 6:15-17. 1976.

"Lankhmar and lands around," Anduril No. 1:16-21. April 1972.

"Literary Copernicus," in: Joshi, S. T., ed. H. P. Lovecraft: Four Decades of Criticism. Athens, OH: Ohio University Press, 1980. pp. 40-62.

"Living From Writing? Sober on the Coast. My Life and Writings, 5," Fantasy Review 7(2): 6-7, 42. March 1984.

"New Purposes and the Cinvention; Alcohol and the Writer; My Life and Writings, Part 3," Fantasy Newsletter 6(7): 14-15. August 1983.

"Not Much Disorder and Not So Early Sex: An Autobiographical Essay," in: Leiber, Fritz. The Ghost Light. New York: Berkley, 1984. pp. 251-368.

"On Fantasy: How I Grew Up to Write Horror Stories; My Life and Writings, Part 1," Fantasy Newsletter 6(3): 10-11. March 1983.

"On Fantasy: Lost Fantasies," Fantasy Newsletter 5(8): 7-9. September 1982.

"On Fantasy: Midlife Crossroads; My Life and Writings, Part 4," Fantasy Newsletter 6(9): 6-7. October/November 1983.

"On Fantasy: Sex and the Fantasist, II," Fantasy Newsletter 5(6): 5-7. July 1982.

"On Fantasy: Sex and the Fantasist," Fantasy Newsletter 5(4): 13-15. April/May 1982.

"On Fantasy; Naming the Moons: Part II," Fantasy Newsletter 6(1): 6-7. January 1983.

"Pearl Harbor Vampire: How I Came to Write Science Fiction: My Life and Writing, Part 2," Fantasy Newsletter 6(5): 22-23. May 1983.

"Profession of science fiction: XII: Mysterious islands, The," Foundation 11/12:29-38. March 1977.

"San Francisco: New Beginnings; My Life and Writings, Part 8, Conclusion," Fantasy Review 7(8): 7-8, 42. September 1984.

"Through Hyperspace with Brown Jenkin: Lovecraft's Contribution to Speculative Fiction," in: Joshi, S. T., ed. H. P. Lovecraft: Four Decades of Criticism. Athens, OH: Ohio U. P., 1980. pp. 140-152.

"Through hyperspace with Brown Jenkin: Lovecraft's contribution to speculative fiction," in: Lovecraft, H. P. The Dark Brotherhood and Other Pieces. Sauk City, Wisconsin: Arkham House, 1966. pp. 164-178.

"Time and Nth dimensions," in: Ash, Brian, ed. Visual Encyclopedia of Science Fiction. New York: Harmony, 1977. pp. 144-153.

"Titivated romance," in: De Camp, L. S., ed. Blade of Conan. New York: Ace, 1979. pp. 189-203.

Leiber, Fritz (Continued)

"To Arkham and the stars," in: Lovecraft, H. P. _The Dark Brotherhood and Other Pieces_. Sauk City, Wisconsin: Arkham House, 1966. pp. 153-163.

"Travails of the fantasy novel: a project unborn," _Foundation_ 17:12-26. September 1979.

"Ups and Downs; Return to Alcohol; My Life and Writings, Part 6," _Fantasy Review_ 7(4): 13, 42. May 1984.

"Utopia for poets and witches," _Riverside Quarterly_ 4(3): 194-205. June 1970.

"Way-out science," _National Review_ pp. 289-291. April 5, 1963. (Book reviews)

Leiber, Justin

"Fritz Leiber and eyes," _Starship_ 16(3):9-18. Summer 1979.

"Fritz Leiber and Eyes," in: Smith, Nicholas D., ed. _Philosophers Look At Science Fiction_. Chicago: Nelson-Hall, 1982. pp. 165-193.

"Introduction," in: Leiber, Fritz. _Worlds of Fritz Leiber_. Boston: Gregg, 1979. pp. v-xii.

"On Science Fiction and Philosophy," _Philosophical Speculations on Science Fiction and Fantasy_. 1(1): 5-11. March 1982.

"Science Fiction Worlds," _Philosophical Speculations in Science Fiction and Fantasy_. 2: 52-60. Summer 1981.

Leiber, Leslie

"Science on a spree," _New York Herald Tribune. This Week Magazine_. April 27, 1947. 2 p.

Leiby, Joan

Burrough's Science Fiction, With an Analytical Subject and Name Index, by R. R. Kudlay and Joan Leiby. Geneseo, NY: SLIS, State University College of Arts and Sciences, 1973. 234 p.

Leighton, Peter

Moon Travellers: A Dream That is Becoming a Reality. London: Oldbourne, 1960. 240 p.

Leiner, F.

"Perry Rhodan. Eine Untersuchung uber Wesen, Wirkung, und Wert der Science Fiction Literatur," _Blatter fur den Deutschlehrer_ 12:65-80. 1968.

Leiner, Friedrich

Science fiction. Texte und Materialien zum Literatur Unterricht. Frankfurt: Diesterweg, 1972. 88 p.

Science Fiction: eine Textsammlung fuer die Schule, by Friedrich Leiner and Juergen Gutsch. Frankfurt: Diesterweg, 1973. 158 p.

Science Fiction: Materialien und Hinweise, by Friedrich Leiner and Juergen Gutsch. Frankfurt: Diesterweg, 1980. 114 p.

Leinster, Murray

"Writing science fiction today," _Writer_ 81(5):16-18. May 1968. also in: Burick, A. S., ed. _Writer's Handbook_. Boston: Writer, 1969. pp. 515-520.

Leiper, E. M.

"Green Fields; Barren Stretches," _Empire For the SF Writer_ 32: 25-27. Winter 1984.

Leith, Linda

"Marion Zimmer Bradley and Darkover," _Science-Fiction Studies_ 7(1): 28-35. March 1980.

Lem, Stanislaw

Fantastyka i futurologia. Krakow: Wydawn. Literackie, 1970. 2 volumes, 292 p and 458 p.

Microworlds: Writings on Science Fiction and Fantasy, ed. by Franz Rottensteiner. San Diego: Harcourt, 1984. 182 p.

Phantastik und futurologie. Frankfurt: Insel, 1977. 2 vols, 480 p. and 670 p.

"About the Strugatskys' _Roadside Picnic_," _Science Fiction Studies_ 10(3): 317-332. November 1983.

"Anhang: _Ubik_ als SF," _Quarber Merkur_ 29:35-39. January 1972.

"Art Credo," _Quarber Merkur_ 31:25-27. July 1972. also in: _Polaris I_. Frankfurt: Insel, 1973. pp. 86-88.

"Bemerkungen zur franzosischen science fiction," _Quarber Merkur_ 44:52-60. July 1976.

Lem, Stanislaw (Continued)

"Cosmology and science fiction," Science Fiction Studies 4(2):107-110. July 1977. Comment, SFS 4(3):316-317. November 1977. Reply, SFS 5(1):92-93. March 1978.

"Cosmology and Science Fiction," in: Lem, Stanislaw. Microworlds. San Diego: Harcourt, 1984. pp. 200-208.

"Erfolg," Quarber Merkur. 50:44-48. February 1979.

"Erotik and sexualitat in der science fiction," Insel Almanach auf das Jahr 1972. Pfade ins Unendliche. Hg. Franz Rottensteiner. Frankfurt: Insel, 1971. pp. 23-60.

"Lebensriss, in Miniaturausgabe," Quarber Merkur 31:27-29. July 1972.

"Looking down on science fiction," Science Fiction Studies 4(2):127-128. July 1977.

"Lost opportunities," SF Commentary No. 24:22-24. November 1971. Reply, No. 26:90-92. April 1972.

"M. K. Joseph's Roman The Hole in the Zero," Quarber Merkur 27:22-26. July 1971.

"Metafantasia: The Possibilities of Science Fiction," Science-Fiction Studies. 8(1): 54-71. March 1981.

"On the structural analysis of science fiction," Science Fiction Studies 1(1):26-33. Spring 1973.

"On the Structural Analysis of Science Fiction," in: Lem, Stanislaw. Microworlds. San Diego: Harcourt, 1984. pp. 31-44.

"Philip K. Dick: a visionary among the charlatans," Science Fiction Studies 2(1):54-67. March 1975.

"Philip K. Dick: A Visionary Among the Charlatans," in: Lem, Stanislaw. Microworlds. San Diego: Harcourt, 1984. pp. 106-135.

"Profession of science fiction: XV: answers to a questionaire, The," Foundation 15:41-50. January 1979.

"Reflections on My Life," in: Lem, Stanislaw. Microworlds. San Diego: Harcourt, 1984. pp. 1-30.

"Reflexionen 1974," Quarber Merkur 38:60-63. November 1974.

"Remarks occasioned by Dr. Plank's essay 'Quixote's Mills'," Science Fiction Studies 1(2):78-83. Fall 1973. Response, Science Fiction Studies 1(2):83-84. Fall 1973.

"Roboter in der science fiction," in: Barmeyer, Eike, ed. Science fiction: theorie und geschichte. Munchen: Fink, 1972. pp. 163-185.

"Roboter in der science fiction," in: Rottensteiner, Franz, ed. Quarber Merkur. Frankfurt: Suhrkamp, 1979. pp. 40-64.

"Robots in science fiction," in: Clareson, T. D., ed. SF: The Other Side of Realism. Bowling Green, Ohio: Bowling Green University Popular Press, 1971. pp. 307-325.

"Science and reality in Philip K. Dick's Ubik," in: Chauvin, Cy, ed. Multitude of Visions. Baltimore: T-K Graphics, 1975. pp. 35-39.

"Science fiction strukturalis meghatarozoi," Helikon 18(1): 55-72. 1972. (From: Fantastyki i futurologia.)

"Science fiction und kosmologie," in: Rottensteiner, Franz, ed. Quarber Merkur. Frankfurt: Suhrkamp, 1979. pp. 33-39.

"Science fiction," Tworczosc No. 2:112-138. 1959.

"Science fiction: a hopeless case, with exceptions," SF Commentary 35/36/37:7-36. September 1973.

"Science Fiction: A Hopeless Case, with Exceptions," in: Lem, Stanislaw. Microworlds. San Diego: Harcourt, 1984. pp. 45-105.

"Science fiction: strukturalistisch gesehen," in: Rottensteiner, Franz, ed. Quarber Merkur. Frankfurt: Suhrkamp, 1979. pp. 17-32.

"Sex in science fiction," Quarber Merkur 25:41-58. January 1971.

"SF: Ein hoffnungsloser Fall mit Ausnahmen," Quarber Merkur 29:11-35. January 1972. Also in: Rottensteiner, Franz, ed. Polaris I. Frankfurt: Insel, 1973. pp. 11-60.

"SF: Pornographie und Phantomatik," Quarber Merkur 28:18-24. November 1971.

"Strukturalische S-F Betrachtung," Quarber Merkur 23:6-15. May 1970.

"Time travel story and related matters of SF structuring, The," Science Fiction Studies 1(3):143-154. Spring 1974.

"Time-Travel Story and Related Matters of Science Fiction Structuring, The" in: Lem, Stanislaw. Microworlds. San Diego: Harcourt, 1984. pp. 136-160.

"Todorov's fantastic theory of literature," Science Fiction Studies 1(4):227-237. Fall 1974. Comment, SFS 2(2):166-167. July 1975. Comment, SFS 2(2):167-169. July 1975. Reply, SFS 2(2):169-170. July 1975.

Lem, Stanislaw (Continued)

"Todorov's Fantastic Theory of Literature,"
in: Lem, Stanislaw. <u>Microworlds</u>. San Diego:
Harcourt, 1984. pp. 209-232.

"Two Ends of the World," <u>Missouri Review</u>
7(2): 238-242. 1984.

"Uber Grotesken," <u>Quarber Merkur</u> 31:29-30.
July 1972.

"Unitae Oppositorum: Das Prosawerk des J. L.
Borges," <u>Quarber Merkur</u> 25:26-30. January
1971.

"Unitas Oppositorum: The Prose of Jorge Luis
Borges," in: Lem, Stanislaw. <u>Microworlds</u>.
San Diego: Harcourt, 1984. pp. 233-242.

"Vorwort zur fussischen Ausgabe vor <u>Solaris</u>,"
<u>Quarber Merkur</u> 38:48-49. November 1974.

"Zulawski's Silver Globe," <u>Science Fiction
Studies</u> 12(1): 1-5. March 1985.

"Zur Entstehung meines Romans <u>Wizja Lokalna</u>,"
<u>Quarber Merkur</u> 61: 59-63. July 1984.

Leman, Grahame

"Science fictional imagination, The,"
<u>Foundation</u> 3:31-34. March 1973.

Lemelin, Robert

"Bellamy and Howells; social justice in the
American utopian novel," <u>The Reprint
Bulletin: Book Reviews</u> 27(2):1-5.
March/April 1972.

Lemieux, Jacques

"Utopias and social relations in American
science fiction, 1950-1980," <u>Science Fiction
Studies</u> 12(2): 148-155. July 1985.

LeMire, E. D.

"H. G. Wells and the world of science fiction,"
<u>University of Windsor Review</u> 2:59-67.
Spring 1967.

Lemonnier, Leon

"Edgar Poe et le roman scientifique francaise,"
<u>La grand revue</u> 133:214-223. September
1930.

L'Engle, Madeleine

<u>Walking on Water: Reflections on Faith and
Art</u>. New York: Bantam, 1982. 198 p.

"Childlike wonder and the truths of science
fiction," <u>Children's Literature Annual</u> 10:
102-110. 1982.

"What is real," <u>Language Arts</u>
55(4):447-451. April 1978.

Lennartz, Michael

"La planlingva ideo kaj la scienc-fikcia
literaturo en Germana D. R.," <u>Kontakto</u>
2:14-16. 1981.

Lense, Edward

"Sauron is watching <u>you</u>; the role of the
great eye in <u>The Lord of the Rings</u>,"
<u>Mythlore</u> 4(1):3-6. 1976.

Lentz, H. M., III

<u>Science Fiction, Horror, & Fantasy Film and
Television Credits</u>. Jefferson,NC: McFarland,
1983. 2 v. 1374 p.

Lenz, C. W.

"Pferd am Schwanz, Das," <u>Science Fiction
Times</u> (Germany) 26(4):15-16. April 1984.

Lenz, J.

"Geometry and other science fiction,"
<u>Mathematics Teacher</u> 66(6):529. October 1973.

Lenz, J. M.

"Manifest Destiny: Science Ficton and Classical
Form," in: Slusser, George E., ed.
<u>Coordinates</u>. Carbondale: Southern Illinois
University Press, 1983. pp. 42-48.

Lenz, Millicent

"Alternate Worlds and a Multiplicity of
Futures," by Millicent Lenz and R. M. Mahood.
in: Lenz, Millicent, and Mahood, Ramona, eds.
<u>Young Adult Literature</u>. Chicago: American
Library Association, 1980. pp. 415-448.

Leo, W. T.

<u>Order in the Fictional Works of J. R. R.
Tolkien</u>. Ph. D. Dissertation, University of
Edinburgh, 1980. 254 p.

Leonard, W. T.

"Superman," in: Leonard, W. T. <u>Theatre:
Stage to Screen to Television</u>. Metuchen, NJ:
Scarecrow, 1981. pp. 1492-1503.

Lerner, Fred

Annotated Checklist of Science Fiction Bibliographical Works, An. East Paterson, New Jersey: by the compiler, 1969.

Modern Science Fiction and Its Reception by the American Literary and Educational Communities, 1926-1970. Ph. D. Dissertation, Columbia, 1981. 387 p. (DAI 44A(10):3069)

Modern Science Fiction and the American Literary Community. Metuchen, NJ: Scarecrow, 1985. 325 p.

"Cataloging and Classifications of Science Fiction Collections," _Special Collections_ 2(1/2): 151-170. Fall/Winter 1982.

"Conference of the bibliography of science fiction," _AB Bookman's Weekly_ 45:1444. April 27, 1970.

"Fan at the MLA, A," _Science Fiction Times_ No. 463:2. February 1969.

"First conference: bibliography of science fiction," _Extrapolation_ 11(1):4-5. December 1969.

"George Orwell and Modern Science Fiction," _Voice of Youth Advocates_ 7(1): 19-20, 60. April 1984.

"Keeping Up: The Science Fiction Reader's Guide to Science Magazines," _Amazing_ 58(1): 50-57. May 1984.

"Popularity of Science Fiction," _Voice of Youth Advocates_ 5(4): 25-27, 34. October 1982.

"Religion Looks at Science Fiction," _Niekas_ 25: 33-34. February 1981.

"Science fiction library," _Special Libraries_ 64(1):3-6. January 1973.

"Science fiction vs. science fact," _New Scientist_ 1454:38. May 2, 1985.

"Syracuse University," _Special Collections_ 2(1/2): 59-62. Fall/Winter 1982.

Lessing, Doris

"Vonnegut's responsibility," _New York Times Book Review_ p. 35. February 4, 1973. (Book review)

Lester, Colin

International Science Fiction Yearbook 1979, The. New York: Quick Fox, 1978. 394 p.

Letson, Russell

"Dragon Masters, The," in: Magill, Frank N., ed. _Survey of Science Fiction Literature_, Vol. 2. Englewood Cliffs, NJ: Salem Press, 1979. pp. 600-604.

"Dying Earth, The," in: Magill, Frank N., ed. _Survey of Science Fiction Literature_, Vol. 2. Englewood Cliffs, NJ: Salem Press, 1979. pp. 665-670.

"Fantasy Magazine," in: Tymn, M. B. and Ashley, Mike. _Science Fiction, Fantasy, and Weird Fiction Magazines._ Westport, CT: Greenwood, 1985. pp. 268-270.

"Great God Pan, The," in: Magill, Frank N., ed. _Survey of Modern Fantasy Literature_, Vol 2. Englewood Cliffs, NJ: Salem Press, Inc., 1983. pp. 642-645.

"Lovers, The," in: Magill, Frank N., ed. _Survey of Science Fiction Literature_, Vol. 3. Englewood Cliffs, NJ: Salem Press, 1979. pp. 1289-1293.

"Novarian Series, The," in: Magill, Frank N., ed. _Survey of Modern Fantasy Literature_, Vol 3. Englewood Cliffs, NJ: Salem Press, Inc., 1983. pp. 1132-1136.

"Odyssey," in: Tymn, M. B. and Ashley, Mike. _Science Fiction, Fantasy, and Weird Fiction Magazines._ Westport, CT: Greenwood, 1985. pp. 441-444.

"Riverworld Series," in: Magill, Frank N., ed. _Survey of Science Fiction Literature_, Vol. 4. Englewood Cliffs, NJ: Salem Press, 1979. pp. 1809-1816.

"Terror, The," in: Magill, Frank N., ed. _Survey of Modern Fantasy Literature_, Vol 4. Englewood Cliffs, NJ: Salem Press, Inc., 1983. pp. 1895-1897.

"Three Imposters, The," in: Magill, Frank N., ed. _Survey of Modern Fantasy Literature_, Vol 4. Englewood Cliffs, NJ: Salem Press, Inc., 1983. pp. 1922-1925.

"Worlds of Fantasy (1968-1971)," in: Tymn, M. B. and Ashley, Mike. _Science Fiction, Fantasy, and Weird Fiction Magazines._ Westport, CT: Greenwood, 1985. pp. 771-773.

"Faces of a thousand heroes: Philip Jose Farmer, The," _Science Fiction Studies_ 4(1):35-41. March 1977.

"Falling through many trapdoors: Robert Silverberg," _Extrapolation_ 20(2):109-117. Summer 1979.

"Introduction," in: Farmer, P. J. _The Green Odyssey._ Boston: Gregg, 1978. pp. v-xv.

"Portraits of Machine Consciousness," in: Dunn, Thomas P., ed. _The Mechanical God._ Westport: Greenwood, 1982. pp. 101-108.

Letson, Russell (Continued)

"Returns of Lazarus Long, The," in: Olander, Joseph D. and Martin Harry Greenberg, eds. <u>Robert A. Heinlein</u>. New York: Taplinger, 1978. pp. 194-221.

"Short fiction of Machen, The," in: Magill, Frank N., ed. <u>Survey of Modern Fantasy Literature</u>, Vol 4. Englewood Cliffs, NJ: Salem Press, Inc., 1983. pp. 1633-1639.

"Worlds of Philip Jose Farmer, The," <u>Extrapolation</u> 18(2):124-130. May 1977.

Letts, Doug

"Preliminary notes on an axiom system for plot," <u>Foundation</u> 1:54-59. March 1972.

Levack, D. J. H.

<u>Amber Dreams: A Roger Zelazny Bibliography</u>. Columbia, PA: Underwood/Miller, 1983. 151 p.

<u>De Camp: An L. Sprague de Camp Bibliography</u>, by Charlotte Laughlin and D. J. H. Levack. Columbia, PA: Underwood/Miller, 1983. 328 p.

<u>Fantasms II: a Bibliography of the Literature of Jack Vance</u>, compiled by Kurt Cockcrum, D. J. H. Levack, and Tim Underwood. Riverside, California: K. Cockrum, 1979. 99 p.

<u>Fantasms: A Bibliography of Jack Vance</u>. San Francisco: Underwood/Miller, 1978. 91 p.

<u>PKD: A Philip K. Dick Bibliography</u>. Columbia, PA: Underwood/Miller, 1981. 158 p.

"Jack Vance: A Bibliography," <u>Science Fiction: A Review of Speculative Literature</u> 4(2): 82-84. June 1982.

"Stephen King, a Bibliography," by Marty Ketchum, D. J. H. Levack, and Jeff Levin. in: Underwood, Tim, and Miller, Chuck, eds. <u>Fear Itself</u>. Columbia, PA: Underwood/Miller, 1982. pp. 231-246.

Leverance, W. J.

"<u>Cat's Cradle</u> and traditional American humor," <u>Journal of Popular Culture</u> 5(4):955-963. Spring 1972.

Levin, A.

"Science fiction and the schoolchild," by A. Levin and A. Velikovich. <u>Soviet Review</u> 11(3):250-257. Fall 1970.

Levin, A. E.

"English-language SF as a socio-cultural phenomenon," <u>Science Fiction Studies</u> 4(3):246-256. November 1977.

Levin, Harry

"Science and Fiction," in: Slusser, George E., ed. <u>Bridges to Science Fiction</u>. Carbondale: Southern Illinois University Press, 1980. pp. 3-21.

Levin, Jeff

"Art of Leo and Diane Dillon," <u>Shayol</u> 1(4): 39-44. Winter 1980.

"Bibliographic checklist of the works of Ursula K. Le Guin," in: Le Guin, U. K. <u>Language of the Night</u>. New York: Putnam, 1979. pp. 237-270.

"Stephen King, a Bibliography," by Marty Ketchum, D. J. H. Levack, and Jeff Levin. in: Underwood, Tim, and Miller, Chuck, eds. <u>Fear Itself</u>. Columbia, PA: Underwood/Miller, 1982. pp. 231-246.

"Ursula K. Le Guin; a select bibliography," <u>Science Fiction Studies</u> 2(3):204-208. November 1975.

Levin, Rob

"World of science fiction," <u>Bloomsbury Review</u> 1(5):10. July/August 1981.

Levine, George

<u>Endurance of Frankenstein: Essays on Mary Shelley's Novel</u>, ed. by George Levine and U. C. Knoepflmacher. Berkeley: University of California Press, 1979. 341 p.

Levine, R. A.

"Downward journey of purgation: notes on an imagistic leitmotif in <u>The Narrative of Arthur Gordon Pym</u>, The," <u>Poe Newsletter</u> 2:29-31. 1969.

Levinson, Paul

"Science fiction: fantasy rooted in fundamental concerns," <u>Media & Methods</u> 15(8):26-28,53. April 1979.

Levinthal, R. E.

"Laws of time travel, The," by S. J. Jakiel and R. E. Levinthal. <u>Extrapolation</u> 21(2):130-138. Summer 1980.

Levitin, Alexis

J. R. R. Tolkien's The Lord of the Rings.
Masters Thesis, Columbia, n.d.   109 p.

Levitis, Ruth

"Need, nature, and nowhere," in: Utopias,
ed. by Peter Alexander and Roger Gill. London:
Duckworth, 1984. pp. 19-30.

Levitt, L.

"Letter to the miscellaneous man, A,"
Miscellaneous Man No. 7:14-15. June 1950.
(Reply by William J. Margolis)

Levy, F. A.

"Possession," Cinefantastique 12(5/6):4.
July/August 1982.

"Spengler on Superman," Cinefantastique
11(2):4-7. Fall 1981.

"Versions of Arrakis you'll never see," by P.
M. Sammon, Stephen Jones and F. A. Levy.
Cinefantastique 14(4/5):32-34. September
1984.

Levy, M. M.

Transformations of Oberon: The Use of Fairies
in Seventeenth-Century Literature.   Ph. D.
Dissertation, University of Minnesota, 1982.
261 p.

Levy, Maurice

"De la Specificite du text fantastique,"
Recherches Anglaises et Americaines 6:3-13.
1973.

Lewicki, Stefan

"Feminism and Science Fiction," Foundation
32: 45-59. November 1984.

"Work in Progress," Vector 105: 16-18.
December 1981.

Lewis, A. O., Jr.

"Anti-utopian novel: preliminary notes and
checklist, The," Extrapolation 2(2):27-32.
May 1961.

"History of the SFRA Pilgrim Award," SFRA
Newsletter. 85: 2S-10S. October 1980.
(Supplement to the Newsletter)

"Pilgrim award: presentation speech, The," in:
Remington, T. J., ed. Selected Proceedings
of the 1978 SFRA National Conference. Cedar
Falls, Iowa: University of Northern Iowa,
1979. pp. 241-242.

"Utopian Hero," in: Roemer, Kenneth M., ed.
American As Utopia. New York: Franklin,
1981. pp. 133-147.

Lewis, A. R.

Concordance to Cordwainer Smith.   Boston:
NESFA Press, 1984. 90 p.

Lewis, Al

"LASFS history: the Evans Freehafer Award,"
in: Patten, Fred. The Best of APA-L, 1966.
Los Angeles: F. Patten, 1966. pp. 22-24.

Lewis, Anthony

"SF magazines, 1969 statistical wrapup,"
Locus No. 49:8. February 23, 1970.

Lewis, C. S.

Experiment in Criticism, An. New York:
Cambridge University Press, 1961. 142 p.

Of Other Worlds; Essays and Stories, by C. S.
Lewis and ed. by Walter Hooper. New York:
Harper, 1966. 147 p.

"On science fiction," in: Rejser i tid og
rum. En Bog om science fiction, ed. by Tage
La Cour. Copenhagen: Stig Verdelkaer, 1973.

"On SF," in: Lewis, C. S. Of Other Worlds.
Harcourt, 1966. pp. 9-73. also in: Lewis, C.
S. Experiment in Criticism. Cambridge Univ.
Press, 1965. pp. 108-111; and Knight, D., ed.
Turning Points. Harper, 1977. pp. 119-131.

"Religion and rocketry," in: Lewis, C. S.
The World's Last Night. New York: Harcourt,
1973. pp. 83-92.

"Sometimes Fairy Stories May Say Best What's to
Be Said," in: Boyer, R. H. and Zahorski, K.
J. Fantasists on Fantasy. New York: Avon
Discus, 1984.   pp. 111-118.

"Unreal estates," in: Lewis, C. S. Of
Other Worlds; Essays and Stories. New York:
Harcourt, 1966. pp. 86-96.

Lewis, David

"Death of the Dragon, The," in: Magill,
Frank N., ed. Survey of Science Fiction
Literature, Vol. 1. Englewood Cliffs, NJ:
Salem Press, 1979. pp. 508-512.

Lewis, David (Continued)

"Inter Ice Age 4," in: Magill, Frank N., ed. Survey of Science Fiction Literature, Vol. 3. Englewood Cliffs, NJ: Salem Press, 1979. pp. 1040-1044.

"Kaitei Gunkan," in: Magill, Frank N., ed. Survey of Science Fiction Literature, Vol. 3. Englewood Cliffs, NJ: Salem Press, 1979. pp. 1106-1109.

"Rashomon and Other Stories," in: Magill, Frank N., ed. Survey of Modern Fantasy Literature, Vol 3. Englewood Cliffs, NJ: Salem Press, Inc., 1983. pp. 1304-1306.

"Sanreizan Hiroku," in: Magill, Frank N., ed. Survey of Science Fiction Literature, Vol. 4. Englewood Cliffs, NJ: Salem Press, 1979. pp. 1854-1858.

"Sword of the Demon," in: Magill, Frank N., ed. Survey of Modern Fantasy Literature, Vol 4. Englewood Cliffs, NJ: Salem Press, Inc., 1983. pp. 1869-1871.

"Japanese SF," in: Barron, Neil, ed. Anatomy of Wonder. 2nd ed. New York: Bowker, 1981. pp. 467-496.

"Japanese update," Locus 12(4):4. May 1979.

"Paradoxes of Time Travel," American Philosophical Quarterly. 13(2): 145-152. April 1976. (Reprinted: Miller, F. D. and Smith, N. D., eds. Thought Probes. Prentice-Hall, 1981.)

"Science fiction in Japan," Foundation 19: 19-29. June 1980.

"SF in Japan," Locus 14(10):14. November 1981.

Lewis, Flora

"Writer of and for the times," Chicago Sun-Times p. 22. January 5, 1971. (not seen)

Lewis, Joan

Utopia as Alternative Futures. Menlo Park, CA: Stanford Research Institute, 1970. 50 p. (Research Memorandum, No. EPRC-6747-7.)

Lewis, Naomi

Fantasy Books for Children. London: National Book League, 1975. 61 p.

Lewis, Peter

George Orwell: The Road to 1984. New York: Harcourt, 1981. 122 p.

Ley, Willy

"Geography for time travelers," in: Greenberg, M. H., ed. Coming Attractions. New York: Gnome, 1957. pp. 70-103.

"Letter to the Martians, A," in: Greenberg, M. H., ed. Coming Attractions. New York: Gnome, 1957. pp. 18-37.

"Space travel: science fiction and science fact," Publisher's Weekly 164(17):1742-1748. October 24, 1953.

"Space war," in: Greenberg, M. H., ed. Coming Attractions. New York: Gnome, 1957. pp. 158-185.

Leydon, Joe

"Dune Meets Art Deco (Review)," Houston Post p. 1F-4F. December 13, 1984.

"Film: Return of the Jedi," Houston Post p. 8B. May 25, 1983.

"Pare and Allen, Off Camera," Houston Post Sec. 3, p. 1. August 3, 1984.

"Ron Howard: Happy Days as a director," Boston Post June 16, 1985. in: NewsBank. Film and Television. 2:D7-D9. July 1985.

Lhoest, C.

Litteratures de science fiction: catalogue, collections communales et provinciales, by C. Lhoest and C. Bailly. Liege: Bibliotheque Centrale de la Ville de Liege, 1976. 91 p.

Liapunov, Boris

V mire fantastiki: obzor nauchno-fantasticheskoi i fantasticheskoi literatury. 2nd ed. revised and expanded. Moscow: Kniga, 1975. 207 p.

V mire mechty. Moscow: Kniga, 1970. 213 p.

"Bibliografiia," in Britikov, A. F. Russkii sovetskii nauchnofantasticheskii roman. Leningrad: Nauka, 1970. pp. 363-436.

"Science puts a rein on fiction," USSR No. 1 (88): 47. January 1964.

"Sovetskaia fantastika (Opyt bibliografii) 1946-1956 godov," in Fantastika-71. Moskva: Molodaia gvardiia, 1971. pp. 350-380.

Liapunova, Izabella

"Sovetskaia fantastika (Opyt bibliografii 1961-1964 gg.)," in Fantastika 73-74. Moskva: Molodaia gvardiia, 1975. pp. 309-349.

Liapunova, Izabella (Continued)

"Sovetskaia fantastika (Opyt bibliografii, 1957-1960 gody)," in Fantastika-72. Moskva: Molodaia gvardiia, 1972. pp. 314-348.

Liat, Kwee Swan

"Natuur versus techniek in de Science Fiction," Restant (Belgium) 10(2): 167-181. Spring 1982.

Libby, Anthony

"Merwin's Planet: Alien Voices," Criticism 24(1): 48-63. Winter 1982.

Libby, E. F.

"Demographic, intellectual, and personality characteristics of science fiction fans," by C. G. Waugh, E. F. Libby and C. L. Waugh. Paper presented at the Science Fiction Research Association Annual Meeting, November 1975. 22 p.

Lichtenberg, Jacqueline

"Karma and Sunsigns and SF stories," Empire: For the SF Writer 3(1): 14-15. June 1977.

"Science Fiction Writers of America and the Nebula Award," in: Cowart, David, ed. Twentieth Century American Science Fiction Writers. Detroit: Gale, 1981. v. 2, pp. 295-297.

Lichtenstein, Allen

"Science Fiction Book Versus Movie Audiences: Implications for the Teaching of Science Fiction," Extrapolation 24(1): 47-56. Spring 1983.

Lieb, Laurie

"Body & mind in That Hideous Strength," CSL: The Bulletin of the New York C. S. Lewis Society 5(11):10-12. September 1974.

Lien, Dennis

"Uncanny Tales (Canadian)," Megavore (Science Fiction Collector) 9:25-37. June 1980.

"Curtis Books," Science Fiction Collector 14: 5-14. May 1981.

Lifton, R. J.

"Image of 'The End of the World': A Psychohistorical View," Michigan Quarterly Review 24(1): 70-90. Winter 1985.

"Kurt Vonnegut: duty-dance with death," American Poetry Review 1:41. January/February 1973.

Lightman, H. A.

"Blade Runner: production design and photography," by H. A. Lightman and Richard Patterson. American Cinematographer 63(7):684-687,715-725. July 1982.

"Filming 2001: A Space Odyssey," American Cinematographer 49(6):412-414,442-447. June 1968.

"Filming 2001: A Space Odyssey," in: Johnson, William, ed. Focus on the Science Fiction Film. Englewood Cliffs, NJ: Prentice Hall, 1972. pp. 126-133.

"Filming Marooned," American Cinematographer 50(10):974-976, 1003-1005. October 1969.

"Filming Planet of the Apes," American Cinematographer 49(4):256-259,278. April 1968.

"Front projection for 2001," American Cinematographer 49(6):420-422,441,445-456. June 1968.

"My close encounter with Close Encounters of the Third Kind," American Cinematographer 59(1):28-29, 56-57,88-91. January 1978.

"On location with H. G. Wells' The Island of Dr. Moreau," American Cinematographer 58(7):846-851,860-861. August 1977.

"Very special effects for Star Trek: The Motion Picture," American Cinematographer 61(2):144-145,174-175,193-197. February 1980.

Limmer, W.

"Phantasmagorien des atomzeitalters. Zur Jack Arnold Retrospektive im Munchner ABC," Suddeutsche Zeitung No. 186:8- . 1974.

Linaweaver, Brad

"Conversation with Michael Shaara," by Brad Linaweaver and W. A. Ritch. Amazing 28(7): 20-26. September 1982.

"Interview With William Tenn, part 1," Riverside Quarterly 7(2): 82-93. March 1982.

"Interview With William Tenn, part 2," Riverside Quarterly 7(3): 150-159. May 1983.

Linaweaver, Brad (Continued)

"Interview with William Tenn, part 3," Riverside Quarterly 7(4): 232-239. December 1985.

Linckens, H. P.

"Interview mit Robert Sheckley," Science Fiction Times (Germany) 26(11):5-8. November 1984.

Lindau, Hans

"Kurd Lasswitz und seine modernen Marchen," Nord und Sud pp. 315-333. September 1903.

"Kurd Lasswitz," Kant-Studien 16(1):1-4. 1911.

Lindboe, Ole

Virkelige eventyr, ed. by Ole Lindboe and Svend K. Moller. Copenhagen: Spar Knaegt, 1978. 168 p.

Lindborg, H. J.

"Venus Plus X: Sturgeon's Rite of Passage," Extrapolation 24(3): 234-240. Fall 1983.

Linden, William

"Tormance and C. S. Lewis," CSL: The Bulletin of the New York C. S. Lewis Society 5(7):4-5. May 1974.

Linder, Heidi

"1984 and Lord of the Flies: The Wages of Evil," in: The Future in Peril: 1984 and the Anti-Utopians. College Station: Honors Program, Texas A&M University, [1985]. pp. 19-23.

Lindsay, Cecile

"Topography of (Science) Fiction: Claude Ollier's Life on Epsilon," Science-Fiction Studies 11(1): 39-44. March 1984.

Lindsay, Clarence

"H. G. Wells, Viktor Shklovsky, and Paul de Man: the subversion of romanticism," in: Collins, R. A., ed. Scope of the Fantastic: Theory, Technique, Major Authors. Westport: Greenwood, 1985. pp. 125-134.

Lindsey, Robert

"Scientology Chief Got Millions, Ex-Aides Say," New York Times p.1, 10. July 11, 1984.

Lindskoog, Kathryn

"C. S. Lewis: reactions from women," Mythlore 3(4):18-20. June 1976.

"Getting it together: Lewis and the two hemispheres of knowing," Mythlore 6(1): 43-45. Winter 1979.

Lingfeld, Norbert

Roboter und Gartenlaube, Ideologie und unterhaltung in der science-fiction-literatur, by Michael Pehlke and Norbert Lingfeld. Munchen: Hanser, 1970. 158 p.

Linwood, G. D.

"Out-of-this-world special effects for Star Trek," by H. A. Anderson, G. D. Linwood, and Joseph Westheimer. American Cinematographer 48:714-717. October 1967.

Linzner, Gordon

"Space and Time," by Mike Ashley and Gordon Linzner. in: Tymn, M. B. and Ashley, Mike. Science Fiction, Fantasy, and Weird Fiction Magazines. Westport, CT: Greenwood, 1985. pp. 582-584.

Lippi, Giuseppe

Guida alla fantascienza, by Vittorio Curtoni and Guiseppe Lippe. Milan: Gammalibri, 1978. 221 p.

"Opinion: fantascienza e letteratura popolare," Robot: rivista de fantascienza. 1(1):111-117. April 1976.

Lipsett, Edward

"SF in Japan: An Overview," by Yoshio Kobayashi and Edward Lipsett. Locus 17(3): 21. March 1984.

"Science Fiction in Japan," by Yoshio Kobayashi, T. Maki, and Edward Lipsett. Locus 18(1): 31-32. January 1985.

Lipski, J. M.

"Literature of the unknowable," in: Collins, R. A. and H. D. Pearce, eds. The Scope of the Fantastic: Theory, Technique, Major Authors. Westport, CT: Greenwood Press, 1985. pp. 113-121.

Lipton, Lawrence

"Illustrated Man: Ray Bradbury," Intro Bulletin 1(6/7): 9, 11. March/April 1956.

Little, D. P.

Historical Survey and Analysis of a Selected Number of Science Fiction Titles. Masters Thesis, Atlanta University, 1962.

Little, Edmund

Fantasts. Amersham, Eng.: Avebury, 1984. 136 p.

Littlefield, Emerson

"Mythologies of Race and Science in Samuel Delany's The Einstein Intersection and Nova," Extrapolation 23(3): 235-242. Fall 1982.

Livingston, Dennis

"Inventory of science fiction stories relevant to public policy issues, An," World Future Society. Supplemental Program 6 p. 1971. (with World Future Society Bulletin. October 1971.)

"Science fiction & futurology: some observations at a science fiction convention," The Futurist 2(3):47-48. June 1968.

"Science fiction as a source of forecast material," Futures 1(3):232-238. March 1969.

"Science fiction as an educational tool," in: Toffler, Alvin, ed. The Role of the Future in Education. New York: Random House, 1974. pp. 235-256.

"Science fiction in the teaching of futurology," World Future Society. Bulletin 4(12):4-6. December 1971.

"Science fiction is valuable means to physically prepare for the future," Trend 7:15,26. Spring 1971.

"Science fiction models of future world order systems," International Organization 25(2):254-270. Spring 1971. also in: Somit, Albert, ed. Political Science and the Study of the Future. Hinsdale, IL: Oryden, 1974.

"Science fiction taught as futurology," Extrapolation 14(2):152-156. May 1973.

"Study of SF as a forecasting methodology," in: Japan Society of Futurology. Challenges From the Future: Proceedings of the Int. Future Research Conference. 4 v. Tokyo: Kodansha, 1970. 1:71-79. (not seen)

"Utility of science fiction, The," in: Fowles, Jib, ed. Handbook of Futures Research. Westport, Connecticut: Greenwood Press, 1978. pp. 163-178.

Ljungquist, K. P.

"Mardi and a Voyage Thither," in: Magill, Frank N., ed. Survey of Modern Fantasy Literature, Vol 2. Englewood Cliffs, NJ: Salem Press, Inc., 1983. pp. 976-979.

"Short fiction of Poe, The," in: Magill, Frank N., ed. Survey of Modern Fantasy Literature, Vol 4. Englewood Cliffs, NJ: Salem Press, Inc., 1983. pp. 1665-1678.

Llewelyn, J. J.

World of the Dark Crystal, by Brian Froud, J. J.Llewelyn, and Rupert Brown. New York: Knopf, 1983. 128 p.

Lloyd, P. M.

"Role of warfare and strategy in The Lord of the Rings," Mythlore 3(3):3-7. 1976.

Lloyd, Rosemary

Baudelaire et Hoffmann: Affinities et Influences. London: Cambridge University Press, 1979. 395 p.

Lobdell, Jared

England and Always: Tolkien's World of the Rings. Grand Rapids, MI: Eerdmans, 1981. 94 p.

Tolkien Compass, A. La Salle, Illinois: Open Court, 1975. 201 p. Reprinted, New York: Ballantine, 1980. 216 p.

"Thornton Wilder as Fantasist and the Science Fiction Antiparadigm: The Evidence of The Skin of Our Teeth," in: Hassler, Donald M. Patterns of the Fantastic II. Mercer Island, WA: Starmont, 1984. pp. 29-38.

Lochhead, Marion

Renaissance of Wonder: The Fantasy Worlds of C. S. Lewis, J. R. R. Tolkien, George MacDonald, E. Nesbit and others. San Francisco: Harper, 1980. 169 p.

Lochte, Dick

"Clockwork Orange: Elevating Sadism and Violence," Los Angeles Free Press p. 10. January 14, 1972.

Lochte, Dick (Continued)

"Interview with the Star of 'A Clockwork Orange'," _Los Angeles Free Press_ p. 7. January 21, 1972.

"Silent Running," _Los Angeles Free Press_ Part 1, p. 15. March 10, 1972.

"Slaughterhouse Five," _Los Angeles Free Press_ Part 1, p. 19, 21. March 31, 1972.

Lock, Owen

"Judy-Lynn del Rey, 1943-1986," _SFWA Bulletin_ 20(1): 28-30. Spring 1986.

Locke, George

Ferret Fantasy's Christmas Annual for 1972. London: Ferret Fantasy, 1972. 76 p.

Ferret Fantasy's Christmas Annual for 1973. London: Ferret Fantasy, 1974. 54 p.

Land of Dreams: A Review of the Work of Sidney H. Sime, 1905 to 1916. London: Ferret Fantasy, 1975. 64 p.

Science Fiction First Editions. London: Ferret, 1978. 96 p.

Spectrum of Fantasy: The Bibliography and Biography of a Collection of Fantastic Literature. London: Ferret, 1980. 246 p.

Voyages in Space: A Bibliography of Interplanetary Fiction 1801-1914. London: Ferret Fantasy, 1975. 80 p.

"Annotated addendum, The," in: Locke, George. _Ferret Fantasy's Christmas Annual._ London: Ferret Fantasy, 1972. pp. 29-70.

"English science fiction magazine, 1919, An," _Science Fiction Studies_ 6(3):304-308. November 1979.

"Wells in three volumes? A sketch of British publishing in the 19th century," _Science Fiction Studies_ 3(3):282-286. November 1976.

Lockwood, G. B.

"Science Fiction and High School Students' Attitudes Toward Science," by P. A. Rubba, G. B. Lockwood, and G. J. Fleming. _Hoosier Science Teacher_ 7(3): 85-88. February 1982.

Lofficier, J. M.

"Adventure in the Nightmare of 'Dreamscape'," by Randy Lofficier and J. M. Lofficier. _Starlog_ 81: 28-30. April 1984.

"Bill Norton: bringing up Baby," by Randy Lofficier and J. M. Lofficier. _Starlog_ No. 93:51-53. April 1985.

"Call Him D. A. R. Y. L," by Randy Lofficier and J. M. Lofficier. _Starlog_ No. 97: 34-35. August 1985.

"Candy Clark: Rolling Through Blue Thunder," by Randy Lofficier and J. M. Lofficier. _Starlog_ 79: 28-29. February 1984.

"Cruising the galaxy with Barbarella," by Randy Lofficier and J. M. Lofficier. _Starlog_ No. 92:38-39. March 1985.

"Dean Stockwell, the traitor of Dune," by Randy Lofficier and J. M. Lofficier. _Starlog_ No. 90:34-36,65. January 1985.

"Dennis Lawson: surviving Star Wars," by Randy Lofficier and J. M. Lofficier. _Starlog_ No. 93:54-56. April 1985.

"Exploring director Joe Dante," by Randy Lofficier and J. M. Lofficier. _Starlog_ No. 98:28-32. September 1985.

"Inside War Games," by Randy Lofficier and J. M. Lofficier. _Starlog_ 74: 42-45, 69. September 1983.

"Interview: David Lynch," by Randy Lofficier and J. M. Lofficier. _Twilight Zone_ 4(6):44-45. January/February 1985.

"Interview: George Miller," by Randy Lofficier and J. M. Lofficier. _Starlog_ No. 98:59-63. September 1985.

"Interview: Joe Dante," by Randy Lofficier and J. M. Lofficier. _Twilight Zone_ 4(4):46-49. September/October 1984.

"Joe Dante's Explorers," by Randy Lofficier and J. M. Lofficier. _Starlog_ No. 97: 48-50. August 1985.

"Long, long road to Dune," by Randy Lofficier and J. M. Lofficier. _Twilight Zone_ 4(6):48-54. November/December 1984.

"Luc Besson on 'Le Dernier Combat'," by Randy Lofficier and J. M. Lofficier. _Starlog_ 85: 24-25, 65. August 1984.

"Marc Singer," by Randy Lofficier and J. M. Lofficier. _Starlog_ 84: 24-25, 95. July 1984.

"Meet the Jetsons," by Randy Lofficier and J. M. Lofficier. _Starlog_ No. 101:38-39. December 1985.

"Mel Gibson: the man who is Mad Max," by Randy Lofficier and J. M. Lofficier. _Starlog_ No. 97: 29-32, 62. August 1985.

Author Entries

Lofficier, J. M. (Continued)

"Noah Hathaway: Boy Hero," by Randy Lofficier and J. M. Lofficier. Starlog 86: 59-60. September 1984.

"On location with Mad Max: Beyond Thunderdome," by Randy Lofficier and J. M. Lofficier. Starlog No. 95: 44-48. June 1985.

"On the Set of 'V': The Conclusion," by Randy Lofficier and J. M. Lofficier. Starlog 83: 28-29, 65. June 1984.

"One Hundred Most Important People in Science Fiction/Fantasy: DeForest Kelley," by J. M. Lofficier and Randy Lofficier. Starlog No. 100: 33. November 1985.

"One Hundred Most Important People in Science Fiction/Fantasy: Jack Williamson," by J. M. Lofficier and Randy Lofficier. Starlog No. 100: 30. November 1985.

"One Hundred Most Important People in Science Fiction/Fantasy: Karel Capek," by J. M. Lofficier and Randy Lofficier. Starlog No. 100: 30. November 1985.

"One Hundred Most Important People in Science Fiction/Fantasy: Olaf Stapledon," by J. M. Lofficier and Randy Lofficier. Starlog No. 100: 39-40. November 1985.

"One Hundred Most Important People in Science Fiction/Fantasy: Robert A. Heinlein," by J. M. Lofficier and Randy Lofficier. Starlog No. 100:40-41. November 1985.

"One Hundred Most Important People in Science Fiction/Fantasy: Robert Bloch," by J. M. Lofficier and Randy Lofficier. Starlog No. 100: 80. November 1985.

"One Hundred Most Important People in Science Fiction/Fantasy: Robert Sheckley," by J. M. Lofficier and Randy Lofficier. Starlog No. 100: 74. November 1985.

"One Hundred Most Important People in Science Fiction/Fantasy: Robert Silverberg," by J. M. Lofficier and Randy Lofficier. Starlog No. 100: 74-75. November 1985.

"One Hundred Most Important People in Science Fiction/Fantasy: Robert Wise," by J. M. Lofficier and Randy Lofficier. Starlog No. 100: 44-45. November 1985.

"One Hundred Most Important People in Science Fiction/Fantasy: Samuel R. Delany," by J. M. Lofficier and Randy Lofficier. Starlog No. 100: 32. November 1985.

"One Hundred Most Important People in Science Fiction/Fantasy: Stanislaw Lem," by J. M. Lofficier and Randy Lofficier. Starlog No. 100: 53. November 1985.

"Raffaella De Larentiis: The Mastermind of Dune," by Randy Lofficier and J. M. Lofficier. Starlog 88: 25-28. November 1984.

"Starlog Interview: DeForest Kelley, Part 1," by Randy Lofficier, J. M. Lofficier, and Julius Fabrini. Starlog 87: 18-20, 67. October 1984.

"Starlog Interview: DeForest Kelley, Part 2," by Randy Lofficier, J. M. Lofficier, and Julius Fabrini. Starlog 88: 22-23. November 1984.

"Starlog Interview: Drew Barrymore," by Randy Lofficier and J. M. Lofficier. Starlog 84: 90-92. July 1984.

"Starlog Interview: Ian McDiarmia," by Randy Lofficier and J. M. Lofficier. Starlog 82: 26-29, 67. May 1984.

"Starlog Interview: Kyle MacLachlan," by Randy Lofficier and J. M. Lofficier. Starlog 89: 42-46. December 1984.

"Starlog interview: Tina Turner," by Randy Lofficier and J. M. Lofficier. Starlog No. 96: 19-21. July 1985.

"Starlog Profile: Richard Matheson," by J. M. Lofficier and Randy Lofficier. Starlog No. 100: 71-73, 93. November 1985.

"Sting: man, myth, and monster," by Bertrand Borie, Randy Lofficier and J. M. Lofficier. Starlog No. 101:16-18. December 1985.

"Terry Hayes, creating the Mad Max myth," by Randy Lofficier and J. M. Lofficier. Starlog No. 99:15-18. October 1985.

Lofficier, Randy

"Adventure in the Nightmare of 'Dreamscape'," by Randy Lofficier and J. M. Lofficier. Starlog 81: 28-30. April 1984.

"Bill Norton: bringing up Baby," by Randy Lofficier and J. M. Lofficier. Starlog No. 93:51-53. April 1985.

"Call Him D. A. R. Y. L," by Randy Lofficier and J. M. Lofficier. Starlog No. 97: 34-35. August 1985.

"Candy Clark: Rolling Through Blue Thunder," by Randy Lofficier and J. M. Lofficier. Starlog 79: 28-29. February 1984.

"Cruising the galaxy with Barbarella," by Randy Lofficier and J. M. Lofficier. Starlog No. 92:38-39. March 1985.

"Dean Stockwell, the traitor of Dune," by Randy Lofficier and J. M. Lofficier. Starlog No. 90:34-36,65. January 1985.

Lofficier, Randy (Continued)

"Dennis Lawson: surviving Star Wars," by Randy
Lofficier and J. M. Lofficier. Starlog No.
93:54-56. April 1985.

"Doctor Who Captures American Imagination,"
San Antonio Express-News December 5, 1982.
in: NewsBank. Film and Television. 61:
C2-3. January 1983.

"Exploring director Joe Dante," by Randy
Lofficier and J. M. Lofficier. Starlog No.
98:28-32. September 1985.

"Inside War Games," by Randy Lofficier and J.
M. Lofficier. Starlog 74: 42-45, 69.
September 1983.

"Interview: David Lynch," by Randy Lofficier
and J. M. Lofficier. Twilight Zone
4(6):44-45. January/February 1985.

"Interview: George Miller," by Randy Lofficier
and J. M. Lofficier. Starlog No. 98:59-63.
September 1985.

"Interview: Joe Dante," by Randy Lofficier and
J. M. Lofficier. Twilight Zone 4(4):46-49.
September/October 1984.

"Joe Dante's Explorers," by Randy Lofficier
and J. M. Lofficier. Starlog No. 97:
48-50. August 1985.

"Long, long road to Dune," by Randy Lofficier
and J. M. Lofficier. Twilight Zone
4(6):48-54. November/December 1984.

"Luc Besson on 'Le Dernier Combat'," by Randy
Lofficier and J. M. Lofficier. Starlog 85:
24-25, 65. August 1984.

"Marc Singer," by Randy Lofficier and J. M.
Lofficier. Starlog 84: 24-25, 95. July
1984.

"Meet the Jetsons," by Randy Lofficier and J.
M. Lofficier. Starlog No. 101:38-39.
December 1985.

"Mel Gibson: the man who is Mad Max," by Randy
Lofficier and J. M. Lofficier. Starlog No.
97: 29-32, 62. August 1985.

"Noah Hathaway: Boy Hero," by Randy Lofficier
and J. M. Lofficier. Starlog 86: 59-60.
September 1984.

"On location with Mad Max: Beyond Thunderdome,"
by Randy Lofficier and J. M. Lofficier.
Starlog No. 95: 44-48. June 1985.

"On the Set of 'V': The Conclusion," by Randy
Lofficier and J. M. Lofficier. Starlog 83:
28-29, 65. June 1984.

"One Hundred Most Important People in Science
Fiction/Fantasy: DeForest Kelley," by J. M.
Lofficier and Randy Lofficier. Starlog No.
100: 33. November 1985.

"One Hundred Most Important People in Science
Fiction/Fantasy: Jack Williamson," by J. M.
Lofficier and Randy Lofficier. Starlog No.
100: 30. November 1985.

"One Hundred Most Important People in Science
Fiction/Fantasy: Karel Capek," by J. M.
Lofficier and Randy Lofficier. Starlog No.
100: 30. November 1985.

"One Hundred Most Important People in Science
Fiction/Fantasy: Olaf Stapledon," by J. M.
Lofficier and Randy Lofficier. Starlog No.
100: 39-40. November 1985.

"One Hundred Most Important People in Science
Fiction/Fantasy: Robert A. Heinlein," by J. M.
Lofficier and Randy Lofficier. Starlog No.
100:40-41. November 1985.

"One Hundred Most Important People in Science
Fiction/Fantasy: Robert Bloch," by J. M.
Lofficier and Randy Lofficier. Starlog No.
100: 80. November 1985.

"One Hundred Most Important People in Science
Fiction/Fantasy: Robert Sheckley," by J. M.
Lofficier and Randy Lofficier. Starlog No.
100: 74. November 1985.

"One Hundred Most Important People in Science
Fiction/Fantasy: Robert Silverberg," by J. M.
Lofficier and Randy Lofficier. Starlog No.
100: 74-75. November 1985.

"One Hundred Most Important People in Science
Fiction/Fantasy: Robert Wise," by J. M.
Lofficier and Randy Lofficier. Starlog No.
100: 44-45. November 1985.

"One Hundred Most Important People in Science
Fiction/Fantasy: Samuel R. Delany," by J. M.
Lofficier and Randy Lofficier. Starlog No.
100: 32. November 1985.

"One Hundred Most Important People in Science
Fiction/Fantasy: Stanislaw Lem," by J. M.
Lofficier and Randy Lofficier. Starlog No.
100: 53. November 1985.

"Raffaella De Larentiis: The Mastermind of
Dune," by Randy Lofficier and J. M.
Lofficier. Starlog 88: 25-28. November
1984.

"Starlog Interview: DeForest Kelley, Part 1,"
by Randy Lofficier, J. M. Lofficier and Julius
Fabrini. Starlog 87: 18-20, 67. October
1984.

"Starlog Interview: DeForest Kelley, Part 2,"
by Randy Lofficier, J. M. Lofficier and Julius
Fabrini. Starlog 88: 22-23. November 1984.

"Starlog Interview: Drew Barrymore," by Randy
Lofficier and J. M. Lofficier. Starlog 84:
90-92. July 1984.

"Starlog Interview: Ian McDiarmia," by Randy
Lofficier and J. M. Lofficier. Starlog 82:
26-29, 67. May 1984.

Lofficier, Randy (Continued)

"Starlog Interview: Kyle MacLachlan," by Randy Lofficier and J. M. Lofficier. Starlog 89: 42-46. December 1984.

"Starlog interview: Tina Turner," by Randy Lofficier and J. M. Lofficier. Starlog No. 96: 19-21. July 1985.

"Starlog Profile: Richard Matheson," by J. M. Lofficier and Randy Lofficier. Starlog No. 100: 71-73, 93. November 1985.

"Stephen King talks about Christine," Twilight Zone 3(6):73-74. January/February 1984.

"Sting: man, myth, and monster," by Bertrand Borie, Randy Lofficier and J. M. Lofficier. Starlog No. 101:16-18. December 1985.

"Terry Hayes, creating the Mad Max myth," by Randy Lofficier and J. M. Lofficier. Starlog No. 99:15-18. October 1985.

Lofts, W. G.

"Master Thriller Series," by Mike Ashley and W. G. Lofts. in: Tymn, M. B. and Ashley, Mike. Science Fiction, Fantasy, and Weird Fiction Magazines. Westport, CT: Greenwood, 1985. pp. 404-406.

Logan, Darlene

"Battle Strategy in Perelandra: Beowulf Revisited," Mythlore 9(3): 19, 21. Autumn 1982.

Logan, G. M.

The Meaning of More's Utopia. Princeton, NJ: Princeton University Press, 1983. 296 p.

Loggem, M. V.

"Amerikanische Zukunftsgeschichte oder die Science Fiction," Akzente 4:412-424. 1967.

Lohle-Tart, Louis

"Temps et la science-fiction, Le," Cahiers de l'Institut de Linguistique de Louvain. (Belgium) 7(1/2): 61-97. 1982.

Loiseau, J. C.

"Science fiction's expanding universe," World Press Review 27(11): 62. November 1980.

Lokke, V. L.

"American utopian anti-novel, The," in: Browne, Ray, ed. Frontiers of American Culture. Lafayette, Indiana: Purdue University Studies, 1968. pp. 123-149.

London, John

Jack London: A Bibliography, by H. C. Woodbridge, John London and G. H. Tweney. Georgetown, California: Talisman Press, 1966. 385 p. Milwood, New York: Kraus Reprint, 1973. Enlarged edition, 554 p.

Loney, J. D.

Reality, Truth and Perspective in the Fiction of C. S. Lewis. Ph. D. Dissertation, McMaster University, 1983. (DAI 44(A):3072-3073)

Long, F. B.

Howard Phillips Lovecraft: Dreamer on the Nightside. Sauk City, Wisconsin: Arkam House, 1975. 237 p.

"Kline on Burroughs," Oak Leaves 1(7):3-4. Spring 1972.

Longyear, B. B.

Science Fiction Writer's Workshop I: An Introduction to Fiction Mechanics. Philadelphia: Owlswick, 1980. 161 p.

"How to Write Good," Empire: For the SF Writer 5(1):4-5, 12-13. Winter 1979.

"Salty," Empire For the SF Writer 32: 22-24. Winter 1984.

"Science fiction in the primary school," in: Williamson, Jack, ed. Teaching Science Fiction: Education for Tomorrow. Philadelphia: Owlswick, 1980. pp. 75-81.

Longyear, R. B.

"Surviving the Ides of April," Empire: For the SF Writer 6(1): 11, 14. Winter 1980.

"Surviving the Ides of April," Empire: For the SF Writer. 23: 17, 19. Spring 1981.

Lonker, Fred

"Infantiles Utopia: Bemerkungen zu H. W. Frankes 'Sirius Transit'," in: Ermert, Karl, ed. Neugier oder Flucht? Stuttgart: Klett, 1980. pp. 126-136.

Loock, T. M.

Lesebuch der deutschen Science Fiction 1984, ed. by H. J. Alpers and T. M. Loock. Meitingen: Corian, 1983. 264 p.

"H. G. Francis im Gespraech," by H. J. Alpers and T. M. Loock. Science Fiction Times (Germany) 25(8):5-9. August 1983.

"Michael Weisser im Gesprach," by H. J. Alpers and T. M. Loock. Science Fiction Times (Germany) 25(10):5-12. October 1983.

"Reinmar Cunis im Gesprach," by H. J. Alpers and T. M. Loock. Science Fiction Times (Germany) 25(2):6-12. February 1983.

Loohaus, Jackie

"Rod Serling," Milwaukee Journal December 5, 1982. in: NewsBank. Film and Television. 69: D6-7. January 1983.

Lord, Glenn

Fiction of Robert E. Howard: A Pocket Checklist, by Dennis McHaney and Glenn Lord. s.l.: McHaney, 1975. 21 p.

Howard Collector. New York: Ace, 1979. 267 p.

Last Celt: A Bio-bibliography of Robert Ervin Howard, The. West Kingston, Rhode Island: Donald M. Grant, 1976. 416 p.; New York: Berkley, 1976. 416 p.

"Gent from Cross Plains," in: De Camp, L. S., ed. Blade of Conan. New York: Ace, 1979. pp. 107-112.

"Howard's detective stories," in: De Camp, L. S., ed. Blade of Conan. New York: Ace, 1979. pp. 123-126.

"Kline-Howard collaboration?" by Glen Lord and O. A. Kline. Oak Leaves 1(10):13. Winter 1972/73.

"Robert E. Howard: an introduction to the creature of Conan," ERB-dom No. 9:6-7. March 1964.

"Robert E. Howard: professional writer," in: Herron, Don, ed. Dark Barbarian: The Writings of Robert E. Howard, a Critical Anthology. Westport, CT: Greenwood, 1984. pp. 135-148.

Lorenzen, J. A.

20 Years of Analog/Astounding Science Fiction-Science Fact. Avon Lake, OH: Locomotive Workshop, 1971. 40 p.

Lorrah, Jean

"Shamanistic vision in fantastic poetry, The," in: Collins, R. A., ed. Scope of the Fantastic: Culture, Biography, Themes, Children's Literature. Westport: Greenwood, 1985. pp. 199-204.

Lorraine, Lilith

"Not an escape but a challenge," Miscellaneous Man 1(3):13-14. Winter 1954.

Los Angeles City Schools.

Far Out: Some Approaches to Teaching the Speculative Literature of Science Fiction and the Supernatural. Los Angeles: Los Angeles City Schools, Instructional Planning Division, 1974. 120 p.

Lothamer, Eileen

"Science and pseudo-science in George Eliot's 'The Lifted Veil'," Extrapolation 17(2):125-132. May 1976.

Loudermilk, Shawn

"More on P. K. Dick," Paperback Quarterly 5(3): 51-54. Fall 1982.

Louit, Robert

"Quatorze stations sur la ligne du present," Magazine Litteraire 88:12-16. May 1974.

Love, G. B.

Best of Trek, The, ed. by Walter Irwin and G. B. Love. New York: Signet, 1978. 239 p.

Best of Trek, No. 2, The, ed. by Walter Irwin and G. B. Love. New York: Signet, 1980.

Best of Trek, No. 3, The, ed. by Walter Irwin and G. B. Love. New York: Signet, 1981. 196 p.

Best of Trek, No. 4, The, ed. by Walter Irwin and G. B. Love. New York: Signet, 1981. 214 p.

Best of Trek, No. 5, The, ed. by Walter Irwin and G. B. Love. New York: Signet, 1982. 201p.

Best of Trek, No. 6, The, ed. by Walter Irwin and G. B. Love. New York: Signet, 1983. 191 p.

Best of Trek, No. 7, The, ed. by Walter Irwin and G. B. Love. New York: Signet, 1984. 205 p.

Love, G. B. (Continued)

Best of Trek, No. 8, The, ed. by Walter Irwin and G. B. Love. New York: Signet, 1985. 221 p.

Best of Trek, No. 9, The, ed. by Walter Irwin and G. B. Love. New York: Signet, 1985. 207 p.

Best of Trek, No. 10, The, ed. by Walter Irwin and G. B. Love. New York: Signet, 1986. 198 p.

Lovecraft, H. P.

Autobiography: Some Notes on a Nonentity. Sauk City, Wisconsin: Arkham House, 1963. 17 p.

Ec'h Pi El Speaks: An Autobiographical Sketch by H. P. Lovecraft. Saddle River, New Jersey: Gerry de la Ree, 1972. 12 p.

Lovecraft at Last, by H. P. Lovecraft and Willis Conover. Arlington, Virginia: Carrollton, Clark, 1975. 272 p.

Selected Letters. Sauk City, Wisconsin: Arkham House, 1965-1976. 5 volumes.

Supernatural Horror in Literature. New York: Ben Abramson, 1945. 111 p. Reprinted, New York: Dover Publications, 1973.

"Introduction to Supernatural Horror in Literature," in: Boyer, Robert H. and Zahorski, Kenneth J. Fantasists on Fantasy. New York: Avon Discus, 1984. pp. 31-40.

Lovell, A. C. B.

"Counterblast to science fiction," New Statesman 47(1201):319-320. March 13, 1954. Discussion, 47(1202):357-358. March 20, 1954.

Lovell, Glen

"Making Alien; behind the scenes; interviews," by M. P. Carducci and Glen Lovell. Cinefantastique 9(1):10-39. Fall 1979.

"Salem's Lot," Cinefantastique 9(3/4):69-70. Spring 1980.

"Tobe Hooper's Funhouse," by Bill Kelley and Glenn Lovell. Cinefantastique 10(3):26-31. Winter 1980.

Loveman, A.

"Clearing House: scientific novels," Saturday Review of Literature 16(13):17. July 24, 1937.

Lowe, Nick

"So, You Fancy Yourself as a Writer?" Focus: An SF Writer's Magazine 9: 16-23. Autumn 1984.

Lowell, A. D.

"Production design for E.T.," American Cinematographer 64(1):50-53. January 1983.

Lowell, Priscilla

"Interview: Alexis Gilliland," Thrust 22: 23-24, 32. Spring/Summer 1985.

"Interview: Jack Chalker," Thrust 20: 17-19. Spring/Summer 1984.

Lowentrout, Peter

"Evocation of Good in Tolkien," Mythlore 10(4): 32-33. Spring 1984.

"Rags of Lordship, The: science fiction, fantasy, and the reenchantment of the world," Mythlore 11(3): 47-51, 57. Winter/Spring 1985.

Lowins, Evelyne

"Agression miniaturisee, L'. Sur Bug et Phase IV," Cinema D'aujourd'hui. No. 7:85-90. Spring 1976.

"Films d'aujourd'hui sur des themes de maintenant," by J. P. Andrevon, Pierre Gires, and Evelyne Lowin. Cinema D'aujourd'hui. No. 7:91-98. Spring 1976.

Lowndes, R. A. W.

Three Faces of Science Fiction. Boston: NESFA Press, 1973. 96 p.

"Magazine of Horror delayed again by printer," Science Fiction Times No. 422:3-4. December 1964.

"Scientific Detective Monthly," in: Tymn, M. B. and Ashley, Mike. Science Fiction, Fantasy, and Weird Fiction Magazines. Westport, CT: Greenwood, 1985. pp. 556-562.

"Cycles," Fantasy Times No. 254:17-18. September (1) 1956.

"James Blish: a profile," Magazine of Fantasy and Science Fiction 42(4):66-71. April 1972.

"James Blish: an appreciation," Locus No. 179:4-5. September 27, 1975.

Lowndes, R. A. W. (Continued)

"Standards in science fiction," _Famous Science Fiction_ 1(2):6-9,113-122. Spring 1967.

Lowry, Brian

"Animating the Black Cauldron," _Starlog_ 97: 65-67, 71. August 1985.

"Anthony Daniels: Was it hot in the costume?" _Starlog_ 99: 23-26, 72. October 1985.

"Chris Columbus Dreaming up Gremlins," _Starlog_ 86: 51-53, 66. September 1984.

"Eric Luke: exploring his dreams," _Starlog_ No. 99:44-46. October 1985.

"Ice Pirates Defrosted," _Starlog_ 82: 44-46. May 1984.

"Interview: William Katt," _Starlog_ No. 94:59-60,66-67. May 1985.

"Interview: Yaphet Kotto," _Starlog_ No. 94:63-65. May 1985.

"Jonathan Betuel: SF fan, SF filmmaker," _Starlog_ 95: 16-18. June 1985.

"Making of 'The Last Starfighter,'" _Starlog_ 80: 34-37. March 1984.

"On the set of My Science Project," _Starlog_ No. 98:16-18. September 1985.

"On the set of Warning Sign," _Starlog_ No. 98:64-66. September 1985.

"One Hundred Most Important People in Science Fiction/Fantasy: Edgar Allan Poe," _Starlog_ 100: 30. November 1985.

"One Hundred Most Important People in Science Fiction/Fantasy: Vincent Price," _Starlog_ 100: 39. November 1985.

"Paul Smith," _Starlog_ No. 97: 23-25, 28. August 1985.

"Profile: Anthony Daniels," _Starlog_ No. 99:23-26,72. October 1985.

"Profile: Hal Barwood," _Starlog_ No. 101:42-44. December 1985.

"Richard Fleischer: Directing Conan the Destroyer," _Starlog_ 85: 18-21, 66. August 1984.

"Starlog Interview: Arnold Schwarzenegger: The Complete Barbarian," _Starlog_ 82: 51-53. May 1984.

"Starlog Interview: Dan O'Herlihy," _Starlog_ 86: 27-29, 65. September 1984.

"Starlog Interview: Nick Castle," _Starlog_ 87: 62-65. October 1984.

"Starlog interview: Stanley Mann," _Starlog_ No. 90:24-26. January 1985.

"Starlog Profile: Hal Barwood," _Starlog_ 101: 42-44. December 1985.

Lu, Chin-po

K'o Huan wen husch. 1980. 142 p. (CF Library of Congress. Books:Subjects.)

Lubienski, Tomasz

"Przepowiednie Lema," _Tworczosz_ No. 7:121-123. 1959.

Lubow, Arthur

"Star wars war: I, a space iliad, The," _Film Comment_ 13(4):20-21. July/August 1977.

Lucas, George

Filmmaker: A Personal Diary. Los Angeles, CA: Direct Cinema, 1983. 16mm, 33 min., color.

"On Star Wars," _Science Fiction Review_ 7(1):16. February 1978.

Lucas, T. R.

"Old Shelley Game, The: Prometheus & Predestination in Burgess' Works," _Modern Fiction Studies_ 27(3): 465-478. Autumn 1981.

Lucas, Tim

Your Movie Guide to Science Fiction/Fantasy Video Tapes and Discs. s.l.: Publications International, 1985. 128 p.

Your Movie Guide to Horror Video Tapes and Discs. s.l.: Publications International, 1985. 128 p.

"Clash of the Titans (review)," _Cinefantastique_ 11(2):51. Fall 1981.

"David Cronenberg's The Dead Zone," _Cinefantastique_ 14(2):24-31,70. December 1983/January 1984.

"David Cronenberg's Videodrome," _Cinefantastique_ 14(2):32-39. December 1983/January 1984.

"Friday the 13th (review)," _Cinefantastique_ 10(2):42. Fall 1980.

"Funhouse (review)," _Cinefantastique_ 11(2):49. Fall 1981.

Lucas, Tim (Continued)

"Ghost Story (review)," *Cinefantastique* 12(2/3):82. April 1982.

"Jerry Cornelius: The Last Days of Man on Earth," *Cinefantastique* 4(2):4-7,38. Summer 1975.

"Thing (review)," *Cinefantastique* 13(1):49. September/October 1982.

"V (review)," *Cinefantastique* 13(6)/14(1):106. September 1983.

"Videodrome (review)," *Cinefantastique* 13(4):4-5. April/May 1983.

"Videodrome," *Cinefantastique* 12(2/3):4-7. April 1982.

Luck, Hartmut

Deformierte Zukunft, Die: untersuchungen zur Science Fiction, by Reimer Jehmlich und Harmut Luck. Munchen: Goldmann, 1974. 208 p.

Fantastik, science fiction, utopie: das realismusproblem der utopisch-fantastischen literatur. Giessen: Focus, 1977. 355 p.

"2001: Ankunft in Ithaka?" *Quarber Merkur* 31:3-17. July 1972.

"Aleksandr Bogdanov zwischen Revolution und Illusion," in: Rottensteiner, Franz, ed. *Quarber Merkur*. Frankfurt: Suhrkamp, 1979. pp. 82-92.

"Echo aus der zukunft. Ein sowjetischer science fiction autor uber die Volksrepublik China," *Sozialistische Zeitschrift fur Kunst und Gesellschaft* 8/9:132- . October 1971.

"Sowjetische wissenschaftlick fantastische Literatur. Aus Frage literarischer utopien in sozialistischen ubergangsgesellschaften," *Sozialistische Zeitschrift fur Kunst und Gesellschaft* 18/19:63-105. July 1953.

Luckiesh, M.

"Scientific fortune teller: past and future through a super-telescope," *North American Review* 233(5):438-444. 1932.

Lucks, Naomi

"Shoplifters will be eaten by the Balrog," *San Francisco Bay Guardian* 12(14):12-13. January 19, 1978.

Ludlam, Harry

Biography of Dracula: The Life Story of Bram Stoker, A. London: Fireside Press, 1962. 200 p.

Ludwig, Albert

"Von zeit und raum: ein beitrag zur psychologie der phantastischen dichtung," *Quarber Merkur* 47:35-48. December 1977. (originally published: *Archiv fur das Studium der Neucren Sprachen und Literaturen* 128:1-18. 1912.)

Ludwin, Carol

"Image of science and scientists in science fiction films, The," by Carol Ludwin and L. A. Pope. Presented at the 1978 Annual Meeting of the Midwest Sociological Society. 1978.

Luk, A. N.

"O Vzaimoot noshedii nauchnogo i khudozhestvennogo tvorchestva," *Voprosy Filosofii* 32, 11, p. 142-150. November 1978.

Lukes, Steven

"Marxism and Utopianism," in: *Utopias*, ed. by Peter Alexander and Roger Gill. London: Duckworth, 1984. pp. 153-168.

Lund, O. A., Jr.

"SF in the classroom : II. SF as an undergraduate elective," *Science Fiction Studies* 15(2):143-148. May 1974.

Lund, R. D.

"Pope's monsters: satire and the grotesque in *The Dunciad*," in: Collins, R. A., ed. *Scope of the Fantastic: Culture, Biography, Themes, Children's Literature*. Westport: Greenwood, 1985. pp. 61-78.

Lundquist, James

Kurt Vonnegut. New York: Ungar, 1977. 124 p.

Lundstrom, Henry

"Var beredskap ar god: SF seminariet, 1-2 mars 1980," *Filmrutan* 23(1):11-15. 1980.

Lundwall, S. J.

Bibliografi over science fiction och fantasy 1830-1961. Stockholm: s. n., 1962. 58 p.

Illustrerad Bibliografi over Science Fiction and Fantasy 1741-1973. Stockholm: Lindqvist, 1974. 338 p.

Science Fiction: An Illustrated History. New York: Grossett and Dunlap, 1978 (c. 1977). 208 p.

Lundwall, S. J. (Continued)

Science Fiction: What It's All About. New York: Ace Books, 1971. 256 p.

Science fiction: fran begynnel sen till vara dagar. Stockholm: Sveridgers Radio Verlag, 1969. 188 p.

"Autre Monde, Un," by Grandville and Taxile Delord in: Magill, Frank N., ed. *Survey of Science Fiction Literature*, Vol. 1. Englewood Cliffs, NJ: Salem Press, 1979. pp. 105-108.

"Begum's Fortune, The," in: Magill, Frank N., ed. *Survey of Science Fiction Literature*, Vol. 1. Englewood Cliffs, NJ: Salem Press, 1979. pp. 153-156.

"Heart of a Dog, The," in: Magill, Frank N., ed. *Survey of Science Fiction Literature*, Vol. 2. Englewood Cliffs, NJ: Salem Press, 1979. pp. 956-959.

"Kallocain," in: Magill, Frank N., ed. *Survey of Science Fiction Literature*, Vol. 3. Englewood Cliffs, NJ: Salem Press, 1979. pp. 1110-1113.

"Mao ch'eng chi," in: Magill, Frank N., ed. *Survey of Science Fiction Literature*, Vol. 3. Englewood Cliffs, NJ: Salem Press, 1979. pp. 1344-1347.

"Omega: The Last Days of the World," in: Magill, Frank N., ed. *Survey of Science Fiction Literature*, Vol. 4. Englewood Cliffs, NJ: Salem Press, 1979. pp. 1592-1595.

"Oxygen och Aromasia," in: Magill, Frank N., ed. *Survey of Science Fiction Literature*, Vol. 4. Englewood Cliffs, NJ: Salem Press, 1979. pp. 1637-1640.

"Roadside Picnic," in: Magill, Frank N., ed. *Survey of Science Fiction Literature*, Vol. 4. Englewood Cliffs, NJ: Salem Press, 1979. pp. 1817-1820.

"Adventures in the pulp jungle," *Foundation* 34: 5-16. Autumn 1985.

"Jules Verne, 1828-1905," *Proxima* No. 19, sect.2:37-41. March 1979.

"Science Fiction in Schweden," *Science Fiction Times* (Germany) 24(8):4-7. August 1982.

Lupoff, R. A.

Barsoom: Edgar Rice Burroughs and the Martian Vision. Baltimore: Mirage Press, 1976. 161 p.

Edgar Rice Burroughs: Master of Adventure. New York: Canaveral Press, 1965. 297 p. New York: Ace Books, 1968 (revised edition). Reprinted, 1975. 317 p.

"Edward Elmer Smith, 1890-1965," *Science Fiction Times* No. 433:2-4. November 1965.

"Forty-five years and five months," by R. A. Lupoff and J. M. Elliot. *Questar* 3(1):18-20,53-56. October 1980.

"Interview with Stanton A. Coblentz," by Lawrence Davidson and R. A. Lupoff. *Locus* 12(11):10-11. December 1979.

"Introduction," in: Dick, P. K. *A Handful of Darkness.* Boston: Gregg, 1978. pp. v-xviii.

"Introduction," in: Douglass, Ellsworth. *Pharoah's Broker.* Boston: Gregg, 1976. pp. v-xvii.

"Legend in Poughkeepsie," *Locus* 10(2):4-5. February 1977.

"Letter; on publishing, magazines, etc.," *Science Fiction Times* No. 427:2,7. April 1965.

"Realities of Philip K. Dick, The," *Starship* 16(3):29-33. Summer 1979.

"Science fiction hawks and doves: whose future will you buy?" *Ramparts* 10(8):25-30. February 1972.

"SF novel, 1979," *Science Fiction Chronicle* 1(9):10. June 1980.

"Very near to my heart," *Algol* 17(2):31-34. Spring 1980.

"What's left of the science fiction market?" *Writer* 69(5):165-167. May 1956. Reply, I. Asimov. 69(8):218. August 1956.

"Whole truth: Richard Lupoff interviews Roger Elwood, The," *Algol* 11(2):19-22. May 1974.

Luserke, Uwe

"David A. Hardy: der exakte Visionar," *Heyne Science Fiction Magazin* 4: 155-168. 1982.

"Jack Williamson Bibliography," *Megavore* 13: 29-41. March 1981.

"Klarkash-ton: Poet des Monstroesen: Leben und Werk des Clark Ashton Smith," *Science Fiction Times* (Germany) 27(3):4-7. March 1985.

Lussier, N. J.

"Science fiction," *Progressive Teacher* p. 10. April/May 1971.

Luther, E.

"Wissenschaftlich-phantastische Literatur in Bulgarien," *Zeitschrift fur Slawistik* 26(5): 730-735. 1981.

Luttrell, Lesleigh

"Mysterious Wilson Tucker, The," SF Commentary 43:15-25. August 1975.

"Philip K. Dick Forum, Part 1: The Really Real," SF Commentary 62/66: 18-20. June 1981.

Luzi, M.

"Letteratura fantastica. Qualche considerazione sulla letteratura fantastica" Letteratura 67/68:167-169. genn-apr, 1964.

Lyles, W. H.

Mary Shelley: An Annotated Bibliography. New York: Garland Publishing, 1975. 297 p.

Putting Dell On the Map: A History of the Dell Paperbacks. Westport, CT: Greenwood, 1983. 178 p.

"First in SF?" Publishers Weekly 224(3): 10. July 15, 1983.

"Science Fiction and Fantasy in the Dell Mapbacks," Paperback Quarterly 5(4): 40-49. Winter 1982.

Lyman, Rick

"Fortune's at Stake in the Fate of 'Dune'," Philadelphia Inquirer in: NewsBank. Film and Television. 66: E11-E12. January 1905.

Lynch, David

Dune: An Interview with Frank Herbert, by Frank Herbert and David Lynch. Stamford, CT: Waldentapes, 1984. 1 cassette, 50 min.

Lynch, James

"Literary banquet and the eucharistic feast: tradition in Tolkien," Mythlore 5(2): 13-14. Autumn 1978.

Lynn, E. A.

"Best of Sci-Fi and Fantasy," San Francisco Examiner December 5, 1982. in: NewsBank. Film and Television. January 1983. 55: B7-8.

"Close Encounters of the Third Kind, a review," Locus 10(10):7,9. December 1977.

"Introduction," in: Brackett, Leigh. The Sword of Rhiannon. Boston: Gregg, 1979. pp. v-xiii.

"Introduction," in: Gotleib, Phyllis. Sunburst. Boston: Gregg, 1978. pp. v-xv.

"Women in, of, and on Science Fiction," Top of the News 39(1): 72-75. Fall 1982.

Lynn, R. L.

Cthulhu Mythos in the Writings of H. P. Lovecraft. Masters Thesis, University of Rhode Island, 1974. 64 p.

Lynn, R. N.

Fantasy for Children: An Annotated Checklist. 2nd. ed. New York: Bowker, 1983. 444 p.

Fantasy for Children: an Annotated Checklist. New York: Bowker, 1979. 208 p.

Lyon, David

"Arthur Penty's post-industrial utopia," World Future Society Bulletin 17(1): 7-14. January/February 1983.

Lyubimova, A. F.

"Tema evolyutsii v sotsial'no-fantasticheskom romane rannego H. Wells.") Uchenye zapiski Perskii universitet (270):133-45. 1973.

M

Mabbott, T. O.

"H. P. Lovecraft: An Appreciation," in: Joshi, S. T., ed. H. P. Lovecraft: Four Decades of Criticism. Athens, OH: Ohio University Press, 1980. pp. 43-45.

Macarthur, D. M.

Ecology: Science and Science Fiction. Worcester, MA: Undergraduate Report, Worcester Polytechnic Institute, 1982. Report No. 82B0191. 65 p.

MacAvoy, R. A.

"Writing hystericals," Empire for the SF Writer 9(3): 8-9. Spring 1985.

MacDermott, K. A.

"Ideology and Narrative: The Cold War and Robert Heinlein," Extrapolation 23(3): 254-269. Fall 1982.

MacDonald, Andrew

"Teaching Western Culture Through Science Fiction," by Andrew MacDonald and Gina MacDonald. Extrapolation 23(4): 315-320. Winter 1982.

MacDonald, D.

"Charles Addams, his family, and his friends," Reporter 9:37-40. July 21, 1953.

MacDonald, George

"Fantastic Imagination, The," in: Boyer, Robert H. and Zahorski, Kenneth J. Fantasists on Fantasy. New York: Avon Discus, 1984. pp. 11-22.

MacDonald, Gina

"Teaching Western Culture Through Science Fiction," by Andrew MacDonald and Gina MacDonald. Extrapolation 23(4): 315-320. Winter 1982.

MacDonald, Greville

George MacDonald and His Wife. London: Allen & Unwin, 1924. 575 p.

MacDonald, Peter

"Geoffrey Unsworth, BSC and the photography of Superman," American Cinematographer 60(1):32-35,66-67,84-85. January 1979.

Macdonnel, A. P.

"John A. Mitchell's Drowsy: 'A most unusual country'," Extrapolation 12(2):99-105. May 1971.

Mace, Scott

"BBS for Science Fiction Fans Debuts," Infoworld 4(29): 6. July 26, 1982.

"Novelists Inspire Games," InfoWorld 6(25): 42-45. June 18, 1984.

Macek, Carl

"Alien: three perspectives: Giger, Scott, and Weaver," Questar 2(1):20-25. November 1979.

MacGregor, Loren

"Technology in a Way of Life," Aurora SF 8(1): 28-29. Summer 1982.

Machen, Arthur

Far Off Things. London: Secker, 1922. 158 p.

Macherey, Pierre

"Jules Verne ou le recit en defaut," in: Macherey, Pierre. Pour une Theorie de la Production Litteraire. Paris: Maspero, 1966. (Eng. Tr. in his Theory of Literary Production. Routledge, 1978.)

"Jules Verne: the faulty narrative," in: Macherey, P. Theory of Literary Production. Routledge, 1978. pp. 159-248. (Tr. of "Jules Verne ou le Recit en Defaut." in his Pour une theorie de la production litteraire. 1966.)

Maciag, Wlodzimierz

"Lem: publicysta," Tworczosc No. 6. 1962.

"Who is transmitting the signal? Qui nous appelle?" Polish Literature/Litterature Polonaise 2 Jahrgang Nr. 3(5), p. 20-23. Autumn 1969.

MacKenzie, I.

"Science ficton, sublimation or prophecy?" Student World 59(4):399-405. 1966.

Mackenzie, Jeanne

Time Traveller: The Life of H. G. Wells, The, by Norman and Jeanne Mackenzie. London: Weidenfeld and Nicolson, 1973. 487 p. Reprinted: H. G. Wells: A Biography. New York: Simon and Schuster, 1973.

Mackenzie, Norman

Time Traveller: The Life of H. G. Wells, The, by Norman and Jeanne Mackenzie. London: Weidenfeld and Nicolson, 1973. 487 p. Reprinted: H. G. Wells: A Biography. New York: Simon and Schuster, 1973.

MacKenzie, Ursula

"John Barth's Chimera and the structures of reality," Journal of American Studies 10:91-101. April 1976.

Mackerness, E. D.

"Zola, Wells, and 'The Coming Beast'," Science-Fiction Studies 8(2): 143-148. July 1981.

Mackey, D. A.

"Chthon," in: Magill, Frank N., ed. Survey of Science Fiction Literature, Vol. 1. Englewood Cliffs, NJ: Salem Press, 1979. pp. 354-357.

"Eye in the Sky," in: Magill, Frank N., ed. Survey of Science Fiction Literature, Vol. 2. Englewood Cliffs, NJ: Salem Press, 1979. pp. 744-748.

"Science fiction and Gnosticism," Missouri Review 7(2): 112-120. 1984.

"Short Fiction of James Tiptree, Jr., The," in: Magill, Frank N., ed. Survey of Science Fiction Literature, Vol. 4. Englewood Cliffs, NJ: Salem Press, 1979. pp. 1999-2002.

MacLean, Katherine

"Alien minds and nonhuman intelligences," in: Bretnor, Reginald, ed. The Craft of Science Fiction. New York: Harper, 1976. pp. 136-158.

"Alien Sort of War, An," in: Bretnor, Reginald, ed. The Future at War: Vol. 3: Orion's Sword. New York: Ace, 1980. pp. 107-116.

"Expanding Mind, The," in: Greenberg, Martin H., ed. Fantastic Lives: Autobiographical Essays by Notable Science Fiction Writers. Carbondale: Southern Illinois University Press, 1981. pp. 79-101.

Maclean, Marie

"Metamorphoses of the Signifier in 'Unnatural' Language," Science-Fiction Studies 11(2): 166-173. July 1984.

MacRae, Donald

"World grown fantastic, A," New Society pp. 23-24. July 1, 1971.

Macvey, J. W.

Space Weapons/Space War. New York: Stein & Day, 1979. 245 p.

Madan, Falconer

Lewis Carroll Handbook: Being a New Version of the Literature of the Rev. C. L. Dodgson...Brought up to 1960 by Roger Lancelyn Green, The, by S. H. Williams and Falconer Madan. London: Oxford University Press, 1962. 307 p.

Madanpotra, S. K.

"Literature and science," Indian Literature 16(3-4):89-92. July-December 1973.

Maddern, Philippa

"True stories: women's writing in science fiction," Meanjin 44(1): 111-123. March 1985.

Maddison, M.

"Case against tomorrow," Political Quarterly 36(2):214-227. April/June 1965.

Maddocks, Melvin

"Defrocking the new theologians, once called science fiction writers," Houston Post p. C-3. February 7, 1978.

"New note: the novel as sci-non-fi," Life 66:15. May 30, 1969. (Book review)

Madle, Bob

"This is the PSFS," Science Fiction Adventures 1(4): 52-58. May 1953.

Madle, R. A.

"Stardust (1940)," by R. A. Madle and Mike Ashley. in: Tymn, M. B. and Ashley, Mike. Science Fiction, Fantasy, and Weird Fiction Magazines. Westport, CT: Greenwood, 1985. pp. 606-607.

Madsen, A. L.

"That starlit corridor; science fiction," English Journal 53(6):405-412. September 1964.

Madsen, Axel

"2001: a space odyssey," Cinema 4(2):58-59. Summer 1968.

"Year of Vonnegut," Sight and Sound 40(4):190-191. Autumn 1971.

Magill, F. N.

Science Fiction: Alien Encounters. Englewood Cliffs, NJ: Salem Softbacks, 1982. 376 p.

Survey of Modern Fantasy Literature. Englewood Cliffs, NJ: Salem, 1983. 5 v.

Survey of Science Fiction Literature. Englewood Cliffs, NJ: Salem Press, 1979. 5 v.

Magistrale, Tony

"Inherited haunts: Stephen King's terrible children," Extrapolation 26(1): 43-49. Spring 1985.

Maglin, Arthur

"Science fiction in the age of transition," Radical America 3:4-11. July/August 1969.

Mahaffey, Bea

"I remember Ray," Locus 10(7):10. September 1977.

Mahanti, J. C.

"Beyond yes and no: the novels of John Cowper Powys," International Fiction Review 2(1):77-79. January 1975.

Mahapatra, G. N.

"Science fiction today, reality tomorrow," Vidura 12(4):241-243. October/December 1975.

Maher, Charles

"Did Tarzan and Mate Live in Treehouse Sin?" The Eagle (Bryan, TX) p. 10. January 1, 1962.

Mahieu, J. A.

"Imagfic-82: Terror e emaginacion," Cuadernos Hispanoamericanos. 386: 374-381. August 1982.

Mahon, R. L.

"Elegiac elements in The Lord of the Rings," CEA Critic 40(2):33-36. January 1978.

Mahoney, Lawrence

"Poison their minds with humanity," Tropic: The Miami Herald Sunday Magazine pp. 8-10,13,44. January 24, 1971.

Mahood, R. M.

"Alternate Worlds and a Multiplicity of Futures," by Millicnet Lenz and R. M. Mahood. in: Lenz, Millicent, and Mahood, Ramona, eds. Young Adult Literature. Chicago: American Library Association, 1980. pp. 415-448.

Maisky, I. M.

Iz vospominanii o Bernard Shaw i Herbert Wells. Moscow: Pravda, 1974. 64 p.

Maitre, Doreen

Literature and Possible Worlds. London: Middlesed Polytechnic Press, 1983. 128 p.

Majuk, Irene

"DAW celebrates 5 million: Interview with Don Wollheim," Fantasy Review 9(6)(eg v. 8 #6): 39-41. June 1985.

Maki, S.

"Science Fiction in Japan," by Yoshio Kobayashi, S. Maki, and Edward Lipsett. Locus 18(1): 31-32. January 1985.

Makkai, Laszlo

"A gepek es az ember," SF Tajekoztato p. 2-7. July 1971.

Maksimova, V.

"Billi Pilgrim puteschestvuet y proshloe," Vercherniaia Moskva February 9-10, 1976.

Malaguti, Ugo

"Mappe della fantascienza italiana," Nova Speciale No. 1. 1977.

Malcohn, Elissa

"Ouch! Writing through upheaval," Empire for the SF Writer 9(3): 16-17. Spring 1985.

Malec, A. B.

"Participant past imperfect; science fiction characters," Writer 82(8):19-21. August 1969.

Malik, Rex

Future Imperfect: Science Fact and Science Fiction. London: Francis Pinter, 1980. 219 p.

"Interview with Arthur C. Clarke," in: Malik, Rex, ed. Future Imperfect. London: Pinter, 1980. pp. 115-122.

Mallardi, Bill

Double: Bill Symposium, by Bill Bowers and Bill Mallardi. Akron, OH: D:B Press, 1969. 111 p.

Malmgren, C. D.

"Philip Dick's Man in the High Castle and the Nature of Science-Fictional Worlds," in: Slusser, George E., ed. Bridges to Science Fiction. Carbondale: Southern Illinois University Press, 1980. pp. 120-130.

Malmquist, Allen

"Dark Crystal (review)," Cinefantastique 13(4):59. April/May 1983.

"Indiana Jones and The Temple of Doom," Cinefantastique 15(2):40-42. May 1985.

"Monty Python's The Meaning of Life (review)," Cinefantastique 13(5):57-58. June/July 1983.

"Saga time at the old Bijou," Cinefantastique 15(4):32-33,58. October 1985.

"Superman III (review)," Cinefantastique 13(6)/14(1):100. September 1983.

"Thriller (review)," Cinefantastique 14(3):60. May 1984.

Maloff, S.

"Tarzan, son of Kala," Newsweek 69:100. April 10, 1967. (Book review)

Malone, Nancy

"Star alien," Read pp. 6-9. March 15, 1968.

Malone, William

"Robby: a star is built," Questar 3(3): 47-50. February 1981.

Malzberg, B. N.

Engines of the Night. Garden City, NY: Doubleday, 1982. 198 p.

"...And a Chaser," in: Greenberg, Martin H., ed. Fantastic Lives: Autobiographical Essays by Notable Science Fiction Writers. Carbondale: Southern Illinois University Press, 1981. pp. 102-117.

"A. Bertram Chandler," Science Fiction Chronicle 5(11):4. August 1984.

Malzberg, B. N. (Continued)

"Ah Tempora! Ah Portions! Ah Mores! Ah Outlines!" Empire: For the SF Writer 6(1): 15. Winter 1980.

"Ah tempora! Ah portions! Ah mores! Ah outlines!" in: Malzberg, B. N. Engines of the Night. Garden City, NY: Doubleday, 1982. pp. 49-52.

"All-time, prime-time, take-me-to-your-leader science fiction plot," in: Malzberg, B. N. Engines of the Night. Garden City, NY: Doubleday, 1982. pp. 147-158.

"Anonymity and empire," in: Malzberg, B. N. Engines of the Night. Garden City, NY: Doubleday, 1982. pp. 14-18.

"At the divining edge," in: Malzberg, B. N. Engines of the Night. Garden City, NY: Doubleday, 1982. pp. 58-61.

"Circumstance as policy: the decade of Ursula K. Le Guin," in: De Bolt, Joe, ed. Ursula K. Le Guin: Voyager to Inner Lands and to Outer Space. Port Washington, New York: Kennikat, 1979. pp. 5-9.

"Come fool, follify," in: Malzberg, B. N. Engines of the Night. Garden City, NY: Doubleday, 1982. pp. 170-173.

"Con Sordino," Patchin Review 1: 4-5, 26. July 1981.

"Con sordino," in: Malzberg, B. N. Engines of the Night. Garden City, NY: Doubleday, 1982. pp. 177-181.

"Cornell George Hopley Woolrich: December 1903-September 1968," in: Malzberg, B. N. Engines of the Night. Garden City, NY: Doubleday, 1982. pp. 108-113.

"Corridors," in: Malzberg, B. N. Engines of the Night. Garden City, NY: Doubleday, 1982. pp. 182-198.

"Cutting edge," in: Malzberg, B. N. Engines of the Night. Garden City, NY: Doubleday, 1982. pp. 136-142.

"Engines of the night," in: Malzberg, B. N. Engines of the Night. Garden City, NY: Doubleday, 1982. pp. 174-175.

"Engines of the Night: Selected Essays," Science Fiction Review 10(1): 6-10. February 1981.

"Engines of the Night: Selected Essays," Science Fiction Review 10(3): 18-22. August 1981.

"Few hard truths for the troops, A," in: Malzberg, B. N. Engines of the Night. Garden City, NY: Doubleday, 1982. pp. 114-117.

"Fifties, The," in: Bova, Ben, ed. Analog Yearbook. New York: Ace, 1978 (c. 1977). pp. 231-244.

"Fifties, The," in: Malzberg, B. N. Engines of the Night. Garden City, NY: Doubleday, 1982. pp. 30-43.

"Fifties, The: recapulation and coda," in: Malzberg, B. N. Engines of the Night. Garden City, NY: Doubleday, 1982. pp. 44-48.

"Flashpoint: Middle," Science Fiction Review 13(2): 24-26. May 1984.

"Give me that old-time religion," in: Malzberg, B. N. Engines of the Night. Garden City, NY: Doubleday, 1982. pp. 162-164.

"Grandson of the true and terrible," in: Malzberg, B. N. Engines of the Night. Garden City, NY: Doubleday, 1982. pp. 159-161.

"Guest Editorial: Is the Most Speculative Form of Literature Afraid to Gamble Anymore...?" Amazing 28(1): 4-6. July 1981.

"I could have been a contender, part one," in: Malzberg, B. N. Engines of the Night. Garden City, NY: Doubleday, 1982. pp. 11-13.

"I don't know how to put it love but I'll surely try," in: Malzberg, B. N. Engines of the Night. Garden City, NY: Doubleday, 1982. pp. 19-25.

"I don't want her, you can have her," in: Malzberg, B. N. Engines of the Night. Garden City, NY: Doubleday, 1982. pp. 85-88.

"Introduction: Philip K. Dick," in: Greenberg, Martin H., ed. Philip K. Dick. New York: Taplinger, 1982. pp. 7-12.

"John W. Campbell: June 8, 1910 to July 11, 1971," in: Malzberg, B. N. Engines of the Night. Garden City, NY: Doubleday, 1982. pp. 71-74.

"Kris Neville: an appreciation," Locus 13(12):24,26. December 1980/January 1981.

"L'etat c'est moi," in: Malzberg, B. N. Engines of the Night. Garden City, NY: Doubleday, 1982. pp. 6-10.

"Mark Clifton, 1906-1963," in: Malzberg, B. N. Engines of the Night. Garden City, NY: Doubleday, 1982. pp. 126-131.

"Memoir from Grub Street," in: Malzberg, B. N. Engines of the Night. Garden City, NY: Doubleday, 1982. pp. 26-29.

"Number of the beast," in: Malzberg, B. N. Engines of the Night. Garden City, NY: Doubleday, 1982. pp. 1-5.

"Onward and upward with the arts, part II," in: Malzberg, B. N. Engines of the Night. Garden City, NY: Doubleday, 1982. pp. 89-92.

Malzberg, B. N. (Continued)

"Onward and upward with the arts, part III," in: Malzberg, B. N. Engines of the Night. Garden City, NY: Doubleday, 1982. pp. 118-122.

"Richard Nixon, John B. Mitchell, Spiro Agnew blues," in: Malzberg, B. N. Engines of the Night. Garden City, NY: Doubleday, 1982. pp. 104-107.

"Science fiction and the academy: some notes," in: Malzberg, B. N. Engines of the Night. Garden City, NY: Doubleday, 1982. pp. 53-57.

"Science fiction as Picasso," in: Malzberg, B. N. Engines of the Night. Garden City, NY: Doubleday, 1982. pp. 123-125.

"Science fiction of science fiction, The," in: Malzberg, B. N. Engines of the Night. Garden City, NY: Doubleday, 1982. pp. 77-84.

"September 1973: what I did last summer," in: Malzberg, B. N. Engines of the Night. Garden City, NY: Doubleday, 1982. pp. 132-135.

"SF forever," in: Malzberg, B. N. Engines of the Night. Garden City, NY: Doubleday, 1982. pp. 165-166.

"Some notes toward the true and the terrible," in: Malzberg, B. N. Engines of the Night. Garden City, NY: Doubleday, 1982. pp. 62-66.

"Son of the true and terrible," in: Malzberg, B. N. Engines of the Night. Garden City, NY: Doubleday, 1982. pp. 143-146.

"Tell me doctor if you can that it's not all happening again," in: Malzberg, B. N. Engines of the Night. Garden City, NY: Doubleday, 1982. pp. 93-103.

"What I won't do next summer, I guess," in: Malzberg, B. N. Engines of the Night. Garden City, NY: Doubleday, 1982. pp. 167-169.

"Wrong rabbit," in: Malzberg, B. N. Engines of the Night. Garden City, NY: Doubleday, 1982. pp. 67-70.

Manchel, Frank

Album of Great Science Fiction Films. Rev. ed. New York: Watts, 1982. 87 p.

Mandel, P.

"Tarzan of the paperbacks," Life 55(22):11-12. November 29, 1963.

Mandel, S.

"Myth of science fiction," by S. Mandel and P. Fingesten. Saturday Review 38(35):7-8. August 27, 1955.

Mandelbaum, Howard

"Just imagine: fantasy and futurism," by Howard Mandelbaum and Eric Myers. in: Mandelbaum, Howard and Eric Myers. Screen Deco. New York: St. Martins, 1985. pp. 163-168.

Mandell, Paul

"Altered States of 'Altered States,'" Cinefex 4: 32-71. April 1981.

"Beast Within (review)," Cinefantastique 12(2/3):83. April 1982.

"Laser Blast," Cinefantastique 6(4)/7(1):4-7. Spring 1978.

"Making Star Wars," Cinefantastique 6(4)/7(1):8-31,66-95. Spring 1978.

"One Hundred Most Important People in Science Fiction/Fantasy: Dick Smith," Starlog 100: 76. November 1985.

"One Hundred Most Important People in Science Fiction/Fantasy: George Pal," Starlog 100: 75-76. November 1985.

"One Hundred Most Important People in Science Fiction/Fantasy: Rick Baker," Starlog 100: 40. November 1985.

"One Hundred Most Important People in Science Fiction/Fantasy: Rod Serling," Starlog 100: 45. November 1985.

"One Hundred Most Important People in Science Fiction/Fantasy: William Cameron Menzies," Starlog 100: 74. November 1985.

"One Hundred Most Important People in Science Fiction/Fantasy: Willis H. O'Brien," Starlog 100: 84. November 1985.

"Open letter to Universal and Dino de Laurentiis," Cinefantastique 5(1):40-43. Spring 1976.

"Photography and visual effects for Dune," American Cinematographer 65(11): 50-61. December 1984.

"Poltergeist: Stilling the Restless Animus," Cinefex 10: 4-39. October 1982.

"Preproducing The Primevals," Cinefantastique 8(1):4-11,38-47. Winter 1978.

"SFX Part XLI: Effective Careers in Retrospect, No. 1: David S. Horsley, ASC," Starlog 59: 48-51, 64. June 1982.

"Starlog Interview: David Lynch," Starlog No. 87: 46-49, 59. October 1984.

"Tauntauns, Walkers and Probots," Cinefex 3: 4-41. December 1980.

Mandell, Paul (Continued)

"TV's Superman Remembered, Part 1," Starlog 75: 25-27. October 1983.

"TV's Superman Remembered, Part 2," Starlog 76: 60-63, 88. November 1983.

"TV's Superman Remembered, Part 3," Starlog 77: 54-58. December 1983.

Manganiello, Dominic

"Artist as Magician, The: Yeats, Joyce, and Tolkien," Mythlore 10(2): 13-15. Summer 1983.

Mank, G. W.

It's Alive! The Classic Cinema Saga of Frankenstein. San Diego: Barnes, 1981. 196 p.

Mank, Greg

"Doctors and the Devils," by Greg Mank and Janrae Frank. Cinefantastique 15(5):28-30. January 1986.

"Val Lewton's The Body Snatchers," Cinefantastique 15(5):30-31,58-61. January 1986.

Mankin, Eric

"Science Fiction Addicts Gather for an Afternoon in Another World," Los Angeles Herald Examiner September 1, 1984. in: NewsBank. Social Relations. SOC 64:C2-C3. 1984.

Manley, Seon

"Frankenstein's Mother," by Seon Manley and Susan Belcher. in: Manley, Seon, and Belcher, Susan, eds. O, Those Extraordinary Women. Philadelphia: Chilton, 1972. pp. 31-56.

Manlove, C. N.

Impulse of Fantasy Literature. Kent, OH: Kent State University Press, 1983. 174 p.

Modern Fantasy: Five Studies. Cambridge, Massachusetts and London: Cambridge University Press, 1975. 308 p.

"Conservatism in the Fantasy of Le Guin," Extrapolation 21(3): 287-297. Fall 1980.

"Fantasy as witty conceit: E. Nesbit," Mosaic 10(2):109-130. Winter 1977.

"Flight to Aleppo: T. H. White's The Once and Future King," Mosaic 10(2):65-83. Winter 1977.

"On the Nature of Fantasy," in: Schlobin, Roger C., ed. The Aesthetics of Fantasy Literature and Art. Notre Dame, IN: University of Notre Dame Press, 1982. pp. 16-35.

"Terminus non est: Gene Wolfe's The Book of the New Sun," Kansas Quarterly 16(3): 7-20. Summer 1984.

Mann, Herbert

"Welt im Nebengleis. Zu Bruno Schulz' Prosa," in: Thomsen, C. W., ed. Phantastik in Literatur und Kunst. Darmstadt: Wissenschaftliche Buchgesellschaft, 1980. pp. 299-313.

Mann, Jim

"Course in science fiction, A," Guying Gyre 11/12:81-84. January 1979.

Mann, Philip

"Rocking of the Boat," Focus: An SF Writers' Magazine No. 8: 22-23. Autumn 1983.

Mann, Roderick

"Hamill: From Skywalker to Elephant Man to Mozart," Los Angeles Times December 26, 1982. in: NewsBank. Film and Television 75: C13. 1982/1983.

Manna, Sal

"Film For Those Folks Who Voted to Freeze Nukes," Los Angeles Herald Examiner November 4, 1982. in: NewsBank. Film and Television. 49:C1-2. December 1982.

"Gary Kurtz Teams Up With Jim Henson on 'Dark Crystal'," Los Angeles Herald Examiner December 14, 1982. in: NewsBank. Film and Television. 61: A7-8. January 1983.

"Ivan Reitman," Starlog No. 85: 45-46, 51. August 1984.

"Starlog Interview: Ralph McQuarrie," Starlog 75: 36-39, 60. October 1983.

"Starlog Interview: The Enigma of Max von Sydow," Starlog 82: 36-40. May 1984.

Manning, A. D.

"Significance of sound in names," Leading Edge No. 7:14-21. undated.

Manning, A. S.

Bradbury's Works. Lincoln, Nebraska: Cliffs Notes, 1977. 91 p.

Mannix, George

"Peter Weir: Master of Unease; Interview," by Terry Dowling and George Mannix. Science Fiction: A Review of Speculative Literature 3(1): 7-27. January 1981.

"Timewinds: Terry Dowling and George Mannix talk with Dennis Collins and Mark Salwowski," by Terry Dowling and George Mannix. Science Fiction: A Review of Speculative Literature 2(1):67-73. May 1979.

Manolescu, Florin

Literatura S. F. Bucuresti: "Univers", 1980. 301 p.

Mansell, Mark

"Conan capers, The," Science Fiction Review 6(4):47. November 1977.

Manser, A. R.

"Alien sociology," Advancement of Science 22(98):204-207. August 1965. also in: Listener 73:56-58. January 14, 1965.

Manson, Margaret

Item 43: Brian W. Aldiss: A Bibliography 1954-1962. Birmingham: Dryden Press, 1962. 24 p.

Manuel, F. E.

Utopian Thought in the Western World, by F. E. Manuel and F. P. Manuel. Cambridge, MA: Harvard University Press, 1979. 896 p.

Manuel, F. P.

Utopian Thought in the Western World, by F. E. Manuel and F. P. Manuel. Cambridge, MA: Harvard University Press, 1979. 896 p.

March, Eric

"Joe Haldeman and the SF alternative," Starlog 17:45-47. October 1978.

Marchesani, Diane

"Tolkien's lore: the songs of Middle Earth," Mythlore 7(1):3-5. March 1980.

Marchesani, J. J.

"Dynamic Science Stories," in: Tymn, M. B. and Ashley, Mike. Science Fiction, Fantasy, and Weird Fiction Magazines. Westport, CT: Greenwood, 1985. pp. 198-199.

"Infinity Science Fiction," in: Tymn, M. B. and Ashley, Mike. Science Fiction, Fantasy, and Weird Fiction Magazines. Westport, CT: Greenwood, 1985. pp. 352-355.

"Marvel Science Stories (1934-1935)," in: Tymn, M. B. and Ashley, Mike. Science Fiction, Fantasy, and Weird Fiction Magazines. Westport, CT: Greenwood, 1985. pp. 398-401.

"Two Complete Science Adventure Books," in: Tymn, M. B. and Ashley, Mike. Science Fiction, Fantasy, and Weird Fiction Magazines. Westport, CT: Greenwood, 1985. pp. 679-681.

"'What If...?' Galaxy's Editorials and the Ideology of Science Fiction," Pennsylvania English 10(2): 35-45. Spring 1984.

"Chalkdust on the Stars: Learning to Teach Science Fiction," Extrapolation 23(2): 185-188. Summer 1982.

"Horace L. Gold, an Editor with English," in: Wolfe Gary, ed. Science Fiction Dialogues. Chicago: Academy Chicago, 1982. pp. 71-82.

Marcus, Ton

"SF in der neueren rumanischen Veroffentlischungen," Quarber Merkur 41:52-54. September 1975.

Margolis, W. J.

"Letter to the Miscellaneous Man. L. Levitt. Reply by William J. Margolis," Miscellaneous Man (Berkeley, California) No. 7:14-15. June 1956.

Margot, J. M.

Bibliographie documentaire sur Jules Verne. Catalogue par mots-cles et par auteurs. Paris: Societe Jules Verne, 1977. 142 p.

Marks, Dorothy

"When children write science fiction," Language Arts 62(4): 355-361. April 1985.

Marks, G. H.

"Teaching biology with science fiction," American Biology Teacher 40(5):275-279. May 1978.

Markus, Manfred

"Science fiction jugendbuch in der Bundesrepublik ab 1970," Blatter fur den Deutschlehrer pp. 67-82. 1974.

Marmor, Paula

"Etymological excursion among the Shire folk," Mythlore 2(3):4. Winter 1971.

"Wielders of the three and other trees," Mythlore 2(4):5-8. Winter 1972.

Maronie, S. J.

"'Triffids' Revisited," by S. J. Maronie and Scott Davis. Starlog 56: 46-47. March 1982.

"John Stears," Starlog 48: 82-85. July 1981.

"Lost in space," Fanfare No. 2:53-57. Winter 1978.

"On the Set With 'Escape From New York'," Starlog 45: 28-30. April 1981.

"Return to the Vortex," Starlog 56: 18-19, 48-49. March 1982.

"Starlog Interview: David Cronenberg," Starlog 43: 24-28. February 1981.

"Starlog Interview: Jerry Goldsmith," Starlog 51: 52-54. September 1981.

"Starlog Interview: Joe Alves," Starlog 46: 48-51. May 1981.

"Starlog Interview: Peter Barton," Starlog 52: 34-37. November 1981.

Marple, A.

"Off the cuff; social satire," Writer 69(5):147-148. May 1956.

Mars, J. R.

"Trim your own," Fantasy Times No. 100:13-15. February (2) 1950.

Marsh, R. J.

Soviet Fiction Since Stalin: Science, Politics, and Literature. Totawa, NJ: Barnes and Noble, 1986. 338 p.

Marshack, A.

"How kids get interested in science," Library Journal 83(8):1253-1255. April 15, 1958. also in: Junior Libraries 4(8):13-15. April 1958.

"Science fiction Soviet style: Ships From the Stars, by I. A. Yefremov," Saturday Review 39(22):20-21,36. June 2, 1956.

Marshall, D. F.

"That great curriculum in the sky," Colloquy: Education in Church and Society 4(5):32-33. May 1971. also in: Varlejs, Jana, ed. Young Adult Literature in the Seventies. New York: Scarecrow, 1978. pp. 327-331.

Marshall, Gene

"Index to the Health Knowledge magazines, An," by Gene Marshall and C. F. Waedt. Science Fiction Collector 3:3-39. 1977.

Marshall, Vikki

"Dreams of the Dreamer: an Interview with Tim Kirk," Shayol 2: 27-37. February 1978.

Marti-Ibanez, Felix

"Tell Me a Story," in: Boyer, Robert H. and Zahorski, Kenneth J. Fantasists on Fantasy. New York: Avon Discus, 1984. pp. 119-124.

Martin, Adrian

"Fantasy," in: Murray, Scott, ed. The New Australian Cinema. London: Elm Tree, 1980. pp. 97-111.

Martin, Andrew

"Entropy of Balzacian Tropes in the Scientific Fiction of Jules Verne," Modern Language Review 77(1): 51-62. January 1982.

Martin, Bob

"I Remember Max: The Road Warrior,(Review)" Starlog 64: 73-76. November 1982.

Martin, Carter

"Fantastic pairing: Edward Taylor and Donald Barthelme," in: Collins, R. A., ed. Scope of the Fantastic: Theory, Technique, Major Authors. Westport: Greenwood, 1985. pp. 183-190.

Martin, Christopher

"Sorceress (review)," _Cinefantastique_ 13(4):56. April/May 1983.

Martin, D. T.

Religious Dimensions of Representative Science Fiction. Ph.D. Dissertation, Ohio State University, 1979. 132 p.

Martin, G. R. R.

"'If Howard Waldrop is such a good writer, how come he isn't rich and famous?' story, or, 'Waiter, I'll have disgusting bird on rye'," _Othercon Program Book._ College Station, TX: Othercon, September 1979.

"First, sew on a tentacle (recipes for believable aliens)," in: Grant, C. L., ed. _Writing and Selling Science Fiction._ Cincinnati, Ohio: Writers Digest, 1976. pp. 147-168.

"Secret of Being a Sci-Fi Guy, The," _Shayol_ No. 5: 20-23. Winter 1982.

"Sins of the Reviewers," _Starship_ 18(1): 25-29. Spring 1981.

"Writer's Conferences", by Gene Wolfe and G. R. R. Martin. _Empire: For the SF Writer_ 4(1): 11-14. July 1978.

"Writer's natural enemy: editors, A," _Science Fiction Review_ No. 33:28-31. November 1979.

Martin, J. C.

"Interview with Evangeline Walton Ensley," _Arizona Daily Star._ May 16, 1977.

Martin, Lisa

"Sci-fi Fans Descend on Kenner Hotel," _New Orleans Times-Picayune_ Sec. A, p. 19. August 11, 1984.

Martin, Mick

"Matheson: a name to conjure with," _Cinefantastique_ 3(1):7-19. Spring 1974.

Martin, Robert

"Max's myth maker," _Twilight Zone_ 5(4): 51-55. October 1985.

"Outland: Interview," _Twilight Zone_ 1(3): 53-56. June 1981.

"TZ Profile: Richard Donner," _Twilight Zone_ 1(4): 48-56. July 1981.

Martin, W. C.

Science Fiction as Social Movement: Ideology and Resource Mobilization in Cultural Production and Reproduction. Winston-Salem, N.C., Oct. 16-18, 1980. 18 p. ERIC ED 200 405.

Martinelli, E. A.

"Photographing The Invisible Man," _American Cinematographer_ 56(7):774-777, 805,814. July 1975.

Martini, Emanuela

"Da dove viene e dove puo' portare L'escalation del 'Fantastico'" _Cineforum_ 19(3):103-117. March 1979.

Martins, Walter

"Science Fiction in Brasilien," _Quarber Merkur_ 26:26-29. February 1971.

Martinson, T. L.

"Most Perfect Example of an Alien Ecology Ever Constructed," _Professional Geographer_ 32(4): 471-477. November 1980.

"Science fiction for geographers: selected works," by G. S. Elbow and T. L. Martinson. _Journal of Geography._ 79(1):23-27. January 1980.

Marton, Tonda

"2001: film poetry," _Cinefantastique_ 4(1):44-45. Spring 1975.

Martos, Joseph

"Religious Imagination and Imagined Religion," by A. J. Frisch and Joseph Martos. in: Reilly, Robert, ed. _The Transcendent Adventure._ Westport: Greenwood, 1984. pp. 11-26.

Marx, Jacques

Tiphaigne de la Roche: Modeles de l'imaginaire au XVIIIe siecle. Brusseles: Editions de l'Universite de Bruxelles, 1981. 107 p.

Marx, Wolfgang

"Entlegene Zeiten der Erde," _Science Fiction Times_ (Germany) 28(1):14-15. January 1986.

"Teufels Skinnerbox, Des," _Science Fiction Times_ (Germany) 27(4):10-11. April 1985.

Marx, Wolfgang (Continued)

"Zwei Essays," <u>Science Fiction Times</u> (Germany) 27(5):4-6. May 1985.

Marxen, Jim

"University collects, stores old science fiction," <u>Fullerton Tribune</u> (CA) p. A-13. October 18, 1979.

Marzin, F. F.

<u>Stanislaw Lem: An den Grenzen der Science Fiction und darueber hinaus.</u> Meitingen: Corian, 1985. 323 p.

"Beurteilung Gustav Meyrinks in der Literatur, 1. Teil," <u>Quarber Merkur</u> No. 59: 8-30. August 1983.

"Helliconia: die Liebe zum Detail," <u>Science Fiction Times</u> (Germany) 27(9/10):4-8. September/October 1985.

"Innenansicht der Deutschen Science Fiction: von aussen Gesehen," <u>Science Fiction Times</u> (Germany) 26(5):20-21. May 1984.

"Romane Gustav Meyrinks, Die: 2. Teil," <u>Quarber Merkur</u> No. 60: 3-22. December 1983.

"Romane Gustav Meyrinks, Die: 3. Teil," <u>Quarber Merkur</u> No. 61: 28-36. July 1984.

"Von Jerusalem's Lot/Maine nach Boulder/Colorado," <u>Science Fiction Times</u> (Germany) 27(11):10-13. November 1985.

Mascall, E. L.

"Out of the silent planet," <u>Theology</u> 38:303-304. April 1939. (Book review)

Masloski, Daniel

"Frankenstein: The True Story," <u>Cinefantastique</u> 3(1):28. Spring 1974.

Maslowski, Igor

"Anticipation scientifique, L'" <u>Mystere Magazine</u> 66. July 1953.

Mason, Cyn

"SFU method for successful writing," by Cyn Mason and Frank Catalano. <u>Science Fiction Chronicle</u> 4(2):14. November 1982.

Mason, Dave

"Fire the critic: the undistributed middle," <u>Inside and Science Fiction Advertiser</u> No. 12: 5-9. November 1955.

Mason, John

"Climate of the future, The," <u>PHP</u> (Japan) 11(5):6-20. May 1980.

Masse, Michelle

"All You Have to Do is Know What You Want: Individual Expectations in <u>Triton</u>," in: Slusser, George E., ed. <u>Coordinates</u>. Carbondale: Southern Illinois University Press, 1983. pp. 49-64.

Masse, P.

"Rosny aine et la prehistorie," by J. Morel and P. Masse. <u>Mercure de France</u> 168:5. 1923.

Massey, Kathleen

"<u>Sylva</u>," in: Magill, Frank N., ed. <u>Survey of Modern Fantasy Literature</u>, Vol 4. Englewood Cliffs, NJ: Salem Press, Inc., 1983. pp. 1872-1874.

"<u>Zotz!</u>" in: Magill, Frank N., ed. <u>Survey of Modern Fantasy Literature</u>, Vol 5. Englewood Cliffs, NJ: Salem Press, Inc., 1983. pp. 2214-2216.

Massey, Sara

"Importance of fantasy, The," <u>Today's Education</u> 64(1):42-43. January/February 1975.

Masson, D. I.

"Part II: the light of imagination," <u>Foundation</u> 10:66-76. June 1976.

Masson, Keith

"Tom Bombadil: a critical essay," <u>Mythlore</u> 2(3):7-8. Winter 1971.

Mateo, Maggey

"Cabell and <u>The Mabinogion</u>," <u>Kalki</u> 7(2):47-50. 1976.

Matheison, Kenneth

<u>Influence of Science Fiction in Contemporary American Writing.</u> Ph.D. Dissertation. University of East Anglia, Norwich. 1983.

Mathews, Jack

"Novelist Loves His Nightmares," _Detroit Free Press_ November 12, 1982. in: _NewsBank. Literature_. 43:E10-11. December 1982,

Mathews, Patricia

"C. L. Moore's Classic Science Fiction," in: Staicar, Tom, ed. _The Feminine Eye_. New York: Ungar, 1982. pp. 14-24.

Mathews, Richard

Aldiss Unbound: The Fiction of Brian W. Aldiss. San Bernardino: Borgo, 1977. 64 p.

Clockwork Universe of Anthony Burgess, The. San Bernardino, California: Borgo Press, 1978. 64 p. (_Popular Writers of Today_, Vol. 19)

Introductory Guide to the Utopian and Fantasy Writing of William Morris. London: William Morris Centre, 1976. 18 p.

Lightning From a Clear Sky: Tolkien, The Trilogy and The Silmarillion. San Bernardino, California: Borgo Press, 1978. 63 p. (The Milford Series: Popular Writers of Today, 15)

Worlds Beyond the World: The Fantastic Vision of William Morris. San Bernardino, California: Borgo Press, 1978. 64 p.

"Cat's Cradle," in: Magill, Frank N., ed. _Survey of Science Fiction Literature_, Vol. 1. Englewood Cliffs, NJ: Salem Press, 1979. pp. 313-317.

"Donovan's Brain," in: Magill, Frank N., ed. _Survey of Science Fiction Literature_, Vol. 2. Englewood Cliffs, NJ: Salem Press, 1979. pp. 579-582.

"Haunted Woman, The," in: Magill, Frank N., ed. _Survey of Modern Fantasy Literature_, Vol 2. Englewood Cliffs, NJ: Salem Press, Inc., 1983. pp. 701-709.

"Last Castle, The," in: Magill, Frank N., ed. _Survey of Science Fiction Literature_, Vol. 3. Englewood Cliffs, NJ: Salem Press, 1979. pp. 1144-1150.

"Lord of the Rings, The," in: Magill, Frank N., ed. _Survey of Modern Fantasy Literature_, Vol 2. Englewood Cliffs, NJ: Salem Press, Inc., 1983. pp. 897-915.

"Return, The," in: Magill, Frank N., ed. _Survey of Modern Fantasy Literature_, Vol 3. Englewood Cliffs, NJ: Salem Press, Inc., 1983. pp. 1307-1310.

"Sundering Flood, The," in: Magill, Frank N., ed. _Survey of Modern Fantasy Literature_, Vol 4. Englewood Cliffs, NJ: Salem Press, Inc., 1983. pp. 1854-1858.

"T zero," in: Magill, Frank N., ed. _Survey of Science Fiction Literature_, Vol. 5. Englewood Cliffs, NJ: Salem Press, 1979. pp. 2223-2228.

"Well at the World's End, The," in: Magill, Frank N., ed. _Survey of Modern Fantasy Literature_, Vol 5. Englewood Cliffs, NJ: Salem Press, Inc., 1983. pp. 2090-2096.

"Wood Beyond the World, The," in: Magill, Frank N., ed. _Survey of Modern Fantasy Literature_, Vol 5. Englewood Cliffs, NJ: Salem Press, Inc., 1983. pp. 2165-2170.

Mathewson, J.

"Hobbit habbit," _Esquire_ 66:130-131. September 1966.

Mathieson, K. G.

"Images of the (im)possible," _Times Higher Eduction Supplement_ 496: 12. May 7, 1982.

Mathieson, Kenneth

"Influence of Science Fiction in the Contemporary American Novel," _Science Fiction Studies_ 12(1): 22-32. March 1985.

Mathis, F.

"Science fiction et mythes modernes", _Revue des questions scientifiques_, 1959, p. 416-438.

Matter, W. W.

"Utopian tradition and Aldous Huxley, The," _Science Fiction Studies_ 2(2):146-151. July 1975.

Matter, William

"On _Brave New World_," in: Rabkin, Eric S., et. al., eds. _No Place Else_. Carbondale: Southern Illinois University Press, 1983. pp. 94-109.

Matthew, Robert

Origins of Japanese Science Fiction. Brisbane: Department of Japanese, University of Queensland, 1978. 43 p.

Matthews, Becky

Texas Fandom 1981. Dallas: Becky Matthews, 1981. 62 p.

Matthews, Dorothy

"Psychological journey of Bilbo Baggins, The," in: Lobdell, Jared, ed. <u>A Tolkien Compass</u>. New York: Ballantine/Del Rey, 1980. pp. 29-43.

Matusevich, V. P.

"Tarkovsky's Apocalypse," <u>Sight and Sound</u> 50(1): 8-9. Winter 1980/81.

Maugh, T. H.

"Media, The; the image of the scientist is bad," <u>Science</u> 200(4337):37. April 7, 1978.

Mauk, Susan

"Riding the crest of renewed science fiction popularity," <u>San Francisco</u> 20:32,69-71. April 1978.

Mauzy, Peter

"Gor Novels, The," in: Magill, Frank N., ed. <u>Survey of Modern Fantasy Literature</u>, Vol 2. Englewood Cliffs, NJ: Salem Press, Inc., 1983. pp. 631-634.

Maxfield, Malinda

"Fantasy's Popularity," <u>Humanities in the South</u> 47: 4-5. Spring 1978.

Maximovic, Gerd

"Einige Anmerkungen zu E. A. Poe," <u>Science Fiction Times</u> (Germany) 27(4):5-9. April 1985.

Maxwell, J. G.

"Why of Wyndham," <u>Australian Science Fiction Review</u> No. 12:20-21. October 1967.

May, J. R.

"Vonnegut's humor and the limits of hope," <u>Twentieth Century Literature</u> 18(1):25-36. January 1972. also in: <u>Toward a New Earth</u>. Notre Dame: Notre Dame University Press, 1972. pp. 191-200.

May, Julian

<u>Pliocene Companion</u>. Boston: Houghton Mifflin, 1984. 219 p.

Mayer, F. J.

"Clark Ashton Smith, Artist and Sculptor," <u>Fantasy: A Forum for Science Fiction and Fantasy Artists</u>. 2(4): 8-11. Winter 1980.

Mayer, Jan

"Science Fiction Reading Class Eliminated," <u>Denver Post</u> Sec. G, p. 8. December 22, 1982.

Mayer, Lester, Jr.

"Films, radio and TV of 1950," <u>Fantasy Times</u> No. 138:11-12. September (2) 1951.

Mayersberg, Paul

"SF films turn respectable," <u>New Society</u> 7(181):22. March 17, 1966.

"Story so far: 'The Man Who Fell to Earth;' a commentary by the screenwriter," <u>Sight and Sound</u> 44(4):225-231. Autumn 1975.

Mayhar, Ardath

"Let us have stories in verse again," <u>Fantasy Review</u> 8(2): 7, 41. February 1985.

"Terra Incognita," <u>Fantasy Review</u> 7(8): 18. September 1984.

"Why of it (SF vs. fantasy), The," <u>Empire for the SF Writer</u> 9(3): 5, 28. Spring 1985.

Mayhew, A. J.

"Thrust Interview: Sharon Webb," by A. J. Mayhew and J. R. McHone. <u>Thrust</u> 23: 22-24. Fall/Winter 1985.

Mayhew, P. C.

"Science in science fiction minicourse," <u>Science Teacher</u> 43:36-37. April 1976.

Maynard, Richard

"Galaxy of science fiction films, A," <u>Scholastic Teacher</u> 102:27-28. November 1973.

Maynard, Temple

"Landscape of <u>Vathek</u>, The," <u>Transactions of the Samuel Johnson Society of the Northwest</u> 7:79-98. 1974.

Mayo, Clark

Kurt Vonnegut: The Gospel From Outer Space. San Bernardino, CA: Borgo, 1977. 64 p.

"Changeling and Madwand," in: Magill, Frank N., ed. Survey of Modern Fantasy Literature, Vol 1. Englewood Cliffs, NJ: Salem Press, Inc., 1983. pp. 228-231.

"Jack of Shadows," in: Magill, Frank N., ed. Survey of Modern Fantasy Literature, Vol 2. Englewood Cliffs, NJ: Salem Press, Inc., 1983. pp. 794-797.

"Moon Pool, The," in: Magill, Frank N., ed. Survey of Science Fiction Literature, Vol. 3. Englewood Cliffs, NJ: Salem Press, 1979. pp. 1449-1452.

"Player Piano," in: Magill, Frank N., ed. Survey of Science Fiction Literature, Vol. 4. Englewood Cliffs, NJ: Salem Press, 1979. pp. 1697-1701.

"This Immortal," in: Magill, Frank N., ed. Survey of Science Fiction Literature, Vol. 5. Englewood Cliffs, NJ: Salem Press, 1979. pp. 2260-2263.

"Welcome to the Monkey House," in: Magill, Frank N., ed. Survey of Science Fiction Literature, Vol. 5. Englewood Cliffs, NJ: Salem Press, 1979. pp. 2447-2450.

Mayo, Mike

"1984 (review)," Cinefantastique 15(3):51. July 1985.

"Adventures of Buckaroo Banzai (review)," Cinefantastique 15(2):44. May 1985.

"Baby," Cinefantastique 15(4):40-43. October 1985.

"Dreamscape (review)," Cinefantastique 14(4/5):105. September 1984.

"Frankenweenie," Cinefantastique 15(2):4-5,61. May 1985.

"Greystoke (review)," Cinefantastique 14(4/5):103. September 1984.

"Halloween III: Season of The Witch (review)," Cinefantastique 13(4):57,60. April/May 1983.

"How to make a mermaid," Cinefantastique 14(4/5):92-99. September 1984.

"Ladyhawke (review)," Cinefantastique 15(3):49-50. July 1985.

"Megaforce (review)," Cinefantastique 13(1):45-46. September/October 1982.

"Q (review)," Cinefantastique 13(4):57. April/May 1983.

"Return of the Jedi," Cinefantastique 13(6)/14(1):4,6. September 1983.

"Sender (review)," Cinefantastique 13(4):58,60. April/May 1983.

"Something Wicked This Way Comes (review)," Cinefantastique 13(6)/14(1):103. September 1983.

"Splash," Cinefantastique 14(3):15-17. May 1984.

"Wizards and Warriors (review)," Cinefantastique 13(5):60. June/July 1983.

Mays, M. A.

"Frankenstein, Mary Shelley's black theodicy," in: Clareson, T. D., ed. SF: The Other Side of Realism. Bowling Green, Ohio: Bowling Green University Popular Press, 1971. pp. 171-180.

Mazer, C. L.

Orwell's 1984, Zamyatin's We and the Sociology of Knowledge. Masters Thesis, Texas Technological College, 1968. 59 p.

Mazo, J. H.

"Writer has Small-Town Vision of Future," Dallas Morning News Sec. E, p. 4. March 29, 1981.

McAulay, George

Michael Moorcock: A Bibliography, by Andrew Harper and George McAulay. Baltimore: T-K Graphics, 1976. 29 p.

McBride, D. L.

"Belated interview, A," Fantasy Review 8(5): 10, 32. May 1985.

McCabe, Loretta

"Exclusive interview with Kurt Vonnegut, An," Writers and Artists Yearbook No. 41:93-95,100-105. 1970.

McCabe, Michael

"Rod Serling's 'Twilight Zone' Stays Unwarped Through Time," San Jose Mercury December 14, 1982. in: NewsBank. Film and Television. 61: D3-4. January 1983.

McCaffrey, Anne

"Hitch your wagon to a star: romance and glamour in science fiction," in: Bretnor, Reginald, ed. <u>Science Fiction Today and Tomorrow</u>. New York: Harper, 1974. pp. 278-294.

"On pernography," <u>Algol</u> 16 (1):27-28. Winter 1978/1979.

McCaffrey, Larry

"Form, Formula, and Fantasy: Generative Structures in Contemporary Fiction," in: Slusser, George E., ed. <u>Bridges to Fantasy</u> Carbondale: Southern Illinois University Press, 1982. pp. 21-37.

"Interview with Ursula K. Le Guin," by Larry McCaffrey and Sinda Gregory. <u>Missouri Review</u> 7(2): 64-85. 1984.

McCarthy, A.

"Paralysis of pessimism," <u>Commonweal</u> 105(20):646,671. October 13, 1978.

McCarthy, John

<u>Video Screams 1983: The Offical Source Book to Horror, Science Fiction, Fantasy, and Related Films on Videocassette and Disc</u>. Albany, NY: FantaCo, 1983. 253 p.

McCarthy, P. A.

<u>Olaf Stapledon</u>. Boston: Twayne, 1982. 166 p.

"Science Fiction as Creative Revisionism: The Example of Alfred Bester's <u>The Stars My Destination</u>," <u>Science-Fiction Studies</u> 10(1): 58-69. March 1983.

"Star Maker: Olaf Stapledon's Divine Tragedy," <u>Science-Fiction Studies</u> 8(3): 266-279. November 1981.

"Zamyatin and the Nightmare of Technology," <u>Science-Fiction Studies</u> 11(2): 122-129. July 1984.

McCarthy, Shawna

"Beam Me Up," <u>Annapolis, MD. Capital</u> August 27, 1984. in: <u>NewsBank. Social Relations</u>. SOC 64:C4. 1984.

"Interview with Barry B. Longyear," in: Schochet, Victoria, and John Silbersack, eds. <u>The Berkley Showcase, v. 2</u>. New York: Berkley, 1980. pp. 193-200.

"Wayne D. Barlow," <u>Isaac Asimov's Science Fiction Magazine</u> 5(3): 68-71. March 16, 1981.

McCarthy, Tom

"Harlan Ellison: sci-fi in a jugular vein," <u>Creem</u> 8(3):59-60. August 1976.

McCarty, John

"Fear No Evil (review)," <u>Cinefantastique</u> 11(1):47. Summer 1981.

"Parallel worlds of Jacques Tourneur," <u>Cinefantastique</u> 2(4):20-29. Summer 1973.

McCauley, V. C.

"Bibliography of space literature for boys and girls," <u>Elementary English</u> 36:98-101. February 1959.

McCellon, Venita

"Trekker Keeps the Faith," <u>Focus</u> (Supplement to The Battalion, Texas A&M University.). p. 14. December 11, 1980.

McClatchey, Dennis

<u>Case Study of Science Fiction From 1938 to the Present</u>. Master's Thesis, University of Kansas, 1973.

McClatchey, J.

"Praise and Christian Unity in War in Heaven," <u>Mythlore</u> 8(1): 19-21. Spring 1981.

McClenahan, C. L.

"'Investment Counsellor': Budrys as Critic," in: Budrys, Algis <u>Benchmarks: Galaxy Bookshelf</u>. Carbondale: Southern Illinois University Press, 1985. pp. ix-xvi.

McClintock, M. W.

"<u>Wanderer, The</u>," in: Magill, Frank N., ed. <u>Survey of Science Fiction Literature</u>, Vol. 5. Englewood Cliffs, NJ: Salem Press, 1979. pp. 2396-2401.

"<u>War of the Wing-Men</u>," in: Magill, Frank N., ed. <u>Survey of Science Fiction Literature</u>, Vol. 5. Englewood Cliffs, NJ: Salem Press, 1979. pp. 2411-2415.

McClintock, M. W. (Continued)

"Contemporaneity of Barry N. Malzberg,"
Extrapolation 23(2): 138-149. Summer 1982.

"Poul Anderson," in: Cowart, David, ed.
Twentieth-Century American Science-Fiction
Writers, Part 1: A-L. Detroit: Gale, 1981.
pp. 3-12. (Dictionary of Literary Biography,
v. 8.)

"Some preliminaries to the criticism of science
fiction," Extrapolation 15(1):17-24.
December 1973.

McClure, J. D.

"Devil's Tor: a Rehabilitation of David
Lindsay's "Monster"," Extrapolation 21(4):
367-378. Winter 1980.

"Purely as entertainment? Adventures of
Monsieur de Mailly as a representative work of
David Lindsay," Studies in Scottish
Literature 11(4):226-236. April 1974.

McClusky, Joan

"J. R. R. Tolkien: a Short Biography," in:
Becker, Alida, ed. A Tolkien Scrapbook. New
York: Grossett & Dunlap, 1978. pp. 9-42.

McComas, J. F.

"Spaceman's little nova, The," New York
Times Book Review p. 51. November 20, 1955.

McConnell, Frank

Science Fiction of H. G. Wells. New York:
Oxford University Press, 1981. 256 p.

"Born in Fire: The Ontology of the Monster,"
in: Slusser, George, ed. Shadows of the
Magic Lamp. Carbondale: Southern Illinois
University Press, 1985. pp. 231-237.

"Rough beast slouching: a note on horror
movies," Kenyon Review 32(1):109-120.
1970.

"Song of Innocence: The Creature From the Black
Lagoon," in: Marsden, Michael T., ed.
Movies As Artifacts. Chicago: Nelson-Hall,
1982. pp. 208-217.

McConnell, J. V.

"Scientists in SF: a debate," by P. R. Geffe,
M. A. Rothman, J. W. Campbell, and J. V.
McConnell. in: Knight, Damon, ed. Turning
Points: Essays in the Art of Science Fiction.
New York: Harper, 1977. pp. 175-196.

McCorkell, E. J.

"Chesterton in Canada," Chesterton Review
2(1):39-54. Fall/Winter 1975/1976.

McCormick, David

"Science fiction art 01-295: a college course,"
Cthulhu Calls 5(1): 27-28. July 1977.

"Strange visions: Virgil Finlay (1914-1971),"
Cthulhu Calls 4(4):28-29. April 1977.

McCracken, H. S.

"Return to Oz (review)," Cinefantastique
15(5):51. January 1986.

McCracken, Samuel

"Novel into film; novelist into critic: 'A
Clockwork Orange' . . . again," Antioch
Review 32(3):427-436. June 1973.

McCreight, Cathryn

"Hardware," Colloquy, Education in Church
and Society 4(5):46-47. May 1971.

McCullar, Clardy

"Science fictioners way out yonder: regional
convention," Dallas Morning News Sec. 4,
p. 1. July 5, 1958.

McCullough, D. W.

"Brothers Hildebrandt, The," in: McCullough,
David W. People, Books, and Book People. New
York: Harmony, 1981. pp. 82-84.

"Harlan Ellison," in: McCullough, David W.
People, Books, and Book People. New York:
Harmony, 1981. pp. 51-52.

McCusker, L. G.

"Creative teaching through fiction,"
Education 77(5):276-280. January 1957.

McCutcheon, Kathy

"Science and Fantasy in Science Fiction."
Vector 104: 7-13. October 1981.

McDaniel, Stan

"Coalescence of Minds," in: Smith, Nicholas
D., ed. Philosophers Look at Science
Fiction. Chicago: Nelson-Hall, 1982. pp.
117-126.

McDermott, Mary

"2001 and the literary sensibility," by W. R. Robinson and Mary McDermott. <u>Georgia Review</u> 26(1):21-37. Spring 1972.

McDonald, C. V.

"Reading and writing of utopia in Denis Diderot's <u>Supplement au Voyage de Bougainville</u>, The," <u>Science Fiction Studies</u> 3(3):248-254. November 1976.

McDonald, S. E.

"In It For the Money," <u>Empire: For the SF Writer</u> 4(4): 9, 14. September 1981.

McDonnell, David

"Beastmaster," <u>Prevue</u> 2(9):56-58,72-73. August/September 1982.

"Edward Feldman: guiding young explorers into adventure," by John Sayers and David McDonnell. <u>Starlog</u> 95: 23-25, 72. June 1985.

"Fantasy Films," <u>Starlog</u> 88: 62-68. November 1984.

"Joe Dante Uncaging Gremlins," by David McDonnell and Marc Weinberg. <u>Starlog</u> 85: 37-38, 67. August 1984.

"One Hundred Most Important People in Science Fiction/Fantasy: Philip Jose Farmer," <u>Starlog</u> 100:15-16. November 1985.

"Rick Moranis: Nebbish, Nerd and Famous Hoser," by David McDonnell and John Sayers. <u>Starlog</u> 86: 41-43, 66. September 1984.

"Samurai Cat," <u>Starlog</u> 81: 36-37. April 1984.

"Science Fiction Television 1983-1984," <u>Starlog</u> 84: 44-47. July 1984.

"Starlog Interview: John Lithgow," <u>Starlog</u> 75: 42-44, 71. October 1983.

McDonnell, T. P.

"Cult of science fiction," <u>Catholic World</u> 178(1063):15-18. October 1953. Reply, J. Wilmer, 178:11. January 1954.

McDougal, Dennis

"Bradbury Works Due on National Public Radio," <u>Los Angeles Times</u> Part VI, p. 1, 10. March 27, 1984.

McDowell, Edwin

"Publishing: From BBC Files, Some Orwell Discoveries," <u>New York Times</u> p. 39. September 9, 1984.

"Robert A. Heinlein," <u>New York Times</u> Sec. 7, p. 26. August 24, 1980.

McDowell, J. C.

"Interview: James Doohan," by Jim George and J. C. McDowell. <u>Starlog</u> No. 94:27-29. May 1985.

McEvoy, Seth

<u>Samuel R. Delany</u>. New York: Ungar, 1985, c1984. 142 p.

McFall, R. P.

<u>To Please a Child</u>, by F. J. Baum and R. P. McFall. Chicago: Reilly and Lee, 1962. 284 p.

McFerran, Dave

"Magic of the dying earth, The," <u>Anduril</u> 6:35-38. 1976.

McGarry, M. J.

"Big Aurora ripoff," by Mark McGarry and Scott Edelstein. <u>Empire: For the SF Writer</u> 3(4): 13-15. April 1978.

"Furor Scribendi: The Image of the Beast," <u>Thrust</u> 16: 25-27. Fall 1980.

"Interview: Cecelia Holland," <u>Empire: For the SF Writer</u> 3(3): 13-18. November 1977.

"Interview: Tom Reamy," <u>Empire: For the SF Writer</u> 3(1): 23-26. June 1977.

McGhan, Barry

<u>Index to Science Fiction and Fantasy Book Reviews in Astounding/Analog 1949-1969, Fantasy and Science Fiction 1949-1969, and Galaxy 1950-1969</u>. College Station, TX: SFRA, 1973. 88 p. (SFRA Miscellaneous Publication, 1)

<u>Science Fiction and Fantasy Pseudonymns</u>. Dearborn, MI: Misfit Press, 1980. 77 p.

<u>Science Fiction and Fantasy Pseudonyms</u>. Dearborn Heights, Michigan: Misfit Press, 1976. Revised Edition, 70 p.

<u>Science Fiction and Fantasy Pseudonyms</u>. Dearborn, MI: Misfit, 1971. 34 p. Reissued in 1973 with 21 page "supplement" bound in.

McGhan, Barry (Continued)

Teaching Tomorrow: A Handbook of Science Fiction for Teachers, by Barry McGhan and Elizabeth Calkins. Dayton, Ohio: Plaum Publishing Company, 1972. 103 p.

"Andre Norton: why has she been neglected?" Riverside Quarterly 4(2):128-131. January 1970.

"Science fiction in the high school," by Elizabeth Calkins and Barry McGhan. in: Williamson, Jack, ed. Teaching Science Fiction: Education for Tomorrow. Philadelphia: Owlswick, 1980. pp. 82-96.

"Sociological factors in the use of science fiction in high school," Extrapolation 21(1):31-44. Spring 1980.

"Whither High School Science Fiction?" English Journal 71(3): 54-55. March 1982.

McGhan, H. P.

1978 Awards for Science Fiction and Fantasy, or, The Best of 1977. "Draft Edition." Flint, MI: McGhan, 1978. 136 p.

"Writing Awards, The," in: Tymn, Marshall B., ed. The Science Fiction Reference Book. Mercer Island, WA: Starmont House, 1981. pp. 130-214.

McGhee, R. D.

"There's something sad about retracting: Jane Parker in the Tarzan films of the thirties," Kansas Quarterly 16(3): 101-124. Summer 1984.

McGill, H. M.

"Science fiction and fantasies," by G. B. Cotton and H. M. McGill. in: Fiction Guides, General: British and American. London: Clive Bingley, 1967.

McGillis, Roderick

"Lilith: A Romance," in: Magill, Frank N., ed. Survey of Modern Fantasy Literature, Vol 2. Englewood Cliffs, NJ: Salem Press, Inc., 1983. pp. 880-886.

"Phantasmion," in: Magill, Frank N., ed. Survey of Modern Fantasy Literature, Vol 3. Englewood Cliffs, NJ: Salem Press, Inc., 1983. pp. 1238-1240.

"Sea Lady, The," in: Magill, Frank N., ed. Survey of Modern Fantasy Literature, Vol 3. Englewood Cliffs, NJ: Salem Press, Inc., 1983. pp. 1369-1371.

"Shaving of Shagpat, The," in: Magill, Frank N., ed. Survey of Modern Fantasy Literature, Vol 3. Englewood Cliffs, NJ: Salem Press, Inc., 1983. pp. 1392-1395.

"Soul of Lilith, The," in: Magill, Frank N., ed. Survey of Modern Fantasy Literature, Vol 4. Englewood Cliffs, NJ: Salem Press, Inc., 1983. pp. 1784-1786.

"Fantasy as adventure: 19th century children's fiction," Children's Literature Association Quarterly 8(3): 18-22. Fall 1983.

"George MacDonald and the Lilith legend in the XIXth Century," Mythlore 6(1): 3-11. Winter 1979.

"If you call me Grandmother, that will do," Mythlore 6(3):27-28. Summer 1979.

McGinnis, Wayne

"Arbitrary cycle of Slaughterhouse-Five: a relation of form to theme, The," Critique 17(1):55-68. 1975.

"Names in Vonnegut's fiction," Notes on Contemporary Literature 3(2):7-9. 1973.

McGlathery, J. M.

"Devil's Elixirs, The," in: Magill, Frank N., ed. Survey of Modern Fantasy Literature, Vol 1. Englewood Cliffs, NJ: Salem Press, Inc., 1983. pp. 387-390.

"Kater Murr," in: Magill, Frank N., ed. Survey of Modern Fantasy Literature, Vol 2. Englewood Cliffs, NJ: Salem Press, Inc., 1983. pp. 831-835

"Peter Schlemihl," in: Magill, Frank N., ed. Survey of Modern Fantasy Literature, Vol 3. Englewood Cliffs, NJ: Salem Press, Inc., 1983. pp. 1234-1237.

"'Marble Statue, The'," in: Magill, Frank N., ed. Survey of Modern Fantasy Literature, Vol 2. Englewood Cliffs, NJ: Salem Press, Inc., 1983. pp. 970-972.

"Short fiction of Tieck, The," in: Magill, Frank N., ed. Survey of Modern Fantasy Literature, Vol 4. Englewood Cliffs, NJ: Salem Press, Inc., 1983. pp. 1718-1723.

McGlynn, A.

"Influence of science on painting and literature," Social Studies 36(8):355-356. December 1945.

McGovern, Eugene

"Some notes on Chesterton," _CSL: The Bulletin of the New York C. S. Lewis Society_ 5(7):6-8. May 1974.

McGowan, W. F.

"Is 1984 Here or Is It Coming?" _English Journal_ 72(6): 28-29. October 1983.

McGrade, B. J.

"Participating in enchantment (a review of _The Uses of Enchantment_)," _Children's Literature_ 6:234-238. 1977. (Book review)

McGraw, John

"Through the Land of the Seven Dimensions: A Philosophical Examination of Lilith," _Philosophical Speculations in Science Fiction and Fantasy._ 2: 81-90. Summer 1981.

McGregor, Don

"Interview With Ray Harryhausen," _Starlog_ 51: 24-28, 60. September 1981.

"Megaforce: A Blueprint for Films, Toys, and Weaponry," _Starlog_ 61: 43-46. August 1982.

"Starlog Interview: Maurice Binder, Part One," _Starlog_ 74: 20-23, 60. September 1983.

"Starlog Interview: Maurice Binder, Part Two," _Starlog_ 75: 56-59, 61. October 1983.

"Starlog Interview: The Greatest American Hero's Robert Culp, part 2," _Starlog_ 55: 45-48, 64. February 1982.

"Starlog Interview: The Greatest American Hero's Robert Culp," _Starlog_ 54: 16-19, 64. January 1981.

McGuff, Luke

"Random writing," _Empire: For the SF Writer_ 4(2): 13. February 1979.

"Workshop Reflections," _Empire: For the SF Writer_ 4(3): 7. July 1979.

McGuire, P. L.

Red Stars: Political Aspects of Soviet Science Fiction. Ph.D. Dissertation, Princeton, 1977. 268 p.

"Blue Star, The," in: Magill, Frank N., ed. _Survey of Modern Fantasy Literature_, Vol 1. Englewood Cliffs, NJ: Salem Press, Inc., 1983. pp. 137-142.

"Forever War, The," in: Magill, Frank N., ed. _Survey of Science Fiction Literature_, Vol. 2. Englewood Cliffs, NJ: Salem Press, 1979. pp. 813-818.

"Mindbridge," in: Magill, Frank N., ed. _Survey of Science Fiction Literature_, Vol. 3. Englewood Cliffs, NJ: Salem Press, 1979. pp. 1407-1412.

"Operation Chaos," in: Magill, Frank N., ed. _Survey of Modern Fantasy Literature_, Vol 3. Englewood Cliffs, NJ: Salem Press, Inc., 1983. pp. 1160-1163.

"Phoenix and the Mirror, The," in: Magill, Frank N., ed. _Survey of Modern Fantasy Literature_, Vol 3. Englewood Cliffs, NJ: Salem Press, Inc., 1983. pp. 1250-1256.

"World Soul," in: Magill, Frank N., ed. _Survey of Science Fiction Literature_, Vol. 5. Englewood Cliffs, NJ: Salem Press, 1979. pp. 2506-2510.

"Future History, Soviet Style: The Work of the Strugatsky Brothers," in: Staicar, Tom, ed. _Critical Encounters II_. New York: Ungar, 1982. pp. 104-124.

"Russian SF," in: Barron, Neil, ed. _Anatomy of Wonder_. 2nd ed. New York: Bowker, 1981. pp. 426-454.

"Short fiction of Le Guin, The," in: Magill, Frank N., ed. _Survey of Modern Fantasy Literature_, Vol 4. Englewood Cliffs, NJ: Salem Press, Inc., 1983. pp. 1607-1610.

"Variants: Joe Haldeman's SF novels," _Algol_ 14(3):19-20. Summer/Fall 1977.

"Water into wine: the novels of C. J. Cherryh," _Starship_ 16(4):47-49. Spring 1979.

McGuirk, Carol

"Optimism and the limits of subversion in _The Dispossessed_ and _The Left Hand of Darkness_," in: _Ursula K. Le Guin_, ed. by Harold Bloom. New York: Chelsea House, 1986. pp. 243-258.

McHaney, Dennis

Fiction of Robert E. Howard: A Pocket Checklist, by Dennis McHaney and Glenn Lord. s.l.: McHaney, 1975. 21 p.

McHone, J. R.

"Thrust Interview: Sharon Webb," by A. J. Mayhew and J. R. McHone. _Thrust_ No. 23: 22-24. Fall/Winter 1985.

McInnis, John

"H. P. Lovecraft's immortal culture," in: Yoke, C. B. and Hassler, D. M., eds. <u>Death and the Serpent</u>. Westport, CT: Greenwood, 1985. pp. 125-134.

McIntyre, V. N.

"Rusty paperclips and personalized rejection slips: opportunities for new writers," in: Williamson, Jack, ed. <u>Teaching Science Fiction: Education for Tomorrow</u>. Philadelphia: Owlswick, 1980. pp. 190-193.

"Ursula K. Le Guin: 'using the language with delight'," <u>Encore</u> (Portland) 1:6-7. April/May 1977.

McKay, C. P.

"On Terraforming Mars," <u>Extrapolation</u> 23(4): 309-314. Winter 1982.

McKenna, Richard

"Journey with a little man," in: Knight, Damon, ed. <u>Turning Points: Essays in the Art of Science Fiction</u>. New York: Harper, 1977. pp. 285-300.

McKie, D.

"Journey to the moon," <u>Discovery</u> 18(214):318-322. October 1937.

McKinlay, John

"Science fiction collection at the University of British Columbia Library, The," <u>British Columbia Library Quarterly</u> 34(4):5-19. April 1971.

McKinstry, Lohr

<u>Hero Pulp Index, The</u>, by Robert Weinberg and Lohr McKinstry. Evergreen, Colorado: Opar Press, 1971. Revised edition, 48 p.

McLaughlin, Frank

"Interview with Kurt Vonnegut, Jr., An," <u>Media & Methods</u> 9(9):38-41,45-46. May 1973.

"The Lord of the Rings: a fantasy film," <u>Media & Methods</u> 15(3):14-17. November 1978.

McLaughlin, Jeff

"Isaac Asimov," <u>Boston Globe</u> January 20, 1979. in: <u>NewsBank. Literature</u>. 105: E5-6. 1979.

McLaughlin, Michael

"Rigel Interviews Barry Longyear," <u>Rigel</u> No. 8: 38-43. Summer 1983.

McLean, Susan

"<u>Beginning Place</u>: An Interpretation," <u>Extrapolation</u> 24(2): 130-142. Summer 1983.

"Psychological Approach to Fantasy in the Dune Series," <u>Extrapolation</u> 23(2): 150-158. Summer 1982.

"Question of balance: death and immortality in Frank Herbert's Dune series," in: Yoke, C. B. and Hassler, D. M., eds. <u>Death and the Serpent</u>. Westport, CT: Greenwood, 1985. pp. 145-152.

McLeese, Don

"Star Trek II," <u>Chicago Sun Times</u>. June 13, 1982. in: <u>NewsBank. Film and Television</u>. 7:B6-7. 1982/83.

McLeish, Kenneth

"Rippingest Yarn of All," in: Giddings, Robert, ed. <u>J. R. R. Tolkien: This Far Land</u>. London: Vision, 1983. pp. 125-136.

McLellan, Joseph

"Falcon, Chewbacca and 1,202 humanoids," <u>Washington Post</u> p. B-1. July 10, 1978.

"For love of dragons: Anne McCaffrey," <u>Washington Post</u> p. B-1. April 4, 1978.

"Frodo and the Cosmos: Reflections on The Silmarillion," in: Isaacs, Neil D. <u>Tolkien: New Critical Perspectives</u>. Lexington: University Press of Kentucky, 1981. pp. 163-167.

"Plotting the possible futures," <u>Washington Post</u> p. C1. February 16, 1978.

McLendon, W. L.

"Compatibility of the fantastic and allegory: Potocki's <u>Saragossa Manuscript</u>," in: Collins, R. A., ed. <u>Scope of the Fantastic: Theory, Technique, Major Authors</u>. Westport: Greenwood, 1985. p. 143-150.

McLeod, P. G.

"Frankenstein: unbound and otherwise,"
Extrapolation 21(2):158-166. Summer 1980.

McLuhan, Marshall

"Origins of Chesterton's medievalism, The,"
Chesterton Review 1(2):49-50. 1975.

McMahon, J.

"Science fiction and the future of anarchy:
conversations with Ursula K. Le Guin," by
Charles Bigelow and J. McMahon. Oregon
Times (Portland) pp. 24-29. December 1974.

McMillan, William

"Science Fiction Theater the Moebius Way," by
Jane Bloomquest and William McMillan. in:
Hassler, Donald M. Patterns of the
Fantastic. Mercer Island, WA: Starmont, 1983.
pp. 81-90.

McMurray, C. R.

"Interview: George R. R. Martin," Starship
17(3).19-23. Summer 1980.

McMurray, Clifford

"Interview with Gordon R. Dickson, An,"
Science Fiction Review 26:6-12. July 1978.

"Interview with Joe Haldeman, An," Thrust
11:18-21. Summer 1978.

McNab, James

"Andromeda Strain, The; masterplots outline,"
in: Magill, Frank N., ed. Masterplots
1970 Annual. New York: Salem Press, 1970.
pp. 24-27.

McNabb, Helen

"PLR (Probably Lost to Reason)," Focus: An
SF Writer's Magazine 7: 12-15. Spring 1983.

"Standpoint: Criticism," Vector 100:
30-31. December 1980.

McNally, Owen

"BBC view of nuclear doom goes beyond 'Day
After'," Hartford Courant May 6, 1985.
in: NewsBank. Film and Television.
117:A10-A11. May 1985

McNamara, Eugene

"H. G. Wells as novelist," University of
Windsor Review 2(2):21-30. Spring 1967.

McNay, Michael

"One of nature's spellbinders," Guardian
p. 7. May 24, 1969.

"Twentieth century vox," Guardian p. 8.
September 11, 1970.

McNeese, Gretchen

"Star Trek's enterprising return," Playboy
27(1): 138-144,172, 308-310. January 1980.

McNelly, W. E.

Dune Encyclopedia. New York: Berkley, 1984.
526 p.

Science Fiction: The Academic Awakening.
Shreveport, Louisiana: College English
Association, 1974. 56 p. (CEA Critic, Vol.
37, No. 1. Supplement)

"Beyond Apollo," in: Magill, Frank N., ed.
Survey of Science Fiction Literature, Vol.
1. Englewood Cliffs, NJ: Salem Press, 1979.
pp. 202-206.

"Bill, the Galactic Hero," in: Magill,
Frank N., ed. Survey of Science Fiction
Literature, Vol. 1. Englewood Cliffs, NJ:
Salem Press, 1979. pp. 223-227.

"Canticle for Leibowitz, A," in: Magill,
Frank N., ed. Survey of Science Fiction
Literature, Vol. 1. Englewood Cliffs, NJ:
Salem Press, 1979. pp. 288-293.

"Demolished Man, The," in: Magill, Frank
N., ed. Survey of Science Fiction
Literature, Vol. 2. Englewood Cliffs, NJ:
Salem Press, 1979. pp. 529-532.

"Double Star," in: Magill, Frank N., ed.
Survey of Science Fiction Literature, Vol. 2.
Englewood Cliffs, NJ: Salem Press, 1979. pp.
587-590.

"Dragon in the Sea, The," in: Magill, Frank
N., ed. Survey of Science Fiction
Literature, Vol. 2. Englewood Cliffs, NJ:
Salem Press, 1979. pp. 595-599.

"Dune," by W. E. McNelly and Timothy
O'Reilly. in: Magill, Frank N., ed. Survey
of Science Fiction Literature, Vol. 2.
Englewood Cliffs, NJ: Salem Press, 1979. pp.
647-658.

"Dying Inside," in: Magill, Frank N., ed.
Survey of Science Fiction Literature, Vol. 2.
Englewood Cliffs, NJ: Salem Press, 1979. pp.
671-675.

McNelly, W. E. (Continued)

"Earth Abides," in: Magill, Frank N., ed. Survey of Science Fiction Literature, Vol. 2. Englewood Cliffs, NJ: Salem Press, 1979. pp. 687-691.

"Engine Summer," in: Magill, Frank N., ed. Survey of Science Fiction Literature, Vol. 2. Englewood Cliffs, NJ: Salem Press, 1979. pp. 721-724.

"Fahrenheit 451," by W. E. McNelly and Keith Neilson. in: Magill, Frank N., ed. Survey of Science Fiction Literature, Vol. 2. Englewood Cliffs, NJ: Salem Press, 1979. pp. 749-755.

"Frankenstein Unbound," in: Magill, Frank N., ed. Survey of Science Fiction Literature, Vol. 2. Englewood Cliffs, NJ: Salem Press, 1979. pp. 840-844.

"Last Starship from Earth, The," in: Magill, Frank N., ed. Survey of Science Fiction Literature, Vol. 3. Englewood Cliffs, NJ: Salem Press, 1979. pp. 1156-1160.

"Lord of the Starship," in: Magill, Frank N., ed. Survey of Science Fiction Literature, Vol. 3. Englewood Cliffs, NJ: Salem Press, 1979. pp. 1261-1264.

"Malacia Tapestry, The," in: Magill, Frank N., ed. Survey of Modern Fantasy Literature, Vol 2. Englewood Cliffs, NJ: Salem Press, Inc., 1983. pp. 951-954.

"Man in the High Castle, The," in: Magill, Frank N., ed. Survey of Science Fiction Literature, Vol. 3. Englewood Cliffs, NJ: Salem Press, 1979. pp. 1323-1327.

"Report on Probability, A," in: Magill, Frank N., ed. Survey of Science Fiction Literature, Vol. 4. Englewood Cliffs, NJ: Salem Press, 1979. pp. 1764-1767.

"Rim of Morning, The," in: Magill, Frank N., ed. Survey of Science Fiction Literature, Vol. 4. Englewood Cliffs, NJ: Salem Press, 1979. pp. 1784-1788.

"Tunc and Nunquam," in: Magill, Frank N., ed. Survey of Science Fiction Literature, Vol. 5. Englewood Cliffs, NJ: Salem Press, 1979. pp. 2311-2315.

"Universal Baseball Association, Inc. J. Henry Waugh, Prop., The," in: Magill, Frank N., ed. Survey of Modern Fantasy Literature, Vol 4. Englewood Cliffs, NJ: Salem Press, Inc., 1983. pp. 1995-1998.

"Alfred Bester," in: Bleiler, E. F., ed. Science Fiction Writers. New York: Scribners, 1982. pp. 283-290.

"Archetypal patterns in science fiction," CEA Critic 35(4):15-19. May 1973.

"Bradbury revisited," CEA Critic 31:4,6. March 1969.

"Brian W. Aldiss," in: Bleiler, E. F., ed. Science Fiction Writers. New York: Scribners, 1982. pp. 251-258.

"British SF scene," in: McNelly, W. E., ed. Science Fiction the Academic Awakening. Shreveport, LA: CEA, 1974. pp. 57.

"Frank Herbert," in: Bleiler, E. F., ed. Science Fiction Writers. New York: Scribners, 1982. pp. 377-385.

"In Memoriam: Frank Herbert, 1920-1986," SFWA Bulletin 20(1): 24-28. Spring 1986.

"Kurt Vonnegut as science fiction writer," in: Klinkowitz, Kurt, ed. Vonnegut in America. New York: Delacorte, 1977. pp. 87-96.

"Linguistic relativity in old high Martian," CEA Critic 30(6):4,6. March 1968. also in: Vector 55:3-5. 1970.

"Philip K. Dick manuscripts and books: the manuscripts and papers at Fullerton," Science Fiction Studies 2(1):4-5. March 1975.

"Ray Bradbury," in: Bleiler, E. F., ed. Science Fiction Writers. New York: Scribners, 1982. pp. 171-178.

"Sci-fi: state of the art," America 133(14):304-307. November 8, 1975.

"Science Fiction & Religion," Niekas 25:22-25. February 1981.

"Science fiction and the academe: an introduction," CEA Critic 35:6-9. November 1972.

"Science fiction and the American dream," CEA Critic 36(1):15-19. January 1973.

"Science fiction awards," in: McNelly, W. E., ed. Science Fiction the Academic Awakening. Shreveport, LA: CEA, 1974. pp. 53-56.

"Science fiction novel in 1968, The," in: Anderson, Poul, ed. Nebula Award Stories Four. Garden City, NY: Doubleday, 1969. pp. xiii-xxv.

"Science fiction: the modern mythology," America 123:125-127. September 5, 1970. also in: Clareson, T. D., ed. SF: The Other Side of Realism. Bowling Green, Ohio: Bowling Green Univ. Popular Press, 1971. pp. 193-198.

"Statement is the self, The: Alfred Bester's science fiction," by Jane Hipolito and W. E. McNelly. in: Tolley, M. J., ed. The Stellar Guage. Carleton, Australia: Norstrilia, 1980. pp. 63-90.

McNelly, W. E. (Continued)

"Two views: I, Ray Bradbury...," in: Clareson, T., ed. <u>Voices for the Future</u>, V. 1. Bowling Green, Ohio: Popular Press, 1976. pp. 167-174. also in: Olander, J. and M. Greenberg, eds. <u>Ray Bradbury</u>. Taplinger, 1980. pp. 17-24.

McNutt, D. J.

<u>Eighteenth-Century Gothic Novel: An Annotated Bibliography of Criticism and Selected Texts, The</u>. New York and London: Garland Publishing, 1975. 330 p.

McQuarie, Donald

"Utopia and Trancendence: An Analysis of Their Decline in Contemporary Science Fiction," <u>Journal of Popular Culture</u> 14(2): 242-250. Fall 1980.

McQuay, Mike

"Apples to Oranges," <u>Starlog</u> No. 96: 58-59. July 1985.

McReynolds, D. J.

"Lights in the Sky Are Stars, The," in: Magill, Frank N., ed. <u>Survey of Science Fiction Literature</u>, Vol. 3. Englewood Cliffs, NJ: Salem Press, 1979. pp. 1217-1220.

"Tunnel Through the Deeps, The," in: Magill, Frank N., ed. <u>Survey of Science Fiction Literature</u>, Vol. 5. Englewood Cliffs, NJ: Salem Press, 1979. pp. 2324-2328.

"What Mad Universe," in: Magill, Frank N., ed. <u>Survey of Science Fiction Literature</u>, Vol. 5. Englewood Cliffs, NJ: Salem Press, 1979. pp. 2451-2454.

"Critical Pretensions: Modern Critics and Depression Era Science Fiction," <u>Extrapolation</u> 24(3): 227-233. Fall 1983.

"Short fiction of Bradbury, The," in: Magill, Frank N., ed. <u>Survey of Modern Fantasy Literature</u>, Vol 3. Englewood Cliffs, NJ: Salem Press, Inc., 1983. pp. 1471-1481.

"Short Fiction of Fitz-James O'Brien, The," in: Magill, Frank N., ed. <u>Survey of Science Fiction Literature</u>, Vol. 4. Englewood Cliffs, NJ: Salem Press, 1979. pp. 1944-1947.

"Short Fiction of Fredric Brown, The," in: Magill, Frank N., ed. <u>Survey of Science Fiction Literature</u>, Vol. 4. Englewood Cliffs, NJ: Salem Press, 1979. pp. 1954-1957.

"Short Fiction of Ray Bradbury, The," in: Magill, Frank N., ed. <u>Survey of Science Fiction Literature</u>, Vol. 4. Englewood Cliffs, NJ: Salem Press, 1979. pp. 2042-2045.

McSherry, F. D.

"Checklist of Science Fiction/Fantasy Works Containing Religious Themes or Motifs," by Robert Reilly, F. D. McSherry, and C. G. Waugh. in: Reilly, Robert, ed. <u>The Transcendent Adventure</u>. Westport: Greenwood, 1984. p. 225-248.

McSorley, B. S.

"Buero Vallejo's <u>Mito</u> and <u>El Traguluz</u>: The Twilight Zone of Hope," <u>Science-Fiction Studies</u> 10(1): 81-86. March 1983.

McVitty, Walter

"Response to Red Shift," <u>Labrys</u> No. 7: p. 133-138. November 1981.

McWhorter, G. T.

"Edgar Rice Burroughs: Alive or Dead," <u>Fantasy Review</u> 8(8): 8-10. August 1985.

"Edgar Rice Burroughs: King of Dreams," <u>Library Review</u> (Univ. of Louisville) No. 30: 3-25. May 1980.

Meacham, Beth

<u>Reader's Guide to Fantasy</u>, by Baird Searles, Beth Meacham, and Michael Franklin. New York: Facts on File, 1982. 196 p.

<u>Reader's Guide to Science Fiction, A</u>, by Baird Searles, Martin Last, Beth Meacham and Michael Franklin. New York: Avon, 1979. 266 p.

"Science fiction and fantasy explosion, The," by Tappan King and Beth Meacham. <u>American Bookseller</u> 2(11):42-58. July 1979.

Mead, Margaret

"Image of the scientist among high school students," by Margaret Mead and Rhoda Metroux. <u>Science</u> 126(3270):384-390. August 30,1957.

"Toward more vivid utopias," <u>Science</u> 126:957-961. November 8, 1957.

Mead, Syd

"Bladerunner," <u>Prevue</u> 2(7): 56-57, 67. May 1982.

Meades, Jonathan

"Kurt Vonnegut: fantasist," _Books and Bookmen_ 18(5):34-37. February 1973.

Meadley, R. G.

"Half an Eye and Tono-Bungay," _Foundation_ 27: 71-78. February 1983.

Meadows, Jim, III

"Star Trek Novels: An Overview," _Lan's Lantern_ No. 10: 20-21. June 1980.

Means, H. J.

"Science fiction, fantasy and the occult," _English Journal_ 62(7):1059-1060. October 1973. (Book review)

Means, R. L.

"Ecology and the contemporary religious conscience," _Christian Century_ 86(49):1546-1549. December 3, 1969.

Meckier, Jerome

"Cancer in utopia: positive and negative elements in Huxley's island," _Dalhousie Review_ 54(4):619-633. Winter 1975.

"Coming of age in Pala: the primitivism of _Brave New World_ reconsidered in _Island_," _Alternative Futures_ 1(2):68-90. Summer 1978.

Mecoy, Bob

"Introduction," in: Schmitz, J. H. _The Universe Against Her_. Boston: Gregg, 1981. pp. v-xii.

Medcalf, Stephen

"Tolkien, J. R. R.," in: Woodcock, George, ed. _20th Century Fiction_. Chicago: St. James, 1985. pp. 668-670.

Medd, H. J.

"Scientist in fiction," _Ontario Library Review_ 46:81-83. May 1962.

Meech, Shirley

"Silent Running," by Kay Anderson and Shirley Meech. _Cinefantastique_ 2(2):8-15. Summer 1972.

Meek, S. P.

"Pseudo-scientific story, The," _Writer's Digest_ 11(6):37-39. May 1931.

Meeker, O.

"Screamy-weamies," _Colliers_ 117(2):42,55. January 12, 1946.

Meeter, Glenn

"Vonnegut's formal and moral otherworldliness: _Cat's Cradle_ and _Slaughterhouse-Five_," in: Klinkowitz, Jerome and John Somer, eds. _The Vonnegut Statement_. New York: Delacorte Press/Seymour Lawrence, 1973. pp. 204-220.

Meglin, Nick

"Frank Frazetta at bat," _American Artist_ 40(406):38-45,77. May 1976.

Meheust, Bertrand

Science fiction et soucoupes volantes: une realite mythicophysique. Paris: Mercure de France, 1978. 350 p.

Mei, Francesco

Giungla del futuro: guida al mondo di domani attraverso la fantascienza. Rome: Cooperativa scritori, 1978. 356 p.

Meikle, J. L.

"Other Frequencies: the Parallel Worlds of Thomas Pynchon and H. P. Lovecraft," _Modern Fiction Studies_. 27(2): 287-294. Summer 1981.

Mele, Jim

Isaac Asimov. by Jean Fiedler and Jim Mele. New York: Ungar, 1982. 122 p.

"Asimov's robots," by Jean Fiedler and Jim Mele. in: Riley, Dick, ed. _Critical Encounters: Writers and Themes in Science Fiction_. New York: Ungar, 1978. pp. 1-22.

Mellard, J. J.

"Modes of Vonnegut's fiction: or, _Player Piano_ ousts _Mechanical Bride_ and _The Sirens of Titan_ invade _The Gutenberg Galaxy_, The," in: Klinkowitz, Jerome, ed. _The Vonnegut Statement_. NY: Delacorte Press, 1973. pp. 178-203.

Mello, J. P., Jr.

"Tron: Man in the Computer," _80 Microcomputing_ 30: 124-130. August 1982.

Mellor, A. K.

"On feminist utopias," _Women's Studies_ 9:241-262. 1982.

Mellor, Adrian

"Science fiction and the crisis of the educated middle class," in: Pawling, Christopher, ed. _Popular Fiction and Social Change_. New York: St. Martins, 1984. pp. 20-49.

Mellott, C. M.

"Two Views of the Sentient Computer: Gerrold's _When Harlie Was One_ and Ryan's _Adolescence of P-1_," in: Hassler, Donald M. _Patterns of the Fantastic II_. Mercer Island, WA: Starmont, 1985. pp. 45-50.

Mendelson, M. O.

"Amerikanskii roman psle Khemingueia, Folknera, Steinbeka," _Novyi Mir_ 8:246-263. 1975.

"Kakim vidit mir Kurt Vonnegut?" _SShA: Ekonomika, politika, ideologiia_ 12:79-84. 1974.

Mendelson, Michael

Modernization of Prose Romance: The Radical Form of William Morris and George MacDonald. Ph. D. Dissertation, Washington State University, 1981. 317 p.

"Opening Moves: The Entry Into the Other World," _Extrapolation_ 25(2): 171-179. Summer 1984.

Mengeling, M. E.

"Machineries of joy and dispair: Bradbury's attitudes toward science and technology, The," in: Olander, J. D. and M. H. Greenberg, eds. _Ray Bradbury_. New York: Taplinger, 1980. pp. 83-109.

"Ray Bradbury's _Dandelion Wine_: themes, sources, and style," _English Journal_ 60(7):877-887. October 1971.

Menger, Lucy

Theodore Sturgeon. New York: Ungar, 1981. 180 p.

"Appeal of _Childhood's End_, The," in: Riley, Dick, ed. _Critical Encounters: Writers and Themes in Science Fiction_. New York: Ungar, 1978. pp. 87-108.

Menningen, Jurgen

Filmbuch science fiction. Koeln: DuMont Schauberg, 1975. 190 p.

"Mythos und kolportage. Erscheinungsformen des amerikanischen science fiction films," _Film Studio_ pp. i-XV. October 1967.

"Mythos und kolportage. Erscheinungsformen des amerikanischen science fiction films," _Egoist_ 3:2-16. 1967.

Menville, Douglas

Future Visions: The New Golden Age of the Science Fiction Film, by Douglas Menville and R. Reginald. Van Nuys, CA: Newcastle, 1985. 192 p.; San Bernardino, CA: Borgo, 1985. 192 p.

Historical and Critical Survey of the Science Fiction Film. Master's Thesis, University of Southern California, 1959. 177 p.

Historical and Critical Survey of the Science Fiction Film, A. New York: Arno Press, 1975. 185 p.

Things to Come: An Illustrated History of the Science Fiction Film, by Douglas Menville and Robert Reginald. New York: New York Times Books, 1977. 212 p.

"Looking back on films that look far ahead," by R. Reginald and Douglas Menville. _Science Digest_ 83(2):12-13. February 1978.

Menzel, D. H.

"Space: the new frontier," _PMLA_ 77(2):10-17. May 1962.

Menzies, I. S.

"Changing dream, The," _New Scientist_ 32(526):691-693. December 22, 1966.

"Changing dream," _New Scientist_ pp. 190-194. December 22, 1962.

Menzies, Janet

"Middle-earth and the Adolescent," in: Giddings, Robert, ed. _J. R. R. Tolkien: This Far Land_. London: Vision, 1983. pp. 56-72.

Mercer, Derwent

"Alien communication," Listener 73:13-15. January 7, 1965. also in: Advancement of Science 22(98):200-203. August 1965. (as "Problems of communication with alien intelligent beings")

Meredith, R. C.

"R. C. Meredith: an autobiographical sketch, August 6, 1975," Starship 16(3):44-45. Summer 1979.

Meredith, Sandy

"Refugees on Mars: FDR's Secret Plan," by Sandy Meredith and Bob Sanders. SFWA Bulletin 18(1): 32-33. Spring 1984.

Meredith, William

"Meredith on Vonnegut," Connecticut College Alumni Magazine 54:2. Fall 1976.

Merker, Reinhard

"Am besten embryos: kyborgs in science fiction and popularwissenschaft," Science Fiction Times No. 134:7-9. August 1974.

"Psychodelische ideologie. Teil 1," Science Fiction Times No. 133:30-34. January 1974.

"Psychodelische ideologie. Teil 2," Science Fiction Times No. 134:39-46. August 1974.

Merla, Patrick

"What is real? asked the rabbit one day," Saturday Review 55(45):43-50. November 4, 1972.

Merli, Angela

Utopia e fantascienza in John Wyndham. Thesis, Universita degli Studi di Urbino, 1976/1977.

Merril, Judith

"Memoir and Appreciation," in: Clifton, Mark. The Science Fiction of Mark Clifton, ed. by Barry N. Malzberg and Martin H. Greenberg. Carbondale: Southern Illinois University Press, 1981. pp. vii-xix.

"Summation," in: Merril, Judith, ed. Year's Best SF, 11th Annual Edition. New York: Dell, 1966.

"Summation: SF, 1963," in: Merril, Judith, ed. Year's Best SF, 9th Annual Edition. New York: Dell, 1964.

"Theodore Sturgeon," Magazine of Fantasy and Science Fiction 23(3):46-55. September 1962.

"What do you mean: science? fiction? part II," Extrapolation 8(1):2-19. December 1966. also in: Clareson, T. D., ed. SF: The Other Side of Realism. Bowling Green, Ohio: Popular Press, 1971. pp. 53-95.

"What do you mean: science? fiction?," Extrapolation 7(2):30-46. May 1966. also in: Clareson, T. D., ed. SF: The Other Side of Realism. Bowling Green, Ohio: Popular Press, 1971. pp. 53-95.

Merrill, Robert

"Vonnegut's Breakfast of Champions: the conversion of heliogabalus," Critique 18(3):99-108. 1977.

Merrit, J. D.

"She Pluck'd, She Eat," in: Barr, Marlene S., ed. Future Females. Bowling Green, OH: Bowling Green State University Popular Press, 1981. pp. 37-41.

Merwin, Sam, Jr.

"Nest of strange and beautiful birds, A," The Alien Critic 3(3):18-19. August 1974.

"S-F and s-e-x (or vice versa)," Science Fiction Review 6:18-20. August 1977.

Meschkow, S. Z.

"Synopses of Stephen King's fiction," in: Schweitzer, Darrell, ed. Discovering Stephen King. Mercer Island: Starmont, 1985. pp. 165-204.

Meskys, E. R.

"Random Thoughts," Niekas 25: 30-31. February 1981.

"Science fiction fan magazines; September 1961," Science Fiction Times No. 369:5-6,36. September 1961.

Messent, P. B.

"Breakfast of Champions: the direction of Vonnegut's fiction," Journal of American Studies 8(1):101-114. April 1974.

Author Entries

Metcalf, Norm

Index of Science Fiction Magazines 1951-1965, The. El Cerrito, California: J. Ben Stark, 1968. 253 p.

Methold, Kenneth

"Science fiction," Contemporary Review 1119:170-173. March 1959.

Metroux, Rhoda

"Image of the scientist among high school students," by Margaret Mead and Rhoda Metroux. Science 126(3270):384-390. August 30,1957.

Metzger, Arthur

Guide to the Gormenghast Trilogy, A. Baltimore: T-K Graphics, 1976. 35 p.

Index and Short History of Unknown. Baltimore: T-K Graphics, 1976. 22 p.

Metzl, E.

"Ghosts and things by Meryn Peake," American Artist 19(2):24-29. February 1955.

Metzner, Joachim

"Vieldeutigkeit der Wiederkehr, Die: Literaturpsychologische Überlegungen zur Phantastik," in: Thomsen, C. W., ed. Phantastik in Literatur und Kunst. Darmstadt: Wiss. Buchgesellschaft, 1980. pp. 78-108.

Meunier, Jacques

"Ethnologie et science fiction," Magazine Litteraire 167:20. December 1980.

Meyer, Rex

"Australia news," Fantasy Times No. 175:2,7. April 1953.

Meyers, Jeffrey

George Orwell: The Critical Heritage. London: Routledge, 1975. 392 p.

"Nineteen Eighty-Four: a novel of the 1930s," in: George Orwell and Nineteen Eighty-Four. Washington, DC: Library of Congress, 1985. pp. 79-93.

"George Orwell: a bibliography," Bulletin of Bibliography 31(3):117-121. July/September 1974.

"George Orwell: a selected checklist," Modern Fiction Studies 21(1):133-136. Spring 1975.

Meyers, Richard

For One Week Only: The World of Exploitation Films. Piscataway, NJ: New Century, 1983. 270 p.

S-F 2: A Pictorial History of Science Fiction Films From Rollerball to Return of the Jedi. Secaucus, NJ: Lyle Stuart, 1984. 256 p.

World of Fantasy Films. New York: Barnes, 1980. 195 p.

"Boris: The Fantastic Art of Boris Vallejo," by Ed Naha and Richard Meyers. Future 3: 66-75. July 1978.

"Held Over By Popular Demand: David Cronenberg," In: Winter, Douglas E. Shadowings: The Reader's Guide to Horror Fiction 1981-1982. Mercer Island, WA: Starmont, 1983. pp. 119-124.

"Ray Harryhausen," Starlog 10:52-56. 1977.

"Up, Up, and Away: An Exclusive Talk With Superman Portrayer Christopher Reeve," Future 6: 28-31. November 1978.

Meyers, W. E.

Aliens and Linguists: Language Study and Science Fiction. Athens: University of Georgia Press, 1980. 257 p.

"And Chaos Died," in: Magill, Frank N., ed. Survey of Science Fiction Literature, Vol. 1. Englewood Cliffs, NJ: Salem Press, 1979. pp. 53-57.

"At the Earth's Core," in: Magill, Frank N., ed. Survey of Science Fiction Literature, Vol. 1. Englewood Cliffs, NJ: Salem Press, 1979. pp. 93-96.

"Atlan Series, The," in: Magill, Frank N., ed. Survey of Modern Fantasy Literature, Vol 1. Englewood Cliffs, NJ: Salem Press, Inc., 1983. pp. 66-68.

"Berserker," in: Magill, Frank N., ed. Survey of Science Fiction Literature, Vol. 1. Englewood Cliffs, NJ: Salem Press, 1979. pp. 168-172.

"Book of the New Sun, The," in: Magill, Frank N., ed. Survey of Modern Fantasy Literature, Vol 1. Englewood Cliffs, NJ: Salem Press, Inc., 1983. pp. 154-160.

"Brain Wave," in: Magill, Frank N., ed. Survey of Science Fiction Literature, Vol. 1. Englewood Cliffs, NJ: Salem Press, 1979. pp. 242-246.

Meyers, W. E. (Continued)

"Conjure Wife," in: Magill, Frank N., ed. Survey of Modern Fantasy Literature, Vol 1. Englewood Cliffs, NJ: Salem Press, Inc., 1983. pp. 314-318.

"Fancies and Goodnights," in: Magill, Frank N., ed. Survey of Modern Fantasy Literature, Vol 2. Englewood Cliffs, NJ: Salem Press, Inc., 1983. pp. 520-523.

"First on Mars," in: Magill, Frank N., ed. Survey of Science Fiction Literature, Vol. 2. Englewood Cliffs, NJ: Salem Press, 1979. pp. 787-791.

"Great Divorce, The," in: Magill, Frank N., ed. Survey of Modern Fantasy Literature, Vol 2. Englewood Cliffs, NJ: Salem Press, Inc., 1983. pp. 635-637.

"Greater Trumps, The," in: Magill, Frank N., ed. Survey of Modern Fantasy Literature, Vol 2. Englewood Cliffs, NJ: Salem Press, Inc., 1983. pp. 649-653.

"Grendel," in: Magill, Frank N., ed. Survey of Modern Fantasy Literature, Vol 2. Englewood Cliffs, NJ: Salem Press, Inc., 1983. pp. 675-679.

"High Crusade, The," in: Magill, Frank N., ed. Survey of Science Fiction Literature, Vol. 2. Englewood Cliffs, NJ: Salem Press, 1979. pp. 977-980.

"Land That Time Forgot, The," in: Magill, Frank N., ed. Survey of Science Fiction Literature, Vol. 3. Englewood Cliffs, NJ: Salem Press, 1979. pp. 1130-1134.

"Last Man, The," in: Magill, Frank N., ed. Survey of Science Fiction Literature, Vol. 3. Englewood Cliffs, NJ: Salem Press, 1979. pp. 1151-1155.

"Martian Odyssey and Other Science Fiction Tales, A," in: Magill, Frank N., ed. Survey of Science Fiction Literature, Vol. 3. Englewood Cliffs, NJ: Salem Press, 1979. pp. 1353-1356.

"Merlin Trilogy, The," in: Magill, Frank N., ed. Survey of Modern Fantasy Literature, Vol 2. Englewood Cliffs, NJ: Salem Press, Inc., 1983. pp. 1010-1014.

"Needle," in: Magill, Frank N., ed. Survey of Science Fiction Literature, Vol. 3. Englewood Cliffs, NJ: Salem Press, 1979. pp. 1505-1509.

"Nova Express," in: Magill, Frank N., ed. Survey of Science Fiction Literature, Vol. 4. Englewood Cliffs, NJ: Salem Press, 1979. pp. 1566-1570.

"Orbitsville," in: Magill, Frank N., ed. Survey of Science Fiction Literature, Vol. 4. Englewood Cliffs, NJ: Salem Press, 1979. pp. 1617-1621.

"Pellucidar," in: Magill, Frank N., ed. Survey of Science Fiction Literature, Vol. 4. Englewood Cliffs, NJ: Salem Press, 1979. pp. 1665-1668.

"Plague of Demons, A," in: Magill, Frank N., ed. Survey of Science Fiction Literature, Vol. 4. Englewood Cliffs, NJ: Salem Press, 1979. pp. 1687-1691.

"Rim Worlds Series, The," in: Magill, Frank N., ed. Survey of Science Fiction Literature, Vol. 4. Englewood Cliffs, NJ: Salem Press, 1979. pp. 1789-1793.

"Shadows of Ecstasy," in: Magill, Frank N., ed. Survey of Modern Fantasy Literature, Vol 3. Englewood Cliffs, NJ: Salem Press, Inc., 1983. pp. 1384-1386.

"Space Lords," in: Magill, Frank N., ed. Survey of Science Fiction Literature, Vol. 5. Englewood Cliffs, NJ: Salem Press, 1979. pp. 2122-2126.

"Space Trilogy, The," in: Magill, Frank N., ed. Survey of Modern Fantasy Literature, Vol 4. Englewood Cliffs, NJ: Salem Press, Inc., 1983. pp. 1790-1797.

"Stainless Steel Rat Novels, The," in: Magill, Frank N., ed. Survey of Science Fiction Literature, Vol. 5. Englewood Cliffs, NJ: Salem Press, 1979. pp. 2136-2139.

"That Hideous Strength," in: Magill, Frank N., ed. Survey of Science Fiction Literature, Vol. 5. Englewood Cliffs, NJ: Salem Press, 1979. pp. 2250-2254.

"Traveler in Black, The," in: Magill, Frank N., ed. Survey of Modern Fantasy Literature, Vol 4. Englewood Cliffs, NJ: Salem Press, Inc., 1983. pp. 1963-1965.

"War in Heaven," in: Magill, Frank N., ed. Survey of Modern Fantasy Literature, Vol 5. Englewood Cliffs, NJ: Salem Press, Inc., 1983. pp. 2063-2066.

"Fantasy games as folk literature," in: Magill, Frank N., ed. Survey of Modern Fantasy Literature, Vol 5. Englewood Cliffs, NJ: Salem Press, Inc., 1983. pp. 2481-2491.

"Future history and development of the English language, The," Science Fiction Studies 3(2):130-142. July 1976.

"Pilgrim Award presentation speech, 1985," SFRA Newsletter 133:3-6. August 1985.

"Pilgrim Award Presentation: E. F. Bleiler," SFRA Newsletter 123: 4-6. July/August 1984.

Meyers, W. E. (Continued)

"Short Fiction of Edmond Hamilton, The," in: Magill, Frank N., ed. Survey of Science Fiction Literature, Vol. 4. Englewood Cliffs, NJ: Salem Press, 1979. pp. 1939-1943.

"Short Fiction of Fritz Leiber, Jr., The," in: Magill, Frank N., ed. Survey of Science Fiction Literature, Vol. 4. Englewood Cliffs, NJ: Salem Press, 1979. pp. 1958-1962.

"Short fiction of Kuttner, The," in: Magill, Frank N., ed. Survey of Modern Fantasy Literature, Vol 4. Englewood Cliffs, NJ: Salem Press, Inc., 1983. pp. 1592-1596.

"Silver John Stories, The," in: Magill, Frank N., ed. Survey of Modern Fantasy Literature, Vol 4. Englewood Cliffs, NJ: Salem Press, Inc., 1983. pp. 1744-1748.

Micha, Rene

"Nouvelle litterature allegorique, Une," La Nouvelle Revue Francaise 2(16):696-706. April 1954.

Michaelson, L. W.

"I Am Thinking of My Darling," in: Magill, Frank N., ed. Survey of Science Fiction Literature, Vol. 2. Englewood Cliffs, NJ: Salem Press, 1979. pp. 991-994.

"Amazing interview: a conversation with Stanislaw Lem," Amazing 27(10): 116-119. January 1981.

"Science fiction and the rate of social change," Extrapolation 11(1):25-27. December 1969.

"Science fiction, censorship and pie-in-the-sky," Western Humanities Review 13(4):409-413. Autumn 1959.

"Social criticism in science fiction," Antioch Review 14(4):502-508. December 1954.

Michaud, M. A.

First World Fantasy Convention: Three Authors Remember. West Warwick: Necromonicon Press, 1980. 52 p.

Lovecraft's Library: A Catalogue, by S. T. Joshi and M. A. Michand. West Warwick, RI: Necronomicon, 1980. 92 p.

Michel, Aime

"Prendre au serieux, A: la science fiction," Science et Vie. November 1958.

Michel, J. B.

"Philosophical novels of Olaf Stapledon," Astronaut Science Fantasy 1(2):9-14. Fall 1948. Reprinted from: Alchemist 1(3). Summer 1940.

Michel, J. C.

"50 films cles du cinema de science fiction: dictionnaire critique," by Jacques Goimard, Jean-Claude Michel, and Alain Schlockoff. Cinema d'aujourd'hui. No. 7:65-84. Spring 1976.

"Imagination en liberte, L'. Les films en tourange et en preparation," by J. C. Michel and Alain Schlockoff. Cinema D'aujourd'hui. No. 7:111-116. Spring 1976.

Miesel, Sandra

Against Time's Arrow: The High Crusade of Poul Anderson. San Bernardino, California: Borgo Press, 1978. 64 p. (Popular Writers of Today, Vol. 18)

"Tau Zero," in: Magill, Frank N., ed. Survey of Science Fiction Literature, Vol. 5. Englewood Cliffs, NJ: Salem Press, 1979. pp. 2236-2240.

"Afterword to Fred Saberhagen's Berserker Man: life and death in dreadful conflict strove," in: Saberhagen, Fred. Berserker Man. New York: Ace, 1979. pp. 208-220.

"Afterword, An (to Home From the Shore)," in: Dickson, Gordon R. Home From the Shore. New York: Ace, 1978. pp. 207-221.

"Afterword: the price of buying time," in: Anderson, Poul. A Stone in Heaven. New York: Ace, 1979. pp. 237-255.

"Algol interview: Gordon R. Dickson," Algol 15(2):33-38. Spring 1978.

"Artist in his studio: Frank Kelly Freas, The," Galileo No. 14:8-12. September 1979.

"Challenge and response: Poul Anderson's view of man," Riverside Quarterly 4(2):78-95. January 1970.

"Chronology of Technic Civilization, A," in: Anderson, Poul. A Stone in Heaven. New York: Ace, 1979. pp. 252-255.

"Dreams Within Dreams," in: Schweitzer, Darrell, ed. Exploring Fantasy Worlds. San Bernardino, CA: Borgo, 1985. pp. 35-42.

"I am Joan and I love you," in: Exploring Cordwainer Smith. New York: Algol, 1975. pp. 24-27.

"Il Costo del Guadagnar Tempo," Cosmo informatore 14(1):54-61. Spring 1985.

Miesel, Sandra (Continued)

"Introduction," in: Henderson, Zenna. <u>Pilgrimage: The Book of the People</u>. Boston: Gregg, 1978. pp. vii-xv.

"Introduction," in: Tucker, Wilson. <u>The Year of the Quiet Sun</u>. Boston: Gregg, 1979. pp. v-xv.

"Man in the high tower, The," <u>Starship</u> 16(3):55-57. Summer 1979. also in: Garrett, Randall. <u>Too Many Magicians</u>. Boston: G. K. Hall, 1978 (slightly revised).

"Mana crisis, The," in: Niven, Larry. <u>The Magic Goes Away</u>. New York: Ace, 1978. pp. 195-213.

"Michael Whelan: Interview," <u>Science Fiction Review</u> 10(4): 26-31. November 1981.

"On commissioned imaginations: science fiction's contribution to the NASA fine arts program," <u>Isaac Asimov's Science Fiction Magazine</u> 3(10):49-73. October 1979.

"Plume and the Sword," in: Dickson, Gordon R. <u>Lost Dorsai</u>. New York: Ace, 1980. pp. 242-267.

"Road to the dark tower, The," in: Dickson, Gordon R. <u>Dorsai</u>. New York: Ace, 1980. pp. 273-305.

"Samuel R. Delaney's use of myth in <u>Nova</u>," <u>Extrapolation</u> 12(2):86-93. May 1971.

"Some motifs and sources for Lord of the Rings," <u>Riverside Quarterly</u> 3(2): 125-128. March 1968.

"Some religious aspects of Lord of the Rings," <u>Riverside Quarterly</u> 3(3): 209-213. August 1968.

"Sword-play: an appreciative afterword," in: Saberhagen, Fred. <u>First Book of Swords</u>. New York: Tor, 1983. pp. 289-309.

"Zenna Henderson's people," <u>Starship</u> No. 37:37-39. Winter 1979/1980. Originally published as the "Introduction" to <u>Pilgrimage: The Book of the People</u>. Boston: Gregg Press, 1979.

"Zenna Henderson: an appreciation," <u>Science Fiction Chronicle</u> 4(11):7. August 1983.

Miklos, Gyorgy

"A science fiction meghatarozasa," <u>SF Tajekoztato</u> p. 13-16. September 1971.

Miklovic, Janice

"Bio-bibliography of Lloyd Alexander, with an analysis of some of his fantasy works,"

Research paper, Kent State University, 1973. 65 p.

Miles, Ian

"Alternative Space Futures: The Next Quarter-Century," by Ian Miles and Micheil Schwarz. <u>Futures</u> 14(5): 462-482. October 1982.

Milicia, Joseph

"Dry thoughts in a dry season," <u>Riverside Quarterly</u> 7(4): 208-221. December 1985.

"Introduction," in: Aldiss, B. W. <u>Hothouse</u>. Boston: Gregg, 1976. pp. v-xvii.

"Introduction," in: Dick, P. K. <u>The Man in the High Castle</u>. Boston: Gregg, 1979. pp. v-xxxiv.

"Introduction," in: Stuart, W. J. <u>Forbidden Planet</u>. Boston: Gregg, 1978. pp. v-xvii.

Millar, Natalie

"Future Interview: John Brunner," <u>Future</u> 6: 70-71. November 1978.

Millard, John

"Worldcon Organization: operations at the convention," <u>MidAmerican Progress Report</u> No. 5:49-54. 1976.

Miller, Charlotte

"Two Teachers Look at E. T." by J. M. Roderick and Charlotte Miller. <u>English Journal</u> 72(5): 87-89. September 1983.

Miller, Chuck

<u>Fear Itself: The Horror Fiction of Stephen King</u>, by Tim Underwood and Chuck Miller. Columbia, PA: Underwood-Miller, 1982. 255 p.

<u>Jack Vance</u>, by Tim Underwood and Chuck Miller. New York: Taplinger, 1980. 252 p.

"1983/1984: the market for SF; an overview," <u>AB Bookman's Weekly</u> 74(14):2148-2152. October 1, 1984.

Miller, D. M.

<u>Frank Herbert</u>. Mercer Island, WA: Starmont, 1981. 70 p. (Starmont Reader's Guide, 5)

Miller, D. M. (Continued)

"Narrative pattern in _The Fellowship of the Ring_," in: Lobdell, Jared, ed. _A Tolkien Compass_. New York: Ballantine/Del Rey, 1980. pp. 103-115.

"Toward a Structural Metaphysic: Religion in the Novels of Frank Herbert," in: Reilly, Robert, ed. _The Transcendent Adventure_. Westport: Greenwood, 1984. pp. 145-156.

Miller, Dan

"Science fiction: future perfect turns to past tense," _American Libraries_ 6(3):168-169. March 1975.

Miller, Don

"Nebula Science Fiction: An Index," _SF&F Journal_ 91: NSF1-NSF14. May 1981.

Miller, Edwin

"Dune: Get an Eyeful of the Future," _Seventeen_ 44(1): 45-46, 96. January 1985.

Miller, Faren

"Recommended reading, 1984," _Locus_ 18(2): 23, 26. February 1985.

Miller, Fred, Jr.

"Introduction: The Philosophical Appeal of Science Fiction," by Fred Miller, Jr. and N. D. Smith. in: Smith, Nicholas D., ed. _Philosophers Look at Science Fiction_. Chicago: Nelson-Hall, 1982. pp. 1-19.

Miller, M. M.

Isaac Asimov: A Checklist of Works Published in the United States, March 1939-May 1972. Kent, Ohio: Kent State University Press, 1972. 98 p.

Machine in the Future: Man and Technology in the Science Fiction of Isaac Asimov. Masters Thesis, University of Maryland, 1969. 81 p.

"Social science fiction of Isaac Asimov, The," in: Olander, Joseph D. and Martin Harry Greenberg, eds. _Isaac Asimov_. New York: Taplinger, 1977. pp. 13-31.

Miller, M. Y.

"Hobbit: Or, There and Back Again, The," in: Magill, Frank N., ed. _Survey of Modern Fantasy Literature_, Vol 2. Englewood Cliffs, NJ: Salem Press, Inc., 1983. pp. 732-739.

"Three Damosels Trilogy, The," in: Magill, Frank N., ed. _Survey of Modern Fantasy Literature_, Vol 4. Englewood Cliffs, NJ: Salem Press, Inc., 1983. pp. 1908-1912.

"Green Sun: a study of color in J. R. R. Tolkien's The Lord of the Rings," _Mythlore_ 7(4):3-11. Winter 1981.

Miller, Margaret

"Ideal Woman in Two Feminist Science-Fiction Utopias," _Science-Fiction Studies_ 10(2): 191-198. July 1983.

Miller, Mark

"Dramatic television and agenda setting: the case of 'The Day After'." by Mark Miller and J. P. Quarles. 14 p. August 1984. ERIC ED 245 257.

Miller, Matthew

"In search of the wild Criblecoblis," _Empire: For the SF Writer_ 6(1): 12-14. Winter 1980.

Miller, P. S.

"Basic science fiction library, The," _Astounding Science Fiction_ 50(5):152-157. January 1953.

"Indexing science fiction," _The Indexer_ 6(4):163-164. Autumn 1969. (Reprinted from _Analog_ 83(3):163-165. May 1969.)

"Informal biography of Conan the Cimmerian," by J. D. Clark, P. S. Miller, and L. S. de Camp. in: De Camp, L. S., ed. _Blade of Conan_. New York: Ace, 1979. pp. 9-44.

"John W. Campbell," _Locus_ No. 90:7. July 12, 1971.

"Lord of the black throne," in: De Camp, L. S., ed. _Blade of Conan_. New York: Ace, 1979. pp. 77-82.

"Second guessing the poll," _Astounding Science Fiction_ 58(3):152-156. November 1956.

"Verdict of you all," _Astounding Science Fiction_ 58(2):150-153. October 1956.

Miller, Ron

Worlds Beyond: The Art of Chesley Bonestell, by Ron Miller and F. C. Durant, III. Norfolk: Donning, 1983. 133 p.

"Brief History of Space Art," in: Emme, Eugene M., ed. _Science Fiction and Space Futures_. San Diego: Univelt, 1982. pp. 107-119.

Miller, Ron (Continued)

"Chesley Bonestell: A Birthday Greeting," Starlog 79: 36-37, 67. February 1984.

"Evolution of the Spaceship; Part 1," Starlog 58: 26-27. May 1982.

"Evolution of the Spaceship; Part 2," Starlog 59: 56-57. June 1982.

"Evolution of the Spaceship; Part 3" Starlog 60: 54-55. July 1982.

"Futures Past: Jules Verne," Starlog 56: 54-56. March 1982.

"Portfolio: David Egge," Future Life 28: 58-63. August 1981.

"Portfolio: Ludek Pesek," Future Life 21: 58-63. September 1980.

"Prophecies that Failed," Starlog 57: 28-29. April 1982.

"Ralph 124C41+," Starlog 55: 60-61. February 1982.

"Worlds of Chesley Bonestell," Starlog 61: 34-35, 64. August 1982.

Miller, S. O.

Middle Earth: A World in Conflict. Baltimore: T-K Graphics, 1975. 82 p.

Mithrandir. Baltimore: T-K Graphics, 1974. 47 p.

Miller, S. R.

"Engl. 8284: intro to SF," Citadel 3:7-9. Summer 1971.

Miller, Sister Ignatius

"Visit to the Wade collection at Wheaton College, A," The Bulletin of the New York C. S. Lewis Society 7(12):5-7. 1976.

Millhauser, Milton

"Dr. Newton and Mr. Hyde: scientists in fiction from Swift to Stevenson," Nineteenth Century Fiction 28(3):287-304. December 1973.

Mills, Bart

"Last Starfighter," Sacramento Bee July 7, 1984. NewsBank. Film and Television. FTV 5: F4. 1984.

"Messianic Visions on a Grim Desert Planet," Kansas City Star in: NewsBank. Film and Television. 66:E9-E10. January 1985.

Mills, Nancy

"Film of '1984': The Timing is Perfect," Los Angeles Times June 24, 1984. NewsBank. Film and Television. FTV 6: E4-E5. 1984.

"Lea Thompson looks back at Future," Boston Herald July 5, 1985. in: NewsBank. Film and Television. 1:C3. July 1985.

Mills, R. P.

"Inside notes on F & SF," Fantasy Times No. 254:23-24. September (1) 1956.

Milman, Fern

"Human reactions to technological change in Asimov's fiction," in: Olander, Joseph D. and Martin Harry Greenberg, eds. Isaac Asimov. New York: Taplinger, 1977. pp. 120-134.

Milnes, C. P.

"Analysis of British and American fantasy in childrens literature," Research paper, Long Island University, 1969. 168 p.

Milosz, Czeslaw

"Science fiction and the coming of the antichrist," in: Milosz, Czeslaw. Emperor of the Earth: Modes of Eccentric Vision. University of California Press, 1977. pp. 15-31.

Milward, Peter

"Perchance to touch: Tolkien as scholar," Mythlore 6(4):31-32. Fall 1979.

Minc, R. S.

Fantastico y lo real en la narrativa de Juan Rulfo y Guadalupe Duenas, Lo. New York: Senda Nueva de Ediciones, 1977. 175 p.

Mines, Samuel

"Afterword," in: Walker, Paul. Speaking of Science Fiction. Oradell, New Jersey: Luna Publications, 1978. pp. 417-421.

"Blind or nightmare alley?" Fantasy Times No. 200:25,27-28. June (1) 1954.

Minichiello, Peter

"Introduction," in: Von Harbou, Thea. Metropolis. Boston: Gregg, 1975. pp. v-xv.

Minor, J.

"Luftfahrten in der deutshcen literatur. Ein Bibliographischer versuch," Zeitschrift fur Bucherfreunde N. F. Jg. 1909. Part 2, pp. 64-73.

Miranda, Vincent

"Fantastic Cinema," in: Tymn, Marshall B., ed. The Science Fiction Reference Book. Mercer Island, WA: Starmont House, 1981. pp. 56-62.

Mirlis, A. I.

"O klassifikacii naucno-fantasticeskoj literatury," Izdatel'skoe delo. Knigovedenie 2:4. 1969.

"Osobennosti redaktirovanija naucno-fantasticeskoj literatury," Kniga. Issledovanija i materialy. Moskva, 1971.

Mische, P. M.

"Feminism, militarism, and the need for an alternative world security system," Alternative Futures 4(2/3): 105-121. Spring/Summer 1981.

Mishan, E. J.

"Temple scientists, The," in: Hay, George, ed. The Disappearing Future: A Symposium of Speculation. London: Panther, 1970. pp. 72-78.

Miske, J. C.

"Characterization in imaginative literature," Arkham Sampler 2(2):75-80. Spring 1949.

Missiaja, Gianluigi

Catalogo generale della fantascienza, by Alfio Bertoni and Gianluigi Missiaja. Venezia: CCSF, 1968.

Mistichelli, J. A.

Jules Verne: A Primary and Secondary Bibliography. by E. J. Gallagher, J. A. Mistichelli, and J. A. Van Eerde. Boston: G. K. Hall, 1980. 544 p.

"Science Fiction at the Library of Congress," Special Collections 2(1/2): 9-24. Fall/Winter 1982.

Mitchell, Elizabeth

"Biolog: Jay Kay Klein," Analog 103(1): 49. January 1983.

Mitchell, Greg

"Meeting my maker: a visit with Kurt Vonnegut, Jr., by Kilgore Trout," Crawdaddy pp. 42-51. April 1, 1974.

Mitchell, Milo

"Blade Runner,", Prevue 2(9):32-35. August/September 1982.

"Krull," Prevue 2(12):54-61. June/July 1983.

Mitchell, S. O.

"Alien vision: the techniques of science fiction," Modern Fiction Studies 4(4):346-356. Winter 1958/1959.

Mitchell, Sean

"Will Their Wild Space Caper Play on This Planet?" Los Angeles Herald Examiner August 10, 1984. in: NewsBank. Film and Television FTV 22:A12. 1984.

Mitchell, Steve

"Special effects in 'Space: 1999'," Filmmakers Newsletter 10(1):23-27. November 1976.

Mitchell, T. F.

"John Schoenherr," Cinefantastique 14(4/5):91. September 1984.

"Science fiction illustrations," Missouri Review 7(2): 121-133. 1984.

Mitchison, Naomi

"Profession of Science Fiction, 23: Wonderful Deathless Ditties," Foundation 21: 27-34. February 1981.

Mitgang, Herbert

"Bookends: USSR SF," New York Times Book Review p. 23. July 3, 1977.

Mobley, Jane

Magic is Alive: A Study of Contemporary Fantasy Fiction. Ph.D. Dissertation, University of Kansas, 1974. 268 p.

Mobley, Jane (Continued)

"Fantasy in the college classroom," <u>CEA Critic</u> 40(2):2-6. January 1978.

"Toward a definition of fantasy fiction," <u>Extrapolation</u> 15(2):117-128. May 1974.

Mogen, David

<u>Wilderness Visions: Science Fiction Westerns, Volume 1.</u> San Bernardino, CA: Borgo, 1982. 64 p.

Mogno, Dario

"Trieste: the first science fiction festival," in: Johnson, William, ed. <u>Focus on the Science Fiction Film</u>. Englewood Cliffs, NJ: Prentice Hall, 1972. pp. 104-117.

Mohs, Mayo

"Science fiction and the world of religion (introduction)," in: Mohs, Mayo, ed. <u>Other Worlds, Other Gods; Adventures in Religious Science Fiction</u>. Garden City, New York: Doubleday, 1971. pp. 11-18.

Moir, Mike

"Final ballot for the 1985 BSFA Awards: detail of votes," <u>Matrix</u> 60:7. August/September 1985.

"Nominations for the 1985 BSFA Awards: Analysis of votes," <u>Matrix</u> No. 59: 4-6. June/July 1985.

Molesworth, Charles

"It's not nice to fool Mother Nature: the disaster movie and technological guilt," by Harold Schechter and Chares Molesworth. <u>Journal of American Culture</u> 1(1):44-50. Spring 1978.

Moller, S. K.

<u>Virkelige eventyr</u>, ed. by Ole Lindboe and Svend K. Moller. Copenhagen: Spar Knaegt, 1978. 168 p.

"Niels E. Nielsen. An introduction," by S. K. Moller and Jannick Pedersen. in: Dollerup, Cay, ed. <u>Volve. Scandinavian Views on Science Fiction</u>. Copenhagen: Department of English, Univ. of Copenhagen, 1978. pp. 55-59.

"Science ficiton Magasiner: en Vurdering og oversigt," <u>Proxima</u> No. 7:18-25. March 1976.

Molnar, Thomas

"Myth and utopia," <u>Modern Age</u> 17(1):71-77. Winter 1973.

Molson, F. J.

"<u>Alice's Adventures in Wonderland</u> and <u>Through the Looking-Glass</u>," in: Magill, Frank N., ed. <u>Survey of Modern Fantasy Literature</u>, Vol 1. Englewood Cliffs, NJ: Salem Press, Inc., 1983. pp. 7-16.

"<u>Chronicles of Prydain, The</u>," in: Magill, Frank N., ed. <u>Survey of Modern Fantasy Literature</u>, Vol 1. Englewood Cliffs, NJ: Salem Press, Inc., 1983. pp. 256-261.

"<u>Enchanted Castle, The</u>," in: Magill, Frank N., ed. <u>Survey of Modern Fantasy Literature</u>, Vol 1. Englewood Cliffs, NJ: Salem Press, Inc., 1983. pp. 483-485.

"<u>Psammead Trilogy, The</u>," in: Magill, Frank N., ed. <u>Survey of Modern Fantasy Literature</u>, Vol 3. Englewood Cliffs, NJ: Salem Press, Inc., 1983. pp. 1297-1300.

"Children's Fantasy and Science Fiction," in: Tymn, Marshall B., ed. <u>The Science Fiction Reference Book</u>. Mercer Island, WA: Starmont House, 1981. pp. 19-32.

"Children's Science Fiction," in: Barron, Neil, ed. <u>Anatomy of Wonder</u>. 2nd ed. New York: Barron, 1981. pp. 335-378.

"Earthsea Trilogy, The: ethical fantasy for children," in: De Bolt, Joe, ed. <u>Ursula K. Le Guin: Voyager to Inner Lands and to Outer Space</u>. Port Washington, New York: Kennikat, 1979. pp. 128-149.

"Ethical Fantasy For Children," in: Schlobin, Roger C., ed. <u>The Aesthetics of Fantasy Literature and Art</u>. Notre Dame, IN: University of Notre Dame Press, 1982. pp. 82-104.

"Juvenile science fiction, 1975-1976," <u>Children's Literature</u> 6:202-211. 1977.

"Tom Swift Novels, The," in: Magill, Frank N., ed. <u>Survey of Science Fiction Literature</u>, Vol. 5. Englewood Cliffs, NJ: Salem Press, 1979. pp. 2298-2302.

"Winston Science Fiction Series and the Development of Children's Science Fiction," <u>Extrapolation</u> 25(1): 34-49. Spring 1984.

Monard, Jean

<u>Merveilleux et la fantastique</u>, by Jean Monard and Michel Rech. Paris: Librairie Delagrave, 1974. 127 p.

Mondell, Paul

"Stop-Frame Fever, Post-Animation Blues,"
Cinefex 12: 28-49. April 1983.

Mondelle, S.

"Spider-man: superhero in the liberal
tradition," Journal of Popular Culture
10:232-238. Summer 1976.

Mongini, Giovanni

Storia del cinema di fantascienza. Rome:
Fanuci, 1976/1977. 2 v.

Monk, Patricia

"Frankenstein's Daughters: The Problems of the
Feminine Image in Science Fiction," Mosaic
13(3/4): 15-27. Spring/Summer 1980.

"Future of imperfect conjugation, The: Images
of marriage in science fiction," Mosaic
17(2): 207-222. Spring 1984.

"Syntax of future shock: structure and the
center of consciousness in John Brunner's The
Shockwave Rider," Extrapolation 26(3):
220-230. Fall 1985.

Monod, Jean

"Egy komputer pszichologiaja," by J. P. Dumont
and Jean Monod. Helikon 18(1): 94-104.
1972.

Monsman, Gerald

"Imaginative world of J. R. R. Tolkien, The,"
South Atlantic Quarterly 69:264-278. Spring
1970.

Montanari, Gianni

Fantascienza, La: gli authori e le opere.
Milan: Longanesi, 1978. 218 p.

Ieri, il futuro. Milan: Nord, 1977. 190 p.
(Based on the author's thesis: Prospettive
critiche della science fiction inglese:
1930-1970.)

"Autocrisi," in: Magill, Frank N., ed.
Survey of Science Fiction Literature, Vol. 1.
Englewood Cliffs, NJ: Salem Press, 1979. pp.
102-104.

"C'era una Volta un Planeta," in: Magill,
Frank N., ed. Survey of Science Fiction
Literature, Vol. 1. Englewood Cliffs, NJ:
Salem Press, 1979. pp. 322-324.

"Colonia Felice, La," in: Magill, Frank N.,
ed. Survey of Science Fiction Literature,
Vol. 1. Englewood Cliffs, NJ: Salem Press,
1979. pp. 406-408.

"Come ladro di notte," in: Magill, Frank
N., ed. Survey of Science Fiction
Literature, Vol. 1. Englewood Cliffs, NJ:
Salem Press, 1979. pp. 415-417.

"Dalla Terra alle stelle," in: Magill,
Frank N., ed. Survey of Science Fiction
Literature, Vol. 1. Englewood Cliffs, NJ:
Salem Press, 1979. pp. 465-467.

"Meraviglie del duemila, Le," in: Magill,
Frank N., ed. Survey of Science Fiction
Literature, Vol. 3. Englewood Cliffs, NJ:
Salem Press, 1979. pp. 1380-1382.

"Quando le Radici," in: Magill, Frank N.,
ed. Survey of Science Fiction Literature,
Vol. 4. Englewood Cliffs, NJ: Salem Press,
1979. pp. 1739-1741.

"Satana dei Miracoli," in: Magill, Frank
N., ed. Survey of Science Fiction
Literature, Vol. 4. Englewood Cliffs, NJ:
Salem Press, 1979. pp. 1863-1865.

"Tunnel Sottomarino, IL," in: Magill, Frank
N., ed. Survey of Science Fiction
Literature, Vol. 5. Englewood Cliffs, NJ:
Salem Press, 1979. pp. 2321-2323.

"Italian SF," in: Barron, Neil, ed. Anatomy
of Wonder. 2nd ed. New York: Bowker, 1981.
pp. 455-466.

Monteleone, T. F.

"Editing a SF Anthology, or, How much crap must
one take before it's sold?" Empire: For the
SF Writer 3(3): 32-34. November 1977.

"Fire and ice: on Roger Zelazny's short
fiction," Algol 13(2):9-14. Summer 1976.

"Introduction," in: Geston, M. S. Lords of
the Starship. Boston: Gregg, 1978. pp. v-xvi.

"Science fiction markets: where and to whom?"
in: Grant, C. L., ed. Writing and Selling
Science Fiction. Cincinnati, Ohio: Writers
Digest, 1976. pp. 19-32.

Montesi, A. J.

"John Coyne: the craftsman and the monsters,"
in: Schweitzer, Darrell, ed. Discovering
Modern Horror Fiction I. Mercer Island:
Starmont, 1985. pp. 106-128.

Monti, Alessandro

"Appunti preliminari per un saggio su Wells"
In: Utopia e fantascienza. Torino:
Giappichelli, 1975. p. 99-128.

Montunnas, Stanley

Arkady and Boris Strugatsky: Masters of Soviet
Science Fiction. Masters Thesis, San Diego
State University, 1974. 122 p.

Mooney, E. W.

"Untapped dimension in fiction," Virginia
Journal of Education 47:20-21. September
1953. Condensed, Education Digest 19:32-34.
November 1953.

Mooney, P. F.

Science Fiction Collections in the George
Arents Research Library at Syracuse
University. Syracuse: the library, undated.
11 p.

Moorcock, Michael

Epic Pooh. Essex: The British Fantasy
Society, 1978. 14 p. (BFS Booklet No. 4)

New Worlds: An Anthology. London:
Fontana/Flamingo, 1983. 512 p.

"New Worlds: a personal history,"
Foundation 15:5-18. January 1979.

"3, 2, 1, rip off: (Star Wars)," New
Statesman 94:857. December 16, 1977.

"Aspects of Fantasy," in: Schweitzer,
Darrell, ed. Exploring Fantasy Worlds. San
Bernardino, CA: Borgo, 1985. pp. 7-34.

"Pariotism and the scientific romance,"
London Magazine 15(5):48-59. December
1975/January 1976.

"Real ideas of Philip K. Dick," Vector 39:
7-14. April 1966.

"Starship stormtroopers," Anarchist Review
No. 4:41-44. No date.

"Wit and Humor in Fantasy," in: Boyer,
Robert H. and Zahorski, Kenneth J. Fantasists
on Fantasy. New York: Avon Discus, 1984.
261-276.

"Wit and humour in fantasy," Foundation
16:16-22. May 1979.

Moore, Maxine

"Asimov, Calvin, and Moses," in: Clareson, T.
D., ed. Voices For the Future: Essays on
Major Science Fiction Writers, Vol. 1.
Bowling Green, Ohio: Bowling Green University
Popular Press, 1976. pp. 88-104.

"Use of technical metaphors in Asimov's
fiction," in: Olander, Joseph D. and Martin
Harry Greenberg, eds. Isaac Asimov. New
York: Taplinger, 1977. pp. 59-96.

Moore, Patrick

Science and Fiction. London: G. G. Harrap,
1957. 192 p.

"Fiction to fact: when the writers become
prophets," in: Holdstock, Robert, ed.
Encyclopedia of Science Fiction. London:
Octopus, 1978. pp. 142-151.

"To other worlds," Listener 69:865-866.
May 23, 1963.

Moore, R. E.

"Science fiction in a junior college reading
program," Journal of Reading 9(5):329-332.
April 1966.

Moore, Raylyn

Wonderful Wizard, Marvelous Land. Bowling
Green, Ohio: Bowling Green University Popular
Press, 1974. 213 p.

Moore, Rosalie

"Science fiction and the main stream," in:
Bretnor, Reginald, ed. Modern Science
Fiction: Its Meaning and Its Future. New
York: Coward McCann, 1953. Reprinted,
Chicago: Advent, 1979. pp. 91-118.

Moorman, C. W.

"Heroism in The Lord of the Rings,"
Southern Quarterly 11(1):29-39. October
1972.

Moorman, Charles

"Space ship and grail: the myths of C. S.
Lewis," College English 18(8):401-405.
May 1957.

"Structures of Charles Williams' Arthurian
poetry," Studies in the Literary
Imagination 14(2):95-116. Fall 1981.

Moran, J. C.

F. Marion Crawford Companion. Westport, CT:
Greenwood, 1981. 548 p.

Seeking Refuge in Torre San Cicola: An
Introduction of F. Marion Crawford.
Nashville: Worthies Library, 1980. 86 p.

Moran, J. C. (Continued)

"Khaled: A Tale of Arabia," in: Magill, Frank N., ed. Survey of Modern Fantasy Literature, Vol 2. Englewood Cliffs, NJ: Salem Press, Inc., 1983. pp. 836-838.

"Wandering Ghosts," in: Magill, Frank N., ed. Survey of Modern Fantasy Literature, Vol 4. Englewood Cliffs, NJ: Salem Press, Inc., 1983. pp. 2054-2058.

"Witch of Prague, The," in: Magill, Frank N., ed. Survey of Modern Fantasy Literature, Vol 5. Englewood Cliffs, NJ: Salem Press, Inc., 1983. pp. 2136-2138.

Moreau, J. M.

"Appel des nebuleuses, L': fluidite des esperances dans la science fiction," Studies in Religion/Sciences Religieuses 7:335-345. 1978.

Moreau, P. F.

Recit utopique, Le, droit naturel et roman de l'etat. Paris: Presses universitaires de France, 1982. 142 p.

Morel, J.

"Rosny aine et la prehistorie," by J. Morel and P. Masse. Mercure de France 168:5. 1923.

"Rosny aine et le merveilleux scientifique," Mercure de France 187:82. 1926.

Morgan, Chris

Fritz Leiber: A Bibliography, 1934-1979. Birmingham, England: Morgenstern, 1979. 36 p.

Shape of Futures Past: The Story of Prediction. Exeter, Eng.: Webb & Bower, 1980. 208 p.

"Atlantis," in: Magill, Frank N., ed. Survey of Modern Fantasy Literature, Vol 1. Englewood Cliffs, NJ: Salem Press, Inc., 1983. pp. 71-73.

"Book of Wonder, The," in: Magill, Frank N., ed. Survey of Modern Fantasy Literature, Vol 1. Englewood Cliffs, NJ: Salem Press, Inc., 1983. pp. 161-163.

"Broken Sword," in: Magill, Frank N., ed. Survey of Modern Fantasy Literature, Vol 1. Englewood Cliffs, NJ: Salem Press, Inc., 1983. pp. 173-177.

"Duncton Wood," in: Magill, Frank N., ed. Survey of Modern Fantasy Literature, Vol 1. Englewood Cliffs, NJ: Salem Press, Inc., 1983. pp. 436-440.

"Ghost Stories," in: Magill, Frank N., ed. Survey of Modern Fantasy Literature, Vol 2. Englewood Cliffs, NJ: Salem Press, Inc., 1983. pp. 605-606.

"Kingdoms of Elfin," in: Magill, Frank N., ed. Survey of Modern Fantasy Literature, Vol 2. Englewood Cliffs, NJ: Salem Press, Inc., 1983. pp. 855-858.

"Quest of Excalibur, The," in: Magill, Frank N., ed. Survey of Modern Fantasy Literature, Vol 3. Englewood Cliffs, NJ: Salem Press, Inc., 1983. pp. 1301-1303.

"Shardik," in: Magill, Frank N., ed. Survey of Modern Fantasy Literature, Vol 3. Englewood Cliffs, NJ: Salem Press, Inc., 1983. pp. 1387-1391.

"Three Hearts and Three Lions," in: Magill, Frank N., ed. Survey of Modern Fantasy Literature, Vol 4. Englewood Cliffs, NJ: Salem Press, Inc., 1983. pp. 1913-1917.

"Till We Have Faces," in: Magill, Frank N., ed. Survey of Modern Fantasy Literature, Vol 4. Englewood Cliffs, NJ: Salem Press, Inc., 1983. pp. 1933-1937.

"Unlimited Dream Company, The," in: Magill, Frank N., ed. Survey of Modern Fantasy Literature, Vol 4. Englewood Cliffs, NJ: Salem Press, Inc., 1983. pp. 2002-2004.

"Alien encounter: the catalytic, ageless force," in: Holdstock, Robert, ed. Encyclopedia of Science Fiction. London: Octopus, 1978. pp. 104-121.

"Cordwainer Smith," in: Bleiler, E. F., ed. Science Fiction Writers. New York: Scribners, 1982. pp. 519-524.

"Hal Clement," in: Bleiler, E. F., ed. Science Fiction Writers. New York: Scribners, 1982. pp. 321-327.

"He That Plays the King: Colin Kapp Interview," Vector 108: 18-23. 1982.

"Incomplete Enchanter Series, The," in: Magill, Frank N., ed. Survey of Modern Fantasy Literature, Vol 2. Englewood Cliffs, NJ: Salem Press, Inc., 1983. pp. 768-772.

"Interview: Anne McCaffrey," Science Fiction Review 11(3): 20-24. August 1982.

"Judith Merril," in: Bleiler, E. F., ed. Science Fiction Writers. New York: Scribners, 1982. pp. 433-439.

"Robert Sheckley," in: Bleiler, E. F., ed. Science Fiction Writers. New York: Scribners, 1982. pp. 497-503.

"Short fiction of Anderson, The," in: Magill, Frank N., ed. Survey of Modern Fantasy Literature, Vol 3. Englewood Cliffs, NJ: Salem Press, Inc., 1983. pp. 1417-1419.

Morgan, Chris (Continued)

"Short fiction of Buchan, The," in: Magill, Frank N., ed. Survey of Modern Fantasy Literature, Vol 3. Englewood Cliffs, NJ: Salem Press, Inc., 1983. pp. 1482-1484.

"Short fiction of Pain, The," in: Magill, Frank N., ed. Survey of Modern Fantasy Literature, Vol 4. Englewood Cliffs, NJ: Salem Press, Inc., 1983. pp. 1662-1664.

Morgan, Dan

"Novacon 5 Guest-of-Honor speech," Vector 72: 5-13. February 1976.

Morgan, Edwin

"Unconcerned," New Statesman p. 545. April 15, 1966. (Book reviews)

Morgan, Ellen

"Alienation of the woman writer in The Golden Notebook," Contemporary Literature 14(4):471-480. Autumn 1973.

"Feminist novel of androgynous fantasy, The," Frontiers 2(3):40-49. Fall 1977.

Morgan, W. J.

"New novels," New Statesman p. 708. November 5, 1960. (Book reviews)

Morganti, Adolfo

Poul Anderson, tecnocrate e bardo. Pescara: "L'Altro Regno," 1981. 42 p.

Morgenstern, Joseph

"Kubrick's cosmos," Newsweek 71:97-100. April 15, 1968.

Morley, J.

"Science and literature," Nature 85:446-448. February 2, 1911. also in: Scientific American Supplement No. 1841:227-228. April 15, 1911.

Morley-Mower, G. F.

"Cabell under fire," Kalki 7(1):5-13. 1975.

"James Branch Cabell's flirtation with Clio: the story of a collaboration," Yale University Library Gazette 47(1):15-27. 1973. also in: Kalki 6(2):39-53. 1972.

Morressy, John

"SF in the classroom: a first attempt at Franklin Pierce," Extrapolation 20(2):129-132. Summer 1979.

Morris, Ann

"Counting Little Stars," Vector 116: 22-26. September 1983.

Morris, Christine

"Indians and other aliens; a native American view of science fiction," Extrapolation 20(4):301-307. Winter 1979.

Morris, E. G.

Science Fiction in the Tales of Edgar Allan Poe. Master's Thesis, University of South Carolina, 1948. 51 p.

Morris, Gerald

"Star Trek: The Motion Picture," Future 4: 34-35. August 1978.

Morris, Gregory L.

World of Order and Light: The Fiction of John Gardner. Athens: University of Georgia Press, 1984. 259 p.

Morris, Oswald

"Photographing The Dark Crystal," American Cinematographer 64(12): 1290-1291, 1312-1316. December 1982.

Morrison, Alasdair

"Uses of Utopia," in: Utopias, ed. by Peter Alexander and Roger Gill. London: Duckworth, 1984. pp. 139-152.

Morrison, Benjamin

"Hitch Hiker's Should Please...Others," New Orleans Times Picayune Sec. 2, p. 4. September 1, 1982.

Morrison, Bill

"Spaced out doctor visits Chapel Hill," Raleigh News and Observer. July 13, 1983. in: NewsBank. Film and Television. 12:A12-13. 1983.

Morrison, Henry

"John W. Campbell," <u>Locus</u> No. 91:9. July 22, 1971.

Morrison, John

"Obedience and surrender in Narnia," <u>CSL: The Bulletin of the New York C. S. Lewis Society</u> 7(12):2-4. 1976.

Morrison, L. D.

<u>J. R. R. Tolkien's The Fellowship of the Ring: A Critical Commentary</u>. New York: Monarch Press, 1976. 98 p.

Morrison, Michael

"Clive Barker: the delights of the dead," <u>Fantasy Review</u> 8(2): 35-37, 47. February 1985.

Morrissey, T. J.

"Armageddon From Huxley to Hoban," <u>Extrapolation</u> 25(3): 197-213. Fall 1984.

Morsberger, K. M.

"<u>Chronicles of the Canongate</u> and 'Wandering Willie's Tale'," in: Magill, Frank N., ed. <u>Survey of Modern Fantasy Literature</u>, Vol 1. Englewood Cliffs, NJ: Salem Press, Inc., 1983. pp. 262-265.

"<u>Clockwork Orange, A</u>," in: Magill, Frank N., ed. <u>Survey of Science Fiction Literature</u>, Vol. 1. Englewood Cliffs, NJ: Salem Press, 1979. pp. 396-401.

"<u>Land That Time Forgot, The</u>," by K. M. Morsberger and R. E. Morsberger. in: Magill, Frank N., ed. <u>Survey of Modern Fantasy Literature</u>, Vol 2. Englewood Cliffs, NJ: Salem Press, Inc., 1983. pp. 873-879.

"<u>Nineteen Eighty-Four</u>," in: Magill, Frank N., ed. <u>Survey of Science Fiction Literature</u>, Vol. 3. Englewood Cliffs, NJ: Salem Press, 1979. pp. 1531-1536.

"<u>Northanger Abbey</u>," in: Magill, Frank N., ed. <u>Survey of Modern Fantasy Literature</u>, Vol 3. Englewood Cliffs, NJ: Salem Press, Inc., 1983. pp. 1127-1131.

"<u>Slaughterhouse-Five</u>," in: Magill, Frank N., ed. <u>Survey of Science Fiction Literature</u>, Vol. 5. Englewood Cliffs, NJ: Salem Press, 1979. pp. 2101-2106.

"<u>Strange Case of Dr. Jekyll and Mr. Hyde, The</u>," in: Magill, Frank N., ed. <u>Survey of Science Fiction Literature</u>, Vol. 5. Englewood Cliffs, NJ: Salem Press, 1979. pp. 2184-2189.

"<u>Short fiction of James, The</u>," in: Magill, Frank N., ed. <u>Survey of Modern Fantasy Literature</u>, Vol 4. Englewood Cliffs, NJ: Salem Press, Inc., 1983. pp. 1568-1574.

Morsberger, R. E.

"<u>13 Clocks, The</u>," in: Magill, Frank N., ed. <u>Survey of Modern Fantasy Literature</u>, Vol 4. Englewood Cliffs, NJ: Salem Press, Inc., 1983. pp. 1904-1907.

"<u>Illustrated Man, The</u>," in: Magill, Frank N., ed. <u>Survey of Science Fiction Literature</u>, Vol. 2. Englewood Cliffs, NJ: Salem Press, 1979. pp. 1008-1013.

"<u>Land That Time Forgot, The</u>," by K. M. Morsberger and R. E. Morsberger. in: Magill, Frank N., ed. <u>Survey of Modern Fantasy Literature</u>, Vol 2. Englewood Cliffs, NJ: Salem Press, Inc., 1983. pp. 873-879.

"<u>She</u>," in: Magill, Frank N., ed. <u>Survey of Science Fiction Literature</u>, Vol. 4. Englewood Cliffs, NJ: Salem Press, 1979. pp. 1908-1912.

"<u>Short Fiction of Herman Melville, The</u>," in: Magill, Frank N., ed. <u>Survey of Science Fiction Literature</u>, Vol. 4. Englewood Cliffs, NJ: Salem Press, 1979. pp. 1989-1993.

"<u>Short Fiction of Nathaniel Hawthorne, The</u>," in: Magill, Frank N., ed. <u>Survey of Science Fiction Literature</u>, Vol. 4. Englewood Cliffs, NJ: Salem Press, 1979. pp. 2035-2041.

"<u>Tarzan of the Apes</u>," in: Magill, Frank N., ed. <u>Survey of Science Fiction Literature</u>, Vol. 5. Englewood Cliffs, NJ: Salem Press, 1979. pp. 2229-2235.

"<u>White Deer, The</u>," in: Magill, Frank N., ed. <u>Survey of Modern Fantasy Literature</u>, Vol 5. Englewood Cliffs, NJ: Salem Press, Inc., 1983. pp. 2118-2121.

"<u>Wonderful O, The</u>," in: Magill, Frank N., ed. <u>Survey of Modern Fantasy Literature</u>, Vol 5. Englewood Cliffs, NJ: Salem Press, Inc., 1983. pp. 2159-2161.

"Edgar Rice Burroughs' Apache epic," <u>Journal of Popular Culture</u> 7(2):280-287. Fall 1973.

"Shakespeare and science fiction," <u>Shakespeare Quarterly</u> 12(2):161. Spring 1961.

"Short fiction of Irving, The," in: Magill, Frank N., ed. <u>Survey of Modern Fantasy Literature</u>, Vol 4. Englewood Cliffs, NJ: Salem Press, Inc., 1983. pp. 1554-1562.

"Short fiction of Thurber, The," in: Magill, Frank N., ed. <u>Survey of Modern Fantasy Literature</u>, Vol 4. Englewood Cliffs, NJ: Salem Press, Inc., 1983. pp. 1712-1717.

Morse, A. R.

M. P. Shiel in Diverse Hands.   Dayton, OH:
J. D. S. Books, 1983. 491 p.

Works of M. P. Shiel: A Study in
Bibliography. Los Angeles: Fantasy
Publishing Company, 1948. 170 p.

Morse, Geraldine

"Vonda McIntyre: an interview,"   Galileo
No. 15:8-11. November 1979.

Morse, R. E.

"Rings of Power in Plato and Tolkien,"
Mythlore 7(3): 38. Autumn 1980.

Morson, G. S.

Boundries of Genre: Dostoevsky's Diary of a
Writer and the Traditions of Literary Utopia.
Austin, TX: University of Texas Press, 1981.
219 p.

"War of the Well(e)s, The,"   Journal of
Communication 29(3):10-20. Summer 1979.

Morton, J. F.

"Few Memories,"   in: Wetzel, George. Howard
Phillips Lovecraft: Memoirs, Critiques, &
Bibliographies. North Tonowonda, NY: SSR,
1955. pp. 8-9.

Morton, Nik

"Auguries of innocence,"   Focus: An SF
Writers' Magazine No. 11: 16-17. 1985.

"We Are Just Statistics,"   Vector 115:
7-14. 1983.

Mosca, Mariangela

"Fantascienza, q.b., nelle prime poere di
William Golding" In: Utiopia e fantascienza.
Torino: Giappichelli, 1975. p. 129-141.

Moser, Cliff

"Interview with Orson Scott Card, An,"
Science Fiction Review No. 32:32-35. August
1979.

Moshcovitz, P. B.

"2001: the media gets the message,"   ERB-dom
No. 36:7,14. July 1970.

"Captain Nemo and the Underwater City
(review),"   Cinefantastique 1(1):30-31.
Fall 1970.

Moshenskaia, L.

"Mir prikliuchenii i literatura,"   Voprosy
Literatury 9: 170-202. September 1982.

Mosig, Dirk

"At the Mountains of Madness," by Dirk Mosig
and D. R. Burleson. in: Magill, Frank N., ed.
Survey of Science Fiction Literature, Vol.
1. Englewood Cliffs, NJ: Salem Press, 1979.
pp. 97-101.

"'The White Ship': a Psychological Odyssey,"
in: Joshi, S. T., ed. H. P. Lovecraft: Four
Decades of Criticism. Athens, OH: Ohio
University Press, 1980. pp. 186-190.

"H. P. Lovecraft: Myth-Maker,"   in: Joshi, S.
T., ed. H. P. Lovecraft: Four Decades of
Criticism. Athens, OH: Ohio University
Press, 1980. pp. 104-112.

"Toward a greater appreciation of H. P.
Lovecraft: the analytical approach," in:
Wilson, Gahan, ed. First World Fantasy
Awards. Garden City, NY: Doubleday, 1977.
pp. 290-301.

Moskowitz, Sam

After Ten Years: A Tribute to Stanley G.
Weinbaum, 1902-1935, ed. by Gerry de la Ree
and Sam Moskowitz. Westwood, New Jersey:
Gerry de la Ree, 1945. 30 p.

Canticle for P. Schuyler Miller, A. Newark,
New Jersey: Moskowitz, 1975. 11 p.

Explorers of the Infinite: Shapers of Science
Fiction. New York: World, 1963. 350 p.

Hugo Gernsback: Father of Science Fiction.
New York: Criterion, 1959. 32 p.

Immortal Storm: A History of Science Fiction
Fandom, The. Atlanta: Burwell, 1951.
Reprinted, Atlanta: Atlanta Science Fiction
Organization Press, 1954. 269 p. Reprinted,
Westport, Connecticut: Hyperion Press, 1974.

Science Fiction by Gaslight: A History and
Anthology of Science Fiction in the Popular
Magazines, 1891-1911. Cleveland: World
Publishing, 1968. 364 p. Reprinted, New York:
Hyperion Press, 1974.

Science fiction in old San Francisco, Volume
1: History of the movement from 1854 to 1890.
West Kingston, RI: Donald M. Grant, 1980.

Seekers of Tomorrow. New York: Ballantine,
1967. 431 p.

Moskowitz, Sam (Continued)

Seekers of Tomorrow: Masters of Modern Science Fiction. Cleveland and New York: World Publishing, 1966. 441 p. Reprinted, Westport, Connecticut: Hyperion Press, 1974.

Strange Horizons: The Spectrum of Science Fiction. New York: Scribners, 1976. 298 p.

Under the Moons of Mars: A History and Anthology of 'The Scientific Romance' in the Munsey Magazines, 1912-1920. New York: Holt, Rinehart & Winston, 1970. 433 p.

"Adam Link: Robot," in: Magill, Frank N., ed. Survey of Science Fiction Literature, Vol. 1. Englewood Cliffs, NJ: Salem Press, 1979. pp. 22-27.

"Edison's Conquest of Mars," in: Magill, Frank N., ed. Survey of Science Fiction Literature, Vol. 2. Englewood Cliffs, NJ: Salem Press, 1979. pp. 698-702.

"Ghost Stories: neglected repository of supernatural fiction," ERB-dom No. 30:37-39. 1970.

"Girl in the Golden Atom, The," in: Magill, Frank N., ed. Survey of Science Fiction Literature, Vol. 2. Englewood Cliffs, NJ: Salem Press, 1979. pp. 878-882.

"30 years ago today," SF Times No. 329:x4,x6. December (2) 1959.

"A. E. Van Vogt," in: Moskowitz, Sam. Seekers of Tomorrow. New York: Ballantine, 1967. pp. 215-224.

"All our yesterdays have light, fool," Science Fiction Times No. 345:11-15. September (1) 1960.

"Anatomy of a Collection: The Sam Moskowitz Collection," Special Collections 2(1/2): 79-110. Fall/Winter 1982.

"Around the worlds with Jules Verne," in: Moskowitz, Sam. Explorers of the Infinite: Shapers of Science Fiction. New York: World, 1963. pp. 73-87.

"Arthur C. Clarke," in: Moskowitz, Sam. Seekers of Tomorrow. New York: Ballantine, 1967. pp. 371-387.

"Arthur Conan Doyle: a study in science fiction," in: Moskowitz, Sam. Explorers of the Infinite: Shapers of Science Fiction. New York: World, 1963. pp. 157-171.

"Barsoom (and Amtor) revisited," ERB-dom No. 23:3-5. April 1968.

"Better the world below than the world above," in: Moskowitz, Sam. Strange Horizons. New York: Scribners, 1976. pp. 92-106.

"Blish on Blish, a book review," Australian Science Fiction Review No. 16:3-7. June 1968.

"By the Waters of Lethe," Fantasy Times 1(10):2-5. December 1945.

"C. L. Moore," in: Moskowitz, Sam. Seekers of Tomorrow. New York: Ballantine, 1967. pp. 303-317.

"Case for science fiction, The," Arkham Sampler 2(1):35-40. Winter 1949.

"Clifford D. Simak," in: Moskowitz, Sam. Seekers of Tomorrow. New York: Ballantine, 1967. pp. 267-282.

"Comparisons are odious," Fantasy Times No. 2:5-6. October 1941.

"Cyrano de Bergerac: swordsman of space," in: Moskowitz, Sam. Explorers of the Infinite: Shapers of Science Fiction. New York: World, 1963. pp. 17-32.

"Dawn of fame: the career of Stanley G. Weinbaum," in: Moskowitz, Sam. Explorers of the Infinite: Shapers of Science Fiction. New York: World, 1963. pp. 296-312.

"Day of the Messiah, The," in: Moskowitz, Sam. Strange Horizons. New York: Scribners, 1976. pp. 22-49.

"E. E. Smith, Ph.D.," in: Moskowitz, Sam. Seekers of Tomorrow. New York: Ballantine, 1967. pp. 17-33

"Edmond Hamilton," in: Moskowitz, Sam. Seekers of Tomorrow. New York: Ballantine, 1967. pp. 73-89.

"Eric Frank Russell," in: Moskowitz, Sam. Seekers of Tomorrow. New York: Ballantine, 1967. pp. 137-153.

"Fabulous fantast: Fitz-James O'Brien, The," in: Moskowitz, Sam. Explorers of the Infinite: Shapers of Science Fiction. New York: World, 1963. pp. 62-72.

"Fantasy may come and fantasy may go," Fantasy Times 1(10):9-10. December 1945. (Reprinted from Sun Spots, Summer 1940.)

"Fritz Leiber," in: Moskowitz, Sam. Seekers of Tomorrow. New York: Ballantine, 1967. pp. 283-301.

"From Sherlock to spaceships," in: Moskowitz, Sam. Strange Horizons. New York: Scribners, 1976. pp. 122-159.

"Frome finale, The," Science Fiction Studies 12(3): 347-348. November 1985.

"Future in present tense," in: Moskowitz, Sam. Explorers of the Infinite: Shapers of Science Fiction. New York: World, 1963. pp. 334-350.

Moskowitz, Sam (Continued)

"Gernsback magazines no one knows," Riverside Quarterly 4(4): 272-274. March 1971.

"Ghosts of prophecies past, or, Frank Reade, Jr., and 'Forgotten Chapters in American History'," in: Moskowitz, Sam. Explorers of the Infinite: Shapers of Science Fiction. New York: World, 1963. pp. 106-127.

"Henry Kuttner," in: Moskowitz, Sam. Seekers of Tomorrow. New York: Ballantine, 1967. pp. 319-333.

"How science fiction got its name," Magazine of Fantasy and Science Fiction 12(2):65-77. February 1957.

"How science fiction gots its name," in: Moskowitz, Sam. Explorers of the Infinite: Shapers of Science Fiction. New York: World, 1963. pp. 313-333.

"Hugo Gernsback: 'Father of Science Fiction'," in: Moskowitz, Sam. Explorers of the Infinite: Shapers of Science Fiction. New York: World, 1963. pp. 225-242.

"I Remember Derleth," Starship 18(1): 7-14. Spring 1981.

"Immortal Storm, Part 18: XLII, Opinion Rallies," Fantasy Commentator 3(6): 172-182. Spring/Summer 1952.

"Immortal Storm: A History of Science-Fiction Fandom, Part 4," Fantasy Commentator 1(11): 288-299. Summer 1946.

"In giro intorno ai Mondi con Jules Verne," Cosmo informatore 14(2):23-32. Summer 1985.

"Invasion of the incredible headshrinkers, The," in: Moskowitz, Sam. Strange Horizons. New York: Scribners, 1976. pp. 107-121.

"Isaac Asimov," in: Moskowitz, Sam. Seekers of Tomorrow. New York: Ballantine, 1967. pp. 251-266.

"Jack Williamson," in: Moskowitz, Sam. Seekers of Tomorrow. New York: Ballantine, 1967. pp. 91-106.

"Jew in science fiction, The," Worlds of Tomorrow 4:109-122. November 1966.

"John W. Campbell," in: Moskowitz, Sam. Seekers of Tomorrow. New York: Ballantine, 1967. pp. 35-53.

"John Wyndham," in: Moskowitz, Sam. Seekers of Tomorrow. New York: Ballantine, 1967. pp. 123-136.

"Karel Capek, manden som opfandt roboter," in: Rejser i tid og rum. En Bog om science fiction, ed. by Tage La Cour. Copenhagen: Stig Verdelkaer, 1973.

"Karel Capek: the man who invented robots," in: Moskowitz, Sam. Explorers of the Infinite: Shapers of Science Fiction. New York: World, 1963. pp. 208-224.

"L. Sprague de Camp," in: Moskowitz, Sam. Seekers of Tomorrow. New York: Ballantine, 1967. pp. 155-169.

"Lester del Rey," in: Moskowitz, Sam. Seekers of Tomorrow. New York: Ballantine, 1967. pp. 171-198.

"Lo! The poor Forteans," in: Moskowitz, Sam. Strange Horizons. New York: Scribners, 1976. pp. 218-248.

"Lore of H. P. Lovecraft, The," in: Moskowitz, Sam. Explorers of the Infinite: Shapers of Science Fiction. New York: World, 1963. pp. 243-260.

"Marvelous A. Merritt, The," in: Moskowitz, Sam. Explorers of the Infinite: Shapers of Science Fiction. New York: World, 1963. pp. 189-207.

"More on the OAK-ERB feud," Oak Leaves 1(7):3. Spring 1972.

"Murray Leinster," in: Moskowitz, Sam. Seekers of Tomorrow. New York: Ballantine, 1967. pp. 55-72.

"Negro in science fiction, The," Worlds of Tomorrow 4(4):40-54. May 1967.

"Newly discovered letters reinforce Gernsback's claim to have coined the term science fiction," Science Fiction Times No. 448:1-2. November 1967.

"Nolacon report," Fantasy Times No. 137:2-4. September (1) 1951.

"OAK-ERB feud," Oak Leaves 1(4):8-10. Summer 1971.

"Olaf Stapledon: cosmic philosopher," in: Moskowitz, Sam. Explorers of the Infinite: Shapers of Science Fiction. New York: World, 1963. pp. 261-277.

"Olaf Stapledon: The Man Behind the Works," Fantasy Commentator 4(1): 3-26, 32-34. Winter 1978-79.

"On Nils Frome and Blish, Lovecraft, et al," Science Fiction Studies 12(2): 229-236. July 1985.

"Peace and Olaf Stapledon," Fantasy Commentator 4(2): 72-81. Winter 1979-80.

"Philip Jose Farmer," in: Moskowitz, Sam. Seekers of Tomorrow. New York: Ballantine, 1967. pp. 389-405.

Moskowitz, Sam (Continued)

"Pilgrim's Progress: Prelude and Postscript to the Publication of J. O. Bailey's Pilgrims Through Space and Time," in: Wolfe, Gary, ed. Science Fiction Dialogues. Chicago: Academy Chicago, 1982. pp. 181-190.

"Portraitist of prescience," in: Moskowitz, Sam. Strange Horizons. New York: Scribners, 1976. pp. 249-270.

"Prophetic Edgar Allan Poe, The," in: Moskowitz, Sam. Explorers of the Infinite: Shapers of Science Fiction. New York: World, 1963. pp. 46-61.

"Ray Bradbury in France," Riverside Quarterly 3(3): 226-228. August 1968.

"Ray Bradbury," in: Moskowitz, Sam. Seekers of Tomorrow. New York: Ballantine, 1967. pp. 351-370.

"Real Earth satellite story, The," in: Moskowitz, Sam. Explorers of the Infinite: Shapers of Science Fiction. New York: World, 1963. pp. 88-105.

"Realizing the Impossible Dream: The First Science Fiction Course in Academe," Fantasy Commentator 5(1): 1-25, 40-43. Winter 1983.

"Remembrance of Paul," Science Fiction Times Vol. 3a:3-4. November 1963.

"Research in progress," Science Fiction Studies 5(1):88. March 1978.

"Road to Avalon: the grand old man of science fiction, Dr. David H. Keller," Fantasy Times No. 58:2-5. November 1947.

"Robert A. Heinlein," in: Moskowitz, Sam. Seekers of Tomorrow. New York: Ballantine, 1967. pp. 191-214.

"Robert Bloch," in: Moskowitz, Sam. Seekers of Tomorrow. New York: Ballantine, 1967. pp. 335-349.

"Rockets to green pastures," in: Moskowitz, Sam. Strange Horizons. New York: Scribners, 1976. pp. 50-69.

"Science fiction and films," in: SF Symposium, Instituto Nacional de Cinema, Brazil, 1969.

"Science fiction market survey, 1956," in: Science Fiction Yearbook, 1957 Edition. Vol. 1. Patterson, NJ: Fandom House, 1957. pp. 25-39.

"Science fiction upswing: a cyclic condition," Fantasy Times No. 200:7-8. June (1) 1954.

"Secret of Warner Van Lorne solved," Science Fiction Times No. 399/400:21-23. January/February 1963.

"Significance of the first post-war science fiction convention," Fantasy Times 1(12):3-7. June 1946.

"Sons of Frankenstein, The," Satellite 2(6):112-121. August 1958.

"Sons of Frankenstein, The," in: Moskowitz, Sam. Explorers of the Infinite: Shapers of Science Fiction. New York: World, 1963. pp. 33-45.

"Space opus: Philip Wylie," in: Moskowitz, Sam. Explorers of the Infinite: Shapers of Science Fiction. New York: World, 1963. pp. 278-295.

"Space, God, and science fiction," in: Moskowitz, Sam. Strange Horizons. New York: Scribners, 1976. pp. 3-21.

"Starburst," in: Moskowitz, Sam. Seekers of Tomorrow. New York: Ballantine, 1967. pp. 407-424.

"Sturgeon, Nolan and me," Science Fiction Times No. 452:6. March 1968.

"Superman," in: Moskowitz, Sam. Seekers of Tomorrow. New York: Ballantine, 1967. pp. 107-122.

"Theodore Sturgeon," in: Moskowitz, Sam. Seekers of Tomorrow. New York: Ballantine, 1967. pp. 231-249.

"This is the ESFA," Science Fiction Adventures 1(6): 74-81. September 1953.

"Thomas S. Gardner dead at 55," Science Fiction Times No. 409/410:13-15. December 1963.

"Thoughts About C. L. Moore," Fantasy Commentator 4(2): 85-90. Winter 1979-80.

"Time stream," Fantasy Times No. 100:17-19. February (2) 1950. (Reprint)

"Time stream: polls, polls, polls, part 1," Fantasy Times No. 9:1-4. May 1944.

"Time stream: polls, polls, polls, part 2 (resume' of science fiction polls)," Fantasy Times No. 10:1-4. June 1944.

"Time waits for no one; an editorial," Fantasy Times 1(10):1. December 1945.

"To Barsoom and back with Edgar Rice Burroughs," in: Moskowitz, Sam. Explorers of the Infinite: Shapers of Science Fiction. New York: World, 1963. pp. 172-188.

"Tom Swift and the syndicate," in: Moskowitz, Sam. Strange Horizons. New York: Scribners, 1976. pp. 160-181.

"Tribute to Walter Sullivan," Fantasy Times 1(12):2-3. June 1946.

Moskowitz, Sam (Continued)

"Twenty-first anniversary of science fiction magazines," <u>Fantasy Times</u> No. 46:38-39. April 13, 1947.

"Unprodigal publisher returns," <u>Fantasy Times</u> 1(12):1. June 1946.

"Virgil Finley: an appreciation," in: Finley, Virgil. <u>Virgil Finlay</u>. West Kingston, RI: Grant, 1971. pp. 66-94.

"Voice of science fiction, The," <u>Fantasy Times</u> No. 254:32-38. September (1) 1956.

"Voyagers Through Eternity: A History of Science-Fiction From the Beginnings to H. G. Wells, Part II," <u>Fantasy Commentator</u> 4(4): 206-212, 259-265. Winter 1982.

"Voyagers Through Eternity: A History of Science-Fiction From the Beginnings to H. G. Wells, Part I," <u>Fantasy Commentator</u> 4(3): 127-145, 190-192. Winter 1981.

"Voyagers Through Eternity: A History of Science-Fiction From the Beginnings to H. G. Wells, Part III," <u>Fantasy Commentator</u> 5(1): 55-64. Winter 1983.

"Warriors of if," in: Moskowitz, Sam. <u>Strange Horizons</u>. New York: Scribners, 1976. pp. 182-217.

"When women rule," in: Moskowitz, Sam, ed. <u>When Women Rule</u>. New York: Walker, 1972. pp. 1-27.

"When women rule," in: Moskowitz, Sam. <u>Strange Horizons</u>. New York: Scribners, 1976. pp. 70-91.

"Why editors get gray," <u>Fantasy Times</u> No. 63:1. March 1948.

"Wonders of H. G. Wells, The," in: Moskowitz, Sam. <u>Explorers of the Infinite: Shapers of Science Fiction</u>. New York: World, 1963. pp. 128-141.

"World, the devil, and M. P. Shiel, The," in: Moskowitz, Sam. <u>Explorers of the Infinite: Shapers of Science Fiction</u>. New York: World, 1963. pp. 142-156.

Moslander, P. E.

"Kiss the blood off my other sword: part II of an examination of John Norman's Gor books," <u>PSFQ</u> (Cupertino, California) No. 3/4:22-25. 1978/1979.

"Kiss the Blood Off My Sword: Dominence-Questing Through Gor, part 1," <u>PSFQ</u> (Cupertino, California) 2: 18-21. Summer 1978.

Moss, Anita

<u>Children and Fairy Tales: A Study in Nineteenth Century British Fantasy</u>. Ph. D. Dissertation, Indiana University, 1979. 387 p.

"'Felicitous Space' in the Fantasies of George MacDonald and Mervyn Peake," <u>Mythlore</u> 8(4): 16-17, 42. Winter 1982.

"Crime and Punishment; Or Development; in Fairy Tales and Fantasy," <u>Mythlore</u> 8(1): 26-28. Spring 1981.

"Pastoral and heroic patterns: their uses in children's fantasy," in: Collins, R. A., ed. <u>Scope of the Fantastic: Culture, Biography, Themes, Children's Literature</u>. Westport: Greenwood, 1985. pp. 231-238.

Mothner, I.

"Those clean-living all American monsters," <u>Look</u> 28(18):50. September 8, 1964.

Motz, Lloyd

"Space books: which and why," by Lloyd Motz and M. R. Motz. <u>Top of the News</u> 17(4):7-15. May 1961. (deals with nonfiction only)

Motz, M. R.

"Space books: which and why," by Lloyd Motz and M. R. Motz. <u>Top of the News</u> 17(4):7-15. May 1961. (deals with nonfiction only)

Mounin, Georges

"Kommunikacio a vilagurrel," <u>Helikon</u> 18(1): 89-93. 1972.

"Poesie ou science fiction?" <u>Les Temps Modernes</u> No. 119:740-746. November 1955.

Moura, Irineu de

"Evolucao de monstros na ficcao cientifica," <u>Vozes</u> 72(8):68-70. October 1978.

"Ficcao cientifica francesa no Brasil," <u>Vozes</u> 71(2):51-58. March 1977.

Moylan, Tom

"Gladiator-at-Law," in: Magill, Frank N., ed. <u>Survey of Science Fiction Literature</u>, Vol. 2. Englewood Cliffs, NJ: Salem Press, 1979. pp. 894-898.

Moylan, Tom (Continued)

"Triton," in: Magill, Frank N., ed.
Survey of Science Fiction Literature, Vol. 5.
Englewood Cliffs, NJ: Salem Press, 1979. pp.
2307-2310.

"Beyond Negation: The Critical Utopias of
Ursula K. Le Guin and Samuel R. Delany,"
Extrapolation 2(1): 236-253. Fall 1980.

"Idealogical contradiction in Clarke's The
City and the Stars," Science Fiction
Studies 4(2):150-157. July 1977. Comments,
5(1):88-90. March 1978. 5(3):303-304.
November 1978. 5(3):304-306. November 1978.

"Locus of Hope: Utopia Versus Ideology,"
Science-Fiction Studies 9(2): 159-166. July
1982.

"Someday the Gross Repair Will be Done: History
and Utopia in Marge Piercy's Woman on the Edge
of Time," in: Wolfe, Gary, ed. Science
Fiction Dialogues. Chicago: Academy Chicago,
1982. pp. 133-140.

Moynihan, Martin

"Cocoon," Albany N. Y. Times Union June
16, 1985. in: NewsBank. Film and
Television. 2:C13-C14. July 1985.

Muchnic, Suzanne

"Apocalyptic visions on view," Los Angeles
Times July 6, 1985. in: NewsBank. Fine
Arts and Architecture 1:B14. July 1985.

Mueller, Joachim

"Interview mit Martin Eisele," Science
Fiction Times (Germany) 27(11):5-9. November
1985.

"Interview mit Roland Emmerich," Science
Fiction Times (Germany) 27(9/10):9-11.
September/October 1985.

Mulcahy, Kevin

"Avram Davidson," in: Cowart, David, ed.
Twentieth-Century American Science-Fiction
Writer, Part 1: A-L. Detroit: Gale, 1981.
pp. 109-112. (Dictionary of Literary
Biography, v. 8)

Mullaney, M. M.

"Alexandra Kollontai and the vision of a
socialist feminist utopia," Alternative
Futures 4(2/3): 73-84. Spring/Summer 1981.

Mullen, R. D.

Science Fiction Studies: Selected Articles on
Science Fiction 1973-1975, ed. by R. D.
Mullen and Darko Suvin. Boston: Gregg Press,
1976. 304 p.

"Sunken World, The: also two visions in
one," Science Fiction Studies
1(4):292-297. Fall 1974.

"23 'classics' of SF: the Hyperion reprints,"
Science Fiction Studies 1(4):300-305. Fall
1974.

"Arno reprints, The," Science Fiction
Studies 2(2):179-195. July 1975.

"Blish, Van Vogt, and the uses of Spengler,"
Riverside Quarterly 3(3): 172-186. August
1968.

"Books and principal pamphlets of H. G. Wells:
a chronological survey, The," Science
Fiction Studies 1(2):114-135. Fall 1973.

"Books of H. Rider Haggard: a chronological
survey, The," Science Fiction Studies
5(3):287-291. November 1978.

"Books, stories, essays," Science Fiction
Studies 2(1):5-8. March 1975.

"Edgar Rice Burroughs and the fate worse than
death," Riverside Quarterly 4(3): 186-191.
June 1970.

"Garland library of science fiction, The,"
Science Fiction Studies 2(3):280-288.
November 1975.

"Gregg Press science fiction series, The,"
Science Fiction Studies 2(3):274-278.
November 1975.

"H. G. Wells and Victor Rouseau Emanuel: When
the Sleeper Wakes and The Messiah of the
Cylinder," Extrapolation 8(2):31-63. May
1967.

"H. G. Wells: the old orthodoxy and the new,"
Riverside Quarterly 3(1): 66-68. August
1967.

"Hyperion reprints: addenda, The," Science
Fiction Studies 2(1):95-97. March 1975.

"I could not love thee, dear, so much,"
Science Fiction Studies 4(2):143-144. July
1977.

"I told you so: Wells' last decade,
1936-1946," in: Suvin, Darko and Robert M.
Philmus, eds. H. G. Wells and Modern Science
Fiction. Lewisburg: Bucknell University
Press, 1977. pp. 116-125.

"Index to American mass-market paperbacks, An,"
Science Fiction Studies 1(3):222-223.
Spring 1974. (Book reviews)

Mullen, R. D. (Continued)

"No time for evolution," <u>Science Fiction Studies</u> 6(2):209-215. July 1979. (Book review)

"Prudish prurience of H. Rider Haggard and Edgar Rice Burroughs (part two), The," <u>Riverside Quarterly</u> 6:134-146. 1974.

"Prudish prurience of H. Rider Haggard and Edgar Rice Burroughs, The," <u>Riverside Quarterly</u> 6:4-19. 1973.

"Undisciplined imagination: Edgar Rice Burroughs and Lowellian Mars, The," in: Clareson, T. D., ed. <u>SF: The Other Side of Realism</u>. Bowling Green, Ohio: Bowling Green University Popular Press, 1971. pp. 229-247.

Muller, Al

"Mote in God's Eye, The," in: Magill, Frank N., ed. <u>Survey of Science Fiction Literature</u>, Vol. 3. Englewood Cliffs, NJ: Salem Press, 1979. pp. 1463-1467.

"Science Fiction and Fantasy Series Books," by Al Muller and C. W. Sullivan, III. <u>English Journal</u> 69(7): 71-74. October 1980.

Muller, H. J.

"Note on utopia, A," in: Muller, Herbert J. <u>The Children of Frankenstein: A Primer on Modern Technology and Human Values</u>. Bloomington: Indiana University Press, 1970. pp. 369-384.

"Science fiction as an escape," <u>The Humanist</u> 17(1):333-337. January/ February 1957. also in: Muller, H. J. <u>Man's Future Birthright</u>. pp. 8-22.

Mumford, David

"Tomorrowland 1986," by Bruce Gordon and David Mumford. <u>Starlog</u> 99: 50-53. October 1985.

Mumford, Lewis

<u>Story of Utopias, The</u>. New York: Boni & Liveright, 1922. 315 p.

Mumper, Mark

"Sf: a literature of humanity," <u>Extrapolation</u> 14(1):90-94. December 1972.

Munn, H. W.

"To Saint Joan," <u>Fantasy Newsletter</u> 2(12): 7-9. December 1980.

Munsky, Wolfgang

"Welt als Schreckenkabinett," in: Thomsen, C. W., ed. <u>Phantastik in Literatur und Kunst</u>. Darmstadt: Wissenschaftliche Buchgesellschaft, 1980. pp. 471-491.

Munson, Brad

"Brainstorm: getting the cookie at the end," <u>Cinefex</u> No. 14:26-49. October 1983.

"Final voyage of the Starship Enterprise," <u>Cinefex</u> No. 18:42-67. August 1984.

"Greg Jein: Miniature Giant," <u>Cinefex</u> 2: 24-49. August 1980.

"Return to Oz," <u>Cinefex</u> No. 22:4-41. June 1985.

"Something Wicked This Way Comes: Adding the Magic," <u>Cinefex</u> 12: 4-27. April 1983.

Munson, Ronald

"Clockwork future: dystopia, social planning, and freedom, The," in: Kaplan, Sylvan J., ed. <u>Ecology and the Quality of Life</u>. Springfield, Illinois: Charles C. Thomas, 1974. pp. 26-38.

"Sf: the literature of possibility," <u>Extrapolation</u> 15(1):35-41. December 1973.

Murall, Lorris

"Chevaliers et des sorciers, Des," <u>Magazine Litteraire</u> 88:23-25. May 1974.

Murat, Napoleon

"Reve et creation chez Lovecraft," in: <u>H. P. Lovecraft</u>. Paris: Editions de l'Herne, 1969. pp. 126-132.

Murdoch, B.

"Overpopulated wasteland: myth in Anthony Burgess' 'The Wanting Seed', The," <u>Revue des Langues Vivantes</u> 39(3):203-217. 1973.

Muren, Dennis

"Jedi Journal," by Richard Edlund, Dennis Muren, and Ken Ralston. <u>Cinefex</u> 13: 4-67. July 1983.

Murphy, Brian

<u>C. S. Lewis.</u> Mercer Island, WA: Starmont, 1983. 95 p.

Murphy, Brian (Continued)

"News from Nowhere," in: Magill, Frank N., ed. _Survey of Science Fiction Literature_, Vol. 3. Englewood Cliffs, NJ: Salem Press, 1979. pp. 1516-1520.

"Perelandra," in: Magill, Frank N., ed. _Survey of Science Fiction Literature_, Vol. 4. Englewood Cliffs, NJ: Salem Press, 1979. pp. 1669-1673.

"Enchanted rationalism: the legacy of C. S. Lewis," _Christianity and Literature_ 25(2):13-29. 1976.

Murphy, Carol

"Of grace and Gollum," _Approach_ 62:34-37. Winter 1967.

"Theology of science fiction, The," _Approach_ (Rosemont, Pennsylvania) No. 23:2-7. 1957.

Murphy, Laura

"Marion Zimmer Bradley," in: Cowart, David, ed. _Twentieth-Century American Science Fiction Writers, Part 1: A-L_. Detroit: Gale, 1981. pp. 77-80. (Dictionary of Literary Biography, v. 8)

Murphy, Richard

Imaginary Worlds: Notes on a New Curriculum. New York: Teachers and Writers Collaborative, 1974. 110 p.

Murray, Albert

"Social science fiction in Harlem," _New Leader_ 49(2):20-23. January 17, 1966. (not about SF)

Murray, D. C.

"Interview: Arthur C. Clarke," _Science Fiction Chronicle_ 4(9):1,20-21. June 1983.

Murray, Peggy

"Fantasy: A Reader's List," by Terri Lehan and Peggy Murray. _Voice of Youth Advocates_ 5(4): 28-34. October 1982.

Murray, Will

"Secret Agent X," in: Tymn, M. B. and Ashley, Mike. _Science Fiction, Fantasy, and Weird Fiction Magazines_. Westport, CT: Greenwood, 1985. pp. 567-568.

"Shadow," by Will Murray and Robert Weinberg. in: Tymn, M. B. and Ashley, Mike. _Science Fiction, Fantasy, and Weird Fiction Magazines_. Westport, CT: Greenwood, 1985. pp. 570-573.

"Sheena, Queen of the Jungle," in: Tymn, M. B. and Ashley, Mike. _Science Fiction, Fantasy, and Weird Fiction Magazines_. Westport, CT: Greenwood, 1985. pp. 575-576.

"Doc Savage returns to radio," _Starlog_ No. 101: 50-51. December 1985.

"Fred Ward: it's hard to be a hero," _Starlog_ No. 101:24-28. December 1985.

"On the set of Remo: The First Adventure," _Starlog_ 99: 65-68. October 1985.

"One Hundred Most Important People in Science Fiction/Fantasy: Edmond Hamilton," _Starlog_ 100: 62. November 1985.

"One Hundred Most Important People in Science Fiction/Fantasy: H. P. Lovecraft," _Starlog_ 100: 76. November 1985.

"Starlog Profile: Fred Ward," _Starlog_ No. 101: 24-28. December 1985.

"Unknown _Unknown_, The (including contents listing)," _Xenophile_ No. 42:11-15. September/October 1979.

Myers, Alan

"Science fiction in the classroom," _Children's Literature in Education_ 9(4):182-187. Winter 1978.

"Some Developments in Soviet SF since 1966," _Foundation_ 19: 38-46. June 1980.

Myers, D. T.

"Brave new world: the status of women according to Tolkien, Lewis and Williams," _Cimarron Review_ No. 17:13-19. October 1971.

"C. S. Lewis' Passages," _Mythlore_ 11(3): 52-56. Winter/Spring 1985.

Myers, David

"Kurt Vonnegut, Jr.: morality-myth in the antinovel," _International Fiction Review_ 3:52-56. 1976.

Myers, Doris

"Sexual politics of Robert A. Heinlein," _Arizona English Bulletin_ 51(1):49-52. October 1972.

Myers, Eric

"Just imagine: fantasy and futurism," by Howard Mandelbaum and Eric Myers. in: Mandelbaum, Howard and Eric Myers. <u>Screen Deco</u>. New York: St. Martins, 1985. pp. 163-168.

Myers, Fred

"Sci-Fi Triumph," <u>Christian Century</u> 85: 844-846. June 1968.

Myers, R. E.

<u>Intersection of Science Fiction and Philosophy: Critical Studies</u>, ed. by Robert E. Myers. Westport, CT: Greenwood, 1983. 262 p.

<u>Jack Williamson: A Primary and Secondary Bibliography</u>. Boston: G. K. Hall, 1980. 93 p.

"Elusive Self and the Intimidating Other," in: Smith, Nicholas D., ed. <u>Philosophers Look at Science Fiction</u>. Chicago: Nelson-Hall, 1982. pp. 127-142.

"Jack Williamson," in: Bleiler, E. F., ed. <u>Science Fiction Writers</u>. New York: Scribners, 1982. pp. 225-231.

"Philosophic insight through science fiction: focusing on human problems," in: Williamson, Jack, ed. <u>Teaching Science Fiction: Education for Tomorrow</u>. Philadelphia: Owlswick, 1980. pp. 177-183.

Myers, Victoria

"Conversational Technique In Ursula K. Le Guin: A Speech-Act Analysis," <u>Science Fiction Studies</u> 10(3): 306-316. November 1983.

N

Nadeau, M.

"Lovecraft superieur a Poe?"
France-Observateur 7.10.1954.

Nadeau, Robert

Readings From the New Book on Nature: Physics and Metaphysics in the Modern Novel.
Amherst: University of Massachusetts Press, 1981. 213 p.

Nagl, Manfred

Einfuehrung in die Analyse von Science Fiction. Tubingen: Narr, 1979.

Science Fiction in Deutschland: Untersuchungen zur Genese, Soziographie und Ideologie der phantastischen Massenliteratur. Tuebingen: Tubeinger Vereinigung fuer Volkskund, 1972. 279 p.

Science Fiction. Ein Segment populaerer Kultur im Medien und Produktverbund. Tubigen: Narr, 1981. 262 p.

"National Peculiarities in German Science Fiction: Science Fiction as a National and Topical Literature," *Science-Fiction Studies.* 8(1): 29-34. March 1981.

"Science Fiction Film in Historical Perspective," *Science Fiction Studies* 10(3): 262-277. November 1983.

"SF, occult sciences, and Nazi myths," *Science Fiction Studies* 1(3):185-197. Spring 1974.

"Unser mann im all. Bemerkungen zu 'Perry Rhodan', der 'grossten science fiction serie der welt'," *Zeitnahe Schularbeit* 22(415):189-208. April/May 1969.

Naha, Ed

Making of Dune, The. New York: Berkley, 1984. 299 p.

Science Fictionary, The: an A-Z Guide to the World of SF Authors, Films, & TV Shows. New York: Seabury, 1980. 388 p.

"'Cat People' Conspiracy," *Starlog* 59: 22-24. June 1982.

"'Krull': A Visit to a Not-so-Small Planet," *Starlog* 76: 48-53, 94. November 1983.

"1980 meets 1941," *Future Life* 22: 51, 67. November 1980.

"Altered States of Moviemaking," *Future Life* 24: 28-31, 67. February 1981.

"Battle Beyond the Stars," *Future Life* 21: 28-32, 57. September 1980.

"Beyond the Star Wars," *Future Life* 19: 26-27, 56. June 1980.

"Black Hole," by David Houston and Ed Naha. *Future Life* 16: 52-55, 63. February 1980.

"Boris: The Fantastic Art of Boris Vallejo," by Ed Naha and Richard Meyers. *Future* 3: 66-75. July 1978.

"Conan the Barbarian," *Starlog* 59: 16-21, 65. June 1982.

"Cosmic Cheesecake," *Future Life* 21: 47-49. September 1980.

"Cosmic Love Story: Altered States," *Future Life* 25: 44-47. March 1981.

"Designing the 23rd Century," *Future Life* 17: 45-47, 81. March 1980.

"Escape From New York," *Future Life* 30: 45-49. November 1981.

"Films of Jules Verne," *Future* 3: 34-39, 47. July 1978.

"Flash Gordon Finds His Roots," *Future Life* 24: 14-19. February 1981.

"Flashy designs," *Future Life* 23: 48-52. December 1980.

"Free enterprise," *Crawdaddy* pp. 42-49. December 1976.

Naha, Ed (Continued)

"Gerry Anderson: the master of space," _Starlog_ 9:30-33. 1977.

"Inside E. T.," _Starlog_ 63: 16-20, 65. October 1982.

"It's Sinbad taste," _Crawdaddy_ pp. 33-35. July 1977.

"Kurt Russell has something on his mind," _Starlog_ 63: 48-51. October 1982.

"Living With Dragons: Anne McCaffrey," _Future_ 6: 22-23, 74. November 1978.

"Making of 'Android', The," _Starlog_ 63: 36-40, 64. October 1982.

"Making of an Empire, The," _Future Life_ 20: 14-19, 68-70. August 1980.

"Metal is a welding of sci-fi and rock," _New York Post_ August 4, 1981. in: NewsBank. _Film and Television_. 25: G4. July/December 1981.

"Molly Ringwald: Starlet Sidekick to a Spacehunter," _Starlog_ 74: 28-29. September 1983.

"Nuclear Disaster in the Cinema," _Future Life_ 19: 30-35, 67. June 1980.

"Outland," _Future Life_ 26: 44-48. May 1981.

"Outland: High Noon in Space," _Future Life_ 27: 28-33. June 1981.

"Quest for Fire," _Starlog_ 55: 26-29, 64. February 1982.

"Remaking of Star Trek, " _Starlog_ 60: 18-23. July 1982.

"Remaking of Star Trek, Part Two," _Starlog_ 61: 16-20. August 1982.

"Scanners: Mind Control With a Heart," _Future Life_ 25: 66-67. March 1981.

"Science fiction," _Creem_ 9(3):48-50. October 1977.

"Shape of things to come, The," by Scott Holton and Ed Naha. _Future_ 2:30-33. 1978.

"Star Trek: The Motion Picture," _Future Life_ 16: 18-24, 66. February 1980.

"Starhunt," _Future Life_ 23: 34-36, 74. December 1980.

"Starlog Interview/Portfolio: Bladerunner's Syd Mead," _Starlog_ 58: 36-39, 61. May 1982.

"Starlog Interview: Phil Kaufman," _Starlog_ 77: 20-24. December 1983.

"Starlog Interview: The Perils of Nancy Allen, a Professional Heroine-in-Trouble," _Starlog_ 75: 66-69. October 1983.

"Superman II," _Future Life_ 28: 28-32. August 1981.

"Sybil Danning: Hollywood's Amazing Amazon," _Starlog_ 76: 82-85. November 1983.

"Time Bandits for those who won't grow up," _New York Post_ November 3, 1981. in: _NewsBank. Film and Television_. 56: B4. July/December 1981.

"Tron (Review)," _Starlog_ 64: 58-62. November 1982.

"Twilight Zone: Rod Serling's dream," _Starlog_ 15:34-51. 1978.

"Video Images: Science Fiction and Fact on Television," _Future_ 1: 22-23. April 1978.

"View From a distant star: Fred Pohl's science fiction world," _Future_ 1: 26-30. April 1978.

"View from the bridge free Enterprise, A! Can Star Trek be put back together?" _Crawdaddy_ pp. 42-49. December 1976.

"Words of George Pal, The," _Starlog_ 10:44-51. 1977.

"Young and the Weightless," _Starlog_ 59: 30-34, 64. June 1982.

Nahin, P. J.

"Computer that writes science fiction, A," _Analog_ 99(2):93-105. February 1979.

Nalle, David

"Paper warriors: SF and fantasy gaming, part 1," _Thrust_ 13:31-32,35. Fall 1979.

"Paper warriors: SF and fantasy gaming, part 2, board games," _Thrust_ No. 15:40-43. Summer 1980.

"Paper warriors: SF and fantasy gaming, part 3, role playing games," _Thrust_ 16: 30-34. Fall 1980.

Nania, J. S.

"Exploding Genres: Stanislaw Lem's Science Fiction Detective Novels," _Extrapolation_ 25(3): 266-279. Fall 1984.

Nardelli, Fred

Frank Frazetta Index. Amsterdam, NY: Nardelli, 1975. 26 p.

Nardo, A. K.

"Decorum in the fields of Arbol: interplanetary genres in C. S. Lewis' space trilogy," Extrapolation 20(2):118-128. Summer 1979.

"Fantasy literature and play: an approach to reader response," The Centennial Review 22(2):201-213. Spring 1978.

Naselli, Carmelina

"Luna nelle credenze popolari e nell'umorismo della fantascienza," Universo, Revista dell'Istituto geografico militare. 51(6):1271-1288. 1971.

Nathan, P. S.

"Books into films; proposed laboratory and information center," Publishers Weekly 161:1783. April 26, 1952.

"Books into films; science fiction," Publishers Weekly 155:2463. June 18, 1949.

"SF goes to the movies," Publishers Weekly 209(24):65. June 14, 1976.

Naujack, P.

"Science fiction: eine neue Literaturgattung?" in: Naujack, P., ed. Roboter. Science Fiction Stories. Zurich, 1965.

Nault, Cynthia

"Fear of Computers as Depicted in Fictional Themes." Worcester, MA: Undergraduate Report. Worcester Polytechnic Institute, 1982. Report No. 82B0164. 78 p.

Navasky, Victor

"In cold print: copyrights," New York Times Book Review p. 22. July 20, 1975.

Neary, John

"Both Sales and Sagas are Fantastic for Stephen Donaldson and His Leper Hero," People Weekly 18(4): 58-62. July 26, 1982.

Nedelkovich, Alexander

"Stellar Parallels: Robert Silverberg, Larry Niven, and Arthur C. Clarke," Extrapolation 21(4): 348-360. Winter 1980.

Nee, David

Michael Bishop: A Preliminary Bibliography. Berkeley, CA: Other Change of Hobbit, 1983. 34 p.

Thomas M. Disch: A Preliminary Bibliography. Berkeley, CA: The Other Change of Hobbit, 1982. 30 p.

Needham, Rodney

"Tarzan of the Apes: A Re-Appreciation," Foundation 28: 20-28. July 1983.

Neeley, Sharlotte

Teaching a Non-Traditional, Honors Anthropology Course. 13 p. ERIC ED 227 050

Nees, Georg

"Orchidee nimmt wahr, Die," in: Rottensteiner, Franz, ed. Polaris 6. Frankfurt-am-Main: Suhrkamp, 1982. pp. 169-205.

Negley, Glenn

Utopian Literature: A Bibliography. Lawrence: Regents Press of Kansas, 1977. 228 p.

Neill, Sam

"Report of the science fiction investigation committee," Ontario Library Review 37(3):187-189. August 1953.

Neilson, Keith

"Boats of 'Glen Carrig', The," in: Magill, Frank N., ed. Survey of Modern Fantasy Literature, Vol 1. Englewood Cliffs, NJ: Salem Press, Inc., 1983. pp. 143-145.

"Camino Real," in: Magill, Frank N., ed. Survey of Modern Fantasy Literature, Vol 1. Englewood Cliffs, NJ: Salem Press, Inc., 1983. pp. 187-189.

"Carrie," in: Magill, Frank N., ed. Survey of Modern Fantasy Literature, Vol 1. Englewood Cliffs, NJ: Salem Press, Inc., 1983. pp. 197-202.

"Collected Ghost Stories of Oliver Onions, The," in: Magill, Frank N., ed. Survey of Modern Fantasy Literature, Vol 1. Englewood Cliffs, NJ: Salem Press, Inc., 1983. pp. 294-299.

"Echoes from the Macabre," in: Magill, Frank N., ed. Survey of Modern Fantasy Literature, Vol 1. Englewood Cliffs, NJ: Salem Press, Inc., 1983. pp. 465-467.

Neilson, Keith (Continued)

"Fahrenheit 451," by W. E. McNelly and Keith Neilson. in: Magill, Frank N., ed. Survey of Science Fiction Literature, Vol. 2. Englewood Cliffs, NJ: Salem Press, 1979. pp. 749-755.

"Firestarter," in: Magill, Frank N., ed. Survey of Modern Fantasy Literature, Vol 2. Englewood Cliffs, NJ: Salem Press, Inc., 1983. pp. 553-556.

"From Evil's Pillow," in: Magill, Frank N., ed. Survey of Modern Fantasy Literature, Vol 2. Englewood Cliffs, NJ: Salem Press, Inc., 1983. pp. 581-584.

"Fury, The," in: Magill, Frank N., ed. Survey of Modern Fantasy Literature, Vol 2. Englewood Cliffs, NJ: Salem Press, Inc., 1983. pp. 590-592.

"Ghost Story," in: Magill, Frank N., ed. Survey of Modern Fantasy Literature, Vol 2. Englewood Cliffs, NJ: Salem Press, Inc., 1983. pp. 607-611.

"Great God Brown, The," in: Magill, Frank N., ed. Survey of Modern Fantasy Literature, Vol 2. Englewood Cliffs, NJ: Salem Press, Inc., 1983. pp. 638-641.

"Haunting of Toby Jugg, The," in: Magill, Frank N., ed. Survey of Modern Fantasy Literature, Vol 2. Englewood Cliffs, NJ: Salem Press, Inc., 1983. pp. 715-717.

"House Next Door, The," in: Magill, Frank N., ed. Survey of Modern Fantasy Literature, Vol 2. Englewood Cliffs, NJ: Salem Press, Inc., 1983. pp. 740-743.

"Man and Superman," in: Magill, Frank N., ed. Survey of Modern Fantasy Literature, Vol 2. Englewood Cliffs, NJ: Salem Press, Inc., 1983. pp. 955-958.

"Mist, The," in: Magill, Frank N., ed. Survey of Modern Fantasy Literature, Vol 3. Englewood Cliffs, NJ: Salem Press, Inc., 1983. pp. 1040-1043.

"Narrative of Arthur Gordon Pym, The," in: Magill, Frank N., ed. Survey of Science Fiction Literature, Vol. 3. Englewood Cliffs, NJ: Salem Press, 1979. pp. 1480-1487.

"Night Land, The," in: Magill, Frank N., ed. Survey of Modern Fantasy Literature, Vol 3. Englewood Cliffs, NJ: Salem Press, Inc., 1983. pp. 1105-1110.

"Night Shift," in: Magill, Frank N., ed. Survey of Modern Fantasy Literature, Vol 3. Englewood Cliffs, NJ: Salem Press, Inc., 1983. pp. 1116-1120.

"Oxrun Station Series, The," in: Magill, Frank N., ed. Survey of Modern Fantasy

Literature, Vol 3. Englewood Cliffs, NJ: Salem Press, Inc., 1983. pp. 1191-1195.

"Rosemary's Baby," in: Magill, Frank N., ed. Survey of Modern Fantasy Literature, Vol 3. Englewood Cliffs, NJ: Salem Press, Inc., 1983. pp. 1338-1342.

"Satanist, The," in: Magill, Frank N., ed. Survey of Modern Fantasy Literature, Vol 3. Englewood Cliffs, NJ: Salem Press, Inc., 1983. pp. 1358-1362.

"Shining, The," in: Magill, Frank N., ed. Survey of Modern Fantasy Literature, Vol 3. Englewood Cliffs, NJ: Salem Press, Inc., 1983. pp. 1402-1406.

"Ubik," in: Magill, Frank N., ed. Survey of Science Fiction Literature, Vol. 5. Englewood Cliffs, NJ: Salem Press, 1979. pp. 2350-2356.

"War of the Worlds, The," in: Magill, Frank N., ed. Survey of Science Fiction Literature, Vol. 5. Englewood Cliffs, NJ: Salem Press, 1979. pp. 2416-2423.

"White Hotel, The," in: Magill, Frank N., ed. Survey of Modern Fantasy Literature, Vol 5. Englewood Cliffs, NJ: Salem Press, Inc., 1983. pp. 2122-2125.

"Wolfen, The," in: Magill, Frank N., ed. Survey of Modern Fantasy Literature, Vol 5. Englewood Cliffs, NJ: Salem Press, Inc., 1983. pp. 2150-2153.

"Science Fiction of Edgar Allan Poe, The," in: Magill, Frank N., ed. Survey of Science Fiction Literature, Vol. 4. Englewood Cliffs, NJ: Salem Press, 1979. pp. 1871-1878.

"Short fiction of Hawthorne, The," in: Magill, Frank N., ed. Survey of Modern Fantasy Literature, Vol 3. Englewood Cliffs, NJ: Salem Press, Inc., 1983. pp. 1536-1543.

"Short fiction of Long, The," in: Magill, Frank N., ed. Survey of Modern Fantasy Literature, Vol 4. Englewood Cliffs, NJ: Salem Press, Inc., 1983. pp. 1616-1620.

"Short fiction of Wells, The," in: Magill, Frank N., ed. Survey of Modern Fantasy Literature, Vol 4. Englewood Cliffs, NJ: Salem Press, Inc., 1983. pp. 1729-1732.

Neisser, H. F.

"Eine Neue Gattung oder eine Stoffgruppe der Unterhaltungsliteratur? Zur Beurteilung von Science Fiction," Buch und Biblioteque 25:127-128. Feb. 1973. Comment, with rejoiner: Buch und Bibl. 25:455-456. May. 1973.

Nelms, Ben

"Farfaring imagination, The: recent fantasy and science fiction," by Ben Nelms and Beth Nelms. English Journal 74(4): 83-86. April 1985.

Nelms, Beth

"Farfaring imagination, The: recent fantasy and science fiction," by Ben Nelms and Beth Nelms. English Journal 74(4): 83-86. April 1985.

Nelson, Gary

"Two Years of Directing 'The Black Hole'," American Cinematographer 61(1): 44-45, 64-65. January 1980.

Nelson, Joyce

"Slaughterhouse-Five: novel and film," Literature/Film Quarterly 1(2):149-153. Spring 1973.

"Vonnegut and 'Bugs in Amber'," Journal of Popular Culture 7(3):551-558. Winter 1973.

Nelson, Marie

"Bird language in T. H. White's The Sword in the Stone," Mythlore 8(2):35-37. Summer 1981.

"Non human speech in the fantasy of C. S. Lewis, J. R. R. Tolkien and Richard Adams," Mythlore 5(1):37-39. May 1978.

Nelson, T. A.

Kubrick: Inside a Film Artist's Maze. Bloomington: Indiana University Press, 1982. 268 p.

Neri, Nicoletta

"Il viaggio nel tempo," in: Utopia e fantascienza. Torino: Giappichelli, 1975. pp. 7-44.

Nesteby, J. R.

"Tarzan of Arabia: American Popular Culture Permeates Yemen," Journal of Popular Culture 15(1): 39-45. Summer 1981.

"Tenuous Vine of Tarzan of the Apes," Journal of Popular Culture 13(3): 483-487. Spring 1980.

Nesvadba, Josef

"Poznamky o sci-fi," Slovenske Pohl'ady na Literature a Umenie 98(4): 101-106. 1982.

"Reason and Rationalism," Vector 122: 12-14. 1984.

"View From Prague," Fountation 30: 48-50. March 1984.

Nettelbeck, U.

"Fleissige Schreiber erobern den Weltraum. Ein uberblick uber die in der Bundesrepublik erscheinenden Science Fiction Reihen," Die Zeit No. 49:7. 1966.

Neuleib, Janice

"Love's alchemy: Jane in That Hideous Strength," Mythlore 7(1):16-17. March 1980.

"Of other worlds: worldly wisdom as it grows in science fiction," Extrapolation 19(2):108-111. May 1978.

"Technology and theocracy: the cosmic voyage of Wells and Lewis," Extrapolation 16(2):130-136. May 1975.

Neumeister, Sebastian

"Aufloesung der Phantastik. Epistemologische Anmerkungen zu Gabriel Garcia Marquez Roman," in: Thomsen, C. W., ed. Phantastik in Literatur und Kunst. Darmstadt: Wissenschaftliche Buchgesellschaft, 1980. pp. 369-386.

Neutzsky-Wulff, Erwin

"Mened & Levninger: Selvbiografiske betragtninger af Erwin Neutzsky-Wulff," Proxima No. 19. sect. I:6-10. March 1979.

"Om science fiction," Proxima No. 5. sect.II. 1975.

"Science fiction: den moderne myte," in: Virkelique Eventyr, ed by Lindboe and Moller. Spar Knaegt, 1978. p. 54- .

Nevans, M. F.

"Writer who appeals to all ages: an interview with Madeleine L'Engle," Bloomsbury Review 2(1):17,19. November/December 1981.

Neville, Kris

"Westercon XVI speech," Inside-Riverside Quarterly p. 11-17. Summer 1964.

New England Science Fiction Association

Index to Perry Rhodan, U.S. Edition 1-25. Boston: NESFA, 1973. 12 p.

Index to Perry Rhodan, U.S. Edition 25-50. Boston: NESFA, 1975. 18 p.

Index to the Science Fiction Magazines, 1966-1970. Cambridge, MA: NESFA, 1971. 82 p.

NESFA Index to the Science Fiction Magazines and Original Anthologies, 1971-1972, The. Cambridge, MA: NESFA, 1973. 42 p.

NESFA Index to the Science Fiction Magazines and Original Anthologies, 1973, The. Cambridge, MA: NESFA, 1974. 30 p.

NESFA Index to the Science Fiction Magazines and Original Anthologies, 1974, The. Cambridge, MA: NESFA, 1975. 43 p.

NESFA Index to the Science Fiction Magazines and Original Anthologies, 1975, The. Cambridge, MA: NESFA, 1976. 36 p.

NESFA Index to the Science Fiction Magazines and Original Anthologies, 1976, The. Cambridge, MA: NESFA, 1977. 38 p.

NESFA Index to the Science Fiction Magazines and Original Anthologies, 1977-1978, The. Cambridge, MA: NESFA, 1983. 73 p.

NESFA Index to the Science Fiction Magazines and Original Anthologies, 1979-1980, The. Cambridge, MA: NESFA, 1982. 90 p.

NESFA Index to the Science Fiction Magazines and Original Anthologies, 1981, The. Cambridge, MA: NESFA, 1982. 60 p.

NESFA Index to the Science Fiction Magazines and Original Anthologies, 1982, The. Cambridge, MA: NESFA, 1983. 64 p.

NESFA Index to the Science Fiction Magazines and Original Anthologies, 1983, The. Cambridge, MA: NESFA, 1984. 68 p.

New, Melvyn

"Orwell and antisemitism: toward 1984," Modern Fiction Studies 21(1):81-105. Spring 1975.

Newcombe, Bryan

"Winston, Hal, and Robotry: 1984 and 2001," in: The Future in Peril: 1984 and the Anti-Utopians. College Station: Honors Program, Texas A&M University, [1985]. pp. 14-18.

Newell, K. B.

"Science fiction and the merging of realism and romance," Extrapolation 14(1):6-12. December 1972.

Newlove, Donald

"Incredible paintings of Frank Frazetta," Esquire 87(6):86-94,149-154. June 1977.

Newman, D. J.

"Dragon Lady author loves her fire-eaters," Chicago Tribune Sec. 2, p. 1-2. July 4, 1978.

Newman, F. R.

"Meeting of the Minds," by Julius Strangepork and F. R. Newman. Muppet Magazine 1(3):17-20. Summer 1983.

Newman, J. R.

"New Maps of Hell, by Kingsley Amis," Scientific American 203:179-180. July 1960. (Book review)

Newman, John

Future War Novels: An Annotated Bibliography of Works in English Published Since 1946, by John Newman and Michael Unsworth. Phoenix: Oryx, 1984. 101 p.

"America at war: horror stories for a society," Extrapolation 16(1):33-41. December 1974.

"Bibliography; novels of post-holocaust America: an annotated bibliography," by John Newman and Donna Leflar. Alternative Futures 1(3/4):110-116. Fall 1978.

"Imaginary war fiction in Colorado State University Libraries: a bibliography," by John Newman and K. J. Kruger. Bulletin of Bibliography and Magazine Notes 35(4):157-168,171. December 1978.

"Part two: America at war: horror stories for a society," Extrapolation 16(2):164-172. May 1975.

Newson, Ted

"Ray Harryhausen story, part 1, the early years, 1920-1958," Cinefantastique 11(4):25-45. December 1981.

Newton, Charles

"Underground man, go home," College English 37(4):337-344. December 1975.

Newton, Judith

"Feminism and anxiety in Alien," Science-Fiction Studies 7(3): 293-297. November 1980.

Nichol, Charles

"Bretnor returns: science fiction: today and tomorrow," Science Fiction Studies 1(3):220-221. Spring 1974.

Nicholas, Joseph

"Future Is All We've Got Left: Gregory Benford Interviewed," Vector 111: 6-14. 1982.

"Guns of the Timberland," Vector 99: 8-9. October 1980.

"Shape of Things to Come," Vector 101: 6-14. April 1981.

"Singing for Supper," Vector 109: 6-12. 1982.

"Two-Foot Square of Gene Wolfe; Interview," by Judith Hanna and Joseph Nicholas. Vector 118: 5-12. February 1984.

Nicholls, Peter

Infinity, Eternity, and the Pulp Magazines. London: Allen Lane, 1976.

Science Fiction at Large: A Collection of Essays, by Various Hands, About the Interface Between Science Fiction and Reality. London: Gollancz, 1976. 224 p. Reprinted, New York: Harper & Row, 1977. 224 p.

Science Fiction Encyclopedia. Garden City, N.Y.: Doubleday, 1979. 672 p.

Science in Science Fiction, by Peter Nicholls, David Langford and Brian Stableford. London: Joseph, 1982. 208 p.; New York: Knopf, 1983. 208 p.

World of Fantastic Films: An Illustrated Survey. New York: Dodd, 1984. 224 p.

"Camp Concentration," in: Magill, Frank N., ed. Survey of Science Fiction Literature, Vol. 1. Englewood Cliffs, NJ: Salem Press, 1979. pp. 277-282.

"Casey Agonistes and Other Science Fiction and Fantasy Stories," in: Magill, Frank N., ed. Survey of Science Fiction Literature, Vol. 1. Englewood Cliffs, NJ: Salem Press, 1979. pp. 308-312.

"Fifth Head of Cerberus, The," in: Magill, Frank N., ed. Survey of Science Fiction Literature, Vol. 2. Englewood Cliffs, NJ: Salem Press, 1979. pp. 770-775.

"Other Days, Other Eyes," in: Magill, Frank N., ed. Survey of Science Fiction Literature, Vol. 4. Englewood Cliffs, NJ: Salem Press, 1979. pp. 1622-1626.

"Rogue Moon," in: Magill, Frank N., ed. Survey of Science Fiction Literature, Vol. 4. Englewood Cliffs, NJ: Salem Press, 1979. pp. 1821-1826.

"Sound of His Horn, The," in: Magill, Frank N., Ed. Survey of Modern Fantasy Literature, Vol 4. Englewood Cliffs, NJ: Salem Press, Inc., 1983. pp. 1787-1789.

"Star-Bearer Trilogy, The," in: Magill, Frank N., ed. Survey of Modern Fantasy Literature, Vol 4. Englewood Cliffs, NJ: Salem Press, Inc., 1983. pp. 1813-1820.

"Starlight: The Great Short Fiction of Alfred Bester," in: Magill, Frank N., ed. Survey of Science Fiction Literature, Vol. 5. Englewood Cliffs, NJ: Salem Press, 1979. pp. 2163-2167.

"Algis Budrys," in: Bleiler, E. F., ed. Science Fiction Writers. New York: Scribners, 1982. pp. 305-311.

"Anatomy of a romance," Vector 67/68:11-15. Spring 1974.

"Death of James Blish, The," Foundation 9:54-56. November 1975.

"Jerry Cornelius at the atrocity exhibition: anarchy and entropy in New Worlds science fiction 1964-1974," Foundation 9:22-43. November 1975.

"Michael Moorcock," in: Bleiler, E. F., ed. Science Fiction Writers. New York: Scribners, 1982. pp. 449-457.

"Philip K. Dick: A Cowardly Memoir," Foundation 26: 5-10. October 1982.

"Report on Eurocon 1," Foundation 3:3-5. March 1973.

"Richard Matheson," in: Bleiler, E. F., ed. Science Fiction Writers. New York: Scribners, 1982. pp. 425-431.

"Robert A. Heinlein," in: Bleiler, E. F., ed. Science Fiction Writers. New York: Scribners, 1982. pp. 185-196.

"Roger Zelazny," in: Bleiler, E. F., ed. Science Fiction Writers. New York: Scribners, 1982. pp. 563-570.

"Science fiction and the mainstream: part 1: the demolition of pigeonholes," Foundation 3:15-25. March 1973.

Nicholls, Peter (Continued)

"Science fiction and the mainstream: part 2: the great tradition of proto science fiction," Foundation 5:9-44. January 1974.

"Science fiction: the monsters and the critics," in: Nicholls, Peter, ed. Science Fiction at Large. New York: Harper, 1976. pp. 157-184.

"Science fiction: the next phase," Bookseller 3699:2468-2470. November 13, 1976.

Nichols, Bill

"English Cult Hero Has Following Here," Clarion Ledger (Jackson, MI) October 12, 1982. in: NewsBank. Film and Television. 50:G2-3. December 1982.

Nichols, David

"Lights! Camera! Aliens!" by Chuck Cirino and David Nichols. Home Video 2(9): 32-33. September 1981.

Nichols, Lewis

"Isaac Asimov, man of 7,560,000 words," New York Times Book Review pp. 8,28. August 3, 1969.

Nichols, Robert

"Novels of tomorrow," Trans-Pacific 16:5. September 29, 1928. (not seen)

Nichols, Ruth

"Fantasy and escapism," Canadian Children's Literature 4:20-27. 1976.

Nicholson, Bruce

"Composite optical photography for The Empire Strikes Back," American Cinematographer 61(6):562-563, 571,612-614. June 1980.

Nicholson, Peter

"Chat with Peter Cushing about Dracula today," by Chris Knight and Peter Nicholson. Cinefantastique 2(2):5-7. Summer 1972.

Nicholson, Roger

"Indiana Jones and The Temple of Doom (review)," Cinefantastique 14(4/5):100. September 1984.

Nicholson, Sam

"Kinetic lighting for Star Trek: The Motion Picture," American Cinematographer 61(2):148-149,183. February 1980.

Nicholson-Morton, R.

"Hints of Failure..." Focus: an SF Writer's Magazine. 4: 18-19. Spring 1981.

"Inveterate Itch," Focus: an SF Writer's Magazine 6: 23-24. Autumn 1982.

Nicol, Charles

"Ballard and the limits of mainstream SF," Science Fiction Studies 3(2):150-157. July 1976.

Nicolazzini, Piergiorgio

"Appunti sulla Saga dell'esilio del Pliocene," Cosmo informatore 14(4):10-13. Winter 1985.

"Il gregge alza la testa: ovvero manuale per una probabile antodistruzione," Alternativa: per una critica della Science Fiction pp. 21-24. Gennaio 1978.

Nicolson, M. H.

Science and Imagination. Ithaca, New York: Cornell University Press, 1956. 238 p.

Voyages to the Moon. New York: Macmillan, 1948. 297 p.

"Cosmic voyages," English Literary History 7(2):83-107. June 1940.

"Kepler, the Somnium and John Donne," Journal of the History of Ideas 1(3):259-280. June 1940.

Nicot, Stephane

"11th French SF Convention," by Stephane Nicot and P. J. Thomas. Locus 18(1): 30. January 1985.

Niederland, W. G.

"Birth of H. G. Wells' Time Machine, The," American Imago 35(1/2):106-112. Spring/Summer 1978.

Nielsen, N. E.

"Foran fremtidens tskel," in: Rejser i tid og rum. En Bog om science fiction, ed. by Tage La Cour. Copenhagen: Stig Verdelkaer, 1973.

Niewiadomski, Andrzej

"Auseinandersetzung mit der Utopie," Quarber Merkur 61: 37-43. July 1984.

Nikolajeva, Maria

"Function of the Charm," Labrys No. 7: 141-145. November 1981.

Niles, P. H.

Science Fiction of H. G. Wells: a Concise Guide. Clifton Park, NY: Auriga, 1980. 58 p.

Nilon, Charles

"Science Fiction of Samuel R. Delany and the Limits of Technology," Black American Literature Forum 18(2): 62-68. Summer 1984.

Nimon, Maureen

"Science fiction," SMMART Journal No. 3:37-42. 1977.

"Selection of SF for a school library, The," Children's Libraries Newsletter 12(3):88-91. August 1976.

Nimoy, Leonard

I am not Spock. New York: Ballantine/Del Rey, c. 1977. 150 p.

"Conversation with Leonard Nimoy (interview)," Penthouse 10(2):189-193. October 1978.

Nitschmann, L.

"Hochkonjunktur in utopien. 'Science fiction' heute eine modelliteratur mit standig steigenden auflagen," Handelsblatt 13(122):14. 1958.

Nitzsche, J. C.

Tolkien's Art: A Mythology For England. New York: St. Martin's, 1979. London: Macmillan, 1979. 164 p.

Niven, Larry

"Biology, Ecology, Xenology," in: Ellison, Harlan, ed. Medea. New York: Bantam, 1985. pp. 28-33.

"Building The Mote in God's Eye," by Larry Niven and Jerry Pournelle. Galaxy. 37(1):92-113. January 1976. also in: Pournelle, Jerry. A Step Further Out. New York: Ace, 1980. pp. 113-141.

"Equipment, Method and the Rest," in: Wingrove, David, ed. The Science Fiction Source Book. New York: Van Nostrand, 1984. pp. 79-80.

"Future histories," SFWA Bulletin 14(3):15-16. Fall 1979.

"My world, and welcome to it," Foundation 1:48-54. March 1972.

"Telepathy, psionics and ESP," in: Ash, Brian, ed. Visual Encyclopedia of Science Fiction. New York: Harmony, 1977. pp. 204-211.

"Words in science fiction, The," in: Bretnor, Reginald, ed. The Craft of Science Fiction. New York: Harper, 1976. pp. 178-194.

"Writers: Equipment, Method and the Rest," Science Fiction Chronicle 6(5): 26. February 1985.

Nobbe, George

"Anne McCaffrey: exclusive interview with the Queen of science fiction," Science and Living Tomorrow. 1(5): 59-62. December 1980.

Noble, B. J.

"Alburquerque Writer Wins Literary Prize," Albuquerque Journal, May 10, 1981. in: NewsBank. Literature. 97: F11-12. 1980/81.

Noble, W. T.

"Unstuck in time . . . a real Kurt Vonnegut: the reluctant guru of searching youth," Detroit Sunday News Magazine pp. 14-15,18. June 18, 1972.

Noda, Masahiro

(SF kokokan). s. l.: s. n., 1974. 214 p. (LCCN 76-811911)

Nodelman, Perry

"Out there in children's science fiction: forward into the past," Science Fiction Studies 12(3): 285-296. November 1985.

Noel, R. S.

Mythology of Middle-Earth, The. Boston: Houghton Mifflin, 1977. 198 p.

Nohbauer, H. F.

"Jules Verne und die Science Fiction," Epoca No. 11:148- . 1966.

Nolan, C. J., Jr.

"Rhetorical end: 'Venus at St. Anne's', The," _CSL: The Bulletin of the New York C. S. Lewis Society_ 9(1):8-9. 1977.

Nolan, J. E.

"Films on tv; Britain's hammer films," _Films in Review_ 22(3):161-164. March 1971. Reply, A. Gordon, 22:238-240. April 1971.

Nolan, Tom

"Science fiction fever," _Penthouse_ 10(2):62-70,112. October 1978.

Nolan, W. F.

Ray Bradbury Companion: A Life and Career History, Photolog, and Comprehensive Checklist of Writing with Facsimiles from Ray Bradbury's Unpublished and Uncollected Work in all Media, The. Detroit: Gale Research, 1975. 339 p.

Ray Bradbury Review. San Diego: by the author, 1952. 63 p.

"Afterthoughts on Logan's Run," _Science Fiction Review_ 6:32-33. August 1977.

"Bibliography of robot fiction, A," in: Nolan, William F., ed. _Pseudopeople: Androids in Science Fiction_. Los Angeles, California: Sherbourne Press, 1956. pp. 228-238.

"Bradbury in the pulps," _Xenophile_ No. 36:R21-R25,R31. November 1977.

"Bradbury's first book appearances," _Xenophile_ No. 36:R8-R12. November 1977.

"Bradbury: prose poet in the age of space," _Magazine of Fantasy and Science Fiction_ 24(5):7-22. May 1963.

"Chad Oliver's collected science fiction: a basic checklist," in: Oliver, Chad. _The Edge of Forever_. Los Angeles: Sherbourne, 1971. pp. 301-305.

"Index to the works of Ray Bradbury, An," _Magazine of Fantasy and Science Fiction_ 24(5):40-51. May 1963.

"Worlds of Chad Oliver: a biographical introduction," in: Oliver, Chad. _The Edge of Forever_. Los Angeles: Sherbourne, 1971. pp. 11-32.

Nolane, R. D.

"_Docteur Lerne, Le_," in: Magill, Frank N., ed. _Survey of Science Fiction Literature_, Vol. 2. Englewood Cliffs, NJ: Salem Press, 1979. pp. 560-563.

"_Monde est notre, Ce_," in: Magill, Frank N., ed. _Survey of Science Fiction Literature_, Vol. 3. Englewood Cliffs, NJ: Salem Press, 1979. pp. 1435-1438.

"_Naissance des dieux, La_," in: Magill, Frank N., ed. _Survey of Science Fiction Literature_, Vol. 3. Englewood Cliffs, NJ: Salem Press, 1979. pp. 1472-1475.

"_Navigateurs de l'infini, Les_," in: Magill, Frank N., ed. _Survey of Science Fiction Literature_, Vol. 3. Englewood Cliffs, NJ: Salem Press, 1979. pp. 1501-1504.

"_Niourk_," in: Magill, Frank N., ed. _Survey of Science Fiction Literature_, Vol. 4. Englewood Cliffs, NJ: Salem Press, 1979. pp. 1537-1540.

"_Oiel du purgatoire, L'_," in: Magill, Frank N., ed. _Survey of Science Fiction Literature_, Vol. 4. Englewood Cliffs, NJ: Salem Press, 1979. pp. 1588-1591.

"_Star_," in: Magill, Frank N., ed. _Survey of Science Fiction Literature_, Vol. 5. Englewood Cliffs, NJ: Salem Press, 1979. pp. 2146-2149.

"_Temple of the Past, The_," in: Magill, Frank N., ed. _Survey of Science Fiction Literature_, Vol. 5. Englewood Cliffs, NJ: Salem Press, 1979. pp. 2241-2244.

"_Xipehuz, Les_," in: Magill, Frank N., ed. _Survey of Science Fiction Literature_, Vol. 5. Englewood Cliffs, NJ: Salem Press, 1979. pp. 2516-2519.

Nordhjem, Bent

"In quest of Tolkien's Middle-Earth. Interpretation and classification of _Lord of the Rings_," in: Dollerup, C. _Volve. Scandinavian Views on Science Fiction_. Copenhagen: Dept. of English, Univ. of Copenhagen, 1978. pp. 17-42.

Nored, Gary

"The Lord of the Rings: a textual inquiry," _Papers of the Bibliographic Society of America_ 68:71-74. 1974.

Norford, D. P.

"Reality and illusion in Peter Beagle's _The Last Unicorn_," _Critique: Studies in Modern Fiction_ 19(2):93-104. 1977.

Norman, H. L.

"Scientific and the pseudoscientific in the works of Luigi Capuana," _Publications of the Modern Language Association_ 53(3):869-885. September 1938.

Norman, Philip

"Prevalence of hobbits,"   New York Times Magazine pp. 30-31. January 15, 1967.

Norman, R. B.

"Back to basics in science fiction," LJ Special Report No. 6:70-74. 1978.

Norman, R. V.

"Fantasy and science fiction; an examination of the field and suggestions for assembling a basic collection," Mountain Plains Library Association Quarterly 19(4):10-14. Winter 1974.

Normanno, L.

"Letterature e 'fantastique'," Culture francaise 12:39-42. Bari, 1965.

Northrop, F. S. C.

"Literature and science," Saturday Review of Literature 27(32):33-36. August 5, 1944.

Norton, Andre

"Living in 1980 plus," Library Journal 77(16):1463-1466. September 15, 1952.

"On Writing Fantasy," in: Boyer, Robert H. and Zahorski, Kenneth J. Fantasists on Fantasy. New York: Avon Discus, 1984. pp. 151-162.

Norwood, W. D., Jr.

"C. S. Lewis, Owen Barfield and the modern myth," Midwest Quarterly 8(3):279-291. Spring 1967.

"Unifying themes in C. S. Lewis' trilogy," Critique: Studies in Modern Fiction 9(2):76-80. 1967.

Nossack, H. E.

"Proligio. Ein traktat uber die zukunft des menschen," Merkur. Deutsche Zietschrift fur Europaisches Denken 19:601-608. 1965.

Notkin, D. L.

"Stephen King: Horror and Humanity for Our Time," in: Underwood, Tim and Miller, Chuck, eds. Fear Itself. Columbia, PA: Underwood/Miller, 1982. pp. 131-142.

Notkin, Debbie

"Interview: Elizabeth A. Lynn,"   Janus 5(1): 18-19, 25. Spring 1979.

"Recommended reading, 1984,"   Locus 18(2): 26. February 1985.

Nourse, A. E.

"Extrapolations and quantum jumps," in: Bretnor, Reginald, ed. The Craft of Science Fiction. New York: Harper, 1976. pp. 73-88.

"One foot in the Grave: Medicine in Future Warfare," in: Bretnor, Reginald, ed. The Future at War: Vol. 1: Thor's Hammer. New York: Ace, 1979. pp. 297-317.

"Outguessing the Unknown: Psychological Aspects of Future War," in: Bretnor, Reginald, ed. The Future at War: Vol. 3: Orion's Sword. New York: Ace, 1980. pp. 228-241.

"Science fiction and man's adaptation to change," in: Bretnor, Reginald, ed. Science Fiction Today and Tomorrow. New York: Harper, 1974. pp. 116-134.

Novikova, N. V.

"Nazvanie letatel'nykh apparatov v sovremennoi nauchno-fantasticheskoi literature," in: Skvortsov, L. I., ed. Terminologiia i kul'tura rechi. Moscow: Nauka, 1981. pp. 250-258.

"Termin v nauchnoi fantastike,"   Russkaia Rech': Nauchno-Populiarnyi Zhurnal p. 55-58. May-June 1981.

Novitski, Paul

"Starship interview: Vonda N. McIntyre," Starship 34:21-28. Spring 1979.

Novy, Vilem

Veda, technika, fantasie. Praha: Universitni knihovna, 1957. 19 p.

Nudelman, R. I.

"(Soviet science fiction and the ideology of soviet society)", (in Russian) Canadian-American Slavic Studies 18(1/2):5-30. Spring/Summer 1984.

"Approach to the structure of Le Guin's SF," Science Fiction Studies 2(3):210-220. November 1975.

"Conversation in a railway compartment," Science Fiction Studies 5(2):118-130. July 1978.

Nudelman, R. I. (Continued)

"Fantastika i nauchno-teckhnicheskii progress," Angara 38(4):62-67. 1968.

"Gesprach im Coupe," in: Rottensteiner, Franz, ed. Polaris 2. Frankfurt: Insel, 1974. pp. 49-76.

"Science fiction," in: Great Soviet Encyclopedia; A Translation of the Third Edition, Vol. 17. New York: Macmillan, 1978. pp. 677-678.

Null, Edward

"Science for SF writers: eating out; way out," Empire for the SF Writer 9(3): 20-21. Spring 1985.

Nunan, E. E.

"Science Fiction and Teaching: Science, Science Fiction, and a Radical Science Education," by E. E. Nunan and David Homer. Science-Fiction Studies 8(3): 311-330. November 1981.

Nunez Ladeverze, Luis

Utopia y realidad la ciencia ficcion en Espana. Madrid: Ediciones del Centro, 1976. 270 p.

Nurdsany, Michel

"Imagination au pouvoir, L', objectif de la science fiction," Le Figaro Litteraire. Supplement Litteraire du Figaro 1317:10. August 13, 1971.

"Pierre Versins, le collectionneur d'utopies," Le Figaro Litteraire 1396:17. February 17, 1973.

"Science fiction sort de son ghetto, La," Figaro Litteraire No. 1568:13. June 5, 1976.

Nutz, Walter

Trivialroman, Der. Seine Formen und seine Hersteller. Ein Beitrag zur Literatursoziologie. Koln-Opladen, 1962.

Nydahl, Joel

"Early Fictional Futures: Utopia, 1798-1864," in: Roemer, Kenneth M., ed. America As Utopia. New York: Franklin, 1981. pp. 254-291.

"From Millennium to Utopia Americana," in: Roemer, Kenneth M., ed. America As Utopia. New York: Franklin, 1981. pp. 237-253.

Nye, R. B.

The Wizard of Oz and Who He Was, by Martin Gardner and R. B. Nye. East Lansing: Michigan State University Press, 1957. 208 p.

O

O'Brien, M. E.

"Space: 1999," by T. R. Atkins and M. E. O'Brien. Cinefantastique 4(2):44-46. Summer 1975.

O'Brien, R. C.

"Telepsyche; the meeting of minds," Holiday 41(2):8,12-19. February 1967.

O'Brien, Tom

"Very High Sci-Fi," Commonweal 109(14): 442-445. August 13, 1982.

O'Conner, Bill

"Elva Smith: Two days on the set of Cocoon," Akron, OH. Beacon Journal June 30, 1985. in: NewsBank. Film and Television. 2:D3-D4. July 1985.

O'Connor, Debra

"Rest of the Story Behind 'The Wizard of Oz'," Sioux Falls Argus Leader, Apr. 6, 1982. in: NewsBank. Literature. 91: F14-G1. 1981/1982.

O'Connor, Gerard

"Function of time travel in Vonnegut's Slaughterhouse Five," Riverside Quarterly 5(3): 206-207. August 1972.

"Many ways to read an 'old' book, The," Extrapolation 15(1):72-74. December 1973.

"Why Tolkien's The Lord of the Rings should not be popular culture," Extrapolation 13(1):48-55. December 1971.

O'Donnell, Charles

"From Earth to ether: Poe's flight into space," PMLA 77:85-96. 1962.

O'Donnell, K. T.

"How I've survived life with a writer," Empire: For the SF Writer 4(1): 18. July 1978.

O'Donnell, Kevin, Jr.

"Bander Who? Snatch What?" Empire: For the SF Writer 4(3): 10-11. July 1979.

"Organization, quirkiness, and creativity," Empire: For the SF Writer 4(1): 19, 27. July 1978.

"Writer's guide to income tax deductions," Empire: For the SF Writer 3(4):21. April 1978.

O'Donohoe, Nick

"Condemned to life: 'The Mortal Immortal' and 'The Man Who Never Grew Young'," in: Yoke, C. B. and Hassler, D. M., eds. Death and the Serpent. Westport, CT: Greenwood, 1985. pp. 83-90.

O'Hare, Colman

"Hero in C. S. Lewis' space novels, The," Renascence: Essays on Values in Literature 31(3):142-154. Spring 1979.

"On the reading of an 'old' book," Extrapolation 14(1):59-63. December 1972.

O'Malley, Robert

"Index to Planet Stories: part III, An," Xenophile 2(9):48. 1976.

"Index to Planet Stories: part IV, An," Xenophile 3(1):13,80. 1976.

O'Neil, P.

"Barnum of the space age," Life 55(4):62-74. July 26, 1963.

O'Neill, Jill

"One Hundred Most Important People in Science Fiction/Fantasy: C. S. Lewis," Starlog 100: 40. November 1985.

"One Hundred Most Important People in Science Fiction/Fantasy: Ursula K. Le Guin," Starlog 100: 53. November 1985.

O'Neill, P. D.

"Helen Slater: Learning to Fly as Supergirl," Starlog 89: 52-54. December 1984.

"Mark Lenard: Father to Spock," Starlog 86: 30-34. September 1984.

"Martha Coolidge," Starlog No. 98:35-37. September 1985.

"Mary Tamm: a noble Romona," Starlog No. 95: 49. June 1985.

"Michael Ironside: Every Overdog Has His Day," Starlog 74: 66-68. September 1983.

"One Hundred Most Important People in Science Fiction/Fantasy: Frank R. Paul," Starlog 100: 52. November 1985.

"One Hundred Most Important People in Science Fiction/Fantasy: John W. Campbell, Jr.," Starlog 100: 14. November 1985.

"One Hundred Most Important People in Science Fiction/Fantasy: Jules Verne," Starlog 100: 62. November 1985.

"One Hundred Most Important People in Science Fiction/Fantasy: L. Sprague de Camp," Starlog 100: 84. November 1985.

"One Hundred Most Important People in Science Fiction/Fantasy: Michael Whelan," Starlog 100: 39. November 1985.

"Scott Glen: The fast gun astronaut," Starlog 97: 68-69, 71. August 1985.

"Starlog Interview: Anthony Ainley," Starlog 80: 54-55. March 1984.

"Starlog Interview: John Nathan-Turner, Producing Doctor Who," Starlog 82: 30-32. May 1984.

"Starlog Interview: Jon Pertwee," Starlog 79: 24-27, 65. February 1984.

"Starlog Interview: Marc McClure," Starlog 84: 74-76. July 1984.

"Starlog Interview: Patrick Troughton," by Ben Landsman and P. D. O'Neill. Starlog 89: 40-41. December 1984.

"Starlog Interview: Tom Baker," Starlog 77: 27-30. December 1983.

O'Neill, T. R.

Individuated Hobbit: Jung, Tolkien, and the Archetypes of Middle-Earth. London: Thames and Hudson, 1980. 200 p.

O'Quinn, Kerry

"From My Eyes Only," Starlog 64: 94-95. November 1982.

"George Lucas Saga, Chapter 1: A New View," Starlog 48: 25-29. July, 1981.

"George Lucas Saga, Chapter 2: The Cold Fish Strikes Back," Starlog 49: 56-60. August 1981.

"George Lucas Saga, Chapter 3: The Revenge of the Box Office," Starlog 50: 52-56. September 1981.

"One Hundred Most Important People in Science Fiction/Fantasy: Bernard Herrmann," Starlog 100: 24. November 1985.

"One Hundred Most Important People in Science Fiction/Fantasy: Chesley Bonestell," Starlog 100: 53, 62. November 1985.

"One Hundred Most Important People in Science Fiction/Fantasy: David Kyle," Starlog 100: 23-24. November 1985.

"One Hundred Most Important People in Science Fiction/Fantasy: Harve Bennett," Starlog 100: 82. November 1985.

"Starlog Interview: Alan Ladd, Jr.," by Kerry O'Quinn and David Everitt. Starlog 55: 40-43. February 1982.

"Starlog Interview: Inside Gene Roddenberry's Head," Starlog 100: 18-20. November 1985.

O'Reilly, Timothy

Frank Herbert. New York: Ungar, 1981. 216 p.

"Childe Cycle, The," in: Magill, Frank N., ed. Survey of Science Fiction Literature, Vol. 1. Englewood Cliffs, NJ: Salem Press, 1979. pp. 330-336.

"Children of Dune," in: Magill, Frank N., ed. Survey of Science Fiction Literature, Vol. 1. Englewood Cliffs, NJ: Salem Press, 1979. pp. 343-348.

"Dune," by W. E. McNelly and Timothy O'Reilly. in: Magill, Frank N., ed. Survey of Science Fiction Literature, Vol. 2. Englewood Cliffs, NJ: Salem Press, 1979. pp. 647-658.

O'Reilly, Timothy (Continued)

"Dune Messiah," in: Magill, Frank N., ed. Survey of Science Fiction Literature, Vol. 2. Englewood Cliffs, NJ: Salem Press, 1979. pp. 659-664.

"Mind Parasites, The," in: Magill, Frank N., ed. Survey of Science Fiction Literature, Vol. 3. Englewood Cliffs, NJ: Salem Press, 1979. pp. 1401-1406.

"From concept to fable: the evolution of Frank Herbert's Dune," in: Riley, Dick, ed. Critical Encounters: Writers and Themes in Science Fiction. New York: Ungar, 1978. pp. 41-55.

O'Toole, Thomas

Encounters with the Future: A Forecast of Life into the 21st Century, by Marvin Cetron and Thomas O'Toole. New York: McGraw-Hill, 1982.

Oaks, Priscilla

"Cloned Lives," in: Magill, Frank N., ed. Survey of Science Fiction Literature, Vol. 1. Englewood Cliffs, NJ: Salem Press, 1979. pp. 402-405.

"Killer Thing, The," in: Magill, Frank N., ed. Survey of Science Fiction Literature, Vol. 3. Englewood Cliffs, NJ: Salem Press, 1979. pp. 1122-1125.

Oberg, C. H.

Pagan Prophet: William Morris. Charlottesville, VA: University Press of Virginia, 1978. 189 p.

Odenthal, Johannes

"Magritte und das Phantastische," in: Thomsen, C. W., ed. Phantastik in Literatur und Kunst. Darmstadt: Wissenschaftliche Buchgesellschaft, 1980. pp. 439-456.

Odom, B. B.

Anti-Utopian Literature as a Genre: A Study and Evaluation of the Aesthetic Qualities and Rhetorical Techniques of Anti-Utopian Literature. Northwestern State University, Natchitoches, LA: Masters Thesis, 1965. 99 p.

Offord, L. G.

Boucher Portrait: Anthony Boucher as Seen by His Friends and Colleagues . . . and A. (sic) Boucher Bibliography. White Bear Lake, Montana: The Armchair Detective, No date.

Offutt, A. J.

"How it happened: one bad decision leading to another," Science Fiction Studies 4(2):138-143. July 1977.

"Money is valuable: save it," in: Grant, C. L., ed. Writing and Selling Science Fiction. Cincinnatti, Ohio: Writers Digest, 1976. pp. 169-186.

"See you later, Leigh," Locus 11(4):6. May 1978.

Ogan, Jane

"Science fiction selection for junior high," Arizona English Bulletin 51(1):32-36. October 1972.

Ogly, Arab

"Cuchemar cosmique dans la litterature de science fiction, Le," La Pensee 102:68-90. March/April 1962.

Ohlin, Peter

"Dilemma of SF film criticism, The," Science Fiction Studies 1(4):287-290. Fall 1974.

Oinas, Felix

"East European Vampires and Dracula," Journal of Popular Culture 16(1): 108-116. Summer 1982.

Okada, Masaya

Illustrated Index to Air Wonder Stories (Vol. 1 No. 1-Vol. 1 No. 11, July 1929-May 1930). Nagoya, Japan: by the author, 1973. 79 p.

Okrent, Daniel

"Short, sad stay of Kurt Vonnegut, Jr., The," The Michigan Daily (Ann Arbor) p. 2. January 25, 1969.

"Very new kind of WIR, A," The Michigan Daily (Ann Arbor) pp. 1-2. January 21, 1969.

Olander, J. D.

Arthur C. Clarke, ed. by J. D. Olander and M. H. Greenberg. New York: Taplinger, 1977. 254 p.

End of the World by E. S. Rabkin, M. H. Greenberg, and J. D. Olander. Carbondale: Southern Illinois University Press, 1983. 204 p.

Olander, J. D. (Continued)

Index to Stories in Thematic Anthologies of Science Fiction, ed. by M. B. Tymn, M. H. Greenberg, L. W. Currey and J. D. Olander. Boston: G. K. Hall, 1978. 193 p.

Isaac Asimov, ed. by J. D. Olander and M. H. Greenberg. New York: Taplinger, 1977. 247 p.

No Place Esle: Explorations in Utopian and Dystopian Fiction, by E. S. Rabkin, M. H. Greenberg, and J. D. Olander. Carbondale: Southern Illinois University Press, 1983. 278 p.

Philip K. Dick, by M. H. Greenberg and J. D. Olander. New York: Taplinger, 1983. 256 p.

Ray Bradbury, by J. D. Olander and M. H. Greenberg. New York: Taplinger, 1980. 248 p.

Robert A. Heinlein, ed. by J. D. Olander and M. H. Greenberg. New York: Taplinger, 1978. 268 p.

Science Fiction: Contemporary Mythology, ed. by Patricia Warrick, M. H. Greenberg and Joseph Olander. New York: Harper, 1978. 476 p.

Ursula K. Le Guin, ed. by J. D. Olander and M. H. Greenberg. New York: Taplinger, 1979. 258 p.

"Teaching political science fiction," by M. H. Greenberg and J. D. Olander. in: Williamson, Jack, ed. *Teaching Science Fiction: Education for Tomorrow*. Philadelphia: Owlswick, 1980. pp. 145-156.

"Utopias and dystopias," by Frederik Pohl, M. H. Greenberg and J. D. Olander. in: Warrick, Patracia, ed. *Science Fiction: Contemporary Mythology*. New York: Harper, 1978. pp. 393-400.

Oliveira, Maria de Lourdes de

"Ovnis ou os contatos luminoso," *Vozes* 72(7):63-67. September 1978.

Oliver, Chad

They Builded a Tower: The Story of Science Fiction. Masters Thesis, The University of Texas, 1952. 157 p.

Two Horizons of Man: Parallels and Interconnections Between Anthropology and Science Fiction. Paper presented Nov. 21, 1974 to the American Anthropological Assoc. Type draft in Texas A&M University Library SF Research Collection.

"Afterthoughts," in: Oliver, Chad. *The Edge of Forever*. Los Angeles: Sherbourne, 1971. pp. 294-300.

"Chad Oliver and Walter Miller," *Sumermorn* 3: 21-25. Fall 1979.

"North American Science Fiction Convention," *SFWA Bulletin* 19(3): 7-9. Fall 1985.

"Science fiction: what is it and what it isn't," *Texas Ranger* 65(2): 14-15. October 1952.

Oliver-Warden, B. C.

"Peake, Mervyn," in: Woodcock, George, ed. *20th Century Fiction*. Chicago: St. James, 1985. pp. 515-517.

Olivier-Martin, Yves

"Les Noms," by Yves Olivier-Martin and Jacques Goimard. *Europe* 580/581:20-22. August/September 1977.

"Litterature populaire, Une," *Europe* 580/581:127-132. August/September 1977.

Olney, Clark

"Edgar Allan Poe: science fiction pioneer," *The Georgia Review* 12(4):416-421. Winter 1958.

Olsa, Jaroslav, Jr.

"SF in Czechoslovakia," by Jaroslav Olsa, Jr. and Peter Holan. *Locus* 18(3): 25-26. March 1985.

Olsen, A. H.

"Anti-Consolatio: Boethius and *The Last Unicorn*," *Mosaic* 13(3/4): 133-144. Spring/Summer 1980.

Olsen, J. A.

"Extraordinary world of the Nome King," *Cinefantastique* 15(5):46-49,58. January 1986.

Olsen, Lance

"Misfires in Eden: Garcia Marquez and narrative frustration," *Kansas Quarterly* 16(3): 52-61. Summer 1984.

Olson, Douglas

"Flesh Gordon," by Mark Carducci and Douglas Olson. *Cinefantastique* 3(4):4-7,38. Winter 1974.

Olson, R. L.

"Science fiction as forecasting," _SFWA Bulletin_ 10(3): 25-26. Winter 1974/1975.

Olten, Carol

"Dykstra Has a Special Effect on Films," _San Diego (Calif.) Union_ July 25, 1982. _Newsbank. Film and Television_. 22:A10-11. 1982/1983.

Onderdonk, Matthew

"Lord of R'Lyeh, The," in: Wetzel, George. _Howard Phillips Lovecraft: Memoirs, Critiques, & Bibliographies_. North Tonowonda, NY: SSR, 1955. pp. 28-37.

Onesti, Richard

"Mycenae to Mars: science fiction in the ninth grade curriculum," by Keith Bushmaker and Richard Onesti. _Wisconson English Journal_ 18(3):13-14,21. April 1976.

Ordway, F. I., III

"Space Fiction in Film, A: Eight Decades from Melies to Lucas," in: Emme, Eugene M., ed. _Science Fiction and Space Futures_. San Diego: Univelt, 1982. pp. 27-46.

"Space Fiction in Film, B: 2001: A Space Odyssey in Retrospect," in: Emme, Eugene M., ed. _Science Fiction and Space Futures_. San Diego: Univelt, 1982. pp. 47-105.

Orjollet, J. F.

"J.R.R. Tolkien: syllogistique du merveilleux," _Litteratur_ No. 8:41-52. December 1972.

Orlikow, Bill

"Conan the Cinema-ian," _AMRA_ 2(62):4-6. October 1974.

Orlova, R.

"O romane Kurta Vonneguta," Afterword to _Boinya nomer pyat', ili krestovui pokhod detei_, trans. of _Slaughterhouse-Five_. _Novyi Mir_ 4:179-180. 1970.

Orr, David

"Science and sorcerers: a casual look at role (roll) playing," _Leading Edge_ No. 7:93-99. undated.

Orth, M. P.

Tarzan's Revenge: A Literary Biography of Edgar Rice Burroughs. Ph.D. Dissertation, Claremont, 1973. 390 p.

Osielski, M. Y.

Science Fiction: An Annotated Bibliography of Selected Resources in the University Libraries SUNY/Albany. Albany: SUNY Albany University Libraries, 1984. 16 p. (ERIC ED 249 994)

Osipov, A. N.

"Fantastika? Eto ne tak prosto," _Bibliotekar_ No. 4:24-28. 1969.

"Iz istorii bibliografii fantastiki," Soviet Bibliography no 4:44-53. 1975.

"Nauchnaia fantastika," _Bibliotekar_ No. 8:45-50. 1971.

"Nauchnaia fantastika: osobennosti propagandy," _Bibliotekar_ No. 12:46-9. 1971.

"Sovetskaia fantastika (Opyt bibliografii 1965-1967 gg.)," in: _Fantastika 75-76_. Moskva: Molodaia gvardiia, 1976. pp. 370-380.

Ostling, J. K.

C. S. Lewis: an Annotated Checklist of Writings About Him and His Works, by J. R. Christopher and J. K. Ostling. Kent Ohio: Kent State University Press, 1973. 389 p.

"C. S. Lewis: a bibliographic supplement," by J. R. Christopher and J. K. Ostling. _CSL: the Bulletin of the New York C. S. Lewis Society_ 5(8):4-6. 1974.

Ostrowski, Witold

"Fantastic and the realistic in literature, The," _Zagadnienia Rodzajow Literackich_ 9(1):54-74. 1966.

"Imaginary History," _Zagadnienia Rodazjow Literackick_ 3(2):27-38. 1960.

Ostwald, Thomas

Jules Verne: Leben und Werk. Brauschweig: Graff, 1978. 299 p.

Otten, Terry

"Fallen and Evolving Worlds of 2001," _Mosaic_ 13(3/4): 41-50. Spring/Summer 1980.

Otty, Nick

"Structuralist's Guide to Middle-earth," in: Giddings, Robert, ed. J. R. R. Tolkien: This Far Land. London: Vision, 1983. pp. 154-178.

Ounsley, Simon

"Alveric and the time warp," Vector 96:15-19. December 1979/January 1980.

"Deadly Tiger: A Dissident's view of Alfred Bester," Vector 98: 12-15. June 1980.

Overbey, D. L.

"Effets speciaux dans les films allemands de Fritz Lang," Cinema D'aujourd'hui. No. 7:53-58. Spring 1976.

"Festival de Trieste: Echec et Scandale," Cinema D'aujourd'hui. No. 7:99-104. Spring 1976.

Owen, Linda

"Dragons in the classroom," English Journal 73(7):76-77. November 1984.

Owen, T. L.

"Collectors' best bets," Science Fiction Times (Boston) 1(4):7. August 1979.

"Doings in Uchronia," Science Fiction Times (Boston) 1(5):5. November 1979.

Owen, Thomas

"Temoignage," in: H. P. Lovecraft. Paris: Editions de l'Herne, 1969. pp. 137-138.

Ower, J. B.

"Manacle forged minds: two images of the computer in science fiction," Diogenes 85:47-61. Spring 1974.

"Some reflections on the college teaching of science fiction," Journal of English Teaching Techniques pp. 1-10. Fall 1972.

"Vers une axiomatique de la science-fiction," Diogene 85:53-69. 1974.

"Walter M. Miller, Jr.," in: Bleiler, E. F., ed. Science Fiction Writers. New York: Scribners, 1982. pp. 441-448.

Ower, John

"Aesop and the ambiguity of Clifford Simak's City," Science Fiction Studies 6(2):164-167. July 1979.

"Idea and imagery in Herbert's Dune," Extrapolation 15(2):129-139. May 1974.

"Theme and Technique in H. G. Wells' 'The Star'," Extrapolation 18(2):167-175. May 1977.

Ower, Patricia

"R. A. Lafferty," in: Cowart, David, ed. Twentieth-Century American Science-Fiction Writers, Part 1: A-L. Detroit: Gale, 1981. pp. 250-255. (Dictionary of Literary Biography, v. 8)

Owings, Mark

Catalog of Lovcraftiana: The Grill/Binkin Collection, by Mark Owings and Irving Binkin. Baltimore: Mirage, 1975. 71 p.

Electric Bibliograph, Part 1: Clifford D. Simak, The. Baltimore: Alice & Jay Haldeman, 1971.

Index to the Science Fantasy Publishers: A Bibliography of the Science Fiction and Fantasy Specialty Houses, The, by M. Owings and J. L. Chalker. Baltimore: The Anthem Series, 1966. Second Edition, 76 p.

James H. Schmitz: A Bibliography. Baltimore: Croatan House, 1973. 31 p.

Revised H. P. Lovecraft Bibliography. Baltimore: Mirage, 1973. 43 p.

Robert A. Heinlein: A Bibliography. Baltimore: Croatan House, 1973. 23 p.

"Jack Williamson: a bibliography," in: World Science Fiction Convention, 1977. Sun Con Program Book. Miami Beach: Sun Con, 1977. pp. 27-29.

"James Blish: bibliography," Magazine of Fantasy and Science Fiction 42(4):78-83. April 1972.

Oznobikhina, N.

"Utopiya i nauchnya fantastika". Yazyki i literatura: dal'nevostochnyi nauchnyi tsentr AN SSSR 1:3-16. 1973.

Ozolins, Aija

"Dreams and doctrines: dual strands in Frankenstein," Science Fiction Studies 2(2):103-112. July 1975.

"Recent work on Mary Shelley and Frankenstein," Science Fiction Studies 3(2):187-202. July 1976.

P

Pace, D. P.

"Back to the Future," by E. C. Barksdale and D. P. Pace. Cinefantastique 16(1):45,56-57. March 1986.

"Tolkien and Vergil," Mythlore 6(2):37-38. Spring 1979.

Paech, Susanne

Von den Marskanaelen zur Wunderwaffe. Munich: SS. Paech, 1981. 300 p.

"Zur Person: Herbert W. Franke," in: Rottensteiner, Franz, ed. Polaris 6. Frankfurt-am-Main: Suhrkamp, 1982. pp. 316-321.

Pace, J. P.

"Monte-Cristo cibernetico," Vozes 72(2):26-50. March 1978.

Page, Bill

Index to SF Cover Art, Vol. I. Bryan, Texas: by the author, 1979. 14 p.

Index to SF Cover Art, Vol. II. Bryan, TX: Dellwood Press, 1980. 16 p.

Index to SF Cover Art, Vol. III. Bryan, TX: Dellwood Press, 1980. 20 p.

"Under the Lone Star," in: First Occasional Lone Star Science Fiction Convention and Chili Cookoff. Austin: Lone Star Con, 1985. pp. 19-25.

Page, Jerry

"Some notes on Robert E. Howard," Science Fiction Times No. 462:1-3. January 1969.

Pagetti, Carlo

Il senso del futuro: la fantascienza nelle letteratura americana. Rome: Edizioni di storia e letteratura, 1970. 323 p.

"25 years of SF criticism in Italy, 1953-1978," Science Fiction Studies 6(3):320-326. November 1979.

"Convegno di Palermo sulla fantascienza e la critica," L'informatore librario p. 11-15. 1979.

"Dick and meta-SF," Science Fiction Studies 2(1):24-31. March 1975.

"Documenti da Nessun Luogo," Cosmo informatore 14(1):1-8. Spring 1985.

"First men on the moon: H. G. Wells and the fictional strategy of his scientific romances, The," Science Fiction Studies 7(2):124-134. July 1980. Comment: 9(1):103-105. March 1982.

"In cerca di una realta. La terza ondata della fantascienza," Gamma 27. February 1968.

"J. G. Ballard: sperimentalismo e mitologia del futuro," Annali dell'Istituto Unversitario Orientale di Napoli. Sezione Germanica. 21(1/2):99-109. 1978.

"Kurt Vonnegut, tra fantascienza e utopia," Studi Americani (Roma) 12:301-322. 1966.

"Ray Bradbury e la fantascienza Americana," Studi Americani (Roma) 11:409-429. 1965.

"SF: da Swift a Ballard," Nuova presenza No. 37/38:1-9. 1970.

"Terra: Paesaggio alieno," Cosmo informatore 14(2):42-43. Summer 1985.

Paine, D. M.

Guide to Science Fiction: Exploring Possibilities and Alternatives. New York: Bantam, 1974. 72 p. also in: ERIC ED 109 038.

Pal, George

"Galaxy of space music," Music Journal 27(1):48. January 1969.

Pal, Pandi

"A magyar Science Fiction osei," SF Tajekoztato 7:33-36. November 1972.

Palafox Marques, Silvario

"Asimov y Cajal: dos cientificos ante el mismo 'Hobby'," Folia Humanistica 17(193/194):31-45. January/February 1979.

Palei, A.

"Literatura o fantastika," Bibliotekar No. 1:23-27. 1973.

Paleo, Lyn

Uranian Worlds: A Reader's Guide to Alternative Sexuality in Science Fiction and Fantasy, by Eric Garber and Lyn Paleo. Boston: G. K. Hall, 1983. 177 p.

Palmade, Guy

"Perspectives sur l'autotechnique de l'homme," Cahiers du Sud No. 317. June 1953.

Palmer, Bruce

Visions of Paradise in LotR. Baltimore: T-K Graphics, 1976. 29 p.

Palmer, Randy

"New Magic (review)," Cinefantastique 14(4/5):108. September 1984.

Palmer, Ray

"Other Worlds Science Stories: my mag one year from now," Fantasy Times No. 100:7-9. February (2) 1950.

"Circulation figures," Fantasy Times No. 233:4-5. October (2) 1955.

"Paul, a nostalgic memory," Science Fiction Times No. 4-5:7-8. August 1963.

"Prejudice enslaves fans," Science Fiction Times No. 293a:1-2. May 1958.

"Science fiction 15 years ago and today," Fantasy Times No. 254:13-16. September (1) 1956.

Palmer, Raymond

"Vonnegut's major concerns," Iowa English Yearbook No. 14:3-10. Fall 1969.

Palmer, Shirley

"Just one more chapter, please," Christian Herald 101:16-18,20-21. March 1978.

Paludan, Julius

Om Holbergs Neils Klim. Copenhagen: Prior, 1878. 337 p.

Paludan, Poul

"Science fiction i gymnasiet," Meddelelser fra Danskloerer foreningen pp.302-306. 1971.

Palumbo, Donald

"Glass Bead Game, The," in: Magill, Frank N., ed. Survey of Modern Fantasy Literature, Vol 2. Englewood Cliffs, NJ: Salem Press, Inc., 1983. pp. 619-624.

"Naked Lunch," in: Magill, Frank N., ed. Survey of Modern Fantasy Literature, Vol 3. Englewood Cliffs, NJ: Salem Press, Inc., 1983. pp. 1086-1088.

"Trial, The," in: Magill, Frank N., ed. Survey of Modern Fantasy Literature, Vol 4. Englewood Cliffs, NJ: Salem Press, Inc., 1983. pp. 1966-1968.

"Adam Warlock: Marvel Comics' Cosmic Christ Figure," Extrapolation 24(1): 33-46. Spring 1983.

"Comics as Literature: Plot Structure Foreshadowing, and Irony in the Marvel Comics' Avengers Cosmic Epic," Extrapolation 22(4): 309-324. Winter 1981.

"Loving That Machine; or, The Mechanical Egg: Sexual Mechanisms and Metaphors in Science Fiction Films," in: Dunn, Thomas P., ed. The Mechanical God. Westport: Greenwood, 1982. pp. 117-128.

"Modern fantasy and Marvel Comics," in: Magill, Frank N., ed. Survey of Modern Fantasy Literature, Vol 5. Englewood Cliffs, NJ: Salem Press, Inc., 1983. pp. 2464-2480.

"Science Fiction as Allegorical Social Satire: William Burroughs and Jonathan Swift," Studies in Contemporary Satire 9: 1-8. 1982.

"William Burroughs' quartet of science fiction as dystopian social satire," Extrapolation 20(4):321-329. Winter 1979.

"William S. Burroughs," in: Cowart, David, ed. Twentieth-Century American Science-Fiction Writers, Part 1: A-L. Detroit: Gale, 1981. pp. 92-96. (Dictionary of Literary Biography, v. 8)

Panshin, Alexei

Heinlein in Dimension: A Critical Analysis.
Chicago: Advent, 1968. 204 p.

Mondi interiori: storia della fantazcienza,
by Alexei and Cory Panshin. Milan: Nord, 1978.
149 p.

SF in Dimension: A Book of Explorations, by
Alexei Panshin and Cory Panshin. Chicago:
Advent, 1976. 342 p.

"Basic science fiction collection, A,"
Library Journal 95(12):2223-2229. June 15,
1970. also in: Colloquy, Education in Church
& Society 4(5):13-25. May 1971.

"Bibliography of twentieth-century science
fiction, A," by Alexei Panshin and Cory
Panshin. in: Williamson, Jack, ed.
Teaching Science Fiction: Education for
Tomorrow. Philadelphia: Owlswick, 1980. pp.
228-241.

"Books in the field: science fiction,"
Wilson Library Bulletin 44(6):616-620.
February 1970.

"First chapter: the world beyond the hill,"
by Alexei Panshin and Cory Panshin.
Extrapolation 13(2):133-145. May 1972.

"Heinlein in Dimension: part V, content,"
Riverside Quarterly 2(4): 284-297. March
1967.

"John Campbell's vision," by Alexei Panshin
and Cory Panshin. Starship 34:18-20.
Spring 1979.

"Nature of creative fantasy, The," Fantastic
Stories 20(3):100-106. February 1971.

"Nature of science fiction, The," Fantastic
Stories 19(6):119-122. August 1970.

"New paradigm: I, A," Fantastic Stories
20(6):110-113. August 1971.

"New paradigm: II, A," Fantastic Stories
21(1):120-126. October 1971.

"New perspectives," Fantastic Stories
20(5):109-113,125. June 1971.

"On Heinlein in Dimension, S. C. Fredericks,
and SF criticism," Science Fiction Studies
4(2):215-218. July 1977. Response, S. C.
Fredericks, 4(2):218. July 1977.

"Profession of science fiction, XIV: Why I no
longer pretend to write science fiction, The,"
Foundation 14:20-26. September 1978.

"Reading Heinlein subjectively," by Alexei
Panshin and Cory Panshin. The Alien Critic
3(2):4-17. 1974.

"Science fiction and academia," in: Turek,
Leslie, ed. Noreascon Proceedings.
Cambridge, MA: NESFA, 1976. pp. 108-111.

"Science fiction and creative fantasy,"
Fantastic Stories 20(2):124-128. December
1970.

"Science Fiction and the Dimensions of Myth,"
by Alexei Panshin and Cory Panshin.
Extrapolation 22(2): 127-139. Summer 1981.

"Science fiction bibliography and criticism,"
American Libraries 1(9):884-885. October
1970.

"Science fiction in dimension," Fantastic
19(5):125-130. June 1970. also in: Clareson,
T. D., ed. SF: The Other Side of Realism.
Bowling Green, Ohio: Bowling Green University
Popular Press, 1971. pp. 326-333.

"Science fiction, new trends and old," by
Alexei Panshin and Cory Panshin. in: Bretnor,
Reginald, ed. Science Fiction Today and
Tomorrow. New York: Harper, 1974. pp.
217-234.

"SF and academia," Fantastic Stories
21(2):110-113,128. December 1971.

"Short history of science fiction, The,"
Fantastic Stories 20(4):109-115. April 1971.

"Short SF in 1968," in: Blish, James, ed.
Nebula Award Stories Five. Garden City, New
York: Doubleday, 1970. pp. 206-213.

"Twentieth century science fiction writers,"
by Alexei Panshin and Cory Panshin. in:
Williamson, Jack, ed. Teaching Science
Fiction: Education for Tomorrow.
Philadelphia: Owlswick, 1980. pp. 52-64.

"Unbinding science fiction," Fantastic
Stories 20(1):89-97. October 1970.

Panshin, Cory

Mondi interiori: storia della fantazcienza,
by Alexei and Cory Panshin. Milan: Nord, 1978.
149 p.

SF in Dimension: A Book of Explorations, by
Alexei Panshin and Cory Panshin. Chicago:
Advent, 1976. 342 p.

"Bibliography of twentieth-century science
fiction, A," by Alexei Panshin and Cory
Panshin. in: Williamson, Jack, ed.
Teaching Science Fiction: Education for
Tomorrow. Philadelphia: Owlswick, 1980. pp.
228-241.

"First chapter: the world beyond the hill,"
by Alexei Panshin and Cory Panshin.
Extrapolation 13(2):133-145. May 1972.

Panshin, Cory (Continued)

"John Campbell's vision," by Alexei Panshin and Cory Panshin. Starship 34:18-20. Spring 1979.

"Reading Heinlein subjectively," by Alexei Panshin and Cory Panshin. The Alien Critic 3(2):4-17. 1974.

"Science Fiction and the Dimensions of Myth," by Alexei Panshin and Cory Panshin. Extrapolation 22(2): 127-139. Summer 1981.

"Science fiction, new trends and old," by Alexei Panshin and Cory Panshin. in: Bretnor, Reginald, ed. Science Fiction Today and Tomorrow. New York: Harper, 1974. pp. 217-234.

"Twentieth century science fiction writers," by Alexei Panshin and Cory Panshin. in: Williamson, Jack, ed. Teaching Science Fiction: Education for Tomorrow. Philadelphia: Owlswick, 1980. pp. 52-64.

Paraf, Pierre

"Science a travers les cites du bonheur, La," Europe revue mensuelle No. 139/140:28-34. July/August 1957.

Parani, Adam

"Many Faces of Ian Holm, The," Starlog 99: 12-14, 71. October 1985.

Parez, Hertha

"Possible and the Real, The: The Growing Success of Science Fiction," Romanian Review No. 1:77-86. 1981.

Paris, B. J.

"George Eliot, science fiction, and fantasy," Extrapolation 5(2):26-30. May 1964.

Parish, J. R.

Great Science Fiction Pictures, by J. R. Parish and M. R. Pitts. Metuchen, NJ: Scarecrow, 1977. 382 p.

"Christopher Lee; career article," by J. R. Parish and M. R. Pitts. Cinefantastique 3(1):5-23. Fall 1973.

Parish, Margaret

"Fantasy," English Journal 66(7):90-93. October 1977.

"Science fiction," English Journal 67(2):117-119. February 1978. (Book reviews)

Park, M. M.

"Archibald Malmaison: Julian Hawthorne's contribution to gothic fiction," Extrapolation 15(2):103-116. May 1974.

Parker, Amy

"Kindly in the mirror: an interview with Dean Ing," Leading Edge No. 6:10-13. undated.

Parker, Douglass

"Hwaet we Holbytla . . . " Hudson Review 9(4):598-609. Winter 1956/1957.

Parker, H. M.

Biological Themes in Science Fiction. Ann Arbor: UMI Research Press, 1984, c1977. 109 p.

Parkin-Speer, Diane

"Alien Ethics and Religion versus Fallen Mankind," in: Reilly, Robert, ed. The Transcendent Adventure. Westport: Greenwood, 1984. pp. 93-104.

"Leigh Brackett's The Long Tomorrow: a quest for the future America," Extrapolation 26(3): 190-200. Fall 1985.

"Robert A. Heinlein: the novelist as preacher," Extrapolation 20(3):214-222. Fall 1979.

Parkinson, Bob

"Authentic vision: a study of the writings of Arthur C. Clarke," Vector 49: 2-6. June 1968.

"Planet Maker: Hal Clement," Vector 14: 7-10. Winter 1961/1962.

"Ray Bradbury: a short critique," Vector 39: 2-6. April 1966.

Parkinson, R. C.

"Dune: an unfinished tetralogy," Extrapolation 13(1):16-24. December 1971.

Parks, H. B.

"Tolkien and the Critical Approach to Story," in: Isaacs, Neil D. Tolkien: New Critical Perspectives, ed. by Neil D. Isaacs and Rose A. Zimbardo. Lexington: University Press of Kentucky, 1981. pp. 133-149.

Parks, Janis

"'Lathe of Heaven' TV Adaptation Eases Le Guin's mind," _Houston Post_ Sec. AA, p. 12. January 9, 1980.

Parks, Michael

"China: Boom for Science Fiction," _Los Angeles Times_ p. 15-17. February 19, 1982.

Parnell, F. H.

Monthly Terrors: An Index to the Weird Fantasy Magazines Published in the United States and Great Britain, by F. H. Parnell and Mike Ashley. Westport, CT.: Greenwood, 1985. 602 p.

"Adventures in Horror," by Mike Ashley and Frank Parnell. in: Tymn, M. B. and Ashley, Mike. _Science Fiction, Fantasy, and Weird Fiction Magazines_. Westport, CT: Greenwood, 1985. pp. 9-10.

"Black Cat (1970-   )," by Mike Ashley and F. H. Parnell. in: Tymn, M. B. and Ashley, Mike. _Science Fiction, Fantasy, and Weird Fiction Magazines_. Westport, CT: Greenwood, 1985. pp. 149-150.

"Book of Terror," by Mike Ashley and F. H. Parnell. in: Tymn, M. B. and Ashley, Mike. _Science Fiction, Fantasy, and Weird Fiction Magazines_. Westport, CT: Greenwood, 1985. pp. 150-151.

"Fireside Ghost Stories," by Mike Ashley and F. H. Parnell. in: Tymn, M. B. and Ashley, Mike. _Science Fiction, Fantasy, and Weird Fiction Magazines_. Westport, CT: Greenwood, 1985. pp. 273.

"Gripping Terror," by Mike Ashley and F. H. Parnell. in: Tymn, M. B. and Ashley, Mike. _Science Fiction, Fantasy, and Weird Fiction Magazines_. Westport, CT: Greenwood, 1985. pp. 323-324.

"Mind Magic Magazine," by Mike Ashley and F. H. Parnell. in: Tymn, M. B. and Ashley, Mike. _Science Fiction, Fantasy, and Weird Fiction Magazines_. Westport, CT: Greenwood, 1985. pp. 409-410.

"Tales of Crime and Punishment," by Mike Ashley and F. H. Parnell. in: Tymn, M. B. and Ashley, Mike. _Science Fiction, Fantasy, and Weird Fiction Magazines_. Westport, CT: Greenwood, 1985. pp. 643-644.

"Tales of Ghosts and Haunted Houses," by Mike Ashley and F. H. Parnell. in: Tymn, M. B. and Ashley, Mike. _Science Fiction, Fantasy, and Weird Fiction Magazines_. Westport, CT: Greenwood, 1985. pp. 644.

"Tales of Mystery and Detection," by Mike Ashley and F. H. Parnell. in: Tymn, M. B. and

Ashley, Mike. _Science Fiction, Fantasy, and Weird Fiction Magazines_. Westport, CT: Greenwood, 1985. pp. 647-648.

"Tales of Terror," by Mike Ashley and F. H. Parnell. in: Tymn, M. B. and Ashley, Mike. _Science Fiction, Fantasy, and Weird Fiction Magazines_. Westport, CT: Greenwood, 1985. pp. 648-649.

"Tales of Terror From the Beyond," by Mike Ashley and F. H. Parnell. in: Tymn, M. B. and Ashley, Mike. _Science Fiction, Fantasy, and Weird Fiction Magazines_. Westport, CT: Greenwood, 1985. pp. 649.

"Tales of the Uncanny," by Mike Ashley and F. H. Parnell. in: Tymn, M. B. and Ashley, Mike. _Science Fiction, Fantasy, and Weird Fiction Magazines_. Westport, CT: Greenwood, 1985. pp. 650-651.

"Thrills," in: Tymn, M. B. and Ashley, Mike. _Science Fiction, Fantasy, and Weird Fiction Magazines_. Westport, CT: Greenwood, 1985. pp. 671-672.

"Witch's Tales," by Mike Ashley and F. H. Parnell. in: Tymn, M. B. and Ashley, Mike. _Science Fiction, Fantasy, and Weird Fiction Magazines_. Westport, CT: Greenwood, 1985. pp. 742-743.

Parnov, E. I.

Fantastika v ved NTR: ocherki sovremennoja nauchoifantastiki. Moscow: Znanie, 1974. 192 p.

Sovremennoja nauchaja fantastiki. Moscow: Zanie, 1968. 101 p.

"Bezumstra 'Nechistoi' Fantastik," _Literaturnaya Gazeta_ 50, 16, p. 15. April 19, 1978.

"Fantastyka naukowa we wspolczesnym swiecie," in: Kaczmarka, J., ed. _Materialy z Miedzynarodowego Spotkania Pisarzy-Tworcow Literatury Fantastyczno-Naukowej_. Poznan: Wyndawnictwo Poznanskie, 1974. pp. 46-52.

"Koenige und Konstrukteure, _Quarber Merkur_ 27:43-50. July 1971.

"Science fiction against nuclear madness," _Soviet Literature_ 6(447): 180-184. 1985.

Parr, J. G.

"Chesterton and technology," _Chesterton Review_ 3:91-98. 1976.

"H. G. Wells: his significance in 1966," _University of Windsor Review_ 2(2):67-76. Spring 1967.

Parr, Julian

"Ernsting out, then back," _Fantasy Times_ No. 253:5-6. August (2) 1956.

"SF boom on in Germany," _Fantasy Times_ No. 257:3-4. October (2) 1956.

Parrill, William

"Stanley Kubrick," in: May, John, and Bird, Michael, eds. _Religion in Film_. Knoxville: University of Tennessee Press, 1982. pp. 189-195.

Parrinder, Patrick

H. G. Wells. Edinburgh: Oliver and Boyd, 1970. 120 p.

H. G. Wells's Literary Criticism, by Patrick Parrinder and R. M. Philmus. Totowa, NJ: Barnes & Noble, 1980. 261 p.

H. G. Wells: The Critical Heritage. London: Routledge & Kegan Paul, 1972. 351 p.

Science Fiction: A Critical Guide. London: Longmans, 1979. 238 p.

Science Fiction: Its Criticism and Teaching. London, New York: Methuen, 1980. 166 p.

"_News from Nowhere, The Time Machine_, and the break-up of classical realism," _Science Fiction Studies_ 3(3):265-274. November 1976.

"Alien encounter, The: or, Ms. Brown and Mrs. Le Guin," _Science Fiction Studies_ 6(1):46-58. March 1979.

"Black wave: science and social consciousness in modern science fiction, The," _Radical Science Journal_ 5:37-61. 1977.

"Characterization in science fiction: two approaches: the alien encounter: or Ms. Brown and Mrs. Le Guin," in: Parrinder, Patrick, ed. _Science Fiction: A Critical Guide_. New York: Longman, 1979. pp. 148-161.

"Imagining the future: Wells and Zamayatin," _Science Fiction Studies_ 1(1):17-26. Spring 1973. also in: Suvin, Darko, ed. _H. G. Wells and Modern Science Fiction_. Lewisburg: Bucknell Univ. Press, 1977. pp. 126-143.

"Science fiction and the scientific world view," in: Parrinder, Patrick, ed. _Science Fiction: A Critical Guide_. New York: Longman, 1979. pp. 67-88.

"Science Fiction as Truncated Epic" in: Slusser, George E., ed. _Bridges to Science Fiction_. Carbondale: Southern Illinois University Press, 1980. pp. 91-106.

"Siblings in Space: The Science Fiction of J. B. S. Haldane and Naomi Mitchison," _Foundation_ 22: 49-56. June 1981.

"Utopia and Meta-Utopia in H. G. Wells," _Science Fiction Studies_ 12(2): 115-128. July 1985.

Parrington, V. L.

American Dreams: A Study of American Utopias. Providence, Rhode Island: Brown University Press, 1947. 234 p. New York: Russell & Russell, 1964. Second edition, 246 p.

Partridge, Brenda

"No Sex Please: We're Hobbits: The Construction of Female Sexuality in The Lord of the Rings," in: Giddings, Robert, ed. _J. R. R. Tolkien: This Far Land_. London: Vision, 1983. pp. 179-198.

Paskanzer, S. C.

"Case for fantasy, A," _Elementary English_ 52(4):472-475. April 1975.

Paskow, D. C.

"Guest editorial: Star Trek, the turning point," _Science Fiction Times_ No. 458:2. September 1968.

"On TV: SF series, 1968-1969," _Science Fiction Times_ No. 460:3,5. November 1968.

Pastour, Isabelle

"Fantastique en litterature, Du," _Documents et Recherches Lettres_ pp. 25-26. April 1975.

Patai, Daphne

"British and American utopias by women (1856-1979): an annotated bibliography," _Alternative Futures_ 4(2/3): 184-206. Spring/Summer 1981.

"Gamesmanship and Androcentrism in Orwell's 1984," _PMLA_ 97(5): 856-870. October 1982.

"When Women Rule: Defamiliarization and the Sex-Role Reversal Utopia," _Extrapolation_ 23(1): 56-69. Spring 1982.

Patrick, J. M.

"Iconoclasm, the complement of utopianism," _Science Fiction Studies_ 3(2):157-161. July 1976.

"Inside utopia," _Extrapolation_ 8(1):20-24. December 1966.

Patrouch, J. F., Jr.

Science Fiction of Isaac Asimov, The. Garden City: Doubleday, 1974. 283 p.

"Asimov's most recent fiction," in: Olander, J. D. and M. H. Greenberg, eds. Isaac Asimov. New York: Taplinger, 1977. pp. 159-173.

"Harlan Ellison and the formula story," in: Porter, Andrew, ed. The Book of Ellison. New York: Algol Press, 1978. pp. 45-64.

"Harlan Ellison's Use of the Narrator's Voice," in: Hassler, Donald M. Patterns of the Fantastic. Mercer Island, WA: Starmont, 1983. pp. 63-66.

"Robert A. Heinlein," in: Cowart, David, ed. Twentieth-Century American Science Fiction Writers, Part 1: A-L, Detroit: Gale, 1981. pp. 208-228. (Dictionary of Literary Biography, v. 8)

"State of the Art: The Ninety Degree Error," Analog 102(6): 145-149. June 1982.

"Stephen King in Context," in: Hassler, Donald M. Patterns of the Fantastic. Mercer Island, WA: Starmont, 1983. pp. 5-10.

"Unpopularity of science fiction, The," Focus on the University of Dayton 4:14-17. January 1971. (not seen)

Patten, Fred

"Lest Darkness Fall," in: Magill, Frank N., ed. Survey of Science Fiction Literature, Vol. 3. Englewood Cliffs, NJ: Salem Press, 1979. pp. 1198-1203.

"Illustrated history of the world science fiction convention, part 2, An," Midamericon Progress Report 4:38-59. No date.

Patterson, N. L.

"Appreciation of Pauline Baynes," Mythlore 7(3): 3-5. Autumn 1980.

"Banquet at Belbury: Festival and Horror in That Hideous Strength" Mythlore 8(3): 7-14, 42. Autumn 1981.

"Beneath That Ancient Roof: The House as Symbol in Dorothy L. Sayers' Busman's Honeymoon," Mythlore 10(3): 39-46. Winter 1984.

"Bright-Eyed Beauty: Celtic Elements in Charles Williams, J. R. R. Tolkien, and C. S. Lewis," Mythlore 10(1): 5-10. Spring 1983.

"Guardaci Bell: the visionary woman in C. S. Lewis' Chronicles of Narnia and That Hideous Strength, part 2," Mythlore 6(4):20-24. Fall 1979.

"Guardaci Bell: the visionary woman in C. S. Lewis' Chronicles of Narnia and That Hideous Strength, part 1," Mythlore 6(3):6-10. Summer 1979.

"Halfe like a serpent: the green witch in The Silver Chair," Mythlore 11(2):37-47. Autumn 1984.

"Homo monstrosus: Lloyd Alexander's Gurgi and other shadow figures of fantastic literature," Mythlore 3(3):24-28. 1976.

"Host of Heaven, The: Astrological and Other Images of Divinity in the Fantasies of C. S. Lewis, Part 2," Mythlore 7(4): 13-26. Winter 1981.

"Host of Heaven, The: Astrological and Other Images of Divinity in the Fantasies of C. S. Lewis, Part 1," Mythlore 7(3): 19-29. Autumn 1980.

"Letters from Hell: symbolism of evil in the Screwtape Letters," Mythlore 12(1): 47-57. Autumn 1985.

"Narnia and the North: the symbolism of northernness in the fantasies of C. S. Lewis," Mythlore 4(2): 9-16. December 1976.

Patterson, Richard

"Blade Runner: production design and photography," by H. A. Lightman and Richard Patterson. American Cinematographer 63(7):684-687,715-725. July 1982.

"Making of Tron," American Cinematographer 63(8): 792-795, 813-819. August 1982.

"Making The Invisible Woman," American Cinematographer 64(4):42-43,105-123. April 1983.

Patteson, R. F.

"Le Guin's Earthsea Trilogy: the psychology of fantasy," in: Collins, R. A., ed. Scope of the Fantastic: Culture, Biography, Themes, Children's Literature. Westport: Greenwood, 1985. pp. 239-248.

Pattison, Patrick

Collector's Edition: Science Fiction Film Awards, by D. A. Reed and Patrick Pattison. s.l.: ESE California, 1981. 107 p.

Paul, F. R.

"Science fiction, the spirit of youth," Science Fiction Times No. 405:5-7. August 1963.

"What makes a science fiction fan?" Science Fiction Times Vol. 3a:2,5. November 1963.

Paul, Terri

Blasted Hopes: A Thematic Survey of
Nineteenth-Century British Science Fiction.
Ph. D. Dissertation, Ohio State University,
1979. 161 p.

"Worm Ouroboros: Time Travel, Imagination,
and Entropy," Extrapolation 24(3):
272-279. Fall 1983.

"'Sixty Billion Gigabits': Liberation Through
Machines in Frederik Pohl's Gateway and
Beyond the Blue Event Horizon," in: Dunn,
Thomas P., ed. The Mechanical God.
Westport: Greenwood, 1982. pp. 53-62.

Pauly, R. M.

"Moral stance of Kurt Vonnegut, The,"
Extrapolation 15(1):66-71. December 1973.

Pavillard, Dan

"Fantastic author escapes on the typewriter,"
Tuscon Daily Citizen. December 2, 1972.

Pavlet, Robert

Fanzine Index...Listing Most Fanzines From the
Beginning Through 1952 Including Titles,
Editors' Names and Data on Each Issue, ed. by
Robert Pavlat and William Evans. Flushing, New
York: Harold Palmer Piser, 1965. 143 p.

Pawling, Christopher

Popular Fiction and Social Change. New York:
St. Martins, 1984. 246 p.

"Watership Down: Rolling back the 1960s,"
in: Pawling, Christopher, ed. Popular
Fiction and Social Change. New York: St.
Martins, 1984. pp. 212-235.

Pax, K.

"Rezension von 'Die bewohnte Insel'," Science
Fiction Times (Germany) No. 128:28-31. 1972.

Paxson, Diana

"Notes From Elfhill: Varieties of Religious
Experience in Fantasy," Niekas 25: 6-8.
February 1981.

"Tolkien Tradition," Mythlore 11(1):
23-27. Summer 1984.

Payne, Ronald

Last Murray Leinster Interview. Richmond,
VA.: Waves Press, 1983. 12 p.

Payton, Crystal

Space Toys, by Crystal and Leland Payton.
Sedalia, MO: Collector's Compass, 1982. 88 p.
(17 p. Price Guide laid in)

Payton, Leland

Space Toys, by Crystal and Leland Payton.
Sedalia, MO: Collector's Compass, 1982. 88 p.
(17 p. Price Guide laid in)

Pearce, H. D.

Scope of the Fantastic: Culture, Biography,
Themes, Children's Literature, ed. by R. A.
Collins and H. D. Pearce. Westport: Greenwood,
1985. 282 p.

Scope of the Fantastic: Theory, Technique,
Major Authors, ed. by R. A. Collins and H. D.
Pearce. Westport, CT: Greenwood Press, 1985.
295 p.

"Dislocating the fantastic: can this old genre
be mobilized?" in: Collins, R. A. and H. D.
Pearce, eds. The Scope of the Fantastic:
Theory, Technique, Major Authors. Westport,
CT: Greenwood Press, 1985. pp. 95-103.

Pearce, Richard

"Circus, the clown and Coover's Public
Burning, The," in: Collins, R. A., ed.
Scope of the Fantastic: Culture, Biography,
Themes, Children's Literature. Westport:
Greenwood, 1985. pp. 129-136.

Pearson, Bill

"Britain's 'Triffids' To Invade U. S.," by
Bill Pearson and David Hirsch. Starlog 56:
15-17, 64. March 1982.

"Constructing the Miniatures for 'Flash
Gordon'," by Bill Pearson and David Hirsch.
Starlog 44: 48-51. March 1981.

Pearson, Carol

"Coming Home: Four Feminist Utopias and
Patriarchal Experience," in: Barr, Marlene
S., ed. Future Females. Bowling Green, OH.:
Bowling Green State University Popular Press,
1981. pp. 63-70.

"Toward a New Language, Consciousness &
Political Theory: The Utopian Novels of Dorothy
Bryant, Mary Staton, and Marge Piercy,"
Heresies 4:84-87. 1981.

"Women's fantasies and feminist utopias,"
Frontiers: A Journal of Women's Studies
2(3):50-61. Fall 1977.

Pearson, E. J.

Science Fiction: Teacher's Manual, by S. Z. Brodkin and E. J. Pearson. Evanston: McDougal, 1974. 56 p.

Peary, Danny

Omni's Screen Flights/Screen Fantasies: The Future According to Science Fiction Cinema. Garden City, NY: Doubleday Dolphin, 1984. 310 p.

Peary, Gerald

"TZ Interview: John Sayles," Twilight Zone 4(2): 26-30. May/June 1984.

Peay, Pythia

"Magic and the imagination: Stephen R. Donaldson," Bloomsbury Review 3(3):15-19. April/May 1983.

Peck, Claudia

"On the subject of writing and clouds," Empire: For the SF Writer 6(1): 8-9, 17. Winter 1980.

Pecker, J. C.

"Pour un professeur d'astrophysique la science c'est tout de meme autre chose," La Quinzaine Litteraire No. 225:11-13. January 16, 1976.

Pecorino, P. A.

"Philosophy and Science Fiction," in: Myers, R. E., ed. The Intersection of Science Fiction and Philosophy. Westport: Greenwood, 1983. pp. 3-14.

Pedersen, E. M.

"Micro-World of Danish SF," Locus 18(1): 28-29. January 1985.

"Women and the Inner Game... by N. Steffen-Fluer: Comment," Science Fiction Studies 12(1): 105-107. March 1985.

Pedersen, Jannick

"Niels E. Nielsen. An introduction," by S. K. Moller and Jannick Pedersen. in: Dollerup, Cay, ed. Volve. Scandinavian Views on Science Fiction. Copenhagen: Department of English, Univ. of Copenhagen, 1978. pp. 55-59.

Pederson, Ellen

"SF and politics: a discussion between Brian Aldiss, Jon Bing, and John-Henri Holmberg," by E. Pedersen. in: Dollerup, Cay, ed. Volve. Scandinavian Views on SF. Copenhagen: Univ. of Copenhagen, 1978. pp. 66-69.

Pedler, Kit

"Deus ex machina?" in: Hay, George, ed. The Disappearing Future; A Symposium of Speculation. London: Panther, 1970. pp. 25-31.

Peecher, J. P.

Making of Star Wars: Return of the Jedi. New York: Del Rey, 1983. 292 p.

Peek, G. S.

"Negative Exempla: Lust Without Love in Counter-Earth Gor," Extrapolation 25(1): 76-82. Spring 1984.

Peel, E. S.

Both Ends of the Candle: Feminist Narrative Structures in Novels by Stael, Lessing, and Le Guin. Ph. D. Dissertation, Yale, 1982. 284 p. (DAI 43: 3903A)

Peeples, S. A.

"Films on 8 and 10 mm," Films in Review 23(3):185-186. March 1972.

Peeters, Josef

Fanzines in Vlaanderen der Nederland: een inventaris-en inleiding. Kessel-Lo (Belgie): Icon, 1975. 60 p.

Pehlke, Michael

Roboter und Gartenlaube, Ideologie und unterhaltung in der science-fiction-literatur, by Michael Pehlke and Norbert Lingfeld. Munchen: Hanser, 1970. 158 p.

Pei, Lowry

"Poor singletons: definitions of humanity in the stories of James Tiptree, Jr.," Science Fiction Studies 6(3):271-280. November 1979.

Pell, S. W. J.

"Asimov in the classroom," Journal of Reading 21(3):258-261. December 1977.

Pell, S. W. J. (Continued)

"Style is the man: imagery in Bradbury's fiction," in: Olander, J. D. and M. H. Greenberg, eds. Ray Bradbury. New York: Taplinger, 1980. pp. 186-194.

Pelz, Bruce

"TAFF railings, part 1," Locus No. 42:11-12. November 21, 1969.

Pemberton, C.

"Editorial: The Awakening of a Conscience: The Day the Buck Stopped Here," by C. Pemberton and Geoff Rippington. Vector 116: 3-5. September 1983.

Penn, David

"Galactic Cluster," Vector 104: 17-19. October 1981.

Penn, Marcella

Ray Bradbury: An Emersonian Romantic. Masters Thesis, University of Texas, Arlington, 1978. 72 p.

Penning, Dieter

"Begriff der Ueberwirklichkeit. Nerval, Maupassnat, Breton," in: Thomsen, C. W., ed. Phantastik in Literatur und Kunst. Darmstadt: Wissenschaftliche Buchgesellschaft, 1980. pp. 201-218.

"Ordnung der Unordnung, Die: Einer Bilanz zur Theorie der Phantastik," in: Thomsen, C. W., ed. Phantastik in Literatur und Kunst. Darmstadt: Wiss. Buchgesellschaft, 1980. pp. 34-51.

Penzoldt, Peter

Supernatural in Fiction, The. London: Peter Nevill, 1952. 271 p. Reprinted, New York: Humanities Press, 1965.

"From the Supernatural in Fiction," in: Joshi, S. T., ed. H. P. Lovecraft: Four Decades of Criticism. Athens, OH: Ohio University Press, 1980. pp. 63-77.

"Supernatural in science fiction, The," in: The Supernatural in Fiction. London: Peter Nevill, 1952. pp. 49-53.

Peoples, Galen

"Agnostic in the whirlwind: the seven novels of Charles Williams," Mythlore 2(2):10-15. Autumn 1970.

Peplow, M. W.

Samuel R. Delany: a Primary and Secondary Bibliography, by M. W. Peplow and R. S. Bravard. Boston: G. K. Hall, 1980. 112 p.

"Samuel R. Delany: A Selective Primary and Secondary Bibliography, 1979-1983," by M. W. Peplow and R. S. Bravard. Black American Literature Forum 18(2): 75-77. Summer 1984.

"Through a Glass Darkly: Bibliographing Samuel R. Delany," by R. S. Bravard and M. W. Peplow. Black American Literature Forum 18(2): 69-75. Summer 1984.

Peppin, Brigid

Fantasy: The Golden Age of Fantastic Illustration. New York: Watson, 1975. 192 p.

Perakos, P. S.

"George Pal's production of The Disappearance," by P. S. Perakos and F. S. Clarke. Cinefantastique 8(4):4-6. Summer 1979.

"Logan's Run (review)," Cinefantastique 6(3):20,23. Winter 1977.

"Stephen King on Carrie, The Shining, etc.," Cinefantastique 8(1):13-15. Winter 1978.

Percy, Walker

"Walter M. Miller, Jr.'s A Canticle for Leibowitz: a rediscovery," Southern Review 7(2):572-578. Spring 1971.

Perec, G.

"Univers de la SF, L'" Partisans May 1963.

Perelman, S. J.

"Cloudland revisited," New Yorker 26(44):18-21. December 23, 1950.

Perez, G. J.

"Cultivadores, temas y motivos de la ciencia ficcion actual en Espana," Romance Notes 25(2): 102-108. Winter 1984.

Pergameno, Sandro

"Il fantistico regno di Lyonesse, nel mondo delle isole elder," Cosmo informatore 14(1):62-63. Spring 1985.

"L'avventura revisitata da Carolyn J. Cherryh," Cosmo informatore 14(2):10-12. Summer 1985.

Pergameno, Sandro (Continued)

"Quando gli umani si incontrarono con i Thranx," Cosmo informatore 14(1):50. Spring 1985.

"Stregoni, indomiti guerrieri, incantevoli principesse: uno sguardo alla fantasy moderna," Cosmo informatore 14(4):3-8. Winter 1985.

Perkins, Agnes

"Corruption of power, The," by Agnes Perkins and Helen Hill. in: Lobdell, Jared, ed. A Tolkien Compass. New York: Ballantine/Del Rey, 1980. pp. 60-72.

Perkins, J. A.

"MYCROFTXX is alive and well: the ambiguous ending of The Moon is a Harsh Mistress," Notes on Contemporary Literature 5(1):13-15. January 1975.

Perkinson, G. E.

"Conference Report: Science fiction: writers and librarians confer," Library Journal 103(10):1018-1019. May 15, 1978.

Perlman, Martin

"Clan of the Cave Bear," Cinefantastique 15(4):30-31,58. October 1985.

"Terminator," Cinefantastique 15(3):36-39,55. July 1985.

"Terminator: special effects by Fantasy II," Cinefantastique 15(2):47. May 1985.

Perret, Marion

"Rings off their fingers: hands in The Lord of the Rings," Ariel: A Review of International English Literature 6(4):52-66. 1975.

Perret, Patti

Faces of Science Fiction. New York: Bluejay, 1984. unpaged.

Perrin, Noel

"From Russia With Hope," Quest/81 5(6): 42-44, 83. July/August 1981.

"New world for women," Inquiry Magazine 1(14):26-27. May 29, 1978.

Perry, J. E.

Visions of Reality: Values and Perspectives in the Prose of Carlos Castenada, Robert M. Prisig, Ursula K. Le Guin, James Purdy, Cyrus Colter, and Sylvia Plath. Ph.D. Dissertation, University of Wisconsin, 1976. 224 p.

Perry, Nick

"Atrocity exhibition, The," by Nick Perry and Roy Wilkie. Riverside Quarterly 6(3):180-188. August 1975.

"Homo hydrogenesis: notes on the work of J. G. Ballard,: by Nick Perry and Roy Wilkie. Riverside Quarterly 4(2): 98-105. January 1970.

"Undivided self: J. G. Ballard's The Crystal World, The," by Nick Perry and Roy Wilkie. Riverside Quarterly 5:268-277. 1973.

Peruzzolo, A. C.

"A dinamic da fantasia em Ray Bradbury," Vozes 70(1):23-32. January/February 1976.

Pesch, H. W.

Fantasy: Theorie und Geschichte einer Literarischen Gattung. P. D. Dissertation, Universitat zu Koln, 1981. 292 p. (Privately printed: Forchheim, W. Germany, 1982.)

J. R. R. Tolkien: der Mythenschoepher, ed. by H. W. Pesch. Meitingen: Corian, 1984. 192 p.

"Sign of the worm, The: images of death and immortality in the fiction of E. R. Eddison," in: Yoke, C. B. and Hassler, D. M., eds. Death and the Serpent. Westport, CT: Greenwood, 1985. pp. 91-102.

Pesqueur, Jean

"Technique et Aventure: La Science-Fiction," Etudes pp. 48-62. April 1957.

Pesses, Albert et Michele Tonneau

"La science-fiction", by Albert Pesses and Michelle Tonneau. Documents et recherches 13:8-11. 1974.

Pessina, Hector

"It's about time," Argentine Science Fiction Review 1(6):5-9. June/July 1968.

"Letter from Argentina, January 1982," Science Fiction Chronicle 3(4):4. January 1982.

Pessina, Hector (Continued)

"Letter from Argentina, July 1981," <u>Science Fiction Chronicle</u> 2(10):6. July 1981.

"Letter from Argentina, June 1982," <u>Science Fiction Chronicle</u> 3(9):5-6. June 1982.

"Letter from Argentina, March 1980," <u>Science Fiction Chronicle</u> 1(6):3. March 1980.

"Letter from Argentina, March 1981," <u>Science Fiction Chronicle</u> 2(6):3. March 1981.

"Letter from Argentina, March 1982," <u>Science Fiction Chronicle</u> 3(6):4-5. March 1982.

"Letter from Argentina, May 1981," <u>Science Fiction Chronicle</u> 2(8):4-5. May 1981.

"Letter from Argentina, May 1982," <u>Science Fiction Chronicle</u> 3(8):5-6. May 1982.

"Letter from Argentina, September 1980," <u>Science Fiction Chronicle</u> 1(12):3. September 1980.

"Letter from South America, February, 1984," <u>Science Fiction Chronicle</u> 5(5):6. February 1984.

"Letter from South America, March 1983," <u>Science Fiction Chronicle</u> 4(6):5. March 1983.

"Letter from South America, November 1979," <u>Science Fiction Chronicle</u> 1(2):7. November 1979.

"Pendulo," <u>Science Fiction and Fantasy Research Index</u> 2: 72. 1982.

Peters, N. J.

"Backyard Bombs and Invisible Rays: Horror Movies on Television," <u>Cultural Correspondence</u> 10/11:39-42. Fall 1979.

Peters, Ted

"Chariots, UFO's, and the mystery of God: the science and religion of Erich Von Daniken," <u>Christian Century</u> 91:560-563. May 22, 1974.

Petersen, Clarence

"Brace Yourself for 'Psycho II'," <u>Chicago Tribune</u>, May 5, 1982. in: <u>NewsBank. Literature.</u> 92:B1-2. 1981/82.

"Herbert's Solution: Get Out of this World," <u>Chicago Tribune</u>, May 4, 1982. in: <u>NewsBank. Literature.</u> 95:D13-14. 1981/82.

Peterson, C. T.

"Jack London's Sonoma novels," <u>American Book Collector</u> 9(2):15-20. October 1958.

Peterson, Gary

"'In Search of August Derleth' Discovers Priceless Reminiscences," <u>Madison (Wisc.) Capital Times</u> October 3, 1984. in: <u>NewsBank. Film and Television</u> FTV 36:E13. 1984/1985.

Peterson, J. V.

"Gap in continuity," <u>Fantasy Times</u> No. 200:26,28-29. June (1) 1954.

Peterson, K. L.

<u>E. T.: Preschool Children's Perceptions</u>, by Bruce Roscoe and K. L. Peterson. 10 p. 1982. ERIC ED 231 546

Peterson, Karne

"Wizardry of Frank Oz: his 'empire' began pre-Yoda with Miss Piggy, The," by Fred Hauptfuhrer and Karne Peterson. <u>People Weekly</u> 13(23):38-41. June 9, 1980.

Peterson, S. A.

"Science fiction and political thought: <u>The Dispossessed</u>," by S. A. Peterson and Douglas Saxon. <u>Cornell Journal of Social Relations</u> 12(1):65-74. Fall 1977.

Petrafaso, Ginger

"SF in the classroom: science fiction in high school," by Martha Pine and Ginger Petrafaso. <u>Extrapolation</u> 14(2):149-151. May 1973.

Petre, Philippe

<u>Litterature fantastique francaise de Belgique, La: essai de bibliographie des romans et nouvelles publies de 1830 a 1976</u>. Bruxelles: Commission belge de bibliographie, 1979. 180 p.

Petrix, Ester

"Linguistics, mechanics and metaphysics: Anthony Burgess's <u>A Clockwork Orange</u>," in: Morris, R. K. <u>Old Line, New Faces</u>. Rutherford, NJ: Farleigh Dickinson Univ. Press, 1976. pp. 38-52.

Petronio, Guiseppe

Letteratura di massa, Letteratura di consumo. Bari: Laterza, 1979. 159 p.

Petrosky, A. R.

"Effects of reality perception and fantasy on response to literature; the two case studies," Research in the Teaching of English 10(3):239-258. Winter 1976.

Petterson, O. E.

"Bibliotekariske betragtniger," Proxima No. 19, sect.II:48-52. March 1979.

Pettus, David

"Charles Grant: Interview," American Fantasy 1(2): 17-21. May 1982.

"Interview With David Hartwell," by R. A. Collins and David Pettus. Fantasy Newsletter 6(7): 8-10. August 1983.

"Interview with Fred Pohl, An," Fan Plus 1(1):4-7,14. January 1980.

"Interview: Ben Bova," Thrust No. 23: 9 12. Fall/Winter 1985.

"Interview: Doug Chaffee," by David Pettus and R. M. Hester. Parsec No. 1: 39-45. June 1982.

"Interview: Michael Bishop," Thrust No. 20: 5-10, 26. Spring/Summer 1984.

Petty, A. C.

One Ring to Bind Them All: Tolkien's Mythology. University, Alabama: University of Alabama Press, 1979. 122 p.

Petzold, Dieter

J. R. R. Tolkien: Fantasy literature als Wunscherfullung u. Weltdeutung. Heidelberg: Winter, 1979. 126 p.

Pfaelzer, Jean

Utopian Novel in America, 1886-1896: the politics of form. Pittsburgh: University of Pittsburgh Press, 1984. 211 p.

"American Utopian Fiction 1888-1896: The Political Origins of Form," Minnesota Review ns6, 1976. pp. 114-117.

"Impact of Political Theory on Narrative Structure," in: Roemer, Kenneth M., ed. America As Utopia. New York: Franklin, 1981. pp. 117-132.

"Parody and satire in American dystopian fiction of the nineteenth century," Science-Fiction Studies 7(1): 61-72. March 1980.

"State of One's Own: Feminism as Ideology in American Utopias, 1880-1915," Extrapolation 24(4): 311-328. Winter 1983.

Pfaff, H. A.

"Vom warencharakter der science fiction," Quarber Merkur 47:48-60. December 1977.

Pfeiffer, J. R.

Fantasy and Science Fiction: A Critical Guide. Palmer Lake, Colorado: Filter Press, 1971. 64 p.

"Androcles and the Lion: A Fable Play," in: Magill, Frank N., ed. Survey of Modern Fantasy Literature, Vol 1. Englewood Cliffs, NJ: Salem Press, Inc., 1983. pp. 42-44.

"Back to Methuselah: a metabiological pentateuch," in: Magill, Frank N., ed. Survey of Science Fiction Literature, Vol. 1. Englewood Cliffs, NJ: Salem Press, 1979. pp. 120-124.

"Glass Bead Game, The," in: Magill, Frank N., ed. Survey of Science Fiction Literature, Vol. 2. Englewood Cliffs, NJ: Salem Press, 1979. pp. 899-904.

"Metropolis," in: Magill, Frank N., ed. Survey of Science Fiction Literature, Vol. 3. Englewood Cliffs, NJ: Salem Press, 1979. pp. 1383-1386.

"Water-Babies: A Fairy Tale for a Land-Baby, The," in: Magill, Frank N., ed. Survey of Modern Fantasy Literature, Vol 5. Englewood Cliffs, NJ: Salem Press, Inc., 1983. pp. 2074-2078.

"'But dragons have keen ears': on hearing 'Earthsea' with recollections of Beowulf," in: De Bolt, Joe, ed. Ursula K. Le Guin: Voyager to Inner Lands and to Outer Space. Port Washington, NY: Kennikat, 1979. pp. 115-127.

"Aldous Huxley," in: Bleiler, E. F., ed. Science Fiction Writers. New York: Scribners, 1982. pp. 101-108.

"Black American speculative literature: a checklist," Extrapolation 17(1):35-43. December 1975.

"Brunner's novels: a posterity for Kipling," in: De Bolt, Joe, ed. Happening Worlds of John Brunner. Port Washington, NY: Kennikat, 1975. pp. 63-77.

"John Brunner," in: Bleiler, E. F., ed. Science Fiction Writers. New York: Scribners, 1982. pp. 297-304.

Pfeiffer, J. R. (Continued)

"Modern Period, The: 1938-1980," by Joe De Bolt and John Pfeiffer. in: Barron, Neil, ed. Anatomy of Wonder. 2nd ed. New York: Bowker, 1981. pp. 125-334.

"SF in the classroom: 3. USAFA: 'English, special topics 495': Spring 1971," Extrapolation 13(2):116-118. May 1972.

"Shaw/science fiction checklist," Shaw Review 16(2):100-103. May 1973.

Pflieger, Pat

Reference Guide to Modern Fantasy for Children, A. Westport, CT: Greenwood, 1984. 690 p.

Pflock, K. T.

"Interview with Charles Sheffield, part one," Science Fiction Review No. 33:10-15. November 1979.

"Interview with Charles Sheffield, part two," Science Fiction Review 9(1):24-29. February 1980.

Phelan, J. M.

"Men and morals in space; comment on C. S. Lewis' trilogy," America 113(15):405-407. October 9, 1965.

Phelan, Paul

"We're still living in the stone age of space era, writer, inventor feels," Science Fiction Times No. 287:3. January 1958. (Reprinted from NY World Telegraph and Sun, 1958)

Phelps, Donald

"Interview: Frank Belknap Long," Pulpsmith 4(2): 38-42. Summer 1984.

"Interview: Manly Wade Wellman," Pulpsmith 3(3): 18-26. Autumn 1983.

Philip, Neil

Fine Anger: A Critical Introduction to the Work of Alan Garner. New York: Putnam/Philomel, 1981. 192 p.

"Fantasy: double cream or instant whip?" Signal 35: 82-90. May 1981.

"Garner and Shamanism," Labrys No. 7: 99-107. November 1981.

Philip, Richard

"Drawpuncture, Transylvania Style," After Dark 10(11): 62-67. March 1978.

Philips, Michael

Philosophy and Science Fiction. Buffalo, NY: Prometheus, 1984. 392 p.

"Elusive Self: Introduction," in: Philips, Michael, ed. Philosophy and Science Fiction. Buffalo, NY: Prometheus, 1984. pp. 139-142.

"Introduction," in: Philips, Michael, ed. Philosophy and Science Fiction. Buffalo, NY: Prometheus, 1984. pp. 1-5.

"Knowledge and the Meaning of Life: Introduction," in: Philips, Michael, ed. Philosophy and Science Fiction. Buffalo, NY: Prometheus, 1984. pp. 9-15.

"Persons, Minds and the Essentially Human: Introduction," in: Philips, Michael, ed. Philosophy and Science Fiction. Buffalo, NY: Prometheus, 1984. pp. 177-182.

"Trips Through Time and Logical Space: Introduction," in: Philips, Michael, ed. Philosophy and Science Fiction. Buffalo, NY: Prometheus, 1984. pp. 113-115.

Phillips, Fred

"What is a Lovecraftian?" Science Fiction Times No. 450:5-6. January 1968.

Philmus, R. M.

H. G. Wells and Modern Science Fiction, ed. by Dardo Suvin and R. M. Philmus. Lewisburg: Bucknell University Press, 1977. 279 p.

H. G. Wells's Literary Criticism, by Patrick Parrinder and R. M. Philmus. Totowa, NJ: Barnes & Noble, 1980. 261 p.

Into the Unknown: The Evolution of Science Fiction From Francis Godwin to H. G. Wells. Berkeley: University of California Press, 1970. 174 p.

"Island of Doctor Moreau, The," in: Magill, Frank N., ed. Survey of Science Fiction Literature, Vol. 3. Englewood Cliffs, NJ: Salem Press, 1979. pp. 1079-1083.

"Time Machine, The," in: Magill, Frank N., ed. Survey of Science Fiction Literature, Vol. 5. Englewood Cliffs, NJ: Salem Press, 1979. pp. 2287-2292.

"Time Machine, The: or, the fourth dimension as prophecy," PMLA 84(3):530-535. May 1969.

Philmus, R. M. (Continued)

"C. S. Lewis and the fictions of 'scientism'," Extrapolation 13(2):92-101. May 1972.

"Dialogue between ideaphilos and philologos (intended to prove little and clarify much), A," Science Fiction Studies 1(3):214-218. Spring 1974.

"Early science journalism of H. G. Wells: a chronological survey, The," by D. Y. Hughes and R. M. Philmus. Science Fiction Studies 1(2):98-114. Fall 1973.

"Early science journalism of H. G. Wells: addenda, The," by D. Y. Hughes and R. M. Philmus. Science Fiction Studies 2(1):98-99. March 1975.

"H. G. Wells as literary critic for the Saturday Review, with abstracts of 92 reviews, 1895-97," Science Fiction Studies 4(2):166-193. July 1977.

"Language of utopia, The," Studies in the Literary Imagination 6(2):61-78. Fall 1973.

"Revisions of the future: The Time Machine," Journal of General Education 28(1):23-30. Spring 1976.

"Satiric Ambivalence of The Island of Doctor Moreau, The," Science-Fiction Studies 8(1): 2-11. March 1981.

"Shape of science fiction: through the historical looking glass, The," Science Fiction Studies 1(1):37-41. Spring 1973.

"Todorov's Theory of 'The Fantastic': The Pitfalls of Genre Criticism," Mosaic 13(3/4): 71-82. Spring/Summer 1980.

"Wells and Borges and the labyrinths of time," Science Fiction Studies 1(4):237-248. Fall 1974.

Picard, Roger

"Poesie romantique, la science et la revolution industrielle," Romanic Review 35:28-42. 1944.

Pichon, J. C.

"Science fiction ou realisme irrationnel?" Europe revue mensuelle No. 139/140:34-42. July/August 1957.

Pick, J. B.

Strange Genius of David Lindsay, by Colin Wilson, E. H. Visiak and J. B. Pick. London: John Baker, 1970. 183 p. (Reprinted: New York: Gregg, 1979.)

Piechotta, H. J.

"Jorge Luis Borges als Mimetiker des Labyrinthischen," in: Rottensteiner, Franz, ed. Quarber Merkur. Frankfurt: Suhrkamp, 1979. pp. 217-238.

"Karl Moo-R 2 in Weltraum," Quarber Merkur 38:6-9. November 1974.

"TAUSENDEINE NACHT: Das wahre und das falsche Labyrinth, oder Die vielen Hier und Jetzt," Quarber Merkur 42:42-52. December 1975.

"Vorformen des Phantastischen: Tausendund einenacht: ," in: Thomsen, C. W., ed. Phantastik in Literatur und Kunst. Darmstadt: Wiss. Buchgesellschaft, 1980. pp. 111-130.

Pielke, R. G.

"Grokking the Stranger," in: Smith, Nicholas D., ed. Philosophers Look at Science Fiction. Chicago: Nelson-Hall, 1982. pp. 153-163.

"Humans and Aliens: A Unique Relationship," Mosaic 13(3/4): 29-40. Spring/Summer 1980.

"Rejection of Traditional Theism in Feminist Theology and Science Fiction," in: Myers, R. E., ed. The Intersection of Science Fiction and Philosophy. Westport: Greenwood, 1983. pp. 225-235.

"Star Wars vs. 2001: a question of identity," in: Remington, T. J., ed. Selected Proceedings of the 1978 SFRA National Conference. Cedar Falls: University of Northern Iowa, 1979. pp. 178-200.

"Star Wars vs. 2001: A Question of Identity," Extrapolation 24(2): 143-155. Summer 1983.

Pieratt, A. B., Jr.

Kurt Vonnegut, Jr.: A Descriptive Bibliography and Annotated Checklist, by A. B. Pieratt, Jr. and Jerome Klinkowitz. Hamden, Connecticut: Archon Books, 1974. 138 p.

Pierce, Hazel

Literary Symbiosis, A: Science Fiction/Fantasy Mystery. Westport, CT: Greenwood, 1983. 272 p.

Philip K. Dick. Mercer Island, WA: Starmont, 1982. 64 p. (Starmont Reader's Guide, 12)

"Flow My Tears, the Policeman Said," in: Magill, Frank N., ed. Survey of Science Fiction Literature, Vol. 2. Englewood Cliffs, NJ: Salem Press, 1979. pp. 797-801.

Pierce, Hazel (Continued)

"Looking Backward: 2000-1887," in: Magill, Frank N., ed. Survey of Science Fiction Literature, Vol. 3. Englewood Cliffs, NJ: Salem Press, 1979. pp. 1246-1250.

"Elementary, my dear . . . Asimov's science fiction mysteries," in: Olander, J. D. and M. H. Greenberg, eds. Isaac Asimov. New York: Taplinger, 1977. pp. 32-58.

"Pastiche Fantasy," Fantasy Newsletter 6(7): 19-20. August 1983.

"Philip K. Dick's Political Dream," in: Greenberg, Martin H., ed. Philip K. Dick. New York: Taplinger, 1982. pp. 105-135.

"Ray Bradbury and the gothic tradition," in: Olander, J. D. and M. H. Greenberg, eds. Ray Bradbury. New York: Taplinger, 1980. pp. 165-185.

Pierce, J. J.

"Devaluation of values, The," Algol 16:4-11. December 1970.

"New eschatology, The," Foundation 1:21-24. March 1972.

"Revolutionary SF," Reason 8(3):50,56. July 1976.

"Sci-fi," Reason 7(11):39-40. March 1976.

"Science fiction in perspective," Reason 7(9):40-41. January 1976.

"Treasure of the Secret Cordwainer," Science Fiction Review 12(3) 8-14. August 1983.

Pierce, J. R.

"Science and literature," Science 113(2938):431-434. April 20, 1951. Reply, J. S. Huxley, 114:109.

Pieszczachowicz, Jan

"Pokusy fantastyki i grozy futurologii," Miesiecznik Literackie No. 9. 1971.

Pilgrim, John

"Science fiction and anarchism," Anarchy 3(12):361-375. December 1963.

Pilo, Gianni

Catalogo generale della fantascienza in Italia, 1930-1979. Roma: Fanucci, 1980. 475 p.

Pimper, Jeff

"Science Fiction Games: a Discussion From the Point of View of the Science Fiction Fan," Pretentious Science Fiction Quarterly 2: 8-9. Summer 1978.

Pincus, A. R. M.

"Effects of Genre Specific Setting on Causal Chain Comprehension." 1984. 27 p. ERIC ED 258 182.

Pincus, R. E.

"Science fiction," English Journal 64(8):80-83. November 1975. (Book reviews)

Pinder, Steve

"Dragondame: an interview with Anne McCaffrey," Fantasy Media 1(2):3-4. June/July 1979.

Pine, Martha

"SF in the classroom: science fiction in high school," by Martha Pine and Ginger Petrafaso. Extrapolation 14(2):149-151. May 1973.

Pini, Richard

"Warp Graphics-Past, Present, Future (An Informal, Brief But Generally Complete History)," in: Hopkins, Mariane S., ed. Fandom Directory 1982. Newport News, VA: Fandom Computer Services, 1982. pp. l8-13.

Pinkerton, Jan

"Backward time travel, alternate universes, and Edward Everett Hale," Extrapolation 20(2):168-175. Summer 1979.

Piper, David

"Totleigh Barton SF Writing Course 1983," Focus: An SF Writers' Magazine No. 8: 44-46. Autumn 1983.

Pirani, Adam

"Albert R. (Chubby) Broccoli, interview," Starlog No. 99:59-62. October 1985.

"David Tomblin," Starlog 86: 44-46, 58. September 1984.

"Grace Jones vs. 007," Starlog 95: 30-33. June 1985.

Pirani, Adam (Continued)

"Jeannot Szwarc: filming the fantasy of Supergirl," Starlog No. 90:37-41. January 1985.

"John Hurt: Big Brother is watching," Starlog No. 93:37-39,63. April 1985.

"Many faces of Ian Holm," Starlog No. 99:12-14. October 1985.

"On the Set of Doctor Who: Resurrection of the Daleks," Starlog 83: 32-34. June 1984.

"On the set of Dream Child," Starlog 101: 45-48. December 1985.

"Robert Watts: secrets of The Temple of Doom," Starlog No. 94:23-26,62. May 1985.

"Starlog Interview: Christopher Walken," Starlog 97: 12-14. August 1985.

"Starlog interview: David Rappaport," Starlog 96: 25-27, 92. July 1985.

"Starlog Profile: Ridley Scott," Starlog 101: 64-67. December 1985.

"Tanya Roberts; interview," Starlog No. 98:44-45,72. September 1985.

"Warwick Davis: Return of the Ewok," Starlog 101: 29-31. December 1985.

"Welcome to 1984," Starlog 88: 78-80, 87. November 1984.

Pironi, Gualtiero

"Fantastico e la science fiction: cinematografici. 1) approccio e definizioni." Cineforum 19(6/7): 348-357. June/July 1979.

"Fantastico e la science fiction: cinematografici. 2) il reale trasgredito," Cineforum 19(9):515-529. September 1979. (not seen)

Piroue, Georges

"Ce que nous disent les etoiles," Combat April 3, 1955.

Pissin, Raimund

"Kurd Lasswitz," Die Nation 22(10):153-154. December 3, 1904.

Pitcher, E. W. R.

"That Web of Symbolism in Zamyatin's We," Extrapolation 22(3): 252-261. Fall 1981.

Pitman, I. J.

"Lure of horror comics; sub-standard pupils," Times Education Supplement 2066:1136. December 3, 1954.

Pitt, J. C.

"Will a Rubber Ball Still Bounce?" in: Smith, Nicholas D., ed. Philosophers Look at Science Fiction. Chicago: Nelson-Hall, 1982. pp. 57-65.

Pittenger, Norman

"C. S. Lewis: combative in defense," Studies in the Literary Imagination 14(2):13-20. Fall 1981.

Pitts, M. E.

"Motif of the Garden in the Novels of J. R. R. Tolkien, Charles Williams, and C. S. Lewis," Mythlore 8(4): 3-6, 42. Winter 1982.

"Ways of Passage: An Approach to Descent Into Hell," Mythlore 10(2): 9-12. Summer 1983.

Pitts, M. R.

Great Science Fiction Pictures. by J. R. Parish and M. R. Pitts. Metuchen, NJ: Scarecrow, 1977. 382 p.

"Christopher Lee; career article," by J. R. Parish and M. R. Pitts. Cinefantastique 3(1):5-23. Fall 1973.

Pitzer, D. E.

"Collectivism, community, and commitment," in: Utopias, ed. by Peter Alexander and Roger Gill. London: Duckworth, 1984. pp. 119-138.

Pividal, Rafael

"Litterature en ut mineur, Une," Europe 580/581:132-138. August/September 1977.

Pizer, Donald

"Nineteen-twenties fiction of James Branch Cabell," Southern Quarterly 23(2): 55-74. Winter 1985.

Plank, Robert

Emotional Significance of Imaginary Beings: A Study of the Interaction Between Psychopathology, Literature, and Reality in the Modern World, The. Springfield, Illinois: Thomas, 1968. 177 p.

Plank, Robert (Continued)

"1001 interpretations of 2001," Extrapolation 11(1):23-24. December 1969.

"Communication in science fiction," Etc., A Review of General Semantics 11(1):16-20. Autumn 1953. Reprinted in: Hayakawa, S. I., ed. Our Language and Our World. New York: Harper, 1959. pp. 272-278.

"Expedition to the Planet of Paranoia," Extrapolation 22(2): 171-185. Summer 1981.

"From science fiction to life and death: a case history," Science Fiction Studies 5:11-18. March 1978.

"Fruher Theoretiker der SF. Josef Popper-Lynkens: Zur 50. Wiederkehr seines Totestages," Quarber Merkur 28:66-70. November 1971.

"Geography of utopia: psychological factors shaping the 'ideal' location, The," Extrapolation 6(2):39-49. May 1965.

"George Orwell," Quarber Merkur 44:16-32. July 1976.

"Golem and the robot, The," Literature and Psychology pp. 12-28. Winter 1965. (not seen)

"Golems und roboter," Forum: Osterreichische Monatsblatter fur Kulturelle Freiheit. 12:510- . 1965. Also in: Rottensteiner, F., ed. Insel almanach auf das jahr 1972. Pfade ins Unendliche. Frankfurt: Insel. pp. 73-95.

"Hassliche Gotterfunke: Ein Fall vom Voklieke fur das Bose," in: Rottensteiner, Franz, ed. Polaris 1. Frankfurt: Insel, 1973. pp. 243- .

"Herzl's Old New Land and Orwell's 1984 as examples of science fiction shaping collective will," in: Samuelson, D. N. Science Fiction and Future Studies. Bryan, TX: SFRA, 1975. pp. 63-70.

"Lighter than air, but heavy as hate," in: Fiedler, L. A., ed. Art of the Essay. New York: Crowell, 1958. pp. 476-486. also in: Partisan Review 24(1):106-116. Winter 1957.

"Lone Survivor," in: Rabkin, Eric S., ed. The End of the World. Carbondale: Southern Illinois University Press, 1983. pp. 20-52.

"Longing for space travel, The," Air Force and Space Digest 46(8):43-45. August 1963.

"Modern Shrunken Utopia," in: Roemer, Kenneth M., ed. America As Utopia. New York: Franklin, 1981. pp. 206-230.

"Names and roles of characters in science fiction," Names 9(3):151-159. September 1961.

"Omnipotent cannibals in Stranger in a Strange Land," in: Olander, J. D. and M. H. Greenberg, eds. Robert A. Heinlein. New York: Taplinger, 1978. pp. 83-106.

"Omnipotent cannibals: thoughts on reading Robert Heinlein's Stranger in a Strange Land," Riverside Quarterly 5(1): 30-37. July 1971.

"Place of evil in science fiction, The," Extrapolation 14(2):100-111. May 1973.

"Plan des Josef Popper-Lynkeus. Part 1," by F. P. Hellin and Robert Plank. Quarber Merkur 39:14-39. January 1975.

"Plan des Josef Popper-Lynkeus. Part 2," by F. P. Hellin and Robert Plank. Quarber Merkur 40:3-26. March 1975.

"Portraits of fictitious psychiatrists," American Imago 13(3):259-268. Fall 1956.

"Presidency in science fiction, The," Extrapolation 16(2):173-191. May 1975.

"Quixote's mills: the man/machine encounter in SF," Science Fiction Studies 1(2):68-78. Fall 1973.

"Reproduction of psychosis in science fiction, The," International Record of Medicine & G. P. Clinics 167:407-421. July 1954. (not seen)

"Roman als Vorbild eines Lebensstils," Quarber Merkur 51:44-52. November 1979.

"Science fiction and psychology," in: Williamson, Jack, ed. Teaching Science Fiction: Education for Tomorrow. Philadelphia: Owlswick, 1980. pp. 157-167.

"Science Fiction wird 'Science Fact'?" Quarber Merkur. 50:49-52. February 1979.

"Science fiction," American Journal of Orthopsychiatry 30(4):799-810. October 1960.

"Scouring of the Shire: Tolkien's view of fascism, The," in: Lobdell, Jared, ed. A Tolkien Compass. New York: Ballantine/Del Rey, 1980. pp. 116-125.

"Sons and fathers, a. d. 2001," Hartford Studies in Literature 1(1):26-33. 1969. also in: Olander, J. D. and M. H. Greenberg, eds. Arthur C. Clarke. New York: Taplinger, 1977. pp. 121-148.

"Three perspectives of a film," by Morris Beja, Robert Plank and Alex Eisenstein. in: Clareson, Thomas D., ed. SF: The Other Side of Realism. Bowling Green, Ohio: Bowling Green University Popular Press, 1971. pp. 263-271.

Plank, Robert (Continued)

"Ungeheure augenblick, Der. Aliens in der science fiction," in: Barmeyer, Eike, ed. Science fiction: theorie und geschichte. Munchen: Fink, 1972. pp. 186-202.

"Ursula K. Le Guin and the decline of romantic love," Science Fiction Studies 3(1):36-43. March 1976.

"Welt in der Glaskugel, Die," in: Rottensteiner, Franz, ed. Quarber Merkur. Frankfurt: Suhrkamp, 1979. pp. 93-110.

Plank, W. G.

"Imaginary: synthesis of fantasy and reality," in: Collins, R. A. and H. D. Pearce, eds. The Scope of the Fantastic: Theory, Technique, Major Authors. Westport, CT: Greenwood Press, 1985. pp. 77-82.

Platt, Charles

Dream Makers Volume II: The Uncommon Men and Women Who Write Science Fiction. New York: Berkley, 1983. 266 p.

Dream Makers: The Uncommon People Who Write Science Fiction. New York: Berkley, 1980. 284 p.

"A. E. van Vogt," in: Platt, Charles. Dream makers: the uncommon people who write science fiction. New York: Berkley, 1980. pp. 133-144.

"Alfred Bester," in: Platt, Charles. Dream makers: the uncommon people who write science fiction. New York: Berkley, 1980. pp. 93-102.

"Algis Budrys," in: Platt, Charles. Dream makers: the uncommon people who write science fiction. New York: Berkley, 1980. pp. 111-120.

"Alvin Toffler," in: Platt, Charles. Dream Makers: Volume II. New York: Berkley, 1983. pp. 55-61.

"Andre Norton," in: Platt, Charles. Dream Makers: Volume II. New York: Berkley, 1983. pp. 95-102.

"Arthur C. Clarke," in: Platt, Charles. Dream Makers: Volume II. New York: Berkley, 1983. pp. 47-54.

"Arts: Books, The," Omni 7(8): 22, 75. May 1985.

"Barry N. Malzberg," in: Platt, Charles. Dream makers: the uncommon people who write science fiction. New York: Berkley, 1980. pp. 77-86.

"Brian W. Aldiss," in: Platt, Charles. Dream makers: the uncommon people who write science fiction. New York: Berkley, 1980. pp. 269-282.

"Buyers guide to world processing," Locus 13(3):9. March 1980.

"Buyers' guide to word processing, part 2," Locus 13(4):7,11. April 1980.

"Buyers' guide to word processing, part 3," Locus 13(5):7-8. May 1980.

"C. M. Kornbluth," in: Platt, Charles. Dream makers: the uncommon people who write science fiction. New York: Berkley, 1980. pp. 103-109.

"C. M. Kornbluth: a study of his work and interview with his widow," Foundation 17:57-63. September 1979.

"Christopher Priest," in: Platt, Charles. Dream Makers: Volume II. New York: Berkley, 1983. pp. 25-33.

"D. M. Thomas," in: Platt, Charles. Dream Makers: Volume II. New York: Berkley, 1983. pp. 73-83.

"D. M. Thomas: A Profile," Fantasy Newsletter 6(6): 9-11. June/July 1983.

"Damon Knight and Kate Wilhelm," in: Platt, Charles. Dream makers: the uncommon people who write science fiction. New York: Berkley, 1980. pp. 193-204.

"Decline of Fiction," Science Fiction Review 13(2): 20-21. May 1984.

"Do Androids Dream of Philip K. Dick?" Horizon 25(5): 38-42. July/August 1982.

"Donald A. Wollheim," in: Platt, Charles. Dream Makers: Volume II. New York: Berkley, 1983. pp. 229-238.

"E. C. Tubb," in: Platt, Charles. Dream makers: the uncommon people who write science fiction. New York: Berkley, 1980. pp. 227-234.

"Edward Bryant," in: Platt, Charles. Dream makers: the uncommon people who write science fiction. New York: Berkley, 1980. pp. 87-92.

"Edward L. Ferman," in: Platt, Charles. Dream Makers: Volume II. New York: Berkley, 1983. pp. 239-247.

"Fiction They Deserve, The," Science Fiction Review 13(1): 12-13. February 1984.

"Frank Herbert," in: Platt, Charles. Dream makers: the uncommon people who write science fiction. New York: Berkley, 1980. pp. 183-192.

"Frank Herbert: interview," Stardate 1(8): 9, 11-17. October 1985.

"Frederik Pohl," in: Platt, Charles. Dream makers: the uncommon people who write science fiction. New York: Berkley, 1980. pp. 57-67.

Platt, Charles (Continued)

"Fritz Leiber," in: Platt, Charles. Dream Makers: Volume II. New York: Berkley, 1983. pp. 131-139.

"Gregory Benford," in: Platt, Charles. Dream makers: the uncommon people who write science fiction. New York: Berkley, 1980. pp. 251-259.

"Hank Stine," in: Platt, Charles. Dream makers: the uncommon people who write science fiction. New York: Berkley, 1980. pp. 39-47.

"Harlan Ellison," in: Platt, Charles. Dream makers: the uncommon people who write science fiction. New York: Berkley, 1980. pp. 159-169.

"Harry Harrison," in: Platt, Charles. Dream Makers: Volume II. New York: Berkley, 1983. pp. 219-227.

"Ian Watson," in: Platt, Charles. Dream makers: the uncommon people who write science fiction. New York: Berkley, 1980. pp. 235-241.

"Interview mit Jack Vance," Science Fiction Times (Germany) 28(1):5-8. January 1986.

"Interview mit Jerry Pournelle," Science Fiction Times (Germany) 27(8):4-10. August 1985.

"Interview mit Larry Niven," Science Fiction Times (Germany) 27(12):5-9. December 1985.

"Interview mit Theodore Sturgeon," Science Fiction Times (Germany) 27(7):4-9. July 1985.

"Interview with Thomas M. Disch," Foundation 19: 47-53. June 1980.

"Introduction," in: Dick, P. K. The Zap Gun. Boston: Gregg, 1979. pp. v-xii.

"Introduction," in: Lafferty, R. A. The Devil is Dead. Boston: Gregg, 1977. pp. v-xiv.

"Introduction," in: Moorcock, Michael. The Condition of Muzak. Boston: Gregg, 1978. pp. v-xii.

"Isaac Asimov," in: Platt, Charles. Dream makers: the uncommon people who write science fiction. New York: Berkley, 1980. pp. 1-7.

"J. G. Ballard," in: Platt, Charles. Dream makers: the uncommon people who write science fiction. New York: Berkley, 1980. pp. 215-225.

"Jack Vance," in: Platt, Charles. Dream Makers: Volume II. New York: Berkley, 1983. pp. 159-166.

"James Tiptree, Jr.," in: Platt, Charles. Dream Makers: Volume II. New York: Berkley, 1983. pp. 257-272.

"Janet Morris," in: Platt, Charles. Dream Makers: Volume II. New York: Berkley, 1983. pp. 203-210.

"Jerry Pournelle," in: Platt, Charles. Dream Makers: Volume II. New York: Berkley, 1983. pp. 1-14.

"Joan D. Vinge," in: Platt, Charles. Dream Makers: Volume II. New York: Berkley, 1983. pp. 211-217.

"Joanna Russ," in: Platt, Charles. Dream Makers: Volume II. New York: Berkley, 1983. pp. 191-201.

"Joe Haldeman," in: Platt, Charles. Dream Makers: Volume II. New York: Berkley, 1983. pp. 123-130.

"John Brunner," in: Platt, Charles. Dream makers: the uncommon people who write science fiction. New York: Berkley, 1980. pp. 243-249.

"John Sladek," in: Platt, Charles. Dream Makers: Volume II. New York: Berkley, 1983. pp. 63-71.

"Keith Laumer," in: Platt, Charles. Dream Makers: Volume II. New York: Berkley, 1983. pp. 113-122.

"Keith Laumer: A Profile," Science Fiction Review 11(4): 8-11. November 1982.

"Keith Roberts," in: Platt, Charles. Dream Makers: Volume II. New York: Berkley, 1983. pp. 85-91.

"Kit Reed," in: Platt, Charles. Dream Makers: Volume II. New York: Berkley, 1983. pp. 249-255.

"Kurt Vonnegut, Jr.," in: Platt, Charles. Dream makers: the uncommon people who write science fiction. New York: Berkley, 1980. pp. 27-37.

"L. Ron Hubbard," in: Platt, Charles. Dream Makers: Volume II. New York: Berkley, 1983. pp. 177-190.

"Larry Niven," in: Platt, Charles. Dream Makers: Volume II. New York: Berkley, 1983. pp. 15-24.

"Michael Moorcock," in: Platt, Charles. Dream makers: the uncommon people who write science fiction. New York: Berkley, 1980. pp. 205-213.

"Norman Spinrad" in: Platt, Charles. Dream makers: the uncommon people who write science fiction. New York: Berkley, 1980. pp. 49-56.

Platt, Charles (Continued)

"Notes From Baltimore," Science Fiction Review 12(4): 8-10. November 1983.

"Philip Jose Farmer," in: Platt, Charles. Dream makers: the uncommon people who write science fiction. New York: Berkley, 1980. pp. 121-132.

"Philip K. Dick," in: Platt, Charles. Dream makers: the uncommon people who write science fiction. New York: Berkley, 1980. pp. 145-158.

"Piers Anthony," in: Platt, Charles. Dream Makers: Volume II. New York: Berkley, 1983. pp. 103-111.

"Piers Anthony: A Profile," Science Fiction Review 12(4): 35-38. November 1983.

"Poul Anderson," in: Platt, Charles. Dream Makers: Volume II. New York: Berkley, 1983. pp. 151-158.

"Profile of Rudy Rucker," Magazine of Fantasy and Science Fiction 67(6): 18-24. December 1984.

"Profile: Harry Harrison," Isaac Asimov's Science Fiction Magazine. 6(8): 28-40. August 1982.

"Profile: James Tiptree, Jr.," Isaac Asimov's Science Fiction Magazine 7(4): 26-49. April 1983.

"Profile: Janet Morris," Science Fiction Review 12(2): 23-26. May 1983.

"Profile: Joanna Russ," Isaac Asimov's Science Fiction Magazine 7(3): 30-45. March 1983.

"Profile: Larry Niven," Science Fiction Review 12(1): 21-24. February 1983.

"Profile: William Burroughs," Isaac Asimov's Science Fiction Magazine. 6(9): 28-43. September 1982.

"Ray Bradbury," in: Platt, Charles. Dream makers: the uncommon people who write science fiction. New York: Berkley, 1980. pp. 171-182.

"Reality in drag: a profile of Philip K. Dick," Science Fiction Review 9(3):6-11. August 1980.

"Robert Anton Wilson," in: Platt, Charles. Dream Makers: Volume II. New York: Berkley, 1983. pp. 141-150.

"Robert Sheckley," in: Platt, Charles. Dream makers: the uncommon people who write science fiction. New York: Berkley, 1980. pp. 19-26.

"Robert Silverberg," in: Platt, Charles. Dream makers: the uncommon people who write science fiction. New York: Berkley, 1980. pp. 261-268.

"Samuel R. Delany," in: Platt, Charles. Dream makers: the uncommon people who write science fiction. New York: Berkley, 1980. pp. 69-75.

"Self-profile," in: Platt, Charles. Dream makers: the uncommon people who write science fiction. New York: Berkley, 1980. pp. 281-282.

"So you're immortal, so what?" Harper 246(1477):9. June 1973.

"Stephen King," in: Platt, Charles. Dream Makers: Volume II. New York: Berkley, 1983. pp. 273-284.

"Theodore Sturgeon," in: Platt, Charles. Dream Makers: Volume II. New York: Berkley, 1983. pp. 167-176.

"Thomas M. Disch," in: Platt, Charles. Dream makers: the uncommon people who write science fiction. New York: Berkley, 1980. pp. 9-18.

"Viewpoint: In Defense of the Real World," Isaac Asimov's Science Fiction Magazine 7(11):53-66. November 1983.

"What is Harlan Ellison really like?" Science Fiction Review 9(1):16-20. February 1980.

"William S. Burroughs," in: Platt, Charles. Dream Makers: Volume II. New York: Berkley, 1983. pp. 35-46.

Platzer, R. L.

"Mystification of outer space: pseudo-mysticism and science fiction, The," Studia Mystica (California State University) 1(3):44-51. 1978.

Plotz, R. D.

"Face to face with R. D. Plotz, founder of Tolkien Society of America," Seventeen 25(1):153. April 1966.

Plummer, K. C.

"Streamlined moderne," Art in America 62(1):46-54. January/February 1974.

Plummer, Peter

"Unlocked Gate, The," Labrys No. 7: 91-98. November 1981.

Pocsik, John

"Case for Solomon Kane," in: De Camp, L. S., ed. Blade of Conan. New York: Ace, 1979. pp. 131-138.

Podelski, H. W.

"Literaturwissenschaftliche theorien der science fiction," Quarber Merkur 48:49-62. March 1978.

Podhoretz, Norman

"If Orwell Were Alive Today," Harpers 266(1592): 30-37. January 1983.

Podojil, Catherine

"Sisters, daughters, and aliens," in: Riley, Dick, ed. Critical Encounters: Writers and Themes in Science Fiction. New York: Ungar, 1978. pp. 70-86.

Pohl, Frederik

Science Fiction Studies in Film, by Frederik Pohl and Frederik Pohl IV. New York: Ace, 1981. 346 p.

Way the Future Was, The: A Memoir. New York: Ballantine, 1979. 293 p.

"Blowing the Lid Off the Even Number Scandal," Starship 18(2): 25-27. Summer/Fall 1981.

"Burning My Bridges," Starship 17(4):31-35. Fall 1980.

"Cities and cultures," in: Ash, Brian, ed. Visual Encyclopedia of Science Fiction. New York: Harmony, 1977. pp. 164-171.

"Evening With Fritz at the Ipsy Wipsy Institute, An," Fantasy Newsletter 6(7): 12-13, 38. August 1983.

"Felszolalus egy SF konferencian," Helikon 18(1): 112-116. 1972. (Tr. from Extrapolation, May 1969.)

"Fifteen Years of SFWA: Where Will it all End," SFWA Bulletin 15(1): 1, 6. Spring 1980.

"Frederik Pohl on the Budrys Columns," in: Budrys, Algis Benchmarks: Galaxy Bookshelf. Carbondale: Southern Illinois University Press, 1985. pp. xvii-xix.

"From Astonishing to Galaxy to ...," Science Fiction Times No. 369:30-32. September 1961.

"How to count on your fingers," in: Greenberg, M. H., ed. Coming Attractions. New York: Gnome, 1957. pp. 232-249.

"How we work: Frederik Pohl," in: Aldiss, Brian W. and Harry Harrison, eds. Hell's Cartographers: Some Personal Histories of Science Fiction Writers. London: Weidenfeld and Nicholson, 1975. pp. 228-232.

"Information science: fiction or fact?" American Documentation 16(2):101-104. April 1965. (Abbreviated version with title "Long John Nebel and the wood louse," Library Journal 90:4704-4708.)

"Innovators, The," Journal of General Education 28(1):43-49. Spring 1976.

"Introduction: The SF Writer at Work," in: Wingrove, David, ed. The Science Fiction Source Book. New York: Van Nostrand, 1984. pp. 66-69.

"J. R. R. Tolkien," Locus No. 149:3. September 14, 1973.

"John W. Campbell," Locus No. 90:8. July 12, 1971.

"Long John Nebel and the wood louse," Library Journal 90:4704-4708. 1965. (see also his "Information science: fiction of fact?")

"Mack Reynolds," Science Fiction Chronicle 4(7):1,14. April 1983.

"On velocity exercises," in: Wilson, Robin Scott, ed. Those Who Can: A Science Fiction Reader. New York: Mentor/New American Library, 1973. pp. 323-328.

"Pohlemic: Academe revisited," Algol 15(2):49-51. Spring 1978.

"Pohlemic: column: how we put the hype in hyperspace," Algol 16(1):29-32. Winter 1978/1979.

"Pohlemic: copyright futures," Science Fiction Chronicle 5(10):26-30. July 1984.

"Pohlemic: how I'd like to be taught," Algol 15(1):35-36. Winter 1977/1978.

"Pohlemic: the author strikes back," Starship 16(4):37-39. Fall 1979.

"Pohlemic: wars over Star Wars," Science Fiction Chronicle 6(1):24,26. October 1984.

"Pohlemic: Battlefield Hubbard," Science Fiction Chronicle 6(12): 34-36. September 1985.

"Pohlemic: Coming Up On 1984," Starship 20(1): 21-28. Winter 1983/84.

"Pohlemic: The Crickets, Hear How They Chirp," Starship 19(1): 21-24. November 1982.

Pohl, Frederik (Continued)

"Publishing of science fiction, The," in: Bretnor, Reginald, ed. Science Fiction Today and Tomorrow. New York: Harper, 1974. pp. 17-45.

"Ragged claws," in: Aldiss, Brian W. and Harry Harrison, eds. Hell's Cartographers: Some Personal Histories of Science Fiction Writers. London: Weidenfeld and Nicholson, 1975. pp. 144-172.

"Reminiscence: Cyril M. Kornbluth," Extrapolation 17(2):102-109. May 1976.

"Reply to Norman Spinrad," Science Fiction Times pp. 6-7. ca. October 1967.

"Science fiction as social comment," Algol 19:15-17. November 1972.

"Science fiction for the young (at heart)," Children's Literature Annual 10: 111-112. 1982.

"Science fiction professional, The," in: Bretnor, Reginald, ed. The Craft of Science Fiction. New York: Harper, 1976. pp. 292-311.

"SF From the Planet Earth," SFWA Bulletin 16(4): 16-18. May 1982.

"Uses of the future," by Frederik Pohl and Sidney Feinleib. in: Turek, Leslie, ed. Noreascon Proceedings. Cambridge, MA: NESFA, 1976. pp. 128-137.

"Utopias and dystopias," by Frederik Pohl, M. H. Greenberg and J. D. Olander. in: Warrick, Patracia, ed. Science Fiction: Contemporary Mythology. New York: Harper, 1978. pp. 393-400.

"Whale blubber, moonies, and me," Science Fiction Chronicle 3(6):21-24. March 1982.

"What science fiction is," Worlds of If Science Fiction 18(3):4. March 1968.

"Writer in the Year 2001, The," Writer's Digest 50:36-39. January 1970.

"Writers, The: Frederik Pohl," Science Fiction Chronicle 6(9): 38-40. June 1985.

"Xenology, Sociology, Politics, Theology, Mathematics," in: Ellison, Harlan, ed. Medea. New York: Bantam, 1985. pp. 34-43.

Pohl, Joy

"Dualities in David Lindsay's A Voyage to Arcturus," Extrapolation 22(2): 164-170. Summer 1981.

Pohle, B. D.

"Star Ka'at creator: Andre Norton," Cats Magazine 35(8):6-7. August 1978.

Poinsot, M. C.

"J. H. Rosny," Grande Revue 41:449-459, 595-604. 1907.

Polito, Gene

"Westworld: a state of mind," American Cinematographer 54(11):1437-1438, 1474-1477. November 1973.

Pollock, Dale

Skywalking: The Life and Films of George Lucas, the Creator of Star Wars. New York: Ballantine, 1983. 332 p.

"Metropolis," New Orleans Times Picayune Sec. 2, p. 14. May 27, 1984.

"Reprieve for Mr. Spock?" New Orleans Times Picayune Sec. 2, p. 8. May 26, 1982.

"Zone accident focuses attention on safety," Los Angeles Times. Calendar Sec. 6, p. 1,9,10. July 30, 1982.

Pollock, Philip

"On Being a Publisher's Reader," Focus: an SF Writer's Magazine. 4: 18. Spring 1981.

Polman, Dick

"Still a Craze After All These Years," Philadelphia Inquirer July 20, 1984. NewsBank. Film and Television. 1984. FTV 20:A13-A14.

Poncher, Jeff

"Interview with Terry Carr: Author, Editor, Fan," in: Gerds, Erick, ed. FAN-tastic: Filk Songs and Other Fannish Delights. Santa Monica, CA: Dag Design, 1981. pp. 35-38 .

Ponnamperuma, Nirmali

"Look forward to encountering new neighbors, A," by Mark Davidson and Nirmali Ponnamperuma. Science Digest 83(2):8-11. February 1978.

Poore, Charles

"Books of the times," New York Times p. 31. March 29, 1962. (Book review)

Pope, E. M.

"Attic of Faerie," Mythlore 9(1): 8-10. Spring 1982.

Pope, Elizabeth

"Themes for tomorrow," Utah Libraries 13(1):25-30. Spring 1970.

Pope, L. A.

"Image of science and scientists in science fiction films, The," by Carol Ludwin and L. A. Pope. Presented at the 1978 Annual Meeting of the Midwest Sociological Society. 1978.

Popov, Vladimir

"I want to illustrate Ray Bradbury's books," Soviet Life pp. 29-31. October 1975.

Popson, Tom

"Dr. Who vs. the BBC," Chicago Tribune Sec. 7, p. 56. November 29, 1985.

Populi, A. F.

"1983 Hugo Awards Provide Few Surprises," Fantasy Newsletter 6(9): 9. October/November 1983.

Porges, I.

"Mathematics motivated through science fiction," School Science and Mathematics 56(489):1-4. January 1956.

Porges, Irwin

Edgar Rice Burroughs: The Man Who Created Tarzan. Provo, Utah: Brigham Young University Press, 1975. 819 p.

Pornon, C.

Reve et de fantastique dans le cinema francais, Le. Paris: la Nef de Paris Editions, 1959. 210 p.

Portelli, Alessandro

"Jack London's Missing Revolution: Notes on The Iron Heel," Science-Fiction Studies. 9(2): 180-195. July 1982.

"Presente come utopia: la narrativa di Isaac Asimov," Calibano pp. 138-184. 1978.

"Three laws of robotics: laws of the text, laws of production, laws of society, The,"

Science Fiction Studies 7(2):150-156. July 1980.

Porteous, J. D.

"Preliminary landscape analysis of middle earth during its third age," Landscape 19:33-38. January 1975.

Porter, Andrew

Book of Ellison, The. New York: Algol Press, 1978. 196 p.

Experiment Perilous: Three Essays on Science Fiction. New York: Algol Press, 1976. 34 p.

Exploring Cordwainer Smith. New York: Algol Press, 1975. 33 p.

"Susan Wood," (Obituary) Starship 18(1): 41. Spring 1981.

Porter, D. L.

"Politics of Le Guin's opus, The," Science Fiction Studies 2(3):243-248. November 1975.

Porter, E. J.

"Profile: H. M. Hoover," Language Arts 59(6): 609-613. September 1982.

Portoundo, J. A.

"Jules Verne's America," Americas 9(10):30-35. October 1957.

Posey, Linda

"Hobbit Hole, The," Texas Highways 26(4):16-17. May 1979.

Poskanzer, S. C.

"Thoughts on C. S. Lewis and The Chronicles of Narnia," Language Arts 53(5):523-526. May 1976.

Pospieszalska, Nelly

"Zu Glos Pana von Stanislaw Lem," by Nelly Pospieszalska and I. Zimmermann-Gollheim. Quarber Merkur 24:29-52. September 1970.

Post, J. B.

Atlas of Fantasy. Revised Edition. New York: Ballantine, 1979. 210 p.

"Bibliophile and the spaceship," Private Library 2d ser., 3:120-123. Autumn 1970.

Post, J. B. (Continued)

"Cartographic fantasy," <u>Bulletin of the Geography and Map Division, Special Libraries Association</u> 101:12-14. September 1975.

"General principles for reviewers," <u>Science Fiction Times</u> No. 462:12. January 1969.

"Group for serious collectors, A," <u>Science Fiction Times</u> No. 462:10. January 1969.

"Look at sex in SF, A," <u>Science Fiction Times</u> No. 464:10,13. March 1969.

"Toward an atlas of fantasy," <u>Bulletin of the Geography and Map Division, Special Libraries Association</u> 75:11-13. March 1969. also in: <u>SFWA Bulletin</u> 24:3-5. June 1969.

Poster, Mark

"Fourier's Concept of the Group," <u>Minnesota Review</u> ns6, 1976. pp. 76-87.

Potter, Gretchen

"Geometry and science fiction," <u>Mathematics in School</u> 5(2):11-13. March 1976.

Potts, S. W.

"Dialogues Concerning Human Understanding: Empirical Views of God from Locke to Lem," in: Slusser, George E., ed. <u>Bridges to Science Fiction</u>. Carbondale: Southern Illinois University Press, 1980. pp. 41-52.

Pournelle, Jerry

"Arming the incomplete enchanter," in: De Camp, L. S., ed. <u>Blade of Conan</u>. New York: Ace, 1979. pp. 249-259.

"Building <u>The Mote in God's Eye</u>," by Larry Niven and Jerry Pournelle. <u>Galaxy</u>. 37(1):92-113. January 1976. also in: Pournelle, Jerry. <u>A Step Further Out</u>. New York: Ace, 1980. pp. 113-141.

"Building future words; logic and consistency in the craft of science fiction," in: Grant, C. L., ed. <u>Writing and Selling Science Fiction</u>. Cincinnati, Ohio: Writers Digest, 1976. pp. 91-110.

"By what standard?" <u>Mythologies</u> 11:11-15. February 1977.

"Construction of believable societies, The," in: Bretnor, Reginald, ed. <u>The Craft of Science Fiction</u>. New York: Harper, 1976. pp. 104-120.

"Inside the Whale: responses to Christopher Priest's 'Outside the Whale'," by Jack

Williamson, Jerry Pournelle and Jack Chalker. <u>Science Fiction Review</u> 9(4): 18-23. November 1980.

"Lasers, Grasers, and Marxists," in: Bretnor, Reginald, ed. <u>The Future at War: Vol. 1: Thor's Hammer</u>. New York: Ace, 1979. pp. 83-101.

"Living with computers," <u>OnComputing</u> 2(1): 33-36. Summer 1980.

"On historiographing the future," <u>SFWA Bulletin</u> 14(3):52-54. Fall 1979.

"On weapons of choice and/or necessity," in: De Camp, L. S., ed. <u>Blade of Conan</u>. New York: Ace, 1979. pp. 215-218.

"Proposed SFWA Model Royalty Statement: A Commentary," <u>SFWA Bulletin</u> 16(2): 36-40. Spring 1981.

"Rearming the incomplete enchanter," in: De Camp, L. S., ed. <u>Blade of Conan</u>. New York: Ace, 1979. pp. 263-274.

"Son of weapons of choice and/of necessity," in: De Camp, L. S., ed. <u>Blade of Conan</u>. New York: Ace, 1979. pp. 219-226.

"Writer looks at Word Processors," <u>OnComputing</u> 2(1): 83-87. Summer 1980.

Pourroy, Janine

"Backyard adventures: Spielberg style," <u>Cinefex</u> No. 24:38-67. November 1985.

"Behind the lines of Enemy Mine," <u>Cinefex</u> No. 25:4-37. February 1986.

"Fright Night," by Jennifer Benidt and Janine Pourroy. <u>Cinefex</u> No. 25:54-71. February 1986.

"Shape of Dune," by Janine Pourroy and Don Shay. <u>Cinefex</u> No. 21:24-71. April 1985.

Pousner, Howard

"Extrapolator Clarke Flies Into the Future," <u>Atlanta Journal</u> December 26, 1984 in: <u>NewsBank. Literature.</u> 64:G5-G6. January 1985.

Powell, Jerry

"John Barth's <u>Chimera</u>: a creative response to the literature of exhaustion," <u>Critique: Studies in Modern Fiction</u> 18(2):59-72. 1976.

Powell, S. E.

"Edgar Rice Burroughs," <u>The Book Mart</u> 1(9):65,67. December 1977.

Powers, R. G.

"Introduction," in: Sheckley, Robert. The 10th Victim. Boston: Gregg, 1978. pp. v-xiii.

"Introduction," in: Stockton, F. R. The Science Fiction of Frank R. Stockton. Boston: Gregg, 1976. pp. vii-xxii.

"Introduction," in: Waterloo, Stanley. Armageddon. Boston: Gregg, 1976. pp. v-xviii.

"Introduction," in: Winsor, G. M. Station X. Boston: Gregg, 1975. pp. v-xii.

Poyser, Kennedy

"Norwescon 4," Science Fiction Chronicle 2(9):15. June 1981.

Poyser, Kippy

"Profile: Michael Whelan," Fantasy: A Forum for Science Fiction and Fantasy Artists 2(4): 14-17. Winter 1980.

Prasad, R. S.

"Science fiction: an essay in perspective," Madhya Bharati 16(14-16):64-70 (part 1, section a). 1965-1967.

Pratt, C. W.

"SF publishers still discovering life, and profits, on Mars," Chicago Tribune Sec. 7, p. 1,3. July 10, 1977.

Pratt, Fletcher

"Beyond stars, atoms and hell; this spring's offerings in the field of fantasy and science fiction," Saturday Review of Literature 33:32-33. June 17, 1950. (Book reviews)

"Critique of science fiction, A," in: Bretnor, Reginald, ed. Modern Science Fiction: Its Meaning and Its Future. New York: Coward McCann, 1953. Reprinted, Chicago: Advent, 1979. pp. 73-90.

"Fiction flights in space and time; review of current publications," Saturday Review 35(8):20-21,34. February 23, 1952.

"Introduction," in: Gernsback, Hugo. Ralph 24C41+: A Romance of the Year 2660. New York: Frederick Fell, 1950. pp. 19-24.

"Nature of imaginative literature, The," in: Pratt, Fletcher. World of Wonder. New York: Twayne, 1951. pp. 15-21.

"Science fiction & fantasy, 1950," Saturday Review of Literature 33(52):16-17. December 30, 1950.

"Science fiction and fantasy, 1949," Saturday Review of Literature 32(52):7-9,23. December 24, 1949.

"Science fiction's second wind," Saturday Review 37(48):14,34. November 27, 1954.

"Season's science fiction, The," Saturday Review 37(32):14-15,37. August 7, 1954.

"Time, space and literature," Saturday Review 34(30):16-17,27-28. July 28, 1951.

"Trail of the paper comet," Saturday Review 36(10):26-27. March 7, 1953. (Book review)

"What's the world coming to? Prophetic fiction," Saturday Review of Literature 17(23):3-4. April 2, 1938.

Pratter, F. E.

"Mysterious Traveler in the Speculative Fiction of Howells and Twain, The," in: Roemer, Kenneth M., ed. American As Utopia. New York: Franklin, 1981. pp. 78-90.

Predal, Rene

Cinema fantastique, Le. Paris: Seghers, 1970. 353 p.

Prelutsky, Burt

"With Only Five Seconds to Live...," in: White, David M., ed. Popular Culture. New York: New York Times/Arno Press, 1975. pp. 304-305. (Originally published Oct. 15, 1967.)

Prescott, P. S.

"Science fiction: the great escape," Newsweek 86(25):68-72. December 22, 1975.

"You're putting me on, I hope," Look 33:12. June 10, 1969. (Book reviews)

Presley, Horton

"C. S. Lewis: Mythmaker," in: Clareson, Thomas D., ed. Voices For the Future, Vol. 3. Bowling Green: Popular Press, 1984. pp. 127-150.

Preston, M. I.

"Children's reactions to movie horrors and radio crime," Journal of Pediatrics 19(2):147-168. August 1941.

Preuss, Paul

"Cosmos: a preview," Locus 13(8):8,10. August 1980.

"EquiCon world building," Locus 14(5):17. June 1981.

"Fraud, free quarks, and Feyerabend," Locus 15(4):10-11. April 1982.

"It takes guts to build a universe," Locus 14(1):8,14. February 1981.

"PEP and other accelerators," Locus 13(10):7,15. October 1980.

"Recommended reading, 1984," Locus 18(2): 23. February 1985.

Prevot, Jacques

Cyrano de Bergerac romancier. Paris: Belin, 1977. 158 p.

Price, Derek de Solla

"Science fiction as science: why sci-fi zaps," New Republic 175(18):40-41. October 30, 1976.

Price, G. H.

"Otis Adelbert Kline: two memoirs," Oak Leaves 1(2):3-10.. Winter 1970/71.

Price, Meredith

"All Shall Love Me and Despair: The Figure of Lilith in Tolkien, Lewis, Williams and Sayers," Mythlore 9(1): 3-7, 26. Spring 1982.

Price, R. M.

"Christ and Conan: Howard's View of Christianity," Cromlech 1(1): 14-23. Spring 1985.

"Hexes and hoaxes: the curious career of Lovecraft's Necronomicon," Twilight Zone 4(6):59-65. November/December 1984.

"Stephen King and the Lovecraft mythos," in: Schweitzer, Darrell, ed. Discovering Stephen King. Mercer Island: Starmont, 1985. pp. 109-122.

"T. E. D. Klein," in: Schweitzer, Darrell, ed. Discovering Modern Horror Fiction I. Mercer Island: Starmont, 1985. pp. 68-85.

Price, Steven

"Freedom and nature in Perelandra," Mythlore 8(3):38-40,42. Autumn 1981.

Prickett, Stephen

"At the Back of the North Wind," in: Magill, Frank N., ed. Survey of Modern Fantasy Literature, Vol 1. Englewood Cliffs, NJ: Salem Press, Inc., 1983. pp. 63-65.

"Phantastes," in: Magill, Frank N., ed. Survey of Modern Fantasy Literature, Vol 3. Englewood Cliffs, NJ: Salem Press, Inc., 1983. pp. 1241-1245.

"Religious fantasy in the nineteenth century," in: Magill, Frank N., ed. Survey of Modern Fantasy Literature, Vol 5. Englewood Cliffs, NJ: Salem Press, Inc., 1983. pp. 2369-2382.

"Short fiction of MacDonald, The," in: Magill, Frank N., ed. Survey of Modern Fantasy Literature, Vol 4. Englewood Cliffs, NJ: Salem Press, Inc., 1983. pp. 1629-1632.

"Uncle Henry's trousers; or, the metaphysical status of other worlds," in: Collins, R. A. and H. D. Pearce, eds. The Scope of the Fantastic: Theory, Technique, Major Authors. Westport, CT: Greenwood Press, 1985. pp. 57-67.

Pride, Ray

"Road Warrior (review)," Cinefantastique 12(5/6):92. July/August 1982.

Priest, Christopher

"Authentic Voice," Focus: An SF Writers' Magazine 4: 4-5. Spring 1981.

"British science fiction," in: Parrinder, Patrick, ed. Science Fiction: A Critical Guide. New York: Longman, 1979. pp. 187-202.

"Foundation Forum: Part I: science fiction: form versus content," by Christopher Priest and Ian Watson. Foundation 10:55-65. June 1976.

"Into the Arena: the Barrel," Vector 109: 22-25. 1982.

"Landscape artist: the fiction of J. G. Ballard," in: Tolley, M. J., ed. The Stellar Guage. Carleton, Australia: Norstrilia, 1980. pp. 187-196.

"Leave the forgotten to the night," Vector No. 127: 9-10. August/September 1985.

"Meetings with Remarkable Men," Vector 98: 4-11. June 1980.

"Mucking About in Bytes," Focus (BSFA) No. 10: 26-28. February 1985.

"New wave: a radical change in the 1960's," in: Holdstock, Robert, ed. Encyclopedia of Science Fiction. London: Octopus, 1978. pp. 162-173.

Priest, Christopher (Continued)

"Novel Contracts," Focus 6:15-19. Autumn 1982.

"Outside the whale," SF Commentary 59:1-3,15-16. April 1980. also in: Science Fiction Review 9(3):17-21. August 1980.

"Overtures and beginners," Vector 93:10-11. May/June 1979. (Reprinted from Foundation. May 13, 1978. "The profession of science fiction: overtures and beginners.")

"Profession of science fiction, XIII: overture and beginners, The," Foundation 13:51-56. May 1978.

"Short story contracts," SFWA Bulletin 14(1):6-16,56-59. Spring 1979.

"View of suburbia; the Chris Priest column: on book reviewing," Speculation 2:12-14. July/August 1969.

"We do it, too! British SF, 1965-1979," in: World Science Fiction Convention, 1979. Seacon 79 Programme Book. SL: Seacon 1979, 1979. pp. 50-53.

Priestly, J. B.

"They come from inner space," New Statesman and Nation 46(1187):712-714. December 5, 1953. Reply: 46(1189):798. December 19, 1953. Rejoiner: 47(1191):16. January 2, 1954.

"Who goes there," New Statesman 56(1434):268-269. September 6, 1958.

Prieto, F. R.

"Annual report: 1956," in: Science Fiction Yearbook, 1957 Edition. Vol. 1. Patterson, NJ: Fandom House, 1957. pp. 12-13.

"Annual SF paperback report," Science Fiction Times No. 399/400:8-12. January/February 1963.

"Fantasy record, April 1956," Fantasy Times No. 245:4-5. April (2) 1956.

"Fantasy record, April 1957," Fantasy Times No. 268:7. April (1) 1957.

"Fantasy record, December 1956," Fantasy Times No. 260:4. December (1) 1956.

"Fantasy record, February 1957," Fantasy Times No. 265:3. February (2) 1957.

"Fantasy record, January 1957," Fantasy Times No. 262:9. January (1) 1957.

"Fantasy record, June 1956," Fantasy Times No. 249:3. June (2) 1956.

"Fantasy record, March 1957," Fantasy Times No. 266:5. March (1) 1957.

"Fantasy record, November," Fantasy Times No. 235:6. November (2) 1955.

"Fantasy record, September 1956," Fantasy Times No. 254:7. September (1) 1956.

"Fantasy record," Fantasy Times No. 257:5. October (2) 1956.

"Science fiction: 1959," Science Fiction Times No. 345:16-17. September (1) 1960.

Primeau, Ronald

"'It Goes Bang:' structure of rhythms in the poetry of John Brunner," in: De Bolt, Joe, ed. Happening Worlds of John Brunner. Port Washington, NY: Kennikat, 1975. pp. 96-109.

Prince, Gerald

"How New is New," in: Slusser, George E., ed. Coordinates. Carbondale: Southern Illinois University Press, 1983. pp. 23-30.

Pringle, David

Earth is the Alien Planet: J. G. Ballard's Four-Dimensional Nightmare. San Bernardino, California: Borgo Press, 1979. 62 p. (The Milford Series: Popular Writers of Today, Vol. 26)

J. G. Ballard: the First Twenty Years, ed. by James Goddard and David Pringle. Hayes, England: Bran's Head Books, 1976. 99 p.

J. G. Ballard: A Primary and Secondary Bibliography. Boston: G. K. Hall, 1984. 156 p.

Science Fiction: 100 SF Authors. Leeds: Leeds City Libraries, 1978. 24 p.

"Crystal World, The," in: Magill, Frank N., ed. Survey of Science Fiction Literature, Vol. 1. Englewood Cliffs, NJ: Salem Press, 1979. pp. 453-456.

"Aliens for neighbours: a reassessment of Clifford D. Simak," Foundation 11/12:15-28. March 1977.

"Fourfold Symbolism of J. G. Ballard," Foundation 4:48-60. July 1973.

"Interview with J. G. Ballard," Thrust 14:12-19. Winter 1980.

"J. G. Ballard interview," by James Goddard and David Pringle. Vector 73/74:28-29. March 1976.

Pringle, David (Continued)

"Lamia, the jester, and the kings: J. G. Ballard's characters, The," <u>Foundation</u> 16:4-15. May 1979.

"Rats, humans and other minor vermin: an assessment of Brian Stableford's novels," <u>Foundation</u> 15:19-28. January 1979.

"Top Thirty Anglo-American Science Fiction Movies of the 1950s to the 1970s," <u>Vector</u> 114: 33-35. 1983.

Printz-Pahlson, Goran

"Forst pa manens yta," in: Printz-Pahlson, Goran. <u>Slutna Varldar, oppen rymd. Essaer och kritiker 1956-1971</u>. Staffanstorp: Cavefors, 1971. p. 72-81.

"H. G. Wells: den melankoliska utopien," in: Printz-Pahlson, Goran. <u>Slutna Varldar</u>, oppen rymd. Essaer och kritiker 1956-1971. Staffanstorp: Cavefors, 1971. p. 66-71.

"Science fiction," in: in: Printz-Pahlson, Goran. <u>Slutna Varldar, oppenrymd. Essaer och kritiker 1956-1971</u>. Staffanstorp: Cavefors, 1971. p. 82-93.

Prioli, C. A.

"Kurt Vonnegut's duty-dance," <u>Essays in English Literature</u> 1(3):44-50. 1973.

Priore, F. V.

"Evaluating books: the pulps," <u>The Book Mart</u> 1(9):65,68. December 1977.

"Some Thoughts on the Acquisition of Graphic-Story Books," in: Hopkins, Mariane S., ed. <u>Fandom Directory 1982</u>. Newport News, VA: Fandom Computer Services, 1982. pp. 377-380.

"Why Do People Collect Comics?" in: Hopkin, Harry A., ed <u>Fandom Directory 1980</u>. Langley AFB, Virginia: Fandom Computer Services, 1980. pp. 262-264.

Pritcher, E. W. R.

"Frankenstein As Short Fiction: A Unique Adaptation of Mary Shelley's Novel," <u>Studies in Short Fiction</u> 20(1): 49-52. Winter 1983.

Pritchett, V. S.

"Prognosticators," <u>New Statesman</u> 66(1697):360. September 20, 1963.

"Scientific romances, The," in: Pritchett, V. S. <u>The Living Novel</u>. New York: Reynal & Hitchcock, 1947. pp. 122-129.

Proctor, George

"Texas writers on a sci-fi high," <u>Dallas Morning News</u> p. G3. June 13, 1976.

Pronin, Vladislav

"Anatomiya nauchnoj fantastiki," by Vladislav Pronin and Andrej Chernyshev. <u>Detskaya Literatura</u> 4(100):32-37. 1974.

Prosser, H. L.

<u>Teaching Race-Ethnic Relations Through Science Fiction in Senior High School Social Studies</u>. Master's Thesis, Southwest Missouri State University, 1982. 24 p. (ERIC ED 222 408)

"Teaching Sociology With the <u>Martian Chronicles</u>," <u>Social Education</u> 47(3): 212-215. March 1983.

Provost, Sylvie

"Bibliographie selective et indicative de la paralitterature," by C. M. Gagnon and Sylvie Provost. <u>Cahiers de l'institut superieur des sciences humaines</u> (Laval Univ.) No. 24. October 1978.

Pryor, T. M.

"2 ask injunction to bar prize film," <u>New York Times</u> Sec. I, p. 27. March 27, 1957.

Przyrowski, Zbigniew

"Doua secole de literatura stiintifico fantastica poloneza," <u>Colectia "Povestiri Stiintifico-Fantastice"</u> 420:3-7. May 15, 1972.

Pugh, Clifford

"Leiber's Houston, 2112," <u>Houston Post</u> p. B1. September 22, 1980.

Pujante, A. L.

"Mundo de John Wyndham, El (Thesis, University of Barcelona)," cf P. A. Stephensen-Payne in <u>Science Fiction Collector</u> 8:44. October 1979. (not seen)

Pukallus, Horst

"Kosmos und Marktkalkul. Gesprach mit einem Science Fiction Autor," <u>Kurbiskern</u> 1:158-163. 1975.

Pukallus, Horst (Continued)

"Perry Rhodan as a social and idealogical phenomenon," by Sylvia Pukallus, R. M. Hahn and Horst Pukallus. Science Fiction Studies 6(2):190-200. July 1979.

Pukallus, Sylvia

"Perry Rhodan as a social and idealogical phenomenon," by Sylvia Pukallus, R. M. Hahn and Horst Pukallus. Science Fiction Studies 6(2):190-200. July 1979.

Pulvertaft, T.

"Five types of science fiction," Spectator 191:702. December 11, 1953.

Purcell, J. M.

"Stanislaw Lem's science fiction: some religious aspects," Communio: International Catholic Review 5(2):202-207. Summer 1978.

"Tarkovsky's film Solaris (1972): a Freudian slip?" Extrapolation 19(2):126-131. May 1978.

Purcell, Mark

"Sinister researches of C. P. Ransom: a checklist, The," Luna Monthly No. 50:3. Winter 1974.

Purdom, Tom

"Medium & the marketplace, The," Colloquy, Education in Church & Society 4(5):34-36. May 1971.

"Science fiction: sci fi's creative vigor," American Libraries 5(3):141-142. March 1974.

"Who's going to run things in twenty three hundred? And how are they going to do it?" in: Grant, C. L., ed. Writing and Selling Science Fiction. Cincinnati, Ohio: Writers Digest, 1976. pp. 129-146.

Purdy, M. R.

"Battle Hill, places in transition in Charles Williams' Descent Into Hell," Mythlore 7(2):11-12. Summer 1980.

"Symbols of Immortality: A Comparison of European and Elvish Heraldry," Mythlore 9(1): 19-22. Spring 1982.

Purnell, George

"Humour of Chesterton, The," Chesterton Review 2(1):1-21. Fall/Winter 1975/1976.

Purtill, R. L.

C. S. Lewis's Case for the Christian Faith. San Francisco: Harper, 1985. 146 p.

J. R. R. Tolkien: Myth, Morality, and Religion. New York: Harper, 1985. 154 p.

Lord of Elves and Eldils: Fantasy and Philosophy in C. S. Lewis and J. R. R. Tolkien. Grand Rapids, Michigan: Zondervan, 1974. 216 p.

"Heaven and other perilous realms," Mythlore 6(4):3-6. Fall 1979.

"Mind, Matter, and Magic in Fantasy and Science Fiction," in: Reilly, Robert, ed. The Transcendent Adventure. Westport: Greenwood, 1984. pp. 27-35.

Purviance, Jim

"Algol interview: Fritz Leiber," Algol 15(3):23-28. Summer/Fall 1978.

Purvin, George

"Golding's Lord of the Flies: an Alternate Interpretation," Media and Methods 17(1): 53-54. September 1980.

Pusch, Harald

Isaac Asimov: der Tausendjahres-planer, ed. by H. J. Alpers and Harald Pusch. Meitingen: Corian, 1984. 199 p.

"Editorial: statistics," Science Fiction Times (Germany) 26(3):4-7. March 1984.

"Indiziert!" by Harald Pusch and Marcel Bieger. Science Fiction Times (Germany) 26(5):15-17. May 1984.

"Interview mit Jorg Weigand," by Marcel Bieger and Harald Pusch. Science Fiction Times (Germany) 26(5):5-14. May 1984.

"Interview mit Wolfgang Hohlbein," by Marcel Bieger and Harald Pusch. Science Fiction Times (Germany) 25(7):14-15. July 1983.

"Schlagt die Neger tot! Oder der Mensch braucht mehr als Myskik. Gedanken zum Phantastischen Film der letzten Jahre," Science Fiction Times (Germany) 24(11):4-7. November 1982.

"Schluss in den Ofen," Science Fiction Times (Germany) 25(6):13-14. June 1983.

"Sex Wars: Zur Erotik der Star Wars Trilogie," Science Fiction Times (Germany) 27(12):10-11. December 1985.

"Toennies Tage in Kiel," Science Fiction Times (Germany) 27(1):12-13. January 1985.

Pusch, Harald (Continued)

"Woelfe, Drachen und Barbaren," <u>Science Fiction Times</u> (Germany) 24(12):4-8. December 1982.

Putrament, Jerzy

"Taki sobie prob-Lem," <u>Przeglad Kulturalny</u> No. 38:23-29. September 1954.

Putz, Manfred

"Who am I this time: die romane von Kurt Vonnegut," <u>Jahrbuch fur Amerikanstudien</u> 19:111-125. 1974.

Pym, John

"Middle American sky, The," <u>Sight and Sound</u> 47(2):99-100. Spring 1978.

Q

Quantons, R.

"Futur fiction," <u>Petrole-Progres</u> July 1962.

Quarles, J. P.

"Dramatic television and agenda setting: the case of 'The Day After'," by Mark Miller and J. P. Quarles. 14 p. August 1984. ERIC ED 245 257.

Queneau, Raymond

"Nouveau genre litteraire, Un: les science-fictions," <u>Critiuge</u> 46:195-198. 1951.

"Science fiction, La," <u>Arts</u> No. 435:1, 4. October 29, 1953.

Quigley, Winthrop

"Star Trek lives on for its creator," <u>Albuquerque Journal</u> February 29, 1976. in: <u>NewsBank. Film and Television.</u> 12:E2. 1976.

Quina, James

"Science fiction as a mode for interdisciplinary education," by James Quina and M. J. Greenlaw. <u>Journal of Reading</u> 19(2):104-111. November 1975.

Quinn, J. E.

"Whitcon report," <u>Fantasy Times</u> No. 69:15-16. September 1948.

Quinn, P. F.

"Poe's imaginary voyage," <u>Hudson Review</u> 4:562-585. 1952.

Quinn, W. A.

"Science Fiction's Harrowing of the Heavens," in: Reilly, Robert, ed. <u>The Transcendent Adventure</u>. Westport: Greenwood, 1984. pp. 37-54.

Quissell, B. C.

"New World That Eve Made: Feminist Utopias Written by Nineteenth-Century Women," in: Roemer, Kenneth M., ed. <u>America As Utopia</u>. New York: Franklin, 1981. pp. 148-174.

R

Raabe, Juliette

"Lavenir de la SF," <u>Quinzaine Litteraire</u>
1.9.1967.

"Science-fiction, La," by Juliette Raabe and
Francis Lacassin. <u>La bibliotheque ideale des
litteratures d'evasion (La bibliotheque
ideale)</u>. Paris: Ed. universitaires, 1969.
pp. 155-178.

"SF et Jaune Roman," <u>France-Observateur</u>
25.5.1961.

Rabiega, W. A.

<u>Environmental Fiction for Pedagogic Purposes</u>.
Monticello, Illinois: Council of Planning
Librarians, 1974. 21 p.

"Classroom Delphi," <u>The Professional
Geographer</u> 34(1): 71-79. February 1982.

Rabinovitz, Rubin

"Mechanism vs. organism: Anthony Burgess' <u>A
Clockwork Orange</u>," <u>Modern Fiction Studies</u>
24(4):538-541. Winter 1978.

Rabkin, E. S.

<u>Arthur C. Clarke</u>. West Linn, Oregon:
Starmont House, 1979. 80 p. (Starmont
Reader's Guide 1).

<u>Bridges to Fantasy</u>, by G. E. Slusser, E. S.
Rabkin, and Robert Scholes. Carbondale:
Southern Illinois University Press, 1982.
231 p.

<u>Coordinates: Placing Science Fiction and
Fantasy</u>, by G. E. Slusser, E. S. Rabkin, and
Robert Scholes. Carbondale, IL: Southern
Illinois University Press, 1983. 209 p.

<u>End of the World</u>, by E. S. Rabkin, M. H.
Greenberg, and J. D. Olander. Carbondale:
Southern Illinois University Press, 1983.
204 p.

<u>Fantastic in Literature, The</u>. Princeton:
Princeton University Press, 1976. 234 p.

<u>No Place Else: Explorations in Utopian and
Dystopian Fiction</u>, by E. S. Rabkin, M. H.
Greenberg, and J. D. Olander. Carbondale:
Southern Illinois University Press, 1983.
278 p.

<u>Science Fiction: History, Science, Vision</u>,
by Robert Scholes and E. S. Rabkin. New York:
Oxford University Press, 1977. 258 p.

<u>Shadows of the Magic Lamp: Fantasy and Science
Fiction in Film</u>, by George Slusser and E. S.
Rabkin. Carbondale: Southern Illinois
University Press, 1985. 259 p.

"Appeal of the fantastic: Old world for new,"
in: Collins, R. A., ed. <u>Scope of the
Fantastic: Theory, Technique, Major Authors</u>.
Westport: Greenwood, 1985. pp. 3-15.

"Atavism and Utopia," in: Rabkin, E. S., ed.
<u>No Place Else</u>. Carbondale: Southern
Illinois University Press, 1983. pp. 1-10.

"Commentary: Two and a Half Practically New
Universes, John Varley, Prop.," <u>Fantasy
Newsletter</u> 5(4): 10-12, 38. April/May 1982.

"Composite Fiction of Olaf Stapledon,"
<u>Science-Fiction Studies</u> 9(3): 238-248.
November 1982.

"Conflation of genres and myths in David
Lindsay's <u>A Voyage to Arcturus</u>," <u>The
Journal of Narrative Technique</u> 7(2):149-155.
Spring 1977.

"Descent of Fantasy," in: Slusser, George E.,
ed. <u>Coordinates</u>. Carbondale: Southern
Illinois University Press, 1983. pp. 14-22.

"Determinism, free will, and point of view in
<u>The Left Hand of Darkness</u>," in: <u>Ursula K.
Le Guin</u>, ed. by Harold Bloom. New York:
Chelsea House, 1986. pp. 155-170.

"Determinism, free will, and point of view in
Le Guin's <u>The Left Hand of Darkness</u>,"
<u>Extrapolation</u> 20(1):5-19. Spring 1979.

"Fairy Tales and Science Fiction," in:
Slusser, George., ed. <u>Bridges to Science
Fiction</u>. Carbondale: Southern Illinois
University Press, 1980. pp. 78-90.

Rabkin, E. S. (Continued)

"Fantasy literature: gut with a backbone,"
CEA Critic 40(2):6-11. January 1978.

"How Budrys 'Blew it' in His Blast at Academe,"
Fantasy Newsletter 6(6): 39-40. June/July
1983.

"Introduction: Shadows of the Magic Lamp," by
G. E. Slusser and E. S. Rabkin. in: Slusser,
George, ed. Shadows of the Magic Lamp.
Carbondale: Southern Illinois University Press,
1985. pp. xiii-xxii.

"Introduction: the appeal of the fantastic: old
worlds for new," in: Collins, R. A. and H. D.
Pearce, eds. The Scope of the Fantastic:
Theory, Technique, Major Authors. Westport,
CT: Greenwood Press, 1985. pp. 3-15.

"Introduction: Why Destroy the World?" in:
Rabkin, Eric S., ed. The End of the World.
Carbondale: Southern Illinois University Press,
1983. pp. vii-xv.

"Metalinguistics and science fiction,"
Critical Inquiry 6(1):79-98. Autumn 1979.

"Rhetoric of Science in Fiction," in:
Staicar, Tom, ed. Critical Encounters II.
New York: Ungar, 1982. pp. 23-43.

"Science and the human image in recent science
fiction," Michigan Quarterly Review 24(2):
251-264. Spring 1985.

"Science fiction power fantasy: Heinlein's
The Puppet Masters," English Record
29(1):6-8. Winter 1978.

"Science Fiction Women Before Liberation,"
in: Barr, Marlene S., ed. Future Females.
Bowling Green OH: Bowling Green State
University Popular Press, 1981. pp. 9-25.

"Significance of SF as a genre, The," in:
Remington, T. J., ed. Selected Proceedings
of the 1978 SFRA National Conference. Cedar
Falls, Iowa: University of Northern Iowa,
1979. pp. 249-254.

"Technophobia in the Arts and Humanities,"
Essays in Arts and Sciences 9(2): 107-121.
August 1980.

"To fairyland by rocket: Bradbury's The
Martian Chronicles," in: Olander, J. D. and
M. H. Greenberg, eds. Ray Bradbury. New
York: Taplinger, 1980. pp. 110-126.

Rabkin, William

"Amazing Stories of Mick Garris,", Starlog
No. 99:29-31,54. October 1985.

"Lauren Schuler producing Ladyhawke,"
Starlog No. 94:36-40. May 1985.

"Special effects: the love at the heart of
Starman," Starlog No. 92:43-46. March
1985.

"Starlog interview: Harvey Bernhard,"
Starlog 96: 55-57. July 1985.

Racette, Gilles

"Cosmos a l'inconscient, Du" La Presse p.
D23, col 1, art. 1. September 20, 1975.

Raddatz, Leslie

"Star Trek wins the Ricky Schwartz award,"
TV Guide 15(46):25-28. November 18, 1967.

"Me tobi ye, abimi?" TV Guide 24:26.
September 11, 1976. (not seen)

Radford, Elaine

"Science for SF writers: the average alien, a
birdbrain?" Empire for the SF Writer 9(3):
18-19. Spring 1985.

Radford, John

"Science fiction as myth," Foundation
10:28-33. June 1976.

Radian, Sanda

"Receptivity and Perception: Attitudes Toward
Science Fiction in Present-Day Romanian
Criticism," Romanian Review No. 1: 89-97.
1981.

Radway, Janice

"Utopian Impulse in Popular Literature Gothic
Romances and 'Feminist' Protest," American
Quarterly 33(2): 14-162. Summer 1981.

Raffetto, Francis

"Science fiction movies are a convention lure,"
Dallas Morning News sect. C, p. 1.
February 16, 1969.

Raicheva, Eliiana

"Fantastichnoto: edin kliuch kum tainata za
choveka," Literaturen Front (Bulgaria)
38(17): 1, 6. April 1982.

Rainbow, Tom

"Science Fiction Sex-Change, The," Isaac
Asimov's Science Fiction Magazine 9(7):
19-37. July 1985.

Rainbow, Tom (Continued)

"Viewpoint: The Mad Scientist's primer," Isaac Asimov's Science Fiction Magazine 9(10): 26-46. October 1985.

Rait-Kovaleva, Rita

"Kanareika v shakhte," Rovesnik 1:16-19. 1974.

Ralston, Ken

"Jedi Journal," by Richard Edlund, Dennis Muren, and Ken Ralston. Cinefex 13: 4-67. July 1983.

"Mama Eel and the Nebulae," American Cinematographer 63(10): 1035-1037, 1052. October 1982.

Ramras-Rauch, Gila

"Holocaust and the fantastic, The: a negative revelation?" in: Collins, R. A., ed. Scope of the Fantastic: Culture, Biography, Themes, Children's Literature. Westport: Greenwood, 1985. pp. 33-42.

Ramsaye, Terry

"From 'Paul and the Time Machine'," in: Johnson, William, ed. Focus on the Science Fiction Film. Englewood Cliffs, NJ: Prentice Hall, 1972. pp. 18-25.

Rand, C.

"It'll never happen; minicourse for students grades 9-12," by C. Rand and Z. Verner. English Journal 65:65-66. April 1976.

Randall, D. A.

Science Fiction and Fantasy: An Exhibition. Bloomington: Lilly Library, 1975. 69 p.

Randall, Marta

"Just When You Thought It Was Safe to Go Back to the Magazine: New Problems With Copyrights in Contributions to Magazines and Anthologies," SFWA Bulletin 16(1): 26-33. Winter 1981.

Rankin, David

"Orwell's intention in 1984," English Language Notes 12(3):188-192. March 1975.

Ranly, E. W.

"What are people for? Man, fate and Kurt Vonnegut," Commonweal 94(9):207-211. May 7, 1971.

Rapp, Bernard

"Science Fiction: die neuen Chansons de geste," Quarber Merkur 30:3-6. April 1972.

Rapp, Rodger

"E. Pluribus Unicorn: Theodore Sturgeon: 1918-1985," Bloomsbury Review 6(3):23. February 1986.

Rasmussen, Palle

Science Fiction. Copenhagen: Munksgaard, 1974. 32 p.

Rasulis, Norman

"Future of empire, The: conflict in the major fiction of John Brunner," in: De Bolt, Joe, ed. Happening Worlds of John Brunner. Port Washington, NY: Kennikat, 1975. pp. 113-129.

Rateliff, J. D.

"She and Tolkien,", Mythlore 8(2):6-8. Summer 1981.

Rathburn, F. M.

Anatomy of a Best Seller: Form, Style, and Symbol in Stephen King's The Stand. Masters Thesis, Stephen F. Austin State University, 1981. 84 p.

Rato, M. A.

"Ficcion especulativa y realismo psiquedelico," Papeles de Son Armadans (Mallorca) 82:89-107. n. d.

Ratto, Kathleen

"Moon in literature, The," Elementary English 48(8):932-936. December 1971.

Raulet, Gerard

Strategies de l'utopie. Colloque organis'e au Centre Thomas More, by Pierre Furter, and Gerard Raulet. Paris: Editions Galilee, 1979. 269 p.

Rausen, Ruth

"Interview with Madeleine L'Engle, An," Children's Literature in Education No. 19:198-206. Winter 1975.

Rawlins, J. P.

"Confronting the Alien: Fantasy and Anti-Fantasy in Science Fiction Film and Literature," in: Slusser, George E., ed. Bridges to Fantasy. Carbondale: Southern Illinois University Press, 1982. pp. 160-174.

"Linear Man: Jack Vance and the Value of Plot in Science Fiction," Extrapolation 24(4): 356-369. Winter 1983.

Rawls, Melanie

"Arwen, shadow bride," Mythlore 12(1):24-25,37. Autumn 1985.

"Feminine Principle in Tolkien," Mythlore 10(4): 5-13. Spring 1984.

"Rings of power," Mythlore 11(2):29-32. Autumn 1984.

Rawson, Ellen

"Fisher King in That Hideous Strength," Mythlore 9(4): 30-32. Winter 1983.

Ray, P. E.

"Alex Before and After: A New Approach to Burgess' A Clockwork Orange," Modern Fiction Studies 27(3): 479-487. Autumn 1981.

Ray, S. G.

"Science fiction," in: Ray, Shiela G. Children's Fiction: A Handbook for Librarians. Leicester: Brockhampton Press, 1972, second edition. pp. 60-68.

Raybin, Ronald

"Ray Bradbury's The Illustrated Man: reality extrapolated," Wisconsin English Journal 18(3):8,15-18. April 1976.

Raymer, A. C.

"Ship Who Sang, The," in: Magill, Frank N., ed. Survey of Science Fiction Literature, Vol. 4. Englewood Cliffs, NJ: Salem Press, 1979. pp. 1917-1921.

"Time and Again," in: Magill, Frank N., ed. Survey of Science Fiction Literature, Vol. 5. Englewood Cliffs, NJ: Salem Press, 1979. pp. 2283-2286.

Raymond, Francois

Developement des etudes sur Jules Verne, by Francois Raymond and Daniel Compere. Paris: Lettres Modernes, 1976. 93 p.

Jules Verne et les sciences humaines, by Francois Raymond and Simone Vierne. Paris: 10/18 Union generale d'edition, 1979. 443 p.

Raynaud, Jean

"Definitions, Le. b) une impasse: le contenu," Europe 580/581:25-34. August/September 1977.

"Science fiction et critique de l'alienation," Revue Francaise d'Etudes Americaines No. 3:80-92. April 1977.

"Ville dans la science fiction americaine contemporaine, La," Revue Francaise d'Etudes Americaines 6(11): 67-78. November 1981.

Rea, S. X.

"Arthur Clarke Tries Another Space Odyssey," Philadelphia Inquirer November 15, 1982. in: NewsBank. Film and Television. 48: E7-8. January 1983.

Read, Herbert

"Fantasy (Fancy)," in: Boyer, R. H. and Zahorski, K. J. Fantasists on Fantasy. New York: Avon Discus, 1984. pp. 41-58.

Read, J.

"Science, literature and human thought," Journal of Chemical Education 37(3):110-117. March 1960.

Ready, Karen

"Other worlds, other worldiness: science fiction and religion," by Karen Ready and Franz Rottensteiner. Christian Century 90:1192-1195. December 5, 1973.

Reasoner, Harry

"60 minutes," CBS News Transcript 3:14-17. September 15, 1970.

Reaves, Michael

"Saturday Morning Superhero Writer's Grant Program, or, "We're Not Doing Ibsen Here," SFWA Bulletin 16(3): 30-37. March 1982.

Reaves, R. B.

"Orwell's 'Second Thoughts on James Burnham' and 1984," College Literature 11(1): 13-21. 1984.

Rebeaux, Max

"Harlan Ellison vs. James Cameron: The Terminator, no Mr. Nice Guy," Cinefantastique 15(4):4-5,61. October 1985.

"Twilight Zone," Cinefantastique 15(4):13,53. October 1985.

Rebello, Stephen

"Cat People: Paul Schrader Changes His Spots," American Film 7(6): 38-45. 1982.

"CFQ retrospective: Jack Clayton's The Innocents," Cinefantastique 13(5):51. June/July 1983.

"Escape From New York (review)," Cinefantastique 11(3):47. September 1981.

"Introvision," Cinefantastique 13(1):36-43. September/October 1982.

"Making of Paul Schrader's Cat People," Cinefantastique 11(4):20-21. December 1981.

"Philadelphia Experiment: invisible no longer," Twilight Zone 4(4):37-40. September/October 1984.

"Shooting for an 'A' on My Science Project," Cinefex No. 23:54-71. August 1985.

"Something Wicked This Way Comes," Cinefantastique 12(5/6):76-77. July/August 1982.

"Wolfen," Cinefantastique 11(3):38-41. September 1981.

Rech, Michel

Merveilleux et la fantastique, by Jean Monard and Michel Rech. Paris: Librairie Delagrave, 1974. 127 p.

Reckitt, M. B.

"Everlasting man, An," Chesterton Review 1(1):7-10. 1974.

Redd, M. G.

"'Report on the Blind': Sabato's journey into the fantastic," in: Collins, R. A., ed. Scope of the Fantastic: Culture, Biography, Themes, Children's Literature. Westport: Greenwood, 1985. pp. 147-154.

Reddy, A. F.

"Till We Have Faces: 'An Epistle to the Greeks," Mosaic 13(3/4): 153-164. Spring/Summer 1980.

Reddy, John

"Propheten des dritten jahrtausends," Das Beste no. 6:33-38. 1969.

Redekop, E. H.

"Labyrinths in Time and Space," Mosaic 13(3/4): 95-113. Spring/Summer 1980.

Redlin, Ekkehard

"Roboter und die utopiesche literatur, Der," Das Molekularcafe. Geschichten von Robotern und Biomaten. Berlin, 1969.

Wissenschaftliche phantastik: authoren der Deutschen Demokratischen Republik, by Gunther Henry and Ekkehard Redlin. s.l.: Schriftstellerverband der DDR, 1978. 64 p.

Reed, A. K.

"Greatest Adventure Is What Lies Ahead: Problems in Media and Mythology; an Analysis of the Rankin/Bass Production of Tolkien's The Hobbit," Journal of Popular Culture 17(4): 138-146. Spring 1984.

Reed, Charlette

"It'll never happen," by Charlette Reed and Zenobia Verner. English Journal 65(4):65-66. April 1976.

Reed, D. A.

Collector's Edition: Science Fiction Film Awards, by D. A. Reed and Patrick Pattison. s.l.: ESE California, 1981. 107 p.

Reed, G. S.

"Fantasy and Phantasy: Eric Rabin's The Fantastic in Literature," Literature and Psychology 28(3/4):168-169. 1978. (Book Review)

Reed, J. D.

"Postfeminism: Playing for Keeps," Time 121(2): 60-61. January 10, 1983.

Reed, J. R.

Natural History of H. G. Wells. Athens: Ohio University Press, 1982. 294 p.

"Archy and Mehitabel," in: Magill, Frank N., ed. Survey of Modern Fantasy Literature, Vol 1. Englewood Cliffs, NJ: Salem Press, Inc., 1983. pp. 54-56.

"Hell House," in: Magill, Frank N., ed. Survey of Modern Fantasy Literature, Vol 2. Englewood Cliffs, NJ: Salem Press, Inc., 1983. pp. 725-727.

"Plague Dogs, The," in: Magill, Frank N., ed. Survey of Modern Fantasy Literature, Vol 3. Englewood Cliffs, NJ: Salem Press, Inc., 1983. pp. 1268-1270.

"Future according the H. G. Wells, The," North American Review 264(2):53-56. Summer 1979.

"Short fiction of Dinesen, The," in: Magill, Frank N., ed. Survey of Modern Fantasy Literature, Vol 3. Englewood Cliffs, NJ: Salem Press, Inc., 1983. pp. 1501-1503.

"Short fiction of O'Brien, The," in: Magill, Frank N., ed. Survey of Modern Fantasy Literature, Vol 4. Englewood Cliffs, NJ: Salem Press, Inc., 1983. pp. 1657-1661.

Reed, P. J.

Kurt Vonnegut, Jr.. New York: Warner Paperback Library, 1972. 222 p. Reprinted, New York: Thomas Y. Crowell, 1976.

"Later Vonnegut, The," in: Klinkowitz, Kurt, ed. Vonnegut in America. New York: Delacorte, 1977. pp. 150-186.

Rees, David

"Earthsea revisited; Ursula K. Le Guin," in: Rees, David. The Marble in the Water. Boston: Horn Book, 1980. pp. 78-89.

"Hanging in their true shapes; Alan Garner," in: Rees, David. The Marble in the Water. Boston: Horn Book, 1980. pp. 56-67.

Reginald, Robert

See: Burgess, Michael

Reich, Howard

"'Quest for Fire': Probable Prehistory or Plain Fantasy?" Chicago Tribune Sec. 6, p. 20-21. March 7, 1982.

Reichardt, Jasia

Robots: Fact, Fiction, and Prediction. London: Thames and Hudson. New York: Viking, 1978.

Reilly, Charles

"Interview with Kurt Vonnegut, Jr., An," DLR (University of Delaware Student Magazine) pp. 20-27. Spring 1976. (not seen)

Reilly, Robert

Transcendent Adventure: Studies of Religion in Science Fiction/Fantasy. Westport: Greenwood, 1985. 266 p.

"Artistry of Ray Bradbury, The," Extrapolation 13(1):64-74. December 1971.

"Checklist of Science Fiction/Fantasy Works Containing Religious Themes or Motifs," by Robert Reilly, F. D. McSherry, and C. G. Waugh. in: Reilly, Robert, ed. The Transcendent Adventure. Westport: Greenwood, 1984. pp. 225-248.

"Discerning conscience, The," Extrapolation 18(2):176-180. May 1977.

"How Machines Become Human: Process and Attribute," in: Dunn, T. P., ed. The Mechanical God. Westport: Greenwood, 1982. pp. 153-165.

"Introduction," in: Reilly, Robert, ed. The Transcendent Adventure. Westport: Greenwood, 1984. pp. 3-8.

"Secondary Works Dealing with Religion in Science Fiction," in: Reilly, Robert, ed. The Transcendent Adventure. Westport: Greenwood, 1984. pp. 249-251.

Reines, D. F.

"Interplanetary copyright," in: Greenberg, M. H., ed. Coming Attractions. New York: Gnome, 1957. pp. 250-254.

"Shape of copyright to come, The," Library of Congress Information Bulletin 29:A15-17. January 29, 1970.

Reinhold, Robert

"Scripting Kubrick's First Flick," Pulpsmith 3(3): 71-78. Autumn 1983.

"Vonnegut has 15 nuggets of talent in Harvard class," New York Times pp. 49,77. November 18, 1970.

Reinsma, Riemer

"Berichten uit de toekomst als literair genre," Hollands Maandblad 15(314):25-30. 1974.

"De toekomst is bijna volgeboekt: Profetische literatuur in Nederland," Revisor (Netherlands) 8(5): 67-73. October 1981.

Reis, R. H.

George MacDonald. New York: Twayne Publishers, 1972. 161 p.

Reitberger, R. C.

Comics: Anatomie eines Massenmediums, by W. J. Fuchs and R. C. Reitberger. Hamburg: Rowohlt, 1971. 333 p.

Remi-Maure

"Nave, La," in: Magill, Frank N., ed. Survey of Science Fiction Literature, Vol. 3. Englewood Cliffs, NJ: Salem Press, 1979. pp. 1497-1500.

"Quinzinzinzili," in: Magill, Frank N., ed. Survey of Science Fiction Literature, Vol. 4. Englewood Cliffs, NJ: Salem Press, 1979. pp. 1742-1745.

"Univers Vagabond, L'," in: Magill, Frank N., ed. Survey of Science Fiction Literature, Vol. 5. Englewood Cliffs, NJ: Salem Press, 1979. pp. 2362-2365.

"Zecca Lume, A," in: Magill, Frank N., ed. Survey of Science Fiction Literature, Vol. 5. Englewood Cliffs, NJ: Salem Press, 1979. pp. 2534-2537.

"Science Fiction in Chile," Science-Fiction Studies 11(2): 181-189. July 1984.

Remington, T.

"SF as structural fabulation," North American Review 260:53-55. Winter 1975. (Book review)

Remington, T. J.

Selected Proceedings of the 1978 SFRA National Conference. Cedar Falls, Iowa: Univ. of Northern Iowa, 1979. 281 p.

"'The Mirror Up To Nature': Reflections of Victorianism in Samuel Butler's Erewhon," in: Rabkin, Eric S., et. al., eds. No Place Else. Carbondale: Southern Illinois University Press, 1983. pp. 33-55.

"Lagniappe: an informal dialogue with Ursula K. Le Guin," in: Remington, T. J., ed. Selected Proceedings of the 1978 SFRA National Conference. Cedar Falls, Iowa: Univ. of Northern Iowa, 1979. pp. 269-281.

"Niven of Oz: Ringworld as Science Fictional Reinterpretation," in: Wolfe, Gary, ed. Science Fiction Dialogues. Chicago: Academy Chicago, 1982. pp. 99-111.

"Other side of suffering: touch as theme and metaphor in Le Guin's science fiction novels, The," in: Olander, J. D. and M. H. Greenberg, eds. Ursula K. Le Guin. New York: Taplinger, 1979. pp. 153-177.

"Three reservations on the structural road," Science Fiction Studies 4(1):48-54. March 1977.

"Time to Live and a Time to Die: Cyclic Renewal in the Earthsea Trilogy," Extrapolation 21(3): 278-286. Fall 1980.

"Touch of difference, a touch of love: theme in three stories by Ursula K. Le Guin," Extrapolation 18(1):28-41. December 1976.

Renard, J. B.

"Religion, Science-Fiction et Extraterrestres: de la litterature a la croyance," Archives de Sciences Sociales de Religions 50(1): 143-164. July/September. 1980.

"Wild man and the extraterrestrial: two figures of evolutionist fantasy," Diogenes No. 127: 63-81. Fall 1984.

Renard-Cheinisse, Christine

"Problemes religieux dans la litterature dite de science fiction, Les," Archives de sociologie des religions 13:141-152. 1968.

Renaud, Tristan

"Portes de l'autre monde, Les," Les Lettres Francaises p. 9. May 19, 1966.

Renault, Gregory

"Science Fiction as Cognitive Estrangement: Darko Suvin and the Marxist Critique of Mass Culture," Discourse No. 2: 112-141. Summer 1980.

"Speculative Porn: Aesthetic Form in Samuel R. Delany's The Tides of Lust," Extrapolation 24(2): 116-129. Summer 1983.

Renault, Maurice

"Qu'est-ce que la Science-Fiction?" Rapports France-USA 67. October 1952.

Renner, Rudolf

"Science Fiction und Theologie," Zeitschrift fur Religionspadagogik. 27(11/12):323-349. 1972.

Renold, Evelyn

"Ron: Actor/Director," New York Daily News June 23, 1985. in: NewsBank. Film and Television. 5:C7-C8. July 1985.

Rense, Rip

"E. T., Go Home." Los Angeles Herald Examiner December 20, 1982. in: NewsBank. Business and Economic Development. 111: E4-6. December 1982.

"Will this man kill Star Trek's Mr. Spock?" Los Angeles Herald Examiner. November 15, 1981. in: NewsBank. Film and Television. 74:A3-5. May 1982.

Repp, E. E.

"My life," Starship 16(3):42-43. Summer 1979.

Resch, H. W.

"Mann, der Conan war: ein psychogramm Robert E. Howards," Science Fiction Times (Germany) 24(5):14-17. May 1982.

Resnick, M. D.

Official Guide to Fantastic Fiction. Florence, AL: House of Collectibles, 1976. 212 p.

Official Price Guide to Comic and Science Fiction Books. Orlando, FL: House of Collectibles, 1979. 422 p.

Ressmeyer, K. H.

"Interieur und Symbol. Zum Phantastastischen im Werk E. A. Poes," in: Thomsen, C. W., ed. Phantastik in Literatur und Kunst. Darmstadt: Wissenschaftliche Buchgesellschaft, 1980. pp. 150-169.

Reusse, Walter

"Science Fiction in Gruppenarbeit in Klasse 10," Der Deutschunterricht 25(5):106-120. 1973.

Reuter, Madalynne

"Talk with Kirill Bulychev," Publishers Weekly 211(20):34. May 16, 1977.

Reveaux, Anthony

"Right Stuff, The," Cinefantastique 14(2):6-9. December 1983/January 1984.

Revich, Vsevolod

"Realizm fantastiki," Fantastika pp. 270-298. 1968.

Rey, H. F.

"Naissance de l'homme-fiction," France-Observateur 26.12.1957.

"Science ficiton ou science mystification?" La Gazette de Lausanne September 29, 1953.

Rey, P. K.

Nouvelle science fiction americaine, La, by P. K. Rey and P. J. Thomas. Cavignac: Ailleurs & Autres Infos, 1981. May 1981. 64 p. (No. 72 bis.)

Reynolds, J. C.

"Science fiction in the 7-12 curriculum," Clearing House 51(3):122-125. November 1977.

"Teaching Socialization Through Science Fiction," Clearing House 56(9): 404-407. May 1983.

Reynolds, Mack

"Change, SF and Marxism: open or closed universes? What do you mean: Marxism?" Science Fiction Studies 1(4):270-271.

"Last letter to Fredric Brown," Locus No. 111:2-3. April 8, 1972.

"Science fiction and political economy," Science Fiction Review 9(3):34-39. August 1980.

"Science Fiction and Socioeconomics," in: Greenberg, M. H., ed. Fantastic Lives: Autobiographical Essays by Notable Science Fiction Writers. Carbondale: Southern Illinois University Press, 1981. pp. 118-143.

Reynolds, Quentin

"Astounding science fiction," in: Reynolds, Quentin. The Fiction Factory. New York: Random House, 1955. pp. 250-264.

Reynolds, W. D.

"Status of science fiction anthologies and their applicability to teaching, The," 10 p. November 1974. ERIC ED 103 881.

Reynolds, W. J.

"Galaxy of SF Stars," by W. J. Reynolds, and D. A. Fryxell. TWA Ambassador 12(10): 94-95, 124-127. October 1979.

Reynolds, William

"Poetry as metaphore in the Lord of the Rings," Mythlore 4(4): 12-16. June 1977.

Rhetts, Joann

"Child Star's transformation into star director continues with Cocoon," Charlotte N. C. Observer June 23, 1985. in: NewsBank. Film and Television. 2:D1-D2. July 1985.

Rhodes, C. H.

"Experiment as heroic quest in Zelazny's 'For a Breath I Tarry'," in: Collins, R. A., ed. Scope of the Fantastic: Culture, Biography, Themes, Children's Literature. Westport: Greenwood, 1985. pp. 191-198.

"Frederick Winslow Taylor's system of scientific management in Zamiatin's We," Journal of General Education 28(1):31-42. Spring 1976.

"Intelligence testing in utopia," Extrapolation 13(1):25-47. December 1971.

"Method in her madness: feminism in the crazy Utopian vision of Tiptree's courier," in: Barr, Marleen, ed. Women and Utopia. New York: Lanham, 1983. pp. 34-42.

"Tyranny by computer: automated data processing and oppressive government in science fiction," in: Clareson, Thomas D., ed. Many Futures, Many Worlds. Kent, Ohio: Kent State University Press, 1977. pp. 66-93.

Rhodes, J. P.

"Left Hand of Darkness: androgyny and the feminist utopias," in: Barr, Marleen, ed. Women and Utopia. New York: Lanham, 1983. pp. 108-120.

Riccardo, M. V.

Vampires Unearthed: The Complete Multi-Media Vampire and Dracula Bibliography. New York: Garland, 1983. 135 p.

Rice, Paul

"Metaphor as a Way of Saying the Self in Science Fiction," in: Myers, R. E., ed. The Intersection of Science Fiction and Philosophy. Westport: Greenwood, 1983. pp. 133-142.

Rice, Susan

"Slaughterhouse-Five: a viewer's guide," Media & Methods pp. 27-33. October 1972.

"Stanley Kubrick's Clockwork Orange: a viewer's guide," Media & Methods 8(7):39-43. March 1972.

Richards, G. B.

Science Fiction Movies. New York: Gallery, 1984. 80 p.

Richards, Tony

"Are you listening? The contemporary fantasy of Harlan Ellison," Vector 87:24-27. May/June 1978.

Richardson, C. C.

"Reality of fantasy, The," Language Arts 53(5):549-551,563. May 1976.

Richardson, D. C.

"Burroughs, Kline and Farley," Oak Leaves 1(7):4-5. Spring 1972.

"Little Known Fantasy, III: Fantasy and Science Fiction in New Magazine, New Story, and All Around," Fantasy Commentator 3(6): 167-169. Spring/Summer 1952.

Richardson, M. A.

"Dream in the Making," Cinefex 12: 50-71. April 1983.

Richardson, Maurice

"After the apocalypse," New Statesman pp. 554, 556. October 30, 1954. (Book review)

"New novels," New Statesman p. 533. April 9, 1960. (Book review)

Richardson, R. S.

"Space fix," in: Greenberg, M. H., ed. Coming Attractions. New York: Gnome, 1957. pp. 110-157.

Riche, Daniel

Bande dessinee de science fiction americaine, by Boris Eizykman and Daniel Riche. Paris: Michel, 1976. 126 p.

"Science fiction et histoire: une introduction," Change (Paris) 40:9-13. 1981.

Richey, J. A. M.

"Science, with a sense of humor," Catholic World 131:685-688. September 1930.

Richler, Mordecai

"Great comic book heroes, The," Encounter pp. 46-48,50-53. May 1967.

Richter, Anne

"Fantastique belge, Le: de la logique du reve au reve logique," Francais 2000 No. 80/81:25-31. 1975.

"Fantastique, Lointain intereiur," Syntheses 23(267/268):47-48. September/October 1968.

Richter, P. E.

Utopia/Dystopia?. Cambridge, MA: Schenkman, 1975. 151 p.

"Utopia/Dystopia?: threats of hell or hopes of paradise," in: Richter, P. E., ed. Utopia/Dystopia?. Cambridge, MA: Schenkman, 1975. pp. 1-28.

Rickard, Bob

"After Such Knowledge: James Blish's tetralogy," in: Chauvin, Cy, ed. Multitude of Visions. Baltimore: T-K Graphics, 1975. pp. 24-34.

Rickard, Dennis

"Drugs and Clark Ashton Smith," Nyctalops No. 7:31-32. August 1972.

"Through black boughs: the supernatural in Howard's fiction," in: Herron, Don, ed. Dark Barbarian: The Writings of Robert E. Howard, a Critical Anthology. Westport, CT: Greenwood, 1984. pp. 65-99.

Rickey, Carrie

"Hollywood gives elderly a break," Boston Herald June 23, 1985. in: NewsBank. Film and Television. 2:C11-C12. 1985.

Rickman, Greg

Philip K. Dick: In His Own Words. Long Beach, CA: Fragments West, 1984. 255 p.

Philip K. Dick: The Last Testament. Long Beach, CA: Fragments West, 1985. 240 p.

Riddle, Patricia

"Rebel mistress of Dune," Prevue 2(15):38-41. April/May 1984.

Ridley, Olivia

"Future in the Classroom Today," English Journal 72(6): 67-68. October 1983.

Rieder, John

"Embracing the Alien: Science Fiction in Mass Culture," Science Fiction Studies 9(1): 26-37. March 1982.

Riemer, J. D.

"Masculinity and Feminist Fantasy Authors," Fantasy Review of Fantasy and Science Fiction 7(3): 19-21. April 1984.

Riggenbach, Jeff

"Science fiction as will and idea: the world of Alfred Bester," Riverside Quarterly 5(3):168-177. August 1972.

Riggsby, D. S.

"Would you believe? Science fiction," Science & Children 6(3):21-22. November 1968.

Rigsbee, Sally

"Fantasy places and imaginative belief: The Lion, The Witch, and the Wardrobe and The Princesss and the Goblin," Children's Literature Association Quarterly 8(1): 10-11. Spring 1983.

Riha, Karl

"Arthur Machen," Quarber Merkur 27:27-29. July 1971.

"Enthemmung der Bilder und Enthemmung der Sprache. Zu Paul Scheergart und Carl Einstein," in: Thomsen, C. W., ed. Phantastik in Literatur und Kunst. Darmstadt: Wissenschaftliche Buchgesellschaft, 1980. pp. 268-280.

Riley, Dick

Critical Encounters: Writers and Themes in Science Fiction. New York: Ungar, 1978. 184 p.

Riley, R. B.

"Architecture and the sense of wonder," Landscape 15(1):20-24. autumn 1965.

"Dreams of tomorrow," Architectural Forum 126(3):66-67,112-113. April 1967.

Riley, S. T.

"Bibliography of Donald M. Grant Publications, A," Fantasy Crossroads 10/11:36-38. 1977.

"Donald M. Grant interview," Fantasy Crossroads 10/11:25-38. 1977.

"Donald M. Grant, publisher: an informal history and appreciation," PSFQ (Cupertino, California) No. 3/4:9-15. 1978/1979.

Rilla, Wolf

"Boundary of imagination, The," Algol 11(2):13-16. May 1974.

Rimmer, R. H.

"I Write Entopian Novels," in: Roemer, Kenneth M., ed. American as Utopia. New York: Franklin, 1981. pp. 43-51.

Ring, David

"Report on Westercon 22," Mythlore 1(4):15-17. October 1969.

Ringel, Eleanor

"Trouble with Spielberg," Atlanta Journal June 10, 1984. NewsBank. Film and Television. FTV 9:A7-A8. 1984.

Ringel, Harry

"Exorcist (review)," Cinefantastique 3(1):24-25. Spring 1974.

"Terence Ficher; the human side," Cinefantastique 4(3):4-17. Fall 1975.

"Terence Fisher: underlining," Cinefantastique 4(3):18-28. Fall 1975.

Rio, Yyes

"Science fiction et refus de l'histoire," Change (Paris) 40:104-111. 1981.

Rioja, Ines

"Ciencia-ficcion y el arte de la tecnica del miedo," Arbor: Revista General de Investigacion y Cultura No. 365:113-117. May 1976.

Rippington, Geoff

Bob Shaw: British Science Fiction Writers, Volume 1, by Paul Kincaid and Geoff Rippington. Kent, Eng.: British Science Fiction Association, 1981. 38 p.

"B. J. Bayley interviewed," Arena 10:13-19. April 1980.

"Collective pool of the unconscious, part I: an interview with Robert Scheckley, The," Arena 6:4-10. August 1977.

"Editorial: The Awakening of a Conscience: The Day the Buck Stopped Here," by C. Pemberton and Geoff Rippington. Vector 116: 3-5. September 1983.

"Haldeman interview, part one," by Ken Lake and Geoff Rippington. Vector 126: 3-5. June/July 1985.

"Haldeman interview, part two," by Ken Lake and Geoff Rippington. Vector 127: 6-8. August/September 1985.

"Mark Adlard interviewed," by Mike Ashley and Geoff Rippington. Arena 7:8-12. March 1978.

"Robert Holdstock interviewed," Arena 9:18-26. August 1979.

Ritch, W. A.

"Conversation with Michael Shaara," by Brad Linaweaver and W. A. Ritch. Amazing 28(7): 20-26. September 1982.

Ritter, Claus

Anno Utopia; oder, So war die Zukunft. Berlin: Das Neue Berlin, 1982. 352 p.

Start nach Utopolis. Eine Zukunfts-Nostalgie. Berlin: Verlag der Nation, 1978. 366 p.

Ritter, Jess

"Teaching Kurt Vonnegut on the firing line," in: Klinkowitz, Jerome and John Somer, eds. The Vonnegut Statement. New York: Delacorte Press/ Seymour Lawrence, 1973. pp. 31-42.

Riuikov, I. U.

Cherez sto Tysiachu Let. Yelovek Budumego i covegekaya khydozhestvennaya fantastika. Moscow: Iskuestvo, 1961. 111 p.

Rivais, Yak

"Bottom, at last," in: H. P. Lovecraft. Paris: Editions de l'Herne, 1969. pp. 163-176.

Riviere, Francois

"Commence, L'un, l'autre continue," Europe No. 595/596:37-42. 1978.

Riviere, Yves

"On distrait," in: H. P. Lovecraft. Paris: Editions de l'Herne, 1969. pp. 133-134.

Rjubikow, Juri

"Notizen uber die literatur von der zukunft," Sovietliteratur no. 4:135-151. 1960.

Robbins, Bruce

"La Maison d'Ailleurs opens," Science Fiction Review 19:18-19. August 1976.

Robbins, J. C.

"Uses of military history in Lord Kalvan of Otherwhen, The," in: Remington, T. J., ed. Selected Proceedings of the 1978 SFRA National Conference. Cedar Falls, Iowa: Univ. of Northern Iowa, 1979. pp. 75-104.

Robbins, Trina

"Vaughn Bode: an appreciation," Locus No. 177:1-2. August 10, 1975.

Roberts, Frank

"Exclusive interview with Ray Bradbury, pt. 1, An," Writers Digest 47(2):39-44,94-96. February 1967.

"Exclusive interview with Ray Bradbury, pt. 2, An," Writers Digest 47(3):41-44. March 1967.

Roberts, Keith

"Sex and taboos," in: Ash, Brian, ed. Visual Encyclopedia of Science Fiction. New York: Harmony, 1977. pp. 212-221.

"Tongue-twisting as a sport," Foundation 19: 30-37. June 1980.

Roberts, Peter

British Fanzine Bibliography, Part 1: 1936-1950. United Kingdom: Privately printed, 1978. (not seen)

British Fanzine Bibliography, Part 2: 1951-1960. United Kingdom: Privately printed, 1978. (not seen)

Guide to Current Fanzines. United Kingdom: Privately printed, 1978. fifth edition. (not seen)

Peter Roberts' Little Gem Guide to SF Fanzines. London: by the author, 1974. 10 p. (not seen)

Roberts, Robin

"Paradigm of Frankenstein: Reading Canopis in Argos in the Context of Science Fiction by Women," Extrapolation 26(1): 16-23. Spring 1985.

Roberts, T. J.

"Science fiction and the adolescent," in: Butler, Francelia, ed. Children's Literature: The Great Excluded. Storrs, Connecticut: Children's Literature Assn., 1973. Vol. II, pp. 87-91.

Roberts, T. N.

"Unicorn: Creature of Love," Mythlore 8(4): 39-41. Winter 1982.

Roberts, Tom

"Reading science fiction and reading interviews," in: Walker, Paul. Speaking of Science Fiction. Oradell, New Jersey: Luna Publications, 1978. pp. 1-10.

Robertson, J. K.

"Science in literature," Queen's Quarterly 58(1):36-55. Spring 1951.

Robertson, Michael

"Writer Frank Herbert Says His Visions are More Criticism than Prediction," San Francisco Chronicle, April 28, 1982. in: Newsbank. Literature. 95:D11-12. 1981/82.

Robertson, Nan

"Vonneguts: dialogue on a son's insanity, The," New York Times p. 45. October 23, 1975.

Robillard, Douglas

"Uncertain Futures: Damon Knight's Science Fiction," in: Clareson, Thomas D., ed. Voices For the Future, Vol. 3. Bowling Green: Popular Press, 1984. pp. 30-51.

Robin, Christian

"Modernite de Jules Verne," Europe 580/581: 170-175. August/September 1977.

Robin, Doris

In a Faraway Galaxy: A Literary Approach to a Film Saga, by Doris Robin, Lee Vibber, and G. F. Elwood. Pasadena, CA: Extequer Press, 1984. 149 p.

Robin, J. F.

"SF (analyse de qqs livres)," Club (Bulletin du club on Meilleur Livre). April 1954.

"Visiteurs de l'infini," Combat 10.10.1957.

Robins, W. M.

"L. Sprague de Camp," in: Cowart, David, ed. Twentieth-Century American Science Fiction Writers, Part 1: A-L. Detroit: Gale, 1981. pp. 112-119. (Dictionary of Literary Biography, v. 8)

Robinson, David

"Two for the sci-fi," Sight and Sound 35(2):57-61. Spring 1961.

Robinson, Derik

"Hasty Stroke Goes Oft Astray, The: Tolkien and Humor," in: Giddings, Robert, ed. J. R. R. Tolkien: This Far Land. London: Vision, 1983. pp. 108-124.

Robinson, Douglas

American Apocalypses: the Image of the End of the World in American Literature. Baltimore: Johns Hopkins, 1985. 283 p.

Robinson, F. M.

"Cinema survey, 1984," Locus 18(2): 1, 46. February 1985.

"Confessions of a convention addict," Locus 9(13):2-3. October 30, 1976.

"For those who never believed in science fiction," Todays Health 51(4):24-28. April 1973.

"Theodore Sturgeon in Memoriam, 5," Locus 18(7): 25. July 1985.

Robinson, Frank

"Conversation with Robert Heinlein," Oui 1(3): 75-76, 112-116. December 1972.

Robinson, G. S.

"Science in SF: hypertravel," Listener 72:976-977. December 17, 1964.

"Travel in space & time," Advancement of Science 22(98):196-198. August 1965.

Robinson, G. W.

"Warum die Zeitmaschine nicht funktionieren kann. Vom Wahrheitsgehalt der Science Fiction Literatur," Stuttgarter Zeitung. No. 87:79. 1967.

Robinson, Glen

"Constructing a 42 foot superstar," American Cinematographer 58(1):51,83. January 1977.

"Mechanical special effects for Logan's Run," American Cinematographer 57(6):646-649,685. June 1976.

Robinson, Hilary

"Lifting the Lid off XIMOC," by Hilary Robinson and Davy Francis. Focus: An SF Writer's Magazine 9: 37-39. Autumn 1984.

Robinson, K. S.

Novels of Philip K. Dick. Ph. D. Dissertation, University of California, San Diego, 1982. 251 p. (DAI 43A:803.)

Novels of Philip K. Dick, The. Ann Arbor: UMI Research Press, 1984, c1982. 150 p.

Robinson, M.

"Planet parenthood; space shows," Colliers 129(1):30-31,63-64. January 5, 1952.

Robinson, R. N.

"Raymond, I hardly knew ye," Locus 10(7):15-16. September 1977.

Robinson, Richard

"Gene Simmons: a famous monster turns to science," Starlog No. 90:43-45. January 1985.

Robinson, Roger

Science Fiction and Fantasy Magazine
Collector's Checklist 1926-1980.   Harold
Wood, Essex: Beccon, 1984. unpaged.

Writings of Henry Kenneth Bulmer.
Manchester, UK: The Print Centre, 1983. 75 p.

Robinson, Spider

"Robert A. Heinlein: a sermon,"   Destinies
2(3):9-39. Summer 1980.

"Theodore Sturgeon in Memoriam, 8,"   Locus
18(7): 28. July 1985.

Robinson, W. R.

"2001 and the literary sensibility," by W. R.
Robinson and Mary McDermott.   Georgia Review
26(1):21-37. Spring 1972.

Robley, L. P.

"Brazil,"   Cinefantastique 16(1):4-5.
March 1986.

"Computer graphics for Superman III,"
American Cinematographer 64(9):68-70.
September 1983.

"Digital simulation for the Last Starfighter,"
American Cinematographer 65(10): 84-91.
November 1984.

"Dragon's Lair,"   Cinefantastique
13(6)/14(1):22-23.   September 1983.

"Enemy Mine,"   Cinefantastique 15(5):13.
January 1986.

"House,"   Cinefantastique 16(1):10,57.
March 1986.

"Koyaanisqatsi (review),"   Cinefantastique
14(2):50,52. December 1983/January 1984.

"Space Ace,"   Cinefantastique 14(2):22-23.
December 1983/January 1984.

"Starchaser: filming computer animation in 3D,"
Cinefantastique 16(1):47. March 1986.

"Starchaser: The Legend of Orin,"
Cinefantastique 16(1):46. March 1986.

Rochelle, Larry

"Quest: the search for meaning through
fantasy," English Journal 66(7):54-55.
October 1977.

Rochette, Marguerite

Science fiction, La. Paris: Larousse, 1975.
192 p.

Rock, J. A.

Who Goes There? A Bibliographic Dictionary.
Bloomington: Rock, 1979. 201 p.

"Notes on collecting," in: Rock, James A.
Who Goes There? A Bibliographic Dictionary.
Bloomington, Indiana: James A. Rock, 1979. pp.
193-201.

Rocklynne, Ross

"I hope you are shocked," Inside and Science
Fiction Advertiser No. 7: 17-19. January
1955.

"Science fiction simplified,"   Writers
Digest 21(11):25-30. October 1941.

Rockow, Karen

"Funeral customs in Tolkien's trilogy,"
Unicorn 2(3):22-30. 1973.

Rodden, John

"Orwell on religion: the Catholic and Jewish
questions,"   College Literature 11(1):
44-58. 1984.

Roddenberry, Gene

Making of Star Trek, The, by S. E. Whitfield
and Gene Roddenberry. New York: Ballantine,
1968. 414 p.

Star Trek Guide, The. Hollywood, California:
Desilu Studios, No date. (not seen)

"Mr. Spock and Gaan,"   Futurist 19(1):
39-41. February 1985.

Rodenbach, G.

"Rosny, Les,"   Nouvelle Revue 105:289-296.
1897.

Roderick, J. M.

"Two Teachers Look at E. T." by J. M. Roderick,
and Charlotte Miller. English Journal
72(5): 87-89. September 1983.

Rodger, William

"Paper Heroes," Maine Antique Digest 6(2):
24-C. March 1978.

Rodikov, Valeri

"Konstantin Feoktistov: toward the stars," Soviet Literature No. 6(447):167-173. 1985.

Rodnjanskaja, I.

"Zwei Gesichter Stanislaw Lems, Die," Quarber Merkur 38:9-15. November 1974.

Roeder, Larry

"Starguide," Fantasy Research & Bibliography 1/2: 5-23. December 1980/May 1981.

Roehm, Bob

"Thomas Burnett Swann: 1928-1976," Science Fiction Review 5(3):5. 1976.

"Thomas Burnett Swann: an appreciation," Locus 9(7):2,4. May 30, 1976.

Roemer, K. M.

American As Utopia, ed. by Kenneth M. Roemer. New York: Burt Franklin, 1981. 410 p.

Build Your Own Utopia: An Interdisciplinary Course in Utopian Speculation. Lanham, MD: University Press of America, 1981. 111 p.

Obsolete Necessity: America in Utopian Writings, 1888-1890, The. Kent, Ohio: Kent State University Press, 1976. 239 p.

"American utopia literature (1888-1900): an annotated bibliography," American Literary Realism 4:227-255. Summer 1971.

"Defining America As Utopia," in: Roemer, Kenneth M., ed. America As Utopia. New York: Franklin, 1981. pp. 1-15.

"H. G. Wells and the 'Momentary Voices' of a Modern Utopia," Extrapolation 23(2): 117-137. Summer 1982.

"Mixing Behaviorism and Utopia: The Transformations of Walden Two," in: Rabkin, Eric S., et. al., eds. No Place Else. Carbondale: Southern Illinois University Press, 1983. pp. 125-146.

"Selected Checklist of Secondary Sources," in: Roemer, Kenneth M., ed. America As Utopia. New York: Franklin, 1981. pp. 367-374.

"Sex Roles, Utopia, and Change: The Family in Late Nineteenth Century Utopian Literature," American Studies 13(2): 33-47. Fall 1972.

"Utopia and Victorian Culture, 1888-99," in: Roemer, Kenneth M., ed. America As Utopia. New York: Franklin, 1981. pp. 305-332.

"Utopian Studies: A Fiction With Notes Appended," Extrapolation 25(4): 318-335. Winter 1984.

Roessner-Herman, Mikey

"Art show," Locus 14(4):12. May 1981.

Roger, G.

"Bon usage de la science fiction, Du," Europe revue mensuelle No. 139/140:42-49. July/August 1957.

Roger, M. D.

"Ursula K. Le Guin," Wilson Library Bulletin 53(2):166-169. October 1978.

Roger, William

Official 1982 Price Guide to Comic and Science Fiction Books, by T. E. Hudgeons and William Roger. Orlando, FL: House of Collectibles, 1982. 501 p.

Rogers, Alva

Requiem for Astounding, A. Chicago: Advent Publishers, 1964. 224 p.

Rogers, C. B.

"Science fiction and social studies," Social Studies 66(6):261-264. November/December 1975.

"Science fiction in the political science classroom," Teaching Political Science 3(4):401-412. July 1976.

Rogers, D. C.

"Everyclod and everyhero: the image of man in Tolkien," in: Lobdell, Jared, ed. A Tolkien Compass. New York: Ballantine/Del Rey, 1980. pp. 73-81.

Rogers, Deborah

J. R. R. Tolkien, by Deborah Rogers and I. A. Rogers. New York: Hippocrene, 1983. 164 p.

Rogers, I. A.

J. R. R. Tolkien, by Deborah Rogers and I. A. Rogers. New York: Hippocrene, 1983. 164 p.

"Extrapolative cinema," Arts in Society 6(2):287-291. Summer/Fall 1969.

Rogers, I. A. (Continued)

"Physical redemption of reality and the science fiction film," in: Turek, Leslie, ed. Noreascon Proceedings. Cambridge, MA: NESFA, 1976. pp. 111-115.

"Robert Heinlein: folklorist of outer space," in: Olander, J. D. and M. H. Greenberg, eds. Robert A. Heinlein. New York: Taplinger, 1978. pp. 222-240.

"Things that go boomp in the night: redemption of physical reality in the SF film," Extrapolation 13(2):85-91. May 1972.

"Time plays of J. B. Priestley, The," Extrapolation 10(1):9-16. December 1968.

Rogers, K. A.

"Augustinian Evil in C. S. Lewis's Perelandra," in: Reilly, Robert, ed. The Transcendent Adventure. Westport: Greenwood, 1984. pp. 83-91.

"Mirror of the Divine: Christian Platonism in C. S. Lewis," Philosophical Speculations in Science Fiction and Fantasy. 1(1): 18-25. March 1981.

Rogers, Michael

"Grand illusions: in the midst of 'wars' special effects come of age," Rolling Stone 247:49-52. August 25, 1977.

Rogers, Robert

"Psychology of the 'double' in 2001, The," Hartford Studies in Literature 1(1):34-36. 1969.

Rogers, T.

"Of Black Holes, Vulcans, and The Force," Films in Review 31(1): 21-29. January 1980.

Roginski, Jim

"Isaac Asimov (interview)," in: Roginski, Jim. Behind the Covers. Littleton, CO: Libraries Unlimited, 1985. pp. 9-32.

"Jane Yolen (interview)," in: Roginski, Jim. Behind the Covers. Littleton, CO: Libraries Unlimited, 1985. pp. 9-32.

Rogow, Roberta

"Little enterprise, please, A," Voice of Youth Advocates 1(4):15. October 1978.

"Star Trek checklist: for young adult librarians who don't know a Vulcan from a baby doctor, A," Voice of Youth Advocates 1(4):16-18. October 1978.

Rogoz, Adrian

"Vest Arkham, o poarta a infernului," Secolul 20(4):82-84. 1973.

Rohl, W.

"Bruder des dritten Jahrtausends. Perry Rhodan: Marchen fur 40 Millionen," Konkret No. 11:18- . 1969.

Rohmer, E. S

Master of Villany: A Biography of Sax Rohmer, by C. V. Ash and E. S. Rohmer, ed. by R. E. Briney. Bowling Green, OH: Popular Press, 1972. 312 p.

Rojas, Billy

"Futuristics at Massachusetts," Extrapolation 12(1):60. December 1970.

Rolfe, Lee

"Shape of Things to Come (review)," Cinefantastique 9(2):31. Winter 1979.

Roller, Howard

"State of the artless," by Parke Godwin and Howard Roller. Amazing 27(11): 19-23. March 1981.

Rollin, B.

"Return of the (whoosh, there goes one!) superhero," Look 30(1):113-114. March 22, 1966.

Rollin, R. B.

"Beowulf to Batman; the epic hero and pop culture," College English 31(5):431-449. February 1970.

Rolls, Brian

"Flight across Barsoom," Vector 24: 4-9. February 1964.

Rome, J. L.

"Twentieth-century gothic: Mervyn Peake's Gormenghast trilogy," Unisa English Studies 12(1):42-54. 1974.

Romer, Kathy

"SF Course in Kansas," Science Fiction Times (Boston) 1(10): 2-3. 1981.

Romero, G. A.

"Afterword," in: Underwood, Tim and Miller, Chuck, eds. Fear Itself. Columbia, PA: Underwood/Miller 1982. pp. 247-251.

Romero, George

"Scaring people to death on a shoestring," Writers Digest 54(7):24-26. July 1974.

Romey, W. D.

"Science as fiction or non-fiction? A Physical scientist's view from a General Semantics perspective," Et Cetera 37(3): 201-207. Autumn 1980.

Ronan, Margaret

"Following the films: 2001, A Space Odyssey," Senior Scholastic 92:24. May 9, 1968.

"Fright on," Senior Scholastic 97(7):304. October 26, 1970.

Rondinone, Peter

"Starbursts on the Twilight Zone," Twilight Zone 5(5): 4A-5A. December 1985.

Rongione, L. A.

"Science fiction, the psychological aspects can contribute much to bibliotherapy," Catholic Library World 36:96-99. October 1964.

Ronstrom, M. D.

"Fantasy fiction collector," Hobbies 56(9):131-132. November 1951.

Roob, Helmut

Kurd Lasswitz, Handscheiftlicher Nachlass und Bibliographie seiner Werke. Gotha: Veroeffentlichungen der Forschungsbibliothek Gotha, 1981. 165 p.

Rooney, C. J.

Dreams and Visions: A Study of American Utopias, 1865-1917. Westport, CT: Greenwood, 1985. 209 p.

"Post-Civil War, Pre-Looking Backward Utopia: 1865-87," in: Roemer, Kenneth M., ed. American As Utopia. New York: Franklin, 1981. pp. 292-304.

Roos, Richard

"Middle Earth in the classroom; studying J. R. R. Tolkien," English Journal 58(8):1175-1180. November 1969.

Root, J. G.

"Sociology in adolescent science fiction," Arizona English Bulletin 51(1):76-82. October 1972.

Roper, Bill

"Campbellian science fiction: social SF; scientific accuracy," The Chimaeran Review 1(1):8-10. Summer 1974.

Roraback, Dick

"Whole Course Correction to the Infinities of Speculative Fictions," Los Angeles Times. Books p. 3. May 2, 1982.

"Women invade the sci-fi writing field," Los Angeles Times Sec. 4, p. 1,9. June 9, 1975.

Rosar, W. H.

"Music for the Monsters: Universal Pictures' Horror Film Scores of the Thirties," Quarterly Journal of the Library of Congress 40(4): 390-421. Fall 1983.

Roscoe, Bruce

E. T.: Preschool Children's Perceptions, by Bruce Roscoe and K. L. Peterson. 10 p. [1982] (ERIC ED 231 546)

Rose, Barbara

"Deep Space: and Visual Thrills," Vogue 172(10): 557-558, 605. October 1982.

Rose, Carl

"Europe instantly," Atlantic 195(2):88-89. February 1956.

Rose, E. C.

"Briefing for Briefing: Charles Williams' Descent Into Hell and Doris Lessing's Briefing for a Descent Into Hell," Mythlore 4(1):10-13. September 1976.

Rose, L.

"Science fiction og om at se tignes betydning," in: Rejser i tid og rum. En Bog om science fiction, ed. by Tage La Cour. Copenhagen: Stig Verdelkaer, 1973.

Rose, L. V.

"Few Thorns: Comments and Opinions," Fantasy Commentator 4(4): 200-204. Winter 1982.

Rose, Lloyd

"Television: Call the Doctor, please," Film Comment 20(3): 72-73. June 1984.

Rose, Lois

Shattered Ring: Science Fiction and the Quest for Meaning, by Lois Rose and Stephen Rose. Richmond, VA: Knox, 1970. 127 p.

Rose, Mark

Alien Encounters: Anatomy of Science Fiction. Cambridge, MA: Harvard University Press, 1981. 216 p.

Bridges to Science Fiction, by G. E. Slusser, G. R. Guffey, and Mark Rose. Carbondale: Southern Illinois University Press, 1980. 168 p.

Science Fiction: A Collection of Critical Essays. Englewood Cliffs, New Jersey: Prentice-Hall, 1976. 169 p.

"Filling the Void: Verne, Wells, and Lem," Science-Fiction Studies 8(2): 121-142. July 1981.

"Jules Verne: Journey to the Center of Science Fiction," in: Slusser, G. E., ed. Coordinates. Carbondale: Southern Illinois University Press, 1983. pp. 31-41.

"Mark Rose on science fiction (the year's books, part I)," New Republic 177(22):37. November 26, 1977. (Book reviews)

"Science fiction," Yale Review 64(1):122-128. October 1974. (Book review)

"What is science fiction anyhow?" New Republic 175(18):31-33. October 30, 1976.

Rose, Maxine

"Embedding, The," in: Magill, Frank N., ed. Survey of Science Fiction Literature, Vol. 2. Englewood Cliffs, NJ: Salem Press, 1979. pp. 712-716.

Rose, Peter

"Hobby Has Special Effect on Model Maker's Fate," Arizona Republic January 6, 1983. in: NewsBank. Film and Television 79:C1. 1982/1983.

Rose, S.

"Science fiction og om at se tignes betydning," in: Rejser i tid og rum. En Bog om science fiction, ed. by Tage La Cour. Copenhagen: Stig Verdelkaer, 1973.

Rose, Stephen

Shattered Ring: Science Fiction and the Quest for Meaning, by Lois Rose and Stephen Rose. Richmond, VA: Knox, 1970. 127 p.

Roselle, D.

"Teaching about world history through science fiction," Social Education 37(2):94-150. February 1973.

Rosen, Deborah

"Yesterday and tomorrow: a study of the utopian and dystopian vision," by Elaine Keller and Deborah Rosen. Arizona English Bulletin 51(1):5-24. October 1972.

Rosenbaum, Joe

"Can you grok that SF rock (science fiction rock music)," Apartment Life 10:42. June 1978.

"Solitary pleasures of Star Wars," Sight and Sound 46(4):208-209. Autumn 1977.

Rosenbaum, Samuel

"Horrible truth about Frankenstein," Life 64(11):74B-84. March 15, 1968.

Rosenberg, Betty

Genreflecting: A Guide to Reading Interests in Genre Fiction. Littleton, CO: Libraries Unlimited, 1982. 254 p.

Rosenberg, Jerome

"Humanity of Sam Gamgee," Mythlore 5(1):10-11. May 1978.

Rosenfeld, Albert

"Perhaps the mysterious monolithic slab is really Moby Dick," <u>Life</u> 64(14):34-35. April 5, 1968.

Rosenfield, John

"Frankenstein, or how Literary can you get?" <u>Dallas Morning News</u> Sec. 3, p. 4. June 23, 1938.

Rosenthal, B. G.

"Kurt Vonnegut: an annotated bibliography of primary and secondary literature," Research paper, Kent State University, 1972. 51 p.

Rosenthal, D. N.

"Ewoks Tune In," <u>San Jose Mercury News</u> in: <u>NewsBank. Film and Television.</u> 67: B8-B9. January 1985.

"From the Creator of the Muppets, A Movie of Magic," <u>San Jose Mercury</u> December 15, 1982. in: <u>NewsBank. Film and Television.</u> 61: A9. January 1983.

Roshwald, Mordecai

"Addressing the future in ancient and modern times," <u>World Future Society Bulletin.</u> 16(4): 21-29. July/August 1982.

Rosinsky, N. M.

<u>Feminist Futures: Contemporary Women's Speculative Fiction.</u> Ann Arbor: UMI Research Press, 1984, c1982. 147 p.

"Anne McCaffrey," in: Mainiero, Lina, ed. <u>American Women Writers.</u> New York: Ungar, 1982. v. 3, pp. 63-65.

"C. L. Moore's 'Shambleau': woman as alien or alienated woman?" in: Remington, T. J., ed. <u>Selected Proceedings of the 1978 SFRA National Conference.</u> Cedar Falls, Iowa: Univ. of Northern Iowa, 1979. pp. 68-74.

"Catherine Lucille Moore," in: Mainiero, Lina, ed. <u>American Women Writers.</u> New York: Ungar, 1982. v. 3, pp. 212-214.

"Female Man? The 'Medusan' Humor of Joanna Russ," <u>Extrapolation</u> 23(1): 31-36. Spring 1982.

"Judith Merril," in: Mainiero, Lina, ed. <u>American Women Writers.</u> New York: Ungar, 1982. v. 3, pp. 164-166.

Ross, D.

"Fantasy is fun," <u>Writer</u> 66(6):192-193. June 1953.

Ross, S. B.

"Sci-Fi Fans Fly High at 3-day Gathering," <u>St. Louis (Mo.) Globe-Democrat.</u> July 26, 1982. in: <u>Newsbank. Social Relations.</u> 33: F5. 1982.

Ross, W. S.

"Lord of the Rings, The: a new kind of movie," <u>Readers Digest</u> 114(681):72-76. January 1979.

Rossi, L. D.

<u>Politics of Fantasy, The: C. S. Lewis and J. R. R. Tolkien.</u> Ann Arbor: UMI Research Press, 1984, c1972. 143 p.

Rossotti, Renzo

"Spectrum: Tito Salomoni," <u>Questar</u> 3(4): 41-44. June 1981.

Roth, Lane

"<u>Metropolis</u>, the lights fantastic: semiotic analysis of lighting codes in relation to character and theme," <u>Literature/Film Quarterly</u> 6(4):342-346. Fall 1978.

"Ambiguity of Visual Design and Meaning in TV's <u>Battlestar Galactica</u>," <u>Extrapolation</u> 24(1): 80-87. Spring 1983.

"Bergsonian Comedy and the Human Machines in 'Star Wars'", <u>Film Criticism</u> 4(2): 1-8. Winter 1980.

"Dracula meets the Zeitgeist: Nosferatu (1922) as film adaptation," <u>Literature/Film Quarterly</u> 7(4):309-313. 1979.

"Raiders of the Lost Archetype: The Quest and the Shadow," <u>Studies in the Humanities</u> 10(1): 13-21. June 1983.

"Rejection of Rationalism in Recent Science Fiction Films," <u>Philosophy in Context</u> 11: 42-55. 1981.

"Teaching Science Fiction Film Genre: Theory, Form and Theme," <u>The Journal of English Teaching Techniques</u> 11(1): 42-56. Summer 1981.

"Vraisemblance and the western setting in contemporary science fiction film," <u>Literature/Film Quarterly</u> 13(3):180-186. 1985.

Roth, P. A.

Bram Stoker. Boston: Twayne, 1982. 167 p.

Roth, Paul

"Composite optical and photographic effects for Star Wars," by Robert Blalack and Paul Roth. American Cinematographer 58(7):706-708,772. July 1977.

Rothfork, John

New Wave Science Fiction Considered as a Popular Religious Phenomenon: A Definition and an Example. Ph.D. Dissertation: University of New Mexico, 1973. 212 p.

"Memoirs Found in a Bathtub: Stanislaw Lem's critique of cybernetics," Mosaic 17(4): 53-72. Fall 1984.

"Can art still save us if science fails?" Illinois Quarterly 38(4):50-62. Summer 1976.

"Cybernetics and a humanistic fiction: Stanislaw Lem's The Cyberiad," Research Studies (Washington State University) 45(3):123-133. 1977.

"Grokking God: phenomenology in NASA and science fiction," Research Studies (Washington State University) 44(2):101-110. June 1976.

"Having Everything is Having Nothing: Stanislaw Lem Vs. Utilitarianism," Southwest Review 66(3): 293-306. Summer 1981.

"NASA, the sixties, and the American hero," Colorado Quarterly 24(1):102-112. Summer 1975.

"Revitalizing the 'intro to lit' course at a technical institution," Freshman English Resource Notes 2:6. Spring 1977.

Rothman, M. A.

"Scientists in SF: a debate," by P. R. Geffe, M. A. Rothman, J. W. Campbell, and J. V. McConnell. in: Knight, Damon, ed. Turning Points: Essays in the Art of Science Fiction. New York: Harper, 1977. pp. 175-196.

"Writer's Craft Transformed: Word Processing," OnComputing 2(3): 60-62. Winter 1980.

Rothstein, Mervyn

"Best of science fiction," New York Post p. 37. December 9, 1971.

Rotsler, William

"Alien ascendant," Locus 12(5):9. June 1979.

"Art books: 1979," Locus 13(3):11,16. March 1980.

"Judging art shows," Locus 11(9):8-9. November 1978.

"Lord of the Rings: a review," Locus 11(9):6. November 1978.

"Names and Language in SF," SFWA Bulletin 10(3): 16-18. Winter 1974/1975.

"On serendipity," Locus 12(1):9-12. January 1979.

"Recommended reading, 1984," Locus 18(2): 23. February 1985.

Rottenberg, Dan

"Nation of robots," Chicago Magazine pp. 102-103. November 1976.

Rottensteiner, Franz

Fantasy Book: An Illustrated History From Dracula to Tolkien. New York: Collier, 1978. 160 p.

Quarber Merkur: Aufsaetze zur Science Fiction und Phantastischen Literatur. Frankfurt: Suhrkamp, 1979. 261 p.

Science Fiction Book, The: An Illustrated History. New York: Seabury, 1975. 160 p.

Ueber H. P. Lovecraft. Frankfurt: Suhrkamp, 1984. 300 p.

"Berge, Meere and Giganten," in: Magill, Frank N., ed. Survey of Science Fiction Literature, Vol. 1. Englewood Cliffs, NJ: Salem Press, 1979. pp. 163-167.

"Cyberiad, The," in: Magill, Frank N., ed. Survey of Science Fiction Literature, Vol. 1. Englewood Cliffs, NJ: Salem Press, 1979. pp. 457-461.

"Druso," in: Magill, Frank N., ed. Survey of Science Fiction Literature, Vol. 2. Englewood Cliffs, NJ: Salem Press, 1979. pp. 639-643.

"Gelehrtenrepublik, Die," in: Magill, Frank N., ed. Survey of Science Fiction Literature, Vol. 2. Englewood Cliffs, NJ: Salem Press, 1979. pp. 865-868.

"Glos pana," in: Magill, Frank N., ed. Survey of Science Fiction Literature, Vol. 2. Englewood Cliffs, NJ: Salem Press, 1979. pp. 905-908.

Rottensteiner, Franz (Continued)

"Heliopolis," in: Magill, Frank N., ed. Survey of Science Fiction Literature, Vol. 2. Englewood Cliffs, NJ: Salem Press, 1979. pp. 960-964.

"Lesabendio," in: Magill, Frank N., ed. Survey of Science Fiction Literature, Vol. 3. Englewood Cliffs, NJ: Salem Press, 1979. pp. 1193-1197.

"Macht der drei, Die," in: Magill, Frank N., ed. Survey of Science Fiction Literature, Vol. 3. Englewood Cliffs, NJ: Salem Press, 1979. pp. 1304-1307.

"Nabou," in: Magill, Frank N., ed. Survey of Science Fiction Literature, Vol. 3. Englewood Cliffs, NJ: Salem Press, 1979. pp. 1468-1471.

"Nightmare, The," in: Magill, Frank N., ed. Survey of Modern Fantasy Literature, Vol 3. Englewood Cliffs, NJ: Salem Press, Inc., 1983. pp. 1121-1123.

"Other Side, The," in: Magill, Frank N., ed. Survey of Science Fiction Literature, Vol. 4. Englewood Cliffs, NJ: Salem Press, 1979. pp. 1627-1631.

"Shot into Infinity, The," in: Magill, Frank N., ed. Survey of Science Fiction Literature, Vol. 5. Englewood Cliffs, NJ: Salem Press, 1979. pp. 2070-2074.

"Solaris," in: Magill, Frank N., ed. Survey of Science Fiction Literature, Vol. 5, Englewood Cliffs, NJ: Salem Press, 1979. pp. 2107-2112.

"Tunnel, The," in: Magill, Frank N., ed. Survey of Science Fiction Literature, Vol. 5. Englewood Cliffs, NJ: Salem Press, 1979. pp. 2316-2320.

"Two Planets," in: Magill, Frank N., ed. Survey of Science Fiction Literature, Vol. 5. Englewood Cliffs, NJ: Salem Press, 1979. pp. 2334-2338.

"Unheimliche Erscheinungsformen auf Omega XI," in: Magill, Frank N., ed. Survey of Science Fiction Literature, Vol. 5. Englewood Cliffs, NJ: Salem Press, 1979. pp. 2357-2361.

"Zone Null," in: Magill, Frank N., ed. Survey of Science Fiction Literature, Vol. 5. Englewood Cliffs, NJ: Salem Press, 1979. pp. 2538-2542.

"Aesthetic theory of science fiction," Australian Science Fiction Review No. 15:3-12. April 1968.

"Anmerkungen dazu: Zum Verstadnisder Phantastik," Quarber Merkur 41:8-10. September 1975.

"Change, SF, and Marxism: open or close universes? In rebuttal," Science Fiction Studies 1(4):271-272. Fall 1974.

"Change, SF, and Marxism: open or closed universes? On an essay by James Blish," Science Fiction Studies 1(2):84-94. Fall 1973. Comment, Damon Knight. 1(3):219-220. Spring 1974.

"Ein magischer Schriftsteller: Franz Spuda," Quarber Merkur 23:20-29. May 1970.

"Erneuerung und beharrung in der science fiction," in: Barmeyer, Eike, ed. Science fiction: theorie und geschichte. Munchen: Fink, 1972. pp. 340-364.

"European scene: Germany, The," Extrapolation 11(2):82-83. May 1970.

"European science fiction," in: Parrinder, Patrick, ed. Science Fiction: A Critical Guide. New York: Longman, 1979. pp. 203-226.

"European theories of fantasy," in: Magill, Frank N., ed. Survey of Modern Fantasy Literature, Vol 5. Englewood Cliffs, NJ: Salem Press, Inc., 1983. pp. 2235-2246.

"German SF," in: Barron, Neil, ed. Anatomy of Wonder. 2nd ed. New York: Bowker, 1981. pp. 381-398.

"German-language fantasy since 1900," in: Magill, Frank N., ed. Survey of Modern Fantasy Literature, Vol 5. Englewood Cliffs, NJ: Salem Press, Inc., 1983. pp. 2391-2414.

"International news," Science Fiction Times No. 463:4. February 1969.

"International news: from Russia," Science Fiction Times No. 460:5. November 1968.

"International news: Germany," Science Fiction Times No. 460:4. November 1968.

"Introduction to Stanislaw Lem," Vector 59: 2-6. Spring 1972.

"Kurd Lasswitz, a German pioneer of science fiction," in: Clareson, T. D., ed. SF: The Other Side of Realism. Bowling Green, Ohio: Bowling Green University Popular Press, 1971. pp. 289-306.

"Kurd Lasswitz: a German pioneer of SF," Riverside Quarterly 4(1): 4-18. August 1969.

"Literatur uber science fiction. Eine auswahlbibliographie," in: Barmeyer, Eike, ed. Science fiction: theorie und geschichte. Munchen: Fink, 1972. pp. 365-373.

"Ordnungsliebend im weltraum: Kurd Lasswitz," in: Rottensteiner, Franz, ed. Polaris 1. Frankfurt: Insel, 1973. pp. 133-164.

Rottensteiner, Franz (Continued)

"Other worlds, other worldiness: science fiction and religion," by Karen Ready and Franz Rottensteiner. Christian Century 90:1192-1195. December 5, 1973.

"Paul Scheerbart, Fantast of 'Otherness'," Science-Fiction Studies 11(2): 109-121. July 1984.

"Playing around with creation: Philip Jose Farmer," Science Fiction Studies 1(2):94-98. Fall 1973. Comment, Damon Knight. 1(3):219-220. Spring 1974. Reply, 1(4):305. Fall 1974.

"Recent books on science fiction from Germany," Science Fiction Studies 12(2): 209-220. July 1985.

"Reflexive Fiktionen," in: Rottensteiner, Franz, ed. Quarber Merkur. Frankfurt: Suhrkamp, 1979. pp. 156-173.

"Science fiction in Germany," Australian Science Fiction Review No. 14:6-14. February 1968.

"Science Fiction in Osteuropa," Heyne Science Fiction Magazine 4: 219-259. 1982.

"Science fiction: eine einfuhrung," Insel Almanach fuer das jahr 1972. Pfad ins unendliche, ed by Franz Rottensteiner. Frankfurt/M., 1971. pp. 5-21.

"Short fiction of Eliade, The," in: Magill, Frank N., ed. Survey of Modern Fantasy Literature, Vol 3. Englewood Cliffs, NJ: Salem Press, Inc., 1983. pp. 1511-1515.

"Short fiction of Grabinski, The," in: Magill, Frank N., ed. Survey of Modern Fantasy Literature, Vol 3. Englewood Cliffs, NJ: Salem Press, Inc., 1983. pp. 1527-1531.

"Some German writings on science fiction," Science Fiction Studies 6(2):201-209. July 1979.

"Some German writings on SF," Science Fiction Studies 1(4):279-287. Fall 1974.

"Some Recent Writings on SF and Fantasy in Germany," in: Wolfe, Gary, ed. Science Fiction Dialogues. Chicago: Academy Chicago, 1982. pp. 201-205.

"Stanislaw Lem Bibliographie," Quarber Merkur 23:38-59. May 1970.

"Stanislaw Lem Bibliographie. 1. Polnische Ausgabe, 2. Deutsche Buchansgaben, 3. ubersetzungen in andere Sprachen," Quarber Merkur 38:68-81. November 1974.

"Stars of Albion?" Foundation 30: 31-33. March 1984.

"Wissenchaftliche phantastik-eine alternative?" in: Weigand, Jorg, ed. Die Triviale Phantasie. Bonn: Asgard, 1976. pp. 59-72.

"Zur 'Wissenschaftlichen Phantastik' der DDR," Canadian-American Slavic Studies 18(1/2): 112-123. Spring/Summer 1984.

Rotzer, Gerd

"Utopie und gegenutopie," Stimmen der Zeit 174:356-365. 1964.

Roudaut, Jean

"Science fiction. Inventor le futur c'est aussi imaginer le passe," La Quinzaine Litteraire No. 225-3-5. January 16, 1976.

Roush, Matt

"For King, Horror is an Amusement Park of the Mind," Cincinnati Enquirer. September 14, 1980. in: Newsbank. Literature. 28: E12-13. 1980/1981.

"Stephen King is Master of All Things Horrific," Cincinnati Enquirer. September 14, 1980. in: Newsbank. Literature. 28: E10-11. 1980-1981.

Rousseau, F. O.

"Doris Lessing en particulier," Magazine Litteraire 215: 84-89. February 1985.

Rousseau, G. S.

"Literature and science," Isis 69(249):583-591. December 1978.

Rousseau, Yvonne

"Letter, on British SF," Foundation 33: 70-71. Spring 1985.

Routeau, Luc

"Jacobs: narration, science fiction," Communications 24:41-62. 1976.

Rouveyrol, Jacques

"S. F. et utopie. a) La mort de l'homme," Europe 580/581: 57-64. August/September 1977.

Rovin, Jeff

Fabulous Fantasy Films, The. New York: A. S. Barnes, 1977. 271 p.

Rovin, Jeff (Continued)

Fantasy Almanac. New York: Dutton, 1979. 312 p.

Pictorial History of Science Fiction Films. Secaucus, NJ: Citadel, 1975. 240 p.

Science Fiction Collector's Catalog. San Diego, CA: Barnes, 1982. 181 p.

"Star Wars pro and con," by J. K. Klein and Jeff Rovin. Galaxy 38(8):63-72. October 1977.

"Science fiction in the cinema: 1977: who needed it?" in: Bova, Ben, ed. Analog Yearbook. New York: Ace, 1978 (c. 1977). pp. 265-276.

"Starlog Interview: Buster Crabbe; His Last Interview," Starlog 76: 22-25, 95. November 1983.

Rovner, Sandy

"But will it ever be on the right 'Trek'?" Washington Post January 2, 1976. in: NewsBank. Film and Television. 12:D13. 1976.

Rowe, David

"Science fiction: is it entertainment or an attempt to grapple future," Canadian Medical Association Journal 118(10):1296-1298. May 20, 1978.

Rowe, Nigel

History of Science Fiction Fandom in New Zealand. Rothesay Bay, NZ: Rowe, 1981. 28 p.

Rowland, A. Z.

"Interview with Artist Thomas Canty," Fantasy Newsletter 5(10): 16-18. November 1982.

Rowland, S. J.

"With moral passion," Christian Century pp. 640-641. May 25, 1960. (Book review)

Roy, C.

"Psychologie du fantastique," Les Temps Moderne 15:1393-1416. 1959/1960.

Roy, J. F.

ERB-dom: A Guide to Issues No. 1-25, by J. F. Roy, John Harwood, and Camille Cazedessus, Jr. Evergreen, CO: Opar Press, 1964. 23 p.

Guide to Barsoom: Eleven Sections of References in One Volume Dealing with the Martian Stories Written by Edgar Rice Burroughs, A. New York: Ballantine Books, 1976. 200 p.

"Bowdlerizing with Ballantine," ERB-dom No. 19:8-9. December 1966.

Rozanova, A. A.

Sotsialnaia i nauchnaia fantastika v klassicheskow frantsuzskol literature shesnadisatogo semnadtsatogo. Kiev: s. n., 1974. 149 p.

Rubahn, H. G.

"Herbert W. Franke: Eine Stilistische Untersuchung," in: Rottensteiner, Franz, ed. Polaris 6. Frankfurt-am-Main: Suhrkamp, 1982. pp. 206-235.

Rubba, P. A.

"Science Fiction and High School Students' Attitudes Toward Science," by P. A. Rubba, G. B. Lockwood, and G. J. Fleming. Hoosier Science Teacher 7(3): 85-88. February 1982.

Rubens, P. M.

"Descents into private hells: Harlan Ellison's 'psy-fi'," Extrapolation 20(4):378-385. Winter 1979.

Rubenstein, Roberta

"Marriages Between Zones Three, Four, and Five: Doris Lessing's Alchemical Allegory," Extrapolation 24(3): 201-215. Fall 1983.

Rubin, Louis D., jr.

"Southerner in Poictesme, Part II," Texas Quarterly 2(3) Supplement:50-81. Autumn 1981.

Rubin, Steve

"Forbidden Planet," by F. S. Clarke and Steve Rubin. Cinefantastique 8(2/3):4-67. Spring 1979.

"Production: Logan's Run," by F. S. Clarke, Steve Rubin and W. A. Wyss. Cinefantastique 5(2):16-21. Fall 1976.

"Retrospect: Forbidden Planet," Cinefantastique 4(1):5-13. Spring 1975.

"Retrospect: The Day the Earth Stood Still," Cinefantastique 4(4):4-23. Winter 1976.

Rubin, Steve (Continued)

"Retrospect: Them!" _Cinefantastique_ 3(4):22-27. Winter 1974.

"War of the Worlds, a retrospective," _Cinefantastique_ 5(4):4-17,34-47. Spring 1977.

Rubinoff, L. M.

"Utopianism and the Eschatology of Violence," _Thought_ 56(220): 29-43. March 1981.

Rubinstein, R. E.

"Social studies/science; trek to the stars," _Teacher_ 95(2):102,104,107. October 1977.

Rubinstein, W. C.

"Coming Race, The," in: Magill, Frank N., ed. _Survey of Science Fiction Literature_, Vol. 1. Englewood Cliffs, NJ: Salem Press, 1979. pp. 418-422.

Rucker, Rudy

"Life in the Fourth Dimension: C. H. Hinton and His Scientific Romances," _Foundation_ 18: 12-18. January 1980.

"Transrealist manifesto," _SFWA Bulletin_ 17(4): 7-8. Winter 1983.

"What SF writers want," _SFWA Bulletin_ 19(1): 42-49. Spring 1985.

Ruddick, Nicholas

"World Turned Inside Out: Decoding Clarke's _Rendezvous With Rama_," _Science Fiction Studies_ 12(1): 42-50. March 1985.

Rudin, Seymour

"Urban Gothic: From Transylvania to the South Bronx," _Extrapolation_ 25(2): 115-126. Summer 1984.

Rudnev, D.

"'Zaknutj mir' sovremennoj russkoj fantastiki," _Grani_ 78:166-196. 1970.

Rullkoetter, Bernd

Wissenschaftliche Phantastik der Sowjetunion, Die. Eine Vergleichende Untersuchung der spekulativen Literatur in Ost und West. Bern: Lang, 1974. 303 p.

"Bogdanov als phantastik-autor," _Science Fiction Times_ No. 133:13-17. January 1974.

"On Soviet readers and fans of science fiction," _Riverside Quarterly_ 7(1):37-41. March 1980.

Rumpf, Wilfried

"Frau in der englischen Anti-Utopia, Die. Pt. 3," _Quarber Merkur_ 29:3-10. January 1972.

"Frau in der englischen Anti-Utopie, Die. Pt. 1," _Quarber Merkur_ 27:30-42. July 1971.

"Frau in der englischen Anti-Utopie, Die. Pt. 2," _Quarber Merkur_ 28:25-44. November 1971.

"Science Fiction and Literature," _Quarber Merkur_ 30:59-66. April 1972.

Ruosch, Christian

Phantastisch-surreale welt im werke Paul Scheerbart. Bern: Lange, 1970. 136 p.

Rupp, William

"Science fiction and the literary community," _Riverside Quarterly_ 5(3):208-213. August 1972.

Ruppersburg, H. M.

"Keith Laumer," in: Cowart, David, ed. _Twentieth-Century American Science-Fiction Writers, Part l: A-L._ Detroit: Gale, 1981. pp. 255-263. (Dictionary of Literary Biography, v. 8)

Rupprecht, Erich

"Ray Cummmings," in: Cowart, David, ed. _Twentieth-Century American Science-Fiction Writers, Part 1: A-L._ Detroit: Gale, 1981. pp. 105-108. (Dictionary of Literary Biography, v. 8)

"Thomas M. Disch," in: Cowart, David, ed. _Twentieth-Century American Science-Fiction Writers, Part 1: A-L._ Detroit: Gale, 1981. pp. 148-154. (Dictionary of Literary Biography, v. 8)

Rurak, James

"Imaginative power of Utopia: a hermeneutic for its recovery," _Philosophy and Social Criticism_ 8(2):184-206. 1981.

Ruse, G. A.

"Algol profile: Andre Norton," _Algol_ 14(3):15-17. Summer/Fall 1977.

Rush, Beverly

"Piers Anthony," by Stephen Buccleugh and Beverly Rush. in: Cowart, David, ed. Twentieth-Century American Science-Fiction Writers, Part 1: A-L. Detroit: Gale, 1981. pp. 13-15. (Dictionary of Literary Biography, v. 8)

Rush, C. R.

"Always working on a book: an interview with Frederik Pohl," Leading Edge No. 8:39-41. Fall 1984.

Russ, Joanna

"Alien monsters," in: Knight, Damon, ed. Turning Points: Essays in the Art of Science Fiction. New York: Harper, 1977. pp. 132-143.

"Amor Vincit Foeminam: the battle of the sexes in science fiction," Science-Fiction Studies 7(1): 2-15. March 1980.

"Communique from the front: teaching and the state of the art," Colloquy 4(5):28-31. May 1971.

"Dream literature and science fiction," Extrapolation 11(1):6-14. December 1969.

"Frauenbild in der Science Fiction," in: Femistische Utopien: Aufbruch in dei postpatriarchale Gesellschaft, ed. by Barbara Holland-Cunz. Meitingen: Corian Verlag, 1986.

"Image of women in SF, The," in: Cornillon, S. K., ed. Images of Women in Fiction: Feminist Perspectives. Bowling Green, Ohio: Bowling Green University Popular Press, 1972. pp. 79-94.

"Introduction," in: Shelley, Mary W. Tales and Stories. Boston: Gregg, 1975. pp. v-xvii.

"On setting," in: Wilson, R. S., ed. Those Who Can: A Science Fiction Reader. New York: Mentor/New American Library, 1973. pp. 149-154.

"Outta space: women write science fiction," Ms 4(7):109-111. January 1976.

"Recent Feminist Utopias," in: Barr, Marlene S., ed. Future Females. Bowling Green, OH: Bowling Green State University Popular Press, 1981. pp. 71-85.

"SF and technology as mystification," Science Fiction Studies 5(3):250-260. November 1978.

"Speculations: the subjunctivity of science fiction," Extrapolation 15(1):51-59. December 1973.

"Toward an aesthetic of science fiction," Science Fiction Studies 2(2):112-119. July 1975.

"Towards an aesthetik of science fiction," in: Samuelson, D. N. Science Fiction and Future Studies. Bryan, TX: SFRA, 1975. pp. 108-116.

"Wearing out of genre materials, The," College English 31(1):46-54. October 1971. also in: Vector 62:16-25. November/December 1972; SFWA Bulletin 7(5/6):7-16. 1972.

"What can a heroine do? or, why women can't write," in: Cornillon, S. K., ed. Images of Women in Fiction: Feminist Perspectives. Bowling Green, Ohio: Bowling Green University Popular Press, 1972. pp. 3-20.

Russell, Bruce

"Costs put sci-fi out of reach," Chicago Tribune Sec. 2, p. 7. November 30, 1977.

Russell, D. H.

"Place of the Comics," in: Russell, David H. Children Learn to Read. Boston: Ginn, 1949. pp. 260-267.

Russell, E. F.

"Author's lot III," Vector 25: 4-5. March 1964.

Russell, Mariann

"'Northern Literature' and the Ring Trilogy," Mythlore 5(2): 41-42. Autumn 1978.

"Elements of the idea of the city in Charles Williams' Arthurian poetry," Mythlore 6(4):10-16. Fall 1979.

Russell, R. S.

"Modes of Space Travel," Aurora SF 8(3): 9-11. Winter 1982/83.

Russell, Ray

"Buck Rogers and I," Playboy 24(12):77. December 1977.

Russell, W. M. S.

"Folktales and Science Fiction," Folklore 93(1): 3-30. June 1982.

"Life and Afterlife on Other Worlds," Foundation 28: 34-56. July 1983.

Russo, Luigi

Fantascienza e la critica: testi del convegno internazionale di Palermo.   Milan: Feltrinelli, 1980. 262 p.

Vent'anni de fantascienza 1952-1972, ed. by Luigi Russo. Palermo: Nuova Persenza Editrice, 1978. 77 p.

Ruth, Leo

"Scene, The," English Journal 60(9):1243-1251,1271. December 1971.

Rutledge, A. A.

"Fredric Brown," in: Cowart, David, ed. Twenieth-Century American Science-Fiction Writers, Part 1: A-L. Detroit: Gale, 1981. pp. 80-83. (Dictionary of Literary Biography, v. 8)

"Mark S. Geston," in: Cowart, David, ed. Twenieth-Century American Science-Fiction Writers, Part 1: A-L. Detroit: Gale, 1981. pp. 192-193. (Dictionary of Literary Biography, v. 8)

"Star Makers: The Agnostic Quest," Science Fiction Studies 9(3): 274-283. November 1982.

Ruttkowski, Wolfgang

"Science Fiction," in his: Bibliographie der Gattungspoetik fur den Studenten der Literaturwisenschaft. Munchen: Max Huber Verlag, 1973. pp. 192-93.

"Utopie-Zukunftsroman," in his: Bibliographie der Gattungspoetik fur den Studenten der Literaturwisenschaft. Munchen: Max Huber Verlag, 1973. pp. 210-13.

Ruyer, Raymond

Utopie et les utopies. Paris: Presses Universitaires France, 1950. 293 p.

Ryabova, M.

"Space Odyssey-Documentary," by M. Ryabova and M. Sheinia. Soviet Film 79(9):11- . 1979.

Ryan, Alan

"Marsden House in 'Salem's Lot," in: Underwood, Tim and Miller, Chuck, eds. Fear Itself. Columbia, PA: Underwood/Miller, 1982. pp. 169-180.

"North and South of Horror," in: Winter, Douglas E. Shadowings: The Reader's Guide to Horror Fiction 1981-1982. Mercer Island, WA: Starmont, 1983. pp. 50-52.

"Remembering Philip K. Dick," Fantasy Newsletter 5(6): 32-33. July 1982.

"Sandman Will Still Be There," in: Winter, Douglas E. Shadowings: The Reader's Guide to Horror Fiction 1981-1982. Mercer Island, WA: Starmont, 1983. pp. 44-46.

Ryan, Anthony

"Mind of Mr. J. G. Ballard, The," Foundation 3:44-48. March 1973.

Ryan, Desmond

"'50s Comics Inspire a Master of Film Horror," Philadelphia Inquirer November 14, 1982. in: NewsBank. Film and Television. 50:B11-12. December 1982.

"Barbaric land created from his imagination," Philadelphia Inquirer. May 9, 1982. in: NewsBank. Film and Television. 130:E4-5. 1981/82.

"Cocoon unfolds, a talent takes wing," Philadelphia Inquirer June 29, 1985. in: NewsBank. Film and Television. 2:D5-D6. July 1985.

"Director Reaches for the Stars With Computer Aid," Philadelphia Inquirer. in: NewsBank. Film and Television. FTV 15:F11. 1984.

"New 'Star Trek' a Nimoy Triumph," Philadelphia Inquirer. in: NewsBank. Film and Television. FTV 9: A12-A13. 1984.

Ryan, J. S.

"Folktale, Fairy Tale, and the Creation of a Story," in: Isaacs, Neil D. Tolkien: New Critical Perspectives, ed. by N. D. Isaacs and R. A. Zimbardo. Lexington: University Press of Kentucky, 1981. pp. 19-39.

"Saruman, 'Sharkey,' and Suruman: analogous figures of Eastern ingenuity and cunning," Mythlore 12(1):43-44,57. Autumn 1985.

"Tolkien's sources," Orana 13(1):8-11. February 1977.

"Uncouth innocence: some links between Chretien de Troyes, Wolfram von Eschenbach, and J. R. R. Tolkien," Mythlore 11(2):8-13,27. Autumn 1984.

Ryan, Judith

"'Into the Orwell Decade': Gunter Grass's Dystopia Trilogy," World Literature Today 55(4): 564-567. Autumn 1981.

Rybacki, D. J.

"Visions of apocalypse: A rhetorical analysis of 'The Day After'," by K. C. Rybacki and D. J. Rybacki. 21 p. May 1984. ERIC ED 246 516.

Rybacki, K. C.

"Visions of apocalypse: A rhetorical analysis of 'The Day After'," by K. C. Rybacki and D. J. Rybacki. 21 p. May 1984. ERIC ED 246 516.

Rykken, Rolf

"Doctor Who? There's no question he's a cult hero," _Wilmington Evening Journal_. July 18, 1983. in: _NewsBank_. _Film and Television_. 12:A10-11. 1983.

S

Saal, R. W.

"Pick of the paperbacks," _Saturday Review_ 53(13):34. March 28, 1970.

Sabatier, J. M.

Classiques du Cinema Fantastique. Paris: Balland, 1973. 425 p.

Sabatini, Bruno

H. G. Wells: pioniere della fantascienza. Firenze: CDA libri, 1969. 144 p.

Sabella, Robert

"Science fiction by the numbers," _Science Fiction Review_ 14(4): 24. November 1985.

"Who Influenced Science Fiction?" _Thrust_ 20: 25-26. Spring/Summer 1984.

Saberhagen, Fred

"Berserker story, The," _Algol_ 14:33,40. Summer/Fall 1977.

Saciuk, Olena

"Forbidden vision of Berdnyk, The," in: Collins, R. A., ed. _Scope of the Fantastic: Culture, Biography, Themes, Children's Literature_. Westport: Greenwood, 1985. pp. 43-50.

Sackett, S. J.

"Just for fun," _Miscellaneous Man_ 1(3):12-13. Winter 1954.

"Last romantic, The," _Nyctalops_ No. 7:23-25. August 1972.

Sackett, Susan

Making of Star Trek: The Motion Picture. New York: Wallaby, 1980. 221 p.

"Making of Star Trek II: a conversation with Gene Roddenberry, The," _Starlog_ 12:24-29. March 1978.

Sackmary, Regina

"Ideal of three: the art of Theodore Sturgeon, An," in: Riley, Dick, ed. _Critical Encounters: Writers and Themes in Science Fiction_. New York: Ungar, 1978. pp. 132-143.

Sadler, F. O.

Science and Fiction in the Science Fiction Novel. Ph.D. Dissertation, University of Florida, 1974. 197 p.

"Relativity and the universe of fiction," _West Georgia College Review_ 9:8-33. 1977.

Sadoul, Jacques

2000 A.D.: Illustrations from the Golden Age of Science Fiction Pulps. Chicago: Regnery, 1975. 176 p. (Tr. of _Hier L'an 2000_. Paris: Denoel, 1973)

Hier, L'an 2000: L'Illustration de Science Fiction des Annees 30. Paris: Denoel, 1973. 176 p.

Histoire de la science fiction moderne, 1911-1971. Paris: Michel, 1973. 410 p.

Histoire de la science fiction moderne, 1911-1975. Paris: J'ai Lu, 1975. 2 v.

Historia de la ciencia ficcion moderna, 1911-1971. Barcelona: Plaza & Janes, 1975. 352 p. (Tr. of _Historie de la science fiction moderne_.)

"Amazing a Vertex, De," _Magazine Litteraire_ 88:28-29. May, 1974.

"Deux conventions de science fiction," _Magazine Litteraire_ (Paris) 88:30-31. May 1974.

"Fan b. d. s. f.," _Magazine Litteraire_ No. 95:23-24. December 1974.

447

Sadoul, Jacques (Continued)

"Passion selon Satan, La," in: H. P. Lovecraft. Paris: Editions de l'Herne, 1969. pp. 117-120.

"Rio, capitale de la science fiction," Magazine Litteraire No. 31:12-15. August 1969.

"Science fiction in France," Algol 18:17-18. May 1972.

Safford, B. R.

"High Fantasy: An Architypical Analysis of Children's Literature. Ph. D. Dissertation, Columbia, 1983. 298 p. (DAI 44: 2280-2281A)

Safford, Tony

"Alien/Alienation," Science-Fiction Studies 7(3): 297-299. November 1980.

Sagan, Carl

"Growing up with science fiction: 'science fiction has led me to science,' says Cornell University astronomer Carl Sagan," New York Times Magazine pp. 24-30. May 28, 1978.

"Man: a Transitional Animal," in: Bretnor, Reginald, ed. The Future at War: Vol. 2: The Spear of Mars. New York: Ace, 1980. pp. 162-170.

"Science fiction: a personal view," in: Sagan, Carl. Broca's Brain. New York: Random House, 1979. pp. 37-146.

"Science fiction: a personal view," in: Williamson, Jack, ed. Teaching Science Fiction: Education for Tomorrow. Philadelphia: Owlswick, 1980. pp. 1-8.

Sage, Lorna

Doris Lessing. New York: Methuen, 1983. 91 p.

Sageret, J.

"Sociologie de Rosny aine, La," Revue du Mois 9:270-285. 1910.

Saint

See: St.

Sainz Cidoncha, Carlos

Historia de la ciencia ficcion en Espana. Madrid: Organizacion Sala Editorial, 1976. 206 p.

Sale, Jonathon

"Did H. G. Wells and Co. get it right?" Observer Magazine pp. 11,13. December 28, 1975.

Sale, Roger

"Audience in Children's Literature, The," in: Slusser, G. E., ed. Bridges to Fantasy. Carbondale: Southern Illinois University Press, 1982. pp. 59-77.

Saleh, Dennis

Science Fiction Gold: Film Classics of the 50's. New York: McGraw-Hill, 1979. 192 p.

Saler, Mike

"Jove Dares to be Bland," by Mike Saler and A. A. Whyte. Science Fiction Times (Boston) 1(10): 1, 9. 1981.

Sallinger, David

"Dr. Asimov's Future Prescription," Quest/Star 4(1): 23-24. October 1981.

"Stockings stuffed with Hugo Gernsback," Questar 3(3): 45-46, 63. February 1981.

Salmonson, J. A.

"Dark Agnes: A Critical Look at Robert E. Howard's Swordswoman," American Fantasy 1(1): 4-6. February 1982.

"Decline of the Anthology," SFWA Bulletin 17(1): 13-15. Spring 1983.

"Ethics and Editing: Blacklisting," SFWA Bulletin 19(2): 10-13. Summer 1985.

"Fantasy as History: The Parisian Swordswomen as a Model for Swords and Sorcery Amazons," Fantasy Newsletter 5(10): 7-9. November 1982.

"Fantasy With Swordplay," Martial Arts Movies 2(6): 46-50. June 1982.

"Hero as Hedonist: The Early Novels of Doris Piserchia," in: Staicar, Tom, ed. Critical Encounters II. New York: Ungar, 1982. pp. 15-22.

"Literary small press mystique," SFWA Bulletin 17(3): 9-11. Fall 1983.

"Moscon fan guest of honor speech," Thrust 16: 28-29. Fall 1980.

"Simultaneous submissions," SFWA Bulletin 18(4): 11-14. Winter 1984.

Salmonson, J. A. (Continued)

"Trade SF," <u>SFWA Bulletin</u> 16(3): 59-61.
March 1982.

Salter, R. G.

"Through a TV Screen Darkly," by Timothy
Clinton and R. G. Salter. <u>Home Video</u> 2(9):
43-45. September 1981.

Salu, Mary

<u>J. R. R. Tolkien: Scholar and Storyteller</u>,
ed. by Mary Salu and R. T. Farrell.
Ithaca: Cornell University Press, 1979.
325 p.

Salvaggio, Ruth

"Octavia Butler and the Black Science-Fiction
Heroine," <u>Black American Literature Forum</u>
18(2): 78-81. Summer 1984.

Salvestroni, Simonetta

<u>Semiotica dell' imaginazione: Dalla
letteratura fantastica russa alla fantascienza
sovietica.</u> Cagliari: Kalb, 1984.

Salwak, Dale

<u>Literary Voices # 2: Interviews With Britain's
Angry Young Men.</u> San Bernardino: Borgo,
1984. 96 p.

"Bill Hopkins: Looking for the Revolutionary,"
in: Salwak, Dale, ed. <u>Literary Voices # 2:
Interviews.</u> San Bernardino: Borgo, 1984.
pp. 61-66.

"Colin Wilson: The Man Behind <u>The Outsider</u>,"
in: Salwak, Dale, ed. <u>Literary Voices # 2:
Interviews.</u> San Bernardino: Borgo, 1984.
pp. 82-92.

"Interview with Kingsley Amis, An,"
<u>Contemporary Literature</u> 16(1):1-18. Winter
1975.

"John Braine: The Man at the Top," in:
Salwak, Dale, ed. <u>Literary Voices # 2:
Interviews.</u> San Bernardino: Borgo, 1984.
pp. 41-60.

"John Wain: Man of Letters," in: Salwak,
Dale, ed. <u>Literary Voices # 2: Interviews.</u>
San Bernardino: Borgo, 1984.
pp. 67-81.

"Kingsley Amis: Mimic and Moralist," in:
Salwak, Dale, ed. <u>Literary Voices # 2:
Interviews.</u> San Bernardino: Borgo, 1984.
pp. 13-40.

Salza, Guiseppe

"Red Sonja," <u>Cinefantastique</u> 15(3):4-5.
July 1985.

Sammon, P. M.

"Black Hole," <u>Cinefantastique</u> 9(2):4-7,36.
Winter 1979.

"Caveman," <u>Cinefantastique</u> 11(2):38-43.
Fall 1981.

"Close Encounters of the Third Kind: The
Special Edition (review)," <u>Cinefantastique</u>
10(3):35-36. Winter 1980.

"Cobb, the designer," <u>Cinefantastique</u>
12(2/3):65-71. April 1982.

"Conan The Barbarian (review),"
<u>Cinefantastique</u> 12(4):49. May/June 1982.

"Conan The Barbarian," <u>Cinefantastique</u>
12(2/3):28-63. April 1982.

"Conan the Destroyer," <u>Cinefantastique</u>
14(4/5):5-7. September 1984.

"Damnation Alley (review)," <u>Cinefantastique</u>
6(4)/7(1):40-41. Spring 1978.

"David Cronenberg," <u>Cinefantastique</u>
10(4):21-35. Spring 1981.

"David Lynch's Dune: Journal,"
<u>Cinefantastique</u> 14(4/5):28-40,73-90.
September 1984.

"Firefox (review)," <u>Cinefantastique</u>
13(1):45,48. September/October 1982.

"Friday the 13th III (review),"
<u>Cinefantastique</u> 13(2)/13(3):92.
November/December 1982.

"Inside The Black Hole," <u>Cinefantastique</u>
9(3/4):4-63. Spring 1980.

"John Hora and Gremlins," <u>American
Cinematographer</u> 65(10): 74-82. November 1984.

"Making of Blade Runner," <u>Cinefantastique</u>
12(5/6):20-47. July/August 1982.

"Milius, the director," <u>Cinefantastique</u>
12(2/3):22-27. April 1982.

"Never feed them after midnight," <u>Cinefex</u>
No. 19:4-43. November 1984.

"Nine days in Cimmeria: on location with
Conan," <u>Cinefantastique</u> 11(3):16-37.
September 1981.

"On the Set of Twilight Zone," <u>Twilight
Zone</u> 3(4): 27-28. September/October 1983.

"Popeye (review)," <u>Cinefantastique</u>
11(1):44. Summer 1981.

Sammon, P. M. (Continued)

"Road Games (review)," <u>Cinefantastique</u> 11(2):50. Fall 1981.

"Saturn 3 (review)," <u>Cinefantastique</u> 10(1):13. Summer 1980.

"Scanners (review)," <u>Cinefantastique</u> 10(4):45. Spring 1981.

"Shadow and substance," by Don Shay and Paul Sammon. <u>Cinefex</u> No. 14:50-71. October 1983.

"Star Trek III: The Wrath of Khan (review)," <u>Cinefantastique</u> 13(1):50. September/October 1982.

"Turn On Your Heartlight: Inside E. T.," <u>Cinefex</u> 11: 4-49. January 1983.

"TZ Interview: John Landis," <u>Twilight Zone</u> 3(4): 29-38. September/October 1983.

"TZ Preview: Cocoon," <u>Twilight Zone</u> 5(3): 86-89. July/August 1985.

"Versions of Arrakis you'll never see," by P. M. Sammon, Stephen Jones and F. A. Levy. <u>Cinefantastique</u> 14(4/5):32-34. September 1984.

"Visions: Peter Ellenshaw," <u>Cinefantastique</u> 9(3/4):84-92. Spring 1980.

Sammons, M. C.

<u>Guide Through C. S. Lewis' Space Trilogy</u>. Westchester, IL: Cornerstone Books, 1980. 189 p.

<u>Guide Through Narnia</u>. Wheaton, IL: Shaw, 1979. 168 p.

"Christian doctrines transposed in C. S. Lewis' <u>Till We Have Faces</u>," <u>Mythlore</u> 7(1):31-35. March 1980.

"Tolkien on fantasy in <u>Smith of Wooton Major</u>," <u>Mythlore</u> 12(1):3-7,37. Autumn 1985.

Sampson, Bob

"Pulp library: <u>The Black Mask</u>," <u>Xenophile</u> No. 42:131-132. September/October 1979.

Sampson, Robert

<u>Night Master</u>. Chicago: Pulp Press, 1982. 216 p.

<u>Yesterday's Faces: Volume 1, Glory Figures</u>. Bowling Green, OH: Bowling Green University Popular Press, 1983. 270 p.

<u>Yesterday's Faces: Volume 2, Strange Days</u>. Bowling Green, OH: Bowling Green University Popular Press, 1984. 290 p.

Samuel, S. R.

<u>Soviet Science Fiction: New Critical Approaches</u>. Ph. D. Dissertation, Stanford University, 1982. 140 p. (DAI 43A:1167)

Samuels, C. T.

"Age of Vonnegut," <u>New Republic</u> 164(24):30-32. June 12, 1971.

Samuels, L. Q.

"Profile: Madeline L'Engle," <u>Language Arts</u> 58(6): 704-712. September 1981.

Samuelson, D. N.

<u>Arthur C. Clarke: A Primary and Secondary Bibliography</u>. Boston: G. K. Hall, 1984. 256 p.

<u>Science Fiction and Future Studies</u>. Bryan, TX: SFRA, 1975. 134 p. (SFRA Miscellaneous Publication No. 2; copy in Texas A&M University Library Science Fiction Research Collection)

<u>Science Fiction and the Two Cultures: A Study in the Theory and Criticism of Contemporary Science Fiction with Reference to the Cultural Division Between the Sciences and the Humanities</u>. B. A. Thesis, Drew Univ. 1962. (not seen)

<u>Studies in the Contemporary American and British Science Fiction Novel</u>. Ph.D. Dissertation, University of Southern California, 1969. 429 p.

<u>Visions of Tomorrow: Six Journeys From Outer to Inner Space</u>. New York: Arno, 1975. 429 p. (Reprint of Doctoral Dissertation, 1969)

"Beyond This Horizon," in: Magill, Frank N., ed. <u>Survey of Science Fiction Literature</u>, Vol. 1. Englewood Cliffs, NJ: Salem Press, 1979. pp. 207-212.

"<u>Black Easter</u> and <u>The Day After Judgement</u>," in: Magill, Frank N., ed. <u>Survey of Modern Fantasy Literature</u>, Vol 1. Englewood Cliffs, NJ: Salem Press, Inc., 1983. pp. 122-128.

"Briefing for a Descent into Hell," in: Magill, Frank N., ed. <u>Survey of Science Fiction Literature</u>, Vol. 1. Englewood Cliffs, NJ: Salem Press, 1979. pp. 254-259.

"Centaur, The," in: Magill, Frank N., ed. <u>Survey of Modern Fantasy Literature</u>, Vol 1. Englewood Cliffs, NJ: Salem Press, Inc., 1983. pp. 222-227.

Samuelson, D. N. (Continued)

"Childhood's End," in: Magill, Frank N., ed. Survey of Science Fiction Literature, Vol. 1. Englewood Cliffs, NJ: Salem Press, 1979. pp. 337-342.

"Chimera," in: Magill, Frank N., ed. Survey of Modern Fantasy Literature, Vol 1. Englewood Cliffs, NJ: Salem Press, Inc., 1983. pp. 236-241.

"Conditionally Human," in: Magill, Frank N., ed. Survey of Science Fiction Literature, Vol. 1. Englewood Cliffs, NJ: Salem Press, 1979. pp. 423-427.

"Einstein Intersection, The," in: Magill, Frank N., ed. Survey of Science Fiction Literature, Vol. 2. Englewood Cliffs, NJ: Salem Press, 1979. pp. 703-707.

"Gateway," in: Magill, Frank N., ed. Survey of Science Fiction Literature, Vol. 2. Englewood Cliffs, NJ: Salem Press, 1979. pp. 858-864.

"Green Man, The," in: Magill, Frank N., ed. Survey of Modern Fantasy Literature, Vol 2. Englewood Cliffs, NJ: Salem Press, Inc., 1983. pp. 661-665.

"In the Ocean of Night," in: Magill, Frank N., ed. Survey of Science Fiction Literature, Vol. 3. Englewood Cliffs, NJ: Salem Press, 1979. pp. 1026-1030.

"Islandia," in: Magill, Frank N., ed. Survey of Modern Fantasy Literature, Vol 2. Englewood Cliffs, NJ: Salem Press, Inc., 1983. pp. 781-786.

"Limbo," in: Magill, Frank N., ed. Survey of Science Fiction Literature, Vol. 3. Englewood Cliffs, NJ: Salem Press, 1979. pp. 1221-1225.

"Limbo: the great American dystopia," Extrapolation 19(1):76-87. December 1977.

"Man Plus," in: Magill, Frank N., ed. Survey of Science Fiction Literature, Vol. 3. Englewood Cliffs, NJ: Salem Press, 1979. pp. 1328-1332.

"More Than Human," in: Magill, Frank N., ed. Survey of Science Fiction Literature, Vol. 3. Englewood Cliffs, NJ: Salem Press, 1979. pp. 1453-1458.

"Past Through Tomorrow, The," in: Magill, Frank N., ed. Survey of Science Fiction Literature, Vol. 4. Englewood Cliffs, NJ: Salem Press, 1979. pp. 1645-1654.

"Poorhouse Fair, The," in: Magill, Frank N., ed. Survey of Science Fiction Literature, Vol. 4. Englewood Cliffs, NJ: Salem Press, 1979. pp. 1714-1719.

"Stand on Zanzibar," in: Magill, Frank N., ed. Survey of Science Fiction Literature, Vol. 5. Englewood Cliffs, NJ: Salem Press, 1979. pp. 2140-2145.

"Star of the Unborn," in: Magill, Frank N., ed. Survey of Modern Fantasy Literature, Vol 4. Englewood Cliffs, NJ: Salem Press, Inc., 1983. pp. 1807-1812.

"Starship Troopers," in: Magill, Frank N., ed. Survey of Science Fiction Literature, Vol. 5. Englewood Cliffs, NJ: Salem Press, 1979. pp. 2173-2178.

"Stranger in the sixties: model or mirror?" in: Riley, Dick, ed. Critical Encounters: Writers and Themes in Science Fiction. New York: Ungar, 1978. pp. 144-175.

"Stranger in a Strange Land," in: Magill, Frank N., ed. Survey of Science Fiction Literature, Vol. 5. Englewood Cliffs, NJ: Salem Press, 1979. pp. 2195-2200.

"Tales of Neveryon," in: Magill, Frank N., ed. Survey of Modern Fantasy Literature, Vol 4. Englewood Cliffs, NJ: Salem Press, Inc., 1983. pp. 1875-1879.

"Arthur C. Clarke," in: Bleiler, E. F., ed. Science Fiction Writers. New York: Scribners, 1982. pp. 313-320.

"Childhood's end: a median stage of adolescence," Science Fiction Studies 1(1):4-17. Spring 1973. also in: Olander, J. D. and M. H. Greenberg, eds. Arthur C. Clarke. New York: Taplinger, 1977. pp. 196-210.

"Creating a world for The Dark Crystal," by D. W. Samuelson and Ann Tasker. American Cinematographer 64(12):1282-1289,1316-1331. December 1982.

"Creating the fantasy of Krull; interview with Derek Meddings," American Cinematographer 64(8):54-60. August 1983.

"Critical Mass: The Science Fiction of Frederik Pohl," Science-Fiction Studies 7(1): 80-95. March 1980.

"Frederik Pohl," in: Bleiler, E. F., ed. Science Fiction Writers. New York: Scribners, 1982. pp. 475-482.

"From aliens to alienation: Gregory Benford's variations on a theme," Foundation 14:5-19. September 1978.

"Frontier worlds of Robert A. Heinlein, The," in: Clareson, T. D., ed. Voices for the Future: Essays on Major SF Writers, Vol. 1. Bowling Green, Ohio: Popular Press, 1976. pp. 104-152.

Samuelson, D. N. (Continued)

"Frontiers of the future: Heinlein's future history stories," in: Olander, J. D. and M. H. Greenberg, eds. Robert A. Heinlein. New York: Taplinger, 1978. pp. 32-63.

"Introduction," in: Miller, Walter M. The Science Fiction Stories of Walter M. Miller, Jr.. Boston: Gregg, 1978. pp. vii-xxv.

"Inventing the future: science fiction, future studies, and the creative imagination," in: Samuelson, D. N. Science Fiction and Future Studies. Bryan, TX: SFRA, 1975. pp. 117-132.

"Lost canticles of Walter M. Miller, Jr., The," SF Studies 3(1):3-26. March 1976. also in: Clareson, T. D., ed. Voices for the Future, Vol. 2. Bowling Green, Ohio: Univ. Popular Press, 1979. pp. 56-81.

"New wave, old ocean: a comparative study of novels by Brunner and Delaney," Extrapolation 15(1):75-96. December 1973.

"Short Fiction of Frederik Pohl, The," in: Magill, Frank N., ed. Survey of Science Fiction Literature, Vol. 4. Englewood Cliffs, NJ: Salem Press, 1979. pp. 1948-1953.

"Spinning galaxy: a shift in perspective on magazine sf, The," Extrapolation 17(1):44-48. December 1975.

"Three syllibi," by Dave Samuelson, Gary Goshgarian and James Gunn. in: Williamson, Jack, ed. Teaching Science Fiction: Education for Tomorrow. Philadelphia: Owlswick, 1980. pp. 194-202.

"Ursula K. Le Guin," in: Bleiler, E. F., ed. Science Fiction Writers. New York: Scribners, 1982. pp. 409-417.

"Work in progress: a suggestion," Science Fiction Studies 5(2):198-199. July 1978.

Sanchez, M. E.

"View From Inside the Fishbowl: Julio Cortazar's 'Axolotl'," in: Slusser, George E., ed. Bridges to Fantasy. Carbondale: Southern Illinois University Press, 1982. pp. 38-50.

Sanders, Bob

"Refugees on Mars: FDR's Secret Plan," by Sandy Meredith and Bob Sanders. SFWA Bulletin 18(1): 32-33. Spring 1984.

Sanders, J. E.

"O'Brien and monsters from the Id," in: Collins, R. A., ed. Scope of the Fantastic:

Culture, Biography, Themes, Children's Literature. Westport: Greenwood, 1985. pp. 205-220.

Sanders, J. L.

Roger Zelazny: a Primary and Secondary Bibliography. Boston: G. K. Hall, 1980. 126 p.

"A. Merritt's Fantasy Magazine, in: Tymn, M. B. and Ashley, Mike. Science Fiction, Fantasy, and Weird Fiction Magazines. Westport, CT: Greenwood, 1985. pp. 1-6.

"Acolyte," in: Tymn, M. B. and Ashley, Mike. Science Fiction, Fantasy, and Weird Fiction Magazines. Westport, CT: Greenwood, 1985. p. 811.

"Algol/Starship," in: Tymn, M. B. and Ashley, Mike. Science Fiction, Fantasy, and Weird Fiction Magazines. Westport, CT: Greenwood, 1985. p. 812.

"Amazing Stories Science Fiction Novel," in: Tymn, M. B. and Ashley, Mike. Science Fiction, Fantasy, and Weird Fiction Magazines. Westport, CT: Greenwood, 1985. pp. 57-59.

"Amra," in: Tymn, M. B. and Ashley, Mike. Science Fiction, Fantasy, and Weird Fiction Magazines. Westport, CT: Greenwood, 1985. pp. 812-813.

"Arena SF," in: Tymn, M. B. and Ashley, Mike. Science Fiction, Fantasy, and Weird Fiction Magazines. Westport, CT: Greenwood, 1985. pp. 813-814.

"Australian Science Fiction Review," in: Tymn, M. B. and Ashley, Mike. Science Fiction, Fantasy, and Weird Fiction Magazines. Westport, CT: Greenwood, 1985. p. 814.

"Baum Bugle," in: Tymn, M. B. and Ashley, Mike. Science Fiction, Fantasy, and Weird Fiction Magazines. Westport, CT: Greenwood, 1985. p. 814.

"Bulletin of the Science Fiction Writers of America," in: Tymn, M. B. and Ashley, Mike. Science Fiction, Fantasy, and Weird Fiction Magazines. Westport, CT: Greenwood, 1985. pp. 814-815.

"Burning Court, The," in: Magill, Frank N., ed. Survey of Modern Fantasy Literature, Vol 1. Englewood Cliffs, NJ: Salem Press, Inc., 1983. pp. 184-186.

"Cinefantastic," in: Tymn, M. B. and Ashley, Mike. Science Fiction, Fantasy, and Weird Fiction Magazines. Westport, CT: Greenwood, 1985. p. 815.

Sanders, J. L. (Continued)

"Cry of the Nameless," in: Tymn, M. B. and Ashley, Mike. Science Fiction, Fantasy, and Weird Fiction Magazines. Westport, CT: Greenwood, 1985. pp. 815-816.

"Dark Horizons," by Mike Ashley and J. L. Sanders. in: Tymn, M. B. and Ashley, Mike. Science Fiction, Fantasy, and Weird Fiction Magazines. Westport, CT: Greenwood, 1985. pp. 816-817.

"Deal with the Devil, A," in: Magill, Frank N., ed. Survey of Modern Fantasy Literature, Vol 1. Englewood Cliffs, NJ: Salem Press, Inc., 1983. pp. 355-357.

"Delap's F&SF Review," in: Tymn, M. B. and Ashley, Mike. Science Fiction, Fantasy, and Weird Fiction Magazines. Westport, CT: Greenwood, 1985. p. 817.

"Destiny," in: Tymn, M. B. and Ashley, Mike. Science Fiction, Fantasy, and Weird Fiction Magazines. Westport, CT: Greenwood, 1985. p. 817.

"Dilvish Series, The," in: Magill, Frank N., ed. Survey of Modern Fantasy Literature, Vol 1. Englewood Cliffs, NJ: Salem Press, Inc., 1983. pp. 396-400.

"EISFA/Yandro," in: Tymn, M. B. and Ashley, Mike. Science Fiction, Fantasy, and Weird Fiction Magazines. Westport, CT: Greenwood, 1985. p. 818.

"Energumen," in: Tymn, M. B. and Ashley, Mike. Science Fiction, Fantasy, and Weird Fiction Magazines. Westport, CT: Greenwood, 1985. p. 818.

"ERBania," in: Tymn, M. B. and Ashley, Mike. Science Fiction, Fantasy, and Weird Fiction Magazines. Westport, CT: Greenwood, 1985. p. 819.

"ERBdom," in: Tymn, M. B. and Ashley, Mike. Science Fiction, Fantasy, and Weird Fiction Magazines. Westport, CT: Greenwood, 1985. p. 819.

"Extrapolation," in: Tymn, M. B. and Ashley, Mike. Science Fiction, Fantasy, and Weird Fiction Magazines. Westport, CT: Greenwood, 1985. pp. 819-820.

"Fanewscard," in: Tymn, M. B. and Ashley, Mike. Science Fiction, Fantasy, and Weird Fiction Magazines. Westport, CT: Greenwood, 1985. p. 820.

"Fanscient," in: Tymn, M. B. and Ashley, Mike. Science Fiction, Fantasy, and Weird Fiction Magazines. Westport, CT: Greenwood, 1985. pp. 820-821.

"Fantasiae," in: Tymn, M. B. and Ashley, Mike. Science Fiction, Fantasy, and Weird Fiction Magazines. Westport, CT: Greenwood, 1985. p. 821.

"Fantasy Commentator," in: Tymn, M. B. and Ashley, Mike. Science Fiction, Fantasy, and Weird Fiction Magazines. Westport, CT: Greenwood, 1985. p. 822.

"Fantasy Media," in: Tymn, M. B. and Ashley, Mike. Science Fiction, Fantasy, and Weird Fiction Magazines. Westport, CT: Greenwood, 1985. pp. 823-824.

"Fantasy Newsletter/Fantasy Review," in: Tymn, M. B. and Ashley, Mike. Science Fiction, Fantasy, and Weird Fiction Magazines. Westport, CT: Greenwood, 1985. p. 824.

"Fantasy Review/Science Fantasy Review," in: Tymn, M. B. and Ashley, Mike. Science Fiction, Fantasy, and Weird Fiction Magazines. Westport, CT: Greenwood, 1985. pp. 824-825.

"Foundation: The Review of Science Fiction," in: Tymn, M. B. and Ashley, Mike. Science Fiction, Fantasy, and Weird Fiction Magazines. Westport, CT: Greenwood, 1985. p. 825.

"Gothic," in: Tymn, M. B. and Ashley, Mike. Science Fiction, Fantasy, and Weird Fiction Magazines. Westport, CT: Greenwood, 1985. p. 826-827.

"Imagination," in: Tymn, M. B. and Ashley, Mike. Science Fiction, Fantasy, and Weird Fiction Magazines. Westport, CT: Greenwood, 1985. pp. 343-347.

"Imaginative Tales," in: Tymn, M. B. and Ashley, Mike. Science Fiction, Fantasy, and Weird Fiction Magazines. Westport, CT: Greenwood, 1985. pp. 347-350.

"Inside," in: Tymn, M. B. and Ashley, Mike. Science Fiction, Fantasy, and Weird Fiction Magazines. Westport, CT: Greenwood, 1985. pp. 821-822.

"Janus/Aurora, in: Tymn, M. B. and Ashley, Mike. Science Fiction, Fantasy, and Weird Fiction Magazines. Westport, CT: Greenwood, 1985. p. 827.

"Journal of Science Fiction," in: Tymn, M. B. and Ashley, Mike. Science Fiction, Fantasy, and Weird Fiction Magazines. Westport, CT: Greenwood, 1985. pp. 827-828.

"Khatru," in: Tymn, M. B. and Ashley, Mike. Science Fiction, Fantasy, and Weird Fiction Magazines. Westport, CT: Greenwood, 1985. p. 828.

"Lighthouse," in: Tymn, M. B. and Ashley, Mike. Science Fiction, Fantasy, and Weird Fiction Magazines. Westport, CT: Greenwood, 1985. p. 828.

Sanders, J. L. (Continued)

"Locus," in: Tymn, M. B. and Ashley, Mike. Science Fiction, Fantasy, and Weird Fiction Magazines. Westport, CT: Greenwood, 1985. p. 829.

"Lovecraft Studies," in: Tymn, M. B. and Ashley, Mike. Science Fiction, Fantasy, and Weird Fiction Magazines. Westport, CT: Greenwood, 1985. p. 830.

"Luna/Luna Monthly," in: Tymn, M. B. and Ashley, Mike. Science Fiction, Fantasy, and Weird Fiction Magazines. Westport, CT: Greenwood, 1985. p. 830.

"Man Who Died, The," in: Magill, Frank N., ed. Survey of Modern Fantasy Literature, Vol 2. Englewood Cliffs, NJ: Salem Press, Inc., 1983. pp. 959-960.

"Mervyn Peake Review," in: Tymn, M. B. and Ashley, Mike. Science Fiction, Fantasy, and Weird Fiction Magazines. Westport, CT: Greenwood, 1985. pp. 830-831.

"Mythlore," in: Tymn, M. B. and Ashley, Mike. Science Fiction, Fantasy, and Weird Fiction Magazines. Westport, CT: Greenwood, 1985. p. 831.

"New Frontiers," in: Tymn, M. B. and Ashley, Mike. Science Fiction, Fantasy, and Weird Fiction Magazines. Westport, CT: Greenwood, 1985. p. 831.

"Niekas," in: Tymn, M. B. and Ashley, Mike. Science Fiction, Fantasy, and Weird Fiction Magazines. Westport, CT: Greenwood, 1985. p. 832.

"Nyctalops," in: Tymn, M. B. and Ashley, Mike. Science Fiction, Fantasy, and Weird Fiction Magazines. Westport, CT: Greenwood, 1985. p. 832.

"Oak Leaves," in: Tymn, M. B. and Ashley, Mike. Science Fiction, Fantasy, and Weird Fiction Magazines. Westport, CT: Greenwood, 1985. p. 833.

"Outworlds," in: Tymn, M. B. and Ashley, Mike. Science Fiction, Fantasy, and Weird Fiction Magazines. Westport, CT: Greenwood, 1985. p. 833.

"Poe Newsletter/Poe Studies," in: Tymn, M. B. and Ashley, Mike. Science Fiction, Fantasy, and Weird Fiction Magazines. Westport, CT: Greenwood, 1985. pp. 833-834.

"Pulp Era," in: Tymn, M. B. and Ashley, Mike. Science Fiction, Fantasy, and Weird Fiction Magazines. Westport, CT: Greenwood, 1985. p. 834.

"Riverside Quarterly," in: Tymn, M. B. and Ashley, Mike. Science Fiction, Fantasy, and Weird Fiction Magazines. Westport, CT: Greenwood, 1985. pp. 834-835.

"Romantist," in: Tymn, M. B. and Ashley, Mike. Science Fiction, Fantasy, and Weird Fiction Magazines. Westport, CT: Greenwood, 1985. p. 835.

"Saturn: The Magazine of Science Fiction," by Joe Sanders and Mike Ashley. in: Tymn, M. B. and Ashley, Mike. Science Fiction, Fantasy, and Weird Fiction Magazines. Westport, CT: Greenwood, 1985. pp. 497-500.

"Science Fiction and Fantasy Book Review," in: Tymn, M. B. and Ashley, Mike. Science Fiction, Fantasy, and Weird Fiction Magazines. Westport, CT: Greenwood, 1985. pp. 836-837.

"Science Fiction Chronicle," in: Tymn, M. B. and Ashley, Mike. Science Fiction, Fantasy, and Weird Fiction Magazines. Westport, CT: Greenwood, 1985. p. 837.

"Science Fiction Collector/Megavore," in: Tymn, M. B. and Ashley, Mike. Science Fiction, Fantasy, and Weird Fiction Magazines. Westport, CT: Greenwood, 1985. p. 837.

"Science Fiction Commentary," in: Tymn, M. B. and Ashley, Mike. Science Fiction, Fantasy, and Weird Fiction Magazines. Westport, CT: Greenwood, 1985. pp. 837-838.

"Science Fiction Digest/Fantasy Magazine," in: Tymn, M. B. and Ashley, Mike. Science Fiction, Fantasy, and Weird Fiction Magazines. Westport, CT: Greenwood, 1985. p. 838.

"Science Fiction Review," in: Tymn, M. B. and Ashley, Mike. Science Fiction, Fantasy, and Weird Fiction Magazines. Westport, CT: Greenwood, 1985. pp. 838-839.

"Science Fiction Studies," in: Tymn, M. B. and Ashley, Mike. Science Fiction, Fantasy, and Weird Fiction Magazines. Westport, CT: Greenwood, 1985. pp. 839-840.

"Science Fiction Times," in: Tymn, M. B. and Ashley, Mike. Science Fiction, Fantasy, and Weird Fiction Magazines. Westport, CT: Greenwood, 1985. p. 840.

"Science Fiction: A Review of Speculative Literature," in: Tymn, M. B. and Ashley, Mike. Science Fiction, Fantasy, and Weird Fiction Magazines. Westport, CT: Greenwood, 1985. p. 836.

"SF Horizons," in: Tymn, M. B. and Ashley, Mike. Science Fiction, Fantasy, and Weird Fiction Magazines. Westport, CT: Greenwood, 1985. p. 841.

"Shadow Series, The," in: Magill, Frank N., ed. Survey of Modern Fantasy Literature, Vol 3. Englewood Cliffs, NJ: Salem Press, Inc., 1983. pp. 1380-1383.

"Sorcerer's Son," in: Magill, Frank N., ed. Survey of Modern Fantasy Literature, Vol 4. Englewood Cliffs, NJ: Salem Press, Inc., 1983. pp. 1780-1783.

Sanders, J. L. (Continued)

"Surly Sullen Bell, The," in: Magill, Frank
N., ed. Survey of Modern Fantasy
Literature, Vol 4. Englewood Cliffs, NJ:
Salem Press, Inc., 1983. pp. 1863-1865.

"Tales of Terror and the Supernatural," in:
Magill, Frank N., ed. Survey of Modern
Fantasy Literature, Vol 4. Englewood Cliffs,
NJ: Salem Press, Inc., 1983. pp. 1880-1883.

"Thrust: Science Fiction in Review," in:
Tymn, M. B. and Ashley, Mike. Science
Fiction, Fantasy, and Weird Fiction Magazines.
Westport, CT: Greenwood, 1985. p. 843.

"Weird Tales Collector," in: Tymn, M. B.
and Ashley, Mike. Science Fiction, Fantasy,
and Weird Fiction Magazines. Westport, CT:
Greenwood, 1985. p. 844.

"World SF Newsletter," in: Tymn, M. B. and
Ashley, Mike. Science Fiction, Fantasy, and
Weird Fiction Magazines. Westport, CT:
Greenwood, 1985. p. 844.

"WSFA Journal/SF&F Journal," in: Tymn, M.
B. and Ashley, Mike. Science Fiction,
Fantasy, and Weird Fiction Magazines.
Westport, CT: Greenwood, 1985. pp. 844-845.

"Xenophile," in: Tymn, M. B. and Ashley,
Mike. Science Fiction, Fantasy, and Weird
Fiction Magazines. Westport, CT: Greenwood,
1985. pp. 845.

"Xero," in: Tymn, M. B. and Ashley, Mike.
Science Fiction, Fantasy, and Weird Fiction
Magazines. Westport, CT: Greenwood, 1985.
pp. 845-846.

"Zenith Science Fiction/Zenith
Speculation/Speculation," in: Tymn, M. B.
and Ashley, Mike. Science Fiction, Fantasy,
and Weird Fiction Magazines. Westport, CT:
Greenwood, 1985. p. 846.

"Dancing on the tightrope: immortality in Roger
Zelazny," in: Yoke, C. B. and Hassler, D. M.,
eds. Death and the Serpent. Westport, CT:
Greenwood, 1985. pp. 135-144.

"Fantastic Non-fantastic: Richard Condon's
Waking Nightmares," Extrapolation 25(2):
127-137. Summer 1984.

"Passions in the Clay: Mervyn Peake's Titus
Stories," in: Clareson, Thomas D., ed.
Voices For the Future, Vol. 3. Bowling
Green: Popular Press, 1984. pp. 75-105.

"Science fiction and detective fiction: the
case of John D. MacDonald," Science Fiction
Studies 7(2):157-165. July 1980.

"SF reprint series: scholarship and
commercialism, The," Science Fiction
Studies 3(3):305-310. November 1976.

"Short fiction of Bierce, The," in: Magill,
Frank N., ed. Survey of Modern Fantasy
Literature, Vol 3. Englewood Cliffs, NJ:
Salem Press, Inc., 1983. pp. 1436-1440.

"Silverberg: Transformation and Death,"
Science Fiction: A Review of Speculative
Literature 5(3): 90-95. September 1983.

"Tools/Mirrors: The Humanization of Machines,"
in: Dunn, Thomas P., ed. The Mechanical
God. Westport: Greenwood, 1982. pp. 167-176.

"Zelazny's 'Dilvish': Enduring Concerns,"
Fantasy Newsletter 6(8): 31-32. September
1983.

"Zelazny: unfinished business," in:
Clareson, T. D., ed. Voices for the Future:
Essays on Major Science Fiction Writers, Vol.
2. Bowling Green, Ohio: Popular Press, 1979.
pp. 180-195.

Sanders, Scott

"Characterization in science fiction: two
approaches: the disappearance of character,"
in: Parrinder, Patrick, ed. Science
Fiction: A Critical Guide. New York:
Longman, 1979. pp. 131-147.

"Invisible men and women: the disappearance of
character in science fiction," Science
Fiction Studies 4(1):14-24. March 1977.

"Post hoc," Novel 9(2):185-189. Winter
1976. (Book review)

"Woman as Nature in Science Fiction," in:
Barr, Marlene S., ed. Future Females.
Bowling Green, OH: Bowling Green State
University Popular Press, 1981. pp. 42-59.

Sanders, T. E.

"Profile: Bram Stoker," Night Cry
1(5):72-79. Spring 1986.

Sanderson, I. T.

"Forteans and the fictioneers, The," in:
Earley, George W., ed. Encounters with
Aliens: UFO's and Alien Beings in Science
Fiction. Los Angeles: Sherbourne Press,
1968. pp. 23-33.

"Man-made unidentified flying objects,"
Fantastic Universe 10(3):37-49. September
1958.

Sandery, P.

"Science fiction and 'legitimate' science,"
South Australian Science Teachers Journal
731:35-36. April 1973.

Sandrelli, Sandro

"Interplanet story," <u>Robot</u> No. 23. 1978.

Sansweet, S. J.

"Does Mr. Spock Die in the next episode of Star Trek saga?" <u>Wall Street Journal</u> p. 1. October 9, 1981.

Santangelo, Elaine

"Battle Beyond the Stars," <u>Questar</u> 3(1):30-34,56-57. October 1980.

"Interview: Mark Hamill," <u>Questar</u> 2(4): 32-36, 63. August 1980.

"John Chambers: Master of Make-up," <u>Questar</u> 3(2): 44-48, 54. December 1980.

Santiesteban, Dionisio

"Dos libros de ciencia ficcion," <u>Plural</u> 6(77):46-47. February 1978.

Santos, Domingo

"Gloria y miseria de la Anticipacion (Que es fantasia cientifica?)," <u>Anticipacion</u> (Barcelona) 1:123-132. (1967).

Sanz, Jose

<u>SF Symposium/FC Simposio</u>, ed. by Jose Sanz. Rio de Janeiro: Institute do Cinema, 1969. 188 p.

Saparin, V.

"Budusces celovecetva cerez prizmu fantastiki," <u>Kommunist</u> 12: 126- . 1967.

Sapiro, Leland

"Cliches in the old super science story (part one)," <u>Riverside Quarterly</u> 5(1):4-10. July 1971.

"Cliches in the old super science story (part three)," <u>Riverside Quarterly</u> 5(3):192-199. August 1972.

"Cliches in the old super science story (part two)," <u>Riverside Quarterly</u> 5(2):101-108. February 1972.

"Faustus tradition in the early science fiction story," <u>Inside-Riverside Quarterly</u> p. 31-40. Summer 1964.

"Oath for science fiction writers," <u>Writers Digest</u> 45(9):25-26,46. September 1965.

"Over the transom and far away," <u>Riverside Quarterly</u> 5(4):278-286. April 1972.

"Philip Jose Farmer's 'The Lovers'," <u>Riverside Quarterly</u> 4(1): 42-47. August 1969.

"Renaissance: a survey of F. Orlin Tremaine's <u>Astounding Stories</u>, part III, the mystic," <u>Riverside Quarterly</u> 2(4): 270-283. March 1967.

"Technique as creation," <u>Inside</u> No. 1: 4-15. October 1962.

Sarasohn, David

"Timely report on the state of California: escape hatch, A," <u>Coast</u> 17:12-13. October 1976.

Sargeant, Winthrop

"Through the interstellar looking glass," <u>Life</u> 30(21):127-140. May 21, 1951. Comment, 30(24):10-11. June 11, 1951.

Sargent, L. T.

<u>British and American Utopian Literature 1516-1975, an Annotated Bibliography</u>. Boston: G. K. Hall, 1979. 324 p.

"Ambiguous legacy: the role and position of women in the English eutopia," <u>Extrapolation</u> 19(1):39-49. December 1977.

"Ambiguous Legacy: The Role and Position of Women in the English Eutopia," in: Barr, Marlene S., ed. <u>Future Females</u>. Bowling Green, OH: Bowling Green State University Popular Press, 1981. pp. 88-99.

"Anarchist utopia," <u>Anarchy</u> 9(10):316-320. October 1969.

"Capitalist Eutopias in American," in: Roemer, Kenneth M., ed. <u>America As Utopia</u>. New York: Franklin, 1981. pp. 192-205.

"English and American utopias: similarities and differences," <u>Journal of General Education</u> 28(1):16-22. Spring 1976.

"Eutopias and Dystopias in Science Fiction 1950-75," in: Roemer, Kenneth M. <u>America As Utopia</u>. New York: Franklin, 1981. pp. 347-366.

"Images of the future in science fiction," A paper presented to the 1974 Annual Meeting of the American Political Science Association. 1974.

"New Anarchism, A: Social and political ideas in some recent feminist eutopias," in: Barr, Marleen, ed. <u>Women and Utopia</u>. New York: Lanham, 1983. pp. 3-33.

Sargent, L. T. (Continued)

"Note of the other side of human nature in the utopian novel, A," Political Theory 3(1):88-97. February 1975.

"Opportunities for research on utopian literature to 1900," Extrapolation 19(1):16-26. December 1977.

"Themes in utopian fiction in English before Wells," Science Fiction Studies 3(3):275-282. November 1976.

"Utopia and dystopia in contemporary science fiction," The Futurist 6(3):93-98. June 1972.

"Utopia: the problem of definition," Extrapolation 16(2):137-148. May 1975.

"Women in utopia," Comparative Literature Studies 10(4):302-316. December 1973.

Sargent, Pamela

"Aliens," by Pamela Sargent and James Gunn. in: Warrick, Patricia, ed. Science Fiction: Contemporary Mythology. New York: Harper, 1978. pp. 146-157.

"How it happened: a chronology," by Pamela Sargent and George Zebrowski. Science Fiction Studies 4(2):129-134. July 1977.

"Introduction: women in science fiction," in: Sargent, Pamela, ed. Women of Wonder. New York: Vintage, 1974. pp. xiii-lxiv.

"New women of wonder: introduction, The," in: Sargent, Pamela, ed. The New Women of Wonder. New York: Vintage, 1978. pp. xiii-xxxiv.

"Why it happened: some notes and opinions," Science Fiction Studies 4(2):134-136. July 1977.

"Women in science fiction," Futures 7:433-441. October 1975.

"Writing for a Living," Empire: For the SF Writer 23: 9, 19. Spring 1981.

Sarrazin, Bernard

"Enfant prodigue, L': une parabole fantastique de Leon Bloy ou le 'Dens ignotus'," Litteratur No. 8:24- . December 1972.

Sarris, Andrew

"Film fantasies, left and right," Film Culture 34:28-34. Fall 1964.

"Rod Serling Viewed from Beyond 'The Twilight Zone'," Twilight Zone 5(1): 45-49. March/April 1985.

Sarti, R. C.

Man in a Mortal World: J. R. R. Tolkien and the Lord of the Rings. Ph. D. Dissertation, Indiana University, 1984. 205 p. (DAI 45A:1410.)

Sarti, Ronald

"Variations on a theme: human sexuality in the work of Robert A. Heinlein," in: Olander, J. D. and M. H. Greenberg, eds. Robert A. Heinlein. New York: Taplinger, 1978. pp. 107-136.

Satty, H. J.

Olaf Stapledon: A Bibliography, by H. J. Satty and C. C. Smith. Westport: Greenwood, 1984. 168 p.

"Last and First Men," in: Magill, Frank N., ed. Survey of Science Fiction Literature, Vol. 3. Englewood Cliffs, NJ: Salem Press, 1979. pp. 1140-1143.

Saunders, C. R.

"Farmer of the apes," Borealis 1(2):17-19. Spring 1978.

Saunders, T. J.

"Plato's clockwork orange," Durham University Journal 68(New series 37, No. 2):113-117. June 1976.

Saunders, V. D.

Gentle Spirits: Female Writers of the Supernatural. Ph. D. Dissertation, Princeton, 1982. 239 p. (DAI 42A:4462)

Savoy, Maggie

"Ray Bradbury keeping eye on Cloud IX," Los Angeles Times Sec. E, p. 1, 18. March 15, 1975.

Sawyer, Andrew

"Child's play," Arena 6:21-26. August 1977.

Sawyer, Andy

"'With One Bound, Jack Was Free," Vector 115: 21-27. 1983.

"Interim Report From the Archives: The SF of Doris Lessing," Vector 103: 5-12. August 1981.

Sawyer, R. J.

"Interview: Donald Kingsbury," _Science Fiction Review_ 13(2): 9-15. May 1984.

Saxe, Leonard

"Day After, The: report of a survey of effects of viewing and beliefs about nuclear war," by T. P. Cross and Leonard Saxe. 12 p. ERIC ED 260 951.

Saxton, Josephine

"Acknowledging Debts," _Vector_ 110: 30-33. 1982.

"Mutants and symbiotes," in: Ash, Brian, ed. _Visual Encyclopedia of Science Fiction._ New York: Harmony, 1977. pp. 190-203.

"Way Things Are," _Vector_ 106: 16-21. Fall 1982.

Say, Daniel

"Interview with Stanislaw Lem, An," _The Alien Critic_ 3(3):4-14. 1974.

Sayers, John

"Edward Feldman: guiding young explorers into adventure," by John Sayers and David McDonnell. _Starlog_ No. 95: 23-25, 72. June 1985.

"Rick Moranis: Nebbish, Nerd and Famous Hoser," by David McDonnell and John Sayers. _Starlog_ 86: 41-43, 66. September 1984.

Sayre, R. F.

"American myths of utopia," _College English_ 31(6):613-623. March 1970.

Scafella, Frank

"White Sphinx and The Time Machine," _Science-Fiction Studies_ 8(3): 255-265. November 1981.

Scapperotti, Dan

"Black Cauldron (review)," _Cinefantastique_ 16(1):40. March 1986.

"Black Cauldron," _Cinefantastique_ 13(5):26-27. June/July 1983.

"Blue Thunder," _Cinefantastique_ 13(5):5-9. June/July 1983.

"Close Encounters of the Third Kind," by Robert Villard and Dan Scapperotti. _Cinefantastique_ 6:32-39. Spring 1978.

"Day of Dead (review)," _Cinefantastique_ 15(4):48-49,52. October 1985.

"Death Bite," _Cinefantastique_ 12(2/3):88-93. April 1982.

"Douglas Trumball interviewed," _Cinefantastique_ 6(4)/7(1):36-39. Spring 1978.

"Evil Dead," by R. A. Glover and Dan Scapperotti. _Cinefantastique_ 13(6)/14(1):24-27. September 1983.

"Filming F/X," _Cinefantastique_ 16(1):8. March 1986.

"Frankenstein (review)," _Cinefantastique_ 11(1):47. Summer 1981.

"Fugitive From the Empire (review)," by Dan Scapperotti and J. P. Harris. _Cinefantastique_ 11(2):45. Fall 1981.

"Golden Voyage of Sinbad," by Dan Scapperotti and David Bartholomew. _Cinefantastique_ 3(1):4,42-45. Spring 1974.

"Hunger (review)," _Cinefantastique_ 13(5):57. June/July 1983.

"Krull," _Cinefantastique_ 13(2)/13(3):28-47. November/December 1982.

"Last Dinosaur (review)," _Cinefantastique_ 6(1):16. Summer 1977.

"Leonard Nimoy," _Cinefantastique_ 14(3):6-11. May 1984.

"Nightmare on Elm Street," _Cinefantastique_ 15(3):40-42. July 1985.

"No Blade of Grass (review)," _Cinefantastique_ 1(2):28. Winter 1971.

"Oriental fantasy from Daiei," _Cinefantastique_ 1(3):6-11. Summer 1971.

"Raiders of the Lost Ark (review)," _Cinefantastique_ 11(3):49. September 1981.

"Raiders of the lost serials," _Cinefantastique_ 15(2):43. May 1985.

"Ray Harryhausen's Clash of the Titans," _Cinefantastique_ 10(3):4-11,38-45. Winter 1980.

"Remo Man," _Cinefantastique_ 15(4):14,56. October 1985.

"Saturday the 14th (review)," _Cinefantastique_ 12(2/3):83. April 1982.

Scapperotti, Dan (Continued)

"Sinbad and the Eye of the Tiger: Ray Harryhausen interview," _Cinefantastique_ 6(2):4-17. Fall 1977.

"Strange Invaders (review)," _Cinefantastique_ 13(6)/14(1):100,104. September 1983.

"Swamp Thing," _Cinefantastique_ 11(4):16-19. December 1981.

"Terminator, The (review)," _Cinefantastique_ 15(2):46,54. May 1985.

"Tobe Hooper on Lifeforce," _Cinefantastique_ 15(3):6-11. July 1985.

Scarborough, Dorothy

Supernatural in Modern English Fiction, The. New York: Putnam, 1917. 329 p.

"Supernatural science," in: Scarborough, Dorothy, ed. _The Supernatural in English Fiction._ New York and London: G. P. Putman's Sons, 1917. pp. 251-281.

Scarborough, John

"H. Rider Haggard," in: Bleiler, E. F., ed. _Science Fiction Writers._ New York: Scribners, 1982. pp. 19-24.

"John Wyndham," in: Bleiler, E. F., ed. _Science Fiction Writers._ New York: Scribners, 1982. pp. 219-224.

"Stanislaw Lem," in: Bleiler, E. F., ed. _Science Fiction Writers._ New York: Scribners, 1982. pp. 591-598.

Schachterle, Lance

"Checklist of secondary studies on imaginary voyages," by Lance Schachterle and Jeanne Welcher. _Bulletin of Bibliography_ 31(3): 99-100,106,110,116,121. July/ September 1974.

Schaefer, Martin

Science fiction als ideologiekritik? Utopische spuren in den amerikanischen science-fiction literatur 1940-1955. Stuttgart: Metzler, 1977. 329 p. (Amerikastudien, 48)

"Rise and fall of antiutopia: utopia, gothic romance, and dystopia, The," _Science Fiction Studies_ 6(3):287-295. November 1979.

Schafer-Syben, Ethy

"Science Fiction aus der Sicht des Lesers," in: Ermert, Karl, ed. _Neugier oder Flucht?_ Stuttgart: Klett, 1980. pp. 137-145.

Schaftel, O.

"Social content of science fiction," _Science and Society_ 17:97-118. November 2, 1953.

Schakel, P. J.

Reading With the Heart: The Way. Grand Rapids, MI: Eerdmans, 1979.

"Retelling Within a Myth Retold: The Priest of Essur and Lewisian Mythopoetics. _Mythlore_ 9(4): 10-11. Winter 1983.

Schatt, Stanley

Kurt Vonnegut, Jr. Boston: Twayne, 1976. 174 p.

"Kurt Vonnegut checklist, A," by Stanley Schatt and Jerome Klinkowitz. _Critique_ 12(3):70-76. 1971.

"Vonnegut bibliography, The," by Jerome Klinkowitz and Stanley Schatt. in: Klinkowitz, Jerome and John Somer, eds. _The Vonnegut Statement._ New York: Delacorte Press/Seymour Lawrence, 1973. pp. 255-277.

"Waiting for the apocalypse: eschatology in recent American fiction," _Journal of the American Studies Association of Texas_ 4:102-108. 1973.

"Whale and the cross: Vonnegut's Jonah and Christ figures, The," _Southwest Quarterly_ pp. 29-42. Winter 1971.

"World of Kurt Vonnegut, Jr., The," _Critique_ 12(3):54-69. 1971.

Schatzberg, Walter

"Relations of literature and science: a bibliography of scholarship, 1972-1973," _Clio_ 4(1):73-93. October 1974.

"Relations of literature and science: a bibliography of scholarship, 1973-1974," _Clio_ 5(1):97-121. Fall 1975.

"Relations of literature and science: a bibliography of scholarship, 1974-1975," _Clio_ 6(1):71-88. Fall 1976.

"Relations of literature and science: a bibliography of scholarship, 1975-1976," _Clio_ 7(1):135-155. Fall 1977.

"Relations of literature and science: a bibliography of scholarship, 1976-1977," _Clio_ 8(1):97-116. Fall 1978.

Schechter, Harold

"It's not nice to fool Mother Nature: the disaster movie and technological guilt," by Harold Schechter and Chares Molesworth. Journal of American Culture 1(1):44-50. Spring 1978.

Scheck, F. R.

"Augenschein und zunkunft. Der anti-utopische reaktion (Samjatin, Huxley, Orwell)," in: Barmeyer, Eike, ed. Science fiction: theorie und geschichte. Munchen: Fink, 1972. pp. 259-275.

"Relativity," Quarber Merkur 25:31-33. January 1971.

Schecker, Fred

"Science Fiction Emerges from the Twilight Zone," Kansas City (Mo.) Star, December 30, 1982. in: NewsBank. Literature. 88:C6-7. 1981-1982.

Scheele, Mitch

"Interview with Philip Jose Farmer, An," by D. A. Kraft, Mitch Scheele, and R. E. Geis. Science Fiction Review 4(3):7-21. 1975.

Scheick, W. J.

"Fourth dimension in Wells' novels of the 1920's, The," Criticism 20(2):167-190. 1978.

"Reality and the word: the last books of H. G. Wells," English Literature in Transition 12(3):151-154. 1969.

"Thing that is and the speculative if: the pattern of several motifs in three novels by H. G. Wells," English Literature in Transition 11(2):67-78. 1968.

"Toward the Ultra-Science-Fiction Novel: H. G. Wells's Star Begotten," Science Fiction Studies 8(1): 19-25. March 1981.

Scheidt, Jurgen vom

"Descensus ad inferos. Tiefenpsychologische aspekte der science fiction," in: Barmeyer, Eike, ed. Science fiction: theorie und geschichte. Munchen: Fink, 1972 pp. 133-163.

"Liebe und sexualitat in der science fiction: eine psychologische studie," in: Weigand, Jorg, ed. Die Triviale Phantasie. Bonn: Asgard, 1976. pp. 123-142.

"Science fiction, eine Literaturgattung wird serios," Der Junge Buchhandel 23:J93-J104.

1970. (Borsenblatt fur den deutschen buchhandel, 26, 1970.)

"Science Fiction: ein uberblick uber das Genre," Der Junge Buchhandel 25:14- . 1972.

Schellenberger, John

"Science Fiction and 'Mind-Sprung'," Foundation 25: 45-49. June 1982.

Schenkman, Richard

"Barbara Carrera: Making Love (and Death) Means 'Never Say Never Again'," Starlog 75: 20-24, 61. October 1983.

Schepelmann, Wolfgang

Englishche Utopie in Uebergang, Die: von Bulwer-Lytton bis H. G. Wells. Wien: VWG, 1975. 305 p.

Scheps, Walter

"Fairy-tale morality of The Lord of the Rings, The," in: Lobdell, Jared, ed. A Tolkien Compass. New York: Ballantine/Del Rey, 1980. pp. 44-59.

Scherwinsky, Felix

Neologismen in der Modernen Franzosischen Science Fiction. Meisneheim: Hain, 1978. 339 p.

Schickel, Richard

"Black comedy with purifying laughter," Harper's 232:102-106. May 1966. (Book reviews)

Schiff, S. D.

"Glorious Past, Erratic Present, and Questionable Future of the Specialty Presses," in: Jarvis, Sharon, ed. Inside Outer Space. New York: Ungar, 1985. pp. 37-50.

"In search of a Smith library," Nyctalops No. 7:68-69. August 1972.

Schillaci, Peter

"Star Wars: nostalgia in hyperdrive," Media & Methods 14(3):18-21,62-68. November 1977.

Schioler, Carsten

Dansk science fiction indeks 1741-1976. Copenhagen: Science Fiction Cirklen, 1977. 125 p.

Schioler, Carsten (Continued)

Trovaerdig forestillingsverden: focus pa dansk science fiction. Copenhagen: Science Fiction Cirklen 1978. 108 p.

"Freezing Down," in: Magill, Frank N., ed. Survey of Science Fiction Literature, Vol. 2. Englewood Cliffs, NJ: Salem Press, 1979. pp. 845-849.

"Matriarketet," in: Magill, Frank N., ed. Survey of Science Fiction Literature, Vol. 3. Englewood Cliffs, NJ: Salem Press, 1979. pp. 1366-1369.

"Danish scene: Danish science fiction, The," in: Dollerup, Cay, ed. Volve. Scandinavian Views on Science Fiction. Copenhagen: Department of English, University of Copenhagen, 1978. pp. 48-54.

Schirmbeck, Heinrich

"Eros und Weltraum," Planet No. 6:3- . 1970.

"Eros, Weltraum, Science Fiction," Die Formael und die Sinnlichkeit. Munchen, 1964.

Schittecat, F.

"Belgium: notes on science fiction: results of an investigation," Bookbird 14(2):50-52. 1976.

Schjonberg, M. F.

"SF3's WisCon7 means sci-fi fun," Madison State Journal March 6, 1983. in: NewsBank. Social Relations. 9:G7. 1983.

Schlesinger, Arthur, Jr.

"2001: A Space Odyssey. 'A Superb Wreck'," Vogue 151(10): 76. June 1968.

Schlobin, R. C.

Aesthetics of Fantasy Literature and Art. Notre Dame, IN: University of Notre Dame Press, 1982. 288 p.

Andre Norton: A Primary and Secondary Bibliography. Boston: G. K. Hall, 1980. 68 p.

Literature of Fantasy: A Comprehensive Annotated Bibliography of Modern Fantasy Fiction. New York: Garland, 1979. 425 p.

Research Guide to Science Fiction Studies: An Annotated Checklist of Primary and Secondary Sources for Fantasy and Science Fiction, A, ed. by M. B. Tymn, R. C. Schlobin and L. W. Currey. New York: Garland, 1977. 165 p.

Urania's Daughters: A Checklist of Women Science Fiction Writers, 1692-1982. Mercer Island, WA: Starmont, 1983. 79 p. (Starmont Reference Guide, 1)

Year's Scholarship in Science Fiction and Fantasy, 1972-1975, by M. B. Tymn, and R. C. Schlobin. Kent, OH: Kent State University Press 1979. 222 p.

Year's Scholarship in Science Fiction and Fantasy, 1976-1979, by M. B. Tymn, and R. C. Schlobin. Kent, OH: Kent State University Press, 1983. 251 p.

"Here Abide Monsters," in: Magill, Frank N., ed. Survey of Science Fiction Literature, Vol. 2. Englewood Cliffs, NJ: Salem Press, 1979. pp. 969-971.

"Minotaur Trilogy, The," in: Magill, Frank N., ed. Survey of Modern Fantasy Literature, Vol 3. Englewood Cliffs, NJ: Salem Press, Inc., 1983. pp. 1029-1033.

"Star Man's Son 2250 A.D.," in: Magill, Frank N., ed. Survey of Science Fiction Literature, Vol. 5. Englewood Cliffs, NJ: Salem Press, 1979. pp. 2156-2158.

"Andre Norton: Humanity Amid the Hardware," in: Staicar, Tom, ed. The Feminine Eye. New York: Ungar, 1982. pp. 25-31.

"Annotated bibliography of fantasy fiction," CEA Critic 40(2):37-42. January 1978.

"Bibliography of fantasy anthologies," by Neil Barron, Mike Ashley and R. C. Schlobin. in: Magill, Frank N., ed. Survey of Modern Fantasy Literature, Vol 5. Englewood Cliffs, NJ: Salem Press, Inc., 1983. pp. 2532-2538.

"Definitions of Science Fiction and Fantasy," in: Tymn, Marshall B., ed. The Science Fiction Reference Book. Mercer Island, WA.: Starmont House, 1981. pp. 496-511.

"Dragon's Well: Anthologies," Fantasy Newsletter 5(1): 22-23, 26. January 1982.

"Fantasy versus horror," in: Magill, Frank N., ed. Survey of Modern Fantasy Literature, Vol 5. Englewood Cliffs, NJ: Salem Press, Inc., 1983. pp. 2259-2266.

"Farsighted Females: A Selective Checklist of Modern Women Writers of Science Fiction Through 1980," Extrapolation 23(1): 91-107. Spring 1982.

"Fool and the Fantastic," Fantasy Newsletter 4(12): 6-9, 29. December 1981.

"Future Females: A Selected Checklist Through 1979," in: Barr, Marlene S., ed. Future Females. Bowling Green, OH: Bowling Green State University Popular Press, 1981. pp. 179-189.

Schlobin, R. C. (Continued)

"In the looking glasses: the popular and cultural fantasy response," in: Collins, R. A., ed. Scope of the Fantastic: Culture, Biography, Themes, Children's Literature. Westport: Greenwood, 1985. pp. 3-10.

"Introduction: Andre Norton," in: Schlobin, Roger. Andre Norton: A Primary and Secondary Bibliography. Boston: G. K. Hall, 1980. pp. xiii-xxxii.

"Locus amoenus and the fantasy quest," Kansas Quarterly 16(3): 29-34. Summer 1984.

"Masterpieces of Modern Fantasy: An Annotated Core List," in: Tymn, Marshall B., ed. The Science Fiction Reference Book. Mercer Island, WA: Starmont House, 1981. pp. 246-290.

"Modern Fantasy Fiction: A Checklist," in: Schlobin, Roger C., ed. The Aesthetics of Fantasy Literature and Art. Notre Dame, IN: University of Notre Dame Press, 1982. pp. 249-261.

"Scholarship of Incidence: The Unfortunate State of Fantasy Scholarship," Extrapolation 25(4): 335-339. Winter 1984.

"Thomas Burnett Swann's Nixies: Pain and Pleasure," Extrapolation 24(1): 5-13. Spring 1983.

"Whispersoft and Shadowfast," in: Winter, Douglas E. Shadowings: The Reader's Guide to Horror Fiction 1981-1982. Mercer Island, WA: Starmont, 1983. pp. 53-55.

"Witch World Series, The," in: Magill, Frank N., ed. Survey of Modern Fantasy Literature, Vol 5. Englewood Cliffs, NJ: Salem Press, Inc., 1983. pp. 2139-2149.

"Year's scholarship in science fiction and fantasy: 1974, The," by R. C. Schlobin and M. B. Tymn. Extrapolation 18(1):73-96. December 1976.

"Year's scholarship in science fiction and fantasy: 1975, The," by R. C. Schlobin and M. B. Tymn. Extrapolation 19(2):156-191. May 1978.

"Year's scholarship in science fiction and fantasy: 1976, The," by R. C. Schlobin and M. B. Tymn. Extrapolation 20(1):60-99. Spring 1979.

"Year's scholarship in science fiction and fantasy: 1977, The," by R. C. Schlobin and M. B. Tymn. Extrapolation 20(3):238-288. Fall 1979.

"Year's scholarship in science fiction and fantasy: 1978, The," by R. C. Schlobin and M. B. Tymn. Extrapolation 21(1):45-89. Spring 1980.

"Year's Scholarship in Science Fiction and Fantasy: 1979, The," by R. C. Schlobin and M. B. Tymn. Extrapolation 22(1): 25-91. Spring 1981.

Schlockoff, Alain

"50 films cles du cinema de science fiction: dictionnaire critique," by Jacques Goimard, Jean-Claude Michel, and Alain Schlockoff. Cinema d'aujourd'hui. No. 7:65-84. Spring 1976.

"Presentation," Cinema D'aujourg'hui. No. 7:9-10. Spring 1976.

"Rencontre a Hollywood avec Eugene Lourie," Cinema D'aujourd'hui. No. 7:59-64. Spring 1976.

Schlueter, Paul

"Trends in Orwell criticism, 1968-1983," College Literature 11(1): 94-112. 1984.

Schlumbohm, Dietrich

"Zwischen Utopie und science fiction: der Zeitgenossene 'Roman d'anticipation' in Frankreich," Romanistisches Jahrbach 25:186-195. 1975.

Schmerl, R. B.

"Fantasy as technique," Virginia Quarterly Review 43(4):644-656. Autumn 1967. also in: Clareson, T. D., ed. SF: The Other Side of Realism. Bowling Green, Ohio: Popular Press, 1971. pp. 105-115.

"Two future worlds of Aldous Huxley, The," PMLA 77(3):328-334. June 1962.

"Who's afraid of fantasy?" Arts in Society 6(2):177-181. Summer/Fall 1969.

Schmidt, Gottfried

"Sozialdemokratische zukunftsbilder," Quarber Merkur 44:33-51. July 1976.

"Sozialdemokratische zukunftsbilder. Deutsche science fiction im 19 jahrhundert in der tradition von Edward Bellamys roman Looking backward 2000-1887," Quarber Merkur 43:34-49. May 1976.

Schmidt, S. A.

"Science fiction courses: an example and some alternatives," American Journal of Physics 41(9):1052-1056. September 1973.

Schmidt, Stanley

"Editorial," Analog 99(12): 5-10. December 1979.

"Editorial: House Warming," Analog 100(9):5-7. September 1980.

"Portrait of you," Analog 101(5): 5-14. April 27, 1981.

"Science fiction and the science teacher," in: Williamson, Jack, ed. Teaching Science Fiction: Education for Tomorrow. Philadelphia: Owlswick, 1980. pp. 110-120.

"Science in science fiction, The," in: Clareson, T. D., ed. Many Futures, Many Worlds. Kent, Ohio: Kent State University Press, 1977. pp. 27-49.

"Science of Writing Science Fiction," Writer's Digest 63(2): 28-31, 50. February 1983.

"SF in the classroom," Extrapolation 17(2):141-150. May 1976.

Schmidt-Sommer, Irmgard

"Traume, Sterne und Raketen. Anmerkungen zur Science Fiction Literatur," Die Zeit im Buch. 27(4):207-213. 1973.

Schmidtchen, P. W.

"Father of science fiction," Hobbies 76(10):135-136,145. December 1971.

Schmidtke, W. G.

"Aussen seiter des Phantastischen," Science Fiction Times (Germany) 24(9):10-14. September 1982.

Schmiel, M. A.

"Forge of Los: Tolkien and the Art of Creative Fantasy," Mythlore 10(1): 17-22. Spring 1983.

Schmitz, Albert

"Science Fiction: Unterhaltungsliteratur mit Tiefgang?" Zielsprache Englisch n. 2, pp. 14-17, April 1974.

Schmitz, J. H.

"John W. Campbell," Locus No. 90:7-8. July 12, 1971.

Schneider, M.

Litterature fantastique en france, La. Paris: Fayard, 1964. 425 p.

"Science fiction, c'est la liberte, Le," Les Nouvelles Litteraires p. 7. June 4, 1964.

Schodel, S.

"Uber Gustav Meyrink und die phantastische literatur," in: H. O. Burge, ed. Studien zur Trivialliteratur. Frankfurt am Main, 1968. pp. 221- .

Schoenecke, M. K.

Science Fiction of Jack London: Scientific Theories and Three Fictional Extrapolations. Masters Thesis, Central State University, 1979. 150 p.

Schofield, Jack

"Cosmic imagery in A Voyage to Arcturus," Extrapolation 13(2):146-151. May 1972.

Scholes, Robert

Bridges to Fantasy, by G. E. Slusser, E. S. Rabkin, and Robert Scholes. Carbondale: Southern Illinois University Press, 1982. 231 p.

Coordinates: Placing Science Fiction and Fantasy, by G. E. Slusser, E. S. Rabkin, and Robert Scholes. Carbondale, IL: Southern Illinois University Press, 1983. 209 p.

Science Fiction: History, Science, Vision, by Robert Scholes and E. S. Rabkin. New York: Oxford University Press, 1977. 258 p.

Structural Fabulation: An Essay on the Fiction of the Future. Notre Dame: University of Notre Dame Press, 1975. 111 p.

"Afterword," in: Dallard, R. H. W., et al. The Sounder Few. Athens, Georgia: University of Georgia Press, 1971. pp. 186-191. (Reprinted from The Hollins Critic)

"Change, SF, and Marxism: open or closed universes? Novels by Brunner and Levin," Science Fiction Studies 1(3):213-215. Spring 1974.

"Chasing a lone eagle," Summary 1(2):35-40. Autumn 1971.

"Fabulation and satire," in: The Fabulators. New York: Oxford University Press, 1967. pp. 35-53.

Scholes, Robert (Continued)

"Footnote to Russ's 'Recent Feminist Utopias', A," in: Barr, Marlene S., ed. Future Females. Bowling Green, OH: Bowling Green State University Popular Press, 1981. pp. 86-87.

"Good witch of the west, The," The Hollins Critic 11(2):1-12. April 1974.

"Good Witch of the West," in: Ursula K. Le Guin, ed. by Harold Bloom. New York: Chelsea House, 1986. pp. 35-46.

"Mithridates, He Died Old: black humor and Kurt Vonnegut, Jr.," Hollins Critic 3(4):1-12. October 1966. Reprinted in: Dallard, R. H. W., et al. The Sounder Few. Georgia: Univ. of Georgia Press, 1971. pp. 173-185.

"Science fiction as conscience: John Brunner & Ursula K. Le Guin," New Republic 175(18):38-40. October 30, 1976.

"Speaking of books: for non-realistic fiction," New York Times Book Review p. 2. October 22, 1967.

"Stillborn literature," The Bulletin of the Midwest Language Association 7(1):1-12. Spring 1974.

"Talk with Kurt Vonnegut, Jr., A," in: Klinkowitz, Jerome and John Somer, eds. The Vonnegut Statement. New York: Delacorte Press/Seymour Lawrence, 1973. pp. 90-118.

Scholl, P. A.

"Vonnegut's attack of Christendom," Newsletter of the Conference on Christianity and Literature 22:5-11. 1972. (not seen)

Scholl, Ralph

"Science fiction: a selected checklist," Bulletin of Bibliography 22(5):114-115. January/April 1958.

Scholt, Grayce

"Enchantment revisited: or why teach fantasy?" by J. M. Bingham and Grayce Scholt. CEA Critic 40(2):11-15. January 1978.

Scholtz, Carter

"Inside the Ghetto, and Out," in: Jarvis, Sharon, ed. Inside Outer Space. New York: Ungar, 1985. pp. 53-65.

Schorr, Karl

"Nature of Dreams in The Lord of the Rings," Mythlore 10(2): 21, 46. Summer 1983.

"Rewards of reading fantasy," Mythlore 11(3): 9-15. Winter/Spring 1985.

Schott, Webster

"Andromeda strain, The," New York Times Book Review pp. 4-5. June 8, 1969. (Book review)

Schow, D. J.

"In and out of The Outer Limits, part one," Twilight Zone 3(5):82-88. November/December 1983.

"In and Out of the Outer Limits," Twilight Zone 4(1): 82-84. March/April 1984.

"Outer Limits," Twilight Zone 4(6):98-100. January/February 1985.

"Outer Limits: and now a word from censor," Twilight Zone 4(3):82-84. July/August 1984.

"Outer Limits: second season," Twilight Zone 4(6):80-82. November/December 1984.

"Outer Limits: unknowaphobia," Twilight Zone 4(4):80-82. September/October 1984.

"Show by show guide: The Outer Limits, part 3," by D. J. Schow and Jeffrey Frentzen. Twilight Zone 4(2):84-87. May/June 1984.

"Show by show guide: The Outer Limits, part 4," by D. J. Schow and Jeffrey Frentzen. Twilight Zone 4(3):85-88. July/August 1984.

"Show by show guide: The Outer Limits, part 5," by D. J. Schow and Jeffrey Frentzen. Twilight Zone 4(4):83-86. September/October 1984.

"Show by show guide: The Outer Limits, part 6," by D. J. Schow and Jeffrey Frentzen. Twilight Zone 4(6):83-86. November/December 1984.

"Show by show guide: The Outer Limits, part 7," by D. J. Schow and Jeffrey Frentzen. Twilight Zone 4(6):101-104. January/February 1985.

"Show by show guide: The Outer Limits, part one," Twilight Zone 3(6):103-106. January/February 1984.

Schow, Dave

"Man From Atlantis (review)," Cinefantastique 7(2):29. Summer 1978.

Schriber, M. S.

"Bringing Chaos to Order: The Novel Tradition and Kurt Vonnegut, jr.," <u>Genre</u> 10(2): 283-297. Summer 1977.

"You've come a long way, Babbit, from Zenith to Ilium," <u>Twentieth Century Literature</u> 17(2):101-106. April 1971.

Schroeder, Horst

<u>Science Fiction literatur in den USA: vorstudien fur eine materialistische paraliteraturwissenschaft</u>. Giessen: Focus, 1978. 519 p.

Schroth, R. D.

"Lord of the Rings," <u>America</u> 116(7):254. Feburary 18, 1967. (Book review)

Schuhler, C.

"Perry Rhodan: Auf Raketen zuruck in die Zukunft," <u>Kurbiskern</u> 4:588-597. 1970. Also in: Arnold, H., ed. <u>Geschichte der deutschen Literatur aus Methoden: Westdeutsche Literatur von 1945-1971</u>. Bd. 3. Frankfurt, 1972.

Schuldiner, Herbert

"How they filmed '2001: A Space Odyssey'," <u>Popular Science</u> 192:62-67. June 1968.

Schuler, R. M.

<u>English Magical and Scientific Poems to 1700: an Annotated Bibliography</u>. New York: Garland, 1979. 120 p.

Schulman, P. H.

<u>Fantastic Television</u>, by Gary Gerani and P. H. Schulman. New York: Harmony Books, 1977. 192 p.

Schulz, D. G.

"Futuristic humanistic science fiction," Paper presented at the Annual Secondary School English Conference of NCTE, 6 p. April 1975. (ERIC ED 108 208)

Schulz, D. L.

"Uses of science fiction, The," in: <u>The Future in Peril: 1984 and the Anti-Utopians</u>. College Station: Honors Program, Texas A&M University, [1985]. pp. 28-31.

Schulz, M. F.

"Unconfirmed thesis: Kurt Vonnegut, black humor, and contemporary art, The," <u>Critique</u> 12(3):5-28. 1971.

Schumack, S. W.

"Demon Seed (review)," <u>Cinefantastique</u> 6(1):14,17. Summer 1977.

"Evolution: Logan's Run, from novel to screenplay to film: an analysis showing how science fiction gets raped again," <u>Cinefantastique</u> 5(2):10-15. 1976.

"Star Wars (review)," <u>Cinefantastique</u> 6(2):22-23. Fall 1977.

Schuman, Samuel

"Vladimir Nabokov's 'Invitation to a Beheading' and Robert Heinlein's 'They'," <u>Twentieth Century Literature</u> 19(2):99-106. April 1973.

Schurr, G.

"4,000 years of science fiction," <u>Connoisseur</u> 167(672):111. February 1968.

Schuster, M. M.

"Skinner and the morality of melioration," in: Richter, P. E., ed. <u>Utopia/Dystopia?</u>. Cambridge, MA: Schenkman, 1975. pp. 93-108.

Schuyler, W. M., Jr.

"<u>Devil Is Dead, The</u>," in: Magill, Frank N., ed. <u>Survey of Modern Fantasy Literature</u>, Vol 1. Englewood Cliffs, NJ: Salem Press, Inc., 1983. pp. 380-382.

"Could Anyone Here Speak Babel-17?" in: Smith, Nicholas D., ed. <u>Philosophers Look at Science Fiction</u>. Chicago: Nelson-Hall, 1982. pp. 87-85.

"Heroes and History," in: Myers, R. E., ed. <u>The Intersection of Science Fiction and Philosophy</u>. Westport: Greenwood, 1983. pp. 197-210.

"Kai Lung Stories, The," in: Magill, Frank N., ed. <u>Survey of Modern Fantasy Literature</u>, Vol 2. Englewood Cliffs, NJ: Salem Press, Inc., 1983. pp. 827-830.

"Mechanisms of Morality: Philosophical Implications of Selected (A)Moral Science Fiction Machines," in: Dunn, Thomas P., ed. <u>The Mechanical God</u>. Westport: Greenwood, 1982. pp. 177-190.

Schuyler, W. M., Jr. (Continued)

"Novels of Firbank, The," in: Magill, Frank N., ed. Survey of Modern Fantasy Literature, Vol 3. Englewood Cliffs, NJ: Salem Press, Inc., 1983. pp. 1137-1141.

"Recent Developments in the Theory of Spell Construction," in: Schlobin, Roger C., ed. The Aesthetics of Fantasy Literature and Art. Notre Dame, IN: University of Notre Dame Press, 1982. pp. 237-248.

Schwab, Joy

"Interview: Artist, David Willson," by Joy Schwab and Mark Smith. Fantasy Newsletter 5(11): 8-10. December 1982.

Schwartz, Harry

"For class war on Mars," New York Times Magazine pp. 81-82. October 19, 1958.

Schwartz, R. A.

"Fantastic in contemporary fiction," in: Collins, R. A. and H. D. Pearce, eds. The Scope of the Fantastic: Theory, Technique, Major Authors. Westport, CT: Greenwood Press, 1985. pp. 27-32.

"Thomas Pynchon and the Evolution of Fiction," Science Fiction Studies 8(2): 165-172. July 1981.

Schwartz, Sheila

"Science fiction as prophecy," in: Schwartz, Sheila. Teaching Adolescent Literature: A Humanistic Approach. Rochelle Park, New Jersey: Hayden Book Company, 1979. pp. 181-198.

"Science fiction: bridge between the two cultures," English Journal 60(8):1043-1051. November 1971.

"Science fiction: literature for our times," Journal of Popular Culture 5(4):979-988. Spring 1972.

"World of science fiction, The," English Record 21(3):27-40. February 1971. Also in: ERIC ED 053 115.

Schwarz, Micheil

"Alternative Space Futures: The Next Quarter-Century," by Ian Miles and Micheil Schwarz. Futures 14(5): 462-482. October 1982.

Schweickart, P. P.

"Reading a wordless statement: the structure of Doris Lessing's The Golden Notebook," Modern Fiction Studies 31(2): 263-279. Summer 1985.

Schweitzer, Darrell

Conan's World and Robert E. Howard. San Bernardino, California: Borgo Press, 1978. 64 p. (Popular Writers of Today, Vol. 17)

Constructing Scientifiction & Fantasy, by John Ashmead, Darrell Schweitzer, and George Scithers. Lake Geneva, WI: TSR Hobbies, 1982. 31 p.

Discovering Modern Horror Fiction. Mercer Island, WA: Starmont, 1985. 156 p.

Discovering Stephen King. Mercer Island, WA: Starmont, 1985. 219 p.

Dream Quest of H. P. Lovecraft. San Bernardino, CA: Borgo, 1978. 64 p.

Essays Lovecraftian. Baltimore: T-K Graphics, 1976. 114 p.

Exploring Fantasy Worlds. San Bernardino, CA: Borgo, 1985. 112 p.

Lovecraft in the Cinema. Baltimore: T-K Graphics, 1975. 24 p.

Science Fiction Voices #1. San Bernardino, California: Borgo Press, 1979. 63 p. (The Milford Series: Popular Writers of Today, Vol. 23)

Science Fiction Voices #5. San Bernardino, CA: Borgo, 1981. 64 p.

SF Voices. Baltimore: T-K Graphics, 1976. 123 p.

"Alfred Bester," in: Schweitzer, Darrell, ed. Science Fiction Voices #1. San Bernardino, CA: Borgo Press, 1979. pp. 18-25. (An earlier version appeared in Amazing, June 1976.)

"Algol interview: Gardner Dozois," Algol 13(1):21-23. Winter 1976.

"Algol interview: Isaac Asimov," Algol 14:22-26. Fall/Winter 1977.

"Algol interview: Samuel R. Delany," Algol 13(2):16-20. Summer 1976.

"Amazing Interview: Fritz Leiber," Amazing Science Fiction 50(2): 59-75. September 1976.

"Amazing interview: Manly Wade Wellman," Amazing 27(11): 122-126. March 1981.

Schweitzer, Darrell (Continued)

"Clifford D. Simak," in: Schweitzer, Darrell. Science Fiction Voices #5. San Bernardino, CA: Borgo, 1981. pp. 48-55. (Reprinted from Squonk, Summer 1979)

"Collecting Stephen King," in: Schweitzer, Darrell, ed. Discovering Stephen King. Mercer Island: Starmont, 1985. pp. 153-164.

"Conversation with Algis Budrys," Amazing 28(3): 9-17. November 1981.

"David Gerrold: Tribbles, New Wave, Chtorr, & Beyond," Amazing 59(3):69-78. September 1985.

"Edmond Hamilton and Leigh Brackett," in: Schweitzer, Darrell. Science Fiction Voices #5. San Bernardino, CA: Borgo, 1981. pp. 35-41. (Reprinted from Amazing, Jan. 1978)

"Frank Belknap Long," in: Schweitzer, Darrell. Science Fiction Voices #5. San Bernardino, CA: Borgo, 1981. pp. 41-48. (Reprinted from Nyctalops, #11)

"Frederik Pohl," in: Schweitzer, Darrell, ed. Science Fiction Voices #1. San Bernardino, CA: Borgo Press, 1979. pp. 26-32. (An earlier version appeared in Changes, April 1975.)

"Fritz Leiber," in: Schweitzer, Darrell, ed. Science Fiction Voices #1. San Bernardino, CA: Borgo Press, 1979. pp. 37-43. (An earlier version appeared in Amazing, Sept. 1976.)

"Ganz recht, ein Barbarenstaat; das Gesprach fuhrte Darrell Schweitzer," Science Fiction Times (Germany) 24(5):5-8. May 1982.

"Hal Clement," in: Schweitzer, Darrell, ed. Science Fiction #1. San Bernardino, CA: Borgo Press, 1979. pp. 43-52. (An earlier version appeard in Amazing, March 1977.)

"Interview mit Joan D. Vinge," in: Alpers, H. J., ed. Science Fiction Almanach 1981. Moewig, 1980. pp. 347-362. Tr. of "An Interview with Joan D. Vinge," Science Fiction Review 30:8-12. Mar./Apr. 1979.

"Interview with A. Bertram Chandler," Amazing 56(5): 75-81. March 1983.

"Interview with Alexei & Cory Panshin," Thrust 13:33-35. Fall 1979.

"Interview with Clifford D. Simak," Amazing 27(6):16-22. February 1980.

"Interview with Fred Saberhagen," Thrust 12:6-9. Summer 1979.

"Interview with George R. R. Martin, An," Science Fiction Review 5(2):3-26. 1976.

"Interview with George Scithers," Science Fiction Review 25:11-13. May 1978.

"Interview with Joan D. Vinge, An," Science Fiction Review 30:8-12. March/April 1979.

"Interview with Joe Haldeman, An," Science Fiction Review 20:26-30. February 1977.

"Interview With Julian May," in: May, Julian. A Pliocene Companion. Boston: Houghton, 1984. pp. 197-207. (Reprinted from Science Fiction Review, 1984)

"Interview with Lester Del Rey, An," Science Fiction Review 18:6-10. August 1976.

"Interview with Manly Wade Wellman," Amazing 27(11): 122-126. March 1981.

"Interview with R. A. Lafferty," Amazing 57(3): 75-82. September 1983.

"Interview with Ron Goulart," Amazing 27(8): 12-19. August 1980.

"Interview with Theodore Sturgeon, An," Science Fiction Review 20:6-13. February 1977. Also in: Schweitzer, Darrell. Science Fiction Voices #1. San Bernardino, CA: Borgo, 1979. pp. 4-18.

"Interview With Thomas Disch," Thrust 19: 15-18. Winter/Spring 1983.

"Interview with Wilson Tucker," Amazing 27(7): 14-18. May 1980.

"Interview with: L. Sprague de Camp, An," by Darrell Schweitzer and R. E. Geis. Science Fiction Review 4(4):11-14. 1975.

"Interview: C. J. Cherryh," Thrust 11:29-31. Fall 1978.

"Interview: Ramsey Campbell," Fantasy Newsletter 3(4):15-20. April 1980.

"Interview: A Conversation With Charles L. Grant," Amazing 28(6): 16-22. June 1982.

"Interview: Dennis Etchison," Fantasy Newsletter 4(3): 16-19, 30. March 1981.

"Interview: Gene Wolfe," Fantasy Newsletter 5(6): 8-9, 37. July 1982.

"Interview: Gregory Benford," Eternity Science Fiction 1(2): 22-25. 1980.

"Interview: James White," Science Fiction Review 11(2): 8-12. May 1982.

"Interview: Julian May," Science Fiction Review 13(3): 33-36. August 1984.

"Interview: Roger Zelazny: From Myth to Science Fiction," Amazing 58(2): 41-47. July 1984.

"Interview: Somtow Sucharitkul," Thrust 18: 20-24. Winter/Spring 1982.

Schweitzer, Darrell (Continued)

"Interview: Tanith Lee," _Fantasy Newsletter_ 4(11): 12-15. November 1981.

"Interview: Terry Carr," _Starship_ 20(1): 17-20. Winter 1983/84.

"Introduction," in: Schweitzer, Darrell, ed. _Discovering Stephen King_. Mercer Island: Starmont, 1985. pp. 5-8.

"Isaac Asimov," in: Schweitzer, Darrell. _Science Fiction Voices #5_. San Bernardino, CA: Borgo, 1981. pp. 7-14. (Reprinted from _Algol_, Winter 1977)

"Jack Williamson," in: Schweitzer, Darrell. _Science Fiction Voices #5_. San Bernardino, CA: Borgo, 1981. pp. 60-64. (Reprinted from _Starwind_, v. 1, no. 2, 1976)

"James Gunn," in: Schweitzer, Darrell, ed. _Science Fiction Voices #1_. San Bernardino, CA: Borgo Press, 1979. pp. 32-36. (An earlier version appeared in _The Drummer_, October 22, 1974.)

"Jane Yolen: The Pornography of Innocence, An Interview," _Fantasy Newsletter_ 6(8): 12-13, 38. September 1983.

"Karl Edward Wagner and the Haunted Hills (and Kudzu)," in: Schweitzer, Darrell, ed. _Discovering Modern Horror Fiction I_. Mercer Island: Starmont, 1985. pp. 86-91.

"Keeper of the flame," _Algol_ 15(1):22-27. Winter 1977/1978.

"L. Sprague de Camp," in: Schweitzer, Darrell, ed. _Science Fiction Voices #1_. San Bernardino, CA: Borgo Press, 1979. pp. 53-63. (An earlier version appeared in _Squonk_, Summer 1979.)

"Lester del Rey," in: Schweitzer, Darrell. _Science Fiction Voices #5_. San Bernardino, CA: Borgo, 1981. pp. 26-35. (Reprinted from _Science Fiction Review_, #18)

"Lin Carter," in: Schweitzer, Darrell. _Science Fiction Voices #5_. San Bernardino, CA: Borgo, 1981. pp. 14-26. (Reprinted from _Fantastic_, February 1977.)

"Lord Dunsany: grand master of wonder," _The Eildon Tree_ 1(1):4-7. 1974.

"Michael Blaine: TZ's new editor seeks eclectic image," _Fantasy Review_ 8(7): 11-12, 33. July 1985.

"Novels of Lord Dunsany, Part 2," _Mythlore_ 7(4): 39-41. Winter 1981.

"Novels of Lord Dunsany," _Mythlore_ 7(3): 39-42. Autumn 1980.

"On Science Fiction Writing Workshops," _Isaac Asimov's Science Fiction Magazine_ 5(3): 101-108. March 16, 1981.

"Philip Jose Farmer: Riverworld, God and Insect Lover," _Amazing_ 58(4): 70-79. November 1984.

"Prithee, Sirrah, What Dosttou Mean by Archaic Style in Fantasy?" _Science Fiction Review_ 21:27-30. May 1977.

"Realism in fantasy," _Empire for the SF Writer_ 9(3): 6-7. Spring 1985.

"Robert Nathan Checklist," in: Schweitzer, Darrell, ed. _Exploring Fantasy Worlds_. San Bernardino, CA: Borgo, 1985. pp. 94-96.

"Robert Sheckley: An Interview," _Science Fiction Review_ 10(3): 7-9. August 1981.

"Sensible Attire for Fantasy Characters," _Fantasy Newsletter_ 6(1): 35. January 1983.

"SF Novels of William Sloane," _Science Fiction Collector_ 14: 33. May 1981.

"Theodore Sturgeon," in: Schweitzer, Darrell, ed. _Science Fiction Voices #1_. San Bernardino, CA: Borgo Press, 1979. pp. 4-18. (An earlier version appeared in _Science Fiction Review_, 20, Feb. 1977.)

"Vivisector: In Search of a 'Regular" Fantasy Novel; an Experiment in Reading," _Science Fiction Review_ 12(1): 37-41. February 1983.

"Wilson Tucker," in: Schweitzer, Darrell. _Science Fiction Voices #5_. San Bernardino, CA: Borgo, 1981. pp. 55-60. (Reprinted from _Squonk_, Summer 1979)

Schwerter, Werner

"Denksport und himmelszauber. Moglichkeiten und grenzen der science fiction," _Rheinische Post_ No. 257. November 4, 1972.

Schwetman, J. W.

"Russell Hoban's _Riddley Walker_ and the language of the future," _Extrapolation_ 26(3): 212-219. Fall 1985.

Schwonke, Martin

Vom Staatsroman zur Science Fiction: eine Untersuchung uber Geschichte und Funktion der naturwissenschaftlich technischen Utopie. Stuttgart: Enke, 1957. 194 p.

"Einbahnstrabn zum ameisenstaat? Zur kritik der negativen utopie vom totalitaren endzustand," _Atomzeitalter_ 6/8:201-204. 1962.

Schwonke, Martin (Continued)

"Naturwissenschaft und technik im utopischen denken der neuzeit," Futurum 4(3):282-297. 1971. Also in: Barmeyer, Eike, ed. Science fiction: theorie und geschichte. Munchen: Fink, 1972 pp. 57-75.

"Verdorbene schopfung, Die," Atomzeitalter 7:163-165. 1961.

"Vilag kiterjesztse es a modern utopia," Helikon 18(1): 36-42. 1972. (From: Vom Staatsroman zur Science Fiction)

Sciacca, Tom

"James Horner: New Melodies for the Starship Enterprise," Starlog 63: 22-23. October 1982.

"Portrait: Caroline Munro," by P. D. Adomites and Tom Sciacca. Questar 2(3):34-41. June 1980.

"Star Trek: the ultimate voyage," Questar 2(2):56-58. February 1980.

Science Fiction Writers of America

Paranoia and Science Fiction: A Round-Robin Letter Symposium with Alexei Panshin, James Blish and Joanna Russ. Baltimore: SFWA, 1967. 11 p.

Writing and Selling Science Fiction, ed. by C. L. Grant. Cincinnati: Writers Digest, c. 1976. 191 p.

Scigaj, L. M.

"Bettelheim, Castaneda and Zen: The Powers Behind the Force in Star Wars," Extrapolation 22(3): 213-230. Fall 1981.

"Prana and the Presbyterian Fixation: Ecology and Technology in Frank Herbert's Dune Tetralogy," Extrapolation 24(4): 340-355. Winter 1983.

Scithers, George

Conan Grimore, The, ed. by L. S. De Camp and G. H. Scithers. Baltimore: Mirage Press, 1972. 263 p.

Constructing Scientifiction & Fantasy, by John Ashmead, Darrell Schweitzer and George Scithers. Lake Geneva, WI: TSR Hobbies, 1982. 31 p.

On Writing Science Fiction. Philadelphia: Owlswick, 1981. 227 p.

"Will they laugh when you sit down to publish a book?" in: World Science Fiction Convention, 1976. MidAmerican Program Book. Kansas City: MidAmerican, 1976. pp. 159-162.

Scobie, Stephen

"Different mazes: mythology in Samuel R. Delany's The Einstein Intersection," Riverside Quarterly 5(1): 12-18. July 1971.

"Concerning Horses; Concerning Apes," Riverside Quarterly 4(4): 258-262. March 1971.

Scoggin, M. C.

"Science fiction roundup," Horn Book Magazine 31:220-222. June 1955. (not seen)

Scortia, T. N.

"Science fiction as the imaginary experiment," in: Bretnor, Reginald, ed. Science Fiction Today and Tomorrow. New York: Harper, 1974. pp. 135-149.

Scot, Darrin

"Filming The Time Machine," in: Johnson, William, ed. Focus on the Science Fiction Film. Englewood Cliffs, NJ: Prentice Hall, 1972. pp. 118-120.

Scott, A.

"Science fiction best sellers," Instructor 77(7):59, 164. March 1968.

Scott, J. D.

"New books," New Statesman p. 290. September 15, 1951. (Book review)

Scott, J. E.

Bibliography of the Works of Sir Henry Rider Haggard 1856-1925. Takely, Bishop's Stortford, Hertsford, England: Elkin Matthews, 1947. 258 p.

Scott, Jody

"In Memoriam: Theodore Sturgeon," SFWA Bulletin 19(2): 13-14. Summer 1985.

"Lafayette Ronald Hubbard, 1911-1986," SFWA Bulletin 20(1): 30-32. Spring 1986.

Scott, Kelly

"Cocoon: a step up for Steve Guttenberg?" _St. Petersburg Times_ June 21, 1985. in: _NewsBank. Film and Television_. 2:A8. July 1985.

"For Don Ameche, respect for elderly sold him on Cocoon," _St. Petersburg Times_. June 21, 1985. in: _NewsBank. Film and Television_. 2:C4. July 1985.

"Red hot Ron," _St. Petersburg Times_ June 23, 1985. in: _NewsBank. Film and Television_. 5:B12-B14. July 1985.

"You gotta be 98 before you can get in movies," _St. Petersburg Times_ June 21, 1985. in: _NewsBank. Film and Television_. 2:C5-C6. July 1985.

"Zanucks provide family film with all-in-the-family production team," _St. Petersburg Times_ June 21, 1985. in: _NewsBank. Film and Television_. 2:C3. July 1985.

Scott, N. A., Jr.

"Orwell's legacy," in: _George Orwell and Nineteen Eighty-Four_. Washington, DC: Library of Congress, 1985. pp. 104-120.

Scott, R. W.

"Research Libraries of Interest to Fandom (RLIF) 1982," in: Hopkins, Mariane S., ed. _Fandom Directory 1982_. Newport News, VA: Fandom Computer Services, 1982. pp. 60-68.

"Research Libraries of Interest To Fandom (RLIF) 1984," in: Hopkins, Mariane S., ed. _Fandom Directory No. 6, 1984/1985 Edition_. Baltimore, MD: Diamond Distributors, 1984. pp. 47-52.

Scott, Ridley

"Filming of Alien," _American Cinematographer_ 60(8):772-773, 808,842-844. August 1979.

Scott, Roberta

"Catastrophe Fiction, 1870-1914: An Annotated Bibliography of Selected Works in English," by Roberta Scott and Jon Thiem. _Extrapolation_ 24(2): 156-169. Summer 1983.

Scott, Tony

"Romero; an interview," _Cinefantastique_ 2(3):8-13. Winter 1973.

Scott, Vernon

"Fright for the fun of it," _Dallas Morning News. TV Channels_. p. 38. May 28, 1972.

Scott, W. T.

"Parenthesis on Lovecraft as Poet," in: Joshi, S. T., ed. _H. P. Lovecraft: Four Decades of Criticism_. Athens, OH: Ohio University Press, 1980. pp. 211-216.

Scully, M. G.

"Books," _Chronicle of Higher Education_ 7:5. December 18, 1972.

Searles, A. L.

"At Midnight on the 31st of March," in: Magill, Frank N., ed. _Survey of Science Fiction Literature_, Vol. 1. Englewood Cliffs, NJ: Salem Press, 1979. pp. 89-92.

"Ghosts," in: Magill, Frank N., ed. _Survey of Modern Fantasy Literature_, Vol 2. Englewood Cliffs, NJ: Salem Press, Inc., 1983. pp. 612-615.

"Great Victorian Collection, The," in: Magill, Frank N., ed. _Survey of Modern Fantasy Literature_, Vol 2. Englewood Cliffs, NJ: Salem Press, Inc., 1983. pp. 646-648.

"Mightiest Machine, The," in: Magill, Frank N., ed. _Survey of Science Fiction Literature_, Vol. 3. Englewood Cliffs, NJ: Salem Press, 1979. pp. 1396-1400.

"Mr. Limpet," in: Magill, Frank N., ed. _Survey of Modern Fantasy Literature_, Vol 3. Englewood Cliffs, NJ: Salem Press, Inc., 1983. pp. 1044-1046.

"'Plus Ultra': An Unknown Science Fiction Utopia, Part I," _Fantasy Commentator_ 4(2): 51-59. Winter 1979-80.

"'Plus Ultra': An Unknown Science Fiction Utopia, Part II," _Fantasy Commentator_ 4(3): 162-170. Winter 1981.

"'Plus Ultra': An Unknown Science Fiction Utopia, Part IV," _Fantasy Commentator_ 5(1): 44-49. Winter 1983.

"Books on Science-Fiction, 1937-1973: a Critical Evaluation," _Essays in Arts and Sciences_. 9(2): 157-202. August 1980.

"Fantasy in _The Idler_ Magazine: A Bibliography," by W. H. Evans and A. L. Searles. _Fantasy Commentator_ 1(11): 302-304. Summer 1946.

"Forgotten Creators of Ghosts, VI: William Fryer Harvey," _Fantasy Commentator_ 1(11): 276-284. Summer 1946.

Searles, A. L. (Continued)

"Is science overtaking science fiction?"
Fantasy Times 1(12):7-10. June 1946.

"Short fiction of Benet, The," in: Magill,
Frank N., ed. Survey of Modern Fantasy
Literature, Vol 3. Englewood Cliffs, NJ:
Salem Press, Inc., 1983. pp. 1428-1432.

"Short fiction of Benson, The," in: Magill,
Frank N., ed. Survey of Modern Fantasy
Literature, Vol 3. Englewood Cliffs, NJ:
Salem Press, Inc., 1983. pp. 1433-1435.

"Short fiction of Harvey, The," in: Magill,
Frank N., ed. Survey of Modern Fantasy
Literature, Vol 3. Englewood Cliffs, NJ:
Salem Press, Inc., 1983. pp. 1532-1535.

Searles, Baird

Reader's Guide to Fantasy, by Baird Searles,
Beth Meacham, and Michael Franklin. New York:
Facts on File, 1982. 196 p.

Reader's Guide to Science Fiction, A, by
Baird Searles, Martin Last, Beth Meacham and
Michael Franklin. New York: Avon, 1979.
266 p.

Stranger in a Strange Land & Other Works.
Lincoln, Nebraska: Cliffs Notes, 1975. 59 p.

"Confessions of a Tolkien fiend," in: Becker,
Alida, ed. The Tolkien Scrapbook. New
York: Grossett & Dunlap, 1978. pp. 110-119.

"Opening a science fiction shop," SFWA
Bulletin 9(6): 4-6. Summer 1974.

Searles, Jack

"Selling of a Blockbuster," Los Angeles
Herald Examiner October 22, 1982. in:
NewsBank. Film and Television. 48: C11-12.
December 1982.

Searls, David

"Science fiction: will robots marry?"
Technology Review 74(5):8-9. March/April
1972.

Searls, H.

"Astronaut, the novelist and Cadwalder Glotz;
science in fiction," Writer
78(9):24-25,46. September 1965.

Sears, P. B.

"Reflections on science: writing," American
Biology Teacher 34:396-399. October 1972.

Seavey, Ormond

"Introduction," in: Locke, R. A. The Moon
Hoax. Boston: Gregg, 1975. pp. vii-xxxvi.

"Introduction," in: Thomas, Chauncey.
Crystal Button. Boston: Gregg, 1975. pp.
v-xiii.

Secrest, Clark

"'Star Con' '81 Back for Far Out Fun,"
Denver Post Sec. 1, p. 31. June 9, 1981.

See, Lisa

"Onward and Upward with L. Ron Hubbard,"
Publishers Weekly 227(9): 32. March 1, 1985.

Seeber, H. U.

Literarische Utopien von Morus bis Gegenwart,
by K. K. Berghahn and H. U. Seeber.
Koenigstein: Athenaeum, 1983. 308 p.

Seehafer, Klaus

"Theologie in der science fiction: eine
'Begegnung der vierten Art'," Quarber Merkur
19(2):23-37. October 1981.

Seelye, John

"Arrgh. Collected works of Buck Rogers in the
25th century," New Republic 162(8):24-26.
February 21, 1970.

"What the kids are reading," New Republic
163(16):23-26. October 17, 1970.

Sefler, G. F.

"Alternate Linquistic Frameworks:
Communications with Extraterrestrial Beings,"
in: Smith, Nicholas D., ed. Philosophers Look
at Science Fiction. Chicago: Nelson-Hall,
1982. pp. 67-74.

Segal, H. P.

"Appropriate Visions: In Defense of Utopianism
Today," World Future Society. Bulletin
18(2): 24-29. March/April 1984.

"Feminist technological utopia, The: Mary E.
Bradley Lane's Mizora (1890)," Alternative
Futures 4(2/3): 67-72. Spring/Summer 1981.

"Utopia Diversified: 1900-1949," in: Roemer,
Kenneth M., ed. America As Utopia. New York:
Franklin, 1981. pp. 333-346.

Segal, H. P. (Continued)

"Vonnegut's Player Piano: Ambiguous Technological Dystopia," in: Rabkin, Eric S., et. al., eds. No Place Else. Carbondale: Southern Illinois University Press, 1983. pp. 162-181.

"Young west: the psyche of technological utopianism," Extrapolation 19(1):50-58. December 1977.

Segal, J. Z.

Protocols: A Guide to the World of Fanzines. SL: Segal, n.d. 55 p. (an authorized Star Trek Welcommittee Publication)

Understanding Kraith. Pawling, NY: Segal, n.d. 40 p.

Segal, P. D.

Imaginative Literature and the Atomic Bomb. Ph.D. Dissertation, Yeshiva University, 1973. 212 p.

Seidel, K. L.

"Lathe of Heaven, The," in: Magill, Frank N., ed. Survey of Science Fiction Literature, Vol. 3. Englewood Cliffs, NJ: Salem Press, 1979. pp. 1161-1164.

"Picnic on Paradise," in: Magill, Frank N., ed. Survey of Science Fiction Literature, Vol. 4. Englewood Cliffs, NJ: Salem Press, 1979. pp. 1678-1681.

"Woman on the Edge of Time," in: Magill, Frank N., ed. Survey of Science Fiction Literature, Vol. 5. Englewood Cliffs, NJ: Salem Press, 1979. pp. 2488-2491.

Seidenfeld, B. B.

"Erewhon and Erewhon Revisited," in: Magill, Frank N., ed. Survey of Science Fiction Literature, Vol. 2. Englewood Cliffs, NJ: Salem Press, 1979. pp. 729-734.

"Lifted Veil, The," in: Magill, Frank N., ed. Survey of Science Fiction Literature, Vol. 3. Englewood Cliffs, NJ: Salem Press, 1979. pp. 1213-1216.

Seldes, Gilbert

"Review: The Twilight Zone and Alfred Hitchcock Presents," TV Guide 9(45):27. October 29, 1961.

Seligman, Dee

Doris Lessing: An Annotated Bibliography of Criticism. Westport, CT: Greenwood, 1981. 139 p.

Seligson, Tom

"TZ Interview: George Romero," Twilight Zone 1(5): 12-17. August 1981.

Sellach, Brigitte

"Frauen bei Marion Zimmer Bradley," by Uta Enders-Dragaesser and Brigitte Sellach. in: Femistische Utopien: Aufbruch in dei postpatriarchale Gesellschaft, ed. by Barbara Holland-Cunz. Meitingen: Corian Verlag, 1985.

Sellin, Bernard

Life and Works of David Lindsay, The. Cambridge: Cambridge University Press, 1981. 257 p.

Seltzer, Leon

"Dresden and Vonnegut's Creative Testament of Guilt," Journal of American Culture. 4(4): 55-69. Winter 1981.

Semark, D. L.

"C. S. Lewis' Space Trilogy: Metaphysical Theology in Science Fiction/Fantasy. Master's Thesis, Western Michigan University, 1979. 48 p.

Sendaydiego, H. B.

"Metaphysics and science fiction," Journal of the West Virginia Philosophical Society 8/9. Fall 1977. (not seen)

Serafine, Frank

"Sound effects design and synthesis for Tron," American Cinematographer 63(8):807,830-834. August 1982.

"Sound effects for Star Trek: the motion picture, part 1," Audiovisual Product News. 2(9): 88-93. September/October 1980.

"Sound effects for Star Trek: the Motion Picture," Audio Visual Directions 2(10):37-40, 60-62. November/December 1980.

Serling, Carol

"Talking Twilight Zone," Twilight Zone 5(5): 13A-14A. December 1985.

Serres, Michel

Jouvences sur Jules Verne. Paris: Minuit, 1974. 291 p.

"Jules Verne's strange journeys," Yale French Studies 52:174-188. 1975.

Servott, Herman

"Miracle of rare device: Mervyn Peake's Gormenghast trilogy, A," Revue des Langues Vivantes pp. 489-496. 1974.

Sevastakis, Michael

"Cinefantastique," in: Slide, Anthony, ed. International Film, Radio, and Television Journals. Westport, CT: Greenwood, 1985. pp. 47-48.

Severin-Lounsberry, Barbara

"Holden and Alex: a clockwork from the rye?" Four Quarters 22:27-37. 1973.

Sewell, Margaret

"Satellite stimulates science fiction stories," by Margaret Sewell and Martha Irwin. Florida Libraries 8:11. December 1957.

Seymour, Michael

"Out of this world production design," American Cinematographer 60(8):776-777, 804-805,823. August 1979.

Seymour-Smith, Martin

"Two years of science fiction," British Book News pp. 5-7. January 1975.

Shackleton, C. C.

"Give me excess of it, that something snaps," SF Horizons 1:58-62. Spring 1964.

"How are they all on Deneb IV?" SF Horizons 2:61-63. Winter 1965.

Shaftell, O.

"Social content of science fiction," Science and Society 17(2):97-118. Spring 1953.

Shaheen, J. G.

Nuclear War Films. Carbondale: Southern Illinois University Press, 1978. 193 p.

Shalashova, Z. P.

Puteshestiviia, prikliucheniia, fantastika: rekomendatelnyi ukazatel literatury. Moscow: Kniga, 1964. 222 p.

"Mir budushchego v khudozhestvennoi literature," in: Kontury griadushchego. Moskva: Kniga, 1970. pp.107-135.

Shales, Tom

"Creatures the world forgot," Washington Post p. D1,11. September 2, 1974.

"Invasion of the sci-fi writers on the day two worlds collided," Washington Post p. C-1. August 31, 1974.

"We're watching the skies again: sci-fi explores new heights," Washington Post p. H1,3. December 30, 1973.

Shane, A. M.

Life and Works of Evgenij Zamjatin, The. Berkeley: University of California Press, 1968. 302 p.

Shanks, Edward

Edgar Allan Poe. New York: Macmillan, 1937. 176 p.

"Other worlds than ours," New Statesman 35(894):305-306. October 14, 1930.

Shapero, H. M. G.

"Red-Haired Heroes, Brown-Haired Losers," Science Fiction Review 14(1): 33-34. February 1985.

Shapiro, Marc

"Defcon 4 (review)," Cinefantastique 16(1):49. March 1986.

"Tim Burton's Big Adventure," Cinefantastique 16(1):38-39. March 1986.

Sharenov, Evelyn

"Interview: Theodore Sturgeon," Pulpsmith 3(2): 5-13. Summer 1983.

Sharp, Roberta

"What Dreams May Come," in: Magill, Frank N., ed. Survey of Modern Fantasy Literature, Vol 5. Englewood Cliffs, NJ: Salem Press, Inc., 1983. pp. 2112-2114.

Sharp, Roberta (Continued)

"Short fiction of Matheson, The," in: Magill, Frank N., ed. Survey of Modern Fantasy Literature, Vol 4. Englewood Cliffs, NJ: Salem Press, Inc., 1983. pp. 1645-1651.

Sharrett, Christopher

"Hero as pastiche: myth, male, fantasy and simulacra in 'Mad Max' and 'The Road Warrior'," Journal of Popular Film and Television 13(2): 80-91. Summer 1985.

Shatnoff, Judith

"(Reviews of) Planet of the Apes and 2001; a space odyssey," Film Quarterly 22:56-62. Fall 1968.

"Gorilla to remember, A," Film Quarterly 22(1):56-62. Autumn 1968.

Shatzkin, Roger

"Big Sleep, The," Take One 2: 29. January 1979.

Shaw, Bob

"BOSH: Shaw shorts, 2," Locus No. 26:11-12. April 19, 1969.

"BOSH: Shaw shorts," Locus No. 25:3-4. April 10, 1969.

"Extraordinary behavior of ordinary materials," Vector 64: 21-23. March/April 1973.

"My life and space/times: Bob Shaw at Aussiecon Two," Matrix No. 61: 5-8. October/November 1985.

"Profession of science fiction: xi: escape to infinity," Foundation 10:13-19. June 1976.

"Seducers With Staples," Focus (BSFA) 10: 11. February 1985.

"Time travellers among us," Vector 70: 5-9. Autumn, 1975.

"Value of bad SF," Vector 69: 15-21. Summer 1975.

Shaw, L. T.

"Whence asunder, The," Fantasy Times No. 254:29-31. September (1) 1956.

Shay, Don

"Bladerunner: 2020 Foresight," Cinefex 9: 4-71. July 1982.

"Clash of the (Foot-Tall) Titans," Cinefex 5: 20-41. July 1981.

"Close Encounters at future general; interviews," Cinefantastique 7(3/4):30-57,80-95. Fall 1978.

"Close Encounters of the Third Kind; interviews," Cinefantastique 7(3/4):4-20. Fall 1978.

"Close Encounters' extraterrestrials," Cinefantastique 7:4-19. Fall 1978.

"Creating an Alien Ambience," Cinefex 1: 34-71. March 1980.

"Creating the wonder of Cocoon," Cinefex No. 24:4-37. November 1985.

"David Dryer: Never Say Never Again," Cinefex No. 15:4-27. January 1984.

"Filming The Omen," Cinefantastique 5(3):40-47. Winter 1976.

"Into the V'ger Maw with Douglas Trumbull," Cinefex 1: 4-33. March 1980.

"Jupiter revisited: The Odyssey of 2010," by Adam Eisenberg and Don Shay. Cinefex No. 20:4-67. January 1985.

"Microcosmic World of Ken Middleham," Cinefex 3: 58-71. December 1980.

"Of Ice Planets, Bog Planets, and Cities in the Sky," Cinefex 2: 4-23. August 1980.

"Outland," Cinefex 4: 4-31. April 1981.

"Photographs and memories," Cinefex No. 15:50-67. January 1984.

"Richard Donner on Superman," Cinefantastique 8(4):13-17. Summer 1979.

"Shadow and substance," by Don Shay and Paul Sammon. Cinefex No. 14:50-71. October 1983.

"Shape of Dune," by Janine Pourroy and Don Shay. Cinefex No. 21:24-71. April 1985.

"Special Visual Effects: Robert Swarthe," Cinefex 11: 50-71. January 1983.

"Star Trek: The Motion Picture; interview," Cinefantastique 8(2/3):88-95. Spring 1979.

"Star Trekking at Apogee with John Dykstra," Cinefex 2: 50-71. August 1980.

"Steven Spielberg on Close Encounters," Cinefantastique 7(3/4):21-28. Fall 1978.

"Tripping through Ellison wonderland," Cinefantastique 5(1):14-23. Spring 1976.

"Willis O'Brien: Creator of the Impossible," Cinefex 7: 5-70. January 1982.

Shay, Don (Continued)

"Wrath of God...and Other Illusions,"
Cinefex 6: 62-79. October 1981.

Shayon, R. L.

"Interplanetary Spock; Star Trek," Saturday
Review 50(24):46. June 17, 1967.

Shea, J. V.

H. P. Lovecraft: The House and the Shadows.
West Warrick, RI: Necronomicon, 1982. 20 p.

"On the Literary Influences Which Shaped
Lovecraft's Work," in: Joshi, S. T., ed. H.
P. Lovecraft: Four Decades of Criticism.
Athens, OH: Ohio University Press, 1980.
pp. 113-139.

Shearman, Bill

"Attendance at Vul-Con I proves Star Trek
favor," New Orleans Times Picayune Sec. 4,
p. 8. June 22, 1973.

Sheckley, Robert

Futuropolis. New York: A&W Visual Library,
1978. 155 p.

"Lost and parallel worlds," in: Ash, Brian,
ed. Visual Encyclopedia of Science Fiction.
New York: Harmony, 1977. pp. 137-143.

"On working method," Starship 16(3):35-38.
Summer 1979.

"Search for the marvellous, The," in:
Nicholls, Peter, ed. Science Fiction at
Large. New York: Harper, 1976. pp. 185-198.

Sheed, Wilfrid

"Good word: writer as something else, The,"
New York Times Book Review p. 2. March 4,
1973.

"Now generation knew him when, The," Life
67(11):64-66,69. September 12, 1969.

Sheffield, Charles

"Easiest way to become a great SF writer, The,"
Thrust 10:13-14. Spring 1978.

"From the Pictured Urn," Thrust 17: 18-21.
Summer 1981.

"From the pictured urn: writing SF,"
Thrust 13:23-25,50. Fall 1979.

"From the Pictured Urn: Carl Sagan," Thrust
19: 19-21, 38. Winter/Spring 1983.

Sheinia, M.

"Space Odyssey-Documentary," by M. Ryabova and
M. Sheinia. Soviet Film 79(9):11- . 1979.

Shell, R. L.

"Shall the meek inherit the Earth?" in: The
Future in Peril: 1984 and the Anti-Utopians.
College Station: Honors Program, Texas A&M
University, [1985]. pp. 24-27.

Shelomentseva, M.

"Malen'kii chitatel' nauchno-khudozhestvennoi
knigi," Bibliotekar No. 11:40-44. 1972.

Shelton, Robert

"Mars-Begotton Men of Olaf Stapledon and H. G.
Wells," Science-Fiction Studies 11(1):
1-14. March 1984.

Shenker, Israel

"Kurt Vonnegut, Jr., lights comic path of
despair," New York Times sec. 1, p. 41.
March 21, 1969.

"Michael Crichton (rhymes with frighten),"
New York Times Book Review pp. 5,40. June
8, 1969.

Shepard, Lucius

"Viewpoint: How I Spent My Summer Vacation,"
Isaac Asimov's Science Fiction Magazine
9(2): 30-42. February 1985.

Shepherd, L. J.

"Tape to film transforming for The Invisible
Man," American Cinematographer
56(7):778-779, 846-847. July 1975.

Sheppard, R. Z.

"Future Grok," Time 97(13):86,88,90.
March 29, 1971.

Sher, Lanny

"Creating the electronic special effects for
The Invisible Man," American
Cinematographer 56(7):782-783,852. July 1975.

Sherard, R. H.

"Jules Verne at Home: His Own Account of His
Life and Work," McClure's Magazine 2(2):
115-124. January 1894.

Sherbert, Linda

"Avalon's 'Flowers for Algernon' Poignant Without Blooming Fully," _Atlanta Journal_. September 7, 1984. in: _NewsBank. Performing Arts_ PER 36:E2. 1984/1985.

Shibano, Takumi

"History of Japanese SF Fandom, part 2: the rise and fall of the SF boom in Japan," _Maneki-Neko_ No. 3:4-9. August 1967.

"History of Japanese SF fandom," _Maneki-Neko_ No. 2:3-8. May 1967.

"News from Japan," _Science Fiction Times_ No. 462:1,3. January 1969.

"Report on Japanese science fiction," _Worlds of If_ 18:29-33. October 1968.

Shibawov, V.

"O nauchnoi fantastike," _Bibliotekar_ pp. 20-26. August 1958.

Shideler, M. M.

"Excerpts from a letter about Charles Williams," _Mythlore_ 2(2):6. Autumn 1970.

Shiflett, R. C.

"If the Stars Are Gods," in: Magill, Frank N., ed. _Survey of Science Fiction Literature_, Vol. 2. Englewood Cliffs, NJ: Salem Press, 1979. pp. 1004-1007.

"Stochastic Man, The," in: Magill, Frank N., ed. _Survey of Science Fiction Literature_, Vol. 5. Englewood Cliffs, NJ: Salem Press, 1979. pp. 2179-2183.

Shine, Jean

Bibliography of the Published Works of John D. MacDonald With Selected Biographical Materials and Critical Essays, by Walter Shine and Jean Shine. Gainesville: University of Florida, Patrons of the Libraries, 1980. 209 p.

Shine, Walter

Bibliography of the Published Works of John D. MacDonald With Selected Biographical Materials and Critical Essays, by Walter Shine and Jean Shine. Gainesville: University of Florida, Patrons of the Libraries, 1980. 209 p.

Shipler, D. K.

"Vonnegut's _Slaughterhouse-Five_ staged in Moscow," _New York Times_ p. 40. January 13, 1976.

Shipman, G. R.

"How to talk to a Martian," _Astounding Science Fiction_ 52(2):112-120. October 1953.

Shippey, T. A.

Road to Middle-Earth. London: Allen, 1982. 252 p.

"All Hallow's Eve," in: Magill, Frank N., ed. _Survey of Modern Fantasy Literature_, Vol 1. Englewood Cliffs, NJ: Salem Press, Inc., 1983. pp. 17-21.

"Alteration, The," in: Magill, Frank N., ed. _Survey of Science Fiction Literature_, Vol. 1. Englewood Cliffs, NJ: Salem Press, 1979. pp. 43-47.

"Brave New World," in: Magill, Frank N., ed. _Survey of Science Fiction Literature_, Vol. 1. Englewood Cliffs, NJ: Salem Press, 1979. pp. 247-253.

"Charwoman's Shadow, The," in: Magill, Frank N., ed. _Survey of Modern Fantasy Literature_, Vol 1. Englewood Cliffs, NJ: Salem Press, Inc., 1983. pp. 232-235.

"Chronicles of Narnia, The," in: Magill, Frank N., ed. _Survey of Modern Fantasy Literature_, Vol 1. Englewood Cliffs, NJ: Salem Press, Inc., 1983. pp. 248-255.

"Jungle Books, The," in: Magill, Frank N., ed. _Survey of Modern Fantasy Literature_, Vol 2. Englewood Cliffs, NJ: Salem Press, Inc., 1983. pp. 822-826.

"Magician out of Manchuria, The," in: Magill, Frank N., ed. _Survey of Modern Fantasy Literature_, Vol 2. Englewood Cliffs, NJ: Salem Press, Inc., 1983. pp. 948-950.

"Make Room! Make Room!," in: Magill, Frank N., ed. _Survey of Science Fiction Literature_, Vol. 3. Englewood Cliffs, NJ: Salem Press, 1979. pp. 1312-1316.

"No Blade of Grass," in: Magill, Frank N., ed. _Survey of Science Fiction Literature_, Vol. 4. Englewood Cliffs, NJ: Salem Press, 1979. pp. 1541-1544.

"Odd John: A Story Between Jest and Earnest," in: Magill, Frank N., ed. _Survey of Science Fiction Literature_, Vol. 4. Englewood Cliffs, NJ: Salem Press, 1979. pp. 1583-1587.

Shippey, T. A. (Continued)

"Once and Future King," in: Magill, Frank N., ed. _Survey of Modern Fantasy Literature_, Vol 3. Englewood Cliffs, NJ: Salem Press, Inc., 1983. pp. 1149-1157.

"_Peregrine Primus_ and _Peregrine Secundus_," in: Magill, Frank N., ed. _Survey of Modern Fantasy Literature_, Vol 3. Englewood Cliffs, NJ: Salem Press, Inc., 1983. pp. 1224-1226.

"_Tritonian Ring, The_," in: Magill, Frank N., ed. _Survey of Modern Fantasy Literature_, Vol 4. Englewood Cliffs, NJ: Salem Press, Inc., 1983. pp. 1972-1974.

"_War in the Air, The_," in: Magill, Frank N., ed. _Survey of Science Fiction Literature_, Vol. 5. Englewood Cliffs, NJ: Salem Press, 1979. pp. 2407-2410.

"_Water of the Wondrous Isles, The_," in: Magill, Frank N., ed. _Survey of Modern Fantasy Literature_, Vol 5. Englewood Cliffs, NJ: Salem Press, Inc., 1983. pp. 2069-2073.

"_Watership Down_," in: Magill, Frank N., ed. _Survey of Modern Fantasy Literature_, Vol 5. Englewood Cliffs, NJ: Salem Press, Inc., 1983. pp. 2079-2083.

"Cold war in science fiction, 1940-1960, The," in: Parrinder, Patrick, ed. _Science Fiction: A Critical Guide_. New York: Longman, 1979. pp. 90-109.

"Creation from philology in The Lord of the Rings," in: Salu, M. & R. T. Farrell, eds. _J. R. R. Tolkien: Scholar and Storyteller. Essays in Memoriam._ Ithaca, NY: Cornell University Press, 1979. pp. 286-316.

"Golden bough and the incorporations of magic in science fiction, The," _Foundation_ 11/12:119-134. March 1977.

"Histoire dans la science fiction, L'," _Change_ (Paris) 40: 14-20. 1981.

"Magic art and the evolution of words: Ursula K. Le Guin's Earthsea trilogy, The," _Mosaic_ 10(2):147-149. Winter 1977.

"Magic art and the evolution of words: The Earthsea Trilogy," in: _Ursula K. Le Guin_, ed. by Harold Bloom. New York: Chelsea House, 1986. pp. 99-118.

"Science fiction and the idea of history," _Foundation_ 4:4-19. July 1973.

"Science fiction et l'idee d'histoire," _Change_ (Paris) 40: 68-84. 1981.

"Short Fiction of Avram Davidson, The," in: Magill, Frank N., ed. _Survey of Science Fiction Literature_, Vol. 4. Englewood Cliffs, NJ: Salem Press, 1979. pp. 1930-1933.

"Short fiction of Kipling, The," in: Magill, Frank N., ed. _Survey of Modern Fantasy Literature_, Vol 4. Englewood Cliffs, NJ: Salem Press, Inc., 1983. pp. 1586-1588.

"Short Fiction of Rudyard Kipling, The," in: Magill, Frank N., ed. _Survey of Science Fiction Literature_, Vol. 5. Englewood Cliffs, NJ: Salem Press, 1979. pp. 2051-2055.

"Traps of time and space," _Futures_ 9(3):234-240. June 1977.

Shirley, John

"Alien in L. A., An," _Science Fiction Review_ 14(3): 46-47. August 1985.

"Final paranoid critical statement," _Thrust_ 16: 22-24. Fall 1980.

"Love's attacks," _Empire: For the SF Writer_ 4(1): 5-6. July 1978.

"Refuge for the Indolent," _Patchin Review_ 1: 21-23. July 1981.

Shively, J. R.

Fantasy in the Fiction of H. G. Wells. Ph.D. Dissertation, University of Nebraska, 1955. 168 p.

Shober, J. L.

Aldous Huxley: a Bibliography, 1916-1959, by C. J. Eschelbach and J. L. Shober. Berkeley: University of California Press, 1961. 150 p.

Shor, I. N.

Vonnegut's Art of Inquiry. Ph.D. Dissertation, University of Wisconsin, 1971. 288 p.

Shorter, Elliot

"TAFF jottings," _Locus_ No. 66:5-6. October 29, 1970.

Showalter, D. E.

"Heinlein's starship troopers: an exercise in rehabilitation," _Extrapolation_ 16(2):113-124. May 1975.

Shperlin, K. A.

"O zhanre romanov Kurta Vonneguta," _Problemy teorii romana i rasskaza_ Riga: Latviiskii gosudarstvennyi universitet im. Stuchki, pp. 119-134. 1972.

Shreffler, P. A.

H. P. Lovecraft Companion, The. Westport, Connecticut: Greenwood Press, 1977. 199 p.

"Interview with Philip Jose Farmer," Xenophile No. 42:7-8,20. September/October 1979.

Shreve, G. M.

"Jaded eternals: immortality and imperfection in Jack Vance's To Live Forever," in: Yoke, C. B. and Hassler, D. M., eds. Death and the Serpent. Westport, CT: Greenwood, 1985. pp. 185-192.

Shroyer, Frederick

"Journey in Other Worlds, A," in: Magill, Frank N., ed. Survey of Science Fiction Literature, Vol. 3. Englewood Cliffs, NJ: Salem Press, 1979. pp. 1098-1101.

"Lieut. Gullivar Jones: His Vacation," in: Magill, Frank N., ed. Survey of Science Fiction Literature, Vol. 3. Englewood Cliffs, NJ: Salem Press, 1979. pp. 1209-1212.

"C. L. Moore and Henry Kuttner," in: Bleiler, E. F., ed. Science Fiction Writers. New York: Scribners, 1982. pp. 161-167.

Shrum, Edison

"Jules Verne: father of science fiction," Hobbies 82(7):152. September 1977.

Shuldiner, Herbert

"How they filmed 2001: A Space Odyssey," Popular Science Monthly 192(6):62-67,184-186. June 1968.

Shuldner, K. L.

"On Dhalgren and Triton," Riverside Quarterly 7(1):5-14. March 1980.

Shurter, R. L.

"Utopian novel in America, 1888-1900, The," South Atlantic Quarterly 34:137-144. April 1935.

Shwartz, Susan

"Andre Norton: Beyond the Siege Perilous," in: Shwartz, Susan, ed. Moonsinger's Friends. New York: Bluejay, 1985. pp. 1-13.

"Marion Zimmer Bradley's Ethic of Freedom," in: Staicar, Tom, ed. The Feminine Eye. New York: Ungar, 1982. pp. 73-88.

"Other Worlds," Fantasy Newsletter 4(1): 12-15. January 1981.

"Women and Science Fiction," New York Times Book Review p. 11, 26-27. May 2, 1982.

Sibley, A. M.

Charles Williams. Boston: Twayne, 1982. 160 p.

Sibley, Brian

"Man from the October country: Bradbury at sixty," Fantasy Media 2(3): 8-9. August/September 1980.

"Through a darkling glass: an appreciation of Mervyn Peake's illustrations to Alice," The Mervyn Peake Review 6:25-29;7:26-29. 1978.

Siciliano, S. J.

Fictional Universe in Four Science Fiction Novels. Ph.D. Dissertation, University of Iowa, 1975. 234 p.

Siclari, Joe

"Science Fiction Fandom: a History of an Unusual Hobby," in: Tymn, Marshall B., ed. The Science Fiction Reference Book. Mercer Island, WA: Starmont House, 1981. pp. 87-129.

Siclier, J.

Images de la science fiction, by J. Siclier and S. A. Labarthe. Paris: Cerf, 1958. 137 p.

Sidney-Fryer, Donald

Emperor of Dreams: A Clark Ashton Smith Bibliogaphy. West Kingston, Rhode Island: Donald M. Grant, 1978. 303 p.

Last of the Great Romantic Poets, The. Albuquerque: Silver Scarab Press, 1973. 28 p.

"Robert E. Howard: frontiersman of letters," in: Don Herron, ed. Dark Barbarian. Westport, CT: Greenwood, 1984. pp. 17-22.

Siegel, Mark

"Fantastic TV: A Subversive Art?" Fantasy Review 6(1): 31-33. January 1983.

James Tiptree, Jr.. Mercer Island, WA: Starmont, 1985. 89 p.

"Breast, The," in: Magill, Frank N., ed. Survey of Modern Fantasy Literature, Vol 1. Englewood Cliffs, NJ: Salem Press, Inc., 1983. pp. 169-172.

Siegel, Mark (Continued)

"My Life in the Bush of Ghosts," in:
Magill, Frank N., ed. Survey of Modern
Fantasy Literature, Vol 3. Englewood Cliffs,
NJ: Salem Press, Inc., 1983. pp. 1071-1074.

"Rhinoceros," in: Magill, Frank N., ed.
Survey of Modern Fantasy Literature, Vol 3.
Englewood Cliffs, NJ: Salem Press, Inc., 1983.
pp. 1317-1319.

"Trout Fishing in America," in: Magill,
Frank N., ed. Survey of Modern Fantasy
Literature, Vol 4. Englewood Cliffs, NJ:
Salem Press, Inc., 1983. pp. 1979-1982.

"Double souled man: immortality and
transcendence in the fiction of James Tiptree,
jr.," in: Yoke, C. B. and Hassler, D. M.,
eds. Death and the Serpent. Westport, CT:
Greenwood, 1985. pp. 163-174

"Foreigner as alien in Japanese science
fantasy," Science Fiction Studies 12(3):
252-263. November 1985.

"Rocky Horror Picture Show: More Than a Lip
Service," Science-Fiction Studies 7(3):
305-312. November 1980.

"Science fiction and fantasy TV," in: Rose, B.
G., ed. TV Genres. Westport, CT:
Greenwood, 1985. pp. 91-106.

"Science-Fiction Characterization and TV's
Battle for the Stars," Science-Fiction
Studies 7(3): 270-277. November 1980.

"Short fiction of Gogol, The," in: Magill,
Frank N., ed. Survey of Modern Fantasy
Literature, Vol 3. Englewood Cliffs, NJ:
Salem Press, Inc., 1983. pp. 1520-1526.

"Short fiction of Singer, The," in: Magill,
Frank N., ed. Survey of Modern Fantasy
Literature, Vol 4. Englewood Cliffs, NJ:
Salem Press, Inc., 1983. pp. 1686-1691.

"Thomas Pynchon and the Science Fiction
Controversy," Pynchon Notes 7: 38-42.
October 1981.

"Toward an Aesthetics of Science Fiction
Television," Extrapolation 25(1): 60-75.
Spring 1984.

Sieger, James

"Ghost Stories: index by author, part 1,"
ERB-dom No. 30:39. January 1970.

"Ghost Stories: index by author, part 2,"
ERB-dom No. 31:10. February 1970.

"Ghost Stories: index by author, part 3,"
ERB-dom No. 32:7-10. March 1970.

"Ghost Stories: index by author, part 4,"
ERB-dom No. 33:11-18. April 1970.

"Ghost Stories: index by author, part 5,"
ERB-dom No. 34:16-17. May 1970.

Siemon, Frederick

Science Fiction Story Index: 1950-1968.
Chicago: American Library Association, 1971.
275 p.

Siewierski, Jerzy

"Antologia Lemowych mozliwosci," Nowe
Ksiazki No. 15. 1963.

"Basnie o Trurlu i Klapaucjuszu," Nowe
Ksiazki No. 16. 1965.

"Fantastyka, groteska, satyra," Nowe Ksiazki
No. 21: 1298-1299. 1961.

"Jeden ze swiatow Lema," Nowe Ksiazki No.
15. 1965.

"Przygody w pustym wszechswiecie," Nowe
Ksiazki No. 9:531-532. 1959.

Sigman, Joseph

"Death's ecstacies: transformation and rebirth
in George MacDonald's Phantasies," English
Studies in Canada 2:203-226. 1976.

Silbersack, John

"Introduction," in: Leiber, Fritz. The
Change War. Boston: Gregg, 1978. pp. vii-xvi.

Silhol, Robert

"Fantastique existe-t-il?" Recherches
Anglaises et Americaines. 6:14-21. 1973.

Silver, Carole

Romance of William Morris. Athens, OH: Ohio
University Press, 1983. 233 p.

Silverberg, Robert

Drug Themes in Science Fiction. Rockville,
Maryland: National Institute on Drug Abuse,
1974. 55 p.

Mirror of Infinity: A Critic's Anthology,
The. New York: Harper, 1970. 324 p.

"Amazing, astounding journeys into the unknown
and back," Horizon 16(3):47-48. Summer 1974.

"Beyond reality's barriers: new dimensions,"
by Robert Silverberg and Charles Elkins. in:
Warrick, Patricia, ed. Science Fiction:
Contemporary Mythology. New York: Harper,
1978. pp. 92-100.

Silverberg, Robert (Continued)

"Characterization in science fiction,"
<u>Fantastic</u> 18(4):4-5,103. April 1969.

"Eyes of the overworld and The Dying Earth,"
in: Underwood, Tim, and Miller, Chuck, eds.
<u>Jack Vance</u>. New York: Taplinger, 1980. pp.
117-130.

"How we work: Robert Silverberg," in:
Aldiss, Brian W. & Harry Harrison, eds.
<u>Hell's Cartographers: Some Personal Histories
of Science Fiction Writers</u>. London:
Weidenfeld, 1975. pp. 213-217.

"Introduction to 'Sundance'," in: Wilson,
Robin Scott, ed. <u>Those Who Can: A Science
Fiction Reader</u>. New York: Mentor/New
American Library, 1973. pp. 169-175.

"Introduction," in: Russ, Joanna. <u>And
Chaos Died</u>. Boston: Gregg, 1978. pp. v-xi.

"Its no longer for outcasts and weirdos,"
<u>San Francisco Bay Guardian</u> 12(14):9-10.
January 19, 1978.

"Jet propelled bird-bath, The," in: Porter,
Andrew, ed. <u>The Book of Ellison</u>. New York:
Algol Press, 1978. pp. 23-27. Reprinted from
<u>Algol</u>. March 1967.

"John W. Campbell," <u>Locus</u> No. 90:6. July
12, 1971.

"Lou Tabakow: an appreciation," <u>Locus</u>
14(5):19. June 1981.

"Opinion," <u>Amazing</u> 59(3): 4-7. September
1985.

"Opinion: publishing," <u>Galileo</u>
11/12:138-139. 1979.

"Opinion; on writing," <u>Amazing</u> 28(1): 6-7.
July 1981.

"Profession of science fiction: ix: sounding
brass, tinkling cymbal, The," <u>Foundation</u>
7/8:6-37. March 1975.

"Silverberg papers, 2," <u>Algol</u> 17(2):25-30.
Spring 1980.

"Silverberg papers, 3," <u>Starship</u>
17(3):15-17. Summer 1980.

"Silverberg Papers, 4," <u>Starship</u> 19(1):
33-37. November 1982.

"Silverberg Papers, 5," <u>Starship</u> 20(1):
31-34. Winter 1983/84.

"Silverberg papers, 6: word processing,"
<u>Science Fiction Chronicle</u> 5(7):26,28. April
1984.

"Silverberg papers," <u>Starship</u> 37:17-21.
Winter 1979/1980.

"Silverberg Papers: Incorporation," <u>Science
Fiction Chronicle</u> 6(4): 22-24. January 1985.

"Silverberg Papers: September 1985," <u>Science
Fiction Chronicle</u> 6(12): 41-43. September
1985.

"Silverberg that was, The," <u>Science Fiction
Review</u> 6:8-16. November 1977.

"Sounding brass, tinkling cymbal," in:
Aldiss, B. W., ed. <u>Hell's Cartographers:
Some Personal Histories of Science Fiction
Writers</u>. London: Weidenfeld, 1975. pp.
7-45. Also in: <u>Algol</u> 13(1):7-18. 1976.

"Tax breaks for writers," <u>Empire: For the SF
Writer</u> 3(4): 20. April 1978.

"Theodore Sturgeon: An Appreciation, 3,"
<u>Locus</u> 18(6): 50. June 1985.

"Thirty Years of Writing," <u>Science Fiction
Chronicle</u> 6(8): 31. May 1985.

Silverman, S. M.

"Hollywood-Hype Brain Surgery for Battered,
Bruised Buckaroo Banzai," <u>New York Post</u>
October 1, 1984. in: <u>NewsBank. Film and
Television</u> FTV 32:A11. 1984/1985.

"One man's fascination catches 'Fire'," <u>New
York Post</u> February 9, 1982. in: <u>NewsBank.
Film and Television</u>. 92:B1. 1981/1982.

Silverstein, Cathy

"Joanna Russ: author professor," <u>Cthulhu
Calls</u> 3(3):13-16. January 1976.

Silvestri, Armando

"<u>Oltre is cielo</u>, il femomeno," <u>Robot</u> No.
22. 1978.

Simak, C. D.

"Face of science fiction," <u>Minnesota
Libraries</u> 17(7):197-201. September 1953.

"Jenkins would be proud," <u>Algol</u>
14(3):9-10. Summer/Fall 1977.

"John W. Campbell," <u>Locus</u> No. 90:9. July
12, 1971.

"Room enough for all of us," <u>Extrapolation</u>
13(2):102-105. May 1972.

Simecka, Milan

"World with Utopias or without them?" in:
<u>Utopias</u>, ed. by Peter Alexander and Roger
Gill. London: Duckworth, 1984. pp. 169-178.

Simmonds, E. M.

"Worlds to conquer; case for science fiction," Times Educational Supplement 2214:1376. October 25, 1957.

Simms, Norman

"M. K. Joseph and time travel," Pacific Quarterly Moana 4(3):350-351. July 1979.

Simon, Erik

"Letter, on Stanislaw Lem," Foundation 33: 100-101. Spring 1985.

"New wine in old bottles: SF in the German Democratic Republic," Foundation 34: 36-49. Autumn 1985.

Simon, Frank

"Plot for an epoch," Saturday Review of Literature 32:23. December 1949. (Letter)

Simpson, D. J.

"Analogists," Assistant Librarian 53(12):233-238. December 1960.

Simpson, E.

"Outlook tower: science fiction," Horn Book 42:215-217. April 1966. (Book reviews)

Simukov, V.

"Stranstviia Billi Pilgrim," Trud 58:4. March 10, 1976.

Sinclair, Karen

"Solitary being: the hero as anthropologist," in: De Bolt, Joe, ed. Ursula K. Le Guin: Voyager to Inner Lands and to Outer Space. Port Washington, New York: Kennikat, 1979. pp. 50-65.

Singh, Kirpal

Stellar Guage: Essays on Science Fiction, ed. by M. J. Tolley and Kirpal Singh. Victoria, Aust.: Norstrilla Press, c1980. 288 p.

"Science Fiction and the Plight of the Literary Critic," Science Fiction: A Review of Speculative Literature 4(3): 106-109. September 1982.

Siniavskii, A. D.

"No discount (on science fiction)," in: Siniavskii, A. D. For Freedom of Imagination (translated and with an introduction by Laszlo Tikos and Murray Peppard). New York: Holt, Rinehart & Woreton, 1971. pp. 17-36,204-205.

Sinjavskij, A.

"Sovremennuj naucno-fantasticeskij roman," Puti razvitija sovremennogo sovetskogo romana. Moskva: s. n., 1961.

Siodmak, Curt

"Sci-fi or sci-fact," Films and Filming 15(2):63-64. November 1968.

"Science fiction and science," Rehovot 8(4):33-35. 1979.

Sire, J. W.

"Truths too bitter for this world: S. Lem's novels and stories," Christianity Today 23(2):34-37. October 20, 1978.

Sirka, Ann

"Uebergungen zum phantastischen Film am Beispiel vom Stanley Kubricks A Clockwork Orange," in: Thomsen, C. W., ed. Phantastik in Literatur und Kunst. Darmstadt: Wissenschaftliche Buchgesellschaft, 1980. pp. 492-513.

Sirridge, Mary

"J. R. Tolkien and the fairy tale truth," The British Journal of Aesthetics 15:81-92. 1975.

Sisario, Peter

"Study of the allusions in Bradbury's Fahrenheit 451, A," English Journal 59(2):201-205,212. February 1970.

Siskel, Gene

"Ron Howard warns film fans: What you see is what you'll get," Chicago Tribune June 23, 1985. in: NewsBank. Film and Television. 5:C1-C3. July 1985.

Sisson, J. E., III

Fiction of Jack London: A Chronological Bibliography, The, by D. L. Walker and J. E. Sisson, III. El Paso: Texas Western Press, 1972. 40 p.

Skeels, D. R.

"Science fiction as myth," _The Trend in Engineering at the University of Washington_ 23(4):10-15,31. October 1971. also in: _Ashwing_ 9:5-12. December 1971.

Skeeter, P. W.

Sidney H. Sime: Master of Fantasy. Pasadena, CA: Ward Ritchie, 1978. 127 p.

Skinner, B. F.

"Utopia as an Experimental Culture," in: Roemer, Kenneth M., ed. _America As Utopia_. New York: Franklin, 1981. pp. 28-42.

Skinner, V. L.

"Guinevere's role in the Arthurian poetry of Charles Williams," _Mythlore_ 4(3): 9-11. March 1977.

Sklar, Robert

"Tolkien and Hesse: Top of the Pops," in: Lentz, Millicent, ed. _Young Adult Literature: Background and Criticism_. Chicago: ALA, 1980. pp. 418-424.

Sklepowich, E. A.

"Fictive quest: Effinger's _What Entropy Means to Me_, The," _Extrapolation_ 18(2):107-115. May 1977.

Skorodenko, V.

"O bezumnom mire; pozitsii khudozhnika," Afterword to _Kulybel' dyla Koshki_ trans. by Rita Rait-Kovaleva from _Cat's Cradle_ Moscow: Mologdaia gvardiia, 1970. p. 212-233.

Skotak, Robert

Fantastic Worlds, by Scot Holton and Robert Skotak. New York: Starlog, 1978. 98 p.

"Man from Planet X," _Future_ 1: 32-35. April 1978.

Skvorecky, Josef

"Literarni typ Raye Bradburyho," in: Bradbury, Ray. _Martanska kronika_. Praha: Mlada Fronta, 1959. pp. 190-195.

Sky, Kathleen

"Dimension of Miracles," in: Magill, Frank N., ed. _Survey of Science Fiction Literature_, Vol. 2. Englewood Cliffs, NJ: Salem Press, 1979. pp. 539-542.

"Children of the future," _SFWA Bulletin_ 14(3):35-37. Fall 1979.

"Finding Science Fiction Ideas," _Writer_ 94(5): 17-18. May 1981.

Sladek, John

"4-Part List," _Vector_ 112: 16-24. 1983.

"Fossil astronauts," _Foundation_ 4:28-31. July 1973.

"Four reasons for reading Thomas M. Disch," in: Tolley, M. J., ed. _The Stellar Guage_. Carleton, Australia: Norstrilia, 1980. pp. 259-280.

"How I Became a Science Fiction Master in Only 15 Minutes A Day," _Science Fiction Chronicle_ 6(8): 31-32. May 1985.

"How I Became A Science Fiction Master in Only 15 Minutes A Day," in: Wingrove, David, ed. _The Science Fiction Source Book_. New York: Van Nostrand, 1984. pp. 82-83.

"Profession of Science Fiction, 29: Kids! Read Books in Your Spare Time," _Foundation_ 25: 49-52. June 1982.

"Science fiction and pseudoscience," _Vector_ 62: 5-11. November/December 1972.

"Writing Places," _Focus_ 6: 11-15. Autumn 1982.

Slate, Tom

"Edgar Rice Burroughs and the heroic epic," _Riverside Quarterly_ 3(2): 118-123. March 1968.

Slater, Ian

Orwell: The Road to Airstrip One., New York: Norton, 1985. 302 p.

Slater, Joseph

"Fictional values of _1984_, The," in: Kirk, Rudolph and C. F. Main, eds. _Essays in Literary History_. New York: Russell & Russell, 1965. pp. 249-264.

Slater, K. F.

British Science Fiction Book Index. Walsoken, England: n. p., n. d. (not seen)

Slater, K. F. (Continued)

Checklist of Science Fiction, Fantasy and Supernatural Stories Available in Paperback in Britain, January, 1966, A. Wisbeth (Cambs.): Fantast (Medway), 1966. 30 p.

Slavov, A. P.

Prognostika, fantastika, svctogled. Sofiia: Partizdat, 1981. 175 p. 81-148744

Sless, David

"Arthur C. Clarke," in: Tolley, M. J., ed. The Stellar Guage. Carleton, Australia: Norstrilia, 1980. pp. 91-107.

Slethaug, G. E.

"Hawkline Monster, The: Brautigan's 'Buffoon Mutation'," in: Collins, R. A., ed. Scope of the Fantastic: Culture, Biography, Themes, Children's Literature. Westport: Greenwood, 1985. pp. 137-146.

"No exit: the hero as victim in Donaldson," Mythlore 11(2):22-27. Autumn 1984.

Slide, Anthony

"Cinefex," in: Slide, Anthony, ed. International Film, Radio, and Television Journals. Westport, CT: Greenwood, 1985. pp. 48-49.

Sloan, J. P.

"When worlds collide: sci-fi buffs invade Northwestern campus," Chicago Tribune. Book World Sec. 7, p. 2. December 16, 1980.

Slobodnik, Dusan

Geneza poetika science fiction. Bratislava: Miade leta, 1980. 256 p. 81-176492

Slocombe, Douglas

"Through a glass not so darkly," American Cinematographer 62(11):1104-1105,1123. November 1981.

Slocum, R. R.

"Sic Parvis Magna: science, technology, and ecology in John Brunner's science fiction," in: De Bolt, Joe, ed. Happening Worlds of John Brunner. Port Washington, NY: Kennikat, 1975. pp. 147-166.

Slonczewski, Joan

"Writer? Who, Me?" Empire: For the SF Writer 5(1): 10-11. Winter 1979.

Slusser, G. E.

Bradbury Chronicles, The. San Bernardino, California: Borgo Press, 1977. 64 p.

Bridges to Fantasy, by G. E. Slusser, E. S. Rabkin, and Robert Scholes. Carbondale: Southern Illinois University Press, 1982. 231 p.

Bridges to Science Fiction, by G. E. Slusser, G. R. Guffey, and Mark Rose. Carbondale: Southern Illinois University Press, 1980. 168 p.

Classic Years of Robert A. Heinlein. San Bernardino, CA: Borgo, 1977. 63 p.

Coordinates: Placing Science Fiction and Fantasy, by G. E. Slusser, E. S. Rabkin, and Robert Scholes. Carbondale, IL: Southern Illinois University Press, 1983. 209 p.

Delany Intersection: Samuel R. Delany Considered as a Writer of Semi-Precious Words. San Bernardino, CA: Borgo, 1977. 64 p.

Farthest Shores of Ursula K. Le Guin, The. San Bernardino, California: Borgo Press, 1976. 60 p.

Harlan Ellison: Unrepentant Harlequin. San Bernardino, California: Borgo Press, 1977. 63 p. (The Milford Series: Popular Writers of Today, Vol 6)

Robert A. Heinlein: Stranger in His Own Land. San Bernardino, California: Borgo Press, 1976. 60 p.

Shadows of the Magic Lamp: Fantasy and Science Fiction in Film, by G. E. Slusser and E. S. Rabkin. Carbondale: Southern Illinois University Press, 1985. 259 p.

Space Odysseys of Arthur C. Clarke, The. San Bernardino, California: Borgo Press, 1978. 64 p.

"2001: A Space Odyssey," in: Magill, Frank N., ed. Survey of Science Fiction Literature, Vol. 5. Englewood Cliffs, NJ: Salem Press, 1979. pp. 2343-2349.

"Death of the Earth, The," in: Magill, Frank N., ed. Survey of Science Fiction Literature, Vol. 2. Englewood Cliffs, NJ: Salem Press, 1979. pp. 513-518.

"Invincible, The," in: Magill, Frank N., ed. Survey of Science Fiction Literature, Vol. 3. Englewood Cliffs, NJ: Salem Press, 1979. pp. 1050-1056.

Slusser, G. E. (Continued)

"Nasty Swans, The," in: Magill, Frank N., ed. Survey of Science Fiction Literature, Vol. 3. Englewood Cliffs, NJ: Salem Press, 1979. pp. 1488-1496.

"Death and the Mirror: Existential Fantasy," in: Slusser, G. E., ed. Coordinates. Carbondale: Southern Illinois University Press, 1983. pp. 150-176.

"Earthsea Trilogy," in: Ursula K. Le Guin, ed. by Harold Bloom. New York: Chelsea House, 1986. pp. 71-84.

"Fantasy, Science Fiction, Mystery, Horror," in: Slusser, G. E., ed. Shadows of the Magic Lamp. Carbondale: Southern Illinois University Press, 1985. pp. 208-230.

"Harlan Ellison," in: Bleiler, E. F., ed. Science Fiction Writers. New York: Scribners, 1982. pp. 357-368.

"Heinlein's Perpetual Motion Fur Farm," Science Fiction Studies 9(1): 51-67. March 1982.

"Introduction: Shadows of the Magic Lamp," by G. E. Slusser and E. S. Rabkin. in: Slusser, George, ed. Shadows of the Magic Lamp. Carbondale: Southern Illinois University Press, 1985. pp. xiii-xxii.

"J. Lloyd Eaton Collection," Special Collections 2(1/2): 25-38. Fall/Winter 1982.

"Literature and Science," by G. E. Slusser and George Guffey. in: Barricelli, Jean-Pierre, ed. Interrelations of Literature. New York: Modern Language Association, 1982. pp. 176-204.

"Sandman, The," in: Magill, Frank N., ed. Survey of Science Fiction Literature, Vol. 4. Englewood Cliffs, NJ: Salem Press, 1979. pp. 1848-1853.

Small, Christopher

Ariel Like a Harpy: Shelley, Mary and Frankenstein. London: Victor Gollancz, 1972. 352 p. Reprinted, Mary Shelley's Frankenstein: Tracing the Myth. Pittsburgh: University of Pittsburgh Press, 1973.

Road to Miniluv: George Orwell, the State, and God, The. London: Victor Gollancz, 1975. 220 p. Reprinted, Pittsburgh: University of Pittsburgh Press, 1976.

Smelkov, Julii

"Beg na meste? Obzor nauchnoi fantastiki," Literaturnoe Obozrenie 10: 19-23. 1981.

"Drei Ansichten des Films Solaris: Nachtrealisierte Moglichkeiten," Quarber Merkur 38:50-52. November 1974.

Smith, A. C. H.

Dark Crystal. New York: Holt, 1982. 128 P.

Smith, A. R.

"Genesis demo," American Cinematographer 63(10):1038-1039, 1048-1050. October 1982.

Smith, Bernard

"Guiding the Dream," Focus: An SF Writer's Magazine 9: 4-7. Autumn 1984.

Smith, C. A.

Planets and Dimensions: Collected Essays, by C. A. Smith and ed. by C. K. Wolfe. Baltimore: Mirage Press, 1973. 87 p.

"To Howard Phillips Lovecraft," in: Joshi, S. T., ed. H. P. Lovecraft; Four Decades of Criticism. Athens, OH: Ohio University Press, 1980. pp. 227-228.

Smith, C. C.

Olaf Stapledon: A Bibliography, by H. J. Satty and C. C. Smith. Westport: Greenwood, 1984. 168 p.

Twentieth-Century Science Fiction Writers. New York: St. Martins, 1981. 642 p.

"Books of Olaf Stapledon: a chronological survey, The," Science Fiction Studies 1(4):297-299. Fall 1974.

"H. G. Wells' Discovery of the Future," SFWA Bulletin 9(5): 9-12. 1974.

"Horror Versus Tragedy: Mary Shelley's Frankenstein and Olaf Stapledon's Sirius," Extrapolation 26(1): 66-75. Spring 1985.

"Introduction," in: Stapledon, Olaf. To The End of Time. Boston: Gregg, 1975. pp. v-xi.

"Manuscript of Last and First Men: Towards a Variorum," Science-Fiction Studies 9(3): 265-273. November 1982.

"Olaf Stapledon's dispassionate objectivity," in: Clareson, T. D., ed. Voices for the Future: Essays on Major Science Fiction Writers, Vol. 1. Bowling Green, Ohio: Bowling Green Univ. Popular Press, 1976. pp. 44-63.

"Olaf Stapledons zukunftshistorien und tragodien," in: Barmeyer, Eike, ed. Science fiction: theorie und geschichte. Munchen: Fink, 1972 pp. 275-292.

Smith, C. C. (Continued)

"Science fiction, asset or liability,"
Science Teacher 20:233-235. October 1953.
Excerpted: Clearing House 28:371. February
1954.

"William Olaf Stapledon: saint and
revolutionary," Extrapolation 13(1):5-15.
December 1971.

Smith, C. S.

Other Angus Wilson: Fantasy in His Fiction.
Ph. D. Dissertation, Georgia State University
1980. 323 p. (DAI 41:683 A)

"Olaf Stapledon and the immortal spirit," in:
Yoke, C. B. and Hassler, D. M., eds. Death
and the Serpent. Westport, CT: Greenwood,
1985. pp. 103-114.

Smith, Curtis

"Science fiction and the revolution,"
Riverside Quarterly 5(1): 44-45. July 1971.

Smith, E. E.

"Paul," Science Fiction Times No. 405:7.
August 1963.

Smith, Godfrey

"Astounding story! About a science fiction
writer," New York Times Magazine pp.
28,75-77. March 6, 1966.

Smith, Jeanne

"Sampler of science fiction for junior high,"
Arizona English Bulletin 51(1):91-96.
October 1972.

Smith, Jeff

"Short happy life of James Tiptree, Jr.,"
Khatru No. 7: 8-12. 1978.

"Short, happy life of James Tiptree, Jr.," in:
World Science Fiction Convention, 1977.
Suncon Program Book. Miami Beach: Suncon,
1977. pp. 93-94.

"Tiptree/Sheldon Bibliography," Khatru No.
7: 23-25. 1978.

"Women in science fiction: a symposium,"
Khatru 3/4:4-125. November 1975.

Smith, John

"Fair Deal for Dealers," Patchin Review 2:
35-37. September 1981.

"Post STS-1 Fiction," Patchin Review 1:
16-17. July 1981.

Smith, Kenneth

"First science fiction writer?" New
Scientist 76: 778-779. December 22-29, 1977.

"Hegelian stratagems in Calvino's Invisible
Cities," in: Collins, R. A., ed. Scope of
the Fantastic: Theory, Technique, Major
Authors. Westport: Greenwood, 1985. pp.
247-254.

Smith, Kevin

"'It's Not a Cliche, It's a Traditional
Narrative Element' (Notes on Milford U.K. 1981)
Focus 5: 27-31. Spring 1982.

"Editorial: Towards a Critical Standard, Part
III," Vector 101: 4-5, 29. April 1981.

"Towards a Critical Standard, Part II,"
Vector 100: 15-16. December 1980.

"Towards a Critical Standard, Part IV,"
Vector 102: 5-7. June 1981.

"Towards a Critical Standard," Vector 99:
4-6. October 1980.

Smith, L. A.

"In Brief Authority," in: Magill, Frank N.,
ed. Survey of Modern Fantasy Literature,
Vol 2. Englewood Cliffs, NJ: Salem Press,
Inc., 1983. pp. 765-767.

"Little Prince, The," in: Magill, Frank N.,
ed. Survey of Modern Fantasy Literature,
Vol 2. Englewood Cliffs, NJ: Salem Press,
Inc., 1983. pp. 891-893.

"Peter Pan," in: Magill, Frank N., ed.
Survey of Modern Fantasy Literature, Vol 3.
Englewood Cliffs, NJ: Salem Press, Inc., 1983.
pp. 1230-1233.

"Wind in the Willows, The," in: Magill,
Frank N., ed. Survey of Modern Fantasy
Literature, Vol 5. Englewood Cliffs, NJ:
Salem Press, Inc., 1983. pp. 2132-2135.

"Miss Bianca Series, The," in: Magill, Frank
N., ed. Survey of Modern Fantasy
Literature, Vol 3. Englewood Cliffs, NJ:
Salem Press, Inc., 1983. pp. 1037-1039.

Smith, L. S.

Space Voyages, 1591-1920: A Bibliography.
Riverside: University of California, Riverside
Library, 1979. 45 p.

Smith, Lareena

"Sound design for The Black Cauldron," _Cinefantastique_ 16(1):41. March 1986.

Smith, M. K.

"1984 as preventive prophecy," _Leading Edge_ No. 7:71-77. undated.

"Unit outline for a six-week course, introduction to science fiction," _Guying Gyre_ 11/12:90-91. January 1979.

Smith, M. P.

"John Varley: An Interview," by M. P. Smith and John Bartelt. _Rune_ No. 70: 35-44. 1982.

Smith, Marcia

"Force Is With Us Again," _Dallas Times Herald_. Sec. G, p. 1, 4. May 27, 1983.

Smith, Mark

"Interview: Artist, David Willson," by Joy Schwab and Mark Smith. _Fantasy Newsletter_ 5(11): 8-10. December 1982.

Smith, Michael

"Condorman," _Starlog_ 44: 36, 40-41. March 1981.

Smith, Milburn

"Edgar Rice Burroughs' Tarzan Chronicles," _Starlog_ 81: 24-27. April 1984.

"Oscar Winners: Science Fiction, Fantasy, and Horror," _Starlog_ 81: 32-35. April 1984.

Smith, N. D.

Philosophers Look at Science Fiction. Chicago: Nelson-Hall, 1982. 204 p.

"Introduction: The Philosophical Appeal of Science Fiction," by Fred Miller, Jr. and N. D. Smith. in: Smith, Nicholas D., ed. _Philosophers Look at Science Fiction_. Chicago: Nelson-Hall, 1982. pp. 1-19.

Smith, P. E., II

"Evolution of politics and the politics of evolution: social Darwinism in Heinlein's fiction, The," in: Olander, J. D. and M. H. Greenberg, eds. _Robert A. Heinlein_. New York: Taplinger, 1978. pp. 137-171.

"Unbuilding walls: human nature and the nature of evolutionary and political theory in _The Dispossessed_," in: Olander, J. D. and M. H. Greenberg, eds. _Ursula K. Le Guin_. NY: Taplinger, 1979. pp. 77-96.

Smith, R. A.

High Road to the Moon: From Imagination to Reality, the Collected Pictures of R. A. Smith. SL: British Interplanetary Society, 1979. 120 p.

Smith, R. H.

Patches of Godlight: The Pattern of Thought in C. S. Lewis. Athens, GA: University of Georgia Press, 1981. 275 p.

Smith, Sheryl

"Arrive at Easterwine: some arrant roadmapping," in: Chauvin, Cy, ed. _Multitude of Visions_. Baltimore: T-K Graphics, 1975. pp. 40-48.

"Ellison on Byronism," _Khatru_ No. 1: 3-22. February 1975.

"Lafferty's Short Stories: Some Mystagogic Goshwow," _Riverside Quarterly_ 7(2): 73-81. March 1982.

Smith, Tyler

"John Boyd," in: Cowart, David, ed. _Twentieth-Century American Science Fiction Writers, Part 1: A-L_. Detroit: Gale, 1981. pp. 55-58. (Dictionary of Literary Biography, v. 8)

Smith, Wayne

"Behind the scenes of Silent Running," _American Cinematographer_ 53(7):746-749, 786-787, 797-798. July 1972.

Smoriakov, V.

"Science Fiction: Facts and Problems," by A. Balabukh and V. Smoriakov. _Soviet Studies in Literature_ 18(1): 70-79. Winter 1981/1982.

Smuszkiewicz, Antoni

Stereotyp fabularny fantastyki naukowej. Wroclaw: Ossolineum, 1980. 167 p.

"Catastrophe theme in Polish science fiction, 1918-39," _Canadian-American Soviet Studies_ 18(1/2):97-105. Spring/Summer 1984.

Smuszkiewicz, Antoni (Continued)

"Space and time in contemporary Polish science fiction," <u>Science Fiction Studies</u> 6(1):85-91. March 1979.

Smyrniw, Walter

"Theme of Man-Godhood in Oles Berdnyk's Science Fiction," <u>Journal of Ukrainian Studies</u> 6(1): 3-19. Spring 1981.

Smyth, G. T.

"<u>Analog</u> sold to Davis Publications," <u>Science Fiction Times</u> (Boston) 1(7):1. March 1980.

Snee, Dennis

"Beyond Jedi: The Saga Continues," <u>Playboy</u> 30(6): 95, 226. June 1983.

Snelson, Robin

"Portfolio: Adolf Schaller," <u>Future Life</u> 22: 58-63. November 1980.

"Portfolio: John Allison," <u>Future Life</u> 24: 58-63. February 1981.

"Portfolio: Jon Lomberg," <u>Future Life</u> 16: 58-63. February 1980.

"Portfolio: Rick Sternbach," <u>Future Life</u> 17: 70-75. March 1980.

Snipes, K. W.

"Artistic variations on living nightmare: Graves's 'Shout'," in: Collins, R. A., ed. <u>Scope of the Fantastic: Culture, Biography, Themes, Children's Literature</u>. Westport: Greenwood, 1985. pp. 107-114.

Snow, C. P.

"Effect of science on the novel, The," <u>New York Times</u> sec. 7, 1:1. January 30, 1955. Reply, <u>New York Times</u> sec. 7, 2:2. February 13, 1955.

Snow, Malinda

"Gray parody in <u>Brave New World</u>, The," <u>Papers on Language & Literature</u> 13(1):85-88. Winter 1977.

Snowden, John

"Stan Pitt: An Interview," <u>Science Fiction: A Review of Speculative Literature</u>. 5(2): 48-56. June 1983.

Snyder, Gene

"Caution, science friction causes heat," <u>Media & Methods</u> 14(3):28-29. November 1977.

"Dialogue? Of couse. But how? You'll see," in: Grant, C. L., ed. <u>Writing and Selling Science Fiction</u>. Cincinnati, Ohio: Writers Digest, 1976. pp. 45-58.

Snyder, Tom

<u>Transcript of the Tomorrow Show, March 15, 1976, Featuring Guest Harlan Ellison</u>. Portland, Oregon: Foray Press, 1976. 20 p.

Sobchack, Vivian

<u>Limits of Infinity: A Critical Study of Image and Sound in the American Science Fiction Film</u>. Master's Thesis, U. C. L. A., 1976.

<u>Limits of Infinity: The American Science Fiction Film 1950-1975</u>. South Brunswick, N. J.: Barnes, 1980. 246 p.

<u>Screening Space: The American Science Fiction Film</u>. New York: Ungar, 1985.

"Decor as theme: A Clockwork Orange," Literature/Film Quarterly 9(2):92-102. 1981.

"Virginity of Astronauts: Sex and the Science Fiction Film," in: Slusser, George, ed. <u>Shadows of the Magic Lamp</u>. Carbondale: Southern Illinois University Press, 1985. pp. 41-57.

Sobel, Dava

"Cinematic neurosis: scary movies can drive you crazy," <u>Science Digest</u> 80:28-33. December 1976.

Sodre, Muniz

<u>Ficcao do tempo, A: analise da narrativa de science fiction</u>. Pertropolis, Brazil: Vozes, 1973. 126 p.

Sokolsky, Bob

"Radio is No Place for 'Rings'," <u>Philadephia Evening Bulletin</u> January 7, 1982. in: NewsBank. Film and Television. 86:B7. 1981/82.

Solmi, Sergio

"Ancora della fantascienza," in: Solmi, Sergio. <u>Della favola, del viaggio e di altre cose: saggi sul fantasico</u>. Milano: Ricciardi, 1971. p. 117-144.

Solmi, Sergio (Continued)

"Divagazioni sulla 'science-fiction', l'utopia e il tempo," in: Solmi, Sergio. Della favola, del viaggio e di altre cose: saggi sul fantastico. Milano: Ricciardi, 1971. p. 61-109.

"Ray Bradbury," in: Solmi, Sergio. Della favola, del viaggio e di altre cose: saggi sul fantastico. Milano: Ricciardi, 1971. p. 11-115.

Solomon, Eric

"Prophetic war novels," Notes & Queries N.S. 6(1):36-37. January 1959.

Solomon, S.

"Science fiction for the space age: how to stimulate supplementary reading among students of all ability levels," Senior Scholastic (teacher edition) 87:sup. 20-21. January 21, 1966.

Solon, Ben

"Howard's Cthuloid tales," in: De Camp, L. S., ed. Blade of Conan. New York: Ace, 1979. pp. 143-147.

"Lovecraft on the doorstep," Haunted: Studies in Gothic Fiction 1:87-88. June 1968.

"Second thoughts: criticism of criticism," Zenith Speculation 2(1):5-9. July 1966.

Solovgova, Isabella

"Science fiction: from popular science fiction to literature," Soviet Life pp. 50-51. July 1966.

Somay, Bulent

"Towards and Open-Ended Utopia," Science-Fiction Studies 11(1): 25-38. March 1984.

Somer, John

Vonnegut Statement, The, ed. by Jerome Klinkowitz and John Somer. New York: Delacorte Press, 1973. 286 p.

"Geodesic Vonnegut: or, if Buckminster Fuller wrote novels," in: Klinkowitz, Jerome and John Somer, eds. The Vonnegut Statement.

New York: Delacorte Press/Seymour Lawrence, 1973. pp. 221-253.

Somtow, S. P.

"Galactic Garbage Art," Fantasy Review of Fantasy and Science Fiction 7(3): 10, 42. April 1984.

"Worst week of my life," Fantasy Review 8(5): 9. May 1985.

Sontag, Susan

Styles of Radical Will. New York: Farrar, Straus & Giroux, c1969. 36 p.

"Imagination of disaster, The," Commentary 40(4):42-48. October 1965. also in: Sontag, Susan. Against Interpretation. New York: Farrar. pp. 209-225.

Soper, Michael

"Liberation of Fiction," Vector 116: 27-28. September 1983.

Sorensen, Peter

"Computer Imaging: An Apple for the Dreamsmiths," Cinefex 6: 4-29. October 1981.

"Last Starfighter: imagery wrought in the total forge," Cinefex No. 17:54-71. June 1984.

"Tronic imagery," Cinefex No. 8:4-35. April 1982.

Sorenson, Peter

"Movies, computers and the future," American Cinematographer 64(1):69-78. January 1983.

Soriano, Marc

Jules Verne. Paris: Julliard, 1978. 412 p.

Soule, S. W.

"Special effects," Harper 247:128. December 1973.

Sourbut, Elizabeth

"What do we do now that the future is here?" Vector 126: 9-10. June/July 1985.

Souriau, J. M.

"Science et science fiction," La Recherche No. 49:854-865. October 1974.

Southard, Bruce

"Language of Science-Fiction Fan Magazines," American Speech 57(1): 19-31. Spring 1982.

Southard, R.

"Superman grabs chance to teach grammar," America 73:196-197. June 9, 1945.

Southern, Terry

"After the bomb came the ice," New York Times Book Review p. 20. June 2, 1963. (Book review)

Spacks, P. M.

"Myth-maker's dilemma: three novels by C. S. Lewis, The," Discourse 2(4):234-243. October 1959.

Spacu, Marina

"Drei Science-Fiction Bucher," Quarber Merkur 23:16-19. May 1970.

Spaink, A.

Fantasfeer: bibliografie van science fiction en fantasy in het Nederlands, by A. Spaink, G. Gorremans, and R. Goossens. Amsterdam: Meulenhoff, 1979. 279 p.

Sparks, E. K.

"Descent into Hell," in: Magill, Frank N., ed. Survey of Modern Fantasy Literature, Vol 1. Englewood Cliffs, NJ: Salem Press, Inc., 1983. pp. 366-373.

"Forgotten Beasts of Eld, The," in: Magill, Frank N., ed. Survey of Modern Fantasy Literature, Vol 2. Englewood Cliffs, NJ: Salem Press, Inc., 1983. pp. 566-570.

"Princess and the Goblin, The and The Princess and Curdie," in: Magill, Frank N., ed. Survey of Modern Fantasy Literature, Vol 3. Englewood Cliffs, NJ: Salem Press, Inc., 1983. pp. 1280-1285.

"New Wave," in: Cowart, David, ed. Twentieth-Century American Science Fiction Writers. Detroit: Gale, 1981. v. 2, pp. 225-235.

Spatt, H. S.

"Mary Shelley's last men: the truth of dreams," Studies in the Novel 7(4):526-537. Winter 1975.

Spector, J. A.

"Dr. Jekyll and Mrs. Hyde: Gender-Related Conflict in the Science Fiction of Joanna Russ," Extrapolation 24(4): 370-379. Winter 1983.

"Science Fiction and the Sex War: A Womb of One's Own," Literature and Psychology 31(1): 21-32. 1981.

"Walter Miller's A Canticle for Leibowitz: A Parable for Our Time," Midwest Quarterly 22(4): 337-345. Summer 1981.

Speer, D. P.

"Heinlein's The Door into Summer and Roderick Random," Extrapolation 12(1):30-34. December 1970.

Speer, Jack

"Far Future of Science Fiction," Fantasy Commentator 1(11): 271-273, 275, 285, 301. Summer 1946.

Spehner, Norbert

"Science fiction in Quebec: a survey," by Elisabeth Vonarburg and Norbert Spehner. Science Fiction Studies 7(2):191-199. July 1980.

"SF in Quebec: a historical survey," Borealis 1(1):18-20. Summer 1978.

Spelling, Ian

"Star crossed lovers of Cocoon: Tahnee Welch," Starlog No. 98:47-49. September 1985.

Spelman, R. C.

Preliminary Checklist of Science Fiction and Fantasy Published by Ballantine Books (1953-1974), A. North Hollywood, California: Institute for Specialized Literature, 1976. 42 p.

Science Fiction and Fantasy Published by Ace Books (1953-1968). North Hollywood, California: Institute for Specialized Literature, 1976. 62 p.

Spencer, Alan

"Starlog Interview: Allan Arkush," Starlog 52: 26-29, 64. November 1981.

"Things (Review)," Starlog 64: 67-69. November 1982.

Spencer, K. L.

"Chronicles of Torner, The," in: Magill, Frank N., ed. Survey of Modern Fantasy Literature, Vol 1. Englewood Cliffs, NJ: Salem Press, Inc., 1983. pp. 275-281.

"Dancers at the End of Time," in: Magill, Frank N., ed. Survey of Science Fiction Literature, Vol. 1. Englewood Cliffs, NJ: Salem Press, 1979. pp. 468-473.

"Flowers for Algernon," in: Magill, Frank N., ed. Survey of Science Fiction Literature, Vol. 2. Englewood Cliffs, NJ: Salem Press, 1979. pp. 802-806.

"Many Dimensions," in: Magill, Frank N., ed. Survey of Modern Fantasy Literature, Vol 2. Englewood Cliffs, NJ: Salem Press, Inc., 1983. pp. 966-969.

"Place of the Lion, The," in: Magill, Frank N., ed. Survey of Modern Fantasy Literature, Vol 3. Englewood Cliffs, NJ: Salem Press, Inc., 1983. pp. 1262-1267.

"Weapon Shops of Isher, The," in: Magill, Frank N., ed. Survey of Science Fiction Literature, Vol. 5. Englewood Cliffs, NJ: Salem Press, 1979. pp. 2442-2446.

"Where Late the Sweet Birds Sang," in: Magill, Frank N., ed. Survey of Science Fiction Literature, Vol. 5. Englewood Cliffs, NJ: Salem Press, 1979. pp. 2469-2473.

"'The Red Sun is High, the Blue Low': Towards a Stylistic Description of Science Fiction," Science-Fiction Studies 10(1): 35-50. March 1983.

"Exiles and Envoys: The SF of Ursula K. Le Guin," Foundation 20: 32-43. October 1980.

Spencer, Paul

"Devil and the Doctor, The," in: Magill, Frank N., ed. Survey of Modern Fantasy Literature, Vol 1. Englewood Cliffs, NJ: Salem Press, Inc., 1983. pp. 374-376.

"Moon Pool, The," in: Magill, Frank N., ed. Survey of Modern Fantasy Literature, Vol 3. Englewood Cliffs, NJ: Salem Press, Inc., 1983. pp. 1060-1064.

"'Some ladies' and 'Jurgen'," Kalki 7(2):51-57. 1976.

"Ape-man and man-ape," Fantasy Review 8(8): 14-15, 36. August 1985. (Book Review)

"Cabell and the 'comics'," Kalki 7:89-92. 1977.

"Cabell in print," Kalki 6(1):33-34. 1974.

"Cabell in print," Kalki 6(4):145-146. 1975.

"Cabell in print," Kalki 7(1):18,33. 1975.

"Cabell, Fantasist of Reality," in: Schweitzer, Darrell, ed. Exploring Fantasy Worlds. San Bernardino, CA: Borgo, 1985. pp. 97-106.

"Evangeline Walton: an interview," Fantasy Review 8(3): 7-10. March 1985.

"Short fiction of Derleth, The," in: Magill, Frank N., ed. Survey of Modern Fantasy Literature, Vol 3. Englewood Cliffs, NJ: Salem Press, Inc., 1983. pp. 1496-1500.

"Short fiction of Keller, The," in: Magill, Frank N., ed. Survey of Modern Fantasy Literature, Vol 4. Englewood Cliffs, NJ: Salem Press, Inc., 1983. pp. 1581-1585.

Spencer, Theodore

"Symbols of a good and bad England," New York Times Book Review p. 10. July 7, 1946. (Book review)

Spencer, W. T.

"They're not robots, they're cyborgs," New York Times Magazine pp. 40-46. December 14, 1969.

Sperling, Edwardine

"Conquest of space," Clearing House 44:299. January 1970. (Poem)

Speth, Lee

"Cavalier treatment: Anastasia," Mythlore 11(3): 26. Winter/Spring 1985.

"Cavalier Treatment: Curses and Caravans," Mythlore 7(3): 10. Autumn 1980.

"Cavalier Treatment: James Elroy Flecker's King of Alsander," Mythlore 6(1): 17. Winter 1979.

"Cavalier Treatment: King Arthur's Vicar," Mythlore 8(3): 19-20. Autumn 1981.

"Cavalier Treatment: More About Arthur Machen,: Mythlore 8(1): 41-42. Spring 1981.

"Cavalier Treatment: Tolkien the Liberator," Mythlore 9(2): 37. Summer 1982.

Spielberg, Steven

The American Film Institute Seminar With Steven Spielberg Held November 26, 1975. Beverly Hills, CA: Center for Advanced Film Studies, c1978. 85 p. on 1 microfiche.

"Of narrow misses and close calls," American Cinematographer 62(11): 1100-1102, 1138-1142, 1160-1168. November 1981.

"Unsung heroes," American Cinematographer 59(1):68-70,88. January 1978.

Spiller, Nancy

"Apes From Space, Maidens in Peril. It's Baycon '82," San Jose Mercury. November 27, 1982. in: Newsbank. Social Relations. SOC 52: A12-13. 1982.

"Frank Herbert," San Jose Mercury August 5, 1984. in: Newsbank. Literature. 16:A9. 1984.

Spina, Giorgio

Utopia e satira nella fantascienza inglese. Genova: Tilgher, 1974. 119 p.

Spinks, C. W.

Prophecy, Pulp, or Punt: Science Fiction, Scenarios, and Values. 14 p. February 1983. ERIC ED 229 314.

Spinrad, Norman

Staying Alive: A Writer's Guide. Norfolk, VA: Donning, 1983. 162 p.

"Stand on Zanzibar: the novel as film," in: Clareson, T. D., ed. SF: The Other Side of Realism. Bowling Green, Ohio: Bowling Green University Popular Press, 1971. pp. 181-185.

"2001: a space odyssey," Cinema 4(2):59. Summer 1968.

"Blade Runner (Review)," Starlog 64: 55-56. November 1982.

"Bug Jack Barron papers, The," Algol 15:9-14. Spring 1969. Also in: Experiment Perilous: Three Essays on Science Fiction. New York: Algol Press, 1976. pp. 21-28.

"Future of Science Fiction," in: Pohl, Frederik, ed. Nebula Winners Fourteen. New York: Harper, 1980; New York: Bantam, 1982. pp. 111-118.

"Greystoke (review)," Starlog 88: 48-49. November 1984.

"Guest editorial: the death of the SF magazines, or, do editors eat their young?"

Science Fiction Times No. 445:4-7. August 1967.

"How Things Work," Science Fiction Review 11(3): 8-17. August 1982.

"Introduction," in: Moorcock, Michael. The Final Programme. Boston: Gregg, 1976. pp. v-xv.

"Introduction," in: Niven, Larry and Jerry Pournelle. Inferno. Boston: Gregg, 1979. pp. v-xii.

"Jack Barron vs. the black tower," Starlog No. 98:14-15. September 1985.

"Jack Vance and The Dragon Masters," in: Underwood, Tim and Miller, Chuck, eds. Jack Vance. New York: Taplinger, 1980. pp. 13-22.

"Look at sex in SF, part two, A," Science Fiction Times No. 465:5. April 1969.

"On Books: A Matter of Style," Isaac Asimov's Science Fiction Magazine 8(8): 171-176. August 1984.

"On Books: The Generation of 1984," Isaac Asimov's Science Fiction Magazine 8(12): 168-176. December 1984.

"Passing of a giant and an era, The," Los Angeles Free Press p. 9. July 30, 1971.

"Prince from Another Land," in: Greenberg, Martin H., ed. Fantastic Lives: Autobiographical Essays by Notable Science Fiction Writers. Carbondale: Southern Illinois University Press, 1981. pp. 157-174.

"Profession of science fiction: XIX: Where I get my crazy ideas," Foundation 19: 15-18. June 1980.

"Rubber sciences," in: Bretnor, Reginald, ed. The Craft of Science Fiction. New York: Harper, 1976. pp. 54-70.

"SFWA Model Paperback Contract," SFWA Bulletin 12(2): 4-5. March 1977.

"Stanley Kubrick in the 21st century," Cinema 3(4):4-6. December 1966.

"Stayin' alive, #20," Locus 15(5):17. May 1982.

"Stayin' Alive, May 1984," Locus 17(5): 9-11. May 1984.

"Stayin' alive, No. 14," Locus 14(8):7,19. September 1981.

"Stayin' alive, No. 15," Locus 14(10):7,26. November 1981.

"Stayin' alive, no. 19: careers," Locus 15(3):7,20. March 1982.

Spinrad, Norman (Continued)

"Stayin' alive, No. 21," Locus
15(9):10-11. September 1982.

"Stayin' alive, no. 22: publishing," Locus
15(10):7,16. October 1982.

"Stayin' Alive, September 1984," Locus
17(9): 19, 35. September 1984.

"Stayin' alive," Locus 14(11):13,15.
December 1981.

"Stayin' alive: ABA," Locus 18(8): 9, 47.
August 1985.

"Stayin' alive: advances," Locus
12(11):7,12. December 1979.

"Stayin' alive: awards and advertising,"
Locus 13(9):5-16. September 1980.

"Stayin' alive: awards," Locus 13(1):7-8.
January 1980.

"Stayin' alive: books," Locus
15(1):11,16. January 1982.

"Stayin' Alive: Britain and France,"
Locus 18(7): 19-21.
July 1985.

"Stayin' alive: column prospectus,"
Locus 12(7):1,5.
August 1979.

"Stayin' alive: editors," Locus
15(2):12-13. February 1982.

"Stayin' alive: Europe," Locus
12(10):7,13. November 1979.

"Stayin' alive: friendship," Locus
16(4):7,16. April 1983.

"Stayin' alive: Jim Baen," Locus
16(12):7,27. December 1983.

"Stayin' alive: promotions," Locus
13(4):5,11. April 1980.

"Stayin' alive: publishing economics,"
Locus 13(10):9,15. October 1980.

"Stayin' alive: publishing in France,"
Locus 16(2):11,20. February 1983.

"Stayin' alive: publishing trends," Locus
14(5):11-12. June 1981.

"Stayin' alive: publishing," Locus
13(3):7-8. March 1980.

"Stayin' Alive: Publishing," Locus 17(7):
11-13. July 1984.

"Stayin' Alive: publishing," Locus 18(4):
15, 17. April 1985.

"Stayin' alive: SF image," Locus
13(7):7-13. July 1980.

"Stayin' alive: SF publishing," Locus
16(9):7,45. September 1983.

"Stayin' alive: survey of 1984," Locus
18(2): 19, 22-23. February 1985.

"Stayin' alive: Timescape," Locus
16(8):1,13-14. August 1983.

"Stayin' alive: writing the best seller,"
Locus 16(5):7-8. May 1983.

"Staying Alive: Worldcon," Locus 17(12):
17-19. December 1984.

"Viewpoint: Alternate Viewpoint," Isaac
Asimov's Science Fiction Magazine 9(6):
63-69. June 1985.

"Viewpoint: Perchance to Dream, Revisited,"
Isaac Asimov's Science Fiction Magazine
8(7): 33-42. July 1984.

"Why I am not announcing that I am leaving
science fiction," Thrust 8:4-6. Fall 1977.

Spittel, O. R.

"Science fiction der DDR-Schrift-steller: eine
auswahlbibliographie," Canadian-American
Slavic Studies 18(1/2):142-151.
Spring/Summer 1984.

Spitzer, R. W.

"Vega Books checklist, A," Science Fiction
Collector 4:19. July 1977.

Spivak, Charlotte

Ursula K. Le Guin. Boston: Twayne, 1984.
182 p.

"Perilous realm: Phantasy as literature,"
Centennial Review 25(2): 133-149. Spring
1981.

"Researching Science Fiction and Fantasy,"
Literary Research Newsletter 8(1): 3-12.
Winter 1983.

Spivey, Ed, Jr.

"UFO as Archangel," Sojourners. 7(2):
34-38. February 1978.

Spraggs, Gillian

"Lawless World: The Fantasy Novels of Susan
Cooper," Use of English 33(2): 23-31.
Spring 1982.

Spraycar, R. S.

"C. S. Lewis's Mechanical Friends in That Hideous Strength," in: Dunn, Thomas P., ed. The Mechanical God. Westport: Greenwood, 1982. pp. 19-26.

"Mechanism and Medievalism in John Gardner's Grendel" in: Wolfe, Gary, ed. Science Fiction Dialogues. Chicago: Acadamy Chicago, 1982. pp. 141-152.

Spriel, Stephane

"Nuovo genere letterario, Un: La fantascienza," by Sephane Spriel and Boris Vian. in: Petronio, Giuseppe, ed. Letteratura di massa, letteratura de consumo: Guida storica e critica. Bari: Laterza, 1979. pp. 107-119.

Spriel, Stephen

"Astronautique est un reve vecu/Quelques histories du futur, L'" La Nef 2 trim. 1960.

"Jovo hatalomra jutasa," Helikon 18(1): 105-111. 1972. (Tr. from Esprit, May 1953.)

"Nouveau genre litteraire, Un: la science-fiction," by Stephen Spriel and Boris Vian. Les Temps Modernes No. 72:618-627. October 1951.

"Ressac du futur, Le," Cahiers du Sud No. 317:21-25. June 1953.

"Romans de l'age atomique," Les Nouvelles Litteraries No. 1221:1. January 25, 1951.

"Sur la 'science-fiction'," Esprit 202:674-685. May 1953.

Springer, Michael

"Stanislaw Lems phantastische Schreibweise," in: Ermert, Karl, ed. Neugier oder Flucht? Stuttgart: Klett, 1980. pp. 106-115.

Sprout, Monique

"Influence of Poe on Jules Verne, The," Revue de Litterature Comparee 41(1):37-53. 1967.

Squire, Susan

"Star Trek alive and kicking," Los Angeles Herald Examiner. August 30, 1976. in: NewsBank. Film and Television. 57:C9-10. 1976.

Squires, J. D.

"Alraune," in: Magill, Frank N., ed. Survey of Modern Fantasy Literature, Vol 1. Englewood Cliffs, NJ: Salem Press, Inc., 1983. pp. 26-28.

"Xelucha and Others," in: Magill, Frank N., ed. Survey of Modern Fantasy Literature, Vol 5. Englewood Cliffs, NJ: Salem Press, Inc., 1983. pp. 2192-2196.

Squires, R. A.

Private Press of Roy A. Squires, The; A Checklist of Imprints. The author, 1970. 4 p.

"Fiction of Clark Ashton Smith, The; when he wrote it and what remains unpublished," Nyctalops No. 7:65-67. August 1972.

Ssachno, H. V.

"Die stunde des stiers oder sozialistische science-fiction," Suddeutsche Zeitung April 4, 1970.

St. Armand, B. L.

H. P. Lovecraft: New England Decadent. Albuquerque: Silver Scarab Press, 1979. 56 p.

Roots of Horror in the Fiction of H. P. Lovecraft. Elizabethtown, NY: Dragon Press, 1977. 102 p.

"Facts in the case of H. P. Lovecraft," Rhode Island History 31(1):3-19. February 1972.

"Facts in the Case of H. P. Lovecraft," in: Joshi, S. T., ed. H. P. Lovecraft: Four Decades of Criticism. Athens, OH: Ohio University Press, 1980. pp. 166-185.

St. Clair, Christopher

"From the Valley of the Dinosaurs," Focus 6: 19-22. Autumn 1982.

St. Clair, Margaret

"Wight in Space: An Autobiographical Sketch," in: Greenberg, M. H., ed. Fantastic Lives.. Carbondale: Southern Illinois University Press, 1981. pp. 144-156.

Stabb, M. S.

Jorge Luis Borges. Boston: Twayne, 1970. 179 p.

Stableford, B. M.

Clash of Symbols: The Triumph of James Blish, A. San Bernardino, California: Borgo Press, 1979. 62 p. (The Milford Series: Popular Writers of Today, Vol 24)

Masters of Science Fiction. San Bernardino, CA: Borgo Press, 1981. 64 p.

Science in Science Fiction, by Peter Nicholls, David Langford, and B. M. Stableford. London: Joseph, 1982. 208 p.

Scientific Romance in Britain 1890-1950. London: Fourth Estate, 1985. 372 p.

"2018 A.D. or The King Kong Blues," in: Magill, Frank N., ed. Survey of Science Fiction Literature, Vol. 5. Englewood Cliffs, NJ: Salem Press, 1979. pp. 2339-2342.

"334," in: Magill, Frank N., ed. Survey of Science Fiction Literature, Vol. 5. Englewood Cliffs, NJ: Salem Press, 1979. pp. 2274-2277.

"Across the Zodiac: The Story of a Wrecked Record," in: Magill, Frank N., ed. Survey of Science Fiction Literature, Vol. 1. Englewood Cliffs, NJ: Salem Press, 1979. pp. 11-15.

"Angel of the Revolution, The," in: Magill, Frank N., ed. Survey of Science Fiction Literature, Vol. 1. Englewood Cliffs, NJ: Salem Press, 1979. pp. 67-71.

"Aphrodite," in: Magill, Frank N., ed. Survey of Modern Fantasy Literature, Vol 1. Englewood Cliffs, NJ: Salem Press, Inc., 1983. pp. 48-50.

"Arachne," in: Magill, Frank N., ed. Survey of Modern Fantasy Literature, Vol 1. Englewood Cliffs, NJ: Salem Press, Inc., 1983. pp. 51-53.

"Atlantida," in: Magill, Frank N., ed. Survey of Modern Fantasy Literature, Vol 1. Englewood Cliffs, NJ: Salem Press, Inc., 1983. pp. 69-70.

"Back to Methuselah," in: Magill, Frank N., ed. Survey of Modern Fantasy Literature, Vol 1. Englewood Cliffs, NJ: Salem Press, Inc., 1983. pp. 74-77.

"Baron Munchhausen's Narrative of His Marvellous Travels and Campaigns in Russia," in: Magill, Frank N., ed. Survey of Modern Fantasy Literature, Vol 1. Englewood Cliffs, NJ: Salem Press, Inc., 1983. pp. 78-80.

"Before the Dawn," in: Magill, Frank N., ed. Survey of Science Fiction Literature, Vol. 1. Englewood Cliffs, NJ: Salem Press, 1979. pp. 149-152.

"Beleaguered City, A," in: Magill, Frank N., ed. Survey of Modern Fantasy Literature, Vol 1. Englewood Cliffs, NJ: Salem Press, Inc., 1983. pp. 84-86.

"Black Cloud, The," in: Magill, Frank N., ed. Survey of Science Fiction Literature, Vol. 1. Englewood Cliffs, NJ: Salem Press, 1979. pp. 228-232.

"Black Flame, The," in: Magill, Frank N., ed. Survey of Science Fiction Literature, Vol. 1. Englewood Cliffs, NJ: Salem Press, 1979. pp. 238-241.

"Caesar's Column," in: Magill, Frank N., ed. Survey of Science Fiction Literature, Vol. 1. Englewood Cliffs, NJ: Salem Press, 1979. pp. 272-276.

"Children of the Atom," in: Magill, Frank N., ed. Survey of Science Fiction Literature, Vol. 1. Englewood Cliffs, NJ: Salem Press, 1979. pp. 349-353.

"Christmas Stories," in: Magill, Frank N., ed. Survey of Modern Fantasy Literature, Vol 1. Englewood Cliffs, NJ: Salem Press, Inc., 1983. pp. 242-247.

"Citadel of Fear, The," in: Magill, Frank N., ed. Survey of Modern Fantasy Literature, Vol 1. Englewood Cliffs, NJ: Salem Press, Inc., 1983. pp. 287-288.

"Cities in Flight," in: Magill, Frank N., ed. Survey of Science Fiction Literature, Vol. 1. Englewood Cliffs, NJ: Salem Press, 1979. pp. 358-362.

"Clockwork Man, The," in: Magill, Frank N., ed. Survey of Science Fiction Literature, Vol. 1. Englewood Cliffs, NJ: Salem Press, 1979. pp. 392-395.

"Connecticut Yankee in King Arthur's Court," in: Magill, Frank N., ed. Survey of Modern Fantasy Literature, Vol 1. Englewood Cliffs, NJ: Salem Press, Inc., 1983. pp. 319-323.

"Cornelius Chronicles, The," in: Magill, Frank N., ed. Survey of Science Fiction Literature, Vol. 1. Englewood Cliffs, NJ: Salem Press, 1979. pp. 433-437.

"Cosmicomics," in: Magill, Frank N., ed. Survey of Science Fiction Literature, Vol. 1. Englewood Cliffs, NJ: Salem Press, 1979. pp. 438-442.

"Crystal Age, A," in: Magill, Frank N., ed. Survey of Modern Fantasy Literature, Vol 1. Englewood Cliffs, NJ: Salem Press, Inc., 1983. pp. 328-330.

"Darkening Island," in: Magill, Frank N., ed. Survey of Science Fiction Literature, Vol. 1. Englewood Cliffs, NJ: Salem Press, 1979. pp. 480-483.

Stableford, B. M. (Continued)

"Darkness and Dawn," in: Magill, Frank N., ed. Survey of Science Fiction Literature, Vol. 1. Englewood Cliffs, NJ: Salem Press, 1979. pp. 484-487.

"Deep Waters," in: Magill, Frank N., ed. Survey of Science Fiction Literature, Vol. 2. Englewood Cliffs, NJ: Salem Press, 1979. pp. 524-528.

"Deryni Trilogy, The," in: Magill, Frank N., ed. Survey of Modern Fantasy Literature, Vol 1. Englewood Cliffs, NJ: Salem Press, Inc., 1983. pp. 360-365.

"Devil in Crystal, The," in: Magill, Frank N., ed. Survey of Modern Fantasy Literature, Vol 1. Englewood Cliffs, NJ: Salem Press, Inc., 1983. pp. 377-379.

"Dream," in: Magill, Frank N., ed. Survey of Modern Fantasy Literature, Vol 1. Englewood Cliffs, NJ: Salem Press, Inc., 1983. pp. 425-427.

"Drought, The," in: Magill, Frank N., ed. Survey of Science Fiction Literature, Vol. 2. Englewood Cliffs, NJ: Salem Press, 1979. pp. 629-633.

"Elsie Venner," in: Magill, Frank N., ed. Survey of Modern Fantasy Literature, Vol 1. Englewood Cliffs, NJ: Salem Press, Inc., 1983. pp. 475-477.

"Emperor of the If," in: Magill, Frank N., ed. Survey of Science Fiction Literature, Vol. 2. Englewood Cliffs, NJ: Salem Press, 1979. pp. 717-720.

"Fafhrd and the Gray Mouser," in: Magill, Frank N., ed. Survey of Modern Fantasy Literature, Vol 2. Englewood Cliffs, NJ: Salem Press, Inc., 1983. pp. 511-517.

"Fantazius Mallare and The Kingdom of Evil," in: Magill, Frank N., ed. Survey of Modern Fantasy Literature, Vol 2. Englewood Cliffs, NJ: Salem Press, Inc., 1983. pp. 535-538.

"Fear and Typewriter in the Sky," in: Magill, Frank N., ed. Survey of Science Fiction Literature, Vol. 2. Englewood Cliffs, NJ: Salem Press, 1979. pp. 761-765.

"Frankenstein: Or, The Modern Prometheus," in: Magill, Frank N., ed. Survey of Modern Fantasy Literature, Vol 2. Englewood Cliffs, NJ: Salem Press, Inc., 1983. pp. 575-580.

"Gardens of Delight, The," in: Magill, Frank N., ed. Survey of Modern Fantasy Literature, Vol 2. Englewood Cliffs, NJ: Salem Press, Inc., 1983. pp. 593-595.

"Gees Series, The," in: Magill, Frank N., ed. Survey of Modern Fantasy Literature, Vol 2. Englewood Cliffs, NJ: Salem Press, Inc., 1983. pp. 596-600.

"Ghost of Guy Thyrle, The," in: Magill, Frank N., ed. Survey of Science Fiction Literature, Vol. 2. Englewood Cliffs, NJ: Salem Press, 1979. pp. 869-872.

"Ghost Pirates, The," in: Magill, Frank N., ed. Survey of Modern Fantasy Literature, Vol 2. Englewood Cliffs, NJ: Salem Press, Inc., 1983. pp. 601-604.

"Green Isle of the Great Deep, The," in: Magill, Frank N., ed. Survey of Modern Fantasy Literature, Vol 2. Englewood Cliffs, NJ: Salem Press, Inc., 1983. pp. 658-660.

"Green Man, The," in: Magill, Frank N., ed. Survey of Modern Fantasy Literature, Vol 2. Englewood Cliffs, NJ: Salem Press, Inc., 1983. pp. 666-669.

"Green Mansions," in: Magill, Frank N., ed. Survey of Modern Fantasy Literature, Vol 2. Englewood Cliffs, NJ: Salem Press, Inc., 1983. pp. 670-674.

"Hampdenshire Wonder, The," in: Magill, Frank N., ed. Survey of Science Fiction Literature, Vol. 2. Englewood Cliffs, NJ: Salem Press, 1979. pp. 945-949.

"Happy Prince and Other Tales, The and A House of Pomegranates," in: Magill, Frank N., ed. Survey of Modern Fantasy Literature, Vol 2. Englewood Cliffs, NJ: Salem Press, Inc., 1983. pp. 687-689.

"Heads of Cerberus, The," in: Magill, Frank N., ed. Survey of Modern Fantasy Literature, Vol 2. Englewood Cliffs, NJ: Salem Press, Inc., 1983. pp. 718-719.

"Herovit's World," in: Magill, Frank N., ed. Survey of Science Fiction Literature, Vol. 2. Englewood Cliffs, NJ: Salem Press, 1979. pp. 972-976.

"His Monkey Wife: Or, Married to a Chimp," in: Magill, Frank N., ed. Survey of Modern Fantasy Literature, Vol 2. Englewood Cliffs, NJ: Salem Press, Inc., 1983. pp. 730-731.

"Humour and Fantasy," in: Magill, Frank N., ed. Survey of Modern Fantasy Literature, Vol 2. Englewood Cliffs, NJ: Salem Press, Inc., 1983. pp. 760-764.

"Ice," in: Magill, Frank N., ed. Survey of Science Fiction Literature, Vol. 2. Englewood Cliffs, NJ: Salem Press, 1979. pp. 1000-1003.

"Inverted World," in: Magill, Frank N., ed. Survey of Science Fiction Literature, Vol. 3. Englewood Cliffs, NJ: Salem Press, 1979. pp. 1045-1049.

Stableford, B. M. (Continued)

"Jirel of Joiry," in: Magill, Frank N., ed. Survey of Modern Fantasy Literature, Vol 2. Englewood Cliffs, NJ: Salem Press, Inc., 1983. pp. 805-807.

"King in Yellow, The," in: Magill, Frank N., ed. Survey of Modern Fantasy Literature, Vol 2. Englewood Cliffs, NJ: Salem Press, Inc., 1983. pp. 844-847.

"Knights of the Limits, The," in: Magill, Frank N., ed. Survey of Science Fiction Literature, Vol. 3. Englewood Cliffs, NJ: Salem Press, 1979. pp. 1126-1129.

"Kwaidan," in: Magill, Frank N., ed. Survey of Modern Fantasy Literature, Vol 2. Englewood Cliffs, NJ: Salem Press, Inc., 1983. pp. 859-860.

"Legion of Time, The," in: Magill, Frank N., ed. Survey of Science Fiction Literature, Vol. 3. Englewood Cliffs, NJ: Salem Press, 1979. pp. 1178-1182.

"Lensman Series, The," in: Magill, Frank N., ed. Survey of Science Fiction Literature, Vol. 3. Englewood Cliffs, NJ: Salem Press, 1979. pp. 1183-1187.

"Little, Big," in: Magill, Frank N., ed. Survey of Modern Fantasy Literature, Vol 2. Englewood Cliffs, NJ: Salem Press, Inc., 1983. pp. 887-890.

"Lost Continent, The," in: Magill, Frank N., ed. Survey of Modern Fantasy Literature, Vol 2. Englewood Cliffs, NJ: Salem Press, Inc., 1983. pp. 916-919.

"Lost Horizon," in: Magill, Frank N., ed. Survey of Modern Fantasy Literature, Vol 2. Englewood Cliffs, NJ: Salem Press, Inc., 1983. pp. 920-923.

"Lost Traveller, The," in: Magill, Frank N., ed. Survey of Modern Fantasy Literature, Vol 2. Englewood Cliffs, NJ: Salem Press, Inc., 1983. pp. 924-925.

"Lost World, The," in: Magill, Frank N., ed. Survey of Science Fiction Literature, Vol. 3. Englewood Cliffs, NJ: Salem Press, 1979. pp. 1270-1273.

"Lumen," in: Magill, Frank N., ed. Survey of Science Fiction Literature, Vol. 3. Englewood Cliffs, NJ: Salem Press, 1979. pp. 1294-1298.

"Magic Skin, The," in: Magill, Frank N., ed. Survey of Modern Fantasy Literature, Vol 2. Englewood Cliffs, NJ: Salem Press, Inc., 1983. pp. 945-947.

"Master and Margarita, The," in: Magill, Frank N., ed. Survey of Modern Fantasy Literature, Vol 2. Englewood Cliffs, NJ: Salem Press, Inc., 1983. pp. 983-987.

"Moonchild," in: Magill, Frank N., ed. Survey of Modern Fantasy Literature, Vol 3. Englewood Cliffs, NJ: Salem Press, Inc., 1983. pp. 1065-1067.

"Mortgage on the Brain, The," in: Magill, Frank N., ed. Survey of Science Fiction Literature, Vol. 3. Englewood Cliffs, NJ: Salem Press, 1979. pp. 1459-1462.

"Morwyn: Or, The Vengeance of God," in: Magill, Frank N., ed. Survey of Modern Fantasy Literature, Vol 3. Englewood Cliffs, NJ: Salem Press, Inc., 1983. pp. 1068-1070.

"Mr. Weston's Good Wine," in: Magill, Frank N., ed. Survey of Modern Fantasy Literature, Vol 3. Englewood Cliffs, NJ: Salem Press, Inc., 1983. pp. 1047-1051.

"Napolion of Notting Hill, The," in: Magill, Frank N., ed. Survey of Modern Fantasy Literature, Vol 3. Englewood Cliffs, NJ: Salem Press, Inc., 1983. pp. 1089-1091.

"Nephele," in: Magill, Frank N., ed. Survey of Modern Fantasy Literature, Vol 3. Englewood Cliffs, NJ: Salem Press, Inc., 1983. pp. 1096-1098.

"Nightwings," in: Magill, Frank N., ed. Survey of Science Fiction Literature, Vol. 3. Englewood Cliffs, NJ: Salem Press, 1979. pp. 1526-1530.

"On Wings of Song," in: Magill, Frank N., ed. Survey of Modern Fantasy Literature, Vol 3. Englewood Cliffs, NJ: Salem Press, Inc., 1983. pp. 1146-1148.

"One of Cleopatra's Nights," in: Magill, Frank N., ed. Survey of Modern Fantasy Literature, Vol 3. Englewood Cliffs, NJ: Salem Press, Inc., 1983. pp. 1158-1159.

"Other Side of the Mountain, The," in: Magill, Frank N., ed. Survey of Modern Fantasy Literature, Vol 3. Englewood Cliffs, NJ: Salem Press, Inc., 1983. pp. 1179-1182.

"Our Ancestors," in: Magill, Frank N., ed. Survey of Modern Fantasy Literature, Vol 3. Englewood Cliffs, NJ: Salem Press, Inc., 1983. pp. 1183-1187.

"Paradox Men, The," in: Magill, Frank N., ed. Survey of Science Fiction Literature, Vol. 4. Englewood Cliffs, NJ: Salem Press, 1979. pp. 1641-1644.

"Passion of New Eve, The," in: Magill, Frank N., ed. Survey of Modern Fantasy Literature, Vol 3. Englewood Cliffs, NJ: Salem Press, Inc., 1983. pp. 1212-1215.

"Philosopher's Stone, The," in: Magill, Frank N., ed. Survey of Science Fiction Literature, Vol. 4. Englewood Cliffs, NJ: Salem Press, 1979. pp. 1674-1677.

Stableford, B. M. (Continued)

"Poison Belt, The," in: Magill, Frank N., ed. Survey of Science Fiction Literature, Vol. 4. Englewood Cliffs, NJ: Salem Press, 1979. pp. 1702-1704.

"Portrait of Jennie," in: Magill, Frank N., ed. Survey of Modern Fantasy Literature, Vol 3. Englewood Cliffs, NJ: Salem Press, Inc., 1983. pp. 1276-1279.

"Purple Cloud, The," in: Magill, Frank N., ed. Survey of Science Fiction Literature, Vol. 4. Englewood Cliffs, NJ: Salem Press, 1979. pp. 1735-1738.

"Revolt of the Angels, The," in: Magill, Frank N., ed. Survey of Modern Fantasy Literature, Vol 3. Englewood Cliffs, NJ: Salem Press, Inc., 1983. pp. 1313-1316.

"Riddle of the Tower, The," in: Magill, Frank N., ed. Survey of Science Fiction Literature, Vol. 4. Englewood Cliffs, NJ: Salem Press, 1979. pp. 1780-1783.

"Ring Around the Sun," in: Magill, Frank N., ed. Survey of Science Fiction Literature, Vol. 4. Englewood Cliffs, NJ: Salem Press, 1979. pp. 1794-1798.

"Ringstones and Other Curious Tales and The Doll Maker and Other Tales of the Uncanny," in: Magill, Frank N., ed. Survey of Modern Fantasy Literature, Vol 3. Englewood Cliffs: Salem Press, Inc., 1983. pp. 1320-1324.

"Romance of Two Worlds, A," in: Magill, Frank N., ed. Survey of Modern Fantasy Literature, Vol 3. Englewood Cliffs, NJ: Salem Press, Inc., 1983. pp. 1332-1334.

"Rose, The," in: Magill, Frank N., ed. Survey of Science Fiction Literature, Vol. 4. Englewood Cliffs, NJ: Salem Press, 1979. pp. 1832-1836.

"Saragossa Manuscript, The," in: Magill, Frank N., ed. Survey of Modern Fantasy Literature, Vol 3. Englewood Cliffs, NJ: Salem Press, Inc., 1983. pp. 1355-1357.

"Saurus," in: Magill, Frank N., ed. Survey of Science Fiction Literature, Vol. 4. Englewood Cliffs, NJ: Salem Press, 1979. pp. 1866-1870.

"Seed of Light," in: Magill, Frank N., ed. Survey of Science Fiction Literature, Vol. 4. Englewood Cliffs, NJ: Salem Press, 1979. pp. 1884-1887.

"Sinister Barrier," in: Magill, Frank N., ed. Survey of Science Fiction Literature, Vol. 5. Englewood Cliffs, NJ: Salem Press, 1979. pp. 2075-2078.

"Spirite," in: Magill, Frank N., ed. Survey of Modern Fantasy Literature, Vol 4. Englewood Cliffs, NJ: Salem Press, Inc., 1983. pp. 1798-1800.

"St. Leon," in: Magill, Frank N., ed. Survey of Modern Fantasy Literature, Vol 3. Englewood Cliffs, NJ: Salem Press, Inc., 1983. pp. 1347-1349.

"Supermale, The," in: Magill, Frank N., ed. Survey of Modern Fantasy Literature, Vol 4. Englewood Cliffs, NJ: Salem Press, Inc., 1983. pp. 1859-1862.

"Symzonia," in: Magill, Frank N., ed. Survey of Science Fiction Literature, Vol. 5. Englewood Cliffs, NJ: Salem Press, 1979. pp. 2207-2210.

"Syzgy," in: Magill, Frank N., ed. Survey of Science Fiction Literature, Vol. 5. Englewood Cliffs, NJ: Salem Press, 1979. pp. 2218-2222.

"These Mortals," in: Magill, Frank N., ed. Survey of Modern Fantasy Literature, Vol 4. Englewood Cliffs, NJ: Salem Press, Inc., 1983. pp. 1898-1900.

"They'd Rather Be Right," in: Magill, Frank N., ed. Survey of Science Fiction Literature, Vol. 5. Englewood Cliffs, NJ: Salem Press, 1979. pp. 2255-2259.

"Three Immortals, The," in: Magill, Frank N., ed. Survey of Modern Fantasy Literature, Vol 4. Englewood Cliffs, NJ: Salem Press, Inc., 1983. pp. 1918-1921.

"Three Stigmata of Palmer Eldritch, The," in: Magill, Frank N., ed. Survey of Science Fiction Literature, Vol. 5. Englewood Cliffs, NJ: Salem Press, 1979. pp. 2269-2273.

"Through the Looking-Glass," in: Magill, Frank N., ed. Survey of Science Fiction Literature, Vol. 5. Englewood Cliffs, NJ: Salem Press, 1979. pp. 2278-2282.

"Thunder on the Left," in: Magill, Frank N., ed. Survey of Modern Fantasy Literature, Vol 4. Englewood Cliffs, NJ: Salem Press, Inc., 1983. pp. 1930-1932.

"Time of Changes, A," in: Magill, Frank N., ed. Survey of Science Fiction Literature, Vol. 5. Englewood Cliffs, NJ: Salem Press, 1979. pp. 2293-2297.

"Twenty Thousand Leagues Under the Sea," in: Magill, Frank N., ed. Survey of Science Fiction Literature, Vol. 5. Englewood Cliffs, NJ: Salem Press, 1979. pp. 2329-2333.

"Twilight of the Gods, The," in: Magill, Frank N., ed. Survey of Modern Fantasy Literature, Vol 4. Englewood Cliffs, NJ: Salem Press, Inc., 1983. pp. 1986-1988.

Stableford, B. M. (Continued)

"Undine," in: Magill, Frank N., ed. Survey of Modern Fantasy Literature, Vol 4. Englewood Cliffs, NJ: Salem Press, Inc., 1983. pp. 1992-1994.

"Upsidonia," in: Magill, Frank N., ed. Survey of Modern Fantasy Literature, Vol 4. Englewood Cliffs, NJ: Salem Press, Inc., 1983. pp. 2005-2007.

"Vampires of Alfama, The," in: Magill, Frank N., ed. Survey of Modern Fantasy Literature, Vol 4. Englewood Cliffs, NJ: Salem Press, Inc., 1983. pp. 2008-2012.

"Violet Apple and the Witch, The," in: Magill, Frank N., ed. Survey of Modern Fantasy Literature, Vol 4. Englewood Cliffs, NJ: Salem Press, Inc., 1983. pp. 2033-2035.

"Voyage to Faremido and Capillaria," in: Magill, Frank N., ed. Survey of Modern Fantasy Literature, Vol 4. Englewood Cliffs, NJ: Salem Press, Inc., 1983. pp. 2046-2048.

"Wandering Jew, The," in: Magill, Frank N., ed. Survey of Modern Fantasy Literature, Vol 4. Englewood Cliffs, NJ: Salem Press, Inc., 1983. pp. 2059-2062.

"Weigher of Souls, The," in: Magill, Frank N., ed. Survey of Modern Fantasy Literature, Vol 5. Englewood Cliffs, NJ: Salem Press, Inc., 1983. pp. 2084-2086.

"Werewolf of Paris, The," in: Magill, Frank N., ed. Survey of Modern Fantasy Literature, Vol 5. Englewood Cliffs, NJ: Salem Press, Inc., 1983. pp. 2102-2106.

"When the Birds Fly South," in: Magill, Frank N., ed. Survey of Modern Fantasy Literature, Vol 5. Englewood Cliffs, NJ: Salem Press, Inc., 1983. pp. 2115-2117.

"Who?," in: Magill, Frank N., ed. Survey of Science Fiction Literature, Vol. 5. Englewood Cliffs, NJ: Salem Press, 1979. pp. 2474-2477.

"Wind from Nowhere, The," in: Magill, Frank N., ed. Survey of Science Fiction Literature, Vol. 5. Englewood Cliffs, NJ: Salem Press, 1979. pp. 2478-2481.

"Wolf-Leader, The," in: Magill, Frank N., ed. Survey of Modern Fantasy Literature, Vol 5. Englewood Cliffs, NJ: Salem Press, Inc., 1983. pp. 2153-2155.

"Wonderful Visit, The," in: Magill, Frank N., ed. Survey of Modern Fantasy Literature, Vol 5. Englewood Cliffs, NJ: Salem Press, Inc., 1983. pp. 2162-2164.

"World Below, The," in: Magill, Frank N., ed. Survey of Science Fiction Literature, Vol. 5. Englewood Cliffs, NJ: Salem Press, 1979. pp. 2497-2500.

"Worm Ouroboros, The," in: Magill, Frank N., ed. Survey of Modern Fantasy Literature, Vol 5. Englewood Cliffs, NJ: Salem Press, Inc., 1983. pp. 2180-2184.

"Yellow Danger, The," in: Magill, Frank N., ed. Survey of Science Fiction Literature, Vol. 5. Englewood Cliffs, NJ: Salem Press, 1979. pp. 2525-2528.

"Against the New Gods: The Speculative Fiction of S. Fowler Wright," Foundation 29: 10-52. November 1983.

"Algebraic Fantasies, The Science Fiction of Bob Shaw," in: Kincaid, Paul, ed. Bob Shaw, British Science Fiction Writers, Volume 1. Kent, Eng.: British Science Fiction Association, 1981. pp. 6-31.

"Alien Ecologies," in: Wingrove, David, ed. The Science Fiction Source Book. New York: Van Nostrand, 1984. pp. 56-57.

"Aliens," in: Wingrove, David, ed. The Science Fiction Source Book. New York: Van Nostrand, 1984. pp. 34-36.

"Chronology of modern fantasy literature," in: Magill, Frank N., ed. Survey of Modern Fantasy Literature, Vol 5. Englewood Cliffs, NJ: Salem Press, Inc., 1983. pp. 2501-2516.

"Clark Ashton Smith," in: Bleiler, E. F., ed. Science Fiction Writers. New York: Scribners, 1982. pp. 139-144.

"David H. Keller," in: Bleiler, E. F., ed. Science Fiction Writers. New York: Scribners, 1982. pp. 119-123.

"Disasters," in: Wingrove, David, ed. The Science Fiction Source Book. New York: Van Nostrand, 1984. pp. 45-47.

"Edgar Fawcett: ghost in the mansion of science fiction history," Vector 78:13,47-49. November/December.

"Edmond Hamilton and Leigh Brackett: An Appreciation," in: Stableford, B. M. Masters of Science Fiction. San Bernardino, CA: Borgo, 1981. pp. 3-14. (Reprinted from Vector, November/December 1978)

"Eroticism and the supernatural," in: Magill, Frank N., ed. Survey of Modern Fantasy Literature, Vol 5. Englewood Cliffs, NJ: Salem Press, Inc., 1983. pp. 2331-2349.

"ESP," in: Wingrove, David, ed. The Science Fiction Source Book. New York: Van Nostrand, 1984. pp. 42-44.

"Fritz Leiber," in: Bleiler, E. F., ed. Science Fiction Writers. New York: Scribners, 1982. pp. 419-424.

Stableford, B. M. (Continued)

"Future Between the Wars: The Speculative Fiction of John Gloag," Foundation 20: 47-64. October 1980.

"Galactic Empires," in: Wingrove, David, ed. The Science Fiction Source Book. New York: Van Nostrand, 1984. pp. 40-41.

"Inner Space," in: Wingrove, David, ed. The Science Fiction Source Book. New York: Van Nostrand, 1984. pp. 62-64.

"Insoluble problems: Barry Malzberg's career in science fiction," Foundation 11/12:135-141. March 1977.

"Insoluble Problems: Footnotes to Barry Malzberg's Career in Science Fiction," in: Stableford, B. M. Masters of Science Fiction. San Bernardino, CA: Borgo, 1981. pp. 24-31.

"J. G. Ballard," in: Bleiler, E. F., ed. Science Fiction Writers. New York: Scribners, 1982. pp. 277-282.

"L. Sprague De Camp," in: Bleiler, E. F., ed. Science Fiction Writers. New York: Scribners, 1982. pp. 179-184.

"Locked in the slaughterhouse: the novels of Kurt Vonnegut," Arena 8:8-15. October 1978.

"Locked in the Slaughterhouse: The Novels of Kurt Vonnegut," in: Stableford, B. M. Masters of Science Fiction. San Bernardino, CA: Borgo, 1981. pp. 15-23. (Reprinted from Arena, October 1978)

"Machines and Inventions: Deus ex machina, SF and technology, II," Vector 67/68: 51-63, 79. Spring 1974.

"Magic," in: Wingrove, David, ed. The Science Fiction Source Book. New York: Van Nostrand, 1984. pp. 58-59.

"Man and Machine," in: Wingrove, David, ed. The Science Fiction Source Book. New York: Van Nostrand, 1984. pp. 25-27.

"Man-Made Catastrophes in SF," Foundation 22: 56-85. June 1981.

"Man-Made Catastrophes," in: Rabkin, Eric S., ed. The End of the World. Carbondale: Southern Illinois University Press, 1983. pp. 97-138.

"Marriage of science and fiction: the emergence of a new fiction," in: Holdstock, Robert, ed. Encyclopedia of Science Fiction. London: Octopus, 1978. pp. 18-27.

"Marxism, Science Fiction and the Poverty of Prophecy: Some Comparisons and Contrasts," Foundation 32: 5-14. November 1984.

"Media," in: Wingrove, David, ed. The Science Fiction Source Book. New York: Van Nostrand, 1984. pp. 60-61.

"Metamorphosis of Robert Silverberg," in: Stableford, B. M. Masters of Science Fiction. San Bernardino, CA: Borgo, 1981. pp. 32-42. (Reprinted from SF Monthly, v. 3 no. 3)

"Mythology of fairie, The," in: Magill, Frank N., ed. Survey of Modern Fantasy Literature, Vol 5. Englewood Cliffs, NJ: Salem Press, Inc., 1983. pp. 2283-2298.

"Needs and demands of the science fiction reader, The," Vector 83:4-8. September/October 1977.

"Notes toward a sociology of science fiction," Foundation 15:28-41. January 1979.

"Opening minds," Vector 76/77:14-17. August/September.

"Parallel Worlds and Alternate Histories," in: Wingrove, David, ed. The Science Fiction Source Book. New York: Van Nostrand, 1984. pp. 51-53.

"Philip K. Dick," in: Bleiler, E. F., ed. Science Fiction Writers. New York: Scribners, 1982. pp. 337-343.

"Politics of Evolution: Philosophical Themes in the Speculative Fiction of M. P. Shiel," Foundation 27: 35-60. February 1983.

"Realistic Romances of Edgar Fawcett," Foundation 24: 23-48. February 1982.

"Religion and Mythology," in: Wingrove, David, ed. The Science Fiction Source Book. New York: Van Nostrand, 1984. pp. 48-50.

"Robot in science fiction: Deus ex machina; science fiction and technology," Vector 66: 5-20. July/August 1973.

"Science fiction and the image of the future," Foundation 14:26-34. September 1978.

"Science Fiction Between the Wars: 1918-1938," in: Barron, Neil, ed. Anatomy of Wonder. 2nd ed. New York: Bowker, 1981. pp. 88-124.

"Science fiction of James Blish, The," Foundation 13:12-43. May 1978. Comment, R. A. W. Lowndes. 16:22-24. May 1979.

"Sex and Sensuality," in: Wingrove, David, ed. The Science Fiction Source Book. New York: Van Nostrand, 1984. pp. 54-55.

"Short fiction of Balzac, The," in: Magill, Frank N., ed. Survey of Modern Fantasy Literature, Vol 3. Englewood Cliffs, NJ: Salem Press, Inc., 1983. pp. 1420-1422.

Stableford, B. M. (Continued)

"Short fiction of Bloch, The," in: Magill, Frank N., ed. <u>Survey of Modern Fantasy Literature</u>, Vol 3. Englewood Cliffs, NJ: Salem Press, Inc., 1983. pp. 1452-1456.

"Short fiction of Boucher, The," in: Magill, Frank N., ed. <u>Survey of Modern Fantasy Literature</u>, Vol 3. Englewood Cliffs, NJ: Salem Press, Inc., 1983. pp. 1465-1467.

"Short fiction of Heard, The," in: Magill, Frank N., ed. <u>Survey of Modern Fantasy Literature</u>, Vol 3. Englewood Cliffs, NJ: Salem Press, Inc., 1983. pp. 1544-1546.

"Short Fiction of J. G. Ballard, The," in: Magill, Frank N., ed. <u>Survey of Science Fiction Literature</u>, Vol. 4. Englewood Cliffs, NJ: Salem Press, 1979. pp. 1994-1998.

"Short Fiction of Jorge Luis Borges, The," in: Magill, Frank N., ed. <u>Survey of Science Fiction Literature</u>, Vol. 4. Englewood Cliffs, NJ: Salem Press, 1979. pp. 2008-2013.

"Short Fiction of Judith Merril, The," in: Magill, Frank N., ed. <u>Survey of Science Fiction Literature</u>, Vol. 4. Englewood Cliffs, NJ: Salem Press, 1979. pp. 2014-2018.

"Short fiction of Lee, The," in: Magill, Frank N., ed. <u>Survey of Modern Fantasy Literature</u>, Vol 4. Englewood Cliffs, NJ: Salem Press, Inc., 1983. pp. 1597-1599.

"Short fiction of Smith, The," in: Magill, Frank N., ed. <u>Survey of Modern Fantasy Literature</u>, Vol 4. Englewood Cliffs, NJ: Salem Press, Inc., 1983. pp. 1692-1697.

"Short Fiction of William Tenn, The," in: Magill, Frank N., ed. <u>Survey of Science Fiction Literature</u>, Vol. 5. Englewood Cliffs, NJ: Salem Press, 1979. pp. 2065-2069.

"Significance of science fiction, The," <u>Spectrum</u> 148:7-9. 1977.

"Skylark Series, The," in: Magill, Frank N., ed. <u>Survey of Science Fiction Literature</u>, Vol. 5. Englewood Cliffs, NJ: Salem Press, 1979. pp. 2091-2095.

"Social design in science fiction," <u>Amazing</u> 52(1): 4-5, 119-124. February 1979.

"Social role of SF, The," <u>Algol</u> 12(2):23-26. Summer 1975.

"Space Travel," in: Wingrove, David, ed. <u>The Science Fiction Source Book</u>. New York: Van Nostrand, 1984. pp. 37-39.

"Stanley G. Weinbaum," in: Bleiler, E. F., ed. <u>Science Fiction Writers</u>. New York: Scribners, 1982. pp. 145-149.

"Tarzan Series, The," in: Magill, Frank N., ed. <u>Survey of Modern Fantasy Literature</u>,

Vol 4. Englewood Cliffs, NJ: Salem Press, Inc., 1983. pp. 1884-1890.

"Theodore Sturgeon," in: Bleiler, E. F., ed. <u>Science Fiction Writers</u>. New York: Scribners, 1982. pp. 203-208.

"Thomas M. Disch," in: Bleiler, E. F., ed. <u>Science Fiction Writers</u>. New York: Scribners, 1982. pp. 351-356.

"Time Travel," in: Wingrove, David, ed. <u>The Science Fiction Source Book</u>. New York: Van Nostrand, 1984. pp. 31-33.

"Utopia and Dystopia," in: Wingrove, David, ed. <u>The Science Fiction Source Book</u>. New York: Van Nostrand, 1984. pp. 28-30.

"Utopia: and Afterwards; Socioeconomic Speculation in the SF of Mack Reynolds," in: Stableford, B. M. <u>Masters of Science Fiction</u>. San Bernardino, CA: Borgo, 1981. pp. 43-64.

"Utopian dream revisited: socio-economic speculation in the SF of Mack Reynolds, The," <u>Foundation</u> 16:31-54. May 1979. "Afterword" by Reynolds: 16:54-55. May 1979.

"William Wilson's prospectus for science fiction: 1851," <u>Foundation</u> 10:6-12. June 1976.

"Witchcraft," in: Magill, Frank N., ed. <u>Survey of Modern Fantasy Literature</u>, Vol 5. Englewood Cliffs, NJ: Salem Press, Inc., 1983. pp. 2350-2368.

Stableford, Vivien

"<u>Borrowers Series, The</u>," in: Magill, Frank N., ed. <u>Survey of Modern Fantasy Literature</u>, Vol 1. Englewood Cliffs, NJ: Salem Press, Inc., 1983. pp. 164-165.

"<u>Dear Brutus</u>," in: Magill, Frank N., ed. <u>Survey of Modern Fantasy Literature</u>, Vol 1. Englewood Cliffs, NJ: Salem Press, Inc., 1983. pp. 358-359.

"<u>Dreadful Dragon of Hay Hill, The</u>," in: Magill, Frank N., ed. <u>Survey of Modern Fantasy Literature</u>, Vol 1. Englewood Cliffs, NJ: Salem Press, Inc., 1983. pp. 423-424.

"<u>Eric Brighteyes</u>," in: Magill, Frank N., ed. <u>Survey of Modern Fantasy Literature</u>, Vol 1. Englewood Cliffs, NJ: Salem Press, Inc., 1983. pp. 486-488.

"<u>Fair to Middling, The</u>," in: Magill, Frank N., ed. <u>Survey of Modern Fantasy Literature</u>, Vol 2. Englewood Cliffs, NJ: Salem Press, Inc., 1983. pp. 518-519.

"<u>Hadrian the Seventh</u>," in: Magill, Frank N., ed. <u>Survey of Modern Fantasy Literature</u>, Vol 2. Englewood Cliffs, NJ: Salem Press, Inc., 1983. pp. 684-686.

Stableford, Vivien (Continued)

"La-bas," in: Magill, Frank N., ed. Survey of Modern Fantasy Literature, Vol 2. Englewood Cliffs, NJ: Salem Press, Inc., 1983. pp. 861-862.

"Owl Service, The," in: Magill, Frank N., ed. Survey of Modern Fantasy Literature, Vol 3. Englewood Cliffs, NJ: Salem Press, Inc., 1983. pp. 1188-1190.

"Seven Men," in: Magill, Frank N., ed. Survey of Modern Fantasy Literature, Vol 3. Englewood Cliffs, NJ: Salem Press, Inc., 1983. pp. 1378-1379.

"Weirdstone of Brisingmen, The and The Moon of Gomrath," in: Magill, Frank N., ed. Survey of Modern Fantasy Literature, Vol 5. Englewood Cliffs, NJ: Salem Press, Inc., 1983. pp. 2087-2089.

"Zuleika Dobson," in: Magill, Frank N., ed. Survey of Modern Fantasy Literature, Vol 5. Englewood Cliffs, NJ: Salem Press, Inc., 1983. pp. 2217-2219.

Stack, Peter

"Author Has Faith in 'Dune'," San Francisco Chronicle December 11, 1984. in: NewsBank. Literature 66: E8. January 1985.

Stackel, Leslie

"Starlog Interview: Jim Henson," Starlog 85: 26-29. August 1984.

Stacy, Paul

"Cinematic thought," Hartford Studies in Literature 1:124-130. 1969.

Staggers, Anthony

"Now read on . . . " New Statesman 52:64-66. July 21, 1956.

Staicar, Tom

Critical Encounters II: Writers and Themes in Science Fiction. New York: Ungar, 1982. 162 p.

Feminine Eye: Science Fiction and the Women Who Write It, ed. by Tom Staicar. New York: Ungar, 1982. 148 p.

Fritz Leiber. New York: Ungar, 1983. 134 p.

"Harlan Ellison: interview/profile," Amazing 27(9): 5-9. November 1980.

"Interview with Alan Dean Foster," Amazing 27(6): 12-16. February 1980.

"Interview: Harlan Ellison," Twilight Zone 1(9):14-25. December 1981.

"Lloyd Biggle, Jr.: What is a Musicologist Doing Writing Science Fiction?" Amazing 28(4): 6-9. January 1982.

"SF writer's library," Empire: For the SF Writer 4(2): 16-18. February 1979.

Stamm, M. E.

"Dark side of the American Dream: Dennis Etchison, The," in: Schweitzer, Darrell, ed. Discovering Modern Horror Fiction I. Mercer Island: Starmont, 1985. pp. 48-55.

"Harlan Ellison: A Profile," Fantasy Newsletter 4(4): 16-22, 31. April 1981.

Stanbury, C. M., II

"Little magazines and the science fiction world of Marshall McLuhan," Small Press Review 2(2/3):3-5. January 1970.

Standish, David

"Playboy interview," Playboy 20(7):57-74,214-215. July 1973.

Stanford, B.

"Shiva and future shock: contemporary insights from world mythology," English Journal 62(6):919-921. September 1973.

Stanley, Dick

"Space party: science fiction fans gather in their own world," Austin American-Statesman Sec. B, p. 1, 7. September 2, 1985.

"Star Trek's successor taking off," Trenton (NJ) Times. January 24, 1976. in: NewsBank. Film and Television. 12:E1. 1976.

Stanley, Don

"First Came a Desert Planet, Now Comes the Plague," Sacramento Bee, October 3, 1982. in: Newsbank. Literature. 35: G12-13. 1982.

Stanley, John

Creature Features Movie Guide. Pacifica, CA: Creature At Large, 1981. 208 p.

Creature Features Movie Guide. New York: Warner, 1984. 304 p.

Stanley, John (Continued)

"Bold Puppet World Created From Scratch," San Francisco Examiner December 19, 1982. in: NewsBank. Film and Television 73: C10. 1982/1983.

"Second banana spaceman becomes a phenomenon," San Francisco Examiner November 28, 1976. in: NewsBank. Film and Television. 85:G9-G10. 1976.

"Time-Warp, Naval Incident," San Francisco Examiner. in: NewsBank. Film and Television. FTV 18: D6-D7. 1984.

Stannard, Lane

"Annual SF magazine report," Science Fiction Times No. 399/400:13-14. January/February 1963.

"Gains are few in science fiction magazine 1964 circulations," Science Fiction Times No. 424:9-10. February 1965.

"Robert E. Howard's Conan," Fantasy Times No. 150:2,4. March (2) 1952.

"Science fiction is not dead," Science Fiction Times No. 345:7-10. September (1) 1960.

"Science Fiction Magazine Record, February 1962," Science Fiction Times No. 379:4. February 1962.

"Strange saga of Science Fiction Adventures, The," Science Fiction Times No. 369:29. September 1961.

Stansell, John

"Isaac's mysteries," New Scientist 75: 399. August 18, 1977.

Stansky, Peter

"Englishness of George Orwell," in: George Orwell and Nineteen Eighty-Four. Washington, DC: Library of Congress, 1985. pp. 39-53.

"Utopia and Anti-Utopia: William Morris and George Orwell," History Today 33: 33-38. February 1983. (reprinted from Threepenny Review, Summer 1982)

Stanton, M. N.

"Startled muse: Emerson and science fiction, The," Extrapolation 16(1):64-66. December 1971.

Stapledon, Olaf

"Interplanetary Man," Journal of the British Interplanetary Society. 7(6):215. November 1948.

"Man's Future," Fantasy Commentator 4(2): 62-65. Winter 1979-80.

"Remaking of Man," Fantasy Commentator 4(1): 27-29. Winter 1978-79.

Starchild, Adam

Science fiction of Konstaintin Tsiolkavsky, by Konstaintin Tsiolkovsky and Adam Starchild. Seattle: University Press of the Pacific, 1979. 454 p.

Starling, M. L.

"Conan legend began in 1932," Las Vegas Review-Journal. February 25, 1982. in: NewsBank. Film and Television. 102:E10. 1981/82.

"Growing Conan cult jams theater for sneak preview," Las Vegas Review-Journal. February 25, 1982. in: NewsBank. Film and Television. 102:E11. 1981/82.

Starrett, Vincent

Arthur Machen: A Novelist of Ecstasy and Sin. Chicago: Walter M. Hill, 1918. 35 p.

Stathis, Lewis

"Introduction," in: Dick, P. K. Time Out of Joint. Boston: Gregg, 1979. pp. v-xiv.

Stathis, Lou

"'Fantasia' visions of non-reality," Fantastic 27(4):112-120,130. January 1979.

Statuti, Sister J. A.

"SF in the classroom: II. SF in the high school," Extrapolation 17(1):31-34. December 1975.

Stawinski, Julian

"Stanislawa Lema Eden," Nowe Ksiazki No. 17. 1959.

Stecher, L. J., Jr.

"Invasions of Earth," in: Bretnor, Reginald, ed. The Future at War: Vol. 2: The Spear of Mars. New York: Ace, 1980. pp. 59-81.

Steele, J. M.

"Back to the Future," Boise Idaho Stateman
July 2, 1985. in: NewsBank. Film and
Television. 1:C4. July 1985.

Steelman, N. V.

"Science fiction and the community college: a
symbiosis," paper presented at the Sixth
Annual Meeting of the College English
Association, Atlanta, Georgia. April 10-12,
1975. 10 p. (ERIC ED 119 237)

Stefen, Rudolf

"Gewalt in utopia oder was wurde bisher an
phantastischer literatur von der
bundesprufstelle als jugendgefahrdend
indiziert?" in: Weigand, Jorg, ed. Die
Triviale Phantasie. Bonn: Asgard, 1976. pp.
143-154.

"Violence in SF, and censorship in West
Germany," Science Fiction Studies
4(3):271-276. November 1977.

Steffan, Dan

"Bullshit artist: SF art," Thrust
12.32-33. Summer 1979.

Steffen-Fluhr, Nancy

"Women and the Inner Game of Don Siegel's
Invasion of the Body Snatchers,"
Science-Fiction Studies 11(2): 139-153.
July 1984.

"Women and the Inner Game...: Response to
Pedersen," Science Fiction Studies 12(1):
109-110. March 1985.

Stein, E.

"Thirteen voyages of Ray Harryhausen," Film
Comment 13(6):24-28. November/December 1977.

Stein, Gerard

"Dracula ou la circulation du 'sans',"
Litteratur No. 8:84-99. December, 1972.

Stein, Heinrich

"Sowjetische 'bibliotek der modernen
phantastik.' Ein uberblick," Quarber Merkur
43:14-33. May 1976.

Steinbach, Victor

"Aliens in Hollywood," Twilight Zone 5(1):
61-64. March/April 1985.

Steinbrunner, Chris

Cinema of the Fantastics, by Chris
Steinbrunner and Burt Goldblatt. New York:
Saturday Review Press, 1972. 282 p.

"On TV: a sci-fi launch-in," Science Fiction
Times No. 462:6. January 1969.

"Science fiction movies on television,"
Science Fiction Times No. 454:6. May 1968.

Steiner, George

"Imagining science," Listener
86(2225):686-688. November 18, 1971.

Steinhoff, William

George Orwell and the Origins of 1984. Ann
Arbor: University of Michigan Press, 1975.
288 p.

"Utopia Reconsidered: Comments on 1984,"
in: Rabkin, Eric S., et. al., eds. No Place
Else. Carbondale: Southern Illinois
University Press, 1983. pp. 147-161.

Steinmuller, Karlheinz

"Digit oder nicht digit," by Karlheinz
Steinmuller and Michael Weisser. Quarber
Merkur 62: 3-10. December 1984.

Stolzmann, R. A.

"Verlorene utopie: das werk Vonneguts und die
Amerikanische Jugend," Naus Hochland
66:271-280. 1974.

Stephan, Halina

"Aleksei Tolstoi's Aelita and the inauguration
of Soviet science fiction,"
Canadian-American Soviet Studies
18(1/2):63-75. Spring/Summer 1984.

"Changing Protagonist in Soviet Science
Fiction," in: Birnbaum, Henrik, ed. Fiction
and Drama in Eastern and Southeastern Europe.
Columbus, OH: Slavica, 1980. pp. 361-378.

"Fairy Tale and Folklore in Soviet Science
Fiction," Mosaic 16(3): 1-10. Summer 1983.

"Wissenschaftliche Fantastik und fantastische
Parabel in der sowjetischen
Gegenwartsliteratur," Osteuropa 29(11):
877-892. 1979.

Stephenson, A. M.

"Let Us Now Re-Appraise Famous Men," Vector
100: 26-27. December 1980.

Stephenson-Payne, Philip

"Civilization and savagery: two novels by Robert Holdstock," <u>Vector</u> 86:22-23. April 1978.

"John Wyndham checklist, A," <u>Science Fiction Collector</u> 8:31-44. October 1979.

Steranko

"Conan,", <u>Prevue</u> 2(7):26-32,39. April/May 1982.

"Return of the Jedi," <u>Prevue</u> 2(12):42-53,73. June/July 1983.

"Sandahl Bergman," <u>Prevue</u> 2(9): 41-46, 73. August/September 1982.

Sterling, E. K.

<u>Science Fiction in the Narrative Worlds of Boris Vian</u>. Ph.D. Dissertation, University of Kansas, 1979. 271 p.

Stern, Michael

"From technique to critique: knowledge and human interests in Brunner's <u>Stand on Zanzibar</u>, <u>The Jagged Orbit</u>, and <u>The Sheep Look Up</u>," <u>Science Fiction Studies</u> 3(2):112-130. July 1976.

"Making Culture into Nature: or, Who Put the 'Special' into 'Special Effects'," <u>Science-Fiction Studies</u> 7(3): 263-269. November 1980.

Sternberg, Jacques

<u>Une succursale du fantastique nommee science fiction</u>. Paris: Terrain Vague, 1958. 160 p.

"Science fiction rebute les francais autant que le surrealisme, La," <u>Magazine Litteraire</u> No. 31:25-27. August 1969.

"Science fiction reste en France un genre mineur, La," <u>Arts</u> January 8, 1958.

Sterritt, David

"Close encounters (review)," by David Sterritt and J. G. Boyum. <u>Science Digest</u> 83(2):16-18. February 1978.

Stevens, C. D.

"Short Fiction of Harlan Ellison, The," in: Magill, Frank N., ed. <u>Survey of Science Fiction Literature</u>, Vol. 4. Englewood Cliffs, NJ: Salem Press, 1979. pp. 1978-1988.

"High fantasy versus low comedy: humor in J. R. R. Tolkien," <u>Extrapolation</u> 21(2):122-129. Summer 1980.

Stevens, David

"Big Time, The," in: Magill, Frank N., ed. <u>Survey of Science Fiction Literature</u>, Vol. 1. Englewood Cliffs, NJ: Salem Press, 1979. pp. 218-222.

"Level Seven," in: Magill, Frank N., ed. <u>Survey of Science Fiction Literature</u>, Vol. 3. Englewood Cliffs, NJ: Salem Press, 1979. pp. 1204-1208.

"On the Beach," in: Magill, Frank N., ed. <u>Survey of Science Fiction Literature</u>, Vol. 4. Englewood Cliffs, NJ: Salem Press, 1979. pp. 1603-1607.

"Three Hearts and Three Lions," in: Magill, Frank N., ed. <u>Survey of Science Fiction Literature</u>, Vol. 5. Englewood Cliffs, NJ: Salem Press, 1979. pp. 2264-2268.

"Incongruity in a world of illusion: patterns of humor in Peter Beagle's <u>The Last Unicorn</u>," <u>Extrapolation</u> 20(3):230-237. Fall 1979.

"Short fiction of Tolkien, The," in: Magill, Frank N., ed. <u>Survey of Modern Fantasy Literature</u>, Vol 4. Englewood Cliffs, NJ: Salem Press, Inc., 1983. pp. 1724-1728.

"Trolls and dragons versus pocket handkerchiefs...The Hobbit," in: Collins, R. A., ed. <u>Scope of the Fantastic: Culture, Biography, Themes, Children's Literature</u>. Westport: Greenwood, 1985. pp. 249-256.

Stevens, M. F.

"Visit to a pulpy planet," <u>Science Fiction Review</u> 4(2):27-32. May 1975.

Stevens, Mark

"Andromeda Strain (review)," <u>Cinefantastique</u> 1(3):24-25. Summer 1971.

Stevenson, Lionel

"Artistic problem: science fiction as romance, The," <u>Extrapolation</u> 4(2):17-22. May 1963. also in: Clareson, T. D., ed. <u>SF: The Other Side of Realism</u>. Bowling Green, Ohio: Popular Press, 1971. pp. 96-104.

"Purveyors of myth and magic," in: <u>Yesterday and After: The History of the English Novel</u>. New York: Barnes & Noble, 1967. pp. 111-154.

Stewart, A. D.

"Fred Saberhagen: cybernetic psychologist," Extrapolation 18(1):42-51. December 1976.

"Jack Williamson: the comedy of cosmic evolution," in: Clareson, T. D., ed. Voices for the Future: Essays on Major Science Fiction Writers, Vol. 1. Bowling Green, Ohio: Popular Press, 1976. pp. 14-43.

Stewart, Alex

"For Love or Money," Focus: An SF Writer's Magazine 10: 3-4. February 1985.

Stewart, Bhob

"Day of the Locust (review)," Cinefantastique 4(3):34-35. Fall 1975.

"Do Androids Dream of Philip K. Dick?" Comics Journal 76: 121-134. October 1982.

"Man Who Fell to Earth (review)," Cinefantastique 5(2):28-29,31. Fall 1976.

"Solaris (review)," Cinefantastique 6(1):15,17. Summer 1977.

"Space: 1999 (review)," Cinefantastique 4(4):24. Winter 1976.

Stewart, Garrett

"Close encounters of the fourth kind," Sight and Sound 47(3):167-174. Summer 1978.

"Videology of Science Fiction," in: Slusser, George, ed. Shadows of the Magic Lamp. Carbondale: Southern Illinois University Press, 1985. pp. 159-207.

Stewart, Robert

"Shaping tomorrow, today: a rationale for the teaching of science fiction," Arizona English Bulletin 51(1):25-26. October 1972.

Stimpson, C. R.

J. R. R. Tolkien. New York: Columbia University Press, 1969. 48 p. (Columbia Essays on Modern Writers No. 41)

Stine, G. H.

"Defending the Third Industrial Revolution," in: Bretnor, Reginald, ed. The Future at War: Vol. 1: Thor's Hammer. New York: Ace, 1979. pp. 29-52.

"How to get along with an extraterrestrial ... or your neighbor," Analog 100(2):39-47. February 1980.

"Science fiction is still too conservative," Analog 105(1): 89-96. January 1985.

"Science fiction is too conservative," Analog 67(3):83-99. May 1961.

"To make a Star Trek," Analog 80:70-85. February 1968.

"Wizard Warriors: Computers and Robots in Future Warfare," in: Bretnor, Reginald, ed. The Future at War: Vole. 3: Orion's Sword. New York: Ace, 1980. pp. 276-295.

Stinner, Arthur

"Physics of Star Trek," by Arthur Stinner and Ian Winchester. New Scientist 1285/1286: 884-887. December 24/31, 1981

Stinson, J. J.

"Anthony Burgess: novelist on the margin," Journal of Popular Culture 7(1):136-151. Summer 1973.

"Better to Be Hot or Cold: 1985 and the Dynamic of the Manichean Douverse," Modern Fiction Studies 27(3): 505-516. Autumn 1981.

"Manichee world of Anthony Burgess, The," Renascence: Essays on Values in Literature 26(1):37-47. Autumn 1973.

"Nothing like the sun: the faces in Bella Cohen's mirror," Journal of Modern Literature 5(1):131-147. February 1976.

"Waugh and Anthony Burgess: some notes toward an assessment of influence and affinities," Evelyn Waugh Newsletter 10(3):11-12. 1976.

Stites, Richard

"Fantasy and revolution: Alexander Bogdanov and the origins of Bolshevik science fiction," in: Bogdanov, A. Red Star. Bloomington: Indiana University Press, 1984. pp. 1-16.

Stock, S. H.

Twenty All-Time Great Science Fiction Films, by Kenneth von Gunden and Stuart Stock. New York: Arlington House, 1982. 250 p.

Stockill, Peter

"2001: the Creation of a Modern Mythology," Vector 110: 25-29. 1982.

Stockton, H. G.

"Science fiction today," Assistant Librarian 47(7):124-126. August 1954.

Stoddard, William

"Critical Approach to Fantasy; With Application to The Lord of the Rings," Mythlore 10(3): 8-13. Winter 1984.

Stoff, Andrzej

Powiasci Fantastyczno-Naukowe Stanislawa Lema. Warsaw: Panstwowe Wydawnictwo Naukowe, 1983. 179 p.

Stoltzfus, Ben

"Subversive Play: Fantasy in Robbe-Grillet's Films," in: Slusser, George, ed. Shadows of the Magic Lamp. Carbondale: Southern Illinois University Press, 1985. pp. 30-40.

Stolzenbach, M. M.

"Water Babies: an appreciation," Mythlore 8(2):20. Summer 1981.

"Machen's Hallows," Mythlore 11(3): 28-38. Winter/Spring 1985.

Stone, Graham

Australian Science Fiction Index, 1925-1967, comp. by Graham Stone. Canberra City: Australian Science Fiction Association, 1968. 158 p.

Australian Science Fiction Index, Supplement, 1968-1975, comp. by Graham Stone. Sydney: Australian Science Fiction Association, 1976. 48 p.

Index to British Science Fiction Magazines 1934-1953, Vol. Two, Author Index. Sydney: Australian Science Fiction Association, 1980. 174 p.

Index to the British Science Fiction Magazines, Vol 3: Title Index. Sydney, Australia: Australian Science Fiction Association, 1979. 221 p.

"American Science Fiction Magazine," by Graham Stone and Mike Ashley. in: Tymn, M. B. and Ashley, Mike. Science Fiction, Fantasy, and Weird Fiction Magazines. Westport, CT: Greenwood, 1985. pp. 59-60.

"Future Science Fiction (1953-1955)," in: Tymn, M. B. and Ashley, Mike. Science Fiction, Fantasy, and Weird Fiction Magazines. Westport, CT: Greenwood, 1985. pp. 284-286.

"Popular Science Fiction," in: Tymn, M. B. and Ashley, Mike. Science Fiction, Fantasy, and Weird Fiction Magazines. Westport, CT: Greenwood, 1985. pp. 481-482.

"Science Fiction Monthly (1955-1957)," in: Tymn, M. B. and Ashley, Mike. Science Fiction, Fantasy, and Weird Fiction Magazines. Westport, CT: Greenwood, 1985. pp. 537-539.

"Selected Science Fiction Magazine," in: Tymn, M. B. and Ashley, Mike. Science Fiction, Fantasy, and Weird Fiction Magazines. Westport, CT: Greenwood, 1985. pp. 569.

"Thrills, Incorporated," in: Tymn, M. B. and Ashley, Mike. Science Fiction, Fantasy, and Weird Fiction Magazines. Westport, CT: Greenwood, 1985. pp. 672-674.

Stone, M. D.

"Beyond first contact," Analog 100(6): 57-67. June 1980.

Storm, Jannick

Vor tids eventyr: katastrofe-omradet, udvalgete science fiction rapporter 1963-1977. Copenhagen: Swing, 1978. 77 p.

Storm, M. G., Jr.

"Thematic parallelism in Tono-Bungay: 'Night and the Open Sea'; as structural device," Extrapolation 18(2):181-184. May 1977.

Stott, J. C.

"Anatomy of a masterpiece: The Borrowers," Language Arts 53(5):538-544. May 1976.

"Midsummer Night's Dream: fantasy and self-realization in children's fiction," The Lion & the Unicorn 1(1):25-39. 1977.

Stout, William

"Movie poster art of Frank Frazetta, The," Fanfare 2:33-42. Winter 1978.

Stovall, T.

"Fiction yes, but science?" Science and Technology 79:10-11. July 1968.

Stover, L. E.

Science fiction americaine: essai d'anthropologie culturelle. Paris: Montaigne, 1972. 187 p.

"Anthropology and science fiction," Cultural Anthropology 14(4):471-473. October 1973.

"Is Jaspers beer good for you? Mass society and counter culture in Herbert's Santaroga Barrier," Extrapolation 17(2):160-167. May 1976.

Stover, L. E. (Continued)

"Science fiction and the research revolution,"
in: Williamson, Jack, ed. Teaching Science
Fiction: Education for Tomorrow.
Philadelphia: Owlswick, 1980. pp. 33-37.

"Science fiction, the research revolution, and
John Campbell," Extrapolation
14(2):129-148. May 1973.

"Social science fiction," in: Williamson,
Jack, ed. Teaching Science Fiction:
Education for Tomorrow. Philadelphia:
Owlswick, 1980. pp. 137-144.

"Social science fiction," in: McNelly, W. E.,
ed. Science Fiction the Academic Awakening.
Shreveport, LA: CEA, 1974. pp. 21-23.

Strachey, Barbara

Journeys of Frodo: An Atlas of J. R. R.
Tolkien's The Lord of the Rings. New York:
Ballantine, 1981. ca. 110 p. (Reprint of the
1981 Unwin edition.)

Straczynski, J. M.

"Show by show guide to Night Gallery, part 1,"
by K. M. Drennan and J. M. Straczynski.
Twilight Zone 5(1): 54 60. March/April 1985.

"Show by show guide to Night Gallery, part 2,"
by K. M. Drennan and J. M. Straczynski.
Twilight Zone 5(2): 83-89. May/June 1985.

"Show by show guide to Night Gallery, part 3,"
by K. M. Drennan and P. M. Straczynski.
Twilight Zone 5(3): 78-85. July/August 1985.

"Show by show guide to Night Gallery, part 4,"
by J. M. Straczynski and K. M. Drennan.
Twilight Zone 5(4): 74-80. October 1985.

"Show by show guide to Night Gallery, part 5,"
by K. M. Drennan and J. M. Straczynski.
Twilight Zone 5(5): 82-87. December 1985.

"Show by show guide to Night Gallery, part 6,"
by K. M. Drennan and J. M. Straczynski.
Twilight Zone 5(6): 72-75. February 1986.

Strangepork, Julius

"Meeting of the Minds," by Julius Strangepork
and F. R. Newman. Muppet Magazine 1(3):
17-20. Summer 1983.

Straubhaar, Joe

"Science Fiction and Mormonism," by Sandy
Straubhaar and Joe Straubhaar. Sunstone
6(4): 52-56. July/August 1981.

Straubhaar, Sandy

"Science Fiction and Mormonism," by Sandy
Straubhaar and Joe Straubhaar. Sunstone
6(4): 52-56. July/August 1981.

Straus, Tomas

"Art et sa fonction d'anticipation, L'" Revue
d'Esthetique 24:39-48. January/March 1971.

Strauss, E. S.

Complete Guide to Science Fiction
Conventions. Port Townsend, WA: Loompanics
Unlimited, 1983. 56 p.

MIT Science Fiction Society's Index to the SF
Magazines, 1951-1965, The. Cambridge,
Massachusetts: The MIT Science Fiction
Society, 1965. 207 p.

Strauss, Sylvia

H. G. Wells and America. Ph.D. Dissertation,
Rutgers, 1968. 282 p.

Street, Douglas

"Wonderful Wiz that was: the curious
transformation of The Wizard of Oz,"
Kansas Quarterly 16(3): 91-98. Summer 1984.

Streier, E. M.

Bedrohung des Menschen durch Naturwissenschaft
und Technologie? Antwortne im Romanwerke
(1952-69) von Kurt Vonnegut, jr. Frankfurt:
Lang, 1984. 279 p.

Strempel, Fritz

"1984 und danach. Barbarella oder Barbarie,"
Twen 12(9):10-16. 1970.

Stresau, Norbert

"2010: Die Fortsetzung," Science Fiction
Times (Germany) 27(2):17. February 1985.

"Christine," Science Fiction Times
(Germany) 26(3):14-15. March 1984.

"Conan the Destroyer," Science Fiction
Times (Germany) 26(10):14-15. October 1984.

"Dead Zone," Science Fiction Times (Germany)
26(5):23. May 1984.

"Dune," Science Fiction Times (Germany)
26(12):10-11. December 1984.

Stresau, Norbert (Continued)

"Ein Aufang immerhin: Das Arche Noah Prinzip,"
Science Fiction Times (Germany)
26(4):17-18. April 1984.

"Grosse Manipulator, Der: Brian de Palma und
seine Filme," Science Fiction Times
(Germany) 26(8):5-9. August 1984.

"Keep, The," Science Fiction Times
(Germany) 26(7):16-17. July 1984.

"Man with Two Brains, The," Science Fiction
Times (Germany) 26(7):16-17. July 1984.

"Mehr Blut! David Cronenberg und seine Filme,"
Science Fiction Times (Germany)
27(8):11-14. August 1985.

"Schaumgebremster superpanarisionsstrip,"
Science Fiction Times (Germany) 26(2):11.
February 1984.

"Something Wicked This Way Comes," Science
Fiction Times (Germany) 26(7):16-17. July
1984.

"Superman 3," Science Fiction Times
(Germany) 26(3):13. March 1984.

"Unendliche Geschichte," Science Fiction
Times (Germany) 26(5):22. May 1984.

"Wanna see something really scary?" Science
Fiction Times (Germany) 26(1):16-17. January
1984.

Strick, Philip

Science Fiction Movies. London: Octopus
Books, 1976. 160 p.

"Fantascienza," Sight and Sound
37(4):183-184. Autumn 1968.

"Monster and the city...," Artforum 21(9):
61-66. May 1983.

"Philip K. Dick and the Movies," Foundation
26: 15-21. October 1982.

"Reporting on possibilities," Vector 63:
32-34. January/February 1973.

"Science fiction and London University,"
Foundation 2:58-59. June 1972.

"SF at Trieste," Sight and Sound
34(4):174-175. Autumn 1965.

"SF Movies," Artforum 21(9): 61-66. May
1983.

"Shape of monsters to come, The," Futures
11(4):342-343. August 1979.

"Time, transplants and Arthur C. Clarke,"
Sight and Sound 40(4):190. Autumn 1971.

"Who Goes There: John W. Campbell," Monthly
Film Bulletin 49(583): 158-160. August 1982.

"Zardoz and John Boorman," Sight and Sound
43(2):73-77. Spring 1974.

Strickland, A. W.

Collection of great science fiction films.
Bloomington: T. I. S. Incorporated, 1979. 179
p.

Reference Guide to American Science Fiction
Films, Volume 1, by A. W. Strickland and F. J.
Ackerman. Bloomington, IN.: T. I. S., 1981.
397 p.

Stross, Charles

"Expressing Myself," Focus: An SF Writer's
Magazine 10: 22-24. February 1985.

Stroupe, J. H.

"Poe's imaginary voyage: Pym as hero,"
Studies in Short Fiction 4:315-321. 1967.

Struendel, Dieter

"Phantastik bei Lewis Carroll. Realitaet und
Mechanismus," in: Thomsen, C. W., ed.
Phantastik in Literatur und Kunst.
Darmstadt: Wissenschaftliche Buchgesellschaft,
1980. pp. 237-254.

Strugatsky, Arkady

"Kakie zvezdy svetiat fantastike?" by Arkady
Strugatsky, Dmitrii Bilenkin, and Igor
Bestuzhev-Lada. Literaturnoe obozrenie No.
8:100-106. 1977. in: Soviet Studies in
Literature 14(4):3-26. Autumn 1978.

"Kobo Abe on science fiction," by Arkady and
Boris Strugatsky. Soviet Literature
11:171-175. 1968.

"Soviet science fiction," USSR Soviet Life
Today 6:62-63. June 1963.

"Uber die Gegenwart in die Zukunft," by Arkady
Strugatsky and Boris Strugatsky. Quarber
Merkur 23:3-5. May 1970.

"What stars gleam in SF?" by A. Strugatsky, D.
Bilenkin and I. Bestuzhev-Lada. Soviet
Studies in Literature 14(4):3-26. Aut. 1978.
(tr. of "Kakie zuezdy Svetiat fantastike?"
Literaturnoe Obozrenie 8:100-106. 1977.)

Strugatsky, Boris

"Kobo Abe on science fiction," by Arkady and
Boris Strugatsky. Soviet Literature
11:171-175. 1968.

Strugatsky, Boris (Continued)

"Uber die Gegenwart in die Zukunft," by Arkady Strugatsky and Boris Strugatsky. Quarber Merkur 23:3-5. May 1970.

Strupp, Peter

"Interview with Stephen King," Science Fiction Review 14(3): 32. August 1985.

Stuart, Dee

"Exclusive interview with Newbery Award winning author Lloyd Alexander, An," Writers Digest 53(4):32-35,58-59. April 1973.

Stuffel, F. W.

Science in Science Fiction. Masters Thesis, Southwest Texas State Teachers College, 1957. 134 p.

Stump, Debra

"Matter of choice, A: King's Cujo and Malamud's The Natural," in: Schweitzer, Darrell, ed. Discovering Stephen King. Mercer Island: Starmont, 1985. pp. 131-140.

"Stephen King with a twist: the E. C. influence," in: Schweitzer, Darrell, ed. Discovering Stephen King. Mercer Island: Starmont, 1985. pp. 91-101.

"Two-For Sale," Media Sight 3(1): 36-37. Summer 1984.

Stumpf, Edna

"Jonathan Carroll: Galen to Vienna to the world," in: Schweitzer, Darrell, ed. Discovering Modern Horror Fiction I. Mercer Island: Starmont, 1985. pp. 129-134.

"Why it's all right now," Colloquy, Education in Church & Society 4(5):10-12. May 1971.

Stupple, A. J.

Utopian Humanism in American Fiction, 1888-1900. Ph.D. Dissertation, Northwestern University, 1971. 249 p.

"Martian Chronicles, The," in: Magill, Frank N., ed. Survey of Science Fiction Literature, Vol. 3. Englewood Cliffs, NJ: Salem Press, 1979. pp. 1348-1352.

"Literature against the future: a study of contemporary American science fiction," in: Samuelson, D. N. Science Fiction and Future Studies. Bryan, TX: SFRA, 1975. pp. 22-30.

"Science fiction: a literature against the future," American Scholar 46:215-220. Spring 1977.

"Short Fiction of Murray Leinster, The," in: Magill, Frank N., ed. Survey of Science Fiction Literature, Vol. 4. Englewood Cliffs, NJ: Salem Press, 1979. pp. 2030-2034.

"Toward a defination of anti-utopian literature," in: McNelly, W. E., ed. Science Fiction the Academic Awakening. Shreveport, LA: CEA, 1974. pp. 24-29.

"Two views: II. The past, the future, and Ray Bradbury," in: Olander, J. D. and M. H. Greenberg, eds. Ray Bradbury. New York: Taplinger, 1980. pp. 24-32.

"Two views: II. The past, the future, and Ray Bradbury," in: Clareson, T. D., ed. Voices for the Future: Essays on Major Science Fiction Writers, Vol. 1. Bowling Green, Ohio: Popular Press, 1976. pp. 175-184.

Sturgeon, Theodore

"Anthologies: the old and the new," National Review pp. 594-596. May 30, 1967. (Book review)

"Anyone for . . . ?" National Review pp. 1074-1075. December 1, 1964. (Book review)

"Beginning with the nineteenth century," National Review pp. 320-322. April 5, 1966. (Book reviews)

"Brace, three singles, and a ten strike, A," National Review pp. 478-480. May 17, 1966. (Book reviews)

"Chromium quaint: and an oddment," National Review pp. 693-694. August 11, 1964. (Book reviews)

"Fine fat packages," National Review pp. 76-77. January 25, 1966. (Book reviews)

"From Terra to TANSTAAFL," National Review 18:1278. December 13, 1966.

"Future writers in a future world," in: Bretnor, Reginald, ed. The Craft of Science Fiction. New York: Harper, 1966. pp. 89-103.

"I list in numbers," National Review pp. 266-267. March 10, 1970. (Book reviews)

"It takes all kinds," National Review pp. 835-836. September 21, 1965. (Book reviews)

"Jackets and footnotes," National Review pp. 244-245. March 26, 1963. (Book reviews)

"John W. Campbell," Locus No. 91:8. July 22, 1971.

"Last Starfighter (review)," Starlog 88: 46-47. November 1984.

Sturgeon, Theodore (Continued)

"Literati vs. cognoscenti," <u>National Review</u> pp. 231-232. October 23, 1962. (Book reviews)

"Men, monsters and moondust," <u>National Review</u> 11:421-422. December 16, 1961. (Book reviews)

"Merril-ly we wave along," <u>National Review</u> 21:1174-1175. November 18, 1969. (Book reviews)

"Momento mori: et seq.," <u>National Review</u> pp. 39-40. January 12, 1971. (Book reviews)

"Nebula Award science fiction, 1965-1970: the fiction," in: Biggle, Lloyd, ed. <u>Nebula Award Stories Seven</u>. New York: Harper, 1973. pp. 274-277.

"Next great name is Smith, The," <u>National Review</u> pp. 471-472. June 1, 1965. (Book reviews)

"Not science fiction, but 'if' fiction," <u>New York Times Book Review</u> pp. 24-25. January 9, 1972. (Book review)

"Odd couple of Hugo and Edgar, The," <u>National Review</u> pp. 743-744. July 14, 1970. (Book reviews)

"Of storytelling: how and what," <u>National Review</u> pp. 689-690. July 12, 1966. (Book reviews)

"Of times and tithes," <u>National Review</u> 12(16):298,301. April 24, 1962.

"One prize, one pleasure," <u>National Review</u> pp. 246-247. March 24, 1964. (Book reviews)

"Science and song," <u>National Review</u> pp. 25-26. July 16, 1963. (Book reviews)

"Science fiction and index," <u>National Review</u> pp. 200-201. March 9, 1965. (Book reviews)

"Science fiction, morals, and religion," in: Bretnor, Reginald, ed. <u>Science Fiction Today and Tomorrow</u>. New York: Harper, 1974. pp. 98-115.

"Science fiction: a function for fable," <u>National Review</u> pp. 201-202. September 23, 1961. (Book reviews)

"Science fiction: books about it," <u>National Review</u> 23(43):1245-1246. November 5, 1971. (Book reviews)

"Science fictionist, The," <u>National Review</u> pp. 403-404. November 20, 1962. (Book reviews)

"Speech, Nov. 18, 1961 (Excerpt)," <u>Locus</u> 18(7): 26-27. July 1985.

"Titanic tome from the tic-toc man," <u>National Review</u> pp. 456-458. May 7, 1968. (Book review)

"Viewpoint, a dewpoint, A," <u>National Review</u> pp. 119-120. February 12, 1963. (Book reviews)

"Why so much syzygy?" in: Knight, Damon, ed. <u>Turning Points: Essays in the Art of Science Fiction</u>. New York: Harper, 1977. pp. 269-272.

"Will Jenkins: an appreciation," <u>Locus</u> No. 175:1-2. June 24, 1975.

Stuttaford, Geneviere

"Report from the con: Lunacon," <u>Publishers Weekly</u> 209(24):50. June 14, 1950.

Subotsky, Milton

"Super Science Fiction," in: Tymn, M. B. and Ashley, Mike. <u>Science Fiction, Fantasy, and Weird Fiction Magazines</u>. Westport, CT: Greenwood, 1985. pp. 629-631.

Sucharitkul, Somtow

"Certain Slant of I," <u>Fantasy Newsletter</u> 6(1): 29-30. January 1983.

"Certain Slant of I: Consulting the Oracle," <u>Fantasy Newsletter</u> 6(2): 36-38. February 1983.

"Children's Corner," <u>Fantasy Newsletter</u> 5(10): 27-28. November 1982.

"No Tickee, No Washee and Other Rebuttals," <u>Fantasy Newsletter</u> 5(8): 29-31. September 1982.

"Theodore Sturgeon in Memoriam, 9," <u>Locus</u> 18(7): 28-29. July 1985.

"What March?" <u>Isaac Asimov's Science Fiction Magazine</u> 6(2): 86-97. February 15, 1982.

Suchy, Viktor

"Zukunftsvisionen des 20. jahrhunderts. Der utopische roman der gegenwart als diagnose der zeit," <u>Wissenschaft und Weltbild</u> 5:18-30, 338-363. 1952.

Sudbery, Tony

"Considering how to run," <u>Vector</u> 45: 10-15. July 1967.

"Science or fiction," <u>Vector</u> 69: 22-25. Summer 1975.

Suderman, E. F.

"Mennonite culture in a science fiction novel,"
Mennonite Quarterly Review 49:53-56.
January 1975.

Suedfeld, Peter

"Dark trends; psychology, science fiction and
the ominous consensus," by Peter Suedfeld and
L. M. Ward. _Futures_ 8(1):22-39. February
1976.

Suerbaum, Ulrich

Science Fiction: Theorie und Geschichte.
Themen und Typen, Form und Weltbild, by Ulrich
Suerbaum, Ulrich Broich, and Raimund Borgmeier.
Stuttgart: P. Reclam, 1981. 215 p. 81-137889

"John Brunner: The Windows of Heaven," in:
Goller, K. H. und Gerhand Hoffman, eds. _Die_
Englische Kurzgeschichte. Dusseldorf, 1973.
pp. 337-348.

Suits, Bernard

"Grasshopper, The: Posthoumous reflections on
Utopia," in: _Utopias_, ed. by Peter Alexander
and Roger Gill. London: Duckworth, 1984. pp.
197-210.

Sukenick, Lynn

"Feeling and reason in Doris Lessing's
fiction," _Contemporary Literature_
14(4):515-535. Autumn 1973.

Suldner, K. L.

"On Dhalgren and Triton," _Riverside_
Quarterly 7(1):5-14. March 1980.

Sullivan, A. T.

"Ray Bradbury and fantasy," _English Journal_
61(9):1309-1314. December 1972.

Sullivan, C. W., III

"Alas, Babylon," in: Magill, Frank N., ed.
Survey of Science Fiction Literature, Vol.
1. Englewood Cliffs, NJ: Salem Press, 1979.
pp. 38-42.

"Beyond the Golden Stair," in: Magill,
Frank N., ed. _Survey of Modern Fantasy_
Literature, Vol 1. Englewood Cliffs, NJ:
Salem Press, Inc., 1983. pp. 87-89.

"Child Buyer, The," in: Magill, Frank N.,
ed. _Survey of Science Fiction Literature_,
Vol. 1. Englewood Cliffs, NJ: Salem Press,
1979. pp. 325-329.

"Driftglass," in: Magill, Frank N., ed.
Survey of Science Fiction Literature, Vol. 2.
Englewood Cliffs, NJ: Salem Press, 1979. pp.
625-628.

"Fates of the Princes of Dyfed, The and Book
of the Three Dragons," in: Magill, Frank N.,
ed. _Survey of Modern Fantasy Literature_,
Vol 2. Englewood Cliffs, NJ: Salem Press,
Inc., 1983. pp. 539-542.

"Jewels of Aptor, The," in: Magill, Frank
N., ed. _Survey of Modern Fantasy_
Literature, Vol 2. Englewood Cliffs, NJ:
Salem Press, Inc., 1983. pp. 798-800.

"Khendiol Novels, The," in: Magill, Frank
N., ed. _Survey of Modern Fantasy_
Literature, Vol 2. Englewood Cliffs, NJ:
Salem Press, Inc., 1983. pp. 839-843.

"Mabinogion Tetralogy, The," in: Magill,
Frank N., ed. _Survey of Modern Fantasy_
Literature, Vol 2. Englewood Cliffs, NJ:
Salem Press, Inc., 1983. pp. 932-937.

"Moon Is a Harsh Mistress, The," in:
Magill, Frank N., ed. _Survey of Science_
Fiction Literature, Vol. 3. Englewood Cliffs,
NJ: Salem Press, 1979. pp. 1439-1443.

"Out of the Silent Planet," in: Magill,
Frank N., ed. _Survey of Science Fiction_
Literature, Vol. 4. Englewood Cliffs, NJ:
Salem Press, 1979. pp. 1632-1636.

"Secret Mountain and Other Tales, The," in:
Magill, Frank N., ed. _Survey of Modern_
Fantasy Literature, Vol 3. Englewood Cliffs,
NJ: Salem Press, Inc., 1983. pp. 1372-1374.

"String in the Harp, A," in: Magill, Frank
N., ed. _Survey of Modern Fantasy_
Literature, Vol 4. Englewood Cliffs, NJ:
Salem Press, Inc., 1983. pp. 1851-1853.

"Evangeline Walton and the Welsh mythos,"
Fantasy Review 8(3): 35-36, 42. March 1985.

"Growing old with Robert A. Heinlein," in:
Yoke, C. B. and Hassler, D. M., eds. _Death_
and the Serpent. Westport, CT: Greenwood,
1985. pp. 115-124.

"Harlan Ellison and Robert A. Heinlein: The
Paradigm Makers," in: Erlich, Richard D., ed.
Clockwork Worlds. Westport, CT: Greenwood,
1983. pp. 97-103.

"Name and Lienage Patterns: Aragorn and
Beowulf," _Extrapolation_ 25(3): 239-246.
Fall 1984.

"Science Fiction and Fantasy Series Books," by
Al Muller and C. W. Sullivan, III. _English_
Journal 69(7): 71-74. October 1980.

Sullivan, Chip

"Sixth annual Conference on the Fantastic," Fantasy Review 8(4): 6-7. April 1985.

Sullivan, D. C.

"Possessed sociology and Le Guin's Dispossessed: from exile to anarchism," by L. L. Tifft and D. C. Sullivan. in: De Bolt, Joe, ed. Ursula K. Le Guin: Voyager to Inner Lands.... Port Washington: Kennikat, 1979. pp. 180-197.

Sullivan, E. D. S.

Utopian Vision: Seven Essays on the Quincentennial of Sir Thomas More. San Diego: San Diego State University Press, 1983. 265 p.

Sullivan, Jack

"Essential writers: L. P. Hartley," Twilight Zone 2(10):56-59. December 1982.

"Essential writers: the haunted mind of Shirley Jackson," Twilight Zone 4(3):71-74. July/August 1984.

"H. R. Wakefield: the last of his breed," Twilight Zone 4(4):68-69. September/October 1984.

"Ramsey Campbell: No Light Ahead," in: Winter, Douglas E. Shadowings: The Reader's Guide to Horror Fiction 1981-1982. Mercer Island, WA: Starmont, 1983. pp. 79-86.

Sullivan, John

G. K. Chesterton: A Bibliography. London: University of London Press, 1958. 208 p. Reprinted, Westport, Connecticut: Greenwood Press, 1974.

G. K. Chesterton: A Centenary Appraisal. New York: Barnes & Noble, 1974. 243 p.

"Chesterton bibliography continued," Chesterton Review 3:141-147. 1976.

"Chesterton bibliography continued," Chesterton Review 2:267-272. Fall/ Winter 1975-1976.

Sullivan, Kathryn

"First Contact: Science Fiction in the Library, 1920-1949," 1977. 27 p. ERIC ED 194 080.

Sullivan, Robert

"'Z. P. G.': A Wrong Step," Los Angeles Free Press Part 1, p. 15. May 26, 1972.

Sullivan, T. R.

"Clockwork Worldcon," Fantasy Review 7(9): 7-8. October 1984.

"Interview: Gardner Dozois," Fantasy Review 8(11): 7, 40. November 1985.

"JuJu, Inc.," Fantasy Review 7(4): 7-9. May 1984.

"TZ is Year's Best Fantasy Film," Fantasy Newsletter 6(8): 33. September 1983.

Summerfield, Geoffrey

"Making room for fantasy," Times Educational Supplement 3179:26-27. May 7, 1976.

Summers, Alphonse

Gothic Bibliography, A. London: Fortune Press, 1941. 620 p. Reprinted, New York: Russell & Russell, 1964.

Sumner, Carolyn

"Meditation on Star Wars," Southwest Review 65(3): 304-310. Summer 1980.

Sunesen, Bent

"Utopian science fiction and the concept of models," in: Dollerup, Cay, ed. Volve. Scandinavian Views on Science Fiction. Copenhagen: Department of English, University of Copenhagen, 1978. pp. 79-88.

Suplee, Curt

"In the Strange Land of Robert Heinlein," Washington Post p. B1, B4. September 5, 1984.

Surmacz, G. A.

"Anatomy of a horror film," Cinefantastique 4(1):15-27. Spring 1975.

Sussex, Lucy

"Germ Growers; an early Australian SF novel," Science Fiction: a Review of Speculative Literature. 2(3): 229-233. August 1980.

"Long versus Short SF: The Examination of a Fix-up," Foundation 28: 28-33. July 1983.

Sussman, H. L.

Victorians and the Machine: The Literary Response to Technology. Cambridge, MA: Harvard University Press, 1968. 261 p.

Sussman, H. L. (Continued)

"Machine and the future: H. G. Wells, The," in: Sussman, H. L. Victorians and the Machine: The Literary Response to Technology. Cambridge, MA: Harvard University Press, 1968. pp. 162-193.

"Production of art in the machine age: William Morris," in: Sussman, H. L. Victorians and the Machine. Cambridge, MA: Harvard University Press, 1968. pp. 104-134.

Sussman, Rudolf

"Trivialkultur und politische Bildung am Beispiel der Science fiction," Politische Studien 31(249):91-96. January/February, 1980.

Sutherland, J. A.

"American science fiction since 1960," in: Parrinder, Patrick, ed. Science Fiction: A Critical Guide. New York: Longman, 1979. pp. 162-186.

Sutherland, R. C.

Inklings, ed. by R. C. Sutherland. Atlanta: Georgia State University Press, 1981. 119 p.

Sutherland, Zena

"In defense of science fiction," Saturday Review 53(14):36. April 18, 1970.

Sutton, Marilyn

"Science fiction as mythology," by T. C. and Marilyn Sutton. Western Folklore 28:230-237. October 1969.

Sutton, T. C.

"Science fiction as mythology," by T. C. and Marilyn Sutton. Western Folklore 28:230-237. October 1969.

Suvin, D. R.

"Eightie-Foure is Icummen in: Lhude Sing Goddam!; or: 1948-1984-2084," Foundation 32: 60. November 1984.

Suvin, Darko

H. G. Wells and Modern Science Fiction, ed. by Dardo Suvin and R. M. Philmus. Lewisburg: Bucknell University Press, 1977. 279 p.

Metamorphoses of Science Fiction: On the Poetics and History of a Literary Genre. New Haven, Connecticut: Yale University Press, 1979. 336 p.

Pour und poetique de la science fiction: etudes en theorie et en historie d'un genre litteraire. Montreal: Presses de l'Universite du Quebec, 1977. 228 p.

Russian Science Fiction 1956-1974: A Bibliography. Elizabethtown, New York: Dragon Press, 1976. second edition, 73 p.

Russian Science Fiction Literature and Criticism, 1956-1970: A Bibliography. Toronto: Secondary Universe 4, 1971. 35 p.

Science Fiction Studies: Selected Articles on Science Fiction 1973-1975, ed. by R. D. Mullen and Darko Suvin. Boston: Gregg Press, 1976. 304 p.

Victorian Science Fiction in the UK: The Discourses of Knowledge and Power. Boston: G. K. Hall, 1983. 461 p.

"Andromeda," in: Magill, Frank N., ed. Survey of Science Fiction Literature, Vol. 1. Englewood Cliffs, NJ: Salem Press, 1979. pp. 58-62.

"Time Machine versus Utopia as a Structural Model for Science Fiction," Comparative Literature Studies 10(1): 334-351. March 1973.

"'Utopian' and 'Scientific': Two Attributes for Socialism from Engels," Minnesota Review ns6, 1976. pp. 59-75.

"Abriss der sowjetischen science fiction," in: Barmeyer, Eike, ed. Science fiction: theorie und geschichte. Munchen: Fink, 1972 pp. 318-339.

"Alternate islands: a chapter in the history of SF, with a bibliography on the SF of antiquity, the Middle Ages, and the Renaissance, The," Science Fiction Studies 3(3):239-248. November 1976.

"Anticipating the Sunburst: Dream and Vision: The Exemplary Case of Bellamy and Morris," in: Roemer, Kenneth M., ed. America As Utopia. New York: Franklin, 1981. pp. 57-77.

"Artifice as Refuge and World View: Philip K. Dick's Foci," in: Greenberg, Martin H., ed. Philip K. Dick. New York: Taplinger, 1982. pp. 73-95. (Reprint from SF Studies, March 1975.)

"Bibliography of general bibliographies of SF literature, A," by Irena Zantovska-Murray and Darko Suvin. Science Fiction Studies 5(3):271-286. November 1978.

"Cognition and estrangement: an approach to SF poetics," Foundation 2:6-16. June 1972.

Suvin, Darko (Continued)

"Communication in quantified space: the utopian liberalism of Jules Verne's science fiction," Clio 4(1):51-71. October 1974.

"Criticism of the Strugatsky brothers work," Canadian-American Slavic Studies 6(2):286-307. Summer 1972.

"Defining the Literary Genre of Utopia: Some Historical Semantics, Some Geneology, A Proposal, and a Plea," Studies in the Literary Imagination 6(2): 121-145. Fall 1973.

"Grammar of form and a criticism of fact: The Time Machine as a structural model for science fiction, A," in: Suvin, D. and R. M. Philmus, eds. H. G. Wells and Modern Science Fiction. Bucknell Univ. Press, 1977. pp. 90-115.

"H. G. Wells and earlier SF," SF Studies 1(3):221-222. Spr. 1974. Comment (A. Eisenstein) & reply 1(4):305-307. Comments, A. C. Clarke, T. N. Hamilton & R. D. Mullen. 2(2):195-196. July 1975.

"Introduction," in: Capek, Karel. War With the Newts. Boston: Gregg, 1975. pp. v-xviii.

"Introduction: the development of the Strugatskys' fiction," in: Strugatsky, Boris and Arkady. The Snail on the Slope. New York: Bantam, 1980. pp. 1-20.

"Jack London and his science fiction: a select bibliography," Science Fiction Studies 3(2):181-187. July 1976.

"James Blish, 1921-1975," Science Fiction Studies 2(3):294-295. November 1975.

"Kritik zum Werk der Bruder Strugatsky," Quarber Merkur 40:26-44. March 1975.

"Literary opus of the Strugatsky brothers, The," Canadian-American Slavic Studies 8(3):454-463. Fall 1974.

"Narrative Logic, Ideological Domination, and the Range of Science Fiction: a Hypothesis with a Historical Test," Science Fiction Studies 9(1): 3-25. March 1982.

"Not only but also: reflection on cognition and ideology in science fiction and SF criticism," by Marc Angenot and Darko Suvin. Science-Fiction Studies 6(2):168-179. July 1979.

"On the poetics of the science fiction genre," College English 34(3):372-382. December 1972.

"On what is and is not, an SF narration," Science Fiction Studies 5(1):45-57. March 1978.

"Open-ended parables of Stanislaw Lem and Solaris, The," in: Lem, Stanislaw.

Solaris. New York: Walker, 1970. pp. 205-216.

"Other worlds, other seas: science fiction from socialist countries," in: Suvin, Darko, ed. Other Worlds, Other Seas. New York: Berkley, 1970. pp. 11-38.

"P. K. Dick's opus: artifice as refuge and world view," Science Fiction Studies 2(1):8-22. March 1975.

"Parables of de-alienation: Le Guin's widdershins dance," Science Fiction Studies 2(3):265-274. November 1975.

"Playful Cognizing, or Technical Errors in Harmonyville: The Science Fiction of Johanna and Gunter Braun," Science-Fiction Studies 8(1): 72-79. March 1981.

"Preface," Autres mondes, autres mers (Presence du futur, 174). Paris, Denoel, 1973. pp. 13-45.

"Preface: on this book, on SF, and on utopianism," in: Suvin, Darko, ed. Other Worlds, Other Seas: Science Fiction Stories From Socialist Countries. NY: Random House, 1970. pp. xi-xxxiii.

"Preliminary reflections on teaching science fiction critically," by Charles Elkins and Darko Suvin. Science Fiction Studies 6(3):263-270. November 1979.

"Radical rhapsody and romantic recoil in the age of anticipation: a chapter in the history of SF," Science Fiction Studies 1(4):255-269. Fall 1974.

"Raymond Williams and SF," Science Fiction Studies 1(3):216-217. Spring 1974.

"Riverside trees, or SF and utopia: degrees of kinship," The Minnesota Review 2/3:108-115. Spring 1974.

"S. F. et utopie. b) Deux arbres au bord du fleuve de l'historie," Europe 580/581: 65-72. August/September 1977.

"Science fiction and the genological jungle," Genre 6(3):251-273. September 1973.

"Science Fiction Karel Capeks und 'Der Krieg mit den Molchen'," Quarber Merkur 41:31-40. September 1975.

"Science fiction mufaj poetikaja," Helikon 18(1): 43-54. 1972.

"Second Supplement to Russian Science Fiction 1956-1974: A Bibliography," Canadian-American Slavic Studies 15(4): 533-544. Winter 1981.

"Select bibliography on Russian SF from the beginnings to 1959, A," Modern Language Review 66(1):156-159. January 1971.

Suvin, Darko (Continued)

"Seventy-four more Victorian books that should be excluded from science fiction bibliographies," Science Fiction Studies 7(2):207-212. July 1980.

"SF et la jungle des genres, La, un voyage extraordinaire," Litterature (La Rousse) No. 10:98-113. May 1973.

"SF novel in 1969, The," in: Blish, James, ed. Nebula Award Stories Five. Doubleday, 1970. pp. 193-205.

"SF theory: internal and external delimitations and utopia (summary)," Extrapolation 19(1):13-15. December 1977.

"Significant context of SF: a dialogue of comfort against tribulation, by A, B, and C, The," Science Fiction Studies 1(1):44-50. Spring 1973.

"Significant themes in the criticism of Soviet science fiction to 1965, with a selected bibliography," Extrapolation 11(2):44-52. May 1970.

"Sociology of science fiction: introduction to this special issue, The," Science Fiction Studies 4(3):223-227,318-319. November 1977.

"Soziale Bewusstsein der Science Fiction: angelsachsisches, russisches und mitteleuropaisches," Quarber Merkur 39:57-62. January 1975.

"Soziale bewusstsein der science fiction: AngloAmerican, Russland und Mitteleuropa," Science Fiction Times (Germany) 24(10):3-7. October 1982.

"Stanislaw Lem und das mitteleuropaische bewusstsein der science fiction," in: Berthel, Werner, ed. Insel Almanach auf das Jahr 1976. Frankfurt: Insel, 1976. (not seen)

"Stanlislaw Lem's Parabel Solaris," Quarber Merkur 25:64-67. January 1971.

"State of the art in science fiction theory: determining and defining the genre, The," Science Fiction Studies 6(1):32-45. March 1979.

"Strugatskys and their Snail on the Slope, The," Foundation 17:64-75. September 1979.

"Supplement to Russian science fiction 1956-1974: a bibliography," Canadian-American Slavic Studies 14(1):88-90. Spring 1980.

"Three world paradigms for science fiction: Asimov, Yefremov, Lem," Pacific Quarterly Moana 4(3):271-283. July 1979.

"Three world paradigms for SF: Asimov, Yefremov, Lem," in: Remington, T. J., ed.

Selected Proceedings of the 1978 SFRA National Conference. Cedar Falls, Iowa: Univ. of Northern Iowa, 1979. pp. 1-8.

"Utopian tradition of Russian science fiction, The," Modern Language Review 66(1):139-159. January 1971.

"Utopische Tradition der russischen Science Fiction," in: Rottensteiner, Franz, ed. Polaris 2. Frankfunt: Insel, 1974. pp. 209-248.

"Victorian Science Fiction, 1871-85: The Rise of the Alternative History Sub-Genre," Science-Fiction Studies 10(2): 148-169. July 1983.

"Wells as the turning point of the SF tradition," Minnesota Review 4:106-115. Spring 1975.

"Wissenschaft und Literatur in der science fiction: Zur Definition," Quarber Merkur 23:30-37. May 1970.

"Zur poetik des literarischen genres science fiction," in: Barmeyer, Eike, ed. Science fiction: theorie und geschichte. Munchen: Fink, 1972. p. 86-105.

Svilpis, J. E.

"Lord Darcy Stories, The," in: Magill, Frank N., ed. Survey of Modern Fantasy Literature, Vol 2. Englewood Cliffs, NJ: Salem Press, Inc., 1983. pp. 894-896.

"Authority, autonomy and adventure in juvenile science fiction," Children's Literature Association Quarterly 8(3): 22-26. Fall 1983.

"Science Fiction Magazine Illustration: A Semiotic Analysis," Science Fiction Studies 10(3): 278-291. November 1983.

"Short fiction of Stevenson, The," in: Magill, Frank N., ed. Survey of Modern Fantasy Literature, Vol 4. Englewood Cliffs, NJ: Salem Press, Inc., 1983. pp. 1698-1702.

Swain, D. V.

"Mack Reynolds, 1917-1983," SFWA Bulletin 17(2): 15-18, 24. Summer 1983.

Swain, Michael

"Science Fiction Reflects Computerphobia," InfoWorld 3(31): 7. December 21, 1981.

Swanson, D. R.

"Uses of tradition: King Arthur in the modern world, The," CEA Critic 36(3):19-21. 1974.

Swanson, R. A.

"Love is the function of death: Forster, Lagervist, and Zamyatin," _Canadian Review of Comparative Literature_ 3(2):197-211. Spring 1976.

"Nabakov's _Ada_ as science fiction," _Science Fiction Studies_ 2(1):76-88. March 1975.

"Spiritual Factor in _Odd John_ and _Sirius_," _Science Fiction Studies_ 9(3): 284-293. November 1982.

"True, the false, and the truly false: Lucian's philosophical science fiction, The," _Science Fiction Studies_ 3(3):228-239. November 1976.

Swartzel, S. B.

Futile Benevolence in Three Vonnegut Novels: The Sirens of Titan, Cat's Cradle, and God Bless You, Mr. Rosewater. Master's Thesis, Florida Atlantic University, 1983. 105 p.

Swecker, S. L.

"Toward a theology of the fantastic," _Christian Century_ 91(2):40-43. January 16, 1974.

Sween, R. D.

Bibliography of Science Fiction. Milwaukee, Wisconsin: Wisconsin Council of Teachers of English, 1974. 28 p.

Fan Publishing Record; A Current Awareness Listing of the Contents of Non-commercial Science Fiction and Fantasy Publication. Platteville, Wisconsin: by the author. n.d.

Reference Sources for the Study of Speculative Literature. SL: Sween, n.d. 47 p.

Speculative Literature Used in U.S. Academic Courses. Plattville: Karrmann Library, n.d. 40 p.

"Discovering fanzines," _Wisconsin English Journal_ 18(3):19-21. April 1976.

"Library in future fiction: not hardware but social and personal impact," _Wisconsin Library Bulletin_ 70:129-130. May/June 1974.

Sweetser, W. D.

Bibliography of Arthur Machen, A, by Adrian Goldstone and Wesley Sweetser. Austin: University of Texas, 1965. 180 p.

"Arthur Machen: a bibliography of writings about him," _English Literature in Transition_ 11(1):1-33. 1968.

"Machen, Arthur," in: Woodcock, George, ed. _20th Century Fiction._ Chicago: St. James, 1985. pp. 410-412.

Swenson, L. S., Jr.

"Mailer's moon: aquarius vs. apollo," _Journal of the American Studies Association of Texas_ 4:65-73. 1973.

Swerdloff, Peter

"After Tolkien: what?" _Mademoiselle_ 77:161-162. June 1973.

Swiatek, E. H.

"Epp," in: Magill, Frank N., ed. _Survey of Science Fiction Literature_, Vol. 2. Englewood Cliffs, NJ: Salem Press, 1979. pp. 725-728.

"Sagan om den stora datamaskine," in: Magill, Frank N., ed. _Survey of Science Fiction Literature_, Vol. 4. Englewood Cliffs, NJ: Salem Press, 1979. pp. 1844-1847.

"Termush, Atlanterhavskysten," in: Magill, Frank N., ed. _Survey of Science Fiction Literature_, Vol. 5. Englewood Cliffs, NJ: Salem Press, 1979. pp. 2245-2249.

"Danish scene: Anglo American science fiction and fandom, The," in: Dollerup, Cay, ed. _Volve. Scandinavian Views on Science Fiction._ Copenhagen: Dept. of English, University of Copenhagen, 1978. pp. 43-48.

Swigart, L. K.

Harlan Ellison: A Bibliographical Checklist. Dallas: Williams, 1973. 117 p.

"Harlan Ellison: a nonfiction checklist," in: Porter, Andrew, ed. _The Book of Ellison._ New York: Algol Press, 1978. pp. 177-191.

"Harlan Ellison: A Bibliographical Checklist, second edition," _Fantasy Research & Bibliography_ 1/2: 24-94. December 1980/May 1981.

Swinden, David

"Art of Course Writing," _Focus_ 6: 36-40. Autumn 1982.

Swinfen, Ann

Sub-Creative Art: An Examination of Some Aspects of the use of Fantasy, Principally in English Children's Literature, 1945-1975. Thesis, University of Dundee, 1979. 409 p.

Swingle, L. J.

"Frankenstein's monster and its romantic relatives: problems of knowledge in English romanticism," Texas Studies in Literature and Language 15(1):51-56. Spring 1973.

Swires, Steve

"Bill Langcaster on Scripting 'The Thing' or 'The Bad News Beast'," Starlog 58: 18-19. May 1982.

"Caroline Munro: Fantasy Films' First Lady," Starlog 57: 52-56. April 1982.

"Checking in With Chekov: Walter Koenig on Star Trek II," Starlog 61: 22-24. August 1982.

"Grab what you can get: the screenwriter as journeyman plumber," Films in Review 27(7):413-421. August 1976.

"Irish McCalla, Sheena, Queen of the TV Jungle," Starlog 89: 30-33, 55. December 1984.

"John Carpenter on Starman: romancing the clone, part one," Starlog No. 92:19-22. March 1985.

"John Carpenter: Directing the Thing," Starlog 60: 26-28. July 1982.

"John Sayles: from Hoboken to Hollywood, part two," Starlog No. 94:43-46. May 1985.

"Kenneth Tobey: From Hawks to Harryhausen-Hollywood's First 1950's SF Hero," Starlog 62: 45-47. September 1982.

"Lorenzo Semple, jr.: Having Fun with James Bond," Starlog 74: 24-27. September 1983.

"Michael Laughlin: Attack of the Killer Cliches," Starlog 78: 58-63. January 1984.

"Paul Aratow: The Troubles with 'Sheena'," Starlog 83: 44-46, 67. June 1984.

"Starlog Exclusive: Leslie Nielsen," Starlog 54: 26-29. January 1982.

"Starlog Interview" Lorenzo Semple, Jr.," Starlog 75: 45-47, 54. October 1983.

"Starlog Interview: David Prowse," Starlog 87: 22-23. October 1984.

"Starlog Interview: David Warner," Starlog 64: 80-83. November 1982.

"Starlog Interview: Irvin Kershner," Starlog 79: 40-42, 67. February 1984.

"Starlog Interview: John Carpenter," Starlog 48: 73-76. July 1981.

"Starlog Interview: John Sayles," Starlog 86: 38-40. September 1984.

"Starlog interview: Peter Cushing," Starlog 96: 60-63, 96. July 1985.

"Starlog Interview: Ray Harryhausen," Starlog 100: 34-37. November 1985.

"Starlog Interview: Stuart Cohen," Starlog 61: 56-58. August 1982.

"Starlog Interview: Tanya Roberts: A Blonde Goddess Named Sheena," Starlog 86: 61-63, 65. September 1984.

"Starlog Interview: The Stars of 'Escape From New York': Kurt Russell and Adrienne Barbeau," Starlog 49: 17-19, 61. August 1981.

"Starlog Interview: William Shatner, part 1: The Once and Future Kirk," Starlog 51: 18-20. September 1981.

"Starlog Interview: William Shatner, part 2: I Am Kirk," Starlog 52: 44-46. November 1981.

"Starlog Interviews: Fiona Lewis." Starlog 79: 16-18. February 1984.

"Starlog Preview: The Creature Wasn't Nice," Starlog 52: 47-49. November 1981.

"Starlog Profile: John Carpenter, part two," Starlog 100: 46 49. November 1985.

"Starlog Profile: Leonard Nimoy," Starlog 100: 54-56. November 1985.

"Starlog Profile: Peter Cushing, Part Two," Starlog 100: 89-92. November 1985.

"Stuff, The," Starlog No. 91:25-27,67. February 1985.

Swycaffer, J. P.

"Historical Motivations for the Siege of Mina Tirith," Mythlore 10(1): 47-49. Spring 1983.

Sykes, W. J.

"Is Wells among the prophets?" Queens Quarterly 49(3):233. Autumn 1942.

Sykora, W. S.

"Torcon report, part 1," Fantasy Times No. 68:3-8. August 1948.

"Torcon report, part 2," Fantasy Times No. 69:9-11. September 1948.

Szabo, P. S.

"Science fiction and the SF movement in Hungary," Hungarian Book Review 16(3): 18-19. July/September 1974.

Szacki, Jerzy

Spotkania z Utopia.   Warsaw: Iskry, 1980.
220 p.

Szalay, Jeff

"Gene Roddenberry: The Years Between, the Years
Ahead,"   Starlog 51: 36, 40-42. September
1981.

"Megaforce,"   Starlog 57: 16-19. April
1982.

"Reach For The Sun: Public Broadcasting Goes
Way Out for a Message That Hits Close to Home,"
Starlog 46: 40-41. May 1981.

"Special Effects of Heartbeeps,"   Starlog
53: 16-21. December 1981.

"Starlog Exclusive: Leonard Nimoy,"   Starlog
63: 30-33, 64. October 1982.

"Starlog Interview: Ray Bradbury,"   Starlog
53: 35-39. December 1981.

Szavai, Janos

"Vision et metamorphose: Deux aspects de la
litterature fantastique,"   Acta Litteraria
Academiae Scientiarum Hungaricae 22(1/2):
73-83. 1981.

Szeemann, Harald

Science fiction, du 28 novembre 1967 au 26
fevier 1968, Musee des arts decoratifs, Paris.
Paris: Musee des arts decoratifs, 1967. 56 p.

Szentmihalyi-Szabo, Peter

"A sci-fi es az isten,"   SF Tajekoztato pp.
44-47. September 1971.

"Some aspects of Hungarian science fiction
since 1945,"   SF Tajekoztato 18:10-12.
1976.

Szpakowska, Malgorzata

"Flucht Stanislaw Lem, Die," in: Barmeyer,
Eike, ed. Science fiction: theorie und
geschichte. Munchen: Fink, 1972. pp.
293-303. Also in: Polnische perspektiven
1(11):23-32. November 1971.

"O wrozeniu z fusow i moralnej
odpowiedxialnosci," Tworczosc No. 8. 1971.

"Stanislaw Lem: immer weiter weg von der
literatur," Quarber Merkur 38:63-67.
November 1974.

"Vom Weissagen aus dem Kaffeesatz und der
moralischen Verantwortung," Quarber Merkur
31:31-35. July 1972. Also in: Rottensteiner,
Franz, ed. Polaris I. Frankfurt: Insel,
1973. pp. 89-96.

"Writer in no-man's-land, A,"   Polish
Perspectives 14(10):29-37. October 1971.

T

Tagashira, Gail S.

"Bogeyman King has Unconventional Fun With Fans," San Jose (Calif.) Mercury November 3, 1981. in: Newsbank. Literature. 45:C4-5. 1981/1982.

Taggart, Patrick

"'Empire Strikes Back': Tune in Next Year..." Austin American Statesman Show World. p. 1, 38-39. May 18, 1980.

"'Force' Snares Austin," Austin American Statesman Sec. 1, p. 1. May 21, 1980.

"Evil One: Even a Villain can Love," Austin American Statesman Sec. E, p. 1. May 23, 1980.

"Force is Definitely With The Empire as it Strikes, The," Austin American Statesman Sec. D, p. 7. May 21, 1980.

"Good Guys: Being a Hero is Hot Work," Austin American Statesman. Sec. E, p. 1. May 23, 1980.

"Return of the Jedi Hits With Strong Cast, Lucas Magic," Austin American Statesman p. C1. May 25, 1983.

Tait, Steven

"Implications of 'Battle Language' in the Dune Universe, The," P*S*F*Q (Cupertino, CA) 6: 15. Fall 1981.

Takeo, Okuno

"Japanese SF," SF Horizons 2:51-52. Winter 1965.

Tamamchenko, E.

"(Science fiction and the model of revolution)" (in Russian) Canadian-American Slavic Studies 18(1/2): 31-41. Spring/Summer 1984.

Tanner, Tony

"Uncertain messenger: a study of the novels of Kurt Vonnegut, Jr., The," Critical Quarterly 11(4):297-315. Winter 1969. also in: City of Words. New York: Harper & Row, 1971. pp. 181-201.

Tanzy, Eugene

"Contrasting views of man and the evolutionary process: Back to Methuselah and Childhood's End," in: Olander, J. D. and M. H. Greenberg, eds. Arthur C. Clarke. New York: Taplinger, 1977. pp. 172-195.

Taormina, Agatha

Hero, The Double, and the Outsider: Images of Three Archetypes in Science Fiction. Ph. D. Dissertation, Carnegie-Mellon University, 1980. 212 p. DAI #81-14638

Tappen, Rowland

"Beware Mutations," Focus: an SF Writers' Magazine 4: 17-18. Spring 1981.

Tarrant, Desmond

"James Branch Cabell: wizard of the unconscious," Kalki 7:93-99. 1977.

Tarratt, Margaret

"Monsters from the id: an examination of the science fiction film genre, part 1," Films and Filming 17(3):38-42. December 1970.

"Monsters from the id: an examination of the science fiction film genre, part 2," Films and Filming 17(4):40-42. Summer 1971.

Tashlik, P.

"Science fiction: an anthropological approach," English Journal 64(1):78-79. January 1975.

Science Fiction and Fantasy Reference Index, 1878-1985

Tasker, Ann

"Creating a world for The Dark Crystal," by D. W. Samuelson and Ann Tasker. _American Cinematographer_ 64(12): 1282-1289, 1316-1331. December 1982.

"Ray Harryhausen Talks About His Cinematic Magic," _American Cinematographer_ 62(6): 556-558, 600-615. June 1981.

Tatara, W. T.

"Effect of novels on ideas about the scientist," _Journal of Educational Research_ 58(1):3-9. September 1964.

Tate, J. M.

"Sexual bias in science fiction for children," _Elementary English_ 50(7):1061-1064. October 1973.

Tatsumi, Takayuki

"Interview with Darko Suvin, An," _Science Fiction Studies_ 12(2): 202-220. July 1985.

Taurasi, J. V.

"1956 World Con," by J. V. Taurasi and Ray Van Houten. in: _Science Fiction Yearbook, 1957 Edition_. Vol. 1. Patterson, NJ: Fandom House, 1957. pp. 8-10.

"Annual fantasy report," _Fantasy Times_ No. 242:1-2. March (1) 1956.

"Cosmic reporter; magazines," _Fantasy Times_ No. 10:7. June 1944.

"Editorial: conventions and profit," _Fantasy Times_ No. 42:26. March 16, 1947.

"FT 15 years from now," _Fantasy Times_ No. 254:16-18. September (1) 1956.

"Notes from the editor: Worldcon bids," _Science Fiction Times_ No. 420:4,9. October 1964.

"Outside the U.S.," by J. V. Taurasi and Ray Van Houten. in: _Science Fiction Yearbook, 1957 Edition_. Vol. 1. Patterson, NJ: Fandom House, 1957. pp. 7-8.

"Ray Van Houten dead at 44," _Science Fiction Times_ No. 409/410:16-17. December 1963.

"Science fiction, 1956," by J. V. Taurasi and Ray Van Houten. in: _Science Fiction Yearbook, 1957 Edition_. Vol. 1. Patterson, NJ: Fandom House, 1957. pp. 3-7.

"State of fandom: 1956," by J. V. Taurasi and Ray Van Houten. in: _Science Fiction_

Yearbook, 1957 Edition. Vol. 1. Patterson, NJ: Fandom House, 1957. pp. 10-11.

"Twenty-one years of science fiction in pulp magazines," _Fantasy Times_ No. 45:34. April 6, 1947.

"World Convention seventeen years old today," _Fantasy Times_ No. 250:1,6. July (1) 1956.

Tautovic, Radojica

Hefest u Svemiru. Ogledi o nauchoj fantastici. Krusevac: Bagdala, 1973. 240 p.

Tavormina, M. T.

"Physics as Metaphor: The General Temporal Theory in The Dispossessed," _Mosaic_ 13(3/4): 51-62. Spring/Summer 1980.

Taylor, Agatha

"_Spider Kiss_ Recalled by Ace," _Paperback Quarterly_ 5(2): 25-27. Summer 1982.

Taylor, Angus

Philip K. Dick & the Umbrella of Light. Baltimore: T-K Graphics, 1975. 52 p.

"Can God fly? Can He hold out His arms and fly? The fiction of Philip K. Dick," _Foundation_ 4:48-60. July 1974.

"Chinese parallels in Le Guin's work," _Arena_ 9:17. August 1979.

"Dougle-edged sword meets the socio-economic root, The," _Foundation_ 11/12:113-118. March 1977.

"Pilgrim of Hope: William Morris on the Way to Utopia," _Foundation_ 32: 15-22. November 1984.

"Politics of space, time and entropy, The," _Foundation_ 10:34-43. June 1976.

"Science fiction: the evolutionary context," _Journal of Popular Culture_ 5(4):858-866. Spring 1972.

Taylor, Frank

"Jack Pierce: Forgotten make-up genius," _American Cinematographer_ 66(1): 33-41. January 1984.

"Makeup: creating the visitors for V," _American Cinematographer_ 65(1):69-74. January 1984.

Taylor, John

"Science thought in fiction and in fact," in: Nicholls, Peter, ed. Science Fiction at Large. New York: Harper, 1976. pp. 57-72.

Taylor, Keith

"From prophecy to prediction: Saint-Simon and the conquest of the future," Futures 9(1):58-64. February 1971.

"Politics as Harmony: utopian responses to the impact of Industrialism, 1830-1848," Alternative Futures 2(1): 60-75. Winter 1979.

Taylor, Martyn

"Art of Good Movie Watching, The," Vector 118: 24-28. February 1984.

"SF on U. K. Television," Vector 102: 8-17. June 1981.

Taylor, Robert

"Kurt Vonnegut," Boston Globe Sunday Magazine pp. 10-12. July 20, 1969.

Teilhet, D. L.

"Tarzan: ape-man into industry," Vanity Fair 43(5):22-23,64. January 1935.

Teitelbaum, Sheldon

"America 3000," Cinefantastique 16(1):7,52. March 1986.

"SF in Israel," Locus 14(11):11-12. December 1981.

Teitler, S. A.

"In Search of Zion: An Annotated Bibliography of Ten Lost Tribes of Israel in Utopia," in: Roemer, Kenneth M., ed. America As Utopia. New York: Franklin, 1981. pp. 186-191.

"Introduction," in: Lane, Mary E. B. Mizora: A Prophecy. Boston: Gregg, 1975. pp. v-x.

"Projected bibliography: 'by the world forgot', A," Extrapolation 12(2):106-108. May 1971.

Telotte, J. P.

Dreams of Darkness: Fantasy and the Films of Val Lewton. Urbana: University of Illinois Press, 1985. 223 p.

"'The Dark Side of the Force': Star Wars and the Science Fiction Tradition," Extrapolation 24(3): 216-226. Fall 1983.

"Human Artifice and the Science Fiction Film," Film Quarterly 36(3): 44-51. Spring 1983.

"Through a Pumpkin's Eye: The Reflexive Nature of Horror," Film/Literature Quarterly 10(3): 139-149. July 1983.

Temple, W. F.

"Talking about John Wyndham: plagiarism in SF," Australian Science Fiction Review No. 12:16-21. October 1967.

Tenn, William

"Fiction in SF, The," Science Fiction Adventures 2(2):66-78. March 1954.

Tepper, M. B.

Asimov Science Fiction Bibliography, The. Santa Monica, California: by the author, n. d. 90 p.

Tepperman, Jay

"Research scientist in modern fiction, The," Perspectives in Biology and Medicine 3(4):547-559. Summer 1960.

Ternes, Hans

"Fantastic in the works of Franz Kafka," in: Collins, R. A. and H. D. Pearce, eds. The Scope of the Fantastic: Theory, Technique, Major Authors. Westport, CT: Greenwood Press, 1985. pp. 221-228.

Terrace, Vincent

"Science fiction shows on radio and television," in: Parish, J. R. Great Science Fiction Pictures. Metuchen, NJ: Scarecrow, 1977. pp. 367-376.

Terrell, Carre

"What Does the Future Hold?" in: The Future in Peril: 1984 and the Anti-Utopians. College Station: Honors Program, Texas A&M University, [1985]. pp. 32-37.

Terry, P. A. M.

"King's cross in orbit: Edmond Hamilton and Leigh Brackett in Sydney," Australian Science Fiction Review No. 14:25-31. February 1968.

Teunissen, J. J.

Other Worlds: Fantasy and Science Fiction Since 1939. Winnipeg, Canada: University of Manitoba, 1980. 225 p. (Also published as Mosaic v. 13, no. 3/4, 1982.

"Pieta as Icon in The Golden Notebook," by E. J. Hinz and J. J. Teunissen. Contemporary Literature 14(4):457-470. Autumn 1973.

Texas A&M University Library

Announcing the Future. College Station: the library, 1974. 14 p.

Thale, Jerome

"Orwell's Modest Proposal," Critical Quarterly 4(4):365-368. Winter 1962.

Thaler, Heiner

"Entdeckungen in 'Fra Mauro'," in: Rottensteiner, Franz, ed. Polaris 6. Frankfurt-am-Main: Suhrkamp, 1982. pp. 311-315.

Theall, D. F.

"Art of social-science fiction: the ambiguous utopian dialects of Ursula K. Le Guin, The," Science Fiction Studies 2(3):256-264. November 1975.

"On Science Fiction as Symbolic Communication," Science-Fiction Studies 7(3): 247-262. November 1980.

Themal, H. F.

"Veterans romp through latest roles," Wilmington, Del. Evening Journal. June 23, 1985. in: NewsBank. Film and Television. 2:B14-B15. July 1985.

Theys, Cornelia

"Eye of the Basilisk," by Steve Theys and Cornelia Theys. Fantasy Newsletter 5(11): 15. December 1982.

"Eye of the Basilisk: Buying Original Art Work," by Steve Theys and Cornelia Theys. Fantasy Newsletter 6(5): 34-35. May 1983.

"Eye of the Basilisk: Marketing Art," by Steve Theys and Cornelia Theys. Fantasy Newsletter 6(4): 32-33. April 1983.

"Eye of the Basilisk: Other Worlds Than Ours," by Steve Theys and Cornelia Theys. Fantasy Newsletter 6(2): 32. February 1983.

"Eye of the Basilisk: Prints," by Steve Theys and Cornelia Theys. Fantasy Newsletter 6(1): 27. January 1983.

"Eye of the Basilisk: Rulemakers Exclude Most Professionals From Worldcon Art Show," by Steve Theys and Cornelia Theys. Fantasy Review 7(6): 31. July 1984.

"Eye of the Basilisk: Why We Ain' Got No Respect," by Steve Theys and Cornelia Theys. Fantasy Review 7(1): 34, 50. January 1984.

Theys, Steve

"Eye of the Basilisk," by Steve Theys and Cornelia Theys. Fantasy Newsletter 5(11): 15. December 1982.

"Eye of the Basilisk: Buying Original Art Work," by Steve Theys and Cornelia Theys. Fantasy Newsletter 6(5): 34-35. May 1983.

"Eye of the Basilisk: Marketing Art," by Steve Theys and Cornelia Theys. Fantasy Newsletter 6(4): 32-33. April 1983.

"Eye of the Basilisk: Other Worlds Than Ours," by Steve Theys and Cornelia Theys. Fantasy Newsletter 6(2): 32. February 1983.

"Eye of the Basilisk: Prints," by Steve Theys and Cornelia Theys. Fantasy Newsletter 6(1): 27. January 1983.

"Eye of the Basilisk: Rulemakers Exclude Most Professionals From Worldcon Art Show," by Steve Theys and Cornelia Theys. Fantasy Review 7(6): 31. July 1984.

"Eye of the Basilisk: Why We Ain' Got No Respect," by Steve Theys and Cornelia Theys. Fantasy Review 7(1): 34, 50. January 1984.

Thiem, Jon

"Catastrophe Fiction, 1870-1914: An Annotated Bibliography of Selected Works in English," by Roberta Scott and Jon Thiem. Extrapolation. 24(2): 156-169. Summer 1983.

Thiesse, Frank

Perry Rhodan: untersuchen einer science fiction heftromanserie, by Beate Ellerbrock, Jurgend Ellerbrock, and Frank Thiesse. Giessen: Anabas, 1976. 152 p.

Thiessen, J. G.

"Astonishing Stories (Canadian)," in: Tymn, M. B. and Ashley, Mike. Science Fiction, Fantasy, and Weird Fiction Magazines. Westport, CT: Greenwood, 1985. pp. 122-123.

Thiessen, J. G. (Continued)

"Brief Fantastic Tales," by Grant Thiessen and Mike Ashley. in: Tymn, M. B. and Ashley, Mike. Science Fiction, Fantasy, and Weird Fiction Magazines. Westport, CT: Greenwood, 1985. pp. 152-153.

"Eerie Tales," in: Tymn, M. B. and Ashley, Mike. Science Fiction, Fantasy, and Weird Fiction Magazines. Westport, CT: Greenwood, 1985. pp. 203-204.

"Girl from U. N. C. L. E. Magazine," in: Tymn, M. B. and Ashley, Mike. Science Fiction, Fantasy, and Weird Fiction Magazines. Westport, CT: Greenwood, 1985. pp. 318-319.

"Haunt of Horror," in: Tymn, M. B. and Ashley, Mike. Science Fiction, Fantasy, and Weird Fiction Magazines. Westport, CT: Greenwood, 1985. pp. 325-336.

"Man From U. N. C. L. E. Magazine," in: Tymn, M. B. and Ashley, Mike. Science Fiction, Fantasy, and Weird Fiction Magazines. Westport, CT: Greenwood, 1985. pp. 396-397.

"Mind, Inc.," by Mike Ashley and Grant Thiessen. in: Tymn, M. B. and Ashley, Mike. Science Fiction, Fantasy, and Weird Fiction Magazines. Westport, CT: Greenwood, 1985. pp. 407-409.

"Uncanny Tales (1940-1943)," by Mike Ashley and Grant Thiessen. in: Tymn, M. B. and Ashley, Mike. Science Fiction, Fantasy, and Weird Fiction Magazines. Westport, CT: Greenwood, 1985. pp. 685-688.

"A. E. Van Vogt: a brief checklist," Science Fiction Collector 8:7-22. October 1979.

"Ace Book alpha-numerical checklist," Science Fiction Collector 1:5-20. 1976.

"Ace Books author index," Science Fiction Collector 1:21-45. 1976.

"Ace Books: a personal appraisal," Science Fiction Collector 1:5. 1976.

"Ace science fiction specials," by J. G. Thiessen and William Trojan. Science Fiction Collector 5:21-23. September 1977.

"Additions and errata to the Ace checklist; more Ace books of associational interest," Science Fiction Collector 2:35-39. 1976.

"Avalon Books," Science Fiction Collector 5:29-36. September 1977.

"Best of phenomenon, The," Science Fiction Collector 4:32-37. July 1977. addendum, 5:47-48. September 1977.

"Fredric Brown: an appreciation; with bibliography of book appearances," Science Fiction Collector 2:26-33. 1976.

"Galaxy Science Fiction Novels," by S. W. Wells, III and J. G. Thiessen. Science Fiction Collector 3:44-48. 1977.

"Golden amazon, by John Russell Fearn, The," Science Fiction Collector 2:24-25. 1976.

"Gone but not forgotten: indexes to defunct paperback lines," Science Fiction Collector 2:6-23. 1976.

"How to file your SF collection," Science Fiction Collector 2:42-45. 1976.

"Interview with A. E. Van Vogt, An," Science Fiction Collector 8:4-7. October 1979.

"James H. Schmitz Bibliography," Megavore 12: 13-19. December 1980.

"Philip Jose Farmer: an appreciation," Science Fiction Collector 5:3-4. September 1977.

"Super science stories (Canadian series)," Science Fiction Collector 4:21-25. July 1977.

"Tarzan and his imitators," Science Fiction Collector 4:26-27. July 1977.

Thiry, Marcel

"Roger Callois et le fantastique," Bulletin de l'Academie Royale de Langue et de Litterature francaises. Bruxelles. 52(3/4):249-259. 1974.

Thole, Karel

Visionen des Unwirklichen: Die phantastichen Bilder des Karel Thole. Munich: Heyne, 1982. 97 p.

Thomas, Bill

Keep Watching the Skies! American Science Fiction Movies of the Fifties. Volume 1, 1950-1957, by Bill Warren and Bill Thomas. Jefferson, NC: McFarland, 1982. 467 p.

Thomas, E. M.

"Real Conversations III: A Dialogue Between Frank R. Stockton and Edith M. Thomas," McClure's Magazine 1(6):467-477. November 1893.

Thomas, L. V.

Civilisation et diagnations: mort, fantasmes, science-fiction. Paris: Payot, 1979. 285 p.

"Catastrophisme et Science-Fiction," Archives de Science Sociales des Religions 27(53): 69-85. January/March 1982.

Thomas, P. J.

Nouvelle Science Fiction Americaine   Rey,
Pierre K.; Thomas, Pascal J.   Cavignac: A&A
Infos, 1981. 64 p. (A & A Infos, NO. 72, Mai
1981.)

"11th French SF Convention," by Stephane Nicot
and P. J. Thomas. Locus 18(1): 30. January
1985.

"Another view (Denvention)," Locus
14(9):17,19-20. October 1981.

"Conversation with John Varley, A," Science
Fiction Times (Boston) 1(4):1,14. August
1979.

"Fiction," Science Fiction and Fantasy
Research Index. 2: 70. 1982.

"French SF and the legacy of Philip K. Dick,"
Foundation 34: 22-36. Autumn 1985.

"Galaxie," Science Fiction and Fantasy
Research Index. 2: 71. 1982.

"Interview: Gregory Benford," Thrust 18:
8-11. Winter/Spring 1982.

"John Varley interview, continued," Science
Fiction Times (Boston) 1(5):4. November 1979.

"L.A. con Programming," Locus 17(12):
2628. December 1984.

"Opzone," Science Fiction and Fantasy
Research Index 2: 72. 1982.

"Philippe Curval: Between Surrealism and
Science Fiction," by P. J. Thomas and Francis
Valery. Science Fiction Times (Boston)
1(10): 7. 1981.

"Report from France, December 1985," Locus
18(12): 24, 33. December 1985.

"Report from France, January 1985," Locus
18(1): 30. January 1985.

"Report from France, March 1984," Locus
17(3):17. March 1984.

"Report from France, May 1985," Locus
18(5): 22-23. May 1985.

"Report from France, October 1984," Locus
17(10):28-29. October 1984.

"Report from France, October 1985," Locus
18(10): 17, 32, 35. October 1985.

"Report from France: short fiction," Locus
17(8):26-27. August 1984.

"SF in France, April 1981," Locus 14(3):9.
April 1981.

"SF in France, July 1981," Locus
14(6):19-20. July 1981.

"SF in France, October 1979," Locus
12(9):6-7. October 1979.

"Some French Science Fiction Trends," A
Foreign Fanzine 4: 7-12. August 1981.

Thomas, Phil

"Growing sales puzzle writer," Ann Arbor
News p. 41. December 12, 1971.

Thomas, W. K.

"Underside of utopias, The," College
English 38(4):356-372. December 1976.

Thomason, Sue

"Living Water: Archetypal Power in 'Dune' and
'The Drowned World'," Vector 119: 33-34.
April 1984.

"SF Poetry," Focus: An SF Writer's Magazine
7: 37-39. Spring 1983.

"Strange New Language, A," Vector 113:
11-13. 1983.

Thompson, Bill

"Conan's Masters," Houston Post p. 7E.
May 28, 1982.

Thompson, D.

"Science fiction editors, writers pitch in to
launch Higbee's new SF department," by D.
Thompson and M. Thompson. Publishers Weekly
209:48. April 19, 1976.

Thompson, D. C.

Grokking the Future: Science Fiction in the
Classroom, by Bernard Hollister and D. C.
Thompson. S. L.: Pflaum/Standard, 1973.
167 p.

Thompson, E. P.

William Morris: Romantic to Revolutionary.
New York: Pantheon, 1977. 829 p.

Thompson, G. H.

"Early reviews of books by J. R. R. Tolkien,
part I," Mythlore 11(2):56-60. Autumn
1984.

"Early reviews of books by J. R. R. Tolkien,
part II," Mythlore 11(3): 59-63.
Winter/Spring 1985.

Thompson, G. H. (Continued)

"Early reviews of books by J. R. R. Tolkien, part III: The Return of the King," Mythlore 12(1): 58-63. Autumn 1985.

Thompson, G. R.

"Apparition of This World, The: Transcendentalism and the American 'Ghost' Story," in: Slusser, George E., ed. Bridges to Fantasy. Carbondale: Southern Illinois University Press, 1982. pp. 90-107.

Thompson, Hilary

"Doorways to Fantasy," Canadian Children's Literature 21: 8-16. 1981.

Thompson, M.

"Science fiction editors, writers pitch in to launch Higbee's new SF department," by D. Thompson and M. Thompson. Publishers Weekly 209:48. April 19, 1976.

Thompson, R. H.

Gordon R. Dickson: A Primary and Secondary Bibliography. Boston: G. K. Hall, 1983. 108 p.

Return From Avalon, The: A Study of the Arthurian Legend in Modern Fiction. Westport, CT: Greenwood, 1985. 206 p.

"Astonishing Stories," by Milton Wolfe and R. H. Thompson. in: Tymn, M. B. and Ashley, Mike. Science Fiction, Fantasy, and Weird Fiction Magazines. Westport, CT: Greenwood, 1985. pp. 117-122.

"Comet," in: Tymn, M. B. and Ashley, Mike. Science Fiction, Fantasy, and Weird Fiction Magazines. Westport, CT: Greenwood, 1985. pp. 163-166.

"Cosmic Stories," in: Tymn, M. B. and Ashley, Mike. Science Fiction, Fantasy, and Weird Fiction Magazines. Westport, CT: Greenwood, 1985. pp. 168-169.

"Science Fiction," by Mike Ashley and R. H. Thompson. in: Tymn, M. B. and Ashley, Mike. Science Fiction, Fantasy, and Weird Fiction Magazines. Westport, CT: Greenwood, 1985. pp. 511-519.

"Stirring Science Stories," in: Tymn, M. B. and Ashley, Mike. Science Fiction, Fantasy, and Weird Fiction Magazines. Westport, CT: Greenwood, 1985. pp. 617-620.

"Super Science Stories (Canadian)," in: Tymn, M. B. and Ashley, Mike. Science Fiction, Fantasy, and Weird Fiction Magazines. Westport, CT: Greenwood, 1985. pp. 635-637.

"Super Science Stories," in: Tymn, M. B. and Ashley, Mike. Science Fiction, Fantasy, and Weird Fiction Magazines. Westport, CT: Greenwood, 1985. pp. 631-635.

"Arthurian legend and modern fantasy," in: Magill, Frank N., ed. Survey of Modern Fantasy Literature, Vol 5. Englewood Cliffs, NJ: Salem Press, Inc., 1983. pp. 2299-2315.

"Commentary: King Arthur in modern fantasy," Fantasy Review 8(12): 12-13. December 1985.

"Enchanter awakes, The: Merlin in modern fantasy," in: Yoke, C. B. and Hassler, D. M., eds. Death and the Serpent. Westport, CT: Greenwood, 1985. pp. 49-56.

"Humor and irony in modern Arthurian fantasy: Thomas Berger's Author Rex," Kansas Quarterly 16(3): 45-49. Summer 1984.

"Modern Fantasy and Medieval Romance," in: Schlobin, Roger C., ed. The Aesthetics of Fantasy Literature and Art. Notre Dame, IN: University of Notre Dame Press, 1982. pp. 211-225.

"Shai Dorsai! A study of the hero figure in Gordon R. Dickson's Dorsai," Extrapolation 20(3):223-229. Fall 1979.

Thompson, W. A.

"Interview: Joan D. Vinge," Starship 19(1): 15-18. November 1982.

Thompson, W. B.

"Interview: Roger Zelazny," Future Life 25: 40-42. March 1981.

"Starlog Interview: Alan Dean Foster," Starlog 81: 51-53, 67. April 1984.

Thomsen, C. W.

Phantastik in Literatur und Kunst, by C. W. Thomsen and J. M. Fischer. Darmstadt: Wissenschaftliche Buchgesellschaft, 1980. 563 p.

"Holden jungfrauen, urigen monstren und reisenden gentlemen des Hans Carl Artmann," by C. Thomsen and G. Brandstetter. in: Thomsen, C. W. Phantastik in Literatur und Kunst. Darmstadt: Wiss. Buchgesellschaft, 1980. pp. 333-368.

"Psivilisation und Chemokratie: Stanislaw Lems Phantastik Konzeption . . .", in: Thomsen, C. W., ed. Phantastik in Literatur und Kunst. Darmstadt: Wissenschaftliche Buchgesellschaft, 1980. pp. 353-368.

Thomsen, C. W. (Continued)

"Robot Ethics and Robot Parody: Remarks on Isaac Asimov's I, Robot and Some Critical Essays and Short Stories by Stanislaw Lem," in: Dunn, T. P., ed. The Mechanical God. Westport: Greenwood, 1982. pp. 27-39.

Thomson, Amy

"Aussiecon II: A Fan's Perspective," Locus 18(11): 1, 23-25. November 1985.

Thomson, Ian

"Roger Elwood interview," by Martin Hatfield, Christopher Fowler, and Ian Thomson. Vector 79: 10-14. January/February 1977.

Thorp, M. B.

"Dynamics of Terror in Orwell's 1984," Brigham Young University Studies 24(1): 3-17. Winter 1984.

Thorpe, B. J.

"Psycho," Cinefantastique 16(1):27-28. March 1986.

Thorson, Stephen

"Brief introduction to the history and origin of the Holy Gail motif," Mythlore 6(1): 23-24. Winter 1979.

"Thematic implications of C. S. Lewis' Spirits in Bondage," Mythlore 8(2):26-30. Summer 1981.

Thron, E. M.

"Outsider from inside: Clarke's aliens, The," in: Olander, J. D. and M. H. Greenberg, eds. Arthur C. Clarke. New York: Taplinger, 1977. pp. 72-86.

Thurber, Bart

"Toward a Technological Sublime," in: Myers, R. E., ed. The Intersection of Science Fiction and Philosophy. Westport: Greenwood, 1983. pp. 211-224.

Thurber, James

"Tempest in a Looking Glass," in: Boyer, Robert H. and Zahorski, Kenneth J. Fantasists on Fantasy. New York: Avon Discus, 1984. pp. 67-74.

"Wizard of Chitenango, The," in: Boyer, Robert H. and Zahorski, Kenneth J. Fantasists

on Fantasy. New York: Avon Discus, 1984. pp. 59-66.

Thurogood, Brian

"Interview with Brian Aldiss, An," Noumeneon 24:10-13. August 1978. also in: Vector 94:7-9. July/August 1979.

Thurston, Robert

"Introduction," in: Dick, P. K. The Game-Players of Titan. Boston: Gregg, 1979. pp. v-xix.

"Introduction," in: Galouye, D. F. Dark Universe. Boston: Gregg, 1976. pp. v-xiv.

"Introduction," in: Zelazny, Roger. Today We Choose Faces. Boston: Gregg, 1978. pp. v-xix.

Tidmarsh, Andrew

"Barry Malzberg's Herovit's World," Vector 78:55-58. November/December.

Tiedman, Richard

Jack Vance: Science Fiction Stylist. Wabash, Indiana: by the author, 1965. (not seen)

"Jack Vance: science fiction stylist," in: Underwood, Tim and Miller, Chuck, eds. Jack Vance. New York: Taplinger, 1980. pp. 179-222.

Tierney, R. L.

"Lovecraft and the Cosmic Quality in Fiction," in: Joshi, S. T., ed. H. P. Lovecraft: Four Decades of Criticism. Athens, OH: Ohio University Press, 1980. pp. 191-195.

Tifft, L. L.

"Possessed sociology and Le Guin's Dispossessed: from exile to anarchism," by L. L. Tifft and D. C. Sullivan. in: De Bolt, Joe, ed. Ursula K. Le Guin: Voyager to Inner Lands.... Port Washington, NY: Kennikat, 1979. pp. 180-197.

Tilove, Jonathan

"Faraway Friends Meet at Space Convention," Springfield (Mass.) Republican, Aug. 1, 1982. in: NewsBank. Social Relations, 37: G3-4. 1982.

Tilsner, Thomas

"Interview mit Michael Klett," by Thomas Tilsner and Joachim Kafer. Andromeda Science Fiction Magazine. 103: 5-9. 1981.

"Perry Rhodan: Anmerkungen zu einer Heftserie," Andromeda Science Fiction Magazine. 103: 10-12. 1981.

Timmerman, J. H.

"Fantasy literature's evocative power," Christian Century 95(18):533-537. May 17, 1978.

"Logres and Britain: the dialectic of C. S. Lewis That Hideous Strength," CSL: The Bulletin of the New York C. S. Lewis Society 9(1):1-8. 1977.

"Tolkien's crucible of faith: the subcreation," Christian Century 91(22):608-611. June 5, 1974.

Timpone, Anthony

"Anthony Michael Hall plays with weird science," Starlog No. 98:38-39. September 1985.

"Merritt Butrick: the search for David," Starlog 95: 28-29, 72. June 1985.

"One Hundred Most Important People in Science Fiction/Fantasy: Alfred Bester," Starlog 100: 80. November 1985.

"One Hundred Most Important People in Science Fiction/Fantasy: Bela Lugosi," Starlog 100: 38. November 1985.

"One Hundred Most Important People in Science Fiction/Fantasy: Boris Karloff," Starlog 100: 76. November 1985.

"One Hundred Most Important People in Science Fiction/Fantasy: Christopher Lee," Starlog 100: 33. November 1985.

"One Hundred Most Important People in Science Fiction/Fantasy: Forrest J. Ackerman," Starlog 100: 39. November 1985.

"One Hundred Most Important People in Science Fiction/Fantasy: Hugo Gernsback," Starlog 100: 41. November 1985.

"One Hundred Most Important People in Science Fiction/Fantasy: Lon Chaney, Sr.," Starlog 100:24. November 1985.

"One Hundred Most Important People in Science Fiction/Fantasy: Nigel Kneale," Starlog 100: 30. November 1985.

"One Hundred Most Important People in Science Fiction/Fantasy: Orson Welles," Starlog 100: 63, 74. November 1985.

"One Hundred Most Important People in Science Fiction/Fantasy: Roger Corman," Starlog 100: 22-23. November 1985.

"One Hundred Most Important People in Science Fiction/Fantasy: Stanley Kubrick," Starlog 100: 22. November 1985.

"One Hundred Most Important People in Science Fiction/Fantasy: Stephen King," Starlog 100: 44. November 1985.

"One Hundred Most Important People in Science Fiction/Fantasy: Steven Spielberg," Starlog 100:38. November 1985.

Tinkel, Bruce

"Science Fiction Adventures (1952-1954)," by Ted Krulik and Bruce Tinkel. in: Tymn, M. B. and Ashley, Mike. Science Fiction, Fantasy, and Weird Fiction Magazines. Westport, CT: Greenwood, 1985. pp. 520-524.

Tiptree, James, Jr. (pseud. of Alice Sheldon)

"Everything but the name is me," Starship 16(4):31-34. Fall 1979.

"Everything but the signature is me," Khatru No. 7: 12-17. 1978.

Tischler, N. M.

Dorothy L. Sayers: A Pilgrim Soul. Atlanta: Knox, 1980. 167 p.

Titcomb, Molly

"Movie of The Lord of the Rings?" Mythlore 1(1):11-13. January 1969.

Titow, German

"Wege zum Unerlebten," Quarber Merkur 31:18-21. July 1972.

Tobias, Andrew

"Battle for King Kong, The," New York Magazine 9:38. February 23, 1976.

Tobin, Jean

"Introduction," in: Beagle, P. S. The Last Unicorn. Boston: Gregg, 1978. pp. v-xxiv.

"Introduction," in: Russ, Joanna. We Who Are About To. Boston: Gregg, 1978. pp. v-xxvi.

Todd, Richard

"Masks of Kurt Vonnegut, Jr., The," New York Times Magazine pp. 16-17,19,22,24,26,30-31. January 24, 1971.

Todorov, Tzvetan

Fantastic: A Structural Approach to a Literary Genre, The, by Tzvetan Todorov and Richard Howard. Cleveland and London: The Press of Case Western Reserve University, 1973. 179 p.

Introduction a la litterature fantastique. Paris: Seuil, 1970. 187 p.

Toepfer, Susan

"Little Star That Could, The," New York Daily News August 5, 1984. NewsBank. Film and Television. FTV 11: A8-A9. 1984.

Toffler, Alvin

"Science fiction and change," in: Nicholls, Peter, ed. Science Fiction at Large. New York: Harper, 1976. pp. 115-118.

Toft, Palle

"Erwin Neutzsky-Wulff, an introduction," in: Dollerup, Cay, ed. Volve. Scandinavian Views on Science Fiction. Copenhagen: Department of English, University of Copenhagen, 1978. pp. 59-63.

Tolkien, Christopher

Letters of J. R. R. Tolkien, by Humphrey Carpenter and Christopher Tolkien. Boston: Houghton, 1981. 453 p.

Tolkien, J. R. R.

Monsters and the Critics and Other Essays. Boston: Houghton Mifflin, 1984. 240 p.

"Fantasy," in: Boyer, Robert H. and Zahorski, Kenneth J. Fantasists on Fantasy. New York: Avon Discus, 1984. pp. 75-84.

"Guide to the names in The Lord of the Rings," in: Lobdell, Jared, ed. A Tolkien Compass. New York: Ballantine/Del Rey, 1980. pp. 168-216.

"On fairy-stories," in: Tolkien, J. R. R. Tree and Leaf. London: Unwin Books, 1964. pp. 11-70.

"To W. H. Auden," in: Boyer, Robert H. and Zahorski, Kenneth J. Fantasists on Fantasy. New York: Avon Discus, 1984. pp. 85-94.

Tolley, M. J.

Stellar Gauge: Essays on Science Fiction, by Michael Tolley and Kirpal Singh. Victoria, Aust.: Norstrilla Press, 1980. 288 p.

"Beyond the enigma: Dick's questors," in: Tolley, M. J., ed. The Stellar Gauge. Victoria, Australia: Norstrilia, 1980. pp. 197-237.

Tomalin, Ruth

W. H. Hudson, a Biography. London: Faber, 1981. 314 p.

Toman, M. D.

"Joan C. Holly, 1932-1982," SFWA Bulletin 17(2): 12-14. Summer 1983.

Tompkins, H. G.

"Jules Verne, uncanny prophet," Coronet 27(3):152-159. January 1950.

Tonkin, Humphrey

"Utopias: notes on a pattern of thought," Centennial Review 14(4):385-395. Fall 1974.

Tonsor, Stephen

"Image of science and technology in utopian literature and science fiction, The," Modern Age 20(1):86-93. Winter 1976.

Toothaker, R. E.

"What's your fantasy I. Q.?" Language Arts 54(1):11-13,24. January 1977.

Torgeson, Roy

1977 Science Fiction and Fantasy Magazine Checklist and Price Guide, by Howard Frank and Roy Torgeson. Port Washington, NY: Science Fiction Resources, 1977. 50 p.

Toth, R. C.

"Science fiction: villain or paradox," New York Herald Tribune. June 2, 1958. (not seen)

Touponce, W. F.

Ray Bradbury and the Poetics of Reverie: Fantasy, Science Fiction, and the Reader. Ann Arbor: UMI Research Press, 1984, c1981. 131 p.

Touponce, W. F. (Continued)

<u>Ray Bradbury and the Poetics of Reverie: A Study of Fantasy, Science Fiction, and the Reading Progress</u>. Ph. D. Dissertation, University of Massachusetts, 1981. 381 p. (DAI 41:5093A)

"Existential Fabulous, The: a Reading of Ray Bradbury's The Golden Apples of the Sun," <u>Mosaic</u> 13(3/4): 203-218. Spring/Summer 1980.

"Some Aspects of Surrealism in the Work of Ray Bradbury," <u>Extrapolation</u> 25(3): 228-238. Fall 1984.

Touttain, P. A.

<u>Jules Verne</u>, ed. by P. A. Touttain. Paris: l'Herne, 1974. 366 p.

"Au dela des apparences," <u>Les Nouvelles Litteraires</u> (Paris) 2444:7. July 29, 1974.

"Dossier de la science-fiction, Le," <u>Les Nouvelles Litteraires</u> No. 2153:6-7. December 26, 1968.

"Litterature fantastique, La," <u>Les Nouvelles Litteraires</u> 2135:6-7. August 22, 1968.

"Science fiction se porte bien, la," <u>Les Nouvelles Litteraires</u> (Paris) 2413:8. December 24, 1974.

Townsend, Alan

"Soviet science fiction," <u>Listener</u> 70(1804):645-646. October 24, 1963.

Townsend, J. R.

"Alan Garner," in: Townsend, J. R. <u>A Sense of Story</u>. Philadelphia: Lippencott, 1971. pp. 108-119.

"Andre Norton," in: Townsend, J. R. <u>A Sense of Story</u>. Philadelphia: Lippencott, 1971. pp. 143-153.

"John Christopher," in: Townsend, J. R. <u>A Sense of Story</u>. Philadelphia: Lippencott, 1971. pp. 48-53.

"Madeleine L'Engle," in: Townsend, J. R. <u>A Sense of Story</u>. Philadelphia: Lippencott, 1971. pp. 120-129.

Toyoda, Aritsune

(Anata mo SF sakka ni nareru wake de wa nai) s.l.: s.n., 1979. 228 p.

Trachentenberg, Stanley

"Vonnegut's cradle: the erosion of comedy,"

<u>Michigan Quarterly Review</u> 12(1):66-71. Winter 1973.

Traschen, I.

"Modern literature and science," <u>College English</u> 25(4):248-255. January 1964.

Trask, Margaret

<u>Fantasy, Science Fiction, Science Materials: papers presented at the School of Librarianship, Univ. of New South Wales, 16th-19th May 1972</u>. Kensington: Univ. of New South Wales, School of Librarianship, 1972. 204 p.

Tredell, Nicholas

<u>Novels of Colin Wilson</u>. Totowa, NJ: Barnes and Noble, 1982. 157 p.

Trefz, Linda

"Brother From Another Planet,", <u>American Cinematographer</u> 65(11):43-48. December 1984.

Treguboff, Z. L.

<u>Study of the Social Criticism in Popular Fiction: A Content Analysis of Science Fiction</u>. Ph.D. Dissertation, UCLA, 1955. 248 p.

Tremaine, F. Orlin

"Decade in STF, A," <u>Fantasy Times</u> No. 138:5-6. September (2) 1951.

"World of tomorrow today," <u>Fantasy Times</u> No. 100:11,15. February (2) 1950.

Tremaine, Louis

"Historical Consciousness in Stapledon and Malraux," <u>Science-Fiction Studies</u> 11(2): 130-138. July 1984.

"Olaf Stapledon's Note on Magnitude," <u>Extrapolation</u> 23(3): 243-253. Fall 1982.

Tremor, M. F.

<u>Adult Educator's Guide to Future Fiction</u>. Ph.D. Dissertation, Florida State University, 1974. 567 p.

Tressler-Hauschultz, A. M.

"Nuclear Nightmare in Popular Fiction, The," unpublished paper, 12-4-80. (Copy in Science Fiction Collection, Texas A&M University)

Trevor, William

"New novels," The Listener p. 273. February 18, 1965. (not seen)

Trimble, Bjo

On the Good Ship Enterprise: My 15 Years with Star Trek. Norfolk, VA: Starblaze, 1983. 286 p.

Star Trek Concordance. New York: Ballantine, 1976. 256 p.

"All of the Filkers are Singing," Starlog 54: 23-24. January 1982.

"Fan Scene: The 10-Foot 'Star Trek' Poll," Starlog 65: 40-41. December 1982.

"Futuristic Philosophy of Theodore Sturgeon, The: 'Ask the Next Question!'" Future Life 16: 26-28. February 1980.

"Hal Clement: S. F. Craftsman," To The Stars 2: 6-8, 37-38. 1984.

"John W. Campbell," Locus No. 91:9. July 22, 1971.

Trimble, Sankey

"Science Fiction Writer is a Working Rocket-Man, Too," The Eagle (Bryan, TX) Sec. 1, p. 4. August 19, 1958.

Tritt, Michael

"Byron's 'Darkness' and Asimov's 'Nightfall'," Science-Fiction Studies 8(1): 26-28. March 1981.

Trojan, William

"Ace science fiction specials," by J. G. Thiessen and William Trojan. Science Fiction Collector 5:21-23. September 1977.

Tropp, Martin

Mary Shelley's Monster. Boston: Houghton Mifflin, 1976. 192 p.

"It came from inner space: science fiction and the self," The CEA Critic 42(4):20-24. May 1980.

Trott, Walt

"Quest for Fire took 4 years to make," Madison Capital Times. March 8, 1982. in: NewsBank. Film and Television. 109:G10-11. 1981/82.

Trousson, Raymond

Voyages aux Pays de nulle pari. Brussels: Editions de l'Universite de Bruxelles, 1975. 298 p.

Troutner, Moanne

"Trekking with science fiction," Audiovisual Instruction 22(8):46-48. October 1977.

Troy, Carol

"Carol Troy interviews Kurt Vonnegut," Rags pp. 24-26. March 1971.

Truchaud, Francois

"Dream-quest of Howard Phillips Lovecraft," in: H. P. Lovecraft. Paris: Editions de l'Herne, 1969. pp. 15-25.

Truesdale, D. A.

"Interview with Andrew J. Offutt, An," Science Fiction Review 32:14-23. August 1979.

"Interview with Andrew J. Offutt, part 1, An," Science Fiction Review 31:10-14. May 1979.

"Interview with Leigh Brackett and Edmond Hamilton, An," Science Fiction Review 21:6-15. May 1977.

"Robert A. Heinlein: interview," Science Fiction Review 9(3):49-51. August 1980.

Truffaut, Francois

"A bas la science fiction," Arts. April 16, 1958.

Trumbull, Douglas

"Creating special effects for 2001," American Cinematographer 49(6):416-420,451-453. June 1968.

"Creating the photographic special effects for Close Encounters," American Cinematographer 59(1):72-83,96-97. January 1978.

Trussell, R. C.

"Final Toast to 'Rocky Horror', A," Kansas City Star July 23, 1984. NewsBank. Film and Television. FTV 20:A11-A12. 1984.

Author Entries

Trzynadlowski, Jan

"Proba poetyki science fiction," in: Budzyk, K., ed. Z teorii i historii literatury. Warsaw: Ossolineum, 1963.

Tschernyschewa, T.

"Mensch und milieu in der modernen wissenschaftlich-phantastischen literatur," Sowjetwissenschaft, Kunst und Literatur. 19(1):60-77. 1971.

"Uber die Kosmisierung des kunstlerischen Denkens und uber die wissenschaftliche Phantastik," Quarber Merkur. 45:3-12. December 1976.

Tsiolkovsky, Konstaintin,

The science fiction of Konstaintin Tsiolkavsky, by Konstaintin Tsiolkovsky and Adam Starchild. Seattle: University Press of the Pacific, 1979. 454 p.

Tuchman, Mitch

"Bradbury: Shooting Haiku in a Barrel," Film Comment 18(6): 39-41. November/December 1982.

Tuck, D. A.

"Cordwainer Smith: a bibliography," Australian Science Fiction Review No. 11:20-21. August 1967.

Tuck, D. H.

Author's Works Listing. Hobart, Tasmania: by the author, 1960-1962. 121 p.

Authors' Books Listing. Lindisfarne, Australia: by the author, 1975. 32 p.

Encyclopedia of Science Fiction and Fantasy Through 1968, Volume 1: Who's Who, A-L; Volume 2, Who's Who: M-Z; Volume 3, Miscellaneous. Chicago: Advent, 1974-1982. 3 volumes.

Handbook of Science Fiction and Fantasy, A. Hobart, Tasmania: by the author, 1954. 151 p.

Handbook of Science Fiction and Fantasy: A Collection of Material Acting as a Bibliographic Survey to the Fields of Science Fiction and Fantasy . . . to December 1957. Hobart, Tasmania: Tuck, 1959. 2nd edition, 2 vols., 396 p.

"Robert Silverberg: bibliography," Magazine of Fantasy and Science Fiction 46(4):81-88. April 1974.

Tucker, Bob

Fantasy Fan Index, The. Bloomington, IL: Author, 1945. 13 p.

Neo-Fan's Guide to Science Fiction Fandom. Hartford City, IN: Coulson, 1966. 16 p.

"Irrepressible Fan, The: An Appreciation," Locus 18(3): 50. March 1985.

"Shasta turned down Dianetics," Fantasy Times No. 111:1-2. August (1) 1950.

"Time Machine," Locus No. 110:14-15. March 25, 1972.

"Time Machine: fans," Locus No. 37:8a-b. September 10, 1969.

"Time machine: fans," Locus No. 58:2a-b. July 1, 1970.

"Time Machine: inflation," Locus No. 33:4a-b. July 21, 1969.

"Time machine: jokes," Locus No. 81:4c-d. April 22, 1971.

"Time machine: Midwestcon 1971," Locus No. 92:4a-b. July 30, 1971.

"Time machine; Fuggheads," Locus No. 64:15-17. September 30, 1970.

"Via Pullman to Portland," Fantasy Times No. 100:23-24. February (2) 1950.

Tucker, F. H.

"Iron Heel, The," in: Magill, Frank N., ed. Survey of Science Fiction Literature, Vol. 3. Englewood Cliffs, NJ: Salem Press, 1979. pp. 1068-1072.

"Magic, Inc.," in: Magill, Frank N., ed. Survey of Modern Fantasy Literature, Vol 2. Englewood Cliffs, NJ: Salem Press, Inc., 1983. pp. 942-944.

"Memoirs Found in a Bathtub," in: Magill, Frank N., ed. Survey of Science Fiction Literature, Vol. 3. Englewood Cliffs, NJ: Salem Press, 1979. pp. 1370-1374.

"Next Chapter, The," in: Magill, Frank N., ed. Survey of Science Fiction Literature, Vol. 3. Englewood Cliffs, NJ: Salem Press, 1979. pp. 1521-1525.

"Major political and social elements in Heinlein's fiction," in: Olander, J. D. and M. H. Greenberg, eds. Robert A. Heinlein. New York: Taplinger, 1978. pp. 172-193.

"Patterns in German science fiction," Extrapolation 19(2):149-155. May 1978.

Tucker, F. H. (Continued)

"Soviet science fiction: recent development and outlook," <u>Russian Review</u> 33(2):189-200. April 1973.

Tucker, Ken

"Unpretentious Kind of Horror," <u>Philadelphia Inquirer</u> August 22, 1982. <u>Newsbank. Literature.</u> 18: C10-11. 1982/1983.

Tucker, P. G.

"2001 (revisited; construction in space)," <u>Construction Specifier</u> 33(1):121-130. January 1980.

Tudor, Andrew

"Future by proxy, The," <u>New Society</u> pp. 142-143. October 21, 1976.

Tuggle, Thomas

"New Worlds at the library," <u>Interface</u> (Univ. of Georgia Libraries Newsletter) 6(8): 1-3. November/December 1919. (Reprinted, <u>Southeastern Librarian</u>, summer 1981.)

"New Worlds at the Library," <u>Southeastern Librarian</u> 31(2): 65-67. Summer 1981.

Tulloch, John

<u>Doctor Who: The Unfolding Text</u>, by John Tulloch and Manuel Alvarado. New York: St. Martins, 1983. 342 p.

Tuma, G. W.

"Biblical myth and legend in <u>Tower of Glass</u>: man's search for authenticity," <u>Extrapolation</u> 15(2):174-191. May 1974.

Tunley, R.

"Unbelievable but true," <u>Saturday Evening Post</u> 233(15):30,90-92. October 8, 1960.

Tunnell, James

"Kesey and Vonnegut: preachers of redemption," <u>Christian Century</u> 89:1180-1183. November 22, 1972.

Turan, Kenneth

"Barbarian in Babylon: Conan's greatest challenge, The," <u>New West</u> 4(18):16-25. August 27, 1979.

Turek, Leslie

<u>Noreascon Proceedings: The Twenty-Ninth World Science Fiction Convention</u>, Boston, Massachusetts, September 3-6, 1971. Cambridge, MA: NESFA, 1976.

Turian, Catherine

"S-F, Le? Une representation fantasmatique de l'Enfance," <u>La Quinzaine Litteraire</u> No. 225:16. January 16, 1976.

Turner, A. K.

"Chronology," in: <u>Exploring Cordwainer Smith</u>. New York: Algol, 1975. pp. 28-30.

"Clarke interviewed," <u>Algol</u> 12(1):14-16. November 1974.

"Harlan Ellison," <u>Publishers Weekly</u> 207:8-9. February 10, 1975.

Turner, C. C.

<u>Primordial Format: Archetypal Symbols of the Unconcious in a Science Fiction Television Series</u>. Ph.D. Dissertation, New York University, 1973. 451 p.

Turner, D. G.

<u>First Editions of Andre Norton, The</u>. Menlo Park, California: by the author, 1974. 12 p.

Turner, G. E.

"Academy visual effects nominees," <u>American Cinematographer</u> 66(4):54-55. April 1985.

"Creative realism for The Day After," <u>American Cinematographer</u> 65(2):56-60. February 1985.

"E.T.: The Extraterrestrial," <u>American Cinematographer</u> 64(4):67-68. April 1983.

"Making the Flash Gordon serials," <u>American Cinematographer</u> 64(6):56-62,117-122. June 1983.

"Spacehunter," by G. E. Turner and Nora Lee. <u>American Cinematographer</u> 64(7):56-59,88-91. July 1983.

"Steven Spielberg and E.T.," <u>American Cinematographer</u> 64(1):46-49,80-85. January 1983.

"Visual effects for Indiana Jones and the Temple of Doom," <u>American Cinematographer</u> 65(7):61-75. July 1984.

Turner, George

"Australian SF, 1950-1980," Science Fiction: A Review of Speculative Literature 5(1): 4-11. March 1983.

"Frederik Pohl as a creator of future societies," in: Tolley, M. J., ed. The Stellar Gauge. Carleton, Australia: Norstrilia, 1980. pp. 109-134.

"God, Frank Herbert, and the Concept of Deity in Science Fiction," SF Commentary 62/66: 16-18. June 1981.

"Nothing to lose but the chains," Australian Science Fiction Review No. 12:22-26. October 1967.

"Overseas scene: an Australian viewpoint, The," Algol 19:21-25. November 1972.

"Profession of Science Fiction, 27: Not Taking It All too Seriously," Foundation 24: 49-58. February 1982.

"Retrospective: Howard Hawks' The Thing," Cinefantastique 12(5/6):78-85. July/August 1982.

"Retrospective: Val Lewton's Cat People," Cinefantastique 12(4):22-27. May/June 1982.

"Science fiction as literature," in: Ash, Brian, ed. Visual Encyclopedia of Science Fiction. New York: Harmony, 1977. pp. 257-262.

"Science fiction in Australia," Arena 9:4-17. August 1979.

"SF: death and transfiguration of a genre," Meanjin Quarterly 32(3):328-334. September 1973.

"What Australian Critics Should Be Talking About," Science Fiction: A Review of Speculative Literature 5(3): 88-89. September 1983.

"Who needs a definition of science fiction? And why?" Science Fiction: A Review of Speculative Literature 2(2):161-174. December 1979.

"Why they'll never equal the original Kong," Los Angeles 21(3):83-85,168-169. March 1976.

Turner, James

"H. P. Lovecraft: a mythos in his own image," Foundation 33: 55-61. Spring 1985.

Turner, S. M.

"Life is sure funny sometimes . . . and sometimes it isn't . . . a guide to understanding Kurt Vonnegut, Jr.," The Thoroughbred (Univ. of Louisville) 2(2):43-46. Spring 1971.

Tuttle, G. E.

Problems in the Pulps: A Study of Special Collections in Pulp Magazines. 33 p. 1983. ERIC ED 249 989.

Tuttle, Lisa

"By the Pricking of My Thumbs," Vector 121: 5-11. August 1984.

"Confessions of a Collaborator," Focus: an SF Writer's Magazine 4: 16-17. Spring 1981.

"Face to face; an interview," Seventeen 31:313. August 1972.

"How I Write," in: Wingrove, David, ed. The Science Fiction Source Book. New York: Van Nostrand, 1984. pp. 83-84.

"Interview: Colin Wilson," Twilight Zone 3(1): 24-28. March/April 1983.

"Interview: James Herbert," Twilight Zone 4(6):37-42. November/December 1984.

"TZ Interviews: Colin Wilson," Twilight Zone 3(1): 24-28. April 1983.

Tuzet, Helene

Cosmos et l'imagination, Le. Paris: Corti, 1965. 541 p.

Tuzinski, Konrad

"Kultur und gesellaschaftskritik im modernen englischen zukunstsroman," Literatur Kultur Gesellschaft. Aspekte und Forschungsbeitrage. Gerhard Muller-Schwefe and Konrad Tuzinski, ed. Frankfurt/M., 1966. pp. 278-298.

Tweet, R. D.

"Clifford D. Simak," in: Bleiler, E. F., ed. Science Fiction Writers. New York: Scribners, 1982. pp. 513-518.

"Philip Jose Farmer," in: Bleiler, E. F., ed. Science Fiction Writers. New York: Scribners, 1982. pp. 369-375.

"Poul Anderson," in: Bleiler, E. F., ed. Science Fiction Writers. New York: Scribners, 1982. pp. 259-265.

Tweney, G. H.

Jack London: A Bibliography, by H. C. Woodbridge, John London and G. H. Tweney. Georgetown, California: Talisman Press, 1966. 385 p. Milwood, New York: Kraus Reprint, 1973. Enlarged edition, 554 p.

Tyler, J. E. A.

Tolkien Companion, The. London: Macmillan, 1976. 531 p. Reprinted, New York: St. Martin's Press, 1976.

Tymn, M. B.

American Fantasy and Science Fiction; Toward a Bibliography of Works Published in the United States 1948-1973. West Linn, Oregon: Fax, 1979. 228 p.

Basic Reference Shelf for Science Fiction Teachers, A. Monticello, Illinois: Council for Planning Librarians, 1978. Exchange bibliography no. 1523. 13 p.

Fantasy Literature: A Core Collection and Reference Guide, by M. B. Tymn, K. J. Zahorski, and R. H. Boyer. New York: Bowker, 1979. 273 p.

Index to Stories in Thematic Anthologies of Science Fiction, ed. by M. B. Tymn, M. H. Greenberg, L. W. Currey and J. D. Olander. Boston: G. K. Hall, 1978. 193 p.

Recent Critical Studies on Fantasy Literature: An Annotated Checklist. Monticello, IL: Council of Planning Librarians, n. d. Exchange bibliography no. 1522. 21 p.

Research Guide to Science Fiction Studies: An Annotated Checklist of Primary and Secondary Sources for Fantasy and Science Fiction, A, ed. by M. B. Tymn, R. C. Schlobin and L. W. Currey. New York: Garland, 1977. 165 p.

Science Fiction Reference Book. Mercer Island, WA: Starmont, 1981. 536 p.

Science Fiction, Fantasy, and Weird Fiction Magazines, ed. by M. B. Tymn and Mike Ashley. Westport, CT: Greenwood, 1985. 970 p.

Survey of Science Fiction Literature Bibliographical Supplement. Englewood Cliffs, NJ: Salem, 1982. 183 p.

Teacher's Guide to Science Fiction. s.l.: s.n., 1981. 54 p.

Year's Scholarship in Science Fiction and Fantasy, 1972-1975, by M. B. Tymn and R. C. Schlobin. Kent, OH: Kent State University Press 1979. 222 p.

Year's Scholarship in Science Fiction and Fantasy, 1976-1979 by M. B. Tymn and R. C.

Schlobin. Kent, OH: Kent State University Press, 1983. 251 p.

Year's Scholarship in Science Fiction, Fantasy and Horror Literature, 1980. Kent, OH: Kent State University Press, 1983. 110 p.

Year's Scholarship in Science Fiction, Fantasy and Horror Literature, 1981. Kent, OH: Kent State University Press, n.d. 103 p.

Year's Scholarship in Science Fiction, Fantasy and Horror Literature, 1982. Kent, OH: Kent State University Press, n.d. 107 p.

"Annotated bibliography of critical studies and reference works on fantasy," CEA Critic 49(2):43-47. January 1978.

"Appendix: Critical studies in horror literature: a selected, annotated bibliography," in: Schweitzer, Darrell, ed. Discovering Modern Horror Fiction I. Mercer Island: Starmont, 1985. pp. 135-145.

"Bibliographic Control in Fantastic Literature: An Evaluation of Works Published 1941-1981," Special Collections 2(1/2): 131-149. Fall/Winter 1982.

"Bibliography of Fantasy Scholarship," in: Collins, R. A., ed. Scope of the Fantastic: Theory, Technique, Major Authors. Westport: Greenwood, 1985. pp. 277-280.

"Bibliography of fantasy scholarship: history and culture, themes...author studies, children's literature," in: Collins, R. A., ed. Scope of the Fantastic: Culture...Children's Literature. Westport: Greenwood, 1985. pp. 267-270.

"Bibliography of fantasy scholarship: theory and aesthetics...," in: Collins, R. A. and H. D. Pearce, eds. The Scope of the Fantastic: Theory, Technique, Major Authors. Westport, CT: Greenwood Press, 1985. pp. 277-279.

"Checklist of American critical works on SF: 1972-1973, A," Extrapolation 17(1):78-96. December 1975.

"Classroom Aids," in: Barrron, Neil, ed. Anatomy of Wonder 2nd ed. New York: Bowker, 1981. pp. 575-589.

"Critical Studies and Reference Works," in: Tymn, Marshall B., ed. The Science Fiction Reference Book. Mercer Island, WA: Starmont House, 1981. pp. 63-83.

"Directory of Specialty Publishers," in: Tymn, Marshall B., ed. The Science Fiction Reference Book. Mercer Island, WA: Starmont Houst, 1981. pp. 493-495.

"Fantasy Reference Works: A Survey," Analytical and Enumerative Bibliography. 5(1): 25-34. 1981.

Tymn, M. B. (Continued)

"Guide to AV Resources in Science Fiction and Fantasy," _Media & Methods_ 16(3): 40-43, 56-59. November 1979.

"Guide to resource materials for science fiction and fantasy teachers," _English Journal_ 68(1):68-74. January 1979.

"Guide to Science Fiction and Fantasy Scholarship, 1980-1982," in: Wolfe, Gary, ed. _Science Fiction Dialogues_. Chicago: Academy Chicago, 1982. pp. 215-227.

"Jack Vance: a bibliography," in: Underwood, Tim and Miller, Chuck, ed. _Jack Vance_. New York: Taplinger, 1980. pp. 227-234.

"Masterpieces of Science Fiction Criticism," _Mosaic_ 13(3/4): 220-222. Spring/Summer 1980.

"Modern Critical Studies and Reference Works on Fantasy," in: Schlobin, Roger C., ed. _The Aesthetics of Fantasy Literature and Art_. Notre Dame, IN: University of Notre Dame Press, 1982. pp. 262-270.

"Philip K. Dick: A Bibliography," in: Greenberg, Martin H., ed. _Philip K. Dick_. New York: Taplinger, 1982. pp. 241-249.

"Ray Bradbury: a bibliography," in: Olander, J. D. and M. H. Greenberg, eds. _Ray Bradbury_. New York: Taplinger, 1980. pp. 227-242.

"Reference sources for science fiction," by L. W. Currey and M. B. Tymn. _A. B. Bookman's Weekly_ 76(18):3062-3100. October 28, 1985.

"Resource materials for science fiction and fantasy teachers," _Arizona English Bulletin_ 19:54-58. 1977.

"Resources for Teaching Science Fiction," in: Tymn, Marshall B., ed. _The Science Fiction Reference Book_. Mercer Island, WA: Starmont House, 1981. pp. 453-479.

"Science Fiction and Fantasy Periodicals," in: Tymn, Marshall B., ed. _The Science Fiction Reference Book_. Mercer Island, WA: Starmont House, 1981. pp. 225-229.

"Science Fiction and Fantasy Scholarship 1982: The Year in Review," _Fantasy Review_ 7(1): 52-54. January 1984.

"Science Fiction in the Classroom," in: Jarvis, Sharon, ed. _Inside Outer Space_. New York: Ungar, 1985. pp. 87-104.

"Science Fiction Organizations and Societies," in: Tymn, Marshall B., ed. _The Science Fiction Reference Book_. Mercer Island, WA: Starmont House, 1981. pp. 489-492.

"Science fiction research: the state of the art," in: Remington, T. J., ed. _Selected Proceedings of the 1978 SFRA National Conference_. Cedar Falls, Iowa: Univ. of Northern Iowa, 1979. pp. 201-221.

"Science fiction," in: Inge, M. Thomas, ed. _Handbook of American Popular Culture_. Westport, Connecticut: Greenwood Press, 1979. pp. 251-273.

"Stephen King: a bibliography," in: Schweitzer, Darrell, ed. _Discovering Stephen King_. Mercer Island: Starmont, 1985. pp. 205-209.

"Ursula K. Le Guin: a bibliography," in: Olander, J. D. and M. H. Greenberg, eds. _Ursula K. Le Guin_. New York: Taplinger, 1979. pp. 241-246.

"Year's scholarship in science fiction and fantasy: 1974, The," by R. C. Schlobin and M. B. Tymn. _Extrapolation_ 18(1):73-96. December 1976.

"Year's scholarship in science fiction and fantasy: 1975, The," by R. C. Schlobin and M. B. Tymn. _Extrapolation_ 19(2):156-191. May 1978.

"Year's scholarship in science fiction and fantasy: 1976, The," by R. C. Schlobin and M. B. Tymn. _Extrapolation_ 20(1):60-99. Spring 1979.

"Year's scholarship in science fiction and fantasy: 1977, The," by R. C. Schlobin and M. B. Tymn. _Extrapolation_ 20(3):238-288. Fall 1979.

"Year's scholarship in science fiction and fantasy: 1978, The," by R. C. Schlobin and M. B. Tymn. _Extrapolation_ 21(1):45-89. Spring 1980.

"Year's scholarship in science fiction and fantasy: 1979, The," by M. B. Tymn and R. C. Schlobin. _Extrapolation_ 22(1): 25-91. Spring 1981.

"Year's scholarship in science fiction, fantasy, and horror literature, 1983," _Extrapolation_ 26(2): 85-142. Summer 1985.

Tyre, R. H.

"_Watership Down_: a tale of survival," _Media & Methods_ 15(5):79. January 1979.

"You can't teach Tolkien," _Media & Methods_ 15(3):18-20,54. November 1978.

Tyrrell, W. B.

"Star Trek as myth and TV as mythmaker," in: Nachbar, Jack, ed. _The Popular Culture Reader_. Bowling Green: Popular Press, 1978. pp. 79-88. Reprinted from _Journal of Popular Culture_ 10(4):711-719. 1977.

Tyrrell, W. B. (Continued)

"Star Trek's myth of science,"   Journal of
American Culture 2(2):288-296. 1979.

Tyson, Kim

"E. T. invades Austin,"   Austin American
Statesman. July 15, 1982. in: NewsBank.
Business and Economic Development. 65:B10.
1982.

Tyson, Peter

"2001 prophecy quiz, The," by Robert Weil and
Peter Tyson. Omni 7(10):38-40, 90-94. July
1985.

U

Ueding, Gert

"Utopia liegt ganz in der Nahe,"   in: Ermert, Karl, ed. Neugier oder Flucht? Stuttgart: Klett, 1980. pp. 18-32.

Ugolnik, Anthony

"Wordhord Onleac: the medieval sources of J. R. R. Tolkien's linguistic aesthetic," Mosaic 10(2):15-31. Winter 1977.

"Godzilla and the Real World,"   Commonweal 109(20): 619-621. November 19, 1982.

Ulanov, Barry

"Science fiction and fantasy," in: Ulanov, Barry. The Two Worlds of American Art. New York: Macmillan, 1965. pp. 298-308.

Underwood, Marylyn

"Reflections on Science Fiction Writers, Part I," Kaleidoscope (Victoria College, TX) 9(1): 1-2. Fall 1979.

"Reflections on Science Fiction Writers, Part II," Kaleidoscope (Victoria College, TX) 9(2): 6-7. Spring 1980.

Underwood, Tim

Fantasms II: a Bibliography of the Literature of Jack Vance, compiled by Kurt Cockcrum, D. J. H. Levack, and Tim Underwood. Riverside, California: K. Cockrum, 1979. 99 p.

Fear Itself: The Horror Fiction of Stephen King, by Tim Underwood and Chuck Miller. Columbia, PA: Underwood-Miller, 1982. 255 p.

Jack Vance, by Tim Underwood and Chuck Miller. New York: Taplinger, 1980. 252 p.

Underwood, Tom

"Empire Strikes Back,"   Cinemascore 9: 12-16. October 1981.

Unger, Art

"Kurt Vonnegut, Jr.: class of 71,"   Ingenue pp. 14-18. December 1971. (not seen)

Unger, Arthur

"Exploring the universe to understand ourselves,"   Christian Science Monitor p. 19. January 28, 1980.

Unsworth, Michael

Future War Novels: An Annotated Bibliography of Works in English Published Since 1946, by John Newman and Michael Unsworth.   Phoenix: Oryx, 1984. 101 p.

Uphaus, R. W.

"Expected meaning in Vonnegut's dead-end fiction,"   Novel 8(2):164-174. Winter 1975.

Urang, Gunnar

Shadows of Heaven: Religion and Fantasy in the Writings of C. S. Lewis, Charles Williams, and J. R. R. Tolkien. Philadelphia: Pilgrim Press, 1971. 186 p.

Urban, A. A.

Fantastika i nash mir. Moscow: s. n., 1972. 255 p.

Urban, Laszlo

"Beginnings of the Hungarian science fiction literature, The," SF Tajekoztato 18:3-10. 1976.

"Fantasztikus irodalom: Mult, jelen, jovo," SF Tajekoztato pp. 2-13. September 1971.

"Literatur der Phantasie," Quarber Merkur 29:56-65. January 1972.

Urban, Laszlo (Continued)

"Science Fiction und Phantastik," <u>Quarber Merkur</u> 36:14- . 1973.

"Ursprunge der ungarishchen SF-literatur," <u>Quarber Merkur</u> 47:13-22. December 1977.

Urbanek, Hermann

"Interview mit Hugh Walker," <u>Andromeda</u> 102: 6-11. July 1980.

Urbanowicz, C. F.

"Cultures: fact or fiction,", <u>Anthrotech: A Journal of Speculative Anthropology</u> 1(1):6-9. Fall 1976.

Urbanowicz, Victor

"Personal and political in <u>The Dispossessed</u>," in: <u>Ursula K. Le Guin</u>, ed. by Harold Bloom. New York: Chelsea House, 1986. pp. 145-154.

"Personal and political in Le Guin's <u>The Dispossessed</u>," <u>Science Fiction Studies</u> 5(2):110-117. July 1978.

Urgosikova, Blazena

<u>Sci-fi: vedecko-fantasticky film od Meliese k Tarkovskemu</u>. Praha: Cs. filmovy ustav, 1974. 36 p.

Urrutia, Benjamin

"Some Notes to the Letters of J. R. R. Tolkien," <u>Mythlore</u> 9(2): 28, 46. Summer 1982.

Utter, Virgil

<u>Catherine Lucille Moore and Henry Kuttner: A Working Bibliography</u>, by Virgil Utter and Gordon Benson, Jr. Albuquerque: Galactic Central, 1986. 45 p.

V

Vacano, Jost

"Neverending Story," _American Cinematographer_ 65(8): 64-69. August/September 1984.

Valentine, K. B.

"Motifs from nature in the design work and prose romances of William Morris (1876-1896)," _Victorian Poetry_ 13(3-4):83-89. Fall/Winter 1975.

Valery, Francis

Bibliographie des revues specialisees, vol. 1: Fiction. Cavignac: A&A, 1979. 14 p.

"Philippe Curval: Between Surrealism and Science Fiction," by P. J. Thomas and Francis Valery. _Science Fiction Times (Boston)_ 1(10): 7. 1981.

Valis, N. M.

"Martian Chronicles, The and Jorge Luis Borges," _Extrapolation_ 20(1):50-59. Spring 1979.

Valla, Riccardo

"Daimon," in: Magill, Frank N., ed. _Survey of Science Fiction Literature_, Vol. 1. Englewood Cliffs, NJ: Salem Press, 1979. pp. 462-464.

"Sepoltura, La," in: Magill, Frank N., ed. _Survey of Science Fiction Literature_, Vol. 4. Englewood Cliffs, NJ: Salem Press, 1979. pp. 1896-1897.

"Fantascienza di Poe: l'antilogica come copertura," in: Ruggero Bianchi, ed. _E. A. Poe: dal gotico alla fantascienza_. Milan: Mursia, 1978. pp.285-298.

"Introduzione a Ballard," _Nuova Presenza_ No. 37/38:21-25. 1970.

"Science fiction in Italia," in: Sadoul, Jacques. _Storia della Fantascienza_. Milan: Garzanti, 1975. pp. 357-363.

Vallentin, Antonina

H. G. Wells: Prophet of Our Day. New York: John Day, 1950. 338 p.

Valli, Luigi

Shakespeare and Fantasy: Modern Theories and Interpretations of the Genre. Ph. D. Dissertation, Bowling Green State University, 1981. 153 p. (DAI 42A:4464)

Vallorani, Nicoletta

"Foto di futura con Signora," _Cosmo informatore_ 14(2):36-42. Summer 1985.

Van Becker, David

"Time, space and consciousness in the fantasy of Peter S. Beagle," _San Jose Studies_ 1,ii:52-61. (rev. art.) February 1975.

Van Der Veer, Frank

"Composite scenes for King Kong using the blue screen technique," _American Cinematographer_ 58(1):56-57, 74-75,91. January 1977.

Van Eerde, J. A.

Jules Verne: A Primary and Secondary Bibliography, by E. J. Gallagher, J. A. Mistichelli and J. A. Van Eerde. Boston: G. K. Hall, 1980. 544 p.

Van Herp, Jacques

Panorama de la science fiction: le themes, le genres, les ecoles, les problemes. Verviers: Gerard, 1973. 430 p.

Van Herp, Jacques (Continued)

"Aventures Extraordinaires d'un Savant Russe," in: Magill, F. N., ed. Survey of Science Fiction Literature, Vol. 1. Englewood Cliffs, NJ: Salem Press, 1979. pp. 109-112.

"Caroline, O Caroline," in: Magill, Frank N., ed. Survey of Science Fiction Literature, Vol. 1. Englewood Cliffs, NJ: Salem Press, 1979. pp. 294-297.

"Guerre au XXe siecle, La," in: Magill, Frank N., ed. Survey of Science Fiction Literature, Vol. 2. Englewood Cliffs, NJ: Salem Press, 1979. pp. 932-935.

"Prisonnier de la planete Mars, Le," in: Magill, Frank N., ed. Survey of Science Fiction Literature, Vol. 4. Englewood Cliffs, NJ: Salem Press, 1979. pp. 1726-1729.

"Voyageur imprudent, Le," in: Magill, Frank N., ed. Survey of Science Fiction Literature, Vol. 5. Englewood Cliffs, NJ: Salem Press, 1979. pp. 2389-2391.

"Cinema et Lovecraft, Le," in: H. P. Lovecraft. Paris: Editions de l'Herne, 1969. pp. 185-190.

"Date de naissance, il y a plusieurs S. F., La," Europe 580/581:22-25. August/September 1977.

"Date de naissance, La. c) Il y a plusieurs S. F.," Europe 580/581:43-48. August/September 1977.

"Source de Lovecraft, le diable au XIXe siecle, Une," in: H. P. Lovecraft. Paris: Editions de l'Herne, 1969. pp. 141-146.

"Univers d'H. P. Lovecraft, L'," in: H. P. Lovecraft. Paris: Editions de l'Herne, 1969. pp. 147-156.

Van Hise, James

Art of Al Williamson. San Diego, CA: Blue Dolphin, 1983. 144 p.

"Blade Runner Screenwriters: Hampton Francher and David Peoples," Starlog 58: 22-24. May 1982.

"Blade Runner's Sean Young," Starlog 61: 38-40. August 1982.

"Bladerunner," Starlog 52: 17-21. November 1981.

"Close encounters with Star Wars," Questar 1:27-30. 1978.

"Gene Winfield: Custom Design and Execution From Star Trek to Bladerunner," Starlog 53: 26-29, 64. December 1981.

"Interview mit Philip K. Dick," Science Fiction Times (Germany) 24(6):15-18. June 1982.

"Interview: Philip K. Dick," Heyne Science Fiction Magazine 4: 39-52. 1982. (Translated from English-Source not identified)

"Philip K. Dick on Bladerunner," Starlog 55: 19-22. February 1982.

"Poltergeist," Cinefantastique 13(2)/13(3):76-87. November/December 1982.

"Road Warrior," Starlog 61: 30-33, 64. August 1982.

"Rutger Hauer," Starlog 63: 43-45. October 1982.

"Scimitar of 4333 Costello," Oak Leaves 1(11):5-9. 1975.

"Star Trek Bloopers, Part 1," Starlog 54: 48-49. January 1982.

"Star Trek Bloopers, Part 2," Starlog 55: 17. February 1982.

"Star Trek Bloopers, Part 3," Starlog 56: 50-51. March 1982.

"Starlog Interview/Portfolio: Ron Cobb," by James Van Hise and Dennis Fisher. Starlog 57: 30-33, 64. April 1982.

"Starlog Interview: Walker Edmiston," Starlog 58: 20-21. May 1982.

Van Horne, H.

"Space rocket kick," Theatre Arts 35(12):40-41,77. December 1951.

Van Houten, Ray

"1956 World Con," by J. V. Taurasi and Ray Van Houten. in: Science Fiction Yearbook, 1957 Edition. Vol. 1. Patterson, NJ: Fandom House, 1957. pp. 8-10.

"Down? or up?" Science Fiction Times No. 369:33-36. September 1961.

"First step into space poses problem for science fiction," Fantasy Times No. 229:1-2,5-6. August (2) 1955.

"Outside the U.S.," by J. V. Taurasi and Ray Van Houten. in: Science Fiction Yearbook, 1957 Edition. Vol. 1. Patterson, NJ: Fandom House, 1957. pp. 7-8.

"Science fiction, 1956," by J. V. Taurasi and Ray Van Houten. in: Science Fiction Yearbook, 1957 Edition. Vol. 1. Patterson, NJ: Fandom House, 1957. pp. 3-7.

Van Houten, Ray (Continued)

"State of fandom: 1956," by J. V. Taurasi and Ray Van Houten. in: _Science Fiction Yearbook, 1957 Edition_. Vol. 1. Patterson, NJ: Fandom House, 1957. pp. 10-11.

"V-Mail interviews, part 1: The Shaver Hoax," _Fantasy Times_ No. 52:63. May 25, 1947.

"World of tomorrow today," _Fantasy Times_ No. 56:6-7. September 1947.

Van Loggem, Manuel

"Amerikanische zukunftgeschichte oder die sache der science fiction," _Akzente_ 4(5):412-424. October 1957.

Van Nouhuys, Dirk

"Micro and the professional writer," _Interface Age_ 6(10):46-47. October 1981.

Van Tokken, Herman

"Rebirth of Burroughs, The," _Science Fiction Times_ No. 398:7-8. December 1962.

Van Troyer, Gene

"Poem in Process," _Empire For the SF Writer_ 32: 13-15. Winter 1984.

Van Valey, T. L.

"Teaching population through science fiction," _Population Index_ 40(3):439-440. July 1974.

Van Vogt, A. E.

Professional Writer. Guilford, CT: Jeffrey Norton, 1984. 1 cassette, 60 min.

Reflections of A. E. Van Vogt: The Autobiography of a Science Fiction Giant, with a Complete Bibliography. Lakemont, Georgia: Fictioneer Books, 1975. 136 p.

"Development of a science fiction writer: III, The," _Foundation_ 3:26-30. March 1973.

"Inner space," in: Ash, Brian, ed. _Visual Encyclopedia of Science Fiction_. New York: Harmony, 1977. pp. 237-247.

"Inventing New Worlds II," in: Malik, Rex, ed. _Future Imperfect_. London: Pinter, 1980. pp. 81-87.

"John W. Campbell," _Locus_ No. 90:8. July 12, 1971.

"Joys of Science Fiction," _SFWA Bulletin_ 9(4): 8-11. Fall 1973.

"My Life Was My Best Science Fiction Story," in: Greenberg, Martin H., ed. _Fantastic Lives_. Carbondale: Southern Illinois University Press, 1981. pp. 175-215.

Van Wert, W. F.

"Film as science fiction: Nicholas Roeg's _The Man Who Fell to Earth_," _Western Humanities Review_ 33(2):141-148. Spring 1979.

Vance, Michael

"C. J. Cherryh: The Quiet Berserker," _Fantasy Review_ 7(2): 9-10, 22. March 1984.

"C. J. Cherryh: The Quiet Berserker; Interview," _Media Sight_ 3(1): 22-25. Summer 1984.

"Interview With Roger Zelazny," _Fantasy Newsletter_ 6(1): 8-10. January 1983.

"Interview: Stephen R. Donaldson," _Fantasy Review_ 8(11): 8-10, 14. November 1985.

"Roger Zelazny: The New Wave King of Science Fiction," by Michael Vance and Bill Eads. _Media Sight_ 3(1): 39-42. Summer 1984.

Vandel, J. G.

"Defense de la science fiction," _Mystere Magazine_ 58. 1er Novembre 1952.

Vandenberg, S. C.

"Great expectations, or, the future of psychology as seen in science fiction," _American Psychologist_ 11(7):339-342. July 1956.

Vanderbilt, Scott

"Caveman: The Real Stars," _Cinefex_ 5: 54-71. July 1981.

Vanderwerken, D. L.

"Pilgrim's dilemma: _Slaughterhouse Five_," _Research Studies_ (Washington State University) 42(3):147-152. June 1974.

Vanlint, Derek

"Alien and its photographic challenges," _American Cinematographer_ 60(8):768-771, 806,812-813. August 1979.

Vardeman, R. E.

"Money, Money," _SFWA Bulletin_ 15(1): 13-14. Spring 1980.

Varley, John

"1955," <u>SFWA Bulletin</u> 14(3):56-63.
Fall 1979.

Vasbinder, S. H.

<u>Scientific Attitudes in Mary Shelley's
Frankenstein</u>. Ann Arbor: UMI Research Press,
1984, c1976. 111 p.

"Allan Quatermain Saga, The," in: Magill,
Frank N., ed. <u>Survey of Modern Fantasy
Literature</u>, Vol 1. Englewood Cliffs, NJ:
Salem Press, Inc., 1983. pp. 22-25.

"Brood of the Witch Queen," in: Magill,
Frank N., ed. <u>Survey of Modern Fantasy
Literature</u>, Vol 1. Englewood Cliffs, NJ:
Salem Press, Inc., 1983. pp. 178-180.

"Golem, The," in: Magill, Frank N., ed.
<u>Survey of Modern Fantasy Literature</u>, Vol 2.
Englewood Cliffs, NJ: Salem Press, Inc., 1983.
pp. 628-630.

"People of the Mist, The," in: Magill,
Frank N., ed. <u>Survey of Modern Fantasy
Literature</u>, Vol 3. Englewood Cliffs, NJ:
Salem Press, Inc., 1983. pp. 1221-1223.

"Aspects of Fantasy in Literary Myths About
Lost Civilizations," in: Schlobin, R. C., ed.
<u>The Aesthetics of Fantasy Literature and
Art</u>. Notre Dame, IN: University of Notre Dame
Press, 1982. pp. 192-210.

"Deathless humans in horror fiction," in:
Yoke, C. B. and Hassler, D. M., eds. <u>Death
and the Serpent</u>. Westport, CT: Greenwood,
1985. pp. 71-82.

"Meaning of 'foma' in <u>Cat's Cradle</u>, The,"
<u>Riverside Quarterly</u> 5:300-302. 1973.

Vax, Louis

<u>Art et la litterature fantastique</u>. 3rd. ed.
Paris: Presses Universitaires de France, 1970.
128 p.

<u>Art et la litterature fantastique</u>. 4th. ed.
Paris: Presses Universitaires de France, 1974.
128 p.

<u>Art et la litterature fantastique</u>. Paris:
Presses Universitaires de France, 1960. 125 p.

<u>Art et la litterature fantastique</u>. Paris:
Presses Universitaires de France, 1963. 127 p.

<u>Arte y literatura fantasticas</u>. Buenos Aires:
Editorial Universitaria, 1973. 127 p. (Tr. of
Art et litterature fantastiques.)

<u>Chefs d'ouvre de la litterature fantastique,
Les</u>. Paris: Presses Universitaires de France,
1979. 230 p.

<u>Seduction de l'etrange: etude sur la
litterature fantastique</u>. Paris: Presses
Universitaires de France, 1965. 313 p.

"Art de faire peur, L'" <u>Critique</u>
15:915-942, 1026-1048. 1959.

Veeder, William

"Technique as recovery: <u>Lolita</u> and <u>Mother
Night</u>," in: Klinkowitz, Kurt, ed.
<u>Vonnegut in America</u>. New York: Delacorte,
1977. pp. 97-132.

Vegetti, Ernesto

<u>Repertory of the Italian Professionals in
Science Fiction and Fantasy 1981</u>. Milan:
World SF Italy, 1981. 44 p.

<u>Repertory of the Italian Professionals in
Science Fiction And Fantasy 1982-1983</u>.
Milan: World SF-Italy, 1984. [114 p.]

"I Libri di fantascienza e fantasy usciti
Italia ne 1954," <u>Cosmo informatore</u>
14(1):9-15. Spring 1985.

Veilleux, Jim

"Warp Speed and Beyond," <u>American
Cinematographer</u> 63(10): 1030-1034, 1054-1058.
October 1982.

Veix, D. B.

"Teaching a censored novel:
<u>Slaughterhouse-Five</u>," <u>English Journal</u>
64(7):25-33. October 1975.

Vejchar, Alfred

"First Perry Rhodan Worldcon held," <u>Science
Fiction Chronicle</u> 2(6):10-12. March 1981.

Velasco, R. L.

<u>Guide to the Star Wars Universe</u>. New York:
Ballantine, 1984. 215 p.

Velikovich, A.

"Science fiction and the schoolchild," by A.
Levin and A. Velikovich. <u>Soviet Review</u>
11(3):250-257. Fall 1970.

Ven, These

"Updated Farmer, or, What you never knew about
Richard Wentworth...," <u>Xenophile</u> No.
42:17-19. September/October 1979.

Venaissin, Gabriel

"Science Fiction contre la roman policier, La?" La Gazette de Lausanne 29 Sept. 1953.

"Utopie, humour, poesie et puissance," Esprit 21:700-718. May 5, 1953.

Verheiden, Mark

"Closed Mondays (review)," Cinefantastique 4(2):32. Summer 1975.

"Making of Closed Mondays," Cinefantastique 4(3):40-45. Fall 1975.

Verner, Zenobia

"It'll never happen; minicourse for students grades 9-12," by Charlette Reed and Zenobia Verner. English Journal 65(4):65-66. April 1976.

Vernier, J. P.

"Evolution as a literary theme in H. G. Wells' science fiction," in: Darko, Suvin and Robert M. Philmus, eds. H. G. Wells and Modern Science Fiction. Lewisburg: Bucknell University Press, 1977. pp. 70-89.

"H. G. Wells at the turn of the century: from science fiction to anticipation," H. G. Wells Society. Occasional Papers 1:10. 1973.

"Science-fiction von J. H. Rosny dem Alteren, Die," in: Rottensteiner, Franz, ed. Polaris 4. Suhrkamp, 1978. pp. 56-71. (Tr. From Science Fiction Studies V.2 No. 2 July 1975.)

"SF of J. H. Rosny the elder," Science Fiction Studies 2(2):156-163. July 1975.

Verniere, James

"Doctor and the Devils, The," Twilight Zone 5(5): 80-81. December 1985.

"Interview: David Cronenberg," Twilight Zone 3(5):55-58. November/December 1983.

"Interview: Leonard Nimoy," Twilight Zone 4(3):55-56,60. July/August 1984.

"Interview: Ridley Scott," Twilight Zone 2(10):18-23. December 1982.

"TZ Preview: Lifeforce," Twilight Zone 5(3): 49-54. July/August 1985.

Vernon, D. R.

What is Science Fiction and Why Is It Popular? Master's Thesis, Pacific Lutheran University, 1979. 44 p. (Not seen.)

Vernon, W. D.

"Charles L. Harness, The Paradox Man," Science Fiction Collector 14: 25-32. May 1981.

"On the Edge: An Interview With Rudy Rucker," Foundation 27: 24-31. February 1983.

Vernon, William

Sound of Wonder: Interviews From "The Science Fiction Radio Show," Volume 1, by Daryl Lane, William Vernon and David Carson. Phoenix: Oryx, 1985. 203 p.

Sound of Wonder: Interviews From "The Science Fiction Radio Show," Volume 2, by Daryl Lane, William Vernon and David Carson. Phoenix: Oryx, 1985. 203 p.

Verrengia, J. B.

"Return of the Jedi film recovered in FBI sting," Kansas City Star. July 29, 1983. in: NewsBank. Film and Television. 16:C13. 1983.

Versins, Pierre

Encyclopedie de l'utopie, des voyages extraordinaires et de la science fiction. Lausanne: l'Age d'Homme, 1972. 999 p.

Encyclopedie des l'Utopie, des Voyages Extraordinaires et de la Science Fiction. Revised ed. Lausanne: L'Age d'Homme, 1984. 997 p.

"Contact," in: Knight, Damon, ed. Turning Points: Essays in the Art of Science Fiction. New York: Harper, 1977. pp. 163-167.

"Date de naissance, Le. a) Depuis que l'homme est l'homme," Europe 580/581:34-38. August/September 1977.

"Debuts de Lovecraft dans Weird Tales," by Pierre Versins. in: H. P. Lovecraft. Paris: Editions de l'Herne, 1969. pp. 26-27.

"Lovecraft et l'indicible," in: H. P. Lovecraft. Paris: Editions de l'Herne, 1969. pp. 39-46.

"Marges, Les," Les Lettres Nouvelles 3(27):778-781. May 1955.

"Porte pent etre ovverte et fermee, Une," Fiction No. 140/141/142. July/August/September 1965.

"Surhumaine tragedie, une," in: H. P. Lovecraft. Paris: Editions de l'Herne, 1969. pp. 28-38.

Versins, Pierre (Continued)

"Vie et aventure do Cora et entretion sur la science fiction avec Francois Le Lionnais et Daniel Drode," in: Arnand, Noel, ed. Entretiens sur la paralitterature. Paris: Plon, 1970. pp. 252-285.

Vessely, T. R.

"In defense of useless enchantment: Bettelheim's appraisal of the fairy tales of Perrault," in: Collins, R. A., ed. Scope of the Fantastic: Culture...Themes, Children's Literature. Westport: Greenwood, 1985. pp. 221-230.

Vetter, Ingeborg

"Femme fatale, Die," Quarber Merkur 51:14-37. November 1979.

"Formen der Verwandlung in deutschen 'Horror-Geschechten' um 1900," Quarber Merkur 50:3-21. February 1979.

Vetter, J. E.

"Lovecraft's illustrators," in: Lovecraft, H. P. The Dark Brotherhood and Other Pieces. Sauk City, Wisconsin: Arkham House, 1966. pp. 268-301.

Vian, Boris

Cinema Science-Fiction, ed. by Noel Arnaud. Paris: Christian Bourgois, 1978. 214 p.

"Aimex-vous la Science Fiction? Si Peau d'ane vous est conte...," La Gazette de Lausanne November 28/29, 1953.

"Architecture et science fiction," College de Pataphysique, dossier no. 6, pp. 80-82.

"Nouveau genre litteraire, Un: la science-fiction," by Stephen Spriel and Boris Vian. Les Temps Modernes No. 72:618-627. October 1951.

"Nuovo genere letterario, Un: La fantascienza," by Stephane Spriel and Boris Vian. in: Petronio, Giuseppe, ed. Letteratura di massa, letteratura de consumo: Guida storica e critica. Bari: Laterza, 1979. pp. 107-119.

"Pierre Kast et Boris Vians' entretiennent de la science fiction," L'Ecran No. 1. January 1958.

"Science-fiction et le cinema," L'Age d'Or No. 1. June 1964.

"Sur certains aspects actuels de la science fiction," La Parisienne 11:1541-1544. Novembre 1953.

Viatte, A.

"Fantastique dans la litterature francaise, Le," Revue de l'Universite Laval (Quebec) 19:715-720. 1964/1965.

Vibber, Lee

In a Faraway Galaxy: A Literary Approach to a Film Saga, by Doris Robin, Lee Vibber, and G. F. Elwood. Pasadena, CA: Extequer Press, 1984. 149 p.

Vidal, Gore

"Novel on the age of science, The," Quarterly Journal of the Library of Congress 22(4):289-299. October 1965.

"Tarzan revisited," Esquire 60:192-193. December 1963. Reprinted, 80:281-283. October 1973.

Vidal, J.

"Enfants terribles du cosmos," Liberation. 17. 22. 8. 1962.

Vierne, Simone

Jules Verne et les sciences humaines, by Francois Raymond and Simone Vierne. Paris: 10/18 Union generale d'edition, 1979. 443 p.

Viggiano, Michael

Science Fiction Title Changes: A Guide to the Changing Titles of Science Fiction and Fantasy Stories Published in Magazines and Books, by Michael Viggiano and Donald Franson. Seattle: National Fantasy Fan Federation, 1965. 47 p.

Viktorov, Richard

"Problems of the Golden Asteroid," Soviet Film 82(1): 23. 1982.

Villadier, Pierre

"Science fiction et litterature d'anticipation," La Nouvelle Critique No. 56:44-58. June 1954.

"SF et litterature d'Anticipacion, 2," Nouvelle Critique July 1954.

Villani, Jim

"Woman Science Fiction Writer and the Non-Heroic Male Protagonist," in: Hassler, D. M. Patterns of the Fantastic. Mercer Island, WA: Starmont, 1983. pp. 21-30.

Villard, Robert

"Close Encounters of the Third Kind," by
Robert Villard and Dan Scapperotti.
Cinefantastique 6:32-39. Spring 1978.

"Steven Spielberg interviewed,"
Cinefantastique 6(4)/7(1):33-35. Spring
1978.

Villemur, A. M.

63 auteurs: bibliographie de science fiction.
Paris: Temps Futurs, 1976. 195 p.

Vilmar, Fritz

"Relevanz und irrelevanz futurologischer
literatur. Dargestellt am beispiel der
sachbuchreihe 'modelle fur eine neue welt'"
Futurum 3:32-45. 1970.

Vinay, J.

"Look at science fiction and fantasy: from the
author's view," by J. Vinay and Marilyn Auer.
Bloomsbury Review 1(5):17-18,20.
July/August 1981.

"Look at science fiction and fantasy: from the
publishing point of view," by Tom Auer and J.
Vinay. Bloomsbury Review 1(5):17,19.
July/August 1981.

Vincent, Mal

"George Lucas Brings the Ewoks to TV Tonight,"
Norfolk Virginian-Pilot November 52, 1984.
in: NewsBank. Film and Television. 67:
B10-B11. January 1985.

"Hawk is no Hamlet, But It's a Living,"
Norfolk Virginian-Pilot August 20, 1984.
In: NewsBank. Names in the News 2:B6.
1981/1982.

Vinge, J. D.

"Open Letter to Andre Norton, An," in:
Shwartz, Susan, ed. Moonsinger's Friends.
New York: Bluejay, 1985. pp. 336-342.

Vinicoff, Eric

"Brief introduction to literary copyrights,"
Empire: For the SF Writer 3(4): 19. April
1978.

Vinograde, A. C.

"Soviet translation of Slaughterhouse-Five,
A," Russian Language Journal 93:14-18.
1972.

Vinz, Ruth

"1984: Intricate Corridors Within a Barren
World," English Journal 72(6): 39-41.
October 1983.

Visiak, E. H.

Strange Genius of David Lindsay, by Colin
Wilson, E. H. Visiak and J. B. Pick. London:
John Baker, 1970. 183 p. (Reprinted: New
York: Gregg, 1979.)

Vitiello, Greg

"Time and Timbuktu," Image 9:6-9. March
1972.

Viviani, Gianfranco

"L'illustrazione di fantascienza and fantasy in
Italia," Cosmo informatore 14(1):48-49.
Spring 1985.

Vivicoff, E.

"Macro-cosmic explorers: books about science
fiction," Booklegger Magazine 1(6):13-15.
1974.

Vlasopolos, Anca

"Frankenstein's Hidden Skeleton: The
Psycho-Politics of Oppression,"
Science-Fiction Studies 10(2): 125-136.
July 1983.

Von Bondy, M.

"Untergang der utopie," in: Die Gegenwart
5(15):13-15. 1950.

Von Everlien, Walter

"Buecherleser: Fragen an eine
Spiegeldokumentation," Science Fiction
Times (Germany) 28(1):9-13. January 1986.

Von Glahn, G. A.

"World of difference: Samuel Delany's The
Einstein Intersection, A," in: Riley, Dick,
ed. Critical Encounters: Writers and Themes
in Science Fiction. New York: Ungar, 1978.
pp. 109-131.

Von Momorzynski, Egon

"Bucher uber Geistergeschichten, Vampyre, und
Robinsonaden," by Rudolf Furst, Egon von
Momorzynski, and Carl Enders. Quarber Merkur
39:51-55. Jan. 1975.

Science Fiction and Fantasy Reference Index, 1878-1985

Vonarburg, Elisabeth

"Femme et la science fiction, La," <u>Requiem</u>
3(5):10-15. 1977.

"Science fiction in Quebec: a survey," by
Elisabeth Vonarburg and Norbert Spehner.
<u>Science Fiction Studies</u> 7(2):191-199. July
1980.

"Science-fiction, pedagogie de l'avenir, La,"
<u>Reseau</u> 6(6):6-7. 1975.

Vonnegut, Kurt

"Only kidding, folks?" <u>Nation</u> 226:575.
May 13, 1978.

"Science fiction," in: Brown, Ernest. <u>Page
2: The Best of 'Speaking of Books' from the New
York Times Book Review</u>. Holt, 1969. pp.
117-120.

"Sleeping beauty," <u>Achitectural Digest</u>
41(6): 30-36. June 1984.

"Why Are You Banning My Book?" <u>Oregon
Education</u> 56: 14. February/March 1982.

Vormweg, Heinrich

"Science Fiction als gegenwartige Literatur.
Eine aktuelle ubersicht," <u>Universitas:
Zeitschrift fur wissenschaft, kunst, und
literatur</u>. 30(4):345-354. 1975.

"Wo die Zukunft schon gegonnen hat. Science
Fiction ist auch in der Bundesrepublik in Mode
Gekommen," <u>Suddeutsche Zeitung</u> No. 68.
1972. (Beilage 'Buch und Zeit')

Vozdvizhenskaia, A.

"Prodolzhaia spory o fantastike," <u>Voprosy
Literatury</u> 8: 200-212. 1981.

W

Wachhorst, Wyn

"Time-Travel Romance on Film: Archetypes and Structures," <u>Extrapolation</u> 25(4): 340-359. Winter 1984.

Wachler, Dietrich

"Deutsches Fehlurteil: uber die Indizierung von Norman Spinrads 'Der Staehlorne Traum'," <u>Science Fiction Times</u> (Germany) 24(12):8-9. December 1982.

"Experiment mit dem Menschen, Das," <u>Science Fiction Times</u> (Germany) 26(12):4-7. December 1984.

"Gefangen der Zeit: Das literarische Experiment mit dem Unmoeglichen," <u>Science Fiction Times</u> (Germany) 25(7):5-11. July 1983.

"Gutachten uber die Behandlung des Nationalsozialismus in Wissenschaft, Literatur und in Norman Spinrad's Der Stahlerne Traum," <u>Science Fiction Times</u> (Germany) 24(5):8-13. May 1982.

"Nachrichten von Nirgendwo, part 1," <u>Science Fiction Times</u> (Germany) 26(1):10-14. January 1984.

"Nachrichten von Nirgendwo, part 2," <u>Science Fiction Times</u> (Germany) 26(2):12-15. February 1984.

"Nachrichten von Nirgendwo, part 3," <u>Science Fiction Times</u> (Germany) 26(3):21-24. March 1984.

"Nachrichten von Nirgendwo, part 4," <u>Science Fiction Times</u> (Germany) 26(4):25-28. April 1984.

"Praexistenz und das Boese: Technik und Magie im Werk von Howard Phillips Lovecraft," <u>Science Fiction Times</u> (Germany) 24(9):4-9. September 1982.

"Wirklichkeit der Phantoms. Uber den Realitatskrise in der Science-fiction," <u>Sprache im technischen Zeitalter</u> 20(73):15-27. 1980.

"Wirklichkeit des Phantoms," <u>Heyne Science Fiction Magazin</u> 4: 121-146. 1982.

Wade, James

"On being scared out of one's knickers: Carl Claudy's Kane-Dolliver juveniles," <u>Riverside Quarterly</u> 7(1):44-53. March 1980.

Waedt, C. F.

"Index to the <u>Health Knowledge</u> magazines, An," by Gene Marshall and C. F. Waedt. <u>Science Fiction Collector</u> 3:3-39. 1977.

Wagar, W. W.

<u>H. G. Wells and the World State.</u> New Haven, Connecticut: Yale University Press, 1961. 301 p. Reprinted, Freeport, New York: Books for Libraries Press, 1971.

<u>Terminal Visions: The Literature of Last Things.</u> Bloomington: Indiana Univerity Press, 1982. 241 p.

"H. G. Wells and the genesis of future studies," <u>World Future Society Bulletin</u> 17(1): 25-29. January/February 1983

"H. G. Wells and the radicalism of despair," <u>Studies in the Literary Imagination</u> 6(2):1-10. Fall 1973.

"Rebellion of Nature," in: Rabkin, Eric S., ed. <u>The End of the World.</u> Carbondale: Southern Illinois University Press, 1983. pp. 129-186.

"Round Trips to Doomsday," in: Rabkin, Eric S., ed. <u>The End of the World.</u> Carbondale: Southern Illinois University Press, 1983. pp. 73-96.

"Science fiction and the Apocalypse," in: Samuelson, D. N. <u>Science Fiction and Future Studies.</u> Bryan, TX: SFRA, 1975. pp. 56-62.

"Steel-grey savior, The: Technocracy as utopia and ideology," <u>Alternative Futures</u> 2(2): 38-54. Spring 1979.

Wagar, W. W. (Continued)

"Toward a World Set Free: The Vision of H. G. Wells," Futurist 27(4): 24-31. August 1983.

"Utopian studies and utopian thought definitions and horizons," Extrapolation 19(1):4-12. December 1977.

Wages, J. D.

"Isaac Asimov's debt to Edgar Allan Poe," Poe Studies 6(1):29. June 1973.

Waggoner, Diana

Hills of Faraway: A Guide to Fantasy. New York: Atheneum, 1978. 326 p.

Wagner, Jeff

"In the world he was writing about: the life of Philip K. Dick," Foundation 34: 69-96. Autumn 1985.

Wagner, K. E.

"Celluloid S&S: Boon or Menace?" Fantasy Newsletter 4(11): 6-8. November 1981.

"Dennis Etchison: The Unknown Writer," In: Winter, Douglas E. Shadowings: The Reader's Guide to Horror Fiction 1981-1982. Mercer Island, WA: Starmont, 1983. pp. 87-91.

"Fan Madness," Fantasy Newsletter 5(9): 5-6. October 1982.

"In Memoriam: Lee Brown Coye," Fantasy Newsletter 5(1): 8-11. January 1982.

"Lost Turkeys of the Ether Waves," Fantasy Review 7(1): 8-9. January 1984.

"On Fantasy," Fantasy Newsletter 6(2): 8-10. February 1983.

"On Fantasy: The Decline But Not Yet Fall of the Anthology," Fantasy Newsletter 6(8): 9-11, 38. September 1983.

"On Fantasy: '...And Others' (David Drake)," Fantasy Newsletter 6(6): 6-7. June/July 1983.

"On Fantasy: Hold the Bologna on Mine," Fantasy Newsletter 5(11): 6-7, 38. December 1982.

"On fantasy: more swell stuff (but cheaper)," Fantasy Review 8(7): 13-14. July 1985.

"On Fantasy: Reality, Assassin of Myth," Fantasy Newsletter 5(5): 5-7, 34. June 1982.

"On Fantasy: Roscoes, Geeks, and Rayguns," Fantasy Review 7(6): 7-9. July 1984.

"On fantasy: swell stuff," Fantasy Reveiw 8(4): 8, 45. April 1985.

"On Fantasy: The Invisible Assassins," Fantasy Newsletter 5(7): 11-13. August 1982.

"On Fantasy: The Lurkers From Across the Pond," Fantasy Newsletter 6(4): 13-14. April 1983.

"On fantasy: yet more swell stuff," Fantasy Review 8(10): 35-36. October 1985.

"Once and Future Kane," Shayol 1: 11-13. November 1977.

Wagner, L. W.

"Heroic fantasies of Frank Frazetta, The," Philadelphia Inquirer May 26, 1985. in: NewsBank. Fine Arts and Architecture. 72:A5-A7. June 1985.

Wagner, Martin

"Interview: Theodore Sturgeon," Mathom 2(2): 9-14. March/April 1982.

Wahlstrom, B. J.

"Alice Mary Norton," in: Mainiero, Lina, ed. American Women Writers. New York: Ungar, 1982. v. 3, pp. 278-281.

"Joanna Russ," in: Mainiero, Lina, ed. American Women Writers. New York: Ungar, 1982. v. 3, p. 521-522.

Wakefield, Dan

"In Vonnegut's Karass," in: Klinkowitz, Jerome and John Somer, eds. The Vonnegut Statement. New York: Delacorte Press/Seymour Lawrence, 1973. pp. 55-70.

Walbridge, E. F.

"Isaac Asimov," Wilson Library Bulletin 27(5):346. January 1953. also in: Current Biography Yearbook pp. 33-34. 1953.

Waldmann, Werner

"Science fiction: Literatur von morgen?" Welt und Wort 27(10):489-491. 1972.

Waldroop, William

"Bill Waldroop Show. Special Guest: Samuel R. Delany," Seldon's Plan 49: 4-12. May 1983.

Waldrop, Howard

"Big-D in '73," <u>Texas Fandom 1981</u>. Dallas: Becky Matthews, 1981. pp. 6-8.

"Little Lisa Tuttle and how she grew some," in: <u>Othercon Program Book</u>. September 1979. 4 p.

"Tom, Tom: A Reminiscence," <u>Trumpet</u> 12: 6, 44. Summer 1981.

Walker, D. L.

<u>Alien Worlds of Jack London, The</u>. Grand Rapids, Michigan: Wolf House Books, 1973. 47 p.

<u>Fiction of Jack London: A Chronological Bibliography, The</u>, by D. L. Walker and J. E. Sisson, III. El Paso: Texas Western Press, 1972. 40 p.

Walker, J. M.

"Demoness and the grail, The: deciphering MacDonald's <u>Lilith</u>," in: Collins, R. A., ed. <u>Scope of the Fantastic: Culture, Biography, Themes, Children's Literature</u>. Westport: Greenwood, 1985. pp. 179-190.

"Myth, exchange, and history in The Left Hand of Darkness," <u>Science Fiction Studies</u> 6(2):180-189. July 1979.

"Myth, exchange, and history in <u>The Left Hand of Darkness</u>," in: <u>Ursula K. Le Guin</u>, ed. by Harold Bloom. New York: Chelsea House, 1986. pp. 171-182.

"Reciprocity and Exchange in <u>A Canticle for Leibowitz</u>," <u>Renascence</u> 33(2): 67-85. Winter 1981.

"Reciprocity and Exchange in Samuel Delany's Nova," <u>Extrapolation</u> 23(3): 221-234. Fall 1982.

"Reciprocity and Exchange in Science Fiction," <u>Essays in Arts and Sciences</u> 9(2): 145-156. August 1980.

"Reciprocity and Exchange in William Golding's The Inheritors," <u>Science-Fiction Studies</u> 8(3): 297-310. November 1981.

"Rites of Passage Today: The Cultural Significance of <u>A Wizard of Earthsea</u>," <u>Mosaic</u> 13(3/4): 179-191. Spring/Summer 1980.

"Science fiction: a commentary on itself as lies," <u>Modern Language Studies</u> 8(3):19-37. 1978.

Walker, M. G.

"Doris Lessing's The Four-Gated City: Consciousness and Community," <u>Southern Review</u> 17(1): 97-120. January 1981.

Walker, M. J.

"Fantastic tale: science fiction at Eastern New Mexico University," <u>Extrapolation</u> 14(1):126-128. May 1973.

"Out of the Closet: Science Fiction at Eastern New Mexico University," <u>Special Collections</u> 2(1/2): 49-57. Fall/Winter 1982.

"Science fiction collections acquired by Eastern New Mexico University," <u>New Mexico Libraries</u> 3:78. Fall 1970.

Walker, Paul

<u>Speaking of Science Fiction</u>. Oradell, New Jersey: Luna Publications, 1978. 425 p.

"Alfred Bester," in: Walker, Paul. <u>Speaking of Science Fiction</u>. Oradell, New Jersey: Luna Publications, 1978. pp. 302-314.

"Andre Norton," in: Walker, Paul. <u>Speaking of Science Fiction</u>. Oradell, New Jersey: Luna Publications, 1978. pp. 263-270.

"Anne McCaffrey," in: Walker, Paul. <u>Speaking of Science Fiction</u>. Oradell, New Jersey: Luna Publications, 1978. pp. 253-262. also in: <u>Luna Monthly</u> 56:1-5. 1974.

"Brian W. Aldiss," in: Walker, Paul. <u>Speaking of Science Fiction</u>. Oradell, New Jersey: Luna Publications, 1978. pp. 397-416.

"Clifford D. Simak," in: Walker, Paul. <u>Speaking of Science Fiction</u>. Oradell, New Jersey: Luna Publications, 1978. pp. 56-67. also in: <u>Luna Monthly</u> 57:1-6. 1975.

"Damon Knight," in: Walker, Paul. <u>Speaking of Science Fiction</u>. Oradell, New Jersey: Luna Publications, 1978. pp. 157-167.

"Edmond Hamilton," in: Walker, Paul. <u>Speaking of Science Fiction</u>. Oradell, New Jersey: Luna Publications, 1978. pp. 361-369. also in: <u>Luna Monthly</u> 60:1-4,12. 1975.

"Frederik Pohl," in: Walker, Paul. <u>Speaking of Science Fiction</u>. Oradell, New Jersey: Luna Publications, 1978. pp. 128-143.

"Fritz Leiber," in: Walker, Paul. <u>Speaking of Science Fiction</u>. Oradell, New Jersey: Luna Publications, 1978. pp. 68-77.

"Harlan Ellison," in: Walker, Paul. <u>Speaking of Science Fiction</u>. Oradell, New Jersey: Luna Publications, 1978. pp. 291-230.

Walker, Paul (Continued)

"Harry Harrison on John W. Campbell," in: Walker, Paul. Speaking of Science Fiction. Oradell, New Jersey: Luna Publications, 1978. pp. 208-212.

"Horace L. Gold," in: Walker, Paul. Speaking of Science Fiction. Oradell, New Jersey: Luna Publications, 1978. pp. 144-156.

"Isaac Asimov," in: Walker, Paul. Speaking of Science Fiction. Oradell, New Jersey: Luna Publications, 1978. pp. 121-127.

"Jack Williamson," in: Walker, Paul. Speaking of Science Fiction. Oradell, New Jersey: Luna Publications, 1978. pp. 384-396.

"James Blish," in: Walker, Paul. Speaking of Science Fiction. Oradell, New Jersey: Luna Publications, 1978. pp. 229-241.

"James Schmitz," in: Walker, Paul. Speaking of Science Fiction. Oradell, New Jersey: Luna Publications, 1978. pp. 85-100.

"Joanna Russ," in: Walker, Paul. Speaking of Science Fiction. Oradell, New Jersey: Luna Publications, 1978. pp. 242-252.

"John Brunner," in: Walker, Paul. Speaking of Science Fiction. Oradell, New Jersey: Luna Publications, 1978. pp. 315-324. also in: Luna Monthly 58:1-5,10. 1975.

"Keith Laumer," in: Walker, Paul. Speaking of Science Fiction. Oradell, New Jersey: Luna Publications, 1978. pp. 101-106.

"Leigh Brackett," in: Walker, Paul. Speaking of Science Fiction. Oradell, New Jersey: Luna Publications, 1978. pp. 370-383.

"Michael Moorcock," in: Walker, Paul. Speaking of Science Fiction. Oradell, New Jersey: Luna Publications, 1978. pp. 213-228. also in: Luna Monthly 59:1-9. 1975.

"Philip Jose Farmer," in: Walker, Paul. Speaking of Science Fiction. Oradell, New Jersey: Luna Publications, 1978. pp. 37-55.

"Poul Anderson," in: Walker, Paul. Speaking of Science Fiction. Oradell, New Jersey: Luna Publications, 1978. pp. 107-120.

"R. A. Lafferty," in: Walker, Paul. Speaking of Science Fiction. Oradell, New Jersey: Luna Publications, 1978. pp. 11-23.

"Robert Bloch," in: Walker, Paul. Speaking of Science Fiction. Oradell, New Jersey: Luna Publications, 1978. pp. 325-339.

"Robert Silverberg," in: Walker, Paul. Speaking of Science Fiction. Oradell, New Jersey: Luna Publications, 1978. pp. 281-290.

"Roger Zelazny," in: Walker, Paul. Speaking of Science Fiction. Oradell, New Jersey: Luna Publications, 1978. pp. 78-84.

"Science fiction, and the people who write it," Media & Methods 15(6):22-24. February 1979.

"Terry Carr," in: Walker, Paul. Speaking of Science Fiction. Oradell, New Jersey: Luna Publications, 1978. pp. 168-207.

"Ursula K. Le Guin," in: Walker, Paul. Speaking of Science Fiction. Oradell, New Jersey: Luna Publications, 1978. pp. 24-36.

"Wilson Tucker," in: Walker, Paul. Speaking of Science Fiction. Oradell, New Jersey: Luna Publications, 1978. pp. 340-360.

"Zenna Henderson," in: Walker, Paul. Speaking of Science Fiction. Oradell, New Jersey: Luna Publications, 1978. pp. 271-280. also in: Luna Monthly 52:1-5,7. 1974.

Walker, R. C.

"Cartography of fantasy," Mythlore 7(4):37-38. Winter 1981.

"Little Kingdom: Some Considerations and Map," Mythlore 10(3): 47-48. Winter 1984.

Walker, S. C.

"IRS as Big Brother; 1984 in 1984," Leading Edge No. 7:61-65. undated.

"Making of a Hobbit: Tolkien's Tantalizing Narrative Technique," Mythlore 7(3): 6-7, 37. Autumn 1980.

"Mooting of the minds: why fans enjoy Tolkien," by N. L. Hayes, Jonathan Langford and S. C. Walker. Leading Edge No. 9:78-84. Winter 1985.

"Tolkien according to Bakshi," Mythlore 6(1): 36. Winter 1979.

Walker, S. L.

"War of the rings treeology," Mythlore 5(1):35. May 1978.

Walling, W. A.

Mary Shelley. New York: Twayne Publishers, 1972. 173 p.

Walmsley, Nigel

"Tolkien and the '60s," in: Giddings, Robert, ed. J. R. R. Tolkien: This Far Land. London: Vision, 1983. pp. 73-86.

Walraven, Ed

"Inner World: The Future in Science Fiction," Windows: Perspectives in Time and Space (Texas A&M Univ.) 2(4): 10-11, 20. Winter 1984.

Walsdorf, J. J.

William Morris in Private Press and Limited Editions: A Descriptive Bibliography of Books by and About William Morris, 1891-1981. Phoenix, AZ: Oryx, 1983. 602 p.

Walsh, Chad

From Utopia to Nightmare. New York and Evanston: Harper & Row, 1962. 191 p. Reprinted, Westport, Connecticut: Greenwood Press, 1972.

Literary Legacy of C. S. Lewis. New York: Harcourt, 1979. 269 p.

"Attitudes toward science in the modern 'inverted utopia'," Extrapolation 2(2):23-26. May 1960.

"Can man save himself," New York Times Book Review p. 4. April 1, 1962. (Book review)

Walsh, J.

"H. G. Wells: he was a seer but a disappointed scientist," Science 155(3759):181-182. January 13, 1967.

Walsh, J. P.

"Lords of time," Quarterly Journal of the Library of Congress 36(2):96-113. Spring 1979.

Walter, E. M.

"Princess Bride, The," in: Magill, Frank N., ed. Survey of Modern Fantasy Literature, Vol 3. Englewood Cliffs, NJ: Salem Press, Inc., 1983. pp. 1286-1290.

Walter, H.

"Lavka snovidenyi," in: Magill, Frank N., ed. Survey of Science Fiction Literature, Vol. 3. Englewood Cliffs, NJ: Salem Press, 1979. pp. 1165-1170.

"Ponedel'nik nachinaetsia v subbotu," in: Magill, Frank N., ed. Survey of Science Fiction Literature, Vol. 4. Englewood Cliffs, NJ: Salem Press, 1979. pp. 1710-1713.

"Solntse zakhodit v Donomage," in: Magill, Frank N., ed. Survey of Science Fiction Literature, Vol. 5. Englewood Cliffs, NJ: Salem Press, 1979. pp. 2113-2116.

Walters, Peter

"Parapsychologische Phanomeme in der Science Fiction Literatur. 2 Teil und Schluss," Quarber Merkur No. 51:55-70. Nov. 1979.

"Parapsychologische Phanomene in der Science Fiction Literatur. 1 Teil," Quarber Merkur. 50:21-44. February 1979.

Walters, Ray

"Paperback Talk," New York Times Book Review p. 19-20. September 5, 1982.

"Paperback talk; R. E. Howard's sword and sorcery fiction," New York Times Book Review pp. 75-76. April 30, 1978.

"Science Fiction Boom: A Shared Passion for 'What If'," New York Times Book Review p. 27-28. February 5, 1984.

Walther, Daniel

"Political SF in France, or, The Long Night of the Fools," Foundation 18: 37-47. January 1980.

Walton, Audrey

"Question: Automation, the automation revolution," Vector 48: 9-12. February 1968.

Walton, Evangeline

"Celtic myth in the twentieth century," Mythlore 3(3):19-22. 1976.

Walton, H.

"How TV tricks take you space traveling," Popular Science 161:106-108. September 1952.

Waltz, G. H., Jr.

Jules Verne: The Biography of an Imagination. New York: Holt, 1943. 223 p.

Waples, Douglas

"Relationship of subject and interest to actual reading, The," Library Quarterly 2(1):42-70. January 1932.

Warburton, Robert

"Screwtape Letters, The," in: Magill, Frank N., ed. Survey of Modern Fantasy Literature, Vol 3. Englewood Cliffs, NJ: Salem Press, Inc., 1983. pp. 1363-1368.

"Short fiction of Malamud, The," in: Magill, Frank N., ed. Survey of Modern Fantasy Literature, Vol 4. Englewood Cliffs, NJ: Salem Press, Inc., 1983. pp. 1640-1644.

Ward, C. M.

"George Alec Effinger," in: Cowart, David, ed. Twentieth-Century American Science-Fiction Writers, Part 1: A-L. Detroit: Gale, 1981. pp. 155-160. (Dictionary of Literary Biography, v. 8)

Ward, H. H.

"Religion 2101 A. D.: who or what will be god?" Christian Century p. 1114. December 3, 1975. (Book review)

Ward, Henri

"Anticipation scientifique, L'" Arts December 26, 1956.

Ward, Jonathan

"Algol interview: Ursula K. Le Guin," Algol 12(2):6-10. Summer 1975.

Ward, L. M.

"Dark trends; psychology, science fiction and the ominous consensus," by Peter Suedfeld and L. M. Ward. Futures 8(1):22-39. February 1976.

Ward, L. R.

"Innocence of G. K. Chesterton, The," Modern Age 19(2):146-156. Spring 1975.

Warner, Frank

"Sounds of silence," American Cinematographer 59(1):44-45,92-94. January 1978.

Warner, Harry, Jr.

All Our Yesterdays: An Informal History of Science Fiction Fandom in the Forties. Chicago: Advent, 1969. 336 p.

"25 years ago," Locus No. 181:4-5. November 17, 1975.

"Ace in the whole," Unpublished note, written for "Ace D-Series Checklist," Danielle Dobbs, compiler. No date. (in Texas A&M University Library SF Research Collection)

"Decisions, decisions," Locus No. 135:5-6. March 3, 1973.

"End of an era," Locus No. 148:7-8. September 12, 1973.

"Everything you always wanted to know about being a Guest of Honor," Locus No. 100:4a-b. November 11, 1971.

"Fan writing," Locus No. 123:7-8. September 22, 1972.

"Fanorama," Speculation 2(1)(whole #13):22-23. July 1966.

"Fanzine explosion," Locus No. 116:7-8. July 8, 1972.

"Hagerstown outlook," Locus No. 110:15-16. March 25, 1972.

"Harry Warner column, August 1974," Locus No. 163:7. August 20, 1974.

"Harry Warner column, November 1974," Locus No. 167:6. November 20, 1974.

"Lunar recollections," Locus No. 61:2a-b. August 5, 1970.

"Most unforgettable fan I never met," Locus No. 105:3-4. January 22, 1972.

"Pocus," Locus No. 58:2c-d. July 1, 1970.

"Remembrance of things past: indexing," Locus No. 65:5-6. October 20, 1970.

"Secret of the ages revealed," Locus No. 86:4a-b. June 18, 1971.

"Sense of wonder," Locus No. 72:6a-b. January 19, 1971.

"Thanks," Locus No. 81:4a-b. April 22, 1971.

"Tribute to Weird Tales," Locus No. 129:7-8. December 15, 1972.

"Why is a fan? Revisited," Locus No. 141:6-8. May 11, 1973.

Warner, S. T.

T. H. White: A Biography. London: Jonathan Cape, 1967. 352 p.

Author Entries

Warren, Alan

"Has success spoiled Stephen King?" in: Schweitzer, Darrell, ed. <u>Discovering Stephen King</u>. Mercer Island: Starmont, 1985. pp. 15-25.

"Roald Dahl: nasty, nasty," in: Schweitzer, Darrell, ed. <u>Discovering Modern Horror Fiction I</u>. Mercer Island: Starmont, 1985. pp. 120-128.

Warren, Anne

"Sense and Sensibility: Strategic Uses of Sensory Description," <u>Focus: An SF Writers' Magazine</u> 8: 28-30. Autumn 1983.

Warren, Bill

<u>Keep Watching the Skies! American Science Fiction Movies of the Fifties. Volume 1, 1950-1957</u>, by Bill Warren and Bill Thomas. Jefferson, NC: McFarland, 1982. 467 p.

"1980: The Year in Fantastic Films," in: Pournelle, Jerry, ed. <u>Nebula Award Stories Sixteen</u>. New York: Bantam, 1983. pp. 149-167.

"Books," <u>Austin American Statesman</u> p. 127. September 21, 1969.

"Movies and Mr. King," in: Underwood, Tim, and Miller, Chuck, eds. <u>Fear Itself</u>. Columbia, PA: Underwood/Miller 1982. pp. 105-128.

Warren, Eugene

"Philip K. Dick: exile in paradox," <u>Christianity Today</u> 21(16):22-24. May 20, 1977.

"Search for Absolutes," in: Greenberg, Martin H., ed. <u>Philip K. Dick</u>. New York: Taplinger, 1982. pp. 161-187.

Warrick, P. S.

<u>Cybernetic Imagination in Science Fiction</u>. Cambridge, MA: MIT Press, 1980. 282 p. (Based on the author's 1977 Dissertation.)

<u>Science Fiction: Contemporary Mythology</u>, ed. by Patricia Warrick, M. H. Greenberg and Joseph Olander. New York: Harper, 1978. 476 p.

"Circuitous journey in John Barth's <u>Chimera</u>, The," <u>Critique: Studies in Modern Fiction</u> 18(2):73-85. 1976.

"Contrapuntal Design of Artificial Evolution in Asimov's "The Bicentennial Man,"" <u>Extrapolation</u> 22(3): 231-242. Fall 1981.

"Encounter of Taoism and Fascism in <u>The Man in the High Castle</u>," in: Greenberg, Martin H., ed. <u>Philip K. Dick</u>. New York: Taplinger, 1982. pp. 27-52.

"Encounter of Taoism and Fascism in Philip K. Dick's <u>The Man in the High Castle</u>," <u>Science Fiction Studies</u> 7(2):174-190. July 1980.

"Ethical evolving artificial intelligence: Asimov's computers and robots," in: Olander, J. D. and M. H. Greenberg, eds. <u>Isaac Asimov</u>. New York: Taplinger, 1977. pp. 174-200.

"Images of the man-machine intelligence relationship in science fiction," in: Clareson, T. D., ed. <u>Many Futures, Many Worlds</u>. Kent, Ohio: Kent State University Press, 1977. pp. 182-223.

"Introduction: mythic patterns," in: Warrick, Patricia, ed. <u>Science Fiction: Contemporary Mythology</u>. New York: Harper, 1978. pp. xv-xvii.

"Labyrinthian process of the artificial: Dick's androids...," <u>Extrapolation</u> 20(2):133-153. Summer 1979. also in: Remington, T. J., ed. <u>Selected Proc. of the 1978 SFRA Natl. Conf.</u> Univ. of North. Iowa, 1979. pp. 122-132.

"Labyrinthian Process of the Artificial: Philip K. Dick's Androids and Mechanical Constructs," in: Greenberg, Martin H., ed. <u>Philip K. Dick</u>. New York: Taplinger, 1982. pp. 189-214.

"Mack Reynolds: the future as socio-economic possibility," in: Clareson, T. D., ed. <u>Voices for the Future: Essays on Major SF Writers</u>, Vol. 2. Bowling Green, Ohio: Popular Press, 1979. pp. 136-153.

"More than human?: androids, cyborgs and others," by George Zebrowski and Patricia Warrick. in: Warrick, Patricia, ed. <u>Science Fiction: Contemporary Mythology</u>. New York: Harper, 1978. pp. 294-307.

"Now We Are Fifteen: Observations on the Science Fiction Research Association by Its President," <u>Extrapolation</u> 25(4): 360-368. Winter 1984.

"Philip K. Dick's Answers to the Eternal Riddles," in: Reilly, Robert, ed. <u>The Transcendent Adventure</u>. Westport: Greenwood, 1984. pp. 107-126.

"Science fiction aesthetic of complementary perception, A," <u>Pacific Quarterly Moana</u> 4(3):329-336. July 1979.

"Science fiction in a computers and society course," in: Williamson, Jack, ed. <u>Teaching Science Fiction: Education for Tomorrow</u>. Philadelphia: Owlswick, 1980. pp. 121-136.

Warrick, P. S. (Continued)

"Science fiction myths and their ambiguity," in: Warrick, Patricia, ed. Science Fiction Contemporary Mythology. New York: Harper, 1978. pp. 1-9.

"Source of Zamyatin's 'We' in Dostoevsky's Notes From Underground, The," Extrapolation 17(1):63-77. December 1975.

Washburn, Dennis

"Plenty of Action, Special Effects in New 'V' Series," Birmingham News. July 1, 1984. NewsBank. Film and Television. FTV 10:B2-B3. 1984.

Waterlow, Charlotte

"Utopia is coming," Alternative Futures 2(2): 77-83. Spring 1979.

Waterman, D. R.

"Collecting in the outer limits," Book Collector's Market 4(3):10-12. May/June 1979.

Watkins, A. H.

Catalogue of the H. G. Wells Collection in the Bromley Public Libraries. Bromley: London Borough of Bromley Public Libraries, 1974. 196 p.

Watkins, John

"Science fiction authors become subject of book," Bryan-College Station Eagle p. 2E. November 28, 1985.

Watkins, W. J.

"How a science fiction writer teaches science fiction," Media & Methods 14(3):22-24. November 1977.

Watney, John

Mervyn Peake. London: Michael Joseph, 1976. 255 p.

Watson, Andy

"Interview: K. W. Jeter," Science Fiction Review 14(2): 12-16. May 1985.

Watson, C. N.

Novels of Jack London: A Reappraisal. Madison: University of Wisconsin Press, 1983. 304 p.

Watson, Christine

"Bid Time Return," in: Magill, Frank N., ed. Survey of Modern Fantasy Literature, Vol 1. Englewood Cliffs, NJ: Salem Press, Inc., 1983. pp. 90-94.

"Dead Zone, The," in: Magill, Frank N., ed. Survey of Modern Fantasy Literature, Vol 1. Englewood Cliffs, NJ: Salem Press, Inc., 1983. pp. 350-354.

"Dragon and the George, The," in: Magill, Frank N., ed. Survey of Modern Fantasy Literature, Vol 1. Englewood Cliffs, NJ: Salem Press, Inc., 1983. pp. 418-422.

"Dying Earth, The and The Eyes of the Overworld," in: Magill, Frank N., ed. Survey of Modern Fantasy Literature, Vol 1. Englewood Cliffs, NJ: Salem Press, Inc., 1983. pp. 441-446.

"Jonathan Livingston Seagull," in: Magill, Frank N., ed. Survey of Modern Fantasy Literature, Vol 2. Englewood Cliffs, NJ: Salem Press, Inc., 1983. pp. 808-810.

"Land of Unreason," in: Magill, Frank N., ed. Survey of Modern Fantasy Literature, Vol 2. Englewood Cliffs, NJ: Salem Press, Inc., 1983. pp. 870-872.

"Night Life of the Gods, The," in: Magill, Frank N., ed. Survey of Modern Fantasy Literature, Vol 3. Englewood Cliffs, NJ: Salem Press, Inc., 1983. pp. 1111-1115.

"Salem's Lot," in: Magill, Frank N., ed. Survey of Modern Fantasy Literature, Vol 3. Englewood Cliffs, NJ: Salem Press, Inc., 1983. pp. 1350-2354.

"Sword of Shannara, The," in: Magill, Frank N., ed. Survey of Modern Fantasy Literature, Vol 4. Englewood Cliffs, NJ: Salem Press, Inc., 1983. pp. 1866-1868.

"Well of the Unicorn, The," in: Magill, Frank N., ed. Survey of Modern Fantasy Literature, Vol 5. Englewood Cliffs, NJ: Salem Press, Inc., 1983. pp. 2097-2101.

"Master Books, The," in: Magill, Frank N., ed. Survey of Modern Fantasy Literature, Vol 2. Englewood Cliffs, NJ: Salem Press, Inc., 1983. pp. 988-992.

"Short fiction of Ellison, The," in: Magill, Frank N., ed. Survey of Modern Fantasy Literature, Vol 3. Englewood Cliffs, NJ: Salem Press, Inc., 1983. pp. 1516-1519.

"Short fiction of Jackson, The," in: Magill, Frank N., ed. Survey of Modern Fantasy Literature, Vol 4. Englewood Cliffs, NJ: Salem Press, Inc., 1983. pp. 1563-1567.

Watson, Ian

"Crudities of science fiction, The," _Arena_ 7:4-7. March 1978.

"Forest as metaphor for mind: _The Word for World is Forest_ and 'Vaster Than Empires and More Slow'," in: _Ursula K. Le Guin_, ed. by Harold Bloom. New York: Chelsea House, 1986. pp. 47-56.

"Forest as metaphor for mind: _The Word for World is Forest_ and 'Vaster Than Empires and More Slow'," _Science Fiction Studies_ 2(3):231-237. November 1975.

"Foundation Forum: Part I: science fiction: form versus content," by Christopher Priest and Ian Watson. _Foundation_ 10:55-65. June 1976.

"Into the Arena, I: Down in the Mine," _Arena_ 12: 24-27. Summer 1981.

"Into the Arena: Shrines and Ratholes," _Vector_ 117: 15-18. December 1983.

"Journey to Chekhov," _Focus: An SF Writers' Magazine_ 8: 15-17. Autumn 1983.

"Le Guin's _Lathe of Heaven_ and the role of Dick: the false reality as mediator," _Science Fiction Studies_ 2(1):67-75. March 1975.

"Meet the editor: Malcolm Edwards," _SFWA Bulletin_ 17(4): 18-19. Winter 1983.

"Money for Authors From Library Loans," _SFWA Bulletin_ 17(1): 8-9. Spring 1983.

"Money for Authors From Library Loans: The Moment of Truth," _SFWA Bulletin_ 18(1): 26-28. Spring 1984.

"One Finger at a Time," _Focus: an SF Writer's Magazine_. 4: 20. Spring 1981.

"Rhetoric of recognition: the science fiction of Michael Bishop," _Foundation_ 19: 5-14. June 1980.

"SF idea capsules for art students," _Foundation_ 5:56-62. January 1974.

"SFWA Overseas Regional Meeting," _SFWA Bulletin_ 18(2): 24. Summer 1984.

"Toward an Alien Linguistics," _Vector_ 71: 14-23. December 1975.

"W(h)ither science fiction," _Vector_ 78:5-10. November/December.

"Who Can Believe in the Hero(ine)?" _SFWA Bulletin_ 16(3): 42-45. March 1982.

Watson, J. D.

Reader's Guide to C. S. Lewis: His Fiction. Ed. D., East Texas State University, 1981. 135 p. (DAI 42:2692A)

Watson, Judy

"Day in the life of an SF writer's wife," _Vector_ 86:5-6. April 1978.

Watson, Keith

"Local Fan Devotion Helps in Bringing 'Dr. Who' To Channal 8," _Houston Post_ Sec. 3, p. 4. June 25, 1984.

"Spielberg to be Executive Producer of NBC Series Set to Debut in 1985," _Houston Post_ Sec. E, p. 6. July 31, 1984.

Watt, Donald

Aldous Huxley: The Critical Heritage. London: Routledge & Kegan Paul, 1975. 493 p.

"Burning bright: _Fahrenheit 451_ as symbolic dystopia," in: Olander, J. D. and M. H. Greenberg, eds. _Ray Bradbury_. New York: Taplinger, 1980. pp. 195-213.

"Galaxy full of people: characterization in Asimov's major fiction, A," in: Olander, J. D. and M. H. Greenberg, eds. _Isaac Asimov_. New York: Taplinger, 1977. pp. 135-158.

"New Worlds Through Old Tools: Some Traditional Critical Tools for Science Fiction," _Essays in Arts and Sciences_ 9(2): 131-137. August 1980.

"View from Malacandra, The," _CSL: The Bulletin of the New York C. S. Lewis Society_ 6(8):3-5. June 1975.

Watt-Evans, Lawrence

"Conan, The Destroyer (review)," _Starlog_ 88: 43-45. November 1984.

Waugh, C. G.

"Checklist of Science Fiction/Fantasy Works Containing Religious Themes or Motifs," by Robert Reilly, F. D. McSherry, and C. G. Waugh. in: Reilly, Robert, ed. _The Transcendent Adventure_. Westport: Greenwood, 1984. pp. 225-248.

"Demographic, intellectual, and personality characteristics of science fiction fans," by C. G. Waugh, E. F. Libby and C. L. Waugh. Paper presented at the Science Fiction Research Association Annual Meeting, November 1975. 22 p.

Waugh, C. G. (Continued)

"Here's looking at you, kids: a profile of SF fans," by C. G. Waugh and D. J. Schroeder. Anthro-Tech: A Journal of Speculative Anthropology 3(1):12-19. Fall 1978.

"Influence of science fiction upon scientific and technological innovations," in: Samuelson, D. N. Science Fiction and Future Studies. Bryan, TX: SFRA, 1975. pp. 37-52.

Waugh, C. L.

"Demographic, intellectual, and personality characteristics of science fiction fans," by C. G. Waugh, E. F. Libby and C. L. Waugh. Paper presented at the Science Fiction Research Association Annual Meeting, November 1975. 22 p.

Waugh, R. H.

"Drum of A Voyage to Arcturus," Extrapolation 26(2): 143-151. Summer 1985.

Weales, Gerald

"Reader to rider," Commonweal 74(10):253-255. June 2, 1961.

"What ever happened to Tugboat Annie?" The Reporter 35:50,52-56. December 1, 1966. (Book reviews)

Weatherly, Joan

"Death of Big Sister: Orwell's tragic message," College Literature 11(1): 22-33. 1984.

Weaver, E. K.

"Relationship of science fiction reading to reasoning abilities," by E. Black and E. K. Weaver. Science Education 49(3):293-296. April 1965.

Webb, Bryan

"First Deltacon," Locus 18(11): 29. November 1985.

"Taxman Cometh," Locus 17(7): 19. July 1984.

Webb, H. A.

"Science fiction writers: prophets of the future," Library Journal 80:2884-2885. Dec. 15, 1955. also in: Junior Libraries 2:6-7. Dec. 15, 1955; Robinson, E. R., ed. Readings About Children's Literature. NY: McKay 1966.

Webb, J. B.

Utopian Fantasy and Social Change 1600-1665. Ph. D. Dissertation, State University of New York at Buffalo, 1982. 313 p. (DAI 43:174A)

Webb, Joseph

"OTR Primer," in: Hopkins, Harry A., ed. Fandom Directory 1980. Langley AFB, Virginia: Fandom Computer Services, 1980. pp. 278-281.

Weber, Rosemary

"Folklore and fantasy: mix or match?" Paper presented at the Pennsylvania School Librarians Conference, Seven Springs, Pennsylvania, April 28-29, 1978. 11 p. ERIC ED 154 424.

Webre, Alfred

"Arthur C. Clarke," Starlog 65: 30-33. December 1982.

Weedman, J. B.

"Dream Millennium, The," in: Magill, Frank N., ed. Survey of Science Fiction Literature, Vol. 2. Englewood Cliffs, NJ: Salem Press, 1979. pp. 614-617.

Weedman, Jane

Samuel R. Delany. Mercer Island, WA: Starmont, 1982. 79 p. (Starmont Reader's Guide, 10)

"Art and the Artist's Role in Delany's Works," in: Clareson, Thomas D., ed. Voices For the Future, Vol. 3. Bowling Green: Popular Press, 1984. pp. 151-185.

"Delany's Babel-17: the powers of language," Extrapolation 19(2):132-137. May 1978.

"Music and cultures of Delany's The Einstein Intersection, The," in: Remington, T. J., ed. Selected Proceedings of the 1978 SFRA National Conference. Cedar Falls, Iowa: Univ. of Northern Iowa, 1979. pp. 114-121.

Weeks, John

"He's a superman of letters," Sun Telegram (San Bernardino) sec. C, pp. 1,11. July 17, 1977.

Weger, W. W.

"H. G. Wells and the genesis of future studies," World Future Society Bulletin 17(1): 25-29. January/February 1983.

Wehmeyer, L. B.

Images in a Crystal Ball: World Futures in Novels for Young People. Littleton, CO: Libraries Unlimited, 1981. 211 p.

"Futuristic children's novels as a mode of communication," Research in the Teaching of English 13(2):137-152. May 1979.

Weibel, Jurg

"Verharmloste Jules Verne," Quarber Merkur. 45:52-62. December 1976.

Weil, Robert

"2001 prophecy quiz, The," by Robert Weil and Peter Tyson. Omni 7(10): 38-40, 90-94. July 1985.

Weiler, A. H.

"Scanning some small wonders," New York Times Sec. II, p. 1. August 23, 1953.

Weimberg, Gary

"Dragonslayer: Camelot Liberalism," Jump Cut 26: 1, 18. December 1981.

Weinberg, Marc

"Charles Martin Smith: alien investigator," Starlog No. 91:28-30. February 1985.

"Joe Dante Uncaging Gremlins," by David McDonnell and Marc Weinberg. Starlog 85: 37-38, 67. August 1984.

"Profile: Kevin Peter Hall," Starlog No. 101:32-33. December 1985.

"Starlog Interview: Hoyt Axton," Starlog 88: 14-16. November 1984.

"Starlog interview: Matthew Broderick," Starlog 95: 68-69. June 1985.

"Steve Railsback," Starlog 97: 52-53, 62. August 1985.

"Villains of Dune," Starlog No. 91:33-39. February 1985.

"Zach Galligan; me and my gizmo," Starlog No. 92:24-25. March 1985.

Weinberg, Robert

Annotated Guide to Robert E. Howard's Sword & Sorcery, The. West Linn, Oregon: Starmont House, 1976. 152 p.

Hero Pulp Index, The, by Robert Weinberg and Lohr McKinstry. Evergreen, Colorado: Opar Press, 1971. Revised edition, 48 p.

Man Behind Doc Savage: A Tribute to Lester Dent, The. Oak Lawn, Illinois: by the author, 1974. 127 p.

Reader's Guide to the Cthulhu Mythos, by Robert Weinberg and E. P. Berglund. Albuquerque: Silver Scarab Press, 1973. Revised edition, 88 p.

Weird Tales Story, The. West Linn, Oregon: Fax Collector's Editions, 1977. 134 p.

"Captain Hazzard," in: Tymn, M. B. and Ashley, Mike. Science Fiction, Fantasy, and Weird Fiction Magazines. Westport, CT: Greenwood, 1985. pp. 158.

"Captain Zero," in: Tymn, M. B. and Ashley, Mike. Science Fiction, Fantasy, and Weird Fiction Magazines. Westport, CT: Greenwood, 1985. pp. 158-159.

"Doc Savage," in: Tymn, M. B. and Ashley, Mike. Science Fiction, Fantasy, and Weird Fiction Magazines. Westport, CT: Greenwood, 1985. pp. 183-185.

"Doctor Death," in: Tymn, M. B. and Ashley, Mike. Science Fiction, Fantasy, and Weird Fiction Magazines. Westport, CT: Greenwood, 1985. pp. 186-187.

"Dr. Yen Sin," in: Tymn, M. B. and Ashley, Mike. Science Fiction, Fantasy, and Weird Fiction Magazines. Westport, CT: Greenwood, 1985. pp. 187-188.

"Dusty Ayres and His Battle Birds," in: Tymn, M. B. and Ashley, Mike. Science Fiction, Fantasy, and Weird Fiction Magazines. Westport, CT: Greenwood, 1985. pp. 194-196.

"G-8 and His Battle Birds," in: Tymn, M. B. and Ashley, Mike. Science Fiction, Fantasy, and Weird Fiction Magazines. Westport, CT: Greenwood, 1985. pp. 289-290.

"Jules de Grandin Series, The," in: Magill, Frank N., ed. Survey of Modern Fantasy Literature, Vol 2. Englewood Cliffs, NJ: Salem Press, Inc., 1983. pp. 811-816.

"Jungle Stories," in: Tymn, M. B. and Ashley, Mike. Science Fiction, Fantasy, and Weird Fiction Magazines. Westport, CT: Greenwood, 1985. pp. 365-366.

"Ka-Zur," in: Tymn, M. B. and Ashley, Mike. Science Fiction, Fantasy, and Weird Fiction Magazines. Westport, CT: Greenwood, 1985. pp. 368-369.

"Mysterious Wu Fang," in: Tymn, M. B. and Ashley, Mike. Science Fiction, Fantasy, and Weird Fiction Magazines. Westport, CT: Greenwood, 1985. pp. 414-416.

Weinberg, Robert (Continued)

"Octopus," in: Tymn, M. B. and Ashley, Mike. Science Fiction, Fantasy, and Weird Fiction Magazines. Westport, CT: Greenwood, 1985. pp. 440-441.

"Operator #5," in: Tymn, M. B. and Ashley, Mike. Science Fiction, Fantasy, and Weird Fiction Magazines. Westport, CT: Greenwood, 1985. pp. 448-451.

"Scorpion," in: Tymn, M. B. and Ashley, Mike. Science Fiction, Fantasy, and Weird Fiction Magazines. Westport, CT: Greenwood, 1985. pp. 565-566.

"Shadow," by Will Murray and Robert Weinberg. in: Tymn, M. B. and Ashley, Mike. Science Fiction, Fantasy, and Weird Fiction Magazines. Westport, CT: Greenwood, 1985. pp. 570-573.

"Spider," in: Tymn, M. B. and Ashley, Mike. Science Fiction, Fantasy, and Weird Fiction Magazines. Westport, CT: Greenwood, 1985. pp. 602-604.

"Strange Stories," in: Tymn, M. B. and Ashley, Mike. Science Fiction, Fantasy, and Weird Fiction Magazines. Westport, CT: Greenwood, 1985. pp. 623-625.

"Strange Tales of Mystery and Terror," in: Tymn, M. B. and Ashley, Mike. Science Fiction, Fantasy, and Weird Fiction Magazines. Westport, CT: Greenwood, 1985. pp. 626-628.

"Terence O'Leary's War Birds," in: Tymn, M. B. and Ashley, Mike. Science Fiction, Fantasy, and Weird Fiction Magazines. Westport, CT: Greenwood, 1985. pp. 659-660.

"Uncanny Stories," by Mike Ashley and Robert Weinberg. in: Tymn, M. B. and Ashley, Mike. Science Fiction, Fantasy, and Weird Fiction Magazines. Westport, CT: Greenwood, 1985. pp. 683-684.

"Weird Tales," in: Tymn, M. B. and Ashley, Mike. Science Fiction, Fantasy, and Weird Fiction Magazines. Westport, CT: Greenwood, 1985. pp. 727-736.

"Collecting Fantasy," Fantasy Newsletter 4(5): 14-16. May 1981.

"Collecting Fantasy: Famous Fantastic Mysteries," Fantasy Newsletter 4(10): 7-9, 35. October 1981.

"Collecting Fantasy: collectable items," Fantasy Newsletter 3(11): 16-18. November 1980.

"Collecting Fantasy: Fantasy Press," Fantasy Newsletter 4(2): 14-17. February 1981.

"Collecting Fantasy: Gnome Press," Fantasy Newsletter 5(9): 10-12. October 1982.

"Conan Series, The," in: Magill, Frank N., ed. Survey of Modern Fantasy Literature, Vol 1. Englewood Cliffs, NJ: Salem Press, Inc., 1983. pp. 300-307.

"Fantasy pulps," in: Magill, Frank N., ed. Survey of Modern Fantasy Literature, Vol 5. Englewood Cliffs, NJ: Salem Press, Inc., 1983. pp. 2447-2463.

"Robert E. Howard: From the Pulps to the Silver Screen," American Fantasy 1(2): 8-15. May 1982.

"Science Fiction Specialty Publishers," Special Collections 2(1/2): 119-130. Fall/Winter 1982.

Weinig, M. A.

"Exchange, complementarity, coinherence: aspects of community in Charles Williams," Mythlore 7(2):27-29. Summer 1980.

Weinkauf, M. S.

"Breaking the discipline barriers; practical uses of science fiction," Delta Kappa Gamma Bulletin 41:32-38. Spring 1975.

"Daughters of Frankenstein: women and science fiction," Cthulhu Calls 5(1):22-26. July 1977.

"Edenic motifs in utopian fiction," Extrapolation 11(1):15-22. December 1969.

"Escape from the garden, The," Texas Quarterly 16(3):66-72. Autumn 1973.

"Five spokesmen for dystopia," Midwest Quarterly (Pittsburgh, Kansas) 16(2):175-186. Winter 1975.

"Frank Reade Library," Riverside Quarterly 7(2): 109-110. March 1982.

"God figure in dystopian fiction, The," Riverside Quarterly 4(4):266-271. March 1971.

"God motif in dystopian fiction, The," Foundation 1:25-29. March 1972.

"Growing old in Utopia," SFWA Bulletin 9(6): 9-14. Summer 1974.

"Indian in science fiction, The," Extrapolation 20(4):308-320. Winter 1979.

"So much for the gentle sex," Extrapolation 26(3): 231-239. Fall 1985.

"Theme for SF: aesthetics and overpopulation," Extrapolation 13(2):152-164. May 1972.

Weinstein, Howard

"Search for Spock, (review)," _Starlog_ 88:
33-35. November 1984.

Weinstock, Matt

"Way to write is to write," _Los Angeles
Mirror News_ p. 10. July 11, 1955.

Weir, Arthur

"No Monroe in Lothlorien," in: Becker, Alida,
ed. _The Tolkien Scrapbook_. New York:
Grossett & Dunlap, 1978. pp. 120-123.

Weisburd, Mel

"Science fiction: from escape to freedom,"
Coastlines 1(3):25-35. December 1955.

Weiser, Deborah

"Female image in speculative fiction, The,"
in: Nachbar, Jack, Deborah Weiser and J. L.
Wright, eds. _The Popular Culture Reader_.
Bowling Green, Ohio: Bowling Green University
Popular Press, 1978. pp. 168-173.

Weisser, Michael

"_Digit_ oder nicht digit," by Karlheinz
Steinmuller and Michael Weisser. _Quarber
Merkur_ 62: 3-10. December 1984.

"Pladoyer fur die Verbindung von Kunst und
Wissenschaft," in: Rottensteiner, Franz, ed.
Polaris 6. Frankfurt-am-Main: Suhrkamp,
1982. pp. 236-270.

Weiximann, Joe

"Octavia E. Butler Bibliography," _Black
American Literature Forum_ 18(2): 88-89.
Summer 1984.

Welch, D. M.

"Breaking the barriers: Theodore Sturgeon's
More Than Human," _Illinois English
Bulletin_ 72(2): 56-63. Winter 1985. (ERIC
ED 252 860)

Welch, D. R.

Science Fiction Bibliography. Austin, TX:
Science Fiction Syndicate, 1935. 12 p.

Welcher, Jeanne

"Checklist of secondary studies on imaginary
voyages," by Lance Schachterle and Jeanne

Welcher. _Bulletin of Bibliography_
31(3):99-121. July/September 1974.

Wellbank, J. H.

"Utopia and the constraints of justice," in:
Richter, P. E., ed. _Utopia/Dystopia?_.
Cambridge, MA: Schenkman, 1975. pp. 29-42.

Wellman, Harold

"King Kong: then and now," _American
Cinematographer_ 58(1):66-67. January 1977.

Wells, Frank

"Organic Theatre's 'Warp' a Sci-Fi Adventure
Blast," _Torch_ (Chicago) p. 13. May 22,
1972.

Wells, G. H.

_Works of H. G. Wells 1887-1925: A
Bibliography, Dictionary, and Subject-Index_.
London: Routledge, 1926. 274 p. Reprinted,
New York: Burt Franklin, 1970.

Wells, G. P.

Last Books of H. G. Wells, The. Tiptree,
Essex: The H. G. Wells Society, 1968. 84 p.

Wells, H. G.

"Mr. Wells reviews a current film, Metropolis,"
New York Times p. 4, 22. April 17, 1927.

"Utopias," _Science-Fiction Studies_ 9(2):
117-121. July 1982.

"Woman and Primitive Culture,"
Science-Fiction Studies 8(1): 35-37. March
1981.

Wells, J. A.

_Of Time, Space and Magic: Selected Works of
Kurt Vonnegut, Jr. and Tom Robbins_. Masters
Thesis, University of Georgia, 1979. 62 p.

Wells, Jeffrey

"Creepshow crawlers can cause creepy cold
chills," _New York Post_ September 3, 1981.
in: _NewsBank. Film and Television_. 21: E6.
July/December 1981.

Wells, L. G.

Fictional Accounts of Trips to the Moon.
Syracuse, NY: Syracuse University Library,
1962. 26 p.

Wells, Mark

"Orycon '80 Convention Four-Way Telephone Conversation: Arthur C. Clarke, Harlan Ellison, Fritz Leiber, Mark Wells," Science Fiction Review 10(3): 12-17. August 1981.

Wells, R. W.

"From textbook to checkbook," Milwaukee Journal. September 14, 1980. in: NewsBank. Literature. 28:E14. 1980.

Wells, S. W., III

Science Fiction and Heroic Fantasy Author Index. Duluth: Purple Unicorn, 1978. 186 p.

"Galaxy Science Fiction Novels," by S. W. Wells, III and J. G. Thiessen. Science Fiction Collector 3:44-48. 1977.

Welsh, J. M.

"Modern Apocalypse: The War Game," Journal of Popular Film and Television 11(1): 25-41. Spring 1983.

Welsh, John

"Flight from the Heart of Being," Vector 100: 31-33. December 1980.

Wendell, Carolyn

Alfred Bester. Mercer Island, WA: Starmont, 1982. 72 p. (Starmont Reader's Guide, 6)

"Alien species: a study of women characters in the Nebula Award winners, 1965-1973, The," Extrapolation 20(4):343-354. Winter 1979.

"Miss Forsyte is dead: long live the sci-fi lady," in: Williamson, Jack, ed. Teaching Science Fiction: Education for Tomorrow. Philadelphia: Owlswick, 1980. pp. 102-109.

"Responsible Rebellion in Vonda N. McIntyre's Fireflood, Dreamsnake, and Exile Waiting," in: Staicar, Tom, ed. Critical Encounters II. New York: Ungar, 1982. pp. 125-144.

Wendland, Albert

Science, Myth, and the Fictional Creation of Alien Worlds. Ann Arbor: UMI Research Press, 1984, c1980. 200 p.

Went, F. W.

"Size of man, The," American Scientist 56(4):400-413. Winter 1968.

Wentworth, C. I.

"Charles L. Harness," in: Cowart, David, ed. Twentieth-Century American Science-Fiction Writers, Part 1: A-L, Detroit: Gale, 1981. pp. 204-205. (Dictionary of Literary Biography, v. 8)

Wentz, W. J.

A. Merritt: A Bibliography of Fantastic Writings. Roseville, California: George A. Bibby, 1965. 33 p.

Wenzel, Dietmar

"Kurd Lasswitz: Prophet des Buergertums," Science Fiction Times (Germany) 27(2):11-16. February 1985.

Werner, Nancy

Flights of Fancy: A Bibliography of Fanciful Literature. 35 p. ERIC ED 025 401.

Werth, L. F.

"Siddhartha and Slaughterhouse Five," in: Myers, R. E., ed. The Intersection of Science Fiction and Philosophy. Westport: Greenwood, 1983. pp. 45-54.

Wertham, Frederic

World of Fanzines: A Special Form of Communication, The. Carbondale: Southern Illinois University Press, 1973. 144 p.

Wescott, A. S.

Relation of Science Fiction to Myth. Master of Philosophy, Council for National Academic Awards, 1982.

Wescott, R. W.

"Libration and liberation: thoughts on living beyond the Earth," Anthrotech: A Journal of Speculative Anthropology 1(3):3-7. Spring 1977.

Wesotowska, D.

"Jezyk fantastyczny w utworach Lema," Jezyk Polske 43:13-27.

Wessel, Dieter

Welt im chaos: Sturkture und Funktion des Weltkatastrophenmotivs in der neueren science fiction. Frankfurt: Akademische Verlagsgesellschaft, 1974. 332 p.

West, Anthony

H. G. Wells: Aspects of a Life. New York: Random House, 1984. 480 p.

"Dark world of H. G. Wells, The," Harper's 214:68-73. May 1957.

"Man and ideas (XII): H. G. Wells," Encounter 41:52-59. February 1967.

West, Donald

"Right Sort of People," Foundation 21: 17-27. February 1981.

West, R. C.

Tolkien Criticism: An Annotated Checklist. Kent, OH: Kent State University Press, 1970. 73 p.

Tolkien Criticism: An Annotated Checklist. Kent, OH: Kent State University Press, 1981. 177 p.

"Annotated bibliography of Tolkien criticism, An," Extrapolation 10(1):17-49. December 1968.

"Interlace structure of The Lord of the Rings, The," in: Lobdell, Jared, ed. A Tolkien Compass. New York: Ballantine/Del Rey, 1980. pp. 82-102.

"Sign of the unicorn: the unicorn motif in selected works of modern fantasy, The," in: Remington, T. J., ed. Selected Proceedings of the 1978 SFRA National Conference. Cedar Falls: Univ. of Northern Iowa, 1979. pp. 45-54.

West, R. H.

"Science fiction and its ideas," Georgia Review 15(3):276-286. Fall 1961.

Westall, Robert

"Hunt for Evil," Signal 34: 3-13. January 1981.

Westerfield, J. K.

"Sky's no limit, The," Writers Digest 20(2):13-19,42. January 1940.

Westerlund, Lois

"It all depends on the point of view: C. S. Lewis' Out of the Silent Planet," CSL: The Bulletin of the New York C. S. Lewis Society 8(12):2-5. 1977.

Westheimer, Joseph

"Out-of-this-world special effects for Star Trek," by H. A. Anderson, G. D. Linwood, and Joseph Westheimer. American Cinematographer 48:714-717. October 1967.

Westling, Louise

"Dialogue with Ursula K. Le Guin," by George Wicks and Louise Westling., Northwest Review 20(2/3):147-159. 1982. (also published in Dialogues with Northwest Writers)

Weston, Peter

"Ashes to ashes, rust to rust: the robot in science fiction," Galileo 1:10-11,68-69,79. No date.

"Just thinking out loud," Galileo 4:12-17. July 1977.

"Temi classici della SF: in viaggio verso le stelle, (1 parte)" Robot: rivista de fantascienza 1(1):103-110. April 1978. Translation of "On the way to the stars: getting off the ground."

Weston, R. L.

"Cold Beyond Hearing," In: Winter, Douglas F Shadowings: The Reader's Guide to Horror Fiction 1981-1982. Mercer Island, WA: Starmont, 1983. pp. 56-58.

Wetzel, G. T.

Howard Phillips Lovecraft: Memoirs, Critiques, & Bibliographies, ed. by George Wetzel. North Tonowanda, NY: SSR Publications, 1955. 83 p.

Lovecraft Collectors Library, The, Volume VI. Commentaries. North Tonawanda, New York: SSR Publications, 1955. 37 p.

"Amateur Press Works," in: Wetzel, George. Howard Phillips Lovecraft: Memoirs, Critiques, & Bibliographies. North Tonowonda, NY: SSR, 1955. pp. 41-57.

"Cthulhu Mythos: A Study," in: Wetzel, George. Howard Phillips Lovecraft: Memoirs, Critiques, & Bibliographies. North Tonowonda, NY: SSR, 1955. pp. 18-27.

"Edward Lucas White: Notes for a Biography, Part I," Fantasy Commentator 4(2): 94-114. Winter 1979-80.

"Edward Lucas White: Notes for a Biography, Part II," Fantasy Commentator 4(3): 178-182. Winter 1981.

Wetzel, G. T. (Continued)

"Edward Lucas White: Notes for a Biography, Part IV," _Fantasy Commentator_ 5(1): 67-70. Winter 1983.

"Lovecraft's Literary Executor," _Fantasy Commentator_ 4(1): 34-43. Winter 1978-79.

"Pseudonymous Lovecraft, The," _Xenophile_ 3(4):3-5,73. 1976.

"Weaver of Nightmares," _Fantasy Commentator_ 3(6): 161-166. Spring/Summer 1952.

Wexelblatt, Robert

"Mad Scientist," _Midwest Quarterly_ 22(3): 269-278. Spring 1981.

Weyn, Suzanne

"Jill Bauman," _Starlog_ 53: 42-45. December 1981.

"Walter Velez," _Starlog_ 44: 43-45, 53. March 1981.

Weyr, Thomas

"Starship interview: Ian & Betty Ballantine," _Starship_ 37:23-25. Winter 1979/1980. Originally published in _Publishers Weekly_. December 12, 1977.

Whalen, Kathryn

"What's a heaven for?, or, science fiction in the junior high school," _Arizona English Bulletin_ 51(1):85-90. October 1972.

Whall, H. M.

"James E. Gunn," in: Cowart, David, ed. _Twentieth-Century American Science-Fiction Writers, Part 1: A-L_. Detroit: Gale, 1981. pp. 194-197. (Dictionary of Literary Biography, v. 8)

Wheat, Kim

"Dungeons and Dragons," in: Hopkins, Harry A., ed. _Fandom Directory 1981_. Langley AFB, Virginia: Fandom Computer Services, 1981. pp. 62-65.

Wheat, Linda

"Eve future, L'," in: Magill, Frank N., ed. _Survey of Science Fiction Literature_, Vol. 2. Englewood Cliffs, NJ: Salem Press, 1979. pp. 735-738.

Wheatley, Barbara

"Teaching linguistics through science fiction and fantasy," _Extrapolation_ 20(3):205-213. Fall 1979.

Wheeler, C. F.

"How to shoot a space picture; in no space," _American Cinematographer_ 53(7):750-753,792-797. July 1972.

Wheelock, A. S.

"Dark mountain: H. P. Lovecraft and the 'Vermont Horror'," _Vermont History_ 45(4):221-228. Fall 1977.

Whetmore, Edward

"Female Captain's Enterprise: The Implications of Star Trek's 'Turnabout Intruder'," in: Barr, Marlene S., ed. _Future Females_. Bowling Green, OH: Bowling Green State University Popular Press, 1981. pp. 157-161.

Whetton, Betty

"Out in third field with Robert A. Heinlein," by Betty Whetton and Annette Dowelson. _Arizona English Bulletin_ 51(1):97-105. October 1972.

Whitaker, Cornelia

Science Fiction. Carmichael, California: San Juan Unified School District, 1974. 50 p. (Fearon Pitman Curriculum Development Library, No. ELA 9-023)

Whitaker, M. A.

"'Hollow Hills': a Celtic Motif in Modern Fantasy," _Mosaic_ 13(3/4): 165-178. Spring/Summer 1980.

White, A. G.

Science Fiction and Architecture: A Selected Bibliography. Monticello, Illinois: Vance Bibliographies, 1979. 11 p. (Vance Bibliographies, A-74)

"Urban futures: science fiction and the city," Council of Planning Librarians, Exchange Bibliography no. 418, 1973. 5 p.

White, D. E.

"Medical Morals and Narrative Necessity," in: Myers, R. E., ed. _Intersection of Science Fiction and Philosophy_. Westport: Greenwood, 1983. pp. 185-194.

White, D. E. (Continued)

"Profile: Jane Yolen," Language Arts 60(5): 652-660. May 1983.

White, D. L.

"Poetics of horror: more than meets the eye, The," Cinema Journal 10(2):1-18. Spring 1971.

White, J. J.

"Mathematical imagery in Musil's Young Torless and Zamyatin's We," Comparative Literature 18:71-78. Winter 1966.

White, J. W.

Ethical Imperative in Recent Science Fiction: Analog, 1965-1970. Masters Thesis, Mississippi State University, 1973. 283 p.

White, James

"Biologies and environments," in: Ash, Brian, ed. Visual Encyclopedia of Science Fiction. New York: Harmony, 1977. pp. 90-99.

White, Jonathan

"Collectible science fiction magazines," AB Bookman's Weekly 74(14):2109-2130. October 1, 1984.

"PW Interviews: Brian Aldiss," Publishers Weekly 227(16):83-84. April 19, 1985.

White, M. D.

"Ellison's Harleqiun: irrational moral action in static time," Science Fiction Studies 4(2):161-165. July 1977.

White, T. I.

"Opposing necessity and truth: the argument against politics in Doris Lessing's utopian vision," in: Barr, Marleen, ed. Women and Utopia. New York: Lanham, 1983. pp. 134-147.

White, Ted

"Baycon and the art show," Science Fiction Times No. 453:2,4. April 1968.

"Harlan Ellison," in: Porter, Andrew, ed. The Book of Ellison. New York: Algol Press, 1978. pp. 15-24. Reprinted from Algol. March 1967.

"Look at sex in SF, A," Science Fiction Times No. 464:10-13. March 1969.

White, V. L.

"Bright the Hawk's Flight: The Journey of the Hero in Ursula Le Guin's Earthsea Trilogy," Ball State University Forum 20(4): 34-45. Autumn 1979.

White, William

"Ernest Bramah (Smith) in periodicals, 1890-1972," Bulletin of Bibliogaphy 32(1):33-34,44. January/March 1975.

Whitehead, Harriet

"Reasonable fantastic: some perspectives on scientology, science fiction, and occultism," in: Zaretsky, I. I. and M. P. Leone, eds. Religious Movements in Contemporary America. Princeton Univ. Press, 1974. pp. 547-587.

Whitehurst, C. A.

"Images of the sexes in science fiction," Internation Journal of Women's Studies 3(4): 327-337. July/August 1980.

Whiteside, T.

"Onward and upward with the arts: Tom Corbett, space cadet," New Yorker 28(2):32-57. March 1, 1952.

Whitfield, S. E.

Making of Star Trek, The, by S. E. Whitfield and Gene Roddenberry. New York: Ballantine, 1968. 414 p.

Whitman, C. H.

"Discourse on fantasy," in: Whitman, C. H. Aristophanes and the Comic Hero. Cambridge: Harvard University Press, 1964. pp. 259-280. (Martian Classical Lectures, Vol. 19)

Whitney, John

"Creating special effects for Westworld," American Cinematographer 54(11):1477-1483. November 1973.

Whitney, Paul

"Philip Jose Farmer: a checklist," Science Fiction Collector 5:4-20. September 1977.

Whyte, A. A.

New SF Bulletin: Index to SF Books 1974. Boston: Paratime Press, 1974. 42 p.

Whyte, A. A. (Continued)

"Jove Dares to be Bland," by Mike Saler and A. A. Whyte. Science Fiction Times (Boston) 1(10): 1, 9. 1981.

Wiater, Stanley

"Evening with Arthur C. Clarke," ERB-dom No. 36:8-9. July 1970.

"Interview: Gahan Wilson," Fantasy Newsletter 6(9): 11-12, 46. October/November 1983.

"Interview: Robert Bloch," Fantasy Newsletter 5(4): 19-20, 35. April/May 1982.

"Shades of evil: Les Daniels, an interview," Fantasy Review 8(2): 5-6, 40. February 1985.

"Thrust Profile: Jane Yolen," Thrust No. 23: 16-17. Fall/Winter 1985.

Wible, C. B.

"Wrestling with Superman," Journal of Education 132(7):190-191. October 1949.

Wicher, Linda

"Power and progress: themes in fiction for a technological age," English Journal 74(4): 64-66. April 1985.

Wicks, George

"Dialogue with Ursula K. Le Guin," by George Wicks and Louise Westling., Northwest Review 20(2/3):147-159. 1982. (also published in Dialogues with Northwest Writers)

Widdershins, K. U. F.

"Cereal music," Australian Science Fiction Review No. 5:3-9. December 1965.

Wiegand, Jorg

Triviale Phantasie, Die: beitraege zur 'Verwertbarkeit' von Science Fiction, ed. by Jorg Wiegand. Bonn: Asgard, 1976. 160 p.

Vorbildliches Morgen: Experten stellen ausgewaehlte Science Fiction stories vor. Bonn: Asgard, 1978. 132 p.

"Fiction: Anmerkungen zu einem Magazin fur science fiction und Phantastik," in: Rottensteiner, Franz, ed. Polaris 4. Suhrkamp, 1978. pp. 153-164.

"'Ich mochte das Bewusstsein der Leute verandern...'," in: Ermert, Karl, ed. Neugier oder Flucht? Stuttgart: Klett, 1980. pp. 77-82.

"Es gibt eine Deutsche Science Fiction," Science Fiction Times (Germany) 26(2):8-10. February 1984.

"Es ist unsere aufgabe, kunstler zu sein...: Zum selbstverstandis der science fiction autoren," Medien-& Sexualpadagogik 4:16-19. 1975.

"Interview mit Hans Joachim Alpers," Science Fiction Times (Germany) 25(4):5-8. April 1983.

"Literatur uber science fiction: eine ausgewahlte bibliographie," in: Weigand, Jorg, ed. Die Triviale Phantasie. Bonn: Asgard, 1976 pp. 155-158.

"Sehnsucht nach Hoherem," in: Ermert, Karl, ed. Neugier oder Flucht? Stuttgart: Klett, 1980. pp. 60-69.

"Workshop Interview mit einem science fiction autor: Walter Ernsting," in: Weigand, Jorg, ed. Die Triviale Phantasie. Bonn: Asgard, 1976. pp. 73-84.

Wiener, Don

"Keep the Movies Clean," Daily Planet p. 1. March 10, 1972.

Wigler, Stephen

"TV cassettes boost Trek stars to new heights," Chicago Tribune Sec. 5, p. 5. June 7, 1985.

Wilcox, Robert

"Spectroscope," Amazing 27(6): 89-90. February 1980.

Wilder, Cherry

"Zeitgeist and Other Timely Ghosts: Notes from West Germany," SFWA Bulletin 16(4): 43-45. May 1982.

Wilgus, Neal

"Algol interview: Suzy McKee Charnas," Algol 16(1):21-25. Winter 1978/1979.

"Down to earth," Samisdat 20:25-28. 1976.

"Interview with Fred Saberhagen, An," Science Fiction Review 35:15-16. May 1980.

"Interview with Jack Williamson," Science Fiction Review 10(1): 26-29. February 1981.

Wilgus, Neal (Continued)

"Interview with Robert Anton Wilson, An,"
Science Fiction Review 5(2):30-34. 1976.

"Interview with Stephen R. Donaldson, An,"
Science Fiction Review 30:26-29.
March/April 1979.

"Interview: Darrell Schweitzer, Part 1,"
Science Fiction Review 12(4): 26-31.
November 1983.

"Interview: Darrell Schweitzer, Part 2,"
Science Fiction Review 13(3): 13-20. August
1984.

"Interview: L. Neil Smith," Science Fiction
Review 14(1): 8-14. February 1985.

"Interview: Robert E. Vardeman," Science
Fiction Review 14(2): 40-44. May 1985.

"Interview: Robert Shea," Science Fiction
Review 14(3): 6-13. August 1985.

"Interview: Roger Zelazny," Science Fiction
Review 9(3):14-16. August 1980.

"Man With the Cosmic Triggerfinger: an
Interview with Robert Anton Wilson," Science
Fiction Review 9(4): 6-9. November 1980.

"Saberhagen's New Dracula: The Vampire as
Hero," in: Schweitzer, Darrell, ed.
Discovering Modern Horror Fiction I. Mercer
Island: Starmont, 1985. pp. 92-98.

"Technology assessment through science
fiction," Spark pp. 22-25. Fall 1974.

Wilhelm, Kate

"Introduction: Nebula Award Stories Nine,"
in: Wilhelm, Kate, ed. Nebula Award Stories
Nine. New York: Harper, 1975. pp. xiii-xxvi.

"On characters," in: Grant, C. L., ed.
Writing and Selling Science Fiction.
Cincinnati, Ohio: Writers Digest, 1976. pp.
33-44.

"On point of view," in: Wilson, Robin Scott,
ed. Those Who Can: A Science Fiction
Reader. New York: Mentor/New American
Library, 1973. pp. 250-255.

"Something happens," in: Williamson, Jack,
ed. Teaching Science Fiction: Education for
Tomorrow. Philadelphia: Owlswick, 1980. pp.
184-189.

"Uncertain Edge of Reality," Arena Science
Fiction 11: 4-12. November 1980.

"Uncertain edge of reality," Locus
13(9):7-8,17. September 1980.

Wilkens, H. G.

"Phantastik und Warenaesthetik. Die Bilder
Rene Magrittes in der Werbung," in: Thomsen,
C. W., ed. Phantastik in Literatur und
Kunst. Darmstadt: Wissenschaftliche
Buchgesellschaft, 1980. pp. 457-470.

Wilkie, Roy

"Atrocity exhibition, The," by Nick Perry and
Roy Wilkie. Riverside Quarterly
6(3):180-188. August 1975.

"Homo hydrogenesis: notes on the work of J. G.
Ballard,: by Nick Perry and Roy Wilkie.
Riverside Quarterly 4(2): 98-105. January
1970.

"Undivided self: J. G. Ballard's The Crystal
World, The," by Nick Perry and Roy Wilkie.
Riverside Quarterly 5:268-277. 1973.

Wilkins, A. N.

"Robert Paltock and the Bishop of Chester,",
Notes & Queries N.S. 5(10):438-440. October
1958.

Wilkinson, R. G. A.

"Science Fiction Art," Vector 101: 19-20.
April 1981.

Willard, Mark

"Tschai: four planets of adventure," in:
Underwood, Tim and Miller, Chuck, eds. Jack
Vance. New York: Taplinger, 1980. pp.
103-116.

Willard, N.

"Angel in the parlor: the reading and writing
of fantasy," Antioch Review 35(4):426-437.
Fall 1977.

Willett, Ralph

"Moorcock's achievement and promise in the
Jerry Cornelius books," Science Fiction
Studies 3(1):75-79. March 1976.

Williams, Bill

"Man in the future," Listener
71(1833):779-781. May 14, 1964.

Williams, C. T.

"Majesty of Kindness: Dialectic of Cordwainer Smith," by G. K. Wolfe and C. T. Williams. in: Clareson, Thomas D., ed. Voices For the Future, Vol. 3. Bowling Green: Popular Press, 1984. pp. 52-74.

Williams, David

"Wilgefortis, patron saint of monsters, and the sacred language of the grotesque," in: Collins, R. A., ed. Scope of the Fantastic: Culture, Biography, Themes, Children's Literature. Westport: Greenwood, 1985. pp. 171-178.

Williams, G. L.

"Italian Science Fiction in the 1980's," Extrapolation 22(2): 191-195. Summer 1981.

Williams, Gurney, III

"Modern fantasy," by J. I. Glazer and Gurney Williams, III. in: Glazer, Joan I. and Gurney Williams, III. Introduction to Children's Literature. New York: McGraw-Hill, 1979. pp. 258-301.

Williams, L. T.

Journeys to the Center of the Earth: Descent and Initiation in Selected Science Fiction. Ph. D. Dissertation, Indiana University, 1983. 329 p. (DAI 44: 746-747A)

Williams, Norma

"Science in science fiction," Australian Science Fiction Review No. 5:10-13. December 1965.

Williams, P.

"Science fiction mags," Library Journal 87(22):4593-4595. December 15, 1962.

Williams, P. N.

"Black perspectives on Utopia," in: Richter, P. E., ed. Utopia/Dystopia?. Cambridge, MA: Schenkman, 1975. pp. 43-56.

Williams, Pat

"Ulysses in space," Books and Bookmen 12:17-18. July 1967.

Williams, Paul

"Introduction," in: Heinlein, R. A. I Will Fear No Evil. Boston: Gregg, 1978. pp. v-xix.

"Introduction," in: Sturgeon, Theodore. The Dreaming Jewels. Boston: Gregg, 1978. pp. v-xxxviii.

"Theodore Sturgeon: An Appreciation, 1," Locus 18(6): 49-50. June 1985.

"True stories of Philip K. Dick, The," Rolling Stone p. 45-50, 88, 91-94. November 6, 1975.

Williams, R. R.

"Repo Man (review)," Cinefantastique 14(4/5):102. September 1984.

Williams, Raymond

George Orwell: A Collection of Critical Essays. Englewood Cliffs, New Jersey: Prentice-Hall, 1974. 182 p.

"Utopia and science fiction," Science Fiction Studies 5(3):203-214. November 1978. also in: Parrinder, Patrick, ed. Science Fiction: A Critical Guide. New York: Longman, 1979. pp. 52-66.

"Utopia and science fiction," in: Williams, Raymond. Problems in Materialism and Culture. London: Verso Editions, 1980. pp. 196-212.

Williams, S.

"'Wall of Silence' Helps Madeleine L'Engle Write," Courier-Journal. March 7, 1982. in: NewsBank. Literature. 85:E2-3. 1981/82.

Williams, S. H.

Lewis Carroll Handbook: Being a New Version of the Literature of the Rev. C. L. Dodgson...Brought up to 1960 by Roger Lancelyn Green, The, by S. H. Williams and Falconer Madan. London: Oxford University Press, 1962. 307 p.

Williams, Tony

"Female oppression in Attack of the 50-Foot woman," Science Fiction Studies 12(3): 264-273. November 1985.

Williams, W. T.

"Alien biology," Listener 72(1865):1003-1004. December 24, 1964.

Williams, W. T. (Continued)

"Problems in alien biology," _Advancement of Science_ 22(98):198-200. August 1965.

Williamson, Chet

"Early Tales: Stephen King and _Startling Mystery Stories_, The," in: Schweitzer, Darrell, ed. _Discovering Stephen King_. Mercer Island: Starmont, 1985. pp. 46-54.

Williamson, J. N.

"In a glass darkly: Horrible dictu," _Riverside Quarterly_ 7(4): 246-247. December 1985.

Williamson, Jack

H. G. Wells: Critic of Progress. Baltimore: Mirage Press, 1973. 162 p.

Science Fiction Comes to College; A Preliminary Survey of Courses Offered. Portales, New Mexico: by the author, 1971. 19 p.

Study of the Sense of Prophecy in Modern Science Fiction. Masters Thesis, Eastern New Mexico University, 1957. 146 p.

Teaching Science Fiction: Education for Tomorrow. Philadelphia: Owlswick Press, 1980. 261 p.

Teaching SF. Portales, NM: Williamson, 1972. 40 p.

Wonder's Child: My Life in Science Fiction. New York: Bluejay, 1984. 276 p.

"City and the Stars, The," in: Magill, Frank N., ed. _Survey of Science Fiction Literature_, Vol. 1. Englewood Cliffs, NJ: Salem Press, 1979. pp. 374-377.

"First Men in the Moon, The," in: Magill, Frank N., ed. _Survey of Science Fiction Literature_, Vol. 2. Englewood Cliffs, NJ: Salem Press, 1979. pp. 782-786.

"Invisible Man, The," in: Magill, Frank N., ed. _Survey of Science Fiction Literature_, Vol. 3. Englewood Cliffs, NJ: Salem Press, 1979. pp. 1057-1061.

"When the Sleeper Wakes," in: Magill, Frank N., ed. _Survey of Science Fiction Literature_, Vol. 5. Englewood Cliffs, NJ: Salem Press, 1979. pp. 2459-2462.

"Amazing Story," _Amazing_ 28(8): 55-59. November 1982.

"Apocalypse," by Jack Williamson and David Ketterer. in: Warrick, Patricia, ed.

Science Fiction: Contemporary Mythology. New York: Harper, 1978. pp. 435-441.

"As I knew Hugo," _Extrapolation_ 11(2):53-55. May 1970.

"Campbell era, The," _Algol_ 12(2):19-22. Summer 1975.

"Case against the critics, The," _Analog_ 100(4):160-165. April 1980.

"Critic as Conquistador," _Extrapolation_ 25(4): 302-305. Winter 1984.

"Edmond Hamilton: an appreciation," _Locus_ 10(1):2. January 30, 1977.

"Exploration and colonics," in: Ash, Brian, ed. _Visual Encyclopedia of Science Fiction_. New York: Harmony, 1977. pp. 78-89.

"H. G. Wells: critic of progress, conclusion," _Riverside Quarterly_ 4(1): 24-33. August 1969.

"H. G. Wells: critic of progress, part 1," _Riverside Quarterly_ 3(1): 6-31. August 1967.

"H. G. Wells: critic of progress, part 2," _Riverside Quarterly_ 3(2): 96-117. March 1968.

"H. G. Wells: critic of progress, part 3," _Riverside Quarterly_ 3(2): 187-207. August 1968.

"H. G. Wells: critic of progress, part 4," _Riverside Quarterly_ 3(4): 272-293. March 1969.

"H. G. Wells: the man who discovered tomorrow," _Saturday Review_ 55:12-15. January 1, 1972.

"Infinity connection, The," in: Williamson, Jack, ed. _Teaching Science Fiction: Education for Tomorrow_. Philadelphia: Owlswick, 1980. pp. 9-18.

"Infinity Connection," _Journal of English Teaching Techniques_ 10(2): 2-12. 1981.

"Inside the Whale responses to Christopher Priest's 'Outside the Whale'," by Jack Williamson, Jerry Pournelle, and Jack Chalker. _Science Fiction Review_ 9(4): 18-23. November 1980.

"Me and my humanoids," _New Mexico Humanities Review_ 1(1):37-42. January 1978.

"Modes of science fiction," _Science Fiction Times_ 455:9. June 1968.

"On SF and the marketplace," _Fantasy Review_ 8(12): 14, 29. December 1985.

"Plotting 'Jamboree'," in: Wilson, Robin Scott, ed. _Those Who Can: A Science Fiction Reader_. New York: Mentor/New American Library, 1973. pp. 12-18.

Williamson, Jack (Continued)

"Profession of Science Fiction, 30: The Way It Was, 1933-1937," <u>Foundation</u> 26: 46-55. October 1982.

"Science fiction comes to college," <u>Extrapolation</u> 12(2):67-78. May 1971.

"Science fiction in a robot's eye," <u>Astounding</u> 60(3):70-74. November 1957.

"Science fiction, teaching, and criticism," in: Bretnor, Reginald, ed. <u>Science Fiction Today and Tomorrow</u>. New York: Harper, 1974. pp. 309-330.

"Science fiction: an art of the possible," <u>Liberal Arts Review</u> pp. 3-18. Fall 1974.

"Science fiction: emerging from its exile in limbo," <u>Publishers Weekly</u> 200(1):17-20. July 5, 1971.

"SF & I," <u>Starship</u> 16(2):9-16. Spring 1979.

"SF Abroad," <u>SFWA Bulletin</u> 16(4): 47-50. May 1982.

"SF in the classroom," in: McNelly, W. E., ed. <u>Science Fiction the Academic Awakening</u>. Shreveport, LA: CEA, 1974. pp. 11-14.

"SF in Yugoslavia," <u>Locus</u> 13(1):8-9. January 1980.

"SF in Yugoslavia," <u>Science Fiction Chronicle</u> 1(6):12,14. March 1980.

"SF: education for the future," <u>Cthulhu Calls</u> 2(3):26-32. April 1975.

"Short stories and novelettes," in: Bretnor, Reginald, ed. <u>The Craft of Science Fiction</u>. New York: Harper, 1976. pp. 195-215.

"Will academe kill science fiction?" <u>Isaac Asimov's Science Fiction Magazine</u> 2(2):61-73. March/April 1978.

"Years of wonder, The," in: Clareson, T. D., ed. <u>Voices for the Future: Essays on Major Science Fiction Writers</u>, Vol. 1. Bowling Green, Ohio: Popular Press, 1976. pp. 1-13.

"Youth against space: Heinlein's juveniles revisited," in: Olander, J. D. and M. H. Greenberg, eds. <u>Robert A. Heinlein</u>. New York: Taplinger, 1978. pp. 15-31. also in: <u>Algol</u> 14:9-15. Spring 1977.

Willis, D. C.

<u>Horror and Science Fiction Films II</u>. New York: Scarecrow, 1982. 488 p.

<u>Horror and Science Fiction Films III</u>. Metuchen, NJ: Scarcrow, 1984. 334 p.

<u>Horror and Science Fiction Films: A Checklist</u>. Metuchen, New Jersey: Scarecrow Press, 1972. 612 p.

<u>Variety's Complete Science Fiction Reviews</u>. New York: Garland, 1985. 479 p.

Willis, J. A.

"Quiet Master," <u>Megavore</u> 13: 26-29. March 1981.

Willis, M. S.

"Frozen Sunlight and the Mutants," <u>Teachers & Writers</u> 14(3):1-4. January 1983.

Wills, D. D.

"Non-Western women of tomorrow," <u>Alternative Futures</u> 4(2/3): 85-104. Spring/Summer 1981.

Willson, K. E.

"Beastmaster: An Inverview with Sylvia Tabet," <u>Starlog</u> 63: 52-57. October 1982.

Wilner, Norman

"Extraspecial vocal chords that link E. T. with Marin," <u>San Francisco Examiner</u>. October 10, 1982. in: <u>NewsBank</u>. <u>Film and Television</u>. 39:F6. 1982.

Wilson, A. M.

<u>August Derleth: A Bibliography</u>. Metuchen, NJ: Scarecrow, 1983. 229 p.

Wilson, Colin

<u>Science Fiction as Existentialism</u>. Hayes, Middx.: Bran's Head Books, 1978. 16 p.

<u>Strange Genius of David Lindsay</u>, by Colin Wilson, E. H. Visiak and J. B. Pick. London: John Baker, 1970. 183 p. (Reprinted: New York: Gregg, 1979.)

<u>Strength to Dream: Literature and the Imagination, The</u>. Boston: Houghton Mifflin, 1962. 277 p. Reprinted, Westport, Connecticut: Greenwood Press, 1973.

<u>Tree by Tolkien</u>. Santa Barbara, CA: Capra, 1974. 47 p.

"A. E. Van Vogt," in: Bleiler, E. F., ed. <u>Science Fiction Writers</u>. New York: Scribners, 1982. pp. 209-217.

"Colin Wilson: the Outsider," by Colin Wilson and J. M. Elliot. <u>Fantasy Newsletter</u> 3(11): 4-7, 31. November 1980.

Wilson, Colin (Continued)

"H. P. Lovecraft," in: Bleiler, E. F., ed. <u>Science Fiction Writers</u>. New York: Scribners, 1982. pp. 131-137.

"Tree by Tolkien," in: Becker, Alida, ed. <u>The Tolkien Scrapbook</u>. New York: Grossett & Dunlap, 1978. pp. 74-88.

"Vision of science, The," in: <u>The Strength to Dream: Literature and Imagination</u>. London: Gollancz, 1962. pp. 94-117.

Wilson, David

"Play it like the Word of God," <u>Los Angeles Times</u> Sec. 4, p. 23-24. June 16, 1978.

Wilson, Edmund

"Oo, those awful orcs," in: Becker, Alida, ed. <u>The Tolkien Scrapbook</u>. New York: Grossett & Dunlap, 1978. pp. 50-55.

"Tales of the Marvellous and the Ridiculous," in: Joshi, S. T., ed. <u>H. P. Lovecraft: Four Decades of Criticism</u>. Athens, OH: Ohio University Press, 1980. pp. 46-49.

Wilson, F. P.

"Look What They've Done To My Song, Ma," <u>Science Fiction Review</u> 13(2): 7-8. May 1984.

Wilson, Gahan

"How to write a science fiction novel," <u>Omni</u> 1(9):107. June 1979.

Wilson, J. J.

"Conventions," in: Hopkins, Harry A., ed. <u>Fandom Directory 1980</u>. Langley AFB, Virginia: Fandom Computer Services, 1980. pp. 28-31.

Wilson, J. T.

"Is utopia possible?" <u>English</u> 20(107):51-54. Summer 1971.

Wilson, R. A.

"Making It As a Writer," <u>Starship</u> 18(2): 32. Summer/Fall 1981.

Wilson, R. H.

"Some recurrent symbols in science fiction," <u>Extrapolation</u> 2(1):2-4. December 1960.

Wilson, R. J.

"Asimov's mystery story structure," <u>Extrapolation</u> 19(2):101-107. May 1978.

"James Blish," in: Cowart, David, ed. <u>Twentieth-Century American Science Fiction Writers, Part 1: A-L</u>, Detroit: Gale, 1981. pp. 40-53. (Dictionary of Literary Biography, v. 8)

Wilson, R. K.

"Stanislaw Lem's fiction and the cosmic absurd," <u>World Literature Today</u> 51(4):549-553. Autumn 1977.

Wilson, R. S.

"Bridging the gap between technology and the humanities," in: Williamson, Jack, ed. <u>Teaching Science Fiction: Education for Tomorrow</u>. Philadelphia: Owlswick, 1980. pp. 38-43.

"Clarion science fiction workshop, The," <u>Extrapolation</u> 10(1):5-8. December 1968.

"Clarion Writer's Workshop," <u>Pennsylvania English</u> 10(2): 25-26. Spring 1984.

"Point of view: the quick-change artist in the typewriter," in: Wilson, Robin Scott, ed. <u>Those Who Can: A Science Fiction Reader</u>. New York: Mentor/New American Library, 1973. pp. 269-274.

Wilson, Richard

"Charles Brockden Brown: the broken-hearted look," <u>Algol</u> 18:24-26. May 1972.

"George Pal: an appreciation," <u>Locus</u> 13(6):11. June 1980.

"How Not to Write Science Fiction," <u>Science Fiction Review</u> 12(1): 18-21. February 1983.

"Syracuse University's science fiction collection," <u>Worlds of Tomorrow</u> 4:99-104. May 1967.

Wilson, S. S.

"Dragonslayer," <u>Cinefex</u> 6: 32-61. October 1981.

"Land of the Lost," <u>Cinefantastique</u> 6(1):38-48. Summer 1977.

"Planet of the Dinosaurs," <u>Cinefantastique</u> 8(4):40-47. Summer 1979.

Wilson, Sharon

"Doctrine of Organic Unity: E. R. Eddison and the Romantic Tradition," _Extrapolation_ 25(1): 12-19. Spring 1984.

Wilson, Simon

"Empire of Charles Williams," _Mythlore_ 1(4):50-53. October 1969.

Wilson, W. G., Jr.

"Battlestar Galactica," _Questar_ 1(3):18-20. March 1979.

"Disney's calculated risk: _The Black Hole_," by W. G. Wilson, Jr. and Kevin Hyde. _Questar_ 2(2):17-21. February 1980.

"His fruit not bread: Francis Thompson, prophet of science," _Quarterly Review_ 548:273-286. April 1941. (does not apply)

"Spectrum: Harrison Ellenshaw," _Questar_ 2(4): 39-41. August 1980.

Wilt, Judith

"Imperial Mouth: Imperialism, the Gothic, and Science Fiction," _Journal of Popular Culture_ 14(4): 618-631. Spring 1981.

Wilton, S. M.

"Juvenile Science Fiction Involves Reluctant Readers," _Journal of Reading_ 24(7): 608-611. April 1981.

Winandy, Andre

"Twighlight zone; imagination and reality in Jules Verne's strange journeys," _Yale French Studies_ 43:97-110. 1969.

Winchester, Ian

"Physics of Star Trek," by Arthur Stinner and Ian Winchester. _New Scientist_ 1285/1286: 884-887. December 24/31, 1981

Windsor, John

"Fi in the sci," _Guardian_ p. 14. April 7, 1972. (not seen)

Wingrove, David

Science Fiction Film Source Book. Harlow: Longman Green, 1985. 312 p.

Science Fiction Source Book, ed. by David Wingrove. New York: Van Nostrand, 1984. 320 p.

"All time rental figures for SF films," in: Wingrove, David. _Science Fiction Film Source Book_. Harlow: Longman Green, 1985. pp. 311.

"Brahmin awakening: Phil Dick & the metaphysical picaresque," _Vector_ 85:6-12. January/February 1978.

"Chronology of important films," in: Wingrove, David. _Science Fiction Film Source Book_. Harlow: Longman Green, 1985. pp. 10-18.

"Collective pool of the unconscious, part II: an enquiry into the work of Robert Sheckley, The," _Arena_ 6:11-20. August 1977.

"Confronting Professor Greatrex; Michael G. Coney," _Vector_ 80:10-11. March/April 1977.

"Creators of SF on screen," in: Wingrove, David. _Science Fiction Film Source Book_. Harlow: Longman Green, 1985. pp. 272-295.

"Frank Herbert," _Noumenon_ 26:8-12. October/November 1978.

"Glossery of special effects terms," in: Wingrove, David. _Science Fiction Film Source Book_. Harlow: Longman Green, 1985. pp. 309-310.

"I am a bill collector disguised as a tree, said the bill collector disguised as a tree: an interview with Robert Sheckley," _Vector_ 89:10-20. September/October 1978.

"Interview with Bob Shaw, An," by James Corley and David Wingrove. _Vector_ 91:10-12. January/February 1979.

"Interview with Frank Herbert, An," _Vector_ 88:5-17. July/August 1978.

"Interview with Frederik Pohl, An," _Vector_ 90:5-20. November/December 1978.

"Interview with Ian Watson," _Vector_ 86:6-11. April 1978.

"Interview with Richard Cowper, An," _Vector_ 92:3-8. March/April 1979.

"Legerdemain; the fiction of Christopher Priest," _Vector_ 93:3-9. May/June 1979.

"Literary Scene: Books into film," in: Wingrove, David. _Science Fiction Film Source Book_. Harlow: Longman Green, 1985. pp. 295-300.

"Novels of Ian Watson," _Vector_ 86:12-21. April 1978.

"Rest is dreams: the work of Richard Cowper, The," _Vector_ 92:9-15. March/April 1979.

"Saving the Tale," _Vector_ 101: 21-29. April 1981.

Wingrove, David (Continued)

"Science fiction cinema: a brief history," in: Wingrove, David. Science Fiction Film Source Book. Harlow: Longman Green, 1985. pp. 10-18.

"Science Fiction Magazines," in: Wingrove, David, ed. The Science Fiction Source Book. New York: Van Nostrand, 1984. pp. 274-287.

"SF Criticism," in: Wingrove, David, ed. The Science Fiction Source Book. New York: Van Nostrand, 1984. pp. 293-308.

"SF serials 1913-1956," in: Wingrove, David. Science Fiction Film Source Book. Harlow: Longman Green, 1985. pp. 271-272.

"Song in the depth of the galaxies," Vector 80:4-8,25-29. March/April 1977.

"Understanding the Grasshopper: Leitmotifs and the Moral Dilemma in the Novels of Philip K. Dick," Foundation 26: 21-40. October 1982.

Winnick, Gary

"Rigel Interviews Poul Anderson," Rigel 6:17-20. Winter 1982.

Winogura, Dale

"20,000 Leagues Under the Sea (review)," Cinefantastique 1(4):38-39. Fall 1971.

"Battle for the Planet of the Apes (review)," Cinefantastique 3(1):29. Fall 1973.

"Conquest of the Planet of the Apes (review)," Cinefantastique 3(1):29. Fall 1973.

"Dark Star," Cinefantastique 3(4):40-42. Winter 1974.

"Dialogues on apes, apes and more apes," Cinefantastique 2(2):16-37. Summer 1972.

"Doc Savage: The Man of Bronze," by D. S. Johnson and Dale Winogura. Cinefantastique 3(3):4-5,38. Fall 1974.

"Mephisto Waltz (review)," Cinefantastique 1(3):21-22. Summer 1971.

"Moon Child," Cinefantastique 2(1):6-7. Spring 1972.

"Omega Man (review)," Cinefantastique 2(1):37. Spring 1972.

"Parallax View (review)," Cinefantastique 3(4):29. Winter 1974.

"THX 1138 (review)," Cinefantastique 1(3):20. Summer 1971.

"Wendkos: the importance of concept," Cinefantastique 2(1):20-27. Spring 1972.

Winson, J. A.

"What in SF can you believe? Interview with M. Kaku," Science Digest 84:26-29. August 1978.

Winston, David

"Iambulus' Islands of the Sun and the Hellenistic literary utopias," Science Fiction Studies 3(3):219-227. November 1976.

Winston, Joan

Making of the Trek Conventions, The. New York: Playboy Press, 1979. 254 p.

Winter, D. E.

Shadowings: The Reader's Guide to Horror Fiction 1981-1982. Mercer Island, WA: Starmont, 1983. 148 p.

Stephen King. Mercer Island, WA: Starmont, 1982. 128 p.

Stephen King: The Art of Darkness. New York: New American Library, 1984. 272 p.

"Art of Darkness," in: Winter, D. E. Shadowings: The Reader's Guide to Horror Fiction 1981-1982. Mercer Island, WA: Starmont, 1983. pp. 3-23.

"Charles L. Grant: A Profile," Science Fiction Review 14(4): 6-9. November 1985.

"Charles Platt," in: Platt, Charles. Dream Makers: Volume II. New York: Berkley, 1983. pp. 293-300.

"Collecting King," Twilight Zone 5(6): 32-33, 97. February 1986.

"David Morrell: Tasting First Blood," In: Winter, D. E. Shadowings: The Reader's Guide to Horror Fiction 1981-1982. Mercer Island, WA: Starmont, 1983. pp. 92-105.

"Forgotten Words: Spoken By Forgotten Ancestors," In: Winter, D. E. Shadowings: The Reader's Guide to Horror Fiction 1981-1982. Mercer Island, WA: Starmont, 1983. pp. 47-49.

"Horror and the Limits of Violence: A Forum of Interviews," In: Winter, D. E. Shadowings: The Reader's Guide to Horror Fiction 1981-1982. Mercer Island, WA: Starmont, 1983. pp. 125-134.

"I Want My Cake: Thoughts on 'Creepshow' and E. C. Comics," In: Winter, D. E. Shadowings: The Reader's Guide to Horror Fiction 1981-1982. Mercer Island, WA: Starmont, 1983. pp. 135-138.

Winter, D. E. (Continued)

"In Memoriam: John Gardner," Fantasy
Newsletter 5(11): 22. December 1982.

"In Night Journeys of Stephen King," in:
Underwood, Tim, and Miller, Chuck, eds. Fear
Itself. Columbia, PA: Underwood/Miller, 1982.
pp. 183-229.

"Interview: Charles L. Grant, Part II,"
Fantasy Newsletter 5(2): 29-32, 38.
February 1982.

"Interview: Charles L. Grant," Fantasy
Newsletter 5(1): 12-15, 34. January 1982.

"Interview: Michael McDowell: From Harvard to
Horror," Fantasy Newsletter 5(11): 23-28.
December 1982.

"John Coyne: a profile," Fantasy Review
8(10): 12-14, 33. October 1985.

"Mostly, I Want to Break Your Heart," by S. M.
Charnas and D. E. Winter. Fantasy Review
7(8): 5-6, 41. September 1984.

"Notes on the 7th World Fantasy Convention,"
Fantasy Newsletter 5(1): 16-17, 25. January
1982.

"Profile: Charles Platt," Science Fiction
Review 12(2): 26-29. May 1983.

"Profile: David Morrell," Fantasy
Newsletter 5(8): 23-28. September 1982.

"Profile: Paul Hazel," Fantasy Newsletter
6(8): 5-8, 38. September 1983.

"Some Words With Stephen King," Fantasy
Newsletter 6(2): 11-14. February 1983.

"Stephen King, Peter Straub and the quest for
the talisman," Twilight Zone 4(6):62-68.
January/February 1985.

"T. E. D. Klein: the reluctant ghoulie,"
Fantasy Review 8(7): 7-10, 42. July 1985.

"Talking terror with Stephen King," Twilight
Zone 5(6): 16-22. February 1986.

"Thoughts on Creepshow & EC Comics," Fantasy
Newsletter 6(2): 33-34. February 1983.

"V. C. Andrews: a profile," Fantasy Review
8(9): 6-10. September 1985.

Winter, F. H.

"Frau im Mond: Fritz Lang's surprising, silent
space travel classic," Starlog 43: 39-41,
62. January 1981.

Winter, Michael

Compendium Utopiarum: Typologie und
Bibliographie literarischer Utopien. Erster
Teilband: Von der Antike bis zur deutschen
Fruhaufklarung. Stuttgart: Metzler, 1978.
287 p.

Winternitz, Felix

"Author Asimov Enjoys His Fame," Wilmington
Evening News, Dec. 10, 1981. in: NewsBank.
Literature. 38:E4-5. 1981/82.

Wintle, Justin

"Alan Garner," in: Wintle, Justin. The
Pied Pipers. New York: Paddington, 1974. pp.
221-235.

"Lloyd Alexander," in: Wintle, Justin. The
Pied Pipers. New York: Paddington, 1974. pp.
208-220.

"Madeleine L'Engle," in: Wintle, Justin.
The Pied Pipers. New York: Paddington, 1974.
pp. 249-262.

"Richard Adams," in: Wintle, Justin. The
Pied Pipers. New York: Paddington, 1974. pp.
132-146.

Wintrebert, Joelle

"S. F. et normalite," Europe
580/581:138-145. August/September 1977.

Wirpsza, Witold

"Fantaszja-nie fantazaja," Nowa Kultura No.
14. 1956.

Wirth, Suzanne

"Books for children and young people: science
fiction, 1966 and 1967," Wisconsin Library
Bulletin 63(5):331-333. September 1967.

Wirtz, Heinrich

"Aliens (Ausserirdische Lebensesen) in der
science ficiton. 2. teil," Quarber Merkur
43:3-13. May 1976.

"Aliens (Ausserirdische Lebewesen) in der
Science Fiction," Quarber Merkur 42:53-61.
December 1975.

Wise, Deborah

"World Famous Author Isaac Asimov Converts to
Word Processing," InfoWorld 4(1): 15.
January 11, 1982.

Author Entries

Wise, S.

Darkover Dilemma: Problems of the Darkover Series, The. Baltimore; T-K Graphics, 1976. 28 p.

Wisehart, Bob

"Ray Bradbury," Sacramento Bee July 2, 1985. in: NewBank. Film and Television. 1:G11-G12. July 1985.

"Science Fiction Rides Again in 'V'," Channels. Bryan-College Station Eagle. p. 7. August 26, 1984.

"Star Wars Earnings Will Be Out of This World," New Orleans Times Picayune January 26, 1983. in: NewsBank. Film and Television 79:C2. 1982/1983.

Wiser, Barbara

"Sampling of stories from The Wind's Twelve Quarters," Illinois English Bulletin 72(2): 46-52. Winter 1985. (ERIC ED 252 860)

Witucke, Virginia

"Treatment of Fantasy and Science Fiction in Juvenile and Young Adult Literature Texts," Top of the News 39(1): 77-91. Fall 1982.

Wixon, D. W.

"Pecking Order," Digressions No. 4: 11-13. February 1980.

Wohlfeil, A. W.

"Science fiction stories in the social studies," Clearing House 44(5):300-304. January 1970.

Wolf, J. C.

"Disney World: America's vision of utopia," Alternative Futures 2(2): 72-76. Spring 1979.

"Science fiction and the fallacy of hope," Extrapolation 17(2):151-152. May 1976.

Wolf, Jose

"Um dia, talvez, outros se lembrarao de nossos sonhos," Vozes 72(7):60-63. September 1978.

Wolf, M. D.

"Creating a prehistoric world for The Age of Mammals," American Cinematographer 62(1):36-39,72-73. January 1981.

Wolf, Mark

"Sinbad and the Eye of the Tiger: special visual effects," Cinefantastique 6(2):40-47. Fall 1977.

"Special effects of Flesh Gordon," Cinefantastique 5(2):40-45. Fall 1976.

"Stop frame: history and technique of fantasy film animation," Cinefantastique 1(2):6-20. Winter 1971.

"Stop frame: history and technique of fantasy film animation," Cinefantastique 2(1):9-17. Spring 1972.

Wolf, R. E.

"Star Wars: the background," Vector 82:6-9,29. July/August 1977.

Wolf, William

"Kurt Vonnegut: still dreaming of imaginary worlds," Insight: Sunday Magazine of the Milwaukee Journal pp. 15-18. February 27, 1972.

Wolfe, G. K.

David Lindsay. Mercer Island, WA: Starmont, 1982. 64 p. (Starmont Reader's Guide, 9)

Known and The Unknown: The Iconography of Science Fiction. Kent, OH: Kent State University Press, 1979. 250 p.

Planets and Dimensions: Collected Essays, by C. A. Smith and ed. by C. K. Wolfe. Baltimore: Mirage Press, 1973. 87 p.

Science Fiction Dialogues. Chicago: Academy Chicago, 1982. 227 p.

"Best of Cordwainer Smith, The," in: Magill, Frank N., ed. Survey of Science Fiction Literature, Vol. 1. Englewood Cliffs, NJ: Salem Press, 1979. pp. 186-190.

"Circus of Dr. Lao, The," in: Magill, Frank N., ed. Survey of Modern Fantasy Literature, Vol 1. Englewood Cliffs, NJ: Salem Press, Inc., 1983. pp. 282-286.

"Devil's Tor," in: Magill, Frank N., ed. Survey of Modern Fantasy Literature, Vol 1. Englewood Cliffs, NJ: Salem Press, Inc., 1983. pp. 391-395.

"E Pluribus Unicorn," in: Magill, Frank N., ed. Survey of Science Fiction Literature, Vol. 2. Englewood Cliffs, NJ: Salem Press, 1979. pp. 676-680.

Wolfe, G. K. (Continued)

"House on the Borderland, The," in: Magill, Frank N., ed. Survey of Modern Fantasy Literature, Vol 2. Englewood Cliffs, NJ: Salem Press, Inc., 1983. pp. 744-748.

"Long Tomorrow, The," in: Magill, Frank N., ed. Survey of Science Fiction Literature, Vol. 3. Englewood Cliffs, NJ: Salem Press, 1979. pp. 1242-1245.

"Medusa," in: Magill, Frank N., ed. Survey of Modern Fantasy Literature, Vol 2. Englewood Cliffs, NJ: Salem Press, Inc., 1983. pp. 993-997.

"Midwich Cuckoos, The," in: Magill, Frank N., ed. Survey of Science Fiction Literature, Vol. 3. Englewood Cliffs, NJ: Salem Press, 1979. pp. 1391-1395.

"Other Passenger, The," in: Magill, Frank N., ed. Survey of Modern Fantasy Literature, Vol 3. Englewood Cliffs, NJ: Salem Press, Inc., 1983. pp. 1173-1175.

"Ralph 124C 41+," in: Magill, Frank N., ed. Survey of Science Fiction Literature, Vol. 4. Englewood Cliffs, NJ: Salem Press, 1979. pp. 1751-1754.

"Re-Birth," in: Magill, Frank N., ed. Survey of Science Fiction Literature, Vol. 4. Englewood Cliffs, NJ: Salem Press, 1979. pp. 1755-1758.

"Santaroga Barrier, The," in: Magill, Frank N., ed. Survey of Science Fiction Literature, Vol. 4. Englewood Cliffs, NJ: Salem Press, 1979. pp. 1859-1862.

"Seedling Stars, The," in: Magill, Frank N., ed. Survey of Science Fiction Literature, Vol. 4. Englewood Cliffs, NJ: Salem Press, 1979. pp. 1888-1891.

"Shadows in the Sun," in: Magill, Frank N., ed. Survey of Science Fiction Literature, Vol. 4. Englewood Cliffs, NJ: Salem Press, 1979. pp. 1898-1901.

"Skin of Our Teeth, The," in: Magill, Frank N., ed. Survey of Modern Fantasy Literature, Vol 4. Englewood Cliffs, NJ: Salem Press, Inc., 1983. pp. 1760-1762.

"Something Wicked This Way Comes," in: Magill, Frank N., ed. Survey of Modern Fantasy Literature, Vol 4. Englewood Cliffs, NJ: Salem Press, Inc., 1983. pp. 1769-1773.

"Voyage of the Space Beagle, The," in: Magill, Frank N., ed. Survey of Science Fiction Literature, Vol. 5. Englewood Cliffs, NJ: Salem Press, 1979. pp. 2378-2382.

"Voyage to Arcturus, A," in: Magill, Frank N., ed. Survey of Modern Fantasy Literature, Vol 4. Englewood Cliffs, NJ: Salem Press, Inc., 1983. pp. 2039-2045.

"Word for World Is Forest, The," in: Magill, Frank N., ed. Survey of Science Fiction Literature, Vol. 5. Englewood Cliffs, NJ: Salem Press, 1979. pp. 2492-2496.

"Autoplastic and Alloplastic Adaptations in Science Fiction: 'Waldo' and 'Desertation'," in: Slusser, George E., ed. Coordinates. Carbondale: Southern Illinois University Press, 1983. pp. 65-79.

"CAS: a note on the aesthetics of fantasy," Nyctalops No. 7:19-20. August 1972.

"Contemporary theories of fantasy," in: Magill, Frank N., ed. Survey of Modern Fantasy Literature, Vol 5. Englewood Cliffs, NJ: Salem Press, Inc., 1983. pp. 2220-2234.

"David Lindsay and George MacDonald," Studies in Scottish Literature 12(2):131-145. October 1974.

"Encounter With Fantasy," in: Schlobin, Roger C., ed. The Aesthetics of Fantasy Literature and Art. Notre Dame, IN: University of Notre Dame Press, 1982. pp. 1-15.

"Eudiche: Theodore Sturgeon," Fantasy Review 8(5): 8. May 1985.

"Fairy tales, Marchen, and modern fantasy," in: Magill, Frank N., ed. Survey of Modern Fantasy Literature, Vol 5. Englewood Cliffs, NJ: Salem Press, Inc., 1983. pp. 2267-2282.

"Frontier myth in Ray Bradbury, The," in: Olander, J. D. and M. H. Greenberg, eds. Ray Bradbury. New York: Taplinger, 1980. pp. 33-54.

"Iconography of Science Fiction Art," in: Cowart, David, ed. Twentieth Century American Science Fiction Writers. Detroit: Gale, 1981. v. 2, pp. 245-254.

"Instrumentalities of the Body: The Mechanization of Human Form in Science Fiction," in: Dunn, Thomas P., ed. The Mechanical God. Westport: Greenwood, 1982. pp. 211-224.

"Known and the unknown: structure and image in science fiction, The," in: Clareson, T. D., ed. Many Futures, Many Worlds. Kent, Ohio: Kent State University Press, 1977. pp. 94-116.

"Limits of science fiction, The," Extrapolation 14(1):30-38. December 1972.

"Majesty of Kindness: Dialectic of Cordwainer Smith," by G. K. Wolfe and C. T. Williams. in: Clareson, Thomas D., ed. Voices For the Future, Vol. 3. Bowling Green: Popular Press, 1984. pp. 52-74.

"Murray Leinster," in: Cowart, David, ed. Twentieth-Century American Science-Fiction Writers, Part 1: A-L. Detroit: Gale, 1981. pp. 290-297. (Dictionary of Literary Biography, v. 8)

Wolfe, G. K. (Continued)

"Mythic structures in Cordwainer Smith's 'The Game of Rat and Dragon'," _Science Fiction Studies_ 4(2):144-150. July 1977.

"Nuclear Rhetoric in Del Rey's _Nerves_," _Foundation_ 32: 68-75. November 1984.

"Ray Bradbury," in: Cowart, David, ed. _Twentieth-Century American Science Fiction Writers, Part 1: A-L_. Detroit: Gale, 1981. pp. 61-76. (Dictionary of Literary Biography, v. 8)

"Remaking of Zero: Beginning of the End," in: Rabkin, E. S., ed. _The End of the World_. Carbondale: Southern Illinois University Press, 1983. pp. 1-19.

"Right of things to come, The," in: Remington, T. J., ed. _Selected Proceedings of the 1978 SFRA National Conference_. Cedar Falls, Iowa: Univ. of Northern Iowa, 1979. pp. 255-259.

"Rocket and the hearth, The," in: Remington, T. J., ed. _Selected Proceedings of the 1978 SFRA National Conference_. Cedar Falls, Iowa: Univ. of Northern Iowa, 1979. pp. 22-29.

"Science fiction film," _Arizona English Bulletin_ 51(1):66-75. October 1972.

"Short Fiction of Arthur C. Clarke, The," in: Magill, Frank N., ed. _Survey of Science Fiction Literature_, Vol. 4. Englewood Cliffs, NJ: Salem Press, 1979. pp. 1926-1929.

"Short fiction of Borges, The," in: Magill, Frank N., ed. _Survey of Modern Fantasy Literature_, Vol 3. Englewood Cliffs, NJ: Salem Press, Inc., 1983. pp. 1457-1464.

"Short Fiction of Hoffmann, The," in: Magill, Frank N., ed. _Survey of Modern Fantasy Literature_, Vol 4. Englewood Cliffs, NJ: Salem Press, Inc., 1983. pp. 1547-1553.

"Short fiction of Serling, The," in: Magill, Frank N., ed. _Survey of Modern Fantasy Literature_, Vol 4. Englewood Cliffs, NJ: Salem Press, Inc., 1983. pp. 1684-1685.

"Special problems of science fiction," _Writer_ 89(5):12-14. May 1976.

"Symbolic fantasy," _Genre_ 8(3):194-209. September 1975.

"To borrow or not to borrow: Benford and Faulkner," _Fantasy Review_ 8(4): 9-10, 12. April 1985.

"Vonnegut and the metaphor of science fiction: _The Sirens of Titan_," _Journal of Popular Culture_ 5(4):964-969. Spring 1972.

Wolfe, Gene

"Aussiecon II," _SFWA Bulletin_ 19(3): 4-6. Fall 1985.

"Few Points About Knife Throwing," _Fantasy Newsletter_ 6(4): 6-7. April 1983.

"Helioscope," _Empire: For the SF Writer_ 6(1): 4-5. Winter 1980.

"How Science Will Conquer the World for Fantasy," _Fantasy Newsletter_ 5(3): 5-7. March 1982.

"On the Tolkien toll-free Fifties freeway," _Vector_ 75: 7-11. July 1975.

"Organizing a life to write," _Empire: For the SF Writer_ 4(2): 25-26. February 1979. (Reprinted from _Empire_ No. 9.)

"Our Young Gamer," _Vector_ 118: 21-23. February 1984.

"Profession of Science Fiction, XVII," _Foundation_ 18: 5-11. January 1980.

"Special Problems of Science Fiction," in: Burick, A. S., ed. _The Writer's Handbook_. Boston: Writer, 1978. pp. 475-479.

"What do they mean, SF?" _Writer_ 93(8):11-13,45-46. August 1980. also in: _SFWA Bulletin_ 16(1):20-25. Winter 1981.

"Where I Get My Ideas," in: Wingrove, David, ed. _The Science Fiction Source Book_. New York: Van Nostrand, 1984. pp. 84-85.

"Writer's Conferences", by Gene Wolfe and G. R. R. Martin. _Empire: For the SF Writer_ 4(1): 11-14. July 1978.

"Writers: Where I Get My Ideas," _Science Fiction Chronicle_ 6(4): 20-22. January 1985.

Wolfe, Milton

"Amazing Stories Annual," in: Tymn, M. B. and Ashley, Mike. _Science Fiction, Fantasy, and Weird Fiction Magazines_. Westport, CT: Greenwood, 1985. pp. 49-51.

"Amazing Stories Quarterly," in: Tymn, M. B. and Ashley, Mike. _Science Fiction, Fantasy, and Weird Fiction Magazines_. Westport, CT: Greenwood, 1985. pp. 51-57.

"Astonishing Stories," by Milton Wolfe and R. H. Thompson. in: Tymn, M. B. and Ashley, Mike. _Science Fiction, Fantasy, and Weird Fiction Magazines_. Westport, CT: Greenwood, 1985. pp. 117-122.

Wolff, Eva

Utopie und Humor. Aspekte der Phantastik im Werk Paul Scheerbarts. Frankfurt: Laing, 1982. 331 p.

Wolff, Heinz

"Future is Further Off Than You Think," in: Malik, Rex, ed. Future Imperfect. London: Pinter, 1980. pp. 55-67.

Wolff, R. L.

Golden Key: A Study of the Fiction of George MacDonald, The. New Haven: Yale University Press, 1961. 425 p.

"Are we the coming race?" Atlantic Monthly 228(3):104-106. September 1971.

Wolfhohl, Clarence

"William Morris' The Wood Beyond the World: the Victorian world vs. the mythic eternities," Mythlore 6(3):29-32. Summer 1979.

Wolfson, Jill

"'Last Unicorn' Is Alive, Well and Casting His Spell," San Jose Mercury, August 29, 1982. in: NewsBank. Literature. 39:A1-2. 1981/82.

Wolicki, Krzysztof

"Przed powrotem na Ziemie," Tworczosc No. 1. 1966.

Wolinsky, Richard

"Rigel Interviews Anne McCaffrey," by Richard Wolinsky and Laurence Davidson. Rigel Science Fiction 3: 19-24. Winter 1982.

Wolk, Anthony

"On the Le Guin issue (of Science Fiction Studies)," Science Fiction Studies 3(1):95-96. March 1976. Reply, Darko Suvin, 3(2):211-212. July 1976.

"Sunstruck Forest: A Guide to the Short Fiction of Philip K. Dick," Foundation 18: 19-34. January 1980.

Wolkoff, L.

"Science fiction," Best Sellers 35:147-148. August 1975. (Book reviews)

Wollheim, D. A.

Universe Makers: Science Fiction Today, The. New York: Harper & Row, 1971. 122 p.

"Guest of honor speech, Lunacon 1968," Niekas 20:25-29. Fall 1968.

"Introduction: the best from the rest of the world," in: Wollheim, Donald A., ed. The Best From the Rest of the World. Garden City, New York: Doubleday, 1976. pp. xi-xix.

"Jack Chandler: a memoir," Science Fiction Chronicle 5(11):4. August 1984.

"News from nowhere," Science Fiction Chronicle 2(6):8-9. March 1981.

"Tolkien influence Italian right," Science Fiction Chronicle 2(6):12. March 1981.

"Valsagban a Wells-kovetok," Helikon 18(1): 117-118. 1972. (Tr. from The Universe Makers.)

Wolter, Charlotte

"Battletruck (review)," Cinefantastique 12(5/6):90. July/August 1982.

"Brainstorm," by Charlotte Wolter and Kyle Counts. Cinefantastique 14(2):16-21,54-59. December 1983/January 1984.

"Cocoon," Cinefantastique 15(3):24-25,54. July 1985.

"Iceman (review)," Cinefantastique 14(4/5):107. September 1984.

"Metalstorm," Cinefantastique 13(6)/14(1):74-83. September 1983.

"Peter Hyams on directing 2010: Odyssey II," Cinefantastique 15(2):50,56. May 1985.

"Starflight (review)," Cinefantastique 13(5):58,60. June/July 1983.

Wong, H. K.

"SF Scene in Hong Kong and Taiwan," Locus 17(3): 24-25. March 1984.

Wood, Charles

"Vonnegut effect: science fiction and beyond, The," by Karen Wood and Charles Wood. in: Klinkowitz, Jerome and John Somer, eds. The Vonnegut Statement. New York: Delacorte Press/Seymour-Lawrence, 1973. pp. 133-157.

Wood, Denis

"Empire's New Clothes," Film Quarterly 34(3): 10-16. Spring 1981.

Wood, Denis (Continued)

"Growing up among the stars: <u>Lord of the Rings</u>, <u>Once and Future King</u>, <u>The Hobbit</u>, <u>The Book of Merlyn</u> and <u>Star Wars</u>," <u>Literature/Film Quarterly</u> 6(4):327-341. Autumn 1978.

"Stars in our hearts: a critical commentary on George Lucas' <u>Star Wars</u>, The," <u>Journal of Popular Film</u> 6(3):262-279. 1978.

Wood, Edward

<u>SF Bibliographies: an Annotated Bibliography of Bibliographical Works on Science Fiction and Fantasy Fiction</u>, by R. E. Briney and Edward Wood. Chicago: Advent Publishers, 1972. 49 p.

"1958 in science fiction, part 1," <u>Science Fiction Times</u> No. 309:1-2. February 1959.

"1958 in science fiction, part 2," <u>Science Fiction Times</u> No. 310:1-2. March 1959.

"1959 in science fiction," <u>Science Fiction Times</u> No. 330:1-4. January (1) 1960.

"1960 in science fiction," <u>Science Fiction Times</u> No. 356:1-5. February (2) 1961.

"1961 in science fiction," <u>Science Fiction Times</u> No. 380:1-3. February (2) 1962.

"1962 in science fiction," <u>Science Fiction Times</u> No. 399/400:3-6. January/February 1963.

"1963 in science fiction," <u>Science Fiction Times</u> No. 412:3-8. February 1964.

"1964 in science fiction," <u>Science Fiction Times</u> No. 424:3-6,9. February 1965.

"1966 in science fiction," <u>Science Fiction Times</u> No. 461:20,26-27. December 1968.

"Science fiction magazines: a selective prospective," <u>Science Fiction Times</u> No. 369:10-12. September 1961.

Wood, Karen

"Vonnegut effect: science fiction and beyond, The," by Karen Wood and Charles Wood. in: Klinkowitz, Jerome and John Somer, eds. <u>The Vonnegut Statement</u>. New York: Delacorte Press/Seymour-Lawrence, 1973. pp. 133-157.

Wood, Michael

"Kiss tomorrow hello," <u>American Film</u> 2(6):14-17. April 1977.

"Sinister pastoral," <u>New Society</u> 2:646. May 2, 1968.

"Tolkien's fictions," in: Tucker, Nicholas, ed. <u>Suitable for Children: Controversies in Children's Literature</u>. Berkeley: Univ. of California Press, 1976. pp. 165-172. (Repr. from <u>New Society</u>, Mar. 27, 1969.)

Wood, Robin

"On Nosferatu," <u>Film Comment</u> 12(3):4-9. May/June 1976.

Wood, Susan

<u>Language of the Night: Essays on Fantasy and Science Fiction, The</u>, by U. K. Le Guin and ed. by Susan Wood. New York: Putnam, 1979. 270 p.

"Discovering worlds: the fiction of Ursula K. Le Guin," in: Clareson, T. D., ed. <u>Voices for the Future: Essays on Major Science Fiction Writers</u>, Vol. 2. Ohio: Bowling Green Univ. Popular Press, 1979. pp. 154-180.

"Discovering Worlds: the fiction of Ursula K. Le Guin," in: <u>Ursula K. Le Guin</u>, ed. by Harold Bloom. New York: Chelsea House, 1986. pp. 183-210.

"Fandom is a way of life," in: World Science Fiction Convention, 1976. <u>MidAmerican Program Book</u>. Kansas City: MidAmerican, 1976. pp. 85-88.

"Introduction," in: Compton, D. G. <u>Continuous Katherine Mortenhoe</u>. Boston: Gregg, 1980. pp. v-xx.

"James Tiptree, Jr.," in: Bleiler, E. F., ed. <u>Science Fiction Writers</u>. New York: Scribners, 1982. pp. 531-541.

"Kate Wilhelm as a Writer," <u>Starship</u> 17(4): 7-16. Fall 1980. (Originally Published as the introduction to: Wilhelm, Kate. <u>The Mile-Long Spaceship</u>. Boston: Gregg Press, 1980.)

"Women and science fiction," <u>Algol</u> 16(1):9-18. Winter 1978/1979.

"Women and science fiction," in: Williamson, Jack, ed. <u>Teaching Science Fiction: Education for Tomorrow</u>. Philadelphia: Owlswick, 1980. pp. 65-72.

"Year in fantasy: 1978, The," in: Carr, Terry, ed. <u>The Year's Finest Fantasy</u>, Vol. 2. New York: Berkley/Putnam, 1979. pp. 269-277.

Woodbridge, H. C.

<u>Jack London: A Bibliography</u>, by H. C. Woodbridge, John London and G. H. Tweney. Georgetown, California: Talisman Press, 1966. 385 p. Milwood, New York: Kraus Reprint, 1973. Enlarged edition, 554 p.

Woodburn, J. H.

"Science fiction as a factor in science education," by E. H. Gross and J. H. Woodburn. Science Education 43(1):28-31. February 1959.

Woodcock, George

"Darkness violated by light: a revisionist view of H. G. Wells, The," Malahat Review: An International Quarterly of Life and Letters (Victoria, Canada) 26:144-160. 1973.

"Darkness Violated by Light: A Revisionist View of H. G. Wells," Malahat Review No. 26: 144-160. April 1973.

"Equilibrations of freedom, part 1, The," Georgia Straight p. 5,9. October 21-28, 1976.

"Equilibrations of freedom, part 2, The," Georgia Straight (Vancouver, British Columbia) 10:6. October 28-November 4, 1976.

"Huxley, Aldous," in: Woodcock, George, ed. 20th Century Fiction. Chicago: St. James, 1985. pp. 318-321.

"Orwell, George," in: Woodcock, George, ed. 20th Century Fiction. Chicago: St. James, 1985. pp. 507-509.

"Utopias in negative," Sewanee Review 64(1):81-97. Winter 1956.

Woodcock, John

"Garden in the machine: variations on spaceship Earth, The," Michigan Quarterly Review 18(2):308-317. Spring 1979.

"Literature and science since Huxley," Interdisciplinary Science Reviews 3(1):31-45. 1978.

"Science fiction and the real future," Alternative Futures 2(2):25-37. Spring 1979.

"Teaching science fiction: unique challenges," Science Fiction Studies 6(3):249-262. November 1979. (Proceedings of the MLA special session, December 1978)

Woodman, Tom

"Science fiction, religion and transcendence," in: Parrinder, Patrick, ed. Science Fiction: A Critical Guide. New York: Longman, 1979. pp. 110-130.

Woods, Bob

"Alien World of Wayne Barlowe," Future Life 31: 58-63. December 1981.

Woods, K. P.

"Edward Bellamy: Author and Economist," The Bookman 7(5): 398-401. July 1898.

Woods, L. D.

"Speculating on speculative fiction," AB Bookman's Weekly 74(14):2153-2154. October 1, 1984.

Woods, Richard

"Figure of Taliesin in Charles Williams' Arthuriad," Mythlore 10(1): 11-16, 29. Spring 1983.

Woodson, W.

"Movie dragons," Nature Magazine 41(9):461-463. November 1948. (does not apply)

Woodward, Kathleen

"On Aggression: William Golding's Lord of the Flies," in: Rabkin, E. S., et. al., eds. No Place Else. Carbondale: Southern Illinois University Press, 1983. pp. 199-224.

Woolever, J. D.

"Science fiction for science students," Science Education 35(5):284-286. December 1951. Same, condensed: Education Digest 17:46-47. April 1952.

Wooley, Chuck

"History of the SF comic book," Science Fiction Times (Boston) 1(7):11. March 1980.

Woolfolk, Steve

"Checklist of Monarch Books," Science Fiction Collector 14: 34-37. May 1981.

Woolston, Stan

"NFFF news," Science Fiction Times No. 462:6. January 1969.

World SF Convention

Proceedings of the 20th World Science Fiction Convention; Chicon III. Chicago: Advent, 1963. 208 p.

Wright, F. W., jr.

"When rejections are rampant," Empire for the SF Writer 9(3): 9. Spring 1985.

Wright, Gene

Science Fiction Image: The Illustrated Encyclopedia of Science Fiction in Film, Television, Radio and the Theater. New York: Facts on File, 1983. 336 p.

Wright, J. W.

"TV's Star Trek; how they mix science fact with fiction," Popular Science 191(6):72-74. December 1967.

Wrobel, Carsten

"Atlan: im auftrag des imperialismus," Science Fiction Times No. 134:10-12. August 1974.

Wrzos, Joseph

"Girl, the Gold Watch, & Everything, The," in: Magill, Frank N., ed. Survey of Science Fiction Literature, Vol. 2. Englewood Cliffs, NJ: Salem Press, 1979. pp. 883-887.

"Needle in a Haystack: In Search of Robert Duncan Milne," Fantasy Commentator 4(4): 195-200. Winter 1982.

"On reading the past," Inside-Riverside Quarterly p. 5. Summer 1964.

Wu, W. F.

Yellow Peril: Chinese Americans in Fiction, 1850-1940. Handem, CT: Shoe String, 1982. 241 p.

"Another View," Locus 17(12): 28. December 1984.

"Asian as Alien: Fantasy's Yellow Peril," Fantasy Newsletter 5(5): 25-26, 37. June 1982.

"Dr. Wu"s Lost & Found Emporium," Fantasy Newsletter 6(8): 30. September 1983.

"Producing the model 'A': science fiction in China," Amazing 58(3):50-53. September 1984.

Wuntch, Philip

"Arrogance With a Smile," Dallas Morning News August 29, 1984. in: NewsBank. Film and Television FTV 22: A14. 1984.

Wurfel, Clifford

Introduction to the J. Lloyd Eaton Collection of Science Fiction and Fantasy. Riverside: University of California, Riverside Library, 1979. 13 p.

Wuth, Evelyn

"Science fiction in Denver's Kennedy High School," Cthulhu Calls 4(2)8-12. January 1977.

Wyatt, K. K.

"BEMS (Bug-Eyed Monsters) and Reality," Christian Science Monitor p. 22. November 20, 1981.

Wyckoff, P. C.

"Douglas Adams," Houston Post April 21, 1985. in: NewsBank. Literature.. 100:A8-A9. May 1985

Wydmuch, Marek

"Dichter des Abstellgleises, Der: Stefan Grabinski," in: Rottensteiner, Franz, ed. Quarber Merkur. Frankfurt: Suhrkamp, 1979. pp. 183-208.

Wyka, Marta

"Przygody kosmicznego Guliwera," Tworczosc No. 4 1962.

Wykes, Alan

H. G. Wells in the Cinema. London: Jupiter, 1977. 175 p.

Wylie, Philip

"Science fiction and sanity in an age of crisis," in: Bretnor, Reginald, ed. Modern Science Fiction: Its Meaning and Its Future. New York: Coward McCann, 1953. Reprinted, Chicago: Advent, 1979. pp. 221-242.

Wymer, T. L.

Intersections: The Elements of Fiction in Science Fiction, by T. L. Wymer et al. Bowling Green, OH: Popular Press, 1978. 130 p.

Twentieth Century American Science Fiction Writers, by David Cowart and Thomas Wymer. Detroit: Gale Research, 1981. 2 v. (Dictionary of Literary Biography, 8)

"Cordwainer Smith: satirist or male chauvinist," Extrapolation 14(2):157-162. May 1973.

"Machines and the Meaning of Human in the Novels of Kurt Vonnegut, Jr.," in: Dunn, T. P., ed. The Mechanical God. Westport: Greenwood, 1982. pp. 41-52.

Wymer, T. L. (Continued)

"Naturalism, Aestheticism and Beyond: Tradition and Innovation in the Work of Thomas M. Disch," in: Clareson, T. D., ed. <u>Voices For the Future, Vol. 3</u>. Bowling Green: Popular Press, 1984. pp. 186-219.

"Perception and value in science fiction," <u>Extrapolation</u> 16(2):103-112. May 1975.

"Perception and value in science fiction," in: Clareson, T. D., ed. <u>Many Futures, Many Worlds</u>. Kent, Ohio: Kent State University Press, 1977. pp. 1-14. (revised)

"Philip Jose Farmer," in: Cowart, David, ed. <u>Twentieth-Century American Science-Fiction Writers, Part 1: A-L</u>. Detroit: Gale, 1981. pp. 169-182. (Dictionary of Literary Biography, v. 8)

"Philip Jose Farmer: the trickster as artist," in: Clareson, T. D., ed. <u>Voices for the Future: Essays on Major Science Fiction Writers</u>, Vol. 2. Bowling Green, Ohio: Popular Press, 1979. pp. 34-55.

"Speculative fiction, bibliographies, and Philip Jose Farmer," <u>Extrapolation</u> 18(1):59-72. December 1976.

"Swiftian satire of Kurt Vonnegut, Jr., The," in: Clareson, T. D., ed. <u>Voices for the Future: Essays on Major Science Fiction Writers</u>, Vol. 1. Bowling Green, Ohio: Popular Press, 1976. pp. 238-262.

Wyss, W. A.

"Conception: Logan's Run," <u>Cinefantastique</u> 5(2):6-9. Fall 1976.

"Production: Logan's Run," by F. S. Clarke, Steve Rubin and W. A. Wyss. <u>Cinefantastique</u> 5(2):16-21. Fall 1976.

Wytenbroek, Jacqueline

"Science Fiction and Fantasy," <u>Extrapolation</u> 23(4): 321-332. Winter 1982.

Y

Yaffe, James

"Modern trend toward meaningful Martians," Saturday Review 43(17):22-23. April 23, 1960. (Book reviews)

"On fission and fish," Saturday Review pp. 14,16. April 20, 1961. (Book reviews)

"Well-trod way to holocaust, The," Saturday Review p. 21. June 4, 1960. (Book reviews)

Yagyu, Nozomyu

Narnia no Kuni wa Tooku nai: C. S. Lewis no Fantasy no Sckai. Tokyo: Shinkyo, 1981. 270 p.

Yamagata, Kazumi

"G. K. Chesterton-Kai: the Chesterton Society in Japan," Chesterton Review 2(1):92-93. Fall/Winter 1975/1976.

Yamano, Koichi

"English Literature and British Science Fiction," Foundation 30: 26-30. March 1984.

Yandell, Steven

"Transcosmic journeys in The Chronicles of Narnia," Mythlore 12(1):9-23. Autumn 1985.

Yankelovich, Skelly & White, Inc.

Omni Reader Involvement Study. s.l.: Yankelovich, Skelly & White, Inc., 1980. 33 p.

Yarbro, C. Q.

"Cinderella's Revenge: Twists on Fairy Tale and Mythic Themes in the Work of Stephen King," in: Underwood, Tim, and Miller, Chuck, eds. Fear Itself. Columbia, PA: Underwood/Miller 1982. pp. 45-55.

"This is another fine mess you've got us into: an essay on suspense techniques in science fiction," PSFQ (Cupertino, California) 3/4:6-8. 1978/1979.

Yarrow, Ralph

"Consciousness, the fantastic, and the reading process," in: Collins, R. A., ed. Scope of the Fantastic: Theory, Technique, Major Authors. Westport: Greenwood, 1985. pp. 83-94.

Yefremov, I. A.

Sooi Efremov, Ivan

Yep, Lawrence

"Attack of the Giant Teenage Space Dogs: Notes of a Science Fiction Film Fan," Top of the News 39(1): 92-94. Fall 1982.

"Fantasy and reality," Horn Book 54:136. April 1978.

Yerkes, Susan

"His Vision Probes 21st Century," Witchita Eagle-Beacon in: NewsBank. Literature. 64:G7-G8. January 1985.

Yershov, Peter

Science Fiction and Utopian Fantasy in Soviet Literature. New York: Research Program on the U.S.S.R., 1954. 66 p.

Yoke, C. B.

Death and the Serpent: Immortality in Science Fiction and Fantasy, by C. B. Yoke and D. M. Hassler. Westport, CT: Greenwood, 1985. 235 p.

Roger Zelazny. Mercer Island, WA: Starmont, 1979. 111 p.

Roger Zelazny and Andre Norton: Proponents of Individualism. Columbus: State Library of Ohio, 1979. 26 p.

Yoke, C. B. (Continued)

"Amber Series, The," in: Magill, Frank N., ed. Survey of Modern Fantasy Literature, Vol 1. Englewood Cliffs, NJ: Salem Press, Inc., 1983. pp. 29-35.

"Behold the Man," in: Magill, Frank N., ed. Survey of Science Fiction Literature, Vol. 1. Englewood Cliffs, NJ: Salem Press, 1979. pp. 157-162.

"Brak the Barbarian," in: Magill, Frank N., ed. Survey of Modern Fantasy Literature, Vol 1. Englewood Cliffs, NJ: Salem Press, Inc., 1983. pp. 166-168.

"Burn Witch Burn!" in: Magill, Frank N., ed. Survey of Modern Fantasy Literature, Vol 1. Englewood Cliffs, NJ: Salem Press, Inc., 1983. pp. 181-183.

"Dark Universe," in: Magill, Frank N., ed. Survey of Science Fiction Literature, Vol. 1. Englewood Cliffs, NJ: Salem Press, 1979. pp. 474-479.

"Dream Master, The," in: Magill, Frank N., ed. Survey of Science Fiction Literature, Vol. 2. Englewood Cliffs, NJ: Salem Press, 1979. pp. 608-613.

"Lord of Light," in: Magill, Frank N., ed. Survey of Science Fiction Literature, Vol. 3. Englewood Cliffs, NJ: Salem Press, 1979. pp. 1251-1256.

"Mask of Circe, The," in: Magill, Frank N., ed. Survey of Modern Fantasy Literature, Vol 2. Englewood Cliffs, NJ: Salem Press, Inc., 1983. pp. 980-982.

"Ship of Ishtar, The," in: Magill, Frank N., ed. Survey of Modern Fantasy Literature, Vol 3. Englewood Cliffs, NJ: Salem Press, Inc., 1983. pp. 1407-1411.

"Slaves of Sleep," in: Magill, Frank N., ed. Survey of Modern Fantasy Literature, Vol 4. Englewood Cliffs, NJ: Salem Press, Inc., 1983. pp. 1763-1765.

"From Alienation of Personal Triumph: The Science Fiction of Joan D. Vinge," in: Staicar, Tom, ed. The Feminine Eye. New York: Ungar, 1982. pp. 103-130.

"List of works on immortality in science fiction," in: Yoke, C. B. and Hassler, D. M., eds. Death and the Serpent. Westport, CT: Greenwood, 1985. pp. 209-222.

"Personality metamorphosis in Roger Zelazny's 'The Doors of His Face, the Lamps of His Mouth'," Extrapolation 21(2):100-121. Summer 1980.

"Precious Metal in White Clay," Extrapolation 21(3): 197-208. Fall 1980.

"Roger Zelazny's Bold New Mythologies," in: Staicar, Tom, ed. Critical Encounters II. New York: Ungar, 1982. pp. 73-89.

"Roger Zelazny's form and chaos philosophy," Science Fiction: A Review of Speculative Literature 2(2):129-150. December 1979.

"Vinge and Vegetation," Fantasy Newsletter 5(10): 24-26. November 1982.

"What a Piece of Work is Man: Mechanical Gods in the Fiction of Roger Zelazny," in: Dunn, Thomas P., ed. The Mechanical God. Westport: Greenwood, 1982. pp. 63-74.

"Why was I born if it wasn't forever?" in: Yoke, C. B. and Hassler, D. M., eds. Death and the Serpent. Westport, CT: Greenwood, 1985. pp. 7-18.

"Zelazny's Damnation Alley: hell noh," Extrapolation 15(1):6-16. December 1973.

Yolen, Jane

Touch Magic: Fantasy, Faerie and Folklore in the Literature of Childhood. New York: Philomel/Putnam, 1981. 96 p.

"Dealing With Dragons," Horn Book 60(3):380-388. June 1984.

"Here There Be Dragons," Top of the News 39(1): 54-56. Fall 1982.

"Modern mythmakers, The," Language Arts 53(5):491-495. May 1976.

"Tough magic," Top of the News 35(2):183-187. Winter 1979.

"Wood between the worlds, The," Mythlore 11(3): 5-7. Winter/Spring 1985.

Yong-Lie, Ye

"1982: foreign SF in Chinese," Locus 16(7):15. July 1983.

"Chinese SF translations," Locus 15(8):15,19. August 1982.

"Chinese SF," in: Barron, Neil, ed. Anatomy of Wonder. 2nd ed. New York: Bowker, 1981. pp. 497-506.

"Development of SF in China," Foundation 34: 57-69. Autumn 1985.

"Robert A. Heinlein in Shanghai," Locus 16(1):1,19. January 1983.

"SF in China," Locus 14(10):1,15,18. November 1981.

"SF magazines in China," Locus 16(5):13. May 1983.

Yong-Lie, Ye (Continued)

"Shanghai meeting," <u>Locus</u> 16(10):23. October 1983.

Young, B. A.

"Space time," <u>Punch</u> p. 820. June 1, 1966. (Book reviews)

Young, R. V., Jr.

"<u>Love in the Ruins</u>," in: Magill, Frank N., ed. <u>Survey of Science Fiction Literature</u>, Vol. 3. Englewood Cliffs, NJ: Salem Press, 1979. pp. 1278-1283.

"<u>Men Like Gods</u>," in: Magill, Frank N., ed. <u>Survey of Science Fiction Literature</u>, Vol. 3. Englewood Cliffs, NJ: Salem Press, 1979. pp. 1375-1379.

"<u>Planet of the Apes</u>," in: Magill, Frank N., ed. <u>Survey of Science Fiction Literature</u>, Vol. 4. Englewood Cliffs, NJ: Salem Press, 1979. pp. 1692-1696.

Young, Stephen

"Question: automation, a utopia," <u>Vector</u> 40: 7-9. February 1968.

Youngberg, Karin

"Job and the gargoyles: a study of <u>The Man Who Was Thursday</u>," <u>Chesterton Review</u> 2:240-252. 1976.

Youngberg, R. T.

<u>Dorothy L. Sayers: A Reference Guide</u>. Boston: G. K. Hall, 1982. 178 p.

Youngblood, Gene

"Free Press Interview: Arthur C. Clarke," <u>Los Angeles Free Press</u> p. 42-43, 47. April 25, 1969. (<u>Underground Newspaper Collection</u>, Reel 21, Title 3)

Yuan, Frederick

"Immortality and Robert Silverberg," in: Tolley, M. J., ed. <u>The Stellar Gauge</u>. Victoria, Australia: Norstrilia, 1980. pp. 239-258.

Yunji, Tan

"SF in China: A Brief Historical Review," <u>Foundation</u> 26: 72-78. October 1982.

Z

Zadig (Pseud.)

"J. H. Rosny," _Revue Bleue_ 13:533-535.
1900.

Zador, Leslie

"George Pal: father of modern science
fiction," by Leslie Zador and Mike Hyatt.
Los Angeles Free Press p. 36. August 20,
1971.

Zahorski, K. J.

_Fantasists on Fantasy: A Collection of
Critical Reflections_, by R. H. Boyer and K. J.
Zahorski. New York: Avon Discus, 1984. 287 p.

_Fantasy Literature: A Core Collection and
Reference Guide_, by M. B. Tymn, K. J.
Zahorski, and R. H. Boyer. New York: Bowker,
1979. 273 p.

_Lloyd Alexander, Evangeline Walton Ensley,
Kenneth Morris: A Primary and Secondary
Bibliography_ by K. J. Zahorski and R. H.
Boyer. Boston: G. K. Hall, 1981. 291 p.

"On fantasy," by R. H. Boyer and K. J.
Zahorski. in: Tymn, Marshall B., Kenneth J.
Zahorski, and Robert H. Boyer. _Fantasy
Literature: a Core Collection and Reference
Guide_. New York: Bowker, 1979. pp. 3-83.

"Science fiction and fantasy literature:
clarification through juxtaposition," by R. H.
Boyer and K. J. Zahorski. _Wisconsin English
Journal_ 18(3):2-8. April 1976.

"Secondary Worlds of High Fantasy, The," by K.
J. Zahorski and R. H. Boyer. in: Schlobin,
Roger C., ed. _The Aesthetics of Fantasy
Literature and Art_. Notre Dame, IN:
University of Notre Dame Press, 1982. pp.
56-81.

Zajong, R. B.

"Some effects of the 'space' serials," _The
Public Opinion Quarterly_ 18(4):367-374.
Winter 1954.

Zak, M. W.

"_Grass is Singing_: a little novel about
emotions," _Contemporary Literature_
14(4):481-489. Autumn 1973.

Zakharchenko, Vasil

"Future as artists see it, The," _Soviet
Life_ pp. 24-27. April 1975.

Zamiatin, Evengii

"Autobiography," in: Zamiatin, Yevgeny. _A
Soviet Heretic: Essays of Yevgeny Zamiatin_,
ed. by Mirra Ginsburg. Chicago: University of
Chicago Press, 1970. pp. 3-14.

"H. G. Wells," in: Zamiatin, Yevgeny. _A
Soviet Heretic: Essays of Yevgeny Zamiatin_,
ed. by Mirra Ginsburg. Chicago: University of
Chicago Press, 1970. pp. 259-290.

"H. G. Wells," in: Ginsburg, Mirra, ed. _A
Soviet Heretic: Essays by Yevgeny Zamgatin_.
Chicago and London: University of Chicago
Press, 1971. pp. 259-290.

Zander, A. R.

"Science and fiction; an interdisciplinary
approach," _American Journal of Physics_
43(1):9-12. January 1975.

Zanger, Jules

"_Five Plays_ and _Plays of Gods and Men_,"
in: Magill, Frank N., ed. _Survey of Modern
Fantasy Literature_, Vol 2. Englewood Cliffs,
NJ: Salem Press, Inc., 1983. pp. 557-560.

"_Gods of Pegana, The_," in: Magill, Frank
N., ed. _Survey of Modern Fantasy
Literature_, Vol 2. Englewood Cliffs, NJ:
Salem Press, Inc., 1983. pp. 625-627.

"_Rose and the Ring, The_," in: Magill, Frank
N., ed. _Survey of Modern Fantasy
Literature_, Vol 3. Englewood Cliffs, NJ:
Salem Press, Inc., 1983. pp. 1335-1337.

Zanger, Jules (Continued)

"Three Mulla-Mulgars, The," in: Magill, Frank N., ed. Survey of Modern Fantasy Literature, Vol 4. Englewood Cliffs, NJ: Salem Press, Inc., 1983. pp. 1926-1929.

"Goblins, morlocks, and weasels: classic fantasy and the industrial revolution," Children's Literature in Education 8(4):154-162. Winter 1977.

"Heroic Fantasy and Social Reality: ex nihilo nihil fit," in: Schlobin, R. C., ed. The Aesthetics of Fantasy Literature and Art. Notre Dame, IN: University of Notre Dame Press, 1982. pp. 226-236.

"Poe's 'Bernice': philosophical fantasy and its pitfalls," in: Collins, R. A. and H. D. Pearce, eds. The Scope of the Fantastic: Theory, Technique, Major Authors. Westport, CT: Greenwood Press, 1985. pp. 135-142.

Zaniello, T. A.

"'Our Future Tends to be Prehistoric' Science Fiction and Robert Smithson," Arts Magazine 52(9): 114-117. May 1978.

Zaniello, Thomas

"Outopia in Jorge Luis Borges' fiction," Extrapolation 9(1):3-17. December 1967.

Zanotto, Piero

Fantascienza, La. Padova: 1967. 63 p.

"Cartoons e fantascienza," Fantascienza Minoro No. 1. 1967. (CF: World Encyclopedia of Comics.)

Zantovska-Murray, Irena

"Bibliography of general bibliographies of SF literature, A," by Irena Zantovska-Murray and Darko Suvin. Science Fiction Studies 5(3):271-286. November 1978.

Zasadinski, Eugene

"Using Science Fiction to Build Research Skills," English Journal 72(4): 69-70. April 1983.

Zavala, I. M.

"Dreams of Reality: Enlightened Hopes for an Unattainable Spain," Studies in Eighteenth-Century Culture, Vol. 6, 1977. pp. 459-470.

Zavgorodny, B. A.

"Letter from Russia," Locus 18(8): 33. August 1985.

"News from the Soviet Union," Locus 18(12): 20-28. December 1985.

Zebrowski, George

"Dreaming again," by Jack Dann and George Zebrowski. in: Dann, Jack and George Zebrowski, eds. Faster Than Light. New York: Ace, 1976. pp. xiii-xviii.

"Herding Words: A Journal," Foundation 28: 5-20. July 1983.

"How it happened: a chronology," by Pamela Sargent and George Zebrowski. Science Fiction Studies 4(2):129-134. July 1977.

"More than human?: androids, cyborgs and others," by George Zebrowski and Patricia Warrick. in: Warrick, Patricia, ed. Science Fiction: Contemporary Mythology. New York: Harper, 1978. pp. 294-307.

"Science fiction and the visual media," in: Bretnor, Reginald, ed. Science Fiction Today and Tomorrow. New York: Harper, 1974. pp. 46-65.

"Why it happened: some notes and opinions," Science Fiction Studies 4(2):136-137. July 1977.

Zelazny, Roger

"Author's Choice," Vector 65: 42-44. May/June 1973.

"Burnt-out case, A?" SF Commentary 54:22-28. November 1978. (Transcript of Zelazny's guest of honor speech at Unicon (Australia), Easter 1978)

"Cordwainer Smith," Riverside Quarterly 3(3): 232-233. August 1968.

"Forum: some science fiction parameters: a biased view," Galaxy 36(6):6-11. July 1975.

"J. R. R. Tolkien," Locus No. 149:3. September 14, 1973.

"On writing and stories; guest editorial," Science Fiction Times pp. 5-6. ca. October 1967.

"Parts that are only glimpsed: three reflexes," Empire: For the SF Writer 4(2): 4-5. February 1979. (Reprinted from SFWA Bulletin No. 67.)

"Process of Composing, The," in: Wingrove, David, ed. The Science Fiction Source Book. New York: Van Nostrand, 1984. pp. 85-86.

Zelazny, Roger (Continued)

"Science fiction and how it got that way," _The Writer_ 84(5):15-18. May 1971.

"Writers: The Process of Composing, The," _Science Fiction Chronicle_ 6(4): 22. January 1985.

Zettl, Guenter

"Franz Rottensteiner im Gespraech," _Science Fiction Times_ (Germany) 25(1):14-16. January 1983.

"Interview mit Frederik Pohl," _Science Fiction Times_ (Germany) 26(6):5-9. June 1984.

"Interview mit Peter Schatt-Schneider," _Science Fiction Times_ (Germany) 26(9):5-8. September 1984.

"Osten in Brighton; Seacon 1984," _Science Fiction Times_ (Germany) 26(6):10-12. June 1984.

Zeugner, J. F.

"American fantasy of Japan in the 1890's and 1970's, The," in: Collins, R. A., ed. _Scope of the Fantastic: Culture, Biography, Themes, Children's Literature_. Westport: Greenwood, 1985. pp. 11-22.

Zgorselski, Andrzej

Fantastyka, utopia, science fiction: ze studiow nad rozwojem gatunkow. Warsaw: Panstwowe Wydawn. Nauk., 1980. 203 p. 80-149438.

"(Types of a presented world in fantastic literature)," _Zagadnienia Rodzajow Literackich_ 10(2):116-127. 1968.

"Begriff des Aquivalentes in der Literatur forschung," _Quarber Merkur_ 40:45-51. March 1975.

"Is science fiction a genre of fantastic literature?" _Science Fiction Studies_ 6(3):296-303. November 1979.

"Nachbemerkung zu dem Aufsatz 'Sum Verstandnis der Phantastik'," _Quarber Merkur_ 41:54-55. September 1975.

"Typen der in der phantastischen Literatur dargestellten Welt," _Quarber Merkur_ 39:40-47. January 1975.

"Types of a presented world in fantastic literature, The," _Problems of Literary Genres_ 10(2):120. 1968.

"Zum Verstandnis der Phantastik," _Quarber Merkur_ 41:3-8. September 1975.

Zicree, M. S.

Twilight Zone Companion. New York: Bantam, 1982. 447 p. (also appeared in _Twilight Zone_, 1981-1983.)

Ziegler, Dale

"Ring-Wraiths: or therein Bakshi again," _Mythlore_ 6(1): 37-38. Winter 1979.

Ziegler, Gilette

"Science fiction dans les collections populaires, La," _Europe Revue Mensuell_ No. 139/140:87-92. July/August 1957.

Ziegler, J. D.

"Primitive, Newtonian, and Einsteinian fantasies: Three worldviews," in: Collins, R. A., ed. _Scope of the Fantastic: Theory, Technique, Major Authors_. Westport: Greenwood, 1985. pp. 69-78.

Ziegler, Thomas

Zeit der Stasis. Munchen: Heyne, 1979. 251 p.

"Science Fiction made in Germany: Anthologien aus Deutschland," _Science Fiction Times_ (Germany) 25(5):5-8. May 1983.

Zillig, Werner

"Trends in der deutscher Science Fiction Szene," _Science Fiction Times_ (Germany) 25(6):9-12. June 1983.

Zimbardo, R. A.

Tolkien and the Critics: Essays on J. R. R. Tolkien's The Lord of the Rings, ed. by N. D. Isaacs and R. A. Zimbardo. Notre Dame, Indiana: University of Notre Dame Press, 1968. 296 p.

Tolkien: New Critical Perspectives, by N. D. Isaacs and R. A. Zimbardo. Lexington: University Press of Kentucky, 1981. 175 p.

"Medieval-Renaissance Vision of the Lord of the Rings," in: Isaac, N. D., ed. _Tolkien: New Critical Perspectives_. Lexington: Univ. Press of Kentucky, 1981. pp. 63-71.

Zimmerman, D. J.

"Maza and Ma Gong: the serial vs. the book version," _Oak Leaves_ 1(6):4-7. Winter 1971/72.

Zimmerman, D. J. (Continued)

"Swordsman of Mars: serial vs. book version," Oak Leaves 1(9):3-20. Fall 1972.

Zimmerman, Errol

"Study of science fiction: is 'future' worth the time?" Arizona English Bulletin 51(1):1-4. October 1972.

Zimmerman, Howard

"Art & Mind of Murray Tinkelman," Starlog 76: 41-45. November 1983.

"Constellation: the 41st Annual World Science Fiction Convention," Starlog 79: 44-46. February 1984.

"Gary Kurtz says farewell to the Empire," Starlog 43: 16-21. February 1981.

"Harlan Ellison: science fiction's last angry man," Starlog 8:22-27,48. 1977.

"Lastword: We've come a long way . . . or have we?," Starlog No. 100: 96-97. November 1985.

"Magic on the Edge," Starlog 80: 59-62. March 1984.

"World Fantasy Convention: Sixty Years of Weird Tales," Starlog 81: 42-43. April 1984.

Zimmerman, Manfred

"Early Glimpses of Middle-earth," Mythlore 8(4): 15. Winter 1982.

"Miscellaneous remarks on Gimli and on rhythmic prose," Mythlore 11(3): 32. Winter/Spring 1985.

"Origin of Gandalf and Josef Madlener," Mythlore 9(4): 22, 24. Winter 1983.

"Rendering of Tolkien's alliterative verse," Mythlore 8(2):21. Summer 1981.

Zimmerman-Gollheim, I.

"Zu Glos Pana von Stanislaw Lem," by Nelly Pospieszalska and I. Zimmermann-Gollheim. Quarber Merkur 24:29-52. September 1970.

Ziolkowski, Theodore

"Otherworlds: fantasy and the fantastic," Sewanee Review 86(1):121-129. Winter 1978.

Zipes, Jack

"Liberating potential of the fantastic projection in fairy tales for children, The," in: Collins, R. A., ed. Scope of the Fantastic: Culture, Biography, Themes, Children's Literature. Westport: Greenwood, 1985. pp. 257-266.

"Mass Degradation of Humanity and Massive Contradictions in Fahrenheit 451," in: Rabkin, Eric S., et. al., eds. No Place Else. Carbondale: Southern Illinois University Press, 1983. pp. 182-198.

Zito, Stephen

"George Lucas goes far out," American Film 2(6):8-13. April 1977.

Zivkovic, Z.

"Future without a future, The; an interview with Stanislaw Lem," Pacific Quarterly Moana 4(3):255-259. July 1979.

Zjawin, Dorothy

"Close encounters of the classroom kind: how to use science fiction in all subject areas," Instructor 87(9):54-57,102-107. April 1978.

Zondergeld, R. A.

Lexikon der phantastischen Literatur. Frankfurt: Suhrkamp, 1983. 314 p.

" 'Es ware falsch, uber die zukunft zu schrieben (J. G. Ballard im gesprach mit Jorge Kirchbaum und Rein A. Zondergeld," by Jorg Kirchbaum and Rein A. Aondergeld. Quarber Merkur 44:60-68. July 1976.

"Daemonie und Verfuehrung. Zu einem grundmotiv im Erzaehlwerk Joseph Sheridan Le Fanus," in: Thomsen, C. W., ed. Phantastik in Literatur und Kunst. Darmstadt: Wissenschaftliche Buchgesellschaft, 1980. pp. 170-181.

"Die sehnsucht der sirene nach dem wasser. Die welt des Maurice Renard," by Jorg Kirchbaum and R. A. Zondergeld. Quarber Merkur 43:50-58. May 1976.

"Proteus im Land der Strueme und des Regens," in: Rottensteiner, Franz, ed. Quarber Merkur. Frankfurt: Suhrkamp, 1979. pp. 209-216.

"Zwei Versuche der Befreiung: Phantastisch und erotische Literatur," Quarber Merkur 41:49-52. September 1975.

Zorkaga, N.

"Drei Ansichten des Films Solaris: Solaris
von Andreij Tarkowskij," Quarber Merkur
38:52-56. November 1974.

Zornow, Edith

"Fantasy," by R. M. Goldstein and Edith Zornow.
in: Goldstein, R. M. and Zornow, Edith. The
Screen Image of Youth: Movies About Children
and Adolescents. Metuchen, NJ: Scarecrow,
1980. pp. 271-278.

Zorza, V.

"Polizeistaat auf einem planeten," Die Zeit
July 26, 1969.

Zorzi, R. M.

Utopia e letteratura nell'ottocento
americano. Brescia, Piadeia. 155 p.

Zsigmond, Vilmos

"Lights! Camera! Action! for Close Encounters
of the Third Kind," American
Cinematographer 59(1):30-33, 64-65,90-104.
January 1978.

Zuber, Bernie

"Magic of middle-earth from J. R. R. Tolkien to
Ralph Bakshi, The," Fanfare 2:22-27.
Winter 1978.

Zuercher, Walter

Science Fiction, ed. by Sergius Golowin and
Walter Zuercher. Gurtendorf: Zuercher, 1967.
68 p.

Zukrowski, Wojciech

"Dociekanie, drazenie," Nowe ksiazki No. 6.
1968.

"Masturbatorek mozgowy," Nowe Ksiazki No.
16. 1971.

Zverev, A.

"De profundis Kurta Vonneguta,"
Inostrannaia literatura 8:265-268. 1970.

"Skazki tekhnicheskogo veka [Tales of the
technological age]" Voprosy literatury 2:
32-66. 1975.